Casablanca
Colonial Myths and Architectural Ventures

Casablanca
Colonial Myths and Architectural Ventures

Jean-Louis Cohen and Monique Eleb

THE MONACELLI PRESS

To Jo and Lucie Eleb,
passionate Casablancans

To Marcel Cohen,
explorer of Judeo-Muslim
convergences

Published with the support of the Centre National des Lettres and of the Direction de l'Architecture et du Patrimoine of the French Ministry of Culture and Communication, as part of the Librairie de l'Architecture et de la Ville, also thanks to grants from the Bureau de la Recherche Architecturale and the Caisse des Dépôts et Consignations.

Originally published as *Casablanca: Mythes et figures d'une aventure urbaine*, © 1998 Éditions Hazan

First published in the United States of America in 2002 by
The Monacelli Press
902 Broadway, New York, New York 10010

Copyright © 2002 by The Monacelli Press, Inc.

All rights reserved under International and Pan-American Copyright Conventions. No part of this book may be reproduced or utilized in any form or by any means, electronic or mechanical, including photocopying, recording, or by any information storage and retrieval system, without permission in writing from the publisher. Inquiries should be sent to The Monacelli Press, Inc.

Library of Congress Cataloging-in-Publication Data
Cohen, Jean-Louis.
  [Casablanca. English]
  Casablanca: colonial myths and architectural ventures / Jean-Louis Cohen and Monique Eleb.
    p. cm.
  Includes bibliographical references and index.
  ISBN 1-58093-087-5
  1. Architecture—Morocco—Casablanca—20th century. 2. City planning—Morocco—Casablanca—History—20th century. 3. Casablanca (Morocco)—Buildings, structures, etc. I. Eleb, Monique, 1945– II. Title.

NA1590.2.C37 C6513 2002
720'.964'3—dc21   2002022576

Printed and bound in Hong Kong
Designed by *Abigail Sturges*

Contents

11 **Introduction**

21 **A Bad Start for a City of Adventure: From Anfa to Casablanca**

51 **Henri Prost's Plan (1914–1917): A Flexible Approach**

89 **The Rule and The Monument — Planning Casablanca after 1920**

135 **Living in the *Ville Nouvelle* in the 1920s**

169 **1930–1940: From Art Deco to Modernism in Residential Construction**

215 **Building the New Medina and Housing the Workers**

251 **Building Modern Leisure Facilities**

275 **The Post-1945 Golden Age and Its Dark Side**

301 **Michel Écochard's Controversial Urbanism (1950–1952)**

325 **"Culture-Specific" Housing for Muslims: The Age of Large-Scale Projects**

365 **Housing the Europeans**

393 **Villas, Beachside Resorts, and Movie Theaters: Hedonism at Work**

441 **Epilogue**

446 Research Methodology
448 Manuscript Sources
449 Bibliography
461 Filmography
462 Biographies of Architects Active in Casablanca
473 Abbreviations and Institutional Acronyms
473 Glossary of Moroccan Terms
474 Index
480 Illustration Credits

Acknowledgments

Had we known that this book would draw us into nine years of research, we would doubtless have paid more attention to the path that—from photograph to sketch, and from manuscript to conversation—led us to conceive, during the summer of 1989, a project whose breadth has at times overwhelmed us. Returning to Casablanca, twenty-five years after having left it, in order to study its intimate history, or discovering it after having analyzed its inventive urbanism from afar, was bound to involve us in a priori unimaginable adventures. The attribution of certain buildings turned into a detective story, as tenuous clues led us from manager to tenant, following long and sometimes false trails. More than once, dating a project implied traveling a sinuous pathway between boxes of archival documents and building permit registers, which, like the chaotic and muddled city, reached us in the greatest disarray.

The research and the writing of the first manuscript was a joint enterprise: Jean-Louis Cohen wrote the drafts for "A Bad Start," "Henri Prost's Plan," "The Rule and the Monument," and "Michel Écochard's Controversial Urbanism"; Monique Eleb wrote the drafts for "Living in the *Ville Nouvelle* in the 1920s," "From Art Deco to Modernism," "'Culture-Specific' Habitat for Muslims," and "Housing the Europeans." The introduction, the epilogue, and the chapters "Building the New Medina," "The Post-1945 Golden Age," "Building Modern Leisure Facilities," and "Villas, Beachside Resorts, and Movie Theaters" were joint endeavors. The final version of the text was completed in a close cooperation of the two authors.

Immersion in the history of a city as emotionally charged as Casablanca meant first and foremost discovering a human environment without which this book would have been unthinkable and undoable. Extraordinary encounters compensated, happily, for the aridity of the archives and the pitfalls of the terrain. It is unfortunately impossible for us to pay homage to all of the inhabitants of apartment buildings and housing developments who steered us in the direction of certain discoveries, but we must express our gratitude to all of those without whom this book would not exist.

It is fitting to evoke the architects who built Casablanca and whom we had the privilege to interview. Our gratitude extends thus to Élie Azagury, who sustained us with his friendship and his memories, and who rightly deserves his alphabetical pre-eminence, and to his companion Martine Delattre, as well as to Dominique Basciano, Gaspare Basciano, Georges Candilis, Gaston Jaubert, Pierre Mas, Léonard Morandi, Giulio Pediconi, Brian Richards, Louis Riou, Alison and Peter Smithson, Éliane and Henri Tastemain, André Studer, and Jean-François Zevaco.

We thank the families and friends of deceased architects, artists, and contractors who provided us with irreplaceable documents and information: Madame Bohin-

Perrotte, Madame Pierre Coldefy, Madame India Heyder-Bruckner, Madame Schmidt-Honegger, Madame Françoise Landowski, Madame Charlotte Maddalena, Mario Milone, Claire and Pierre Suraqui, Cécile Benmussa, and Marion Tournon-Branly. Marc Lacroix, photographer and to some extent active member of the brotherhood of 1950s Casablancan architects, lent and then gave us his collection.

We also thank our Moroccan colleagues and friends as well as the institutions that have helped us in this endeavor. At the Agence urbaine de Casablanca, Governor Abdelfettah Moujahid understood the meaning of our project and lent his aid. Mohammed Saïdi and Latifa Ouadi contributed to this assistance, while Abdellah Bouhaya provided generous and sustained support. We were granted access to building permits preserved in the storerooms of the Wilaya of Greater Casablanca by Lahcen Yahya and the team composed of Lahcen Belouali, Abddelatif Boukait, and Idriss Khmass. At the Chambre de commerce et d'industrie, we were able to study the *Bulletin municipal officiel* thanks to the kindness of Noureddine Ben el Fellah.

In Rabat, the Bibliothèque générale et archives opened its collections to us, thanks to its head librarians Mohammed Ben Cherifa and Ahmed Toufiq, and with the help of Mohammed Rochdi. The Ministère de l'habitat granted us access to its library, thanks to Fatima-Zohra Khaji, and to its photograph collection, thanks to Abderrahman Slimani, because its Secretary General, Abdessatar El Amrani, understood our project. At the Centre cinématographique marocain, Director General Souheil Benbarka and archivists Fatima and Naima Darsi enabled us to find rare reels. At La Source library, Father Levrat afforded us access to collections of rare periodicals. At the Office national des chemins de fer marocains, Director Driss Hamri provided us with the plans of the Casablanca-Voyageurs station.

Our fieldwork led us to meet the owners and managers of many buildings and establishments who gave us access or provided us with plans and photographs: Sylvie and Patrice Anselin (Tahiti swimming pool); Carlos Bendayan (Lévy-Bendayan apartment block); Omar Benjelloun (Volvo garage); Mustapha Fannan (AFCA transactions); Mohammed Mninouche (L'Entente); Mustapha Sadrane (Soceca); Georges Noulellis and Henri Oleggini (Immobilière L'Océan). We were able to visit remarkable houses thanks to the hospitality of Michèle and John-Dick Ansado, Madame Souad Bennani, Madame Anne Boukobza, Danièle Cohen-Olivar, Monsieur Aziz Lazrak, Monsieur and Madame Jacques Mélia, Madame Niddam, as well as Monsieur and Madame Jacques Robelin. In Paris, Madame Sété Guetta shared with us her memories of the home built by her father, Raphaël Benazéraf. Useful advice and discreet assistance was lavished on us by Amelia Benzaquen, Saïd Lahbabi, Monsieur and Madame André Peter, Jérome Peter, Léandre and Jo Pola, and Isabelle Sahyoun.

Moroccan colleagues kindly lent or gave us useful documents at certain moments during our research: Meryem Alami-Bennis, Ahmed Alaoui-Fdili, Rachid Ben Brahim Andaloussi, Hafid El Awad, Jabrane El Bezzi, Baadi El Mokhtar, and Rachid Ouazzani. Michel Nachef made the reproductions in Rabat. North of the Mediterranean, Myriam Boccara, Alexandre Chemetoff, Jean Dethier, Daniel Le Couédic, Roland Crétegny, and Marida Talamona provided us with precious information and materials. Francis Rumpf, whose passing has left us inconsolable, gave us original photographs of the 1907 campaign.

Our urban explorations in Morocco would not have been possible without the affectionate enthusiasm of rediscovered friends such as Rosine and Victor Elbaz and Gilles and Sophie Benzaquen, as well as precious new friends such as Jacqueline Alluchon (who brought us significant aid in certain Casablancan mazes), Jamal Boushaba, Gérard Falandry, and Valérie Moréno and Saïd Mouline (who provided efficient support in Rabat). In Paris, our research was welcomed at the Archives d'architecture du XXe siècle, thanks to Maurice Culot, Gilles Ragot, David Peyceré, and Guillaume Marchand;

at the Académie d'Architecture, thanks to Claudine Devaulchier and Pieter Uyttenhove; and at Boulogne-Billancourt's Musée des Années 30, through Michèle Lefrançois. In Nantes, Bruno Ricard, Françoise Maxence, and Germain Blanchard facilitated our access to the Moroccan files of the Archives du Ministère des affaires étrangères.

At the Eidgenössische Technische Hochschule Zurich, Jos Bosman granted us access to as-of-yet uncatalogued C.I.A.M. materials. Fran Terpak flushed out rare photographs from the mysterious collection of the Getty Research Institute for the History of Art and the Humanities, which permitted us, thanks to the hospitality of Kurt W. Forster, Thomas F. Reese, and Herbert Hymans, to assemble a portion of our source materials. Stuart Ng granted us access to the Warner Bros. archives at the University of Southern California School of Cinema-Television. Mary Norris opened the Burbank Public Library Warner Research Collection to us. Rosemarie Haddad provided us with documents held at the Canadian Centre for Architecture. The late Ernest Pascucci mentioned Lettrist publications to us. Michael Gilsenan drew our attention to complementary works on Moroccan agriculture and Richard Klein to Marcel Desmet's early Flemish career.

The École d'Architecture Paris-Villemin provided an institutional framework for our research, thanks to resources allocated by the Bureau de la Recherche Architecturale and the Plan Construction et Architecture. The school's director, Sylvie Clavel, created a favorable atmosphere for this work, while Raphaël Salzedo produced invaluable photographic reproductions. The research project's administrative coordinator, Joëlle Trouvé, facilitated the organization of trips and assured the daily operation of the accounting logistics.

The generosity of Michel Laugier of Akzo-Nobel Maroc convinced us that big business could be attentive to culture and to architectural invention.

Students in "Le projet architectural et urbain, théories et dispositifs" DEA program must also be thanked for their patient attention in courses based on our work whose clarification was greatly facilitated by the efficient assistance of Jean-Louis Violeau (for supporting biographical research), and of Sylvain Le Stum, Cristiana Mazzoni, and Philippe Simon (for building drawings and maps featured in this book). Anne Debarre and Alexander Waintrub in Los Angeles, as well as Tami Hausman in New York, periodically completed the collection of bibliographic and iconographic documents.

Attentive readers and unfailing friends Raymond Benhaïm, François Chaslin, Jean-Charles Depaule, Jean-Charles Eleb, Yves Lion, and Yannis Tsiomis convinced us to retain expositions that seemed at times needlessly detailed and encouraged us with their comments. During the publication phase, the transformation of an excessively long and over abundantly illustrated manuscript into a still too dense book was the work of Nicolas Druet, Isabelle Garel, Juliette Hazan, and, of course, Éric Hazan, who spared no effort to bring to fruition a book that aspired to combine historical precision with visual relevance. The English-language translation was carried out scrupulously by Sarah Parsons. We thank most warmly Ariela Katz, who took care of the painstaking translation of footnotes and appendices; Gwendolyn Wright, who nearly rewrote the introduction; and Elisabeth Essaïan and Emily Bills, who contributed to last-minute checks. The dedication of Andrea Monfried, Ron Broadhurst, Steve Sears, Elizabeth Kugler, and of course the enthusiasm of Gianfranco Monacelli allowed for what amounts, thanks also to the rigorous yet supple layout of Abigail Sturges, to an entirely new book.

Finally, we must pay homage to those who, for more than nine years, were the victims of our Casablancan obsession—in countless conversations, dinners, and other everyday moments. Foremost among these, as they know all too well, are our daughters Elsa, Laetitia, and Mathilde.

Casablanca city center and port, view from the air, c. 1953. The medina is to the left of the Avenue du IVe-Zouaves leading to the sea, and the newly opened Avenue de la République is on the right. In the foreground, the Vox movie theater and Galerie Lafayette department store, both demolished. Agricolavia, Rabat.

Introduction

A city is more than a place in space. It is a drama in time.

Patrick Geddes, 1904[1]

The name Casablanca resounds hauntingly in songs and movies. A place of adventure, a "strange and unsettling city" where anything can happen, yet also a locus of invention and modernity—such is the myth that for decades clung to Casablanca. Evoked in films, pop songs, and newspaper articles from all over the world, even among those who know little of the city's past or its present,[2] the aura of Morocco's commercial capital derives partly from Michael Curtiz's melodrama of 1946, *Casablanca*—even though the city itself is never shown in that film.[3] This rise to fame through cinema served to enhance Casablanca's image, which had been projected until then in paeans to the "outpouring of distinctly French energy" in Morocco, to quote the writer Pierre Mac Orlan,[4] paeans that reappeared in popular novels such as *Le conquérant* by Émile Nolly and Claude Farrère's *Les hommes nouveaux*.[5]

If Casablanca was featured in literature and screenplays, it resounded no less forcefully in the chronicle of modern urban planning and architecture, where it was portrayed as an exceptional testing ground for new building practices and innovative landscapes. Until 1960 the city was praised effusively in treatises on urbanism and applauded in architectural magazines. By contrast, today's tourist guidebooks treat Casablanca as a place of no particular note, for this product of the twentieth century does not fit into their romantic models of classical and medieval Morocco. "Don't bother staying there, there's nothing to see" seems to be the advice they give visitors, who are then sent directly on to Marrakech or Fès. Yet for two-thirds of a century this supposed "nothing" captured the attention of journalists, critics, and architects, who saw in it both the promises and the threats of the modern metropolis—a "blueprint for the future," as it were.[6]

As analysts of French cities and domestic architecture, why did we devote ten or so years to studying Casablanca? Quite simply because we were struck by its beauty and originality. The public does not seem to see this side of Casablanca, perhaps because they feel confused by its twentieth-century forms. We therefore wanted to render it justice. That being said, however, we did not consciously decide to embark on the writing of this book. In the summer of 1989, when we started examining the buildings, photographing them, classifying them by type, and identifying them

1 Patrick Geddes, "Civics: as Applied Sociology I," in *The Ideal City*, ed. Helen Meller (Leicester: Leicester University Press, 1979), 79. First published in *Sociological Papers 1904* (1905).

2 In his song "Casablanca," recorded in 1946, Danish-born singer Georges Ulmer alludes to a "strange and unsettling" city. Alain Souchon recorded a song of the same title in 1983.

3 Among other films, one might cite Marcel L'Herbier, *Les hommes nouveaux*, 1936, with Harry Baur; Archie Mayo, *A Night in Casablanca*, 1946, with the Marx Brothers; and Bernard Borderie, *La Môme vert de gris*, 1952, with Eddy Constantine.

4 Pierre Mac Orlan, "Bousbir," in *Rues secrètes* (Paris: Gallimard, 1934), 64

5 Émile Nolly [Captain Détanger, pseud.], *Le conquérant, journal d'un "indésirable" au Maroc* (Paris: Calmann-Lévy, 1915); Claude Farrère, *Les hommes nouveaux* (Paris: Flammarion, 1922); and Robert Brasillach, *La Conquérante* (Paris: Plon, 1943). This last is a transparent reference to Nolly. A very general (if rather deceptive, as far as Casablanca is concerned) overview of Morocco's literary success can be found in Abdeljlil Lahjomri, *L'image du Maroc dans la littérature française (de Loti à Montherlant)* (Algiers: Société Nationale d'Édition et de Diffusion, 1973).

6 Gabriel Bertrand, "Casablanca d'hier et d'aujourd'hui; un brouillon pour demain," *La France indépendante* (Paris), August 5, 1950, 2.

[7] Léandre Vaillat, *Le visage français du Maroc* (Paris: Horizons de France, 1931), 6.

[8] Paul Rabinow, "Techno-Cosmopolitanism: Governing Morocco," in *French Modern, Norms and Forms of the Social Environment* (Cambridge: MIT Press, 1989); idem, "France in Morocco: Technocosmopolitanism and Middling Modernism," *Assemblage* no. 17 (April 1992): 53–57; and Gwendolyn Wright, *The Politics of Design in French Colonial Urbanism* (Chicago: University of Chicago Press, 1991).

[9] This is suggested by the title of the volume in which we published our first articles on this theme. Jean-Louis Cohen, "Casablanca: de la 'cité de l'énergie' à la ville fonctionnelle," and Monique Eleb, "Casablanca, de l'immeuble de rapport à l'unité d'habitation," in *Architectures françaises outre-mer*, eds. Maurice Culot and Jean-Marie Thiveaud (Paris: Institut Français d'Architecture; and Liège: Pierre Mardaga, 1992), 104–45.

as the work of architects as yet largely unknown to us, the book decided on us in a way; the city had us in its grip. A number of questions began to arise, which were too systematic to be discounted as idle curiosity. Why did such a pioneering new town spring up so rapidly, and why in this particular spot? Why, in contrast to the supposed "nothing" of today, did it inspire such a flood of commentaries and mythical incarnations? When measured against all of those novels, songs, movies, and colonialist pamphlets, what was post-1900 urban life in Casablanca really like? Where did those architectural forms, which were deemed innovative from their earliest beginnings, originate? And, as the final paradox, how did this bustling commercial city, suffering from a housing shortage and populated by displaced and often oppressed social groups, arouse instant and fierce loyalty on the part of its successive inhabitants?

To recount Casablanca's astonishing story, which contrasts so sharply with the rather mixed fortunes of other twentieth-century new towns, meant understanding how and why the city took the form it did. This task required analyzing the guiding principles of successive urban plans as well as their specific effects on urban design and development. Equally important, it entailed a close analysis of domestic architecture, identifying who had commissioned various groups of dwellings and what factors shaped people's home lives. Indeed, was there one specific way of life in Casablanca, or several? Did climatic, ethnic, and cultural features generate particular needs, tastes, and behavioral patterns? In addition, we wanted to understand the courses of action adopted by Casablanca's architects, who acted as mediators between local traditions and European doctrines. And lastly, we sought to unravel how social relationships within a fast-growing colonial city were adapted to a terrain that had already been subdivided, and how these relationships translated into built forms.

A Modern Urban Myth

While it is true that Casablanca developed as a port city well before the French landings of 1907, it is unquestionably a twentieth-century metropolis, one that ranks among the most significant urban creations of the epoch. As a major metropolis during the French Protectorate (1912–1956), it of course served to aid and abet colonial practices that were often quite ruthless. Yet the remarkable teams of architects and planners, whose clients were eager for innovation and modernization, also made Casablanca a laboratory for legislative, technological, and cultural experimentation. In 1929 the Parisian critic Léandre Vaillat declared, not without a hint of pique, "Casablanca is boldly constructing new projects that Paris is too timid to try,"[7] clearly implying that even the very capital of the Empire had much to learn from this new kind of city. The prevailing myth of the 1920s focused on General Lyautey's modernization of Casablanca as the epitome of French "energy," in contrast to the lethargy that prevailed on the mainland. This soon evolved into a more substantive hypothesis, the premise that Morocco constituted a full-scale laboratory for French urbanism.[8] One of our initial aims was to test this hypothesis. We therefore had to prove that the colonial experiment had indeed been analyzed and then transferred back to France. Our assumption was largely borne out by the work undertaken in Casablanca by several outstanding planners, including Henri Prost and Michel Écochard, and by architects such as Auguste Perret and Georges Candilis, who came across from France to put their theories into practice. Nevertheless, we had to piece together the actual experiments that were carried out and then study them in detail.

Another prevalent myth portrays Casablanca as an "overseas French city" whose form and way of life sought to mirror that of metropolitan France.[9] In truth, Casablanca has always been both an international and a Moroccan city—a mestizo city, characterized by a pooling of national and regional skills. It can thus be regarded as a collective endeavor that combined the professional know-how of European engineers, architects, and landscapers with the skills of Moroccan *m'allemîn* (master masons, carpenters, tilers, sculptors, and gardeners). Furthermore, as well as forming a mosaic of Mediterranean cultures from Tunisia, Algeria, Spain, and Italy, it also served as fertile ground for an early Americanization process that was triggered by the Allied landings of 1942. This is confirmed by the artist Wyndham Lewis, who wrote, "Casablanca is a city upon the American model then; it is semi-skyscraping"; this is further corroborated by the journalist Bernard Newman, according to whom, "[Casablanca] rather resembles a Frenchman's idea of Chicago, complete with skyscrapers and Galeries Lafayette."[10] Social, national, and cultural blending occurred in tandem with segregation policies, carried out with considerable sensitivity in the new medina but with vicious disdain in the shantytowns. France's "civilizing methods" may have been less destructive in Morocco than elsewhere, given Lyautey desire to distance himself from previous colonial practices; yet the Protectorate's attitude toward "indigenous" arts, including architecture, was nonetheless based on a condescension that Muslim Moroccans inevitably experienced as an assault on their sovereignty.

Piecing Together an Urban Puzzle
The transformation of Casablanca occupies a far from negligible place in the literature about modern Morocco. Prolific quantities of colonial propaganda provide useful research material, including repeated proclamations of a rather disgusting type of colonial ideology. Municipal archives reveal more conflicting accounts. Important works of scholarship include André Adam's invaluable study of Westernization in Morocco, by far the most comprehensive example of the genre; Jean-Louis Miège's writings on the early history of European settlement in Morocco; and Daniel Rivet's analysis of French administrative policies under the Protectorate system.[11]

Nonetheless, a substantial gulf separates historical, anthropological, and sociological works from the still preliminary study of spatial changes at various scales, in various epochs. Monographs published decades ago were often our sole means of tracking the evolution of particular neighborhoods. Ideological writings celebrating the "greatness" of the colonial undertaking were then counterbalanced in the 1950s and 1960s by French texts that were far more sympathetic to an independent Morocco, although not wholly free of bias either. Since then, scientific and critical analyses have often been eclipsed by a stereotypical anti-colonialist discourse. A strange inversion of the earlier triumphalist colonial rhetoric thus appeared, no less mythologizing in its own terms, which drew principally from the 1950s studies of shantytowns. More recently, a theoretical criticism has emerged that addresses various forms of colonial representation. However, these texts, based on seminal works by Maxime Rodinson and Edward Said,[12] concentrate on the analysis of discourse, bypassing the complexity of spatial and social factors, despite their centrality to any thorough understanding of colonization.

In short, up until now, all accounts of Casablanca's history have been reduced to a focus on two players: on the one hand, the Protectorate, with all its administrative trappings, and on the other hand, newly urbanized Muslims whose organizational methods were rather more spontaneous. Very often, these studies fail to include intermediary social groups and classes involved in colonization, such as the Spanish working class and the French lower middle classes.[13] Similarly, they omit the active role of Moroccan feudal lords and prosperous merchants within the sphere of real estate, and they do not incorporate the Jewish population, whose contribution to the city's devel-

10 Wyndham Lewis, *Journey into Barbary: Morocco Writings and Drawings* (Santa Barbara: Black Sparrow Press, 1983), 73; Bernard Newman, *Morocco Today* (London: Robert Hale, 1953), 121.

11 André Adam, *Casablanca: essai sur la transformation de la société marocaine au contact de l'Occident*, 2 vols. (Paris: Éditions du CNRS, 1968); idem, *Histoire de Casablanca (des origines à 1914)* (Aix en Provence: Ophrys, 1968); Jean-Louis Miège, *Le Maroc et l'Europe (1830–1894)*, 4 vols. (Paris: 1961–63); and Daniel Rivet, *Lyautey et l'institution du Protectorat français au Maroc 1912–1925*, 3 vols. (Paris: L'Harmattan, 1988).

12 Maxime Rodinson, *Europe and the Mystique of Islam* (Seattle: University of Washington Press, 1987; reprint, Paris: L'Harmattan, 1988); and Edward Said, *Orientalism* (New York: Pantheon Books, 1978); idem, *Culture and Imperialism*, (New York: Knopf, 1993).

13 See certain chapters in Yvonne Knibiehler, Geneviève Emmery, and Françoise Leguay, *Des Français au Maroc* (Paris: Denoël, 1992).

14 The most pertinent observations in this regard remain those of Doris Bensimon-Donath, *Évolution du judaïsme marocain sous le Protectorat français, 1912–1956* (Paris and The Hague: Mouton et Cie, 1968).

15 André Adam, *Casablanca*, 1:15.

16 Decoration is the main concern in Zurfluh's early book. Jean-Michel Zurfluh, *Casablanca* (Casablanca: Soden, 1985); and Nathalie de Chaisemartin, "Perspective de recherche sur le décor des façades des habitations privées dans le centre de Casablanca 1880–1930," in *Actes du colloque de Casablanca* (Casablanca: Publications de la Faculté des Lettres et des Sciences de Casablanca, 1983), 15–34.

17 François Béguin, with Gildas Baudez, Denis Lesage, and Lucien Godin, *Arabisances, décor architectural et tracés urbains en Afrique du Nord 1830–1950* (Paris: Dunod, 1983).

opment was as varied as their own geographical and class origins.[14] As Adam himself points out, the "primary target" of his work on Casablanca was the study of its "Muslim society," not of its European and Jewish communities.[15]

This type of bias has distorted an analytical understanding of Casablanca's urban spaces and buildings. Favored sites mentioned repeatedly in celebrative colonial discourse, such as the port and the Place de France, have simply been replaced by other favored sites, such as the *bidonvilles* (shantytowns) and the Habous quarter, which was already amply described in the 1930s. Completely ignored—except when they are reduced to mere decorative schemes—are the thousands of apartment buildings constructed in the city center and the innumerable villas in the residential neighborhoods.[16] The notion of *Arabisance* (i.e., French architects borrowing architectural decoration from Moorish buildings), while useful in its day, cannot fully encompass the processes of modernity in Morocco or the various architectural forms that emerged.[17] By the same token, the corpus of Casablanca's urban plans has been reduced to those that were drawn up by such legendary figures as Prost (1915) and Écochard (1951), and which were subsequently widely published in urban design handbooks. True, these plans are of primary importance, yet there also exist a number of earlier documents (such as the Tardif plan drafted in 1912 and the Courtois plan of 1944) that have been completely left by the wayside, even though the solutions they envisioned were implemented at a later stage. Furthermore, Casablanca's extraordinary street system of wide avenues planted with palm trees, boulevards lined with porticoes, shopping areas, and distinctive squares has hardly been studied at all. Lastly, need we mention that in order to understand Moroccan building practices in Casablanca, it is essential to be extremely familiar with European and American architecture, including all the accompanying ideals, doctrines, methods, and institutions. This approach contrasts sharply with the narrow bilateral attitude prevalent in most studies, focused solely on the relationship between Paris and Casablanca. Indeed, the key to Casablanca's architectural enigmas can often be found not only in Paris, but also in Berlin, Rio de Janeiro, or even Los Angeles.

Coming to Grips with Casablanca's Urban Lifestyles

Obviously, a project of this scale entailed far more than studying postcard collections. We had to gain access to the city's archives, including those for building permits and subdivision plans. Only by examining all the various maps, administrative reports, and publications were we able to measure the discrepancy between the plans and the ever-changing face of reality. We pored over surveys of streets, courtyards, and housing, past and present. Only first-hand experience—personal testimonies (including those of novelists), interviews with people who had been on the scene, and our own visits inside the dwellings in question, both avant-garde villas and single-room housing blocks for workers—could provide a sense of the texture of people's lives, their ideas, their variety.

Intuitively, we realized at an early stage that the dominant role reportedly played by French speculators and industrialists had to be relativized with regard to the involvement of Muslim and Jewish Moroccans, as well as in relation to other immigrants. From this perspective, the population categories as defined by the different administrations under the Protectorate proved false, despite the fact that the planners often endorsed these categories in their programs. In terms of housing policy, three apparently clear-cut population segments were specified—European, Muslim, and Jewish. Today these categories can be seen as openly racist: the Moroccans were divided by religion (Muslim and Jewish), and the Europeans were treated as a whole, despite considerable social and cultural differences between each nationality. By researching how these groups were distributed through the city, and by analyzing the Moroccans' reactions to a Western urban lifestyle (especially in the form of housing), we began to reflect on the various kinds of acculturation experienced by the colonized populations.[18] Moreover, we noted that there had been an inverse acculturation process through which many colonial settlers and officials in turn adopted Moroccan customs.[19]

Surveying architectural objects, government policies, and professional cultures led to an analysis that encompassed social, cultural, and geographical dimensions of urban history. We considered urban and architectural space as simultaneously cultural artifacts and creative explorations. Within this broad historical framework, we emphasized three conceptual frameworks: *distribution* (layout plan), *dispositif* (spatial arrangement), and *régulation* (public regulation of private construction). The layout plans of buildings reveal how housing types are adapted to traditions and customs, and point up switches in attitude and tastes.[20] At every scale, from that of a dwelling to that of a district, plan layouts show how various dwelling types adapt to traditions and custom, even as they reveal changes in attitudes and tastes; they articulate social spaces and lifestyles, architectural aesthetics and cultures. Our close study of plans also looks for underlying systems: ways of grouping and classifying various components and people, usually in an effort to produce particular kinds of social behavior. The concept of *dispositif,* or arrangement, central to the work of Michel Foucault, among others, can be analyzed on any scale—from that of a city to that of a square—that seeks to govern relations between various individuals and groups. In turn, the concept of regulation helps trace the rapport between official urban plans and actual daily practices in a city. The history of cities is less a matter of implementing (or resisting) specific plans and building designs and more an ongoing negotiation between government bureaucrats or other public authorities and myriad private actors.[21] Especially in a city like Casablanca, this history of regulation moves between the prescriptive policies of the state and the more tumultuous throes of the private market, straddling the grandiose gestures of official planners and the pragmatic actions of developers. We therefore decided to focus our study on *unique* buildings, which demonstrate the distinctive character of this complex interaction, as well as *generic* buildings, mutually accepted types that are repeated or reproduced with multiple variations.

Constructing a Time Frame

It was no easy task to define the time span this book should cover. If we chose to frame the political history of modern Morocco, this would have meant beginning with 1907 (the initial French landings), or with 1912 (the year of the treaty that established the French Protectorate), and ending with 1956 (the year in which Morocco regained its independence). We deliberately decided against such an option for two main reasons. First, recent interpretations by historians of twentieth-century architecture have clearly demonstrated how major shifts in architectural culture have coincided with political shifts, sometimes extremely brutal ones—the Revolution of 1917 and the fall of the Third Reich, for instance. Second and perhaps more significantly, the history of Morocco, and of Casablanca in particular, reveals that European "penetration" commenced well before 1907. We thus decided to set the initial episode of the book in the late nineteenth century, at the time of Casablanca's commercial revival.

The concluding date of our study was rather more difficult to define. We chose not to align with the obvious political cutoff point of 1956, but rather with the complex transition that occurred during the early 1960s. Colonial policies of urban policy and professional practice persisted after the change in government, even after the departure of many European architects and clients.[22] Two specific events helped

18 The term *acculturation* designates "the complex processes of cultural contact through which societies or groups assimilate or see imposed on themselves traits or groups of characteristics originating in other societies." Pierre Bonte and Michel Izard, *Dictionnaire de l'ethnologie et de l'anthropologie* (Paris: PUF, 1991). Nathan Wachtel includes the reciprocal action in his definition: "The word, which first appeared in Anglo-American anthropological literature at the end of the nineteenth century, designates all the phenomena of inter-reaction resulting from the meeting of two cultures." Nathan Wachtel, *The Vision of the Vanquished: The Spanish Conquest of Peru through Indian Eyes, 1530–1570* (New York: Barnes and Noble, 1977; reprint, Paris: Gallimard, 1971), 4.

19 Regarding these two terms, see Albert Memmi, *The Colonizer and the Colonized* (New York: Orion Press, 1965; reprint, Paris: Corréa, 1957, and Payot, 1973).

20 Previous research on domestic architecture in France is useful in this regard. See Monique Eleb and Anne Debarre-Blanchard, *Architectures de la vie privée: maisons et mentalités XVIIe–XIXe siècles* (Brussels: Archives d'Architecture Moderne, 1989).

21 Such issues have been addressed in Jean-Louis Cohen and André Lortie, *Des fortifs au périf: Paris, les seuils de la ville* (Paris: Pavillon de l'Arsenal/Picard, 1992).

22 Later French foreign aid workers consolidated the policies pursued by the veterans of Écochard's team and Moroccan architects. Archives of the Housing Ministry (*Ministère de l'Habitat*) at Rabat strongly attest to this continuity.

23 See our appended methodological note.

24 Certain actors were present simultaneously in both of these realms. However, the nature of the archives consulted, the documents analyzed, and the projects' scalar diversity (ranging from a small villa to an entire region) called for a more precise examination of what was at stake in each project.

25 The reign of Sultan Moulay Abd-el-Aziz (1894–1908) was followed by those of Moulay Hafid (1908–12); Moulay Youssef (1912–27); and Mohammed V (1927–61). Following the administration of General (later Marshal) Lyautey (1912–25) were the residencies of Théodore Steeg (1925–29); Lucien Saint (1929–33); Henry Ponsot (1933–36); Marcel Peyrouton (March–September 1936); Charles Noguès (1936–43); Gabriel Puaux (1943–46); Eirik Labonne (1946–47); Alphonse Juin (1947–51); Augustin Guillaume (1951–54); Francis Lacoste (1954–55); Gilbert Granval (July–August 1955); Pierre Boyer de la Tour du Moulin (August–November 1955); and finally André Dubois (1955–56).

break this thread. First, the reconstruction program for Agadir after the 1960 earthquake led Moroccan architects and planners to shift the bulk of their design work toward the south; here they gradually distanced themselves from the functionalist issues of the 1950s, as if modern architecture had run out of steam. Second, who can deny that the death of Mohammed V in 1961 and the early years of Hassan II's reign began a new political cycle in Morocco? Moreover, in the realm of research methodology, the regular publication of periodicals and the accessibility of archival material, twin bases for our inquiry into architecture before 1960, were simply no longer available.[23] In any case, it should perhaps be left to Moroccan scholars to interpret this later historical epoch, no longer so markedly defined by European involvement—sometimes quite forcible—in Morocco's national culture.

Having established our overall time frame, we needed to divide it in order to verify the hypothesis of the central point of our work, namely that Casablanca had served as an urbanistic laboratory. It would have been particularly difficult to adopt a linear approach, since there is no real synchronicity between the time when urban planning strategies were drawn up and the time when housing and other buildings in Casablanca were actually built. Moreover, broad cycles can be identified in the city's urban regulations, as well as in the changes in domestic architecture and the ways in which housing was actually used.[24] Similarly, the time frame of Moroccan history and even the Protectorate system itself was marked by differences between various French resident-generals and their administrations, as well as the distinct epochs of the interwar years and the post-1945 epoch.[25] These cycles marked out the framework governing architectural culture and politics.

The first stage of this saga, between 1907 and the late 1920s, encompasses the French conquest, with Lyautey's teams of experts creating the first significant public works and attempting to regulate the haphazard urban development that had already occurred. This was the aim of Prost's interventions. The early development of the new town saw archetypal French housing patterns adapted to the Moroccan setting. Behind the facades of bourgeois dwellings in a neo-Provençal or Hispanic mode and faintly Parisian apartment buildings with prominent roofs or conspicuous corner entrances were floor plans, decors, and openings to the outside that represent new hybrid adaptations. The main players assumed two roles in this urban adventure: on the one hand, enterprising and creative spirits; on the other, oppressive agents of colonialism.

The 1930s saw a second stage, marked by more regulated urban growth and methodical expansion of the city in a context of economic uncertainty. A central business district was proposed and major industries began to play a more central role. Domestic architecture emphasized the need for hygiene, public health, and new standards of comfort, both for the European new town and the new Moroccan medina. Sleek white buildings announced a streamlined aesthetic with more than a hint of monumentality. With housing difficult to find for all groups, Casablanca began to suffer from its success, and social, spatial, and ethnic polarization worsened.

Between the Allied landing in 1942 and independence in 1956, the third stage can be characterized as a decade-long crisis. Reform-minded resident-general Eirik Labonne launched new public initiatives that included public housing. Both projects and completed buildings suggest a more radical concept of modern life. Middle-class villas adopted Mediterranean, Scandinavian, and Californian motifs and incorporated the latest household appliances from the United States. Working-class housing followed the precepts of the Congrès Internationaux d'Architecture Moderne (C.I.A.M.), even as they stirred debates about regionalism within this organization.

Casablanca thus became an arena for battles between private investors, municipal authorities, and the colonial government. It was also a common ground, even a crucible, for interaction between different cultures: a hegemonic (not predominant) group of French settlers (itself by no means uniform, hailing mostly from Provence, Gascony, and Corsica), together with Arabs, Berbers, Moroccan Jews, Sicilians, and Andalucians. If mixtures are above all evident in the interiors and facades of buildings, cultural pluralism did extend into other domains of urban life. Thus the use of courtyards, alleys, and sidewalks show Moroccan cultures mixing with different Mediterranean and Iberian practices. From another perspective, Casablanca shows the Parisian apartment house being exported abroad, where it too would undergo subtle transformations, in a process of cultural transfer and appropriation that is only now being explored.[26]

Most texts about Casablanca—whether celebratory tracts of the colonial era or anti-imperialist pamphlets—have tended to oversimplify the fluidities and ambiguities of urban life into rigid, indeed crystalline, models. Fortunately, such oversimplification seems to have declined; since 1990 both Moroccan and French writers have taken a new, more literary approach.[27] Yet Casablanca has not yet found a Louis-Sébastien Mercier to paint a picture of the city in all its glory, nor a Walter Benjamin to piece together the most significant parts of its puzzle, nor a Reyner Banham to extract its joyful essence and juxtaposed "ecologies."[28] Our aim was not to attempt the impossible task of providing an exhaustive history; rather, we sought to contribute to the major studies that have already been undertaken on Casablanca by recounting the saga of a torn yet endearing city. We have thus focused just as much on Casablanca's diverse social fabric as its layered urban space.

An Unexpected Moroccan Response

We have been able to assess preliminary response to our research and findings through the French edition of the present book, which was published in fall 1998. In addition, an exhibition deriving from our research opened in spring 2000 in Casablanca, allowing us to further gauge how the work had generally been received. We found that most Moroccan readers perceived the episodes related in the book as narrowly colonial, but they nonetheless felt that these formed part of a history with which they could identify. As a result, we realized that it is not merely architects and planners who have strong emotional ties with the city's architectural history, but rather a much broader circle of the population. We noted that the book has enabled a large number of Casablancans to rediscover the beauty inherent in their city, helping them to understand more clearly why they are so strongly attracted to its shape and texture. It has also made them aware of certain urban forms hitherto unknown to them, and has demonstrated how these forms were the product of specific strategies.

Over and above urban and social issues, one main point of discussion in various Moroccan institutions and many private gatherings has been how the work has bestowed on the city a certain historical legitimacy. For despite the fact that it is a chief contributor to the national economy, Casablanca is often looked down upon by citizens of Fès, Marrakech, and Rabat, who regard it as a city deprived of all history. In some respects, this can be compared to the condescending attitude adopted by Bostonians toward Los Angeles. It would seem, therefore, that the Casablancans' pride in their city has been restored, perhaps because they now have tangible proof of the creative genius that went into its making. Moreover, it has been made apparent to them that Casablanca is a city of international renown, not least because of its urban structure and features. It is to be sincerely hoped that all these factors will play a major role in preserving the built heritage that is documented in the following pages.

[26] Consider, for example, the dissemination of the bungalow type, superbly analyzed in Anthony King, *The Bungalow: The Production of a Global Culture* (London: Routledge & Kegan Paul, 1984). Regarding the Parisian apartment building, see André Lortie, ed., *Paris s'exporte: architecture modèle ou modèles d'architecture* (Paris: Pavillon de l'Arsenal/Picard, 1995).

[27] Nineteen-fifties Casablanca was the theater of the sentimental education that constitutes the framework of Michel Chaillou's *Mémoires de Melle* (Paris: Seuil, 1993). See also the varied perspectives of writers and photographers assembled in Alain Bourdon and Didier Folléas, eds., *Casablanca, fragments d'imaginaire* (Casablanca: Institut français de Casablanca, Éditions Le Fennec, 1997).

[28] Louis-Sébastien Mercier, *Tableau de Paris* (Paris: Mercure de France, 1994; reprint, Hamburg: Virchaux; Neufchâtel: S. Fauche, 1781); Walter Benjamin, *The Arcades Project* (Cambridge, Mass.: Belknap Press, 1999); and Reyner Banham, *Los Angeles, the Architecture of Four Ecologies* (Harmondsworth: Penguin Books, 1971). See also the work done on two other North-African metropolises: Zeynep Çelik, *Urban Forms and Colonial Confrontations: Algiers under French Rule* (Berkeley: University of California Press, 1997); and Mohamed Scharabi, *Kairo: Stadt und Architektur im Zeitalter des europaischen Kolonialismus* (Tübingen: Wasmuth, 1989).

Casablanca
Colonial Myths and Architectural Ventures

A Bad Start for a City of Adventure: From Anfa to Casablanca

The myth perpetuated by proponents of colonialism that Casablanca is a product of the French conquest must be dispelled *de facto*, for in reality the city boasts a deep-seated urban legacy. In addition, it is to be noted that Casablanca began its journey down the road of modernization well before the *Galilée* landed on August 5, 1907, an event that triggered the conflict and repression leading to the declaration of the French Protectorate in 1912. Accounts by nineteenth-century travelers may portray the town as a godforsaken spot, but the truth is that trade fever had already firmly set in, generating a turnaround in the fortunes of a settlement that had been practically wiped off the map for three centuries.[1]

Reviving a Forgotten Port (1770–1900)

Apart from a tower once struck by lightning, a fairly well preserved Moorish bath, and an apparently unfinished mosque, there seems to be nothing but half-buried ruins to remind visitors that they are standing in ancient Anefa, for many years one of the wealthiest cities in this part of the Maghreb ... Time has apparently turned everything to dust.

Narcisse Cotte, 1860[2]

The first reference to a populated area known as Anfa can be traced back to the eleventh century, although no plausible explanation can be assigned to its etymology. It is believed that the city's founders were Zenata Berbers,[3] despite claims of Roman and Phoenician ancestry championed respectively by the Muslim traveler Johannes Leo Africanus and the Spanish national Luis Marmól Carvajal, who was imprisoned in the town during the sixteenth century. It was a bustling and influential hub that spawned both soldiers and men of letters, surviving attacks by Almoravid and Almohad invaders to grow into a thriving center of trade under the Merinide dynasty between the thirteenth and fifteenth centuries.[4] Around this time it attracted Italian and Portuguese ships, which local sailors would ambush with their small fast craft. As punishment for such harmful sport, Infante Don Fernando (brother of the Portuguese king, Alphonse V) landed a fleet of fifty vessels carrying ten thousand men and razed the city walls. The Portuguese planned another attack in 1515, but abandoned this venture after their out-and-out defeat at the hands of

Opposite
The medina. Photographed from a hot-air balloon in 1907. At right in photo: Grand Socco and Wadi Bouskoura. In the foreground: the mellah.

[1] The climate is generally considered hospitable, despite the coastal humidity. L. d'Anfreville de la Salle, "Essai sur la climatologie et la démographie de Casablanca," *Bulletin de la Société de pathologie exotique* 12, no. 8 (August 1919): 525–30; Dr. Charbonneau, "Casablanca est-elle une ville humide ou non?" *L'Intransigeant marocain* 1, 3 (April 27, 1945; and A. Le-Det, "Éléments du climat de Casablanca," *Revue de géographie marocaine* 3, 4 (1963): 137–41.

[2] Narcisse Cotte, *Le Maroc contemporain* (Paris: Charpentier, 1860), 27–28.

[3] Other names, such as El-Anfa, Anafa, or Anaffa, Anafe, Anife, Anifee, Nafe, or Nafee, are also mentioned. The spelling of Arabic terms used in this text follows a simplified version of the transliteration conventions used by André Adam in *Casablanca*. As most archival documents and publications used throughout the book are based on this standard of French transliteration, we have chosen to adhere to it in the present English translation.

[4] In the early fourteenth century, it ranked seventh among the country's cities in terms of taxes paid to the sultan. Adam, *Histoire de Casablanca*, 42.

The ruins of Anfa, in Georg Braun and Franz Hogenberg, *Civitates orbis terrarum* (Cologne, 1572).

the Merinides during the battle of Mamora.[5] Johannes Leo Africanus rather flatteringly describes the site he then discovered:

> The city was once extremely civilized and prosperous due to its highly fertile land. Indeed, it is the finest site in the whole of Africa, being surrounded on all sides by a plain of some eighty miles, except in the north, which is coastal. Judging from its ruins, Anfa formerly possessed many temples, handsome shops and lofty palaces.[6]

This ghost town subsequently served as a port of call for Dutch sailors seeking to replenish their fresh water supply. The earliest existing illustration of Anfa is a sorry picture, though probably false: on a plate published in 1572 by Braun and Hogenberg, a handful of lopped towers watch forlornly over a flat expanse of land dotted with ruins, foregrounded by two ships moored in rocky creeks.[7] Johannes Leo Africanus was moved to tears when gazing on this town, whose pitiful state seemed to curtail any hope of it being inhabited ever again.[8] A whitewashed building did, however, stand tall over the ruins of the city walls, doubtless giving rise to the new name of *Dar el-Beida*, bestowed on the town during the seventeenth century and used until roughly 1860.[9]

Around 1770 the Alouite sultan Sidi Mohammed Ben Abdallah decided to restore the city walls, at a time when Louis de Chénier (then French consul in Rabat) remarked that Anafé, or Dar el-Beida, was "occupied by just a few Moors living in huts."[10] The sultan's plan was to create a stronghold to resist European forays into Mazagan and Rabat, arming the town with a battery, or *sqala*.*[11] Yet he also had commercial ideas in mind. According to Mohammed al-Duayf, a contemporary chronicler, the sultan "was incredulous at the way in which his port was generally perceived" and "reproached the *R'bati** for continually decrying it, although this was because in truth they clearly feared the people of Dar el-Beida." Furthermore, he "authorized many Christians to load up grain there."[12] In 1786, Juan Manuel Salmón, the Spanish consul, reported on the "sizable construction works" under-

5 Manuel Pablo Castellanos, *Historia de Maruecos*, 3rd ed. (Tangiers: Impr. Hispano-Arábiga de la Mision Católico-Española, 1898). Sixteenth-century chronicles report the intention of King Manuel of Portugal (1495–1521) to build a fortress at Anafe. Damião de Goís, *Les Portugais au Maroc de 1495 à 1521*, trans. and intro. Robert Picard (Rabat: F. Moncho, 1937), 150.

6 Johannes Leo Africanus, *Description de l'Afrique*, trans. A. Épaulard (Paris: Adrien-Maisonneuve, 1956), 1:160.

7 Georg Braun and Franz Hogenberg, *Civitates orbis terrarum* (The towns of the world) (Cologne: Bertram Buchholtz, 1572) vol. 1, plate 58.

8 Leo Africanus, *Description de l'Afrique*, 1:161.

9 Based on heretofore neglected texts by late-eighteenth-century Moroccan historians, the Spanish historian Lourido Diaz contests André Adam's view that the name *Casa branca* was first bestowed on the city by the Portuguese. Ramón Lourido Diaz, "Documentos ineditos sobre el nacimiento de Dar-al-Bayda' (Casablanca) en el siglo XVIII," *Hespéris-Tamuda* (1974): 119–46; idem, "De nuevo sobre la creación de la ciudad marroquí Dar-al-Bayda' (Casablanca)," in *Homenaje al Prof. Dario Cabanelas Rodriguez, OFM con motivo de su LXX aniversario* (Granada: Universidad de Granada, 1987), 405–17.

10 Louis de Chénier, *Recherches Historiques sur les Maures et histoire de l'Empire du Maroc* (Paris, 1787), 3:33. Chénier was in Morocco from 1767 to 1782.

11 Italicized terms identified by an asterisk are translated and defined in the glossary located at the back of the book.

12 Mohammed al-Duayf, *Ta'rij al-Duayf*, ca. 1800 (unpublished manuscript), quoted in Ramón Lourido Diaz, "Documentos ineditos," 139. The sultan apparently visited the city in February–March 1785.

taken to rebuild the walls and to build a "college for studies" as well as a "good" mosque, which would become the *Jama-el-kebir*.* Describing this site "as one of the best cities in the entire Kingdom," Salmón details three dwellings owned by himself, the governor, and the ambassador of Tripoli, which contrasted sharply with the "huts" and "remains of bygone times."[13]

This rapid takeoff swiftly soared to further heights through the Spanish-Moroccan treaty signed in 1799,[14] resulting in the city's reintegration into the Atlantic economic circuit. Around 1790, the English traveler William Lempriere spoke of a "bay where vessels of considerable size can readily drop anchor, except when buffeted by strong northwesterly winds," but remarked that Dar el-Beida is a "sad-looking town."[15] In 1834, Jacopo Gråberg di Hemsö saw it as a "mediocre, walled town with a spacious bay and rather an unsafe port."[16]

Early European Settlements

Europeans gradually began to put down roots in this small township of just one thousand inhabitants, which acquired a permanent customs office in 1836. Cypriot-born J. B. M. Rey, resident in Tangiers, restored a building to house his shop, and later the Frenchman Prosper Ferrieu settled there in 1839 with a view to obtaining wool for the Lodève factories. At the same time, French and *R'bati* merchants set about organizing the export of those raw materials that were crucial to European industry.[17] From 1854 onward, grain produced in the inland Chaouia Plain similarly began to be exported, with French merchants apparently playing a predominant role. European exports increased sharply in the 1850s, when steamships first started being used, and companies such as the Marseilles-based Bazin & Gay and Cohen & Cie began filling their holds with merchandise to be sold on arrival in order to avoid sending empty ships across from France. Despite the coastline being labeled a ship's graveyard, other companies followed suit and opened up offices in town, notably Paquet, which also acquired tracts of rural land.

Henceforth, Casablanca's foreign trade climbed steadily, owing to the standardizing of customs tariffs stipulated in the 1856 Anglo-Moroccan treaty, and to a gradual shift of trade from Rabat, which found itself handicapped by higher prices. In spite of frequent economic setbacks, the port's commercial links with the hinterland expanded, and an increasingly reliable transport network developed. According to Jean-Louis Miège, the town grew into more of a "collection and distribution center" than a transit point for wool and grain; in other words, it functioned as a large warehouse of sorts, to the detriment of Gibraltar. Furthermore, it became home to an increasing number of European vice-consuls (such as the English and French in 1857 and 1865, respectively) who moved there from Mazagan, Mogador, and Rabat.

Whereas a city's demographic shifts are dictated by labor demand, its physical framework is slower to take shape. Even as late as 1844, a certain J. B. M. Rey spoke about "a tide of ruins" lying in the wake of "a fissured, tottering rampart," inhabited by a hundred or so Moorish and Jewish families living in "tents woven with goat and sheep hair or thatched reed huts covered in a layer of clay and lime."[18] Narcisse Cotte, who arrived in the mid-1850s, admits to having "a lump in his throat at such a scraggy spectacle of dilapidated huts, ramshackle dwellings, and squalid hill sites answering to the name of *Dar el-Beida*," among which he searched in vain for the remains of a more glorious past.[19] Cotte would take an active interest in the future of this small town sited on the road between Fès and Marrakech, believing it could play host to a profitable hotel business. However, he doubted that the "*White House* would ever evolve into a large population center," since its inhabitants "prefer to live higgledy-piggledy in smoky tents and huts than to pick up the stones scattered

13 Juan Manuel Salmón, letter to Count Floridablanca, Dar-el-Bayda, January 3, 1786, quoted in Ramón Lourido Diaz, "Documentos ineditos," 144. See also Ricardo Ruiz Orsatti, *Relaciones hispano-marroquies: un gran amigo de España, el Sultán Mohammed-ben-Abdalá* (Madrid: Instituto de Estudios Politicos, 1944), 57–60. Sidi Mohammed Ben Abdallah (1757–90) was the founder of the port of Mogador and helped bring about the commercial development of Morocco.

14 The city's commerce was entrusted to a quartet of merchants from Cádiz in 1782 and, fifteen years later, to the Cincos Gremios Mayores company of Madrid.

15 William Lempriere, *Voyage dans l'empire de Maroc et le royaume de Fez, fait pendant les années 1790 et 1791* (Paris: Tavernier 1801), 56; in English: *A Tour from Gibraltar to Tangier, Sallee, Mogodore, Santa Cruz, Taroudant, and thence over Mount Atlas to Morocco, including a particular account of the Royal Harem, etc.* (London: printed by J. Walter and sold by J. Johnson, 1791), quoted in Adam, *Histoire de Casablanca*, 67.

16 Jacapo Gråberg di Hemsö, *Specchio geografico e statistico dell'impero di Marocco* (Genoa: Dalla tip. Pellas, 1834), 53.

17 Jean-Louis Miège, "Les origines du développement de Casablanca au XIXe siècle," *Hespéris* (1st and 2nd Trimester 1953): 204–5.

18 J. B. M. Rey, *Souvenirs d'un voyage au Maroc* (Paris: n.p., 1844), 12–13, quoted in Adam, *Histoire de Casablanca*, 85.

19 Cotte, *Le Maroc contemporain*, 28.

Remains of the Portuguese prison c. 1900.

around them to make comfortable shelters." Yet in 1858, Beaumier records an "incredible transformation" that gave rise to "a pretty little Moroccan town with white walls and fully renovated thoroughfares." In this settlement, "good dwellings" and "large shops" owned by merchants stood beside workers' "small stone houses."[20] In 1867, the vice-consul to France spoke of reviving a "well-situated" town whose inhabitants then numbered eight thousand: "Over the past ten years or so, Casablanca has experienced a complete turnaround, marked by a steady influx of European merchants. The huts that formerly littered the town have been progressively replaced by proper dwellings, as well as by storage buildings that house goods intended for export."[21]

An Emerging European City

The town's growth was spurred by the "protection" of some Moroccan citizens by foreign powers—a system initiated by the Spanish-Moroccan agreement signed in 1861 whereby such beneficiaries no longer had to answer to the *Makhzen** (the sultan's administration). This system, which effectively kindled loyalty toward each protector state, was widely developed in Casablanca.[22] Additionally, the 1864 mission undertaken by the British philanthropist Moses Montefiore prompted many Jews to migrate from the hinterland to the Atlantic ports, Casablanca in particular.[23]

Many rural-based Muslims were also driven to the town by famine and the promise of work, constructing huts outside the town walls on their arrival. Somewhat surprisingly, though, shops set up as early as 1830 by important Fassi families were slow to develop and totaled no more than twenty by 1907.[24] In 1876, the French consul registered "around thirty completed or practically completed major buildings granted by the Makhzen to European merchants."[25] The formerly predominant French populace was now neck and neck with the Germans and had even been outstripped by the Spanish, who constituted the largest colony until 1907,[26] though growth was cut short by outbreaks of cholera and fever in 1878 and 1879.

Several late-nineteenth-century descriptions paint intimate portraits of the town. In 1878, the British botanist Joseph Dalton Hooker commented that it was "owing to the French merchants" that the "handful of white dwellings" conveyed a certain prestige, but nevertheless considered it "difficult to envisage a less attractive place than Casablanca."[27] Ten years later, the Belgian officer Auguste Lahure reported coming across a "godforsaken hole that has no signs of life." Nonetheless, it shone forth brightly when viewed from the sea thanks to "the layer of whitewash that reigns throughout the whole of Islam" and which "covers the entire town, composed of houses, monuments, crenelated walls, and towers."[28] In his *Nouvelle géographie universelle*, Élysée Reclus sums up these observations, likening Casablanca to a "European coastal settlement" and declaring it to be "desolate and extremely unhealthy."[29]

Again in the late nineteenth century, German journalist Gerhard Rohlfs affirmed, "The town has important trade links with Europe, but is so well positioned and boasts such a bounteous hinterland that it is to be wondered why its development has not been even more pronounced."[30] As for British-born Walter Harris, he deemed it "of but little interest and, comparatively modern" in that it is "clean, nicely laid out and half European in appearance"; its importance, he said, "is owing principally to the fact that there are many Europeans there, engaged in trade."[31] In 1904, Paul Mohr, another German, wrote that it was "the largest commercial town [in Morocco] and home to the greatest number of Europeans after Tangiers."[32]

---

20 Beaumier, quoted in Jean-Louis Miège and Eugène Hugues, *Les Européens à Casablanca au XIXème siècle (1856–1906)*: Institut des Hautes Études Marocaines: Notes et documents 14 (Paris: Librairie Larose, 1954), 214. See the more pessimistic contemporary description in James Richardson, *Travels in Morocco* (London: Charles J. Skeet, 1860), 17–128.

21 J. Gilbert, "Note sur la province de Chaouia," *Bulletin de la Société de Géographie* 13 (March 1867): 326–27. Gilbert recalls past destruction, which he blames on "a prince named El-Kheer, who came from Sudan at the head of well-armed legions." Ibid., 326.

22 In 1909, 5,300 Europeans "protected" 18,000 Moroccans in the Chaouia region. On this system for granting privileges, see Leland Louis Bowie, "The Protégé System in Morocco 1880–1904" (Thesis, University of Michigan, 1970).

23 Between 1856 and 1866, the Jewish population grew from 500 to 1,800. Coming from Tangiers and Rabat, as well as from Algeria, their numbers grew to 5,000 (one-quarter of the total population) by 1900. Miège and Hugues, *Les Européens à Casablanca*.

24 Adam, *Histoire de Casablanca*, 100–101; and Roger Le Tourneau, *Fès avant le Protectorat, étude économique et sociale d'une ville de l'occident musulman* (Casablanca: Société marocaine de librairie et d'édition, 1949), 445.

25 Sultan Moulay Hassan's 1876 visit to the city was indicative of the importance of the European presence at the time. Adam, *Histoire de Casablanca*, 97.

26 The overall population grew from 4,000 in 1866 to 8,000 in 1878; 14,000 in 1890; and 24,000 in 1905. Miège and Hugues, *Les Européens à Casablanca au XIXe siècle*, 20–36. The Spaniards came from the south, most notably from Andalusia.

27 Joseph Dalton Hooker and John Ball, *Journal of a tour in Morocco and the great Atlas* (London: Macmillan and Co., 1878), 67–68. Ten years later, Hugh Stutfield remarked, "Dar el Beida is not an interesting place, but it is one of the most important on the coast from a commercial point of view." Hugh Stutfield, *El Maghreb: 1200 miles' ride through Marocco* (London: Sampson Low, Marston, Searle and Rivington, 1886), 194.

28 Colonel Baron Auguste Lahure, *Lettres d'Afrique Maroc et Sahara Occidental* (Brussels: Oscar Lamberty, 1905), 29.

29 Élysée Reclus, *Nouvelle géographie universelle, la terre et les hommes* (Paris: Hachette, 1886), 11: 753.

30 Gerhard Rohlfs, "Casablanca und der Deutsche Neumann," *Deutsche Rundschau für Geographie und Statistik* 17, no. 4 (November 1895): 156.

31 Walter B. Harris, *The Land of an African Sultan: Travels in Morocco 1887, 1888, and 1889* (London: Sampson Low, Marston, Searle, and Rivington, 1889), 254.

32 Paul Mohr, "Casablanca in Marokko," *Deutsche Rundschau für Geographie und Statistik* 27, no. 2 (November 1904): 71. Miège and Hugues note the preponderance of southern French and the virtual absence of Algerian French in the population before 1909. Miège and Hugues, *Les Européens à Casablanca*, 46. The British were often Gibraltarians of Spanish origin—a trajectory illustrated by the Lapeen (La Peña) family evoked in this study. For a comparison of Casablanca's rate of growth with that of other coastal cities, see *Les Européens à Casablanca*, 36.

Spanish army surveyors, plan of Casablanca, 1895.

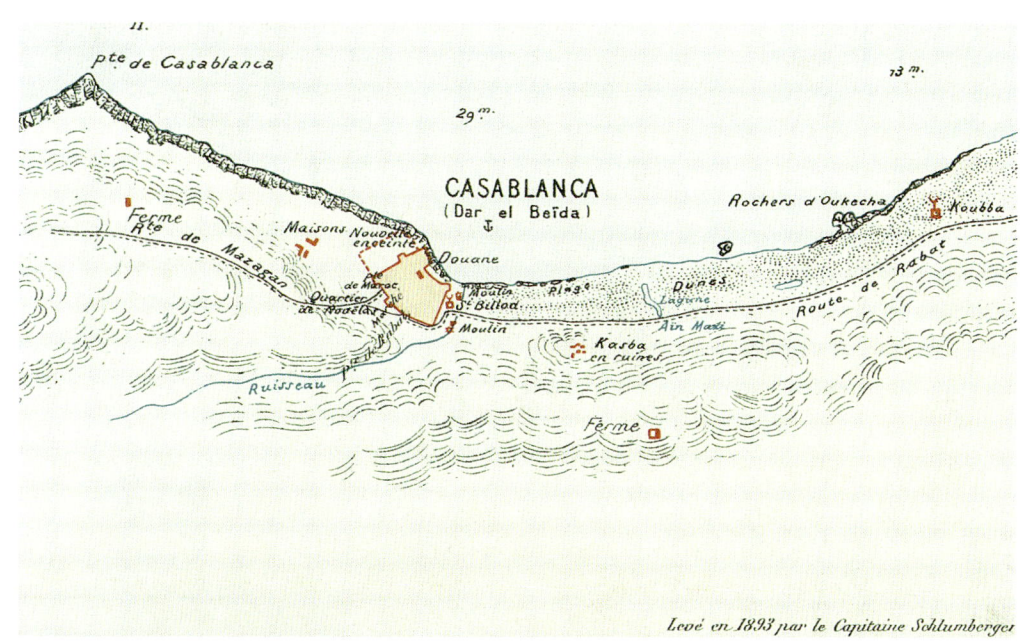

Captain Schlumberger, plan of Casablanca and harbor, 1893.

33 Dr. Félix Weisgerber, *Trois mois de campagne au Maroc, étude géographique de la région parcourue* (Paris: Ernest Leroux, 1904), 21.

34 Charles Penz and Roger Coindreau, *Le Maroc: Maroc français, Maroc espagnol, Tanger* (Paris: Société d'éditions géographiques, maritimes et coloniales, 1949), 126.

35 Jacques Ladreit de Lacharrière, "L'œuvre française en Chaouia," *Renseignements Coloniaux et documents publiés par le comité de l'Afrique Française et le comité du Maroc* 20, no. 9 (September 1910): 264.

36 Captain Schlumberger, "Notes sur les ports de la côte atlantique du Maroc" (Rabat, May 1893, Service historique de la Marine, Vincennes, BB4, carton 2458, dossier 4, 14). This document is discussed in F. Gendre, "Les plans de Casablanca," *Revue de géographie marocaine* (May 1939): 236; and Jean-Louis Miège, "Deux plans inédits de Casablanca à la fin du XIXe siècle," *Notes marocaines*, no. 3 (1953): 1–2.

37 Weisgerber spent a year in the city in 1897, before going to court to treat the Grand Vizier Bâ Ahmed. He recounts his adventures in Weisgerber, "En campagne avec l'armée chérifienne; notes de voyage d'un médecin du Grand Vizir," *L'Illustration* no. 3134 (March 21, 1903): 178–82. On doctors' role as scouts, before 1907, see James Albert Paul, "Professionals and Politics in Morocco: A Historical Study of the Mediation of Power and the Creation of Ideology in the Context of European Imperialism," (Ph.D. diss., New York University, 1975): 101–6.

Interior view of the city, in *L'Illustration*, 1907.

Casablanca Circa 1900— A "Picturesque" but "Squalid" Town

Whereas Casablanca appears somewhat forbidding and hostile from the sea, it could not present a more welcoming picture to those traveling from inland. Its leafy gardens are topped by willowy palm trees, crenelated walls, flat roofs, and whitewashed minarets dazzling in the African sun; all this offers a striking backdrop against the deep blue of the natural haven that cradles svelte yachts and burly black and red steamboats.

Félix Weisgerber, 1904[33]

For many years, the French peddled the condescending image of a "dilapidated port . . . set beside a pitiful vegetating town," seeking to underscore Casablanca's "miraculous" development under the Protectorate.[34] The "disappointment" experienced by travelers was underlined as early as 1910 by Jacques Ladreit de Lacharrière:

All that can be seen is a jumble of white houses on flat land edging a treeless region—a site that bears none of the customary attractive features of Arab towns. Only a few minarets stand out here and there against the sky, together with a few masts heralding the flapping consulate flags, which make the town look like the Arab section of a colonial exhibition.[35]

To Lacharrière's mind, "Casablanca is no town in the Moroccan sense of the term," unlike Rabat, Tétouan, and Fès, but rather "a stopping place along the Fès-Marrakech road, a sort of Casbah analogous with Bouznika or Fédala, whose role as a major center of trade is due solely to its geographic position." The land survey conducted in 1893 by Schlumberger, a captain in the French navy, conveys the image of a compact "middling" town, clipped onto the coastal rocks and joined to the land by two dirt tracks.[36]

A Tripartite Settlement

Despite the above accounts, the finely detailed plan drawn up by Weisgerber in 1900 nevertheless clearly reveals the layout of an actual town.[37] Weisgerber produced carefully measured drawings accompanied by a number of openly racist comments:

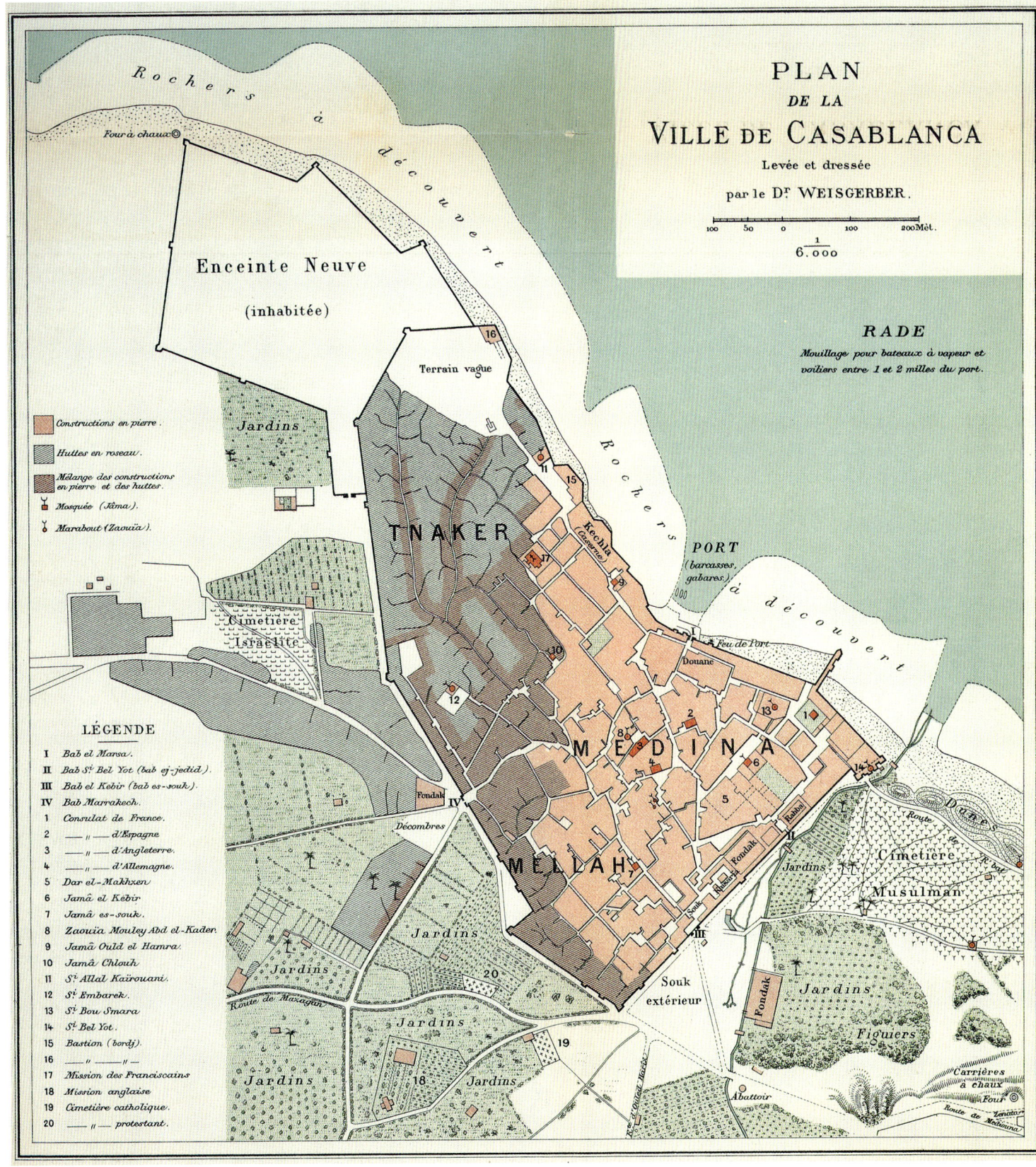

Dr. Félix Weisgerber, plan of Casablanca (Algiers, 1900).

View of the mellah (postcard, c. 1912).

A *noualla,* or straw hut, in the Tnaker neighborhood (postcard, c. 1910).

38 Weisgerber, *Trois mois de campagne au Maroc*, 22.

39 Weisgerber, *Trois mois de campagne au Maroc*, 23. In an early use of the notion in Francophone literature, the word *médina* (a generic term signifying "city" in Arabic) is used in a restrictive fashion here to denote the dense area inhabited by Muslims. On the structure of Moroccan and North African cities, see Le Tourneau, *Fès avant le Protectorat*; and, although Morocco was never part of the Ottoman Empire, André Raymond, *Grandes villes arabes à l'époque ottomane* (Paris: Sindbad, 1985).

40 This was one of six "secondary conditions" described in the eleventh century by Al Mawardi and cited in André Chouraqui, *La condition juridique de l'Israélite marocain* (Paris: Presse du livre français, 1950), 51.

Like most oriental towns, Casablanca is not what it makes itself out to be. On entering one of its four gates, the visitor encounters a tangled web of streets lined with banal houses that are neither Spanish nor Moorish in style. One's eye is greeted by pitiful shop booths, reed huts, and sheds crammed with grain, animal skins, and wool transported by caravan from inland sites. Filled with dust in summer and fetid black mud during the rainy season, many of these constructions resemble nothing other than refuse-strewn pigsties.[38]

According to Weisgerber's plan, the polygonal area occupied by the town measured barely fifty hectares and was girded by a crenelated wall peppered with square towers standing between eight and eleven meters high. This wall rose up against the shoreline, which it bordered for approximately a thousand meters before branching out to the southeast, embracing three of the town's constituent parts, namely the medina, the mellah, and the *Tnaker** quarter.

Though described by Lahure as the "aristocratic" district, according to Weisgerber the medina "boasts neither prestigious Moorish dwellings nor artistic monuments," and "the mosques, marabouts, and Moorish baths of *Dar-el-Makhzen** are the most basic of structures."[39] Although Weisgerber noted that the mellah was not "as strictly contained as in most Moroccan towns," the Jewish population did not escape their condition of *dhimmi*, i.e., protégés of the Muslim community, as prescribed in the Koran for the "People of the Book." The protection codes notably stated that *dhimmi* "must not build their houses higher than Muslim ones," nor must their synagogues "rise above the minarets and mosques."[40] The mellah, composed of brightly colored stone houses, was lined with *nouallas* (straw huts) that covered practically the entire Tnaker and spilled out beyond the western wall, among the cemeteries and gardens skirting the town.

A Drab and Dreary Site

At the time, the wall of the town was pierced by four main gates: *Bab** el-Mersa on the seafront, Bab el-Kebir (or Bab es-Souk) and Bab sidi Belyout (or Bab ej-Jdid) on the east, and Bab Marrakech on the west. It also had two ancillary gates. To the north of the town lay the empty enclosure of Sour-ej-Jdid, built in 1892 by Moulay Hassan to house European settlements, although the designated residents considered it too far from their workplaces; instead, it served occasionally as an encamp-

The city wall on the seaside. Photographed in 1995.

Bab es-Souk, c. 1907, in *Le Tour du Monde,* 1911.

41 Schlumberger notes, "Unfortunately, the location is poorly chosen, on marshy terrain, and hardly tempts future occupants." Schlumberger, "Notes sur les ports," 14.

42 Georges Bourdon, *Ce que j'ai vu au Maroc: les journées de Casablanca* (Paris: Pierre Lafitte, 1908), 112.

43 Reginald Rankin, *In Morocco with General d'Amade* (London: Longmans, Green, 1908), 239–340.

44 This market was lauded by Paul Mohr in "Casablanca in Marokko," 77–78.

45 S. L. Bensusan, *Morocco* (London: Adam & Charles Black, 1904), 24.

ment zone.[41] Following the French landings in 1907, Georges Bourdon sorrowfully described the town's "squalid carapace." In the vein of Louis-Sébastien Mercier describing eighteenth-century Paris, he strongly warned those tourists who "have a love of beauty and suave fragrances" against the town's "repugnant filth" and "seedy quarters":

> O thin pale crest edging the horizon of a yellow land, you resemble a worm warming itself in the sun. Flat and monotonous, sprawled like a dab against the flat landscape, one has to come close to perceive you clearly. Slumped in a hill-less setting, the minarets of your mosques, the ridges of your miradors, and the platforms of your terraces jut out jaggedly against the silver sky, revealing nothing but a sawtooth facade. You are devoid of grace, Casablanca. You evoke neither the languid voluptuousness of Tunis or Bône, nor the stark majesty of Kairouan. You seem alien to this land of Islam, for which you serve as front sentry, though you might well be the rear guard.[42]

Casablanca's bland features continued to be invoked throughout the Protectorate, accompanied by development proposals. However, Reginald Rankin, correspondent for the *London Times*, drew parallels between Casablanca and "those towns that form the backdrop to Massacio paintings," to the point of seeing a reincarnation of Dante's Florence "when the crowd gathers in celebration of the Aid, clad in their dazzling green, pink, blue and orange djellabas, splashed with crimson here and there."[43]

Two main markets served as the trading place for agricultural produce harvested in the Chaouia region. The smaller of these (*Jutiya**) stood inside the city, in Bab el-Kebir square, while the larger one lay outside the gates, along Wadi Bouskoura.[44] In 1904, the British traveler S. L. Bensusan wrote in disgust about the "muddy lanes whose rickety paving stones barely cover up the drains," though he also asserted that the town's market offered "as oriental an image as any Westerner might wish to see."[45] In addition, there was the grain market (*er-Rah'ba**), located beside Bab sidi Belyout. The medina's main street formed the hub of European life, diagonally linking Bab es-Souk with Bab el-Mersa, passing by the Place du Commerce near the customs office. Even today, the *Jama-el-kebir** in Rue Dar-el-Makhzen still forms the largest mosque in the medina, although as Weisgerber pointed out, "The mosque bearing the most finely detailed architecture" was the *Jama-ould-el-hamra*,* situated next to the *Kechla** (army barracks) on Rue de la Marine, bordering the walls along the sea. The tomb of Sidi Belyout, protector of

The Jutiya, c. 1914.

Jama-el-kebir mosque, 1915.

Sidi Kairouâni Qubba, c. 1915, in *Villes et tribus du Maroc* (Paris, 1915).

46 André Adam dates the current construction to 1881. Adam, *Casablanca*, 1:34.

47 Émile Lapeyre and E. Marchand, *Casablanca, la Chaouia* (Paris: Larose, 1918), 94.

48 E. Déchaud, "Une croisière de reconnaissance commerciale au Maroc," *Renseignements coloniaux et documents publiés par le comité de l'Afrique française* 14, no. 4 (April 1904): 111. As of 1890, the building industry also became more structured. Miège and Hugues, *Les Européens à Casablanca*, 91.

49 Rankin, *In Morocco with General d'Amade*, 226.

50 Paul Azan, *Souvenirs de Casablanca* (Paris: Hachette, 1911), 107.

51 Rankin, *In Morocco with General d'Amade*, 218–19.

52 Lahure, *Lettres d'Afrique*, 35.

53 A. Henri Dyé, "Les ports du Maroc," *Bulletin de la Société de Géographie commerciale de Paris* 30 (May–June 1908), 194–95.

54 De Chaisemartin, "Perspective de recherche," 15–34.

An entrance door in the medina, 1915.

Casablanca, lies in the southeast corner of the town[46] while the *kissaria*,* an indoor cloth market, sat beside Bab el-Kebir.

*Fonduks**—large, rectangular courtyards girded by high walls, containing housing and shops—sprang up on the town's outskirts.[47] Industrial buildings were erected in the late nineteenth century with the first steam mill set up by the American John Cobb, followed by a German-owned soap factory, a tobacco plant that opened in 1900, water bottling factories and buildings for carpet manufacturing.[48] The consulates of the major European powers, i.e., France, Germany, England, and Spain, took up residence in the medina (where the Franciscans constructed a church consecrated in 1891), while the Protestant North Africa Mission set up its premises south of the town. Following an outbreak of cholera in 1878, the European consuls launched a program to develop a basic street-cleaning service and a sewage system, which they put in place in 1884 and 1888.

Public buildings opened in the 1890s, including the Spanish Franciscan school, the French-speaking Alliance Israélite Universelle, the Spanish Circle, and the Anfa International Club, instituted in 1894. This last was "a building constructed in the time-honored Moorish style, containing a glazed courtyard colored with bright Rabat tiles; this courtyard is flanked by game- and reading-rooms, where daily news is discussed in all the languages of Babel."[49] In 1909, Paul Azan remarked that the club had no French members, despite it being "tastefully decorated " and "very well laid out."[50] Like the Germans, the French nationals preferred to set up their own associations. Apart from three tennis courts and a polo ground on the town's outskirts, leisure pursuits were rare in this already "cosmopolitan" town, as termed by Rankin, who deplored the fact that it lacked a race course, that cricket and football were unknown, and that plans for a golf course had been stymied by the war.[51]

Houses and Gardens

Traces of elegantly decorated door surrounds testify to the fact that Muslim dignitaries lived in luxury dwellings, although no description of the interiors has been handed down to us. An interesting exception, however, is Lahure's depiction of the Dar-el-Makhzen (house of the caid, or sultan's representative), in the east of the medina: "The house and verandah with Moorish arches sit at the back of a large courtyard shaded by groves of locust and palm trees. There are green slatted blinds and fine rugs adorning the flagstones and cushions on which the Caid reclines in dignified fashion, with the Cadi and two other swanky Arabs at his side."[52] Lahure also refers to the house of Xantopoulos, a Greek merchant from Dakar: "a pretty [dwelling], built in a Moorish and Spanish style, with a patio or inner courtyard in its center." He points out the "picturesque" quality of the more modest dwellings belonging to the various population groups and notes that those houses with balconies were owned by Jews or Europeans. Yet according to the French navy hydrographer A. Henri Dyé, "The patio houses peppered randomly in the tangled web of streets are characterless." With their paved inner courtyards, Dyé said, these houses looked exactly the same as those in Seville, Cadiz, and Malaga. He apparently searched in vain for "fine examples of Moorish houses" in this chaos of disparate buildings.[53] It is true that the medina's urban fabric is an assembly of several generations of building types. There are cubelike houses dating from the first half of the nineteenth century; these are folded back around patios and can occasionally be singled out by the design of their street-facing entrance door.[54] Then there are Mediterranean house types such as hotels and low-rise apartment blocks with balconies, as well as merchants' dwellings comprising storage rooms on the ground floor. According to Rankin, "The town's European houses are better than might be expected," since modern building methods had been used in some cases: "Several

Benjelloun house, junction of Rue de la Marine and Rue de Larache, 1896. View of the main room. Photographed in 1997.

The Rue de Mogador in the medina. Photographed in 1999.

Jews have built huge apartment blocks which would not be out of place in Tübingen or in the suburbs of Cologne. They contain a number of fine apartments furnished in the Stuttgart and Bremen style, with sweeping views of the port."[55]

As early as the sixteenth century, Johannes Leo Africanus had pointed out the abundance of gardens around Anfa.[56] In 1893, the Protestant mission set up a farm, and a German-born merchant named Neumann purchased a smallholding one league outside town and initiated suburban development.[57] Harris speaks of "large private gardens, prettily laid out, some belonging to natives and a few to Europeans" that bordered the town.[58] Adopting a similar vein, Mohr refers to the "heavenly profusion" of gardens owned by Europeans and the "wondrous" vineyards of some Muslims. In 1908, Rankin noted, "His garden is the chief interest of the consul or merchant at Casablanca, for, in that land of glare, the sight of a tree and the cool dark shadows beneath its branches are even more precious to the Englishman or to the German than they are to the Moor." Drawing particular attention to those belonging to Mr. Lamb and to Edmund Fernau, he noted that these contained features that were more Italian than Andalusian.[59] And as a final anecdote, revealing the scarcity of planted areas, in 1909, Captain Azan remarked that there was such a shortage of timber that the whole of Chaouia could have been purchased in return for the wood used in the French military camps.[60]

The French Invasion—A Predictable Happening

Behind me lay the crescent-shaped bay in all its blue luminosity, harboring thirty smoldering moored ships. On my right was the port where I had landed; on my left stood huge piles of packages and crates topped by the steel frames of a huge dock. I looked out, overwhelmed, to the horizon, but my view was obstructed by Casablanca's ramparts, those reddish, tawny-hued walls of a feudal city standing some thirty feet high, composed of adobe and rubble stone pierced with loopholes and slits. Through these could be glimpsed a chaotic jumble of dwellings made up of dazzling white and bright blue cubes—dwellings belonging to the Arab and Jewish people, the first settlers in this land.

Émile Nolly, 1915[61]

The development of steamships caused estuary ports such as Rabat-Salé to become redundant, and provided the perfect opportunity for Casablanca to take center stage. Hence, by 1906 it had become Morocco's busiest port, outstripping even Tangiers. Nonetheless, access to this "harborless port," as Casablanca was known, was by no means easy.[62] Furthermore, boats were often grounded at low tide in the fifty-meter-wide naval dock adjacent to Bab el-Mersa.

Difficult Coastal Access

Casablanca's poor port facilities made unloading goods and passengers an enterprise rather akin to acrobatics, even in the most favorable weather conditions. The situation was much worse, though, whenever storms hit the coast, since very few craft could approach the shore due to the high breakers.[63] Weisgerber noted, "In bad weather, especially in winter, the town is frequently cut off for several days in a row, and ships often have to turn back into the open sea to avoid being run aground on the razor-sharp reefs lining the coast."[64] The port was further congested by a lack of unloading craft—a consequence of the Makhzen monopoly.

In 1910, Lacharrière commented that ships would sometimes remain "in the harbor for thirty or forty days." He also underlined the fact that the town's access road "passes through a narrow gate, continually clogged by two-way traffic. In addi-

---

[55] Rankin, *In Morocco with General d'Amade*, 225.

[56] Leo Africanus, *Description de l'Afrique*, 1:11.

[57] Rohlfs, "Casablanca und der Deutsche Neumann," 156.

[58] Harris, *The Land of an African Sultan*, 254.

[59] Rankin, *In Morocco with General d'Amade*, 219.

[60] Azan, *Souvenirs de Casablanca*, 15.

[61] Nolly, *Le conquérant*, 27.

[62] Adam, *Casablanca*, 14.

[63] Henri Croze, *Souvenirs du vieux Maroc* (Paris: Éditions des Deux Mondes, 1952), 16, 46–49.

[64] Dr. Félix Weisgerber, "Études géographiques sur le Maroc, 1. La province de Chaouia, 2. Casablanca," *Bulletin de la Société de Géographie de Paris* 1 (1st semester, 1900): 448.

Bab el-Mersa, in Otto C. Artbauer, *Kreuz und quer durch Marokko* (Stuttgart, 1911).

tion, the warehouses are cramped, causing crates and goods of all shapes and sizes to be piled up in the streets, hindering circulation."65 As a buzzing commercial town, Casablanca was flooded with agricultural produce during good harvests, and "caravans weighted down with crops [came] to unload the earth's riches in huge warehouses." Two to three thousand camels would arrive daily, cluttering the town with "sacks of wheat, corn, chickpeas, and barley."66

In his report of 1893, Captain Schlumberger declared that constructing a port in Casablanca would prove difficult and extremely costly. He thus envisaged such a possibility only if "Europeans [settled] along the whole coast"67—a scenario that ended up becoming reality. This "most Moorish of seaports," to quote Bensusan, underwent initial redevelopment in 1904, when the Makhzen commissioned the Compagnie Marocaine to build a pier and two jetties to protect a small, twenty-hectare expanse of water from the swell.68 J. Renaud, chief engineer of the navy's hydrographic section, executed a design study in 1905 for "a small-scale port," as well as for a "powerful unloading device operated by barges and tugs."69 His scheme was for a polygonal basin, encompassing the naval port and a pier built by the Portuguese in 1850. The basin was to be protected by two 300-meter-long breakwaters set perpendicular to the shore.

Work got under way in May 1907, closely supervised by the French authorities.70 Although France had not obtained a Tunisian-type Protectorate, which led to

65 Ladreit de Lacharrière, "L'œuvre française en Chaouia," 351. The lengthy stay of the steamers in the harbor was due to the reduced number of small craft available: nine in 1909.

66 Lahure, *Lettres d'Afrique*, 29. Dessigny confirmed this situation, "which did considerable damage to commerce and cleanliness in the town." Commandant Dessigny, "Casablanca, notice économique et administrative," *Bulletin de la Société de géographie d'Alger et d'Afrique du nord*, 16 (3rd trimester, 1911): 317.

67 Schlumberger, "Notes sur les ports," 18.

68 The Compagnie Marocaine was set up by Schneider in April 1902, after the purchase of the Gautsch company, which had been long established in Morocco. Gaston de Caqueray, *Note pour l'histoire de Casablanca et de son port* (Paris: Publications du Comité de l'Afrique Française, 1937), 5–12; and Pierre Guillen, "Les milieux d'affaires français et le Maroc à l'aube du XXe siècle: la fondation de la Compagnie Marocaine," *Revue Historique* 229 (April–June 1963): 397–422.

69 J. Renaud, "À propos du port de Casablanca" (letter to the editor), *L'Afrique française* 20, no. 12 (December 1910): 392.

70 The port's construction was supervised by Michel Schmidt, a graduate of the *École centrale*, one of France's foremost civil engineering schools.

71 On Moroccan reactions, see Edmond Burke III, *Prelude to Protectorate in Morocco; Precolonial Protest and Resistance, 1860–1912* (Chicago and London: University of Chicago Press, 1976).

72 In a meticulous account of the "incidents," the writer Georges Bourdon highlights neighboring tribes' desire for plundering the "rich and abundant city," the "diamond of the Chaouia." At the same time, he emphasizes the desire for adventure among the officers of the *Galilée*. Bourdon, *Ce que j'ai vu au Maroc,* 16–20.

Moroccan trade being handed over to the Europeans, under the Act of Algesiras, the agreement clearly stipulated that a French inspector be appointed to ensure that customs officials collected commodities, securing the loan granted in 1904 to the Makhzen. It likewise specified that port facilities needed to be improved.[71] Around four hundred workers were hired for the task, and a narrow-gauge Decauville railroad was laid to supply the building site with aggregate from the Ain Mazi quarry east of the town. The patronizing manner in which the French handled the customs office, combined with their ruthless and sacrilegious act of running the railroad through the Muslim cemetery, churning up piles of bones, sparked off an angry reaction by the Chaouia tribes.[72]

The 1907 Military Campaign

On July 30, 1907, nine European laborers were killed in an attack against the *Babor* (*Babor,* or vapor in Spanish, was a popular term for the steam locomotive carrying building materials for the port, and a symbol of the foreign invasion). The French responded immediately by dispatching their *Galilée* battleship on August 5 from Tangiers to Casablanca, carrying a landing party under the command of Sub-

The derailed locomotive and scene of attack that served as a pretext for the French landings of August 1907.

The mellah after looting in August 1907, in *L'Illustration,* 1907.

Plan of the land troop movements on August 19, 1907, in *L'Illustration*, 1907.

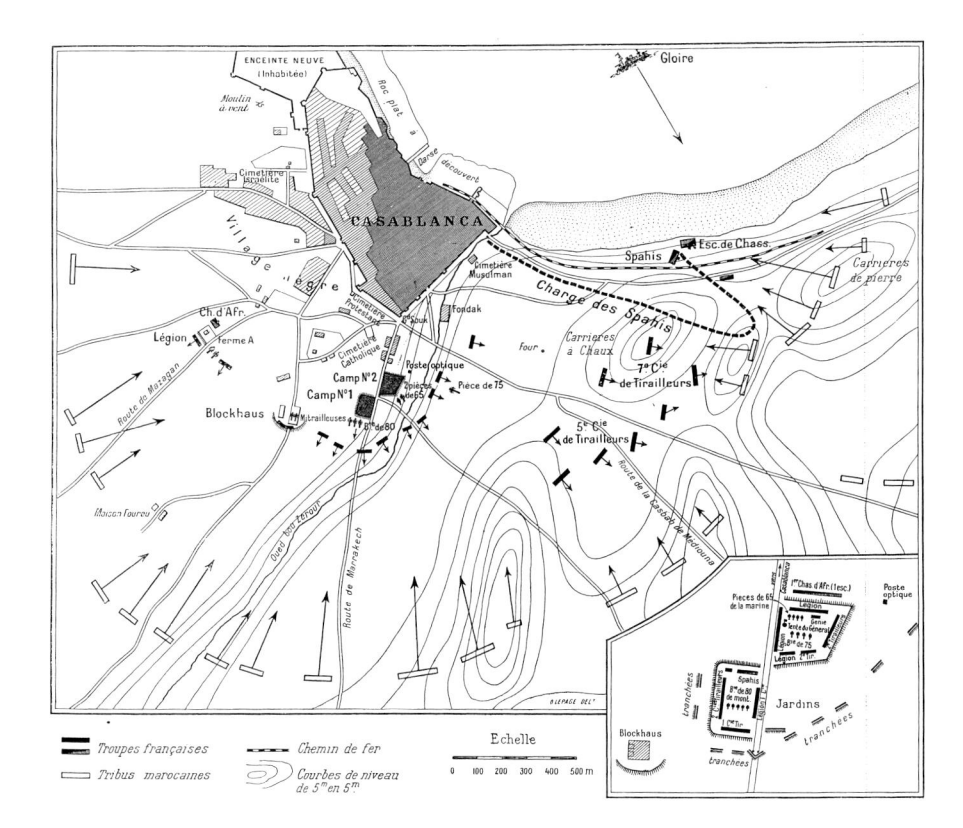

Lieutenant Ballande.[73] Yet in fact, ever since 1905, the French army had been toying with the idea of establishing a bridgehead on the Atlantic coast, since pressure exerted by the navy on the northern shore adjacent to Algeria had not in any way intimidated the Makhzen.[74] The troops proceeded to bombard Casablanca from the ship, provoking a violent reaction from the tribes and triggering pillage and arson, targeted mainly at European dwellings and the mellah.[75]

On August 7, more troops were brought in, led by General Drude and Major Mangin, and they took firm control of the town.[76] The combined effects of pillage and bombing, "conducted to a high degree of perfection,"[77] resulted in extensive damage to the medina, a fifth of which was burnt. The victims (at least 600 and possibly even as many as 1,500) were Jews and Muslims for the most part. Drude subsequently encircled Casablanca with defense forces and organized forays into the neighboring region. General D'Amade's column carried on the slaughter into early 1908, drawing on numerous troops and heavy artillery, with the result that Chaouia was crushed by a sort of deadly spinning top, as described by Daniel Rivet.[78]

The French authorities took hold of the reins again, and "the world's most fertile agricultural region grew prosperous once more." On June 7, 1908, troops filed past "on the slope leading to the shore." D'Amade glimpsed "the very soul of France . . . in this magnificent setting composed of tawny hills, a sea dotted with ships and a white town resplendent with gardens."[79] The entire venture was presented as one that aimed to "bring wealth and civilization to Morocco" and was recounted in all French bourgeois families. Jules Chancel wrote an epic volume in his series *Les enfants à travers l'histoire*, in which the events of 1907 are related through the eyes of Lulu, a young Parisian child.[80] Having entered the annals of patriotic literature for all ages, Casablanca became a familiar name throughout Europe, thus partly explaining the rather unexpected waves of immigration.

[73] Adam, *Histoire de Casablanca*, 103–35.

[74] Note of the Ministère de la Guerre, August 27, 1905, quoted in Douglas Porch, *The Conquest of Morocco* (New York: Knopf, 1983), 149. The French held maneuvers outside Tangiers in December 1906 and occupied Oujda in April 1907. Alfred Le Châtelier writes of the "methodical provocation" of the French in "Au Maroc, la politique nécessaire," *La Revue bleue* 10 (1908): 419.

[75] In November 1907, Alexandre Ribot declared to the *Chambre des députés*, "It is unfortunate that the *Galilée* was so hasty in unloading those sixty heroes who crossed the beach." Alexandre Ribot, *Journal Officiel de la République française* (November 13, 1907). The landing's premeditation is vaunted in the memoires of the diplomat who conducted the operations from Tangiers. Auguste Félix Charles de Beaupoil, Comte de Saint-Aulaire, *Confession d'un vieux diplomate* (Paris: Flammarion, 1953), 173–86.

[76] An illustrated account of the conflict was serialized in *L'Illustration*. "Les événements du Maroc, à Casablanca," *L'Illustration*, no. 3363 (August 10, 1907): 83–85; and "Les événements du Maroc," *L'Illustration*, no. 3364 (August 17, 1907): 98–101. See also André Adam, "Sur l'action du Galilée à Casablanca en août 1907," *Revue de l'Occident Musulman et de la Méditerranée* 6 (1st and 2nd semester, 1969): 9–22.

[77] Bourdon, *Ce que j'ai vu au Maroc*, 109.

[78] Rivet, *Lyautey et l'institution du Protectorat français*, 1:55. On this campaign see General D'Amade, *Campagne de 1908–1909 en Chaouia*, ed. Captain Broussaud, (Paris: R. Chapelot, 1911); Captain Alphonse-Louis Grasset, *À travers la Chaouia* (Paris: Hachette, 1912), a report serialized under the title "Journal du corps de débarquement de Casablanca à travers la Chaouia," in *Le Tour du Monde* (April–May 1911); Rankin, *In Morocco with General d'Amade*; and Azan, *Souvenirs de Casablanca*.

[79] D'Amade, *Campagne de 1908–1909 en Chaouia*, 160.

[80] Jules Chancel, *Lulu au Maroc*, illustrated by L. Bombled (Paris: C. Delagrave, 1913). Among other feats, Lulu fires the first shot from the *Galilée*'s cannon.

French infantry encampment south of Casablanca, August 1907.

Military Rule and Creative Developers

Deals were done on the terrace of the Roi de la bière *café. Casablanca had turned into a dive. Brokers with maps in their pockets went around each table proposing various plots for sale. There was incredible overbidding. For instance, land in Edmond Doutté square in Rue Lassalle, which could not even sell for two francs a meter in 1910, now fetched twenty to thirty francs ... At each crossroads there were large panels displaying land subdivisions, such as those of Fayolle (Boulevard Leclerc), Comptoir Lorrain, the Nathan brothers (Rue de Briey, Rue de Nancy, and Boulevard de Lorraine), Mers-Sultan, Haim Cohen, Racine, Oasis, Anfa-Supérieure, and Roches Noires.*

Christian Houel, 1954[81]

Once the hostilities had ended, Mangin ordered soldiers and prisoners to set about clearing up the debris.[82] He also wrote out an inventory of ransacked goods and ensured that all stolen objects were replaced. As early as the summer of 1907, Mangin expressed concern about the running of the town, given that the Makhzen had no "available funds."[83] The French built several army facilities, both as part of the landings operation and to control clashes with neighboring tribes, which continued for several months; some of these structures would, in fact, remain standing until independence. For instance, army tents and reed houses that had been erected by Drude in the south of the town were reinforced, and two forts were built using existing buildings; one overlooked the Route de Mediouna and was named in tribute to Major Provost, while the other, along the road to Marrakech, was dedicated to Captain Ihler. They stood five meters high, were built of stone to a square twenty-meter plan, and were girded by barbed wire. An army hospital and camp facilities were also constructed in the Sour ej-Jdid.[84]

France's territorial hold in Chaouia led to lengthy debate regarding Casablanca's destiny. In D'Amade's view, the town center clearly had a crucial role to play in terms of the turnaround in the relationship between Morocco and the north, which in reality had begun decades earlier[85]: "Casablanca's communication links with Marrakech and Fès, allied with its rich agricultural hinterland and the fact that it will soon constitute the country's sole Atlantic port, all point to the logic

81 Christian Houel, *Mes aventures marocaines* (Casablanca: Éditions Maroc-Demain, 1954), 234–35. Place names are those in use after 1945. The *Matin*'s reporter in Casablanca, Houel, was to create *La Vigie marocaine*.

82 A Spanish contingent was likewise stationed in Casablanca.

83 Commandant Mangin, "Note au commandant des troupes de débarquement," August 22, 1907, SHAT, carton 3H, 568.

84 The site was ceded by the sultan to the War Ministry on February 20, 1908. Chef de Bataillon Benoist, chef du Génie, Étude sur le domaine militaire de la chefferie du Génie de Casablanca, August 25, 1922, Archives du Génie, CDG Maroc, Carton 1. In fact, this land was kept as collateral by the Mendelssohn Bank, creditor of the Makhzen.

85 Jean-Louis Miège, M'hammad Benaboud, and Nadia Erzini, *Tétouan: ville andalouse marocaine* (Paris: CNRS Éditions, 1996), 74.

Provost and Ihler forts (postcard, c. 1908).

Geographic division of the French army, land survey of the medina, c. 1910. Note the location of the public garden in the northwest.

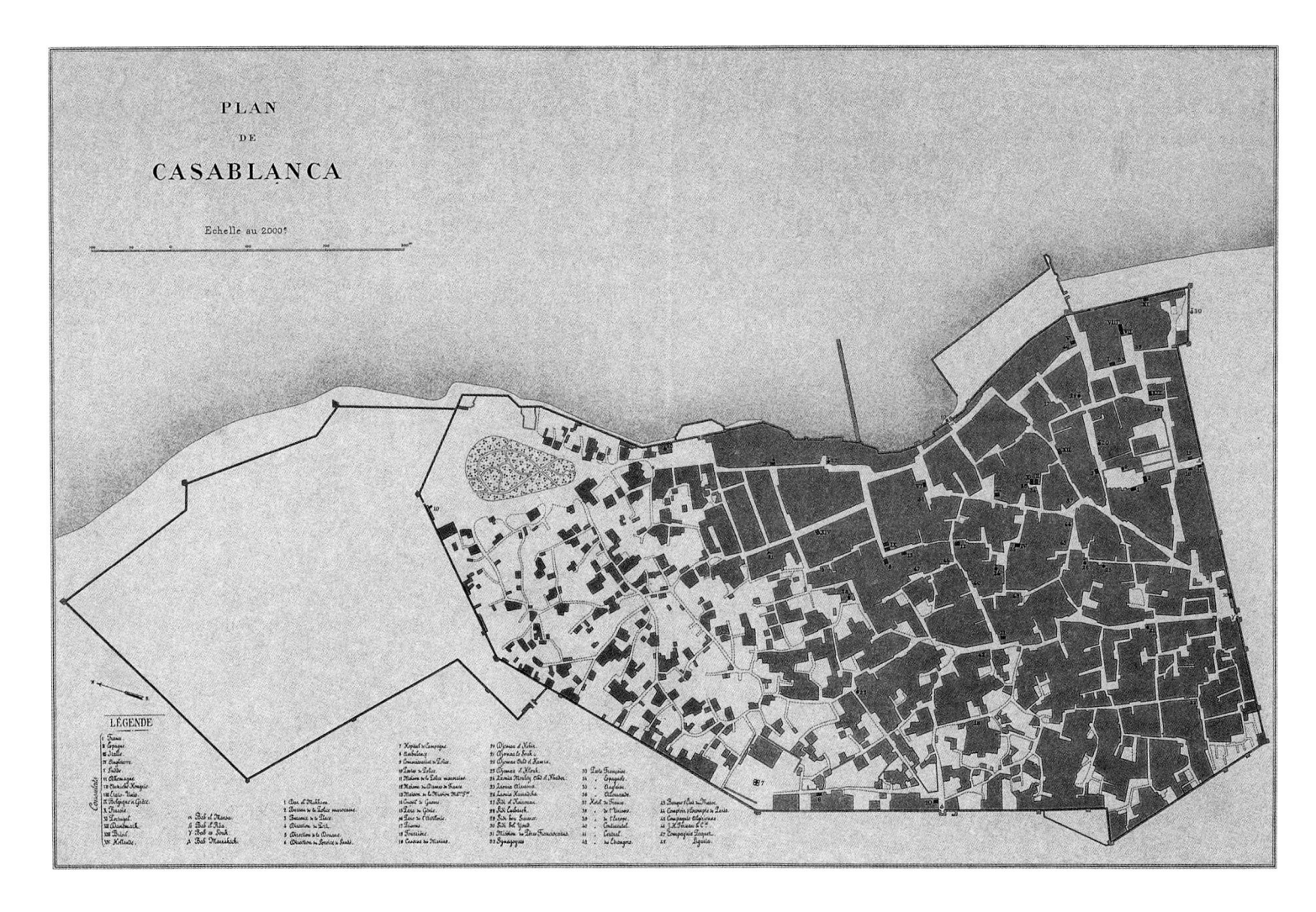

The city and the camps, photographed by Lieutenant Étévé from a hot-air balloon on March 23, 1910.

86 D'Amade, *Campagne de 1908–1909 en Chaouia*, 380.

87 General Moinier, "Note au Ministre de la Guerre," Fort Gurgens, April 17, 1909, SHAT, carton 3H 568. Moinier is, of course, referring to the presidios (enclaves in hostile territory) of Ceuta and Melilla.

88 D'Amade, *Campagne de 1908–1909 en Chaouia*, 280.

89 Otto C. Artbauer, *Kreuz und quer durch Marokko, Kultur- und Sittenbilder aus dem Sultanat des Westens* (Stuttgart: Strecker und Schröder, 1911), 102–4.

90 Azan, *Souvenirs de Casablanca*, 11, 106.

of it accommodating the country's largest railroad network. Indeed, this is an essential requirement in order for the town to cope with its already substantial level of trade, which is likely to attain vast proportions in the near future."[86] General Moinier, who replaced D'Amade in February 1909 as commander of the landing forces, was strongly against the idea of evacuating Chaouia and concentrating the population in one city center. Furthermore, he wondered whether Casablanca was not running the risk of "becoming a presidio similar to the one set up centuries ago by our neighbors on the Moroccan coast, from which they have never succeeded in extracting themselves."[87] The army, headed by General D'Amade, subsequently launched a firm agricultural colonization policy in Chaouia; each military detachment was allotted the task of collecting information about land ownership and drawing up "land registers" as a preliminary to a land survey. D'Amade pointed out that the French "possess enough financial resources . . . to make speculative purchases of land outside the towns, such as along the routes of future railroads, and to wait for these sites to gain added value."[88]

Military presence was strong in the south of the town as well as in the medina, where soldiers sought entertainment. In 1911, the German national Otto Artbauer denounced the French troops' aggressive attitude as well as their "cultural" activities, namely frequenting the many cafés that offered abundant supplies of "absinthe, Pernod, and Dutch gin," everything, in other words, "except coffee."[89] Mercié, the opera singer who had performed in front of European audiences up until 1907, was replaced by the Bijou-Concert, which in turn swiftly had as its neighbor the Parisiana-Bar, an "American bar" whose decor reminded Paul Azan of Maxim's and which had been set up by a "young man from Montmartre in Paris."[90] Cabarets sprang up under the famous banners of the Eden-concert and the Moulin-Rouge. Émile Nolly refers to a music hall attended just as much by the upper crust of Casablanca as by "the scum of the huge wave that has come crashing down on the shores of this new country": "Everyone, whether from Provence, Gascony, Lyons, or greater Paris, can be immediately recognized by their accent. Whether they be French, Italian, Spanish, Maltese, Greek, German, English, or Levantine, I can see unavowed anguish in them all, a feverish battle burning in their eyes, rendering their features taut and strained."⁹¹

As regards administrative issues, by far one of the most important steps taken by the French authorities was its decision in July 1908 to set up a public facilities department, headed by Captain Charles Dessigny, an intelligence expert.⁹² One of Dessigny's first initiatives was to take over the project launched by Mangin to install a drainage system. He also coordinated work on public hygiene, the road system, and policing; he developed port access thoroughfares, opened up routes through the city walls, created a two-hectare public garden, put in place lighting facilities, redeveloped the markets and the slaughterhouse, and instituted a municipal budget system. In so doing, he ensured "effective, judicious, and impartial"

91 Nolly, *Le conquérant*, 19–20.

92 Dessigny had served fifteen years in the *Service des Affaires indigènes d'Algérie*, most notably at Ain Sefra, where Lyautey had served. He was initially settled in a *cagibi* at the entrance to the medina.

Public garden; general view showing surrounding buildings, c. 1913.

A Bad Start for a City of Adventure 41

administration of the town.[93] Lieutenant Marie François Segonds describes the city as a "tidy, clean, and healthy" place, with sewers that were regularly "inspected and repaired." The roads were well laid out and lighting was seen to by soldiers who had taken on the "dual role of policemen and site supervisors."[94] These early alterations to the urban fabric fed literary accounts such as *L'Odyssée d'un écumeur*, by Marcel Frager, in which the action is set in "Darbeda, a friendly bustling port" whose gradual metamorphosis is compared to the changes in the "lascivious" nature of its inhabitants: "Just as ladies of pleasure became more exacting, acquiring a more elegant and refined air, the cafés adopted a semideluxe style, and a real auditorium was incorporated into the cinema-cum-concert hall. And so the town developed, its appearance taking on an increasingly European quality."[95]

Health Risks and Conflicts over Land Ownership

Public hygiene still posed a major problem, despite the construction of a health center and slaughterhouses for the Muslim and Jewish populations, as well as a new hospital set up by Doctor Henri de Rothschild in 1909, a year after arriving in Casablanca. Dessigny stressed the urgent need for a fresh water supply and a drainage system, stating that the streets, "paved in sea pebbles which are forever being dislodged," should be "made level" and "laid with sandstone."[96] In 1909, the army set about giving a more orderly visual structure to the medina by numbering the houses and marking the street names in French and Arabic at each crossroads. In addition, the "primitively narrow" lanes were widened by reclaiming the space "taken over by residents."[97]

Within this framework of economic growth and urban expansion, the issue of land ownership assumed a central role. As the town had been reconquered and rebuilt by the sultan during the eighteenth century, in 1907 a large part of the land in Dar el-Beida belonged to the Makhzen.[98] Corruption and mismanagement resulted in property becoming increasingly run-down. In August 1907, land prices started to climb, attaining levels almost on a par with Paris. Europeans and Muslims who owned plots outside the town (notably next to the souk) began to speculate, as did the Jewish population who had previously been authorized to engage in property transactions concerning only their own dwellings and were prevented from trading land. The army similarly became involved in land ownership issues, not only in order to retain control of their buildings, but also to clarify such matters as land ownership rights and property tax. In 1908, D'Amade suggested purchasing the land given over to the army camps "to avoid speculation surprises"; he also recommended that the town's European citizens be taxed and that a land register be drawn up to "determine land rights" (a move that would imply the sultan was in agreement). Lastly, he put forward the idea of setting up a French mortgage bank.[99]

France brought increasing pressure to bear on the Makhzen, which it deemed incapable of instilling order and overseeing tax collection. This pressure was further intensified after the Franco-German agreement was signed on November 4, 1911, which accorded France free rein. The Protectorate treaty of March 30, 1912, charted Casablanca's destiny as a commercial stronghold and seat of colonial power, proving false the all-too-hasty prediction made by Georges Bourdon on the heels of the 1907 hostilities:

> Littered with corpses, Casablanca is slowly returning to its former humdrum existence and is starting out on the road to oblivion. It is once again cloaked in the monotony of mean-minded and gloomy disharmony, having been captured and carved up by a troop of Spanish and Algerian mercenaries as in so many other Islam cities, whose sullied souls are melting pots of Eastern flaws and European vices, all crumbling under the hand of civilization.[100]

---

[93] This praise came in support of Dessigny's request to remain in his post, despite a promotion. General Moinier, "Note au Ministre de la Guerre," Casablanca, October 11, 1909, SHAT, carton 3H 87. His appointment confirmed by Lyautey in October 1912; Dessigny remained in his post until March 1913. General Hubert Lyautey, Service Note, Rabat, October 15, 1912, SHAT, carton 3H 330. The activity of the department was first placed under the supervision of the French vice-consul, and later under that of the consul himself, where it remained until March 1914, when it came under the supervision of the residency.

[94] Lieutenant Marie François Segonds, "Casablanca, monographie de la Chaouia," *Bulletin de la Société de géographie d'Alger et d'Afrique du Nord* 15 (3rd trimester, 1910): 369. Segonds was in Casablanca from December 1907 to October 1908. See also Joseph Goulven, "L'histoire d'une ville; la création du port de Casablanca," *Le Maroc catholique*, no. 9 (September 1924): 453. A lawyer and writer, Goulven was the secretary of the Casablanca Chamber of Commerce.

[95] Marcel Frager, *La ville neuve: odyssée d'un écumeur*, preface by Jean-José Frappa (Paris: Ollendorf, 1924), 112–13.

[96] Dessigny, "Casablanca, notice économique et administrative," 316–17.

[97] One of the first orders, issued in 1909, decreed that the "streets, squares, and other public routes of Casablanca are to be left entirely free for circulation, to which no obstacle should be presented." Casablanca, decree no. 11, July 15, 1909, MAE, series A Tanger, carton 667.

[98] This despite various families' more or less authorized appropriation of a *zrîba** (enclosure) and its adjacent streets.

[99] Note on General D'Amade's December 13, 1908, Report on Real Estate in Chaouia, Paris, March 18, 1909, SHAT, carton 3H 78.

[100] Bourdon, *Ce que j'ai vu au Maroc*, 388.

Clock tower and Grand Socco, 1911.

The tower stretched thirty meters high (as did the one previously built by Dessigny at Ain-Sefra in the Algerian Atlas mountains) and comprised a square central part, loggia, and cupola. Deemed "rickety" in 1948 it was subsequently demolished. A replica was erected on a nearby site in 1993.

Commercial Boom (1907–12)

The town is spilling beyond its confines. A Negro neighborhood, comprising a heap of squalid structures, has sprung up in the vicinity of Bab-Marrakech, while warehouses and shops have sprouted around the market gate. The inner quarters are essentially Arabic in style, although at times reveal glimpses of semimodern fragments. Winding thoroughfares with rickety paving, or sometimes no paving at all, turn into quagmire at the very first drop of rain. Tiny narrow squares are wedged between low, flat-roofed houses totally lacking in any kind of architectural appeal. Apart from the mosques, a handful of private dwellings, and the German consulate, no monument whatsoever can be said to attract the visitor's gaze.

Lieutenant Segonds, 1910[101]

The first buildings constructed in the *ville nouvelle* were a response to the trade boom that had been accelerated by the French landings.[102] The engineer corps started work on general amenities, such as the clock tower built by Dessigny in 1910 near the city wall, on the right of Bab el-Kebir.[103] According to Lacharrière, "As in Tangiers, [it used to be impossible] to know the right time in Casablanca, since the Muslims, the Spanish Franciscans, and the battleships all operate to a different clock."[104] The tower served as an indicator that the town was henceforth linked to air and land networks and was therefore expected to function at the same pace as industrial civilization. The French signal tower similarly proved that the city had stepped into the modern age. Built on the western beach in 1908 for the Compagnie Française de TSF by the engineer Henri Popp, it was "in direct contact with the Eiffel Tower."[105]

Shops that had previously been contained in the inner courtyards of housing now invaded the medina lanes. Christian Houel describes how the buildings were "gutted to make way for commercial booths," "shifting" the bustle of life into the streets.[106] Muslim and Jewish butchers set up in Rue du Capitaine Ihler, and a string of outlets peppered Rue du Commandant Provost, which was the new name given

[101] Segonds, "Casablanca, monographie de la Chaouia," 345–46.

[102] Passing through Casablanca in 1911, Gouraud noted that the city "has developed enormously . . . but, alas, not in beauty!" Henri Joseph Eugène Gouraud, *Au Maroc, 1911–1914: souvenirs d'un Africain* (Paris: Plon, 1949), 110.

[103] Charles Ducatel, "Histoire de la tour de l'Horloge," *La Tribune des vieux Marocains* (February 1948): 11. Dessigny was assisted by his deputy, Engineer Corps Captain Bouillot and by Senior Master Sergeant Brèthes.

[104] Ladreit de Lacharrière, "L'œuvre française en Chaouia," 350.

[105] Segonds, "Casablanca, monographie de la Chaouia," 369. This post enabled communications independent of emitters mounted on Marine cruisers.

[106] Houel, *Mes aventures marocaines*, 133.

A Bad Start for a City of Adventure 43

Aerial view, 1911 (shot taken using a military "photographic kite").

107 Two hundred nineteen developed European properties and 624 appropriated but undeveloped hectares were inventoried in 1912. A. Tarriot, *Monographie de Casablanca de 1907 à 1914* (Casablanca: Imprimerie du Petit Marocain, 1924), 42–43.

108 Croze, *Souvenirs du vieux Maroc*, 29.

109 It was thanks to the resale of the scrap from the cargo ship *La Nive* that Lendrat was able to launch his operation. Houel, *Mes aventures marocaines*, 149.

110 Dessigny noted, "'Rooms' measuring 4 to 5 meters long at most, by 2 1/2 to 3 meters wide, are rented for 10 to 15 francs per month. A very modest little apartment rents for 50 to 80 francs per month; these are quite rare. A small apartment consisting of three rooms, a kitchen, *cabinet d'aisances*, and a cistern costs between 100 and 150 francs per month. A large apartment is rented for 200 to 300 francs per month . . . A small gardener's house or cottage costs about 6,000 francs to build. A little house with a garden: 15,000 francs. A middle-class house with a garden: 30,000 francs. A large elegant villa, with an attractive garden: 50,000 francs . . . By 'garden' one must understand a more or less large plot located near the residence which must be fully planted." Dessigny, "Casablanca, notice économique et administrative," 323.

111 The track was extended to the customs service platform in late 1908. Its transformation into a 1.05-meter-wide road (a project involving the *Union des mines marocaines*) was discussed in 1910, alongside a plan to extend the Decauville rail line linking the port to Bab Marrakech as far as Sour Jdid. Project, SHAT, carton 3H 114. Mule traction reminds Gouraud of the zoological garden. Gouraud, *Au Maroc*, 112.

to the town's main street. Housing and commercial outfits mushroomed in Casablanca's outskirts, including slaughterhouses opposite Bab es-Souk along with a livestock market slightly further off.[107] Farms were converted into suburban dwellings and cafés were shunted out, such as the Glacier located on the Socco. The Fernaus, Butler, and Lamb launched residential programs, and, in 1909, the banker Antoine Mas commissioned the first apartment house. The year 1908 saw construction of the Grand Socco Factory on the edges of Wadi Bouskoura, a project that was initiated by the pharmacist Gabriel Veyre and which combined a flour and saw mill, a water distilling factory, and an icehouse. Meanwhile, with no building codes, private dwellings were constructed haphazardly along the shoreline. Housing developments began to see the light of day amid the rush for land, the first being commissioned by the Fernaus.[108] The Place de France, situated at the crossing point of the old and new towns, rapidly became a densely built-up area where roads intersected and tradesmen gathered. It was here that the first electric lighting pylon was erected.

Dessigny officially delineated the civic boundaries on December 23, 1911. Commercial companies, such as the one owned by the German trader Karl Ficke, set up their fonduks along the Route de Médiouna, while Eugène Lendrat, a former grocery boy and founder of the Union des Travailleurs (a trade union), spurred growth by commissioning the Roches Noires housing development near the shore.[109] Hostility expressed by the Socialist members of parliament prior to the Protectorate triggered doubts as to how long the French would remain in Chaouia, though this did little to dampen investors' drive. Despite the increase in real-estate supply, housing prices were still at a premium due to the steady rise in demand generated by the continual influx of Europeans, many of whom settled permanently.[110]

New land links served to connect the port with the rest of Morocco. A mule-hauled tramway mainly dedicated to military use (as this alone complied with the Act of Algesiras) was built between May and September 1908, joining Casablanca with Berrechid, a "regional military base" that stretched out to the army camp south of the town.[111] A more ambitious and permanent network was established in late 1911, in the form of a railroad linking Rabat with Casablanca, and a main station was built on a polygonal site edging the beach in the east of the town. In addition, a 188-meter-long timber bridge was flung across Wadi Nfifikh, marking the first step toward improving coastal links with the north.[112] Civil aviation likewise made its appearance in 1911, when the newspaper *Le Petit Journal* organized an "air expedition" from Casablanca to Fès.[113]

A Mosaic of Populations

The Porte de la Marine, now a historical site, is home to the oddest types of fellows: burly businessmen on flying visits to meet with Europeans who bought up land prior to 1907; personae non grata *who are endeavoring to adopt a new image by donning gaiters and carrying a revolver or cosh; aspiring officers peering out from beneath their helmets or wide-rimmed gray trilbies; and former deserters who will be hired as valets to consuls or some other high-ranking official.*

Joseph Goulven, 1924[114]

The clarity with which the town took shape was counterbalanced by the diverse population groups that began to settle in Casablanca. The French chargé d'affaires to Morocco notified General Charles Moinier about the Council of Ministers' concern regarding "the arrival in Morocco of unauthorized penniless people who are turning up in droves and who have already penetrated deep into the town." He then went on to request an "urgent clean-up."[115] A new policy was introduced once France enforced its plan for a long-term Protectorate on the Makhzen. Although Casablanca's expansion cannot be attributed solely to the institution of a modern state system and the stable environment that grew out of French rule, it is true that the new economic framework did bring about radical changes. The combined development of the town and port created employment opportunities coupled with access to a modern lifestyle both for newcomers to Morocco and for Moroccans themselves. Given its role as a dual threshold—an urban entranceway of sorts—Casablanca not only evolved into an increasingly important transit hub, equipped with all the requisite technical, commercial, and cultural facilities, but also into an ethnic and financial nerve center.

Half a century after the 1907 landings, Casablanca would continue to accommodate myriad population groups. In addition to the French (the largest European populace), it was also home to Spaniards and Italians, as well as to some Portuguese, Russians, Poles, Swedes, Britons, Swiss, and Americans, whose numbers swelled after World War II. These groups did not lead segregated lives; on the contrary, they intermixed on both a social and urban level. Closer study of the background of the French population in Casablanca toward the end of the Protectorate reveals that its members came chiefly from major cities or port towns in the south of France. They formed a young and dynamic community, in which newcomers arriving directly from the metropolis (and hence completely unfamiliar with North African lifestyle) stood out among "acclimatized" migrants from Algeria and Tunisia. The latter included many Jews, enticed by Casablanca's promise of wealth. Sicilians and Andalusians also made up a seasoned segment of the population, given their Mediterranean origins. By far the most dynamic and influential of these groups, however, were the architects, contractors, and their clients, all of whom contributed to the process of devising new daily lifestyles and housing environments. It was they who communicated innovative building styles and practices to the former metropolitan dwellers.

Moroccans also felt the pull of Casablanca, which they generally regarded as the gateway to modernity. Georges Vidalenc speaks of "Muslims who are flocking to the center in search of work," as well as Jews "forced out of the overpopulated mellahs

112 It would be named after Engineer Corps Lieutenant Blondin, who died of typhoid fever during its construction.

113 René Lebaut, *De Casablanca à Fez en aéroplane* (Paris: Librairie du Petit Journal, 1911), 32.

114 Joseph Goulven, "L'histoire d'une ville: Le développement de Casablanca avant la guerre," *Le Maroc catholique*, no. 11 (November 1924): 556–61.

115 Auguste Félix Charles de Saint-Aulaire, French chargé d'affaires in Morocco, note on the "mesures de police à l'égard des gens sans aveu au Maroc," December 20, 1911, Tangiers, SHAT, carton 3H 330.

116 Georges Vidalenc, "La croissance de Casablanca et les problèmes de la construction," *La Terre marocaine illustrée*, no. 51 (March 15, 1930): 2017.

117 Nonetheless, certain Muslim notables were in a position to participate in the pursuit of land on the periphery. Among these was Si Omar Tazi, who in 1911 built three rental villas near the Compagnie Française de TSF tower. On this very Europeanized family, closely tied to the sultan, see "L'évolution du Makhzen, la famille Tazi," *Bulletin du comité de l'Afrique française*, no. 2 (February 1904): 50–51.

118 Pierre Léris, "Histoire immobilière de Casablanca," *La Terre marocaine*, no. 2 (March 1, 1928): 26. Until then, the Jews had essentially owned no properties *extra muros*.

119 See correspondence cited in Michael M. Laskier, *The Alliance Israélite Universelle and the Jewish Communities of Morocco: 1862–1962* (Albany: State University of New York Press, 1983), 68.

by the French authorities."[116] New shifts began to take place inside the town. Its modern quarters were closed to the majority of Muslims, even though no regulation as such forbade them from living there. This gave rise to "Arab villages," such as the neighborhood known as Bousbir, which took up roughly three hundred square meters of land on the western outskirts of the city. The medina grew stiflingly dense, and was occupied by the lower classes who either worked in the medina itself or who were employed by companies that had set up in the east of the town.[117] Between the French landings and World War I, Casablanca's tripartite split as defined by Weisgerber in 1900, namely the heavily populated medina, the mellah, and the Tnaker, was replaced by a more complex array of ethnic and social groups. In the early years, Moroccan Jews were more attracted than Muslim Moroccans to the *ville nouvelle*, and the wealthier of them moved out of the mellah. Furthermore, as of 1907, numerous Moroccan Jews succeeded in converting the security pledged by their Muslim debtors into real estate; this included not only buildings (the initial mortgage), but also the *harim*—the surrounding vacant land.[118] D'Amade's early championing of the Alliance Israélite Universelle, which he deemed would be useful for French "infiltration" into Casablanca, also proved helpful to the Jewish population.[119]

Professional players soon took a hold over construction and the running of the town, though military presence would remain strong, with army facilities even being used in later urban development. Intelligence officers previously responsible for public facilities were replaced by engineers, while land surveyors who also played the role of property developers, such as Tardif and Buan, were put in charge of reporting on urban growth. Several contractor-architects (Barbedor and Tonci, for example) opened design offices to meet the needs of the authorities and of wealthy investors.

The built plots initially stretched out like fingers along the main roads, the urban backbone itself being formed by the bottleneck thoroughfare that connected Sidi Belyout cemetery with the army camps. European neighborhoods sprang up in clusters around the military land, presumably due to the protection this offered in the increasingly unlikely event of a raid by Chaouia tribes. Further out, buildings

Place du Commerce, c. 1912. Land subdivision plans on the wall opposite the Café du Commerce.

Grand Café de Paris, c. 1912.

were erected essentially for agricultural use; two-thirds of these were French-owned, while the remainder belonged to the Germans.[120] By late 1912, Casablanca was home to some 46,000 inhabitants, including 25,000 Muslims and 9,000 Moroccan Jews. A detailed property breakdown reveals a high proportion of British- and German-owned buildings,[121] while a comparative analysis of French-owned land (largely taken up by the military camps) clearly explains the focus on peripheral development over the ensuing years.[122]

An El Dorado for Developers

Dar el-Beida, descendant of the small sixteenth-century Portuguese town of Anfa, has in turn been swallowed up and transfigured by a ville nouvelle. *The old town has no real history to speak of and there is no trace of the Portuguese influence, while the new town has no past at all. Only recently spawned, it changes slightly every day. A multitude of boulevards (which are already too narrow) have stepped into the old dirt tracks, and a mass of luxury apartment houses are springing up at an incredible rate, eating both into the stark countryside and into the* derbs* *(native slum areas), which were cobbled together after the conquest out of assorted pieces of debris.*

L. d'Anfreville de Jurquet de la Salle, 1930[123]

In short, then, by the time Lyautey was appointed resident-general of the French administration[124] on April 26, 1912, Casablanca's development was already in full swing. The city's growth was thus not underpinned by *creation* as such, but rather by *controlled extension*. In the years following the 1907 landings, building space was there for the taking, engendering unbridled construction of industrial structures in the vicinity of the port, as well as disparate private venture schemes and random housing developments commissioned by real-estate firms based in the city center. Land prices increased twentyfold, even as early as 1907,[125] and land speculation began to play an

120 Joseph Goulven, "Villes d'Afrique, Casablanca la commerçante," *Renseignements coloniaux et documents publiés par le Comité de l'Afrique française et le Comité du Maroc* 14, no. 2 (February 1914): 75–81. Prunier, "Étude sur le territoire de Casablanca-banlieue," *Bulletin économique du Maroc*, no. 4 (1914): 5.

121 French residents numbered 7,000; Spaniards 2,500; and Italians 2,200. The British owned seventy-five buildings *intra muros* and 80 hectares *extra muros* (for one hundred nationals); the Germans owned eighteen buildings and 48 hectares (for two hundred nationals); the French owned sixty-five buildings and 489 hectares; the Spaniards owned fifty-eight buildings and 9 hectares; and the Italians owned two buildings. Tarriot, *Monographie de Casablanca*, 42, 49.

122 The structure of land ownership is legible on maps produced between 1912 and 1918. See that of the surveyor and developer Georges Buan, published in the appendix to Léon Guigues, *Guide de l'Exposition franco-marocaine* (Casablanca: Imprimerie rapide, 1915). See also Tardif's map and an undated map produced by the Comptoir lorrain du Maroc (in all likelihood made in 1917), both in IFA, Fonds Perret, as well as that of Agache, in the collection of the authors (to be discussed later on).

123 L. d'Anfreville de Jurquet de la Salle, "Une grande ville vient de naître!", *La Géographie* 53 (January–February 1930): 30. Laden here with racist or at least condescending connotations, the term *native* is elsewhere used to designate Muslims or Jews born in Morocco. It is in this sense that we employ the two terms of *native* and *indigenous* in the rest of our text. We share the point of view of André Adam, who sees "no reason to reject the use of this term [*indigène*], whose meaning is very clear, because certain Europeans disqualified it by loading it with contempt. Contempt is in men's mind, not in words." Adam, *Casablanca*, 36.

124 For the purposes of this publication, the French central authorities based in Rabat are referred to as the administration.

125 Tarriot, *Monographie de Casablanca de 1907 à 1914*, 43.

Place du Commerce and Café du Commerce, c. 1912.

126 Gillet, "La construction au Maroc au début du Protectorat," 28; Croze, *Souvenirs du vieux Maroc*, 29.

127 Claude Farrère, *Les hommes nouveaux*, 2nd ed., color woodcuts by G. Géo-Fourrier, engraved by Auguste Mathieu (Paris: Horizons de France, 1928), 46. See also the article published by the novelist upon his return from Morocco: idem, "Une ville-champignon," *L'Ouest* (Angers), December 12, 1920.

128 Born in Casablanca in 1866, Prosper Ferrieu became General D'Amade's political adviser in 1907.

129 General representative of L'Union Insurance and an active developer, Tardif was responsible for Casablanca's land survey.

130 Edmond Joyant, "Législation des plans d'aménagement urbain du Maroc," *Annales des Ponts et Chaussées*, 11th series, 1, no. 4 (1921): 106.

131 Tardif tried in vain to secure the transfer of a lot at the corner of the Mazagan road from the developers Racine & Cie. This addition would have enabled the expansion of the road to thirty meters, and the creation of a circular public square measuring seventy meters in diameter. He also revealed himself to be preoccupied by the "intensity of the circulation," and "the conveying of goods by camels that encumber circulation routes," as well as by the need to plan for the eventual installation of a tramway. Commandant Dessigny, "Note au Consul de France," Casablanca, April 17, 1913, MAE, series A Tanger, carton 666.

increasingly important role. The Café du Commerce, located at the intersection of Rue du Commandant Provost and Rue de la Douane, served as the general trading area due to a shortage of office space. According to Houel, the café replaced "the public town square or forum" where "vacant land and old houses were bought and sold."[126] Claude Farrère's highly evocative *Les hommes nouveaux*, written in the early 1920s, paints a colorful picture of adventurers enticed by the colonial lifestyle; these are personified by Amédée-Jules Bourron, "the man from Casablanca":

> It was all a matter of converting a bleak and desolate place into a civilized country, and land in civilized countries is traded at a specific price per square meter. That much I knew. I was the first to realize we had to buy up as many square meters as we could at the best possible price—and fast—because then we would be able to sell them for an incredibly high sum. In 1912, I had three hundred thousand French francs. By 1914 I had twelve hundred thousand. I bought here, there, and everywhere, in Casa, Rabat, Fès, and so on. I also acquired shops, where I stocked everything everyone required. After all, it's important to help each other out when colonizing a place![127]

Investors such as Lendrat, the Fernaus, and Ferrieu subsequently "grew in importance," to use one of Bourron's favorite expressions, building shops and houses without any concern for architectural quality. A study of Casablanca's place names reveals the charisma of some of these entrepreneurs—Ferrieu, for example, whose father had propelled Casablanca into the commercial ranks of the wool trade. Bousbir, the name allotted to the new Muslim district whose narrow lanes bounded the west side of the public garden, is, in fact, a phonetic distortion of Prosper, Ferrieu's first name.[128]

Tardif's Extension Plan

The plan drawn up in 1912 by the surveyor Albert Tardif provides clear insight into the town's growth after 1907. This early scheme, which marked out the city's future, has been completely disregarded in all historical analyses of Casablanca, and most of its features were in fact later credited to Henri Prost.[129] It meticulously illustrates the siting of buildings, revealing the early urban efforts of the army and the Protectorate Public Works Department. It sewed together a number of randomly placed structures and set out several road system proposals with a view to providing a main thread for Casablanca's urban fabric. The first such proposal was for Rue du Marché, whose first section ran out to the Bab es-Souk area around the clock tower; later, though, the name of this road would be changed to Rue de l'Horloge (meaning clock). In the face of opposition from landowners, Dessigny had no option but to map out a winding road that followed the "broken route enforced by the buildings and property boundaries."[130]

Tardif designed a seven-kilometer circular boulevard, though purchasing the land for this project engendered heated negotiations between Dessigny and real-estate developers.[131] Additionally, Tardif stepped up urbanization in the southeast by way of an "extension plan," which encompassed roads and subdivisions straddling the boulevard as well as a park that had been created in 1907 in tribute to a British tradesman named Murdoch.

Although still somewhat sprawling, the town nonetheless began to adopt a polycentric structure stamped with three specific sectors. First, the Roches Noires quarter along the eastern shoreline, occupying land owned by the real-estate developer Eugène Lendrat. Second, a new plot earmarked for the railroad station in the southeast, as well as a subdivision scheme funded by the Société pour le Développement de Casablanca that lay between the station and the road to Rabat, traversed by an attractive, meandering thoroughfare. And third, the

Anfa quarter on the western side of the city, though on the eve of World War I this was no more than a project on which bets were being hedged: "Some see it as becoming Casablanca's future 'privileged district,' convinced that the town's well-to-do residents and major industrialists will come to the cool hills of Anfa-Supérieure, seeking to escape the sweltering summer heat. In fact, in just a few years all these parcels of land that currently lie vacant and undeveloped may well be covered with chic villas nestled in delightful gardens."[132] By 1914, plans for a large theater and a Palace Hotel were already under way for this district dedicated to "luxury and recreation" that was slowly starting to take shape.[133]

[132] Goulven, "Villes d'Afrique," 75–81.

[133] *L'essor industriel de Casablanca, enquête sur les entreprises industrielles de Casablanca faite par la "Vigie marocaine"* (Casablanca: Éditions de La Vigie marocaine, 1914), 118. The initial buyer is L. Julien.

Albert Tardif, extension plan for Casablanca, 1912. The written annotations are by Auguste Perret, who used this copy in 1913 for siting his building projects.

A Bad Start for a City of Adventure 49

The Magasins Paris-Maroc and the crowd on Place de France, c. 1914.

Henri Prost's Plan (1914–1917):
A Flexible Approach

Morocco's Natural Haven

There is no reason why Casablanca cannot be dealt with in the same way as other ports, such as Saint-Jean de Luz and Leixões, whose seas are just as problematic... To abandon the port project would signal Casablanca's immediate and unequivocal downfall. A detailed analysis is thus urgently required, for although it has been deemed difficult to upkeep large breakwaters, it would be even more complicated to maintain a small, unprotected inner harbor. Should the latter course be adopted, then Casablanca would have no port, either large or small.

Gaston Delure, letter to General Lyautey, February 8, 1913[1]

It was by no means certain at the outset that Casablanca would be cast in the role of French Morocco's main port. The navy was particularly hostile to such a scheme, having set its heart on Mazagan, or even Fédala. Georges and Jean Hersent, two brothers active in technology and finance, had even purchased one thousand hectares of land in Fédala, expecting this town to win the selection process.[2] In 1907, though, an ambitious project had been launched for developing the port of Casablanca, and work was in progress to build a new breakwater near the town's northernmost bastion. In 1910, when exploring the various options for Casablanca's growth, Lacharrière had thought of creating a "fast motorized wagon service" that would enable warehouses to be set up on the outskirts of Casablanca, one of the ideas behind this project being to rid the town of its fonduks. Yet the most pressing concern was the increasingly congested port; for instance, in 1912 it apparently took almost six months to load up grain. A large portion of the funds raised by Lyautey's Protectorate lobbying campaign therefore went toward developing new facilities for the port.

In 1913, Paul Tirard, Protectorate secretary general, spoke out against those officers who "taking a sailor's standpoint, i.e., disregarding economic interests, consider Casablanca to be one of the most unfavorable sites for a major seaport."[3] Thus the determining factor in the selection of Casablanca as the country's "economic hub" over other older ports, notably Rabat, lay not in its sea access, but in its land links with the rest of "usable" Morocco, where there were already numerous European settlements. As the capital of Chaouia, Casablanca was a "natural storage

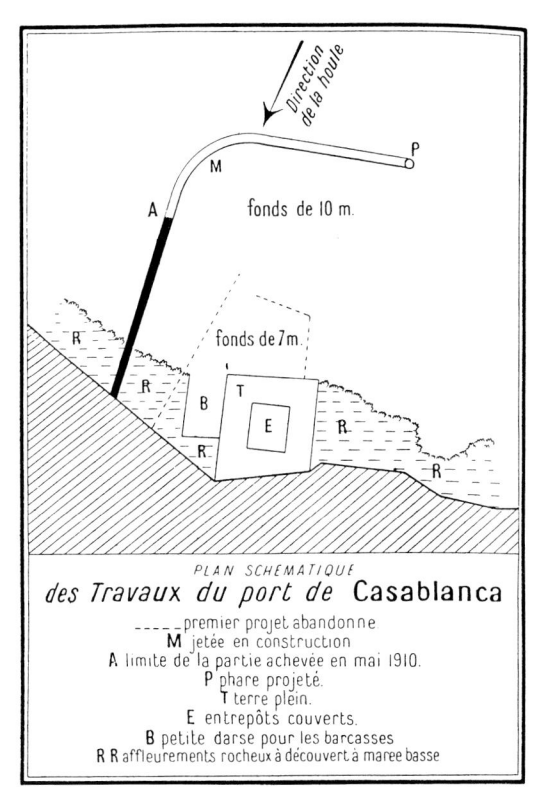

Schematic plan drafted in 1910 for the port development, in *Renseignements coloniaux et documents publiés par le comité de l'Afrique française et le comité du Maroc*, 1910.

[1] Gaston Delure to General Lyautey, February 8, 1913, AN, 475 AP/52.

[2] Dyé had challenged this alternative as early as 1908, believing that "Fédala will one day be a small port worthwhile for fishing and for exporting the agricultural products of Zénata," but that "Casablanca will remain the outlet of the greater Chaouia region, like Alexandria, Tunis, and Bordeaux were in no way dethroned by Port Said, Bizerte, and La Pallice." A. Henri Dyé, "Les ports du Maroc," 199. In 1914, the Hersent brothers managed to convince the Protectorate to open Fédala to maritime traffic, in the guise of a backup to Casablanca. The pressure of German firms, which had various installations nearby, strengthened their point. Memo from the Inspecteur général des Ponts-et-Chaussées, technical adviser of the Ministry of Foreign Affairs, August 31, 1913, SHAT, box 3H 114.

[3] Paul Tirard to General Lyautey, February 5, 1913, AN, 475 AP/52.

General view of
the wharves, 1913.
Right: new customs
warehouses; ships
moored in the harbor
waiting to be unloaded
by small craft.

The port lashed by
a storm, 1913.

"The breakwater assailed by waves on a stormy day in Casablanca" in *L'Illustration*, 1913.

site for the surrounding regions."[4] As the journalist André Colliez pointed out, "Casablanca possesses such a panoply of advantages that it is unthinkable for it not to be the capital." Its jewel in the crown, though, was its geographical position, which meant that it could easily develop into a "gigantic, sprawling, spidery city," ready to "lay its web at the crossroads of land and sea routes."[5] After arriving in Casablanca on May 13, 1912, Lyautey informed a French gathering of businessmen that he intended "to be able to enter his house," that is, "to open up the ports." When he learned of the navy's reticence early the following year, he expressed concern over the "outcry that would ensue in Casablanca" should another port be chosen.[6]

The port expansion project was drafted by the civil engineer A. François and was overseen by Gaston Delure, Protectorate director general for the Department of Public Works.[7] The works contract was awarded in Tangiers on March 25, 1913, to a group composed of the French industrial firm Schneider, the Compagnie Marocaine, and the Hersent brothers, who were called in at the last minute. The group immediately got down to the task at hand, under the watchful eye of Paul

[4] Berthe Georges-Gaulis, *La France au Maroc (l'œuvre du général Lyautey)* (Paris: Armand Colin, 1919), 284.

[5] André Colliez, Notre protectorat marocain: la première étape 1912–1930 (Paris: Marcel Rivière, 1930), 369, 208. Also in 1930, Colliez would advocate the establishment of the capital at Casablanca, deploring the fact that a "brain city" had been created alongside the business city—something like establishing "Washington alongside Chicago," ibid., 209.

[6] General Lyautey to Gaston Delure, February 5, 1913, AN, 475 AP/52. Regarding this issue, see Daniel Rivet, *Lyautey et l'institution du Protectorat français au Maroc 1912–1925* (Paris: L'Harmattan, 1988), 1:247. Coming at the end of a period of difficult weather, the winter 1913 tidal wave provided added justification for Casablanca's detractors. As for Delure, he noted that these storms "caused only slight harm to the built works, comparable to that suffered by any maritime construction," and stood by his argument in favor of Casablanca. Delure to General Lyautey, February 8, 1913.

[7] In French public administration, a *directeur général*, or director general, heads a wide spectrum of different services put under the authority of their respective *directeurs*. The career of Gaston Delure (1877–1926) had taken him, most notably, to Argentina and Bayonne. It culminated, after 1918, in the directorship of the "Commerce and Mines of Alsace-Lorraine." Galatoire-Malégarie, "Note sur l'œuvre marocaine de M. Gaston Delure, inspecteur général, ancien directeur général des Travaux publics du Maroc," *Annales des Ponts et Chaussées* 97, no. 4 (July–August 1927): 7–12.

Henri Prost's Plan (1914–1917)

Chaix, an engineer who had trained at the École Centrale in Paris.[8] The brief was to develop a 160-hectare area, and this was to include a 1,900-meter breakwater, some 300 meters of which had already been built as part of the earlier project. It was to be extended northeast before curving around to run parallel to the shore. Another 1,400-meter-long horizontal jetty was designed to section off a harbor able to hold ships with a ten-meter draft.[9]

The reasons for selecting Casablanca were well founded and were henceforth generally accepted, even though the damage caused by the Atlantic swell continued to incite "empty and negative criticism" on the part of "pessimists, detractors, and gloomy souls."[10] Observers strongly berated the analysis published in 1912 by the head of the navy's hydrographic department who had asserted that it was "impossible to build a port on the west coast of Morocco that will be accessible under all weather conditions," since "incredibly long jetties would be required to get past the breakers that build up during storms."[11] As it was, these marine difficulties would be heralded as an example of Lyautey's "daring," Delure's "perseverance," and the project's "grand scale."[12] Work on the main breakwater got under way swiftly, due to a 50-million-franc advance out of an overall 170-million-franc loan granted to Lyautey on March 16, 1914, by the Chamber of Deputies. The outbreak of World War I slowed construction, but it did not by any means bring it to a standstill, although the project was threatened on a number of occasions by hikes in building material prices.[13]

Land use and layout in the *ville nouvelle* were affected by the designs of the port drafted by Delure's department. The main breakwater had no real impact in this respect, but the secondary, orthogonal breakwater ran almost parallel to the medina. It was this segment of the seafront, which was previously a beach, that was to handle all trade between Morocco's chief port and the rest of the world. The Muslim cemetery still ran along roughly half the waterfront of the town, opposite the Bab sidi Belyout marabout, and blocked practically all access to the town from the port. As early as 1913, it thus became clear that a road system would have to be laid to join together the still sparsely populated areas that immediately surrounded the medina.

Incisive Urbanity

To speak of rational development and analytical organization in a town like Casablanca is tantamount to holding forth on the wealth and opulence of a native's cottage... Casablanca bears the burden of being the offspring of chance spawned in mediocrity. Appallingly neglected at an early age, its excessively rapid growth has resulted in physiological flaws which must be removed at all costs if we wish to see it develop into a robust adult capable of fruitful labor.

Victor Cambon, 1917[14]

Following the 1919 Cornudet Law, development, extension, and redevelopment plans began to be drawn up for a large number of French towns and cities.[15] Some of these urban experiments served as a point of reference for planners; this was true for Morocco, which, in terms of urbanization, was often compared with Germany and America. In his *Urbanism Handbook*, published in 1924, Edmond Joyant, a civil engineer and deputy director of the Protectorate Department of Public Works, demonstrates the process whereby "a small, sleepy Moorish town evolved into a major modern commercial city" by virtue of strict zoning and modern land ownership policy.[16]

It would therefore seem that the urban development policy advocated under Lyautey clearly responded to one of the Protectorate's main objectives, which was to "regenerate" France by pulling her out of slippery decline.[17] In attempting to

---

8 The cost of construction was 46 million francs. Gaston de Caqueray, "Pourquoi et comment Casablanca eut son port," in Paul Bory (ed.), *Le port de Casablanca et la naissance d'une grande ville*, Notre Maroc 10 (June 1952): 5–12.

9 Sheltered by this jetty, the construction of seven hundred meters of docks and sixteen hectares of platforms was planned. Furthermore, jetties to the east and west of the small port were yet to be completed. A. C., "Les travaux du port de Casablanca (Maroc) et l'emprunt marocain," *Le Génie civil* 44, no. 23 (April 4, 1914): 458–60. It is important to remember that the port had barely fifty meters of docks in 1913.

10 Georges Toutlemonde, "Le port de Casablanca," *Le Génie civil* 105, no. 8 (August 25, 1934): 162–63.

11 Account of "the eminent hydrographic engineer, director of the navy hydrographic service, who wrote in the *Revue générale des sciences*, in 1912," reported by M. Normandin in, "Les ports marocains," *Annales des Ponts et Chaussées* 104, no. 3 (May–June 1934): 305.

12 "Le port de Casablanca," *Revue générale des sciences pures et appliquées* (April 15, 1914): 332–36.

13 E. L. Guernier, "Casablanca, grand port de la côte occidentale d'Afrique," *France-Maroc*, no. 8 (August 15, 1917): 12–18.

14 Victor Cambon, "L'aménagement et l'extension des villes," in *Conférences franco-marocaines* (Paris: Plon, 1917), 2:203.

15 See Jean-Pierre Gaudin, *L'avenir en plan: technique et politique dans la prévision urbaine, 1900–1930* (Seyssel, Champ Vallon, 1985).

16 Edmond Joyant, "Casablanca," in *Traité d'urbanisme*, 2nd ed. (Paris: Eyrolles, 1928), 2:95. See also idem, "Le plan d'aménagement de Casablanca (Maroc)," *Le Génie Civil* no. 2036 (August 20, 1922): 161–67; and idem, "L'Urbanisme au Maroc," *La Technique sanitaire et municipale* (April 1922): 88–103. The Prost plan is also one of the fundamental examples evoked by René Danger in his *Cours d'urbanisme* (Paris: Eyrolles, 1933), figs. 232–34. The centrality of the Moroccan experience for the French developments is discussed by Hélène Vacher in *Projection coloniale et ville rationalisée: le rôle de l'espace colonial dans la constitution de l'urbanisme en France, 1900–1931* (Aalborg: Aalborg University Press, 1997).

17 Regarding the marshal's action, see General Hubert Lyautey, *Paroles d'action—Madagascar, Sud-Oranais, Oran, Maroc (1900–1926)* (Paris: Armand Colin, 1927); and Max Leclerc, *Au Maroc avec Lyautey* (Paris: Armand Colin, 1921).

A row of houses and depots in the city center, c. 1911.

House in Rue 15 (Bousbir quarter), 1918. Extract from the building permit.

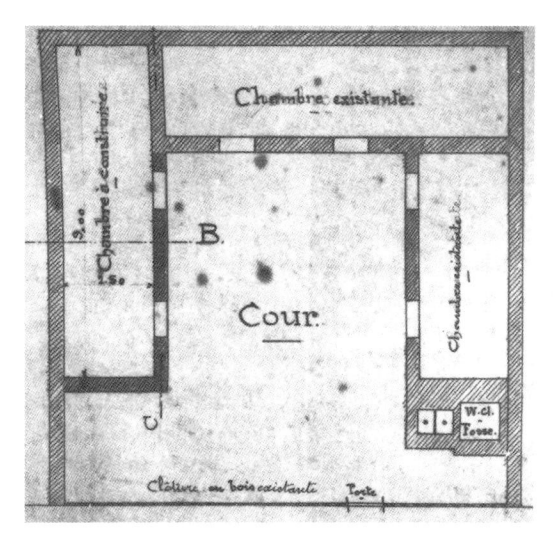

recharge the batteries of a war-ravaged nation, the resident-general could not fail to draw on the newly emerging discipline of urban planning.[18] The Moroccan example was to play a considerable role in French postwar reconstruction efforts as well as in the heated debate preceding ratification of the Cornudet Law. When Victor Cambon put forward his postwar program for France in 1916, he adopted Lyautey's viewpoint, asserting that Casablanca, the "offspring of chance" that had "started out so badly," was truly developing into a "well laid out French city with decent standards of health and hygiene."[19]

Casablanca's First Layer of Buildings

According to Joseph Goulven, the different ethnic groups living in Casablanca in 1912 were clearly divided by geographic zone: "Bousbir was inhabited by Arabs, the Route de Médiouna by Jews [and] the Liberté quarter by Europeans."[20] Some Muslims built very basic dwellings on narrow plots running parallel to Bousbir. These traditional abodes contained long rooms set in L and U shapes around a courtyard and they had a 3.5-meter ceiling height. This housing type was characteristic of the working class quarters, until inhabitants began to systematically add on parts, causing the demise of the courtyard. Meanwhile, rapid trade expansion resulted in fonduks mushrooming around Casablanca's new "life force," namely the Route de Médiouna: "The fonduks are being ousted from the flourishing center ... they have been taken over by cafés, banks, and shops that have been built by the Europeans along the old road formerly used by caravans for transporting grain from fertile Chaouia to Dar el-Beida."[21]

Tardif's extension plan targeted the area known as Mers-Sultan, along the Route de Médiouna. It was here that caravanserai owners settled in villas, having been driven out of their more central abodes.[22] This site was close to the city

[18] As in Tunisia and every French protectorate, France's highest representative in the country held the title of *résident général*. For more on Lyautey's enterprises, see the short work by Alfred de Tarde, *Le Maroc école d'énergie* (Paris: Plon, 1923). Regarding the administrative mechanism of the Protectorate, see Alan Scham, *Lyautey in Morocco, Protectorate Administration, 1912–1925* (Berkeley, Los Angeles, and London: University of California Press, 1970); and Abdellah Ben Mlih, *Structures politiques du Maroc colonial* (Paris: L'Harmattan, 1990).

[19] Victor Cambon, "Au Maroc," in *Notre avenir* (Paris: Payot, 1916), 242. Son of Ambassador Jules Cambon, the author was an engineer and graduate of the *École centrale*. He was an attentive observer, prior to 1914, of the progress of "modern countries." His publications include *L'Allemagne au travail* (Paris: Pierre Roger, 1910); *Les derniers progrès de l'Allemagne* (Paris: Pierre Roger, 1914); and *États-Unis-France* (Paris: Pierre Roger, 1917).

[20] Joseph Goulven, "L'histoire d'une ville; chapitre 2," *Le Maroc catholique*, no. 12 (December 1924): 598–607.

[21] Goulven, "Villes d'Afrique," 77. In Fès, the fonduks "are used ... to house animals and travelers," as in the caravanserais of the East, or "for storing merchandise and for various industrial and commercial uses." Le Tourneau, *Fès avant le Protectorat*, 190–91.

[22] The architect Pierre Jabin explains that "the rampant speculation" forced "many people of modest means to move away from centers that were too expensive for them and to create on more calm and outlying sites neighborhoods that, given their distance from the center, could not expect to accommodate rental properties, and thus became villa districts." Pierre Jabin, "Villas modernes à Casablanca," *Chantiers nord-africains* (January 1929): 85–86. The subdivisions were the work of the Nathan brothers' Comptoir lorrain (to the north), of the German Frédéric Brandt, and of Haïm Cohen.

Henri Prost's Plan (1914–1917)

Banon house and Ifergan house on Avenue Général Moinier and Boulevard de Paris, built c. 1910. Photograph taken in 1994.

23 Joseph Goulven, "Les biens austro-allemands à Casablanca," *Le Maroc catholique*, no. 6 (June 1924): 318–24.

24 Particularly Rue Chevandier de Valdrôme, Boulevard d'Anfa, and Avenue du Général Moinier.

center, "on the airy plain of Mers-Sultan with commanding views of the city, sea, and countryside" and was said to be steeped in "charm and beauty."[23] It adjoined the Liberté quarter and was divided into plots to the southeast of the army camps, as defined in a plan drawn up by Comptoir lorrain. Its ethnic zoning was not as contained as Goulven makes out, notably with respect to the area neighboring the old town: far from confining themselves to the Route de Médiouna, where a number of their shops were located, the Jews settled along the roads of the new town leading to the mellah.[24] For instance, in 1910, the Banon and Ifergan Jewish families built a group of five houses arranged around a garden overlooking the entrance to one of the aforementioned roads; even in the late 1990s these dwellings still provide insight into the scale and texture of the initial urban fabric.

Small box-shaped houses with ground-floor terraces lined with balusters constituted a "preliminary layer" of sorts for the *ville nouvelle*. These are encircled by small gardens and open onto the street by means of verandahs whose friezes and columns display a variety of vocabularies. This diverse repertoire is, in fact, the sole means of distinguishing the dwellings from one another. The early central buildings are fairly stark in design. Apt examples include the Central Hotel, built in 1912, and

"The French town under construction," c. 1914, in *Villes et tribus du Maroc* (Paris, 1915).

Row of houses in the new town, c. 1913.

Henri Prost's Plan (1914–1917) 57

Ansado house, Avenue du Général Drude, 1912. Main room. Photographed in 1998.

Ulysse Tonci, "Grand colonial villa," c. 1913. Ground-floor plan, in *L'Architecture usuelle*, 1913–14.

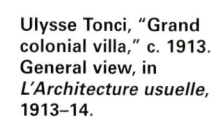

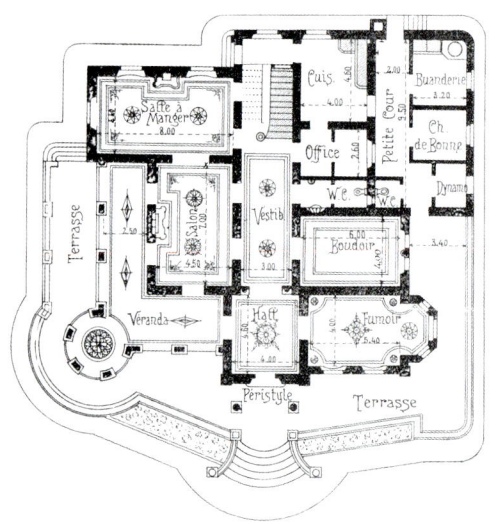

Ulysse Tonci, "Grand colonial villa," c. 1913. General view, in *L'Architecture usuelle*, 1913–14.

Karl Ficke's house, corner of Avenue de Londres and Traverse de Médiouna, 1913. Photographed in 1996.

the Ansado-Gautier-Lapeen house, constructed around the same period at the intersection of Rue Roget and Avenue du Général Drude, and whose facade is stamped by only the occasional *azulejo*.

One of the earliest building types in Mers-Sultan was the "grand colonial villa," designed by the architect-contractor Ulysse Tonci in 1913. This type was the first in Casablanca to receive Parisian press coverage, and its design was praised by the otherwise harsh critic Émile Rivoalen: "There is no artificial luxury in these constructions, just vibrant life both inside and out, with verandahs and terraces bedecking the ground floor and upper stories. They are roomy and opulent, and the servants' quarters have been clearly separated by grouping the ancillary areas to the rear and to the left of the ground floor."[25] Certain traits of contemporary Parisian mansions and French Riviera villas can be detected in Tonci's plan. Yet it was not the originality of these dwellings that Rivoalen was applauding as much as the architect's highly commendable skill in managing to "produce buildings in a country where construction materials are scarce, given that demand outstrips supply and that the port is still badly equipped." Karl Ficke's "grand" house was built in a similar style and dominated the city from the Mers-Sultan hill.[26] Goulven speaks highly of its outbuildings, which included "a garage with a bedroom, a stable, stalls," and other premises.[27]

Construction materials were indeed in short supply. Bricks, which had initially been imported from Malaga or Marseilles, were replaced by artificial stone produced

25 "Grande villa coloniale à Casablanca: Ulysse Tonci," *L'Architecture usuelle* (ca. 1913–14): 223–24. On Rivoalen, see Monique Eleb and Anne Debarre, *L'invention de l'habitation moderne: Paris, 1880–1914* (Brussels: Archives d'Architecture Moderne; Paris: Hazan, 1995).

26 Below the hill, alongside the Circular Boulevard, the contractor Pappalardo would build, in 1930, a villa in the same vein.

27 Joseph Goulven, "Les biens austro-allemands à Casablanca," 318–24.

Henri Prost's Plan (1914–1917)

F. M. Barizon apartment, Rue de l'Amiral Courbet, c. 1911. Photographed in 1996.

The structure of the building is of reinforced concrete. The semicircular arcade pattern was hardly ever used again.

28 Georges Gillet, "La construction au Maroc au début du Protectorat," *Notre Maroc* 10 (December 1950): 27–40. Dyé evokes the use of iron. A. Henri Dyé, "Les ports du Maroc," 194–95.

29 C. Dantin, "La centrale à ciment de Casablanca," *Le Génie civil* 68, no. 18 (April 29, 1916): 273–77. Construction had begun in 1913.

30 In 1901, the city had three hotels. In 1911 Dessigny noted "six to seven hotels and four or five European restaurants." This seemed "sufficient" to him. To the houses that had been transformed since 1907 was added the Hôtel de Cuba, built near the TSF on the coast. Dessigny affirmed, though, that "a hotel equipped with modern comforts is desirable and would be assured of a good clientele." Commandant Dessigny, "Casablanca, notice économique et administrative," 321.

in the Magnier factory that had been set up in El Hank in 1912. The early houses contained limestone rubble walls, wooden beams, and floors covered with cement tiles from Marseilles and Spain. Iron girders imported from Belgium were used for a while, but were eschewed in favor of reinforced concrete due to Casablanca's high level of humidity.[28] Binder would be imported up until the opening of the Roches Noires lime and cement factories in 1915.[29]

The Magasins Paris-Maroc and the Excelsior Hotel

The first two buildings constructed by the architect Hippolyte Delaporte were located in the vicinity of the medina and can be read as a response to new priorities. Design work on the Magasins Paris-Maroc (a department store demolished in the 1970s) began in March 1912, and its completion symbolized how Morocco had opened up to French trade. The Excelsior Hotel was built on the site of the slaughterhouse and fit well with Commandant Dessigny's action plan in that it marked the arrival of a new category of traveler to Casablanca. Both buildings were conceived as six-story structures, signaling a turnaround in scale with respect to the nearby medina. The department store was slotted in between wings accommodating deluxe apartments, and its main nave was topped by a glazed roof.

The Excelsior marked an important step forward in terms of modern comfort and elegance.[30] According to Henry Dugard, it embodied the metamorphosis of "a

Place de France, c. 1918. Left in photo: Excelsior hotel. The Magasins Paris-Maroc is in the background, and the clock tower is at right.

Hippolyte Delaporte, Excelsior hotel, Place de France, 1914–16. Construction work, looking from the clock tower about 1915.
Note the Banque d'État du Maroc on the left of Rue de l'Horloge.

Henri Prost's Plan (1914–1917)

Hippolyte Delaporte in association with the Perret brothers, Magasins Paris-Maroc, Place de France, (1913–14). Sketch of facade overlooking the square, 1913.

Hippolyte Delaporte in association with the Perret brothers, Magasins Paris-Maroc, Place de France, (1913–14). Facade elevation on Avenue du Général d'Amade, 1913.

31 Henry Dugard, *Le Maroc au lendemain de la guerre* (Paris: Payot, 1920): 155–56.

32 Farrère, *Les hommes nouveaux*, 121–25.

rough and unrefined monster" into a civilized city.[31] The building had a concrete frame, but Delaporte nonetheless drew discreetly on neo-Moorish decorative themes that were popular in Algeria and Tunisia at the time, notably in his treatment of the friezes and balconies. The Excelsior swiftly replaced the Café du Commerce as the hub of speculation, and its brasserie became a new meeting place where Bourron and his cronies carried out their wheelings and dealings.[32] These two milestones in the *ville nouvelle* not only broke new ground in terms of their height, but also triggered a long string of architectural innovations due to early use of reinforced concrete.

Meanwhile, construction on the Magasins Paris-Maroc got under way in 1913 and the building was inaugurated on November 17 the following year. From a struc-

Hippolyte Delaporte in association with the Perret brothers, Magasins Paris-Maroc, Place de France, (1913–14). Main staircase. Photographed c. 1914.

Hippolyte Delaporte in association with the Perret brothers, Magasins Paris-Maroc, Place de France, (1913–14). Plan of the first and second floors, 1913.

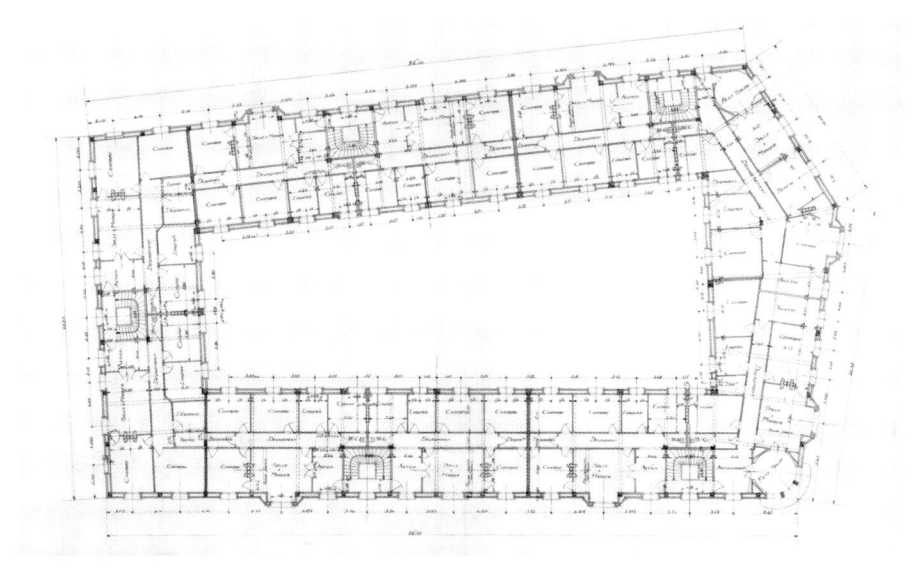

tural perspective, it was designed along stricter lines than the hotel, and its detailing was more deeply rooted in geometric abstraction, since it contained Arabic-Andalusian features.[33] The architectural components were designed by Delaporte, but the structural elements were assigned to the Perret brothers, who had already worked on projects in Oran. It is noteworthy that the start of Casablanca's construction phase coincided with the completion of the Théâtre des Champs-Elysées, which won Auguste Perret much acclaim in the Parisian architectural scene. Rather than remaining in a purely consulting role, Perret took an extremely active interest in Casablanca up until 1920, to the point of designing housing for his own workers, which will be dealt with in a later chapter. He constructed the Wallut warehouse between 1914 and 1916, echoing the duality between the facade mask and the

33 See the dossier des dessins d'exécution, fonds Perret, IFA. Perret also produced studies for a branch of the store in Tangiers. The Tardif plan that he owned is dated June 16, 1913, and no doubt corresponds to his first visit to Morocco. The Magasins Paris-Maroc later became the Magasins Modernes, and ultimately, Galeries Lafayette. It was razed in the 1970s. The hold of the Moroccan experience is perceptible even in the title of Auguste Perret's article: "Ce que j'ai appris à propos des villes de demain: c'est qu'il faudrait les construire dans des pays neufs" (What I have learned about the cities of tomorrow: that they must be built in new countries), *L'Intransigeant* (November 25, 1920).

Perret brothers, Wallut warehouses, Circular Boulevard and Route de Médiouna, 1914–16. Perspective cross section of the storage buildings.

Perret brothers, Wallut warehouses. General view, c. 1920.

Perret brothers, Wallut warehouses. Angle photo by the U.S. Army, April 1943.

64 Casablanca

interior structural clarity that characterizes the Théâtre des Champs-Elysées. The store camouflaged the warehouse behind, whose roof contained highly innovative lightweight concrete shell vaults.[34] This warehouse facility, along with several others based on the same design principle, was widely applauded in the 1920s, especially by the historian Sigfried Giedion, who praised its "extreme lightness" and its "membranelike thinness."[35] As of 1919, Le Corbusier would in turn draw on these "vast eggshell naves" when designing his Monol houses.[36]

Public Health Crisis

Public hygiene had been one of the administration's central preoccupations since the 1907 hostilities.[37] Outbreaks of plague had been a cause for concern right from the outset of the occupation, and had led to the creation of a Public Health Commission in November 1913. Headed by Laronce, the consul at the time, its members included a number of French doctors and "native Moroccan dignitaries."[38] The administration introduced health centers and kept a close eye on the livestock market and slaughterhouse "from where blood ran right down to the beach"[39]; in addition, the Public Health Commission set up a quarantine center on the windswept tip of El Hank to the west of the city.[40] An increasing number of studies were conducted in response to the spread of typhoid, smallpox, and, above all, malaria. According to a Doctor Bienvenu, very few cases of malaria had been reported prior to the city's "huge development," since it had formerly "benefited from extremely favorable conditions of health and hygiene." The new districts of Fernau and Ferrieu, together with the area beside the medina, were described as infested slums with open cisterns placed adjacent to cesspools, and garbage stagnating in the street gutters. The way in which the outlying districts were constructed also came under fire as malaria took a heavy toll on workers' lives.[41]

Providing a fresh water supply and, more notably, improving health and hygiene in the lanes of the medina and in the *ville nouvelle* were absolute priorities. "Foul" smells resulting from a lack of public lavatories, combined with putrifying animal corpses and dust blown into the city, complete the overall apocalyptic picture. Bienvenu stressed the urgent need for running water, a sewage system, and a highway maintenance service to "transform one of the unhealthiest places in western Morocco into a clean and healthy city." However, as the Jewish representative on the Public Health Commission pointed out, "The mellah lanes are too narrow for street cleaning carts and, in any case, it would be impossible to find workers willing to carry out such a task." While remaining vague as to how a project of this type would be financed, the French did not beat around the bush when it came to the educative aspects of the scheme, bluntly requesting that "the Muslim gentlemen of the Commission kindly encourage the fellow members of their religious community to promote the most basic principles of public health and cleanliness."[42]

Bienvenu's analyses were confirmed by several epidemics, including an outbreak of smallpox in November 1913 that once again turned "some parts of Casablanca into mass graves" and revealed the "useful role" that a housing authority could play. The French greatly feared that the contagion would spread to the European community,[43] though it was not until March 1914, when a typhus epidemic claimed 4,000 lives out of a total 45,000 inhabitants, that the Protectorate finally took action.

In Search of a City Center

Dessigny worked up plans for the rather nebulous space that had been formerly taken up by the souk and which had been renamed the Place du Grand Socco. Dessigny's intention was to create a proper square lined with shops backing onto the wall of the mellah.[44] The plot had been cleared during the typhus epidemic, and

---

34 An importer of McCormick agricultural machines, Wallut would be among Perret's French clients. Perret would also build the Rabat road warehouse of the wholesaler Hamelle, whose president, Pierre Grand, was to play a critical role in the city's industrial development. In 1920, for the Paris-Maroc company, Perret would design a small annex on the circular boulevard, adorned with neo-Moorish details. He would build their warehouse on Rue de Libourne in the same year. Regarding Perret's oeuvre, see the analyses of Joseph Abram. *Perret et l'école du classicisme structurel (1910–1960)* (Villers-les-Nancy: École d'Architecture de Nancy, 1985). See also the material gathered in Roberto Gargiani, *Auguste Perret, la théorie et l'œuvre* (Paris: Gallimard-Electa, 1994).

35 Sigfried Giedion, *Building in France, Building in Iron, Building in Ferro-Concrete*, trans. J. Duncan Berry (Santa Monica, Calif.: The Getty Center for the History of Art and the Humanities, 1995), 157, 159. First published as *Bauen in Frankreich, bauen in Eisen, bauen in Eisenbeton* (Leipzig and Berlin: Klinkhardt & Biermann, 1928).

36 Le Corbusier pointed out the impact of "architectural reserves," or stocks of ideas, developed by Perret in Casablanca on the church at Raincy. Le Corbusier, *Une maison—un palais* (Paris: G. Crès & Cie, 1928), 44.

37 The rapid development of the urbanism movement in France was inseparable from the consolidation of public health policies, confirmed by the adoption of the public health law of 1902.

38 The Public Health Office was backed up by a Public Health Commission or Council. MAE, series A Tanger, box 775. In October 1910, all doctors, both civil and military, as well as the entire consular corps, were mobilized due to a suspicious death in the mellah.

39 French Consul to Director of the Municipal Services, January 5, 1913, MAE, series A Tanger, box 667.

40 Regarding this point, the Public Health Office noted, "Until now, Casablanca has been dependent on the Tangiers Public Health Council. We will be able to gain our independence only when we have obtained the means to execute primary prophylactic measures locally, namely isolation and disinfection." Public Health Office, minutes of the November 16, 1912, meeting, MAE, series A Tanger, box 775.

41 Doctor Bienvenu, report on "l'hygiène de la ville de Casablanca et de sa banlieue," July 5, 1913, MAE, series A Tanger, box 775.

42 Public Health Council, minutes of the July 26, 1913, meeting, MAE, series A Tanger, box 775. Émile Klein notes, "The native left to his own devices is dirty." Émile Klein, untitled article in *La Presse médicale*, quoted in *La Nature* supplement to no. 30 (March 1912): 141.

43 "Everywhere the ground is prepared for sowing, germinating, and growing the seed." Doctor Azémar (chief physician of the Casablanca region), to the French consul, November 11, 1913, MAE, series A Tanger, box 775.

44 The defense perimeter, still defined by the ramparts, was moved back toward the exterior or strategic points, and the construction was thus authorized. Telegram of the resident-general, December 7, 1912, MAE, series A Tanger, box 666.

Aerial view of the medina, c. 1914. Note the port development and extension of the city in the southwest.

Aerial view of Place de France, 1919.
In the foreground: the market and start of Boulevard de la Gare.

the facade of the Magasins Paris-Maroc provided an axis of symmetry for the entire scheme:

> This square ... occupies a central site in relation to the old town and the eastern and southern extensions. It is thus essential that it be accorded the greatest possible ground area ... The shops and indoor market that run on either side of it, along with the Magasins Paris-Maroc currently under construction on its south side, will result in a decent and attractive arrangement. In any event, it will be infinitely preferable to the city wall that currently stands there and whose dilapidated poster-clad surface offers nothing in the way of aesthetic quality.[45]

Another major challenge was the extension of Rue de l'Horloge. This project had been initially proposed in early 1914 by De Cazanove, the newly appointed head of municipal services. De Cazanove severely criticized the narrowness of the "arterial road" that was "meant to act as the main thoroughfare connecting the town with the railway station and which was supposed to serve as an overflow for the Rabat road so that the latter might be used solely for heavy traffic." It was in the context of this scheme that concerns about the "town's aesthetic nature" were expressed for the first time.[46] Despite opposition from owner-occupiers, Edmond Joyant, then assistant director of the Public Works Department, managed to persuade the Municipal Council to exchange a tract of land (the future Place de France) for a plot near Rue de l'Horloge. This parcel of land would be earmarked

[45] Commandant Dessigny, memorandum, March 8, 1913, MAE, series A Tanger, box 666. A livestock market had been created in September–October 1912. In 1914 the Municipal Council removed the last obstacle to the envisioned improvements by requiring the relocation of the railroad tracks bisecting the Place du Grand Socco. Municipal Council, resolution, March 7, 1914, MAE, series A Tanger, box 667.

[46] C. de Cazanove to the resident-general, Casablanca, January 23, 1914, BGA, SGP, Bureau des municipalités, Casablanca, 1913–26. De Cazanove was to be discharged after the typhus epidemic.

Henri Prost's Plan (1914–1917)

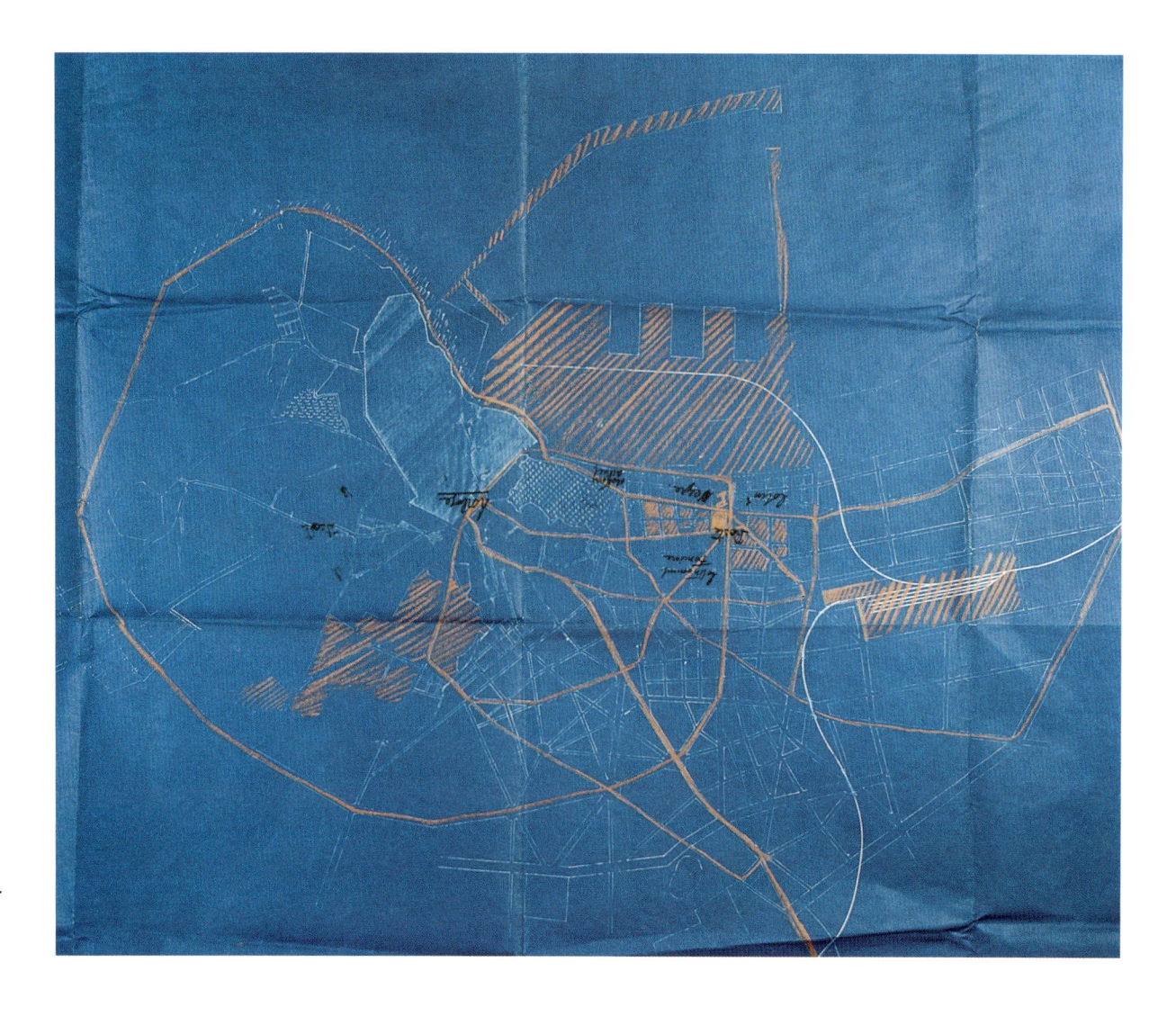

Claude Favrot, sketch for an administrative center along Route de Rabat, 1913.

for the Franco-Moroccan exhibition of 1915, before becoming the permanent site for the central market.[47]

Trade, however, formed but one area of policy within the wider quest for an urban core. For instance, property developers and the administration clashed over the site for the post office, which was the first major civic building to be erected. The official story is that the final site (the Place Administrative) was the only plot selected, but the ins and outs of the whole project were in fact far more complex. In late 1912, the municipal authority suggested slotting the building into the triangle formed by D'Amade and Moinier avenues,[48] while the lawyer Claude Favrot, acting on behalf of the Syndicat Français des Intérêts de Casablanca, proposed that it be located at the junction of the Circular Boulevard and the Route de Rabat. He put forward the idea of creating a main public square, claiming that "a well-turned-out city is one that is judiciously arranged," and that "since we are making a city from scratch, it will cost no more to come up with something artistic than it will to create something trite and ugly."[49]

In March 1913, Dessigny suggested building a girls' secondary school as well as two junior high schools and three district schools.[50] This civic program was rather more complex than anything that had come before and corresponded to a new step in Casablanca's urban development, being underpinned by semipublic, semiprivate investment. Meanwhile, the official inauguration of the Municipal Council on

47 Permission was granted on July 29, 1914. A. Tarriot, *Monographie de Casablanca*, 54.

48 Memorandum (with sketch), November 15, 1912, MAE, series A Tanger, box 666. These lots belonged to a consortium of the landowners Fernau, Lamb, and Braunschvig, as well as to Bendahan. The tax administrator Martin approved this solution.

49 Claude Favrot, on behalf of the Syndicat français des intérêts de Casablanca, to the French consul, November 26, 1912, MAE, series A Tanger, box 666. Favrot evokes the idea of an architectural competition and draws a network of new roads, in particular new radial roads, in support of a letter whose ideas will be taken up again in Prost's project.

50 Commandant Dessigny, "Programme de travaux municipaux à exécuter dans la ville." Certain schools were commissioned from the architect-contractor Barbedor.

September 25, 1913, marked the end of military control.[51] The council began to tackle central issues relating to urban planning and housing, and intervened in questions of "public morality," such as setting up a "vice squad" to clamp down on "registered prostitutes."[52] Casablanca's shady character is conveyed through legislation drawn up at the time pertaining to surveillance of alcohol sales and nightlife premises, as well as countless orders issued against a number of bars and the granting of rights to certain individuals to bear weapons. All of this gives substance to the image of an African Far West as peddled by journalists at the time.

Although the council played an active role in instituting building legislation, it was merely one of many channels used by businessmen to get their ventures off the ground.[53] This was largely due to the fact that the council was primarily concerned with the city's daily operations, whereas organizations such as the Chamber of Commerce, Industry, and Agriculture were involved in broader programs. For instance in 1914, it pushed to have Casablanca designated as capital:

> There are many reasons why the country's administrative services should be grouped in Casablanca, making it the very nerve center of the entire colony. First, its rapid pace of development . . . Second, its central geographic position within Morocco. Third, the fact that it is to be the future terminus of the Moroccan railroad network . . . And lastly, its seaport, currently under construction, which is expected to boost Casablanca's prosperity to such an extent that the city will very likely rival even the largest cities in France.[54]

It was around this time that the close working relationship struck up between contractors and the military was interrupted by the arrival of several urban planners—a recently founded professional body whose ambitions were all the stronger given their newly acquired status. A number of these planners turned their attention to Casablanca's future—that "ugly, intelligent creature so adept at stirring up fiery feelings," to quote Long, who was a reporter for the Chamber of Commerce's foreign affairs commission.[55]

---

51 The council included Prosper Ferrieu, Antoine Philip, and Gabriel Veyre, among others. The former city administration's lack of popular support is highlighted by its fiscal difficulties: In May 1912 Tardif resigned from his post of administrator responsible for urban taxation because 50 percent of the French did not pay their municipal taxes. Regarding relations with the Moroccan administration see William A. Hoisington, *Lyautey and the French Conquest of Morocco* (New York: St. Martin's Press, 1995), 135–62.

52 Decree no. 13 of October 19, 1913, regulated camel traffic (forbidden except between 4:00 and 9:00 A.M. and 12:00 and 2:00 P.M.); decree no. 92/4 of July 29, 1914, prohibited stationing herds of livestock within the limits of the Circular Boulevard; decree no. 14 of October 19, 1913, organized car traffic. MAE, series A Tanger, box 667.

53 A decree of March 4, 1914, created a commission for "identifying and visiting insalubrious lodgings," "evaluating their hygienic condition," and proposing "measures that would be appropriate to impose, in both the general and specific interest, on the owners or tenants of these establishments." The municipality established the regulation regarding the naming of streets and the numbering of houses on June 25, 1914.

54 Resolution of the Casablanca Chamber of Commerce, Industry, and Agriculture, n.d. [early 1914], MAE, series A Tanger, 668.

55 *L'essor industriel de Casablanca*, 33–35.

Early omnibus service, 1913.

Blondel La Rougerie, map of Casablanca and vicinity, 1923, based on surveys by the geographic division of the French army. Scale: 1/50000.

ZENATA
Oukacha
El Aouinet
Feux des Roches Noires
Route Nº 1
Route Nº 106
Poste de T.S.F.
Gare
Tit Mellil
Usine
El Ghelem
Dahar en Nouala
Er Refifida
Mars Mohammed
Olad Khania
Olad Haddou
Olad Bessabbou
Hafer Chifa
Koudiat Dahar el Akkar
OULAD MERCHICH
OULAD EL MJATIA
Bled el Mekki ben Larbi
Guetaa el Hadj Ahd b. Derouich
Lalla Khedidja
Mzarat St el Ahsen
Fme Garenne
Fme La Vallonnée
St Ahmed
St bou Ziane
St Otmane
Vers Rabat
11°00'
37°30'
37°20'

The Musée Social Enters the Fray: Forestier and Agache in Casablanca

Casablanca had reached fever pitch. It was a city that had shot up out of the ground, Far West style. Plots of land changed hands three or four times a day, between five and seven in the evening, on café terraces. Star-shaped subdivisions sprang up everywhere, each owner intent on making his small web of streets the hub of the future city. Naturally, everyone looked after his own interests without thinking of his neighbors. There was no cohesion linking the flights of fancy of the so-called property developers, only bustle, exchange premiums, and chaos. With just a scrap of paper from their respective consuls, Englishmen, Spaniards, Germans, or native Moroccans under German protection could, if they so wished, build right in the middle of an avenue that the French had tagged for development. A handful of roads had begun to be laid out, but these tended to follow a zigzag path before finally running into a dead end. Such was the case for "Rue de l'Horloge," the pride and joy of Casablancans in 1914. In short, then, anarchy prevailed, but it was superbly organized, as was only fitting, since it was high-ranking diplomats who had seen to the making of this city.

Albert Laprade, 1928[56]

Laprade, a young architect recently arrived from France, did not mince words when describing Casablanca as he perceived it in 1915. He employed the same type of self-justifying terms as Lyautey's euologists, and at the same time was clearly directing a slight dig at Tardif.

French investors were buying up more and more of the city, making merchants and industrialists much less powerful than they had been prior to 1907.[57] The proponents of "French interests," headed by André Colliez and Claude Favrot, who had criticized the decision to set up the capital of the Protectorate in Rabat, urged Lyautey to "rapidly put in place an extension plan for Casablanca." They felt the city "was going up too haphazardly . . . meticulously respecting all the twists and turns of the former caravan tracks," despite various measures adopted by the engineer corps.[58] Tardif's plan, which could be "tailored to suit needs," was thus deemed "an incontestable mark of progress."[59] It was, however, major property developers and investors who called for a long-term plan, intent as they were on obtaining Moroccan-owned land under the best conditions and on edging out smaller developers to capitalize on the added value created by new roads:

> Anarchy, disorder, and indifference are the elements that currently govern Casablanca, and if we are not careful they will be carved in stone, for a city is made but once . . . Let order therefore be established in Casablanca; in other words, let the administration draw up a cohesive city plan. All is not lost; the city's future can still be salvaged. Let us capitalize on the lay of the land, which is highly favorable to building a great city. And let us make it great. Let there be squares, civic buildings, and broad avenues to meet the needs of modern traffic.[60]

On March 1, 1914, a meeting was held at the Eldorado music hall and measures of health and hygiene were called for in view of the typhus epidemic. This at last forced Lyautey to urge the municipality to come up with a viable project.[61] Meanwhile, in 1913 in Paris, the Musée Social addressed the wider issue of extension plans for Moroccan towns, with Casablanca at the top of the list. The Musée's Committee for Urban and Rural Hygiene, set up in 1908, was campaigning for the city walls of Paris to be replaced by a belt of parks, and for legislation to be enacted promoting compulsory urban development plans.[62] This generated a significant volume of correspondence between Georges Risler, Lyautey, and André Colliez. On his return from Morocco, Colliez informed the committee of the resident-

---

56 Albert Laprade, "Lyautey urbaniste," *Revue hebdomadaire* 37, no. 9 (September 1928): 220.

57 This was particularly true of the Société foncière marocaine, the Société pour le développement de Casablanca, and the Société Agricole.

58 Claude Favrot, for the Parisian *Syndicat des intérêts français de Casablanca*, "Pétition à Monsieur le Résident Général pour l'exécution d'urgence d'un plan d'extension de la ville de Casablanca," n.d. [September 1912], 1–2, AN, 475 AP/52. Composed of representatives of numerous companies active in Morocco and directed by André Colliez, this organization was created on September 27, 1912. Favrot emphasized that the engineer corps had sabotaged the Public Works Department project for a thirty-meter-wide circular boulevard.

59 Claude Favrot, memorandum to General Lyautey, Casablanca, 15 October 1912, 1–2, AN, 475 AP/52.

60 Claude Favrot, memorandum to General Lyautey, 13.

61 See the petition and the police report, AN, 475 AP/52. See also Christian Houel, *Mes aventures marocaines*, 239.

62 The Musée social, created in 1894, joined reform-minded politicians and professionals in the fight for affordable housing and social modernization. Its Urban and Rural Hygiene Section, established on January 14, 1908, united urban specialists, Parisian civil servants, physicians, politicians, businessmen, and figures committed to the progress of urbanism, around its founder, the parliamentary representative and mayor of Le Havre, Jules Siegfried. See Anne Cormier, "Extensions-limites-espaces libres, les travaux de la section d'Hygiène urbaine et rurale du Musée social" (postgraduate thesis, École d'Architecture Paris-Villemin, Paris, 1987); Giovanna Osti, "Il Musée social di Parigi e gli inizi dell'urbanistica francese (1894–1914)" (master's thesis, Instituto Universitario di Architettura di Venezia, 1983; and Janet R. Horne, "Republican Social Reform in France: The Case of the Musée Social, 1894–1914" (Ph.D. diss., New York University, 1992).

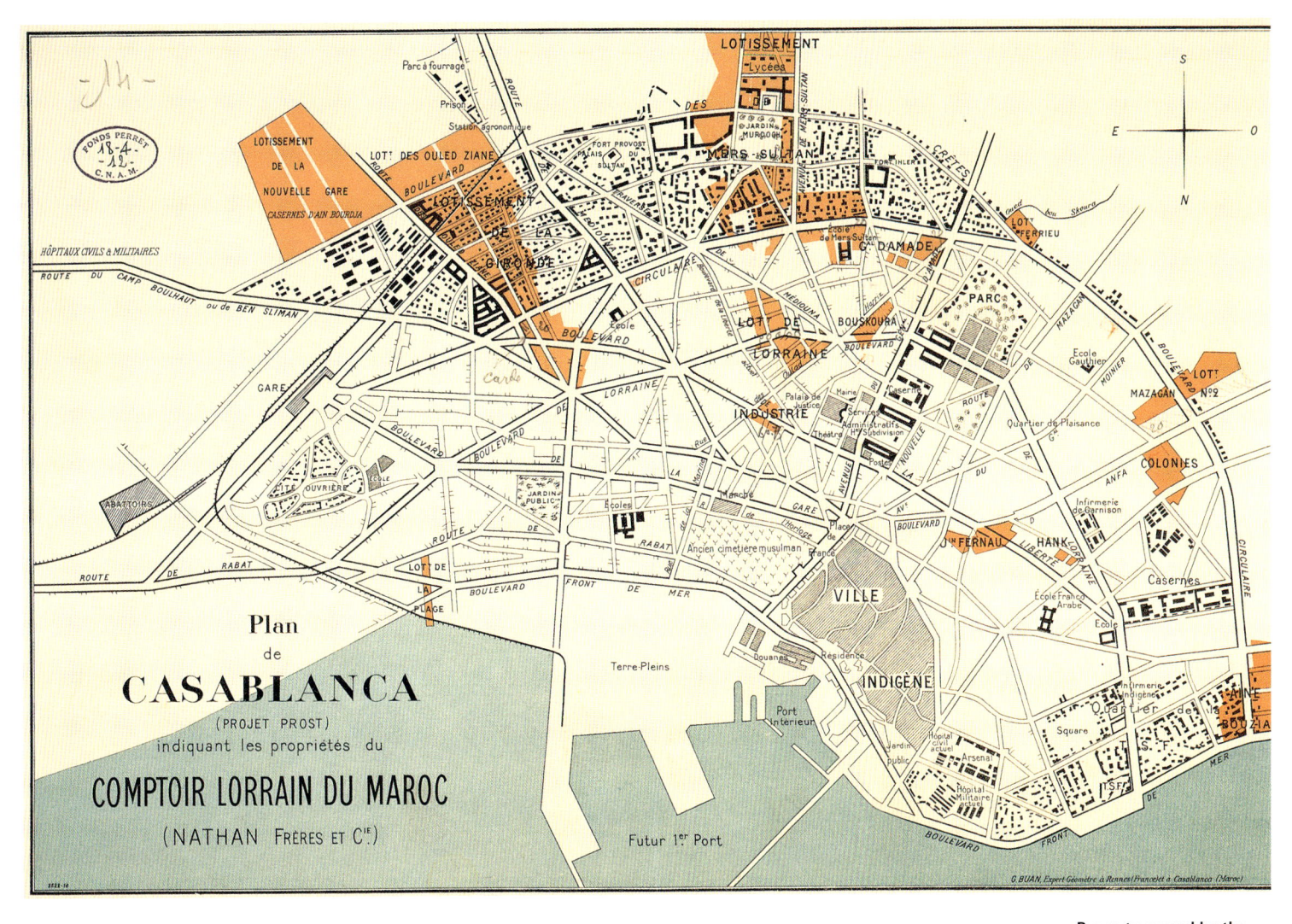

Plan de CASABLANCA (PROJET PROST) indiquant les propriétés du **COMPTOIR LORRAIN DU MAROC** (NATHAN Frères et Cⁱᵉ)

Property owned by the Comptoir lorrain du Maroc, c. 1920.

general's intention to set up a project dealing with the land ownership situation in Casablanca. Risler suggested that a competition be held, or that the authorities consider "calling on the services of Henri Prost, the recent competition winner of the Antwerp extension plan." Risler argued, "Not only has Prost drawn up a remarkable reconstruction plan for Constantinople, but he is also very much au fait with matters relating to the Orient and to Islam."[63] On February 13, 1913, Delure gave a presentation on the construction work that had already been carried out, making Tardif's extension plan his own:

> The French authorities arrived too late to be able to inject any kind of aesthetic quality into the town, and it is now difficult to rectify the construction plans of certain individuals who have built haphazardly without any agreements being established in advance. What we can do, however, is create a 30-meter-wide Circular Boulevard one kilometer outside the walled town running along the station facade. This road would also border the seafront. We could thus preserve the old town and in the surrounding area (the *ville nouvelle*) we would mark out arterial roads leading to an exterior thoroughfare. We could set up a pleasant residential neighborhood for Casablanca in the vicinity of the station and build villas on the flanks of the port's hillocks.[64]

63 Georges Risler, memorandum on a meeting of the Rural and Urban Hygiene Section of the Musée social, *Revue mensuelle du Musée social* (1913): 114.

64 Delure, comments to the Urban and Rural Hygiene Section of the Musée social (presented at the February 13, 1913, meeting), ibid., 115–16. Risler had asked Lyautey to "come to one of the meetings" and "to bring along maps of Casablanca and Rabat upon which we could trace an urban renewal and extension plan."

Jean Claude Nicolas Forestier, streets designed for towns in Morocco. Illustration in *Des réserves à constituer au dedans et aux abords des villes capitales du Maroc* (Paris, 1914).

65 Jean Claude Nicolas Forestier, "Des réserves à constituer au dedans et aux abords des villes capitales du Maroc; remarques sur les jardins arabes et de l'utilité qu'il y aurait à en conserver les principaux caractères" (December 1913), in Jean Claude Nicolas Forestier, *Grandes villes et systèmes de parcs: suivi de deux mémoires sur les villes impériales du Maroc et sur Buenos Aires* (Paris: Norma, 1997): 159–219.

66 Albert Laprade, "L'urbanisme en Afrique du Nord," *L'Architecture d'aujourd'hui*, no. 3 (March 1939): 67.

67 Lyautey's social views are the result of his contacts with Albert de Mun as well as with Eugène-Melchior de Vogüé, a member of the *Société d'économie sociale* founded by the sociologist Frédéric Le Play, whose ideas also permeated the Musée social. Regarding the colonial activity of the "leplaysiens," see Catherine Bruant, "L'Orient de la science sociale," *Revue du monde musulman et de la Méditerranée* 73–74, no. 3–4 (1994): 296–310.

68 Lyautey invokes his "gratitude" toward Risler for "having given Morocco the invaluable gift" of having summoned Prost. General Lyautey to Henri Prost, Vichy, January 17, 1916, quoted in Jean Royer, "Henri Prost, urbaniste," *Urbanisme* 34, no. 88 (1965): 12. See also the opinion of one of the advocates of Prost's recruitment, Georges Risler, "Les villes d'aujourd'hui et de demain (notes sur l'urbanisme)," *France-Maroc*, no. 3 (March 1930): 62–65. Prost was notified of his new assignment by Tirard, secretary general of the Protectorate, on February 21, 1914. Paul Tirard, memorandum to Henri Prost defining his mission in Morocco, Rabat, February 21, 1914, AA, Henri Prost estate. He arrived on April 13, 1914.

69 Winner of the second prize in the competition for a plan for Canberra (1911), Agache designed an extension plan for Dunkirk (1912). Catherine Bruant, "Donat-Alfred Agache (1875–1959), l'architecte et le sociologue," *Les Études sociales*, no. 122 (1994): 23–61; and idem, "Un architecte à 'l'école d'énergie,' Donat-Alfred Agache, du voyage à l'engagement social," *Revue du monde musulman et de la Méditerranée*, 73–74, no. 3–4 (1994): 100–17. Colliez, who met Agache through the Musée social, would continue to use his theories as a reference point fifteen years later. Colliez, *Notre protectorat marocain*, 195–96.

70 The dissension among Agache's clients—the Société foncière marocaine and the Société agricole du Maroc, both founding members of the Syndicat des Intérêts français de Casablanca and the Société pour le développement de Casablanca (owner of land abutting the projected train station)—would prevent him from pursuing this project any further.

71 General Hubert Lyautey, manuscript note, n.d., AN, 475 AP/52.

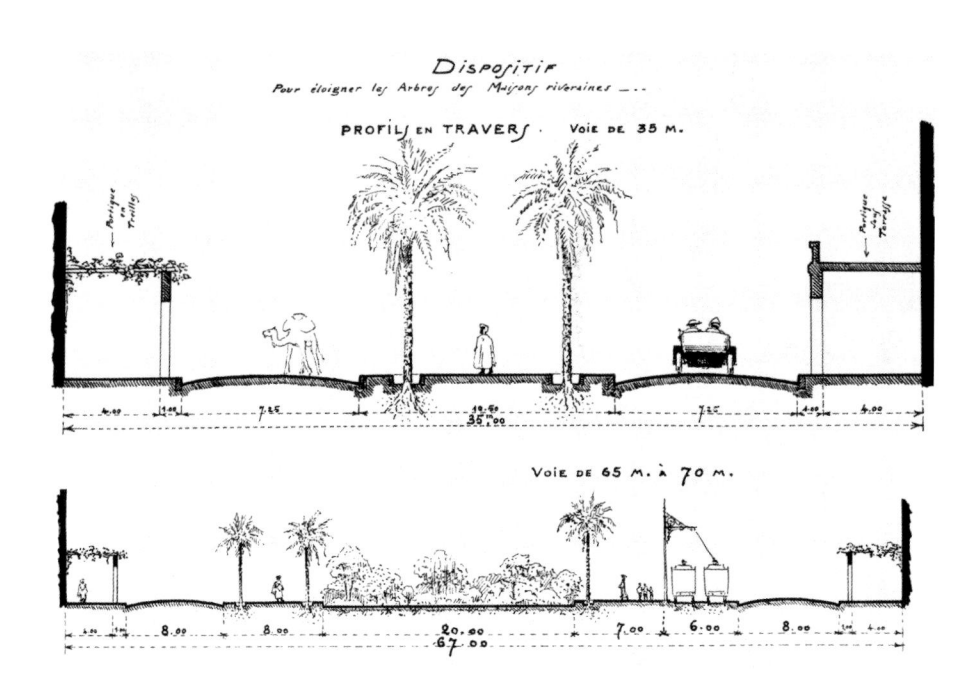

In 1913, Secretary General Tirard invited Jean Claude Nicolas Forestier to manage the issue of "open spaces" in Morocco. Forestier was a major theorist of urban planning as well as a landscape architect managing the western gardens and promenades of Paris. After attending Delure's presentation in February 1913, he began to map out roads and gardens for the existing towns of Fès, Marrakech, and Rabat. Some of his suggestions for the road system and the new neighborhoods would later be adopted by the Protectorate, which also put him in charge of designing the garden for the sultan's residence in Casablanca.[65] Laprade would later pay lukewarm tribute to Forestier's "somewhat odd report, filled with landscaping recommendations but insufficiently precise to serve as a true basis for future urban development."[66] On his return from Morocco, Forestier communicated his findings to the Committee for Urban and Rural Hygiene and, like Risler, suggested that Lyautey call on Prost.[67]

Hence, 1914 saw Prost appointed to the Service spécial d'architecture et des plans de villes (Department of Architecture and City Planning)—the first department set up by French institutions to be specifically devoted to urban planning issues. He began by tackling the problem of Casablanca.[68] Meanwhile, the Syndicat Français des Intérêts de Casablanca requested a plan from Donat-Alfred Agache, who was also a member of the Committee for Urban and Rural Hygiene.[69] Agache does not seem to have been given the right resources for such a task though, since the only extant documentation of his work is an inventory of the land he "surveyed." This inventory is largely dedicated to the major properties owned both by the Makhzen and by French companies. It is therefore difficult to ascertain whether Agache was seeking simply to improve the road system or whether he had more far-reaching objectives.[70] What is clear from his assignment, though, is that developers were serious about getting their private schemes off the ground. Prost's commission went further than this in that it covered the whole of Morocco, though Casablanca in particular. Lyautey recommended that "before establishing a final plan, Prost should reach an agreement with the parties concerned." This can be interpreted as an acknowledgment of the pressure that real-estate developers had brought to bear on him over the previous months.[71]

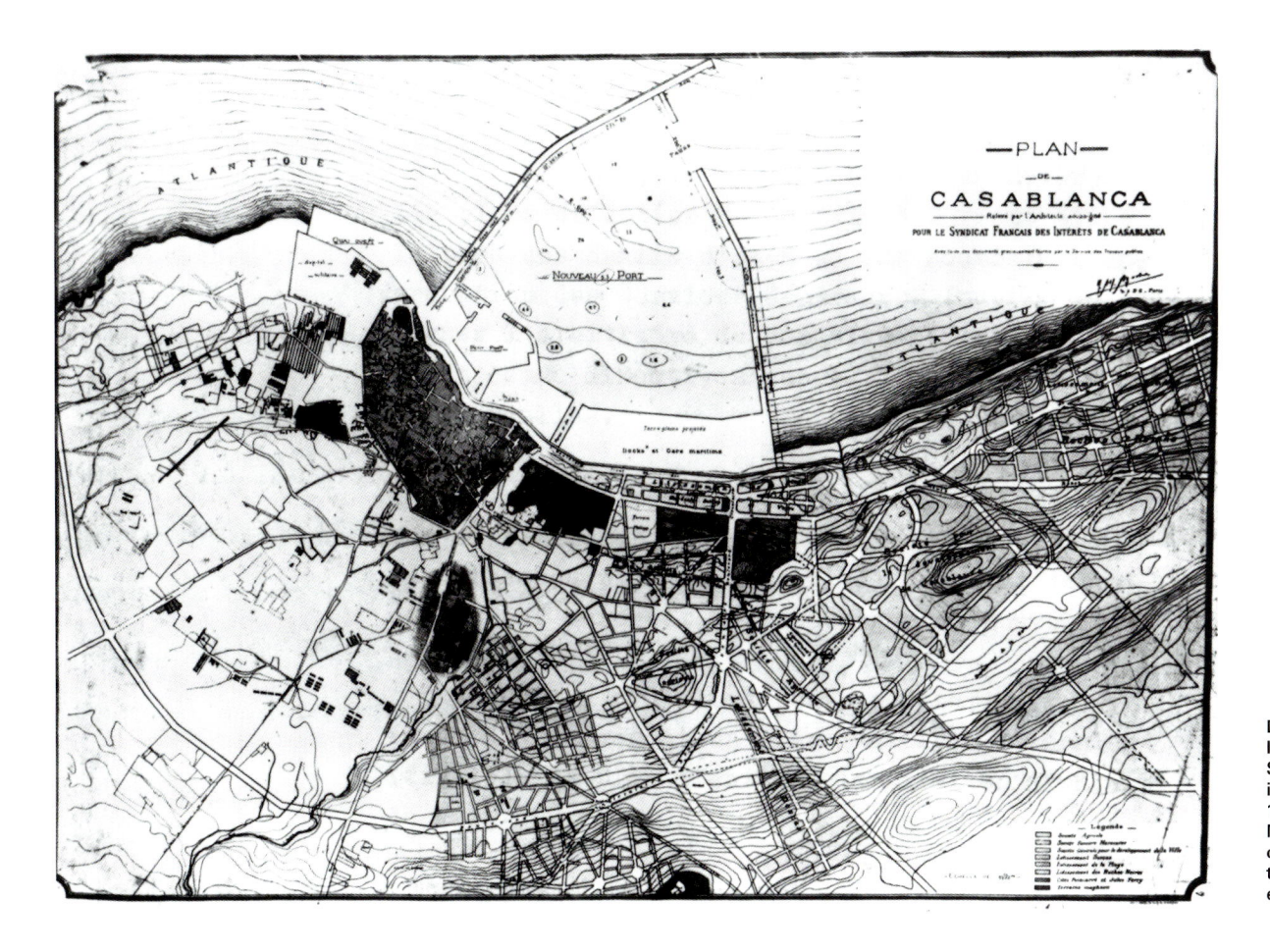

Donat-Alfred Agache, land survey for the Syndicat français des intérêts de Casablanca, 1914.
Note the growth of the city eastward and the fact that encampments still existed in the south.

Georges Buan, plan showing the subdivisions of Casablanca, in Léon Guigues, *Guide de l'Exposition Franco-Marocaine* (Casablanca, 1915).

Henri Prost Sets the City in Order

72 Henri Prost, "Le plan de Casablanca," *France-Maroc* (August 15, 1917): 5.

73 Cambon, "L'aménagement et l'extension des villes," 203.

74 Prost's "*envoi*" from Rome is a reconstruction of Hagia Sophia in Constantinople, elaborated through careful drawings in which a clear interest in structure, as well as a concern for situating the edifice in its urban context, are evident. Joseph Marrast, ed., *L'Œuvre de Henri Prost architecture et urbanisme* (Paris: Académie d'Architecture, 1960), 13–27.

75 Joining, via Eugène Hénard, the study of an extension plan for Paris undertaken by the Musée social in 1910, Prost won the competition for an improvement plan for Antwerp's fortifcations in the same year.

Henri Prost, preliminary layout of roads, as featured in the development and extension plan of 1917.

By early 1914, the small native Moroccan town was drowned amid an extraordinary mix of fonduks and dwellings of all shapes and sizes—basic wooden shacks, villas, and six-story apartment buildings, all scattered several kilometers away from the city walls. At first sight, it represented a picture of incredible chaos, curtailing all hope of establishing any kind of road system, so rapidly had development sprung up in all directions. Vast housing subdivisions had sprouted on all sides, all vying with one another to become the vital center of the ville nouvelle . . . *In the face of these well-meaning yet disorganized efforts, it was a difficult task indeed to define an urban shape capable of responding to so many diverging interests.*

Henri Prost, 1917[72]

Choosing Prost to mastermind the reshaping of a town that Cambon termed a "lost cause," "a bad start,"[73] was to prove a wise move. Awarded the Grand Prix de Rome in 1902, Prost had made his debut under the dual banner of the East (having spent several years in Constantinople)[74] and urban planning. Like Tony Garnier and Léon Jaussely, he was a staunch supporter of the new discipline of urban planning that offered so much more than the narrow boundaries laid down by Beaux-Arts large-scale composition.[75] In Morocco, his task was made slightly easier by the guidelines

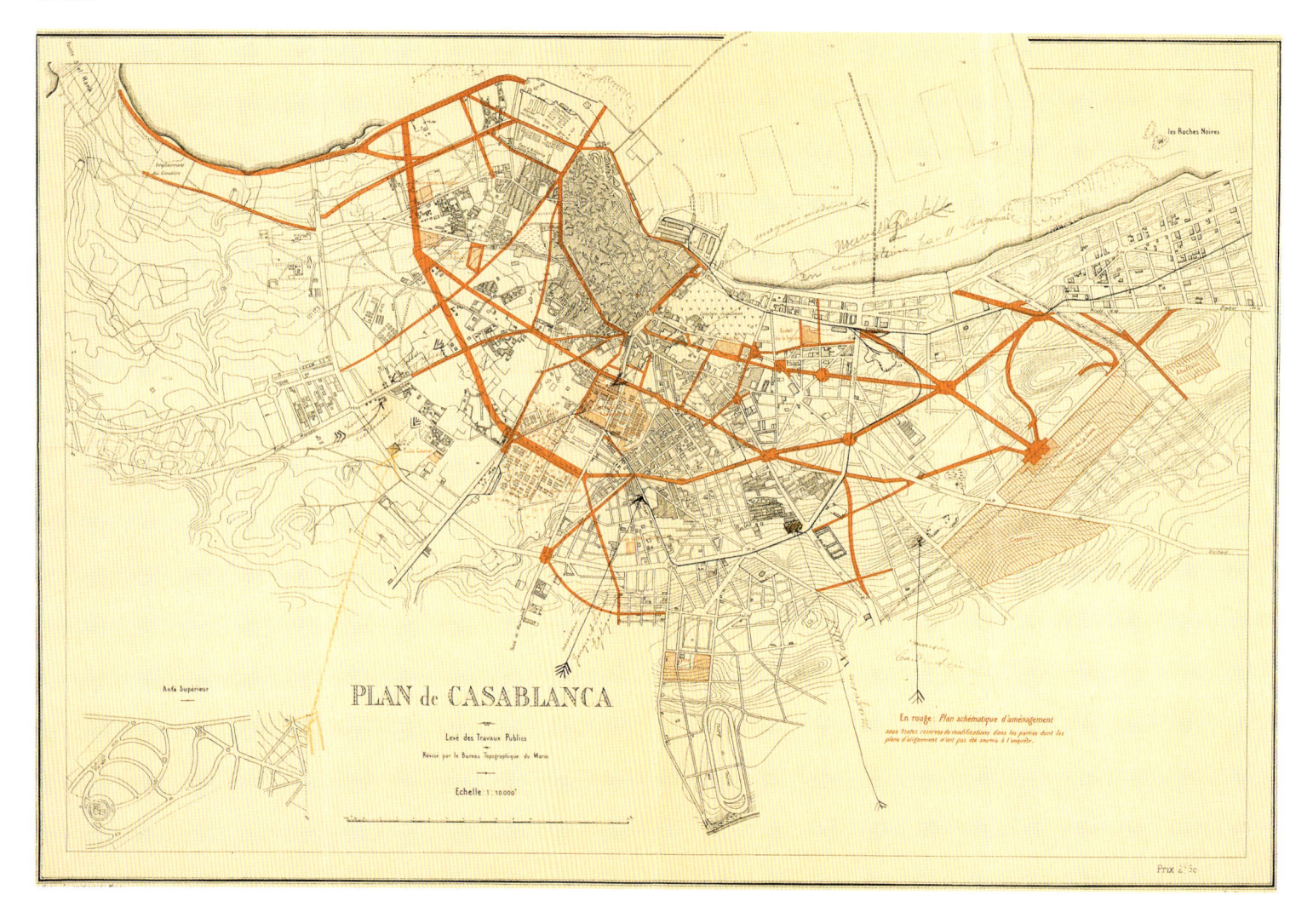

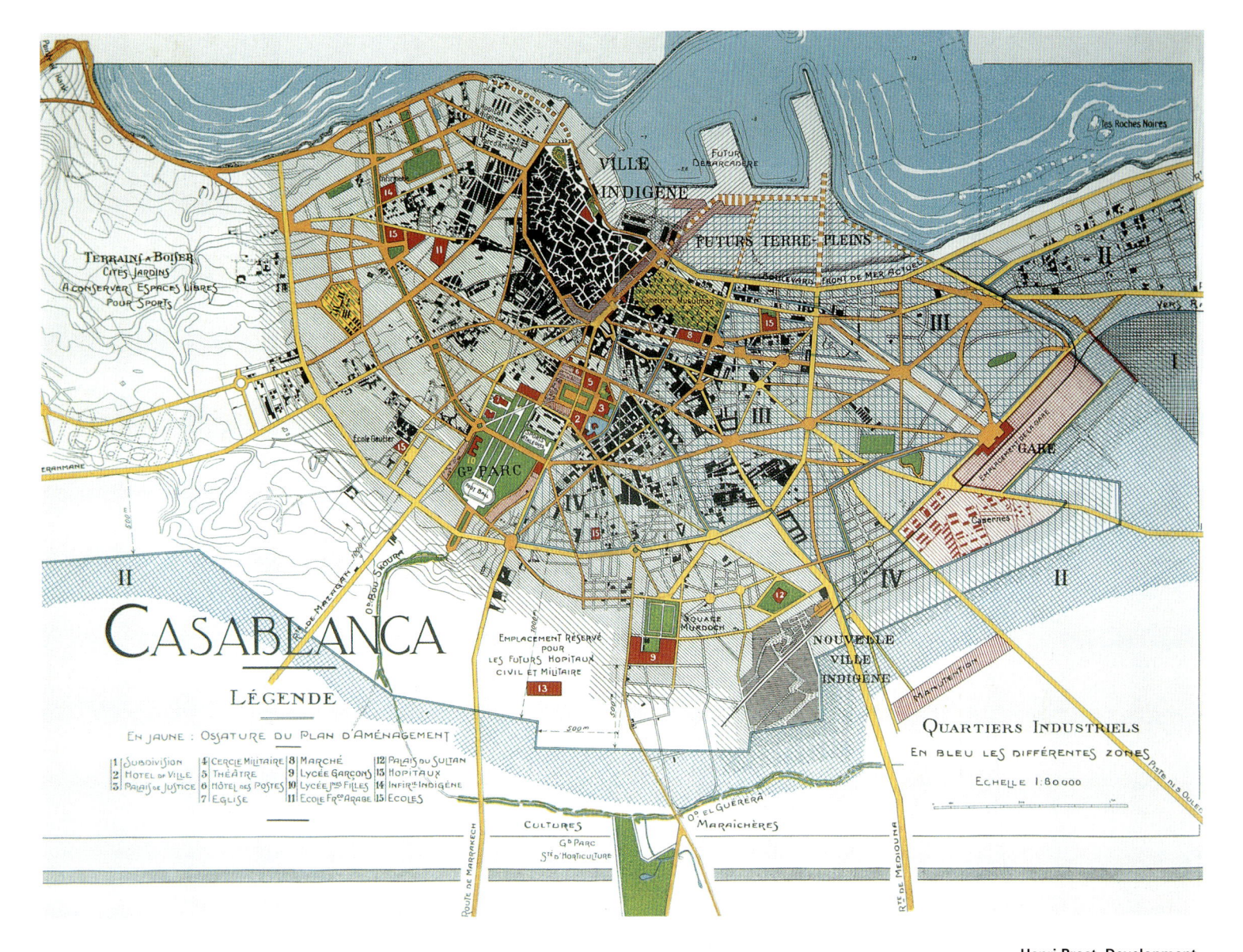

Henri Prost, Development and extension plan of 1917 for Casablanca, in *France-Maroc*, 1917.

that had already been drawn up by Forestier and, more important, by the legal system that had been put in place by Paul Tirard and Guillaume de Tarde.[76] The *dahir** of August 12, 1913, governing land ownership registration had a significant impact on planning insofar as it regulated the real-estate market, though it left the door open to brutal confiscation of Moroccan-owned land. Nonetheless, it did enable an extremely precise land survey to be implemented and it also instigated the creation of a Land Conservation Department.

Within the sphere of urban planning itself, the *dahir** of April 16, 1914, pertaining to "alignments, road maintenance, road taxes, and development and extension plans," can be deemed a milestone. It stipulated that plans should henceforth indicate not only the layout of roads and parks (in accordance with Forestier's report), but that they should also show neighborhood boundaries, as well as sewage networks and leisure facilities. This law, which also stipulated that building permits were compulsory, was in many ways much more advanced than the French one passed on March 14, 1919. It was complemented by the *dahir* of August 31, 1914, which authorized expropriation by zone and enabled the municipalities to levy a certain amount of taxes on speculative gains, causing a general outcry among colonial

[76] Prost met this lawyer and junior civil servant with the French consul on the ship carrying him to Morocco.

Henri Prost's Plan (1914–1917) 77

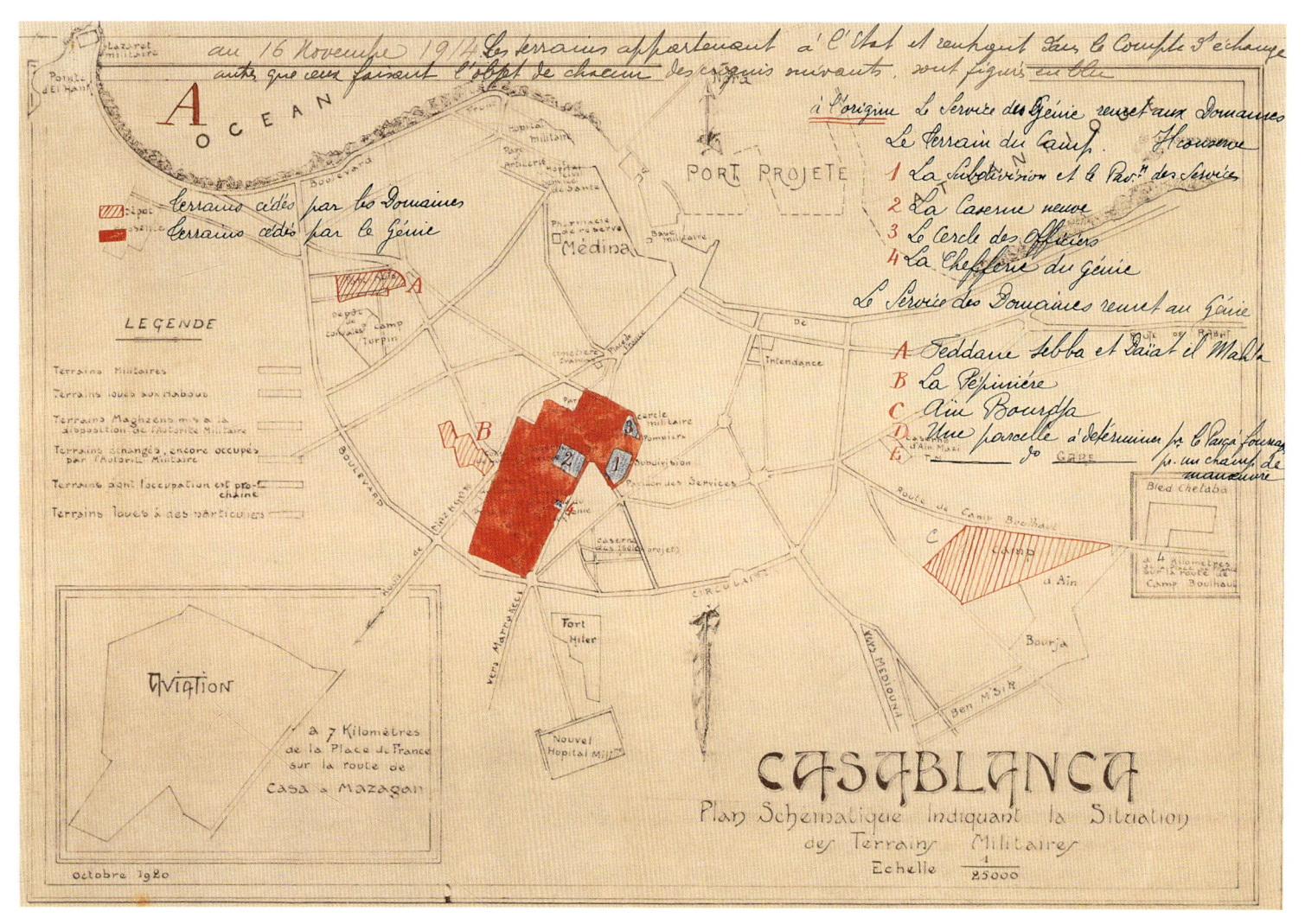

French army's Engineer Corps, plan drafted in 1921 showing exchange of land as part of the Place Administrative development scheme—a pivotal element in Prost's plan. Situation as of November 1914. The French army exchanged central tracts of land for lots owned by the Colonial administration on the outskirts of the town.

77 Rivet, *Lyautey et l'institution*, 1:235.

78 Defined for the first time in the law of January 21, 1865, real-estate owners' associations in France were only admitted within the urban perimeter in 1938, under the law-decree of June 14 regarding the hygienic clearance of insalubrious areas, and with the laws of October 11, 1940, and July 12, 1941, which governed in the context of wartime reconstruction.

79 Regarding Lyautey's urban policy, see Janet L. Abu-Lughod, *Rabat, Urban Apartheid in Morocco* (Princeton: Princeton University Press, 1980); Paul Rabinow, "Techno-Cosmopolitanism: Governing Morocco," in Paul Rabinow, *French Modern*, 277–319; Gwendolyn Wright, "Tradition in the Service of Modernity: Architecture and Urbanism in French Colonial Policy, 1900–1930," *Journal of Modern History* 59 (June 1987): 291–316; idem, *The Politics of Design*. Among recent analyses of the case of Casablanca, see Raffaele Cattedra, "Nascita e primi sviluppi di una città coloniale: Casablanca," *Storia urbana* 14, no. 53 (October–December 1990): 127–80.

80 Henri Prost, "L'urbanisme au Maroc," unpublished handbook, n.d. [ca. 1920], AA, Henri Prost estate, E6 15.

settlers.[77] Another *dahir* was passed on November 10, 1917, ruling that landowner associations could be set up and land redevelopment schemes put in place, provided consensus was reached between the various parties concerned.[78]

Based in Rabat from April 1914 onward, Prost encountered a totally different scenario in Casablanca than he had in cities such as Fès, Rabat, Marrakech, and Meknes, where he could readily apply Lyautey's principle of dividing the ethnic communities.[79] As Casablanca was "already extremely built up and subdivided, but devoid of any kind of master plan," Prost's self-declared aim was merely to arrange the town "as best he could."[80] Fifteen years down the line, Laprade, who sided with Prost throughout the project, related the conditions they had faced initially:

> The task was horrendously difficult. There was no legislation, no land surveys, nor any information on existing constructions . . . The only step we could take to establish some sort of a plan was to halt construction in order to harness the town's feverish chaotic growth, albeit at the risk of rioting. Gradually, with the aid of volunteers, wounded soldiers from the French front, and the most basic resources, we were able to set up workers' brigades and an embryonic planning office. The air force supplied us from the outset with invaluable aerial views, allowing us to see how things looked in the gaps between the streets. And Prost achieved the impossible in creating huge

arterial roads that are crucial to modern circulation, while barely touching any of the major housing blocks which would have been far too costly to pull down.[81]

Prost's plan of 1915 can be read less as a full-scale urban creation than as a *restructuring process* modeled on prototypes of circulation flows such as those advocated at the time in Paris by Eugène Hénard. The first course of action was to deal with the typhus threat by marking out a course for the major roads[82]; this was carried out by the spring of 1914. These roads were laid and imposed on the developers even before the master plan for Casablanca was finalized. There were three major objectives underpinning this master plan. First, to develop a structured road network so as to create some order out of the random subdivisions. Second, to institute zoning regulations with respect to height restrictions and public health and hygiene. Lastly, to set out the boundaries of major functional zones, in line with practices initiated by German planners.[83] Prost concentrated less on formulating a theoretical urban model than on laying down rules and regulations, as is signaled by Françoise Choay.[84]

A unifying scheme was drafted to "steer" the growth of what was from the beginning a multipolar city.[85] The road system project jeopardized schemes drawn up by the army and implied quashing certain housing developments. Prost's first battle was to prevent the engineer corps from constructing permanent garrisons, which would have blocked off the city in the southeast. He was, however, powerless to prevent a number of subdivisions from being built, since they fell under Tardif's extension plan, and he had to "abdicate his rights" over the Liberté quarter, which had gone up "so quickly yet so badly."[86] Prost's road system for Casablanca was without a doubt one of the first to fully take into account infrastructural and industrial concerns, which at the time had still not been properly addressed in metropolitan France. Furthermore, it responded to the needs created by early use of cars in Morocco; by 1914, some five hundred cars were registered in Casablanca, i.e., one for every ninety inhabitants.[87] The city's major roads were designed on a scale appropriate to the size of the cars and provided rapid links between the fairly remote luxury residential districts, the commercial quarter, and the factories. Meanwhile, garages took on the status of major urban monuments.[88]

Functional Zoning Upstages Aesthetic Improvements

Shaping a new city does not involve simply laying out roads, neighborhoods, parks, and public gardens. Nor is it a matter of merely preserving historical sites and monuments or designating sites for administrative buildings such as schools, post offices, public health facilities, and so forth. It is also a question of rationally shaping the urban block in a way that is appropriate to its end use.

Henri Prost, ca. 1920[89]

Prost's methodological perspectives can be clearly detected in his planning handbook for Moroccan towns and cities, which he drew up while he was working on the master plan for Casablanca.[90] This work criticizes French practices and sets out construction principles based primarily on German experience:

Everything produced in France is invariably centered around an aesthetic goal dictated by existing or planned buildings that serve to bound squares and crossroads, or which act as a backdrop to rectilinear perspectives, as is finely illustrated by our capital itself. Indeed, Paris has hypnotized our entire generation. In the suburbs, however, there are no existing or planned major monuments that can frame squares or crossroads or act as a backdrop for sweeping perspectives. And yet no one has

Drawing by Henri Prost of a theoretical layout for urban blocks, preparatory study for a handbook on urbanism, c. 1912.

81 Albert Laprade, "Lyautey urbaniste," *La Revue hebdomadaire* 37 (September 1928): 224.

82 Goulven, "L'histoire d'une ville: chapitre 2," 601.

83 Whereas Agache was capable neither of resolving contradictions between major developers nor of contesting military implantations, the insertion of Prost into the administration and the *dahir* on landownership associations made the essential choices of his plan possible. The precision and the fervor with which, beginning in 1915, Favrot reports on the Prost project clearly indicate that the defenders of Casablanca's "interests" had been closely linked to its development. Claude Favrot, "Une ville française moderne," in *Conférences franco-marocaines* (Paris: Plon, 1917) 2:224–225.

84 Françoise Choay, *The Rule and the Model: On the Theory of Architecture and Urbanism* (Cambridge, Mass.: M.I.T. Press, 1996).

85 Its development was to begin concurrently from the medina's eastern and southern boundaries, the Roches Noires industrial sector to the north, and the Anfa villa district to the west. Anfa district developers spared no effort in trying to have it linked to the urban perimeter. As early as 1914, Julien successfully lobbied to have his property included. See the relevant correspondence in MAE, Casablanca, box 856.

86 Étienne Lambert, "La construction à Casablanca," *La Terre marocaine*, no. 16–17 (October 1–15, 1928): 312, 317.

87 At the time, France contained one car for every 450 inhabitants. Christophe Studeny, *L'invention de la vitesse: France, XVIIIe–XXe siècle* (Paris: Gallimard, 1995), 307, 328.

88 Regarding these major arteries, Prost seems to have envisioned once again calling on Forestier to establish a program for green spaces. Jean Royer, "Henri Prost, urbaniste," 12.

89 Prost, "L'urbanisme au Maroc," AA, Henri Prost estate, dossier E6 37. Prost's method was based not on the design of single buildings but rather on delineating a zoning envelope for entire groups of city blocks.

90 Since before 1910, Prost's preoccupations were evident in urban surveys and comparisons of urban planning regulations executed, along with Jaussely, at the request of Paul Léon, who had asked the two young architects to prepare a work on city plans. See Maria-Ida Talamona, "Henri Prost architecte et urbaniste (1874–1959)" (postgraduate thesis, École des hautes études en sciences sociales, 1983); and idem, "Henri Prost, du projet au zoning 1902–1912," in *L'usine et la ville: 150 ans d'urbanisme 1936–1986*, ed. Jean-Pierre Épron (Paris: Institut Français d'Architecture/Culture technique, 1986), 51–55.

91 Prost, "L'urbanisme au Maroc," AA, fonds Henri Prost, dossier E6 31-32 (minutes, partly typescript, partly manuscript).

92 Prost, "L'urbanisme au Maroc," AA, Henri Prost estate, dossier E6 36–37.

93 The Swiss source is explicitly mentioned in M. de Montauzan, "L'organisation des villes nouvelles au Maroc," *La Construction moderne* 24 (December 30, 1923): 148.

94 Regarding German zoning procedures, see Franco Mancuso, *Le vicende dello zoning* (Milan: Il Saggiatore, 1978).

95 The zoning developed with finesse by Jaussely is sustained all the way down to his color coding. Manuel Torres-Capell, *Inicis de la urbanistica municipal de Barcelona 1750–1930* (Barcelona: Ajuntament de Barcelona, Corporacio metropolitana de Barcelona, 1985), 2140.

thought of establishing a plan to bring together these plots of land containing housing blocks that are chiefly occupied by the poorer strata of society. When building cities, the French have always focused on monumental avenues rather than housing, despite the scope of creation offered by the latter.[91]

The land ownership policies pursued by German municipalities also inspired legislation on urban redistribution and were to form an integral part of Casablanca's road system. Yet as illustrated in the above quote, Prost's view was that creating a modern city required more than just road layout. Above all, it called for the construction of "housing and other functional buildings, as well as parks and gardens":

> Streets are for circulating and buildings are for working and living in. Furthermore, the landform accommodating these constructions constitutes a crucial component of any new city, for it is on these sites that apartment buildings, factories, shops, and villas will be built, spawning the urban core. The proportions and dimensions of these tracts of land have a profound impact on public health, optimal land use, and district boundaries.[92]

The majority of Prost's manual was based on building codes drawn up for the Lausanne region and is dedicated to defining "urban blocks."[93] Prost identified a range of block types of varying density and eaves height yet geared to overall morphological homogeneity. He succeeded in putting these concepts into practice in Casablanca both in the city's road system (by defining the typical section profile of buildings) and in the depth of construction plots. However, his most innovative step, at least in pragmatic terms, was to introduce zoning practices already employed in Germany and the United States, which had resulted in heated debate at the Musée social.[94] Prost's work here was in fact in a continuum with the Barcelona master plan drawn up in 1905 by his friend Léon Jaussely.[95] Two patterns

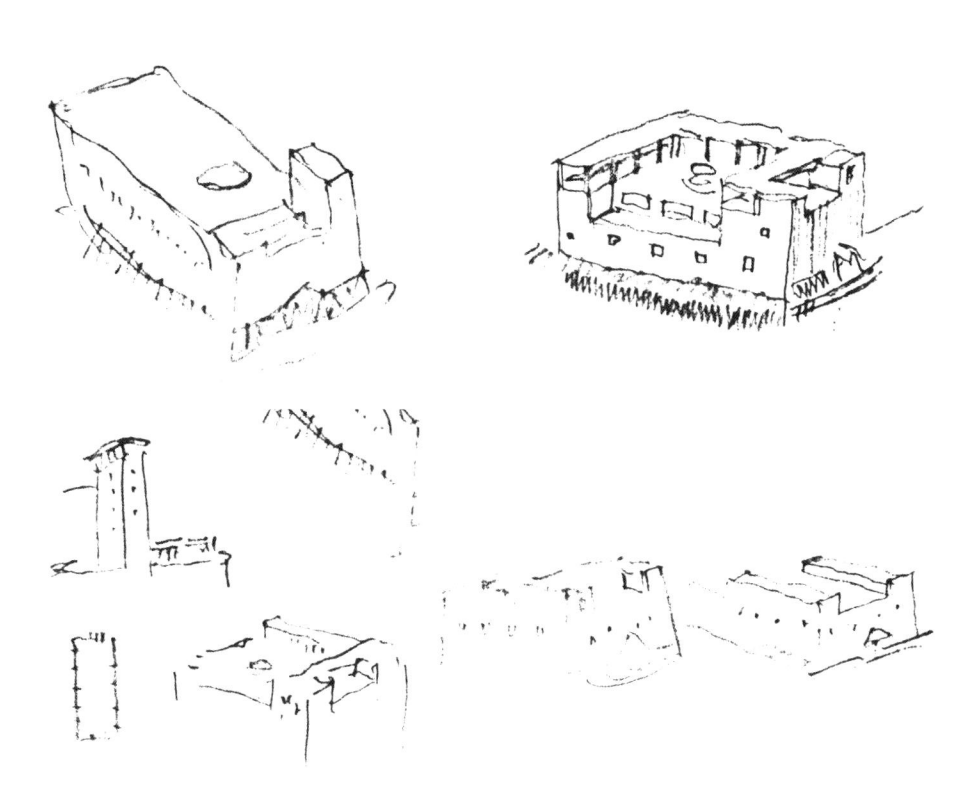

Henri Prost, sketches of the "blocks to be constructed." Design study for a treaty on Moroccan urbanism, c. 1918.

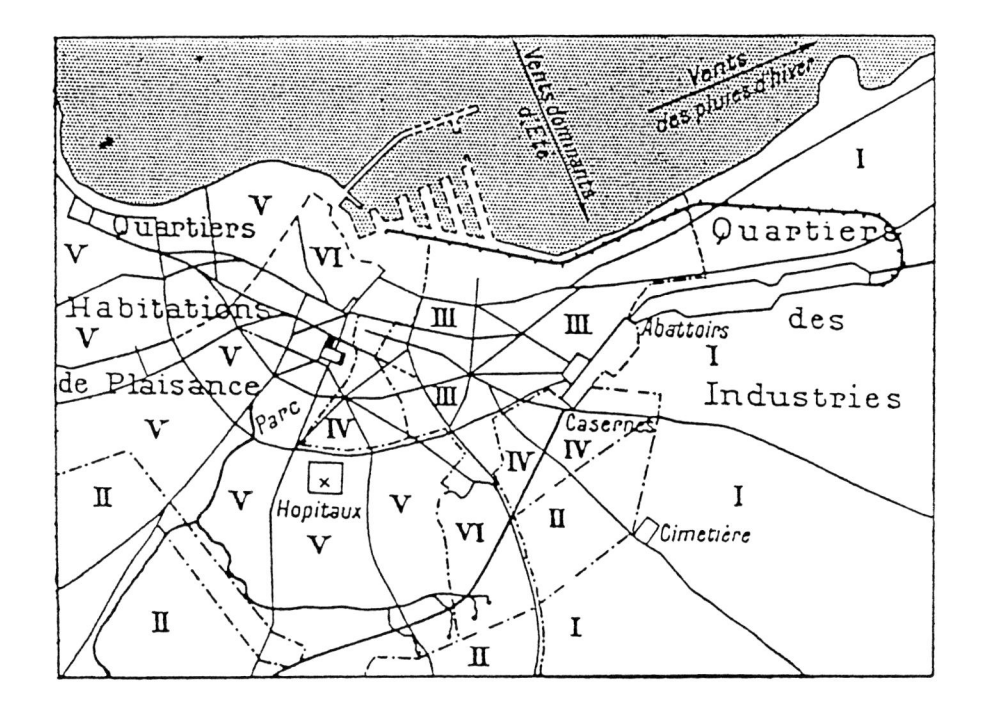

Henri Prost, zoning plan for Casablanca, in Edmond Joyant, *Le Génie civil*, 1922.

I. Any type of industrial firm allowed

II. All offensive odors and smoke prohibited

III. As in Zone II, plus prohibition of fire hazards

IV. All kinds of smoke prohibited (including machines run on steam)

V. All kinds of smoke and noisy industry prohibited

VI. Indigenous quarters (as in Zone IV plus specific building code)

of zoning were devised for Casablanca. First, three zones were defined for the European section; these comprised "central," "industrial," and "residential" areas (the last composed of villas and single-family dwellings) and had to comply with "requirements related to public health, circulation, and aesthetic features." Second, six zones were created to improve levels of hygiene and to contain the environmental risks connected with industry.⁹⁶

Prost considered the medina to be "devoid of artistic interest" and "ill-suited to the requirements of European trade." He therefore sought to demolish this "indigenous area" altogether, especially as his long-term aim was for the *ville nouvelle* to "connect directly with the port on all sides." Two types of new districts based on studies of European and American cities were selected to make Casablanca "a healthy and practical city." The first was a "business center," a concept that had yet to reach metropolitan France. The second was residential neighborhoods composed of individual dwellings—"the sole form of housing that provides a sound basis for healthy living conditions":

> As a reaction to the development of rapid transport links, modern cities in America, England, Belgium, and Germany tend to have a sparsely populated business center, containing practically nothing but offices, shops, and banks. Rather than enclosing themselves in abominable modern "caravanserai" with sparse amounts of space, air, and light, inhabitants instead seek accommodations in greener surroundings, where land prices are low. In Casablanca, too, we shall perhaps witness a similar growth in single-family houses, sited either on individual plots or grouped together amid the greenery outside the city center.⁹⁷

The partial freeze on real estate occasioned by the war proved to be an auspicious context in which to implement the Prost plan.⁹⁸ Widespread expropriation rights authorized by Protectorate legislation enabled work on the new road system to get under way rapidly, and although speculation was not brought to an end altogether, it was at least considerably reduced thanks to the project's focus on communal interests which in effect *equalized* profit opportunities.

96 City of Casablanca, "Ville de Casablanca, règlement de voirie du 26 mai 1920," quoted in Joyant, *Traité d'urbanisme*, 1:201.

97 Prost, "Le plan de Casablanca," 11.

98 Joseph Goulven, "Casablanca pendant un an de guerre," *Renseignements coloniaux et documents publiés par le comité de l'Afrique française et le comité du Maroc*, no. 8 (August 1915): 133.

The sultan of Morocco visits the Franco-Moroccan exhibition of 1915.

The Franco-Moroccan Exhibition of 1915

All the architects have managed to retain the local flavor of the Exhibition by respecting the Moorish style, expressed through white facades and terraces, high cupolas, vast arches, and minarets jutting out against the sky. In the evening, everything takes on a magical air in this Oriental setting where all races rub shoulders and where artificial sunlight picks out the pavilion profiles and illuminates the flora.

Léon Guigues[99]

The Franco-Moroccan Exhibition was staged by Lyautey in the war-torn year of 1915. The underlying objective was to convince French colonial settlers and Moroccans alike that, despite its sufferings at home, France was determined to see through the venture it had embarked on in 1912. Around one hundred temporary structures were displayed on sites between Rue de l'Horloge and the Route de Médiouna; the fact that they were temporary reflected the urban fabric of the city itself, which at the time resembled little more than a huge encampment.[100] In addition, the exhibition provided a showcase in which the municipal authority and French and Moroccan industrialists could present their different ventures.[101] Rapidly assembled using the forced labor of German prisoners, the exhibited structures served as a metaphor of the orderly development that might one day characterize Casablanca.

The French pavilion was built to a design by Jean de Montarnal, architect for the French exhibitions commission, who oversaw the whole event.[102] A model of the wharf was made to illustrate the port development project, and a number of draw-

99 Guigues, *Guide de l'Exposition Franco-Marocaine*, 75.

100 Maurice Tranchant de Lunel, director of the Beaux-Arts, coordinated the exhibition, whose general curator was Victor Berti. The latter had been inspector of the Moroccan debt in 1904.

101 The technical services were directed by Captain Louis Brau, chief civil engineer of the Casablanca region, assisted by Mantoux, Vimort, Beaunet, and Prévot. *Exposition franco-marocaine de Casablanca, rapport général et rapport des sections* (Paris: Plon, 1918); and Charles Mourey, "Le Maroc pendant la guerre et l'exposition de Casablanca," *Annales de Géographie* 23–24, no. 132 (November 15, 1915): 437–42. Under the aegis of Louis Bonnier, the city of Paris exhibited the 1913 low-rent housing competition, schools, and metro stations, as well as plans for the center of the capital. The exhibitors were chosen by a committee including Edmond Coignet, Jean and Georges Hersent, Charles Letrosne, and Édouard Redont, among others. *Exposition franco-marocaine de Casablanca 1915: Catalogue général officiel et liste des récompenses* (Paris: Plon, 1919), 45–51.

102 The municipal architect Bousquet produced the Casablanca and Chaouia pavilions. Bride built the pavilions for the Compagnie Transatlantique, Tabacs, and Société d'Études. Gourdain was responsible for the pavilions for the Paquet company and for Algeria. Naturally, Delaporte built the Magasins Modernes pavilion. Guigues, *Guide de l'Exposition*, 127. Projects by Fougère, Noblet, Oustry, and Wolf were also presented.

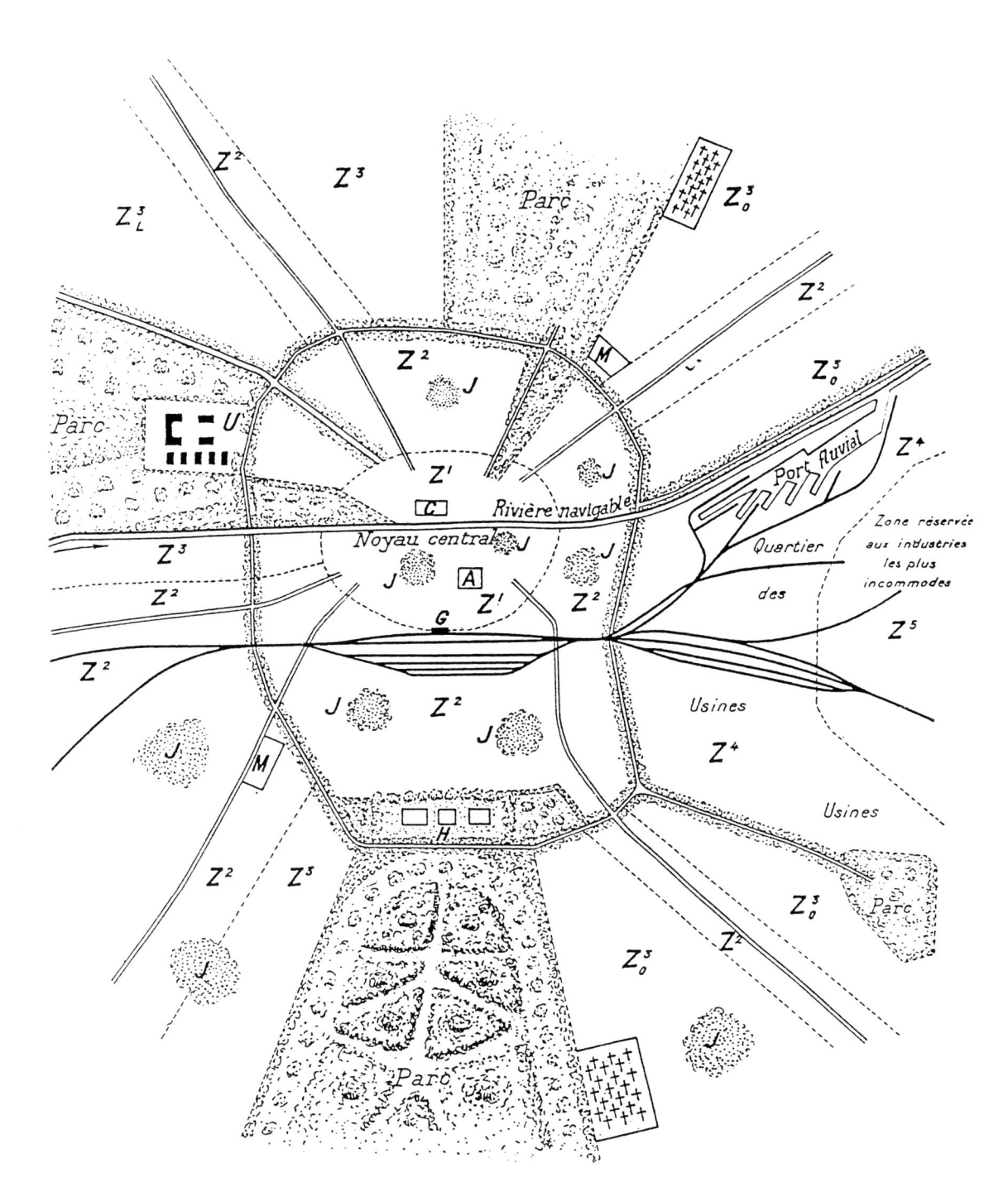

Edmond Joyant, "Schematic drawing of a city and its diverse areas," in *Traité d'urbanisme,* 1923.
This theoretical diagram would seem to be a symmetrical copy of Prost's plan for Casablanca. The axis of symmetry is the railroad, which follows the same type of course as in Casablanca. The seaport has been replaced by a river port.

══════ Grandes routes.	Z^1 Zône centrale _ Quartiers d'affaires et d'administration. Constructions hautes et denses.
▓▓▓▓▓ Avenues _ Promenades.	Z^2 Zône des habitations collectives. Constructions bloquées, densité moindre que Z^1
──────── Chemins de fer.	Z^3 Zône des habitations individuelles.
---------- Limites de zones.	Z^4 Zône des Usines.
✝✝✝✝ Cimetières.	Z^5 Zône réservée aux usines les plus incommodes.
	Z^3_0 Quartiers de population ouvrière.
	Z^3_L Quartiers des villas de luxe.

G Gare principale.
A Centre des affaires (Place du Marché, de la Bourse....)
C Centre civique (Place de l'Hôtel de Ville, de la Préfecture....)
J Jardins de quartiers. Squares.
M Casernes et Établissements militaires.
H Hôpitaux.
U Universités.

Henri Prost's Plan (1914–1917) 83

Town plans for Morocco, displayed at the Colonial Exposition in Marseilles, 1922.
The Casablanca plan is hung in the center.

103 The damage was to earn Laprade, barely off the boat, a memorable dressing-down by Lyautey. Albert Laprade, "Souvenirs du temps de la guerre: contribution à la future histoire de Casablanca et de Rabat," *Le Maroc catholique* (September 1928): 500.

104 Cambon, "L'aménagement et l'extension des villes," 214–15.

105 It would be accompanied in this migration by a small building occupied by the Horticultural Society. Gillet, "La construction au Maroc au début du Protectorat," 34.

106 See the numerous documents attesting to the renumeration, by the residency, of journalists and chroniclers who reported on the French "effort" in Morocco. BGA, bureau de la Presse de la Résidence générale, uncatalogued.

ings and photos showing construction of the port were presented in several pavilions. Prost's urban plans were exhibited in a temporary structure which unfortunately flooded.[103] Casablanca's city councilors saw to it that the works of local architects were suitably displayed, while the veteran Tonci presented a three-dimensional model of the city. Not surprisingly, the exhibition's industrial section was dedicated to the building trade and construction materials. In total, some 120,000 visitors attended this sixty-two-day architectural event that was advertised as an extension of local tradition. Victor Cambon, a journalist and a member of the exhibition jury, recalled how the structures of the Paris exhibitions of 1878, 1889, and 1900 had later been rendered permanent, and went on to suggest that Prost's plan for Casablanca include "a tree-lined square, a public garden filled with flowers, a museum, and an assembly room . . . in tribute to this magnificent exhibition and the great Frenchman behind it."[104] As it was, the exhibition structures were to be replaced by the central market, and the metal-frame pavilion that had been designed by P. Gosset for the city of Rabat would be transported to the Parc Lyautey to serve as a meeting hall.[105]

The 1915 exhibition was not the only indicator of Lyautey's desire to promulgate his ideas. He also sent countless invitations to journalists and writers urging them to visit Morocco, occasionally offering to cover all their expenses.[106] The Prost plan provided an expedient propaganda vehicle in this respect. For instance, even as early as 1913, Lyautey used the plan in the presentation on Casablanca's development that Auguste Terrier and Jacques Ladreit de Lacharrière gave, at Lyautey's initiative, during a town planning exhibition in Ghent.[107] Reports were written praising the "greatness" of the undertaking,[108] and outspoken proponents of the Protectorate's urban policy, such as Edmond Joyant and H. de la Casinière, took advantage of the congress held by the Société française des urbanistes in Strasbourg in 1923 and the Colonial Urban Planning Congress in 1931 to detail the scope of work being carried out in Casablanca.[109]

Urbanists Respond to Prost's Plan

When establishing a plan for a new town, to be set up on virgin land, it is a gross mistake to seek to hinge this plan on the geometric outline formed by a network of public roads designed a priori. *Before marking out this network, it is important to draw up some sort of site plan for the future town, characterized by specific quarters. It is only once these quarters have been established in the plan and the ensuing circulation requirements defined that the road network intended to access them can be mapped. Furthermore, these quarters must not be spread out in arbitrary fashion, for even if the town is to be built from scratch, the land is never bare and flat like a sheet of drawing paper.*

Edmond Joyant[110]

Prost's work in Casablanca coincided with reconstruction programs launched for France's war-ravaged regions. However, due to the wartime suspension of French architectural reviews, it was not until 1919 that precise information regarding Prost's urban achievements actually reached professional circles. Yet this lapse of time in fact proved useful in that the complex process could be described as a whole, revealing how the previously disparate land subdivisions had been brought together in one orchestrated stroke. In this respect, Prost's influence was far-reaching, notably following the Cornudet Law passed in France in 1919. For instance, in Edmond Joyant's *Urbanism Handbook*, which focused chiefly on recommending "different building codes" for each neighborhood, the author provided "a zoning layout for a city" that closely resembled Prost's zoning plan for Casablanca.[111]

Prost's Moroccan solutions were likewise studied by French and Italian planners in Syria and Libya, respectively, thereby confirming the experimental nature of the exercise undertaken by the Protectorate.[112] In fact, the presentation of Casablanca's master plan in 1923 at the Musée social seemed to resemble a group study of a successful protocol.[113] Prost pursued the research he had undertaken in Morocco in his urban design for greater Paris, which he completed in 1934 and in which he attempted to "create a backbone" for the city in the same way as for Casablanca. At the request of Mustapha Kemal Atatürk, then president of Turkey, Prost went on to work on a city plan for Istanbul between 1936 and 1954, bringing together the main design principles that had developed since the latter half of the nineteenth century. He ruthlessly modernized Istanbul's existing urban fabric to a degree far beyond that in Casablanca, which goes to show how much he had been held back by Lyautey in Morocco. In the end, his master plan for Casablanca was viewed as a benchmark by both journalists and specialists right up until the Vichy period[114] and served to put the city on the urban design map. Prost became a well-known individual in Casablanca (though not necessarily always a hero) and would be remembered by the public for his founding layout of the city in much the same way as Haussmann's name is connected with Paris.

---

[107] Tarriot, *Monographie de Casablanca*, 62. Documents destined for the *Exposition comparée des villes* were delivered by Dessigny.

[108] M. Bousquet, "Le Port et la Ville de Casablanca," *La Construction moderne* 20 (December 7, 1919): 76–78, pl. 39 and 40. This refers to the first publication of the Prost project in France, following its presentation in *France-Maroc* in 1915.

[109] H. de la Casinière, "Les plans d'extension des villes et l'urbanisme au Maroc," in Société française des urbanistes, *Où en est l'urbanisme en France et à l'étranger?* (Paris: Eyrolles, 1923), 202–11; idem, "La législation de l'Urbanisme au Maroc," in Jean Royer, ed., *L'urbanisme aux colonies et dans les pays tropicaux* (Paris: Éditions d'Urbanisme, 1935), 2:103–8.

[110] Joyant, *Traité d'urbanisme*, 1:68

[111] Joyant, *Traité d'urbanisme*, 1:pl. 253.

[112] Frank Fries, "Les plans d'Alep et de Damas: un banc d'essai pour l'urbanisme des frères Danger," *Revue du monde musulman et de la Méditerranée* 73–74, no. 3–4, (1994): 311–25; Maria Gubiena Fuller, *Colonizing Constructions: Italian Architecture, Urban Planning, and the Creation of Modern Society in the Colonies, 1869–1943* (Ph.D. diss., University of California, Berkeley, 1994).

[113] Edmond Joyant and Henri Prost, "Communication sur les plans d'aménagement et d'extension des villes au Maroc," report presented to the Urban and Rural Hygiene Section of the Musée social, June 23, 1922 (typescript), Musée Social Archives, Paris.

[114] The Moroccan press is sensitive to the echo that Prost's urbanism encounters in France. See "Comment on nous juge à Paris," *Travaux publics et bâtiments* (Paris, July 20, 1931). Under Vichy, Jacques Gréber would recall Lyautey's actions in order to demand an urbanism program. Jacques Gréber, "Urbanisme," in André Bellessort et al., *France 1941: la Révolution nationale constructive, un bilan et un programme* (Paris: Alsatia, 1941), 490. At the same moment, Laprade would invoke Casablanca's zoning as a model for reconstruction. Albert Laprade, "De la discipline de tous naît la prospérité de chacun," *L'Illustration* (May 22, 1941): n.p. In 1942, discussing Vichy's plan for Paris, Édouard Crevel, head of the architecture department of the Paris region, expressed hope that "the team for the plan of the Paris region will based on the one that existed for Morocco, in better times," Comité d'aménagement de la région parisienne, February 17, 1942, AN, 820774/19 (information provided by Tami Hausman). Finally, Prost's work is elevated to the status of a paragon by Pierre Lavedan in *Histoire de l'urbanisme: Époque contemporaine* (Paris: Henri Laurens, 1952), 261–62.

Geographic division of the French army, plan of the road system and buildings, c. 1922. Scale: 1/5000.

PLAN DE CASABLANCA

ECHELLE 1:5000

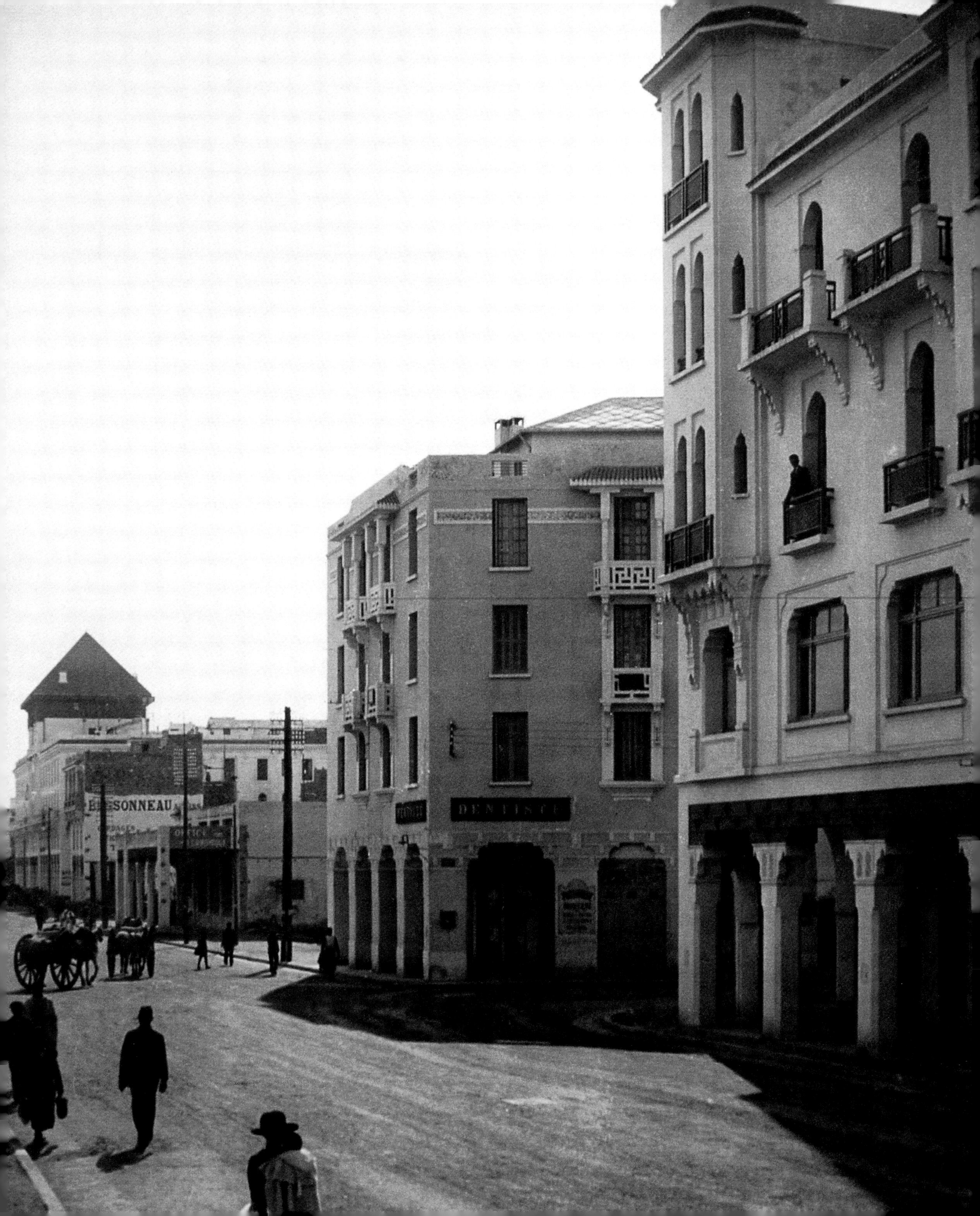

The Rule and the Monument — Planning Casablanca after 1920

A City That Mushroomed

There in front of him stood the modern city—a handful of buildings, pylons, factory stacks, half-finished avenues petering out in mud pools, dwellings set in gardens on hilly slopes, a jumble of tents, corrugated iron shacks, huts and old wagons, a leper zone assailing the hospital, and then beyond that . . . the shabby grandeur of conquest.

Robert Brasillach, 1943[1]

Picture a city in the making, unsure of its path and lacking in traditions, a city with a fiery, mixed, and defiant population caught up in struggle and toil. Imagine a people's entire strength concentrated violently and exclusively not on well-being—they are long used to sleeping on hard mattresses in rickety huts—but on the money they are hoarding away in the bank. Envisage a host of nationalities all seeking to stamp their individuality on a budding conurbation.

***France-Maroc*, April 1917**[2]

R estored to its prewar state of booming expansion, Casablanca of the 1920s was a hub of ambitions, strategies, conflicts, and ideologies. Having witnessed their country thrust into turmoil by the Protectorate, the Moroccans were now looking to benefit from the spin-offs of growth and wealth generated by the country's modernization. All the radical progress was related in eyewitness reports as early as 1918. It was one "huge buzzing building site" set in high-speed motion by a populace with consuming ambition and great confidence. In *France-Maroc*, R. A. Griffel noted, "The only thing stopping these self-confident people [from achieving the impossible] is financial resources." In his view, "Casablancans are characterized by the assurance they feel in themselves and in their city. It is all a matter of daringly forging ahead."[3]

The mushroom metaphor and the equally popular expression of "sprouting city" prove that Casablanca had not yet passed its "awkward growth phase."[4] Historical tags were already being attached to "this new Eldorado." In 1928, for instance, Pierre Léris distinguished three stages within the city's development: the pastoral phase, the speculative phase, and the construction phase. The "former

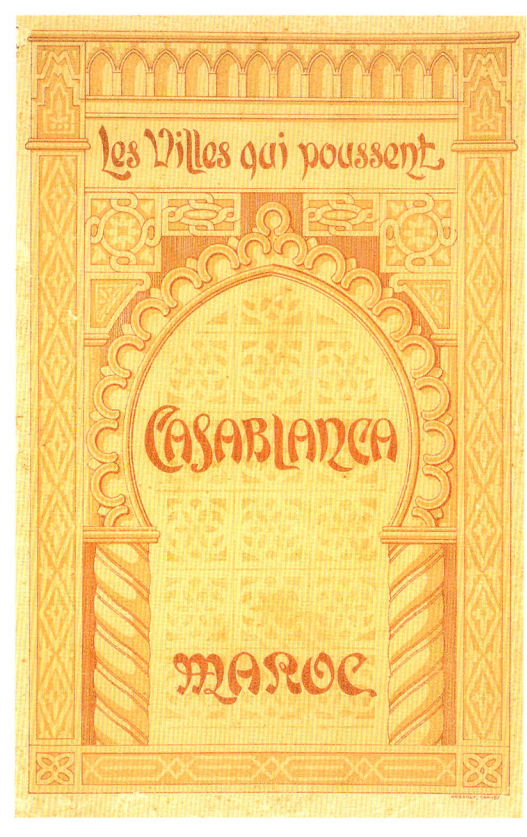

Opposite
Boulevard de la Gare, c. 1917.
At left in photo: Hubert Bride's Bessonneau apartment building.

Les Villes qui poussent (Mushrooming Cities). Brochure, 1922.

1 Robert Brasillach, *La conquérante* (Paris: Plon, 1943), 113. Rightist writer Brasillach was raised in Morocco. His pro-German views would lead him to the firing squad after France's liberation.

2 "La vie au Maroc, le mouvement intellectuel à Casablanca," *France-Maroc* 2, no. 4 (April 15, 1917): 35–36.

3 R. A. Griffel, "La croissance de Casablanca," *France-Maroc* 5, no. 5 (May 1920): 106–7.

4 Trinquier, *Les villes qui poussent: Casablanca* (Cannes: Impr. Robaudy, n. d. [ca. 1922]), 2. Trinquier was the deputy head of the municipal services.

5 Léris, "Histoire immobilière de Casablanca," 25–27.

6 Built during the war, the Opéra-Comique had a troupe composed of conscripts who later left the city. It was subsequently demolished. In 1919, the School of Dramatic and Musical Art was created. Louis Delau, "Casablanca: problèmes du temps présent," *France-Maroc* 3, no. 7 (July 15, 1919): 194–95.

7 Lambert, "La Construction à Casablanca," 315. Here we adopt the typology of populations, used at the time, which blends national and religious criteria. Thus, non-Moroccan Jews are not enumerated separately.

8 The public administration numbered 6,500 jobs in 1925 and 19,300 in 1932. John P. Halstead, *Rebirth of a Nation: The Origins and Rise of Moroccan Nationalism, 1912–1944* (Cambridge, Mass.: Harvard University Press, 1967), 56.

9 See the comparison of densities presented by André Adam in *Casablanca*, 1:125.

outer-city vegetable gardens" had apparently been replaced by "feverish building of housing developments and hastily assembled military camps," followed by "wide roads lined with monumental apartment buildings made from reinforced concrete."[5] The Protectorate appointed a promotional squad to ward off the image of Casablanca as a cynical city concerned only with making a quick dollar or two, while journals, reviews, literary associations, and even a "people's library" were launched in 1917 with the aim of redeeming profiteers who were apparently just as uncultured as they were ambitious:

> Five years ago, Casablanca was a town of speculation; it was home to all sorts of daring ventures, and all sorts of successes too. You got off the boat with several thousand francs in your pocket and a fortnight later were either rich or bankrupt. A blacksmith one day, you could be rigged out in superb glory the next, with a cane tucked under your arm, gray hat tilted over one eye—a dazzling sight to behold. It was the golden age. Since then, the city has taken shape and grown. Science came first and then the arts slipped into place, with theaters such as the *Eldorado* and *Opéra-Comique* appearing on stage.[6]

Social Division of Urban Space

Development of the *ville nouvelle* bred new spatial, social, and cultural differences among a population that shot from 63,000 in 1916 to 120,000 in 1927, when census figures revealed that half the population was Muslim Moroccan, one-third European (half of whom were French), and one-sixth Jewish.[7] The newcomers' origins, social station, and family lifestyle were closely correlated to the various building types and neighborhoods, which means that today we can gain a clear picture of the city's overall social history by studying one type of dwelling or quarter. The French who arrived in the immediate postwar period at first cautiously moved into small central apartments; they embarked with their families, or had their families join them once they were established. Having made their fortune, they built private dwellings in the most sought-after parts of town, such as Mers-Sultan or along Boulevard d'Anfa, near the city center. The privileged class' penchant for sweeping views from the Anfa hill became apparent as of 1920. The bourgeoisie occupied country villas or single-family dwellings similar to those in the Parisian suburbs; tradesmen lived in roomy apartments close to their centrally located premises, rather than in out-of-town villas; and low wage earners took up residence in more remote, yet nonetheless accessible districts such as Roches Noires, which was populated chiefly by French and Italians. Another point worthy of interest is the upsurge in administrative staff during the interwar period; this is a clear indicator of the increasing number of cogs in the Protectorate wheel, engendering a rise in housing demand.[8]

The areas primarily inhabited by Jewish and Muslim Moroccans grew overpopulated, whereas European quarters remained low in density,[9] except for the Maarif working-class district, which was occupied by the poorer members of the Spanish and Italian communities; these people were generally mechanics by trade who had become builders or who had set up their own small building firms. The Spaniards, some of whom lived in central apartment buildings, constituted the largest foreign population after the French.

Rural Moroccans took on odd jobs, settling first in *noualla* villages (which were then located mostly in Bidonville and in Derb Ghallef), before seeking out more stable living conditions. Some of these newcomers, together with residents who had been expelled from the old quarters, managed to find accommodation either in the new medina, whose construction had got under way in 1918, or in workers' housing that had begun to be financed (albeit somewhat grudgingly) by

Georges Vimort, Bank of British West Africa, Place Edmond Doutté, 1919. Photographed in 1922.

employers. This carving out of specific neighborhoods in line with social rank underscores the class antagonism that prevailed at the time.[10] Whatever the people's nationality or religion, though, housing supply was generally tight, especially among single people[11]; this situation never eased, except after the 1929 crash, which triggered a slight drop in European demand.[12] Nonetheless, there was a huge chasm between the harsh lifestyle of the lowest stratum of society and Casablanca's most affluent city-dwellers, Moroccans included, who were aspiring to modernity. The coexistence of these two extreme social categories perhaps explains the preoccupation with sculpting a new, modernized profile for the city.

The low-income segment of Moroccan Jews initially occupied the mellah, which was the convergence point for those arriving from coastal towns hit by Casablanca's expansion. The more affluent Jews settled along Boulevard d'Anfa and the Place de Verdun, near the synagogues, schools, and cemetery, creating "a handsome district of

10 The "dualistic character of the city" was still noticeable in 1971. *Les grandes villes d'Afrique et de Madagascar, Casablanca, Notes et études documentaires* no. 397–98 (Paris: La Documentation française, 1971), 21.

11 French men would be more numerous than French women for a long time. In Morocco as a whole, there were 94 women for every 100 men in 1926, and 90 in 1931. Among non-French Europeans, women were more numerous: 105 for every 100 men in 1926. *Recensement général de la population, 1951–1952* (Rabat, 1953), 2:10.

12 René Gallissot, "Le Maroc et la Crise," *Revue française d'histoire d'outre-mer* 63 (3rd and 4th trimesters, 1976): 477–91.

Portraits of architects and contractors in *Le Maroc* in 1932:

a. Marius Boyer
b. Albert Greslin
c. Edmond Gourdain
d. Élias Suraqui
e. Joseph Suraqui
f. Aldo Manassi
g. Jean Balois
h. Marius Pappalardo
i. Fernand Baille

private dwellings" in the area lying between the military camp and the medina.[13] By 1926, Casablanca had become the "largest Jewish town in Morocco."[14] Westernized Jews previously living in the port towns of Morocco, Tunisia, and Algeria were traders, craftsmen, or landed folk who had set up businesses; they lived in the *ville nouvelle*, as the new neighborhoods included in Prost's plan were named, and they owned many of the central buildings.[15] Yet written sources on Casablanca's population groups seldom refer to the Jewish category; instead, they focus on the lower classes who were generally of rural stock and who had been "rescued" by the Protectorate from their status of Muslim protégés.[16]

Hardly any of the Casablancans had lived in a large town before. Hence they found themselves thrust into a lifestyle structured by trade and industry and burgeoning with modernist ideals. Compelled to adapt to the city's values and daily pace, people clung firmly to the values and ideologies of their own origins, which accounts for the staunch microsocieties that sprang up in Casablanca. Religion was paramount among these various communities, although not everyone was necessarily a practicing believer. Parishes functioned as a forceful urban structure, in a similar way to mosques and synagogues. Religious days were also an opportunity for different communities and neighborhoods to get together; for instance, on Rosh Hashanah a Muslim Moroccan would bring a gift or pay a visit to a Jew, who would reciprocate on Aid el Kebir. Each neighborhood was therefore characterized by ethnic, religious, and social differences. Finally, it is interesting to note that many inhabitants were members of sports, philanthropic, or musical associations. One of the primary aims of these associations was social networking, and consequently such groups played a key role in architectural commissions.

After World War I, the French were particularly harsh in their revenge against their previous competitors. *Vae victis* became their program. Although not all the Germans in Casablanca were shot as "spies," as was the case for Karl Ficke, whose

13 Lambert, "La construction à Casablanca," 313.

14 Adam, *Casablanca*, 1:186. The Moroccan portion of this population, the only part to be enumerated as such, comprised 18.2 percent of the population (i.e., 19,500 inhabitants) in 1926. With the massive influx of Muslims from that point onward, this percentage diminished steadily.

15 Building permit registers mentioning the name of the first owner attest to this. See Permis de construire de Casablanca, 1918–1950, fonds de microfiches, Agence urbaine de Casablanca; and Permis de construire de Casablanca, 1916–1960, fonds de microfiches et dossiers, Wilaya du Grand Casablanca.

16 Joseph Goulven, *Les mellahs de Rabat-Salé* (Paris: Librairie orientaliste Paul Geuthner, 1927). For a long time chroniclers of the colonial epic, beginning with the very anti-Semitic Goulven and occasionally joined by certain contemporary ethnologists, saw only the down-and-out and uprooted peasants in the midst of this very diverse population. Doris Bensimon-Donath describes the process whereby mellahs emptied of their most affluent inhabitants only to fill with more recently arrived poor migrants. Bensimon-Donath, *Évolution du judaïsme marocain*, 52–53.

f
g
h
i

house served for a while to intern his compatriots, their property was nevertheless confiscated, then sold off in 1924.[17] German-owned suburban market gardens were sold to future retirees, as well as to tree growers and young couples interested in purchasing a patch of land for a beach cottage. As for the agricultural land owned by the Manesmann brothers between Casablanca, Fédala, and Camp-Boulhaut, it was seized by the state.[18]

A prewar hotel on Rue de la Douane—a building protruding above the harbor side of the medina walls—was auctioned off. The same fate awaited Karl Ficke's two flagship properties, namely his fonduk, complete with tennis courts and garden on Boulevard du IVe-Zouaves, and his villa in Mers-Sultan, that "jewel in the crown, that monument to Germany's glory which, from its commanding hilltop position, seeks to crush Casablanca beneath its feet."[19] The villa was acquired by the public authorities in the late 1920s, after which it was turned into the Pauline Kergomard Orphanage.[20]

Architects and Clients

The Casablancan bourgeoisie carefully charted the course of innovation and "modern" amenities, keen to see their city propelled to the status of an avant-garde metropolis. Private investors played a more prominent role during this phase of Casablanca's history than institutional bodies or the Protectorate. The speculation fever characterizing the early years gave way to a sense of panic instilled by the housing crisis, while alleviation of the rent freeze imposed in 1918 generated a hike in market prices. Nouveau riche Europeans, Moroccan feudal lords, and upper-class North African Jews all built their own private dwellings and central apartment buildings, calling on French architects who had teamed with Italian contractors. In addition, a number of contractors purchased many fine apartment blocks both in the city center and in flourishing residential districts.[21]

17 See the accounts of German eyewitnesses: Edmund Nehrkorn (Ficke's nephew), *Die Hölle von Casablanca: Erlebnisse eines Marokkodeutschen* (Berne: Ferd. Wyss Verlag, 1918), 10–17; and Gustav Fock, *Wir Marokko-Deutschen in der Gewalt der Franzosen* (Berlin and Vienna: Ullstein, 1916), 63–65.

18 The French also did a lucrative business in the villa developments created by Frédéric Brandt in the Mers-Sultan district, and the lands owned by Walter Opitz between the center and the new station.

19 Goulven, "Les biens austro-allemands à Casablanca," 312. A subdivision facing the dense part of the Maarif, between the Mazagan road and Boulevard Claude Perrault, was also put up for sale at a low price.

20 *Bulletin municipal officiel* (hereafter referred to as *BMO*), March 15, 1926. Published bimonthly and sometimes monthly by the Casablanca municipality, the *BMO* featured legal texts and proceedings from the Municipal Council. Pagination was not systematic.

21 Among these were, notably, Baille, Rivollet, and Sidoti, as well as the Italians' Liscia, Ferrara, and Selva.

Storehouse for Spanish tiles on Route de Rabat in Roches Noires, c. 1920. Photographed in 1996.

22 Henri Prost, "Note au secrétaire général du Protectorat au sujet des architectes agréés par le gouvernement," December 3, 1922, AA, Henri Prost estate. See the biographical appendices.

23 Brasillach, *La conquérante*, 111–12.

From the very outset, several businessmen and property owners sought a culture-specific style devoid of pastiche. In short, they were anxious not to reproduce the textbook errors of other North African countries—a sentiment shared by their architects. Early examples thus reveal an ambition to marry Moroccan features with rational architecture. Hubert Bride and Hippolyte Delaporte, who had been working on the *ville nouvelle* since 1913, chose to employ the local syntax, adapting imported references to the Moroccan vernacular. Delaporte and Edmond Gourdain were the first architects to arrive on the scene, though they were rapidly joined by scores of others. Among these figured Marius Boyer, according to Prost a recipient of countless awards from the Ecole des Beaux-Arts, who came over as a lieutenant with the engineer corps during the war. Auguste Cadet also formed part of the ranks; after being swiftly hired by the Protectorate's Department of Architecture, he went into partnership with Edmond Brion and Aulier. Georges Vimort arrived during the exhibition of 1915, and at the same time René Fougère came over from Tangiers.[22] Albert Laprade and Joseph Marrast entered the arena in 1915 and early 1916, respectively. The appeal of making a quick buck attracted a flock of technicians, and Prost had to struggle daily against the grasping greed of certain selfish Protectorate officials. This particular type of huckster is personified in Robert Brasillach's novel *La conquérante*, published in 1943, in which the hero is "a qualified architect, although naturally not state-recognized, who contributed to the corruption of Casablanca."[23] Opportunities under the Protectorate acted like a magnet for architects who were unable to make it in metropolitan France. These individuals were rarely the offspring of landed families, and therefore generally harbored nonconformist ideas with regard to "progress." They were attracted by the opportunities that Casablanca offered and worked in a climate of freedom that spawned a string of innovative projects.

Job applications filed with the administration in the early 1920s reveal that the number of architects in Casablanca was double that of Algiers and three times that of Tunis, with an even higher headcount of contractors when calculated on a relative scale.[24] They came from widely diverse backgrounds,[25] and their design solutions were rooted not only in rationalism but also in eclecticism, which was a sure means, apparently, of safeguarding their conceptual freedom.[26] As analyzed in a later chapter, the effect of Parisian and European theoretical debate can be read in the plans and facades of the buildings, though this emphasis soon shifted after leading architectural proponents discovered the country's ancient edifices, as reported by Antoine Marchisio, who was to head the Protectorate's Architecture Department after Prost:

> The dwellings and palaces they discovered in Morocco showed them the truths they had been instinctively seeking. They felt that these buildings were the outcome of a lengthy and meticulous gestation phase in which set formulae had been clearly shunned. How elegant it all was! What refined concern for comfort! It was a lesson by no means wasted on minds that had long doubted the teaching they had received in their official schools. Imbued with such an atmosphere of creation and spurred by invaluable tutelary encouragement from spiritual chiefs, the young team of French architects was ripe for fomenting an architectural renaissance of sorts.[27]

In addition, many Italian and French contractors had already experienced the life and climate of the Maghreb.[28] Not only quick to recognize the skills of Moroccan *m'allemîn** and to capitalize on these, the various teams also pooled their respective cultural experiences and know-how. George Vidalenc notes that these contractors were assisted by "jobbers and masons from Sicily or from Limousin and Valence in France," who managed to make their fortune "through sheer hard work, perseverance, and stringent saving." He marvels at how easily the Moroccans adapted to new and unfamiliar building methods, pointing out "how quickly they assimilated the use of reinforced concrete," and remarks that many companies made a point of employing only native workers, apart from the site supervisor, who was always European.[29] Yet it took merely one good agricultural year, as in 1928, for the country folk to return to their land. Grown wise to this, building firms realized they had better quickly introduce mechanized construction methods.

The Place Administrative— A Manifesto of Civic Architecture

This piece of land, which has now been vacated by the army, will be devoted to an administrative square containing all the military and civic organs of the modern city . . . Casablanca's two main limbs (the business quarter and the residential district) will henceforth be jointed by public buildings, as well as by sports facilities and areas for promenading. It is here that the law courts, military command office, city hall, post office, officers' club, and so forth shall be constructed, with a view to grouping Casablanca's key edifices.

Henri Prost, 1917[30]

This creation of an institutional square—the Place Administrative—can be considered the most spectacular venture undertaken as part of the Prost plan. In a city dedicated to trade and business, such a scheme was clearly intended to underscore the influence of the Protectorate in its role as judicial and administrative powerhouse. The program for a hub of official civilian and military leisure activities was not solely Prost's brainchild, since it responded to the plan drawn up by Dessigny in March 1913, which brought together the post office and law courts in an institutional square.[31] The Place Administrative, initially called Grand'Place, then Place de

---

24 Rivet, *Lyautey et l'institution du Protectorat français*, 18–21.

25 The Pertuzio brothers were born in Algeria and trained in Tunis, while their compatriots Jabin, Arrivetx, and Cottet studied in Algeria. Born in Oran, the Suraqui brothers had only a geometer's training. Manassi was a graduate of the Accademia di Brera in Milan, while the Frenchman Curton was trained in Berlin.

26 Regarding the formulation of these doctrines in early-twentieth-century France, see Émile Rivoalen, *Maisons modernes de rapport et de commerce* (Paris: Ed. Fanchon, 1906), 234.

27 Antoine Marchisio, "L'architecture moderne au Maroc," *Aguedal* (Rabat) (May 1936): 63.

28 Italians such as Ferrara, the Selva brothers, Biagio, Battaglia, and Pappalardo, as well as French such as Baille, Gouvernet, and Lorentz, had previously been in Tunisia or Algeria. Regarding the itinerary of Italian architects of this period, see "Amate Sponde: Presence of Italy in the Architecture of the Islamic Mediterranean," *Environmental Design* 9–10 (1990); and Giuliano Gresleri, Pier Giorgio Massaretti, and Stefano Zagnoni, eds., *Architettura italiana d'oltremare 1870–1940* (Venice: Marsilio, 1993).

29 Vidalenc, "La croissance de Casablanca et les problèmes de construction," 2017–18.

30 Prost, "Le plan de Casablanca," 10.

31 Commandant Dessigny, "Programme de travaux municipaux à exécuter dans la ville," March 8, 1913, MAE, series A Tanger, box 666.

Henri Prost, preliminary sketch of the Place Administrative, November 1914.

32 Jaussely's *Place du peuple dans la métropole d'un grand état démocratique* project received the Chenavard prize in 1900. It was known to Prost, whose 1911 project for Antwerp echoes it. *Les concours Chenavard (Section d'architecture) à l'École Nationale des Beaux-Arts, 1894 à 1900* (Paris: A. Vincent, 1909), pl. 16 and 17. This place where the masses would have been able to "demonstrate freely"(ibid., pl. 17) was of socialist inspiration, like the central spaces of Tony Garnier's *Cité industrielle*.

33 Camillo Sitte, *City Planning according to Artistic Principles*, trans. George and Christiane Collins (New York: Random House, 1965). First published as *Die Städtebau nach seinen künstlerischen Grundsätzen* (Vienna: C. Graeser & Co., 1889). In French, this book appeared as *L'Art de bâtir les villes: notes et réflexions d'un artiste*, trans. and annot. Camille Martin (Geneva: Ch. Eggiman; Paris: H. Laurens, 1902).

34 In exchange for approximately forty-one very central hectares, ceded to the Protectorate, a series of parcels were allocated to the engineer corps. Engineer Corps of Casablanca, "Résumé des modifications relatives à l'échange des terrains des camps de Casablanca," Archives du Génie, CDG Maroc, carton 16, dossier 1 (note accompanied by drawings).

35 Reduced to a group of plates with minimal commentary, the only relatively comprehensive publication about the square is Henri Descamps, *L'architecture moderne au Maroc*, vol. 1, *Édifices publics* (Paris: Librairie de la Construction moderne, 1930), pl. 32–46. Although its very small scale does not permit one to draw definitive conclusions, see also Henri Prost, "Plan d'aménagement et d'extension de Casablanca," in *France-Maroc* 2, no. 8 (August 15, 1917): unpaginated insert.

36 For a comparative discussion of nineteenth- and early-twentieth-century architecture and urbanism in colonial North Africa, see François Béguin et al., *Arabisances: décor architectural et tracé urbain en Afrique du Nord 1830–1950* (Paris: Dunod-Bordas, 1983).

la Victoire, materialized into a global project that stood apart from the traditional garrison square or the *plaza mayor* of Spanish colonial towns. It formed a pragmatic vehicle of the expression for turn-of-the-century design studies conducted by Léon Jaussely and Tony Garnier, Prost's fellow Beaux-Arts students.[32] Interestingly, the combination it formed with the commercial Place de France can be seen as a direct translation of the ideas developed by Camillo Sitte in his *City Planning according to Artistic Principles*, the French version of which was a key source for early-twentieth-century planners in France.[33]

Thanks to Lyautey's direct intervention, Prost was able to use the rectangular plot of the former military camps, whose site formed an ideal articulation point not only for the business quarters and the medina, but also for the dense housing districts in the east and the more airy neighborhoods in the west.[34] Prost drew up the program for the square in 1915 and assigned its general layout to Joseph Marrast.[35] A major component of this initial project was the theater, which was intended to add a picturesque touch to the northern part of the square. Prost's team worked closely with Lyautey, whose role seems to have gone far beyond that of mere client; they broke with Algerian and Tunisian precedents by rejecting preliminary eclectic sketches, which were no doubt based on a didactic concern to illustrate the diverse character of each building. Like the 1920s civic architecture of Kemalist Turkey, the design process did not consist simply of coming up with typical Beaux-Arts plans and layouts with a hint of Moorish style; rather, it focused on endowing the core buildings with a modern yet distinctly symmetrical and hierarchical layout, punctuated sporadically with stark ancillary facilities.[36]

The alliance between modern architectural schemes rooted in tradition and Islamic art as perceived by Prost's team proved to be a fertile one. A new interpretation of local syntax emerged, comparable to Josef Hoffmann's sketches of rural houses in Campania, or to Paul Klee's and August Macke's designs of Tunis and

Djerba, which they drafted around 1914. The team concentrated on creating simple volumes with sharp edges, rather than focusing on decorative aspects.[37] Lyautey himself acted as spokesman for this approach, having probably been duly drilled by his public servants:

> We are rather proud of the fact that we have kept one of the best features of Arab construction, that is, plain exteriors. In Algeria there have been too many past examples, notably during the period of bad taste in the romantic vein, of endeavoring to re-create Arabic art by loading buildings with external ornamentation. This is pure heresy. It is a point of honor in Arab construction that nothing should be revealed on the outside, save the profile, contours, and facades.[38]

As resident-general, Lyautey would seize every opportunity to promulgate this line of thinking and to promote the design solutions put forward by Maurice Tranchant de Lunel, head of the Beaux-Arts Department (the office charged with preserving historical monuments and local crafts), though these were not always accepted readily. In a memorandum written in 1920, Lyautey recommended that construction of the administrative buildings be carefully monitored, so as not to "deface" the sites. He advised "complying strictly with the solutions, plans, and profiles whose fundamental value resides in their very simplicity."[39] His chief concern was that the civic buildings should "present a united front," forming "a harmonious ensemble around squares and gardens." This vision was based on his intimate knowledge of the scheme built in Nancy by Emmanuel Héré de Corny for Stanislas Leczinsky:

> These structures must be based on France's great eighteenth- and nineteenth-century architectural layout of streets and squares (Place Royale, Place Vendôme, Place de la Concorde in Paris, Versailles, Nancy, etc.), though obviously they will be designed in a different style. In other words, there must be perfect harmony between the road pattern, the flora, and the scale and features of the monuments. This can only be achieved by adopting one single approach.[40]

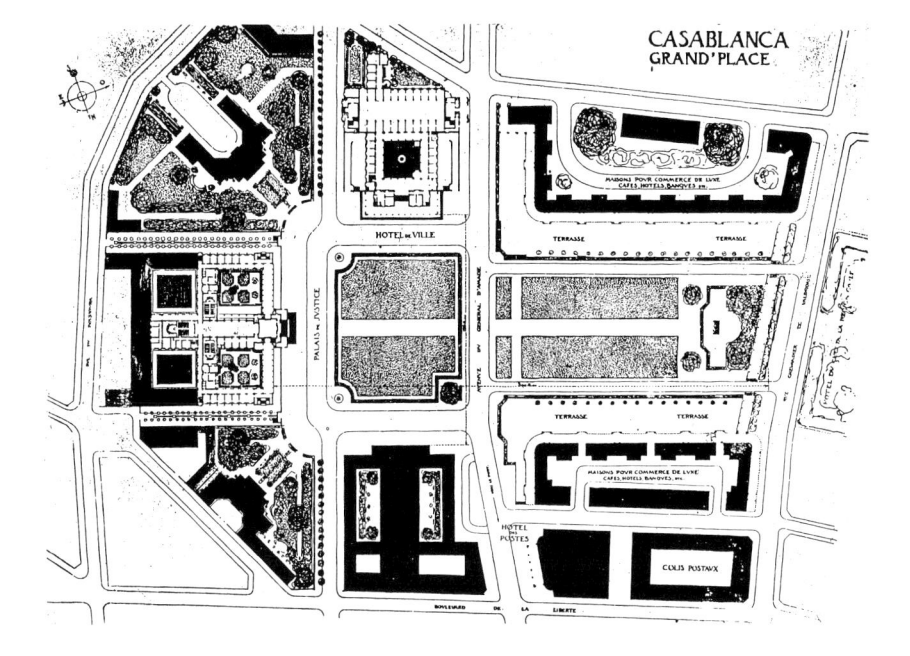

37 A synthetic Mediterranean architecture of this kind can be found in the San Diego and La Jolla work of Irving Gill between 1905 and 1915. Esther McCoy, *Five California Architects* (New York: Reinhold, 1960), 59–102.

38 General Hubert Lyautey, *Paroles d'action*, 450.

39 General Hubert Lyautey, "Note au sujet du Service des Beaux-Arts," Rabat, March 25, 1920, *Lyautey l'Africain: lettres et textes du maréchal Lyautey* (Paris: Plon, 1957), 4:76.

40 General Hubert Lyautey, "Une note de service de Lyautey," *L'Architecture d'aujourd'hui* 7, no. 3 (March 1936): 59. For Lyautey, "It is in losing sight of this principle that, despite the merit of each structure taken on its own, the juxtaposition of the Grand, the Petit Palais and the Pont Alexandre III forms such an unsatisfying ensemble."

Joseph Marrast, general plan for the Place Administrative (1920), in Descamps, *L'Architecture moderne au Maroc* (Paris, 1930).

Opposite
Aerial view of the Place Administrative looking south, c. 1924. From left to right in photograph: the law courts, military circle, and theater.

Prost's primary task was thus to endow the site with overall unity, both from an artistic and a functional perspective, since the buildings could be erected only in successive phases, dictated by the rate at which the military huts were vacated.[41] He achieved this by combining a main square bounded by civic and military facilities with a secondary and narrower space, which he lined with residential mansions. It was a similar strategy to the one adopted by Héré in Nancy, where the institutional Place Stanislas and the bourgeois Place de la Carrière are clearly differentiated from one another. Another point worthy of interest is that some of the major buildings are placed at the end of the diagonals of the Place Administrative, echoing the location of fountains and gratings in Nancy.

Early Buildings in the Square

The first building to be completed in the Place Administrative was the post office, constructed between 1918 and 1920 by Adrien Laforgue, who had been appointed to the Architecture Department in Rabat upon arriving in Morocco.[42] According to Albert Laprade, the final scheme "[is] paradigmatic in every respect; it is clear, concise, and practical and will make any Frenchman turn green with envy."[43] The stepped level overhang is trimmed with tiles, forming a continuous band around the building, neatly capping the additional story on the side wings.[44] The facade overlooking the square incorporates two sets of round arches fulfilling very different roles. The ground-floor arches offer glimpses through a shady loggia containing mailboxes set into a handsome wall section covered in *zillij*, or tiles of cut enameled ceramic; sight lines are then channeled beyond this into the main hall, which is domed by a cupola edged with glazing. The smaller arches on the upper floor conceal the more prosaic spaces of Casablanca's telephone exchange, which was conceived as a "veritable factory" to meet the needs of the growing city.[45]

The law courts were built between 1921 and 1922 to a design by Marrast and received Lyautey's personal backing, following Marrast's rejection of Prost's sketch for a sort of Doge's Palace with a central courtyard. The scheme was more ambitious than that of the post office, both in terms of plot size and the building's monumental treatment.[46] Like Laprade's residency building in Rabat, it was to serve as a yardstick for the public edifices reflecting the power of the Protectorate:

> The parti adopted takes into account both climatic differences and Morocco's judicial system. The main entrance is flanked by interior patio gardens and along its facade are arches that provide sweeping views of the square. There are also lush gardens in which lawyers and litigants can relax.[47]

Viewed from the square, the law courts are dominated by the vertical arrangement of the entrance portico; this entrance is sculpted with traditional motifs covered with green *zillij*[48] and is topped by the visor of a tiled roof canopy. The open portico facade unveils views of the *piano nobile*, which is linked to the square via sweeping steps typical of French judicial buildings but without the customary rustication. The building is encircled by a sculpted frieze, which meets up with the main entrance, and its base accommodates a number of services. According to Laprade, it forms a "magnificent backdrop to the square and its style fits well with Moroccan legal procedures, which are logical and stripped of all the complexities of the French system."[49]

In 1916, Laprade launched the construction phase for a military administration building in the southeast corner of the Place Administrative, even though a group of huts still occupied the land separating this plot from the post office. Descamps notes, "The building was intentionally conceived as a delicate structure to highlight the imposing profile of the law courts."[50] The Military Circle, designed by Marius Boyer in association with the engineer corps, was set in the northern corner. The

---

[41] The Belgian architect Brunfaut noted how successful this "enormous labor" was, and the degree to which the skillful recourse to local forms conferred quality on Prost's work. Jules Brunfaut, "L'urbanisme au Maroc," *Bulletin de la Classe des Beaux-Arts, Académie Royale de Belgique* 6, no. 10–12 (1925): 91–92. On the other hand, Louis Delau was very critical. See Delau, "Casablanca," *L'architecture au Maroc*, n.p.

[42] A first project was defined by Laprade. Laprade estate, AN, 403 AP.

[43] Laprade, "Lyautey urbaniste," 225.

[44] According to one anecdote, at the end of construction Lyautey insisted that red roof tiles already in place be replaced by green tiles that were more in keeping with Moroccan practices.

[45] Gaston Loth, "L'architecture des bâtiments administratifs au Maroc. I. Les postes et télégraphes," *L'Architecture* (August 10, 1924): 183–87.

[46] According to Paul Landowski, Lyautey said to Prost, "Make me a facade and shove anything at all behind it! The bureaucrats will always find a way to settle in comfortably, but we will not always have the opportunity to make a pretty facade." Paul Landowski, journal, May 19, 1921, archives Françoise Landowski, Sèvres.

[47] Descamps, *L'architecture moderne au Maroc*, vol. 1, *Édifices publics*, 2.

[48] *Zillij*, enameled pieces of baked clay hand cut to suit a given design, are specifically Moroccan. Rooms in traditional houses are paved or paneled with them. They are also used to decorate facades, cupolas, and building entrances. See André Paccard, *Le Maroc et l'artisanat traditionnel islamique dans l'architecture* (Saint-Jorioz: Éditions Atelier 74, 1980); and John Hedgecoe and Salma Samar Damluji, *Zillij: The Art of Moroccan Ceramics* (Reading: Garnet, 1992).

[49] Laprade, "Lyautey urbaniste," 225.

[50] Descamps, *L'architecture moderne au Maroc*, vol. 1, *Édifices publics*, 2.

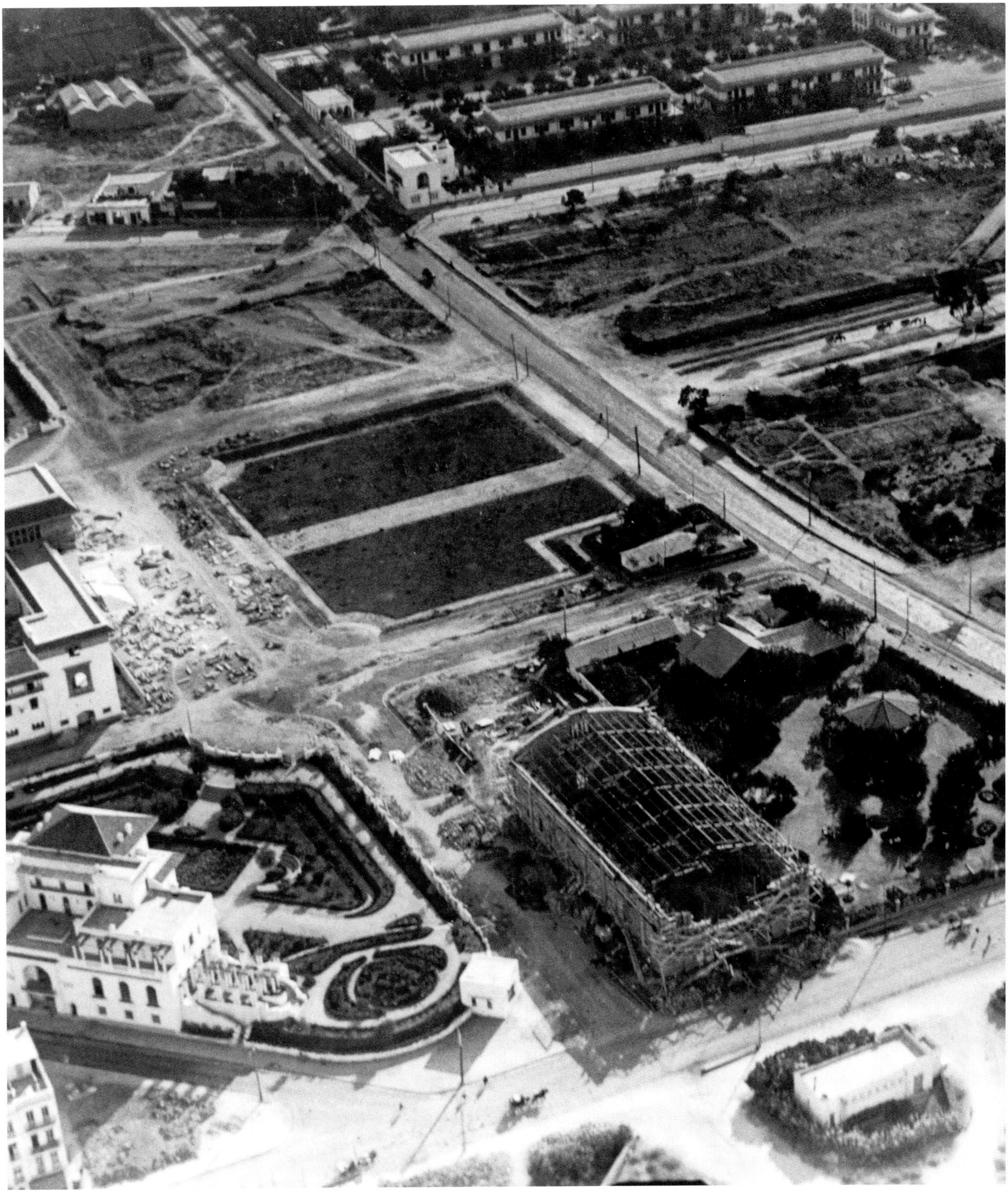

Adrien Laforgue, central post office, 1918–20, study of the main facade.

Adrien Laforgue, central post office, 1918–20, facade elevation showing the portico with *zillij* tiles.

100 Casablanca

Adrien Laforgue, central post office, 1918–20, general view.

Adrien Laforgue, central post office, 1918–20, teller hall.

The Rule and the Monument 101

Henri Prost, sketch for the front of the law courts, c. 1920.

Joseph Marrast, law courts, c. 1923, view through the ground-floor gallery. Photographed in 1991.

Joseph Marrast, law courts, c. 1923, facade overlooking the Place Administrative. Photo taken in 1993 showing detail of the main entrance.

Joseph Marrast, law courts, c. 1923, general view of the facade overlooking the Place Administrative. Photographed in 1991.

Hippolyte Delaporte, Temporary theater, 1922. Early color photo, 1926.

Albert Laprade, competition design for the theater of Casablanca, 1922 (elevation sketch).

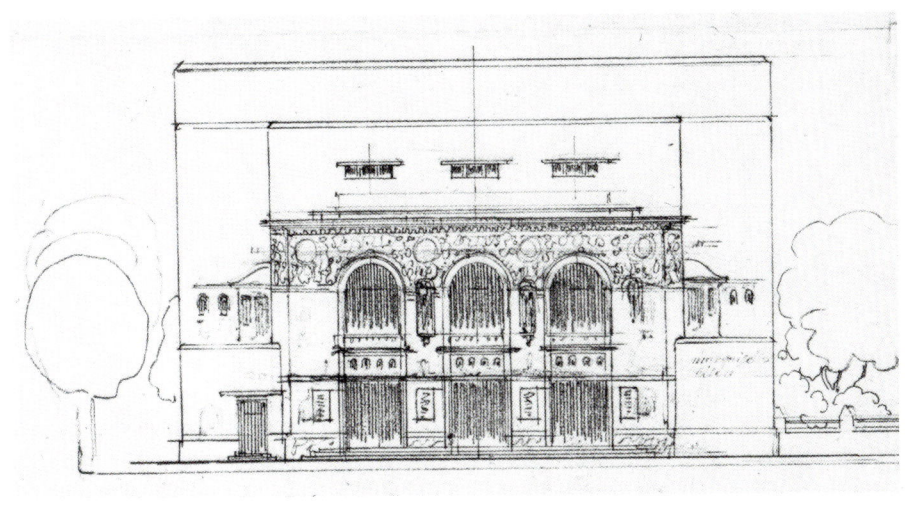

year 1922 also saw Laprade and the engineer Haller participating in a competition for a temporary theater that could seat a thousand; the initial design idea was that the theater should resemble a structure along the lines of the law courts, but with a fly tower. However, the project was scrapped, and at Public Works Director Joyant's insistence the ground plan was finally restricted to only half of that planned by Prost, with the other half given over to a small public garden.[51] This "temporary" theater, built by Delaporte in just ninety days, would in fact remain standing for fifty years or so.[52]

51 Municipality of Casablanca, program of the Casablancan architects' competition for the construction of a temporary theater, 1922, Laprade estate, AN, 403 AP (typescript).

52 Boyer and Buan also participated in the competition. The theater was demolished in the early 1980s.

The Rule and the Monument 103

Landowski's Ambiguous Monument

In 1919, the Casablancan war veterans' association organized a competition for a monument commemorating French victory in World War I, which was produced between 1921 and 1923 by the sculptor Paul Landowski, with whom Prost had struck up a friendship in Rome. Set along the axis of the law courts, the work offered a rather one-sided interpretation of the French-Moroccan alliance, with a French cavalryman and a Moroccan spahi saluting one another on either side of a hillock covered in olive branches.[53] It stands somewhat apart among Landowski's postwar monuments and obscures the brutality of a mechanized war in which the Moroccan troops were used as cannon fodder. At the time, however, it was viewed in rather a different light:

> Why mask Victory under the African skies? Why hide the warrior spirit when the oriental perception of fighting is, after all, a sort of bellicose celebration, a gigantic fantasia? Such reasoning is reflected in French North Africa, where sculptural works tend to be designed to colossal proportions, featuring the motif of the robed Arab and a thoroughbred in a blend of ornamental beauty and intense color. As for French-Moroccan alliance, this is illustrated through the theme of cavalrymen facing one another—one a Frenchman, the other a native Moroccan—of which a splendid example can be found in Casablanca.[54]

Many Moroccans perceived the bowed head of the spahi's horse as an intolerable symbol of submission, perhaps explaining why the work was hurriedly shipped to Senlis in France after Morocco regained its independence. Several similar designs were executed by Laprade for an equestrian statue of Lyautey, sculpted by François-Victor Cogné after the marshal's death in 1934. It was allotted pride of place in the square and was inaugurated by Antoine Marchisio in 1938.[55] Yet the crowning piece within this commemorative ensemble evoked neither the war nor the *ville nouvelle*'s founding father, but rather Casablanca's radical reform under the French. The piece was none other than the "wooden shack" used as a shelter by General Drude in 1907—a vestigial structure closely linked to the origins of the new town and preserved "on a small hillock in the shade of a fig tree."[56]

The Hôtel de Ville and Backstage Buildings

The final building constructed in the square was the Hôtel de Ville, or city hall, entrusted to competition winner Marius Boyer in 1927 and inaugurated in 1937. A Venetian design had already been sketched by Prost in 1914 and was initially reworked by Marrast, who stretched the building back around a single courtyard and opened it up by introducing wider arcades. Prost's design for the campanile evoked the Tour Hassan in Rabat, whereas Marrast drew inspiration from the towers of Tuscan civic buildings.[57] Boyer's scheme, however, was much more Moroccan, as is graphically borne out by the main facade. It is interesting to note that his competition version shows a portico entrance made up of pointed arches, while the completed work comprises a row of architrave columns.[58] Boyer inserted three sculpted double windows into the upper level, along with a set of three inner patios, which form the very core of the structure and lend the building an extremely spacious feel, despite its closed exterior appearance. The main staircase is flanked by two major works by the painter Jacques Majorelle, depicting the religious festivals of the *Moussem* and the *Haouache*.[59]

The programs for the western edge of the square with its arcade-lined private mansions are clearly defined in Prost's preliminary design sketch and in Marrast's plan. The latter corresponds to two blocks of "upmarket shops, cafés, hotels, and banks," though the initial scheme shows a building with four stories plus an attic story, punctuated at regular intervals by porticoes. The program, which was

---

53 The motif that had inspired the sculptor was, by his own admission, borrowed from an image of herdsmen of the Roman countryside. The siting on the square is the result of a choice made jointly by Prost and Landowski. Landowski, journal, May 19, 1921.

54 Raymond Isay, *Paul Landowski* (Paris: Librairie de France, 1931), 12. See also Bruno Foucart, Michèle Lefrançois, and Gérard Caillet, *Paul Landowski* (Paris: Éditions Van Wilder, 1989). Remember that of the 34,000 Moroccans sent to the German front, 9,000 were killed and 17,000 were wounded.

55 Cogné (1870–1945), a specialist in busts and statues of soldiers and statesmen, is the sculptor of the statue of Clémenceau located on the Champs-Élysées (1932).

56 L. D'Anfreville de Jurquet de la Salle, "Une grande ville vient de naître," *La Géographie* (January–February 1930): 30.

57 A minute illustration of the project's main elevation is published in Descamps, *L'architecture moderne au Maroc*, vol. 1, *Édifices publics*, pl. 38A. See also Marrast's letters to Prost, AA, Henri Prost estate, file A5. Drawings for this project are kept in the archive of the architect (private collection). Endowed with secondary towers in the competition version, the clocktower would be given a sleeker form by Gaspare Basciano. Gaspare Basciano, interview by the authors, Casablanca, December 13 and 14, 1990.

58 "L'hôtel de ville de Casablanca," *La Construction moderne* 42, no. 3 (April 1927): 318–20. D., "Le nouvel hôtel de ville de Casablanca," *Chantiers nord-africains* 4, no. 1 (January 1931): 69–73.

59 Son of the cabinetmaker Louis Majorelle, Jacques (1886–1962) had settled in Marrakech in 1917.

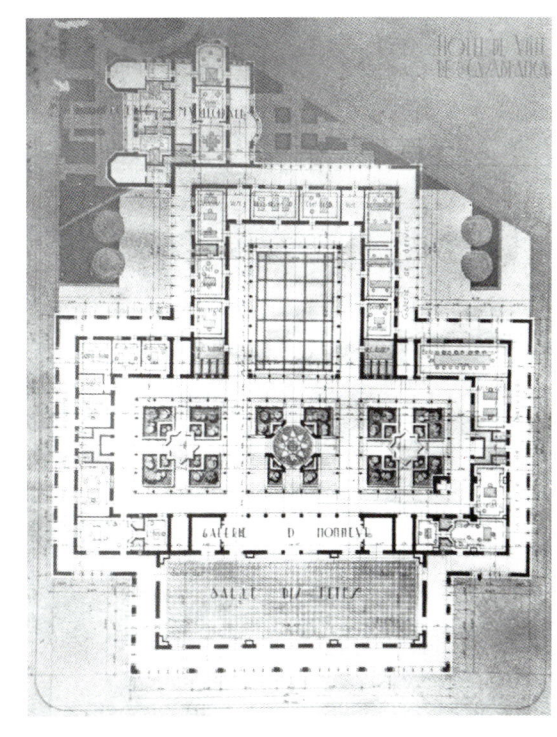

Opposite:
Paul Landowski,
Memorial to the Fallen,
Place Administrative,
1922.

Albert Laprade, design for a commemorative statue of Lyautey, 1924 (perspective drawing).

This page:
Marius Boyer, city hall, 1928–36, general view. Photographed in 1997.

Marius Boyer, city hall, 1928–36, the patios. Photographed in 1997.

Marius Boyer, city hall, 1928–36, second-floor plan.

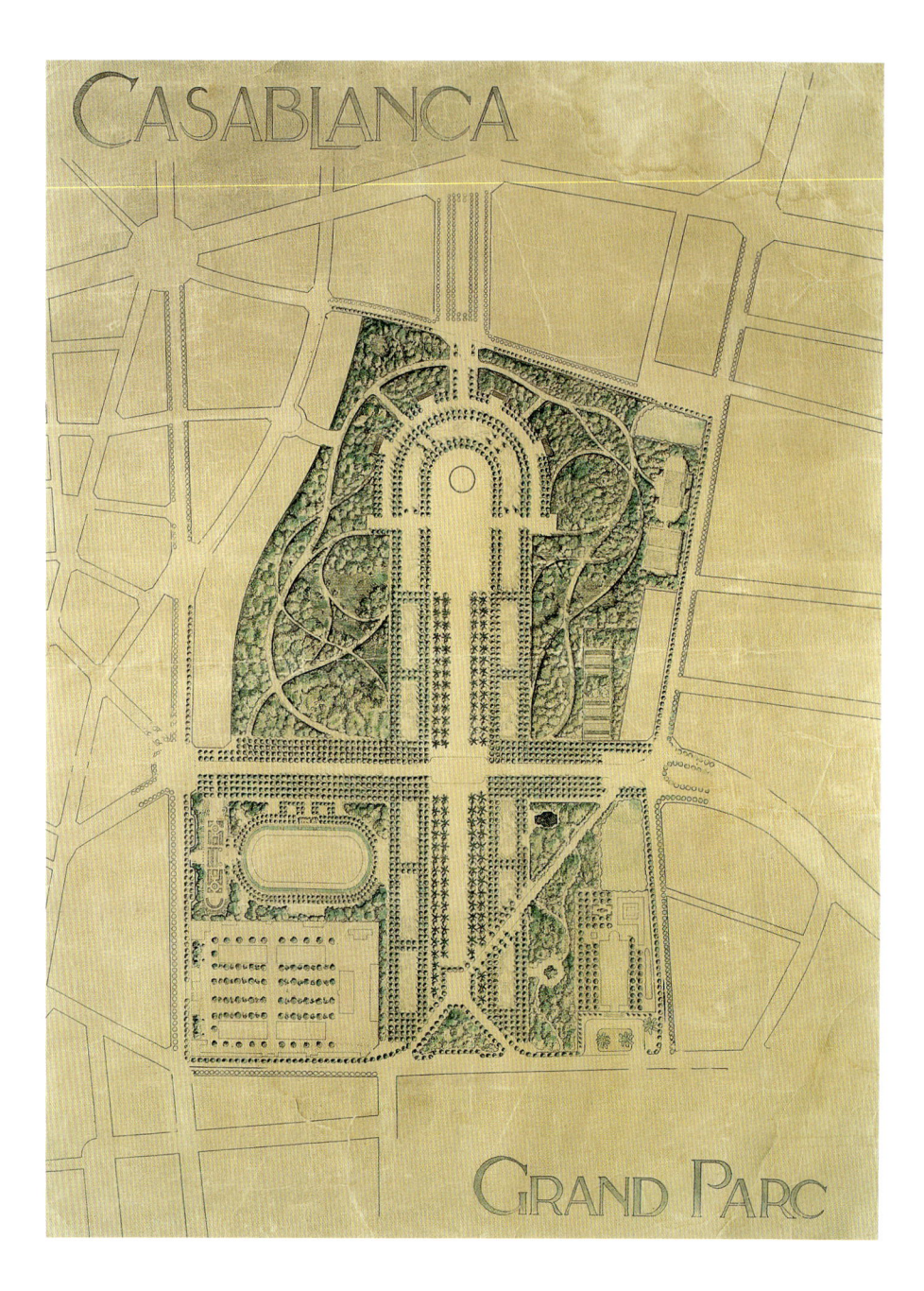

Albert Laprade, general plan for Parc Lyautey. Watercolor dated 1922, prepared for the Marseilles Colonial Exposition.

60 General Lyautey, quoted in André Maurois, *Lyautey* (Paris: Plon, 1931), 315. For reasons no doubt linked to the softness of the speculative real-estate market, the administration would be constrained to retain this land. Ultimately, the austere offices of the General Treasury and the Real Estate Property Registry, built after World War II, would face this site.

scrapped in 1925, would have offered a striking contrast between the grand civic buildings and the residential blocks. André Maurois relates Lyautey's bitter reaction to the project being abandoned:

> Here [jumping onto the base of the monument], here I wanted to create something like the Palais-Royal gardens. Think of that. A beautiful planted square, framed by long symmetrical buildings. Only when I was ill, very ill, and was absent for two years, they ruined everything. I flew into a mad rage. But what could I do? The deed had been done. Personally, I always accept the irreversible.[60]

The design for the central park was drafted by Laprade on behalf of the Architecture Department and was derived from proposals included in Forestier's 1913 report. Sited more or less on the city outskirts in Prost's early plans, the park swiftly became more of an inner-city nature reserve than a link between Casablanca and the rural hinterland. It was granted a plot southwest of the square, but was

View of the main avenue in Parc Lyautey by Albert Laprade, 1919. Photographed in 1991.

Reassembled remains of the Portuguese prison. Photographed in 1991.

Side alley in Parc Lyautey by Albert Laprade, 1919. Photographed in 1991.

The Rule and the Monument 107

Paul Tournon, Sacré-
Cœur cathedral, 1930–52.
Photographed in 1956.

61 *Casablanca, parc central, place, services administratifs*, master plan, Laprade estate, AN, 403 AP.

62 Laprade, "Souvenirs du temps de la guerre," 547.

63 D'Anfreville de Jurquet de la Salle, "Une grande ville vient de naître," 31–32.

64 "La future cathédrale de Casablanca," *Chantiers nord-africains* 2, no. 5 (May 1929): 349. Étienne Branly, Tournon's brother-in-law, was director of finances for the Protectorate.

65 D'Anfreville de Jurquet de la Salle, "Une grande ville vient de naître," 32. This initial project (whose prints are kept in the BGA, Archives du contrôle des municipalités) grew out of a 1925 study for the Sainte-Jeanne d'Arc church in Paris, and led to the 1928 Saint-Esprit church, built on Avenue Daumesnil in Paris. See *Paul Tournon architecte 1881–1964* (Paris: Éditions Dominique Vincent, 1976), 95–102.

separated from the latter by the new barracks with which it connected diagonally. The park is encircled by a major road linking the regional tax office to a large stadium and is extended south beyond the Circular Boulevard—Casablanca's largest road, which curves around the *ville nouvelle*—by a short parkway called Boulevard Claude Perrault. The second largest road, the final section of Boulevard Moulay-Youssef, was set at right angles to this and was designed as another parkway linking the center with the new quarters in the northwest.[61] Laprade used the labor of German prisoners of war to dig two huge trenches, which were then planted with palm trees.[62] He also erected several porticoes made from reclaimed stone in the park, maintaining that these were "the last remains of the former Makhzen prison," symbolizing how the French had shut down all the "old Gehennas."[63]

Paul Tournon's Cathedral Design

The cathedral of Casablanca, whose striking form distinguishes it from the other buildings in the city, was built to a design by Paul Tournon, winner of the Prix de Rome, for the forty thousand Catholics supposedly residing in Casablanca at the time. It is bordered by the porticoes in the park and is set quite a way back from the square, as though the residency were seeking to tone down religion in the city center.[64] The preliminary scheme, which was drafted during the second half of the 1920s, reveals a large surbased cupola joined to two towers, resulting in the same "Byzantine style" that characterizes Prost's initial sketch perspective.[65] In the

Paul Tournon, Sacré-Cœur cathedral, 1930–52. Interior perspective, 1930.

completed version, however, the building's white envelope is the only feature that matches the architectural language of the square. The built structure, conceived by Tournon as a five-nave basilica, corresponds to a 75-by-36-meter rectangle topped by lightweight vaults, and the main facade sports twin towers, even though Lyautey had recommended a single bell tower to echo the mosque minarets. The building's profile is emphasized by stepped concrete pinnacles, though Tournon chose to deliberately conceal the geometrical stained-glass windows. A number of French critics picked up on the architect's rebuttal of a potentially reassuring historicism,[66] though in the 1960s, Paul Bowles rather cruelly noted, "The cathedral looks like something invented by a clever child using a set of expensive German building blocks; it has no style whatsoever."[67]

Construction work was split into lengthy phases. Only three of the nave spans were actually built, and it took Tournon until 1953 to complete the nave and choir. This resulted in the edifice resembling a lone bookend for some time, though it should be noted that Tournon was simultaneously working on the churches for Rabat and Ifrane. Raymond Subes's entrance gate, Elisabeth Branly's paintings, and the stained-glass windows by Florence Tournon-Branly, Jean Mamez, and Louis Barillet, testify to Tournon's attempts to draw artists into the sphere of reinforced-concrete design. The cathedral, which according to Laprade endowed the city with "all the grandeur of a capital,"[68] therefore emerged as a collective artwork marking the end to an overall campaign to endorse Casablanca's central role.

66 Charles Imbert, "L'Église du Sacré-Cœur à Casablanca," *Chantiers nord-africains* 5, no. 7 (July 1932): 579–72—first published in *La Technique des travaux* (May 1932): 259–63; "Église du Sacré-Cœur à Casablanca," *L'Architecture française*, no. 131–32 (April 1953): 79–81; and "Église du Sacré-Cœur de Casablanca," *Travaux*, no. 244 (February 1955): 250–52.

67 Paul Bowles, "Casablanca," illustrations by Ronald Searle, *Holiday* 4, no. 3 (1966): 121.

68 Laprade, "Lyautey urbaniste," 226.

The Rule and the Monument 109

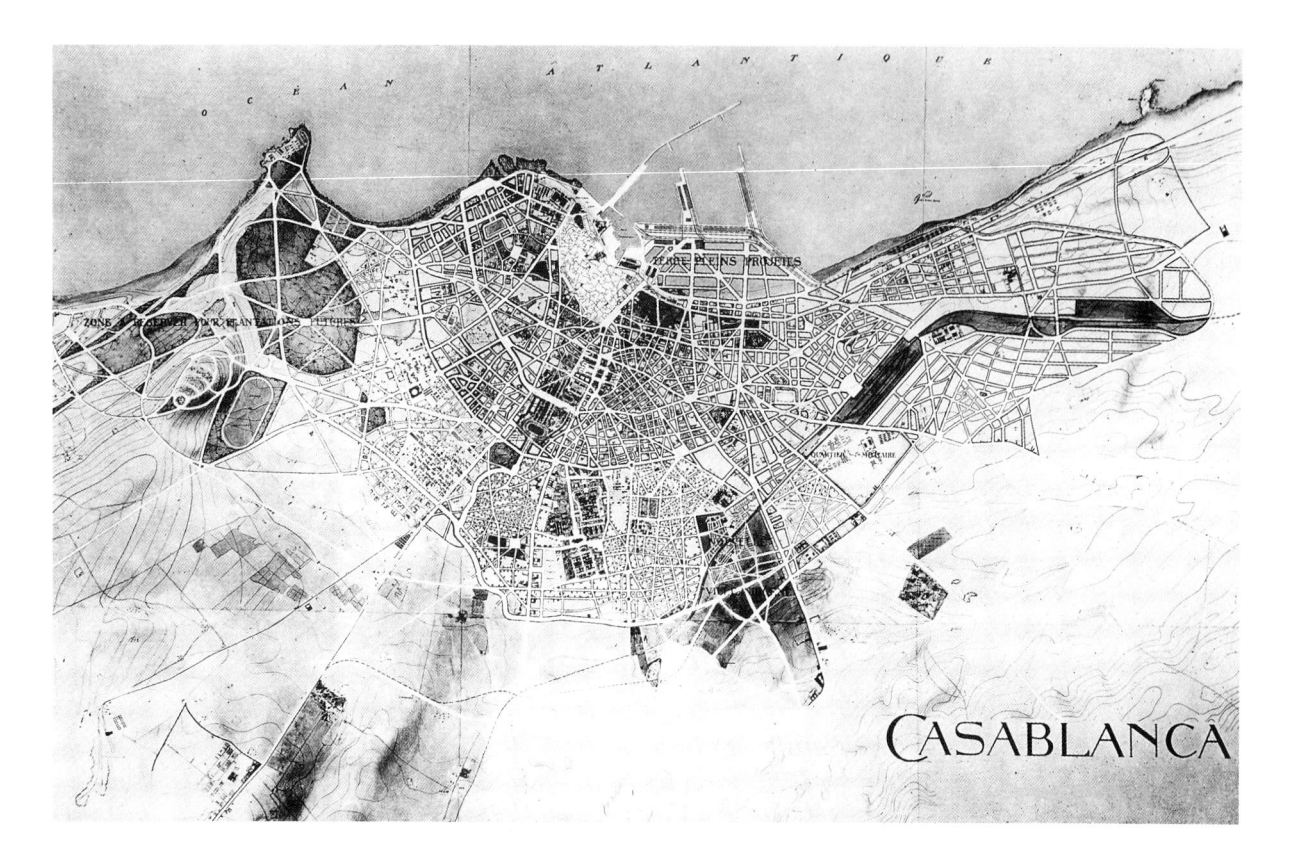

Henri Prost, development and extension plan for Casablanca. Layout of the road system, c. 1925.

Architectural Layout and Land Regulation

Prost's regime is no dictatorship; it is a partnership between the administration and the landowners. The latter are usually more active in taking the initiative, and are often held back by the authorities. In any event, the parameters are now being defined. Landowners have set up their own associations in each specific area and major boulevards are slowly creeping further from the center. Everything needs to be reshuffled or even knocked down.

Étienne Lambert, 1928[69]

The war had cleaned up Casablanca's real-estate market, and the city's postwar development hinged primarily on the construction of hefty civic buildings, due to the municipality's increasingly autonomous role.[70] Besides Prost's master plan and zoning scheme, which would be reworked in 1932,[71] design guidelines were imposed on individual builders with regard to constructing private schemes alongside the newly opened streets. Meanwhile, the city's profile was changing rapidly. The Tour de l'Horloge (clock tower) was the first sign that Casablanca had entered the world of modern networks. This was followed by the El Hank lighthouse, which was constructed by the city authorities—apart from the crowning decoration, that is, which was designed in 1916 by Albert Laprade, who modeled his scheme on the superstructures of Moroccan minarets.[72] Henceforth, the lighthouse, the station tower (1922), and the Hôtel de Ville (1936) together formed an aerial triangle that soared over the city center.

By 1923, the year Prost left Morocco, most of the urban infrastructure had therefore already been mapped out.[73] Contrary to the rather false picture that the planner Michel Écochard would paint after 1945 of his immediate predecessors, the two decades that elapsed between Prost's departure and the Courtois plan of 1944 did not merely revolve around sluggishly implementing the guidelines established

---

69 Étienne Lambert, "La construction à Casablanca," *La Terre marocaine*, no. 16–17 (October 1–15, 1928): 313.

70 As an exception to the general rule established in the Municipal Charter governing all of Morocco (*dahir* of April 8, 1917), the Casablanca Municipal Commission was the only one granted deliberative powers (*dahir* of June 1, 1922).

71 *Service des études législatives* (hereafter referred to as SEL), regulation regarding provisions relative to construction in different quarters of the city, July 30, 1932, BGA, SGP, *Service des études législatives*, plan of Casablanca, 1931–32, no. 211. The public inquest regarding this regulation exposed the hostility of the real-estate industry to any form of regulatory action on the part of the administration. Ibid.

72 The sketch showing two variants is in the Laprade estate, AN, 403 AP. The more folkloric variant would be chosen by the chief of public works of Casablanca, François.

73 Developed at the scale of 1:10,000 and of 1:5,000, the Prost plan was implemented in each of the demarcated districts with the help of 1:1,000 or 1:500 scale neighborhood plans, in which the exact lot outlines appeared. Joyant, "Le plan d'aménagement de Casablanca," 166. The abundant correspondence regarding each district plan is kept at the BGA, SGP, bureau des Municipalités, Casablanca; travaux, aménagement de rues et bâtiments, II 1913–26.

74 Jean-Claude Delorme's analysis is an example of a schematic, if well-intentioned, approach to this history. Jean-Claude Delorme, "Casablanca de Henri Prost à Michel Écochard," *Architecture, mouvement, continuité,* no. 42 (June 1977): 5–12.

Albert Laprade, lighthouse, El Hank. Photographed in 1916.

in 1915.[74] It was a period that saw the creation of some highly diverse architecture, both in terms of types and forms, with initial urban touchstones being respected. Building codes were based on the functional zoning plan and differed from neighborhood to neighborhood. In major urban spaces such as the Place Administrative, schemes fell entirely under the supervision of the administration. Elsewhere, buildings had to blend with their architectural setting, or, more often, a building permit was required. Although in theory this involved stringent procedures, in practice these were often flouted.

Attempts to ensure overall architectural coherence and high standards of building design bestowed a twofold sense of continuity and diversity on the city, expressed most notably in the variety of centrally located public spaces branching out into porticoes and shopping arcades. The Prost plan laid down guiding princi-

Town Planning Department, architectural guidelines along Boulevard de Paris, c. 1924. Avenue du Général d'Amade lies between the two buildings. Note the difference in style between the apartments and the Citroën garage, which was eventually allocated the whole of the corner site.

The Rule and the Monument 111

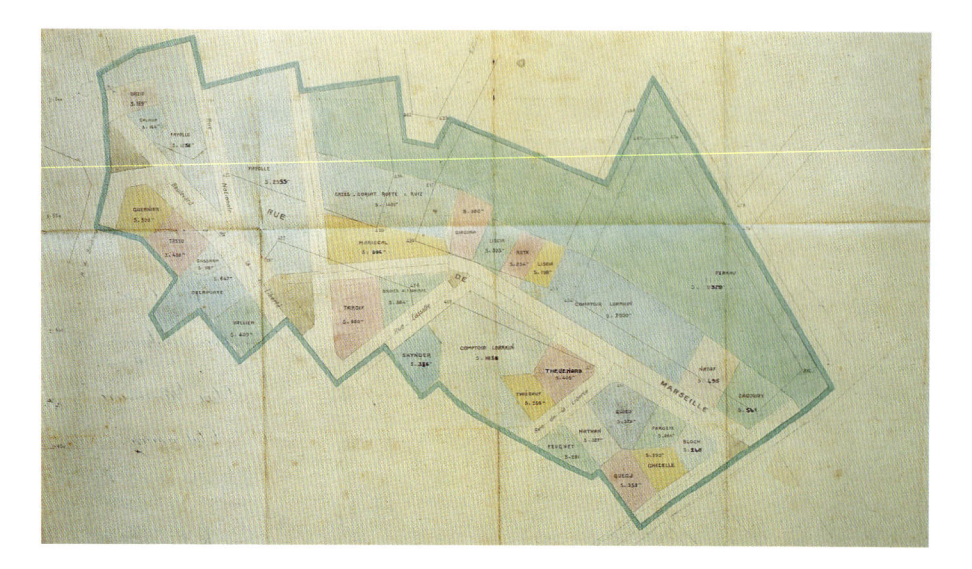

Town Planning Department, Boulevard de Marseille, lot division before land consolidation, August 1919.

Town Planning Department, Boulevard de Marseille, lot division after land consolidation, August 1919.

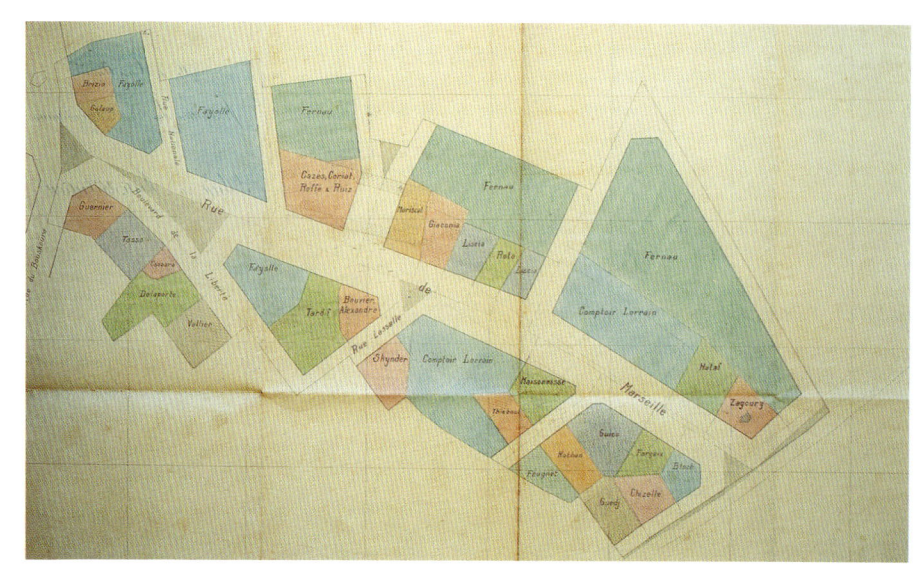

75 Those foreseen as the starting point of the Boulevard d'Anfa and for a diagonal road that would have directly linked the station and the port by way of the military station were not built.

76 Édouard Sarrat, "Les architectes et les entrepreneurs qui ont construit Casablanca," in "Le Maroc en 1938," *L'Afrique du Nord illustrée,* special issue (1938): 86.

77 In 1924 this was applied to the Place Administrative and the Place de France, as well as for the Boulevard du IVe- Zouaves. Subsequently, the process extended to the following (listed in chronological order of the decisions made between November 1925 and October 1928): Rue de Marseilles; Avenue du Général d'Amade; Boulevard de Lorraine; Boulevard Moulay-Youssef; Rue de Paris; Avenue du Général Drude; Avenue du Parc and Avenue du Général Gouraud; the western end of Rue d'Alger; and Avenue Mers-Sultan. Direction générale de l'instruction publique, des Beaux-Arts et des Antiquités, *Historique 1912–1930* (Rabat: Résidence Générale, 1931), 287.

78 Formulated by Louis Bonnier, the 1902 ordinance reacted against the monotony of the Haussmannian streetscape by introducing provisions for variety and imaginativeness in facade design. Louis Bonnier, *Les règlements de voirie* (Paris: Charles Schmid, 1903). The main work regarding the heated Parisian debate triggered by Bonnier's ordinance is Charles Lortsch, *La beauté de Paris et la loi*, preface by André Hallays (Paris: Sirey, 1913).

79 From 1897, a yearly "Concours de façades" took place in Paris, with prizes awarded to the building that had the best designed and most original facade completed during the corresponding year. See Monique Eleb, *L'invention de l'habitation moderne*, 464–78

ples with respect to portico arrangements and made them a compulsory feature of some roads, such as Boulevard de la Gare, Rue Gallieni, the initial stretch of Avenue du General d'Amade, and part of Rue Georges Mercié.[75]

New ground was broken with the creation of a "watchdog committee for aesthetic construction," instigated by Lyautey himself.[76] Additionally, the *dahir** of April 1, 1924, put the Beaux-Arts Department in charge of monitoring unity in the layout of roads and squares, and the department gradually drew up typical facades and specific building codes for the structures along a dozen or so of the roads in the city center.[77] Casablanca's major avenues were thus shaped by negotiations between the authorities, the architects, and the developers. Prost supported the view formulated in Paris in reaction to the ordinance passed in 1902, declaring that he believed street layout should be governed by legislation.[78] Yet the press nonetheless ran an article in 1920 proposing that an annual facade competition be staged along the lines of the one that had been organized in Paris since the 1890s.[79]

The formation of landowner associations—voluntary groups enabling reshuffling of land boundaries on an amicable basis—paved the way for twenty-three neighborhood plans, each of which was implemented. Yet the administration found it extremely difficult to apply this innovative procedure on a broader scale.[80] At the outset, not one single landowner seemed to understand the underlying function of these associations, nor did any of the public servants seem capable of explaining it. The Protectorate asked the director of Casablanca's Municipal Facilities Department to make use of his "personal influence" to "assuage misgivings and gently guide recalcitrants along the right path." Some landowner associations, such as those for the Horloge and Foncière districts, whose plans were approved in 1916, were set up only after cautious groundwork.[81] However, as is clearly indicated by the work carried out in Rabat, this did not lessen their importance in the development of other cities that fell under Protectorate rule, nor within metropolitan France itself: "The new formula we are attempting to introduce into Morocco is of enormous significance, as it will allow for rational urban development without entailing the costly burden of expropriation."[82]

Henri Prost would continue to track Casablanca's development from the time he left Morocco in 1923 until the mid-1930s. Commenting on events several years after they occurred, he raised the issue of land consolidation. In particular, he deplored the width of the roads because, as he saw it, they generated "overwhelming problems since they suck up almost all the private land, without this [loss] being offset elsewhere."[83] In fact, land consolidation slowed after Prost's departure, though his successors were hardly sparing in their criticism of landowners' attitudes, and two decades worth of disparaging memos piled up in the residency offices. By 1932, the landowner associations had "fulfilled their role" and from then on they began to be disbanded.[84]

Aside from the complications caused by owner-occupiers, the architects themselves expressed discontent about the "discipline" forced on them by the authorities. Fernand Benoit referred to this in 1930 in a comparison between Casablanca and Rabat:

> The question is why this discipline was not respected in Casablanca, which is a city that has expanded too rapidly beyond the confines of its port, spreading haphazardly, full of palaces and bombastic facades loaded with motifs and ornamentation. The answer assuredly resides in the very character of the two cities. Such discipline was, generally speaking, more readily acceptable in Rabat given that the city serves as the country's administrative seat and so it is the brawny civic buildings that set the urban tone. Conversely, since Casablanca is a seaport and trade center, it was inevitable that businessmen would want to give free rein to their fanciful ideas there.[85]

Arterial Roads in the *Ville Nouvelle*

Look at that street—it's the main road in my city. It will lead straight to the sea. I want passengers to step off the boat right into the hub of life. The city walls? They're going. They're ugly. I'll just keep this little marabout, which is sacred. Someone said to me, "But you've got low houses on one side and tall ones on the other." And I replied, "That's right. On the left there's the native Moroccan facade—an Arab fonduk—and on the right there's the European facade composed of large, French-style buildings. It's perfect.

Hubert Lyautey, April 1925[86]

The first issue to be broached concerning the road system was how to link the wharves and the warehouses, since this meant passing through the medina alleys and along a narrow track winding around the city walls. As early as 1915, Claude Favrot put forward solutions to join the city to the port and the station, which made up the two urban backbones. He suggested widening the "crack" between the

---

80 Examples of regulations are presented in Joyant, *Traité d'urbanisme*, 2:105.

81 The fact that the residency was unwilling to discipline European businessmen was deplored in a vigorous anti-Lyautey pamphlet. H. Labadie-Lagrave, *Le mensonge marocain: contribution à l'histoire "vraie" du Maroc* (Casablanca: Imprimerie ouvrière, 1925), 143.

82 Secrétaire général du Protectorat, memorandum to the head of the Casablanca municipal authority, March 1916, BGA, SGP, bureau des Municipalités, Casablanca; travaux, aménagement de rues et bâtiments, II, 1913–26.

83 Henri Prost, "L'urbanisme au Maroc," *Chantiers nord-africains* 5, no. 2 (February 1932): 119.

84 Casablanca Municipal Authority, "Dissolution des associations syndicales: Rue de Tours, boulevard de la Gare, Gautier, quartier est de la place Administrative," *BMO*, October–November 1932. The credit surplus generated by their activity, a result of the difference between income from the sale of land and expenses related to land acquisition and construction, was turned over to road-building operations.

85 Fernand Benoît, "100 ans d'urbanisme nord-africain," *L'Architecte* 9, no. 9 (September 1932): 84.

86 Maurois, *Lyautey*, 315.

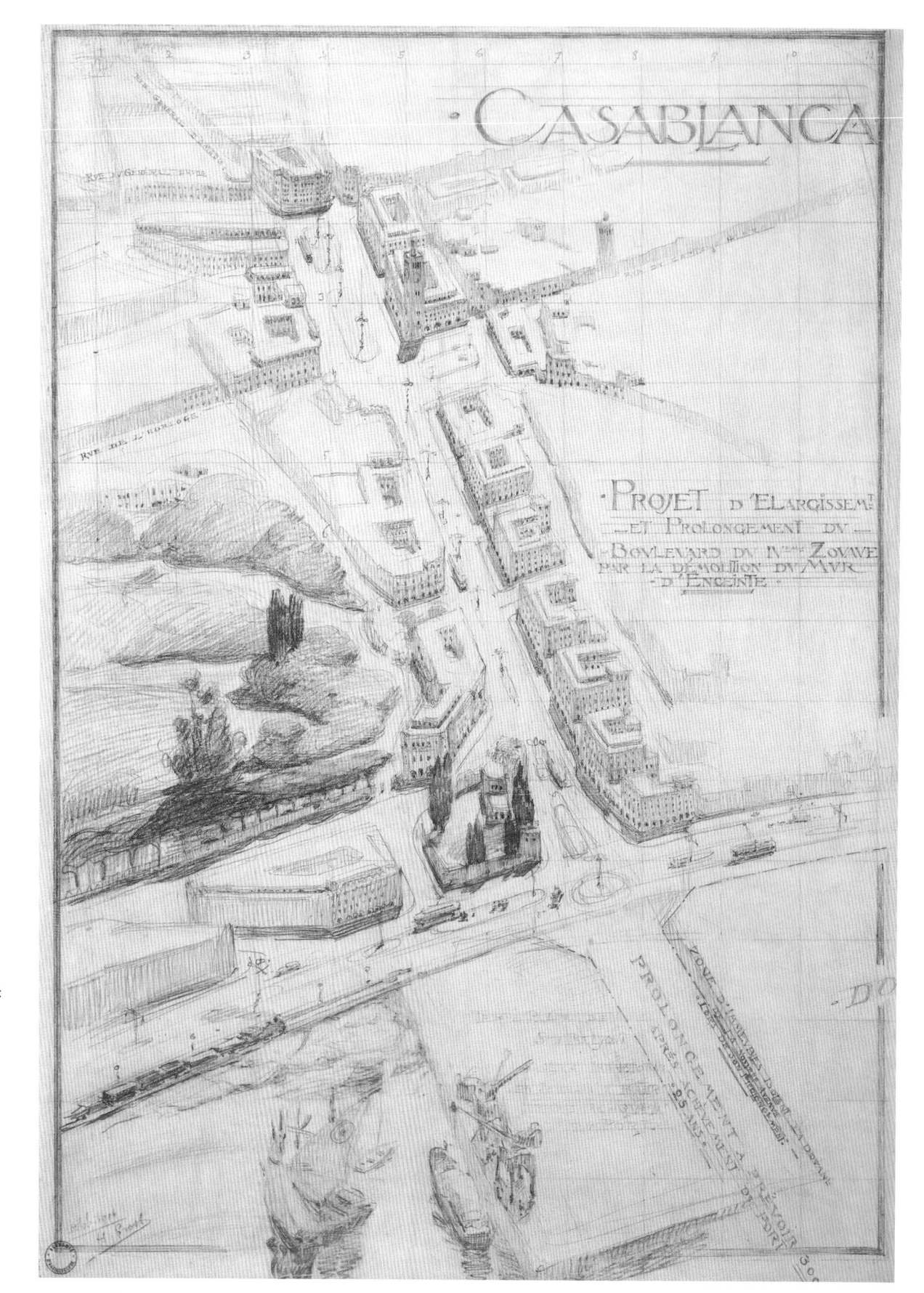

Henri Prost, "Canebière de Casablanca" (sketch, October 1914).
Prost conceived a line of continuity between the future Boulevard du IVe-Zouaves and Place de France. The Magasins Paris-Maroc building is in the background, while on the right, a new built front conceals the preserved parts of the medina.

Boulevard du IVe-Zouaves. Aerial view looking toward the port, c. 1922. Lower right in photo: Excelsior hotel, Compagnie des Transports Marocains, and Banque d'État du Maroc.

medina and the cemetery to make way for a new boulevard that would "run along the port axis" (the "median artery of the new town") leading to the "architectural mass" of the Place Administrative. This road would create a visual tie between "the civic buildings set against a backdrop of foliage" with the "diorama of the port divulging a tangle of masts, ships' funnels, high-brimmed hulls, and an endless horizon of sea and sky."[87]

A Moroccan "Canebière"

On arriving in Casablanca, Prost had sketched out a thoroughfare, which he labeled Casablanca's "Canebière" (after the avenue leading from the center of Marseilles to the harbor).[88] He used aerial photographs to map out the road,

[87] Favrot, "Une ville française moderne," 224–25.

[88] According to Marrast, it was Lyautey who had suggested a similarity between Prost's drawing and the Marseilles thoroughfare. Marrast, "Maroc," in *L'Œuvre de Henri Prost*, 55.

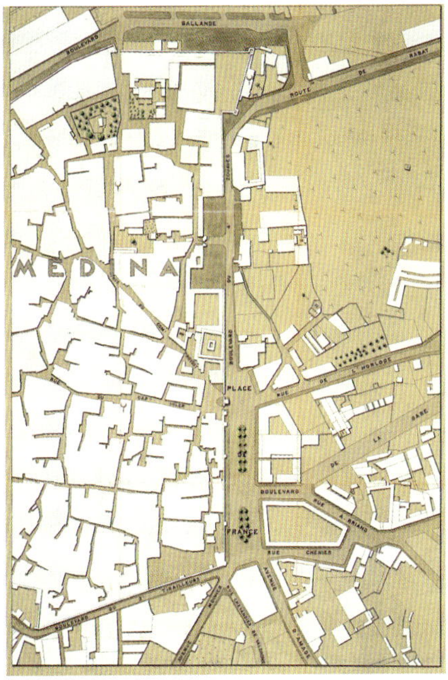

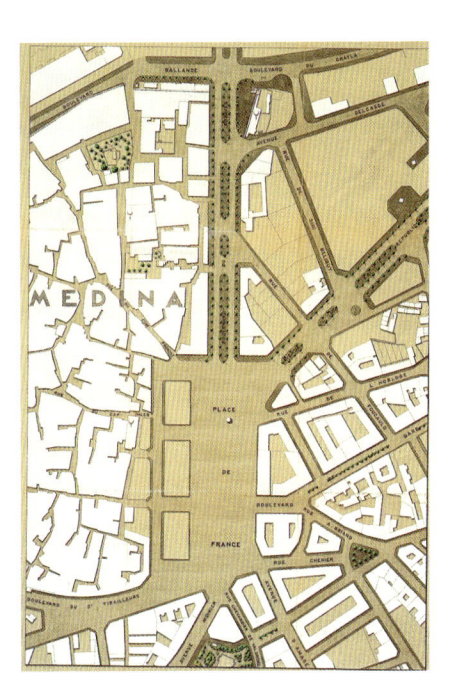

Town Planning Department, Boulevard du IVe-Zouaves, plan in 1920, before restructuring and land consolidation.

Town Planning Department, Boulevard du IVe-Zouaves, plan in 1923, after restructuring and land consolidation.

The Rule and the Monument 115

Henri Prost, extension plan for the city center, c. 1922, set on land reclaimed in the port area. Aerial perspective.

89 A decree regulating the street line of the Boulevard du IVe-Zouaves had been issued by the Municipal Commission on June 22 1914, MAE, series A Tanger, carton 667.

90 The public inquest did not generate any negative observations. See the relevant report in BGA, Études législatives, Plans de villes, Casablanca 1926–27.

91 "La réunion des propriétaires; elle a adopté hier un vœu hostile à la suppression du rempart," *Le Petit Marocain* (December 31, 1921); and "L'élargissement du boulevard du IVe-Zouaves," *La Presse marocaine* (December 31, 1921).

92 General Hubert Lyautey, "Note au sujet de Casablanca," Casablanca, December 5, 1921, *Lyautey l'Africain*, 4:190. Regarding this operation, see L. Sablayrolles, "L'urbanisme au Maroc, les moyens d'action, les résultats" (Ph.D. diss., Faculté de droit, Toulouse, 1925), 62–64.

which was subsequently named in tribute to the Fourth Regiment of the Zouaves and which resulted in an alignment bylaw enacted in 1914.[89] The area surrounding the *Bab sidi Belyout** marabout stood in the way of the road's access to the port, and so in March 1917 it was ordained that expropriation proceedings should commence.[90] This involved demolishing part of the eastern outskirts of the medina to make way for Prost's housing blocks; it also entailed requisitioning land that had been occupied since 1907 by colonial settlers, who put up much resistance to the scheme.[91] It was only due to the planned visit on April 22 of Alexandre Millerand, then president of the French Republic, that Prost's project was able to finally get off the ground. Essentially, Lyautey wanted Millerand to be driven "from the ship to the Place de France along a wide road instead of through narrow, tortuous lanes that currently form the sole means of access to the town, creating a horrendous first impression."

Lyautey was irritated by landowners' reactions, as well as by the breakdown in talks with financial companies that had shown an interest in backing the building schemes; however, he did not withdraw his support of the project, which he considered from the outset to be "remarkably logical and satisfactory." Instead, he proposed dropping the "initial scheme based purely on financial criteria," which was characterized by "an alignment of blocks" and "secondary streets," and suggested directly appealing to the public authorities to rapidly expropriate a narrow band of properties located along the new road's planned route.[92]

The Boulevard du IVe-Zouaves served as a springboard for one of Prost's major design proposals: shifting the shoreline to "reclaim part of the sea." This concept was still only in sketch stage when the 1917 plan was published, but was nonetheless included in aerial perspective views of the city and port. The scheme must have been rejected fairly swiftly, though, as the land that Prost was suggesting should be reclaimed was never actually incorporated into any of the city zones. According to the authorities, such large-scale public investment, which would have involved shunting the railroad station five hundred meters north, was not warranted. Later plans were hence located on *terra firma*.

Boulevard du IVe-Zouaves. View of the section leading into Place de France. At left in photo: Excelsior hotel; at center: clock tower.

General layout of Boulevard de la Gare. Lot division before land consolidation, September 1917 (Town Planning Department).

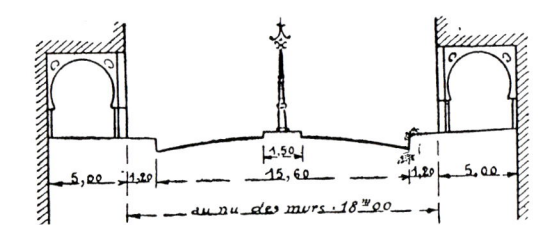

Cross section of Boulevard de la Gare, in Jean Raymond, *L'urbanisme à la portée de tous* (Paris, 1925).

Hubert Bride, Bessonneau apartment block, Boulevard de la Gare, 1916–17. Photographed c. 1922.

93 Louis Delau, "Chronique de Casablanca," *France-Maroc* 4, no. 5 (May 15, 1919): 143.

94 Favrot, "Une ville française moderne," 225.

95 Consolidation was addressed in an area approximately 1,200 meters long and 200 meters wide, encompassing sixty-three tracts that ranged in size from under 400 to over 500 square meters.

96 Claude Favrot to secretary general of the Protectorate, Casablanca, February 11, 1916, BGA, SGP, bureau des municipalités, Casablanca; travaux, aménagement de Rues et bâtiments, II, 1913–26.

Boulevard de la Gare—An Exemplary Road Concept

The second point to be tackled in the plan concerned linking the center to the new station in the southeast of the city. This issue had in fact been addressed as early as 1915, in view of Casablanca's "heavy overspill toward the east."[93] Favrot endeavored to respond to public demand in his program:

> Alas, only a winding, tortuous road—the Rue de l'Horloge—connects the Place de France (in effect the city center) with the station. We will have to cut into its flesh and open up an artery at least twenty-five meters wide. This will form the chief trade and transit road, acting as the very backbone of the city's commercial sector.[94]

The procedures for the consolidation of tracts of land that lay along the boulevard's course are typical of the early land ownership strategies implemented in Casablanca.[95]

Favrot's preoccupation with this road is confirmed by the pressure he exerted on the administration in 1916, during the public inquiry over the development plan. He addressed the issue of assessing indemnity amounts for expropriated owners, notably suggesting that the said indemnity be calculated in proportion to the added value gained by other owners; in addition, he argued for extending the zone of landowner associations, as the new roadway would above all benefit those plots located in the vicinity of the station. In his view, the zone "should assume the general form of a cone, with the planned boulevard serving as its axis."[96]

Guillaume de Tarde, director of civic affairs, followed the proceedings carefully, paying particular attention to land valuation, as did Prost, who firmly rejected most of the observations made in the public inquiry.[97] Prost was especially heedful of market effects, and had no misconceptions about land value:

> Previously, land prices in the subdivisions were based much more on location than on accessibility. This explains why plots of land between the Place de France and the market square are highly valuated, despite their having no access road (which in terms of trade renders them worthless in an organized city). Conversely, the land belonging to the Société Foncière [a real-estate company] bears a much lower value, even though it has a road network, the land for which was ceded by the Société Foncière itself. The former plots have thus benefited from "anticipated value," inasmuch as their owners knew from the outset that there would come a day when the administration would have to lay a road in the central part of Casablanca, and that the plots of land still edging this road would outstrip the value of those owned by the Société Foncière.[98]

Prost stressed the fact that the council was intent on rendering the land functional.[99] Boulevard de la Gare and neighboring thoroughfares were linked by tracts of land that could accommodate monumental corner buildings. The first new structure was the Bessonneau apartment building, constructed by the architect Hubert Bride along the widest section of road, opposite the market. This sturdy structure contains some sixty apartments with individual bathrooms as well as public baths. Pierre Bousquet, the municipal architect, requested that the building's street-facing overhang be scaled down, along with the curve of the green-tiled roof. Prost carefully monitored the scheme, as can be perceived in several remarks of his regarding "a freestanding structure lined with terraces." He accepted the "building's green-tiled roof," saying it "could pass as a decorative element." However, he considered its highly visible porticoes too cumbersome, claiming that they risked dwarfing the shops.[100]

In contrast to the uniform character of Boulevard du IVe-Zouaves, Boulevard de la Gare is lined on both sides with porticoes and is visually linked by a planted central median that grows gradually wider, practically becoming a square on the right-hand side of the market.[101] The design of the crossroads is varied, ranging from simple roundabouts to a large square that contains a garden.[102] The boulevard finally branches out into a host of carefully designed galleries and arcades around the Place de France, providing a fine area for shopping and strolling. As for the facades, they form a continuous sculptural wall due to the layout imposed on the architects.

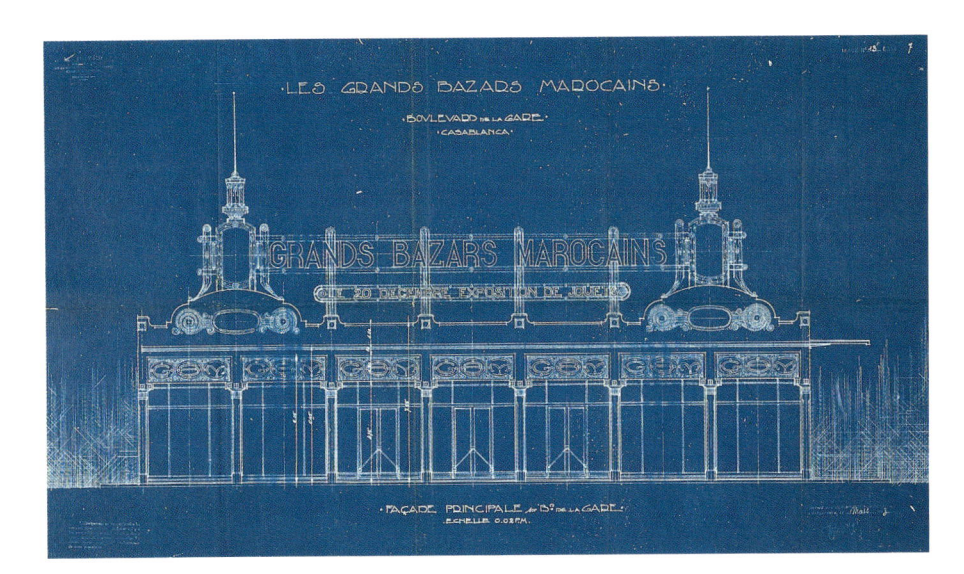

97 Of forty-one landowners situated within the perimeter and affected by the boulevard, thirty-eight belonged to the landowners association, presided over by the head of the municipal authority, Collieaux. Land valuation took account of a coefficient p proportional to the proximity of the Place de France, of the market, and of other roads, as well as of the specific form of the lots and their position within the block—be it on a corner or or between adjoining lots.

98 Henri Prost, "Note à de Tarde," May 8, 1918, BGA, Études législatives. See the redistribution plans in Joyant, *Traité d'urbanisme*, 1: figs. 313 and 314; and H. de La Casinière, *Les municipalités marocaines, leur développement, leur législation* (Casablanca: Librairie Faraire, 1924), pls. I and II.

99 He mentions "buildable forms" in the context of the new roadways. Pertuzio and Cadet, architects in the Casablanca Urban Plan Service, oversaw the negotiations with landowners. Cadet's role is mentioned by Prost in his "Note au secrétaire général du Protectorat."

100 He called "the municipality's attention to the opportunity to reduce the thickness of the pillars along the entire portion of the facade whose construction has not yet begun." Henri Prost, "Note aux Services Municipaux de Casablanca," 1918, BGA, SGP, Bureau des municipalités, Casablanca; travaux, aménagement de rues et bâtiments, II, 1913–26. This building would be the first to benefit from the attention of the Parisian architectural press. "Maisons de rapport au Maroc," *La Construction moderne* 36, no. 6 (November 7, 1920): 44 and pl. 23.

101 The cross section of the wide part of the boulevard, to the right of the central market, is presented as a model of an urban roadway in Jean Raymond, *L'urbanisme à la portée de tous* (Paris: Dunod, 1925), 66; and *idem*, *Précis d'urbanisme moderne* (Paris: Dunod, 1934), 147.

102 Regarding the Boulevard de la Gare, see Amine Alaoui Fdili, "Casablanca 1913–1940, un plan—une percée" (master's thesis, École d'Architecture Paris-Villemin, 1986).

Marius Boyer, Grands Bazars Marocains department store, Boulevard de la Gare, elevation with arcade, 1923.

Edge of the mellah and the Place de France, c. 1925.

103 R. de la Celle, "Place de France," *L'Afrique du Nord illustrée* 30, no. 755 (October 19, 1935): 34–35.

104 Comte Maurice de Périgny, *Au Maroc, Casablanca, Rabat, Meknès* (Paris: Pierre Roger & Cie, 1922), 15–16.

The Mellah Endangered by the Place de France

Work related to the drainage, paving, and widening of the Place de France continued throughout the 1920s, mainly by means of gnawing at the medina's outskirts. The square even came to symbolize the Protectorate's organizing foundation[103]; in 1922, for example, writer Maurice de Périgny viewed "this perfect rectangle" as nothing less than the "city's core."[104] It is true that since the construction of the Excelsior and the Magasins Paris-Maroc, Casablanca's architects had been vying with one another to put their own stamp on this particular spot, sometimes provoking thorny debate. For example, the project to extend the square by demolishing the mellah wall kindled lasting conflict that would only be fully resolved in the

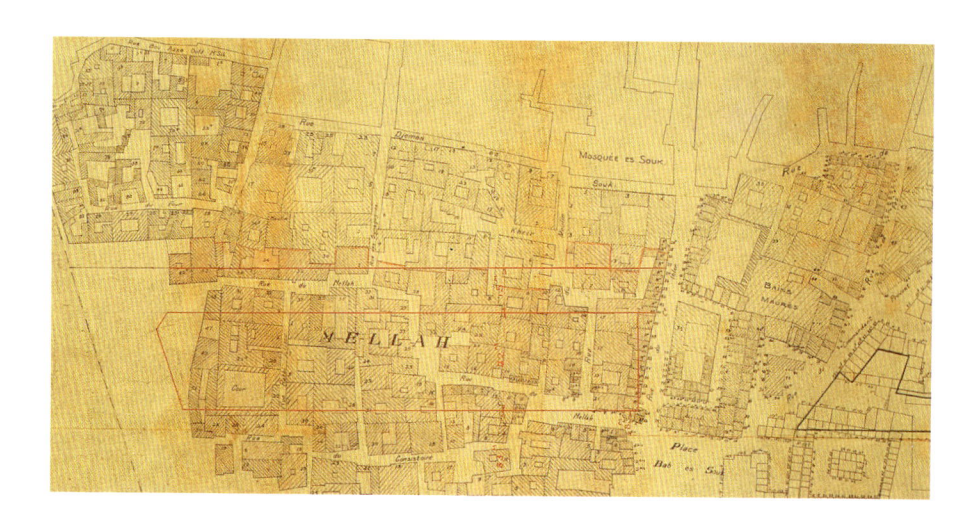

Town Planning Department, expropriation plan drafted in 1922 for the section of the mellah edging the Place de France.
The area devoted to reconstruction is narrower than the one occupied by buildings earmarked for demolition.

1950s. By contrast, there was no opposition whatsoever to plans for turning a plot south of the square into a public garden in tribute to the geologist Louis Gentil. In 1918 Marcel Mirtil described the disparity between the Place de France and the mellah, which "continues to live its past life," severed from the *ville nouvelle* "more by mental barriers than by any material obstacle."[105]

The square's history can be said to emphasize the ambiguous and ever-changing attitude of the Protectorate with respect to the Jewish community. As early as 1921, a preliminary public inquiry was launched concerning the buildings that Prost had earmarked for demolition as part of the Avenue du IVe-Zouaves extension program. A petition was drawn up by the thousand or so targeted families:

> This project consists of gutting the neighborhood, which has been home to our kin for almost a century, in the aim of widening the main street of the new town, the so-called Place de France . . . Never in the entire history of French North Africa has a project of this type been conceived, let alone put into effect . . . In Casablanca, though, the order has been issued to pull down our houses, synagogues, and mausoleums, which for decades past have formed the resting place for the remains of our venerated saints . . . The administration's handsome designs for our poor little mellah may well be far worthier than our tumbledown houses, shop booths and modest temples, but in our eyes, these booths and temples represent an entire century of toil and labor.[106]

The lawyer Armand Bickert and the Banon brothers (whose synagogue was one hundred years old) lent their support to the campaign. They emphasized "the distress that would be caused to Casablanca's Jews should their religious edifices be demolished." Such unprecedented raising of defense shields compelled Lyautey to freeze the project.[107] In November 1922, the municipal council approved a less controversial program, drafted by Pierre Grand, Albert Tardif, and Alfred Tarriot, for extending the square.[108] A limited competition was launched in the spring of 1923, for which the brief specified that an arcade facade should edge the square along the alignment of Boulevard du IVe-Zouaves. Georges Vimort's scheme contained eight apartment buildings carved into a setback arrangement on the mellah side, with a Doric portico in the section overlooking the square.[109] Prost's scheme was more modern and visionary, as it also embraced the Boulevard du IVe-Zouaves. His plan depicts the mellah as clearly divided into three large apartment houses with rows of trees lining the square. Prost was clearly concerned with creating an opposing pull between large volumes and corner buildings, whereas Vimort was seeking facade continuity, as he did in most of his work.[110]

---

105 Marcel Mirtil, "Le Mellah de Casablanca," *France-Maroc* 3, no. 12 (December 15, 1918): 359. Regarding life in the houses of the mellah, see Armand Ettedgui's recollections published in Yaron Tsur and Hagar Hillel, *Yehude Kazablankah: iyunim be-modernizatsyah shel hanhagah Yehudit bi-tefutsah kolonyalit* (Ramat Aviv and Tel Aviv: ha-Universitah ha-Petuhah, 1985), 77–81.

106 The signatories reminded Lyautey that "most of the well-to-do Jews of the mellah left it long ago." They suggested that "the administration confine itself to the ramparts themselves and to a narrow strip of land on the interior." Collective letter to General Lyautey, December 26, 1921, BGA, SGP, Études législatives, Plans de ville, Casablanca, 1926–27.

107 De la Casinière, director of the Service of Civil and Municipal Audits, memorandum of February 13, 1923, BGA, SGP, Études législatives, Plans de ville, Casablanca, 1926–27.

108 Jean Rabaud, head of the municipal authority to the secretary general of the Protectorate, December 9, 1922, MAE, carton 851. The resident general approved the projet "taking into consideration the objections formulated" during the inquest. Resident general to the secretary general, January 29, 1923, BGA. The project was limited to a 32-meter-wide lot and a 15-meter road—in other words, a 177-meter strip that was somewhat less "narrow" than that which had been requested.

109 Vimort cited the example of the Strada del Venti Settembre in Genoa. Georges Vimort and A. L. Cane (business administrator), "Concours en vue de l'élargissement de la place de France," May 31, 1923, MAE, dossier 851 Place de France, 2–3.

110 The declaration of public utility allowing for expropriation issued February 13, 1923, was revoked because it was considered too general. Its text was not specific enough in determining the value of the buildings to be razed. The new text was signed on March 5, 1930, bringing the depth of the holding to 180 meters.

Georges Vimort, development plan for the mellah area, 1923. Elevation on the Place de France.

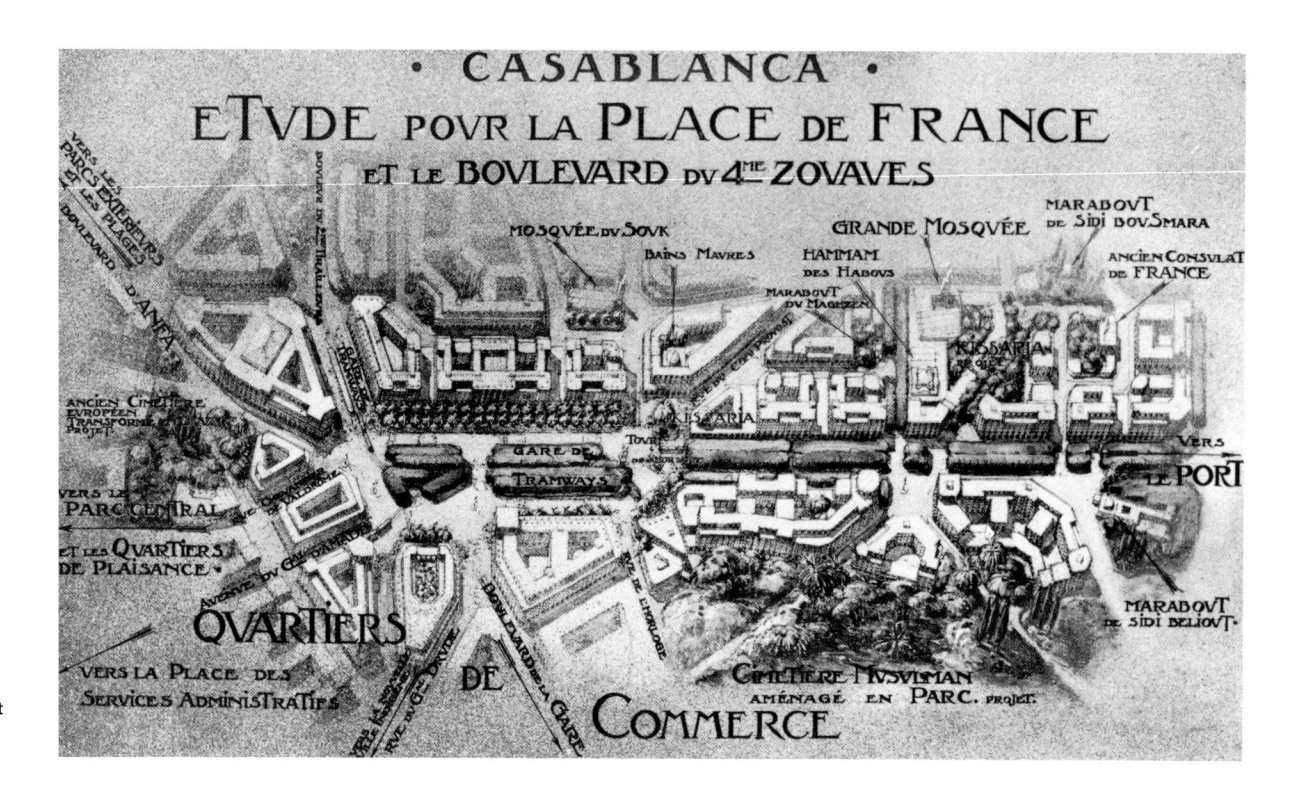

Henri Prost, development plan for the mellah area, 1923. Aerial perspective.

111 Marcel Berthet to the administration, December 1928, BGA, SGP, Études législatives, Plans de ville, Casablanca 1926–27. For the Casablanca Tourist Board, the enclosure's walls had "no artistic cachet." Resolution of December 10, 1928, BGA, SGP, Études législatives, Plans de ville, Casablanca 1926–27. Haïm Bendahan was the major Jewish Moroccan landowner prior to 1914, holding large estates east of the center and in the area near Mers-Sultan.

112 Direction générale de l'instruction publique, *Historique 1912–1930*, 287–88.

113 "Enfin, on démolit...," *L'Avenir illustré* (August 25, 1932). This weekly was published by a group of bourgeois Jews committed to the modernization of the Moroccan community and more reserved with regard to the Zionist project.

114 On June 1, 1933, ninety-one buildings in the mellah were bought and demolished. Thirty-six remained to be demolished and 237 remained to be bought. *BMO* (May–June 1933). The fence was built in 1930 and remodeled in 1937. Regulation of advertising and the aesthetic treatment of this urban curtain were the subjects of many meetings of the Municipal Commission.

115 *BMO* (November–December 1939).

Private firms joined the chorus of dissent, thus slowing proceedings. In 1928, the Algéro-Marocaine company declared that the project went against both the Prost plan and the residency's principle that "old Moroccan towns should retain their original character." The company claimed "it made more sense for the plan to stretch east." Yehia Zagury, the influential inspector of Jewish institutions, proclaimed that the project to exhume the bodies of rabbis buried within the precinct of the Bhira "was unprecedented in the history of Moroccan Judaism." Eugène Tordjman and Georges Terrenoud noted, "Knocking down the rampart would inevitably create an amalgam of the city's native and European parts, impairing the beauty of the Place de France." In essence, they were arguing in favor of "a distinct segregation, which the European community as a whole had been campaigning for since the declaration of the Protectorate." Unlike partisans of the official project, these Europeans believed that "direct contact with the mellah [would not only] generate problems of health and hygiene, but would also daub our fine square." According to the land surveyor Marcel Berthet, "The most handsome part of our city is spilling out toward the east and southwest,to the extent that the southeastern tip of the indigenous town (the filthy mellah) seems to be digging deeper and deeper into the very heart of the central quarter."[111]

In 1929, the Beaux-Arts Department put forward its own scheme for the square, namely creating "setback buildings devoid of inner courtyards to free up more floor area."[112] Meanwhile, demolition programs went ahead and were approved by the local Jewish press, which praised the destruction of those "slums that are the shame of Casablanca, a city that can be justifiably considered the jewel of modern urban planning."[113] The programs were stymied in 1933 due to a lack of expropriation funds, and the municipality had to bail out the Protectorate in order for the venture to be pursued. A fence still stood between the clock tower and the Boulevard du 2^e-Tirailleurs.[114] It was not until late 1939 that new designs reflecting the council's ambitions were submitted by Marchisio, based on arcades rather than streets slotted between the apartment buildings.[115]

Overall, developing the east side of the square was easier. Nonetheless, direct access from Boulevard de la Gare to the square was prevented due to the former market site that was owned by Haïm Bendahan's heirs and which the authorities attempted to expropriate on several occasions, but to no avail.[116] A portico block was eventually constructed, containing the Socifrance and Bendahan apartment buildings. After Prost's site plan was rejected in 1923, he and Marchisio were commissioned to build the Compagnie Algérienne building, in order to link the square with Avenue d'Amade.

The Boulevard Network

Other roads were also laid, though not all on the same scale as those leading off from the Place de France. The Circular Boulevard was one such thoroughfare, built by German prisoners of war prior to the Prost plan:

> The Circular Boulevard ... starts and ends at the sea, delineating a vast curve around the *ville nouvelle*, which it broadly encircles in a greenbelt by way of sweeping tree-lined side lanes. It is a pleasant drive out with no doubling back along the same route, since it intersects all the roads running in from the surrounding countryside to the Place de France.[117]

As the apartment buildings began to delineate stretches of facades, so other boulevards gradually began to take shape. Varied widths and eaves heights, combined with tree-lined schemes, gave rise to myriad styles. Prost focused on major linkages, often in the form of a central pedestrian walk. Two pertinent examples are in Boulevard de la Gare and Boulevard Moulay-Youssef: the walk in the former road is tightly narrow, whereas in the latter it is extremely wide, creating, as mentioned earlier, an extension to the park.

The ground plans and building codes defined by Prost for the land edging Boulevard Moulay-Youssef resulted in the area resembling a low-density residential quarter composed of villas and school buildings not exceeding three stories. The road's meandering course is an uncommon feature in Casablanca; it seems to be an invitation for drivers to slow down and discover each nodal point, such as the intersection with the park and the spot at which it widens into a square, at the junction with Boulevard d'Anfa.

116 De la Casinière, director of the Service of Civil and Municipal Audits to Secretary General of the Protectorate, March 9, 1926, BGA, SGP Études législatives, plan de Casablanca 1926–27.

117 Comte de Périgny, *Au Maroc*, 14–15. Having been dedicated to Foch, Joffre, and Pétain, and subsequently to the Resistance, today the Circular Boulevard bears the name of Mohamed Zerktouni, a victim of French oppression.

Cross-sectional sketches of roads in the city center. Drawings by Philippe Simon.

a. Boulevard de la Gare (standard section)

b. Boulevard de la Gare (central section, in front of the market)

c. Rue Gallieni

d. Rue Georges Mercié

e. Avenue du Général d'Amade

f. Boulevard du IVe-Zouaves

g. Rue des Charmilles (Oasis)

h. Avenue de la Côte d'Émeraude (Anfa)

i. Boulevard du Général Gouraud

j. Allée des Marronniers (Anfa)

k. Avenue du Lido (Anfa)

l. Boulevard Moulay-Youssef

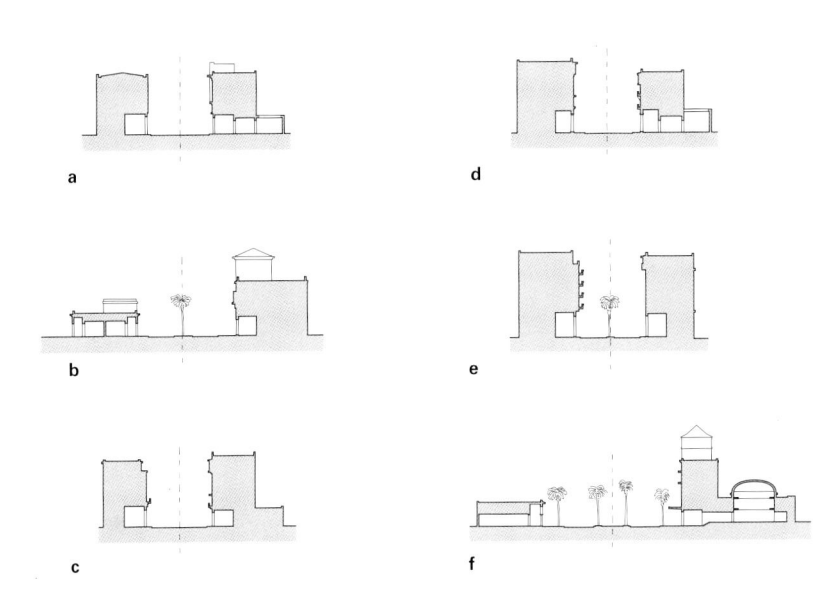

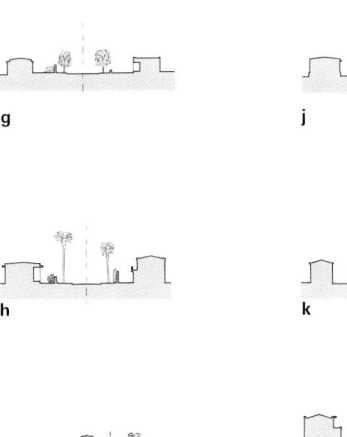

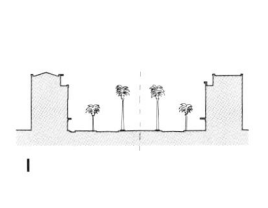

Boulevard Moulay-Youssef. Photographed in 1991.

118 Jacques Berque, *Le Maghreb entre deux guerres* (Paris: Seuil, 1962), 211–12.

119 Reyner Banham, *Los Angeles*, 38.

120 Albert Charton, "La politique des ports du Maroc," *Le Monde colonial illustré* 5, no. 52 (December 1927): 284.

121 General Hubert Lyautey, ed., *Rapport général sur la situation du Protectorat du Maroc au 31 juillet 1914* (Rabat: Résidence Générale de la République française au Maroc, 1916), 371–72. On the history of this project see Jean-Louis Cohen and Monique Eleb, "La constitution du dispositif portuaire urbain de Casablanca" (research paper, Laboratoire ACS/Plan Construction et Architecture, Paris, 1993, typescript).

Unlike the portico-lined boulevards, which were devised for pedestrians to stroll past the shops in shady comfort, the underlying design concept for Boulevard Moulay-Youssef originated essentially in an attempt at synthesis with the Mediterranean landscape, whereby the villas' double screen of palm trees and dense foliage seems to nudge Casablanca's metropolitan features out of the main picture. Once linked to these roads, the various quarters of the *ville nouvelle* underwent rapid expansion, similar to that described by Jacques Berque for North Africa as a whole.[118] An interesting comparison can be drawn between the simultaneous development of Casablanca and Los Angeles, for, like Casablanca, Californian metropolises did not grow steadily outward from the city center, but started from many scattered points of origin, as is aptly pointed out by Reyner Banham.[119]

Battling over the Port

It was truly a battle that had to be fought—a battle against the ocean that had to be tamed by two powerful breakwaters, today Casablanca's pride and joy. It was a battle in the name of trade and communication, enabling Casablanca to develop into French Morocco's major road and rail hub. The port is the lifeblood of this city that is struggling to carve out an existence for itself and whose uncertain future serves as fertile ground for speculation ... Yet this being said, Casablanca is nevertheless a fully formed entity whose pulse beats healthily.

Albert Charton, 1927[120]

By the outbreak of World War I, only 121 meters of the inner harbor's west breakwater and several dozen meters of the main breakwater had been constructed. The Protectorate's progress report provided details of the preliminary work and gave an optimistic outlook regarding the project's "future rate of development."[121]

1900

1926

1912

1935

1917

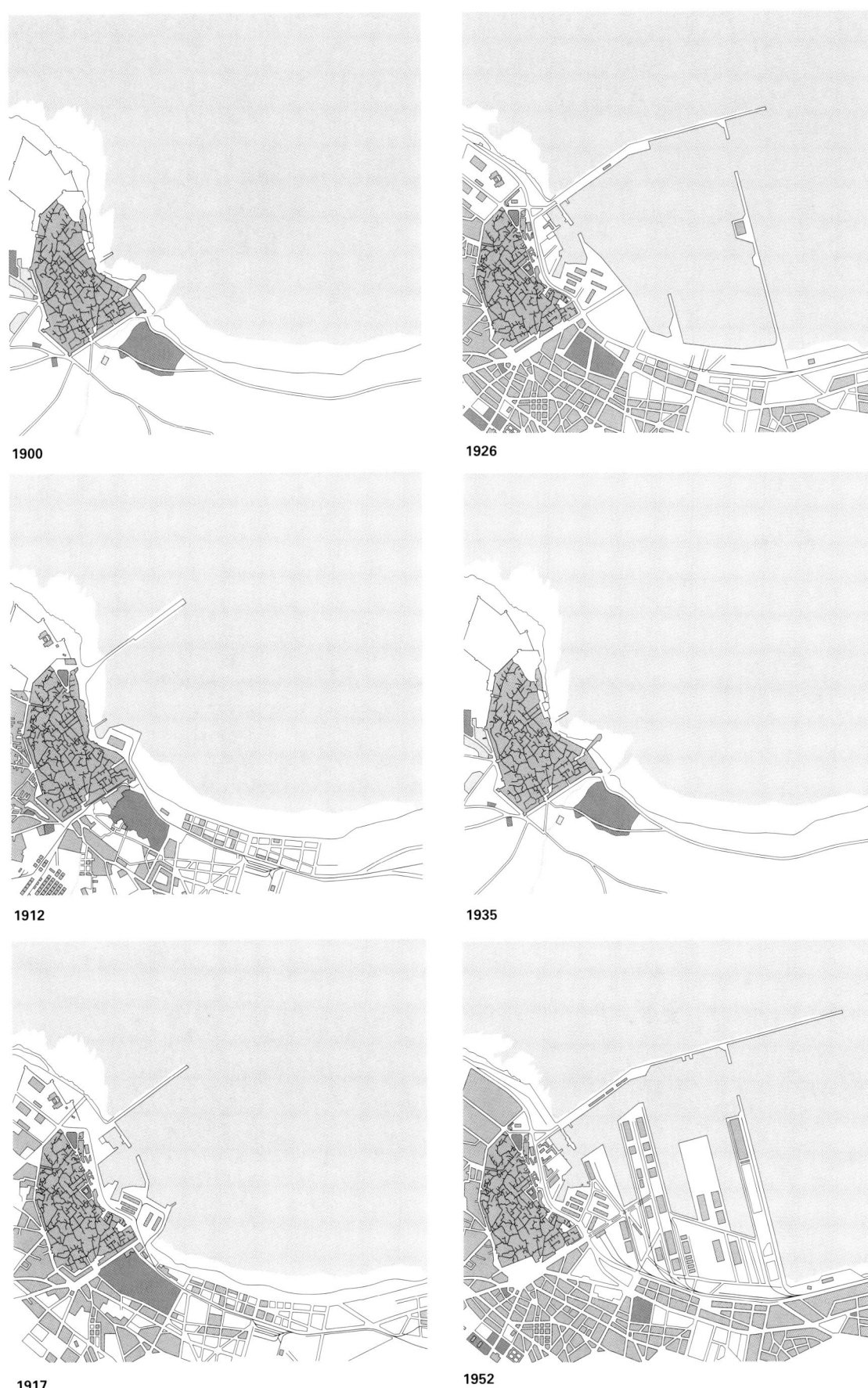

1952

Port development in 1900, 1912, 1917, 1926, 1935, and 1952. Drawings by Philippe Simon.

Camille Boirry, poster advertising Crédit Foncier d'Algérie et de Tunisie, 1920.
The poster shows the west side of the first section of the Delure breakwater in the port of Casablanca.

However, work ground to a halt in late 1914, resuming again in 1915 at a pace dictated by the quantities of cement available. The inner harbor had been completed by 1917, but cargo still had to be unloaded from the ships by small craft.[122] After the war, Delure realized that the size of the initial project outstripped allocated resources; he therefore recommended cutting the length of the main breakwater to 1,300 meters and laying a breakwater crossways toward the west. These could be extended at a later stage, he argued, even though the Casablanca Chamber of Commerce was campaigning for swift completion of the main port.[123]

A more ambitious program was launched in 1920.[124] Platforms were laid between the smaller port and the transverse jetty, and a pier for loading phosphate was run alongside this jetty to handle the burgeoning export trade that was to take off fully in 1922. It was an undertaking that proved fatal for the beach, which had been highly popular until then. By 1923, the main breakwater had reached some 1,900 meters and the Compagnie Paquet's *Doukkala*, along with the Compagnie Générale Transatlantique's *Figuig*, berthed in the port for the first time, side by side.[125] This was a symbolic occasion for Casablancans, signaling a rise in the city's economic clout. It was followed by other port development work, such as extending the main breakwater to 2,450 meters in 1934, along with completion of the transverse jetty and the accompanying pier.[126] The port was equipped with several floating cranes, a twenty-five-ton portal frame, and thirty or so electric cranes, the first few having been brought over from Germany as war trophies. All the appropriate facilities were thus in place to cope with Casablanca's steadily growing trade. In 1939, construction began on a mineral-ore loading wharf running parallel to the shore, and a proposal was put forward for another pier to run alongside the trade pier, as well as for a second transverse jetty to be laid on the right of Roches Noires.[127] In the main, then, the "port battle," as it was referred to by Charton, was won, benefiting the general public, to whom accounts had to be rendered regarding the use of public funds.[128]

Grain, Phosphates, and Sardines

The wharves and piers were packed with dock buildings, and the phosphate loading devices, installed in 1926 on the north wharf of the transverse jetty, were generally held to be the most powerful in the world.[129] Passenger handling (attaining 1,500 when two ships berthed at the same time) was neither centralized in a single terminal as in Le Havre, Naples, and Genoa, nor split into separate terminals such as in Marseilles; instead, passengers were channeled through two buildings at the Delande and Delpit terminals. Delande was the more prestigious of the two, as it was chiefly dedicated to luxury liners, being favorably positioned in relation to Bordeaux. Tall storage facilities were rare, since it was difficult to build on sandy soil. The silo dates from 1933; it was designed by the Chamber of Commerce along the lines of large American structures, but it was built to a symmetrical plan, causing it to resemble some kind of grain cathedral. It was fitted with a fifty-meter-high mechanized loading tower that became the port's vertical landmark and that enabled crops to be loaded quickly, thereby resolving the congestion problem that had clogged the town since the turn of the century.

The fishing port was redeveloped in 1936 to supply the recently opened canning factories and accommodate the rapid expansion of the sardine fleet. The covered fish market, located close to the old medina, was transplanted to the docks of the new fishing port. It was designed by the engineers Bars, Bouquet des Chaux, and Surleau under the direction of the marine section of the Public Works Department and was accorded a functional, modernizing vocabulary. It served both as a public building crossed by a walkway and as a sort of fish factory structured around a system of metal rails to which the fish crates were hung.[130]

---

[122] Jean Eyquem, *Les ports de la zone française du Maroc: leur rôle économique* (Algiers: Imprimerie Heintz, 1933), 43. Between 1915 and 1918, the mobilization of four thousand workers resulted in the construction of 522 meters of the main breakwater (upon which all efforts had been concentrated). By the end of the war it was close to 900 meters long.

[123] Georges Vidalenc, *Une œuvre française: le port de Casablanca* (Casablanca: Librairie Faraire, 1928), 61–64; and Charles Penz, *Trentenaire de la Chambre de commerce et d'industrie de Casablanca 1921–1951* (Casablanca: Imprimerie rapide, 1951).

[124] Aimed at extending the main breakwater to the length of 2,250 meters and constructing 750 meters of dock, it was financed by a portion of the loan incurred in the same year.

[125] Eyquem, *Les ports de la zone française du Maroc*, 45. The construction technique used for the main breakwater was modified, with a core anchored to underwater foundations replacing the loose concrete blocks that had been used initially. "Port de Casablanca," in *Encyclopédie coloniale et maritime* (Paris: Encyclopédie coloniale et maritime, 1942): 330–34.

[126] "L'histoire, l'organisation, l'outillage et l'avenir du port de Casablanca," *Revue de géographie marocaine*, no. 2 (May 1939): 155–78. In July 1926, the initial group, composed of Schneider, the Compagnie Marocaine, and the Hersent brothers, was put in charge of the elongation of the main breakwater to 2,250 meters, the extension of the phosphates pier, and the construction of a "commercial pier." In December 1928, the enlargement of the inner pier and the construction of a coal

dock on the transverse breakwater were initiated. A final construction contract, approved in December 1932, allowed work to be completed.

127 "L'histoire, l'organisation," 168–69; and Henri Couette, *Le port de Casablanca, historique, description, etc.* (Casablanca: Éd. Réalisations, 1938), 55–56.

128 Bouquet des Chaux, "Les ports marocains, 1. port de Casablanca," *Annales des Ponts et Chaussées* 104, no. 3, (May–June 1934): 308–37.

129 In 1939, the commercial pier would accommodate 46,000 square meters of warehouses framed with twenty-meter-span metal roof trusses, judged to be more flexible than reinforced-concrete structures. By that time, the transverse jetty was 1,545 meters long, and the pier was 220 meters wide.

130 "La nouvelle halle aux poissons de Casablanca," *La Pêche maritime* (February 1939): 39–40; and "Le port de pêche de Casablanca et le marché aux poissons de Casablanca," *L'Architecture d'aujourd'hui* 11, no. 3–4 (March–April 1940): 60–62. The fact that there were immediate plans for a large restaurant at this location is an indication of its popularity.

Grain silo in the port, photographed by the U.S. Army in November 1942.

Aerial view of the port, c. 1938, in Henri Couette, *Le Port de Casablanca* (Casablanca, 1938).

The Rule and the Monument 127

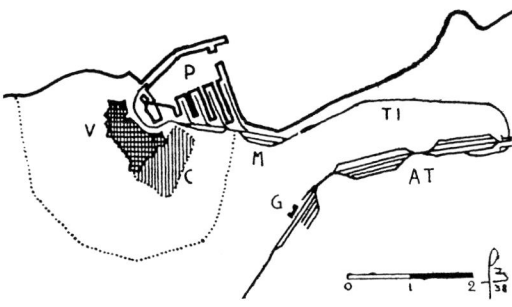

Gaston Bardet, "Casablanca: an excellent example in connecting sea, rail and industrial facilities." Sketch illustrating Bardet's analysis in *Problèmes d'urbanisme* (Paris, 1941).

Casablanca's modern port development was featured in countless articles and reports in which the city was portrayed as a major player of maritime freight, marking a new phase in the history of Morocco's commercial capital.[131] Similarly, Casablanca boasted the second largest French airfield after Le Bourget in the north of Paris, owing to its key position along the airmail routes to Africa and South America.[132] Meanwhile, behind the port, the city itself served as the gateway to "useful" Morocco. Champions of the French colonial epic marveled at the progress made since 1907:

> Once upon a time there was a sort of perilous, barbarian anchorage point. A handful of white houses ringed by ramparts peppered a low and inhospitable coastline swept by the swell of the ocean. Whenever a ship dropped anchor, a vociferous crowd used to drag heavy dark boats into the water, then, pulling with all their might on the oars, they would fling themselves toward the ship amid much clamor ... Gaze upon this calm haven, designed specially for your comfort and safety. Work out how many blocks of concrete had to be sunk to construct those breakwaters and jetties that now form a defense against the ocean, which in its moments of frenzy, sets upon them furiously ... Of all our widely spread interests, whether in Africa, the Ocean Isles, or South American cities, it is here that our ambitions have been best fulfilled. We have transformed that handful of white shacks into a bustling city brimming with life.[133]

The port of Casablanca was clearly regarded as exemplary. This is apparent in the recommendations made by the French planner Gaston Bardet in 1937, when he suggested building an industrial quarter in Rome which "should be accessible both by rail and road, as in Casablanca and Strasbourg."[134]

The Port Quarters in the Shadow of New York

In Casablanca, the hand of the present is so firmly imprinted on the past that the latter has practically ceased to exist, as if it has been wiped out forever ... I told myself that American energy output, to use a stock phrase, could never be rivaled, that its vigor and strength were like an equatorial plant, growing taller and taller with each passing day. But in fact, Morocco has achieved an even greater feat than America, for out of the ten years of colonization, there were those four horrendous ones that paralyzed the majority of Europe.

André Chevrillon, 1922[135]

131 The construction of the port provoked conflicts between the Public Works Department of the Protectorate, which was in charge of port management, and the Service of Municipal Audits, itself having no prerogative regarding the construction of buildings not subject to building permits. See the many memorandums from the Public Works Department in BGA, SGP, Travaux Publics, Ports divers 1932–50, no. 274.

132 Colliez, *Notre protectorat marocain*, 211.

133 Rémy Beaurieux, "Casablanca," *Le Monde colonial illustré* 5, no. 161 (December 1936).

134 Gaston Bardet, *Une nouvelle ère romaine sous le signe du Faisceau: la Rome de Mussolini* (Paris: Massin, 1937), 135.

135 André Chevrillon, "Notes on Morocco," *France-Maroc* 6, no. 67 (June 1922): 184.

136 Jean Eyquem, *Les ports de la zone française du Maroc*, 33–145.

137 Prost, "L'urbanisme au Maroc," 119.

The Protectorate's overriding objective to turn Casablanca into a major port and industrial city had been attained by the mid-1920s.[136] However, Prost's projects for urban expansion toward the sea were curbed by the "insurmountable obstacle" of the Sidi Belyout cemetery, located between the new center of trade and the port itself. The complex issue of shifting the tombs was a sine qua non condition for the project to come to fruition and thus constituted a top planning priority. From then on, the new district planned for the area lying between the Place de France and the ocean took on the status of a business hub, as befitted the image of a fast-developing seaport. Prost himself noted: "When arriving from the sea, Casablanca's panorama is rather depressing: just a dull horizontal line. How much more pleasing a demeanor it would offer to the outside world were five or six tall buildings to rise proudly from the cityscape."[137]

Such an approach refuted all nostalgia for the East and instead cast Casablanca in the role as the New York of Morocco. The aim was to endow the city with a new image, at a time when the whole of Morocco was perceived more as a Far West figure, or as a sort of French California. Lyautey expected high results from the port development that drew on "innovative, youthful methods" from across the Atlantic[138]; even as early as 1914, Casablanca's impulsive growth had resulted in it being likened to "an American city."[139] Walter Berry, chairman of the U.S. Chamber of Commerce in Paris, detected "a distinct Yankee feel" in the early 1920s,[140] a comparison that turned into a cliché in the writings of General d'Amade, who calmly stated in 1928, "By the end of the century, French North Africa will be the United States of today, with Casablanca stepping into the shoes of New York."[141] In contrast, Le Corbusier, a disparaging critic of Prost's work, took advantage of a trip to New York to lambaste the planning projects being conducted in Casablanca. In his view, the city's so-called high-rise construction was inferior, and he noted, not without a hint of racism, that only an upright city like Manhattan "could have instilled respect among the Arabs."[142]

Léandre Vaillat was counting on seeing "a set of *sky-scrapers* rise from the heart of this city of conquerors."[143] He even suggested constructing a 150-meter-tall building on the Place de France, expressing the desire to see "this *sky-scraper* stand on its own individual plot, so that it can be surveyed from all four sides, in the same way as Renaissance towers, minarets, and modern high-rise buildings."[144] This concept was shared by art historian Fernand Benoît, as is illustrated in Benoît's writings on founding a new identity for Casablanca, which he contrasted with the urban identities of Rabat and Algiers[145]:

> The city, buried in the dull flatness of its coastline, seems to have sought out its architectural future through vertical elevation. As much as it would be illogical to push Algiers up by out-of-scale skyscrapers (for Algiers's beauty resides in the horizontal terracing of its boulevards around the bay), so high-rise development for a business city set close to the quays seems natural for Casablanca's future urban countenance . . . The day is assuredly not far off when Casablanca's harbor will be accorded the noble surroundings it currently lacks, when it will be girded by a modest circlet of ten- to fifteen-story buildings, featuring numerous setbacks and terraces and linked by porticoes and gardens, all of which will lend the port a warm and welcoming backdrop.[146]

The Labonne Project

The notion of high-rise development for the port area was inscribed within the framework of architectural Americanism, one of the underlying vehicles for the modernization of European culture. However, the concept took a different turn in the late 1920s, during debate over height restrictions for the Place de France, which formed part of a broader discussion on creating a more complex and tightly knit urban core. In 1930 Eirik Labonne, Protectorate secretary general and a staunch supporter of Morocco's industrialization,[147] submitted to the Municipal Council an ambitious project for reshaping the city center. In Labonne's view, shifting the port eastward rendered Prost's plan null and void. As he saw it, a "modern developing city" meant "layouts, perspectives, plans, and ornamental arrangements." The Protectorate's directive was therefore to create another center, in the form of overflow roads and high-rises:

> By closely linking the current business center with the foreshore port, we will create the sort of city that in any case automatically develops out of a need for contact, grouping, and concentration. As proved by experts, all large towns tend to "self-center" so as to handle their trade more effectively . . . Tall structures facing the port will provide an ordered solution to the current absence of arrangement and balance. They will etch out a setting that shall express the city's commercial power.[148]

Labonne denied that he was acting out of selfish interests, claiming his proposals were merely "objective and valid arguments" for a project that fell within the realm of metropolitan concepts that had been put in place for Chicago, New York,

---

138 General Hubert Lyautey, "A propos du port de Casablanca," Archives Lyautey, AN, 475 AP/Thorey 520. As early as 1920, Prost received a written submission for an "American-style building, containing nothing but commercial offices," which he did not pursue further. J. E. Sacchetti, engineer (on letterhead featuring the address "New York, Paris") to Henri Prost, July 21, 1920, AA, Henri Prost estate, A1 117.

139 L'essor industriel de Casablanca, 35.

140 De Tarde, Le Maroc école d'énergie, 60.

141 General d'Amade, preface to Casablanca de 1889 à nos jours: Album de photographies rétrospectives et modernes montrant le développement de la ville, text by Joseph Goulven, documents collected by the photographer Émilien Flandrin (Casablanca: Éditions photographiques Mars, 1928).

142 Le Corbusier, When the Cathedrals Were White: A Journey to the Country of Timid People, trans. Francis E. Hyslop, Jr. (New York: Reynald & Hitchcock, 1947), 37. First published as Quand les cathédrales étaient blanches: voyage au pays des timides (Paris: Plon, 1937). At the time, Le Corbusier was competing against Prost for the Algiers regional plan project.

143 Vaillat, Le visage français du Maroc, 5.

144 Vaillat, Le périple marocain, 85.

145 Fernand Benoît, "L'évolution des villes et le décor architectural au Maroc," La Renaissance de l'art 14, no. 8 (August 1931): 239–44.

146 Benoît, "L'évolution des villes," 242.

147 He published a polemical work on this theme (using a pseudonym): Eirik Jussiaume, Réflexions sur l'économie africaine (Paris: Klincksieck,1933). Sur son parcours, see Jean Lacouture, Profils perdus: 53 portraits de notre temps (Paris: A. M. Métailié, 1983), 99–103.

148 Eirik Labonne, "Procès-verbal de la réunion officieuse de la Commission Municipale pour échanges de vues sur le projet d'aménagement des quartiers voisins du port," BMO (February–March 1930): 3.

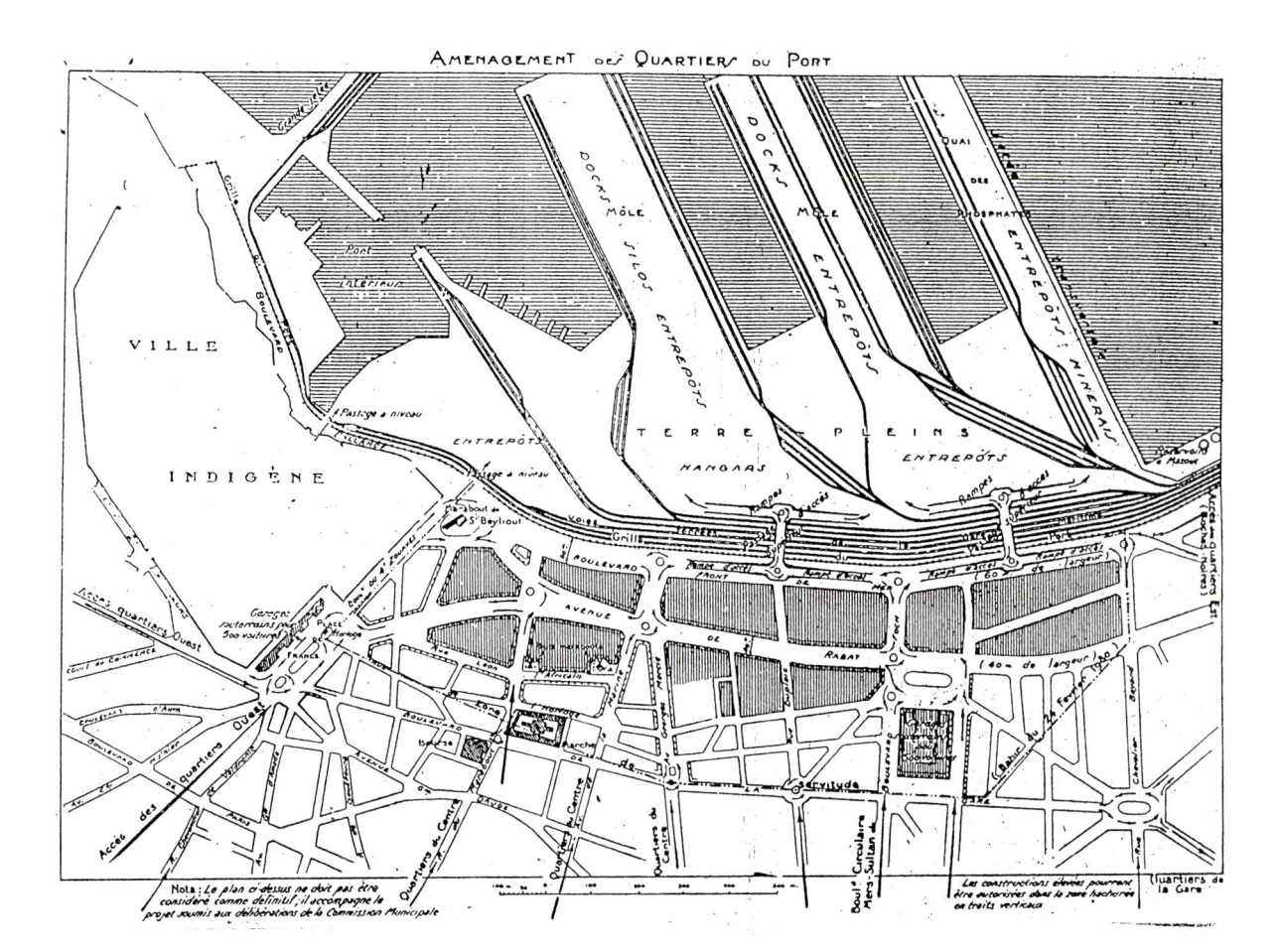

Town Planning Department, development plan for the port district, 1930. Published in *Bulletin municipal officiel*, 1930.

Town Planning Department, plan featuring "changes to the development plan for the port district," December 1931.

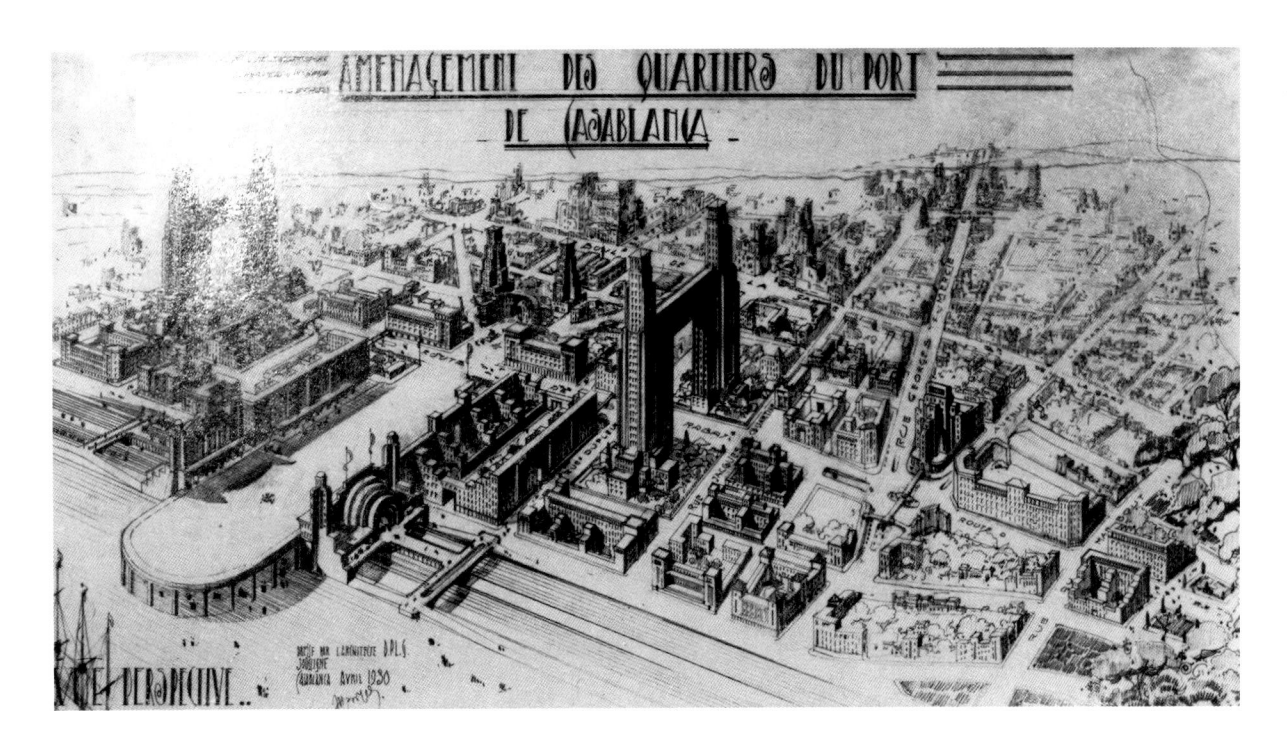

Marius Boyer, development plan for the port district, 1930 (aerial perspective).

Berlin, and Paris over the preceding twenty years. The scheme, drafted by Edmond Joyant, chiefly comprised laying two wide roads running parallel to the coastline; these would be connected to the port by ramps and lined with sixty- to eighty-meter-high buildings as well as with lower structures. Talks with the municipal authority subsequently got under way regarding this "long-term" plan that had the Protectorate's full backing. The architect Georges Grel, along with Marcel Rivollet, a contractor, supported the project, although they expressed doubts over the idea of a skyscraper district; nor did they favor shifting the city's urban core.[149] In April, the council discussed the schemes drawn up by Marius Boyer and Robert Lièvre. Boyer criticized the lack of arterial backbones in the official project and put forward an "architectural plan" whose major feature was a 450-by-250-meter esplanade aligned with the Circular Boulevard: "The proposal is to create a large-scale circulation flow embracing the railroad and motor transport stations, which shall be located near the landing stages. It is likewise recommended that a vast esplanade be built where tourist and freight airplanes can take off and land, and which will be flanked by all the requisite attendant buildings."[150]

In the same way as Le Corbusier in *Ville contemporaine*, Boyer discarded the principle of tall buildings lining the port, recalling Le Corbusier's criticism of the "monumental error of New York." However, he did admit that it might be "extremely worthwhile" to "devise an architectural decor" for this "flat and featureless city." He pictured "a sort of urban amphitheater," with "two portico skyscrapers" flanking low-rise shoreline structures that would tier out into higher structures comprising "modern setback buildings, without courtyards," similar to the ones he was to build in the 1930s.[151]

Lièvre reluctantly accepted the idea of skyscrapers, provided they were designed "not as American blocks, but in the French cruciform shape ... following the same setback arrangement as in Sauvage's work."[152] Overall, he simply incorporated modest-scale changes to the road system and freed up space in "Maître Prost's" plan, which he ardently admired. This plan corresponded more

149 Proceedings of the Municipal Council, *BMO* (March–April 1930): 8–10.

150 Proceedings of the Municipal Council, 12.

151 See the schematic perspective in "Aménagement des quartiers du port," in *Urbanisme, constructions nouvelles* (Casablanca, 1930). Labonne viewed this idea as "new, ingenious, outlining the future," "Procès-verbal de la réunion officieuse de la Commission Municipale": 3.

152 *BMO* (March–April 1930): 17.

Marius Boyer, unbuilt project for a set of four apartments with a portico entrance (Rue Damrémont and Rue de Reims). General perspective.

153 Direction générale de l'instruction publique, *Historique 1912–1930*, 287–88. See also: Service des plans de villes, *Rapport sur l'activité du service de l'administration municipale en 1930* (Rabat: Imprimerie Officielle, 1931). The project was published in *La Construction moderne* (December 14, 1930): 170; and in Léandre Vaillat, *Le visage français du Maroc*, 6–7. Regardless of the North American undertones of Boyer's and Marchisio's projects, their proposals should be seen in the context of Agache's plan for Rio de Janeiro, which conjoins the verticality and a Beaux-Arts composition in the creation of a business center linked to a port.

154 La Société mobilière et immobilière Franco-Marocaine, the Société marseillaise de crédit, and the *Petit Marocain* protested as well. See "Modification au plan d'aménagement des quartiers avoisinant le port," registre d'enquête, January 18–February 18, 1932, BGA, SGP, Études législatives, plan de Casablanca 1931–32, no. 211. The plan modification and the regulation pertaining to the area adjacent to the port were approved on July 25, 1930.

155 Marc, "L'œuvre française au Maroc," 54.

156 Henri Prost, "Rapport de fin de mission au Maroc," Paris, May 1932, MH Rabat, R1, 3.

157 A new permeability was created thanks to the renewed interest manifested by the municipality in 1938, at which time it empowered Desmet to develop a new project. The Municipal Commission declared, "It is of the utmost importance to the city to proceed with the improvement of this roadway, which will enhance the value of land that is jointly owned by the city and the state." Debate on the timeliness of the Avenue Pasteur at the Municipal Commission, *BMO*, July–August 1938.

Antoine Marchisio, development plan for the port district, 1930. View of the model in *La Construction moderne*, 1930.

closely to the municipality's ambitions than did the schemes put forward by Boyer and the city architects, inasmuch as the councillors feared high-rises would saturate the real-estate market. At Labonne's insistence, the Protectorate finally agreed to sell off land gradually to make way for high-rise buildings, and the plan was submitted for approval in May 1930. It was, however, rejected in favor of a scheme by Antoine Marchisio, whose "grand architectural arrangement," including "fifteen-story buildings linked by porticoes and bridges," was endorsed by Prost.[153]

The public inquiry laid bare fierce opposition on the part of land ownership companies that possessed land within the scheme's parameters. The Comptoir Lorrain recognized the "irrefutable need" for wide overflow roads, but remained "fully opposed to any program whose sole aim is to erect high-rise buildings, as these do not reply to any kind of need whatsoever. On the contrary, they run totally counter to this country's customs and traditions, and thus clash with the local surroundings."[154] Jean Marc, a narrow-minded colonialist, deemed that these "fanciful projects that seek to turn Casablanca into some kind of African New York or Chicago" emphasized the secretary general's "open-mindedness" but also revealed the "illusionary side to his character."[155]

In his report of 1932, Prost unreservedly expressed his fear of "an increase in tuberculosis in the light-deprived buildings located at the base of such selfish structures." In addition, he drew attention to the problem of traffic congestion that would result "in roads that are already too narrow and which could not be made any wider when they were originally laid since property agents put up so much opposition."[156] This business center project stagnated in the 1930s, although the roadways connecting the center with the foreshore were nonetheless completed.[157] These early schemes did, however, act as a springboard for the designs drawn up by Alexandre Courtois and Michel Écochard after the program was relaunched in the years following World War II, when Labonne returned to Morocco as if to take up the broken thread of his dreams.

LE PETIT MAROCAIN

CASABLAN[CA]

Voici les projets de M. Boyer pour deux maisons que Casablanca verra s'élever dans quelques mois. (Photos Demeure.)

SOMMES-NOUS A UN TOURNANT DE NOTRE URBANISME ?

Marius Boyer, unbuilt projects for high-rise buildings in central Casablanca. Press clipping from *Le Petit Marocain,* April 3, 1931.

Albert Greslin, IMCAMA building, Rond-point Lyautey, Boulevard de Lorraine and Rue d'Agadir, 1928. Facade overlooking Parc Lyautey. Photographed in 1991.

Living in the *Ville Nouvelle* in the 1920s

Apartment Buildings—Innovation and Mimesis

Having recently done the rounds of your Moroccan hub, I can safely say that Casablanca easily rivals any town in North Africa. That does not, by any means, imply that everything is perfect; that would make the triumph of Beauty too easy, too monotonous. It is a city in full development phase and thus has many faces; yet all in all, it does seem to me to be extremely well constructed.

Letter from a reader to *Chantiers nord-africains*, 1931[1]

In the early days of the Protectorate, Casablanca's urban pattern was nothing but a jumble of construction sites, huts, nebulous tracts of land and buildings set in the middle of nowhere. Flat-roofed structures lined with balusters ran along the commercial streets, waiting in vain to have more stories added. Then, all of a sudden, monumental edifices were springing up on street corners, and deluxe private dwellings and mid-range houses sprouted on the edge of the city. Whatever the European housing type, it became clear from 1920 on that Casablancans had acquired a taste for modern conveniences. This would explain one observer's comment that barely twelve years after "the tricolor flag was raised over Morocco, it is remarkable to see Casablanca basking in a level of comfort and luxury that even Algiers, after ninety years of colonization, cannot claim to enjoy."[2] The following detailed analysis of the design principles for these buildings, together with an appraisal of their layouts and fittings, should provide clearer insight into this phenomenon.

Courtyard Residential Buildings

A prime example of Casablanca's early low-rise buildings is the apartment house constructed by Pierre Ancelle and the Montarnal brothers in 1922 for the Syndicat Immobilier de Casablanca. Situated at the junction of Rue de l'Horloge and Boulevard de la Gare, the building combines ground-floor shops with one story of housing, while its jutting facade, crowned by geometric *zillij* pediments and a small green-tiled awning, displays a traditional Moroccan vocabulary. It is lined with arcades along Boulevard de la Gare, in compliance with the building codes of the time, and is lit by an inner courtyard. For a while it was home to the Galeries Lafayette department store.

Pierre Ancelle and Jean-Marie de Montarnal, Syndicat Immobilier de Casablanca building, Boulevard de la Gare and Rue de l'Horloge, 1922.

[1] "Les innombrables visages de l'architecture casablancaise," *Chantiers nord-africains* 3, no. 10 (October 1931): 989.

[2] Farrère, *Les hommes nouveaux*, 91.

Albert Greslin, IMCAMA building, Rond-point Lyautey, Boulevard de Lorraine and Rue d'Agadir, 1928. Facade overlooking Rue d'Agadir, photographed in 1991.

Albert Greslin, IMCAMA building, 1928. Partial floor plan.

Albert Greslin, IMCAMA building, 1928. Partial floor plan.

Ignace Sansone and Paul Busuttil, Lévi and Charbon building, Avenue de la Marine, Rue de l'Amiral Courbet and Rue de Tours, 1929. Elevation from the building permit.

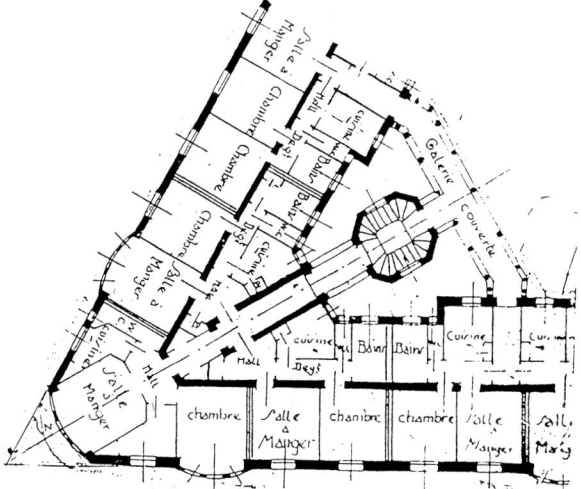

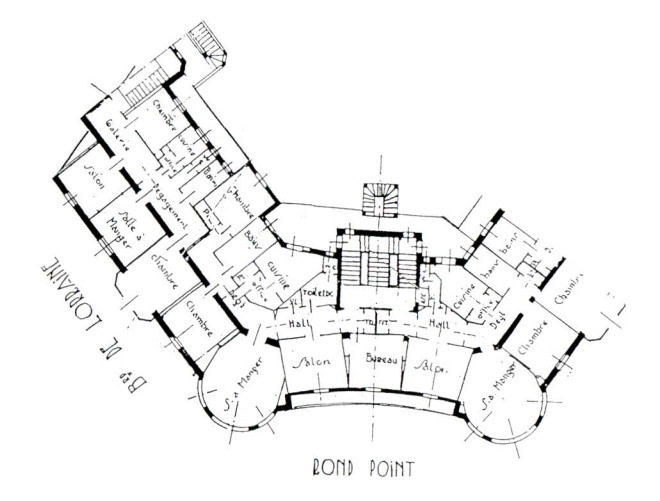

Corner buildings with monumental features were to play a dominant role in Casablanca's urban structuring, following on their success in Paris at the turn of the century. Along with helping to structure public squares, they also serve to punctuate perspective views down the boulevards. Exterior ornamentation such as cupolas, turrets, decorated pediments, and belvederes were designed to provide a showy front for apartments that were often small and designed with a traditional layout. The imposing Lévi and Charbon building, constructed by Sansone and Busuttil along Rue de l'Horloge in 1929, is especially notable in this respect; its cupolas and brown and blue *zillij* mark the corners of a square in a breach of building height restrictions that had long been imposed on Jewish *dhimmi*. Eyewitnesses likened it to "some large Parisian structures in the new western districts which are imitated by the South Americans."[3] However, for all the building's outward display of elegance, it contains only one- and two-bedroom apartments; the dining rooms (occasionally located in the turret part, and featuring bay windows) were designed to function simultaneously as salons. Similarly, the lavishly ornate corner building constructed on Rue Lassalle by Pappalardo, a contractor, has surprisingly small two- and three-bedroom apartments that measure barely fifty square meters in floor area.

The large courtyard building type served as a model for the following generation, having made a timid debut in prewar Paris as part of the low-cost housing program, and, on rarer occasions, as the object of speculation.[4] Each ensemble, which generally groups deluxe buildings, sits on a vast lot surrounded by roads. Urban prestige and interior comfort often went hand in hand, as is clearly confirmed by the spectacular building constructed for the IMCAMA insurance company by Albert Greslin in 1928 along the road intersecting the Parc Lyautey. The structure covers a triangular 2,300-square-meter plot, and its curved facade overlooking the treetops was deemed to be "unpretentiously majestic and designed in the modern spirit."[5] Furthermore, it was delivered with "all the latest technological fittings,"[6] such as a refrigerator in each apartment and a telephone booth inside the entrance hall. The *Afrique du Nord illustrée* quite justifiably considered this edifice to be one of Casablanca's architectural wonders, pointing out that "this building, which contains admirable hygienic facilities, is an exemplar of modern construction."

A Web of Arcades

Some of the housing blocks incorporate shopping arcades that were intended to fulfill an important role in commercial and social life. The first of these dates from 1928 and was designed by Marius Boyer, who emerged as the city's most prolific and innovative architect,[7] in association with Jean Balois. The building in question was commissioned by the Glaoui (the pasha of Marrakech); it is edged by Boulevard de la Gare, Rue Nolly, and Rue de l'Horloge, and is topped by turrets that accommodate the split-level salons of the fifth-floor apartments. In addition to making striking use of these turrets, the architects also included loggias, columns, *zillij*, and geometric forms—motifs that were recycled and reinterpreted, both by Boyer, whose name served as the hallmark of this building type for many years, as well as by several of his admirers. The arcade is pierced with glass blocks and is divided into sequences by rotundas linking up the galleries, which are illuminated by prismatic light fittings.

Arcades were created on the Boulevard de la Gare, near the Place de France, extending the network of covered shopping facilities into blocks located in the busiest part of the city. The development of these luxury shopping spaces in Casablanca paralleled the emergence of a new generation of arcades initiated by Léonard Rosenthal along the Champs-Élysées in Paris. In essence, they mediated between the Moroccan *kissaria** and the arcades incorporated into Parisian

3 "Les innombrables visages de l'architecture casablancaise," 991.

4 Eleb and Debarre, *L'Invention de l'habitation moderne*, 283–87.

5 "Un groupe d'immeubles modernes à Casablanca, A. Greslin, architecte," *Chantiers nord-africains* 3, no. 3 (March 1931): 291–92.

6 "A. Greslin Albert, architecte SAM," "Le Maroc en 1932: 20 années de protectorat français," special issue of *L'Afrique du Nord illustrée*, no. 577 (May 1932): 62.

7 Marius Boyer, *Casablanca: travaux d'architecture* (Strasbourg: Edari, 1933); and "Nécrologie de Marius Boyer," *L'Entreprise au Maroc* (January 1, 1948). See also Myriam Boccara, "Casablanca—histoires d'architectures" (master's thesis, Unité pédagogique d'architecture no. 8, 1985).

Marius Boyer and Jean Balois, El Glaoui building, Boulevard de la Gare, Rue Nolly and Rue de l'Horloge, 1922.

General view.
Photographed in 1992.

The arcade.
Photographed in 1990.

Second-floor plan.
Drawing by Cristiana Mazzoni based on the building permit.
The main staircase provides access to street-facing "through" apartments and a service gallery leads to those on the arcade side.

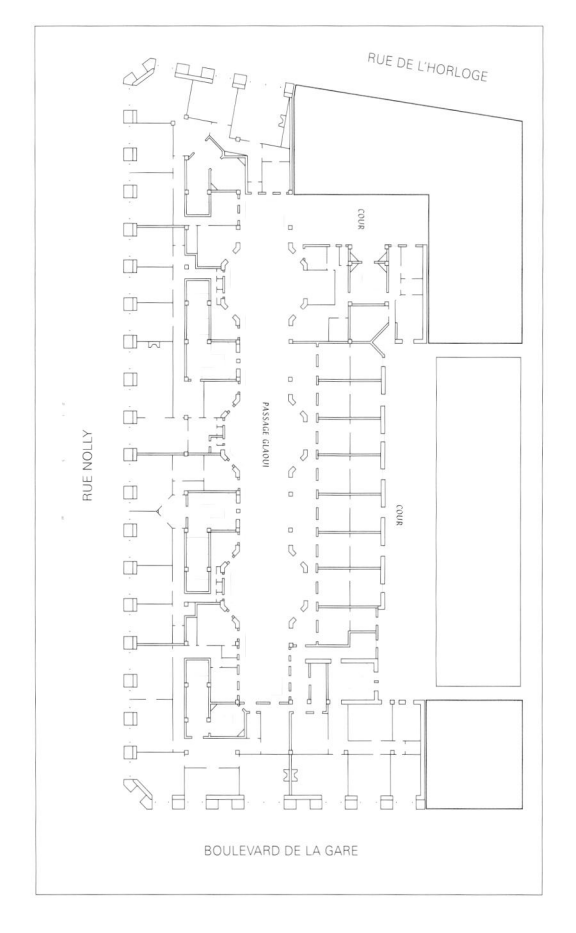

Louis-Paul and Félix-Joseph Pertuzio, El Hadj Omar Tazi building, Rue du Capitaine Maréchal, Rue Poincaré and Avenue Général d'Amade, 1929. Photo taken from inside the arcade in 1990.

Auguste Cadet, Edmond Brion and Marcel Desmet, SUMICA arcade, Boulevard de la Gare, 1932. Published in *Réalisations*, December 1934.

boulevards during the nineteenth century, although they also revealed a certain Eastern influence (Egyptian in particular).[8]

Meanwhile, Auguste Cadet, Edmond Brion, and Marcel Desmet worked together on an art deco complex replacing the former SUMICA edifice.[9] Other less architecturally elaborate arcades were similarly woven through apartment buildings along Boulevard de la Gare and were designed to house fairly standard shops. Alternatively, the arcade built by the Pertuzio brothers in 1929 that cuts through the apartment block commissioned by Omar Tazi (for a time the pasha of Casablanca) sports a fine display of marble on either side of a large rotunda lit by glass blocks at regular intervals.[10]

8 Johann Friedrich Geist, *Arcades: The History of a Building Type* (Cambridge, Mass.: MIT Press, 1983; first published, Munich: Prestel, 1969).

9 The latter had taken the place of Dr. Veyre's flour mill. In 1916, Louis Vigouroux, president of SUMICA, or *Société universelle de mines, industrie, commerce et agriculture* (Universal Mine, Industry, Commerce, and Agriculture Company), complained directly to Lyautey about the pathway of the boulevard. See the relative correspondence in BGA, SGP, bureau des Municipalités, Casablanca; travaux, aménagement de rues et bâtiments, II, 1913–26.

10 Omar Tazi and his brother Abdellatif were successive pashas of Casablanca. Hoisington, *Lyautey and the French Conquest of Morocco*, 141–49.

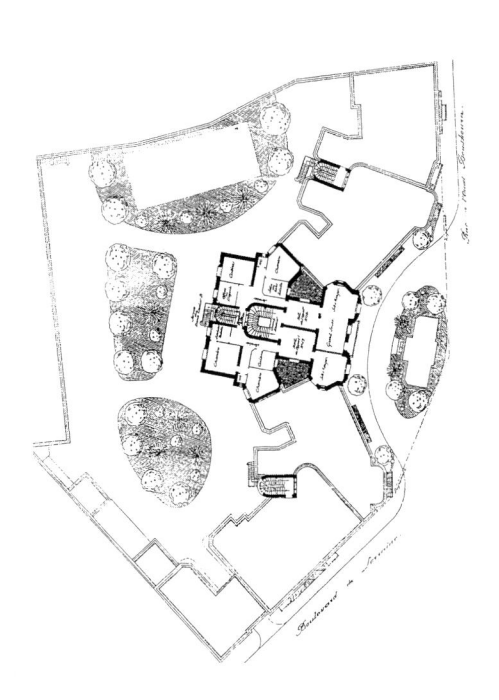

Robert Lièvre, J. Parrain buildings. Second-floor plan from the building permit.
There are six main staircases, all doubled up by service stairs. Three of the main stairs (A, B, and C) lead to the apartments, which were equipped with the latest modern comforts.

Robert Lièvre, J. Parrain buildings, Rue Reitzer, Rue Chapon, and Rue du Lieutenant Bergé, 1928. Facade overlooking Rue Reitzer. Photographed in 1991.

11 See the Parisian buildings of Richard Bouwens van der Boijen (Quai Branly) and the Perret brothers (Rue Franklin), as well as Eugène Hénard's study, *Études sur les transformations de Paris,* ed. with an introduction by Jean-Louis Cohen (Paris: L'Équerre, 1982; first published, Paris: Librairie centrale d'architecture, 1903–9).

From Open Courtyard Buildings to Slabs

New building types emerged in Casablanca in the late 1920s. The complex that Robert Lièvre designed in 1928 is particularly striking in terms of its shape, its vast usable floor area, and its positioning at the intersection of three streets. The scheme fits between two courtyards and combines two types of design: first, narrow slab housing turned inward to form a courtyard and aligned at either end with Rue Reitzer and Rue Lieutenant Bergé; and, second, an open courtyard building marking out a square at the intersection of Rue Reitzer and Rue Chapon. As a design concept, the open courtyard dovetailed with contemporary French thinking on urban issues and hygiene.[11] The most noticeable feature of the building is its extremely linear facade, which creates a well of light in all the main rooms. In addition, the building's narrowness helps to ventilate the secondary rooms and to let in light. An interesting cross-sectional view of contemporary Casablancan society is provided through the scheme's mixed apartment types: these are composed of four-bedroom apartments with salons and dining rooms, studio apartments ("bachelor pads"), and maids' quarters in the communal section above the courtyard.

In 1928, Marius Boyer designed the Lévy-Bendayan building, located at the junction of Boulevard de Marseille and Rue Lassalle. In his scheme, Boyer shunned the enclosed courtyard, thereby demonstrating his sympathy with Parisian hygienist

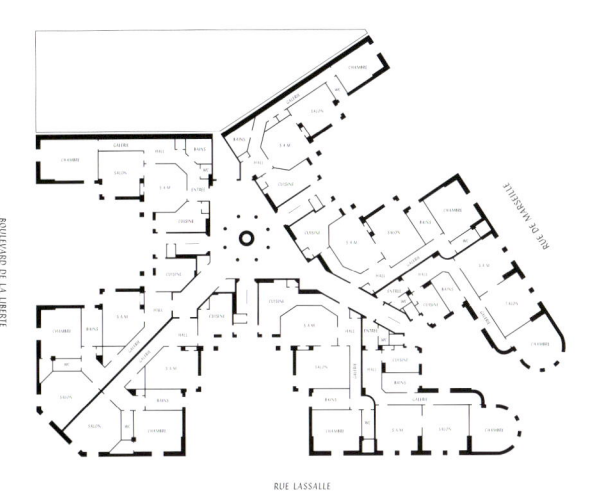

Marius Boyer, Lévy-Bendayan building, 1928.

Typical floor plan. Drawing by Cristiana Mazzoni based on the building permit.

Perspective drawing, 1928.

Elevator shaft. Photographed in 1993.

Corner view. Photographed in 1991.

Living in the *Ville Nouvelle* in the 1920s   141

12 "Trois immeubles modernes à Casablanca," *Chantiers nord-africains* 5, no. 9 (September 1932): 745–51.

13 Goulven, *Casablanca de 1889 à nos jours*, 68.

14 "Groupes d'immeubles à Casablanca, boulevard de la Liberté et Rue du Soldat Jouvencel," *Chantiers nord-africains* 1, no. 9 (September 1929): 524.

15 See the analysis of plan arrangements in buildings of the same type in Eleb and Debarre, *L'invention de l'habitation moderne*, 37–62.

campaigns. Boyer designed the block as a large nine-story structure with three open courtyards and dedicated the four main stories to the structural body, using the building's base as a sort of perch. The building's stark facades were gouged to make way for courtyards, while, from the fifth floor up, the bedrooms and dining rooms run into terraces whose brises-soleil form the building's sole decorative element. The breach in the facade turns the building in on itself, channeling light into the heart of the deepest rooms. Boyer based his design on "American prototype plans," or so it was claimed by *Chantiers nord-africains*, which viewed this building as "Casa's most thought-provoking apartment block." The article spotlights "the building's cruciform plan, namely four bodies of buildings arranged around a main staircase with four setbacks in the facades that replace the inner courtyard."[12] At the time, these "courtyard-less buildings" were heralded as a dominant current in modern Casablancan architecture.

A group of six-story apartment buildings by Pierre Jabin drew attention in 1929. The complex is sited in the Liberté quarter, then in full development phase, and was considered to "rival any district in any European town."[13] It comprises four parallel slab buildings linked by walkways, which can be accessed by elevator from the building facing the street, and it contains some fifty apartments, all of which include rooms with views on both sides of the building. According to *Chantiers nord-africains*, the structure's "reinforced-concrete shell" was a clear sign of modernity: "It can even be said that it is the first apartment house in Morocco that draws on truly modern principles. [The architects] have ingeniously made use of a deep site to create a real chef d'oeuvre."[14] The illustration accompanying this article features the unembellished rear of the building, and not the street facade incorporating Le Colisée movie theater. Inside, the apartments are fairly small and were fitted out with all the requisite modern comforts.

Evenly Distributed Compactness

Centrally located apartments were essentially occupied by the bourgeoisie and complied with tried and tested layout rules, i.e., those deployed in Parisian apartment blocks since the late nineteenth century.[15] The 1919 corner building designed by the Parisian architect Georges Vimort is a case in point: a gallery separates the private and communal parts, while the salon opens onto the dining room, which fea-

Élias and Joseph Suraqui, Coriat building, 58 Rue de l'Aviateur Coli, 1929. Facade overlooking the street. Photographed in 1929.

Élias and Joseph Suraqui, Coriat building. Courtyard. Photographed in 1929.

Élias and Joseph Suraqui, Gallinari building, Boulevard de la Gare and Rue Roget, 1924. General photo taken from the boulevard around 1929.

All the rooms in the apartments receive natural light, including the street-facing bathrooms, the courtyard, and the rear gallery. The main rooms are of regular shape, thanks to careful geometric honing, and the remaining spaces often serve as utility rooms.

Pierre Ancelle, Société Urbaine Marocaine building, Rue Lapérouse, 1930. Elevation from the building permit (computer rendering by Sylvain Le Stum).

Note the garage entrance on the right.

tures a typically Parisian bay window. The master bedroom is located along the main facade, overlooking Boulevard de Paris.

The central Rue Coli apartment house built by Joseph and Élias Suraqui in 1928 was tagged "modern-style Louis XVI" by *Chantiers nord-africains*, summing up the tie between innovation and tradition that characterizes most buildings of that time. In this instance, the layout was designed to follow standard spatial division principles for deluxe apartment buildings with a limited floor area. Visitors step into "an entrance hall, which together with the salon and dining room forms the apartment's 'reception space,' being clearly separated from the private realms."[16] The architects decided to incorporate a garden courtyard into this centrally located building, thereby marrying Hispano-Moorish tradition with a design principle that had been used in France since the turn of the century.

In 1929, Jean Michelet designed the Artaud building at the junction of Rue Védrines and Rue Prom; Michelet overcame the problem posed by the skewed dimensions of the rooms by inserting triangular cupboards.[17] A boudoir leads on from the salon; the apartments originally had no bathrooms, except when the storage room could be suitably converted. In general, very few architects gave in to client pressure to lay out lower-middle-class dwellings in the traditional French mid-nineteenth-century style. Most of the mid-range apartments were usually well equipped, incorporating a lobby with a connecting storage room or a good-sized hall, a naturally lit bathroom (sometimes adjoining a shower room), pantry, linen room, and a laundry either on each floor or on the building's roof terrace. By the same token, the 1930 apartment block built by Pierre Ancelle for the Société Urbaine Marocaine is presented in *Chantiers nord-africains* as containing "all the requisite modern conveniences." Although small, the apartments came with their own "handsomely fitted bathrooms," while the kitchens featured "a storage cupboard, larder, wood unit on wheels, and, more important, a waste disposal system with a specially designed chute."[18] While there may have been a limited number of rooms, it was nonetheless expected that these would be decently fitted out. Local living standards thus differed from metropolitan norms in that modern comforts were not confined exclusively to a privileged minority.

16 "Casablanca cité moderne," *Chantiers nord-africains* 1, no. 4 (April 1929): 273.

17 The art of geometric compensation, which allowed architects to regularize the main rooms of apartments situated on irregular lots, resulted in the creation of small recesses that could be transformed into closets. This art of "recuperation," which in the early twentieth century still signaled the architect's skill, has been lost today.

18 "Les innombrables visages de l'architecture casablancaise," 987–94.

Living in the *Ville Nouvelle* in the 1920s 143

19 Patrick Céleste, "L'apparition de l'automobile individuelle dans l'immeuble urbain d'habitation," in "L'Immeuble," *Cahiers de la recherche architecturale*, no. 22 (1988): 12–19.

As is frequently cited in contemporary reviews, this apartment building type combined traditional elements with more "modern" solutions. For instance, the 1929 Magne-Rouchaud building at the junction of Rue de Bouskoura and Rue Terves was designed in the same style as pre-1914 Parisian corner buildings, its main rooms enlarged by facade projections, and its turret corner accommodating the salons; nonetheless, its art deco architectonic details and naturally lit, sizable bathrooms gave the scheme a modern twist.

It is also striking that, although the apartments echoed French turn-of-the-century principles in their interior layout, they were nonetheless attuned to local climatic conditions. Furthermore, architects had to take into consideration that the colonial settlers had large armies of live-in staff. Thus service areas were clearly divorced from private spaces and reception rooms, and the maids' quarters (which often included a storage room, as in the Guedj apartment building constructed by Boyer in 1919) were set on the roof terrace, next to the laundry. The Public Health Department added a clause in building permits, stipulating that "those rooms marked 'storage' on the roof terrace shall not in any event serve as habitation, as they are not closed off by doors and they fail to comply with the minimum eight-meter floor area requirement." It can therefore be deduced that more than one resident was tempted to lodge servants or subtenants in these cramped spaces.

Organizing Luxury

The interiors of the central deluxe apartments reflect the canonical distribution principles of French bourgeois housing at the time in that public, private, and servant spaces are distinctly separated via corridors or other such devices. Another typical feature is the vast reception hall, which serves as an extension to the more or less interconnecting salon and dining room. This open-plan form was well suited to hosting social events and betokened affluence, as did the numerous service stairways and corridors running from these areas to the servants' rooms. In these buildings, the architects often placed servants' quarters on the same floor as the master bedroom; moreover, a small linen room/bedroom is indicated on many of the plans, which was in all likelihood intended for one of the live-in staff.

The principle of grouping the kitchens, bathrooms, and lavatories seems to have been widely respected. The master bedrooms in the larger apartments had en suite washrooms; the bathroom (often overlooking the courtyard) was placed near the main bedroom; and the kitchen (in the rear of the apartment) was always cut off from the dining room by a corridor or lobby, which was generally positioned near the entrance. Thus, the hierarchic front/rear arrangement for main and secondary water-serviced rooms still constituted a popular design solution, as illustrated by the apartment block that was designed in 1930 by the contractor Belvisi.

As in Paris, apartment buildings on deep sites were sometimes split into two structural parts targeted at two types of residents. Hence, the Tolédano building constructed by the Suraqui brothers on Boulevard de Paris was conceived as two apartment house types: first, a street-facing block with apartments comprising a salon/dining room, accessed by a main staircase and servants' stairs; second, a courtyard building containing smaller apartments with no salon and which are accessed by just one stairway. Also, since cars were becoming steadily more popular, garages started being tucked into the basements of bourgeois apartment buildings as of the late 1920s.[19]

A case in point is the apartment block designed by Ancelle for the Société Urbaine Marocaine, which was built with six garage spaces for a total of thirty-nine, mainly three- and four-bedroom apartments. It should also be noted that most of the buildings of this housing type were fitted with an elevator if they were over four stories.

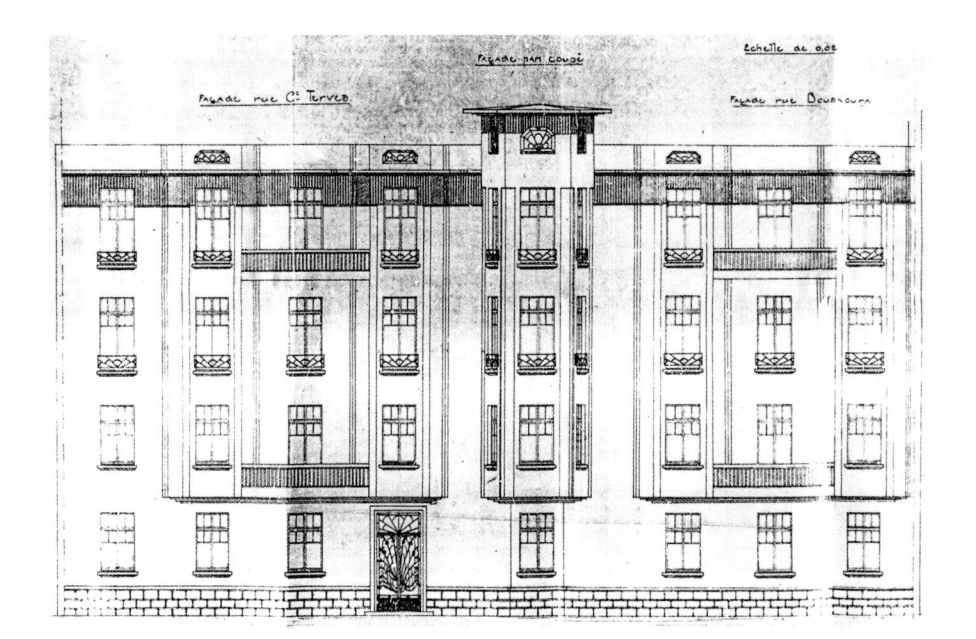

Constant Bonnet, Magne-Rouchaud building, Rue de Bouskoura and Rue du Commandant Terves, 1929. Street-facing elevation as featured in the building permit.

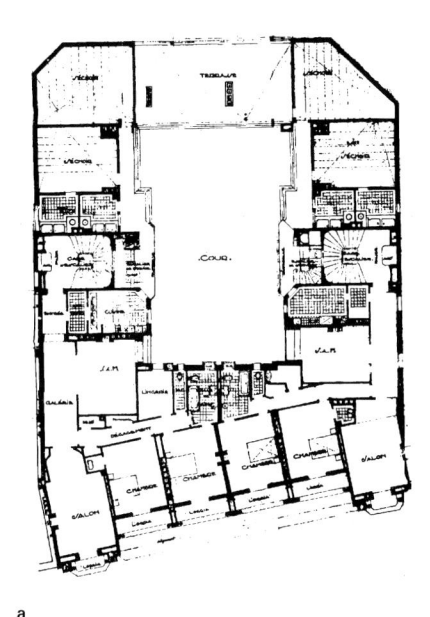

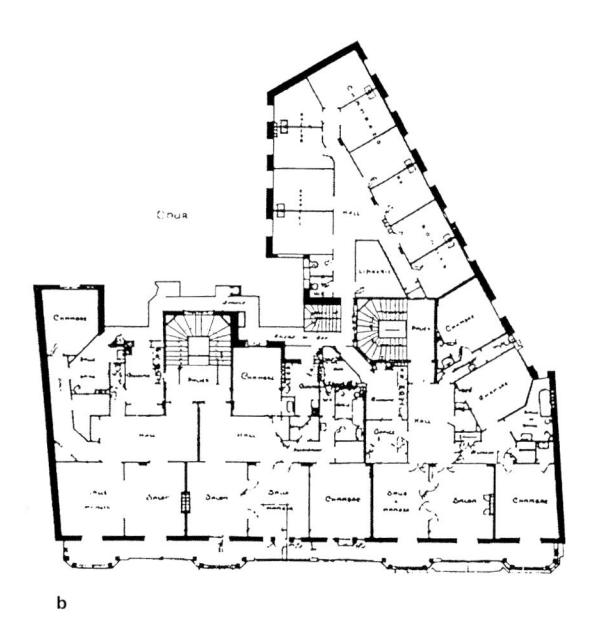

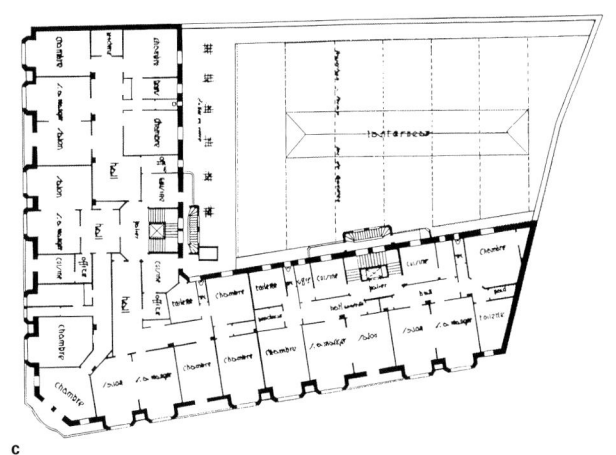

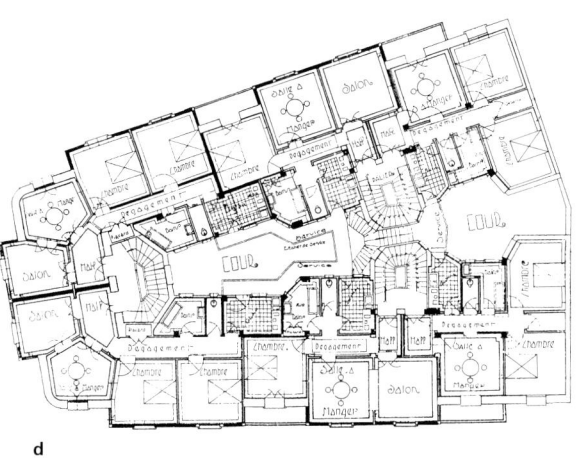

a. Auguste Cadet and Edmond Brion, Grand Socco building, Boulevard de la Gare, 1929. Sixth-floor plan from the building permit (computer rendering by Philippe Simon).
Although the apartments only have three bedrooms, a large amount of space is devoted to service areas: a domestic staircase, bathrooms with adjoining linen rooms, kitchens and pantries, laundry rooms, and a large drying room on the terrace.

b. Élias and Joseph Suraqui, in association with D. Gimenez, G. Braunschwig building, Boulevard de la Gare, 1930. Sixth-floor plan from the building permit (computer rendering by Sylvain Le Stum).
A service gallery runs around the rear and the service staircase leads to a hall that provides access to ten maids' rooms, each fitted with a washbasin. Note the multitude of service areas: utility rooms, pantry, linen room, and cupboards.

c. Aldo Manassi, Banon building, 1928. Standard floor plan from the building permit (computer rendering by Sylvain Le Stum).

d. Belvisi building (unbuilt), c. 1930, Avenue du Général d'Amade and Circular Boulevard. Plan from the building permit (computer rendering by Sylvain Le Stum).
The service stair is in the courtyard and is adjacent to two main staircases. It leads to walkways providing access to the kitchens, which are grouped in a clearly defined service core.

Living in the *Ville Nouvelle* in the 1920s   145

a

b

c

Entrance doors to 1920s apartment buildings.

a. Hubert Bride, Bessonneau building, Boulevard de la Gare, 1916–17.

b. Albert Greslin, IMCA-MA building, Rond-point Lyautey, 1928. Marblework by Léglise and Maria.

c. Apartment building, 57 Boulevard de Lorraine.

d. Marius Boyer, Apartment building, 85 Rue Colbert, 1929.

e. Apartment building, 38 Rue Gallieni.

f. Apartment building, 46 Rue Gallieni.

Marius Boyer and Jean Balois, one of two paired houses (known as Les Tourelles), Rue d'Alger and Boulevard Gourand, c. 1930. Commissioned by the contractors Gouvernet and Lorentz. Photo taken from Rue d'Alger in 1991.

Aerial view of Anfa-Supérieur, c. 1928. Foreground: the racetrack; center: Marius Boyer's Villa El Mokri; right: ochre-colored villa commissioned by M. Teste.
A. Soubreville noted, "The hill is adorned with colored villas, surrounded by white walls, lawns, bougainvillea trees, mimosa, pomegranate trees and *squinus molle* which are on a par with the finest weeping willows in France. This gives rise to a mass of greenery with a touch of the tropical in the form of palm trees and aloes. A remarkable balance has been struck in Anfa, creating an elegant blend of local tradition and cottagelike design."
Chantiers nord-africains, September 1931.

Private Villas: Influences and Adaptation

Given Casablanca's role as Morocco's only major port, and the wheeling and dealing that goes on there, it would be hellish if there weren't somewhere peaceful to escape to, away from the feverish hub. [There is no] site better adapted to such a psychological role than Anfa hill, a neighborhood that has become a relaxation zone, a "rest area" as Le Corbusier would perhaps say. It offers a daily cure for the weary mind, due to its bracing sea breeze and its soothing setting.

Chantiers nord-africains, 1929[20]

Casablanca's residential districts initially stretched from south to west of the city. Handsome thoroughfares near the center, such as Boulevard Moulay-Youssef and Rue d'Alger, rivaled one another and accommodated a host of housing types from upmarket villas to low-scale detached homes. Colonial settlers arriving from rural areas or from medium-sized towns settled in the latter type, whereas the Casablancan bourgeoisie was torn between the benefits of living in Anfa or in Mers-Sultan, in the southeast suburbs. Whereas Mers-Sultan was the first of the two districts to be inhabited, Anfa, which lies further west, became home to luxury private dwellings. The hillside development was basically a response to Prost's concept of "residential neighborhoods" where "businessmen can relax in the family domicile surrounded by greenery." The Casablancans, workaholics that they were, could rest and recharge their batteries in this country setting while still being within reach of the city. The land was parceled out in two directions: from the top of the hill downward and along the shore.[21] Léonard Julien named his housing development

[20] "Villas modernes à Casablanca," *Chantiers nord-africains* 1, no. 1 (January 1929): 85.

[21] Léonard Julien began from above while the bankers Maurice and Théo Teste began from below.

Marius Boyer and Jean Balois, Villa El Mokri, Anfa-Supérieur, c. 1928. General view, c. 1930.

Exterior view from the street, photographed shortly before demolition in 1994.

Marius Boyer and Jean Balois, Villa El Mokri, Anfa-Supérieur, c. 1928. Main facade, c. 1932

22 Léonard Julien, advertisement, in Léon Guigues, *Guide de l'Exposition franco-marocaine*, 120. See also Schulz, "L'effort économique à Casablanca et en Chaouïa," *Bulletin de la Société de géographie commerciale de Paris* 36, no. 2 (1914): 117–18.

23 A. Soubreville, "Villas à Anfa-Supérieur, Robert Lièvre, architecte," *Chantiers nord-africains* 3, no. 9 (September 1931): 907–8.

Anfa-Supérieur, in evocation of the Anfa Club (the social scene for the town's smart set) and the then well-known district of Mustapha-Supérieur in the city of Algiers. The promotion of this quarter was geared both to its location and to the promised amenities:

> There are well-kept sites for private dwellings set in green grounds with sweeping views of the city and ocean. There are hotels, restaurants, chalets, refreshment rooms, recreational activities, tennis courts, and a public garden with an ornamental lake. There is a bus and omnibus service, as well as running water in each residential development. There are no open-air cafés or cabarets . . . and there are rebates for purchasers who wish to build straightaway.[22]

Private property developers played a crucial role here. The Teste brothers, who owned land along the coast, "compelled buyers to build in an attractive style that would not clash with existing structures." The press praised such "salutary dictatorship," which they saw as being "grounded in a concern for homogeneity, aesthetic appeal, healthiness, elegance, greenery, and local style."[23] Yet this slightly tyrannical monitoring of housing and private life guaranteed unity less in terms of architectural style than in terms of social structure. The tracts of land remained out of reach for the native population, apart from the most influential Muslim aristocrats. The outcome was an intersection of social and racial segregation, in contrast to Mers-Sultan, where a more balanced population mix developed. These urban extensions resulted in the city extending out along wide landscaped roads leading to quiet lanes bordered by deluxe houses. Boulevard d'Anfa and the Ain-Diab coastal road are typical in this respect, and they used to be a popular drive out for well-to-do Casablancans:

> Casablanca has no inner suburbs to the south. Leaving Place de France, one seems to enter directly into a realm of perpetual country holidays. One is always drawn by the pleasure of going out to Anfa, along the radiant lanes of Parc Lyautey and the Avenue de l'Hippodrome. There, all is light and harmony.[24]

The first buildings constructed in Anfa-Supérieur were crowned by the turrets of the palatial villa built for Si El Hadj Mohammed el Mokri, who had been grand vizier to the sultan since 1917.[25] Constructed by Boyer and Balois in 1928, the building has *zillij* paneling and loggia adorned with balustrades and arcades set it firmly within the "neo-Moroccan" sphere. It contained state-of-the-art amenities, in line with its overall modernizing style, with a bathroom deemed to be "unique within all Morocco." A typically Casablancan partnership underpinned the project, namely the fruitful association struck up between the grand vizier and the Europeans (the architects and Belvisi, the contractor). This relationship was presented as a paradigm of political cooperation:

> The *œuvre* was conceived and directed by [the grand vizier] himself. He placed total trust in the architects and contractors, demonstrating that stylistic tastes and design ideas can come together in harmony, provided there is a will to reach mutual understanding and agreement. This kind of attitude carries much more weight than any discourse about bringing the two races closer together, thereby confirming that this latter aim may be achieved through the finest of elements—Work.[26]

The early large "colonial" villas are decked in terraces and verandahs reminiscent of French Riviera dwellings, a form that had been widely used as a source of inspiration from the inception of the *ville nouvelle*. These villas were also designed along the lines of Parisian *hôtels particuliers* of the eighteenth century; for instance, specific reception rooms were included, such as parlors, smoking rooms, and grand salons, as well as spaces dedicated to female or male activities, and courtyards and servants' quarters to cater for the large numbers of local live-in servants. In fact, the architect Pierre Jabin wrote an article presenting the Casablancan villa as a specific *type*, as did a number of critics:

> There are wide porches, large windows, entrance halls (the English-style living room is beginning to take hold), generous-sized rooms, and numerous amenities. Nothing has been neglected in the aim to render each villa, whether luxurious or utilitarian, large or small, as pleasant and functional as possible. Likewise, efforts are increasingly being made to eliminate those dreadful long corridors that bear overtones of prisons and strongholds; instead, the doors open onto well-lit, comfortable rooms, as well as onto airy passageways that link the various parts of the villa.[27]

Marius Boyer's 1928 villa for the trader Raphaël Benazéraf (sadly demolished in 1994) provides an explicit example of such an arrangement around a double-height salon and open-plan reception spaces. This true masterpiece contained an arcade that led to a wood-paneled study on one side and to the main entrance lobby on the other, which opened onto the hall complete with a "magnificent curved black marble staircase decorated with gold beading."[28] While the villa's arrangement echoed that of modernized, late-nineteenth-century *hôtels particuliers*, here it was reworked[29]: the Arab salon served as a "small lounge," while the master bedroom with adjoining loggia was flanked by a boudoir and a white marble bathroom. The entrance steps comprised "a set of tiered canopy flags" and led into a "planted patio" with an "oriental fountain . . . forming, in effect, the entrance lobby to the Arab salon."

L'Escale villa—one of the first buildings to be erected on Anfa hill—was given a red-ochre hue, causing it to stand out in the neighborhood. It was built to a Robert

24 Soubreville, "Villas à Anfa-Supérieur," 907–8.

25 El Mokri would remain grand vizier until his death in September 1957, at the age of 105. Regarding el Mokri, see William A. Hoisington, *Lyautey and the French Conquest of Morocco*, 142–43.

26 " Le Palais de son excellence El Mokri, Grand vizir de S.M. le Sultan du Maroc (MM. Boyer et Balois architectes)," *Chantiers nord-africains* 1, no. 7 (July 1929): 467–70. This unique testament to a Moroccan aristocrat's refined art of living was destroyed in 1994, despite vigorous protest.

27 Pierre Jabin, "Villas modernes à Casablanca," *Chantiers nord-africains* 1, no. 1 (January 1929): 86.

28 "Villas à Casablanca (M. Boyer)," *Chantiers nord-africains* 4, no. 8 (August 1932): 651.

29 Monique Eleb, "Le Corbusier et la tradition de l'hôtel particulier," in Jacques Lucan, ed., *Le Corbusier: une encyclopédie* (Paris: CNAC Georges Pompidou, 1987), 174–76.

Marius Boyer, Villa Bénazéraf, Rue d'Alger, 1928. General view. Photographed in 1993.

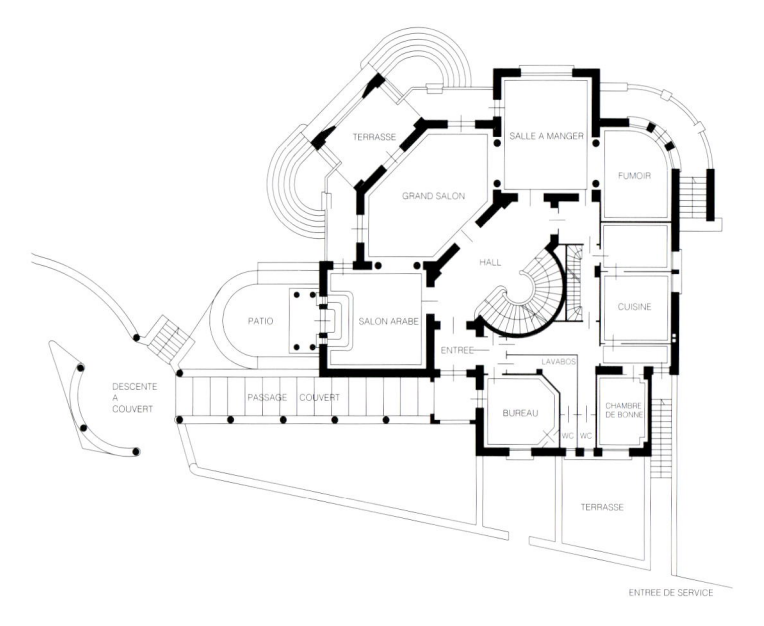

Marius Boyer, Villa Bénazéraf, 1928. First-floor plan. Drawing by Cristiana Mazzoni based on the building permit.
Entrance hall, main lounge, "Arab lounge," dining room and smoking room can form one open space if required.

Marius Boyer, Villa Bénazéraf, 1928. Patio and entrance to the "Arab lounge." Photographed in 1993.

Marius Boyer, Villa Bénazéraf, 1928. Dining room. Photographed in 1985.

Marius Boyer, Villa Bénazéraf, 1928. Master bedroom. Photographed in 1985.

The master bedroom is an apartment in its own right, with a boudoir, bathroom, and linen room. The two other bedrooms have a linen room and are separated by a bathroom.

Marius Boyer, Villa Bénazéraf, 1928. Bathroom. Photographed in 1985.

Living in the *Ville Nouvelle* in the 1920s

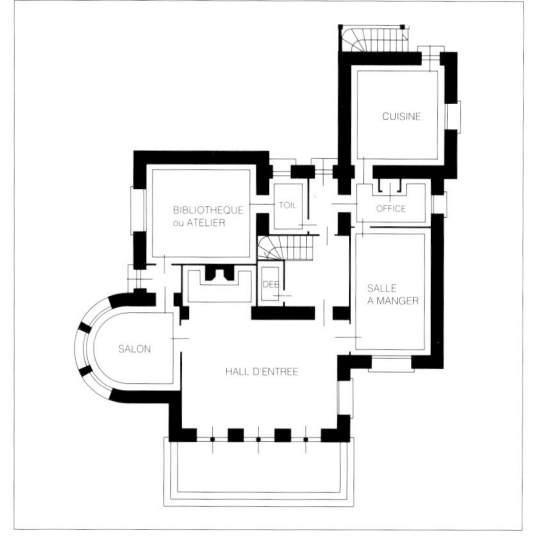

Lièvre design for one of the Teste brothers, with front steps leading into an entrance hall with a fireside area that is similar to Frank Lloyd Wright's much-acclaimed inglenook. A dining room and bay-windowed salon lead off from the hall, and there is also an atelier/library. Jabin stressed the importance of modern comforts and hygiene in the construction of these hillside dwellings: "They are all equipped with bright, airy bathrooms and kitchens, almost all of which are fitted with a waste-disposal system. The rooms are brightly painted or wallpapered, and are easy to keep clean, being laid with hygienic joint-free wood flooring or marble flags."[30]

The Cohen (or Violetta) villa, built by the Suraqui brothers in 1929, features a remarkable bathroom clad in white marble with art deco detailing. Extremely spacious and well lit, it clearly shows how the architects of these types of houses all focused on climate-specific features, modern conveniences, and easy-to-maintain materials rather than seeking to underscore their clients' wealth or social station.

The mid-range houses commissioned by the French and Moroccan bourgeoisie make up the most frequent house type, conceived as a modern interpretation of the Moroccan dwelling. The majority of these are centrally located, such as on Avenue du Général Moinier and Rue d'Alger, but there are also some that stretch up to the city's edges and along the shoreline. The rather small Villa Le Glay is an apt example in this category. Designed by Boyer and Balois in 1928, the house was designed in the form of cubes of varying sizes pierced with the odd window and embellished in places with *zellij*-clad arches and green-tiled awnings. Yet its interior layout is closer to that of a suburban dwelling than a villa, with its ground floor given over to reception space and average-sized rooms, and the bedrooms occupying the upper story.

Interior Decor — A Neo-Moroccan Challenge

In 1931, Léandre Vaillat, a prominent upholder of French regionalism, admitted to a certain fondness for the style adopted by petit bourgeois colonial settlers: "Those systematic red tiles would infuriate me in the French countryside; here, though, they rather touchingly symbolize the settlers' attachment to France, revealing how these people have stubbornly transplanted even the most second-rate elements to neutral ground, clothing them in a parochial French style."[31] Overall, however, 1920s critics showed a clear preference for "neo-Moroccan" villas, a term that referred more to borrowing decorative syntax from the Moroccan repertoire than to specific housing layout. This strategy is clearly demonstrated in the dwelling built by Hippolyte Delaporte for his own use. Similarly, while the Villa Bonan constructed by Boyer

Robert Lièvre, Villa Teste, known as l'Escale, c. 1925. General view. In *Chantiers nord-africains* (September 1931).

Robert Lièvre, Villa Teste, known as l'Escale, c. 1925. Plan (drawing by Cristiana Mazzoni).

A pantry links the dining room with the kitchen, which contains a service staircase. There are three bedrooms with terraces on the second floor; these have a linen room, a washroom, and a shared bathroom.

30 Jabin, "Villas modernes à Casablanca," 85–87.

31 Vaillat, *Le visage français du Maroc*, 24.

32 "Villas à Casablanca (M. Boyer)," 656.

Auguste Perret, project for a villa in Casablanca, 1920. Perspective sketch.

and Balois on Boulevard Moulay-Youssef in 1930 may sport a green-tiled facade and "a Neo-Moroccan style square roof," its interior nonetheless reflects the design principles used in *hôtels particuliers*. It contains a main and secondary staircase, "a fireside area, wrought-iron gates opening onto a conservatory and magnificent pergola, as well as a huge European wood-floored hall with traditional furnishings."[32] The cross section of the earlier Villa Laurent, constructed by Boyer and Balois in 1928 (again on Boulevard Moulay-Youssef), likewise highlights the fusion between neo-Moroccan exterior grammar and interior art deco vocabulary, notably in the wrought-iron gates and fireplace.

Marius Boyer and Jean Balois, Villa Bonan, Boulevard Moulay-Youssef, 1930. General view, in Marius Boyer, *Casablanca, travaux d'architecture*, 1933.

Hippolyte Delaporte, architect's own house, Rue du Parc, c. 1924. Photo of the interior, c. 1935.

Marius Boyer and Jean Balois, Villa Bonan, 1930. View of the hall/lounge, in Marius Boyer, *Casablanca, travaux d'architecture*, 1933.

Marius Boyer and Jean Balois, Villa Bonan, 1930. First-floor plan. Drawing by Cristiana Mazzoni based on the building permit.

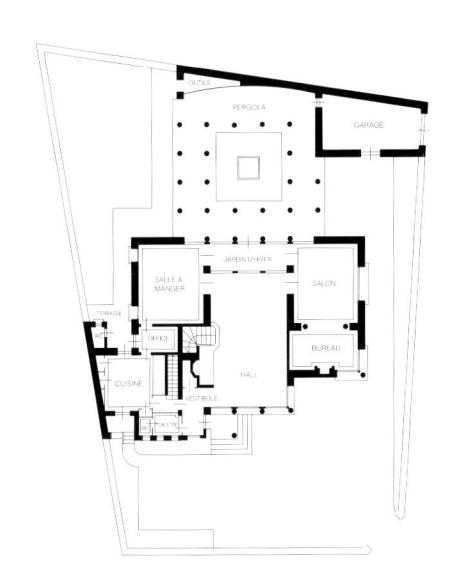

Living in the *Ville Nouvelle* in the 1920s

The Villa Assaban was afforded a surprisingly ornate interior, though its exterior is just like any of the other small houses. The dwelling's two salons paint a telling picture of how its bourgeois Jewish occupants were clearly torn by a cultural divide: one of the salons is a mix between neoclassical furniture and Louis XVI–style trimmings with pilasters and gilding, while the other is of Arabo-Andalusian style and sparkles and glitters in a blend of Moroccan furniture and Viennese armchairs. Yet the neo-Moroccan concept was seemingly in decline by the late 1920s, for numerous dwellings that were included in this category by virtue of their facades in fact had an interior layout and decor à la française. A prime example is the house designed and lived in by Robert Lièvre, who was an advocate of strict geometrical forms. The whole structure was considered to be modeled on the Njjarin fountain in Fès, a masterpiece of the Hispano-Moorish age, and the west facade was considered to be purposefully Moroccan: "[The dwelling's] ochre hue would seem bold anywhere else, but here it fits admirably with its setting. Its wide planar surfaces are pleasing, as are its generous openings that charmingly make way for a small Merinide-style window."[33] However, here again, the large reception hall, "Madame's boudoir," the study, and the master bedrooms all echo late-eighteenth-century Parisian *hôtels particuliers*. Critics were quick to point out this mix of approaches; some spoke highly of new buildings that were successfully attuned to the local style, culture, and climate, and others pointed out the quality of the design solutions, which at times were deemed to be on a par with French seaside resorts. Indeed, Morocco and France were often bracketed together in this respect, as in *Chantiers nord-africains*, which considered the red brick design of the Villa Teste worthy of both Marrakech and Le Touquet-Plage. The villa's varnished brick, "the same used by *m'allemîn* [Moroccan builders]," was praised, as were the various types of opening: "The square windows of our modern Riviera chalets fit well with Hispano-Moorish pointed openings."[34] Writing for *Chantiers nord-africains*, Pierre Jabin referred to the ways in which traditional Moroccan elements could be borrowed on a modest scale for large dwellings in order to produce an innovative result:

> It is not a question of falling into a "neo-Moroccan" style, which requires excessively large proportions for a private dwelling; rather, it is all about creating a style that hinges on sun, light, and flora. Multiple recesses, play on shadow, wide openings, a few green tiles, flower-filled window boxes, a loggia splashed with Etruscan red, a colored base, a touch of mosaic, and everything bathed in light. That is the recipe for joyful harmony.[35]

The North African press devoted a series of articles to the Moorish house and its modern interpretation. Jean Cotereau, who was one of the most prolific critics in Algiers, felt that a number of traditional elements were worth maintaining:

> The green-clad canopies, for instance, that have been so frequently, and generally skillfully, copied. The colored glass screen walls that soften the light, rendering it delightfully iridescent. The *mashrabyas* that, without interfering with air flows, divide up the rooms. The white walls, which are extremely hygienic in hot countries. Then, of course, there are the ceramics. Wall tiling, for example, is highly decorative and at the same time complies with regulations pertaining to hygiene, which accounts for its current widespread use.[36]

Many Europeans were fascinated by the Moroccans' sensual love of life. The country's temperate climate led most Casablancans, whatever their origins, to adopt new behavioral patterns as their senses became pleasurably sharpened by outdoor living. As early as 1912, Eugène Montfort, an author enamored of the Mediterranean shores, wrote:

---

[33] Soubreville, "Villas à Anfa-Supérieur," 907.

[34] Soubreville, "Villas à Anfa-Supérieur," 907.

[35] Jabin, "Villas modernes à Casablanca," *Chantiers nord-africains* (January 1929): 85–87.

[36] Jean Cotereau et al., "La maison mauresque," special issue of *Chantiers nord-africains* 2, no. 6 (June 1930): 602.

Villa Assaban, Boulevard de Bordeaux, c. 1930. Eclectic European lounge. Photographed in 1985.

Villa Assaban, Boulevard de Bordeaux, c. 1930. Moroccan lounge. Photographed in 1985.

Living in the *Ville Nouvelle* in the 1920s   157

Louis-Paul and Félix-Joseph Pertuzio, Sultan's Palace in the new medina, c. 1930. Postcard showing the open-plan reception rooms (1930).

> Someone who knows and loves the Arab people told me this tale: A builder was making a wall; he laid a rose on the foundations, and breathed in its scent each time he bent over to pick up a stone or mortar. This appreciation of sensual delight, this refined love of life, this receptiveness to the outdoors and the ability to draw a thousand pleasures from it, is something at which the Orientals excel. They are wonderful sensualists; they are, each and every one of them, artists.[37]

Referring to the Alhambra in Granada, where shade and coolness come together amid a backdrop of trickling water, Montfort asserts, "In Morocco, one can find similar elements that satisfy the senses." Obviously, though, not all architects and critics felt the same respect as Laprade for Moroccan or Moorish style. Most of them merely drew on those elements that they thought could best be adapted to a more Mediterranean, if not European, architecture. Furthermore, many of them perceived the Moorish house as "gloomy" and thus sought to open it up, as Cotereau recommended: "Architects must endeavor to brighten the countenance of Moorish housing; large openings with handsome windows framed by brightly colored mosaics will work best. However, we also believe that moderate use of miradors and bartizans can contribute to a building's overall harmony, provided that these elements do not encroach on the dwelling's profile." In this article, Cotereau recommends architectural pastiche, though he fails to point out the accompanying risk of distorting the original building type. His chief criticism, however, is implicitly leveled at the lack of sophistication in traditional houses:

> Moorish dwellings whose interiors have not been altered are devoid of all home comforts. They are always dark and dreary, as well as lacking in air, and since almost all the openings look onto the inner courtyard, occupants live practically on top of one another. This is a way of living that runs totally counter to ours.[38]

[37] Eugène Montfort, "Maisons du Maroc," *La Construction moderne* 27, no. 39 (June 23, 1912): 457.

[38] Jean Cotereau, "Vers une architecture méditerranéenne," *Chantiers nord-africains* 2, no. 4 (April 1929): 245–47.

The racism that can be glimpsed here is patent elsewhere. Yet the tone changed considerably depending on whether the subject was a modest Moroccan abode or a sumptuous dwelling. In some cases, such as in the journal *France-Maroc*, the differences between European and Moroccan lifestyles and housing were linked to their being spawned by different civilizations, and specifically to the contrast between the two urban cultures:

> Whereas the European town is largely open to sun and air, offering places for strolling and discovering all its secrets, the Moroccan town is threateningly closed, silent and locked into the shade. There are few windows, and these are placed very high up and are vigilantly barred; as for the doors, these are low and are carefully closed or they open onto corridors that twist and turn like Saracen gates. The European town attracts, just as the Moroccan town repels. But the oddest thing is that this sensation is reversed on entering the dwellings. The most open one is in fact the most disappointing, for it reveals its secret treasures at first glance, and these treasures subsequently seem worthless. All its charm lies in its facade, in its decoration. The Moorish house, however, while revealing nothing seductive on the outside, jealously keeps back all its secrets, surprises, and unsuspected delights for those who are allowed to enter. Everything is bright, roomy, airy, flowery, and fragrant. The courtyards and gardens blend joyfully in subtle simplicity, harboring sleepy pools and babbling fountains surrounded by cool, yet colorfully vibrant rugs and copperware.[39]

Because it drew inspiration from these two traditions, Anfa grew into a seemingly successful hybrid; this was not a hybrid of different populations or of social classes, but rather of northern and southern elements, namely European and African design components.

Issues of Style

Modern Moroccan architecture has traveled down a changing path. Originally a pastiche of Muslim art, it initially featured large white walls bearing so-called Arab motifs—fake Moroccan in other words. A few architects then began imitating Europe, working at Louis XVI style and so on ... Afterward, Marshal Lyautey established "town plans," hired an army of architects, and endowed Morocco with a set of public buildings, giving true artists scope to display their talent. A new style accordingly came into being, in keeping with the local surroundings and gradually freeing itself from Arab motifs to attain an attractively simple and innovative form. This making of a new architecture in Morocco preceded a similar movement in France, brought to the fore in 1925 at the Exposition des Arts Décoratifs.

Henri Descamps, 1930[40]

For the first two or three decades after construction got under way on the *ville nouvelle*, the facades were shaped by a broad range of decorative styles. As Descamps noted, the relatively scant ornamentation of the early buildings was followed by work produced in accordance with two different trends. The first drew on pre-1914 concepts, in which a watered-down version of art nouveau jockeyed with neoclassicism. For instance, along Rue de l'Horloge stand a number of apartment buildings whose facades are loaded with cherubs, fruit baskets, cornucopias, and sprays of flowers; lion heads and shells gaily alternate with one another in some places, while other parts were accorded a more modern repertoire of thistles and creepers, with neoclassical pilasters and balusters underscoring the new road alignments at varying intervals.

The second, more innovative trend corresponded to endeavors to assimilate Moroccan culture, ranging from fusion with the older urban landscape to intentional

39 "Nos villes et nos maisons," *France-Maroc* 2, no. 10 (October 15, 1917): 33. The author of this anonymous article was in all likelihood de Tarde.

40 Henri Descamps, "L'architecture française au Maroc, introduction: la création marocaine," *Chantiers nord-africains* 2, no. 10 (October 1930): 912. First published in *La Construction moderne* 41 (1930): 50–55.

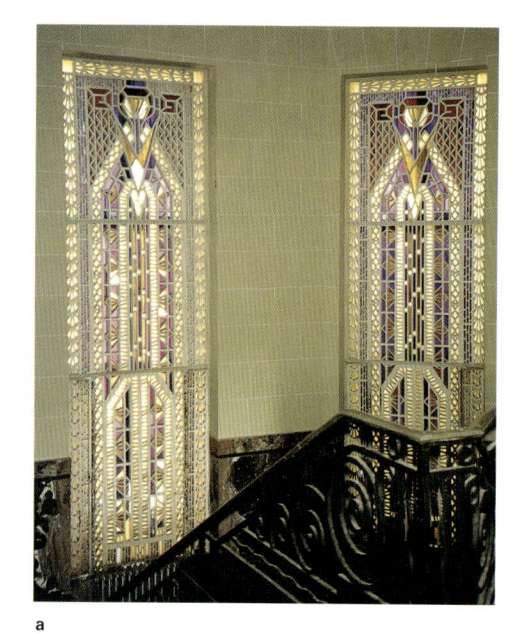

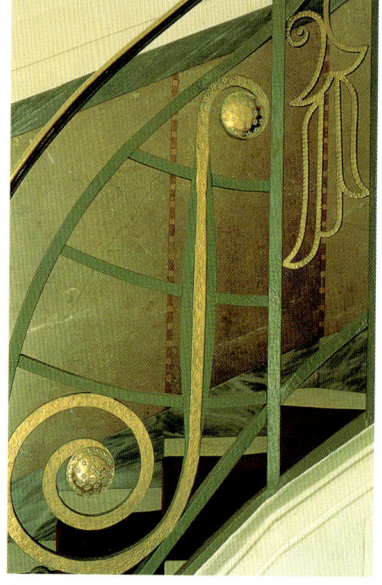

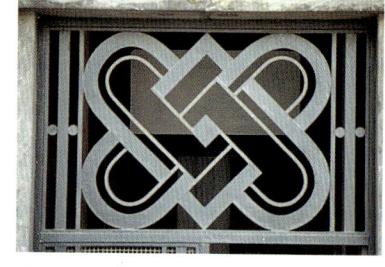

Wrought-iron work and stained-glass windows in 1920s and 1930s buildings.

a. Marius Boyer and Jean Balois, Villa El Mokri, c. 1928. Photo 1994.

b. Élias and Joseph Suraqui, Villa Violetta, Boulevard Moulay-Youssef, c. 1929. Photo 1985.

c. Sauveur Licari, Villa "Petite Source," 20-20 bis Rue de Calais, 1915. Photo 1993.

d. Élias and Joseph Suraqui, Villa Violetta, Boulevard Moulay-Youssef, c. 1929. Photo 1985.

e. Villa, Parc Murdoch, c. 1925. Photo 1993.

f. Marius Boyer, architect's own house, Rue d'Alger, c. 1930. Photo 1993.

g. Aldo Manassi, Bennarosh building, Rue de Bouskoura, 1932. Photo 1994.

h. Aldo Manassi, Bennarosh building, Rue de Bouskoura, 1932. Entrance gate. Photo 1994.

reproduction of foreign forms. These approaches evolved out of *mimeticism*, *pastiche*, or *adaptation*. Unlike most of the European dwellings, where no effort whatsoever was made to merge the new architecture with that of the medina, either in terms of location or style, the houses in the new Muslim quarters, such as the Habous development (analyzed in a later chapter), were based on *mimeticism*, i.e., reproducing typological and architectonic layouts of old housing patterns. Of course, this form of imitation bore only a distant relationship to the reproduction strategy so graphically illustrated in colonial exhibition buildings.[41] The use of *pastiche*, involving near-parodic appropriation of the prototype, was used chiefly in large dwellings, where play on traditional culture was paramount. The most common strategy, though, was that of *adaptation*, whereby European approaches were tailored to local spatial principles, notably with respect to the exterior. In certain cases, *hybrid* configurations also came into being, transcending simple combinations of European and Moroccan forms to constitute genuine innovations.

Overall, it was this plurality of approaches that would characterize Casablancan building output, although metropolitan shifts in architectural ideals did nonetheless induce cyclical changes. For instance, facades were overloaded, then purged, in line with postwar French architectural discourse. Yet whatever their points of reference—art nouveau or neoclassicism in the 1910s, followed by art deco in the 1920s—architects established close links with mosaic craftsmen, ironworkers, and cabinetmakers. This does not, however, imply that "neo-Moorish" or "neo-Moroccan" practices—two terms employed almost indiscriminately—excluded the quest for synthesis with modern themes.

In more general terms, one can deduce that Casablanca's architects gradually acquired a "Moroccan" taste, based on observation and comparison, yet essentially grounded in the broader issue of decoration. The encounter between Moroccan decorative arts and art deco layouts gave rise to original-looking facades in which stark white surfaces were adorned with elements such as geometric colored tiling, finely worked cedar balconies, and clearly defined friezes and panels. These motifs, which grew more widespread due to the impact of the *Exposition des Arts Décoratifs* of 1925, were readily taken up in Morocco; this was facilitated in large part by the fact that use of geometric forms and the insertion of decorative patterns on large blank surfaces were already a familiar feature of local architectural tradition.

A striking similarity can be perceived between the facades of Casablanca's early large apartment blocks and those of contemporary Parisian buildings. *Zillij* in Casablanca echoed the terra-cotta facing used in Paris prior to 1914[42] and were also employed to tile wall panels, decorate pediments and cupolas, underline traditional moldings, or clad reinforced-concrete walls. They prefigured art nouveau and art deco by centuries and, more than any other design element, offered a style specific to Islamic tradition by way of their highly versatile geometric motifs.

In 1928, Laprade—the first architect truly aware of the emergence of "a new Moroccan style"—evoked the "synthesis of our Latin spirit with a love of native art, in which our partiality for simplicity and harmonious volumes fits well with the design of Arab houses."[43]

Georges Rémon viewed Laprade's building in the Place Administrative as fully embodying such an approach, for without reproducing "archeological details," "the style typical of warm climes has, in general, been preserved, and Andalusian-Moroccan components have been discreetly introduced." In addition, Rémon pointed out, "While the building's underlying structural flow is inspired by local tradition," its overall design is modern with "unadorned, large wall planes, sweeping loggias and vast horizontal openings, through which finely worked details can be perceived in the shadow projected by the overhangs."[44]

Aldo Manassi, Ugazio building, Boulevard de la Liberté and Rue Gay-Lussac, 1931. Photographed in 1986.

[41] Homi K. Bhabha, "Of Man and Mimicry," in *The Location of Culture* (London and New York: Routledge, 1993), 85–92.

[42] Regarding the Parisian enameled terra-cotta-clad buildings of Jules Lavirotte, Auguste Perret, André Arfvidson, and Paul Guadet, see Eleb and Debarre, *L'Invention de l'habitation moderne*, 429–48.

[43] Laprade, "Souvenirs du temps de la guerre," 599.

[44] Georges Rémon, "Architecture moderne au Maroc, Albert Laprade, architecte," *Jardins et Cottages* (1926): 172.

Living in the *Ville Nouvelle* in the 1920s

Zillij designs and floor decoration in 1920s and 1930s buildings.

a. Apartment building on Rue d'Alsace. Capping. Photo 1995.

b. Constant Bonnet, Villa Lozana, Rue Jean-Jaurès, 1930. Capping. Photo 1993.

c. Henri Prost and Antoine Marchisio, Compagnie Algérienne building, Avenue du Général d'Amade, 1926. Capping. Photo 1996.

d. Marius Boyer, Villa Le Glay, Avenue Général Moinier, c. 1928. Frieze on the capping. Photo 1990.

e. Jospeh Marrast, law courts, Place Administrative, 1923. Capping. Photo 1991.

f. Apartment building, 57 Boulevard de Lorraine. Entrance frieze. Photo 1995.

g. Apartment building, 57 Boulevard de Lorraine. Terrazzo and mosaic floor. Photo 1995.

h. Élias et Joseph Suraqui, Villa Violetta, Boulevard Moulay-Youssef, c. 1929. Terrazzo floor. Photo 1996.

i. Pierre Jabin, apartment building, Boulevard de Paris, 1930 (detail of the entrance hall). Photo 1996.

d

e

f

g

h

i

Living in the *Ville Nouvelle* in the 1920s 163

Élias and Joseph Suraqui, Hassan and De la Salle building, Avenue Général Moinier, Rue Novo, and Rue Bossuet (postcard, 1926).

45 "Casablanca cité moderne," *Chantiers nord-africains* 1, no. 4 (April 1929): 273.

46 "Immeubles à Casablanca," *Chantiers nord-africains* 1, no. 7 (July 1929): 473–74.

47 "L'immeuble d'un grand hôtel moderne à Casablanca, Louis Jourdan," *Chantiers nord-africains* 3, no. 7 (July 1931): 694.

48 "Immeubles modernes à Casablanca, l'immeuble du Grand Bon Marché (Cadet et Brion, architectes dplg)," *Chantiers nord-africains* 3, no. 8 (August 1931): 801.

The Hassan and De la Salle apartment block, built by the Suraqui brothers on Louis-Gentil Square, offers another interesting example of how art deco and traditional ornamentation were combined: "Constructed to an extremely modern design, [the building] is composed solely of sharply angled wall planes, with curves used only for the decorative parts. The tone is clearly cubist, although the architects have added a local touch by incorporating Moorish green tiling on the fourth floor, as well as varnished tiles known as *zillij*."[45] Gradually, however, *zillij* and tilework became less common, and buildings began to be stretched upward, as did their design components, made up of symmetrical facades with pediments, turrets, and side overhangs. This was chiefly due to the increased emphasis on separating the structure's base, stories, and ridge in markedly tripartite fashion. The Roig apartment building (Rue Gallieni) by Félix and Louis Pertuzio, together with the Ettedgui and Shriqui building, constructed by Aldo Manassi in 1927 (Boulevard de la Gare), illustrate this trend. Conversely, the Noulellis apartment building, constructed around the same time by Manassi at the junction of Rue Védrines and Rue Prom, is a mutant of sorts: the register of floral sculptures adorning the fourth-floor window arches is art nouveau, whereas the geometric strictness of the base, as well as the window design and wrought-iron elements, is extremely art deco. On the other hand, the Escot apartment building, designed by Gustave Cottet in 1929 at the intersection of Rue Oudjari and Rue Coli, is purely geometric in style, its tripartite facade crowned by a large loggia set off by pillars. The contrast between the Noulellis and Escot buildings demonstrates the coexistence of floral decoration, Moroccan elements, and early modern aesthetic strategies—a stylistic combination that did not go unnoticed at the time.[46]

The end of the decade marked widespread concern for "purging structural lines and achieving exterior decorative harmony solely through essential curves—notably in balconies and windows—without resorting to sculptural forms or tilework."[47] Of course, such lack of ornamentation is by no means synonymous with dullness. As *Chantiers nord-africains* noted with respect to the Grand Bon Marché building designed by Cadet and Brion in 1931, "Although the facade is simple," the architects "have managed to inject life into vast, intractable surfaces solely through using straight lines."[48]

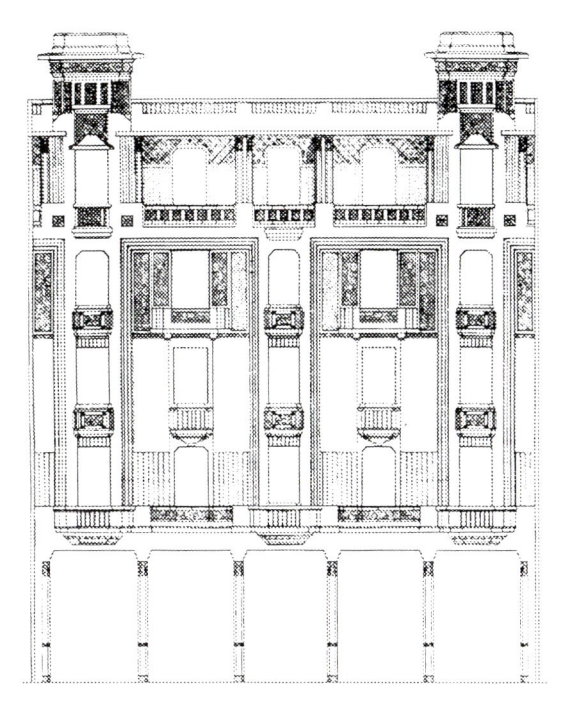

Louis-Paul Pertuzio and Félix-Joseph Pertuzio, Roig building, Rue Gallieni, c. 1927. Elevation from the building permit (computer rendering by Sylvain Le Stum).

Aldo Manassi, Ettedgui and Shriqui building, Boulevard de la Gare, 1927. Elevation from the building permit.

Aldo Manassi, Noulellis building, Rue Védrines and Rue Coli, 1927. Photographed in 1990.

Gustave Cottet, Escot building, Rue Oudjari and Rue Coli, 1929. Photographed in 1990.

Living in the *Ville Nouvelle* in the 1920s   165

From 1930 onward, strict geometrical forms and freely arranged openings were to prevail over ornamental decoration, a development that will be detailed in the following chapter. The steady rise in construction costs fed this tendency, as architects sought to cut down on decoration to meet the local clientele's demands for modern comforts. In addition, the skyscraper craze led architects to concentrate on designing forceful, "skyward" schemes. Whereas Boyer's elegant neo-Moorish designs had attracted attention several years earlier, the architect now recommended starkness, as he himself explained in a lecture in 1929:

> The facades have been rid of their heavy moldings and the walls are now stripped of their deplorably tasteless ornamentation. Colors sing out brightly on healthy, torture-free surfaces, and the building's lines are restored to purity, soothing the eye. Truth, and above all simplicity, carry the day. As with everything else, successful architecture requires honesty.[49]

Lovers of the past feared that the local vernacular would be left by the wayside. A columnist for *Chantiers nord-africains* condemned the fact that the building commissioned to Edmond Gourdain by the Compagnie Générale Transatlantique was the only one of its kind "on Boulevard de la Gare, a road in which, sadly, local motifs are exceedingly rare":

> The architect has taken pains to introduce a measured element of Moroccan art into this modern building: green-tiled festoons; ochre tones in keeping with local housing; ornamental surrounds recalling motifs of plaster sculptures by Fassi craftsmen; a brightly colored base; prismatic marble columns resembling arcades; wide openings of various forms that pattern the facades; stone balusters; modern wrought-iron balconies; and, lastly, pergolas that crown the recessed top floor in delightful fashion.[50]

Other critics deprecated ornamentation when it drew on other cultures or periods, but accepted it when it was rooted in the local vernacular; this was the case for Cadet and Brion's building on Boulevard de la Gare, which is decorated not with "stylized caryatids or parasite moldings," but with "wide ceramic panels that create a perfectly balanced pattern and whose colors recall regional earthenware."[51] However, borrowed references were increasingly decried toward the end of the decade, and critics praised the fact that architects had "wisely given up on persis-

Auguste Cadet and Edmond Brion, Grand Bon Marché building, Boulevard de la Gare, 1929. Photo taken in 1991 showing part of the facade.

49 Marius Boyer, "La construction moderne," lecture presented in Casablanca, 1929, collection of Gaspare Basciano, Casablanca (typescript), 22.

50 "L'immeuble d'une compagnie de navigation à Casablanca, Ed. Gourdain, architecte, B. Nigita entrepreneur," *Chantiers nord-africains* 3, no. 9 (September 1931): 905.

51 "Immeubles modernes à Casablanca, l'immeuble du Grand Bon Marché," 802.

Edmond Gourdain, Compagnie Générale Transatlantique building, Boulevard de la Gare and Avenue de la Marine, 1929. Photograph taken in 1997 showing facade overlooking the boulevard.

Louis Fleurant, Villa Masson, Rue de La Haye and Boulevard de Londres, 1930. Photographed in 1992.

tently reproducing a Moorish style that did not always match 'modern requirements,' notably with respect to health and hygiene."[52]

The notion of a link between interior and exterior was addressed by many critics, including Jean Gallotti, who deemed that "the plan reflects the very soul of the building," a viewpoint that had been upheld by rationalists since 1880. Condemning the "fanciful layout of Parisian houses," Gallotti stressed the "dilemma faced by modern architects in their rejection of ornamentation; they have to choose whether to keep to a simple plan, only producing frozen, lackluster cubes, or else make use of setbacks and projections to distract the gaze, which calls for a complex scheme."[53]

These contrasting strategies, which were all employed with the aim of achieving external simplicity, thus gave rise to original, albeit ambiguous, designs. Consequently, it became clear even to observers far removed from the architectural scene, such as Claude Farrère, that after just two decades of Protectorate administration, Lyautey had won his wager of being able to fashion a Moroccan approach to architecture:

> In short, architects in Morocco were well trained, learning in the school of a certain Maurice de Tolly how to create a construction style hinged on logic. Architecture has to merge with a country's climate and customs. Merely copying native buildings would imply that a Frenchman leads the same lifestyle as an Arab or a Berber. Similarly, transplanting our Parisian boulevard buildings to Mogador and Tangiers would mean that the Parisian climate is the same as in Fès and Marrakech. De Tolly always took this into account, right from the start of the Protectorate.'In so doing, a truly Moroccan architecture has been born, unlike in Algeria and Tunisia, where it is still in an embryonic stage.[54]

[52] "Villas à Casablanca," *Chantiers nord-africains* 1, no. 9 (September 1929): 523.

[53] Jean Gallotti, "Une nouvelle rue à Paris, (la rue Mallet-Stevens)," *L'Art vivant* 4, no. 64 (August 1927): 668. An active contributor to architectural and decorative arts magazines in the 1920s and 1930s, Gallotti had been on staff at the Service des antiquités, Beaux-Arts et monuments historiques (Antiquities, Fine Arts, and Historical Monuments Service) in Rabat when it was headed by Tranchant de Lunel. The character of de Tolly, in *Les hommes nouveaux*, was based on de Lunel.

[54] Farrère, *Les hommes nouveaux*, 91.

Place de France at the corner of Avenue Général d'Amade and Rue du Capitaine Maréchal (postcard, c. 1935). From left to right: the Socifrance, Bendahan, Baille, Tazi, Compagnie Algérienne and Paris-Maroc (Galeries Lafayette) buildings.

1930–1940: From Art Deco to Modernism in Residential Construction

Casablanca is stretching out, expanding, taking up more room. It believes in the future. This city is a fine lesson in optimism for an unsettled world.

R. de la Celle, 1935[1]

The Place de France—on the right, four reinforced-concrete apartment buildings, covering five stories and fitted with central heating; on the left, the filthy adobe of the Moorish rampart, a crenelated gate shrouded in barbed wire, and the flaking minaret of a locked and barred mosque. The Place de France, with buses skidding in the clay, well nigh running over blue-garbed storytellers droning out A Thousand and One Nights, with straying camels diverted from their route by the purr of the landing airmail plane. On closer inspection, though, nothing seemed out of the ordinary, not even the teeming crowds of Europeans, Moors, Arabs, Berbers, Negroes, and rich and poor Jews. No, nothing seemed out of place, not even the mishmash of djellabas, smocks, burnous, jackets, selhams, kaftans, rags, and uniforms. It was just like any other square, Morocco or elsewhere. The only people who marveled at the scene were tourists whose favorite pastime was ordering iced drinks at the Excelsior, served by a Parisian maître d'hôtel in full attire while having their shoes polished by a darkie topped by a tarboosh. What was extraordinary was to be found elsewhere, namely in the direct contact, and conflict, of all the pasts and all the futures within this African land of Maghreb that is home to the Western caliphs. It is a land, moreover, which is fast becoming a New America; in fact, it is more American than Chicago and San Francisco put together. Contact and conflict, then, with the Place de France as the battlefield.

Claude Farrère, 1932[2]

[1] R. de la Celle, "Maroc, place de France," *L'Afrique du Nord illustrée* 30, no. 755 (October 19, 1935): 34.

[2] Claude Farrère, "Les Français au Maroc," in *Histoire populaire des colonies françaises: le Maroc* (Paris: Éditions du Velin d'Or, 1932), 360–61.

[3] De la Celle, "Maroc, place de France," 34.

An African Babel

In contrast to Farrère's observations, the extension of the Place de France in 1935 attracted a crucible of Mediterranean peoples, with "carters cracking their whips amid much swearing in Arabic, Spanish, Maltese, and French."[3] Yet this miniature "Tower of Babel" was in truth a distorted image of the demographic reality, as is illustrated by the 1931 census, in which the public authorities' initial prediction that Casablanca would be mostly "French" was proved wrong; out of the 160,000

4 The European third of the population comprised 35,000 French, 9,500 Spaniards, and 7,200 Italians. "La population de Casablanca (d'après les services municipaux de la ville)," in "Casablanca, grande ville et grand port de l'Empire français," special issue of *Revue de géographie marocaine* 23, no. 1 (1940): 43–45.

5 René Janon, "L'œuvre d'une municipalité marocaine: Casablanca," *Chantiers nord-africains* 4, no. 7 (July 1932): 564.

6 "La population de Casablanca," 45.

7 Bensimon-Donath, *Évolution du judaïsme marocain*, 51.

8 "La population de Casablanca," 45.

9 Louis Delau, "Casablanca et le Casablancais," in "Casablanca, grande ville et grand port de l'Empire français," special issue of *Revue de géographie marocaine* 23, no. 1 (1940): 11.

10 Farrère, *Les hommes nouveaux*, 115.

estimated inhabitants, Muslim Moroccans represented half the figure, and Moroccan Jews—the only Jews to be counted separately—numbered around 20,000. The native population therefore made up two-thirds of the city's residents and this proportion continued to grow with industrialization.[4] Five years later, Casablanca's 260,000 headcount placed it in the same category as Bordeaux and Algiers, and its surface area was comparable to Lyons or inner Paris. The Muslim and Jewish population had doubled, whereas the number of Europeans had risen by only a third. This dramatic increase was a unique situation in colonial Maghreb, and the city authorities began to express some apprehension about it: "The municipal authority is extremely concerned about the population growth that has been induced by large-scale construction works. Their two key concerns are therefore providing housing for the native population and extending the city out toward the sea."[5]

The municipal authority commented on the emergence of "elite traders and craftsmen mostly originating from Morocco's imperial cities." Far from simply cashing in on "the city's flourishing trade," as municipal officials liked to put it, these Muslim Moroccans proactively contributed to Casablanca's development. However, the "manual laborers, who could readily find jobs in the city's various industries" made up a much larger segment of the population.[6] Meanwhile, Moroccan Jews were continuing to migrate from Marrakech, Mogador, Safi, and Agadir. As Doris Bensimon-Donath has pointed out, social groups underwent shifts in location within the city itself: "The most integrated members of the population preferred to move into the heart of the new European districts, and were even involved to a certain extent in the construction of these areas."[7] Recent newcomers took up residence in the apartment buildings that had been preserved in the mellah and part of the old medina; the sedentary population, however, often resettled in the Lusitania and Liberté neighborhoods, as is evidenced by the large number of apartment buildings that were both commissioned and leased by Jews.

The Spaniards played a key role in the city, in view of their building, fishing, and mechanical skills. Unlike the Italians, they tended toward assimilation (as in Algeria), especially after the Spanish civil war. They put down roots in all parts of the *ville nouvelle*, although the poorer among them always clustered in the Maarif district. Members of the Italian community were chiefly concentrated in the Maarif and in Roches Noires, and managed to "maintain close links with home, through schools, patriotic associations, and social events."[8] As previously mentioned, whether contractors or workers, the Italians were extremely active in public works and the building industry. The fact that Casablanca was also home to immigrants from England, the United States, Belgium, Switzerland, Poland, Greece, and even from Japan, China, and India, confirmed that it had "become a great city, in which a host of different nationalities originating from highly varied cultures live side by side in perfect harmony." Yet this rosy picture was nothing but a mere illusion, for in truth there was an underlying hierarchy that dictated daily life, working relations, and social ties.

Portrait of the Typical Casablancan

Despite such diverse populations, a number of authors endeavored to paint portraits of the stereotypical Casablancan. Louis Delau viewed him as a pragmatic Frenchman leading a "hard-working but happy life,"[9] who "may prefer profit to ideas," but paradoxically, was extremely willing to help out his "fellow sufferers," while the image of the superactive Casablancan is portrayed through Bourron in *Les hommes nouveaux*, who is never happier than "when he is selling and buying."[10] As for the German writer Friedrich Sieburg, author of the bestseller *Is God a Frenchman?*, Casablanca represented France's "Fountain of Youth," one of its main characteristics being the inhabitants' drive and energy:

What I felt in Algiers, I feel one hundred times stronger here; France has grown younger in North Africa. This city seems to be saying, "It's not true that France is indolent and dusty; it's not true that our people are lethargic, that the country is made up of Dominican sinners and that the future frightens us." The customary image of the typical Frenchman has been turned on its head. And so it is hardly surprising that the young generation of French Morocco is, in a way, fanatically devoted to Casablanca.[11]

Casablanca's French population certainly "did business," propelled, as Delau observed, "by the need for prosperity." These people were greedy for modern comfort, loved life with zeal, were sporty, and sought travel opportunities, fresh air, and top-notch entertainment. Although more attracted to "outdoor life" than to "any kind of deep and meaningful existence," by the late 1930s they had begun to "increasingly show an interest in the arts, literature, handsome decor, and fine artworks."[12] At the same time, Vincent Berger noted a link between Casablancan lifestyle and house types; in other words, property had become an indicator of social rank:

It was originally the Latin immigrants who not only wanted to build rapidly and on a large scale, but who also sought elegance and grace . . . Casablanca has become an architect's paradise. A technique has been created based on airiness, natural light, and simple design. We have witnessed the birth of a new style. I do not know of any other city that boasts such a varied display of smart villas set amid lush greenery.[13]

Meanwhile, as was commented on by many observers, the Casablancan lower middle class had grown steadily more demanding. Intent on living well and manifesting their success, this group viewed housing as a social springboard.

Clients in Quest of Modern Comforts

New architects entered the arena in the early 1930s. These included Marcel Desmet, Erwin Hinnen, Georges Renaudin, and Paul Perrotte, all graduates of the École des Beaux-Arts in Paris, which had begun to adopt a more modern take on contemporary issues.[14] This influx coincided with a marked shift in the first generation, as it became more receptive to new concepts. It was a turning point that was analyzed in 1939 by Edmond Pauty, then head of the Protectorate's Historical Monuments Department. Pauty particularly stressed the demand for rationality that had been expressed by Casablanca's clientele:

It is all a matter of responding to different needs from those of metropolitan France in a different climate. Our clients, who have grown with the city, have their own tastes and requirements when it comes to modern comforts. They are truly Casablancan. For a long time, architects in Morocco sought ways of reproducing Islamic monuments. A reaction was bound to occur. Forms had to be brought more in line with their function; plans had to become freer . . . Architectural practices were not influenced by the artistic qualities of cities such as Marrakech or Fès, but rather by the expression of European art nouveau, made popular by glossy photographs.[15]

Neo-Moroccan style in housing and civic buildings continued to be rejected throughout the 1930s. From then on, starkness and tempered modernity dictated design vocabulary, and structural qualities prevailed over ornamentation. Simultaneously, less affluent social groups likewise began to call for more modern comforts, which gave rise to up-to-the-minute design solutions for low-income housing. The basements contained garages, and most of the apartments (even the smaller ones) included waste-disposal systems and fitted-out bathrooms, while drying rooms and laundry facilities were now deemed essential. Given that average building height had increased dramatically, each scheme always incorporated elevators and also often comprised freight elevators.

The start of the decade witnessed a rapid rise in new housing schemes for Casablancans who were better off. In 1932, *Chantiers nord-africains* noted, "Last

11 Friedrich Sieburg, "Le rôle économique de Casablanca vu par un écrivain allemand," *Bulletin économique du Maroc* 5, no. 4 (July 1938): 205–7. First published in the *Frankfurter Zeitung* (June 24, 1938). Sieburg had published *Is God a Frenchman? or, the Gospel of St. Joan. A German Study of France in the Modern World*, trans. Alan Harris (London and Toronto: J. Cape, 1931). First published as *Dieu est-il français?* (Paris: Grasset, 1930).

12 Delau, "Casablanca et le Casablancais," 13.

13 Vincent Berger, "Casablanca-Radio-reportage," in "Casablanca, grande ville et grand port de l'Empire français," special issue of *Revue de géographie marocaine* 23, no. 1 (1940): 15–18.

14 See Antonio Brucculeri, "L'École des Beaux-Arts de Paris saisie par la modernité," in Jean-Louis Cohen, ed., *Années 30: l'architecture et les arts de l'espace entre industrie et nostalgie* (Paris: Éditions du Patrimoine, 1997), 219–24.

15 Edmond Pauty, "Tradition et modernisme à Casablanca," *L'Architecture* 52, no. 4 (April 1939): 140.

year's construction market beat all records," and "eyewitnesses are amazed by the building fever that has gripped Casablanca."[16] Nonetheless, the effects of the 1929 recession began to take their toll in the second half of 1931. By 1935, high building output and excessive rents caused housing supply for Europeans to outstrip demand, hitting a 26 percent vacancy rate. Yet this exceptional episode in Casablanca's housing history was not destined to last long, for by 1939 the rate had plummeted to just 5 percent.[17] Construction work slowed as of 1935, despite ongoing waves of immigration, notably an influx of Spanish refugees, followed by a rush of Europeans during World War II. It was clear that the Casablancan middle class had begun to acquire a taste for modernity, which explains why modern conveniences continued to form an integral part of design schemes even after rents came down in 1931:

> It is pleasing to note that construction firms have not altered their policy regarding modern comforts. In fact, it is quite the reverse—these fittings are now the norm for new apartment buildings, whose rent covers electric heating, refrigerators, ovens, running water, fully fitted bathrooms, and waste-disposal devices, either in the form of a chute or incinerator . . . In short, new buildings are geared to providing maximum comfort rather than just providing low-rent accommodation.[18]

This middle-class taste for home comforts points to an ambition to capitalize on the improved living standards offered by cutting-edge technology, as is illustrated in the inventory of new fittings detailed in *Afrique du Nord illustrée*.[19] By the same token, a wider spectrum of building programs emerged. Typical 1920s housing schemes, such as small apartment houses and private dwellings, now shared land with workers' developments and large deluxe apartment buildings containing state-of-the-art conveniences, as well as with low-rent housing for Muslim Moroccans whose numbers, and aspirations, had swelled. Apartment types grew increasingly diverse, and studio apartments for single residents became commonplace. In addition, the vogue for high-rise office construction also began to affect housing.

An Interplay of Solids and Voids

Despite its diversity of style, or rather its nonstyle, Casablanca is nonetheless a stylish city . . . It has been saved by its neat layout, by its elegant yet restrained ornamentation, and by the whiteness of its facades, which must be maintained at all costs, since these frame the city's many gardens. It is vital that Casablanca retain (or perhaps adopt) the Spanish taste for massive structures and planted areas, the French penchant for regulating lines, and the Moroccan love of daring color combinations. More than any other city, it is perfectly suited to expressing the twofold ambition of modern art, that is, drawing on the most basic resources to create a remarkably stark exterior while providing maximum interior comfort.

Louis Delau, 1939[20]

In Casablanca, architectural debate and building design encountered a new form of discourse in the decade leading up to World War II. Casablanca's facades were stripped down, and the buildings took on the shape of offset cubes, creating a new aesthetic based on an open play of solids and voids in which "soothing planar surfaces" formed the ruling element. Vaillat underlined "the city's architectural development, which, having been dominated by so-called rental boxes and heavy Louis XVI–type ornamentation, went through a sort of Neo-Arabian phase . . . before arriving at a style whose entire beauty resides in its consummate ability to adapt to local climate and customs."[21] The obsession with facade decoration that had been the hallmark of the previous decade gave way to a rationalist treatment of volumes.

---

16 "Nouveaux immeubles à Casablanca," *Chantiers nord-africains* 4, no. 3 (March 1932): 231. See also Rouvière, "L'activité immobilière marocaine vue à travers l'essor de Casablanca," *Bulletin économique du Maroc* (July 1935): 214–17.

17 Girard, "L'habitat au Maroc, études et réalisations du Service de l'habitat," in *Compte-rendu des journées de l'habitat* (Casablanca: C.I.F.M., 1950), 4. Following his trip to Casablanca, Léandre Vaillat remarked that rents there were higher than those in Paris. Vaillat, *Le Périple marocain,* 90.

18 "Nouveaux immeubles à Casablanca," 231.

19 De la Celle, "Maroc, Place de France," 34.

20 Delau, " L'Architecture au Maroc. Casablanca," *Le Maroc du Nord au Sud* and *Réalisations,* special joint issue (June 1939).

21 Vaillat, *Le Visage français du Maroc*, 12. Regarding Parisian precedents, see Émile Rivoalen's accounts cited in Eleb and Debarre, *L'Invention de l'habitation moderne,* 429–503.

Hippolyte Delaporte, Maret building, 128 Boulevard de la Gare, 1932. Photographed in 1993.

Adrien Laforgue, SIMAF building, Rue Georges Mercié, 1929. Photographed in 1995.

22 "Les innombrables visages de l'architecture casablancaise," *Chantiers nord-africains* 3, no. 12 (December 1931): 1208. These critiques echoed the accusation, leveled against European modernists, that excessively spare forms threatened the future of the craft of construction.

23 This building is the only one that Laforgue, who lived and practiced in Rabat, built in Casablanca.

Facades were now governed by bay windows, balconies, and corbeled loggias in response to concerns related to new interior layout and spatial arrangements. At the same time, however, fears were expressed over the threat this posed to traditional style and skills.[22]

In 1931 a columnist for *Chantiers nord-africains* noted with some relief, "The last word has not been said on mosaics and *zillij*," and "the 'machine for living in' is finding it difficult to triumph over our Latin tastes." The same columnist recommended a gradual change, taking as his model the building by the Suraqui brothers on Louis-Gentil Square. He envisaged that "sculptural forms, staff, and relief ornamentation will increasingly yield their place to diversely colored walls and measured use of ceramic motifs." Casablancan architectural output of the 1930s was indeed to follow this trend, as is demonstrated in Laforgue's building for the SIMAF company, which denoted a step toward starkness fused with local points of reference.[23]

Vaillat would criticize the city hall's "outdated Hispano-Moorish style," but considered the Laforgue building to be "excellent—a real lesson in style," despite the fact that "only the front [had been] detailed":

1930–1940: From Art Deco to Modernism

Marius Boyer, apartment building, Rue de l'Aviation Française, c. 1933. Photographed in 1989.

M. Vandelle, Hôtel Guynemer, Rue Guynemer, c. 1932. Photographed in 1994.

There is much here to serve as a yardstick for other builders: white plastered walls that create a subtle interplay of shadow and light depending on the time of day (Morocco does not take kindly to colored plaster of the type used in Italy and Spain); marble-clad porticoes on the ground floor, though these may be a trifle high; square windows whose surround is so darkly green it almost verges on black; a gallery that snakes along the entire top floor and whose Pompeii-red recess exudes a sensation of coolness in the excessively bright light (in Morocco, facades should be sculpted with hollows not projections); two overhangs inscribed in the gallery; and lastly, high coping that crowns the building.[24]

In his description of the "ideal solution for the modern family dwelling," Boyer asserts, "The rule should be to banish all ornamental complexity, which is a sign of bad taste, and instead seek effect through color and volumes, combined with a play of shadow and light." Adapted to suit client needs, the building "should include pilotis, hanging gardens, loggias, open balconies, and walls closed off to the north and to the rain."[25]

Even window forms represented a challenge. Portholes and footbridges predominated, though this is not surprising, given Casablanca's role as a port, coupled with the infatuation for ocean liners that then raged throughout the world, from Los Angeles to Tel Aviv.[26] By contrast, it is interesting to note that ribbon windows were not really the order of the day, though they were by no means ruled out altogether, as is evidenced by Natale Girola's Villa Mimran, where they are combined with porthole windows. According to a *Chantiers nord-africains* reader, the windows in Algiers tend to be wide and not high; in Casablanca, Lyautey noted, "Many architects prefer numerous vertical openings grouped in one space rather than single windows."[27] The window scheme for the buildings in the Place Administrative clearly fits this description.

Adapting to the dictates of climate was already an essential method in the research on directional light which was conducted by modern planners. Casablanca is very humid in winter, "a cold country that has a beating sun," to quote Lyautey, so at this time of year unheated dwellings are cold and the contents of cupboards can grow moldy if there is not enough light. According to Vaillat, it was therefore a question of "imitating the native population," who regarded a southeastern orientation as "the most favorable for retaining coolness, since all that is required to block out the blazing summer sun is an overhang above the windows and doors." Furthermore, as the southeast "receives the most sun, in winter the rooms are flooded with slanting light for most of the day."[28] As Descamps noted, climatic concerns in construction obviously hinged more on creating shade than on providing sun-filled spaces: "The European response to climatic considerations has given rise to a profusion of porches, overhangs, balconies, terraces, and porticoes along the shopping streets. This succession of arcades lends Casablanca a certain cachet, thanks to which it has escaped the rather banal character of most large modern cities."[29]

Claustras, or screen walls, which were used often by Perret, became an increasingly popular feature and were widely produced in reinforced concrete. According to the Casablancan interior decorator Kirk Lucien Coste, these "openwork panels are designed to let in faint light from the windows in which they are set,"[30] thereby allowing air to circulate. Like the *mashrabiehs*, used throughout the Arabic world to shield interiors, they also allow occupants to see without being seen, in other words, to be out in the open but concealed from public view.[31]

In Jean Cotereau's opinion, "what is to be learned about Moorish housing plans" is not so much "the aesthetic detail of their columns and arches"—the focus of too many "mediocre" architects—but rather "the way in which arcades, porticoes, and galleries deal with the heat factor."[32] Thus in the 1930s neo-Moroccan

24 Léandre Vaillat, "Le décor de la vie: au Maroc, Casablanca," *Le Temps* (Paris) (February 7, 1932): 4.

25 Boyer, "La construction moderne," 19.

26 Regarding the nautical metaphor in architecture, see Gert Kähler, *Architektur als Symbolverfall: der Dampfermotif in der Baukunst* (Brunswick and Wiesbaden: Vieweg, 1981).

27 "Les innombrables visages de l'architecture casablancaise," 1207–11.

28 Vaillat, *Le visage français du Maroc*, 38. Lyautey's quote belongs to the limitless collection of bons mots credited to the General.

29 Descamps, "L'architecture française au Maroc, introduction: la création marocaine," 911–12.

30 Kirk Lucien Coste, "Le claustra," *Réalisations* 2, no. 4 (February 1936): 111–17. Coste's definition is: "From the Latin *claustrum*, only used as a plural. Arabesque *tourica* of flowers on sculpted plaster and incised *zillij*. Plaster embroidery skillfully freed of its background. It is very easy to find numerous applications for such beautiful decoration in the studios, entrance halls and salons of our modern interiors."

31 Jean-Charles Depaule and Jean-Claude Arnaud, *À travers le mur* (Paris: Centre de création industrielle, 1985).

Decoration, ceramic and *zillij* designs from 1930s buildings

a. Emmanuel Chaine, Villa, Rue Curie, c. 1932. Photo 1996.

b. Biazzo, Liscia building, Boulevard de Paris, 1929. Photo 1991.

c. Apartment building, 47 Rue Dumont d'Urville, c. 1935. Photo 1996.

d. Georges Grel, Apartment building, Avenue Général Moinier, c. 1930. Photo 1993.

e. Kirk Lucien Coste, *zillij* tiles for the church of Léon Dumas' Notre-Dame des Archanges, Rond-point des Sports, 1932. Photo 1996.

f. Pierre Jabin, Villa Cohen, Rue Curie, 1931–32. Photo 1996.

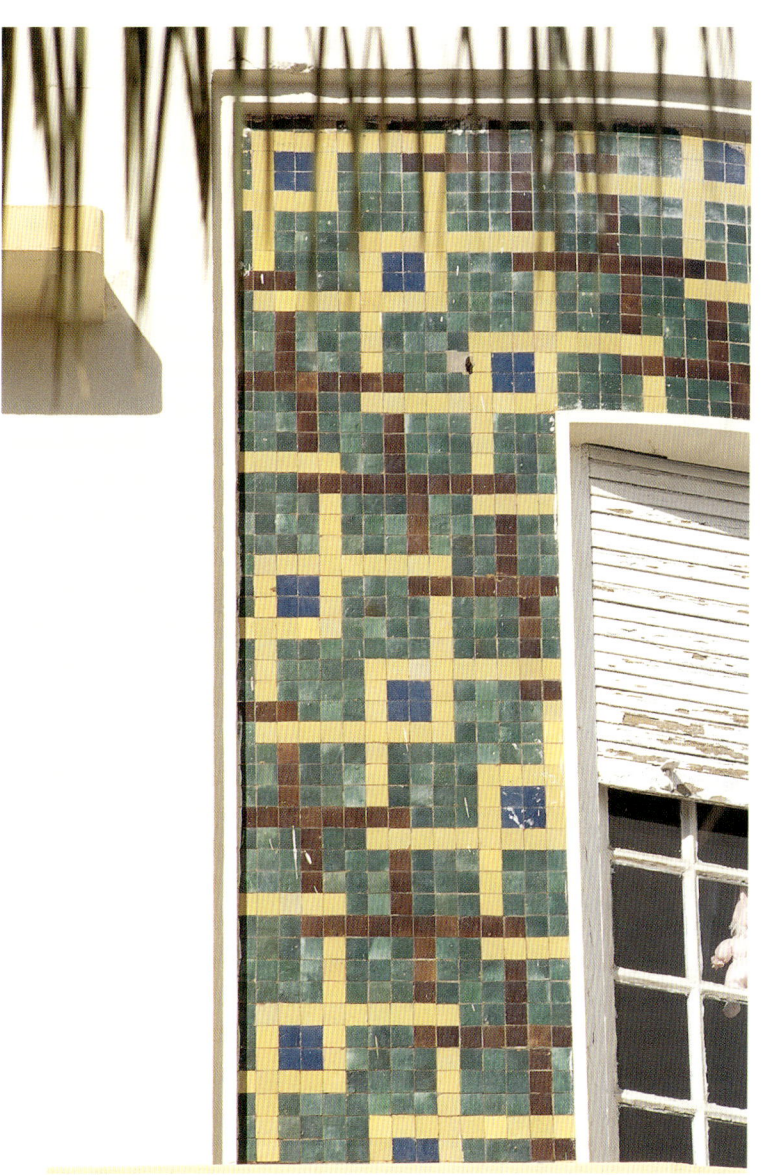

d

e

f

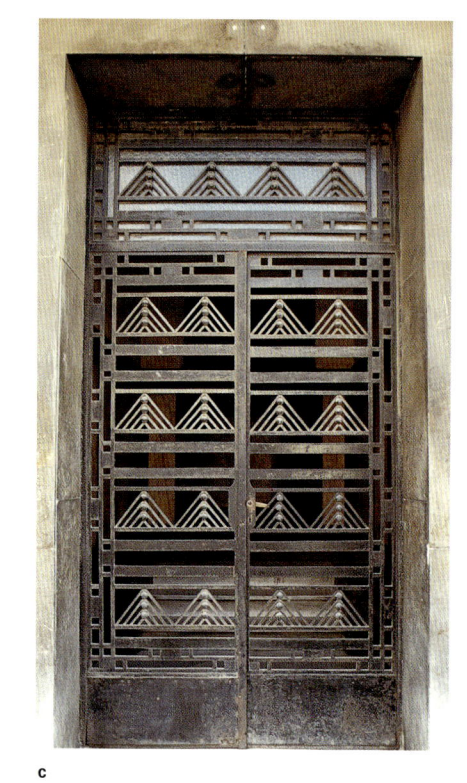

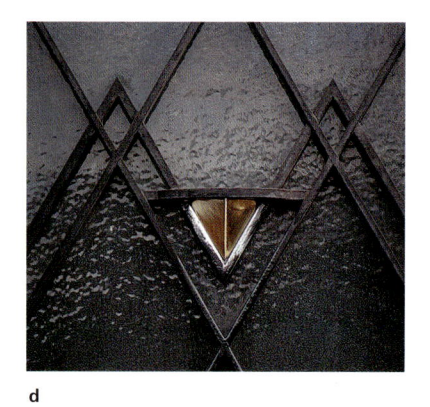

a

b

c

d

e

f

Entrance halls and doors of 1930s buildings

a. Élias and Joseph Suraqui, apartment building, 164 Avenue Mers-Sultan and Rue Condorcet. Photo 1994.

b. Typical 1930s door Place Bel-Air. Photo 1995.

c. Apartment building, 41 Rue Prom. Photo 1994.

d. Xavier Rendu and R. Ponsard, Nationale building, 1930–31. Detail on door facing Avenue du Général d'Amade. Photo 1994.

e. Marcel Desmet, Fraternelle du Nord building (Brazza Group), 1931–32. Entrance on Rue Savorgnan de Brazza. Photo 1990.

f. Marius Boyer, Shell building, Boulevard de la Gare, 1934. Photo 1990.

g. Pierre Jabin, Moretti-Milone building, 1934–35. Entrance on Boulevard du IVe- Zouaves. Photo 1994.

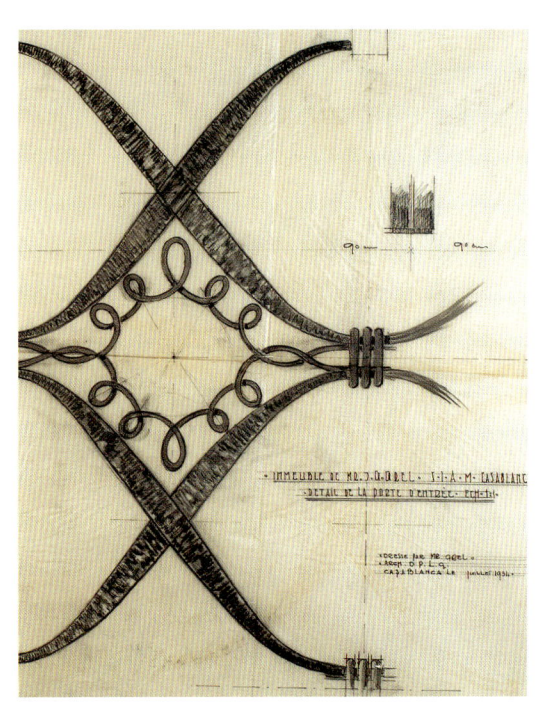

g

Georges Grel, detail of the wrought ironwork for an apartment building. Drawing, c. 1932.

designs were usurped by climate-specific considerations. The villas "include regional elements while bearing contemporary overtones of a 'new' style whose concepts are rooted in more than just fanciful, random extravagance." This modern vocabulary derived "from natural factors: namely climate, landscape, local customs, and sometimes even soil types."[33]

Construction materials were essentially Moroccan, apart from bricks and cement, which were mass-produced locally from the 1920s onward. Gray- and red-veined marble from Wadi Yquem and Wadi Akreuch were used to clad the entrances of deluxe buildings, while the mosaics, *zillij*, glass fixtures, and wrought-iron elements were produced in Casablanca. All these components were assembled together to create unified works of art, such as the entrance halls in the 1930s buildings. The geometric principles governing such design schemes were more often Viennese than Parisian, as exemplified by the large marble slabs that alternate with mosaic strips and terrazzo tile-edged floors, their degree of intricacy reflecting the affluence of the building. Richly decorated buildings vie with one another in a subtle game of hierarchy, the splendor of their marblework, mirrors, and wrought-iron gates demonstrating how marbleworkers such as Léglise, Maria, and Liscia, and ironworkers like the Spécioso brothers left their stamp on this particular building type just as much as the architects did.

[32] Jean Cotereau, "La maison mauresque," *Chantiers nord-africains* 2, no. 6 (June 1930): 602.

[33] "Villas à Casablanca," *Chantiers nord-africains* 1, no. 9 (September 1929): 521–23.

High-Rise Buildings and Block Schemes

Whether designed for offices, housing, or hotels, skyscrapers must be cruciform in plan or based on a derived section, in order to rule out once and for all buildings with interior courtyards and wasted space. The basements should contain storage rooms and garages with access ramps; the ground-floor and mezzanine levels should accommodate shops and public space, and the upper floors should be dedicated to work areas and living space.

Marius Boyer, 1929[34]

In addition to forming a possible design solution for offices in the port area, the skyscraper concept was also appropriated by architects and clients as an alternative to the standard apartment block types. Henri Sauvage's setback apartment building concept was reinterpreted by Boyer, who benefited from more favorable conditions than in Paris, as building codes were less stringent and there was a high demand for buildings with terraces.[35] Casablanca also enjoyed the twofold advantage of having larger building plots than Paris and wealthier clients who were eager to prove that they had a modern outlook. At the time of its construction (1932–33), Boyer's eleven-story Asayag building on Avenue de la Marine rose above Casablanca's other edifices.[36] The main building mass is a triple-tower structure, while setbacks form the terraces to the bachelor apartments and duplexes on the eighth to eleventh stories. Each tower displays a sophisticated design and contains an octagonal core housing the elevator and a glazed cruciform light shaft, channeling light into the domestic quarters.

The Asayag building enabled Boyer to assemble his major themes and vocabularies and propose a scale greater than Casablanca had ever seen. The concept for this work stemmed both from the 1930 port project and from ideas prepared for a lecture Boyer had given in 1929. He originally intended for the skyscraper to be twice the height of the built work and for it to contain avant-garde interior systems, though the scheme had to be dropped on account of the client's lack of daring:

> Each building will include a set of local and express elevators, goods elevators, a heating system, room cooling devices, telephones, and waste-disposal chutes. The top floors will be given over to utility facilities—laundry, drying rooms, and steam rooms—while elsewhere specific spaces will be dedicated to functional amenities, such as restaurants, storage rooms for cleaning equipment, kindergartens, and so forth.[37]

The high-rise race was closely tracked by all the trade reviews. For a while, the low-rent apartment building owned by the businessman Banchi took the lead. It was constructed by Henri Couette at the junction of Boulevard Foch and Rue de Pont-à-Mousson and earned the tag "a modern multiple-story apartment house"; it included studio and one-bedroom apartments as well as setback apartments with terraces on the ninth floor.[38] Barely two months later, though, *L'Afrique du Nord illustrée* designated Lièvre's Lafitte building as Casablanca's tallest structure.[39]

Yet height was not the only yardstick, as is corroborated by the Brazza project, a widely acclaimed housing complex constructed on a 4,000-square-meter triangular plot. Composed of eight seven-story buildings grouped around a triangular courtyard, this "modest-rent apartment house" was built by Marcel Desmet between 1931 and 1932 for the Fraternelle du Nord insurance company. The scheme also incorporated forty shops arranged around a vast "patio," as well as underground garage space for sixty cars located next to the boiler room and accessed by a double ramp. Natural light filters into the buildings through the courtyard, brightening the staircases.[40] Yet by far the most outstanding aspect of

---

[34] Boyer, "La construction moderne," 17.

[35] Vaillat, *Le périple marocain*, 88–89. Regarding the Parisian situation, see François Loyer and Hélène Guéné, *Henri Sauvage: les immeubles à gradins* (Liège: Mardaga, and Paris: IFA, 1987).

[36] Asayag intervened successfully during the public inquest on the Labonne project, rejecting the imposition of arcades alongside the Avenue de la Marine, which would have undermined Boyer's project. Moses Asayag to the director of Municipal Services, Casablanca, February 15, 1932, File: Modification au plan d'aménagement des quartiers avoisinant le port, registre d'enquête, BGA, SGP, Études législatives, plan de Casablanca 1931–32.

[37] Boyer, "La construction moderne," 18–19.

[38] "Nouveaux immeubles à Casablanca: Immeuble Banchi," *Chantiers nord-africains* 4, no. 3 (March 1932): 233.

[39] "Le Maroc en 1932, 20 années de protectorat français," 64.

[40] "Groupe Brazza à Casablanca, Marcel Desmet architecte," *L'Architecture d'aujourd'hui*, no. 3 (March 1936): 66–68.

Marius Boyer, Asayag building. General view. Photographed in 1990.

Marius Boyer, Asayag building, Boulevard de la Marine, Rue de l'Horloge, and Rue Léon l'Africain, 1930–32. Perspective view in Marius Boyer, *Casablanca, travaux d'architecture,* 1933. Twelve two- and three-bedroom apartments occupy the first seven floors. The bachelor apartments, laundry rooms and maids' rooms are on the eighth floor. The top two floors are given over to three duplex apartments with terraces.

Marius Boyer, Asayag building, 1930–32. Photo taken in 1991 showing the superstructures.

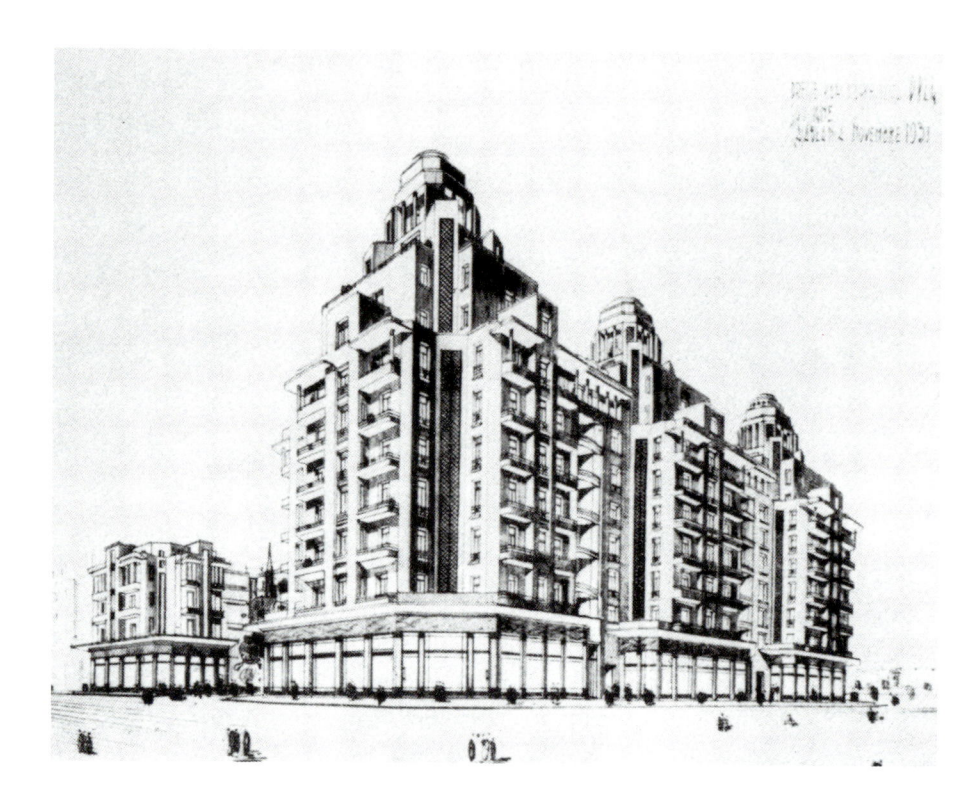

Intersection of Boulevard de la Marine and Rue de l'Horloge (postcard, c. 1932).
Left in photo: Marius Boyer's Asayag building; right: Sansone's and Busuttil's Lévi and Charbon building. The Asayag's duplex apartments are at the top, with views of the port and surrounding *zillij*-clad cupolas.

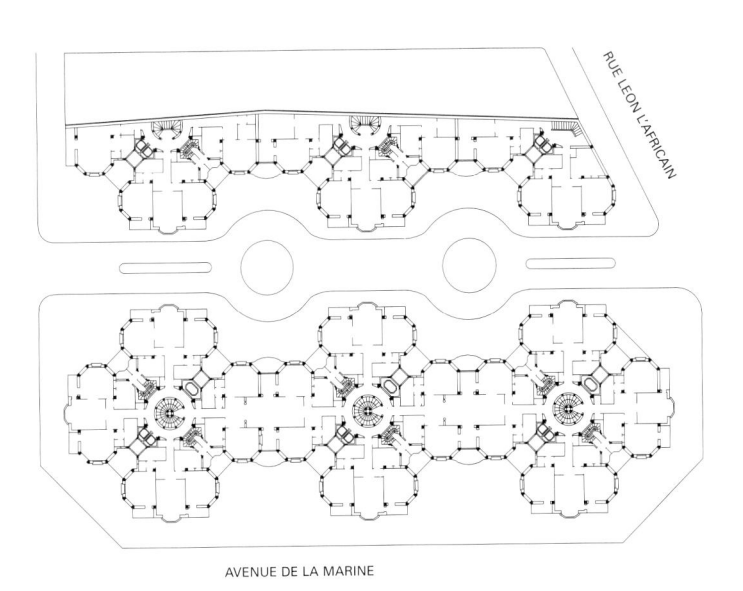

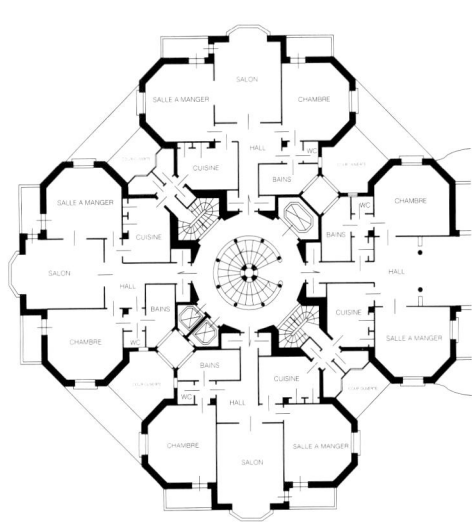

Marius Boyer, Asayag building, 1930–32. General plan (drawing by Cristiana Mazzoni).

Marius Boyer, Asayag building, 1930–32. Second-floor plan (drawing by Cristiana Mazzoni). The towers are both floriform and cruciform in plan, which means that the main rooms, located around the center, are extremely well lit. Special attention was paid to sound insulation between the apartments, which in every case are separated by a service stair, elevator, or storage room. The secondary building—a four-story structure—follows the same principle but is made up of three separate parts shaped like flowers' halves.
An interior street runs between the two buildings, housing underground garage space. The base is dedicated to shops—a vital requirement for a neighborhood that was then in full development.

1930–1940: From Art Deco to Modernism 183

Marcel Desmet, Fraternelle du Nord building (Brazza Group), Boulevard de la Gare, Rue Savorgnan de Brazza, and Rue Jacques Cartier, 1931–32. Photo taken in 1991 from Boulevard de la Gare.

The complex contains 150 units ranging from studio to four-bedroom apartments.

Marcel Desmet, Fraternelle du Nord building (Brazza Group). Photo of the courtyard, in *L'Architecture d'aujourd'hui*, March 1936.

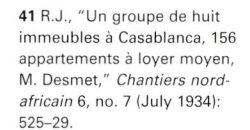

41 R.J., "Un groupe de huit immeubles à Casablanca, 156 appartements à loyer moyen, M. Desmet," *Chantiers nord-africain* 6, no. 7 (July 1934): 525–29.

42 "Immeuble de la Fraternelle, boulevard de la Gare à Casablanca," *Réalisations* 2, no. 2 (October 1935): 42–51.

these spacious apartments was that they provided "quality accommodations at an affordable rent."[41] The fact that the three- and four-bedroom apartments had two bathrooms was equally surprising for this type of housing scheme. Desmet's complex was one of the first to offer mid-income clients modern, comfortable apartments in the city center; furthermore, it provides valuable insight into how some of the best architects and engineers of the period adapted their work to a specific cultural and climatic context:

> The structural frame is entirely in reinforced concrete, with double brick walls as exterior infill. This type of construction process is becoming increasingly widespread in Morocco, given its many advantages. First, since there is a high level of humidity, reinforced-concrete frames are preferable to iron frames for building along the Moroccan coast. Second, native workers—a low-cost labor source—have been well trained in this type of construction method, so they put the buildings up quickly. And lastly, the double exterior partitioning provides maximum protection against external temperature changes.[42]

City-Center Apartment Blocks, or Residential Monuments

The current Moroccan clientele has grown extremely demanding, calling for more home comforts and expecting kitchens and bathrooms to come with all the latest fittings. Residents make their choices entirely on the strength of these criteria, changing homes without a moment's thought.

Edmond Pauty, 1939[43]

43 Edmond Pauty, "Tradition et modernisme à Casablanca," *L'Architecture* (April 1939): 141. The "Moroccans" are, of course, colonists. Pauty, an architect practicing in Rabat, thus adopts a usage widely deployed by Lyautey.

The central apartment buildings occupied by Casablanca's bourgeoisie constituted the city's main monuments. They were known to everyone by the name of their initial owner and functioned as landmarks, since street addresses were not commonly used. By the 1930s, deluxe apartment blocks had sprung up along the main roads, such as the one built by Xavier Rendu and R. Ponsard between 1930 and 1931 along Avenue D'Amade, behind the Place Administrative. The fact that these two

Xavier Rendu and R. Ponsard, Nationale building, Avenue Mers-Sultan and Avenue Général d'Amade, 1930–31. General view. Photographed in 1993. "An elegant profile is created by the two recessed top floors. In addition, a play on mass and void endows the building with a distinguished air, as do the tightly profiled, curved walls." Edmond Pauty, *Tradition et modernisme à Casablanca,* 1939.

Xavier Rendu and R. Ponsard, Nationale building, Avenue Mers-Sultan and Avenue Général d'Amade, 1930–31. View of the roof and the mirador. Postcard, c. 1935.

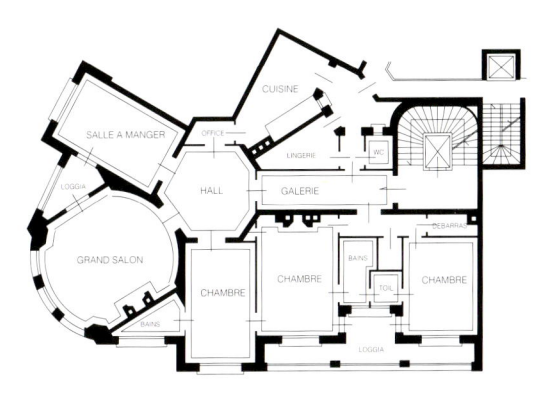

Xavier Rendu and R. Ponsard, Nationale building. Part of the typical floor plan. (Drawing by Cristiana Mazzoni based on the building permit.)
Each floor includes two four-bedroom apartments with a vast lounge in either corner of the building. Some of the larger apartments have a washroom and *cabinet de toilette*. The main bedrooms sometimes occupy a full 22m² in floor area.

1930–1940: From Art Deco to Modernism

44 On-site supervision of the construction of this project, undertaken for La Nationale insurance company, was provided by Joseph Gras.

45 J. Cuénot, "Réalisations électriques, immeuble de La Nationale à Casablanca," *Réalisations* 1, no. 4 (June 1934): 109.

46 Similarly, the use of 35-millimeter-thick fiber-and-cement panels was a first.

Parisian architects were able to take up a key position in an arena already filled with talented players proves just how masterful the scheme was.[44] The white rendering and stone window frames echo the nearby city hall; furthermore, it should be noted that the work features a large number of components that were used in Parisian corner buildings during the same period, notably the apartment block's rounded corner that tapers into a tower. Its marble-clad base accommodates shops and a few apartments, while the main five-story body has varied structural arrangements at each level, and the loggias are separated on either side by a vertical row of windows, which creates a tense pull with the building's marked horizontality. This horizontal aspect is particularly emphasized on the corner, whereas the setback window pattern serves to underscore the rounded volume. The architects capped the recessed top floor with a mirador, and slotted sixteen parking spaces into the basement of the building (entered by a ramp), as well as numerous storage rooms.

Access to the upper stories is via three main staircases or elevators. There are also two freight elevators and two service staircases leading to a service gallery. These facilities are unusual, given that each floor contains only six three- and four-bedroom apartments, each of which measures an average 175 square meters. The entrance corridor leads into a hall, which in some apartments separates the living room from the dining room, thus allowing either room to be extended, depending on the social occasion. The centrally positioned hall often runs out into a loggia, thereby forming a room in its own right. *Réalisations*, a Moroccan architectural review launched in 1933, praised the design of the apartment block:

> The La Nationale building sits like a large liner ready to swathe the Place Administrative . . . Its strict lines, sweeping terraces, and large windows commandingly draw the gaze of passersby . . . In our view, this is one of Casablanca's finest architectural ventures, as well as being the most modern apartment block in town. Furthermore, it is the only building in the whole of Morocco to be fully wired and fitted with electrical appliances.[45]

Although coal-heated, the apartment building was indeed fitted out with all the latest modern conveniences. An electric transformer unit was installed in each basement storage room, and the kitchen fittings were designed to "run fully on electricity," a highly uncommon feature.[46] Everything seemed very avant-garde to the public, especially the "refrigerating units," electric radiators, and washing machines.

Erwin Hinnen, project for the Bendahan building, Place Edmond Doutté, 1932. Perspective from Place de France.

Edmond Brion, Bendahan building, Place Edmond Doutté, 1935. General view (postcard c. 1938). The Bendahan is to the right in this photo, taken from the Baille building.

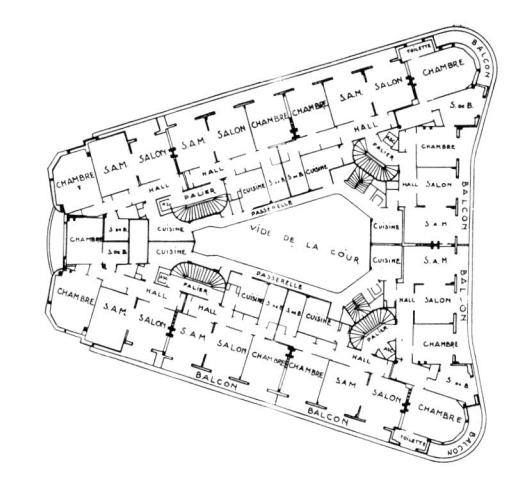

Edmond Brion, Bendahan building, Place Edmond Doutté, 1935. Standard floor plan, in *L'Architecture,* April 1939.

Edmond Brion, Bendahan building, Place Edmond Doutté, 1935. Photo of the rear, taken from Rue Bendahan in 1992.

In 1935, Edmond Brion designed the Bendahan building on Place Edmond Doutté, one of the busiest squares in the *ville nouvelle* and the site of the former market. It juts out like the prow of a ship and became celebrated for its elegance; for instance, Edmond Pauty noted, "The architectural expression conveyed in the facades stems from a simple plan" and "the design solution is remarkable for its starkness."[47] It contains three stories of two- and three-bedroom apartments, and is bounded by three streets. Shops occupy its base, and four staircases take up the corners, providing access to the eight apartments on each floor. The main rooms are situated along the facade, while the secondary ones are located at the rear; these receive light and air from a large inner courtyard. The most favorably positioned rooms are the bedrooms slotted into the building's corners; they even rival the living and dining rooms in size. No less impressive is the apartment that takes up the fifth and sixth stories and which forms a kind of observatory overlooking the square. Reserved by Brion for his personal use, this "studio apartment" includes a double-height reception hall and a staircase leading to the floor above. Five rooms make up the lower level, and the sixth floor was dedicated to intellectual pursuits and physical culture, with a smoking room/library, mirador, gymnasium, and garden terrace. Other terraces were also integrated into this level. The top floor, which would have traditionally been devoted to the maids' rooms, was given over to amenities such as "laundry, drying, and storage rooms." An article published in Paris at the time (one of the rare few to be devoted to Casablancan building output) praised Brion for his twofold skill: on the one hand he was able to design neo-Moroccan workers' settlements and on the other hand he had come up with a modern design vocabulary for the Bendahan building that was "masterly crafted in the free French spirit yet appropriately adapted to its Moroccan setting."[48]

Modernization schemes for the Place de France and the port area got under way in 1935 with Pierre Jabin's building for two Italian-born building contractors, Moretti and Milone. By introducing a break in scale with the lower buildings at the city's entrance, it set the urban tone for Labonne's Boulevard Pasteur even before the road was laid. Observers remarked with some relief, "The fences that currently

[47] Pauty, "Tradition et modernisme à Casablanca," 142.

[48] Pauty, "Tradition et modernisme à Casablanca," 141.

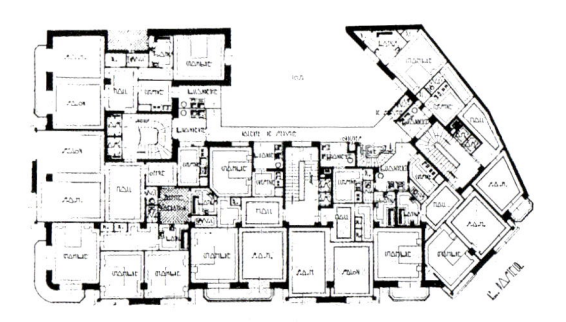

Pierre Jabin, Moretti-Milone building, Boulevard du IVe-Zouaves and Place de France, 1934–35. Photographed in 1993.
The two lower levels are dedicated to offices. Above these are eight floors, orchestrated by sunshades and bay windows, with each floor containing eight apartments. Long balconies stretch along the upper three floors, creating a pattern of black and white, of mass and void, contrasting with the column-lined loggia on the tenth level. The building is crowned with studio, one- and four-bedroom apartments with terraces that overlook the square, medina, and port.

Pierre Jabin, Moretti-Milone building, Boulevard du IVe-Zouaves and Place de France, 1934–35. Standard floor plan.
The main bedrooms (16 to 20m²) are often larger than the lounge or dining room. The latter two rooms are linked to a vast hall and are not separated by partitioning, although they do differ from one another in terms of style (computer rendering by Sylvain Le Stum).

49 "Immeuble place de France à Casablanca, P. Jabin, architecte," *Réalisations* 2, no. 2 (October 1935): 52–53.

50 Mario Milone (owners' grandson), interview by the authors, Casablanca, August 1994.

51 "Immeuble place de France à Casablanca, P. Jabin, architecte," 52.

form the Place de France's sole architectural decoration will soon yield their place to handsome buildings constructed to a modern design."[49]

Jabin's twelve-story building dominates the square from its position on the corner of Boulevard du IVe-Zouaves and the future Boulevard Pasteur. Its rough concrete base houses two levels of offices, while the facade covering the eight stories of apartments ranging from one to four bedrooms displays contrasting patterns. The building permit was initially refused, as the attic floor was "Moroccan in style, with tilework, whereas elsewhere the design lines are distinctly horizontal."[50] The facade that was eventually approved is "characterized by pronounced vertical and horizontal lines formed by the bay windows." Three staircases lead to the apartments, and each of them is coupled with two elevators fitted with a foldaway seat and telephone. There is also a secondary staircase, which was designed to provide access to a service gallery leading to the laundry rooms and servants' lavatories. Cork lining was laid on the ceilings, floors, and walls to insulate the apartments against sound.[51]

This apartment building type was luxurious, not because the apartments were particularly large, but because there were top-notch amenities, as well as a greater number of fast elevators and ancillary facilities that offered extra touches of modern comfort. These included an entrance hall, servants' quarters, and large, well-positioned bedrooms with fine views from terraces or balconies, indicating the high caliber of the building. It should also be noted that one of the rooms in the three-bedroom apartments was labeled a "studio," implying that the apartment was designed for a young couple without children. The tenth floor is given over to ten studio apartments for single residents. They have a private laundry room and often contain a large, bright bathroom overlooking the boulevard.

In 1934, Erwin Hinnen completed the Socifrance building on the east side of the Place de France at the junction of Boulevard de la Gare and Rue Chénier. It contains offices, as well as cafés and shops that are tucked behind the ground-floor arcade. Striped with horizontal lines, it offers an alternating pattern of white spandrels and dark bands that contain regularly spaced windows. This, together with the striated balcony walls, generates a marked geometric play and gives rise to a rather planar facade that bulges on one edge. The Socifrance building signaled an exploration of new inroads in Casablancan building output by breaking with the

Erwin Hinnen, Socifrance building, Place de France, Boulevard de la Gare and Rue Chénier, 1934–35. Photographed in 1991.

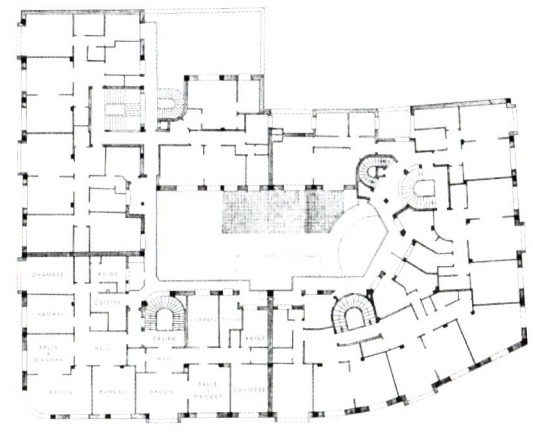

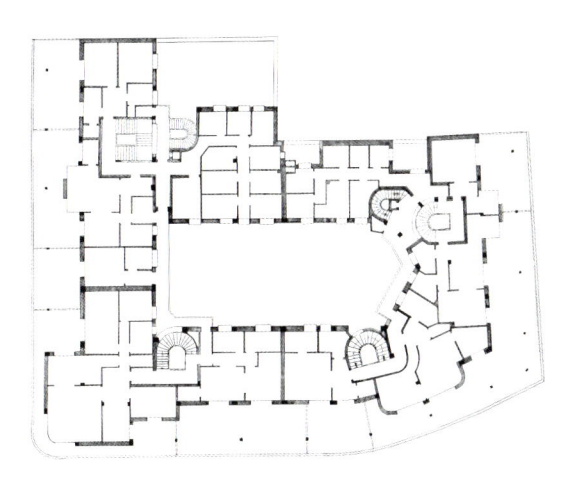

Erwin Hinnen, Socifrance building, Place de France, Boulevard de la Gare and Rue Chénier, 1934–35. Standard floor plan. Drawing by Cristiana Mazzoni, based on the building permit.

Sixth-floor plan from the building permit (computer rendering by Sylvain Le Stum).

Each of the six stories contains ten apartments. The sixth floor includes a large four-bedroom corner apartment, five one-bedrooms, and three studio apartments.

Erwin Hinnen, Socifrance building, Place de France, Boulevard de la Gare and Rue Chénier, 1934–35. View of the staircase. Photographed from the hall in 1995.

1930–1940: From Art Deco to Modernism

52 Furthermore, it is important to remember that at the time it was not expected that each child would have his or her own bedroom.

53 "Les *Studios*, immeuble de rapport, M. Boyer, architecte dplg," *Réalisations* 2, no. 1 (July 1935): 6.

Pierre Jabin, Liscia building (commissioned by the Société Centrale Immobilière), Boulevard de Marseille and Rue de l'Aviateur Prom, 1937. General view. Photographed in 1990.

Pierre Jabin, Liscia building (commissioned by the Société Centrale Immobilière), Boulevard de Marseille and Rue de l'Aviateur Prom, 1937. Standard floor plan from the building permit (computer rendering by Sylvain Le Stum).

tradition of projecting facades, terraces, and applied ornamentation, and introduced a new, slightly Viennese flavor. The sixth floor is composed of a large corner apartment and smaller apartments with terraces, communal laundries, and nine attic rooms—a first for a city like Casablanca, whose population was hardly one that steeped itself in the past. As with many buildings in the city center, most of the apartments are fairly small and were clearly not designed for large families. It would thus appear that in this instance the developers were targeting young couples and single affluent residents.[52]

The Liscia building, erected by Pierre Jabin in 1937 on Boulevard de Marseille, forms another of the city's monuments and was designed along even stricter lines than the Socifrance building. The architect alternated white strips with gray vertical projections at the intersection of Rue Prom and created a continuous strip of windows, which he separated by dark striated panels to enhance the facade's white surfaces. The Lux movie theater was fitted into the base of the building, and shops were built on either side of it; the larger apartments were inserted along the boulevard side, whereas the smaller ones overlook Rue Prom. A four-bedroom apartment, apparently for the owners' use, was placed on the seventh floor, together with a garden terrace and a pergola that caps the building. This design feature was widely copied in later, less striking buildings.

A building that had a profound influence on the Casablancan architectural scene is Les Studios, a corner building constructed by Boyer in 1933 on Avenue D'Amade. Widely acclaimed for its innovative features, it contains duplexes that were initially designed for the artistic and intellectual avant-garde as well as for single residents and young couples. Boyer owned the building, which enabled him to "make something for himself" that would never have gotten by his clients.[53] Despite a skewed and narrow site, he skillfully fashioned the main rooms into rectangular and square shapes; the site is so narrow, in fact, that it makes the facade appear even

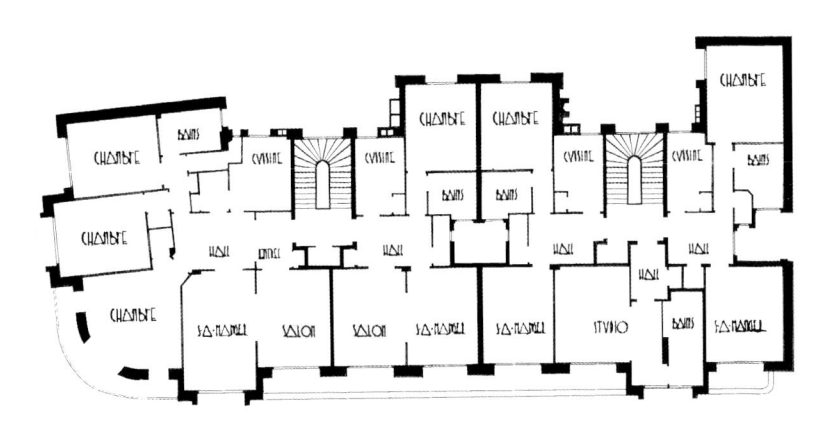

Marius Boyer, Boyer building, known as Les Studios, Avenue Général d'Amade and Rue de Bouskoura, 1935. General view. Photographed in 1990.
The building has a main staircase, elevator and three service stairs, two of which receive light through the side facades.

Plan of the seven-bedroom apartment on the tenth floor. Drawing by Cristiana Mazzoni based on the building permit.
In this building, Boyer used principles and denominations similar to those employed in Parisian apartments of the same type. A lobby leads into the hall, which serves as a pivot between the dining room, lounge, and covered terrace.

Section of the duplexes from the building permit (computer rendering by Sylvain Le Stum).

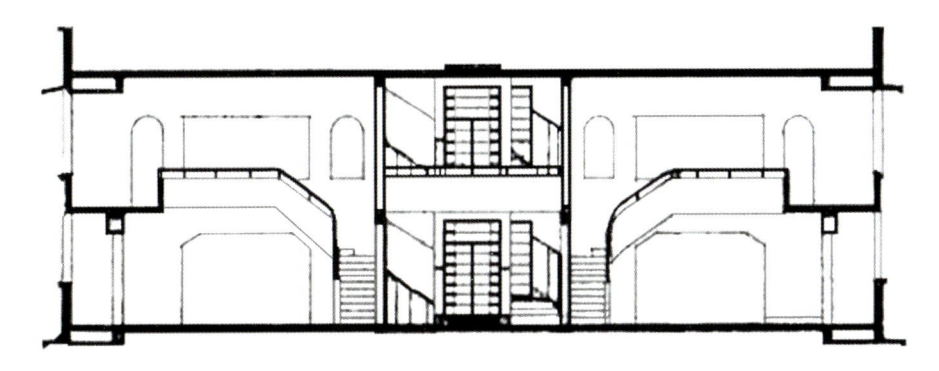

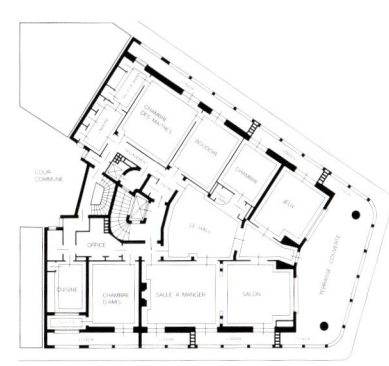

1930–1940: From Art Deco to Modernism

Jean Balois and Paul Perrotte, Ettedgui/Mellul building, Avenue du Général Moinier, 1932. General view. Photographed in 1990. The building contains five stairwells, including three service ones, which lead to each floor composed of four apartments and a bachelor's apartment.

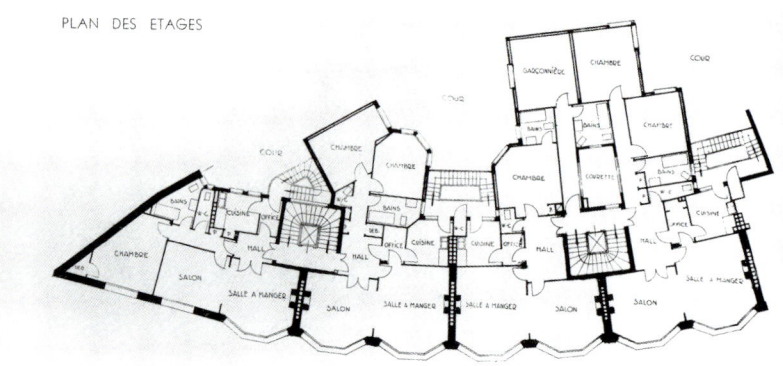

Jean Balois and Paul Perrotte, Ettedgui/Mellul building, Avenue Général Moinier, 1934. Standard floor plan, in *Réalisations*, no.1, February 1935. The lounge and dining room (always the larger of the two) are more or less open plan. Both have a bay window.

Georges Grel and Georges Renaudin, Apartment building, Place des Aviateurs, c. 1935. General view, in *Réalisations*, no. 2, 1935. Two four- and five-bedroom apartments overlook the street on each floor. The dining rooms are regularly proportioned, thanks to a skilful play on geometry, and the main rooms have a bay window with detailed steel joinery.

54 "Immeuble de rapport à Casablanca, J. G. Grel et G. Renaudin, architectes dplg," *Réalisations* 4, no. 2 (September 1937): 47–51. This building was among those published in "Marruecos moderno," *Arquitectura* (Mexico) 5, no. 11 (December 1942): 23.

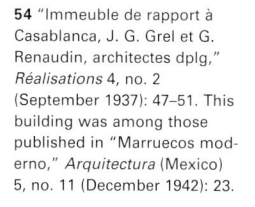

longer than it actually is. Boyer reserved the penthouse apartment for his own use, turning it into a paradigmatic luxury dwelling.

The form, materials, and modern conveniences of the Ettedgui building—a smaller but equally eye-catching edifice by Jean Balois and Paul Perrotte on Avenue du Général Moinier in 1934—are just as elaborate. The gently curved form of the front is underscored by ripples of bay windows, while the entrance is entirely covered in sand-colored *zillij*, framed by strips of darker tiles. The alternating rows of black-and-white tiles along the base are reminiscent of Adolf Loos's project for Josephine Baker, and the ridge is decorated simply with a cornice.

The following year, Georges Grel and Georges Renaudin adeptly capitalized on a long, thin plot on the Place des Aviateurs to create "one of the finest and most comfortable apartment buildings in town,"[54] which they achieved by wedging two blocks around a courtyard and fountain. Living and domestic quarters were neatly separated, and a "hidden" service entry was incorporated on the street side to provide access to the maids' rooms. These look onto a sunken courtyard and were rather surprisingly fitted with showers. The courtyard apartments are bachelor apartments, some with bedrooms, others without; as for the stairwell windows, these overlook the courtyard and are arranged according to an elegant design, their continuous narrow glazing serving as a symmetrical axis for the openings in the apartments.

Standard Apartment Buildings

Whereas Casablanca's small middle-class apartment houses might not be arranged in the same way as the residential buildings described above, their architecture is nonetheless of high quality. In addition, they sometimes came with modern features, such as garages, waste incinerators, and even elevators when the building exceeded five stories. The rooftop terraces are accessible to all residents and include communal laundry rooms and private drying areas, at times sectioned off by claustras. Although the apartments lack a salon, a service stairway was nonetheless fitted into some of the buildings in response to the extensive employment of servants among the lower middle classes and white-collar workers.

This apartment building type was gradually stripped of all ornamentation throughout the 1930s, yet the communal areas remained very stylish, notably the marble entrances and striking staircases. In the Dayan building, for instance, constructed by Paul Manuguerra in 1931, a handsome circular stairway leads to several two-bedroom apartments with a dining room. They do not contain a salon, although they do feature a bathroom that is lit naturally. In 1937, the businessmen Moretti and Milone spurned Jabin, their usual architect, in favor of the more "modern" Hinnen, commissioning him to construct a corner building at the junction of Avenue du Général Moinier and Rue Murdoch.[55] Its highly detailed finishings and luxury fittings were exemplary, and the vast communal areas in the building contrast sharply with the small apartments without salons.

During the 1920s, the Suraqui brothers had received a substantial number of commissions from the Casablancan Jewish bourgeoisie to design apartment buildings with *zillij* pediments and Louis XVI ornamentation in the central quarters and around the Place de France. Despite adopting a new building language in the following decade, the Suraquis continued to produce works that stood out just as forcefully in Casablanca's central cityscape. The Moses Pinto building, for example, which they completed in 1931 at the intersection of Place de Verdun and Rue Lacépède, is particularly noticeable for its austere facade. Some of the bedrooms overlook the square and were perhaps intended to accommodate the parents and a child together. They measure sixteen square meters, making them as large as the salon, which implies that at the time of construction they may have contained other furniture besides the architect-designed double bed. It is also to be noted that there is no dining room, thus clearly demonstrating that more importance was attached to the salon. In fact, the latter may even have been used as a bedroom. These assumptions are not without relevance, given that in large-family neighborhoods such as the one accommodating the Pinto building, children's beds were set up in various places throughout the apartment, whatever the occupants' social rank.

A large number of medium-sized rental apartment blocks were also built during this period. In 1934, *Réalisations* noted, "Following the construction drive that triggered a sharp rise in large buildings, an increasing number of smaller buildings are now being slotted into the empty spaces previously concealed by fencing."[56] The Domerc building, built by Gustave Cottet in 1934 at the intersection of Rue Lapérouse and Rue Bascunano, was deemed emblematic of "an average apartment house type."[57] Each of its four stories contains a studio apartment with a bathroom, as well as two- and three-bedroom apartments, though only the two-bedroom apartment on the corner includes a salon. Some of the bathrooms are arranged along the facade, but this layout would become less common as services began to be increasingly grouped at the rear.

In 1938, Paul Manuguerra wedged his small Joseph Allée building (composed of eight two-bedroom apartments) into one of the gaps that still existed on Rue

55 Meant for rental occupancy, this building had to be durable. Milone, interview.

56 "Immeuble de la Soblanca, Hinnen et Balois architectes," *Réalisations* 1, no. 5 (October 1934): 153–55.

57 *Réalisations* 2 (November 1936): 209.

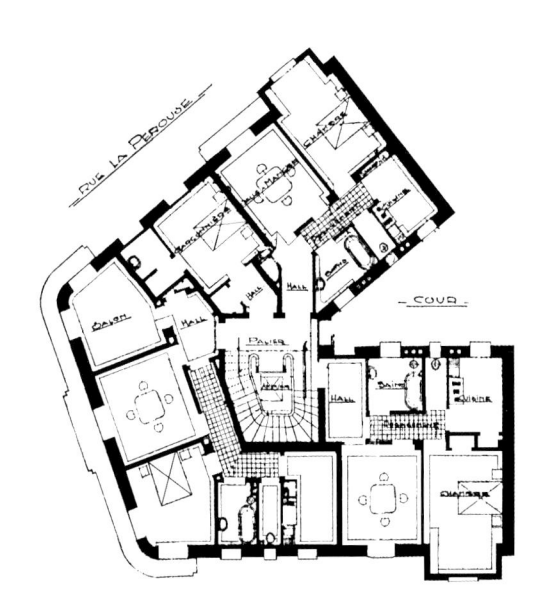

Gustave Cottet, Domerc building, Rue Lapérouse and Rue Bascunano, 1934. Floor plans from the building permit (computer rendering by Sylvain Le Stum).

Jean Michelet, apartment building, Boulevard d'Anfa and Rue de l'Oise, c.1933.
Front of the building. Photographed in 1993.

Jean Michelet, apartment building, Boulevard d'Anfa and Rue de l'Oise, c.1933.
Standard floor plan, in *Réalisations*, June 1934. The smallish smoking room *(fumoir)* adjoins the lounge. It is slotted into the corner of the building, making it the best positioned room, receiving light through three windows.

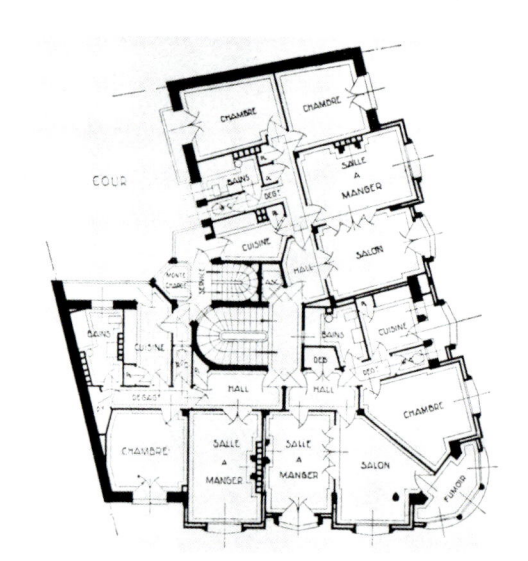

Blaise Pascal in the city center. Manuguerra highlighted the geometric facade by means of setbacks and balconies and incorporated fully fitted bathrooms into the scheme, along with five garage spaces. These features clearly illustrate the rather affluent lifestyle led by the Casablancan petite bourgeoisie during that period, especially if one draws a comparison with Toulouse, a city whose size then equaled Casablanca's. There, most apartment blocks built at the same time for similar classes were not fitted with bathrooms.[58]

Although exterior design changed conspicuously between 1920 and 1940, many architects continued to use traditional layout principles, such as regular-shaped main rooms with a clear separation between public and private space. For example, Jean Michelet chose to tuck a bathroom, cupboards, and even a smoking room into the skewed spaces of his building at the junction of Boulevard d'Anfa and Rue de l'Oise merely to maintain the regular shape of the main rooms. As for the exterior tone of the building, overall it conveys a sense of sobriety despite the "curved bay-window pattern linking the two facades."[59]

Meanwhile, some of the leading architects were producing works that were considered avant-garde in Morocco and France. Marcel Desmet, who had enjoyed a successful career in Lille, France, before practicing in Casablanca, figured among these. The building he designed in 1935 for the SIF company on the Place de la Gare was one of the rare few covered by *L'Architecture d'aujourd'hui*. According to the review, the building's four stories unfold in a highly modern arrangement of interior space above the street arcade imposed by building regulations. Its galleries were praised in the article, even though the use of galleries was generally criticized at the time, and the handsome "entirely cantilevered [spiral] staircase that winds in

[58] Regarding this issue, see Thierry Mandoul, "Architecture domestique," in *Toulouse 1920–1940: la ville et ses architectes* (Toulouse: Ombres-CAUE 31, 1991), 117.

[59] A. Arnone, "Immeuble de rapport, boulevard d'Anfa à Casablanca, J. Michelet, architecte." *Réalisations* 1, no. 4 (June 1934): 99.

Marcel Desmet, SIF building, Place de la Gare, 1935. Facade overlooking the square. Photographed in 1991.

Marcel Desmet, SIF building, Place de la Gare, 1935. Screen walls of the drying rooms. Photographed in 1991. The rooftop laundry rooms are protected by screen walls, while the individual drying rooms are open-air and are surrounded by a "slatted shutter" wall to promote air circulation. *Réalisations*, April 1936.

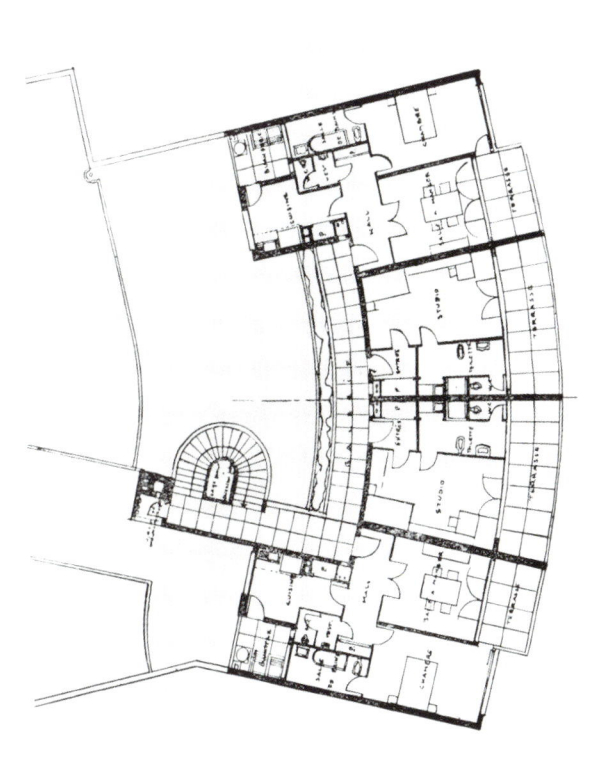

Marcel Desmet, SIF building, Place de la Gare, 1935.
Rear of the building, photographed in 1991. A spiral staircase and walkways fitted with planters provide access to the apartments.

Marcel Desmet, SIF building, Place de la Gare, 1935.
Standard floor plan, in *L'Architecture d'aujourd'hui*, March 1936.
The studio apartments and one-bedrooms are generously lit by floor-to-ceiling windows that open onto a terrace.

1930–1940: From Art Deco to Modernism 195

Pierre Jabin, Moretti-Milone building, 1934–35. Superstructures. Photographed in 1993.

Marius Boyer, Asayag building, 1930–32. Villas and bachelor apartments with terraces. Photographed in 1993.

Edmond Brion, Bendahan building, 1935. Superstructures. Photographed in 1994.

Pierre Jabin, Liscia building, Boulevard de Marseille and Rue de l'Aviateur Prom, 1937. Photo of the brise-soleil taken in 1990.

a semicircle around the void of the elevator shaft" was also applauded.[60] The floors, which are composed of rendered concrete, hollow brick infill, and terrazzo, provide optimal sound insulation and were among the typical solutions of the time.

Due to the restricted space in this standard building type, new forms of layout and design began to be developed, as is exemplified by Georges Renaudin's apartment building at the intersection of Rue Rabelais and Rue Jean Jaurès.[61] By 1930, the term *salon-salle à manger* was widely employed, denoting the fusion of the salon and the dining room, the term *living room* came into common usage at the end of the decade. These name changes, which paralleled shifts in living patterns, and consequently new attitudes among architects, did not go unnoticed in trade journals: "Our new lifestyle has led architects to radically alter their housing plans. Unity and flexibility are now the key programmatic words. Apart from bathrooms and kitchens, purpose-specific rooms are gradually becoming obsolete, whereas terraces and balconies now extend the apartment out into the open air."[62]

Outdoors at Home—Terraces, Loggias, and Pergolas

The tent is a prism, the noualla [hut] is a tapered end, and religious buildings and pleasure pavilions are conceived as tiled tapering prisms. The rooftop terraces of the dwellings and lofty Casbahs create a sharply flat-edged skyline. This is true Morocco. Then the Europeans came in. In the name of Art we have recommended, and, where necessary, enforced roof terraces so that new European structures may blend harmoniously with their surroundings. It is our heartfelt view that terraces have provided modern art with its most communicative vehicle of expression.

Adrien Laforgue, 1939[63]

Living in the open air—on the roof terrace, in the shade of the pergola, or on the balcony—already formed part and parcel of Moroccan culture, especially given the vital role of these outdoor spaces in the domestic and social life of women. The number of buildings with terraces and setbacks had increased significantly by the 1920s, and architects combined metropolitan and Mediterranean styles in response to client requirements. Vast terraces set off the upper stories, as in the Liscia building on Boulevard de Paris, doubling the floor area of the salon and functioning as cool evening reception spaces in summer. They also serve to increase the size of small top-floor apartments, as in the I.P.M. Tolédano building by the Suraqui brothers. In addition, terraces were added to many of the landings, providing pleasant open-air access to the apartments.

The Rendu and Ponsard building is especially striking in that its halls and bedrooms extend out into loggias, which become a living space in themselves; in some cases, these spaces have even been converted into conservatories with views over the park. The Liscia building ends in "marble-clad loggias and, most notably, in a floor set back from the ensemble and fitted with a pergola."[64]

Boyer's Asayag building nonetheless remains the paradigmatic example, with huge terraces leading out from the duplexes and studio apartments, and balconies running alongside the maids' rooms.

The Roof Terrace Becomes a Widespread Feature

Rooftop terraces are such a natural feature of Moroccan building practices that the rare pitched roof immediately catches the eye. Hence, Buan and Beaufils' Faucherot building, which has "a delightful sloping reinforced-concrete roof

---

60 "France d'outre-mer," special issue of *L'Architecture d'aujourd'hui* 7, no. 3 (March 1936): 70.

61 *Réalisations* 5 (May–June 1938): 139–40; "L'architecture au Maroc," *Le Maroc du nord au sud* and *Réalisations*, special joint issue (June 1939).

62 G. Brunon-Guardia, "La décoration des intérieurs en 1935," *Chantiers nord-africains* 7, no. 2 (February 1935): 92–93.

63 Adrien Laforgue, "Notes sur la question des terrasses et des couvertures au Maroc," in *L'Architecture au Maroc*.

64 "Immeubles modernes à Casablanca," *Chantiers nord-africains* 3, no. 8 (August 1931): 809.

Xavier Rendu and R. Ponsard, Nationale building, 1930–31. The loggias. Photographed in 1991.

65 "Immeuble Faucherot, avenue Mers Sultan, rue de Terves, L. Beaufils et G. Buan, architectes," *Chantiers nord-africains* 2, no. 9 (September 1929): 528.

66 "Villas à Casablanca, Cormier, architecte, Gabriel, entrepreneur," *Chantiers nord-africains* 1, no. 11 (November 1929): 649–50.

67 Regarding the scope of this debate in Germany, see Richard Pommer, "The Flat Roof: A Modern Controversy in Germany," *Art Journal* 43, no. 2 (Summer 1983): 158–69.

68 Jean Cotereau, "Vers une architecture méditerranéenne," *Chantiers nord-africains* 2, no. 1 (January 1930): 21.

69 Farrère, *Les hommes nouveaux*, 278. Regarding this practice, see also Fatima Mernissi, *Rêves de femme: Contes d'une enfance au harem* (Casablanca: Éditions Le Fennec, 1997).

70 Jean Cotereau, "Vers une architecture méditerranéenne," 19.

71 Emmanuel de Thubert, "L'aménagement et la décoration des toitures-terrasses," *Chantiers nord-africains* 2, no. 9 (September 1930): 757.

covered with mosaic tiling," was considered "utterly charming," even though it "intentionally breaks with Casablancan tradition."[65] Conversely, a villa with a complex sloping roof structure was singled out by *Chantiers nord-africains* as being incongruous, though it was redeemed by "an unusual setback arrangement" that provides space for "a wide balcony with all the conveniences and pleasant attributes of a terrace."[66] At a time when Europe (France and Germany in particular) was hotly debating the legitimacy of the roof terrace, with opinion divided over sloping and flat roofs,[67] it was generally agreed that this design element was fully suited to Moroccan climate and customs. Algiers-based Jean Cotereau, a fervent champion of Mediterranean architecture, declared, "No matter what form it takes, the rooftop terrace is logical from every angle," and "the country's geographical setting justifies, and even calls for, use of the flat roof."[68]

Writers engaged in the celebration of colonial enterprises, such as Pierre Loti and the Tharaud brothers, carefully listed all the functions of the Arab terrace, and ascribed a certain poetic force to it. Claude Farrère gave an equally detailed description for his readers, most of whom would have been unfamiliar with this design feature:

> Every Moroccan house has a terrace. That is, instead of a roof it has a cemented platformed covering. These terraces slope gently; they have channels for draining rainwater and are edged by low walls that are very easy to cross. Every evening at sunset, the women of the Maghreb come up to them, not so much to breathe in the delightful coolness of dusk, but to call out shrilly to one another from roof to roof, from dwelling to dwelling.[69]

Insisting on international use of the roof terrace seemed ridiculous to architects who appreciated its qualities in a contextual setting. "Although lovers of cubic forms recommend it for any climate," Cotereau condemned the fact that it tended to be overused by modernists. In his view, it is "not suitable for foggy and snowy climes," but is "eminently practical" in the Maghreb.[70] *Chantiers nord-africains* set out the concerns signaled in a competition staged by the Société des Architectes Modernes in Paris, pointing out that detractors of the flat-roof form generally lambasted it because it did not "provide as effective a covering as a normal roof," even though it was now properly weatherproofed.[71] The competition clearly indicated that "young architects [were] endeavoring to create an annex of sorts to the

Jean Michelet, apartment building, Boulevard d'Anfa and Rue de l'Oise, c. 1933. Photo of the terrace, in *Réalisations*, June 1934.

72 Arnone, "Immeuble de rapport, boulevard d'Anfa," 99.

73 This Spanish term for a belvedere was very commonly used in Casablanca.

Robert Lièvre, Lebascle building, Avenue Général d'Amade and Rue du Lieutenant Bergé, 1931. Photographed in 1993.

Robert Lièvre, Lebascle building. Plan of the terrace.

Marcel Desmet, apartment building, 22 Boulevard de la Gare, 1934–35. Photo of the terrace on the seventh floor, in *Réalisations*, October 1935.

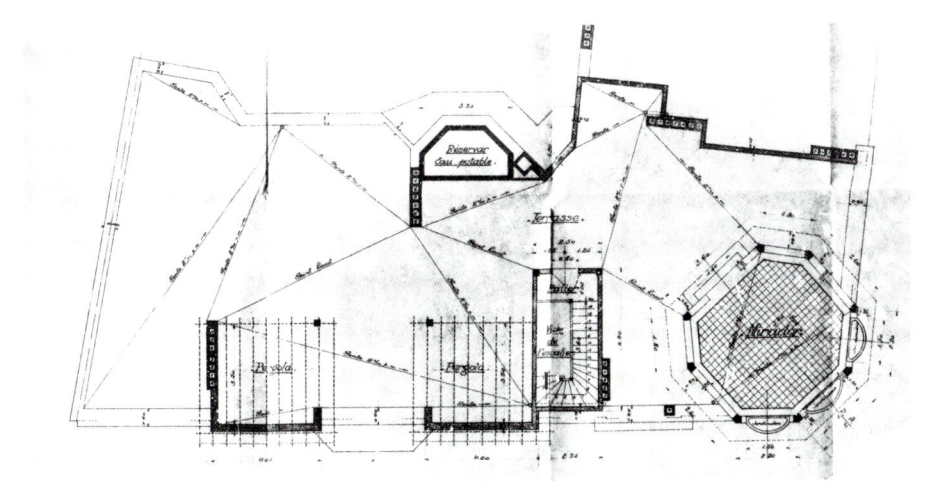

dwelling" by facilitating access, cutting out cumbersome chimney stacks, and sheltering the terraces from wind.

It became standard practice in Casablanca to cleave the flat roof into two sections. Thus, the roof of Jabin's 1939 Décrion building is divided into a communal part, with a laundry room and terrace for residents' use, and a private section, occupied by an apartment with a terrace and hanging garden. The largest apartment in this central block benefits from both these types of outdoor spaces. It was not uncommon for clients to commission their architects to decorate and furnish the terraces, as was the case with the lone apartment (containing a striking hexagonal entry hall) that Jean Michelet placed at the top of his building in Boulevard d'Anfa: "[It is] extended by a pleasant terrace with crisscrossed lattice partitioning that is interwoven with climbing plants. It looks like a miniature garden, embellished with a pergola wedged between the two fully glazed side walls, and an ornamental pool that can hold up to eight hundred liters of water."[72]

Architects and owners often devoted the building's roof terrace to one single apartment. The terrace in the Lebascle building, for example, constructed by Lièvre opposite the Parc Lyautey in 1931, is directly linked to the apartment below and is topped by a *mirador*[73] and pergolas. It is easy to picture how pleasant such a spot must be on summer evenings and festive occasions, or indeed just as a place for

1930–1940: From Art Deco to Modernism 199

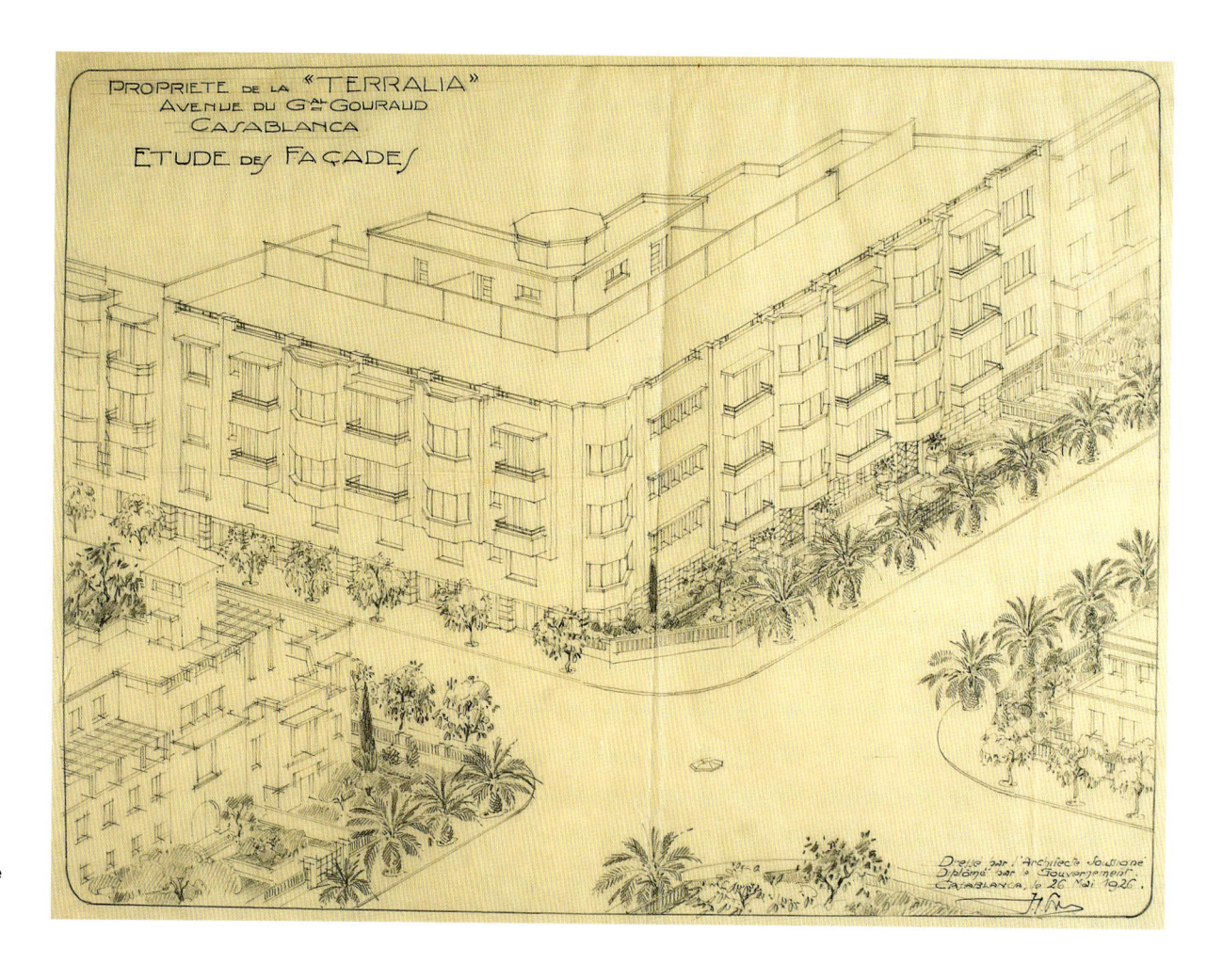

Georges Grel, Terralia building (unbuilt), Avenue Général Gouraud, 1926. Axonometric perspective.

74 In 1951 the architect transformed the roof terrace itself into an apartment, replacing the *mirador* with a large salon. This very well equipped five-room residence would benefit from the presence of the roof garden, whose pergolas were retained.

75 "Immeuble de La Fraternelle, boulevard de la Gare à Casablanca," 51.

76 Cotereau, "La maison mauresque," 602.

77 Cotereau, "La maison mauresque," 559. Cotereau is referring to the holiday of Succoth.

relaxing and breathing in the fresh air.[74] The roof apartment in these buildings is often the most luxurious, since it opens onto vast private terraces serving as summer salons, as in the Banon building. Another example is the seventh floor of the Marcel Desmet building on Boulevard de la Gare, which is made up of apartments overlooking "a large planted terrace with sweeping views over the port."[75] Here, the scheme included a pergola made up of trelliswork and concrete posts as well as gray mosaic flooring and planters.

The roof terraces therefore fulfilled four distinct but compatible functions. First, it was a place for socializing, which meant that it was fitted out with furniture, bars, fountains, and pergolas; it could even be divided up into separate spaces, depending on how large it was. Second, it tied in with physical exercise and well-being, which as many eyewitness accounts confirm, was widely practiced among the Europeans of Casablanca; in particular, it enabled residents to breathe in fresh air while remaining at home and allowed their "lungs to eliminate all the grime of the city."[76] Third, it was also a domestic space, since drying clothes in the sun is supposed to purify the house, ridding it of its germs; this practice has long been part of Moroccan culture, just as it is customary to use the terrace as a second kitchen in summer. And finally, in several neighborhoods, the roof terrace was used on specific religious days. For instance, the Moroccan Jews "installed reed huts on their rooftops" to "practice the complicated rites instituted in commemoration of their flight from Egypt."[77] This practice would be taken into account in the 1950s, when the concept of a "culture-specific habitat" was being developed.

Housing for Singles and Couples without Children

The Casablanca streetscape proves that Casablanca is a city of single people. Its society is newborn and family groups are few and far between, apart from the native Moroccan population... Many businessmen come over here alone to sound out the territory.

Chantiers nord-africains, 1932[78]

Until the 1920s, accommodations for single residents seem to have been built in random fashion, designed to fill up nooks of land, or otherwise they merely took the form of rented rooms within a larger apartment. In the 1930s, however, a more specific, even prestigious, program was established. Those solitary "pioneers" who had come to try out the Moroccan experience needed a particular type of abode, such as in Robert Lièvre's 1932 building in Rue Mouret, which included some twenty-eight bachelor apartments: "Nobody had previously thought of building a purpose-specific bachelors' apartment house. Such a scheme entailed taking a number of risks, and there had to be some certitude that it would prove popular, in other words that the structural form of the apartments and the modern conveniences would respond to the requirements of a 'cultured' bachelor."[79]

By placing the entry lobby in front of the main room, Lièvre skillfully ensured that each apartment was suitably private. These main rooms could also be used as a reception room, since the bed was tucked into an alcove near the service rooms (bathroom, lavatory, and kitchen area). This was a far cry indeed from the "furnished room that is difficult to sublet, being wedged at the rear of an apartment occupied by a family with whining children and without any independent lavatory or entrance."[80] But in a city with an endemic housing crisis, most single people were at the mercy of the real-estate market, and the poorer among them continued to live in sublet accommodations.

Marius Boyer's Les Studios building, completed in 1933, was dedicated to singles and couples without children; it was not, however, a testing ground, since Boyer had already assigned this role to his earlier bachelor apartments with terraces that

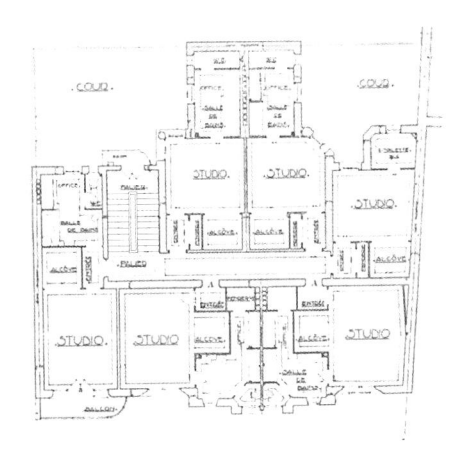

78 R.J., "28 garçonnières dans un immeuble: Architecte Robert Lièvre," *Chantiers nord-africains* 3, no. 2 (February 1932): 151.

79 R.J., "28 garçonnières dans un immeuble," 151.

80 R.J., "28 garçonnières dans un immeuble," 151.

Robert Lièvre, apartment building, Rue Mouret, 1932. Floor plan from the building permit, in *Les Chantiers nord-africains*, February 1932 (computer rendering by Philippe Simon).

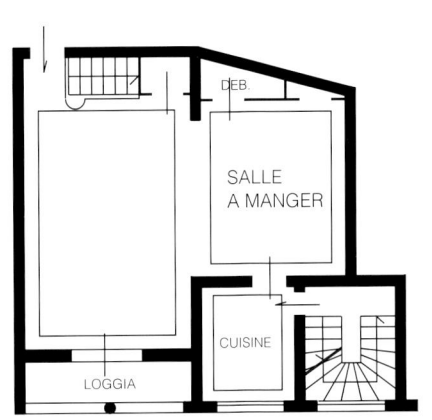

Marius Boyer, Boyer building, known as Les Studios, Avenue Général d'Amade and Rue de Bouskoura, 1935. Photo showing the inside of a two-bedroom corner apartment, in *Réalisations*, July 1935. The interior staircase is in the double-height dining room/lounge, which is extended by a loggia.

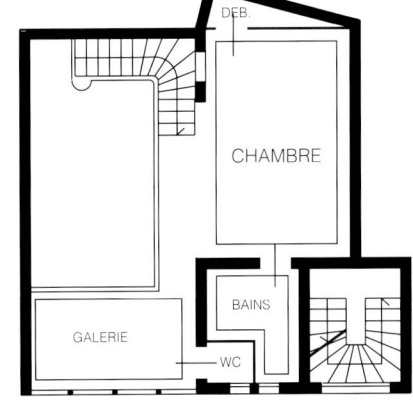

Les Studios, plan of the duplexes (drawing by Cristiana Mazzoni based on the building permit).

81 "Les *Studios*, immeuble de rapport," 7.

82 In 1926, Henri Sauvage built Les Studio building on Rue La Fontaine in Paris.

he had incorporated into the top floor of his Asayag building. The only difference between the Asayag scheme and Les Studios was that the latter signals its status via the name inscribed above the entrance. The double-height apartments were designed to be perceived from the exterior as having "five floors instead of ten"[81] due to the arrangement of four windows and a loggia, which is crowned by a single sunshield. Boyer used the facade windows designed for the Lévy-Bendayan building to light the staircase—an innovative concept for Casablanca, even though it had already been tried and tested in Paris.[82] It must nonetheless be remembered that if Boyer enjoyed a considerable degree of freedom, it was because he owned the building, just as Robert Lièvre owned the bachelors' apartments on Rue Mouret.

Boyer set a wide staircase and elevator in the heart of Les Studios, adjoining these to a service staircase leading to a linen room. Two other sets of stairs provide access to the side wings, as well as to the kitchens—an indisputable indicator of luxury. The lower level of each apartment includes a drum-shaped entrance, kitchen, dining room, and sometimes a linen room, while the upper level contains a bedroom with an en suite bathroom, linen room, lavatory, and a gallery overhanging the dining room. The architect chose to insert windows rather than loggias at this level. The four-room apartments have only one bedroom (as no children's rooms were needed), the other rooms being given over to gender-specific spaces, such as the boudoir and the smoking room adjoining the dining room. These design features were a clear sign that the apartments were upscale and were thus quite distinct from a family home. Modern conveniences included central heating, waste-disposal chutes, and a public telephone booth installed on the mezzanine floor.

Aside from these purpose-specific apartment blocks, the concept of reserving the top floor of standard buildings for studio or bachelor apartments grew in popularity. In 1934, Ignace Sansone and Paul Busuttil constructed the Eyraud building on Boulevard de Marseille, with five stories of spacious apartments and one floor of bachelor apartments. The steady influx of colonial settlers, allied with the type of lifestyle specific to Casablanca, resulted in ongoing demand for single-resident accommodations, with different types of programs offered with each architectural cycle.

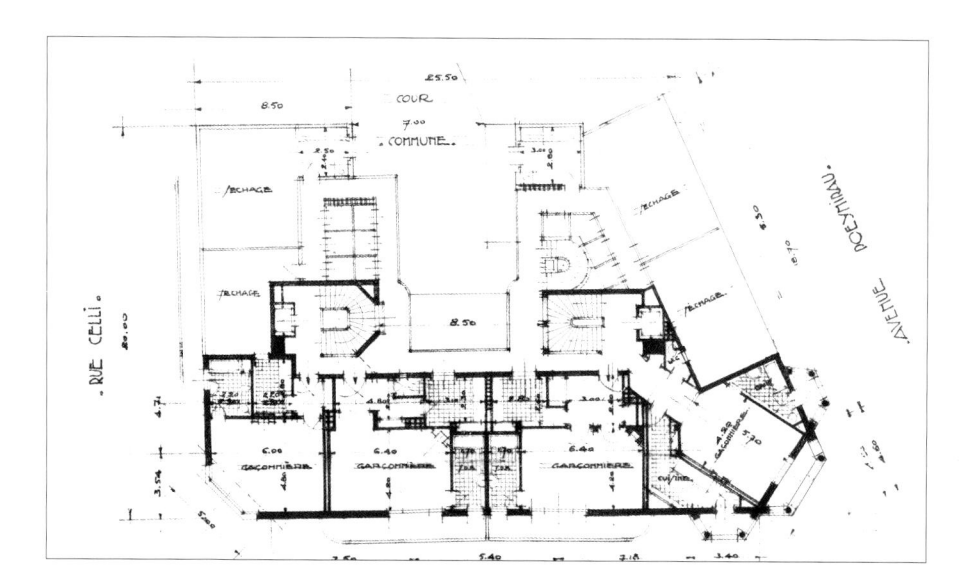

Sansone & Busuttil, Eyraud apartment building, Boulevard de Marseille, 1934. Sixth-floor plan showing bachelor apartments.

Pierre Jabin, Villa Cohen,
Rue Curie, 1931–32.
Street facade,
photographed in 1996.

1930s Villas

An architect from Rabat once gave me a humorous definition of Morocco: "It's a country buzzing with skyscraper talk," he said, "but which only turns out villas."

Chantiers nord-africains, December 1931[83]

The villa types that were produced during this period cover a wide spectrum, ranging from the seemingly orthodox "modern movement" to restrained radicalism, the early pastiches fading by the minute. Yet for the majority of architects and their clients, luxury was still inextricably linked to a combination of French and Moroccan styles. It is no easy task picking out the main themes that knit together the multiple villa types of the 1930s. Stylistic differences continued to be grounded in social issues, which perhaps explains why clients opted for either very traditional or ultramodern solutions, even within the same income group. Yet whatever the solution adopted, breeding either "creations of undeniable originality" or structures "that complied with a set of 'standards' (i.e., low-cost housing prototypes),"[84] the critics were, as a rule, effusive in their praise. The most traditional of these villas resembled French single-family dwellings of the previous decade. They included rooftop terraces and were a tremendous success with the middle classes—"the steady savers, the up-and-coming bourgeoisie," to quote *Chantiers nord-africains*.[85] The Villa Cohen was a typical commission within the category of comfortable bourgeois homes. Built by Pierre Jabin in 1931 with art deco details, the villa features a superb interior staircase that threads into a flowing open-plan sequence of reception rooms ideal for festive occasions. As for the rather austere villa designed by Alexandre Cormier in Rue Monge, it was conceived more along the lines of a private mansion. Cormier introduced elements that echoed the nearby Place Administrative, such as small columns, green tiles, a grouped window scheme, and brise-soleil. This range of motifs was used by many architects at the time.

Despite all the distinctive characteristics mentioned above, the layout of these bourgeois villas remained quite traditional, with the salon, dining room, and kitchen

83 "Villas marocaines," *Chantiers nord-africains* 4, no. 12 (December 1931): 1213.

84 "Villas marocaines," 1215. Fleurant's Villa Masson, discussed above, was given as an example of originality.

85 "Villas marocaines," 1215.

1930–1940: From Art Deco to Modernism

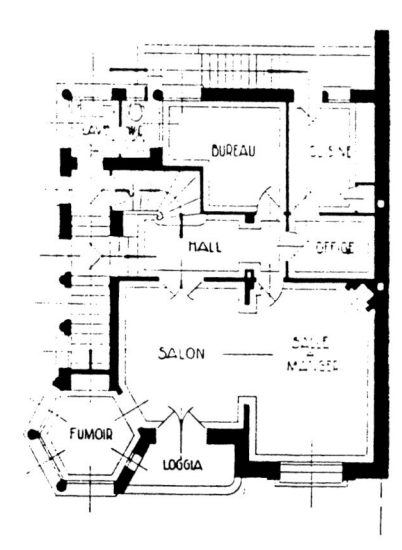

Jean Michelet, Villa F., Boulevard d'Anfa, 1934. Ground-floor plan, in *Réalisations*, June 1934.

86 "Les villas modernes de Casablanca," in "Le Maroc en 1932, 20 années de protectorat français," *L'Afrique du Nord illustrée*, 72.

87 "Villas casablancaises, J. Michelet, architecte," *Bâtir* (December 1932–January 1933): 23. See also the pages of *L'Architecture au Maroc* (June 1939) that are dedicated to this architect.

88 "Villa de M. F., boulevard d'Anfa, J. Michelet," *Réalisations* 1, no. 4 (June 1934): 103–4.

89 Numerous pages of photographs in *L'Architecture au Maroc* (June 1939) are devoted to Hinnen.

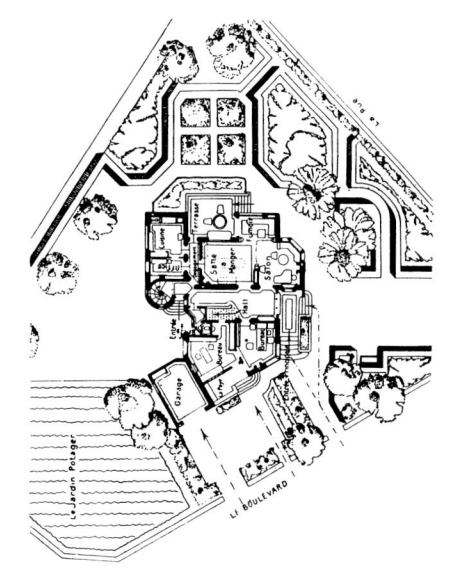

Paul Michaud, Villa Rivollet, Boulevard de la Marne, 1929–30. Ground- and first-floor plans, in Henri Descamps, *L'architecture moderne au Maroc*, 1930.

occupying the first level, and the bedrooms and bathroom taking up the second floor. Conveniently located and often embellished with loggias, pergolas, and canopies, the villas, by their sheer number alone, dominated in terms of architectural style. Architects such as Louis Fleurant and René Arrivetx specialized in this market. Arrivetx in particular constructed around fifty villas for mid-income earners between 1916 and 1932, using a design based on the Garden City; this solution undoubtedly stemmed, in some part at least, from his Algiers origins: "He brought with him the delightful concept of villas coquettishly snuggled into the green Algiers suburbs, and finding the same sun in the Land of Fortune as the one in his native region, he sought to endow his adopted homeland with the same beauty as that which he had recently left behind."[86]

Jean Michelet, another architect specializing in Louis XVI–style villas for clients of modest wealth, was "a key player in making Casablanca the white city it is," to quote the magazine *Bâtir*, whose columnist prided himself on living in a city surrounded by such fine suburbs:

> [Michelet's] villas are extremely varied in form and aspect . . . Just single- or two-story, they are all bright and welcoming, dotted with pergolas and flora gently bathed in the otherwise harsh Moroccan sun. Not only do these dwellings merge with the African light and setting, they also bear the structural and aesthetic hallmark of France, reflecting the origins of both their architect and their owners.[87]

Michelet's villas are indeed derived from climate-specific elements, such as outdoor rooms annexed to glazed salons so that occupants can benefit from the winter sun, as in a villa he designed on Boulevard d'Anfa.[88] In this case, clients' requirements were again carefully thought through; for instance, there is a monumental pergola staircase ending in a turret and small belvedere, and elsewhere there are combinations of jutting cubes with large openings and *brises-soleil*. Erwin Hinnen's prolific output is especially noteworthy within this category, combining as it does Provençal, Spanish, and Moroccan points of reference. From 1935 on, Hinnen became the favorite architect among those members of the bourgeoisie who yearned for France but at the same time wished to put down Mediterranean roots, or at least show that they could adapt to local conditions. Hinnen's works thus teem with pergolas, planted patios, arcades, and wrought ironwork. Well attuned to the North African climate, these houses were built in Anfa or in other upmarket neighborhoods for Europeans who were nostalgic for their native towns.[89]

The villa owned by Marcel Rivollet (a building contractor and an active member of the municipal council) was intended to convey affluence without being showy. It was designed by Paul Michaud between 1929 and 1930 and has a large floor area with office space. Its smooth facades are pierced with multiple loggias and terraces, and are covered with green tiles to impart a local flavor. The main entrance provides direct access from the boulevard into the reception rooms, which are generously lit by a bay window and a terrace as big as the salon. Both the terrace and window overlook the garden. The service access point is on the opposite side of the main entrance and leads into the pantry and kitchen, while a third entry is reserved for business visitors and garage access. The architect based his design for the grounds on medieval gardens and incorporated a vegetable plot close to the servants' quarters.

The Villa S, built by Fleurant in the early 1930s, is an exemplary affluent dwelling built in the modern vein. It has an entrance fitted with a large brise-soleil, chamfered balconies, and a cylindrical design component that encompasses the four first-floor windows and outlines the overhang of a large second-floor terrace. Such motifs grew increasingly common, not just in the top-range villas but at the lower end of the scale, too. The notion of the "modern villa," frequently cited in reviews, was also inextricably linked to provision of up-to-the-minute fittings. The Azogué house, built in 1935

Erwin Hinnen, villa, Anfa, 1938, perspective.

Erwin Hinnen, Villa Theil, Anfa, 1938, perspective from the air.

1930–1940: From Art Deco to Modernism   205

Ignace Sansone and Paul Busuttil, Villa Grégoire, Rue de Malines and Rue de Namur, 1931. General view, in *Chantiers nord-africains*, June 1932.

Louis-Paul and Félix Joseph Pertuzio, Villa Azogué, 1935. General view. Photo published in *Réalisations*, June 1936.

Louis-Paul and Félix Joseph Pertuzio, Villa Azogué, 1935. Bathroom with electric water heater. Photo published in *Réalisations*, June 1936.

90 "Une villa entièrement électrifiée, la villa Azogué à Casablanca, Pertuzio frères, 1935," *Réalisations* 2, no. 6 (June 1936): 163.

by the Pertuzio brothers, was similarly heralded as a model of modernity, not least due to its being "fully wired and fitted with electrical appliances."[90]

Muslim tradesmen had their houses built in the Moroccan tradition, mainly in the vicinity of the sultan's palace. Although these were often constructed without the aid of an architect, some nevertheless contain elements borrowed from the modern, or Western, style. A striking example is a villa in Mers-Sultan, commissioned by the Andaloussi family from Fès to an unknown designer in 1932, after they had lived for ten years or so in the Habous quarter. The dwelling is located in a mainly European neighborhood, and at first glance does not really stand out among the other cubelike villas built in the same period. However, closer study reveals it to be a modernized adaptation of the traditional Fassi house, its large salon acting as a courtyard. The bedrooms and fittings were designed in line with contemporary standards.

Mendeli Moulay Thami house, built in 1932 in the medina (Rue de la Douane). Photo of the lounge, taken in 1997.

Villa Andaloussi, 3 Rue des Cavaliers de Courcy, 1932–36. Main lounge. Photographed in 1997. The interior is traditional, with three lounges of different sizes, two of which are furnished with wall seats. The tall doors are flanked by inside windows, recalling a patio layout. They symbolize the movement from the open courtyard into an enclosed lounge. Local furniture and 1930s European-style furnishings are mixed together.

Villa Andaloussi, 3 Rue des Cavaliers de Courcy, 1932–36. Facade. Photographed in 1997. Note how high and narrow the windows are overlooking the street. By contrast, the openings overlooking the courtyards and gardens are extremely wide. Interestingly, the three high windows in the main lounge open onto the exterior.

1930–1940: From Art Deco to Modernism   207

Marius Boyer, Villa Pierre Grand, Rue Montesquieu, Rue Jean Jaurès, and Rue Alexandre Dumas, 1930.

General perspective. Published in Henri Descamps, *L'architecture moderne au Maroc*, 1930.

View of the salon. Published in Henri Descamps, *L'architecture moderne au Maroc*, 1930.

Marius Boyer chose to work with diverse vocabularies adapted to his clients' requirements. He produced several outstanding villas, the most remarkable being the one he built in 1930 for the entrepreneur Pierre Grand (demolished in 1990). This *ryad** house was situated on Rue Jean Jaurès and had lush gardens, *zillij* ornamentation, and a layout type that can be likened to the enchanting palaces of the Moroccan aristocracy, as described by Claude Farrère:

> *Ryads* are the inner courtyards of Moroccan dwellings. Rectangular in shape, and often girded by a cloister colonnade, they are planted with gardens full of orange, banana, and pomegranate trees, and they always emanate the sweet fragrance of jasmine and roses. *Ryads* are similar to the Andalusian patio, with the same basins, trickling water, fountains, and ornamental ponds; it is just that they are designed on a grander scale.[91]

Boyer consciously chose to mix Arabic-Muslim pomp with the luxury features of Parisian private mansions. The house was a continuous thread, comprising a "Sevillian patio," followed by a summer house, a *ryad*, an ornamental pool, a terrace, and an Arab salon. The Parisian features included a double entrance, master apartment, smoking room, and boudoir, as well as a hall, conservatory, linen room, and pantry. It is interesting to note that the reception rooms had a much larger floor area than the private quarters. Although the villa itself was huge, it only contained two master bedrooms and guestrooms, all of which had an en suite bathroom. The sizable domestic quarters were arranged around the courtyard and were separated from the rest of the house, representing an additional symbol of wealth. Henri Descamps underlines the qualities of this dwelling owned by "a colonial settler who had made his fortune out of determined hard work":

> The house is split into three sections. First, a reception space (hall, reception rooms, smoking room, and conservatory) adjoining a *ryad*, which can be easily converted into a swimming pool. Second, private quarters and the owner's study, which is situated near a Sevillian patio and has a separate entrance. And lastly, clearly segregated servants' quarters, laid out pragmatically around a courtyard. All the outside walls are white, the roof is covered with varnished green tiles, and the high paneling is dressed in *zillij*. The ground-floor level is covered with gray ceramic tilework, while the openings have been judiciously positioned to soften the sun's harsh light and angle its rays into the bedrooms at certain times of the day.[92]

Marius Boyer, Villa Bensimhon, Avenue Mers-Sultan, 1935. Front of the villa in *Réalisations*, June 1936.

Marius Boyer, Villa Bensimhon, Avenue Mers-Sultan, 1935. View of the hall, looking toward the staircase and reception rooms. Photo published in *Réalisations*, June 1936.

The hall, lounge, and dining room are more or less open plan. They are extremely well lit and are extended by a verandah and terrace. The private quarters are accessed by a large staircase that receives natural light through side glazing. This staircase is extended by a gallery overhanging the hall.

91 Farrère, *Les Hommes nouveaux*, 166.

92 Descamps, *L'Architecture moderne au Maroc*, 2:2. The Villa Grand was razed in 1991.

Charles Abella, Villa Pierre Mas, Avenue du Golf, Anfa, 1937. Photo of the main facade, taken in 1943.

93 Gillet was the site architect.

Several years later, Marius Boyer built the Villa Bensimhon, whose remarkable iron and glass work give the facade a modern touch. Although stripped of all neo-Moorish elements, the composition and layout are nonetheless extremely skillful. The double-height, ground-floor hall functions as a salon, reminiscent of Charles Plumet's and Henri Sauvage's halls, and acts as an extension to the dwelling's reception space. The architect drew on vast volumes, overhangs, and galleries to create a *promenade architecturale* that calls into play the various spatial elements.

In 1937, Pierre Mas, owner of *La Vigie marocaine* newspaper, called on the distinguished Parisian architect Charles Abella, to design a sumptuous villa near the racetrack.[93] Conceived to host parties and other social events, it has a large number of salons and small apartments, including one on the pergola terrace. It sits in the heart of a vast garden full of unexpected features, such as wide paths that lead to private, green "chambers." The design vocabulary is composed of extremely high porthole windows and a flat asymmetrical facade broken only by a double cylindrical motif. The overall result echoes Roger-Henri Expert's house schemes in Arcachon, France, as well as Michel Roux-Spitz's buildings in Paris.

The final dwelling worth mentioning is Dar es-Saada, the house in which Franklin Roosevelt stayed during the Anfa conference in 1943, and which is featured in the background of official period photographs. Built in 1937 for Mrs. Besson-Maufrangeas, Dar es-Saada was one of Hinnen's first large villas. Its geometric detailing and large art deco windows are combined with modern elements—a rare feature in Hinnen's work. This mark of modernity is apparent in the entrance, which is not only fitted with a brise-soleil but is also flanked by gray marble-clad posts and topped by a ribbon window. As for the building's cubic section, it adjoins a sort of curved prow accommodating the brightly lit master bedroom. Looking from the wrought-iron and copper gate, views are channeled through the hall and double-height salon into the garden adorned by a fountain. A light wood sliding door serves to separate the entrance from the salon, whose walls are pierced with large openings.

By the eve of World War II, a great many critics firmly believed that Casablanca was the embodiment of modern architecture. Despite the general outcry that ensued when some of the early, handsome buildings began to be demolished, the changes implemented since 1920 were interpreted as follows:

> When our architects began to build European towns in Morocco, it seemed artistically "right" to respect local tradition and style, which would explain why there is such a vast number of conventional Hispano-Moorish buildings. Lyautey even swore he would fire a canon at the first "block" he saw. Today, stumbling across one of these low stucco houses with their pointed windows in the midst of our buildings with their large plate-glass windows and wide wall planes, it is the pseudo-Moorish that stands out as ugly, and justly so, for it represents no more than a sterile effort to resurrect something from the dead.[94]

94 Jean Célérier, "Les conditions géographiques du développement de Casablanca," in "Casablanca, grande ville et grand port de l'Empire français," special issue of *Revue de géographie marocaine* 23, no. 1 (1940): 131–53.

Erwin Hinnen, Villa Dar es-Saada, Anfa, c. 1935. General view from the garden in 1943.

Erwin Hinnen, Villa Dar es-Saada, Anfa, c. 1935. Lounge, photographed in 1994.
The lounge is generously glazed and is flanked by a lower, more intimate, lounge and a bar/library with fine wainscoting. A staircase and gallery edged by a ribbon window lead to the bedrooms.

1930–1940: From Art Deco to Modernism 211

"Modern Architecture at Home in Morocco"

The Arab villa and the modern dwelling share surprising analogies of style and simplicity, stemming from an ambition to restrict all exterior display of wealth. In both cases, white juxtaposed cubes form the underlying design syntax. In both cases, overhangs and recesses, large walls and clear-cut angles give rise to the same aesthetic effects. In both cases, the structure is surmounted by a roof terrace.

Jean Cotereau, 1930[95]

The shift in Casablancan architectural trends derived chiefly from the new approaches being explored in Parisian architecture during the same period. "The rejection of initial pastiches coincides with the campaign pursued by Parisian modernists, confirming that "Le Corbusier's austere design principles do indeed have their place in Morocco's simple and harmonious structural setting."[96] Additionally, subsequent research has borne out the assumption made by more than one writer that modern aesthetics grew out of North Africa. We are now aware of the important formative role played by Mediterranean landscapes in the work of Josef Hoffmann, Tony Garnier, and Le Corbusier. As Léandre Vaillat noted in 1922, referring to Le Corbusier's Ville contemporaine, "its plan unfolds like an Arab town viewed from a minaret."[97] Many eyewitness reports speak of the intimate links between modern and Moroccan architecture. In 1938, Édouard Sarrat claimed he was sure that "modern architecture, which is characterized by a sort of return to antiquity through bare plans and arrangement of volumes, is better suited to Morocco than to the Paris skyline, or any other European capital for that matter."[98] Henri Descamps had made a similar observation as early as 1930: "Local motifs are giving way to a dense form of architecture. Interestingly, the international modern style is eminently suited to Morocco, perhaps even more so than to its country of origin."[99]

On another note, Descamps recalled, "'Modern architecture has been reproached for bearing too many overtones of the Orient,'" and he believed that "it has found its ideal setting in Morocco."[100] Soubreville praised the "starkly modern, sober, and majestic lines" of Moroccan edifices, which he considered were built in true "Hispano-Moorish" style.[101] When Rue Mallet-Stevens opened in 1927, Jean Gallotti was struck by the buildings' resemblance to French Moroccan architecture, in particular the flat roofs, which were uncommon in colder climes.[102] Ten years later, Gallotti returned to the theme of Casablanca's urban structures, which "are suitably modern for lovers of modernity, yet sufficiently Moroccan for those who are partial to an exotic flavor. Moreover, they are undeniably homogenous and of a quality that is lacking in almost all the new quarters of our metropolitan cities." He described how this architectural fabric had been woven spontaneously, seemingly by stitching together a number of stylistic threads:

> Once France brought cubic and schematic architecture (the outgrowth of reinforced concrete) to Morocco in 1925, it was decided to make optimal use of kindred elements between modern art and Muslim secular art. It was a way of deluding everybody, whether lovers of the past, who were led to believe that the aim was to remain faithful to Moroccan style, or lovers of the new art who were convinced that European methods were being deployed. Yet it was also a way of pleasing everyone and, above all, of providing an effective response to the fundamental question of how to preserve North Africa's most precious urban element—white towns dressed in terraces that capture the colored shafts of sunlight.[103]

---

95 Cotereau, "La maison mauresque," 538.

96 R. d'Arcos, "L'urbanisme au Maroc," *Chantiers nord-africains* 1, no. 10 (October 1929): 583–84.

97 Léandre Vaillat, "Le décor de la vie, Au Salon d'Automne, l'art urbain," *Le Temps* (Paris) (November 4, 1922): 3–4.

98 "Les architectes et les entrepreneurs qui ont construit Casablanca," 86.

99 Henri Descamps, "Urbanisme et architecture française au Maroc," *La Cité moderne*, no. 12 (summer 1931): 25.

100 Descamps, "Urbanisme et architecture française au Maroc," 25. It is known that the Weissenhofsiedlung housing development in Stuttgart (1927) was derisively called *Araberdorf* in a photomontage postcard in which it was shown invaded by Bedouins and dromedaries. Richard Pommer and Christian F. Otto, *Weissenhof 1927 and the Modern Movement in Architecture* (Chicago: University of Chicago Press, 1991), ill. 85.

101 A. Soubreville, "Le Maroc, vivant musée d'architecture hispano-mauresque et berbère," *Chantiers nord-africains* 2, no. 12 (December 1930): 1121.

102 Gallotti, "Une nouvelle rue à Paris," *L'Art vivant* 3, no. 64 (August 15, 1927): 668.

103 Jean Gallotti, "L'art moderne adapté au ciel du Maroc," in "L'urbanisme en Afrique du Nord," *Plaisir de France*, no. 54 (March 1939): 43–44.

Marius Boyer, Banque commerciale du Maroc, place Guynemer, 1930. Partial view. Photographed in 1994.

Ambivalent Praise from Algiers

The deliberations set out by Henri Descamps, Léandre Vaillat, and Jean Gallotti form part of multiple studies and reports drawn up on "New Morocco." Visitors to Casablanca were greeted with one huge buzzing building site, as construction still constituted the most important economic activity. These works attracted so much attention that the Algiers-based magazine *Chantiers nord-africains* launched a special column in the late 1920s dedicated to "the many facets of Casablancan architecture" and in which everything seemed to be described in superlative terms:

> We are, most fortunately, witnessing a much higher quality of architectural output than in those huge mushrooming growths of which the Yankees are so proud. There are many architects in Morocco whose talents rival even the most prominent Parisian architects, and whose buildings, whether public or private, are imbued with good taste, order, harmony, and comfort. Not only are these men gifted and brave artists, driven by a modern spirit in its most rational and balanced form, they are masters at adapting to the local environment.[104]

Many of these analyses clearly indicate that Algiers and Casablanca were competitors. Algiers critics were constantly attacking Casablanca's eclecticism and mercenary nature, yet at the same time they acknowledged its technical prowess. After a trip to Morocco, an Algerian architect related: "Casablanca is a large port, peopled with all kinds of races and driven by all sorts of aesthetic conceptions, and is thus confusedly split between diverse stylistic tastes. How can architects impose a sense of discipline on this city when it is the clients who are dictating its making?"[105] Observers were surprised by the quality of construction skills: "All the firms are extremely advanced, and their people are fully qualified to interpret any kind of plan and work on any kind of project." They were similarly impressed during their visits to "major manufacturers of steel frames and decorative wrought iron, as well as to some extremely interesting furniture factories and joinery firms." In addition, they expressed their admiration for several "high-quality ceramic and sculpture workshops that concentrate on adapting certain elements of Morocco's Hispano-Moorish ornamentation to large-scale modern construction; it is to be noted that these workshops are very successful indeed."[106] Overall, the view was that "French Morocco is turning out some highly original, first-rate architecture."[107] Some visitors did express their reservations, however, as is evident in a letter from a *Chantiers nord-africains* reader, written in reaction to the articles cited above:

> The overriding tendency in the external design of tall buildings [is] to somewhat overload the top floors. Galleries, overhangs, projections, balconies, and loggias all jut out from the facades. Elsewhere, heavily ornamented pinnacles abound. Supporting pillars are often spindly, which creates a certain imbalance, especially when the buildings are constructed on a public thoroughfare. In a nutshell, there are many Casablancan buildings that lack a sense of momentum, adopting as they do the form of an inverse pyramid.[108]

This criticism is not unjustified, for the upper sections of Casablanca's buildings are top-heavy. Given that clients all requested terraces, loggias, and pergolas (believing that they could thereby command higher rents), the architects often had no choice but to resort to ostentatious solutions. However, the critical reader received a cutting response from the columnist:

> The reasons that impelled architects to incorporate overhangs on the top floors of apartment buildings were mainly of a practical nature [based on] on the owners' tastes and interests. Furthermore, not all these "inverse pyramids" are disasters... More important, though, [the city's] most recent structures no longer contain such deficiencies.[109]

Gustave Cottet, apartment building, Rond-point Mers-Sultan and Rue Franchet d'Esperey, c. 1932. Photographed in 1991.

Élias and Joseph Suraqui, Suraqui building, Rue Chevandier de Valdrôme, 1930. Front facade. Photographed in 1994.

104 "Villas modernes à Casablanca," *Chantiers nord-africains* 1, no. 1 (January 1929): 85.

105 "Les innombrables visages de l'architecture casablancaise," *Chantiers nord-africains* 3, no. 10 (October 1931): 988–89.

106 "Les innombrables visages de l'architecture casablancaise," 990.

107 "Les innombrables visages de l'architecture casablancaise," 990.

108 "Les innombrables visages de l'architecture casablancaise," *Chantiers nord-africains* 3, no. 12 (December 1931): 1207-1208.

109 "Les innombrables visages de l'architecture casablancaise," 1207.

**The Habous quarter —
a residential street,
c. 1925.**

Building the New Medina and Housing the Workers

The Habous—A Fictitious Quarter

One of the major features that characterizes Casablanca is its ever-growing native population. It is perhaps the only Muslim town in the whole of North Africa where this type of development has occurred... As a consequence, grim suburbs and squalid slums have sprung up, unfortunately squeezed right in between the European quarters.

Henri Prost, 1917[1]

The Arab people have their own lifestyle and traditions, which must be respected, as is finely illustrated in Mr. Prost's plan for a small indigenous town. Our Moroccan protégés will have no cause for complaint; they will be surrounded by their souks, mosques, fountains, and squares; they will be at home in a familiar setting.

Claude Favrot, 1917[2]

Along with large-scale works dedicated to crafting the "European town," successive ventures were undertaken between 1920 and 1940 to provide accommodations for the unexpected influx of Moroccan migrants. The cover of a tourist brochure from the early 1930s clearly indicates Casablanca's new function: glimpsed through the keyhole arch of a traditional gate, the city is portrayed both as the European threshold to Morocco and as the place where rural Moroccans could find work and a certain degree of modernity. To quote Jacques Berque, the commercial capital's rapid expansion was "shaping the country far and wide."[3] Muslims would not however, be allocated housing in the new quarters, but in districts outside town designed for that purpose. They were excluded from the major roads of the new town, in the same way as servants were relegated to the rear of bourgeois apartments.

Creating the New Indigenous Town

Prost's plan included very few projects actually inside the old core of the medina, though in 1915 he did propose that the Ould-el-Hamra mosque square be redeveloped. The medina no longer really had any room for expansion, as it was wedged between the new roads and tightly hemmed in on its western side. Furthermore, its outskirts were gradually being gnawed away to make room for Boulevard du IVe-Zouaves, notably by demolishing the native Moroccan huts, the *kissaria*,* and the

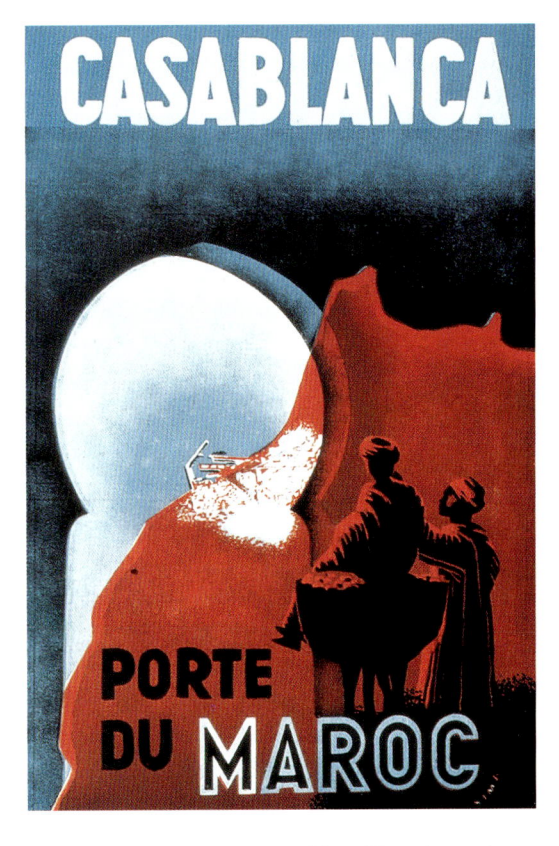

Xima, "Casablanca, the gateway to Morocco." Front cover of a tourist brochure, c. 1930.

1 Henri Prost, "Le plan de Casablanca," 10.

2 Favrot, "Une ville française moderne," 227.

3 Jacques Berque, "Médinas, villeneuves et bidonvilles," *Les Cahiers de Tunisie* no. 21-22 (1st and 2nd Trimesters 1959): 5.

main market, which symbolized the decline of traditional shops to the benefit of French trade. In 1917, Prost claimed that he was convinced the old quarters would be replaced by a "new indigenous town . . . located on the road most frequently used by the native population, not far from the recently built station, the future trade districts, and the sultan's new palace."[4] When presenting his plan to the Musée Social in 1922, he revealed his intention to demolish the medina in its entirety.[5]

Prost's ambition to "shift the working population and pull down the slums" was shared by the lawyer Claude Favrot, his ally, who pictured European workers living "in the east, near the station." He too raised "the problem of housing for the native population," which he declared was specific to [French] African towns."[6] Both men imagined a reassuring "setting" for the Moroccans, away from Casablanca's urban core yet close to its economic hub. In 1922 Maurice de Périgny, like Favrot, envisaged "Moroccan country folk" finding "small rooms [above shops] where at night they can sleep on palm tree matting and in the daytime sit about quaffing large amounts of mint-flavored tea."[7]

Small Muslim neighborhoods began to be carved out next to the quarters bordering the western part of the medina. In 1914 another project was instigated by two Moroccan landowners who developed Derb Ghallef to the west of the Bouskoura road. Yet, as Périgny noted, the plots picked out for the planned housing extension schemes lay chiefly along Avenue du Général Drude, which ran on from the Route de Médiouna (the road to Marrakech). "It is here that all the main *fonduks* can be found, where the tribal population sells its grain, wool, and hides, purchasing imported goods in exchange."[8] This busy commercial street ended in the old city core; as early as 1918, Émile Lapeyre and E. Marchand had been so struck by its pulsating rhythm and lively atmosphere that they had even thought of equipping it with a streetcar line:

> During their stay in Casablanca, Arabs sell their goods or trade them for local and European products. To do so, they have to move about frequently, going "into town" as it were; hence the Avenue du Général Drude bustles with life at certain times of the day . . . It can even be said that it is the liveliest road in Casablanca.[9]

Developing the Habous Quarter

It was decided that the as-yet-undeveloped land situated along the Route de Médiouna would form the site of the new indigenous town, not least because it lay close to major military structures, which reduced the risk of uprisings. Subdivision of the area began in 1916, after the authority in charge of the Habous (a religious foundation under Samuel Biarnay's direction) had been given tracts of land belonging to the Jewish landowner Haïm Bendahan.[10] The land pattern resulting from this complex transaction translated into four distinct segments, with the lot nearest the city center (the site of the former Provost fort) assigned to a new palace for the sultan, clearly indicating that the area was intended to accommodate the Moroccan population. The sultan's mediation was instrumental, since Muslim foundations could not, as a rule, receive a gift from a Jew.[11] Derb Sidna, or Soltane, located southeast of the fort, was earmarked for palace staff lodgings, while Derb el-Hagib was reserved for the residence of the sultan's chamberlain. The remaining land was devoted to the Habous development itself.[12]

The sultan's mansion, built by the Pertuzio brothers, was afforded a sumptuously modern interior, and in September 1916 J. C. N. Forestier designed an ensemble of Mediterranean gardens for it. This was in fact Forestier's sole direct contribution to Casablanca's development.[13] The following year, Laprade drafted a preliminary housing program for low-income Muslims on a four-hectare parcel donated by Bendahan, drawing on observations of ancient Moroccan and

---

4 Henri Prost, "Village indigène," n.d., AA, fonds Henri Prost, A1 1-17 (partially typescript).

5 Joyant and Prost, "Communication sur les plans d'aménagement et d'extension des villes au Maroc," 16.

6 Favrot, "Une ville française moderne," 227.

7 Comte Maurice de Périgny, *Au Maroc*, 17–18.

8 M. Hubert, *L'evolution de Casablanca* (Rabat: Centre des hautes études d'administration musulmane, 1946), 17.

9 Lapeyre and Marchand, *Casablanca*, 94–95.

10 Regarding the role of this institution, see Georg Stöber, "Habous Public," in *Marokko, Zur wirtschaftlichen Bedeutung religiöser Stiftungen im 20. Jahrhundert*, Marburger Geographische Schriften, no.104 (Marburg/Lahn: Marburger Geographische Gesellschaft, 1986); and Sylvie Denoix, ed., "Biens communs, patrimoines collectifs et gestion communautaire dans les sociétés musulmanes," *Revue des mondes musulmans et de la Méditerranée* no. 79–80 (1997).

11 A note by Prost nonetheless indicates that the sale of Bendahan's lands occurred *after* the decision to construct the sultan's residence. Prost, "Village indigène."

12 Hubert, *L'evolution de Casablanca*, 7–8; and Adam, *Casablanca*, 69–70. Driss Chraïbi evoked derb Soltane in "La Maison Blanche," in Bourdon and Folléas, eds., *Casablanca, fragments d'imaginaire*, vol. 3.

13 See the general plan of the garden in Jean-Claude-Nicolas Forestier, *Jardins, carnet de plans et de dessins* (Paris: Émile Paul Frères, 1920). The original drawing is archived in the IFA, fonds Forestier-Leveau. The residence was particularly well equipped, as attested to by the Kelvinator company, which emphasized in recurrent advertisements printed in *La Vie marocaine illustrée* that it was provided with a refrigerator.

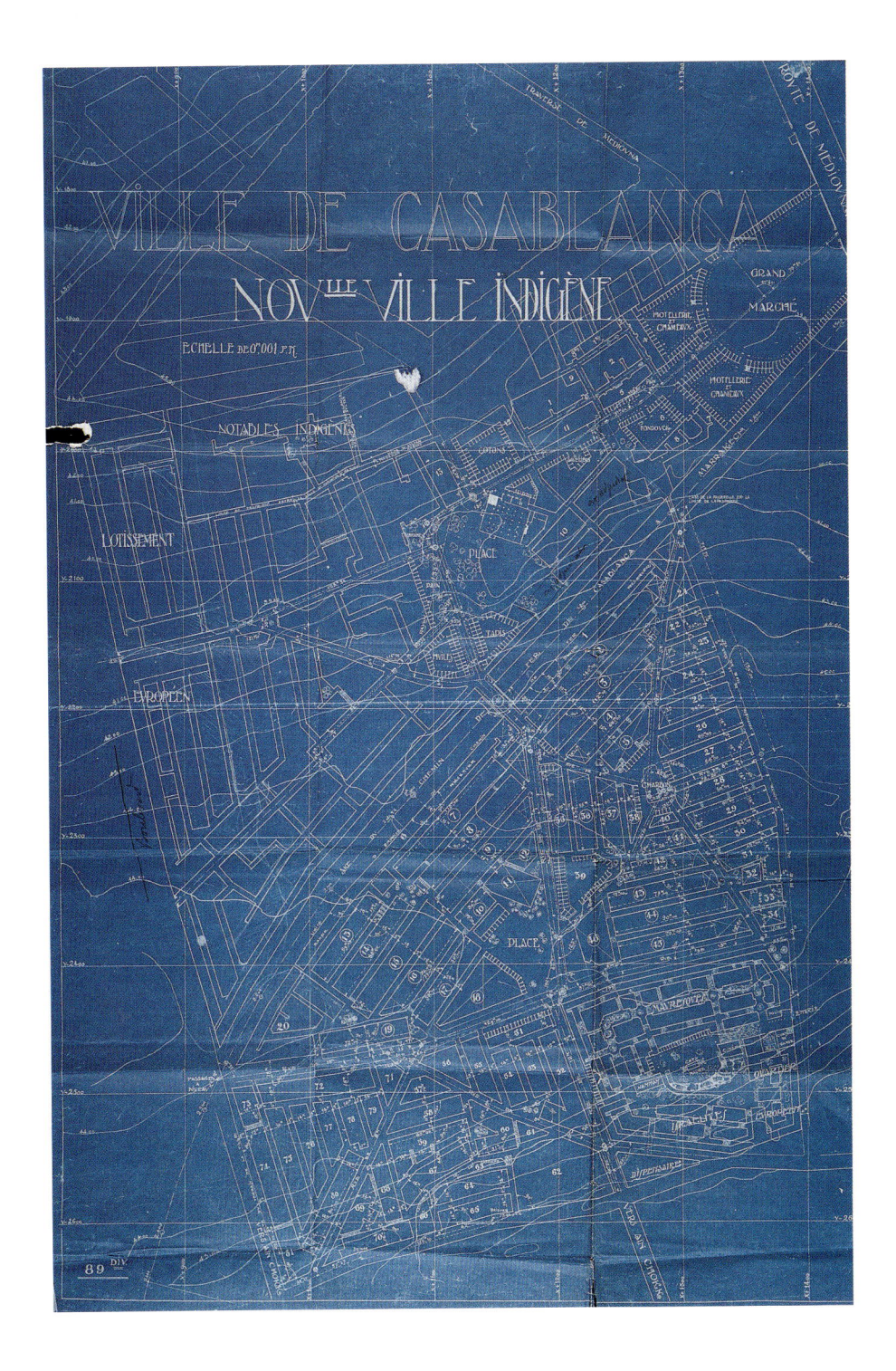

Henri Prost, master plan for the "new indigenous town," c. 1921.

Andalusian architecture.¹⁴ In 1930, Léandre Vaillat declared the Habous to be "an indigenous town or, more precisely, a town built for the native population by French architects in a way that respects local customs and scruples, while offering the additional benefit of French hygienic facilities."¹⁵ Vaillat described the reasons behind the development of this quarter: "Idealists were forever expressing concern about the harsh living conditions of the native population that were induced by the housing shortage. Having come from the countryside to lend their strength to budding industries and large-scale urban development, these workers were packed into

14 Laprade's sketches would reappear in his *Croquis Portugal Espagne Maroc* (Paris: Vincent, Fréal & Cie, 1958), 81–100.

15 Vaillat, *Le visage français du Maroc*, 12.

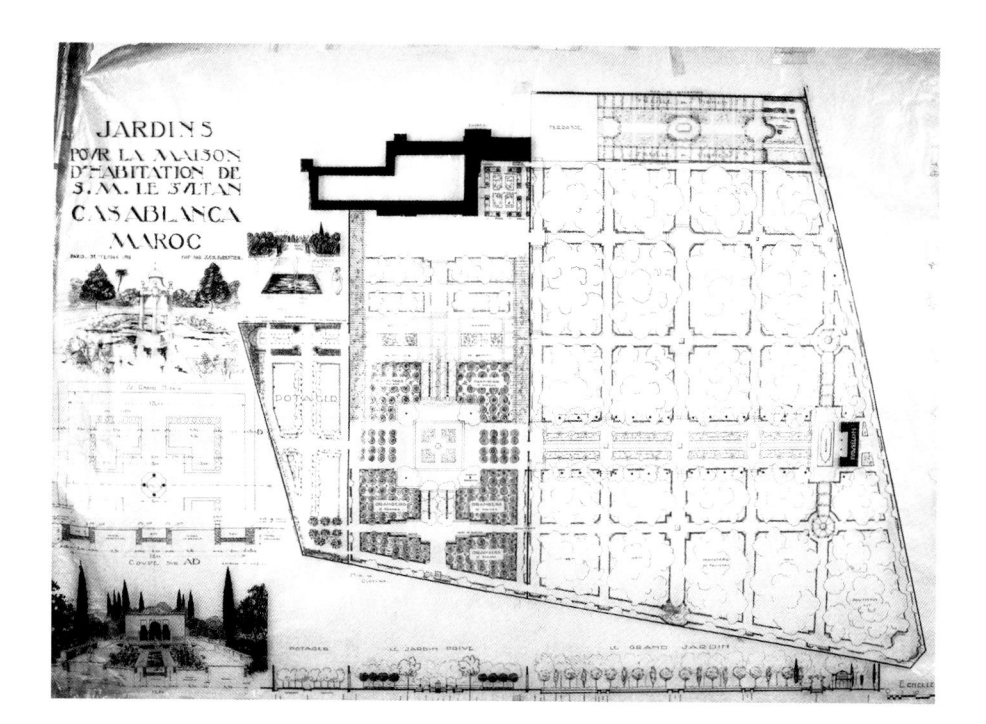

Jean Claude Nicolas Forestier, project for the garden of the sultan's palace, 1916. Master plan, cross section, and perspectives.

16 Léandre Vaillat, "La nouvelle médina de Casablanca," *L'Illustration* no. 4752 (October 18, 1930): 225. The team worked in the building "on Place de France, built by the Perret brothers," in other words, in the Paris-Maroc store.

17 Where he built Lyautey's residence. G. Rémon, "Architecture moderne au Maroc," 161–74.

18 Regarding representations of Islamic architecture in the nineteenth century, see Zeynep Çelik, *Displaying the Orient: Architecture of Islam at Nineteenth-Century World's Fairs* (Berkeley, Los Angeles, and Oxford: University of California Press, 1992).

19 Vaillat, *Le Visage français du Maroc*, 12 and 16.

20 Vaillat, "La nouvelle médina de Casablanca," 225.

21 Albert Laprade, "Une ville créée spécialement pour les indigènes à Casablanca," in Jean Royer, ed., *L'Urbanisme aux colonies et dans les pays tropicaux*, 1: 97–98. See also: Anna Pasquali and Gaetano Arcuri, "Casablanca the Derb el Habous by A. Laprade or how to build in the Arab fashion," *Environmental Design* no. 1 (1985): 14–21.

filthy slums, reed dugouts, and even in petrol drums, without sewage facilities, or indeed hygienic amenities of any kind."[16]

After Laprade left for Rabat,[17] Auguste Cadet and Edmond Brion took over his work on the Habous project, for which the initial construction phase lasted ten years. The scheme did not simply entail reproducing the "Arab sections" featured in world fairs since the mid-nineteenth century[18]; instead, it hinged on an innovative design concept that spurned gratuitous picturesque elements in favor of a play on diversity, both with respect to housing and to the road system. Vaillat hailed the scheme as representing "incisive reflections by European artists on the Oriental lifestyle"[19] and underscored the importance of its traditional slant: "One need not be an architectural expert to note that in native Moroccan towns, one steps from the narrow street straight into a spacious patio, having first passed through a bayonet-type entranceway which so effectively shields the family from public view . . . It is precisely this relationship between the street and the courtyard that underpins the design for the new medina."[20]

Laprade presented his scheme at the colonial urban planning congress held in Paris in 1931. Here he stressed his refusal to take the "easy route," i.e., reproducing hackneyed traditional motifs, and underscored the location of the indigenous town, set between the Route de Médiouna, the palace, and the railroad. He saw it as a "cul-de-sac" where residents could stroll and linger in a way "suited to the country's lifestyle":

> The entrance is marked by a vast square girded by shops and flanked by high-rise hotels to provide lodgings for rural folk from far-off villages . . . The main road starts from here and is lined with an elegant portico shopping arcade. This street leads to the main square, which groups a large mosque, Moorish baths, and bazaars. There are residential streets on the left and right of the main road, yet this thoroughfare contains very few entrances to the dwellings. Small houses are located near the market, the larger ones being situated near the mosque in the quietest part of the district. Care has been taken to ensure that no streets cut through the winding lanes that lead to the houses.[21]

Aerial view of the Habous quarter, c. 1924.

Albert Laprade, project for a market at the entrance to the new indigenous town, 1917. Perspective sketch.

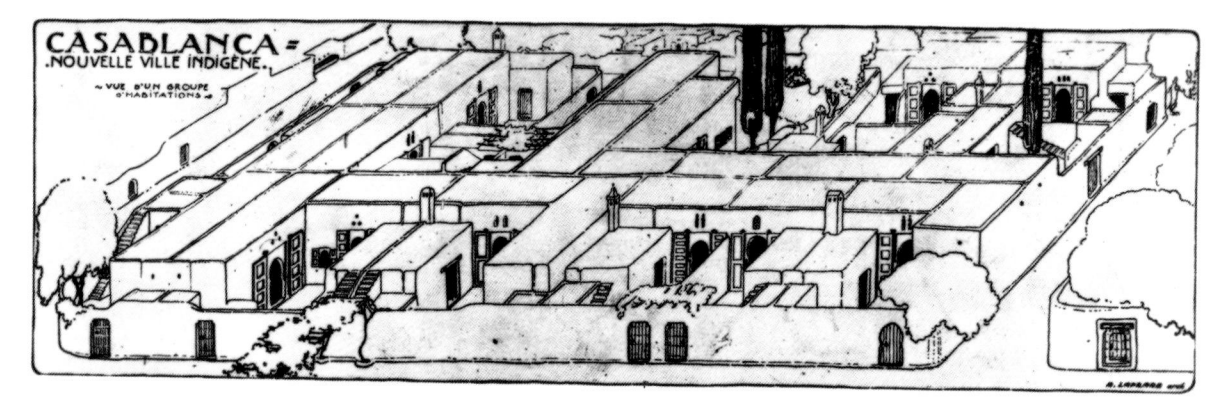

Albert Laprade, project for the new indigenous town, 1917. Housing, axonometric view.

Albert Laprade, project for the new indigenous town, 1917. "Views of various streets."

From a design perspective, the Habous quarter is a skillful combination of shopping arcades and blank walls that make up the housing, which cannot be accessed from the main street. The site itself occupies a skewed rectangle, crossed by the main street and tilted toward a market square shaped in the form of a horseshoe. The road curves slightly a third of the way down, concealing views of the square, around which are all the civic buildings—Koranic school, mosque, and *hammam*, or public bath. Laprade conceived his site plan and axonometry for this "residential neighborhood" as a collage of linear elements (the streets) and horizontal features (the housing units), hyphenated by the *fonduk* courtyards, which he wedged into the kinked angles. His aim was to endow the new native town with all the customary urban facilities, as well as spaces integral to Muslim tradition and religion: mosques, Moorish baths, squares, inns, a market, bazaars, and roughly 150 shop booths, both freestanding and grouped in a *kissaria*. Climbing vines were woven around wooden lathes above the crossroads, although this bears more overtones of Marrakech than of North Morocco or Andalusia. Cadet was put in charge of designing the *hammam*, as well as the main mosque (built "to an Almohad style" according to Laprade) and the principal arcades. Permanent markets and fairs soon sprang up, testifying to the quarter's success.

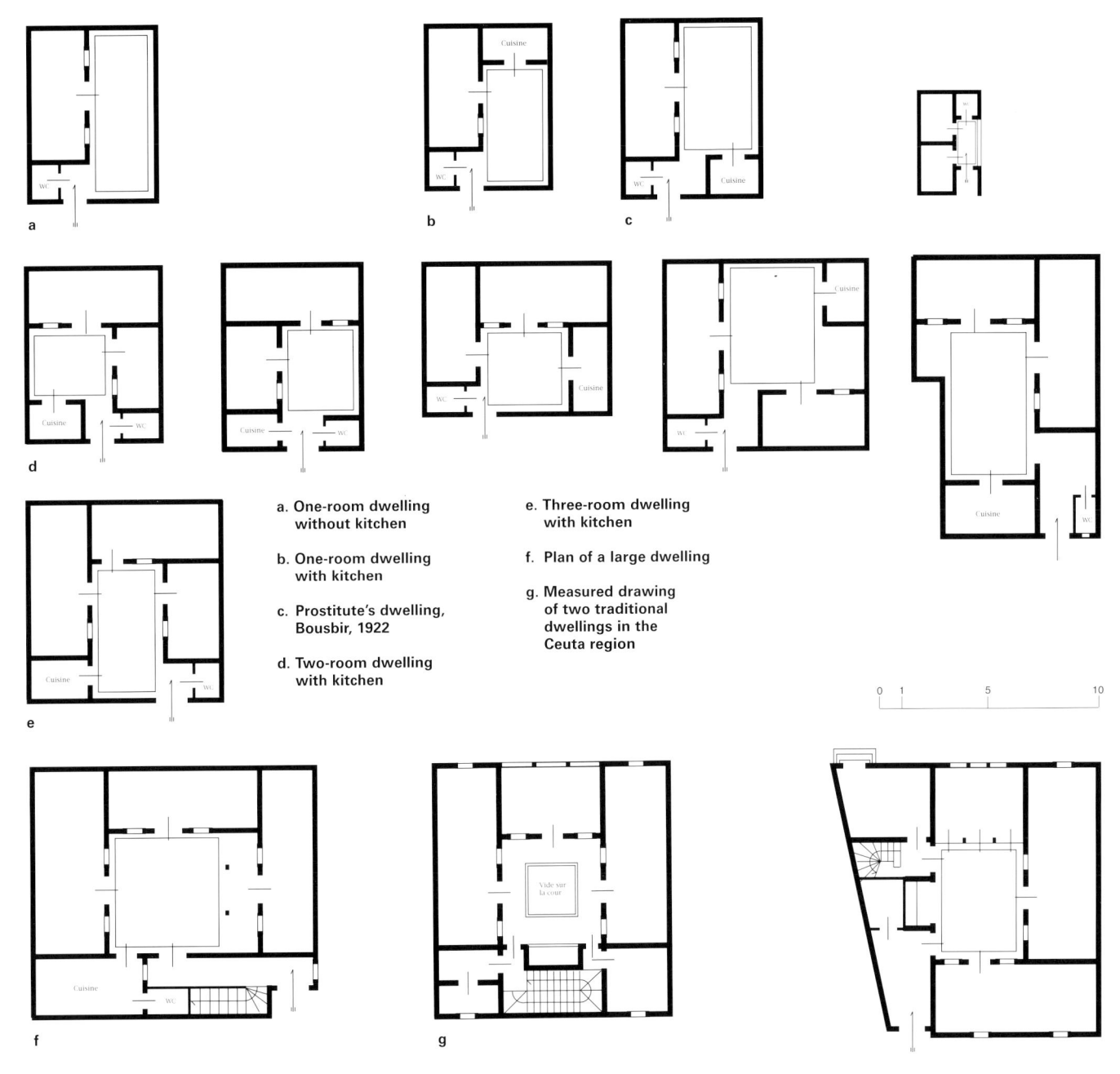

a. One-room dwelling without kitchen

b. One-room dwelling with kitchen

c. Prostitute's dwelling, Bousbir, 1922

d. Two-room dwelling with kitchen

e. Three-room dwelling with kitchen

f. Plan of a large dwelling

g. Measured drawing of two traditional dwellings in the Ceuta region

Housing types in the new medina. Drawings by Cristiana Mazzoni based on Laprade's general plan and various written accounts.

Single-family dwellings are on the ground and first floors. Only the ground-floor plans are shown here.

The layout of the smaller houses (which occupy a ground plan of around 40m²) is based on housing from rural areas and coastal towns. Apart from the one-room dwelling with courtyard, the rooms are usually set out in a square around the courtyard.

On the whole, the rooms are much longer than they are wide (2.4m on average). The entrance is generally of zigzag shape and the kitchen is a room in its own right, except for the one-room dwellings, which have no explicit kitchen area — just the *kanoun,** which has been shifted from the courtyard into the house.

The prostitutes' dwellings were designed using a similar type, though sometimes with two stories.

The larger houses (occupying a ground plan of between 150m² and 200m²) are laid out like bourgeois town houses. They have a courtyard, colonnades and reception room with a central door and side windows, though the rooms are no wider than those in the smaller dwellings, as illustrated in the Dinouri house. (see p. 222)

Despite the good-sized floor area of 150m² to 200m², these houses only have a small number of rooms, which are large and of oblong shape. Some have arches and windows with small columns, creating an air of grandeur.

For the purpose of comparison, see the measured drawings by Alfonso de Sierra of two traditional houses in the Ceuta region, published in *Vivienda Marroqui* (Ceuta: Editorial Cremades, 1960).

Dinouri house, 7 Rue Imam Ghazali, Habous quarter. The courtyard. Photographed in 1994.

22 According to Roger Le Tourneau, the traditional Moroccan houses of Fès are based "on the model of urban residences found throughout North Africa." Le Tourneau, *Fès avant le Protectorat*, 495.

23 Laprade, "Une ville créée spécialement pour les indigènes à Casablanca," 97–98. See also: R. de La Celle, "Casablanca (Dar el-Beïda), ses vieux souks, sa nouvelle médina," *L'Afrique du nord illustrée* 30, no. 751 (September 21, 1935): 2–3.

The dwellings, built by Cadet and Brion, are composed of rectangular units assembled back to back or at right angles, the depth of each block corresponding to two units. The dwellings' dimensions vary according to the residents' social status. In the smaller ones, one or two narrow rooms, generally measuring 2.5 meters long but with a 3.5-meter floor-to-ceiling height, are arranged around a private courtyard, in keeping with tradition. At the time of construction these small units had no kitchen, so the *kanoun** was shifted from the courtyard into the house. The larger houses contain L- and U-shaped rooms that open onto a sizable courtyard. The entrance in these dwellings is usually of zigzag form, and the kitchen takes up an entire room. These larger houses sometimes have two stories with a steep, narrow staircase leading to the bedroom(s) and storage rooms. The architects based the interior layout of these dwellings on that of bourgeois town houses, and included in their scheme a courtyard, colonnades, and a room for receiving guests[22]; in these town houses, the floor area is occasionally enlarged and enhanced by a column-lined gallery.

The smaller houses are located around the market square, whereas the larger ones are positioned near the mosque. Unexpected design features were incorporated into the dwellings, such as rooms on the second floor that straddle the lanes, and terraced structures whose side entries mark a break in the built pattern. The entrances to the dwellings were deliberately positioned so as not to face each other on either side of the street: "There are no direct views between the houses . . . Everything has been meticulously thought through to respect the overriding sense of mystery that envelops the private lives of Muslims."[23] The solutions adopted tied together pre-1914 theories of architects, politicians, and writers with respect to Moroccan housing culture. As early as 1912, Eugène Montfort had claimed that, in a sense, Moroccan dwellings were an artifact of civilization, to coin a contemporary term:

> Architecture . . . is a narrative about customs and traditions, providing insight into religion and beliefs. In accordance with the Koran's prohibition of windows overlooking the street, the towns all present long stretches of blank walls . . . Furthermore, the doors are always closed. Affluent Moroccan abodes all share a similar layout—a courtyard topped by a glazed dome and an ornamental basin in the center with a fountain that babbles constantly. At the rear there is a sort of recess that is accessed by one or two steps and has divans lining the walls. It is here that the host receives his

guests. Opposite this small open salon can generally be found the women's quarters, which are shut off by a Moorish door and tightly closed grille windows. Everything is spick-and-span.[24]

Whereas Montfort forgot to mention the roof terrace—that fundamental annex where women could socialize freely—Cadet and Brion's team was careful to include it. The entire housing scheme was rooted in detailed research into traditional Moroccan houses, the main difference between the model and the built version being that the latter reflected contemporary concerns for health and hygiene. The project also derived from drawings published in Jean Gallotti's book *Moorish Houses and Gardens of Morocco*.[25] Every room was linked up to the sewers, thereby knitting together European housing substructures and "typical features of Arab towns."[26] Henri Descamps furnished an in-depth account of this duality:

> Native customs and traditions have been preserved in the new Arab town: the thoroughfares are narrow, with attractive indents, and the houses turn in on themselves, opening onto the family patio. There have, however, been a few discreet additions

24 Montfort, "Maisons du Maroc," 457.

25 Jean Gallotti, *Moorish Houses and Gardens of Morocco*, 2 vols., illustrations by Albert Laprade, photographs by Lucien Vogel, Félix, VveP. R. Schmitt, G. Faure and Canu (New York: William Helburn, inc., [1926]). (First published as: *Le jardin et la maison arabes au Maroc*. Paris: Éditions Albert Lévy, 1926).

26 A. H. Sabatier, "Les habitations à bon marché au Maroc," *Urbanisme* no. 46 (July–August 1936): 292.

A fountain in the Habous quarter, c. 1925.

Shopping street in the Habous quarter, c. 1925.

with respect to modern science; for instance, the dirt-covered roof terraces and insect-infested beams have been replaced by reinforced concrete, and the lavatories are all connected to the sewers. Electricity and telephones have been provided; the streets are now clean, and although winding, they are wide enough to accommodate street-cleaning vehicles. Yet these new amenities do not in any way encroach on the original spirit of ancient Oriental lifestyle.[27]

In Vaillat's opinion, the "white cubic houses are not coldly severe, but on the contrary are warm and welcoming, having been designed in a sensitive and solicitous fashion." Laprade's scheme "has respected the traditional Muslim house plan, which aside from a few minor differences, can be likened to the ancient Mediterranean dwelling." As Vaillat saw it, Laprade's solutions stemmed from his cultural background and personal tastes: "He was so enamored of Arab houses, which are so basic in design yet so bright and intimate, that from the outset he sought not just to include as many modern conveniences as possible, but above all to keep the walls vibrantly white and loaded with poetical force, so that the future occupants would feel truly at home rather than feeling imprisoned."[28]

Laprade may have based his design on "poor people's housing in Rabat and Salé,"[29] but the rooms of his "Arab house" published in Gallotti's book are depicted in Western terms, even though the whole essence of Moroccan dwellings resides precisely in their multifunctionality. Furthermore, the guest room (*bit el diaf*) is the only room treated in true ornamental fashion. Nonetheless, the skills of the architectural team are clearly apparent in the initial 257 units that were built in the quarter; they are of mixed types and were designed individually in order to reproduce the same quality as their urban and rural prototypes. Eyewitness accounts stress the "authentic" aspect of "the most majestic ancient city in the whole of Morocco," to quote Abdallah Zrika, however ironical this statement may seem.[30] Any risk that the buildings might come across as monotonously similar due to their being built simultaneously was obviated by the variety of the housing types and the way in which exterior spaces were handled. Mosaic fountains, *zillij*-clad benches tucked into niches, and wooden lattices woven with bougainvillaea and jasmine stretching from wall to wall all form part of an intricately designed landscape, as do the ficus, eucalyptus, and palm trees planted during the construction phase.[31]

Laprade did not conceal the project's political objectives: "Peasants, port workers, and factory laborers can trade their goods, pray, and amuse themselves without impinging on the European town." This, he pointed out, "will keep conflict to a minimum."[32] Yet the houses were rapidly occupied by more affluent families than expected—often Fassi shop owners, who had the resources to live in them and ensure their upkeep, and who slipped easily into these dwellings inscribed in their own canonic traditions.[33] By 1932, the new medina was home to three thousand residents, and other districts swiftly sprouted around the initial core. Meanwhile, in the 1920s the "Cité Municipale," or *Derb el-Baladiya*,* was developed ten hectares south of the railroad tracks, inaugurating a different urban policy: it was no longer a question of having finely detailed schemes drafted by architects such as Laprade and Cadet; instead, plots were bought up by the public authorities and leased for a ninety-nine year period traditionally called a *zina*. Dwellings built in keeping with Moroccan practices were erected on these plots, although regulations pertaining to height restrictions and hygienic facilities were of a fairly basic order. One such plot is Derb Carlotti, which developed in the northeast corner bounded by the railroad tracks and the Route de Médiouna; it was originally populated by Fassi shop owners and suburban farmers as well as by former residents of the old medina.[34]

A corner house in the Habous quarter, in Henri Descamps, *L'architecture moderne au Maroc*, 1930.

Albert Laprade, plan of a traditional "Arab house." Illustration published in Jean Gallotti, *Le jardin et la maison arabes au Maroc*, 1926.

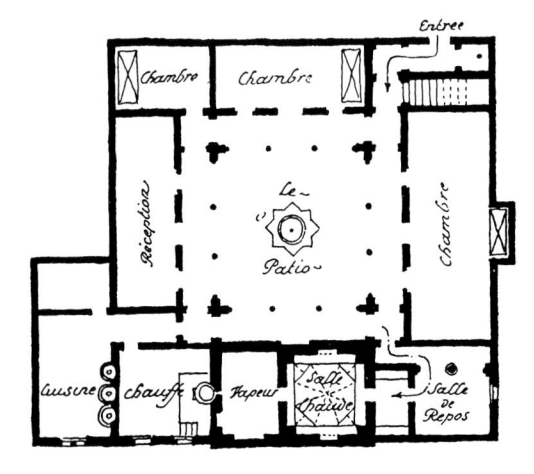

[27] Henri Descamps, *L'Architecture moderne au Maroc*, vol. 2: *Constructions particulières*.

[28] Vaillat, "La nouvelle médina de Casablanca," 225.

[29] Laprade, "Une ville créée spécialement pour les indigènes à Casablanca," 97.

[30] Abdallah Zrika, "La Cité des Habous," in Alain Bourdon, Didier Folléas (dir.), *Casablanca, fragments d'imaginaire*, vol. 11.

[31] Today, most of the inhabitants of the Habous and of Casablanca think that the town is ancient and that it was built by Moroccans in the "good and true tradition." This notion confirms the fact that the district's design respects the way of life of Moroccan Muslims.

[32] Laprade, "Une ville créée spécialement pour les indigènes à Casablanca," 99.

[33] Brian Brace Taylor, "Planned Discontinuity: Modern Colonial Cities in Morocco," *Lotus International*, no. 26 (1980): 60.

[34] Jean-Louis Miège, "La nouvelle médina de Casablanca; le derb Carlotti," *Les Cahiers d'Outre-mer* 6, no. 23 (1953): 244–57.

Bousbir, or Picturesque Debauchery

The 1920s witnessed the creation of one of Casablanca's strangest quarters—a "reserved district" called Bousbir, whose underlying concept originated in cynical and methodical thinking. Prost masterminded the whole scheme, inspired by the Yoshiwara in Tokyo,[35] and claimed that the main objective was to "curb debauchery to prevent it from rotting the darkest depths of the city."[36] Bousbir was the name of a central area that had become known as the "red town," in view of the numerous brothels there.[37] In 1923, these brothels were moved to a purpose-specific quadrangular plot south of Derb Carlotti, and the name of the district migrated with the function.

Laprade's initial plan occupied a rectangular parcel with an orthogonal road pattern. However, in the built scheme, Cadet and Brion continued with their picturesque treatment of traditional forms as in the Habous quarter. Twenty-one housing blocks containing 175 units were laid out inside a polygonal enclosure, around a main road measuring ten meters wide and sixty meters long.[38] A health center, eight cafés, and forty-two shop booths were sprinkled along the street network, which was adeptly designed to follow the site's slope and was accessed by a single, guarded entrance. As many as seven hundred Muslim and Jewish women lived in this prisonlike complex, two to a room:

Bird's-eye view of the new medina, c. 1924. In the foreground: Bousbir. At left: Derb el-Baladiya. At right: Derb Carlotti. In the background are the Habous quarter and sultan's palace.

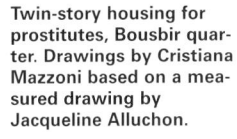

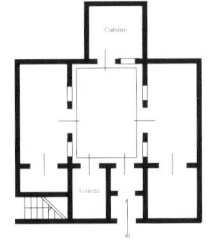

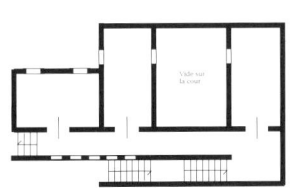

Twin-story housing for prostitutes, Bousbir quarter. Drawings by Cristiana Mazzoni based on a measured drawing by Jacqueline Alluchon.

35 The Japanese reference is mentioned by André Colliez, *Notre protectorat marocain*, 212.

36 Henri Prost, *Village indigène*.

37 On the mythical history of the place, see J. E. Laurent Saint-Aignan, *Bousbir, ville réservée* (Rabat: Éditions d'art J. E. Laurent, 1950).

38 The municipality facilitated the creation of the private La Cressonnière company on the new land, to which it granted a long-term lease and gave the responsibility of realizing the project by the administration.

Auguste Cadet and Edmond Brion, Bousbir quarter, 1922. Postcard showing an interior square, c. 1930.

Auguste Cadet and Edmond Brion, Bousbir quarter, 1922. Watercolor published in Saint-Aignan, J.E. Laurent, *Bousbir, ville réservée*, 1950.

> Each woman's bedroom is built to the same model. Take Khadouj's room, for instance. It is part of a two-story house with an outside staircase leading up to the second floor from a courtyard measuring 3 meters by 3 meters. The stairs end in a gallery that provides access to two rooms. The ground floor similarly comprises two rooms, measuring roughly 2 meters by 5 meters, with no opening other than a door facing the courtyard. A tiny lavatory (1.6 meters by 0.8 meters) and a kitchen (1.6 meters by 1.3 meters) complete the ensemble.[39]

The quarter was intended to provide "integral insight into the Eastern world" through its "picturesque presentation of Moroccan urban planning."[40] Tourist guides did not fail to mention this district—"a favorite with painters and roving amateur photographers"—which so resembled "the pure Moroccan-style houses" of the Habous.[41] Writers and reporters likewise sought out the streets of Bousbir. Albert Londres stayed there for a whole week, and Pierre Mac Orlan dedicated several pages of his *Légionnaires* to it in 1930, followed by an article in 1934 on the world's "backwaters."[42] During the same period, Hendrik de Leeuw ranked Casablanca among the "Western world's towns of sin" and related his visit to Bousbir, which a special bus service linked to the city center in just seventeen minutes:

> I was greeted by a delightful spectacle. Beside the entrance was a souk, with fountains sparkling against the myriad colors of their mosaic setting, nestled amid a mass of lush plants whose leaves rustled in the breeze, echoing the delights of the Côte d'Azur. The French experts had apparently thought of everything in their aim to fashion a modern town out of chaos. There was a Moorish bath, wide and airy boulevards, and a cinema showing erotic films . . . There were shops selling all sorts of exotic products and hundreds of charming houses, while the narrow, refreshingly cool streets were adorned with benches and trees which lent this love market a near-rural air.[43]

Conceived as a heterotopia transplanted outside the center, Bousbir crystallizes the image of colonial Casablanca, as much in its elaborately picturesque decor as in the way it perpetuated the image painted since the nineteenth century of "public women" in North Africa.[44] Simone de Beauvoir figured among the visitors to Bousbir, following "the tradition forged by Gide, Larbaud, and Morand, among many others," and in *La Force de l'âge* describes the "shame" she felt on seeing what seemed to her to resemble "one of those artificial villages displayed in certain exhibitions."[45] This "must" for tourists of all types, including writers, was eventually closed in 1954.

---

39 Jean Mathieu and P. H. Maury, *La Prostitution marocaine surveillée de Casablanca; le quartier réservé* (n.p., [1951]), 44.

40 "Un aspect pittoresque de l'urbanisme marocain," *L'Afrique du Nord illustrée* 25, no. 492 (October 4, 1930): 8.

41 Henri Couette, *Casablanca et sa région* (Casablanca: Éditions Maroc-Presse, 1941), 30. See also: Charles Penz, "Le quartier réservé de Casablanca," in "Le Maroc en 1938," special issue of *L'Afrique du Nord illustrée*, (1938): 70–71.

42 Pierre Mac Orlan, *Légionnaires: à la Légion étrangère espagnole, à la Légion étrangère française* (Paris: Éditions du Capitole, 1930); and "Bousbir," in *Rues secrètes* (Paris: Gallimard, 1934): 64–93.

43 Hendrik de Leeuw, *Sinful Cities of the Western World* (New York: Citadel, 1934), 99–100.

44 Malek Alloula, *The Colonial Harem*, trans. Myrna and Wlad Godzich (Minneapolis: University of Minnesota Press, 1986; First published as: *Le Harem colonial, images d'un sous-érotisme*. (Paris: Garance, 1991).

45 Simone de Beauvoir, *The Prime of Life*, trans. Peter Green (Cleveland: World Publishing Co., 1962). (First published as: *La Force de l'âge*. Paris: Gallimard, 1960), 262.

Early Housing Schemes for Working-Class Europeans

For many months of the year, rainwater stagnates in an impermeable ravine. While the rest of Morocco may lack water, this is certainly not the case for the Maarif—"Casablanca's Venice"—where one requires waders to walk through the streets, ironically named by the administration after mountains: Mt. Blanc, Mt. Cenis, Mt. Cinto, etc. The predominantly Spanish population is chiefly working class.

Jean Marc, 1930[46]

The influx of European manual laborers and bottom-rung office workers caused housing demand to hit a record high in the new European town. Spaniards and Italians, together with French migrants from Algeria and Tunisia, settled in "Spanish" buildings, so called for their courtyards that were converted into service spaces for the dwellings, and for their walkways with wrought-iron railings. Other large courtyard buildings accommodated occupants grouped by origin, such as those from Algeria. Elsewhere, laborers lived side by side with French, Spanish, and Italian craftsmen, these last having often only recently been granted citizenship.

The workers' housing block in Rue du Caporal-Beaux in the Liberté quarter, nicknamed *la caserne* (the barracks) by its residents, can be seen as a local version of the *courée* (a typical courtyard workers' housing scheme), which was a widespread feature in northern France. This configuration—four stories set out around a main courtyard with two openwork side staircases providing access to corridors leading to mostly two- and sometimes three-room units—gave rise to a self-contained community. Cramped living conditions meant that numerous domestic activities spilled out into the galleries and courtyard, generating a true sense of community. In addition, the windows in the tiny kitchens and in some of the rooms overlook the communal access walkways. The atmosphere in this apartment house resembled the "large dwelling" referred to by Mohammed Dib, which could be typically found in Algeria.[47] It functioned as *de facto* workers' housing built without public aid and testifies to the involvement of private companies in low-cost housing schemes, as in pre-1914 France.[48]

Housing "barracks," Rue du Caporal-Beaux, c. 1920. Courtyard and walkways. Photographed in 1994.

---

46 Jean Marc, "L'œuvre française au Maroc: Casablanca la nouvelle," *L'Exportateur français*, (Paris), October 9, 1930: 53.

47 Mohammed Dib, *La Grande maison* (Paris: Seuil, 1952).

48 A. H. Sabatier underlined "the total success of projects undertaken by private companies during the early years of the Protectorate." As an example he cited the Casa Logis building located on Boulevard de Lorraine, a few steps away from the "barracks" where rents are "lower than rents paid in town [thanks to a] rental-sale plan." Sabatier, "Les habitations à bon marché au Maroc," 289.

49 Janine Nicolas, "Un quartier de Casablanca, le Maârif," *Cahiers d'Outre-mer*, no. 63, (July–September 1963): 283.

50 Nicolas, "Un quartier de Casablanca, le Maârif," 298.

The Maarif—An Urban Village

A similar kind of population lived in the Maarif housing subdivision built adjacent to the road leading to Mazagan. Set quite a way from the center, the houses in this quarter resemble working-class suburbs built in previous years in Andalusian coastal towns. Development began in 1911, when three English merchants bought land there "fifty times cheaper than in the center," a price difference that "attracted many Spanish and Italian immigrants [to the quarter], who had arrived with hope-filled hearts but empty pockets."[49] Like the nearby Derb Ghallef, the district's success highlighted the unrealistic side of Prost's plan with regard to housing for the people with the lowest incomes. On a grid pattern that left no room for public spaces, this quarter was for a long time separated from the center by fields, typifying the haphazardly built enclave developments that marked the outskirts of Casablanca. It was chiefly made up of enclosures containing small houses and low buildings with flat roofs and balconies. Janine Nicolas has classified this neighborhood according to three housing types: courtyard dwellings, villas, and small apartment blocks. The first type corresponds to "the so-called Algerian house—a single-story abode adorned with an openwork balustrade" with "small rooms leading to a rear courtyard, similar to the Muslim or Spanish patio."[50] It was primarily built by contractors without the aid of an architect and was widely adopted throughout Casablanca's working-class districts. Small interwar houses with one or two stories make up the second type; these pompously christened "villas" were in fact designed merely as basic dwellings with one communal room, a kitchen, and one or two other rooms opening on to a small garden. The last category evolved out of the practice, adopted from 1925 onward, of adding levels to single-story houses to create apartment buildings, though these seldom exceeded four floors.

The numerous artisan workshops, warehouses, shop booths, and cafés all generated a warm and bustling atmosphere in these working-class streets. A local

Aerial view of the Maarif, c. 1922. Note the first church of the area (center of photo).

A house in the Maarif. Photographed in 1994.

newspaper was launched, and in the 1920s the "Free Commune of Maarif" was established, sparking annual celebrations during the "neighborhood's good old days." There was a strong sense of belonging, and residents even felt that they were more "Maarifian" than Casablancan. A sleepy district in the daytime, it "came alive as soon as the sun went down, as in Seville and Granada,"[51] with a gamut of nationalities thronging the pavements and café terraces. It functioned as a tightly knit, multicultural society (mostly of Mediterranean origins) and was based on a system of mutual cooperation, even though some hierarchical order between classes and nationalities did continue to exist. Poverty was rife, leading to the establishment of philanthropic and religious associations from the outset, together with educational and health facilities, such as medical centers, a hospice, and supply of free milk for infants. Idriss El Khoury, who was a schoolboy in the 1940s in Derb Ghallef, remembers that, far from being "a closed area or guarded by formidable armed policemen," the Maarif was "open to absolutely everyone," unlike the bourgeois residential districts.[52]

Experiments in Low-Cost Housing

At the same time as the Maarif was being energetically injected with a large dose of private initiative, the Protectorate was endeavoring to develop an affordable postwar housing policy. Mortgage funds with thirty-year repayment plans were set up in 1919, as was a housing commission, with a view to constructing modern working-class developments and low-cost housing.[53] The commission was largely modeled on French legislation.[54]

The low-cost housing schemes, or Habitations à bon marché (abbreviated to HBM), benefited from loans at reduced interest and were exempt from city tax until the end of the loan period. The municipal authority was encouraged to acquire shares in these companies, which had to comply with health and hygiene regulations laid down by the Public Health Commission. Legislation took time to be enacted, notably due to high building costs in the city center and to the fact that available suburban plots were difficult to access. The War Veteran Office and Department of Housing, catering to large families, were in charge of selecting the first occupants.

51 Michel de la Varde, *Casablanca ville d'émeutes* (Givors: André Martel, 1955), 13.

52 Idriss El Khoury, "Qui sommes-nous pour ce monde blanc?," in Bourdon and Folléas, eds., *Casablanca, fragments d'imaginaire*, vol. 4.

53 "Crise des logements," *France-Maroc* 3 (June 15, 1919): 25. This commission took on its true scope only in 1929, when it was transformed into the Caisse de prêts immobiliers du Maroc (Mortgage Fund of Morocco) and when loan legislation was recast, especially for villas (under the aegis of the Crédit foncier de France and its affiliate, the Crédit foncier d'Algérie et de Tunisie).

54 The commission's primary functions were "to determine the type of buildings to be created, be they individual or collective, whether susceptible to appropriation by the occupants or not; to distribute the loans of the Caisse de prêts immobiliers between the different low-rent housing companies; and to fix the maximum rents relative to each type of building and location." See *Chantiers nord-africains* 4, no. 2 (February 1932): 151–52. Initial legislation is the *dahir* of December 24, 1919, regarding low-rent housing companies, *BO*, 1919.

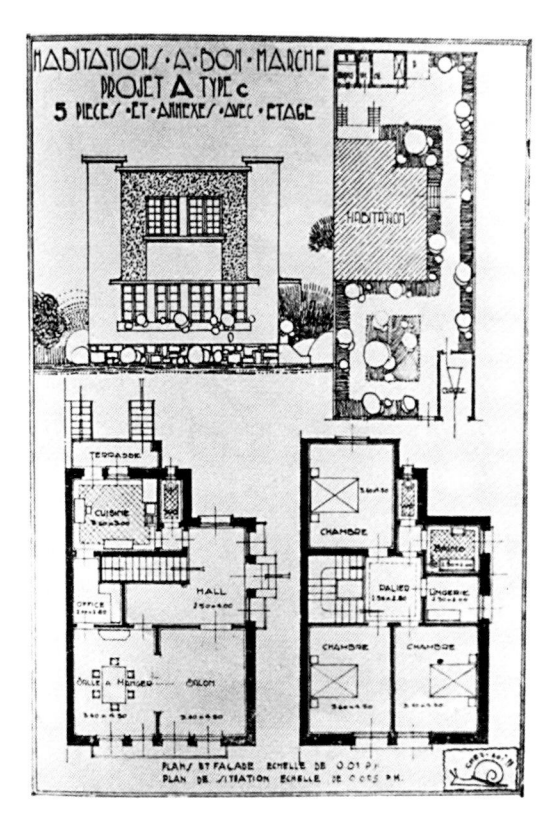

Marius Boyer and Jean Balois, project for a two-bedroom house type with potential extension space, 1928. Published in *Les habitations salubres et à bon marché*, 1928.

55 Moroccan government, *Les Habitations salubres et à bon marché: projets primés au concours des modèles d'habitations (août 1928)* (Casablanca: Imprimeries réunies, 1928).

56 *BMO*, May–June 1928.

57 E. Poix, "L'histoire et l'avenir de Casablanca," *Le Bâtiment* (May 10, 1931), 3.

58 Sabatier, "Les habitations à bon marché au Maroc," 288.

59 "Villas à Casablanca, Arrivetx, architecte," *Chantiers nord-africains* 3, no. 3 (March 1931): 295. See also: Poix, "L'histoire et l'avenir de Casablanca," 3.

60 Sabatier, "Les habitations à bon marché au Maroc," 292. As in most official publications of the time, here the term *Sharifian* stands for Moroccan.

61 "Villas marocaines," *Chantiers nord-africains* no. 12 (December 1931): 1213.

Although it was not to take effect until the following decade, the *dahir** of July 14, 1928, marked a new step in the process by creating specific corporations for salubrious and low-cost housing. At the same time, the Protectorate organized a competition to develop a "low-cost salubrious housing prototype." The competition winners were not only prominent architects, such as Marius Boyer, Jean Balois, and Adrien Laforgue, but also newcomers, including Louis Fleurant and M. Vandelle. All the entrants proposed small houses with two to four rooms, complete with bathroom, garage, and ancillary domestic quarters; extensions could be added in some cases if required.[55] As it was, though, the competition did not result in any built works.

Members of the Casablanca Municipal Council vied with one another in their attempts to drive the Moroccans out of the center. In 1928, Jean Rabaud suggested constructing low-cost housing blocks in Sidi-Belyout, a central quarter, "so that residents would not have to travel long distances, as this is a costly business." Marcel Rivollet remarked, "Barrack-type blocks with appropriate hygienic facilities" constituted the only realistic building type. The chairman of the Crédit Foncier mortgage fund, Grillot, stated a preference for a "residential neighborhood with single-family dwellings, which would be more pleasant for laborers and office workers to live in than multistory buildings." Georges Gillet, a qualified civil engineer, regarded low-cost housing schemes as "pure financial heresy," recommending that legislation be enacted "compelling owners of old apartment blocks to refurbish their property and bring it in line with norms, notably with regard to health and hygiene." He also proposed "setting up public schemes whereby residents could purchase a tract of land and have a house built for very little money."[56] Talks went on for a long time in this vein, without ever coming to anything.

It was still considered top priority in the early 1930s to provide accommodation for public servants and to help the French and other European working-class populations find "affordable salubrious housing."[57] As the judge A. H. Sabatier cynically, or perhaps artlessly, noted in 1936, this objective was rendered all the more urgent by the fact that "while Arab workers may be adept at living in self-built huts, slums and shacks, this is not true for European workers."[58]

A double setback emerged, however. First, the Protectorate dropped its prototype project, after which the municipal authority eliminated its low-cost housing program. Public initiatives were restricted to granting individual mortgages, monitoring health and hygiene, and ensuring that each venture fulfilled certain "artistic" requirements. The majority of "low-cost salubrious housing" in fact comprised modern houses, such as those built by the architect René Arrivetx in conjunction with the Caisse des Prêts Immobiliers, a mortgage fund devoted to war veterans and large families.[59]

Soon after this indirect public intervention program got under way, the government decided to apply the financial brakes. Sabatier noted, "Just before the Sharifian state was forced to freeze all projects in 1934, due to the growing recession, it had been estimated that the housing program (which had broken even thus far) would have resulted in the construction of 1,500 detached houses in Morocco over a five-year period, i.e., one a day."[60] As it was, with the program's abandonment, very few low-cost European housing schemes were realized. However, other observers noted that, if the "low-income housing trend [had] not yet made its mark in Morocco, it [was] because the country [was] too young, its people too mobile."[61]

The programs that did come to fruition were attuned to the local context; furthermore, it is interesting to note that standards governing floor area and modern comforts were higher than in metropolitan France. For instance, apart from the servants' lavatory, the amenities of the low-cost eleven-story housing block built in

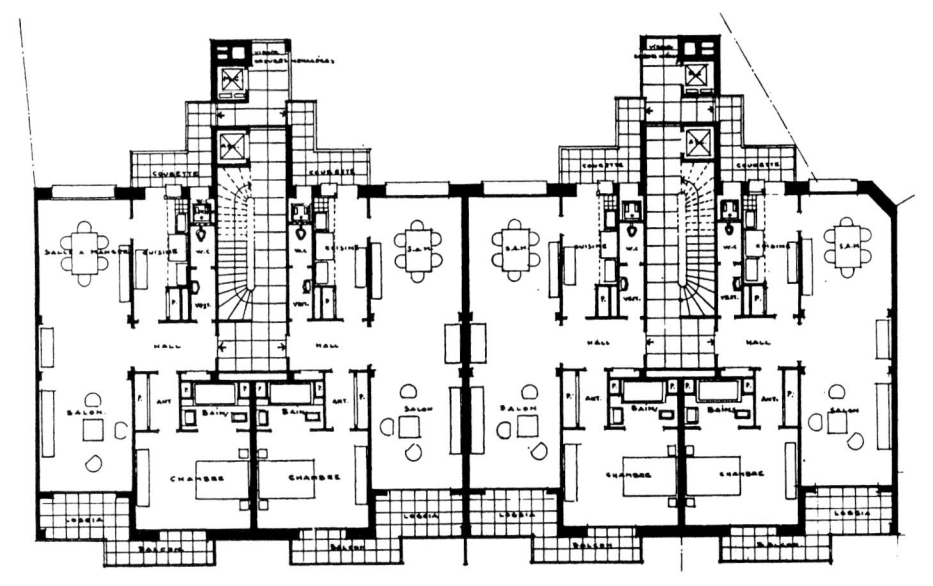

Marcel Desmet, low-rent housing building, 349 Boulevard de la Gare, 1935.

Marcel Desmet, low-rent housing building, 349 Boulevard de la Gare, 1935. Standard floor plan, in *L'Architecture d'aujourd'hui*, March 1936.

The lounge and dining room form a large through room with a loggia leading on from the lounge. There is a long, fitted kitchen that opens on to the dining room and a small courtyard containing a servants' lavatory. The bedrooms have balconies, an antechamber, a cupboard, and a bathroom, as in a hotel room.

1935 by Marcel Desmet on Boulevard de la Gare closely resembled those later designed for French public housing in the 1970s.[62] As *L'Architecture d'aujourd'hui* pointed out, "It is fitted with running hot water, a waste-disposal system, and two main elevators," even though elevators were normally found only in luxury apartment buildings.[63] Additionally, the ground-floor shops were all designed on an individual basis. The cladding is typical of the period: the porticoes along Boulevard de la Gare are covered in red polished marble from Wadi Akreuch, while the entrance is clad in marble and terrazzo. Nevertheless, the scheme can be considered an exception to the rule, given that from 1935 onward European working-class accommodations were financed exclusively by private sources.

Company-Funded Ventures

Many housing projects were undertaken by the private sector, in contrast to the rather cautious policy espoused by the Protectorate. An early example of workers' housing is the design conceived by Auguste Perret for his own company in 1919, when he viewed his venture in Casablanca as a long-term enterprise. The plans reveal a complex of "single-story family dwellings" with courtyards and gardens, with each unit containing a communal room and two bedrooms situated along the symmetrical facade in a layout comparable to French minimum housing of the period, but adapted to local conditions. The bathroom (a first for this housing type) is the same size as the kitchen, while the lavatory and laundry, accessed from the courtyard, are fitted out in the local vernacular.[64] However, the scheme was never actually built, as Perret's Moroccan operations stopped.

Some medium-sized companies also built accommodations for their staff in the form of small blocks outside the city center. This was the case for the "Asayag villas," built in the 1920s in the Racine quarter by an unknown designer and named after the philanthropic employer who commissioned them. The houses are set in

62 Desmet's building contained forty-six one- to three-room apartments and was crowned by four studios with large, covered roof terraces.

63 "HLM, 349 bd de la Gare," *L'Architecture d'aujourd'hui* (March 1936): 74.

64 IFA, fonds Perret.

Ciments Lafarge workers' housing development, Boulevard Laurent Guerrero and Route de Mazagan, 1922-1923. Aerial view, photographed in 1924.

Each house has four rooms. Some of the houses are split, forming two semi-detached dwellings with two rooms each. They all have a small garden with outside lavatories placed between each pair of houses.

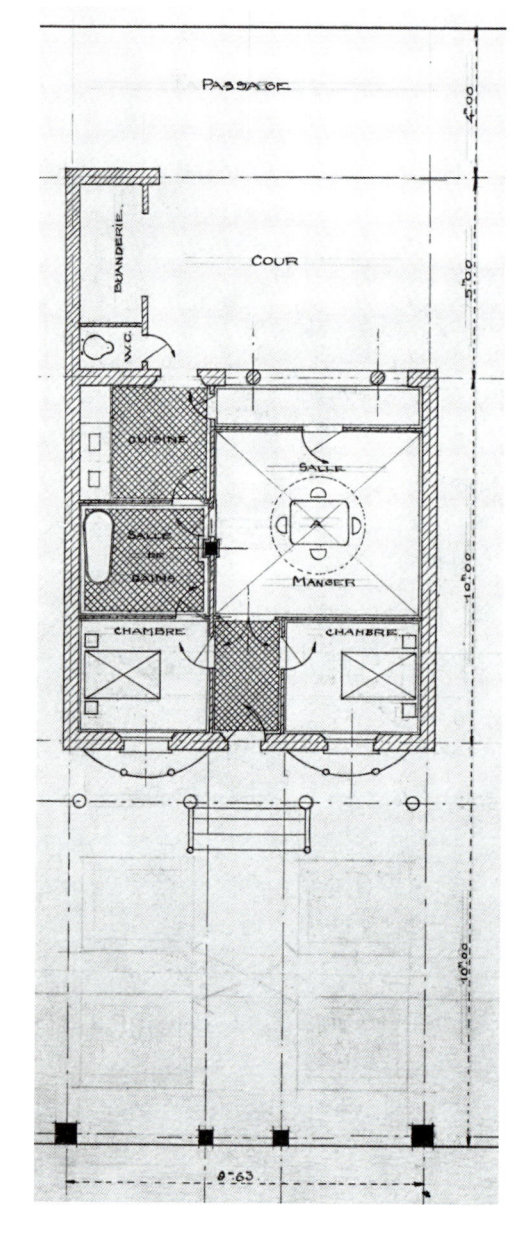

65 De Montarnal et Deloncle to Nacivet, director of the Office du Protectorat in Paris, May 17, 1922 (from the *Gazette financière marocaine*), BGA, Travaux, aménagement de Rues et bâtiments (1921–22). Having expended its budget on slaughterhouses, the municipality rejected the architects' request for funding in August 1922. The housing development was never built.

Auguste Perret, plan for a single-story family dwelling, 1919.

Jean and Jean-Marie de Montarnal and Deloncle, project for a workers' development, Roches Noires, 1921. Perspectives.

three rows parallel to a courtyard; some of them are split in two to accommodate two families, and all came with a kitchen. Another employer-funded housing scheme was set up between 1922 and 1923 in the Maarif extension: each of the twenty-five single-story dwellings in this development is topped by a glazed dome covering a central, top-lit room. Although a clear hierarchy was established between dwellings for blue-collar and white-collar workers, and between single and family accommodations, all these schemes were plainly targeted at Europeans.

The first genuine large-scale workers' housing program was proposed in 1921 by the Parisian architects Montarnal and Deloncle, who designed their project along the lines of Tony Garnier's Cité Industrielle of 1917.[65] The program encompassed five hundred units located south of Roches Noires, between the road to Rabat and the road leading to the station; the units are set on a six-hectare ground plan arranged in the shape of an open V. In addition, the architects applied for pub-

232 Casablanca

Pierre Bousquet, workers' housing for the Chemins de fer du Maroc, Rue Claude Debussy, c. 1926. Photographed in 1993.

lic funding for two-story houses with open porches, grouped back-to-back in rows of ten.[66] Cooperative buildings completed the complex, though the scheme never got beyond project phase.

Meanwhile, in the 1920s the Moroccan railroad company commissioned semidetached housing, also south of Roches Noires. These dwellings, situated beside the tracks, were intended for the company's supervisors and were in the form of cubes.[67] In 1926, the same company asked the municipal architect Pierre Bousquet to design housing for its managerial staff.[68] Working in association with Soblanca (the company in charge of developing the station area), Bousquet and the contractor Ferrara produced a tiered scheme, ranging from semidetached houses to apartment blocks. This prototype would be reproduced in other quarters near the rail tracks, notably in Roches Noires.

Some industrialists also commissioned housing for their Moroccan rural migrant laborers who subsequently vacated their shantytowns and *noualla** districts. The quality of these dwellings was mediocre and their culture-specific features almost nonexistent. The 1913 Chaux et Ciments development (since demolished) was the first scheme of this kind; it accommodated some 150 families, with each dwelling comprising a kitchen and a rectangular room overlooking a courtyard of similar size. More than twenty years after its construction, the hygienist doctors Gaud and Sicaud declared that this housing development offered "magnificent living conditions for the native Moroccans." However, they also noted the following:

> Despite its advantages, the kitchen is never used, and the local women continue to cook outside, come sun or rain. Moreover, they keep a brazier going in the main room when it is cold, which is a much more dangerous practice than lighting a kitchen fire, and the semienclosed courtyard lavatories are often converted into a tiny room. The Chaux et Ciments company commissioned 140 of these new units, set in groups of four, creating an entire village complete with sewage facilities, wells, roads, and a market. It was a fine initiative indeed, and has since been imitated, in general successfully, by other companies.[69]

According to the lawyer Yvonne Mahé, construction began in 1927 on workers' housing built by Pavin-Lafarge, a company specializing in cement. Mahé points out

66 The architects recalled the earlier success of the *compartiment d'Indochine* (Indo-China compartment)—a type of compact residence used during the French colonization of Vietnam. Jean and Jean-Marie de Montarnal and Deloncle, "Création d'une cité ouvrière," BGA, Travaux, aménagement de Rues et bâtiments (1921–22). The land belonged to the Omnium Lyonnais company.

67 They were destroyed in 1996.

68 The first group of villas for company personnel was followed by a school for "children of colonists" and, in 1931, by a "larger" group of staff dwellings. "Le Maroc en 1932," 50.

69 M. Gaud and G. Sicaud, "L'habitat indigène au Maroc," *Bulletin de l'Institut d'hygiène du Maroc*, no. 4 (1937) 85–86. Gaud was the Protectorate's director of Public Health and Hygiene; Sicaud was a doctor.

Edmond Brion, Lafarge workers' development, Rue du Lieutenant Vidal, c. 1932. Main entrance, photographed in 1991.

70 Yvonne Mahé, "L'extension des villes indigènes au Maroc," (Ph.D. diss., Faculté de droit de Bordeaux, 1936), 55–56.

Adrien Laforgue phosphates workers' development, Rue du Lieutenant Bruyant, 1929. Main entrance. Photographed in 1996.

that, unlike its fellow developments, the Pavin-Lafarge complex "is not walled, but is nonetheless sufficiently private." The company's single laborers were housed in "premises near the factory but away from the family area."[70] Pavin-Lafarge did not stop at this scheme—by the 1950s it had constructed three such developments (two of which had shops and a school), accounting for some 347 units in all. Poliet et Chausson, another cement firm, together with J. J. Carnaud, a metal manufacturing company in the slaughterhouse district, also built housing for their workers directly opposite the factories. Poliet et Chausson opted for a complex of eight blocks, each building comprising ten one-room units with a communal kitchen and lavatories, whereas J. J. Carnaud decided on fifteen single-family dwellings containing a bedroom, lavatory, and small courtyard, a solution that would become the norm for this housing type.

The Khouribga phosphate company would later develop the concept of the kitchen-shelter, which was generally heralded as a step forward. During the interwar period, it commissioned Adrien Laforgue to build a small development for its port workers near the company's landing stage. Laforgue, who was already well known for his design of Casablanca's post office and many public buildings in Rabat, came up with another noteworthy architectural experiment here. The overall scheme reads as a walled enclosure, accessed by a monumental gate capped with green tiles. However, the dwellings themselves were spartan, and a health center formed the sole communal facility. As in the other schemes, families and single residents were separated, the latter being housed at the entrance to discourage them from disrupting family life in the core of the development.

Built mostly in the 1920s, these early company-funded ventures reveal the divide between low-cost housing schemes of the period and overall urban policy in Casablanca, especially when one considers the luxury private dwellings that were then being commissioned. The institutional framework resembled that of late-nineteenth-century France and so public aid was limited. Eventually, though, unsanitary conditions began to take their toll, worsened by the massive influx of immigrants in the 1930s; this led to health and hygiene inquiries, the results of which prompted the business community and decision makers to take proper action and set up decent facilities.

From Bidonville to the Beginnings of "Culture-Specific" Housing

Bidonville is synonymous with a tinplate town. Immigrants looking for work used to live in tents set up in camps . . . where the city's garbage lay rotting in heaps. To ward off the high risk of contamination, the public authorities forcibly evicted the occupants and set fire to the place. The people were allocated a field in the suburbs, near a water source. New shelters subsequently sprang up, made of old plates of corrugated iron, bits of tarred crates, and flattened petrol drums, taking on the shape of an actual town. Today, Bidonville is a hideous suburban sprawl, where squares and streets are only slowly beginning to be mapped out.

Friedrich Sieburg, 1938[71]

The concept behind the post-1945 Protectorate policy of adapting mass housing to each ethnic group can be traced back to 1936. This was when A. H. Sabatier differentiated between the "Arab population, who are used to a specific form of construction and interior layout," and "the European populace, which not only requires European-style housing, but also a separate, Mediterranean housing type."[72] This attitude was to form the conceptual baseline for low-cost housing schemes right up until Morocco's independence, with the sole exception of Jewish housing, which was dealt with separately in the belief that Jews formed a distinct ethnic group, despite their Moroccan origins.

Tackling the Bidonville Problem

The new medina may have been carefully designed (given its role as a propaganda vehicle for French audiences), but the site was far too small to accommodate Casablanca's ever-growing population. Moroccan laborers put down roots south of the planned expansion area, around the Carlotti quarries, and, more important, established a huge encampment called Gadoueville (mud town), which became known as Bidonville (oil-drum town) in the late 1920s. Mac Orlan refers to this pile of "petrol drums and corrugated iron" as "the capital of slumland,"[73] and by 1930 the term *bidonville* had become a generic synonym for shantytown even outside Morocco.[74] The various descriptions of this "filthy pit with pestilent cesspools and

[71] Sieburg, "Le rôle économique de Casablanca vu par un écrivain allemand,"206.

[72] Sabatier, "Les Habitations à bon marché au Maroc," 288.

[73] Mac Orlan, "Bousbir," 65.

[74] Marc, "L'œuvre française au Maroc," 54. André Adam places the first use of the term four years later. Adam, *Casablanca*, 1: 86.

Postcard of Bidonville, c. 1932.

The courtyard *kanoun* in workers' housing, c. 1950

dirt tracks" echo early accounts of the city's poor hygiene and evoke the increasing sense of panic instilled by the steady growth of "this indigenous village." In 1938, Sieburg declared he had witnessed "a reverse civilization process" whereby "shepherds and farmers" had turned into "African proletarians penned up on the edges of the town, propelled by new needs."[75] Brasillach describes it as "a sort of nondescript Parisian slum zone, full of unfinished structures, piles of garbage, and shacks, resembling something between a manure field and a fairground."[76]

Reports on the public health threat posed by the "dangerous classes," among whom malaria was rife, took on similar overtones to the reports drafted by late-nineteenth-century Parisian ideologists.[77] The danger was taken seriously by the municipal authority, which throughout the 1930s unceasingly strove to improve the "slumlike derbs" and to raze the *bidonvilles*. This program was devoted to relocating the slum districts in more hygienic sites and to rendering the makeshift structures more robust. At a council meeting in 1930, Rivollet stated, "The native population must at all costs be grouped in specific areas to prevent it from spilling into the city."[78] Likewise, another promunicipality journalist wrote in 1937: "[Concentrating the indigenous populace] in several precise locations facilitates the task of monitoring health and hygiene and of policing the zone, without engendering any of the complexities brought on by high-density schemes."[79]

The municipal authority set about knocking down the wooden shacks in the center of town and around the medina.[80] In February 1931, a bylaw was passed forbidding *nouallas* inside the municipal boundaries—an act that the council firmly believed "would put an end to Bidonville."[81] These efforts to "purge the city" were not, however, particularly radical,[82] and the measures of control soon proved insufficient. Hence, the only effective "remedy," according to the council, was "to speed up construction in the new medina," but this was far too costly. Since it was out of the question to offer all shantytown occupants permanent dwellings, it was suggested that existing shantytowns be fitted with modern amenities.[83] In Casablanca, though, the official go-ahead had scarcely been given for this strategy when it was immediately reversed. The hygienists Gaud and Sicaud subsequently recommended that rather than "ruling out *bidonvilles* as a temporary housing solution for a portion of the new native population, [it might be advisable] to redevelop them as rural housing of sorts but with upgraded facilities."[84] The findings of a survey they conducted in 1937 showed that shantytowns were in fact "an essential step," an observation echoed forty years later by Colette Pétonnet, who defined them as "the acculturation stage" within the urban process.[85] The municipal authority thus had to take this acculturation factor into account and put up with "the necessary evil" of shantytowns for a while:

> The occupants of shacks and *nouallas* are mostly poverty-stricken creatures who cannot afford a permanent dwelling, nor can they ever hope to own even the smallest abode, whatever credit facilities may be offered them. It is also a population that has only recently shed its nomadic skin, and which therefore shuns permanent housing built in bricks and mortar. This has been proved on more than one occasion in the past when, having turned down a landowner's offer of newly built accommodations for a minimal rent, they promptly set about building shacks and *nouallas* in exactly the self-same spot. By the same token, it has been noted that those members of the indigenous community who live in public housing at Derb Baladiya illegally sublet their dwellings to a third party while they themselves go off and live in a shantytown.[86]

Such squalor and poverty roused Dr. Georges Béros's indignation, causing him to speak out against the (relatively) privileged treatment accorded to laborers employed by major industrialists, while the rest of the working class were "scattered in overpopulated *derbs* and shantytowns . . . all lacking hygienic facilities."[87]

---

75 Friedrich Sieburg, "Le rôle économique de Casablanca," 206.

76 Brasillach, *La conquérante*, 121. The zone surrounding Paris featured ten thousand shacks on a ground ruled for many decades by military prescriptions. See: Jean-Louis Cohen, André Lortie, *Des fortifs au périf: Paris, les seuils de la ville* (Paris: Pavillon de l'Arsenal/Picard, 1992).

77 For Vaillat, "a real threat to the European city resides in these 'shantytowns.'" Vaillat, *Le Périple marocain*, 91.

78 Marcel Rivollet, *BMO* 5, no. 4 (April–May 1930).

79 "Un effort d'assainissement: Casablanca va être entourée d'agglomérations indigènes," *Le Petit Casablancais* (Casablanca), July 16, 1938.

80 Bylaw of March 20, 1930, prohibiting residence in the wooden huts on Rue de Safi, *BMO* 5, no. 2 (March–April 1930).

81 Hygiene Subcommission, bylaw of January 22, 1931, *BMO* 6, no. 1 (January–February 1931.) This bylaw was based on a *dahir* of 1915.

82 M. Bon, "Rapport général sur l'assainissement de la Ville de Casablanca, Bidonvilles et derbs, exercice 1938–1939," (February 27, 1939), 21 (typescript). The author was an assistant to the head of municiple services. Subsequently, *noualla*s remained "temporarily" authorized south of the Ben M'Sik garden, between the Médiouna and Ouled Ziane roads.

83 A similar solution was deployed in Rabat, where the Protectorate installed public water closets and lavatories in the *noualla* shantytown of Douar Debagh.

84 Gaud and Sicaud, "L'habitat indigène au Maroc," 96.

85 Colette Pétonnet, *Espaces habités, ethnologie des banlieues* (Paris: Galilée, 1981), 75.

86 Bon, "Rapport général sur l'assainissement," 24.

87 Georges Béros, "La lutte contre les taudis à l'étranger, les projets d'assainissement de la ville de Casablanca," *Le Maroc médical*, no. 202 (April 1939): 145.

Although fairly conservative, he did adopt a rhetoric that was widely used in the discourse of the Popular Front, notably condemning "Casablanca's government-backed wall of money" and urging decision makers to open their eyes to the city's ethnic diversity.[88] Béros distinguished two different classes of Muslims—the "enlightened citizens" and the "seminomads"—just as he differentiated the lower- and middle-class Jews, without forgetting that "those Europeans (notably the Spanish) living in the Ferme-Blanche quarter have just as few hygienic facilities as the indigenous population." According to Béros, such ethnic divides called for culture-specific housing:

> It is a question of housing individuals of different races in dwellings equipped with decent hygienic facilities. And within each race, there are categories that have reached a different stage of evolution. Furthermore, experience has shown that it is impossible to force dwelling types on the native population, since they always, understandably, return to their customary way of living.[89]

Boundaries were thus shifted to merge existing quarters, and in 1932 the administration realigned the shacks and widened the roads in the Ben M'Sick *bidonville*.[90] Markets, Koranic schools, a large mill, and a mosque were built, and a garbage-removal service was provided once every other day. A bus service enabled workers to commute to the factories. In the latter half of the decade, Ben M'Sick was perceived as a way of familiarizing rural migrants with city life, as was the Aviation *bidonville*, which had been opened and sanitized by the municipal authority.[91] The official records for the period reveal how an embryonic form of the Carrières Centrales *bidonville* was already beginning to form in the northeast. At the same time, the municipal authority launched an evacuation campaign of the *derbs*:

> There are a great many *derbs*, covering a total of 54 hectares . . . Some of them have even spilled out around the old medina, which spawned their creation in the first place. We suggest redeveloping the area, dedicating it to housing for the native Moroccans so that the majority of laborers may have accommodations within easy reach of the port and surrounding quarters. We will lay sewers and install all the requisite hygienic facilities.[92]

As early as 1929, Si Mohamed ben Abderrahman Zemmouri, the landowner of Derb Ghallef, had been given formal notice to "provide proper public facilities in the said *derb*, namely, installing sewage pipes that must be linked up to the mains, as well as laying and surfacing roads."[93] However, appropriate measures were not taken until 1938, when an outbreak of typhus in the shantytowns led to a release of credit facilities to lay roads in the "unsafe zones," i.e., in those areas where the dwellers posed a potential threat. The municipal authority noted, "Residents in Ben Jdia and in the Maarif represent the greatest risk," no doubt because they were the most fit for struggle in the big city, and that "Derb Ghallef is slightly less threatening, as are those areas around the Marrakech gate."[94]

The situation was still tense on the eve of World War II. By 1938, 9,500 out of 10,000 shacks had been demolished, but the forty thousand evicted occupants had not yet been allocated permanent accommodations. The new private housing developments erected in the new medina extension and strewn across twelve hectares southeast of the city were but a partial solution to the problem, since building residential developments merely for the creditworthy did not ease the housing shortage faced by the poorer members of the population. It is to be noted though that in these developments, particular attention was paid to improving the technical aspects of "native-built structures."[95] In addition, the new medina's "relatively high" rents made it inaccessible "to low-income laborers and white-collar employees," resulting in "the privileged classes occupying these districts, that is, *chaouchs* (jani-

---

88 This "wall of money" (*mur d'argent*) was the nemesis of the left-wing Front populaire coalition that won the French parliamentary elections in 1936.

89. Béros, "La lutte contre les taudis à l'étranger," 148. Béros was rebuked by the conservative press. See, "À la Commission municipale," *L'Éclaireur marocain* (Casablanca), May 20, 1939.

90 The settlement was built on lands belonging to the children of Si Abd el Kerim Ben El M'sick, former *khalifa* (adjunct) of the pasha of Casablanca.

91 "Le recasement des indigènes; les projets en cours sont-ils suffisants?" *Le Petit Casablancais* (Casablanca) January 28, 1939.

92 Municipal commission, meeting of June 17, *BMO* 13, no. 4 (June–July 1938), 7.

93 Bylaw of May 21, 1929, *BMO* 4, no. 3 (May–June 1929).

94 *BMO* 13, no. 6 (October–November 1938).

95 Access to natural light and air in living spaces was promoted. Bon, "Rapport général sur l'assainissement," 8. Among the private developments were those of Eyraud, Oued Koréa in the industrial district, and Derb el Moghreb.

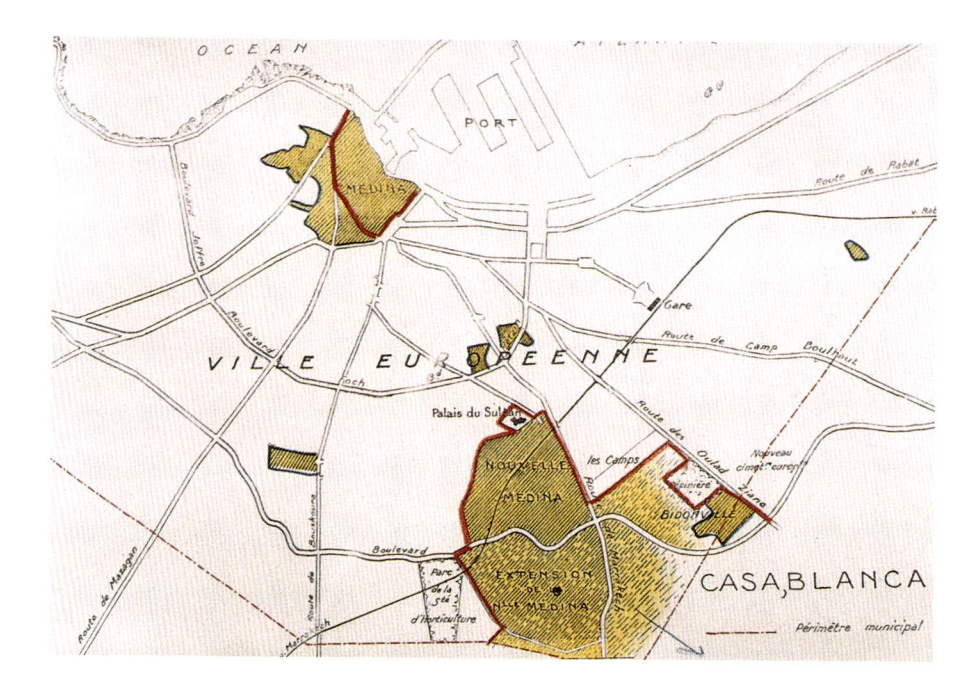

Department of the Interior, map showing the location of Muslim neighborhoods and *bidonvilles* within the city. July 1933.

96 Gaud and Sicaud, "L'habitat indigène au Maroc," 96.

97 Sabatier, "Les Habitations à bon marché au Maroc," 293. Reproduced verbatim in J. G., "Le problème de l'heure: l'habitat indigène, l'expérience marocaine," *Travaux* (Algiers), September 23, 1936.

98 "Une cité ouvrière pour indigènes à Casablanca," *Construire* (February 15, 1939): 1.

99 Report of the Government Council June 20 and 21, 1930, BGA, SGA, dossier Habitat indigène, Casablanca, 1930.

100 *BMO* 7, no.1 (January–February 1932). On August 8, 1930, the socialist delegates from the Chaouia region demanded that the resident general consult them "on the future location of the workers' housing development." Address in BGA, SGA, Habitat indigène, Casablanca, 1930.

101 *BMO* 7, no. 1 (January–February 1932). The administration asked the city to buy land from Mohammed bel Larbi, co-owner with the Bendahan heirs. In connection with the competition, nine additional hectares were bought. The declaration of public property relative to expropriation was provided for by the *dahir* of May 30, 1931.

tors, who classified as civil servants) and administrative personnel."⁹⁶ It was thus decided to focus more on the underlying program of the schemes than on their actual location. With this in mind, the HBM office launched a construction project for more basic rental housing dedicated to the "twenty-seven to thirty thousand working-class [Muslim] families" registered in the 1936 census:

> Different housing types [need to be] developed for those who cannot afford expensive dwellings. First, for low wage earners, we should build houses no larger than fifty square meters arranged around the customary patio, containing at least one bedroom and two other rooms. Three thousand of these are required. And second, for higher wage earners, we should construct the same housing type but with more rooms, covering a greater floor area. Half a dozen of these should suffice.⁹⁷

Having slowed as of 1935, construction practically ground to a halt by 1939, rendering null and void the municipal authority's claim that it still aimed to provide an end solution to the housing problem by "grouping the thousands of native Moroccans previously scattered throughout the *derbs* in one policed neighborhood." Before construction was stifled, the municipal authority had pretended to "slightly improve health and hygiene," and even "remedy the problem of native identity that has already caused so much ink to flow."⁹⁸

Extending the New Medina

The public authorities gradually pieced together their ambitious construction schedule for the "policed neighborhood." The first issue to be tackled was funding. In 1930, the Protectorate offered a five-million-franc loan to the municipal authority, provided it borrowed the same again from other sources.⁹⁹ The second question was where to situate the dwellings. Maurice Roucher, chairman of the Kuhlmann factory and member of the municipal council, suggested the industrial quarters in the east—"the laborers' workplace"—while Marcel Rivollet recommended "grouping the native population in one single area," in the name of "safety" and "hygiene."¹⁰⁰ The latter solution was retained in 1931, and a plan was drafted for a development to be sited south of the new medina. Twenty hectares were expropriated and a competition was organized for "low-cost indigenous housing."¹⁰¹ The program included "plots for stabling cattle," delousing points, a health center, showers,

Marius Boyer, competition project for "affordable indigenous Moroccan dwellings," 1931. Overall perspective, in Marius Boyer, *Casablanca, travaux d'architecture*, 1933.

and a fonduk. A *hammam* and a communal oven were also provided, at the request of the Khalifat.[102] Marius Boyer's entry was voted the winning scheme and is the only one whose plans have been handed down to us; it corresponds to a mixed-use development of collective apartment houses and small courtyard dwellings with shops. The orthogonal road network was cut by sweeping diagonal lines, translating into an open arrangement that could be easily policed, contrasting sharply with the sinuous, picturesque design of the narrow streets.[103]

The competition was not followed through, though the Public Works Department did draw up "low-cost housing plans for native Moroccan laborers" in 1933.[104] The 880 planned units were conceived as "courtyard houses" arranged back to back in long rectangular plots, covering four blocks of increasing size.[105] The shops and facilities, including a *hammam*, were to be set up along the main streets as well as in the corners of the triangular parcels. However, General Mérillon—secretary general of the Protectorate at the time—deemed these municipal plans to be too conservative and also criticized them for being based on outmoded planning methods:

> The problem is, in fact, the scheme's underlying concept, that is, the cellular formula resulting in huge numbers of the native population being crammed into a maze of narrow streets—not at all how Casablanca's future indigenous town should look. Basically, it is a question of correcting a major flaw in the initial plan, which lacked a sufficiently large area for the ever-growing Moroccan population. This requires creating not just one neighborhood, but an entire town that can be continually extended southward if the situation so dictates. After twenty years of experience, we would not be forgiven if we repeated past mistakes.[106]

Preempting Écochard's criticisms of the late 1940s, Mérillon stressed "the pressing need for changes to Moroccan housing." He likewise underscored the shifts in Moroccan lifestyle and, above all, "the want of circulation flows, hygiene, and proper surveillance," all of which, he said, called for "a modern road system linked to the rest of the city network and adapted to the soil type." In 1933, he therefore requested that the Department of Architecture design a satellite town, to be sited along the Route de Médiouna,[107] and whose easternmost segment would have brought laborers closer to the Roches Noires factories.[108] The project was

[102] "Établissement de l'avant-projet relatif aux constructions indigènes," *BMO* 6, no. 1 (February–March 1931), and no. 3, (May–June 1931). The city wished to remain without obligation to the competition winner, and asked for the right to hire a private architect.

[103] Marius Boyer, *Casablanca: travaux d'architecture*, 36–37. On the final results of the competition, see *BMO* 8, no. 1 (February–March 1933.)

[104] The Soblanca real-estate company offered to build the development on the condition that the city provide the land. A joint venture was created in order to realize this project, supported by the Municipal Commission members Grel and Ancelle. *BMO* 8, no. 2 (March–April 1933).

[105] These were to be small single-story residences and "superimposed houses." Every two units shared a courtyard and lavatory, which permitted an embryonic, communal life. The one-story houses were to be built of cement-coated bricks, while the two-story buildings were to have a concrete frame with stuccoed bricks. These had a 2.6-square-meter courtyard with lavatory, as well as a 13-square-meter room (type A) to which an approximately 1.5-square-meter kitchen could be added (type B). In type C buildings, the kitchen acted as an intermediary space linking the main room and the courtyard. Type D houses were equipped with a larger (2.5-square-meter) kitchen and a lavatory. BGA, SGP, dossier Habitat indigène Casablanca, 1930, and Habitat indigène 1936–1950.

[106] Mérillon, secretary general of the Protectorate, to the head of Municpal Services, April 4, 1933, BGA, SGP, dossier Habitat indigène, Casablanca, 1930.

[107] Mérillon to the head of Municipal Services, June 9, 1933, BGA, SGP, dossier Habitat indigène, Casablanca, 1930. The Route de Médiouna remained, as Lapeyre and Marchand remarked in 1919, the "most important arrival point for natives coming from the interior." Lapeyre and Marchand, *Casablanca*, 94.

[108] Mérillon to the head of Municipal Services, October 21, 1933, BGA, SGP, dossier Habitat indigène, Casablanca, 1930.

Maurice Sori, in association with Massot and Grégoire (contractors), native Moroccan houses in the second new medina extension. General view of Lot C, 1938, in *Le Maroc en 1938*.

109 Declaration of the head of Municipal Services. A letter from the developer André Mantout triggered the debate on a long-term plan. André Mantout, "Question de l'habitation à bon marché pour les indigènes à mettre à l'étude dans les plus brefs délais," *BMO* 9, no. 1 (January–February 1934).

110 There were joint submissions: Lot C (architect: Sory, contractor: Massot and Grégoire) was launched in July 1937, lot D (architect: Gourdain, contractor: Baille) in September, and lots A (architect: Fleurant, contractor: Chapon) and B (architects: Balois and Perrotte, contractor: Rivollet) in October. *BMO* 12 (February–March through September–October 1937).

111 *BMO* 12, no. 4 (July–August 1937).

scrapped, however, out of fear of conflict between the administration and the private sector.

In 1934 talks started up again within the municipal council for a large-scale construction program to be funded by private corporations in view of meager public resources. After approving the new medina extension plan, the council set about making land available "to a financial group willing to bear the construction costs," despite uncertainty over whether "laborers would be happy to leave their cheap *nouallas*" for higher rents.[109] Once the urban framework and real-estate structure had been worked out, another competition for building "low-cost indigenous housing" was launched in early 1937. This time things moved swiftly, and the four planned "parcels" were built in just a few months by several teams of architects and contractors.[110] The dwellings were constructed using highly economical building methods and ranged from one-room courtyard houses with a lavatory to one- or two-room dwellings with kitchens that were sometimes slotted beneath an awning. The layout and construction principles set out in 1932 by the Public Works Department seem to have been largely respected, yet despite the thought that went into the scheme, "light only enters [the dwellings] at certain times of the day."[111]

Following the decision not to work to an overall plan, the quarter known as the "new medina extension" grew into a collage of heterogeneous schemes. Built by Brion in the early 1940s, it was designed to accommodate five hundred individual

Town Planning Department, project for the main square in the new medina extension, March 1935. Perspective.

low-cost units for native Moroccan war veterans.[112] The municipal authority likewise launched a housing program, though it was closely monitored by the administration. This program was dedicated "solely to those Muslims who have been evacuated from the *derbs* and shantytowns, provided they begin building housing on the site within a year, and that they live there for a minimum period of five years."[113] As the structures went up, Laprade's vision of Moroccan quarters crossed by arcaded streets, squares, and monumental edifices was lost. Aware of the problem, the Protectorate launched a design study in 1935 for a large portico-lined square, intended to serve as the core of the vast urban area under construction.[114]

Housing design concepts switched course when Charles Noguès became resident general in 1936. He set up a permanent Indigenous Housing Commission with a special section assigned to supervising "the building of indigenous housing projects."[115] Having launched a program in 1939 for a "native Moroccan housing development" in Rabat's Douar Debbagh quarter, the commission set to work on brainstorming the measures that needed to be put in place for Casablanca. This incited praise from the newspaper *Vigie Marocaine*, which commended the initiatives undertaken to meet those needs created by "the huge influx of our protégés who are attracted to the country's major towns by the prospect of work."[116] In 1940, a Sharifian (or Moroccan) Indigenous Housing Office was set up, thereby providing the Protectorate with the means to truly turn its attention to the issue at hand. From then on, a totally different approach was adopted, closely linked to Noguès's measures "to gradually wipe out the *bidonvilles* and replace them with housing that complies with public health regulations."[117] The prototype development embarked on in Rabat was continued in a scheme for Ain Chock, situated in Casablanca's southernmost outskirts; this work set the parameters for a new housing policy, the effects of which would not, however, be truly felt until 1945.

The Cosuma Prototype of Workers' Housing

The press was swift to compare the "plodding" nature of Protectorate ventures with the fast-moving (albeit sporadic) housing programs set up by private entrepreneurs.[118] Edmond Brion's design for Cosuma, a Moroccan sugar producer, stands out most notably among the various workers' developments. Built for the company's

112 Funding came from the Office of War Invalids. "Habitations à bon marché destinées aux anciens combattants indigènes," *BMO* 13, no. 3 (April–May 1938): 23. See also: *Bulletin d'informations et de documentation du Maroc* (January 1, 1941).

113 They were also required "not to be owners of any other structure legally authorized and used for theirown lodging and that of their family." "Gestion du lotissement municipal de la Nouvelle médina extension," *BMO* 13, no. 10 (October–November 1938).

114 The perspective presented at the Paris International Exposition of 1937 has been lost. A reproduction can be found in the photograph archive of the Moroccan Ministry of Housing in Rabat.

115 Founded on October 12, 1937, the commission was presided over by the director of Political Affairs, Sicot. *Bulletin d'informations et de documentation du Maroc* (December 15, 1940), 11.

116 "La commission de l'habitat indigène s'est réunie hier à Rabat," *La Vigie marocaine* (Casablanca), October 24, 1937.

117 "La commission de l'habitat indigène s'est réunie hier à Rabat."

118 See especially R. Lauriac, "Tandis que d'autres cherchent leur voie . . . , la Compagnie sucrière marocaine a depuis longtemps résolu le problème de l'habitation indigène à bon marché," *La Vigie marocaine* (Casablanca), March 8, 1939. The Banque de Paris had a strong presence in the capital of Cosuma.

Edmond Brion, Cosuma workers' development, Boulevard du Commandant Runser, 1932–37. Aerial view, c. 1970.

Edmond Brion, Cosuma workers' development. A bend in the main street. Photographed in 1991.

119 Mahé, *L'Extension des villes indigènes au Maroc*, 56.

120 Pauty, "Tradition et modernisme à Casablanca," 139.

Muslim employees, it was sited in the Roches Noires quarter (close to the factory then under construction) and was a variation on the themes developed earlier by Brion in the Habous project. The construction phase got under way in 1932 and was split into several stages; by 1936 a total of 330 units had been built, accommodating some 1,500 occupants.

A wall was incorporated into the scheme to shield the residents from public view; as in the Habous, this is pierced only by two gates leading to shop-lined squares at either end of the site. Community facilities were provided, including a mosque built in 1937, a Koranic school, a communal oven, and a *kissaria*. The patio houses are protected by high, blank walls and were deliberately designed to open onto blind alleys rather than main streets, with zigzagging entrances to heighten the sense of privacy. Sculpted doors and *zillij*-embellished fountains, coupled with sparse trees placed here and there, led Yvonne Mahé to conclude, "Here for the first time there appears to be a true concern for aesthetic quality."[119] Edmond Pauty also praised the masterful design components:

> Some housing units, reserved exclusively for the native Moroccan population, have been constructed according to the traditional way of life, featuring time-honored design elements that might otherwise be forgotten . . . E. Brion has managed to inject a flavor of the old medina into this new housing development. He has achieved this by incorporating into his plan a capricious web of thoroughfares, crossroads embellished with unexpected fountains, trelliswork spilling over the outer walls, and a thousand and one other tiny details achieved only by long and patient observation of indigenous housing patterns.[120]

A number of private dwellings, again designed by Brion, went up beyond the enclosure wall, by the sports fields, for the use of the company's European employees, including the chairman, Pierre Sahuc. In 1939, Sahuc inaugurated the "plain but pragmatic and sufficiently spacious" workers' dwellings that formed part of a "real little town," noting how Brion "skillfully eschewed the hackneyed effect of mass-produced housing."[121] The interior layout of the seventy units is traditional and was conceived in conformity with the occupants' status.[122] The rooms are not as wide as they are long, and it is their floor area, rather than the number of rooms, that increases in size; for instance, a two-room unit can range from forty to eighty square meters, courtyard included. Despite the scheme's attractive qualities, construction was surprisingly halted in 1939, following the workers' refusal to pay rent. A *bidonville* containing eighty units was subsequently built on the vacant land. The press commented, "In the main, the indigenous population is insensible to home comforts, since they have not had adequate time to adapt to them, and they therefore very readily return to their tents and *nouallas*."[123] Gaud and Sicaud regretfully noted the Moroccans' slowness to adjust to such housing types, yet nevertheless examined the issue from the reverse angle, namely, adapting housing to the lifestyles of an essentially rural population:

> The Moroccan populace has not yet acquired the taste for home living as we understand it. It is therefore somewhat discouraging to see these delightful purpose-built houses, which to us seemed perfectly suited to native customs, falling into such a sorry state within only a few months of occupation. The average working-class Moroccan needs to be educated in this respect, although it will be a gradual process, just as they will only slowly adapt to a more settled and stable way of life. Once our Moroccans better understand the advantages of a home, they will acquire a taste for it; in the same way, when they feel the need for modern comforts, however relative, they will make more of an effort to attain them.[124]

As pointed out by Yvonne Mahé, though, the rents were manifestly too high for most workers. Mahé concludes, "The only conceivable form of housing for this category of laborers is a one-room dwelling with a kitchen and a small courtyard that can be rented for between fifteen and twenty francs a month."[125] A journalist writing for *Réalités* praised the Cosuma development after it had been extended by Brion in 1951, even though "Casablanca's major employers" did not, on the whole, seem "particularly advanced from a philanthropic perspective."[126] Commenting on this, Yvonne Mahé frankly remarked that the developments were built "less out of a concern for humanitarian issues than in the aim of creating an elite rank of workers, or otherwise as an investment strategy."[127] Meanwhile, Brion employed the same design principle as for the Bou Jniba Phosphates development, which he built in 1938 near Khouribga, and for the Ciments Lafarge development in Casablanca. Here, the scheme reads as a web of streets and houses contained within a rectangular enclosure, accessed through a monumental gate.

Other architects similarly reflected on the design and arrangement of housing to create complexes adapted to the traditions and financial means of the city's inhabitants. In 1934, an unknown architect proposed "minimum" housing to wipe out the *bidonvilles*, although the planned houses were in fact much larger than the ones for Cosuma:

> There is just one room and this overlooks the courtyard . . . There is nothing Moroccan about it, other than the interior arrangement required for the harem lifestyle, to which working-class Muslims adhere just as strongly as wealthy upper-class Muslims. Women will thus be protected from public view. All the rooms face south, which is Morocco's most favorable orientation . . . Two or three steps shaped in the form of a bench lead into the room . . . A wide window is pierced into the door to let in southern light, and at the back there are three ventilation openings. The rooms are rectangular, in line with the Moroccan *qaida*,* thereby enabling beds to be

Edmond Brion, Cosuma workers' development. View of the terraces, in *Réalisations*, June 1939.

121 Lauriac, "Tandis que d'autres cherchent leur voie," It is important to note that the question of situating residences and factories, a strategy that contradicted Prost's zoning, was not discussed.

122 This project included four two-room dwellings; fifty-six one-room homes with a kitchen, lavatory, storeroom, and courtyard; and ten row-houses for pairs of single residents. Details provided by Dr. Valade, quoted in Gaud and Sicaud, "L'habitat indigène au Maroc," 92.

123 Gaud and Sicaud, "L'habitat indigène au Maroc," 92.

124 Gaud and Sicaud, "L'habitat indigène au Maroc," 95.

125 Mahé, *L'Extension des villes indigènes au Maroc*, 58.

126 "Casablanca, le développement prodigieux d'une ville en pleine fièvre de croissance," *Réalités* no. 89 (June 1953): 48.

127 Mahé, *L'Extension des villes indigènes au Maroc*, 59.

Building the New Medina and Housing the Workers 243

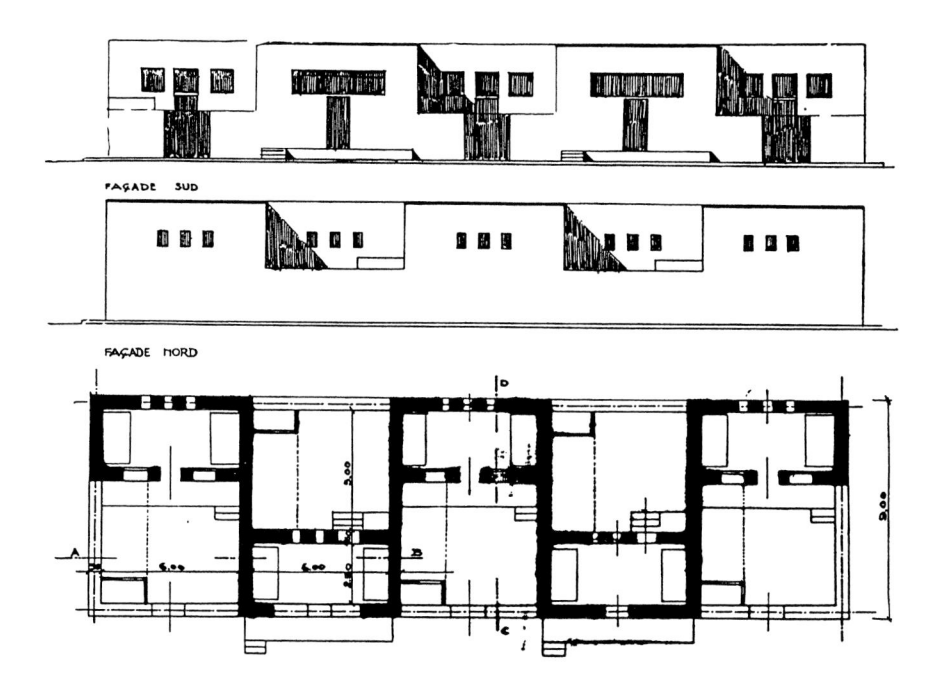

Project for low-cost indigenous housing, 1934. Plan and elevations, in *Chantiers nord-africains,* **August 1934.**

128 "L'habitat indigène au Maroc," *Chantiers nord-africains* 6, no. 8 (August 1934): 649. All the details of this project for above-average-sized houses—the courtyard measured 30 square meters and the bedroom 21 square meters—were carefully worked out. The project may have originated with Cadet (at the time when the practitioner most attentive to Moroccan vernacular architecture) or perhaps with Brion.

129 Report presented to the municipal council by the architect Desmet, the developer Carlotti, and Si Mohamed Touimi, *BMO* 13, no. 1 (January–February 1938). Touimi was one of six Muslims on the council, which included fourteen Frenchmen and two Jewish Moroccans.

130 *BMO* 13, no. 6 (January–February 1939). See also: "À la Commission municipale; la ville de Casablanca prendra des parts dans une société fondatrice d'une cité ouvrière indigène," *Le Petit Marocain* (Casablanca) February 9, 1939; and "Le recasement des indigènes. Quelques précisions sur la cité ouvrière des industriels," *Le Petit Casablancais* (Casablanca), February 18, 1939.

131 The housing built by the Protectorate at Douar Debbagh Rabat was initially meant to serve as a model. Subsequently, a project was commissioned from Arrivetx, long active in the realm of privately funded mass housing. The latter was ousted after having reported on the project to the municipal council, as was Boyer, who was eager to get the commission.

laid at either end and a bench slotted between them. The courtyard . . . has a sheltered space for cooking, which the Moroccans do on the ground in the open air whenever possible. This area comprises three low walls in cement, or bricks abutted against the main wall like an awning. A hole for a squat lavatory takes up one of the corners, and in front of the gardens [wedged between the facades and rear wall] there is an enclosure wall measuring between 1.5 and 2 meters, with an openwork door. Whitewashed walls and blue-painted wood paneling complete the ensemble.[128]

Although this scheme was not taken up at the time, it did serve as the bedrock for the work undertaken after 1945, notably for the housing developments built by Écochard's team.

The Industrialists' City

During the latter half of the 1930s, the public authorities, industrialists, and architects all set about drafting new programs. The main firms located in the east of Casablanca decided to create a joint housing development for their workers, comprising some two thousand units in total. They considered the new medina to be too far away, so requested a sector near the Roches Noires factories, which was a zone forbidden to European dwellings due to unsanitary conditions there. Sabalot was the only member of the municipal council to object to setting up an indigenous housing program on such a site. His colleagues on the council deemed it "difficult to prevent the native population from settling near their workplace." Their sole effort was to ensure that "building codes [were laid down] with regard to indigenous housing constructed in the factory zones."[129]

Although it expressed reservations, the municipal authority nevertheless purchased land between the slaughterhouses and the Poliet et Chausson factory near the Roches Noires district, giving the go-ahead for the construction of 1,600 units covering ten hectares. Talks subsequently got under way as to how to go about developing the "Industrialists' City."[130] In July 1938, the Indigenous Housing Commission decided to use the Cosuma development as a point of reference, and Brion was naturally selected as the architect.[131] The project was taken in hand by one of the most influential entrepreneurs in Casablanca at the time: Édouard

Gouin, head of the French-Moroccan olive oil mill and of the Marseilles-Morocco soap factories. In 1939, Gouin outlined the scheme as follows:

> The proposed units will contain a main room measuring five meters by three meters, together with a kitchen and a lavatory. In front of the houses there will be a cement-laid patio, entirely concealed from public view... An additional room shall be incorporated into a number of houses dedicated either to skilled or semiskilled workers with above-average incomes. No running water shall be supplied, to avoid problems relative to plumbing.[132]

This rather unusual measure lent the project a spurious quality, driving it below par in relation to company-funded schemes built around the same time. That being said, it nonetheless included all the customary facilities, such as a mosque, hammam, Koranic school, mill, oven, and shops. The plots measured fifty meters—larger than the ones in the new medina—and special legislation was enacted so that the administration could "set minimum requirements with respect to ventilation, illumination, and natural lighting of the living quarters."[133] Yet on two occasions, the municipal authority did refuse to allocate more than two public drinking fountains.[134] This did not prevent one local official from proudly declaring that the Casablanca municipal authority was "the first [public authority in Morocco] to introduce a set of specific measures pertaining to the hygiene of indigenous housing that previously only applied to European dwellings."[135] Running water would not, however, be installed in the houses until the early 1950s.

SOCICA (Société pour la construction de la cité des industriels de Casablanca) was founded by twenty private firms, the railroad company, the municipal authority—which granted land—and by Protectorate representatives. It was established in May 1940 under the presidency of Gouin,[136] and rendered employees less dependent on one single employer, for they could keep their dwelling if they were laid off.[137] It was, moreover, a move that relieved modern-thinking industrialists of a hefty burden as the numerous planned developments were intended to bring "thousands of laborers within easy reach of their work, thus cutting out lengthy traveling time during rush hour."[138] Besides, it was "easier for the administration than for employers to spend time picking out the plots."[139] The municipal authority approved a preliminary program for 320 units in March 1940, and ground was broken in December of that year.[140] Brion put himself forward for designing the arcades and the Moroccan detailing of twin windows and wrought-iron grilles. Numerous decorative elements featured in the building permit were not actually included in the built work for financial reasons. Also noteworthy is the comment

132 Édouard Gouin, "Rapport sur la cité ouvrière indigène des Roches-Noires," *Bulletin de liaison des industriels du Maroc* (1939): 10.

133 Bon, *Rapport général sur l'assainissement*, 8.

134 Édouard Gouin, letters of protest to the municipality, 1946, SOCICA Archives, Casablanca.

135 Bon, *Rapport général sur l'assainissement*, 21.

136 Among the companies involved were Carnaud, Shell Maroc, Huileries et savonneries du Maroc, Énergie électrique du Maroc, Brasseries du Maroc and Cosuma.

137 R. Cagnon, "Le problème du logement au Maroc," in "Terres d'Afrique," special issue of *Problèmes humains* (1948): 151–58.

138 Regarding the politics of Casablancan industrialists during this period, see René Gallissot, *Le Patronat européen au Maroc (1931–1942)* (Rabat: Éditions techniques nord-africaines, 1964), 115–52.

139 "Une cité ouvrière pour indigènes à Casablanca." This attention to workers' habitat was not the work of philanthropists. Lefebvre, a Carnaud administrator, insisted that it "served the primary interests of industry and of Morocco," because "workers who were happy in life and in work would increase productivity." Jacques Lefebvre, "L'action des industriels marocains en faveur de leurs collaborateurs indigènes," in "Cinq ans de politique constructive," *Notre Maroc* (April 1942).

140 "Hier à Casablanca la première pierre de la cité ouvrière indigène des Roches-Noires a été posée par le général Noguès," *Le Petit Marocain* (Casablanca), December 30, 1940.

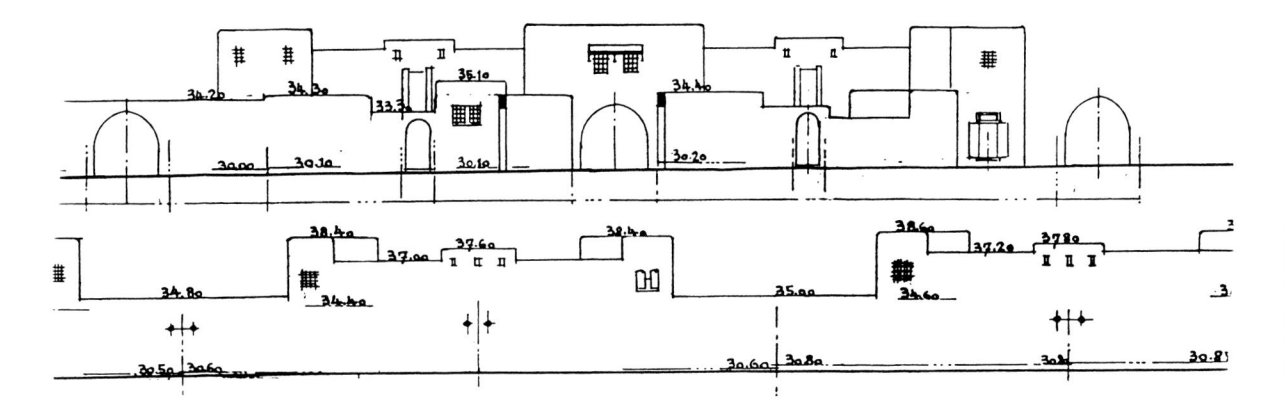

Edmond Brion, SOCICA workers' development, Rue du Lieutenant Campi, 1942. Elevation facing lane No. 5 (1942) as featured in the building permit.

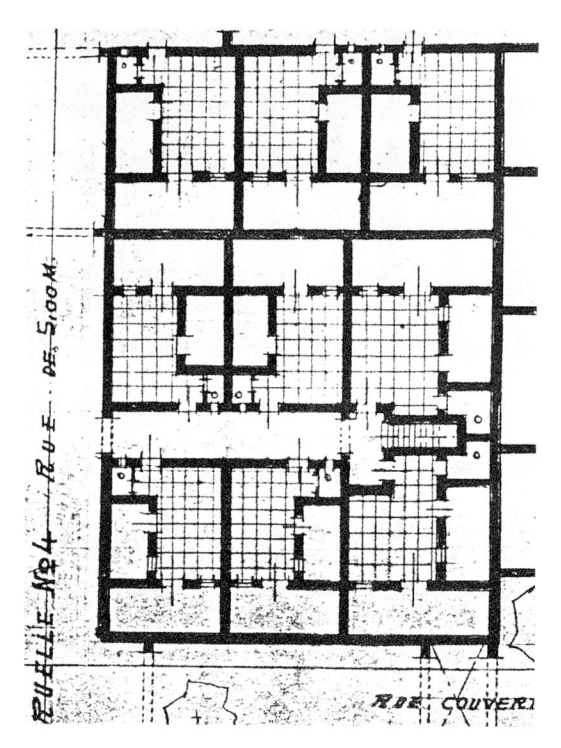

Edmond Brion, SOCICA workers' development, Rue du Lieutenant Campi, 1942. Group of courtyard dwellings, as featured in the building permit.

made by the press that Brion was "the only European" who was willing to act as on-site supervisor for construction work entirely carried out by "Moroccan artisans."[141] Furthermore, the French Contractors' Federation had actually objected to the fact that Moroccan firms had been allowed to submit bids, as it believed this set a dangerous precedent for future tenders.[142]

Severe conflict arose, since the authorities prevented Brion from basing the site plan on native construction, which the architect angrily declared was his usual approach.[143] On top of this, the outbreak of war dramatically reduced the availability of materials, so the development was built on a shoestring budget. Only 15 of the 368 units had two rooms, and these were reserved for supervisory staff; there was thus a total lack of thought as to family size. The dwellings were conceived as single- or two-story dwellings (the latter incorporating a steep staircase) and were delivered with a kitchen and lavatory, as well as a "hidden" patio, though this was always converted into extra living space once the residents moved in.[144] In 1945, the board of directors complained to the resident general that not one of the civic buildings had been constructed, and in 1947, Gouin sadly declared that "the municipality is unable to pursue its initial policy in respect of workers' housing and will not participate in the development's completion, nor in its extension."[145] The municipality's shares were bought up by entrepreneurs, and the projects for workers' housing developments were either transferred *de facto* to the public sector or left to the market. During this time, the mosque, the communal oven, and several fountains were built, but not the hammam.

A comparison of Brion's plans for Muslim housing built between 1920 and 1940 reveals a move toward simplicity and orthogonal form, dictated both by an increasing lack of resources and by a change in Brion's own aesthetic ideals. The Habous design, on which he worked with Laprade and Cadet, is underpinned by a play on contrast and unexpected urban features, as well as by a focus on public spaces. Designed twenty years later, the SOCICA development comprises architectonic details similar to the Habous, but its plan is orthogonal, as is that of the Lafarge development. Only Cosuma comes close to the picturesque qualities of the Habous quarter, but even here the effect is rather spoiled by an overly large surrounding wall.

Plans for Jewish Housing Run Aground

Since the mellah had been partially demolished it became increasingly urgent to set up a specific Jewish housing program, which fueled frequent debate at the municipal level. As early as 1929, the Jewish municipal representative, Tolila, had pushed in vain for a rehousing program to accommodate the 3,000 inhabitants scheduled to be driven out of the Place de France.[146] In 1931, the council finally allocated one million francs out of the five-million-franc workers' housing budget to the Jewish populace; it was a move encouraged by the Protectorate, which expressed concern that "so many of the lower classes [were being] expelled from the mellah."[147] The secretary general subsequently inquired as to whether the municipal authority intended to maintain its project to "reserve a district in the new indigenous town for the Jewish community," in other words, "for the poorest segment of this populace."[148] In 1936, the council at long last agreed in principle to a scheme put forward by "a group of Jewish community members" to create their specific "colony." Some city councilors pointed out "the imbalance between Jewish programs compared to those for other categories of citizens," expressing fear of possible Muslim protest. They also stressed the "inappropriateness of such construction, given the current vacancy rate."[149]

---

141 "Des bidonvilles aux cités nouvelles," *Bulletin d'informations et de documentation du Maroc* (January 1942): 9–11.

142 French companies would denounce, notably, the commission given, with Brion's consent, to a single *m'allem*, Hadj Embarek Ben El Hadj Boualem. Hadj Embarek had already collaborated with Brion on the Bou Jniba Phosphates housing development near Khouribga.

143 Edmond Brion, "Exposé des difficultés rencontrées par l'architecte dans l'étude et la réalisation de cette cité," Note to the president of the SOCICA, March 26, 1941, SOCICA Archives.

144 Édouard Gouin, "L'effort des industriels de Casablanca en faveur de l'habitat indigène de leurs ouvriers," in "Cinq ans de politique constructive," *Notre Maroc* (April, 1942).

145 Édouard Gouin to the head of Municipal Services, June 27, 1947, SOCICA Archives. In 1945, 118 units were opened, while by early 1946, 232 units were complete and 61 remained unbuilt. A final section of 74 new homes would be completed in 1954. After independence, the housing development took the name of SOCECA, the 'I' (for *indigènes*, or 'natives') having been replaced by an 'E' (for *entrepreneurs*, or 'builders').

146 "Habitat des israélites," *BMO* 4, no. 3 (April–May 1929).

147 Emmanuel Durand, director general of Municipal Administration, to the director general of Finance, August 24, 1932, BGA, SGP, dossier Habitat indigène, Casablanca, 1930.

148 Mérillon, to the head of Municipal Services, June 9, 1933, BGA, SGP, dossier Habitat indigène, Casablanca, 1930. The Jewish community press was concerned about the program's slowness. *L'Avenir illustré* remarked, "The population of the European town will continuously increase the pressure on this population, from whom the possibility of better housing is becoming indispensable." He further asked, "What is the situation of the project for low-rent housing?" *L'Avenir illustré* no. 293 (May 1, 1933).

149 *BMO* 9, no. 3 (May–June 1934.)

Edmond Brion, Phosphates workers' development, Khouribga, c. 1936. View of the building site. The technology is similar to that used at the SOCICA development.

Edmond Brion, SOCICA (formerly SOCECA) workers' development.

Enclosure wall and one of the gates along Rue Marinié. Photographed in 1994.

Interior street, photographed in 1991.

Here, there are no monumental entranceways, as there were in other workers' developments. The walls of the dwellings create a near-blank enclosure, with extremely plain doors pierced into the four sides. Geminated windows form the sole ornamentation.

Building the New Medina and Housing the Workers 247

The mellah and Place de France. Photographed c. 1935. Note the demolished outer parts screened by fencing.

150 *BMO* 12, no. 6 (June 1937).

151 To this end, the Jewish community expended 300,000 francs. A subcommission was created, with the clear intent of burying the project. It included Arrivetx, Desmet, Andrieu, Tabet, and Touimi, the Muslim representative."Correspondance au sujet des habitations à bon marché pour la colonie israélite," *BMO* 13, no. 2 (February–March 1938) and "Habitations pour la population israélite," *BMO* 14, no. 3 (April–May 1939).

152 Bon, *Rapport général sur l'assainissement*, 40.

In an attempt to play for time and to fend off criticism of favoritism, the excuse was made that a suitable site for the scheme could not be found. Plots picked out first in the new medina, then west of the mellah, were respectively discarded, and the old health center site in Rue de Tanger that had been proposed in 1937 was also rejected.[150] Moreover, the council sabotaged the efforts of the Jewish community to launch its own program for a site near the mellah, despite appeals by the then Jewish Council representative Tabat that the program at least be "tested."[151] A highly detailed report on Casablanca's "hygienic facilities," drafted in 1939, emphasized the harsh living conditions of migrant Jews, and argued for larger-scale programs. Nonetheless, it ruled out the possibility of grouping these with Muslim quarters:

> It is understood that the scheme cannot be located in the new medina, nor in its extension. One way, however, of "decongesting" the mellah is to construct residential blocks in the European quarter. The administration is currently working to this end in association with qualified members of the Jewish community and it plans to build a low-cost Jewish housing development comprising some 1,000 units. The issues to be addressed concern both financial resources and site selection.[152]

Despite these noble intentions, all loans were suspended in the summer of 1939. With the Protectorate's enforcement of anti-Jewish legislation issued by the Vichy government, the situation worsened in 1941, compelling those Moroccan Jews who had managed to find central accommodations after the mellah's demolition to flee a section of the city that was now firmly restricted to Europeans.

Georges Buan, Ettedgui synagogue, Rue de la Mission in the old medina, c. 1935. Photographed in 1998.

CASA REVUE

THÉÂTRE · CINÉ · SPORTS · TOURISME · MODE

19 SEPT. 1933

Building Modern Leisure Facilities

Movie Theaters, Garages, and Other "Monuments"

Our most remarkable achievement in Morocco is the speed at which we have introduced change. It has triggered a complete turnaround in lifestyle and, while it may sometimes leave the locals a little dizzy, it has unquestionably been, and will continue to be, a pivotal aspect of Moroccan development.

Jacques Ladreit de Lacharrière, 1930[1]

The fact that the Rialto is one of the finest movie theaters in the whole of North Africa would be meaningless if it did not have well-chosen programs to draw the crowds. Aware that the movie industry now wields a large degree of social influence, Rialto's management is sparing nothing to ensure that the most recent and reputed films are shown in its theater at the same time as they are released in Paris, and sometimes even before.

Le Maroc en 38, 1938[2]

Prominent buildings commissioned by private firms or dedicated to public services shaped the *ville nouvelle* in the same way as the apartment houses did, and similarly marked a transition from eclecticism to modernity in terms of building design. Not only were these edifices intended to serve basic urban functions, they also provided the physical framework for the city's economy and for its wide range of commercial facilities. The most ambitious of the early municipal constructions was the slaughterhouse complex built by the Paris-based architect Georges-Ernest Desmarest, whose solution provided a response to the problem of health and hygiene that had formed the focus of debate since 1912. Completed in 1922, it sits in the vicinity of the station, a fair distance from the center, and it used to occupy the largest roofed floor area in Casablanca.[3] It was conceived as a concrete structure, framed by decorative panels tiled with yellow and green *zillij*. By contrast, the Casablanca-Voyageurs railroad station, designed by their in-house architectural office, is very understated in terms of monumental scale. This is surprising given the station's importance within the master plan of the *ville nouvelle*, though is most likely due to the fact that, at the time, another project was under way for a new railroad terminus in the port quarter. Designed as a boxlike structure, Casablanca-Voyageurs is pierced with three central openings that are weighed

Opposite
Front cover of *Casa-Revue*, September 1933.

[1] Ladreit de Lacharrière, *La création marocaine*, 62–63.

[2] "Les beaux cinémas casablancais," in Édouard Sarrat, ed., *Le Maroc en 1938*, 81.

[3] L. Benoist, "Les nouveaux abattoirs de Casablanca (Maroc)," *Le Génie civil* 82, no. 5 (February 3, 1923): 98–100; and Joseph Goulven, "Les abattoirs municipaux de Casablanca," *La Vie urbaine* 5, no. 21–22 (August–October 1923): 311–22.

Georges-Ernest Desmarest, Casablanca's municipal slaughterhouses, 1922. American military photo taken in April 1943.

Architectural Department of the Chemins de Fers Marocains, Casablanca-Voyageurs railway station, c. 1923. Elevation.

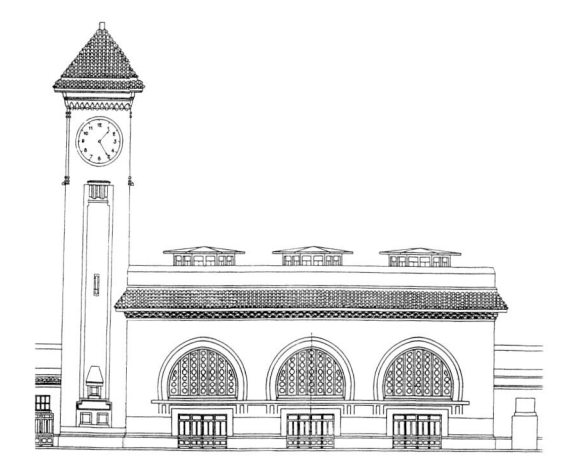

4 "Garage de la société France-Auto Citroën à Casablanca," *Chantiers nord-africains* 11, no. 9 (September 1930): 803–10; and "Casablanca—un garage moderne," *Bâtir*, no. 3 (June 1932). The engineer Georges Gillet coordinated the construction. On the Fiat garage, see "Le garage Fiat à Casablanca, A. Manassi, architecte," *Chantiers nord-africains* 1, no. 9 (September 1929): 525–26.

down slightly by a cornice. It is flanked on one side by a tower capped with green tiles, which the architect deliberately aligned with Boulevard de la Gare in order to inscribe it within the city's new minaret pattern. The main ticket hall, complete with three cupolas and wrought-iron chandeliers, forms the most striking element in the overall scheme.

Although there were still several rail tracks running through the city streets in the mid-1920s, cars began to replace the railroad as the most popular means of transport. The automobile industry soon reached cruising speed, and in the city center garages became just as striking landmarks as the stolid civic buildings. The Citroën garage, for instance, built by Maurice-Jacques Ravazé (Citroën's in-house architect) in the late 1920s at the junction of Avenue D'Amade and Boulevard de Paris, was assigned a monumental slot in the Place Administrative, opposite Laforgue's post office. Any jarring visual effect that could have arisen from such a positioning was smoothed out by Laprade's harmonizing layout scheme. The garage's concrete frame and ramps are enveloped in a facade dominated by long horizontal lines, injecting a radical form of architecture that broke with the modest structures being built by the firm's competitors, such as the Fiat garage by Aldo Manassi.[4] Particularly noteworthy is the monumental Auto-Hall built in 1930; it was designed by Pierre Bousquet for the Moroccan representative of Ford Motors and became the mecca of Casablancan car fanatics. Its facade arrangement, which is punched with a vast entrance that seems more suited to accommodating airships than cars, went beyond the role of an ordinary parking facility to become a genuine urban landmark.

Maurice-Jacques Ravazé and Georges Gillet, Citroen garage, Boulevard de Paris. Published in H. Descamps, *L'Architecture moderne au Maroc*, 1930.

Pierre Bousquet, Auto-Hall garage, Boulevard de Marseille, 1930. Main entrance. Photographed in 1994.

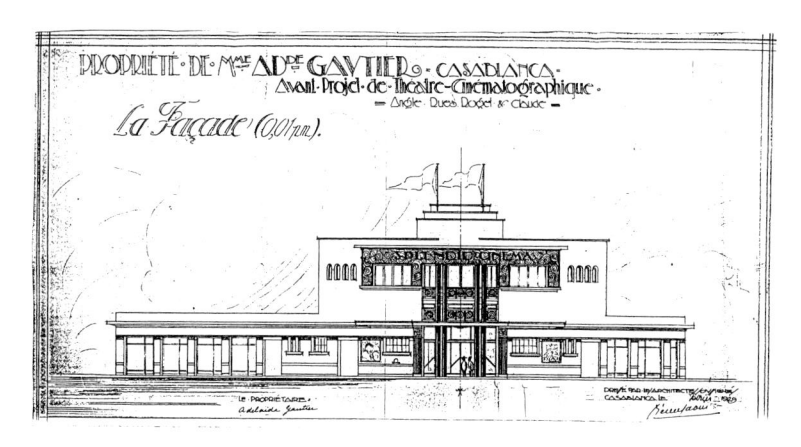

Pierre Jabin, Rialto movie theater (originally called Splendid), Rue de l'Aviateur Roget, 1930. Elevation, as featured in the building permit.

Rialto movie theater. View of entrance hall, in *Le Maroc en 38*.

Rialto movie theater. View of exterior, in *Le Maroc en 38*.

Rialto movie theater. View of the auditorium from the stage, in *Le Maroc en 38*.

Casablanca's expansion not only coincided with the development of the automobile industry, but also with the rapid growth in cinematography. The pre–World War I years saw the opening of early movie halls in the medina, followed by the construction of large theaters in the city center, such as the Empire, the Régent, the Triomphe, and the Colisée, to which Casablanca's young population flocked in open-mouthed wonder. The Rialto was constructed in 1930 by Pierre Jabin and was built to seat 1,350; it features moldings, stained-glass windows, and art deco light fittings, which contrast with its rather stark reinforced-concrete frame and cupola.[5] Another major project was the Vox (since demolished), completed by Marius Boyer in 1935 and heralded as one of the largest movie theaters in Africa. Conceived as a massive freestanding edifice, it was intended to form a monumental counterpart to the Magasins Paris-Maroc, with its "cubic mass," to quote Michel Chaillou, casting long shadows across the ground. The interior was rather less monumental and contained three stacked balconies that could seat up to two thousand. It was lit by indirect lighting and even had its own rudimentary air-conditioning system—a foldaway ceiling—which meant that the audience could breathe the cool evening air.[6]

Casablanca evolved into the very nerve center for the banking sector and the Moroccan press, resulting in various outstanding office schemes. For example, Boyer's 1930 design for the Banque Commerciale du Maroc offered a provocative variation on the monumental theme, its terraces and high-rise blocks locked in dialogue both with the conventional Banque de l'Afrique Occidentale and Prost's Compagnie Algérienne opposite the Magasins Paris-Maroc. According to the press, the originality of this office building/apartment block lay in its "two side towers, the form of its stairwells, its unusual arrangement of cantilevered corner balconies, and its large central setback, which replaces insalubrious inner courtyards." Its similarity to "a bright, light-filled stronghold, or a medieval Casbah in the Atlas mountains, gleaming with sumptuous marble from the Moroccan quarries," did not go unnoticed and demonstrated the strong impact that Boyer's southern travels had apparently made on his work.[7]

Marius Boyer, Vox movie theater, Louis Gentil Square, c. 1935. Aerial photo taken in 1936 showing rear of the Magasins Paris-Maroc.

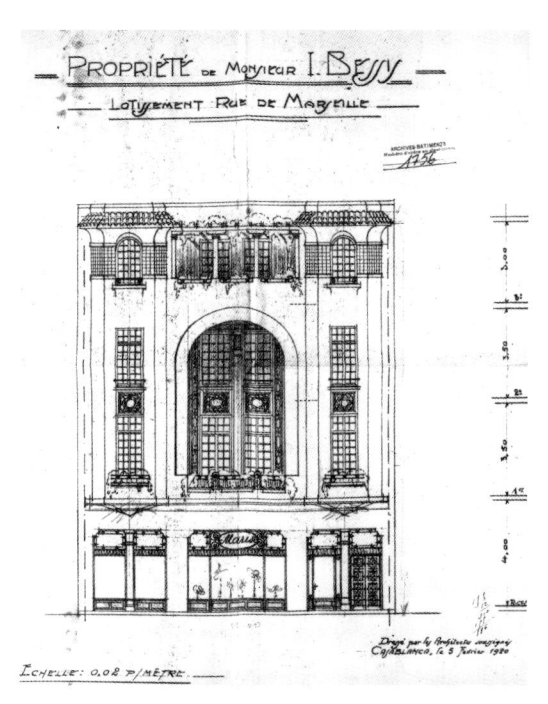

Marius Boyer, Hôtel Volubilis, Rue de l'Aviateur Védrines, 1920. Elevation from the building permit.

Pierre Jabin, La Coupole brasserie, Boulevard de la Gare, c. 1932. Published in *Bâtir*, 1932.

5 "Cinéma-théâtre le Rialto, MM. Jabin et Penicaud architectes," *Chantiers nord-africains* 1, no. 10 (October 1929): 588.

6 Chaillou, *Mémoires de Melle*, 64. See also "Les beaux cinémas casablancais," 79–81.

7 "Casablanca, la Banque commerciale du Maroc," *Bâtir* (January 1933): 15.

Building Modern Leisure Facilities

Marius Boyer, Banque Commerciale du Maroc, Rue Gallieni, 1930. General view. Photographed in 1995.

Henri Prost and Antoine Marchisio, Compagnie Algérienne building, Avenue Général d'Amade and Place de France, 1928. Interior perspective.

8 "Le nouvel immeuble de la Banque d'Etat du Maroc à Casablanca," special issue of *Réalisations*, no. 4 (March 1938): 85–124.

9 "L'immeuble d'un grand quotidien et d'une imprimerie moderne," *Chantiers nord-africains* 4, no. 8 (August 1932): 647–50.

The Banque d'État du Maroc, completed by Edmond Brion in 1937, was built to a more conservative design. It makes up the fourth side of the Place Administrative, its frontage reflecting the scale of the other buildings in the square and its main hall forming one of Casablanca's most successful examples of the covered patio.[8] The cautious style employed by Brion echoes that of the headquarters of the newspaper *La Vigie marocaine*, which were built by Boyer on a corner site of Boulevard de la Gare. The tower of these headquarters was made to break with the eaves' height so that it would enter into the play of the new minarets. Conversely, the headquarters and printing works of *Le Petit Marocain*, designed by the Bern-based architect Seliner, convey a terse architectural language.[9]

Boyer's solutions stand out most within this particular building type. His 1934 scheme for a tobacco factory on the edge of the new medina is especially noteworthy, combining a hierarchically symmetrical language in the office structures with

Edmond Brion, Banque d'État du Maroc, Boulevard de Paris, 1937. Facade overlooking the boulevard and Place Administrative. Photographed in 1992.

Edmond Brion, Banque d'État du Maroc, 1937. Glazed roof in the main hall, in *Réalisations*, March 1938.

an entirely functionalist syntax for the workshops.[10] The Shell building, constructed in the same year, introduced a new note into Boulevard de la Gare, not so much through the design of its window scheme and tectonic elements, which closely resemble certain patterns widely used at the time in Berlin, as through the way it lithely envelopes the boulevard corner. A more fluid urban aesthetic was thus established, replacing the somewhat jerky pattern adopted in the buildings of the earlier period.

Schools in the *ville nouvelle*, along with the boys' high school by Pierre Bousquet on Avenue Mers-Sultan (conceived according to a system of detached pavilions), continued to be constructed according to nonadventurous Protectorate designs.[11] Only the Italians dared to take a more innovative approach, as is finely illustrated by Mario Paniconi and Giulio Pediconi's 1935 scheme for a school in Roches Noires, which is remarkable for its cylindrical tower, harboring an African-

10 Roger Duroudier, "Une manufacture de tabacs à Casablanca," *Chantiers nord-africains* 6, no. 5 (May 1934): 373–77.

11 A. Roby, "Le lycée de garçons de Casablanca," *France-Maroc* (September 1923): 169–70; and Descamps, *L'architecture moderne au Maroc*, 1: pl. 49–50.

Marius Boyer, Shell building, Boulevard de la Gare, 1934. General view from General Patton traffic circle. Photographed in 1991.

Marius Boyer, Hôtel d'Anfa, Anfa quarter, c. 1938. Photo c. 1950, published in *L'évolution du Maroc en 1951*, 1951.

style screen wall.[12] Corbusian elements also made a rather unexpected appearance in Casablanca, as can be seen in the police headquarters designed by Maurice Sori in 1936 and completed in 1939.[13] It is composed of large rows lined with ribbon windows and is organized around an entrance hall surmounted by a large cupola lit with glass blocks. Its frontal openings bear a certain resemblance to those on the ground floor in the Maison Cook, constructed by Le Corbusier in Boulogne in 1926. The main food market, built by Paul Perrotte between 1936 and 1939 to his winning competition design, was afforded similar radical solutions and features a large yet delicate parabolic arch, rather like Émile Maigrot's covered market in Rheims.

External points of reference were not, therefore, lacking in Casablancan construction, though there did develop a propensity toward training homegrown architects, thanks notably to Boyer's proactive involvement. Although he did not officially graduate as an architect until 1932 (the year in which he sent the Villa

12 This building was one of the few in Casablanca that was considered worthy of publication in *L'Architecture d'aujourd'hui*: "Ecole italienne à Casablanca, M. Paniconi et J. Pediconi, architectes," *L'Architecture d'aujourd'hui* 7, no. 3 (March 1936): 75. For the Italian echo, see "Tre scuole all'estero, arch. Mario Paniconi e Giulio Pediconi," *Architettura* (August 1935): 463–74. The commission emanated from the Italian embassy in Rabat. Giulio Pediconi, interview by Jean-Louis Cohen, Rome, June 28, 1997.

13 "Services de la sécurité, Casablanca: Maurice Sori, architecte," *L'Architecture d'aujourd'hui* 16, no. 3 (September–October 1945): 75.

Maurice Sori, central police station, Boulevard Jean Courtin, 1939. Entrance dome, in *L'Architecture d'aujourd'hui,* **1945.**

Paul Perrotte, wholesale market, Rue du Chevalier Bayard, 1936–39. Partial view of the exterior. Photographed in April 1943.

Mario Paniconi and Giulio Pediconi, Italian schools, Rue Eugène Lendrat, Roches Noires, 1935. Partial view from the street.

Boyer's draftsmen, c. 1935.

Grand plans to Paris, as part of his thesis), Boyer had been lecturing since the early 1920s in Casablanca's École des Beaux-Arts, under the directorship of the painter Édouard Brindeau. A two-year program was put in place, together with an annual "Boyer competition" and "debate topics on architectural theory," selected by the *maître* himself. It was here that young professionals such as Gaspare Basciano, Corrado Fichet, Sylvain Chefnoury, and many others learned the rudiments of urban design.[14] At the same time, Boyer opened the doors of his practice (which was then the largest in Casablanca) to young enthusiasts. He would often support them financially and recommend them in a paternal way to the professors heading the ateliers of the École des Beaux-Arts in Paris. Due to Boyer's mediation, then, the École in Paris would appear to have acted as a magnet that drew the major architects of post-1945 Casablanca, such as Élie Azagury and Jean-François Zevaco.[15]

[14] Marius Boyer, "Programme des cours de M. Boyer," École des Beaux-Arts, Casablanca, 1923; see also the programs of studio exercises assigned to students (copied from those given at the École des Beaux-Arts in Paris during the years 1890–1910), Gaspare Basciano personal archives, Casablanca. See also: K. M., "L'École des Beaux-Arts de Casablanca," *France-Maroc* 8, no. 6 (June 1923): 106–7.

[15] Moroccans with French university training were rare at the time. In 1930, they numbered twenty, and were exclusively doctors, lawyers, and teachers. The case of the doctors in this group has been well documented by Paul in "Professionals and Politics in Morocco."

Sidi Belyout beach, seen from a roof terrace in the medina with the new town in the background. Photo c. 1913.

Conquering Casablanca's Beachside

We were sitting side by side in the rough, abrasive grass of the dunes. Sidi Belyout beach curved flatly before us, exposed by the low tide. The afternoon was drawing to a close, and the blinding heat had eased, the sun dipping into the darkening blue sky toward the city's minarets and tiered terraces. It was a Sunday afternoon, so similar to many an afternoon I have spent in Royan and Biarritz, with families slowly making their way back through crackling seaweed. Brightly dressed women were chattering away, perched on the carcass of a gutted rowboat. A yacht floated along in the open sea, its sails puffed out, etching a black-and-white pattern against the deep blue of the ocean.

Émile Nolly, 1915[16]

Casablanca's frenzied inland growth by no means constituted the sole focus of urban development, for, as of 1912, the city's seafront also underwent alterations, based on the need for port facilities and a demand for recreational seaside activities. As early as the turn of the century, the German writer Mohr praised Casablanca's "fine beach" of Sidi Belyout and its bathing amenities.[17] Situated near the city walls, port, and cemetery, this beach had become a favorite swimming spot soon after the 1907 landings, although the nudity of Moroccan men so shocked Anglo-Saxon diplomats that the public authorities had to enforce the wearing of "bathing trunks or some other item of clothing."[18]

A retaining wall was built at the start of the future Boulevard du IVe-Zouaves to shield both the road and the beach, situated just a stone's throw from the Place de France, in the city center. The bathing scenes depicted by Nolly are highly picturesque, even though the Casablancans of today have no recollection whatsoever of this beach. "Dotted with huts and attractions,"[19] it served as a popular summer promenade and leisure facility for the European colony. Rather symbolically, the new ruling power even staged its military parade there on Bastille Day. However, industrial growth and development of the port soon prevented people from using

16 Nolly, *Le conquérant*, 206.

17 Mohr, "Casablanca in Marokko," 78.

18 Bylaw no. 12 of July 13, 1909, on "*décence publique aux bains de mer*" (public propriety at seaside beaches), MAE, consulat Tanger, carton 667. Bathing trunks were obligatory at the port and on the shore up to a distance of three kilometers from the city.

19 Nolly, *Le conquérant*, 30.

Sidi Belyout beach, as seen during the Bastille day 1913 military parade. Published in *Casablanca de 1889 à nos jours*, 1928.

this strip of sand, which lay too close to the city center; thus by 1928 it had already been firmly relegated to the past:

> Our fine beach has gone, replaced by others. Casablanca needs more building space, which explains why the port station project has been put before health and fitness. Fortunately, though, there are two up-and-coming beaches: Ain Diab in the west and Ain Sebaa in the east.[20]

Once the Europeans arrived, other beaches around the city started to be used too. On Tardif's 1912 plan, a narrow stretch of sand bordering the Télégraphi sans fil, or TSF, quarter that had only recently been built west of the medina, is qualified as a beach. It edges an area that was still largely rural at the time but which was quickly swallowed up by the port development. Roches Noires beach (one of the earliest), with an alternating pattern of rocks and fine sand, lies east of Sidi Belyout. A lighthouse and casino were built on this spot, swiftly accompanied by recreational facilities where people could eat and socialize. In their 1918 study of the city's amenities, Lapeyre and Marchand noted that between June and late September, this beach served as "a popular meeting place where bathers come to recharge their batteries and enjoy several hours of coolness to recover from the sun's scorching rays."[21]

Further east, the beach of Ain Sebaa borders an industrial, working-class district that took a fair amount of time to develop, although it was eventually chosen to accommodate a municipal tree nursery and a zoo. It was enlivened by attractions, dance halls, and restaurants, and proved popular with the local French, Spanish, and Italian working classes. To a certain degree, the Roches Noires and Ain Sebaa beaches suffered from their proximity to the city's industrial zone, though they would continue to be used by the local population or by Casablancans seeking a change of scene, just three kilometers from the center.

In the 1920s, the long sandy beach of Fédala, twenty-five kilometers east of Casablanca, became a favorite family bathing area, for not only was it a public beach, but it was also one of the rare few in the region to be protected from the

20 Goulven, *Casablanca de 1889 à nos jours*, 27.

21 Lapeyre and Marchand, *Casablanca, la Chaouïa*, 117.

Building Modern Leisure Facilities 261

Roches Noires beach, postcard c. 1920.

22 Victor Cambon, "Les villes marocaines en 1927," *La semaine coloniale*, special Morocco issue (1927): 21.

sometimes deadly currents. Its three-kilometer stretch was sprinkled with wooden beach huts and canvas structures. Trees were planted on the dunes and a promenade was laid out along the shoreline, on a vast esplanade bounded by the pine forest and the gardens of a large hotel. Writing in 1927, Victor Cambon was struck by "the clearly Portuguese style" of Fédala's buildings and by the number of Casablancans who used the beach: "It is rare in Morocco to find such long beaches sheltered from the waves. Believing it could serve as a summer bathing attraction for the residents of Casablanca, the developers decided to build an elegant and comfortable sea-bathing facility there, together with a casino, hotels, open-air attractions, and a large park with wide paths winding through it."[22]

Café des Roches on Roches Noires beach, postcard c. 1914.

El Hank coastal area, postcard c. 1920.

A Changing Beachscape

In the early 1920s, Casablanca's sedentary upper and middle classes let it be known that they wanted a safe beach equipped with leisure facilities and within easy reach of the city. A more family-oriented lifestyle was taking over, accompanied by "a fondness for the seashore."[23] Although the Casablancan authorities were initially reluctant to set up facilities close to the sea, they nonetheless decided to capitalize on the climate and the ocean. During the period when Morocco had been perceived as a passing-through place, there had been no point in "worrying about a beach,"[24] but now that the Europeans were beginning to put down roots, it was a different story. The Roches Noires beach was too dangerous, owing to the low outcrop of rocks from which the beach's name derives, while Ain Sebaa had become swamped by industry, and Fédala was too far for those Casablancans who did not have a car. The El Hank headland was also inhospitable, and so it was at Ain Diab, a site to the west of Casablanca, that a typically French beach resort was set up for the privileged classes. As Laprade reports, although the beach was fairly remote, it was nonetheless connected to the city by a road that had been laid by General Calmel during the war. The general had used the labor of German prisoners to open up "access to the fine beaches of Sidi Abderrahmane, next to which a strategic road was laid in case of a German submarine attack."[25] "Unearthed" by Croze and Saboulin, the Ain Diab coastal site came into use around 1923, its rapid rise in popularity surprising more than one eyewitness.[26]

Ain Diab was particularly popular with businessmen, since it was a safe place where their families could spend the summer without having to leave the confines of the city. On the other hand, the coastline was arid and barren, with rocky waters and exceedingly high dunes. Moreover, the waves were very powerful there, and there were dangerous crosscurrents and a sandbar. A vast amount of investment was thus required in order to "tame the sea" and make it safe for bathing.

There was no lack of ideas on this score. In response to a request by the Teste brothers in 1920, Laprade drew up a scheme to convert the Ain Diab site into a full-scale seaside resort. His design took the form of a resort neighborhood modeled on the French Riviera with a "Croisette promenade," "municipal casino," hotels

23 Alain Corbin, *Le Territoire du vide: l'Occident et le désir du rivage 1750–1840* (Paris: Aubier, 1988).

24 Joseph Goulven, "La plage de Casablanca, Ain-Diab," *La Terre marocaine* (May 15, 1928): 132.

25 Laprade, "Souvenirs du temps de la guerre," 547.

Thus, in 1928, Joseph Goulven asked, "Who would have predicted the birth of Ain Diab ten years ago?" Goulven, "La plage de Casablanca, Ain-Diab," 132.

Building Modern Leisure Facilities 263

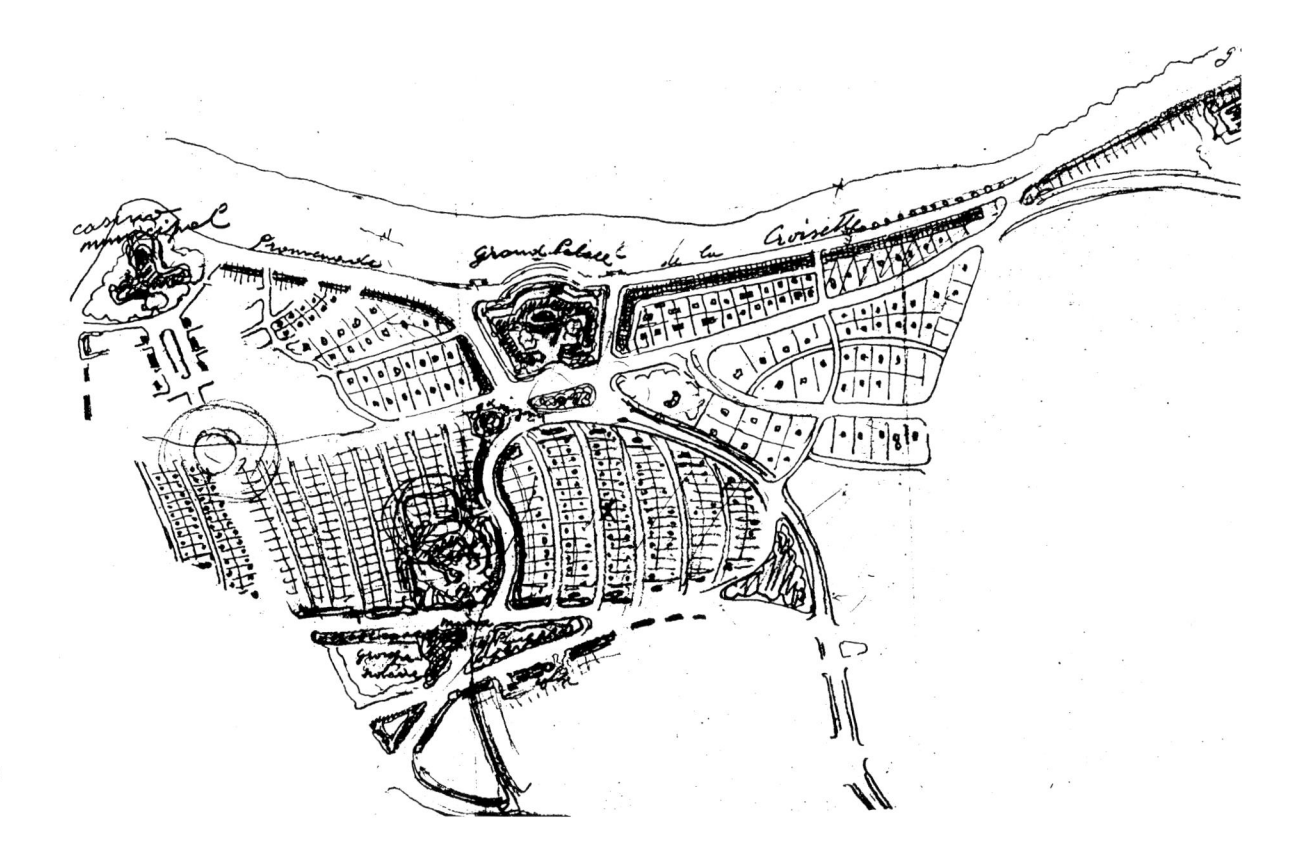

Albert Laprade, development plan for the seafront in Anfa, sketch, 1920.

(including two "major luxury hotels" set just in front of the ocean), deluxe villas, a few apartment buildings, and gardens. He likewise planned for a racetrack, along with a department store, town hall, school, and church. The clients asked Laprade to provide a plan "showing an easily marketable bird's-eye view of their housing development and land in Anfa."[27] They also asked whether it would be possible to set up a market and shops "on the main avenue served by the streetcar,"[28] and suggested creating a "sports complex" in the green tract of land that lay between the Anfa neighborhood and the TSF quarter, "to bring the place alive on Sundays." In the end, though, this highly ambitious project, for which Laprade designed a vast landscaping plan, was shelved, and the site was devoted to prosaic residential subdivisions.

In 1928, Joseph Goulven submitted a proposal to the Public Works Department for a swimming pool and surrounding facilities along the Ain Diab road to compensate for "the lack of a beach close to Casablanca." He marked out the site's boundaries on an aerial photo, entitling it "Ain Diab Village Resort":

> The benefits of developing Ain Diab are clear. Very soon, Casablanca's main beach will have ceased to exist and the public authorities will have to meet the residents' legitimate demands for a local spot where they can relax, have a change of scene, and bathe... In fact, forty buildings have already been constructed to this end for the sum of around two million francs.[29]

Goulven noted that Ain Diab's summer facilities and "the popular walk along the stretch of rocky shoreline are attracting scores of Casablancans." Given the treacherous currents, he suggested "building a major swimming facility nestled among the rocks—an entirely plausible scheme given that the rocks run parallel to the shore." He recommended setting up breakwaters to protect the pool,[30] and advised fitting out the beach in the same way as coastal resorts in western France, namely, "building the beach huts on a raised platform just at the edge of

27 Albert Laprade to Félix Pertuzio, head of the Casablanca City Plan Service, October 9, 1921, fonds Laprade, AN, 403 AP.

28 Maurice and Théo Teste to Albert Laprade, ca. 1920, fonds Laprade, AN, 403 AP.

29 Goulven, proposal for Ain Diab village resort, November 23, 1928, MAE, carton 856, Région de Casablanca, affaires immobilières.

30 Goulven, proposal for Ain Diab Village Resort.

the high-tide line." Fortunately, this second idea was not followed through, nor, rather more unfortunately, was the project to "incorporate shade and greenery along the beach."³¹

While it failed to generate an immediate response, Goulven's scheme did nevertheless serve as the conceptual basis for a public swimming pool on a quieter site closer to the city center (analyzed in a later chapter), as well as for many development projects in Ain Diab itself. Furthermore, in 1928, the Public Works Department ordered access roads to be laid. A bus service was provided, and the Forestry Commission launched an afforestation program to bind the sand dunes. Forty or so buildings, ranging from villas to chalets and huts, sprang up on this site henceforth known as La Corniche. And so it was that in the space of just twenty years, an inhospitable site had been transformed into a prime recreational setting, swinging the focus of summer activity from east to west.

31 Goulven noted that private gardens planted with "eucalyptus, mimosas, araucarias, cypresses, tamarisks, and myoporums demonstrate their resistance to sea breezes" and could thus be used along public thoroughfares. Goulven, "La plage de Casablanca, Ain-Diab," 133.

Georges Renaudin, La Réserve restaurant, Ain Diab, 1933. Photographed in 1994.

Building Modern Leisure Facilities   265

32 Chaillou, *Mémoires de Melle*, 44.

33 "Compte-rendu de la séance du 3 mars 1937," *Bulletin de la Chambre de commerce et d'industrie de Casablanca* 16, no. 177 (March 1937): 149.

34 Richard Klein and Dominique Delaunay, *Le Touquet-Paris-Plage: la Côte d'Opale des années trente* (Paris: Norma, 1994).

35 Situated to the right of the Ain Diab quarter's lower periphery, this site remained uninhabited due to the severity of the sea spray and the nighttime humidity.

36 "Le Lido de Casablanca, Maurice L'Herbier, architecte SFA," *Chantiers nord-africains* 2, no. 9 (September 1930): 799–801. The basin measured thirty meters by fifteen meters.

37 It was named after the head of Regional Administration and president of the Casablanca Municipal Council. "Les piscines municipales à Casablanca," *Bulletin économique du Maroc* (July 1936): 254; "Piscine municipale de Casablanca," *Réalisations* (November 1936): 185–94; "La piscine municipale de Casablanca," *Chantiers nord-africains* 9, no. 12 (December 1937): 529–53; "La piscine de Casablanca et l'électricité," *Réalisations*, supplement to no. 7 (April 1937): 229–38; "La piscine municipale de Casablanca," *Réalisations* (January–February 1938): 82–84; "Parcs et jardins et réalisations dans le domaine des sports," *Revue de géographie marocaine* (May 1939).

38 R. T., "Le vélodrome de Casablanca," *Chantiers nords-africains* (December 1929): 703–4

39 *BMO* 6, no. 5 (September–October 1931).

40 Many contractors' names appear in the numerous articles devoted to this Municipal Works Service project but, strangely enough, no architect's name is mentioned.

41 "Piscine municipale de Casablanca," 186.

Maurice L'Herbier, Lido pool, Anfa-Plage, 1930. General view, in *Chantiers nord-africains*, September 1930.

Georges Orthlieb public swimming pool, Boulevard Calmel, 1934. The diving boards, seen from the café, postcard c. 1936.

Seawater Pools for the Masses

Flat-nosed buses with prehistoric chug-chug engines rattled along the roads in the afternoon sun. Jolting us from side to side, they wound their way toward the beaches and the Orthlieb swimming pool, named after a deceased administrator who was now undoubtedly administrating the waves from up above. At high tide, the ocean's frothy breakers would crash over the long seawall, built to prevent us from swimming out into the open sea. It ranked as the largest swimming pool in the world (the whole world came to rank it) and was situated next to the Georges-Louis competition pool, which was used by the Vallerey brothers and by Alex Jany—the 100-meter freestyle world champion.

Michel Chaillou, 1993[32]

Avid swimmers were allotted training facilities within the port, which were set up by sports associations. The Bathers' Club, located in the harbor along the Delure breakwater, was replaced in 1937 by the swimming section of Casablanca's university racing club.[33] For less experienced swimmers, however, the city's beaches were notoriously dangerous due to their breakers and sandbars; seawater swimming pools became a consistently popular feature, filling at high tide like the one in the channel resort of Le Touquet.[34]

The first such facility set up along La Corniche was the Lido, which opened in the summer of 1930 on the site known as Anfa-Plage.[35] It replaced the Potinière, a restaurant/dance club that had been closed for the previous eight years, and before its opening it was given a complete overhaul by Maurice L'Herbier. A concrete swimming pool was set into the rocky ground, and seawater was pumped into it from a well dug into the rocks.[36] The club's two large terraces were patterned with colonnade pergolas and were lined with approximately forty beach huts arranged in a semicircle; these had just two showers (a minimum requirement that was perhaps acceptable back in 1930). The color scheme was distinctly south Moroccan—red-ochre walls, ivory columns, and blue pergolas—and the exposed brick bar was wittily named Brik's Bar.

The Lido was, however, ousted from center stage after the Georges Orthlieb public swimming pool opened on July 14, 1934.[37] This formed part of a broader project that had been drawn up in 1931 by the Department of Architecture for a large-scale recreational center on the beach in the TSF quarter; the first facility built there was Alexandre Cormier's cycling stadium.[38] The site was set well away from the sewers, at the start of Boulevard Moulay-Youssef, which meant that it benefited from good bus links. The underlying idea of the project was to create a "foreshore swimming pool measuring some three hundred meters by one hundred meters," and "another main pool" as well as a competition pool and "a sandy area for children."[39] A sports ground was also planned. The initial concept was revised in 1932, and the built work was finally reduced to a three-hectare plot, in view of the decision to drop the sports ground scheme and postpone construction of the competition pool.[40]

The first summer was a huge success, with four thousand daily visitors instead of the anticipated one thousand; this was due to the quality of the facilities and to the novelty of a pool linking the city with the sea. Because the rocks were broken up, the pool could be snuggled into the ocean, yet protected from the waves. This was confirmed by observers, according to whom, "One can often see a still expanse of water cradled among the waves that roll in from the open sea and crash onto the breakwaters, which can barely be made out above the water's surface."[41] The overall site measured 5.7 hectares, making it the largest bathing facility in Africa, composed of a large pool, a public pool, and a watersports stadium. The seawater was renewed daily by the rising tide, and a pump was installed to cope with cases of

Georges Orthlieb public swimming pool, Boulevard Calmel, 1934. Photo taken in November 1942 from a USS Ranger-based plane.
The TSF station is in the foreground. The pool was divided into two parts of unequal length. The building to the west housed a café-brasserie, showers, and lavatories on the ground floor, and the first floor was devoted to "one of the best restaurants" in town. The larger building to the east contained the locker rooms and fully fitted beach huts.

Georges Orthlieb public swimming pool, Boulevard Calmel, 1934. Main pool, postcard c. 1936.

Building Modern Leisure Facilities 267

insufficient swell. Some 328,000 visitors were recorded within the first four months of its opening, causing the municipal authority to extend it westward by way of a more "ordinary" pool. This public pool was used mainly by a low-income population that did not know how to swim, which was true not only of most Muslim and Jewish Moroccans, but also of the poorer European classes. Although the pool was some 110 meters long, it went no deeper than 1.5 meters. The locker rooms were shared by men and women and there was only one bar.

The Casablancans felt extremely proud of their modern swimming pool, which became a favorite meeting place for all city dwellers, whatever their station in life. Its features were described in 1950 by American photographer G. E. Kidder Smith, who considered the "Toboggan" of the "enormous ocean-fed swimming pool" an "outstanding design." He saw in this "entertaining structure . . . a clever and capable exposition of French concrete versatility."[42] The primary objective of the pool, which had been to fuse the classes and populaces through sport and play, was thus achieved for a while. Yet the social mix, which worked so well to start with, would later be killed, due to social and ethnic divides, followed by outright racism. The Europeans eventually stopped using the facility, and in 1986 it was filled in to make way for Casablanca's grand mosque.

Casablanca in 1939—Elusive Unity

Our local architecture is frequently lambasted for its lack of homogeneity, and with good reason too, for it seems to be based on a wide spectrum of different design concepts, each architect testing out various styles to suit his jumble of clients. As Mr. Prost told me recently, expressing, it must be said, much sympathy for such architectural chaos, Casablanca's private construction reflects its role as a major port in which ships from all over the world come to dock.

Chantiers nord-africains, 1931[43]

There can be no doubt as to Casablanca's economic and demographic success, just twenty years after the Prost plan was implemented. Its main squares set a clear urban framework, and the port was applauded in all contemporary commentary. Conversely, though, the city center was heavily congested, and its urban fabric was a total mélange of architectural patterns. Despite (or perhaps because of) their sophistication, the initial development principles drafted for the city had been forgotten in the daily routine of bureaucratic urban planning.

The fact that some of the large thoroughfares of the 1917 plan had not yet been built was also problematic, since there were still many bottlenecks in the central quarters. This circulation problem was highlighted by Prost in a report drawn up after an inspection visit in 1932, in which he recommended creating a traffic circle system and even underpasses, such as at the intersection of Boulevard de la Gare and Rue Georges Mercié. He pointed out how it had originally been decided not to align some of the roads—the Route de Médiouna, for instance, and part of Rue du Général Drude—in order "to avoid impinging on Casablanca's trade." In other words, these roads could be widened, and this was now a measure that urgently needed to be applied.[44]

Numerous programs had been launched for building residential neighborhoods and laying wide boulevards, but very few works had actually been completed. In 1926, the economy picked up, and Pierre Léris noted a certain amount of "concentration." That is, "instead of building a splurge of high-rises on the outskirts, stories are being added to existing corner buildings in the central area."[45] An unsigned

42 G. E. Kidder Smith, "Report from Morocco," *The Architectural Forum* 92, no. 6 (June 1950): 64. Beginning in the 1940s, George Everard Kidder Smith (1913–97) published many illustrated books on European and American architecture.

43 "Immeubles modernes à Casablanca, immeubles boulevard de Paris," *Chantiers nord-africains* 3, no. 7 (August 1931): 804.

44 Prost, "Rapport de fin de mission au Maroc," 1.

45 Léris, "Histoire immobilière de Casablanca," 28.

memorandum (undoubtedly written by Brion) condemned the "lack of unity" and even "the anarchy" of Casablanca's "building arrangement," without laying the blame in any way at Prost's door. Although everything sat "in its rightful place," the memorandum went on to say, the original layout plan had been "distorted," due to excessively lenient building codes and "to the fact that private venture always wins over public interest."[46] Brion's acerbic criticism was leveled chiefly at the uneven eaves' height and building sizes along the central thoroughfares; only the first sections of Avenue D'Amade and Boulevard de la Gare escaped reproof, saved by their strict portico arrangement:

> It has to be admitted that unity has been achieved here through a portico arrangement. Yet this is an exception, and visitors must surely be shocked by the sight of other central streets, squares, and crossroads, wondering why, in such a modern, well-laid-out city, property developers have been allowed to give full vent to their tasteless flights of fancy. Next to a standard-height building one can see others that have just one, two, or three stories, depending on the whim of the owner. Casablanca is truly in the destructive grip of eccentric foolery.

Brion laments the lack of a sufficiently influential official body, since the Department of Architecture and City Planning that had wielded such power under Lyautey was now completely ineffectual. Its director, Antoine Marchisio, was the first to agree with "the shortcomings in Casablanca's building principles and guidelines." In his view, "the Department of Architecture set up by Prost in 1913 had been unable to keep abreast of Morocco's rapid urban expansion, Casablanca in particular." He also regretted the fact that developers had been given "free rein to

46 Edmond Brion, "Du manque d'unité dans la présentation immobilière de Casablanca, ses conséquences; exemples, recherche des remèdes," Casablanca, Conseil économique régional consultatif, ca. 1935, MH Rabat, D 242, 1.

Henri Prost's development and extension plan for Casablanca. Zoning plan, c. 1932.
This document shows the proposed extension for the outer areas of the city, which were not incorporated in the plan drawn up in 1917.

Apartment buildings in central Casablanca. Photographed c. 1934. Right: Rue de Pont-à-Mousson; note Avenue du Général d'Amade in the background, with the Studios and IMCAMA building. "The anarchy" that reigned in the city center is illustrated by the contrasts in scale between the buildings.

"An industrial sector in Casablanca," development plan for Roches Noires and the factory quarter, drafted by the Town Planning Department in March 1935. Aerial perspective viewed from the east. The graphic detailing in this drawing resembles the project for the square in the new medina extension. Lower right: the Chaux et Ciments factory.

build as high as they liked," and that regulations governing height restrictions had not been more explicit, in other words, that they did "not impose a *minimum* height." Marchisio also pointed out that sites awaiting construction still contained *derbs*, and declared that "the time it takes to implement a plan once it has been approved is excessive." Consequently, "the city's overall architectural quality risks being permanently marred."[47]

These comments provide explicit insight into Casablanca's contradictory urban mesh. As a result of the preliminary working relationship that was established between the Protectorate, the municipal authority, and private entrepreneurs, building codes were instituted and a complex plan was drawn up, though only partially implemented. However, once the initial street-development phase was completed, the Department of Architecture lost its hold, leaving the land free for lone investors to do as they liked. This situation was aggravated by the fact that freestanding buildings had become the main focus in architectural doctrines and that the municipal council was extremely quick to side with real-estate developers. As early as the 1930s, owners of lots along Boulevard Moulay-Youssef challenged the building codes, notably demanding the right to reduce the sidewalk space and to build alongside the street. Flooded with such requests, the council ended up acquiescing in 1932.[48]

The so-called failures that Michel Écochard attributed to Prost in 1949 when he began work on a new master plan did not, in reality, stem from Prost's urban design. The real problem was that the road system was developed out of step with the apartment buildings and office blocks, since construction of the latter depended on real-estate trends. Yet despite all the criticism, the viewpoint expressed in 1940 by the *Revue de géographie marocaine*—that the Protectorate "has contributed to endowing Casablanca with all the attributes of a modern city rivaling any French agglomeration"—was largely shared on both sides of the Mediterranean.[49]

Construction slowed on the eve of World War II.[50] The housing crisis had peaked, with Casablanca's yearly immigration intake totaling roughly 5,000 Europeans and 20,000 Moroccans. The French subsequently found themselves pressed on several fronts to tackle the issue of Muslim housing in a fair and non-racist manner. It must be remembered, after all, that the Muslim population was confined to spaces that were enclosed either physically (the old medina) or virtually (the new medina, girded by military access roads), unlike the open European town. As Louis Delau noted, "More Muslims live in Casablanca than in any other Moroccan city," yet "many Casablancans have no contact with this ever-growing populace other than with their *fatma* [woman servant] or the street newspaper seller." However, he pointed out that "far-sighted Casablancans mix as much as possible with the Muslims, for these are a cordial, loyal, and courteous people. Furthermore, there are some types of contact that are essential and that are now gradually being established, such as with public servants, traders, and men of letters." He thus called on Casablanca's French population to "face up to its responsibilities toward the Muslim community."[51]

Despite the rising tide of nationalism, architects and planners began to switch course in terms of their approach, many of them firmly believing that Morocco's future could no longer be governed by a repressive and paternalistic colonial system. A final point worthy of interest is that postwar urban design teams, such as Écochard's, resisted the temptation of money-making ventures, and instead picked up the thread of 1930s thinking on "culture-specific housing." In many respects, therefore, the large-scale projects of the postwar period served as a pragmatic vehicle of expression for the urban policy that had been sketched out against the blurred backdrop of conflict between the Protectorate and Casablanca's political and business leaders.

Édouard Brindeau, tourism advertising poster, c. 1930. Note the romantic image attached to the city. It is also interesting to see that only the medina is portrayed, with the clock tower looking as though it were centuries old.

47 Antoine Marchisio, "Note au sujet du rapport de M. Brion sur la ville de Casablanca," Rabat, ca. 1935. It is this response by Marchisio that enables us to identify Brion as the author of "Du manque d'unité."

48 *BMO* 6, no. 2 (March–April 1931). The debate would continue during the following year. *BMO* 7, no. 2 (February–March 1932).

49 "La population de Casablanca," 45.

50 The triennial exemption from direct taxes on new buildings and the freedom granted to rental transactions were not sufficient to jump-start production.

51 Delau, "Casablanca et le Casablancais," 8.

Longitude W
290000m.E.
91
92
93
94
95
485000m.N.
480000m.N.
A T L A N T I C
Pte. d'El Hank
Barracks
El Hank
old Cimar oil storage
To Ain Diab
Anfa Superior
Hippodrome
School
Maarif
Garage
Plateau de Mers Sultan
Old Military Hospital
Chantiers
Jetée Delure
(Grande
Darse Ouest
Petit Port
Port de Pêche
Bassin Delande
Floating Dock
Môle du Commerce
Harbour Police Offices
Bassin Delpit
3 Loading chutes
Grain Silo
Landing Stage
Coal Wharf
Floating Dock
Being Reclaimed
Ancienne Médina
Sidi Belyout
Parc Lyautey
Hôpital Militaire
Nouvelle Médina
Aerial Masts
Boulevard Félix Faure
To Mazagan 60 Miles
To Fouchard 42 Miles
Approximate mean declination 1942
Annual magnetic change decrease
Longitude

Plan of Casablanca (scale: 1/10000) drawn up by the U.S. Intelligence Department in 1942. Based on the French plan of 1935, it was used for the Allied landings.

MAROC 208-I
HABITAT DU PLUS GRAND NOMBRE

Le bidonville

Causes psychologiques
de l'afflux vers les
villes.

Désir de l'individu de
s'émanciper en échappant
au patriarcat rural ?

    Ville = Eldorado ?

Psychological causes
of the movement towards
the towns.

Desire of the individual
to escape from rural
patriarchy ?

    Town = Eldorado ?

"Town = Eldorado?" or "Psychological causes of the movement toward the towns." Display "grid" designed by the Town Planning Department for a presentation given by the Moroccan group at the CIAM held in Aix-en-Provence in 1953.

The Post-1945 Golden Age and Its Dark Side

Concert given by Josephine Baker to U.S. troops at the Rialto movie theater on April 13, 1943.

When the American visitor arrives in Morocco for the first time, often the one city of whose name he is absolutely sure, and which he is determined to see, is Casablanca . . . There was once a film bearing that title, and since then the city has enjoyed the reputation of being a glamorously sinister Oriental labyrinth . . . The visitor comes [but] finds no twisting alleys, no turbaned sheiks conducting international intrigues. Instead, he is confronted with a modern metropolis that looks like a somewhat newer Havana, whose wide boulevards go on for miles, and it is only by chance that he will come upon either an alley or a turban. The place has its share of intrigue and crime, but none of all this is particularly mysterious or Eastern. Casablanca is not Morocco; it is a foreign enclave, an alien nail piercing Morocco's flank.

Paul Bowles, 1966[1]

Casablanca's destiny was transformed by upheavals during World War II. It briefly played the role of a center of French resistance after France's military defeat, when parliamentary members stepped off the *Massilia* on June 24, 1940, led by Georges Mandel. However, Resident General Noguès supported Pétain, and the attempt to create a pocket of resistance in North Africa was doomed.[2]

After the Armistice, Casablanca grew into a naval base of some importance, serving as home to the battleship *Jean Bart*, along with a considerable portion of the French submarine fleet. During the first two years of the Vichy regime, the city was, more than ever before, the hub of relations between France and Africa. It also became a stopover point for people fleeing the unoccupied zone on their way to Latin America and the United States, and was thus a temporary camp for refugees of all origins.

The war brought an end to all civil construction, except infrastructure work.[3] In addition, despite the distance, Casablanca was affected by policies instituted in France. Under instructions from Vichy, Noguès reformed the administration, suspended the elected bodies, and introduced a corporative system.[4] The Protectorate was also quick to enact the two "bylaws" established by Vichy in 1940 and 1941, whereby Jews were excluded from schools and public service positions, and were kept out of important sectors of the economy.[5] Furthermore, the *dahir** of August 22, 1941, prevented them from living in the European quarters. Given that a discriminatory decision in 1937 by the pasha of Casablanca had already barred them

1 Bowles, "Casablanca," 75.

2 Christiane Rimbaud, *L'Affaire du "Massilia"* (Paris: Seuil, 1984).

3 Attention continued to be paid to the port's extension. In April 1942 Noguès sent Vichy a "Ten-Year Improvement Plan for the Ports of Morocco." BGA, SGP, Travaux Publics, Port divers 1932–50, no. 274.

4 William A. Hoisington, *The Casablanca Connection: French Colonial Policy, 1936–1943* (Chapel Hill and London: University of North Carolina Press, 1984).

5 Michel Abitbol, *Les Juifs d'Afrique du Nord sous Vichy* (Paris: Maisonneuve et Larose, 1983), 59–107.

from the new medina,⁶ they were therefore forced either to live crammed into what remained of the mellah or to leave the city.

The Allied landings of 1942 brought about a swift return to business, generating a prosperous climate that would last until Independence. Far from weakening the city, the war substantially reinforced Casablanca's symbolic role and spurred its economic and demographic development.⁷ In its last golden age, the city underwent a radical transformation, buoyed in particular by rapid industrial growth. At the same time, new cultural ideals spread, notably in the form of Americanism, which hit Morocco well before metropolitan France. This was strongly reflected in the general lifestyle and in the architecture of bourgeois housing. It was a process that derived largely from the arrival of the Allied forces, which, in a sense, served as a real-life sequel to the city's cinematographic idealization.

A Dream Made in Hollywood

[Casablanca was Muslim and] during the Second World War it became a way station for refugees fleeing German-occupied Europe to neutral countries. Moreover, it was notoriously corrupt. There was little distinction between the Vichy authorities who were supposed to enforce the laws and the criminals who made a living by breaking them. They were two sides of the same coin and often worked profitably together. As in Saigon of the sixties, anything could be bought and sold on the black market—foreign currency, jewels, visas, girls, even human lives.

Howard Koch, 1973⁸

Operation Torch—the code name given to the long-awaited Allied landings in North Africa—took place on November 8, 1942, having been prepared by American diplomats and specialists who had gone to Casablanca to set up trade agreements between the United States and Vichy France.⁹ In fact, for some time already, U.S. networks had been looking for various ways to topple the French hegemony in Morocco. Fighting broke out, triggered by unexpected resistance from Noguès's forces after General Béthouart failed to engineer a pro-Allied coup, following which the port was bombed simultaneously by U.S. navy ships and by aircraft launched from the U.S.S. *Ranger*.¹⁰

Now occupied by Americans, the city was embroiled once again in the machinations of the war when Roosevelt and Churchill met at the Hôtel d'Anfa from January 12 to 23, 1943. It was an event that was overshadowed, from the French point of view at least, by a serious disagreement that broke out between De Gaulle and Giraud. Given the context, *Life* had no trouble finding material to run a cover story entitled "Date in Casablanca," which recounted the adventures of an American officer and a French woman who had sought refuge in Morocco.¹¹ Yet although the country was Allied territory, the wounds inflicted by Vichy policies continued to fester: refugees were still interned, and Casablancans whose houses had been requisitioned remained, in effect, homeless.

In truth, Casablanca had been taken hostage by Hollywood long before being shelled by the U.S. navy. A certain sense of adventure along the lines of Farrère's *Hommes nouveaux* was already perceptible in the hovels of the fictional Mogador frequented by Marlene Dietrich and Gary Cooper in *Morocco*, directed by Josef von Sternberg in 1938. Then came a movie that stood out from all others. Like the American remake of Julien Duvivier's *Pépé le Moko*, redubbed *Algiers* in the United States, this one was based on the play *Everybody Comes to Rick's* and was renamed *Casablanca*. It provided a great stage for conflict and intrigue for those

---

6 Abitbol, *Les Juifs d'Afrique du Nord sous Vichy*, 35. The sultan made known his sympathy to the Jewish community, a gesture that would win him their almost unanimous gratitude after the war.

7 In 1946 the city numbered 551,000 inhabitants of whom 121,000 were European and 430,000 were Moroccan.

8 Howard Koch, *Casablanca: Script and Legend* (Woodstock, N.Y.: The Overlook Press, 1973), 20.

9 One of these envoys who worked for the OSS (Organization of Secret Services) chronicled the occupation and landings in W. Stafford Reid, "Personal Experience in North Africa from April 4 to the Armistice," National Archives, Washington D.C., OSS, RG 226, box 36, file 183. See also the reminiscences of various agents documented in the "Torch Anthology," National Archives, Washington, D.C., OSS, RG 226, box 39, file 198.

10 Jacques Mordal [Hervé Cras, pseud.], *La Bataille de Casablanca (8, 9, 10 novembre 1942)* (Paris: Plon, 1952), 105–27. Note also the account of two United States Navy pilots shot down over the city. M. T. Wordell and E. N. Seiler, *"Wildcats" over Casablanca* (Boston: Little, Brown, 1943).

11 "Date in Casablanca," *Life* (February 1, 1943).

Opposite
Georges Manzana-Pissaro, U.S. military parade along Rue de l'Horloge in November 1942, oil on canvas, 1942.

Henri Giraud, Franklin D. Roosevelt, Charles de Gaulle, and Winston Churchill at the Anfa conference held from January 12 to 23, 1943. The picture was taken in the garden of Erwin Hinnen's Dar-es-Saada villa—Roosevelt's place of residence during the conference.

The U.S. fleet facing Casablanca, November 1942. Illustration published in *"Wildcats" over Casablanca* by M. T. Wordell and E. N. Seiler, 1943.

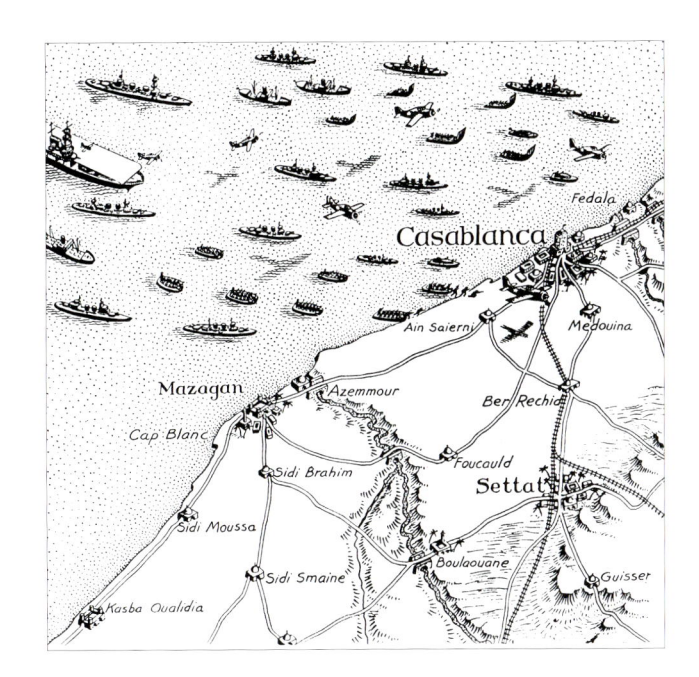

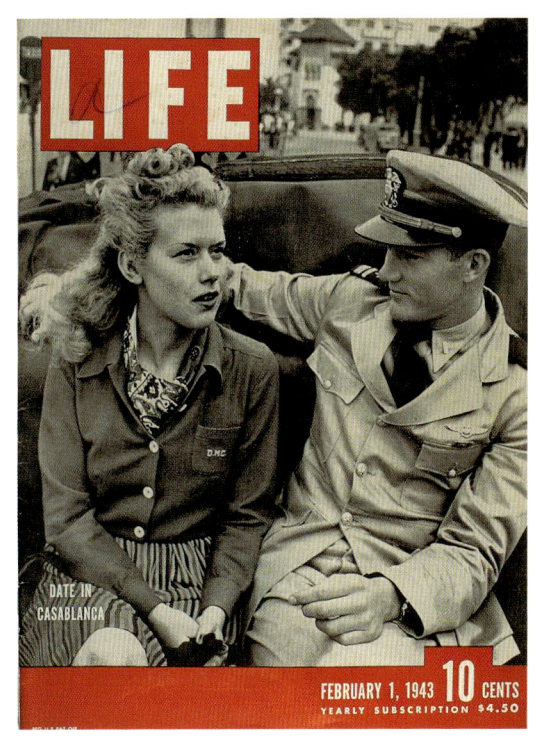

"Date in Casablanca," cover story run by *Life* on February 1, 1943.

U.S. tank on Boulevard du IVe-Zouaves, November 11, 1942. Photographed by the U.S. Navy. The Plaza hotel, Moretti-Milone building and clock tower are on the right.

The Post-1945 Golden Age and Its Dark Side   277

Review of U.S. troops by General Clark and General Patton, Boulevard de la Gare, January 1943. Marcel Desmet's Fraternelle du Nord building is on the left, in the background, and Marius Boyer's Shell building is on the right. The traffic circle would later be named after Patton.

A street in the medina, 1942. Photo taken for the *Casablanca* movie set.

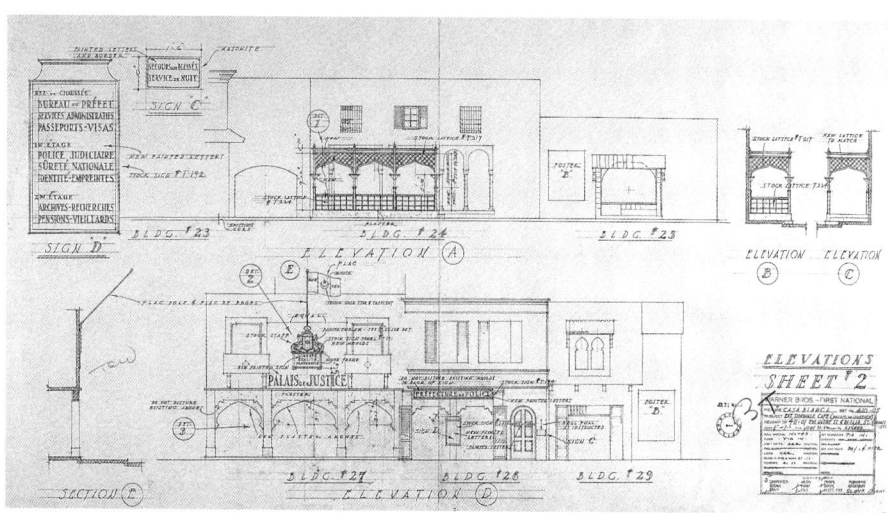

Public buildings in Casablanca. Elevations and plan. Working drawing for the *Casablanca* movie set, 1942.

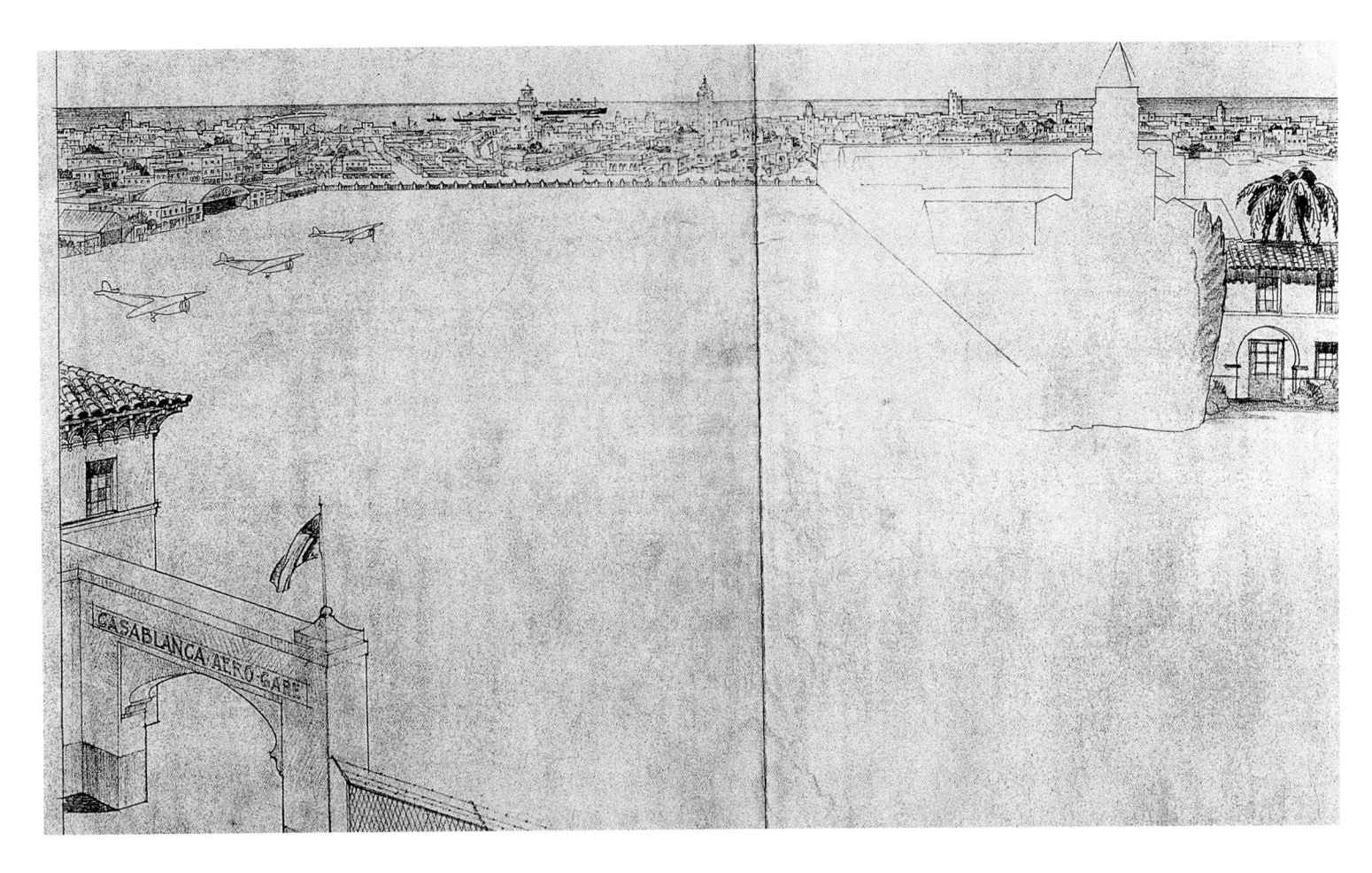

Panoramic view of the city, port, and aerodrome. Preliminary drawing for the movie *Casablanca*, 1942.

scriptwriters who had heard the city was an important stopover point for European refugees on their way to America.[12]

Julius and Philip Epstein worked up the screenplay from clichés better suited to Tangiers than to Casablanca. The audience cannot help but empathize with the café manager, Rick, played by Humphrey Bogart, when he says he was misinformed about the city's location. In the movie's opening scene "the camera pans down the facade of the Moorish buildings to a narrow, twisting street crowded with the polyglot life of a native quarter. The intense desert sun holds the scene in a torpid tranquility."

Renault: And what in heaven's name brought you to Casablanca?

Rick: My health. I came to Casablanca for the waters.

Renault: The waters? What waters? We're in the desert.

Rick: I was misinformed.[13]

The Warner team put together visuals on Casablanca taken from French illustrated periodicals available in Los Angeles[14]; it also flew a consultant over and built a small-scale version of the medina's central streets, complete with reproductions of the street signs. The preparatory drawings show the links created in the movie between the airfield, the city, and the port. Oddly enough, the tower in the Los Angeles aerodrome resembles a superstructure by Marius Boyer.[15] The producer's attachment to the city bearing the movie's name was so great that, in 1946, it took all the irony of Groucho Marx to overcome Warner Brothers' attempts to prevent the Marx brothers from calling their new movie *A Night in Casablanca*. The studio wanted exclusive ownership rights over the city, as though they were the ones who had actually created it.[16] Meanwhile, clothed in its new image, Casablanca now entered another cycle of urban planning under Courtois.

12 Charles Francisco, *You Must Remember This . . . The Filming of Casablanca* (Englewoods Cliffs, N.J.: Prentice Hall, 1980), 39.

13 Julius and Philip Epstein, screenplay for *Casablanca*, 1942, in *Casablanca Script and Legend*, 59.

14 The materials collected from these magazines were pasted into two albums now located in the Burbank Public Library, Warner Research Collection.

15 The set drawings for *Casablanca* are stored in the Warner Bros. archives at the University of Southern California School of Cinema and Television.

16 Groucho Marx, *Groucho and Me* (New York: Bernard Geiss, 1959): 243–47.

Alexandre Courtois, project for a set of skyscrapers on Rond-Point du Général d'Amade, 1944, perspective, collection Alexandre Courtois, Bayonne.

Alexandre Courtois, project for a gate leading to the old medina, Bab Marrakech, 1944, perspective, collection Alexandre Courtois, Bayonne.

Courtois Plans a "Gateway" for Casablanca

Everyone thought that Prost's plan would be good for years. Yet private interests gradually eroded the work of the planner to whom Morocco owes so many successes. Apart from a few wide major roads, which have fortunately survived, the plan was distorted beyond recognition, and nothing could be done about it.

Alexandre Courtois, 1944[17]

17 Alexandre Courtois, "Casablanca, projet d'aménagement et d'extension de la ville," 1944, MH Rabat, R 126, 42. See also Alexandre Courtois, *Studies for the Plan of Casablanca*, unpublished illustrated manuscript, 1943–45, personal archives of Alexandre Courtois, Jr., Bayonne.

18 "Le grandiose projet d'aménagement et d'extension de Casablanca," *La Presse marocaine* (Casablanca), June 1, 1945.

Quite by chance, the war brought Alexandre Courtois, winner of the 1933 Grand Prix de Rome, to Casablanca, where he had a commission to build the Morocco headquarters of a major Parisian bank. In 1943, the Protectorate's Municipalities Administration Department commissioned him to work on "a series of clearly defined schemes for the city of Casablanca, which must be strung together coherently." According to the Casablancan press, his task was therefore "to set out [the department's policy] on paper by drawing up precise plans . . . basing them on the plan drafted by the great Moroccan planner, Prost."[18] However, the scheme Courtois

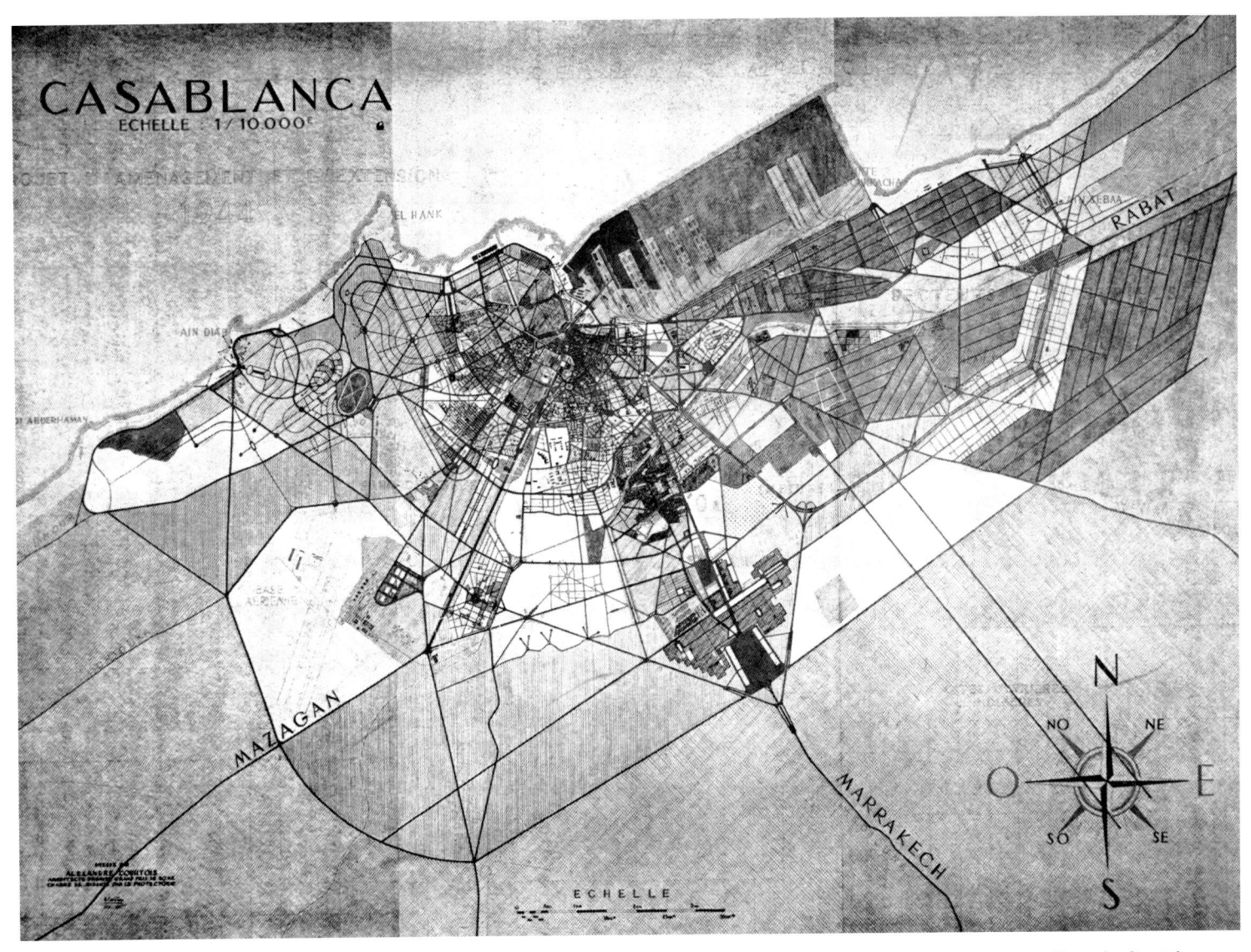

Alexandre Courtois, development and extension plan by for Casablanca, 1944. General plan published in *L'Architecture d'aujourd'hui*, September–October 1945.

presented in November 1944 went far beyond the specifications of the brief, as he "felt there was a need for more sweeping changes to the existing development plans." In his view, "the gateway to the Sharifian empire cannot attain its full potential of development in its present urban state."[19] In his preliminary plan, Courtois therefore recommended extending the layout devised thirty years earlier, but on a scale commensurate with a city that had now reached a population of 500,000.

Courtois began work on modernizing the Place de France and the Place de Verdun with a series of detailed sketches in which shades of 1930s American-style skyscrapers could still be found. Echoing prewar thinking, he spoke of a "sprawling city that gives the illusion of a capital in some places," while "in many others sadly [resembles] a ghost town." He recommended that it be given an overhaul by incorporating tall buildings and more comprehensive landscaping strategies. "It is not a question of extending the city, but rather of containing it, of organizing it, shaping its features, and giving it substance. The issue is how to channel expansion to make a city where art and good taste can flourish while at the same time providing all the requirements of modern city life, such as proper traffic flows."[20]

19 "Mission Courtois," Rabat, Service du contrôle des municipalités, 1945, MH Rabat, D 494, 1.

20 Courtois, "Casablanca, projet d'aménagement et d'extension de la ville," 1–2.

Alexandre Courtois, project for the central square of the new medina, 1944, perspective, collection Alexandre Courtois, Bayonne.

Reorganized Zoning

Courtois was critical of housing subdivisions in remote areas and suggested that "these ridiculous extensions be stopped." He also advocated laying wide thoroughfares in sparsely populated areas rather than widening centrally located streets. In addition, his development plan included changes to the original zoning schemes drawn up by Prost's successors, whom he criticized for "the whimsical manner [in which they] divided up the zones, especially in industrial areas." He denounced "the insufficient space given over to native Moroccan housing in relation to the size of the population," and when it came to the Europeans, he believed that it was "high time housing subdivisions stopped sprouting haphazardly," totally devoid of parks or communal facilities.

The zoning plan introduced significant changes regarding the range and distribution of quarters available to Moroccan newcomers. More industrial areas were created in the east, and housing for the native population in the new medina was extended "indefinitely" southward to include the development planned for Ain

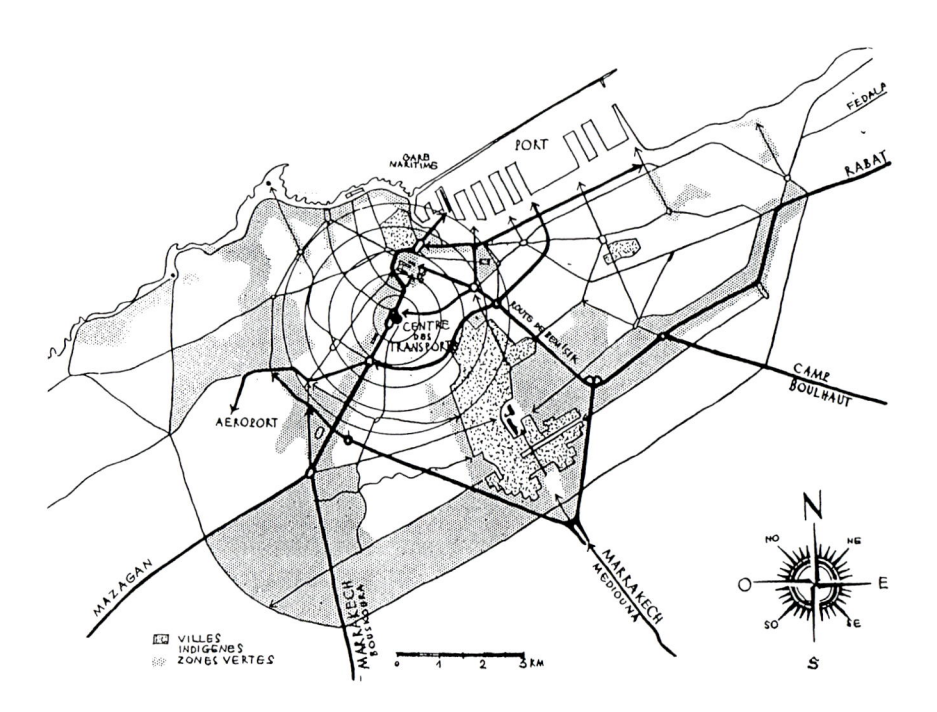

Alexandre Courtois, development plan for Casablanca, 1944. Circulation system, in *L'Architecture d'aujourd'hui*, September–October 1945.

Chock. Courtois decided that the main square should accommodate those districts that had already been planned back in the 1930s. This square, he went on to affirm, "should form the city's architectural focus," especially as it was to be home to the main mosque and a central railroad station. The scheme was modeled on the Djemaa el Fna square in Marrakech. Courtois dedicated the land between Bab Marrakech and the Place de Verdun to an urban "hub," in effect "barring the native population from the Place de France." Along with this policy of excluding Moroccans from the city center came a revival of the parks system.[21]

To meet vehicular needs, Courtois suggested modernizing the junctions and "creating a hierarchy of major access roads." He was adamant about creating a "sort of freeway" close to the greater Casablanca area and connected to a "central transport hub." He also suggested that a "broad straight avenue" be laid between the D'Amade traffic circle and the Place Administrative. He compared this "urban entranceway" with the Avenue du Bois in Paris, but instead of lining it with private mansions as in Paris, he ranged all the buildings along Avenue D'Amade in line with the "maximum eaves' height" of Boyer's Les Studios. Slightly taller "symmetrical elements" were designed to mark the "start of the urban entranceway" on the traffic circle.[22]

Courtois was particularly interested in monumental spaces, which is hardly surprising given his Beaux-Arts background. He thus aimed to make the Place Administrative "heftier and sturdier by fleshing out buildings such as the law courts and the city hall." He also designed a complex for this same square containing "a theater, an exhibition space, a museum, and a library, which can all be linked up with the existing land buildings, thus enabling them to be woven into the [square's] architectural fabric." For the Place de France, he recommended that it be set out "in an architecturally ordered arrangement" and that it be punctuated "with tall buildings [since] this area is the city's business district and is immediately adjacent to the port": "A tower is already up—the Moretti building . . . but this excessively narrow high-rise cannot remain totally secluded. It must be incorporated into a complex of buildings of similar scale that blend with the neighboring

21 The system was redefined in such a way that entrance to the city, from the southern or eastern routes, would be made via parks. Green zones were also planned for Ain Sebaa and Ain Diab. For these districts Courtois, echoing Laprade's sketch, envisioned pools, vacation hotels, and a casino. Courtois, "Casablanca, projet d'aménagement et d'extension de la ville," 9.

22 Courtois, "Casablanca, projet d'aménagement et d'extension de la ville," 26.

Aerial view of Place de France, c. 1952. The BNCI is in the center (separated from the Socifrance building by Boulevard de la Gare) and shows the new eaves' height introduced by Courtois. This is especially noticeable when compared with the Moretti-Milone building on the left. Avenue de la République had not yet been opened.

ones; furthermore, it must be ensured that the resulting urban pattern is not marred by other tall structures, unless they have been specifically designed so as not to detract from the city's skyline."[23]

Edmond Pauty, an architect and critic based in Rabat, viewed Courtois's strategy as being full of "clever combinations," paving the way for "new harmonies."[24] As a companion to the Moretti building, Courtois designed a rather stout "pylon structure," which he sited on the plot of the Magasins Paris-Maroc.[25] He also reworked the old medina in order to "create an architectural mass [opposite the Place Verdun]; although this will not necessarily constitute city walls, it will be broken up occasionally by Muslim architectural elements to facilitate passage to and from the surrounding European buildings." Some importance was attached to the railroad: besides the central passenger station in the European town, another main station for passengers and freight was proposed for the new medina, with a branch railroad leading to the industrial zones and Rabat. Assuming that Garden Cities would be going up "in the southwest suburb along the railroad," Courtois recommended that preliminary plans be drafted for the area beyond that covered in his plan, "encompassing a radius of fifteen to twenty kilometers around the center of Casablanca." Courtois's research would be rewarded later, when he was commissioned to build the station for the port of Casablanca.

Reactions to the Courtois Plan

The Municipalities Administration Department admitted that the project involved "gradual redevelopment, which could take fifty years or more." It concentrated on zoning, which was "a question of special importance with regard to industrial districts and residential neighborhoods for the native population. The relevant locations and areas for expansion should be very clearly marked out so that the specific character of the buildings in these quarters does not adversely affect the city's overall pattern."[26] On the whole, the press reacted favorably when the plan was presented to the municipal council on May 31, 1945. For instance, *La Presse marocaine* commended the option chosen for the Place de France, and applauded the idea of erecting "another skyscraper across from the Moretti building, thereby creating a monumental gateway to Casablanca."[27] *Le Journal du Maroc* also praised this scheme, which, it claimed, would result in "an architectural aesthetic as well as in a modern urban and suburban image in keeping with the stature this large city deserves."[28]

In June 1945, however, the Municipalities Administration Department raised the question of how to finance the "first comprehensive plan undertaken since Henri Prost that provides Casablanca with the means to become truly a great city." Rather than expropriation, it advised setting up landowner associations. The Protectorate's role was to oversee the "essential" aspects of the plan, i.e., "broad circulation flows and public spaces," while the municipal council was responsible for features that were more "local."[29] In fact, the administration was toying with the idea of forcing the plan on the council, "at the risk of conflict," since the latter refused a scheme for widening Boulevard de la Gare, which involved demolishing the central median.

In a sense, then, Courtois's plan can be perceived as a missed opportunity to revise Prost's preliminary proposals, "which were always being overtaken by real-estate development." According to *Le Petit Marocain*, which viewed Casablanca as "a sort of urban monster . . . regarded by both experienced urban planners and stunned tourists as the ugliest city in Morocco . . . major surgery [was] the only answer," and the state could no longer "shirk its share of financial responsibility."[30] The guiding principles of Courtois's plan would in fact often be credited to Écochard, who incorporated them into his proposals of 1951.

Casablanca Viewed as "Chained to Progress"

I used to dislike the abbreviation "Casa"—the slang of busy people looking to make a quick deal. But no sooner do you set foot in Casablanca than you see that it takes too long to use four syllables for a city that is constantly growing, that has a new face every week ... Architects, trying to keep up with a steady stream of commissions, do everything too briskly and with no program. And then of course it's a port. But it's a port with no place for boule players, and I find that encouraging. I urge all young people who want to be their own boss and who believe in the future to go to Casa.

Jacques de Lacretelle, 1949[31]

Anything goes in Casablanca. Casa's straitjacket is bursting apart. It's a city where things happen, things fall apart and change, things go up and tumble down. Bustle and yelling, singing and suffering, laughter and death. Flashy cars, beggars, shoeshine boys, newspaper vendors; drills, desert winds, ocean mist, Jews wearing skullcaps and long coats. Overhead, cranes sway, factory chimneys spew their plumes of smoke, and donkeys bray. There is a scent of oranges, and beside a display of pornographic magazines a Moroccan woman strolls by, veiled and modest, like a hundred thousand others, and living—but for how much longer—like her great-great-grandmother a hundred years ago. From a minaret, the muezzin hails Allah in piercing tones, acting as the speaking clock for this city chained to progress, with its seven hundred thousand inhabitants, its construction sites, its commercial and industrial edifices and its enormous rented homes casting their proud shadows over a few Moroccan hovels.

Jean-Édouard Chable, 1955[32]

During the postwar period, the demographic structure of Casablanca was transformed, as was the case throughout Morocco. Population shifts toward the coast accelerated, and Casablanca became home to a third of the country's urban population.[33] In addition to welcoming an influx of colonial settlers, it had to accommodate ever-growing numbers of rural and sometimes nomadic Moroccans drawn by jobs in the big city.[34] Casablanca stood out as an island of modernity in a largely underdeveloped country, but with each segment of the population presenting a different picture.

Splits in the European Population

Many of the refugees from Vichy France remained after the war because of continuing shortages at home. Then, too, there were the French who feared for their money, sometimes gained from black-market dealings, and who found a more open economy in Morocco than in postwar France. Yet the Europeans in Casablanca were not a homogeneous group by any means. While always a minority in the city, the European population had dwindled to only 19 percent of the total by 1952, while the Moroccan population "doubled every ten years" from 1907 on.[35] The number of French residents increased twofold from 1936 to 1951,[36] and there was a host of different nationalities, including Spaniards, Italians, Algerians, Americans, and Swiss, among many others. A certain amount of racism developed along class lines, as well as along an explicit north-south divide. The situation was worse when Moroccan resistance fighters opposed to the Protectorate placed a bomb at the Mers-Sultan crossroads, killing several civilians. This resulted in a demonstration organized in July 1955 by laborers and *petits blancs*, or lower-class European settlers, who made the racial divisions clear to contemporary observers:

---

31 Jacques de Lacretelle, "Casa," *Le Figaro* (Paris), July 20, 1949.

32 Jean-Édouard Chable, "Lieux dont on parle, Casablanca, édifice monumental et fragile," *La Tribune de Genève*, January 11, 1955.

33 In 1951 Morocco's population numbered 7.5 million Muslims, 200,000 Jews, and 330,000 Europeans.

34 Casablanca had almost 700,000 inhabitants in 1952, a population increase of 85 percent since 1921.

35 Adam, *Casablanca*, 1:150.

36 During that period, the French population rose from 46,400 to 99,000, equivalent to 74 percent of the 133,000 residents; Spanish citizens represented 10 percent and Italians 6 percent of the total. The number of Corsicans was striking: 19.7 of every 1,000 of the *département* of Corsica's population lived in Morocco. See the census information cited by Adam in *Casablanca*, 1:176–78.

Town Planning Department, graph illustrating Casablanca's demographic growth between 1897 and 1950.

37 "Un élément important du problème marocain: le prolétariat européen de Casablanca," *Perspectives*, no. 33 (October 1, 1955).

38 "CIFM, avant-projet de programme de construction pour l'année 56," MH (typescript). See also the data presented in Adam, Casablanca, 1:171.

39 Adam, *Casablanca*, 1:167.

Casablancan Europeans can be divided roughly into two classes. First, the wealthy or affluent class that makes up the French bourgeoisie and other foreign middle and upper classes (for example Swiss, Belgian, Scandinavian, and American). This social category owns or controls the city's main industry and trade. It supplies senior managers for the administration and private companies. Its standard of living is high, and it is proud of its wealth and status. It considers itself indispensable to Morocco, no matter what happens, because it feels that it would take years for it to be replaced by the small and not very sophisticated native elite.

Second, there is the proletariat, which is chiefly made up of Mediterranean peoples (Corsican, Spanish, Italian, Maltese, Algerian, Portuguese, etc.). This segment of the European population tends to be poor. It supplies low-level public servants for the post office, railroad, telephone, water, and electricity companies, as well as employees for municipal services, customs, port services, the police force, and the like. It also provides most of the skilled and semiskilled laborers and white-collar employees for European businesses. In many respects it resembles the mixed working class that has always existed in large Mediterranean cities, but it has little in common with the working-class population of a French city of an equivalent size.[37]

The structure of European households changed during this period. While there had previously been more single people—mainly men—than couples (especially in the French community), developers noted in 1956 that the demand for single-occupant apartments had been falling every year since 1951.[38] This was due to a structural shift that occurred in the early 1950s, which André Adam explains was triggered by the fact that "the French and Spanish grew steadily more sedentary, while the others went back to being pioneers."[39]

A Growing Muslim Majority

A close look at Casablanca's demography, especially after 1945, explodes the myth of it being a "new French city." Between 1907 and 1960, the Muslim Moroccan population rocketed from 19,000 to nearly 850,000. In 1952, 473,000 Muslims represented 69 percent of the city's total population, and there was great diversity in terms of their social station and cultural background. The national liberation movement had to go to some lengths to force the Europeans to stop perceiving themselves as superiors lording over a few Moroccan employees and servants who disappeared into their *derbs* at night. The French no longer felt "at home" and

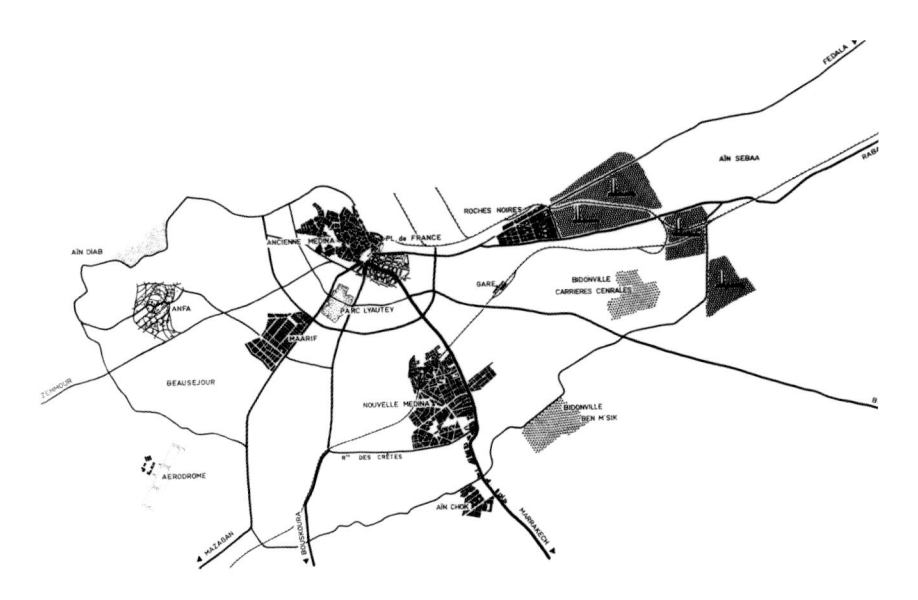

Town Planning Department, plan showing the Muslim housing sectors in Casablanca, c. 1951.

The Ain Chock development is in the south, near the Route de Marrakech.

became aware of their real place in the city. As André Adam notes, the massive increase in the Muslim population gave the Europeans of Casablanca "proof of their numerical inferiority. The overpopulated Moroccan quarters continued to spread until they eventually formed an arc connecting Sidi-Bernoussi, in the east, to Derb Jdid, in the west; this gave the Europeans the "impression of being surrounded," which was particularly disagreeable since it came as something of a surprise.[40] The strong division between the two populations was caused not only by racism, but also by class reflexes that are certainly not exclusive to Casablanca or to that particular period. For instance, the low-income housing developments in La Courneuve are just as foreign today to an upper-class woman from Neuilly, Auteuil, or Passy (Paris's version of New York's Upper East Side) as Ain Chock was at the time to an Anfa housewife.

There had been a wealthy Muslim class even before 1907, and now some of the Muslims owed their fortune to land they possessed near the center. Others were merchants in Fès, who first set up outlets in Casablanca without wanting to settle in the city, but then actually moved there. André Adam explains their social role by the fact that they "alone had retained the traditions of an old urban civilization." Therefore, they "inspired jealousy but were often imitated."[41] Other inland migrants, the *Soussis*,* who owned many shops, especially food stores, were the Fassis' main rivals. These families were very much involved in setting up housing developments and other types of buildings on the outskirts, and in *Le Passé simple*, written in 1954, Driss Chraïbi satirizes the greed of these speculators.[42] Most of Casablanca's Moroccan population was, however, made up of rural people from the Chaouia hinterland who had joined the proletariat with the industrial boom; there were also others who had come from more remote regions. By 1952, 120,000 Moroccans were living in *bidonvilles*, with another 15,000 joining them every year.[43]

Influx of Jewish Migrants

The Jewish population practically doubled between 1936 and 1951, rising from about 38,500 to 75,000, or 10 percent of the total. This population, too, was characterized by strong contrasts. Some were Jews of Andalusian origin from northern cities, such as Mogador or Marrakech, and they constituted the bourgeoisie. They had done business with Europeans for centuries and formed a rather small elite. Communities from the south migrated to Rabat and Casablanca in growing numbers—by 1960, 45 percent of Morocco's Jewish population lived in Casablanca.[44]

40 Adam, *Casablanca*, 1:180.

41 André Adam, "Casablanca, grande ville marocaine," in "À la rencontre de l'Empire chérifien," special issue of *Journal de Genève* (September 4, 1951), 3.

42 Driss Chraïbi, *Le Passé simple* (Paris: Denoël, 1954; reprint, Paris: Folio, 1986), 264.

43 MAE, SGP 237 Urbanisme, Habitat années 1954–55.

44 The southern communities lost one-quarter of their members between 1940 and 1950. Bensimon-Donath, *Évolution du judaïsme marocain*, 36–37.

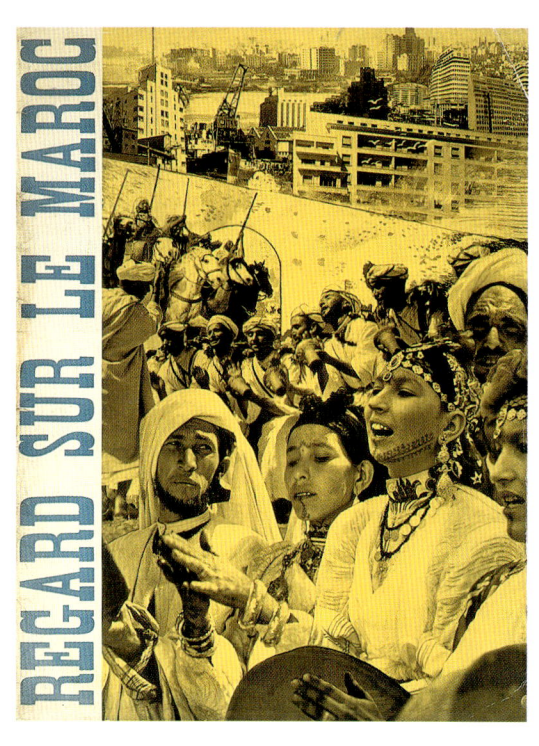

Édy Legrand, cover photomontage of *Regards sur le Maroc*, featuring Casablanca's modern skyline, 1954.

Advertisement for Mills tube scaffoldings, c. 1949, in *Le Maroc*, 1950. In this allegorical image, Casablanca is portrayed as a city under construction. Note the city hall and cathedral in the distance.

These newcomers gave rise to such a large Jewish working class that special housing programs were required. Besides these Moroccan Jews, by 1947 there were an estimated 11,500 "foreigners of Jewish confession" living in the city, a figure that was far from negligible.[45]

The number of both Jewish and Muslim Moroccans increased considerably in the immediate postwar period, while the number of Europeans and Jewish Moroccans declined after 1952. The city's population growth between 1950 and 1960 was due entirely to people flooding in from the countryside or small towns, attracted by the manufacturing jobs that had been created by strong postwar economic expansion. Furthermore, rural Moroccans were drawn by the affluent lifestyle led by the Europeans. Class and cultural differences would also influence the city's structure and future housing schemes. In 1952, Jean-Paul Trystram described the ethnic and work-related hierarchies in Morocco: "The engineer is French, the foreman, Spanish or Italian, and the laborer, Moroccan."[46]

A City of Chaos, Construction, and Danger

From 1945 onward, literary and film representations of Casablanca began to portray a different picture of the city. It no longer symbolized the "driving force" of a slumbering thousand-year-old French empire, but rather trafficking, intrigue, and, even more important, fear in the face of the rising national movement. The city retained its wartime image of a "Nest of Spies"—the title of the awful 1963 remake of *Casablanca*.[47] However, it also became threatening on two counts: first, any attempt to impose order through public regulation seemed doomed to failure because of the city's size, and second, the first bombs began to go off in clashes that would ultimately lead to Independence. All the contradictions in colonial urban planning became explosive in this city, "which having not yet acquired the soul and patina of centuries of history, expresses itself in the youth of its arteries, through which lively new blood flows."[48] Addressing the issue of whether "Casablanca is actually beautiful," the *Journal de Genève* concluded in 1952 that this was not the case, but also noted, "It is quite excusable for a city that has grown thirty-two-fold in forty-five years to develop haphazardly. In fact, such development is moving and captivating."[49]

During this period, many people saw Casablanca as one huge building site. Jacques de Lacretelle aptly summarized the view he was greeted with in 1949 as "a vacant lot yesterday, a construction site today, and tomorrow a building. That is Casablanca in a nutshell."[50] Pierre Drouin, however, was struck by the contrast between the Casablancans' "religion of business" and the places in which it was practiced: "Casablanca's tallest minaret is the silo in the port. The symbols of the religion of business are sad . . . They are merely concrete junk and building sets without instructions, though some grandeur does show through in the city like flashes of sunlight."[51] In his visits to the outskirts of Casablanca, Drouin drew parallels between the shantytowns there and the slums around Paris, saying that the *bidonvilles* "bear certain similarities to the Parisian slum belt or to the society depicted in Steinbeck's *Grapes of Wrath*." Postwar building types gave some areas an entirely new appearance. For example, neighborhoods where villas formerly predominated were now also home to new apartment buildings. The problem was similar in outlying districts, both old and new, where small detached houses sprang up haphazardly.[52]

Even more than the architectural contrasts, it was the opposition of extreme wealth and abject poverty—the elements that fueled the resistance movement—that struck visitors as of 1950. Newspaper reports trickled back to France, Switzerland, and the United States about "Morocco's hub" becoming "a monumental and fragile edifice,"[53] as well as a "city of fear."[54] The tension marking debates over planning and housing issues was in effect the product of this general climate.

Housing—The Protectorate Steps In

Bureaucrats took over from the pioneers.

Jean and Simonne Lacouture, 1958[55]

The grandeur and poverty of Casablanca—an immense city but riddled with pockets of deluxe buildings sitting beside plots of land that will perhaps lie vacant forever.

Léon Dubois, 1950[56]

Thirty years after the Protectorate was established, a new mechanism for public sector intervention was put in place within a political framework that Georges Balandier described as "a technocratic phase of colonization taking over from the [original] politico-administrative phase."[57] A new generation of managerial staff was born, whose approach clashed with the entrenched attitudes of the administration.[58]

These new policies transformed the urban landscape. The strict prewar separation of apartment buildings and villas gave way to an intricate array of collective housing developments, high-rise buildings, and Garden Cities comprising detached houses and small apartment blocks. The scale of the buildings and satellite towns that sprouted on the outskirts clashed with the earlier rows of adjoining buildings. The city's character changed, with a belt of new construction going up, while new centrally located apartment buildings were added to those that had formed part of the Prost plan. Also, more floor area was worked into the designs for deluxe apartment blocks and low-rent housing for Europeans. Yet although the Casablancan economy enjoyed strong growth—the image of a Golden Age was repeatedly evoked at this time—construction funds continued to come mainly from the public sector.

From a Housing Shortage to a Building Boom

As of 1940, quotas on construction materials, an influx of refugees, and population growth caused the chronic housing shortage in Casablanca to worsen. Construction came to a complete standstill during the war, and the authorities requisitioned housing; they also instituted provisions protecting tenants, which frightened off builders of rental properties.[59] Rents for apartments in the *ville nouvelle* were practically frozen at 1939 levels, although they were "raised slightly twice, at the insistence of landlords," while in the new medina, rents were more "standard." For leaseholders, the practice of demanding extortionate sums for "key money" and lease premiums became commonplace.[60]

The situation was hardly a happy one for working-class and lower-middle-class Europeans. Young couples, singles, and newcomers lived in hotels or furnished accommodations, sometimes becoming caretakers of villas.[61] However, construction picked up in 1947, thanks to new strategies such as condominium programs, combined with housing allowance schemes and new financial mechanisms for homeownership. A boom then began, comparable to the one that had lasted from 1912 to 1920. Casablanca underwent a radical shift. The architect Robert Maddalena wrote, "Construction there progressed at breakneck speed, making Casablanca one of the world's fastest-growing cities."[62] The city's built area tripled annually from 1947 to 1952, at a time when metropolitan France was having trouble launching postwar reconstruction. In 1949, a Parisian journalist was surprised to find "more building sites in Casablanca than in France's three largest *départements*,"[63] and Georges Creugnet estimated that Casablanca was "one of the cities with the highest level of construction in the world, with ten billion francs worth of building permits issued in just eight months for villas, apartment buildings, and additional stories."[64] The French minister of reconstruction, Eugène Claudius-Petit, was also stunned by what he saw in 1949.[65]

---

45 Adam, *Casablanca*, 1:196.

46 Jean-Paul Trystram, "Quelques aspects des relations industrielles au Maroc," *Annales Économies, Sociétés, Civilisations* 7, no. 3 (1952): 361–62.

47 Henri Decoin, *Casablanca, nid d'espions*, 1963; see fimography.

48 Étienne Rod, "Casablanca, métropole européenne," *Le Journal de Genève*, September 4, 1951.

49 André Rodari, "Casablanca, l'attrait de la profusion," *Le Journal de Genève*, November 9–10, 1952.

50 De Lacretelle, "Casa."

51 Pierre Drouin, "Visages du Maroc au travail, II: Casablanca, l'Eldorado et son envers," *Le Monde* (Paris), June 5–6, 1949.

52 At issue here are districts such as Ain Diab, Oasis, Aviation, Beauséjour, Franceville, Crêtes, Polo, and Hermitage.

53 F. Paoletti, "Casablanca, plaque tournante du Maroc," in "À la rencontre de l'Empire chérifien," special issue of *Journal de Genève*, September 4, 1951. See also in the same issue "Casablanca, une ville qui a la puissance d'un symbole," and J. E. Chable, "Lieux dont on parle."

54 Barrett McGurn, "Casablanca, City of Fear," *New York Herald Tribune*, April 27, 1955; Noël Barber, "The City of Fear," *Daily Mail* (London), July 15, 1954; and "Casablanca: City under a pull of fear; the once-thriving Moroccan metropolis is stilled by terror, with both Frenchman and Arab dreading new bursts of violence," *New York Times Magazine*, September 11, 1955.

55 Jean and Simonne Lacouture, *Le Maroc à l'épreuve* (Paris: Seuil, 1958), 42.

56 Dubois, "L'évolution de la construction à Casablanca," 67.

57 Georges Balandier, "La situation coloniale: approche théorique," *Cahiers internationaux de sociologie* 11 (1951): 44.

58 Knibiehler, Emmery, and Leguay, *Des Français au Maroc*.

59 BGA, SGP 449, Service du personnel et du Bulletin officiel, Office de l'habitat européen, 1944–48.

60 R. Cagnon, "Le problème du logement au Maroc," *Terre d'Afrique* (1948): 150–51.

61 According to one contemporary account, "Over ten thousand European families are presently without lodging or living in substandard housing. When we say 'without lodging' we mean living in garages or basements, sometimes worse. By 'substandard housing' we simply mean four, five, or six people per room." "Pour un logis humain," *Notre Maroc* (December 1950): 31.

62 Robert Maddalena, "Sur l'évolution de l'architecture et de l'urbanisme au Maroc," in "Le Maroc moderne; architecture et urbanisme," special issue of *Réalités et expansion du Maroc* (1954).

63 "Maroc: constructions à Casablanca et au Maroc," *Arts* (August 1949): 4.

64 Georges Creugnet, "Casablanca, l'une des villes-chantiers les plus actives du monde: 10 milliards d'autorisation de construire en 8 mois," *Travaux nord-africains* (September 20, 1951).

65 "Maroc: constructions à Casablanca et au Maroc," 4.

Pair of semidetached Wates houses, Rue d'Auxerre, 1946. Photographed in 1998.

66 Léon Marchal, delegate to the residency general, memorandum of August 10, 1944, BGA, Habitat indigène, Casablanca, 1930.

67 In the spring of 1945 the cost of work on the Ain Chock indigenous housing development undertaken by the O.C.H. led the Protectorate's finance director, Robert, to threaten to stop funding the O.C.H.'s programs for European housing of this type. Robert, memorandum to the O.C.H., April 23, 1945, BGA, Habitat indigène, Casablanca, 1930.

68 Robert to secretary general of the Protectorate, January 5, 1947, BGA, Habitat indigène, Casablanca, 1930.

69 "Bâtiment et logement de demain," *Construire* (September 16, 1945): 906.

70 *La Vigie marocaine* (Casablanca), November 1, 1945.

71 Memorandum on European housing, MAE, carton Cabinet civil 122, dossier habitat Maroc. A Wates house in Bourgogne is the backdrop for Marie-Thérèse Cuny's novel, *La Petite Fille de Dar-el-Beïda* (Paris: Fixot, 1990). Additional Wates houses were erected at the Ferme bretonne and on Rue de la Participation, at Roches-Noires, and at Ain Sebaa.

The Sharifian Housing Office— The Secular Arm of the Administration

Although the notion of public sector involvement in housing was not totally new, projects were traditionally managed by the municipalities or religious foundations, such as the Habous, with the state acting as no more than a generous trustee. Public and institutional players began to replace enlightened private clients and the one-off official bodies of the prewar period, which were now few and far between. The Protectorate was hesitant about which road to take. After setting up a special commission in 1937 to deal with issues of housing for Moroccans, it went on to create the Office Chérifien de l'Habitat (Sharifian Housing Office), or O.C.H.[66] Essentially, the Protectorate was endeavoring to withdraw from schemes for solvent Europeans so that it could concentrate on providing credit facilities, low-interest loans, and tax relief.[67] In early 1947, the Protectorate's finance director confirmed that the O.C.H.'s role was to coordinate private construction firms and to play a direct part in construction programs. Nonetheless, he expressed doubts as to the latter initiative, since he felt it might well be too costly and difficult to manage.[68]

The administration constantly brought pressure to bear on the O.C.H. to build less and more cheaply. Despite this, the O.C.H. still continued to produce some large-scale works, notably the Ain Chock Muslim satellite town and the Bourgogne Garden City for Europeans, although it did use rapid, rational building methods and inexpensive materials. In 1945, the magazine *Construire* viewed the concept of metal houses as a "partial solution to the current crisis,"[69] and the following year Germain Milan, director of the O.C.H., went to England to study site-management methods there, as well as reconstruction and prefabrication projects.[70] He returned with schemes for several prefabricated Wates concrete houses (sharp-cornered, mass-produced boxes), and the O.C.H. ended up building ninety-five of these dwellings on the southern edge of the Bourgogne neighborhood.[71]

In 1946, the Paris-based architect Jacques Couëlle carried out another experiment in Fédala, using flattened, conelike elements called "ceramic missiles" to build the vaults of a complex of 508 units for Moroccans at a speed that amazed the *Petit*

Jacques Couëlle and Albert Planque (site architect), Housing for Muslims, Fédala, 1947. Photographed in 1947.

Marocain.⁷² This solution, which seemed appropriate given the acute housing shortage, would not be pursued, despite the interest it roused in other countries. For instance, in 1954, the director of Public Works, Girard, was consulted by the United Nations, as it was interested in using the same technique for refugee housing. Yet Girard noted that the system had "turned out to be more expensive than conventional ones and [that] the residents did not like this type of house, as the rooms were vaulted."⁷³

In 1949, the O.C.H.'s duties were transferred to the Housing Section of the Public Works Department, although the total number of construction projects supervised directly by the state was far from enough to meet the housing demand.⁷⁴ The O.C.H. had used up all its resources on building units whose floor areas were considered too spacious compared to France, England, and Sweden.⁷⁵ From then on, the state limited its direct involvement in Moroccan housing since it was "less likely than European housing to benefit from substantial private backing."⁷⁶

C.I.F.M. and C.I.L.M. Programs

In April 1951, a semipublic company was set up called the Compagnie Immobilière Franco-Marocaine (C.I.F.M.). It was assigned the twofold mission of building low-rent housing complexes for Europeans and Moroccans and of managing the rental units. The C.I.F.M. was the only body authorized by the Protectorate to build low-rent housing, and as such it inherited the stock of the O.C.H. and the Housing Section of the Public Works Department.⁷⁷ The complexes were erected on vast tracts of cheap land on the city outskirts and contained around 1,000 units per scheme—a new scale for Morocco.⁷⁸ As is illustrated by the economic and technical studies conducted by the C.I.F.M. design office, the aim was to rationalize building methods and cut construction costs.

Workers' housing in Casablanca accounted for only about a thousand units (approximately one-tenth of the Carrières Centrales *bidonville*), despite the efforts of SOCICA and the Moroccan railroad company.⁷⁹ In 1950, several contractors joined forces, creating the Comité Interprofessionnel du Logement au Maroc (Joint Commission of Industrials for Housing in Morocco), or C.I.L. In December of that

72 "Une maison de deux pièces construite en 6 jours," *Le Petit Marocain* (Casablanca) March 7, 1946. The O.C.H. acted as developer. Albert Planque was the project architect. Initially designed by Jacques Couëlle, the system would also be used in Marseilles by Pouillon. Fernand Pouillon, *Mémoires d'un architecte* (Paris: Éditions du Seuil, 1968), 35–36.

73 Girard (director of Public Works), letter of December 4, 1954, MAE, Cabinet civil 122, dossier Habitat Maroc.

74 André Adam estimated that 16 percent of all housing construction between 1944 and 1960 was state-sponsored. *Casablanca*, 1:101.

75 Girard to the delegate to the residency general, October 22, 1949, MAE, CDRG 131.

76 Lamy, "L'effort financier de l'État marocain pour résorber la crise du logement," in *Compte-rendu du 5e Congrès nord-africain du bâtiment et des travaux publics, 1953* (Casablanca: Éditions Construire, 1953).

77 "Compagnie immobilière franco-marocaine," *Le Maroc moderne: architecture et urbanisme* (n.p.).

78 By December 31, 1955—the eve of independence—the C.I.F.M. had built 7,064 housing units in Casablanca.

79 Adam, *Casablanca*, 1:96.

80 In the case of Ain Sebaa (54 hectares) and Beauséjour (32 hectares), the majority of requests for lots were made by war veterans (138). The remaining petitioners were mainly large families (44) and civil servants (22).

81 The *dahir* of December 19, 1949, facilitated the provision of construction loans to veterans for specified building sizes. These ranged from 65 to 165 square meters and included "living room [of] 15 usable square meters; bedrooms [of] 9 square meters, and kitchen [of] 7 square meters." "Prêts à la construction des Anciens combattants," *Construire* (January 11, 1950). See also the report of the O.C.H. Permanent Committee, January 14, 1944, BGA, SGP, 449, Office de l'habitat européen, 1944–48.

82 See Monique Eleb, *L'Apprentissage du "chez-soi": Paris, le Groupe des maisons ouvrières, 1908* (Marseilles: Parenthèses, 1994), 108.

83 Léon Dubois, "L'évolution de la construction à Casablanca," *Notre Maroc* (December 1950): 55–67.

84 This number included 4,744 French and 3,072 other foreigners, including 350 non-Moroccan Muslim families. Two thousand three hundred sixteen European families lived in the medinas or in Moroccan quarters; 4,000 in garages or basements; and 1,500 in hotels.

85 Grillet, head of Municipal Services, memorandum of December 11, 1952, MAE, Cabinet civil 122, dossier Habitat européen.

86 Department of the Interior, memorandum of September 6, 1955, MAE, Cabinet civil 122, dossier Habitat européen.

87 See the 1960 census tables published in Adam, *Casablanca*, 1:128–31.

88 Eighty percent of dwellings at the time contained fewer than four rooms; 61 percent contained fewer than two.

89 Adam, 1:133.

same year, the Cités C.I.L. companies bought up land in Anfa and Beauséjour. Plots for villas surrounding the collective housing complexes, analyzed in a later chapter, were sold to private companies as well as to private individuals interested in building for their own use.[80] Although this Moroccan initiative drew on tried and tested ventures in France, it served as a model for comparable undertakings in Algeria and Tunisia.

A Chronic Housing Shortage

The shortage of housing for Europeans stemmed from a lack of financial resources, and by 1944 it had become clear that the problem could not be solved by the O.C.H. alone, nor could it be eased through military aid. Measures were therefore introduced to facilitate mortgages and to help mortgage banks build working-class housing. War veterans and large families were regarded as a priority,[81] and numerous steps were taken in 1951 to spur private development, giving rise to complex negotiations regarding landlords' interests and leaseholders' rights.

Real-estate legislation was extended to cover Moroccan quarters. Concerned about insalubrious housing in the *derbs*, one Dr. Sanguy recommended that it be made a legal requirement for small-scale landlords to possess a "residence permit." This was similar to the Siegfried Law, enacted in 1894 in France, which stipulated that builders of low-rent housing comply with bylaws pertaining to health and hygiene.[82] However, for the *bidonvilles* and other insalubrious areas, which housed close to fifty thousand Moroccans, additional measures were also required.[83]

Financially straitened Europeans had to put up with harsh living conditions during the final years of the Protectorate. The riots of December 8, 1952, in Ain Chock revealed that many were living in makeshift housing in Muslim quarters, notably in the Carrières Centrales *bidonville*, and the authorities were under pressure to speed up their inquiries. The 1953 inquiry concluded that 7,816 European families needed to be rehoused.[84] This apparent "discovery" stirred public feeling, and having rejected the idea of temporary "housing camps" in Moroccan quarters, "near defense posts,"[85] the Housing Section of the Public Works Department set about building for the financially straitened populace. The Casablanca Region allocated forty million francs to rehousing schemes such as Bournazel, described in a later chapter, while, as of 1955, French residents began to be evacuated from the medinas for reasons of "safety."[86]

It should be noted that in the 1950s barely three-quarters of the housing units in Casablanca were made out of stone or other long-lasting materials; in 1960, it was recorded that 27 percent of the Muslim Moroccans were living in what statisticians called "basic" dwellings, made of adobe, corrugated iron, and porous masonry, or even in tents and *nouallas*.* These units were densely populated, and it was not uncommon to find six to ten people living in just two rooms in the most primitive conditions.[87] However, it was also documented in 1960 that around 31 percent of Muslim Moroccans owned their own homes, mostly on the outskirts. Moroccan Jews and foreigners, on the other hand, tended to rent accommodations, likewise on the outskirts. Their reluctance to buy stemmed mainly from the likelihood that they would have to vacate the city in view of the political climate. Most of the dwellings were small, with only a handful of villas boasting over ten rooms[88]; that said, they contained all the home comforts, and in 1960, 33 percent were recorded as having a bathtub or shower. This was the same percentage as in the Paris region, but was much higher than in most French cities with over 100,000 inhabitants, where it was reported in 1954 that "only 16.6 percent of dwellings had such an amenity."[89] The fact that Casablanca was a young city filled with contrasting social factors most likely accounts for this swing between progress and uncertainty.

Ain Chock development,
Aerial view.
Photographed in 1952.

Ain Chock—Prototype Housing for Muslims

Ain Chock, the new housing development for the native population, which is intended to gradually "drain" the "shantytowns," already houses some 20,000 people. It's like a Hollywood setting for an Arab movie: aggressively clean, milky-white walls, with wide streets unlike any ever seen in a medina, and each one numbered ... Strolling through it is like being in Wells's Country of the Blind. *All the traditions have been respected. The dwellings deliberately turn their backs on urban life.*

Pierre Drouin, 1949[90]

In 1936, the Protectorate drew up a prototype development to be located in Ain Chock, with the aim of absorbing the Ben M'Sick shantytown.[91] The design process stopped in 1941, but was then resumed in 1944, with the O.C.H. in charge of the work; this entailed building ten thousand dwellings on 210 hectares of land near the intersection of the Route de Marrakesh and Boulevard des Crêtes.[92] The scheme was presented in the press as an autonomous and well-equipped district that would not be a "dull pile of stone cubes, but rather a coherent and harmonious series of buildings specially designed to make up a town in its own right."[93] Antoine Marchisio, head of the Protectorate's architectural office, drafted the site plan as well as the designs for the initial units. The O.C.H. began work on the first blocks in 1945 under the direction of the municipal engineer, Vergnettes, and with help from apprentices of a masonry school set up on-site. The advantages of this working

90 Drouin, "Casablanca, l'Eldorado et son envers."

91 C. Sanguy, "Réflexions sur le problème de l'habitat indigène à Casablanca," *Le Maroc médical* (March 1947): 104–9.

92 The secretary general of the Protectorate would encounter great difficulty in convincing the municipality to become involved in this "project having the character of a social service." For construction to begin, the city had to agree (in November 1944) to assume responsibility for half of the roadwork. See Germain Milan, "La construc-tion de logements indigènes à bas loyers au quartier d'Ain Chock," November 16, 1944, BGA, SGP, 449, Office de l'habitat européen, 1944–48. Regarding the initiation of the first sections of the project, see Paul Couzinet, notes to the secretariat of the Protectorate, October 28, 1944, BGA, SGP, 449, Office de l'habitat européen, 1944–48.

93 Raymond Lauriac, "Une nouvelle ville de 210 ha est en construction à Casablanca. Elle pourra abriter 100.000 Musulmans," *La Vigie marocaine* (Casablanca), November 9, 1945.

Antoine Marchisio, Ain Chock development, initial study, 1945. Sketch of the site plan.

Antoine Marchisio, Ain Chock development, 1946. Project for multistory housing. Partial isometry in *L'Architecture française*, July–August 1946.

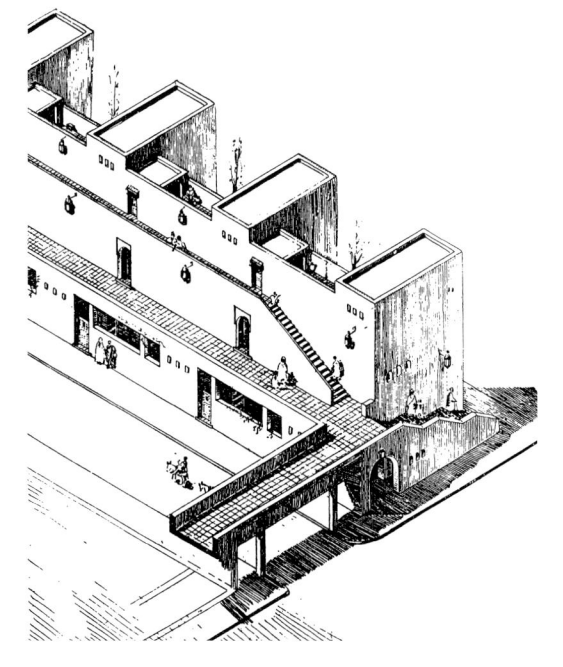

94 Lauriac, "Une nouvelle ville de 210 ha est en construction à Casablanca."

95 Antoine Marchisio, "Ain Chock-habitation à étages," June 1945, BGA, SGP, 449, direction des Affaires politiques.

96 Paul Couzinet, "L'urbanisme au Maroc," *L'Architecture française* 7, no. 60–61 (July–August 1946): 52.

97 This way of organizing public housing has been highly valued by young French architects of the 1990s.

98 Memorandum on Ain Chock, November 1945, BGA, SGP 449, Urbanisme, Office de l'habitat Européen, 1944–48.

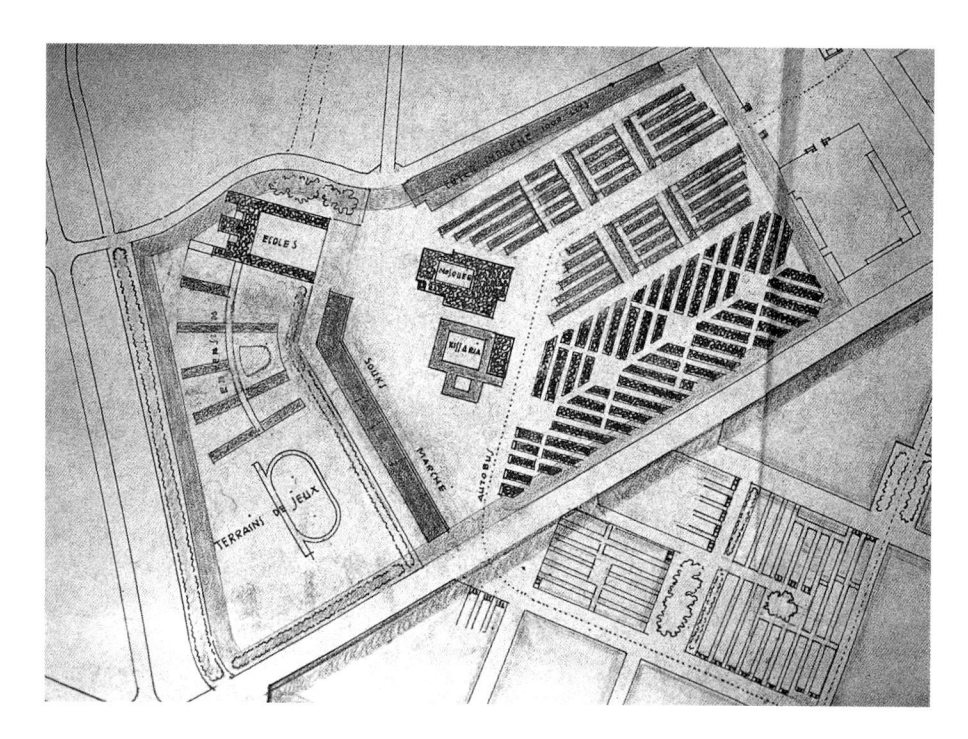

method were set out in *La Vigie marocaine*: "The purpose of centralizing these projects in the Office is to save the Protectorate money by generally keeping construction costs down. Centralization has also been dictated by a shortage of building materials and has meant that urban planning regulations have had to be strictly adhered to, which can only be considered as advantageous for our *protégés*' well-being."[94]

Despite its thorny start, the project marked a new stage in the design of housing for Muslims. Its scale led to savings on the foundations and roof structure, as did the fact that the buildings covered more than one story, although this called for a load-bearing floor. There was one major stumbling block, though: the O.C.H. and Marchisio disagreed on the underlying construction principle, insofar as the architect deemed that O.C.H.'s solution of collective housing was inappropriate for the future residents:

> This scheme serves only to point up the risk of haphazard, incoherent ventures, where the main purpose is to adapt borrowed forms or to come up with something new and absurd . . . Combining single-family dwellings in one building requires a number of communal elements, such as corridors and staircases. For public health reasons, it is important that these be clearly defined in the layout plan, since experience has demonstrated that such communal elements usually tend to be neglected by the residents.[95]

Marchisio therefore suggested a scheme with outdoor staircases "leading to a large terrace that provides access to the units on the first floor." In his initial sketches he proposed "an exterior circulation zone in the form of walkways running along the facades."[96] In essence, the project translates into semicollective housing, with single-family dwellings stacked on top of one another, each with its own outdoor space, a private entrance for the first-floor units and entries along the access walkways for those units on the second floor.[97] Debate arose over where to position the "communal house for the natives," the general street system, and the development's access points.[98] The main road is made up of small buildings joined in forty-five-degree chevrons, resulting in a sawtooth arrangement that lets sunlight into

Antoine Marchisio, project for a group of four dwellings in Ain Chock, 1946. Plan published in *L'Architecture française*, July–August 1946.

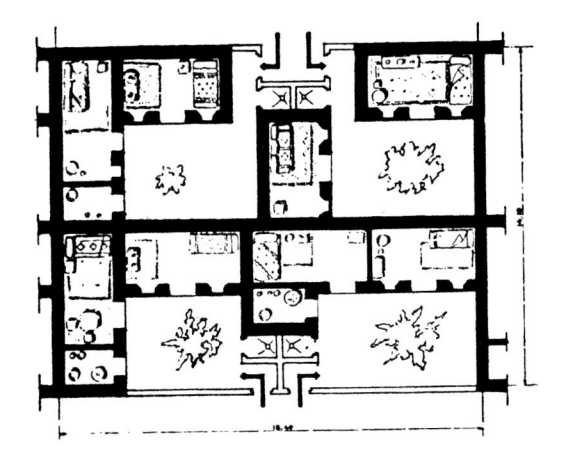

Housing in the first phase of the Ain Chock development, c. 1945. Elevations and cross sections from the building permit.

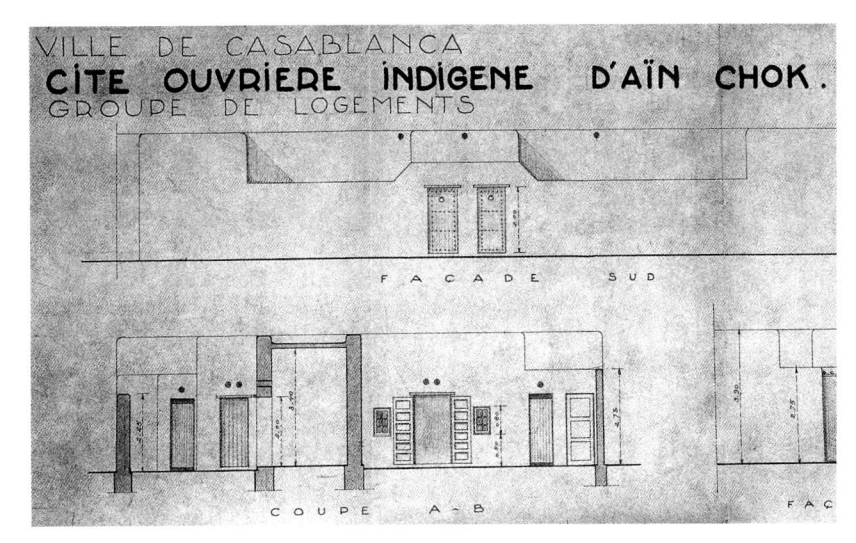

Paul Busuttil, Type D4 housing, Ain Chock. Ground- and first-floor plans, in *La Construction moderne*, September 1952.

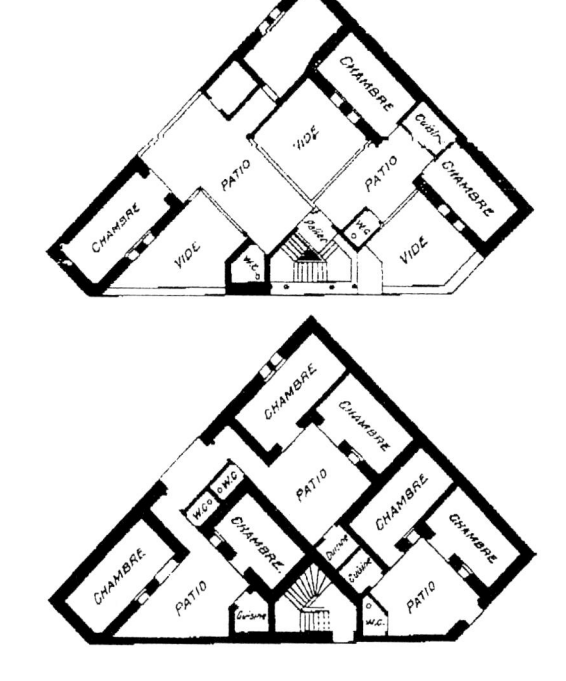

most of the units. In his scheme, Marchisio drew on research conducted on the system of "indents" by Eugène Hénard in 1903 in Paris, and which had been put into practice in the 1920s by Ernst May in Frankfurt.[99] The traditional hierarchic street system of the medinas was maintained, with the houses accessed by blind alleys, and in addition, a five-meter-wide service street was laid adjacent to the twenty-meter-wide main road. A large number of facilities were already available when the first residents arrived in 1946,[100] though it is somewhat surprising that none of the units came with running water; the residents thus had to use the drinking fountains, which were designed as monuments in their own right.

The first complex (built to a seven-phase construction schedule) was designed to contain 650 units, all with private entrances. This first step in collective housing for Muslims was not a high-rise district. Every building was conceived as a single-story detached unit or two units, one above the other, each with a private entrance and a communal portico. The five built types range from one- to four- room units, though the two-room unit is the most common format.[101] Paul Busuttil designed most of the units, faithfully reproducing Marchisio's schemes for some of them "to comply with the established plans,"[102] which, as eyewitnesses noted, contained a number of principles relating to Moroccan housing and lifestyle:

> All the windows in the rooms face the patio, and the enclosure walls are high enough to prevent anyone from seeing in, following the local tradition that women must be hidden from public view. The dwellings seem austere when perceived from the street, yet on entering the lush patio, it is clear that the home is very much the core of Moroccan family life. Sunlight flows into all the rooms through the openings pierced into the southern and eastern walls.[103]

Each unit was delivered with a kitchen, lavatory, and a patio (the women's gathering place), which is screened by a bayonet-type entrance. The dwellings were designed for residents of varying income levels, as is evidenced by the different floor areas, as well as by the ancillary facilities, such as laundries and sheds. Each room has two windows, but at the time of construction there was no bathroom, which ran counter to the fundamental notion of providing healthy living conditions.

99 Eugène Hénard, "Les alignements brisés," in *Études sur les transformations de Paris*, 23–54.

100 Seventy-four shops, four communal ovens, two pharmacies, three Moorish cafés, a cheap restaurant, a laundry, and a drying room were all open to the public.

101 In 1953 Ain Chock had 694 two-room dwellings without kitchens, 1,394 two-room dwellings with kitchens, 12 four-room dwellings, and 263 single-room dwellings. Délégation aux affaires urbaines de Casablanca, memorandum on the Muslim and Jewish habitat in Casablanca, February 1953, MAE, Cabinet Civil 122, dossier Habitat européen.

102 Paul Parinet, quoted in Georges Benoit-Lévy, "Une banlieue-jardin marocaine, Ain Chock," *La Construction moderne* (September 1952): 322. Benoit-Lévy had been the founder of the French Garden City Association in 1903.

103 Pierre Parinet, quoted in Benoît-Lévy, "Une banlieue-jardin marocaine, Ain Chock," 322.

The Post-1945 Golden Age and Its Dark Side

104 "L'œuvre gigantesque de l'OCH," *L'Entreprise au Maroc* (June 24, 1948): 23–24. Note that all of the dwellings built in town were hooked up to the water and electricity networks.

105 *Maroc 1950* (Casablanca: Éditions Fontana, 1950), 156.

A square and fountain in Ain Chock (first phase). Photographed in 1946.

Edmond Brion, housing development for Moroccan war veterans, Ain Chock. Photo c. 1950, in *Dans la lumière des cités africaines*, 1956.

Also, it was recorded in 1953 that only 10 percent of the houses had running water and that no more than 25 percent had electricity.[104] Close to 2,400 dwellings had been completed by 1949, but despite the project's vast scale Busuttil managed to inject the streets with just the right amount of charm, as was noted at the time:

> Few towns in the Islamic world can lay claim to such a delightful countenance and such homogenous facades, whose traditional whiteness and stark lines are entirely in keeping with the Arab style, without being at all monotonous. Their severity is alleviated by awnings and by tall, narrow openings, hidden behind screen walls bearing harmonious decorative motifs. The entrances to the dwellings have shady arches and benches that invite people to linger.[105]

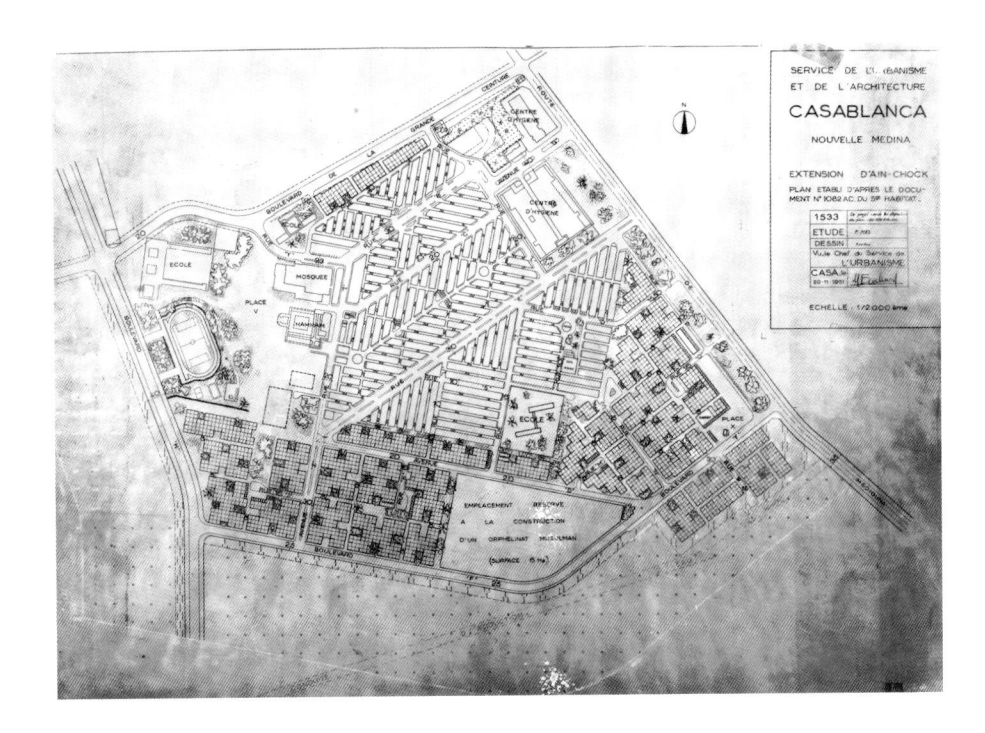

Pierre Mas on behalf of the Town Planning Department, extension plan for the Ain Chock development, 1951. Master plan.

Marcel Parizet and Georges Vargues also built several houses, as well as numerous shops. In 1950, Edmond Brion was put in charge of the fifth construction phase, namely, a fully fitted complex composed of single-story houses for war veterans. The Housing Department, which took over from the O.C.H. in 1949, was responsible for managing the residential units, "to avoid the common practice of speculation when selling and leasing the dwellings."[106]

In 1951, Busuttil built an extension to the scheme, comprising a less expensive road system and less sophisticated dwellings drawn up in keeping with the site plan drafted by Écochard's team. To some extent, these changes seem to have been introduced in response to the 1949 inquiry conducted by the liberal Catholic daily *Maroc-Presse*, which complained that "some houses [were] lying vacant" and called for more economical solutions to be adopted:

> Ain Chock may be trying to pass muster as a low-rent workers' development, but in fact it houses the families of shopkeepers, public servants, and even city dignitaries, who have been selected by the authorities and who can afford to pay 1,400 francs per month in rent. Of course, the idea was too good to be true, too expensive to really pan out, and the upshot is that it has not improved the housing shortage by one iota. What is more, the design of Ain Chock will soon become outdated, and will probably be replaced by *zribas*—small basic houses set along parallel streets, serving as fairly comfortable, cheap and hygienic homes for Moroccans. These might be used as a way of improving the *bidonvilles* and may well even replace them.[107]

The new plans combined dwellings similar to those in the previous phases. In other words, the rooms were laid out around a courtyard, as in earlier housing development schemes, with rows of buildings organized in a way entirely alien to Morocco. This courtyard resembles the backyard of working-class suburban houses, not least due to the fact that it is located at the rear and can only be accessed via the bedrooms.

By 1953, the development's three thousand units, which were linked to the city center by a streetcar, were home to 15,000 residents, who benefited from "all the commercial, cultural, and social facilities of a modern city."[108] Overall, the population was young, and a kindergarten for Muslim children was opened in 1948. This

106 Paul Parinet, quoted in Benoit-Lévy, "Une banlieue-jardin marocaine, Ain Chock," 322.

107 Extract published in *Bulletin d'informations et de documentation du Maroc* (August 15–31, 1949): 12.

108 Pierre Parinet, "L'habitat marocain," *L'Architecture française* 14, no. 131–32 (April 1953): 12.

109 Chemineau would be commissioned to build another daycare center in 1956.

110 "La garderie d'enfants d'Ain Chock," *Bulletin d'information du Maroc*, no. 5 (March 15, 1948): 23–24.

111 Raymond Lauriac, "L'Office de l'Habitat veut éliminer les bidonvilles," *La Vigie marocaine* (Casablanca), November 10, 1945.

112 Fleurant would build a teacher's college in 1957 and elementary schools in 1960.

113 J. D., "A propos de l'inauguration du hammam d'Ain Chock," *Paris* (Casablanca), February 6, 1948: 4.

114 J. D., "A propos de l'inauguration du hammam d'Ain Chock," 4. The Protectorate authorities published the most photogenic views of the scheme's outdoor spaces,

115 Benoit-Lévy, "Une banlieue-jardin marocaine," 319, 324.

was a first for the lower classes and proved highly popular with working women. Unfortunately, however, there was room for just thirty children.[109] Priority was accorded "to children of former military staff" or to "those whose social status deserves particular attention,"[110] a criterion that can be interpreted in any number of ways. Many other civic amenities were provided, given that the town was intended to accommodate 100,000 residents[111]; these facilities include a Franco-Muslim school and Koranic school by Émile Louis,[112] and a mosque by Edmond Brion, whose minaret was deemed at the time to be "the tallest in Morocco." As for Pierre Chassagne's *hammam*, it was considered "the largest and most modern one in Morocco."[113] Paul Busuttil's indoor market built of reinforced concrete is particularly striking, especially due to the twinkling reflection of light produced by the colored glass blocks set into the roof. Moorish cafés and stores were set up to inject life into the square, and the residency launched a publicity campaign extolling the virtues of Ain Chock, including a "new score" composed to the tune of "time-honored melodies."[114] Also as part of this campaign, Georges Benoit-Lévy sang the praises of the new "Moroccan garden suburb," whose houses are laid out in "a herringbone shape":

> A new quarter … has been created in Casablanca containing commercial, social, and religious facilities designed in accordance with age-old traditions and climatic conditions. The native Moroccans have thus found themselves transported, as in a tale from *Arabian Nights*, from the most ghastly hovels into an almost palatial city that is brand-new, but where everything is still based on ancient customs. In other words, its newness is not disorienting; renovation has been achieved without innovation.[115]

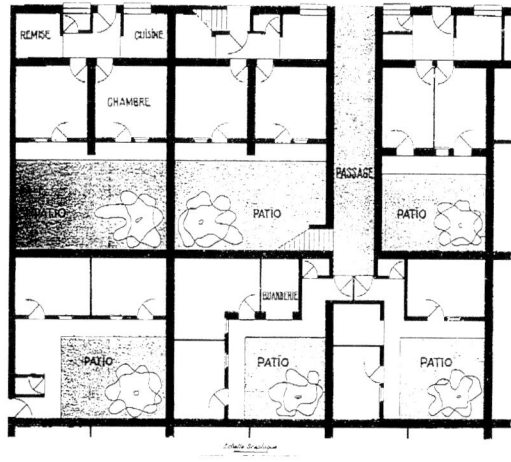

Paul Busuttil, Block B single-story dwellings, Ain Chock, c. 1951. Plan published in *La Construction moderne*, September 1952.

Pierre Chassagne, *hammam*, Ain Chock, 1948.

Paul Busuttil, covered market, Ain Chock, 1950. Photographed in 1996.

Auguste Cadet, the Pasha's Mahakma, Habous quarter, 1941–52. Aerial view, in *La Mahakma de Casablanca,* 1953.

Auguste Cadet, the Pasha's Mahakma, Habous quarter, 1941–52. One of the main patios. Photographed in 1953.

In 1951, American observers saw the development as a rather successful *médinette*.[116] Yet, as *Maroc-Presse* feared, the would-be occupants could not afford to live in the units. Granted, many of the residents of the six hundred dwellings delivered in June 1946 were rural migrants previously living in *bidonvilles*,[117] but by the 1960s, as Adam notes, this population segment represented barely a few hundred of the development's 50,000 residents. Adam also remarks that "the new development was so spacious and comfortable that Europeans had moved in."[118] Although Ain Chock failed to fulfill its social objectives, thus fueling the criticism Écochard leveled at his predecessors, its architectural coherence has provided the Casablancans of today with an image of *déjà là*, of a district predating colonization, of a quarter that is typically Moroccan.

Meanwhile, Auguste Cadet was commissioned by the pasha of Casablanca to build the *Mahakma** (Muslim law courts) in the new medina. Cadet's scheme was anachronistic yet ingenious: he arranged the building around a vast courtyard and two main patios, drawing on the skills of Moroccan craftsmanship to grandiose effect through use of *zillij*, cedar woodwork, and sculpted stone and plaster.[119] Another *Mahakma* was built in 1954—this time by Brion, who was commissioned by the Cadi (the Moroccan municipal authority)—though it was more abstract than Cadet's scheme. Cadet was in fact continuing the work on traditional design that had already been undertaken in the Habous and would later be pursued in Ain Chock.

[116] Ferdinand Tuohy, "Mass Housing in Morocco," *The Sphere* (December 22, 1951).

[117] In order to prevent the migrants' shacks from being inherited by other shantytown dwellers, Philippe Boniface, director of the regional administration, decided to raze them as they were evacuated. Philippe Boniface to Paul Couzinet, April 6, 1945, BGA. SGP 449, Office de l'habitat Européen, 1944–48.

[118] Adam, *Casablanca*, 1:97.

[119] The *Mahakma* replaced the Dar-el-Makhzen, located in the medina. Auguste Cadet, *La Mahakma de Casablanca* (Paris: Paul Hartmann, 1953); and "Mahakma du Pacha de Casablanca, A. Cadet, architecte dplg," *L'Architecture française*, no. 131–32 (April 1953): 84–85.

The Post-1945 Golden Age and Its Dark Side

Ecochard
CASABLANCA
le roman d'une ville

Michel Écochard's Controversial Urbanism (1950–1952)

Just as Morocco seems poised to reach a milestone in its economic and social course, so the development of its cities and rural centers is set to pose problems that will at times be more difficult to deal with than those that spurred the research of the "pioneer" planners.

Gabriel Puaux, 1945[1]

In an official statement on "monitoring urban planning," Puaux, Noguès's successor as resident-general, highlighted the differences between the start of colonization and the postwar period. Following Courtois's report, Michel Écochard had to come up with radical proposals that were suited to Casablanca's major expansion as a port city. Work resumed on the port facilities in 1949, forming part of an ambitious program to rebuild the initial section of the Delure breakwater and extend it to 2,900 meters by raising the underwater structures and creating a jetty for ships in dock.[2] Schneider began to build a 150-meter-long dry dock at the far end of the port, just in front of the Porte de la Marine. Formerly the site of the Portuguese dock, it was now given over to freighters, and observers pointed out that it was the largest on the west coast of Africa, after Dakar.[3] Oil imports had increased after the Allied landings, and the port of Fédala, which had been used for bulk imports since 1923, but was not deep enough to take big tankers, saw its share of overall traffic grow.[4] Meanwhile, new wine warehouses and the development of the fishing trade contributed to Casablanca's rapid expansion. The war of geometry raged on between the port and the city, adopting new forms, and the orientation of the breakwaters became more important than street arrangement in determining the layout of new port buildings.

The Allied forces had reequipped Morocco's airports, which were now handling a large volume of civilian traffic. Although flights between Toulouse and Dakar no longer included a stopover at Camp Cazes, as was the case during the time of Saint-Éxupéry's postal flights, passenger air traffic had outstripped passenger sea traffic by 1947. By the end of the French and American modernization program, Casablanca had three airfields: Camp Cazes to the southwest, which handled commercial traffic; the Tit-Mellil airfield to the southeast, serving light aircraft; and the Nouaceur base, thirty kilometers to the south, out toward Marrakech, which was built in the early 1950s for U.S. air force strategic bombers.[5]

Opposite
Michel Écochard, *Casablanca, le roman d'une ville*, 1955. Front cover. The photo shows the Place de France and vacant land resulting from demolition of the mellah. At the time, this land was used as a parking lot.

1 Gabriel Puaux, "Instruction résidentielle sur le contrôle général de l'urbanisme," October 10, 1945, MAE, carton 131, Habitat et urbanisme, 1948–51. See also Écochard's August 3, 1946, memorandum, portions of which are published in Michel Écochard, "L'urbanisme au Maroc," *L'Architecture d'aujourd'hui* 17, no. 7–8 (September–October 1946).

2 This breakwater was to be located to the right of a new 1,200-meter-long transverse pier. The construction of an intermediate jetty (discussed since the 1930s) was agreed upon. It would be completed in 1953. The enlargement of the phosphates pier was also launched. "Le port de Casablanca," in Albert Monnet, ed., "L'évolution du Maroc en 1951, Casablanca," special issue of *Réalités marocaines* (1951): 17–22.

3 Raymond Lauriac, "L'essor du port de Casablanca doit précéder et non suivre le développement du trafic," in "Le port de Casablanca et la naissance d'une grande ville," ed. Paul Bory, special issue of *Notre Maroc* 10 (June 1952): 27–31. The dock would be completed by mid-1954.

4 In the early 1950s, the consumption of hydrocarbons increased constantly. High-sea docking stations and a 2,700-meter sea-line were created at Fédala. P. Lepanot, "Les moyens de réception des produits pétroliers dans le port de Casablanca," in "Le port de Casablanca et la naissance d'une grande ville," 47–53. Regarding the earliest improvement measures see "Fédhala, le succès de l'urbanisme au Maroc," *Le Monde colonial illustré* (December 1927): 289–90.

5 This base (which employed 7,500 Americans) and the U.S. Air Force bases at Sidi Slimane, Ben Guerir, and Benslimane, as well as the naval and air base of Port-Lyautey, were built following the Franco-American agreements of December 22, 1950. They were ceded to the Moroccans on January 1, 1964. William I. Zartman, *Morocco: Problems of New Power* (New York: Atherton Press, 1964): 23–60.

Port of Casablanca
and cityscape, c. 1960.

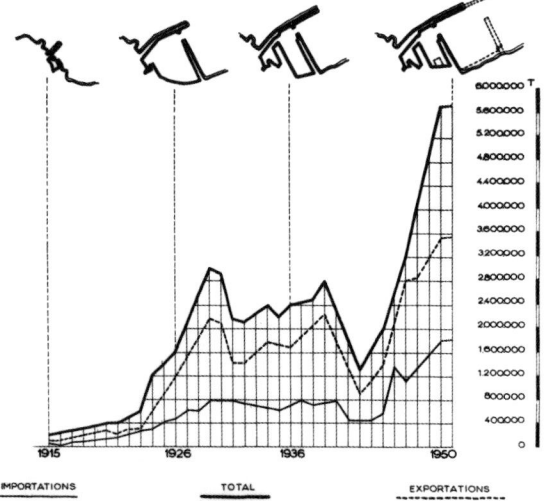

Town Planning
Department, graph of the
growth of Casablanca's
port trade between 1915
and 1950.

Chamber of Commerce
silo in the Port of
Casablanca. Photo c. 1955.

A Functionalist in Morocco

A hodgepodge of knowledge often camouflages nonsense, but if we endeavor to arrange cities according to the four basic functions of the Athens Charter—dwelling, work, recreation, and transportation—we can, with the imagination and love that should go into such a task, solve the serious problems created by our new cities and adapt our old cities to modern life."

Michel Écochard, 1955[6]

Casablanca's urban development process was redefined in 1946 when Eirik Labonne took over from Puaux as resident-general. As mentioned earlier, Labonne had shown a strong interest in the port area between 1929 and 1930, during his term as secretary general of the Protectorate, and new resources were now allocated to health, education, and housing as part of a policy on modernizing and industrializing North Africa. Labonne—in whom Charles-André Julien saw a "peerless proconsul" and a "liberal Resident"[7]—stressed the urgent need to "feed, clothe, and house" the Moroccan populations. This was also perhaps partly due to the increasing pressure brought to bear by the national movement, which had published its manifesto on independence on January 11, 1944, resulting in a clear need to deal with certain expectations that had formerly been ignored. The differences between French liberals and partisans of colonization were growing, with the administration entering into conflict with Philippe Boniface (head of the Casablanca region) and the municipal authority. Both the municipal authority and Boniface were fiercely against making any "concessions" to the Moroccans.[8]

To reform the Protectorate's urban policy, Labonne hired Michel Écochard, who like Prost had started his architectural career in the Far East, and whose point of departure was a radical variety of functional urbanism.[9] Écochard was a charismatic figure of strong convictions and he left his mark not just on Casablanca, but on the whole of Moroccan architectural culture during the postwar era. Having first trained as an architect before becoming an archaeologist, then an urban planner in Syria and Lebanon under the French mandate, he began to adhere to Le Corbusier's thinking and functionalist theories from 1944 on.[10] From 1946 to 1952 he directed the Protectorate's Service de l'Urbanisme (Town Planning Department), drafting plans that diverged dramatically from pre-1939 policies. His teams implemented zoning principles that complied with Le Corbusier's Athens Charter, and they developed housing schemes on an unprecedented scale.[11]

6 Michel Écochard, *Casablanca: le roman d'une ville* (Paris: Éditions de Paris, 1955), 98.

7 Charles-André Julien, *Le Maroc face aux impérialismes: 1415–1956* (Paris: Éditions J. A., 1978): 198. Abdelkebir Khatibi noted that Labonne "tries to join Moroccan entrepreneurs and colonial capitalism." Khatibi, "Note descriptive sur les élites administratives et économiques marocaines," in *Annuaire de l'Afrique du Nord 1968* (Paris: Éditions du CNRS, 1970), 79–90. Regarding industrial policy, see Jacques Lucius, "L'évolution économique récente du Maroc," in *Industrialisation de l'Afrique du nord*, ed. Gaston Leduc (Paris: Armand Colin, 1952), 252–75.

8 Regarding Écochard's politics, see the left-wing Catholic Ignace Lepp, *Minuit sonne au Maroc* (Paris: Aubier, 1954), 200–3; and the analysis by Hervé Bleuchot, *Les libéraux français au Maroc (1947–1955)* (Aix-en-Provence: Éd. de l'Université de Provence-CNRS, 1973). Regarding the fateful role of Boniface (an upper-level colonialist civil servant and director of Political Affairs between 1944 and 1947) see Julien, *Le Maroc face aux impérialismes*, 192–93.

9 It was, no doubt, by way of the Protestant networks frequented by Écochard's wife, Odile Pottecher, that Labonne encountered him. The political significance of Écochard's experiments is addressed in Robert Montagne, *Révolution au Maroc* (Paris: France-Empire, 1953): 290–95.

10 Regarding Écochard's intellectual and professional trajectory, see Vincent Bradel, *Michel Écochard 1905–1985* (Paris: Institut Français d'Architecture/Bureau de la Recherche Architecturale, 1985).

11 The charter was a radicalized version of the fourth CIAM, held in Athens in 1933. Le Corbusier, *La Charte d'Athènes* (Paris: Plon, 1943).

Port of Casablanca and skyline, c. 1960. The slab buildings of Avenue de la République can be seen on the right.

12 Regarding the activity of the Urban Planning Department, see Michel Écochard, "La nouvelle organisation du Service de l'urbanisme au Maroc," *Le Génie civil* (January 15, 1949): 37; idem, "Problèmes d'urbanisme au Maroc," *L'Architecture d'aujourd'hui* 21, no. 35 (May 1951): 9–11; and idem, "Les quartiers industriels des villes du Maroc," *Urbanisme* 20, no. 11–12 (November–December 1951): 26–39.

13 Michel Écochard, "La réorganisation du contrôle général de l'urbanisme," [1946], MAE, CRDG131 Habitat et urbanisme, 1948–51. Department of Municipal Administration, *Organisation du contrôle général de l'urbanisme au Maroc* (Rabat: Imprimerie officielle, 1946). See also Puaux's residential decree, January 10, 1946, regarding the reorganization of the Department of Municipal Administration and Urban Planning.

14 Marcel Lods, "Principes d'urbanisme," *Construire* (December 28, 1949): 928–31; idem, "L'urbanisme et la vie moderne," *Construire* (November 23, 1949): 839. Lods presented his Mayence and Sotteville-lès-Rouen projects—work based on a literal application of the Athens Charter. Bodiansky spoke of "Modern construction procedures."

15 Michel Écochard, "Quelques idées sur la politique de l'urbanisme et du logement au Maroc," [1948], MAE, 131 Habitat et urbanisme, 1948–51. See also the "documentation générale," photograph albums, Photothèque du Ministère de l'Habitat, Rabat. Écochard presented his American experiences in "La planification, condition de l'urbanisme" (paper presented at the American University, Beirut, May 9, 1946), IFA, Fonds Écochard. Regarding the MRU trip that he participated in, see Jean-Louis Cohen, *Scenes of the World to Come: European Architecture and the American Challenge 1893–1960* (Paris: Flammarion; Montreal: Canadian Centre for Architecture, 1995), 171–73.

16 Michel Écochard et al., *Rapport préliminaire sur l'aménagement et l'extension de Casablanca* (Rabat: Direction de l'Intérieur, Service de l'urbanisme, 1951), 25.

17 Écochard, *Casablanca le roman d'une ville*, 11.

18 Michel Écochard, comments made during the Regional Committee of Urban Planning plenary session, February 22, 1950, MAE, carton 848 Région de Casablanca, Comité régional d'urbanisme 1949–52, stenographer's record, 2.

19 Pierre Mas, "Reprendre Casa," *Urbanisme*, no. 211 (January 1986): 56.

20 Écochard et al., *Rapport préliminaire*, 7.

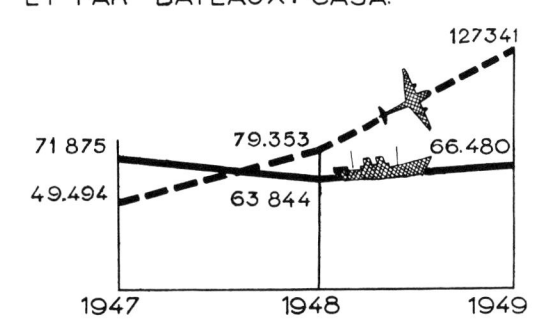

Town Planning Department, graph of Casablanca's air and sea traffic between 1947 and 1949.

These changes in doctrine went hand in hand with a redefinition of the status of urban planning within the Protectorate.[12] The reform introduced in 1946 was based on criticism of the approach adopted by Prost and his successors, and confirmed that "urban planning [had] now become one of the modern sciences." Following the example of French reconstruction, it was recommended that "a new hierarchy of planners" be set up; "regional planning inspections" were established, and an architect was appointed "head of technical services in architecture and planning." Public servants were distrusted, as is evidenced by the fact that recruitment was carried out on a contract basis only, to ensure a degree of "flexibility." In addition, the new recruits "tended to be people who shied away from a hard and fast connection with the administration."[13]

In November 1949, speeches by eminent C.I.A.M. members Marcel Lods and Vladimir Bodiansky revealed the support Écochard enjoyed with respect to his work in Casablanca. Lods extolled the virtues of functional zoning with naive enthusiasm, in the very place where it had first been put into practice by the French.[14] However, the recommendations of the Planning Department fell short of C.I.A.M. precepts. The department's reports contained studies on urban form and infrastructure that drew comparisons between Casablanca and various other projects, such as Swedish zoning experiments, André Lurçat's urban compositions, the mimetic reconstruction of Warsaw, and Richard Neutra's plans for workers' housing. In addition, observations made by Écochard during a memorable trip to the United States in 1945 were expanded, giving rise to numerous analytic drawings of freeway interchanges.[15]

A Linear Industrial City

We have included Fédala in our analysis of Casablanca in order to paint a broader picture of what is known as "rural disintegration." The area between Casablanca and Fédala is industrial. Casablanca accounts for approximately 75 percent of the country's industry, while Fédala boasts a port and cheaper land. Naturally, this has had repercussions on the narrow strip of land that lies between the two cities, and which is connected by road, rail, and sea links.

Michel Écochard, 1951[16]

On arriving in Morocco, Écochard feigned surprise at Casablanca's lack of legible structure and acted as though he had believed that Morocco was "the birthplace of urban planning, that everything was regulated and organized and that the cities and rural areas were developing in perfect harmony."[17] When he saw that Casablanca was a "city that has mushroomed, devoid of any urban planning," and where "the elite are completely out of touch," it was clear in his opinion that the Protectorate was incapable of supervising the development of Morocco's large urban areas. Yet he did perceive in it a certain beauty, saying it was a place where "French and Moroccan genius [had] come together"; nevertheless, he intended to "perform surgery and remove the cancerous parts," or so he asserted, employing a rather hackneyed metaphor.[18]

The Town Planning Department laid down its guidelines and principles for Casablanca in 1950.[19] They employed the tenets of the Athens Charter in their proposals to extend the city regionally, rejecting Courtois's plan of restricting construction to the inner city, stating that "since this plan has not been implemented, it makes no difference whatsoever to the city's development."[20] Écochard did adopt some of Courtois's solutions, though, implicitly making them his own, and he submitted pro-

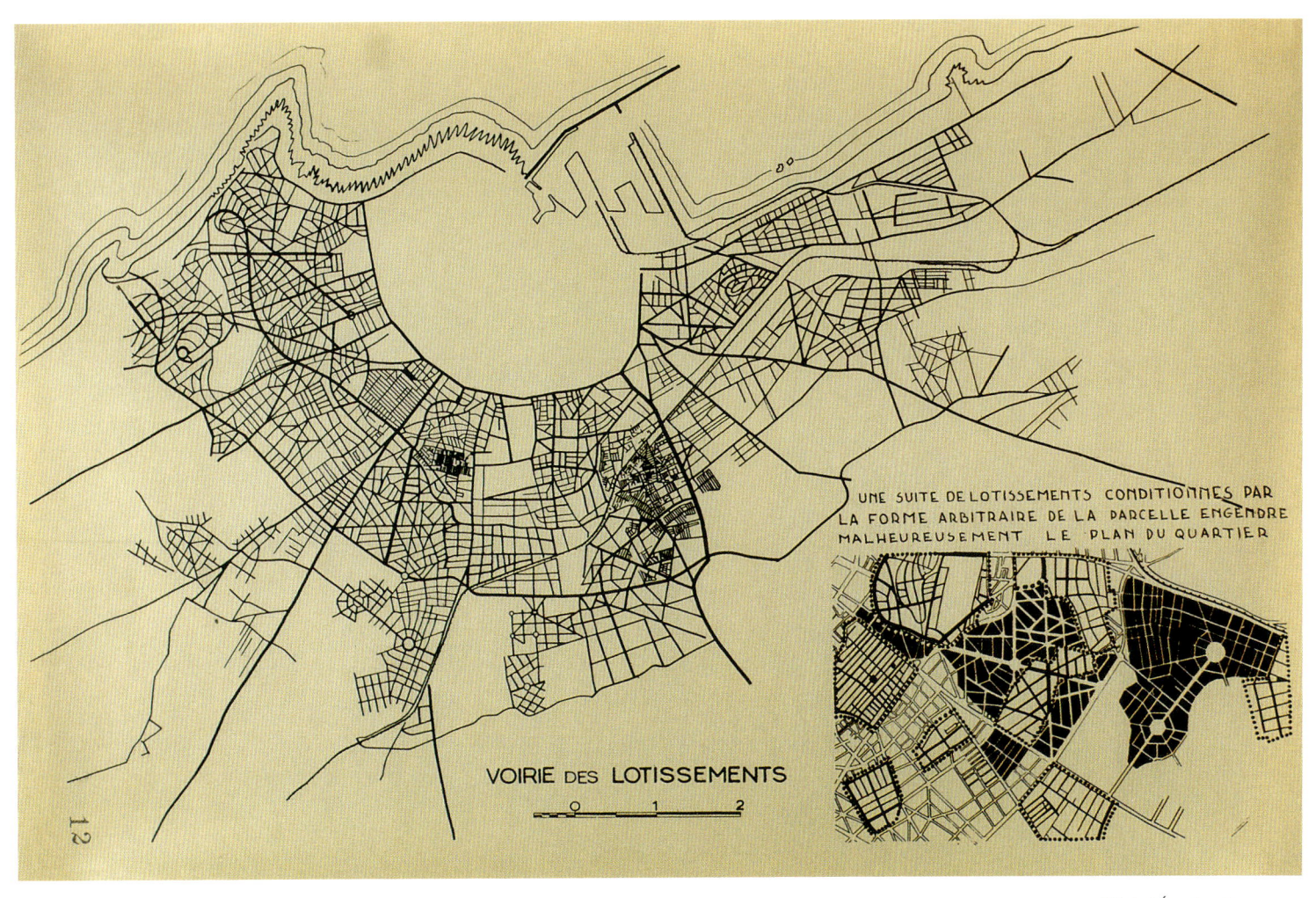

Michel Écochard, graphic critique of the "subdivision system" for Casablanca (1951), in *Rapport préliminaire sur l'aménagement et l'extension de Casablanca*, 1951.

posals to extend Casablanca thirty-five kilometers along the coast, which corresponded to three times the area occupied by the city at the time. This expansion was justified by the fact that port traffic was expected to rise sharply, therefore engendering an increase in trade. In fact, even then the port district—an "economic barometer" and "generator of industry"—was already creeping steadily northwest.[21]

The Casa-Fédala Industrial Complex

Rather than leave it to the naval authorities to decide where to locate the port facilities, Écochard proposed that an "industrial complex" be created to fuse Casablanca and Fédala. This concept, which was not dissimilar to the one underpinning the Soviet five-year plans and certain large-scale American projects, was set out in a report written in 1948 by Admiral Barjot, then commander of the French navy in Morocco, and coincided with the industrial scenario envisaged by Labonne:

> Arguing that the Fédala port was no longer being used for oil shipment, he [Barjot] suggested that the breakwater be turned around to face the same direction as that of Casablanca. Starting with this idea of one single port stretching toward the northeast, he conceived a massive industrial and residential area located immediately behind the port. While we as urban planners did not share the same point of departure, namely a gigantic port, our findings did lead us to the same conclusion concerning industry and housing.[22]

21 Écochard et al., *Rapport préliminaire*, 9.

22 Écochard et al., *Rapport préliminaire*, 25. Active in the Free French Forces, Vice-Admiral Pierre Barjot was the navy commander in Morocco in 1947–48.

Michel Écochard's Controversial Urbanism (1950–1952)

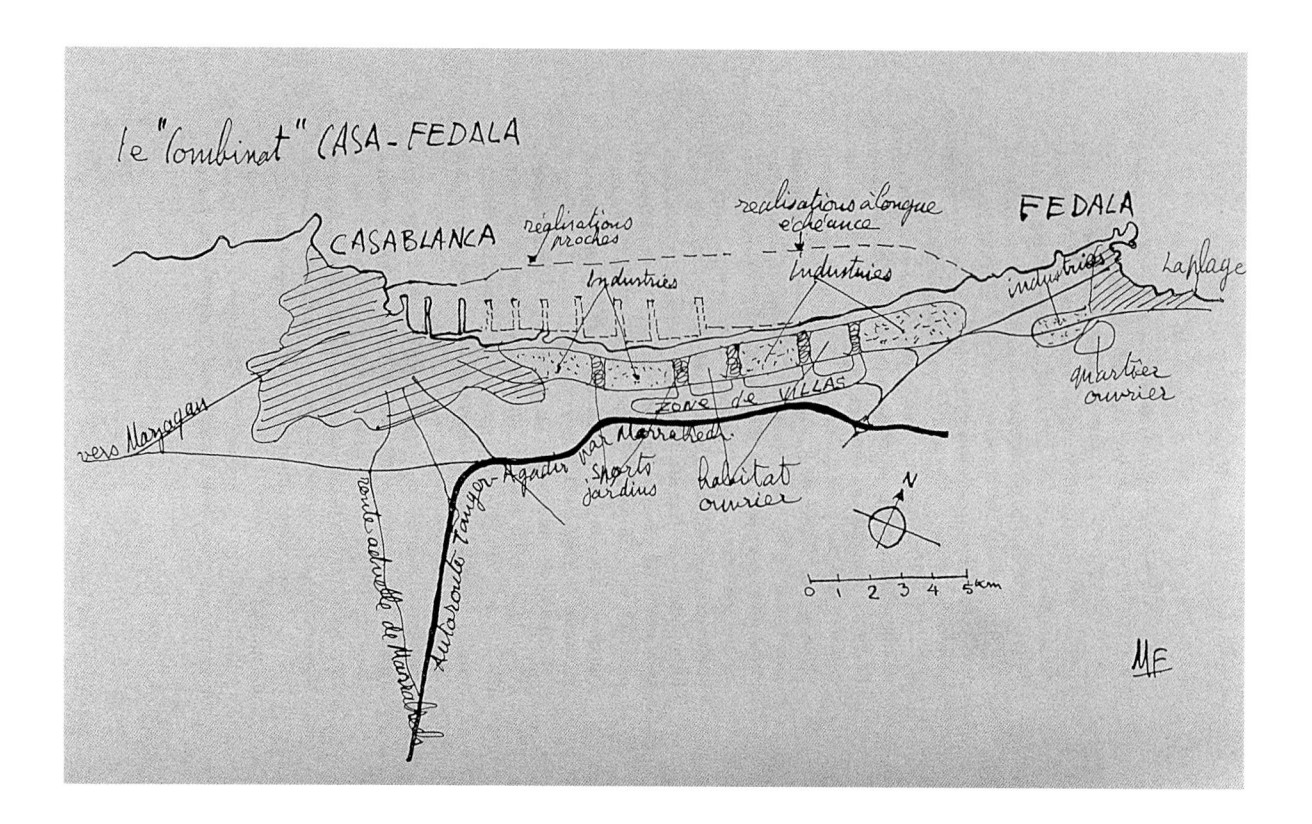

Michel Écochard, sketch for the "Casa-Fédala complex" (1951), in *Rapport préliminaire sur l'aménagement et l'extension de Casablanca*, 1951.

23 Le Corbusier, *Les Trois établissements humains* (Paris: Denoël, 1945). An assembly of agricultural units, linear industrial towns, and "radio-centric" cities of culture and political power, Le Corbusier's concept was derived from Miliutin's and Soria y Mata's models. Nikolai Miliutin, *Sotsgorod: The Problem of Building Socialist Cities* (Moscow: Gos. Izdatelstvo, 1930; reprint, Cambridge, Mass.: MIT Press, 1974); Arturo Soria y Mata, *La cité linéaire: nouvelle architecture de villes* (Madrid: Imprenta de la Ciudad lineal, 1913; reprint, Paris: CERA/ENSBA, 1979). In 1910 Soria had imagined a linear urban development linking Tétouan and Ceuta.

24 Écochard et al., *Rapport préliminaire*, 25.

The port structure was therefore woven into the urban fabric to create a "linear coastal city," the principles of which were borrowed from the "linear industrial city." The latter forms one of the "trois établissements humains" (three human establishments) as defined by Le Corbusier, reworking the ideas set out by Nikolai Miliutin and Arturo Soria y Mata.[23] Unlike Le Corbusier's scheme, though, the kind of development Écochard had in mind was not continuous. It was divided into industrial neighborhoods, which were "fragmented so that the classification yards on which they depend will not become congested" and were combined with individual residential neighborhoods:

> The residential zones will be located as close as possible to the industrial district, so that laborers can be within easy reach of their workplace, yet the area will be protected from noxious fumes and gases ... The extension to the industrial quarter and the various satellite districts that we are planning shall be sited between the railroad and the port, and must be directly linked to the latter. Schematically, then, these zones will be set along a strip running beside the coast between the port of Casablanca and Fédala, with the railroad lying south of this.[24]

After the "industrial and workers' city" came the second "establishment," which was in effect an updated version of Prost's central "business district," located opposite the port. Prost's scheme, however, was minute compared to the new project. The third "establishment" was composed of "the residential area, surrounded by a wooded belt." Écochard's proposal was thus for a genuinely new city, based on a principle that differed fundamentally from that of the Prost plan and which was inextricably linked to the coastal development of the port and industrial quarters.

View of Carrières centrales *bidonville*. On the left is Edmond Brion's Lafarge workers' development. In the background, the cement and sugar factories. "Habitat for the greatest number," detail from the display "grid" presented by the Moroccan group to the C.I.A.M. at Aix-en-Provence, 1953.

"Habitat for the greatest number." Display "grid" presented by the Moroccan group to C.I.A.M. at Aix-en-Provence in 1953. The functions of "dwelling," "work," and "transportation" are laid out parallel to the coast and the Casablanca-Rabat freeway. The sector presented below in schematic form is the same as the one in the previous illustration.

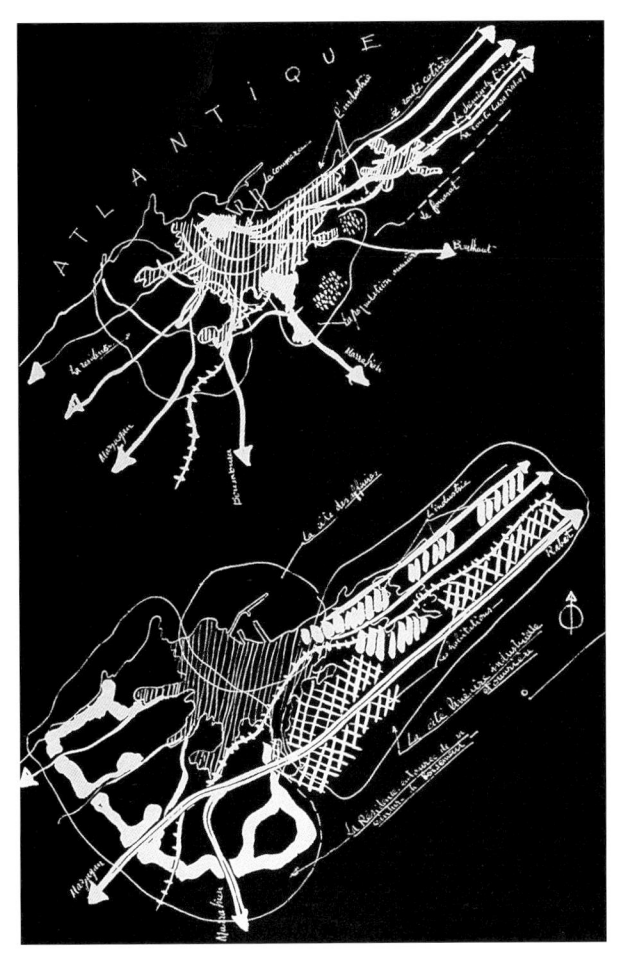

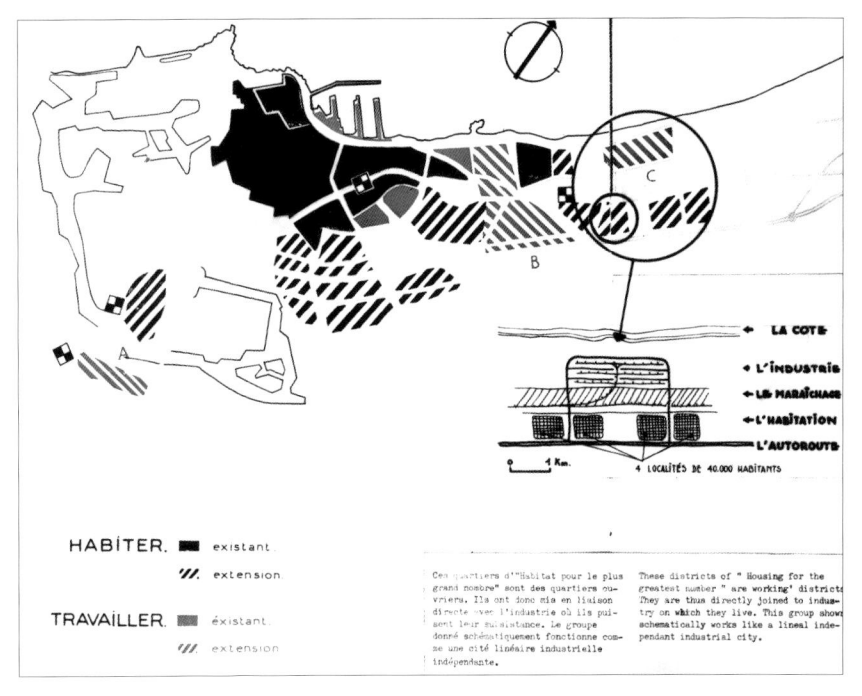

Michel Écochard, development and zoning diagram for "Greater Casablanca," 1951. Published in *Casablanca, le roman d'une ville*, 1955.

Michel Écochard's Controversial Urbanism (1950–1952) 307

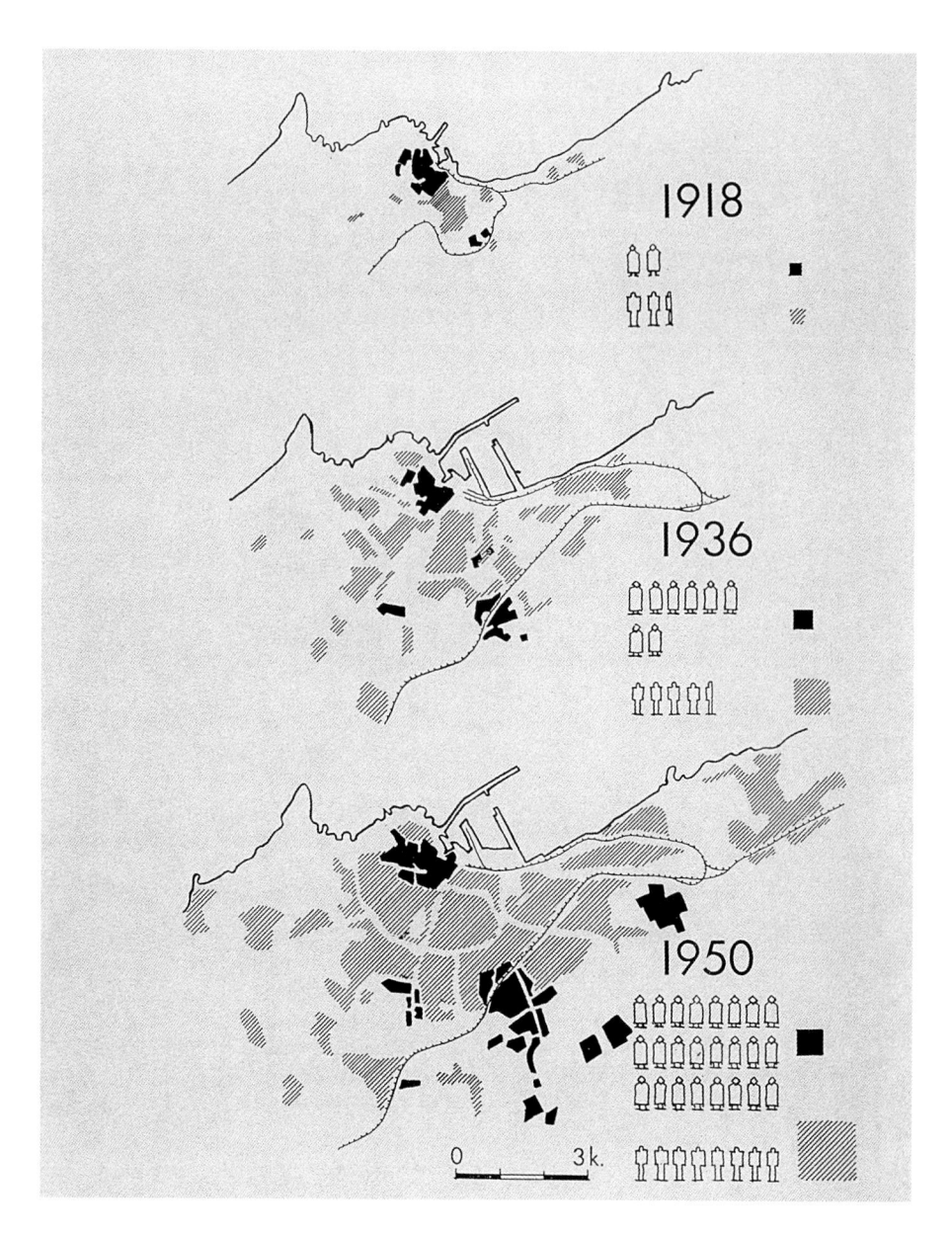

Michel Écochard, areas occupied by various populations of Casablanca from 1918 to 1950, in *Casablanca, le roman d'une ville*, 1955.

"A Monstrous Urban Plan"

War is still being waged over Écochard's proposals, with everyone unanimously agreeing that an incoherent monster of a plan has come into being.

Le Petit Marocain, 1952[25]

25 Jacques Le Prévost, "L'enquête sur le plan Écochard: il reste du terrain pour les millionnaires," *Le Petit Marocain* (Casablanca), February 29, 1952. Owned by the communist-leaning General Labor Confederation between 1945 and 1949, this newspaper subsequently represented the colonialist views of the Mas group.

In addition to talks that took place between 1949 and 1952 on the proposed plan, the administration set up a number of regulatory nets to pin down the Casablanca regional authorities and the municipal council. Despite the tougher line adopted by the residency under General Juin, vestiges of Labonne's policy were still being applied. Vallat, head of interior affairs in Rabat, helped Écochard create a Regional Inspectorate of Urban Planning in 1950, with Georges Godefroy at the helm. This was, however, strongly opposed by Grillet, who was in charge of municipal services.

Talks centered on the city's growth and zoning by social class, and eventually led to the acceptance of Écochard's plan in 1952. For the first time in Casablanca's his-

308 Casablanca

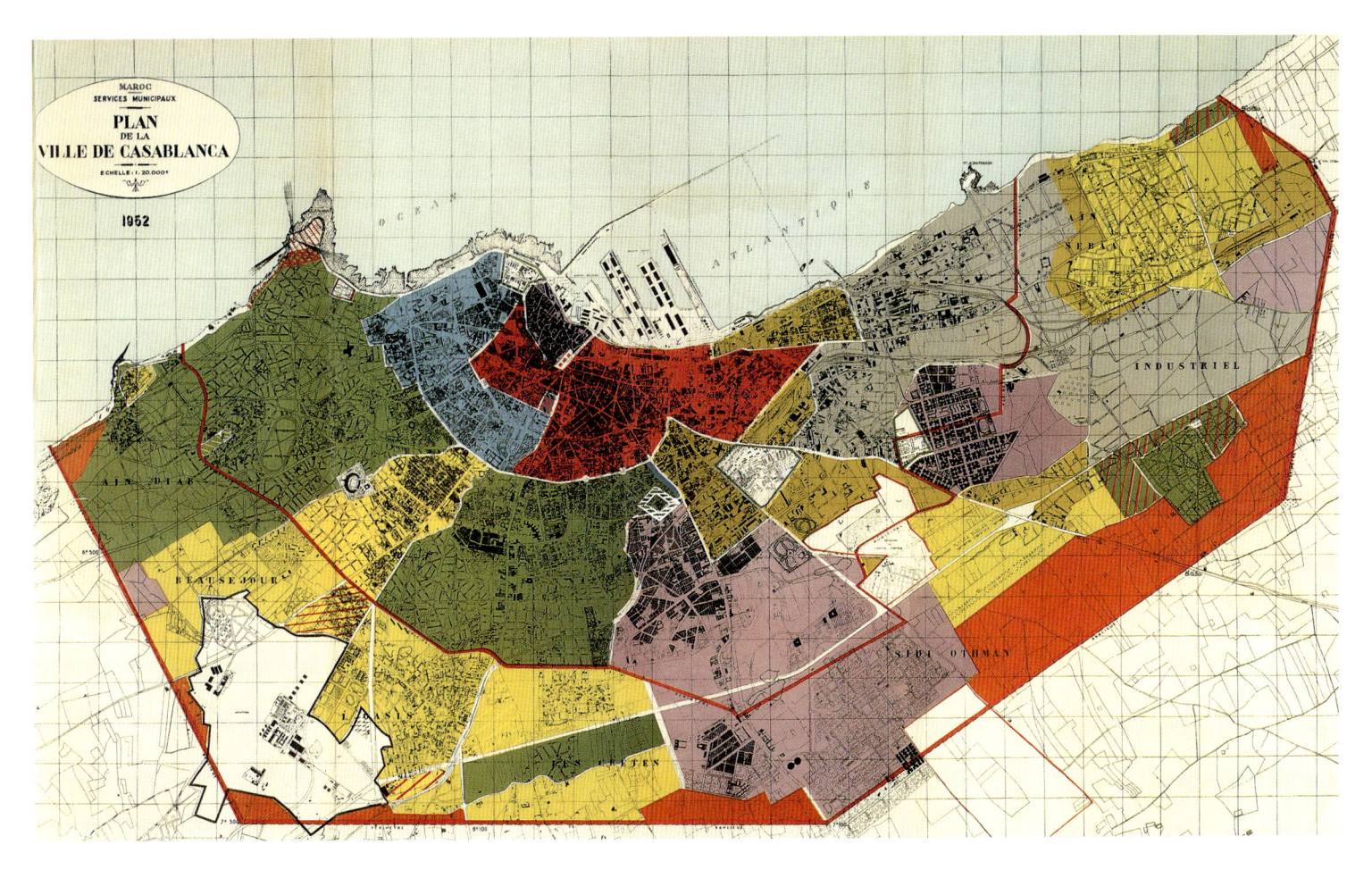

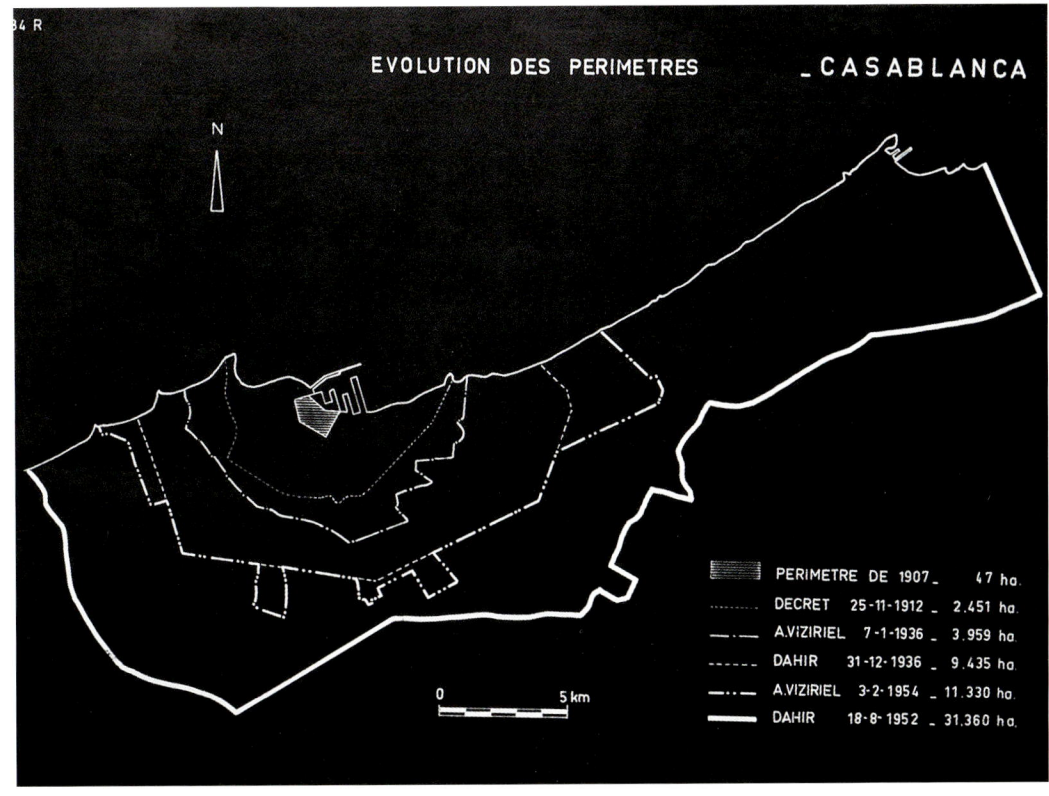

Michel Écochard, zoning plan for Casablanca and suburbs, 1952.

Town Planning Department, diagram showing gradual extension of Casablanca's municipal perimeter, between 1907 and 1952.

tory, the upsurge in rural migrant Moroccans was addressed by incorporating extension areas. Design concepts for these areas were based on an analysis of industrial facilities and of *bidonvilles*, where 100,000 Muslims were crammed into twenty thousand shacks.[26] Backed by the Protectorate's secretary general, Francis Lacoste, Écochard presented the first draft of his plan in 1952 to the Comité regional d'urbanisme (Regional Urban Planning Committee), or C.R.U, which had been headed by Boniface since 1950.[27] Introducing the three concentric areas covered by the bylaws—the outer city, the suburbs, and the greater suburbs, or "greater Casablanca area"—Écochard emphasized the need to reduce congestion and step up expansion, which would "straighten out the suburban belt."[28] As for the inner city, the department recommended that space be freed up and that the number of residential neighborhoods be increased, based on a construction schedule extending from 1950 to 1965. Moreover, it was observed that the existing quarters already harbored an ethnic mix: "The so-called European districts will house a mix of Europeans and Moroccans, since these quarters are occupied by Muslims, accounting for 10 percent, and Jews, who currently represent 12 percent and are soon likely to reach 15 percent."[29]

Écochard accused Grillet of "systematically undermining all the planning projects" and called for his resignation. Many of the participants in the countless meetings held on the subject spoke of the "paralyzing atmosphere of hostility and distrust."[30] The civil inspectors in charge of administering the *bidonvilles* worked on-site and were therefore more accepting of Écochard's projects than the council, where there was little Muslim representation.[31] Grillet blocked Écochard's project for Sidi Belyout, claiming that it ran counter to "the traditions of the Casablancan population," and he granted building permits to private developers for land that had been set aside for the new railroad station.[32] It also became clear at the following meetings of the Regional Committee that the municipal authority was extremely reluctant to finance a fifteen-year plan, nor were they willing to fund access roads to the port. In order for the plan to be approved, the secretary general of the Protectorate had to stress, in 1952, that "the development of the greater Casablanca area was an issue that affected Morocco as a whole," and that, as with the Prost and Labonne plans, the state would not shirk its responsibilities.[33]

A second rift opened between Écochard and the landowners, who made no bones about their objection to the plans.[34] In 1951, the vice-chairman of the municipal council, Marazzani, hypocritically deplored all the publicity given to the Écochard plan, which had led to a hike in land prices, and nostalgically looked back to "the days when town planning went on quietly in offices." His main criticism was leveled against Écochard "for obstructing free exercise of land rights by way of measures that seemed questionable from a legal perspective."[35] Many landlords, especially Édouard Gouin, were critical of collective housing being built in areas like Le Polo, which were zoned for villas. In addition, Gouin, a spokesman for the road system subcommittee, stated in 1952 that the projects drafted by the Planning Department "seriously jeopardized private property."[36] The tedious wrangling ended in an agreement on Ain Sebaa, east of the city; acquiescing to the request of the population, it was decided that only individual dwellings would be built in the area and that industrial development would be restricted to a minimum, even though private firms were extremely hostile to such an idea.

Council members also criticized the decision to maintain the Moroccan housing zone along the Azemmour road. They believed that the *bidonville*, which had been created out of a "raking together of shacks," was "too close to the villa district." However, the administration, which had instigated the zone's creation, calmly stated that it was needed to house "the servants of villas in Anfa."[37] The political

---

26 Minutes of the meeting at the Regional Civil Administration building, presided over by Francis Lacoste, October 27, 1949, MAE, carton 848, Région de Casablanca, Comité regional d'urbanisme, 1949–52.

27 Beginning in 1949, the Greater Casablanca Commission was the forerunner of the Regional Urban Planning Committee. Laraki, an active developer and president of the Moroccan Chamber of Commerce and Industry, had successfully petitioned for membership on the commission, in which Muslims were, as usual, underrepresented.

28 The C.R.U. united the civil administrators of Casablanca, Chaouia, and Fédala; the vice president and five members of the Municipal Council, qualified civil servants and technicians; representatives of the Chambers of Agriculture and Commerce; as well as *a single* Muslim elected official.

29 Urban Planning Department, "Note sur l'évolution démographique et la densité urbaine de Casablanca," February 1, 1950, MAE, carton 848, Comité régional d'urbanisme, 1949–52, 21. Seven hundred fifteen hectares were devoted to the decongestion of Muslim quarters, and 1,255 to their expansion. One hundred ten hectares were given over to the decongestion of Jewish districts, and 125 to their expansion. Seven hundred fifty hectares were earmarked for the expansion of European neighborhoods.

30 Casablanca Urban Affairs Administrator Jean Cousté to Philippe Boniface, March 12, 1951, MAE, carton 848, Comité régional d'urbanisme, 1949–52. Casablanca's municipal survey architect, Henri Souque, confirmed that Écochard was persona non grata at the Municipal Council. Henri Souque, interview by the authors, Paris, November 6, 1996.

31 Pierre Mas, interview by the authors, October 7, 1996.

32 Écochard complained vociferously, so much so that the project was adopted by the Municipal Council. Michel Écochard, memorandum to the Director of the Interior. The director had intercepted this memorandum, addressed to General Juin, February 13, 1951, MAE, carton 849, Comité régional d'urbanisme.

33 Georges Hutin (Protectorate secretary general) to the vice president of the Casablanca Municipal Council, February 19, 1952, MAE, carton 849, Comité régional d'urbanisme.

34 The public inquest registered 136 dissenting voices regarding suburban areas and 211 regarding the greater Casablanca zoning proposals. The latter postulated a minimum lot size of one hectare, in order to avoid processes of excessive speculation and to preserve the "rural character" of the zone." Zoning de la banlieue de Casablanca, Enquête de comodo et incomodo du 28 janvier au 31 mars 1952, rapport de fin d'enquête," Casablanca, 1952, MH, D 253; Comité régional d'urbanisme, réunion du 28 mai 1952, MAE, carton 850, Comité régional d'urbanisme.

35 Emmanuel Marazzani to the Director of the Interior, July 3, 1951, MAE, carton 849, Comité régional d'urbanisme.

36 Hajoui and Nahon were the Muslim and Jewish authors of "Rapport sur les projets d'aménagement et d'extension de Casablanca, étude des propositions de la sous-commission Travaux-voirie-plan d'urbanisme," Casablanca, 1952, MH, R 77. Through his determination, Gouin would manage to ban such buildings from the Crêtes district.

37 Stenographer's record of the October 27, 1949, meeting, MAE, carton 848, Comité régional d'urbanisme; and meeting minutes of the Council on Local Interests of the Casablanca Suburbs, April 9, 1952, MAE, carton 850, Comité régional d'urbanisme.

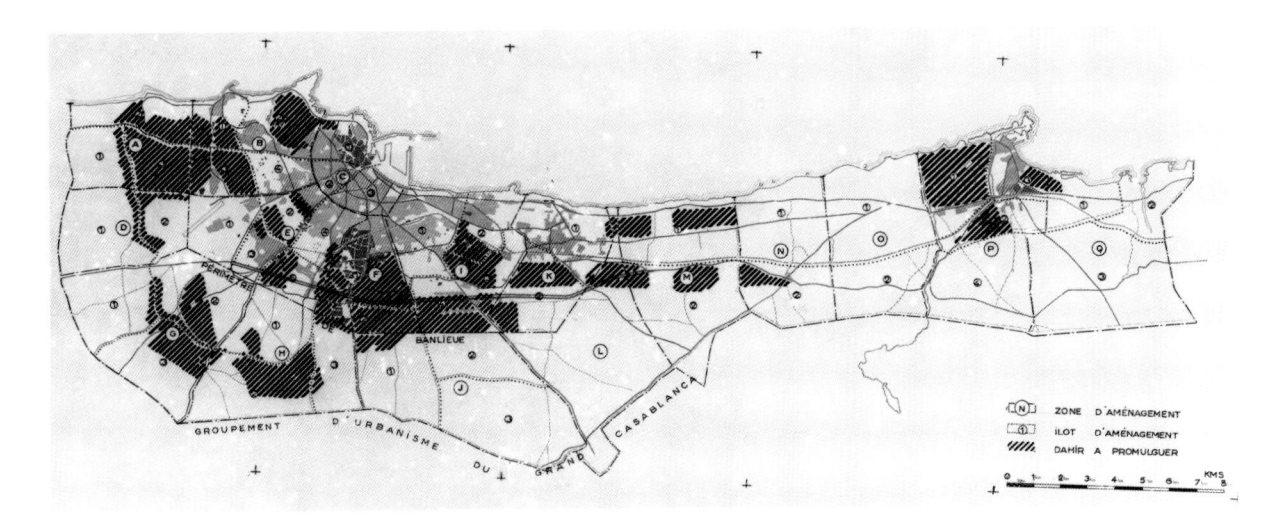

Michel Écochard, development plan for Casablanca, 1951. Functional zoning and areas of development.

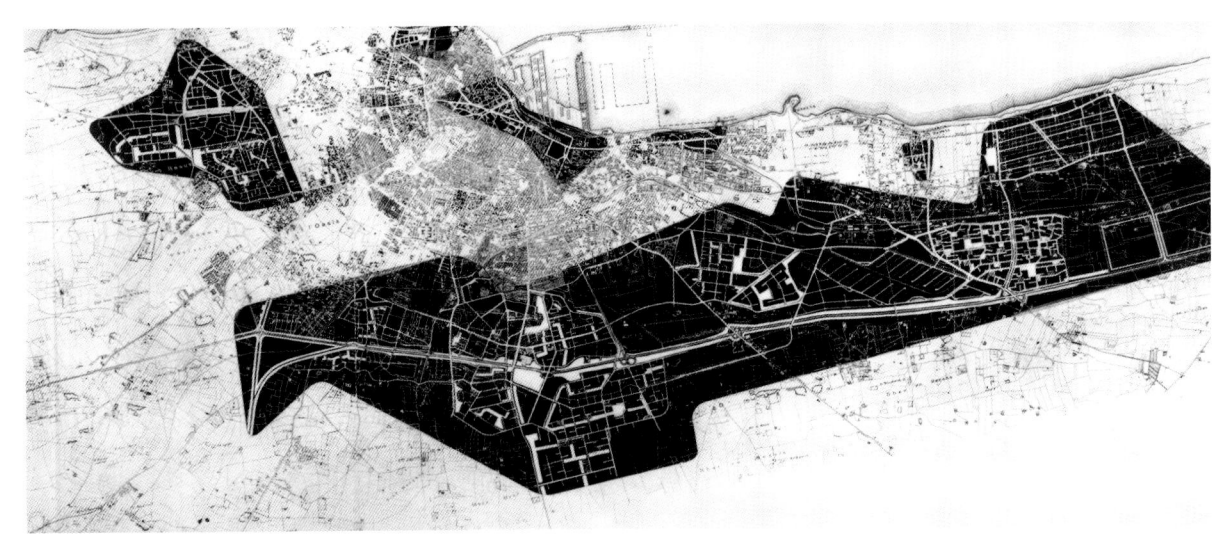

Michel Écochard, development plan for Casablanca, 1951. Proposed residential neighborhoods. Published in *Casablanca, le roman d'une ville*, 1955.

risks of Moroccan housing schemes were also cited, and Secretary General Hutin maintained that "proletarian communities should not be concentrated around the city."[38] The notion of a "red belt" was raised in the press by partisans and critics alike.[39] In the debate over the suburbs, Nahon pointed out that there was no provision in the zoning plan for an area to rehouse the Jews who had been evicted from the mellah as part of the extension program for the Place de France. Responding to these issues of ethnic zoning, Écochard declared, "The areas zoned for Moroccan housing [are] not reserved exclusively for Muslims, but for all Moroccans, regardless of ethnic origin"; however, the objection was raised that "there [is] no ethnic mix in the medinas." Land was hence sought for a "Jewish extension zone" out toward the Boulhaut Camp road, near the Bata factory, and Grillet and the civil inspector Quessada eventually decided on a plot near the El Hank headland.[40] Thus, in addition to the two central zones "corresponding to the main districts already occupied by the Muslim population," there were to be four others on the outskirts, "organized as fully autonomous satellite towns."[41] The zoning of greater Casablanca—which since 1936 included unbuilt land administered by the local authorities—was approved in 1951. In this plan the city's outskirts were divided over a radius of twelve to fifteen kilometers into five sectors that were subject to specific building codes.[42] The suburban zoning plan and its accompanying bylaws were validated in 1952.[43]

38. Stenographer's record of the administration's January 8, 1952, internal working session (which shaped a joint position in preparation of the Regional Committee's plenary session), MAE, carton 849, Comité régional d'urbanisme, 13.

39 Robert Hanztberg, "Le plan Écochard est-il applicable?, 2. Le problème des ceintures rouges," *La Vigie marocaine* (Casablanca), February 26, 1952; and Jacques Le Prévost, "Le Grand Casablanca: nous allons avoir notre ceinture rouge," *Le Petit Marocain* (Casablanca), February 18, 1952.

40 Meeting minutes of the Council on Local Interests of the Casablanca Suburbs, April 9, 1952, MAE, carton 850, Comité régional d'urbanisme.

41 Jacques Delarozière, "L'Urbanisme au Maroc," in *Le Maroc moderne: architecture et urbanisme* (Casablanca: Diffusions d'outre-mer, 1954).

42 Stenographer's record of the C.R.U. plenary session, January 8, 1952, MAE, carton 850, Comité régional d'urbanisme; stenographer's record of the C.R.U. Select Committee meeting, January 15, 1952, MAE, carton 850, Comité régional d'urbanisme. The blocks were, from west to east: the Oulad-Messaoud, Oulad-Haddou, Harraouiyine, Ain-el-Harrouda, and Saint-Jean-de-Fédala sectors.

43 *Dahir* of August 25, 1952, BO (September 12, 1952). This decree approved and endorsed the public utility of the suburban zoning plan and regulations.

44 See Jacques Le Prévost, "Le Service de l'Urbanisme accouche d'un monstre: le Grand Casablanca"; "Un monstre de l'urbanisme: le Grand Casablanca: un retraité à la recherche d'un petit coin tranquille"; "Un monstre de l'urbanisme: le Grand Casablanca: 'car tel est mon bon plaisir'"; "L'enquête publique sur le plan Ecochard prolongée d'un mois; les fantaisies du service de l'urbanisme vivement critiquées;" "L'enquête sur le plan Écochard: il reste du terrain pour les millionnaires;" and "L'enquête sur le Grand Casa: des centaines de protestations condamnent le plan Ecochard." *Le Petit Marocain* (Casablanca), February 17, 20, 21, 27, 29, and March 1, 1952.

45 The lawyer Louis de Saboulin believed that Écochard "did not invent anything." Louis de Saboulin, "À propos du Grand Casablanca, le point de vue juridique," *La Vigie marocaine* (Casablanca), March 4, 1952. See also de Saboulin, "À propos du Grand Casablanca, un précurseur: Me Claude Favrot," *La Vigie marocaine* (Casablanca), February 29, 1952; and de Saboulin, "Sur le front du Grand Casa, la bataille fait rage," *Maroc-demain*, February 23, 1952.

46 See Robert Hanztberg, "Le plan Écochard pour l'aménagement du Grand Casablanca est-il applicable? Un handicap lourd à rattraper: celui d'un passé désordonné et anarchique;" "Le problème des ceintures rouges"; "Les zones d'habitat dispersé: une nouveauté qui suscite une vive opposition"; "Voici ce que seraient les zones d'habitat dispersé si le plan de zoning était adopté"; and "Ce plan présente certainement des défauts." *La Vigie marocaine* (Casablanca), February 25, 26, 27, 28, and 29, 1952.

47 Michel Écochard to Sigfried Giedion, Rabat, ca. January 1948, gta/ETH Zurich, 42-SG-21-7.

48 Le Corbusier had already imagined such a roadway when, during his 1931 trip to Morocco, he wrote in his sketchbook about "classification of Rabat-Casa speeds." Sketchbook B7, in Françoise de Franclieu, ed., *The Le Corbusier Sketchbooks* (New York: Architectural History Foundation; Cambridge, Mass.: MIT Press, 1981), 1:435.

49 Direction de l'urbanisme, "Note sur l'autoroute périphérique de Casablanca, 1953," MH, R8, 17–18. A series of regulatory documents assured the initiation of this project even before debate had ended. Forty percent of the land acquisitions were made as of 1952. The first regulatory measures were: for the western section, a June 1948 decree prohibiting construction on land destined for the freeway; and, for the eastern section, a October 2, 1950, *dahir* on the enlargement of the Ouled Ziane road, followed by a July 7, 1953, *dahir* on improvement plans for Ben M'Sick and Sidi Othman.

50 Marème Dione and André Guillerme, *Techniques et politiques économiques, les travaux publics en Afrique du nord 1953–1962* (Paris: Plan Urbain, 1987).

51 The only green spaces worthy of the title were: the Ben M'Sick nursery (13.9 hectares, acquired in 1916) and its annex (7.4 hectares, acquired in 1922); Parc Murdoch, the first public garden (4.1 hectares, bought by the city in 1921); Parc Lyautey (2.5 hectares, acquired in 1926); Parc de la Société d'horticulture, (17 hectares, acquired in 1927); and the Jardin du Belvédère (1.5 hectares, acquired in 1938).

52 Inspection générale de l'urbanisme, "Les problèmes d'espaces verts de Casablanca," February 1952, MH, R6.

Michel Écochard, development plan for Casablanca, 1951. Casablanca-Rabat freeway.

Michel Écochard, development plan for Casablanca, 1951. Link-up between the Casablanca-Rabat freeway and existing main roads.

Michel Écochard, development plan for Casablanca, 1951. Green areas.

The intensity of the conflicts can be perceived in the many vituperative articles in the Casablancan press concerning the planned development and the various bylaws. *Le Petit Marocain* persisted in its criticism of what it called a "monstrous urban plan," and came down hard on the man behind it, before whom "the prefectures and municipalities have no choice but to keep quiet and obey."[44] When it came to the greater Casablanca area, the battle raged between the "Écochardistes" and their adversaries, who considered the plan too dangerous or positively useless.[45] Écochard's strongest supporter was the journalist Robert Hantzberg, who blamed "the prior lack of urban planning" for Casablanca's "missing center."[46]

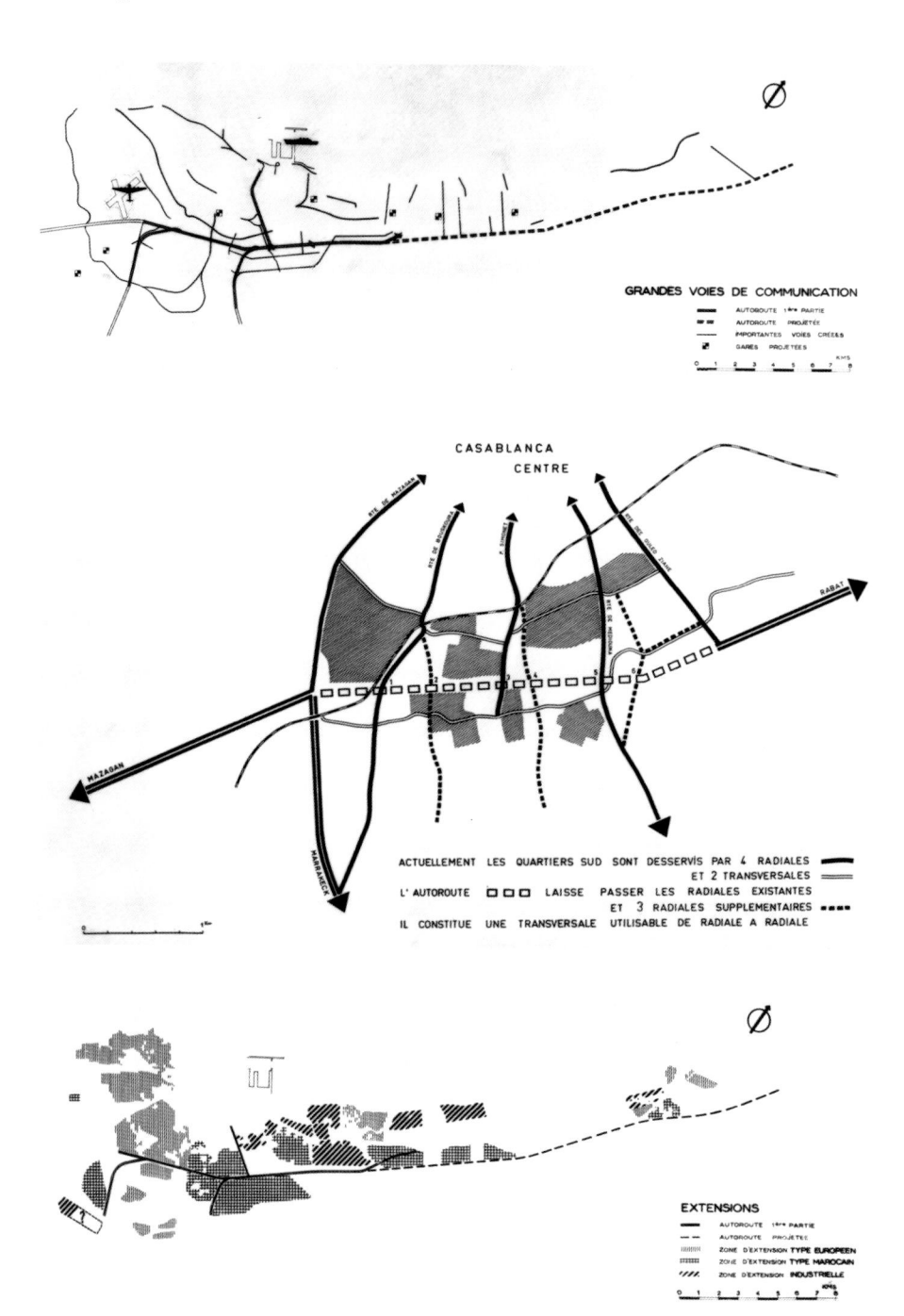

Écochard's Defeat

The work I have conducted in Morocco so far has raised many issues I would like to discuss. An ambitious program has been set up for the expansion and development of Moroccan cities but within it there are several contradictory factors that simply cannot be avoided. By taking into account local traditions, the grid pattern of cities should be improved over time. In addition, there are all sorts of questions indirectly related to urban planning, such as creating processing centers for agricultural products in the countryside so that the rural populations can remain on their farms and thereby prevent certain cities from becoming urban sprawl.

Michel Écochard, 1948[47]

Besides negotiating the plan, the Planning Department was also carrying out studies for the Avenue de la République that was to run through the city center and for the Casablanca-Rabat freeway, the very backbone of the scheme. It was designed as the first section of a "major road with two branches leading to Tangiers-Oujda and Marrakech-Agadir" and ran parallel to the coast, through a string of Moroccan districts.[48] It came under fairly heavy criticism, since it was to be laid "as close as possible to the city core," and since it split the southern neighborhoods in two. The planners argued that "a straight line is the best layout," and compared the road to the scheme for the Boulevard Périphérique [beltway] that was then being drafted for Paris:

> It would be a mistake to consider [this section of the] freeway as just a bypass, for it is key to the entire traffic system for Greater Casablanca and therefore to the development plan as a whole. Diverting the road or making it anything other than a freeway would mean backing down, with serious ramifications for the future. And a city like this cannot back down, just as it cannot give way concerning projects such as the Avenue de la République, which is to run through the medina, for few other modern cities have embarked on anything at all comparable.[49]

It was due to these types of projects, and to the construction methods behind them, that Casablanca maintained its status as a testing ground for new procedures.[50] Conversely, work on the parks fell behind schedule because of the time wasted since Prost and Laprade, and the situation became pressing. There were many complaints that the city was "not green enough," and that Casablanca seemed to be "the most destitute of all new towns built since 1912." The Planning Department ascribed this to the water shortage, the city's rapid growth, and the cost of land, which, since 1938, had been too high for the council to buy plots for public gardens.[51] There were very few parks, and even these were scattered. Nor was there anywhere close by where residents could take a walk, except in the coastal area of Sidi Abderrahmane, to the west, and the "forest park" created during the war in the south, between Bouskoura and Médiouna. In their development plan, Écochard's team included "green spaces" in the new subdivisions; they also recommended constructing large apartment buildings to cope with the growing population and to free up land that could be converted into "green areas on people's doorsteps." A small belt of parks was designed, spreading halfway around the city to the southwest, as if in a posthumous tribute to Forestier's concept of the park system.[52]

The work conducted by the Planning Department covered all aspects of the urban framework and reopened the dusty file on Labonne's central "business district," which was supposed to stretch out along the new Avenue de la République down to the Place de France. Écochard's team rejected the neo-Haussmannian ideas adopted after the skyscraper concept in the Labonne plan was dropped, and instead designed a road lined with large slab buildings that ran into the plot

Michel Écochard, plan for the "main east-west axis" (Avenue de la République), 1949.

Michel Écochard, sketch for the link-up between the "main east-west axis" and Place de France, 1950.

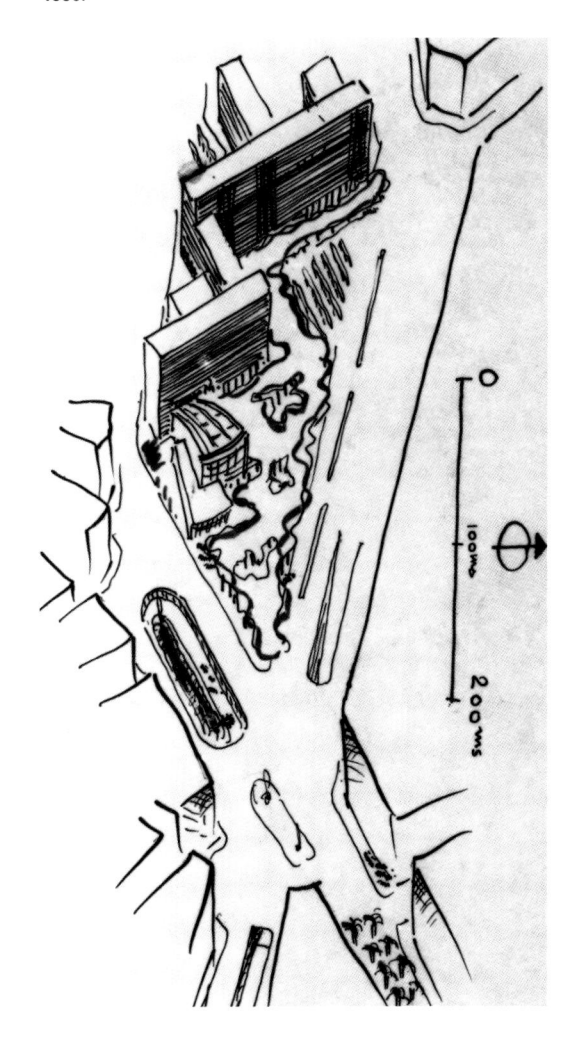

Michel Écochard's Controversial Urbanism (1950–1952) 313

53 The disastrous Hyatt Regency hotel, built in 1985, is the direct descendant of this project.

54 Michel Écochard, comments made during the October 30, 1947, meeting about urban planning questions relative to landmarked medinas; Michel Écochard, memorandum to the Director of the Interior, Rabat, December 16, 1947, MAE, SGP, carton 235, Monuments historiques; and Henri Terrasse, memorandum regarding the preservation of medinas, Rabat, 11 November 1949, MAE, SGP, carton 235, Monuments historiques.

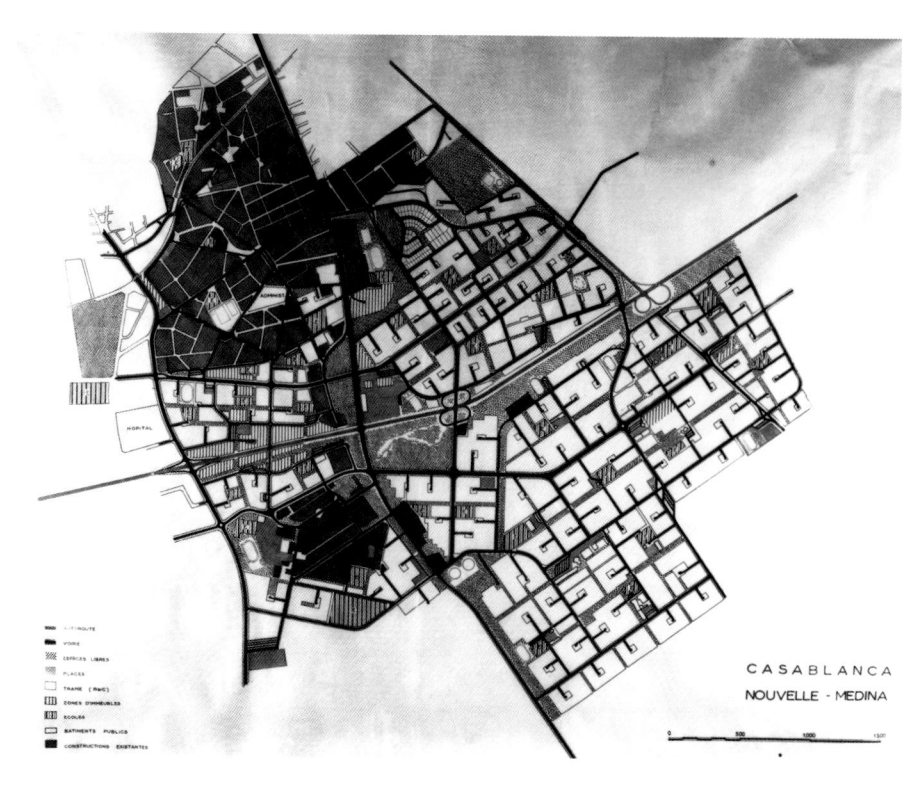

Town Planning Department, extension plan for the new medina, April 1954.

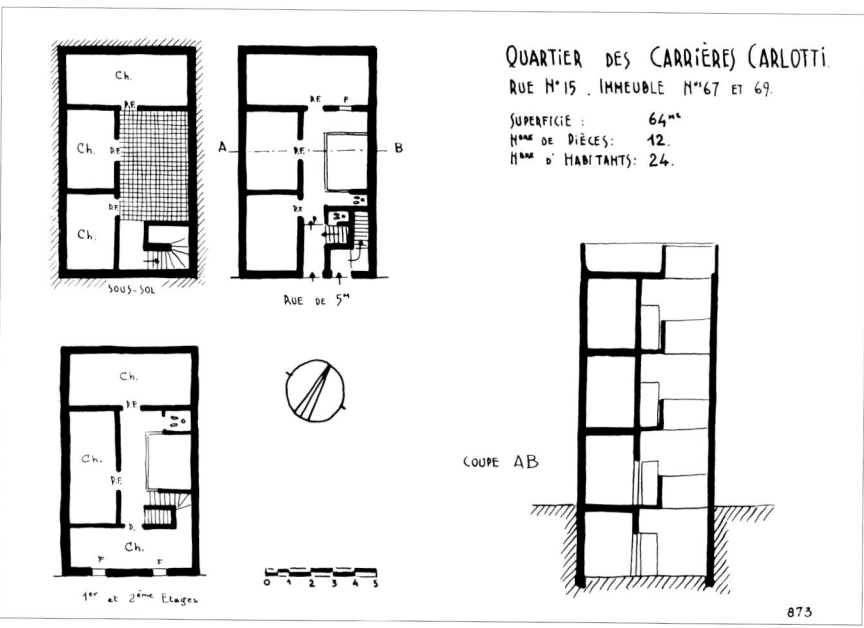

Pierre Mas and Pierre Pelletier, measured drawing of a residential building, Carrières Carlotti neighborhood, 1950.

occupied by the old mellah.⁵³ The avenue was bounded to the east by a strip of offices and apartments, followed by a "comb" of slab units dedicated mainly to hotels. Écochard continued to maintain that Casablanca's medina should be demolished, and from 1947 on this led to violent clashes with the famous historian Henri Terrasse, Inspector of Historical Monuments, Medinas, and Listed Sites. Écochard wanted to "open" the medinas rather than turn them into "tasteless museums with trite medieval reproductions," whereas Terrasse felt that the modernization program for Muslim housing should be targeted mainly at the new medinas.⁵⁴ In 1949, Écochard suggested listing just a few "carefully chosen areas of unquestionable picturesqueness" in the medinas, and refused to let the Historical Monuments team freeze "architectural development" of the centers. As a "modern architect," he was "conscience-bound" to reject "insalubrious architectural forms." He justified his actions on the grounds that "a number of Moroccans [wished] to see the old quarters modernized"; he also invoked the precepts of the Athens Charter, resulting in a schematic discourse that triggered an ironic response from Henri Terrasse about the indisputable virtues of modern urbanism.[55]

The Planning Department thus set about studying possibilities for further extending the "new indigenous town" that had been built in 1920. A survey by Pierre Mas and Pierre Pelletier in 1950 and the census of March 1952 provided precise figures on the density of the neighborhoods in the new medina, where 179,000 inhabitants were packed into 178 hectares of land.[56] Due to such overcrowding, the residents in question lacked "essentials, which [they] had every right to expect as basic municipal facilities." Streets were eating up excessive areas of the neighborhoods; in addition, this "particularly dense and costly street system did no more than carve out long small strips of land measuring ten meters deep with six meters of frontage." Forty-three percent of the surface was paved, and there were no gardens.[57] All in all, then, it can be said that the scope and radical nature of the studies carried out by the planning team demonstrated its commitment and drive to far-reaching objectives that would soon become a thorn in the Protectorate's side.

Post-Écochard Administrative Reforms

In order for Michel Écochard's grand project to be properly implemented, certain administrative aspects needed to be revised. In 1951, Écochard therefore proposed that the planning and construction departments be merged so that funds earmarked for housing by the lending authorities, the Civil Buildings Department, and the Planning Department could be better managed. The idea was for "the overall program, credit facilities management, and technical issues" to be handled by one and the same body, with the underlying concept modeled on the structure of the Ministry of Reconstruction and Urban Planning (M.R.U.) that had been set up in France in 1944.[58] The mission of this new body included coming up with standard plans and establishing new neighborhoods in a way that would "counterbalance

55 Meeting minutes of the advisory committee on the protection of medinas and landmarked zones, November 26, 1949, MAE, SGP, carton 235, Monuments historiques. The final version of this document was subject to numerous interventions through which Écochard attempted to enhance the control of the Urban Planning Department over historic towns. Terrasse would never stop battling this policy. See Henri Terrasse to Protectorate secretary general, January 26, 1950, MAE, SGP, carton 235, Monuments historiques.

56 That is, a population density of 1,020 people per hectare. The principal sectors were: (1) the Habous development, Derb Hajib, and Derb Martinet; (2) Derb Carlotti 1 and 2, Derb Baladiya, the Spagnol and Bel Alia districts, Derb Bouchentouf, and Derb el Miter; (3) Derb Koréa and the Chorfa Tolba quarter; and (4) the Kébir Fassi district and el Afou.

57 Urban Planning Department, "Casablanca, nouvelle médina extension, étude d'aménagement du secteur ouest," April 1953, MH, R 116.

58 Écochard intended to rescind the 1947 split between, on the one hand, the Departments of Municipal Administration and Urban Planning, which had retained the responsibility for substantive projects, and, on the other hand, the Department of Urban Planning and Architecture, which was in charge of general plans.

Resident-General Francis Lacoste inspects the Carrières Centrales building site on June 18, 1954.

Michel Écochard presents his ideas on the future of the city in the movie *Salut, Casa!* directed by Jean Vidal in 1952.

Casablanca press clippings criticizing Écochard, 1952. Montage published in *Casablanca, le roman d'une ville*, 1955.

59 Among such individuals were the Moroccan developers Sadni and Laraki. Michel Écochard, memorandum regarding reform of the Urban Planning Department, 1951, MAE, carton 139, Habitat, logement, urbanisme, 1951–54.

60 Marcel Vallat, memorandum to the Protectorate secretary general regarding reform of the Department of Urban Planning and Architecture, January 15, 1952, MAE, carton 230 Beaux-Arts.

61 With respect to expropriation, indemnities were improved, and lands reserved but not acquired were guaranteed to be returned after a period of ten years. At the same time, "plan preparation bylaws" allowed the administration to prevent transfers of land (and thus speculation) while plans were being developed. *Dahir* regarding urban planning, July 30, 1952, *BO*, September 26, 1952, 1338–40.

62 *Dahir* regarding subdivisions and land parcels, September 30, 1953, *BO*, no. 2142, November 13, 1953, 1620–24.

63 Alexandre Courtois to Protectorate secretary general, June 15, 1952, MAE, carton 230, Beaux-Arts. Privately, Courtois displayed favor toward Écochard's policies and encouraged the training of Moroccan architects. Pierre Mas, letter to authors, October 7, 1996.

64 Town Planning Department, draft reply to Courtois's letter, July 21, 1952, MAE, carton 230, Beaux-Arts.

speculative ventures" and would enable technical assistance to be provided to "deserving" individuals.⁵⁹ Vallat, who strongly supported Écochard, recommended that the Planning Department directly oversee construction, since its plans were "being distorted beyond recognition in the built works and its careful savings were being thrown down the drain."⁶⁰ This led to a Direction de l'Urbanisme et de l'Habitat (Town Planning and Housing Directorate) being instituted under the *dahir* of January 21, 1955.

An urban planning reform was enacted in July 1952 to revise the system introduced under Lyautey, which was deemed too obsolete to "remedy the problems caused by Morocco's ever-expanding cities." Administrative constraints were eased and the "emerging centers," "suburban zones," and "inner and outer peripheries" were taken into account. "Urbanism districts" were set up, such as the one linking Casablanca and Fédala. And more important, urban plans became increasingly diversified so as to include two-year zoning plans and more detailed development schemes.⁶¹

In 1953, talks regarding the metropolitan plan for Casablanca led to stricter legislation pertaining to subdivisions. According to Protectorate officials, "If left to the whim of interested parties, there is a risk that insalubrious, poorly serviced, and badly laid out subdivisions will be created on skewed sites, which will never be able to subsequently form part of any rational city plan."⁶² From then on, developments were to be integrated into the master plan and monitored by the planning authorities. This extension of the legal and technical prerogatives of the Town Planning Department worried some architects. Alexandre Courtois, head of the Conseil Supérieur de l'Ordre (Higher Council of the Order of Architects), spoke out in 1952 against what he considered to be "unfair competition" by Écochard, "who has submitted a number of building permit requests."⁶³ Like the M.R.U. in France, the Planning Department provided builders with "standard plans for low-cost housing" but underscored the fact that "its role was not to supervise or monitor any of the construction work."⁶⁴

Despite, or perhaps because of, his victory in the battles over the Casablanca plan and administrative reshuffling, Écochard made many enemies in the Protectorate. These included landowners and even some of the most reputable architects. Having formed part of the broad-minded team put together by Labonne, he had now become one of the executives pushed onto the sidelines by Juin, Labonne's successor.[65] Despite all the support for him both in Morocco and France, he was dismissed on December 31, 1952, by General Guillaume (resident-general after Juin) on account of his determination not to give into developers and corrupt administrators.[66]

Écochard's record after six years as the head of the Planning Department earned the praise of his successor, Jacques Delarozière, who wrote in 1954 of Écochard's "clear-thinking and courage."[67] Resident-General Gilbert Grandval was in favor of a smooth end to the Protectorate, and during his brief time in office, in 1955, he tried to reinstate Écochard.[68] Furthermore, Écochard was later able to take literary revenge with the publication of his book *Casablanca: le roman d'une ville*, in which he recounts all the battles he was forced to wage.[69] Many of the policies instituted on his initiative were actually followed through after he left office and even after independence. In addition, there can be no denying the interest his projects roused among planners working in Africa and Latin America. Écochard's fate can, in the end, then, be likened to that of the enlightened missionaries. According to Albert Memmi, a critic of colonialism, these "birds of passage, even if animated by considerable energy, never succeed in shattering the appearance, or simply the administrative routine, of colonial headquarters."[70]

C.I.A.M. Discovers Écochard

Écochard's work resounded around the world through the Congrès Internationaux d'Architecture Moderne (C.I.A.M.), when the latter began meeting again in 1947. Far from acting merely as a relay for the Athens Charter, which Le Corbusier drafted after the 1933 congress,[71] the Planning Department took the lead in something of a new phenomenon, the spread of functionalist discourse to the south. C.I.A.M. members began to examine the *habitus* and traditions of rural Moroccans, who had been shunted to the edges of cities, as part of a broader analysis of large

65 Bleuchot, *Les libéraux français au Maroc*, 53.

66 See letters and telegrams of support preserved in the fonds Écochard, IFA. Le Corbusier, who gave encouragement to Écochard and applied pressure on his behalf at the time of his termination, lobbied Nehru to entrust him with a project in India. However, Écochard would ultimately work in Pakistan. Le Corbusier, correspondence with and regarding Michel Écochard, FLC, E 2(1).

67 Jacques Delarozière, "Urbanisme," April 20, 1954, MAE, direction de l'Intérieur, 303, 4.

68 Gilbert Grandval, *Ma mission au Maroc* (Paris: Plon, 1956), 165.

69 Écochard, *Casablanca*, 11–14, 107–22.

70 Albert Memmi, *The Colonizer and the Colonized*, 50.

71 Écochard transmitted the charter to the delegate to the Residency General, in support of the *dahir* regarding urban planning, October 8, 1952, MAE, direction de l'Intérieur, 303.

"Grid" presented by the Morocco group to C.I.A.M. at Aix-en-Provence, 1953. A comparison is made between the courtyard dwellings of the medina in Fès and those in the Carrières Centrales.

72 This perspective had remained central to the analyses documented in the 1933 congress album. See Jose Luis Sert, *Can Our Cities Survive?* (Cambridge, Mass.: Harvard University Press, 1942).

73 At the time, Écochard had presented his studies of Syrian baths to Giedion, who later discussed them in *Mechanization Takes Command: A Contribution to Anonymous History* (New York and Oxford: Oxford University Press, 1948): 636, 639.

74 Sigfried Giedion to Michel Écochard, Zurich, December 17, 1947, gta/ETH, 42-SG-23-386.

75 Jean-Jacques Honegger to Michel Écochard, Geneva, December 29, 1949, gta/ETH, 42-JLS-20-1. See also "Bilan et situation des groupes, période du 13 novembre 1947 au 30 juin 1951," gta/ETH, 42-JLS-19-97/106.

76 The proposal for the new Yacoub el Mansour quarter, prepared for Rabat by Écochard's team and published under the signature of the "Groupe CIAM du Maroc," essentially constituted the group's public birth announcement. See "Rabat Salé, a new satellite town," in *The Heart of the City: Towards the Humanisation of Urban Life*, Jacqueline Tyrwhitt, Jose-Luis Sert, Ernesto N. Rogers, eds. (New York: Pellegrini and Cudahy, 1952): 126–27.

77 In the absence of GAMMA archives, useful documents are preserved in the personal archives of Henri Tastemain and at the Ministry of Housing in Rabat.

cities in Africa, Asia, and Latin America. This thus marked a break with Eurocentric criticism of urban slums and "insalubrious housing blocks."[72]

In the late 1940s, new groups began to take part in the C.I.A.M. meetings, clearly indicating that the debate on modernism had spread well beyond Europe. The Moroccan group was set up thanks to the convergent work of Écochard and Georges Candilis. Sigfried Giedion (C.I.A.M. secretary general) had contacted Écochard in December 1947, two years after they had met in New York,[73] requesting his help in arranging a visit to Morocco. Further to this, on the heels of the Bridgewater conference (the first since the end of the war), Giedion asked Écochard if he would like to contribute to the work of C.I.A.M.[74] Écochard was officially admitted into the C.I.A.M. ranks in 1949, as a "private member at first."[75] The same year, at the Bergamo congress, the Moroccan members were still considered to be "juniors," a category created in Bridgewater for the Algerian group (Pierre-André Emery and Jean de Maisonseul) and for the Tunisian representative (Bernard Zehrfuss).

GAMMA (Groupe d'Architectes Modernes Marocains) was recognized as a branch of C.I.A.M. at the 1951 Hoddesdon congress.[76] However, divisions between the French C.I.A.M. members were felt in Morocco. For instance, within ATBAT-Afrique, which was set up in Casablanca in 1951, Vladimir Bodiansky was affiliated with the Lods group, while Candilis remained closer to Le Corbusier. The young architects in Écochard's team belonged to the third group, La Cité, headed by Roger Aujame. Hence, to a much greater extent than during the interwar period, European and French debates were spilling over onto Moroccan soil.

Young architects working in Morocco—such as Élie Azagury, Jean-François Zevaco, Henri Tastemain, and Jean Chemineau—presented a fair number of built works at the C.I.A.M. meetings in the early 1950s, mainly thanks to the country's prosperity and to the fact that modern architecture was dominant there. This was not the case for the French, since postwar economic conditions in France meant that they were often unable to push their projects past design stage.[77] However, this difference in circumstances alone does not explain the attention that the experiments in Morocco received. In addition, the international acclaim for Écochard's theories on mass housing and the work produced by his team lent his concepts that much more impact within Casablanca itself.

Gaston Jaubert, Georges Candilis and Brian Richards in front of an experimental school by Vladimir Bodiansky, Casablanca, c. 1953.

"Habitat for the Greatest Number"

The principles of the Athens Charter shall now be applied to Morocco. There is virgin soil and it would be inexcusable not to use it for urban redevelopment, in other words, for creating residential neighborhoods that are set out in rows and which benefit from the most favorable orientation.

Arts, August 1949[78]

The Protectorate's postwar policy for Morocco's large cities was not to focus on integration, but instead to come up with individual low-rent housing programs for Muslims, Jews, and Europeans. The policy did not specify any inherent characteristics for distinguishing these groups, which were in fact heterogeneous in origin, urbanization, and culture. It was a categorization that found support in Écochard's programs, and his ideas on the notion of *appropriate housing*, via the recognition of *specific domestic cultures* (as referred to at the time) can be found in the draft housing charter discussed at C.I.A.M. congresses and which was intended as a complement to the Athens Charter. When presenting the principles underlying his projects for Muslim housing, Écochard declared, "Workers' neighborhoods will be organized in the same way as residential districts," and announced that he would create "serviced neighborhood units" that would respect "traditional customs" and would ultimately lead to "a gradual change in lifestyle."[79]

Taking "Secular Traditions" into Account

The theoretical ideas and schemes of the Planning Department evolved out of observations on rural living patterns in villages and *bidonvilles*, as well as out of criticisms of previous work. Architects began analyzing the characteristics of traditional Casbahs in view of studies that the department had been drawing up since 1946 indicating that 40 percent of the immigrants in large cities came from the Atlas Mountains. Equally, ethnologists started to resume their research on these Casbahs, which they had broken off in the 1930s.[80]

Having observed the differences between the three populations in question, Écochard and his colleagues felt that housing should be designed according to the customs in the residents' countries of origin, something that Écochard labeled "secular traditions." Although he refused to make a "distinction between the various population categories," Écochard adopted the Protectorate's categories and in 1946 he applied them, not to people, but to neighborhoods. These were differentiated in a way that might seem to border on racism today. The criteria were inconsistent, being based on religion for the Muslims and Jews and on nationality for the Europeans, who for some reason were perceived as originating from a unified culture. Hidden beneath this differentiation of race and geographic origin were class differences, the real basis for the policies: wealthy Muslims and Moroccan Jews were treated as European, while "appropriate" housing was reserved for the poorer members of both the Muslim and Jewish communities.

Adam would later explain the ambiguities in Écochard's line of action, stating how Écochard realized that "putting an end to segregation required more than merely renouncing the principle of it." Instead, he felt that his concept of "neighborhoods of European-type housing and neighborhoods of Moroccan-type housing" would enable "Moroccans who wished to live like Europeans to be just as comfortable in either type."[81] On arriving, Écochard had called for a change in both the political and urbanistic approach to the problem, drawing attention to the fact that in the early years of French colonial rule in Morocco "the issue of Muslim housing was still in its infancy and no extension area had therefore been planned

Laborers in front of the Lafarge cement works in Roches Noires. Morning scene, 1951.

Robert Montagne, pie charts indicating the ethnic origins of the occupants of Ben M'Sick bidonville. Published in *Naissance du prolétariat marocain*, 1952.

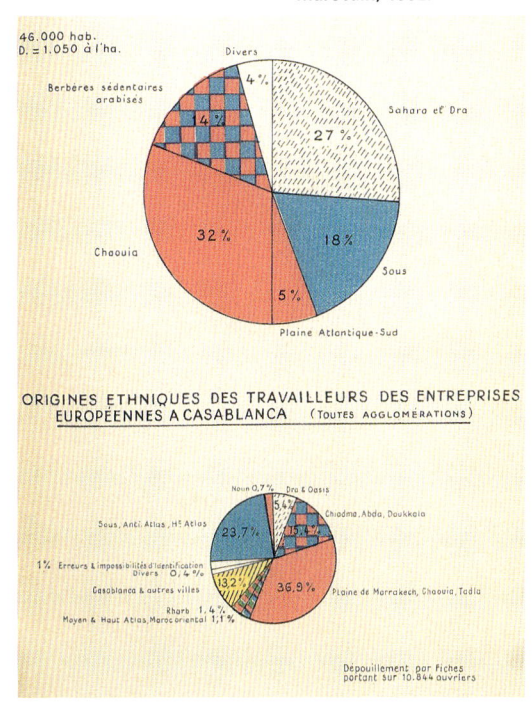

78 "Maroc: constructions à Casablanca et au Maroc."

79 Michel Écochard, "Habitat musulman au Maroc," *L'Architecture d'aujourd'hui* 26, no. 60 (June 1955): 37.

80 The main prewar texts on these structures are: Robert Montagne, *Villages et kasbahs berbères: tableau de la vie sociale des berbères sédentaires dans le sud du Maroc* (Paris: F. Alcan, 1930); and Henri Terrasse, *Kasbahs berbères de l'Atlas et des oasis: les grandes architectures du sud marocain* (Paris: Horizons de France, 1938). Later studies include: Dj. Jacques Meunié, *Greniers-citadelles au Maroc*, preface by Robert Montagne, plans by Paul Mamie based on the author's surveys (Paris: Arts t Métiers Graphiques, 1951); and Jean Orieux, *Kasbahs en plein ciel* (Paris: Flammarion, 1951).

81 Adam, *Casablanca*, 1:105.

82 Écochard, "Habitat musulman au Maroc," 36. In most of his texts, Écochard (like Courtois before him) was silent on the matter of the employers' housing developments discussed above.

83 Michel Écochard, "Urbanisme et construction pour le plus grand nombre" (paper presented at the Casablanca Chamber of Commerce and Industry, February 10, 1950), in *Annales de l'ITBTP* (October 1950): 6

84 Berque, "Médinas, villes neuves et bidonvilles," 6–8.

85 Michel Écochard, memorandum on housing, Direction de l'Urbanisme, 1949, MAE, délégué à la Résidence générale, carton 131, Habitat et urbanisme.

86 Minutes of the July 19, 1949, Housing Commission meeting, MAE, 138, Direction de l'Intérieur, Commission des logements, 1949–52.

87 The approximately 25-square-meter courtyard would be divided into two smaller 12.5-square-meter courtyards that, according to Delarozière, were still livable. Jacques Delarozière, "Urbanisme," 4.

88 Écochard, "Habitat musulman au Maroc," 37.

89 Georges Godefroy, "Problèmes d'habitat de type européen," *L'Architecture d'aujourd'hui* 26, no. 60 (June 1955): 46.

90 André Adam, *Le "bidonville" de Ben M'sik à Casablanca: contribution à l'étude du prolétariat musulman au Maroc* (Alger: La Typo-Litho et Jules Carbonnel, 1950); and Robert Montagne, *Naissance du prolétariat marocain: enquête collective 1948–1950* (Paris: Peyronnet & Cie, n. d.); idem, "Naissance et développement du prolétariat marocain," in Gaston Leduc, ed., *Industrialisation de l'Afrique du nord*, 199–222. Abdelkebir Khatibi sees in Montagne an "activist sociologist," advocating a reformism based on "recalibrating the balance of power" in favor of Moroccans. Abdelkebir Khatibi, "État et classes sociales au Maroc," in *Études sociologiques sur le Maroc* (Rabat: Société d'études économiques, sociales et statistiques, 1971), 5.

Michel Écochard, organization principle for a Moroccan neighborhood, 1949. Published in *Urbanisme et construction pour le plus grand nombre*, 1950. Each neighborhood unit (*unité vicinale*) accommodated 1,800 inhabitants, and five such units constituted a district (*quartier groupe*). Educational facilities (*enseignement*), recreational facilities (*récréation*), administrative buildings (*organismes administratifs et sociaux*) such as the post office and police station, a mosque and Koranic schools (*culte*), and a commercial area (*commerce*) are the major elements.

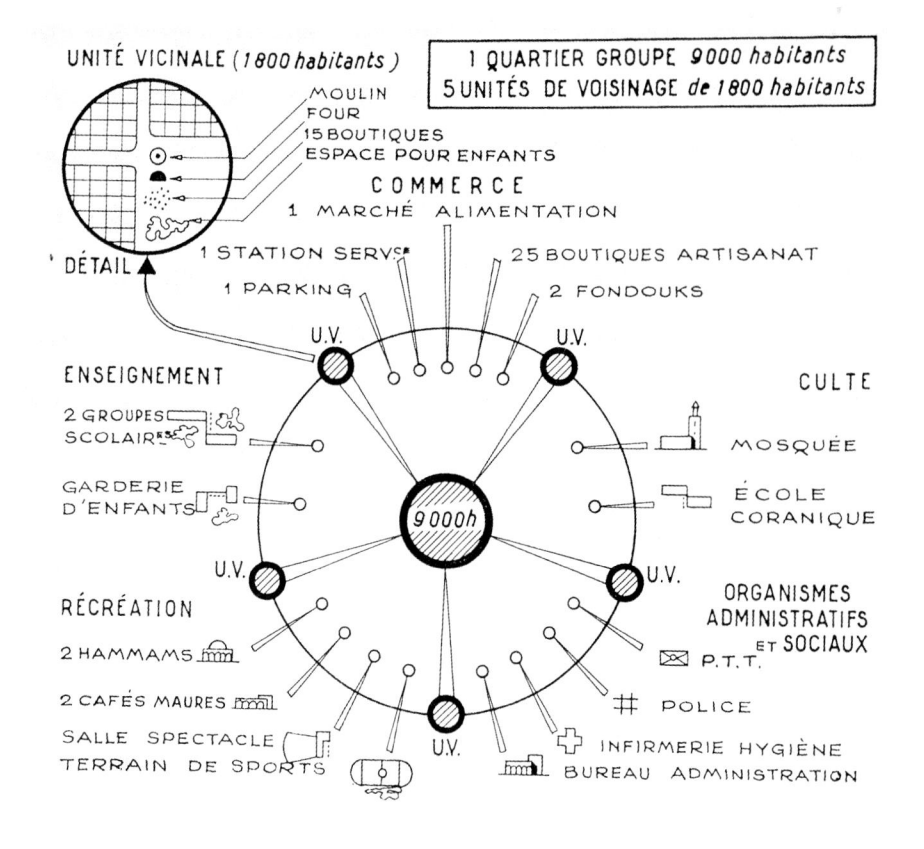

for the medinas outside the city walls (except in Casablanca, where an embryo of a new medina had been built)."[82]

The Neighborhood Unit and the Housing Grid

Mass housing was not just a "crucial problem for Morocco," it was also a "technical and moral problem for France." Écochard gave a talk on the subject in 1950, in which he offered perhaps the best description of his doctrine. He called for new solutions and suggested that "a theoretical guide be created" ("the neighborhood unit") that took into account pedestrian flows and the installation of specific amenities, such as *hammams*, mosques, and Koranic schools.[83] The number of residents was set at precisely 1,800 per unit, and the diagram Écochard presented in his talk showed a large number of community facilities. Écochard did not simply pick 1,800 out of the blue—it was based on research and was later corroborated by Jacques Berque's findings on settlements located around souks and housing in small North African towns.[84]

Écochard insisted on reducing the area inside the unit that was devoted to purposeless streets, which he perceived as anathema. Particular attention was paid to ensuring that children had no major roads to cross and that the distance between their homes and school did not exceed five hundred meters. He also established an eight-meter-square "housing grid" that was designed to allow for all possible "combinations," and which would form the underpinning framework for all the Planning Department's later projects.[85] Initially, "minimal dimensions" of eight by nine meters were proposed, but as the regional urban planning inspector, Jacques Delarozière, explained to the housing commission in 1951, "By tightening things up, we can get down to sixty-four square meters, or eight by eight meters, which will enable us to build dwellings with two standard rooms."[86] It also allowed for 350 occupants per hectare, which was no minor consideration, given the problem of rehousing *bidonville* occupants. Delarozière put forward another, more pragmatic, consideration: since it was impossible to prevent subletting, many of the dwellings would be occupied by two families.[87]

Debate over the dwellings' "minimal dimensions" was accompanied by studies on the principle of collective housing that the new contracting authorities had been working on since 1945, and which had also been taken up by the Écochard team. Two years after leaving Morocco, Écochard summarized his work on housing (described in detail further on):

> [The program] established standardized types to reduce costs. It stipulated that different types of housing be built successively or simultaneously, and that there be an urban grid based on plots measuring at least eight meters by eight meters containing the following forms of housing:
>
> a) temporary rehousing for *bidonville* dwellers;
>
> b) traditional single-story structures (rooms opening onto an enclosed patio);
>
> c) multistory buildings, either of European design, with openings facing the street, or of traditional design, with openings looking onto patios stacked one on top of the other.[88]

Everyone agreed that freestanding multistory buildings had to be set on open land with optimal exposure to the sun. A threefold objective was thus set, namely to "erect plain and well-oriented structures, free up ground space, and provide enough room between the facades to guarantee full sunlight, creating a sort of microclimate."[89]

Low-Cost Culture-Specific Housing

The primary goal of Écochard's team was to create different types of dwellings for the Muslims, so that *bidonville* dwellers could be rehoused in homes with a patio, in keeping with their traditional customs. The point of departure was to cater to the "lifestyle of populations whose civilization is Islamic" and to take up the more recent concern of living conditions in rural housing. There was nothing arbitrary or formalistic about such an approach; on the contrary, it was rooted in the early convergent studies on the living conditions of the new Moroccan proletariat carried out by sociologists such as Robert Montagne and André Adam.[90] Some of Écochard's assistants (Pierre Mas, for example) would further develop these ambitious areas of research.[91] Another innovation in terms of the projects themselves was that they took into account age, marital status, and income levels since they were targeted at Moroccans with limited financial resources, as well at young European couples and single people.

The first housing type to be devised consisted of combinations of eight-by-eight-meter grids intended to accommodate houses with patios. They were based not only on observations of "new forms that have developed in industrial cities," but also on an analysis of the old medinas, in which "privacy at street level is a traditional requirement in Muslim homes." Consideration for this aspect, combined with the principle of collective housing for Muslims, constituted groundbreaking concepts. The situation was very different, though, when it came to interior layout, which was no more than a later version of the earlier "indigenous housing" schemes for the Habous quarter and the Lafarge, Phosphates, and Cosuma developments.[92] It can therefore be said that the focus shifted from architectural considerations to urban structure. This was closely related to the scale of the buildings and to industrialized construction methods, as well as to the fact that these schemes now fell directly under the responsibility of the public authorities.[93]

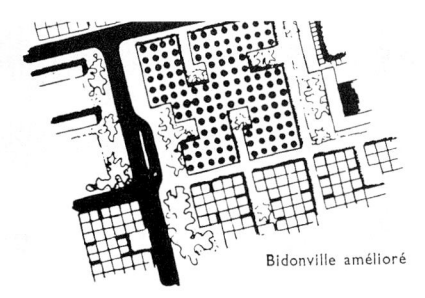

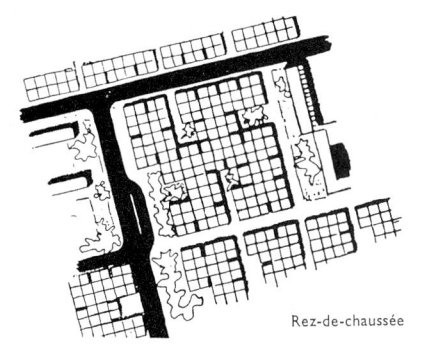

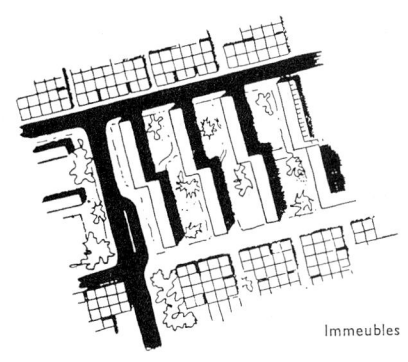

Michel Écochard, phased development of Moroccan neighborhoods (1949). Published in *Urbanisme et construction pour le plus grand nombre*, 1950.

91 Pierre Mas, "L'urbanisation actuelle au Maroc: les 'bidonvilles,'" *La Vie urbaine* (1951): 185–221. Mas's urban planning thesis examined the same themes. Pierre Mas, "Les phénomènes d'urbanisation et les bidonvilles du Maroc" (master's thesis, Institut d'Urbanisme, Paris, 1950).

92 The very notion of minimum housing was the subject of a proposal published in 1934 in *Chantiers nord-africains* (discussed earlier in this text): "L'habitat indigène au Maroc."

93 Construction programs were financed by the municipalities, public organizations, and, above all, by the state. Projects were managed by the Housing Department, which provided the plans to interested private builders. See Michel Écochard, *Situation de l'habitat à Casablanca en 1952 et établissement d'un programme d'État* (Rabat: Ministère des travaux publics, Circonscription de l'urbanisme et de l'habitat, 1953).

Plan of Casablanca, 1952.
Scale: 1/10,000.

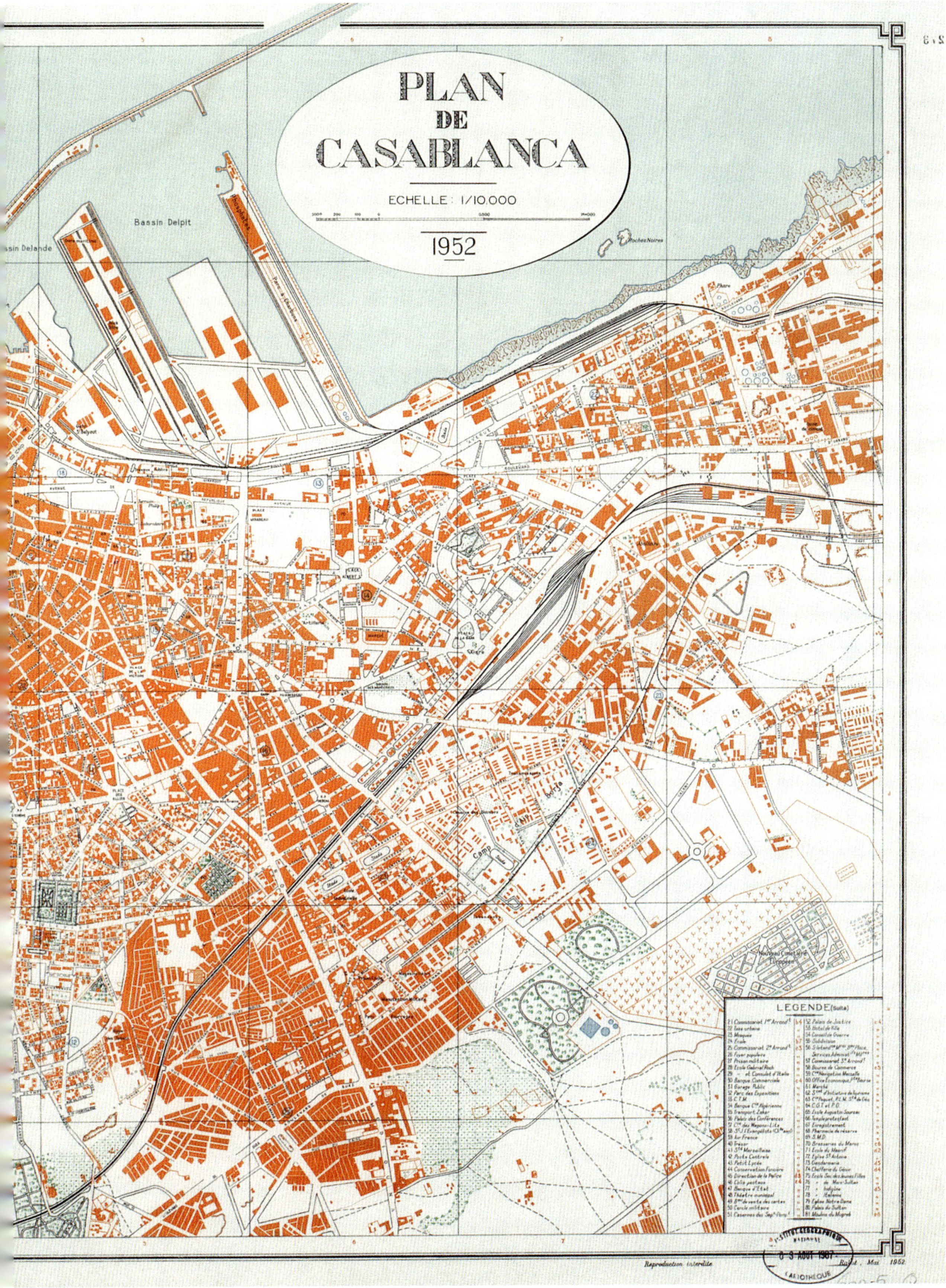
PLAN
DE
CASABLANCA
ECHELLE: 1/10.000
1952
Bassin Delpit
LEGENDE (suite)
Reproduction interdite

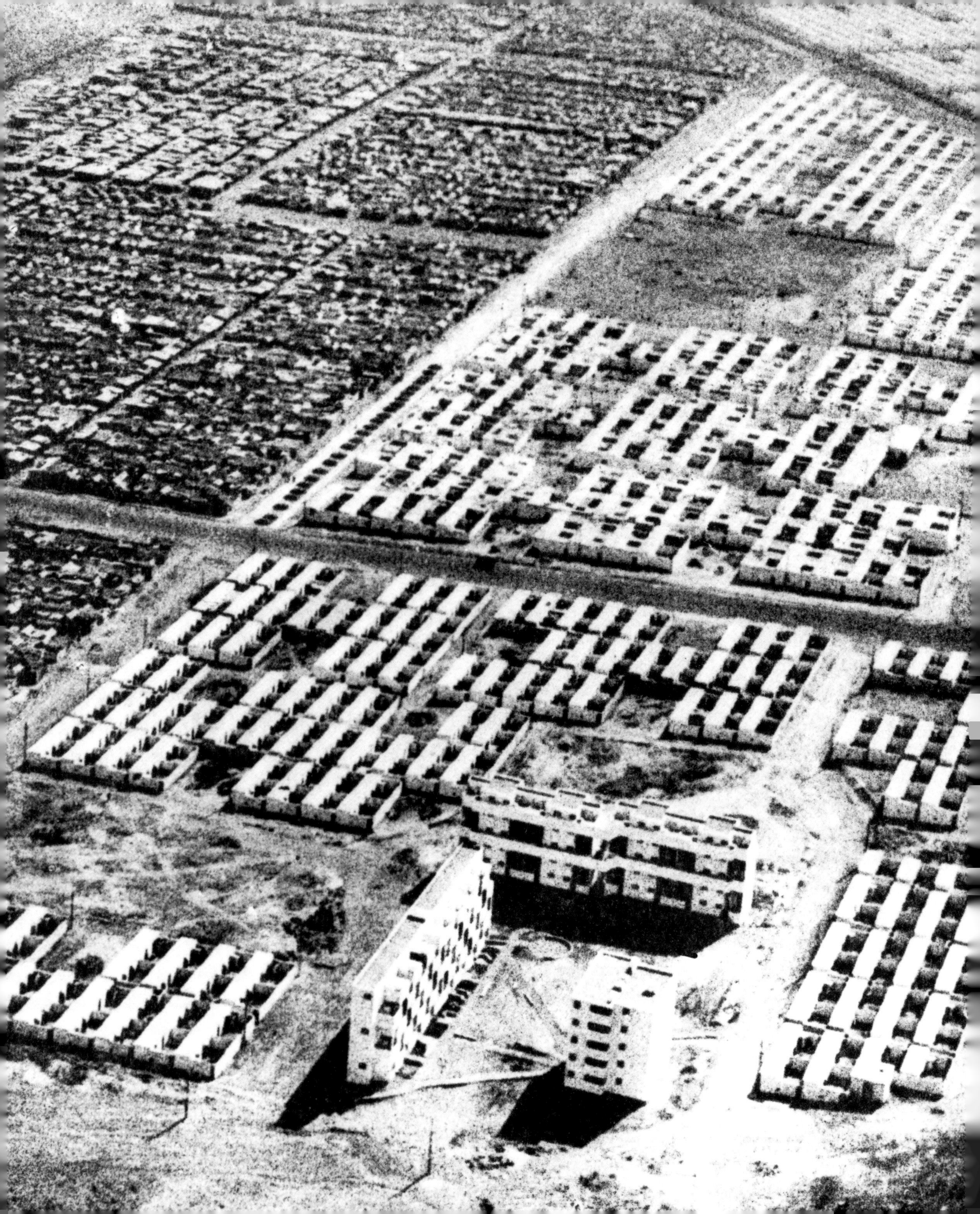

"Culture-Specific" Housing for Muslims: The Age of Large-Scale Projects

Minimum Courtyard Dwellings

Unlike European slums, bidonvilles *do not directly imply a deficient social state. However, while they may not necessarily be the outgrowth of poverty, it cannot be denied that they propagate an abject standard of living. The attraction of city life has caused many Moroccans from the southern part of the country and the Atlas Mountains to break with the framework of their rural and familial lives. In moving to* bidonvilles *they lose contact with their tribes and villages, and the communal support of these social structures is replaced by a feeling of isolation amid chronic overcrowding. Rural migrants subsequently find it difficult to integrate, for although they are often welcomed in the city and factories, no provision is made for them in the way of housing or public facilities.*

Michel Écochard, 1950[1]

The pious, outraged reports drawn up in 1930 on conditions in the Bidonville area were considered outmoded twenty years later, even though the census of March 1947 indicated that 19 percent of Casablancan Muslims lived in bidonvilles.[2] Jean Robert, an intern from the École nationale d'administration, which had been created after 1945 to train high-profile public servants, noted in 1952 that these shantytowns were "considered an investment opportunity, especially by the Moroccan elite who remain skeptical about the future of Moroccan housing projects." Rental returns were even greater given that the five- to seven-square-meter shacks and attendant ten- to fifty-square-meter *zriba** (enclosure) were closely packed together.[3] Other observers believed that simply viewing bidonvilles as social disasters overlooked their important role as areas of transition between the rural and urban environments, anticipating views that are still maintained by some ethnologists today.[4]

Although Robert was by no means idealizing substandard housing, he did nonetheless believe that "*bidonvilles* were an improvement on traditional rural housing" for some migrants. He further added, "Contrary to popular belief, bidonvilles can in several respects be considered preferable to housing in the medinas."[5] In support of this observation, he drew attention to the reduced incidence of infantile tuberculosis, linking it to the low levels of natural light and poor ventilation in the medinas. This conclusion was also corroborated by a study undertaken by the Town Planning Department on public health risks in the medina, which arose when residents covered their courtyards and added extra stories.[6]

Opposite
Aerial view of Carrières Centrales housing (1951–55). Photographed in 1958.

Note the mix of individual patio houses, the three collective housing buildings by ATBAT-Afrique, and the *bidonvilles*.

1 Écochard, "Urbanisme et construction pour le plus grand nombre," 5.

2 In other words, 75,600 out of 383,000 people.

3 Jean Robert, "Vers une politique populaire de l'habitat marocain; bilan critique," internship report, École nationale d'administration, Fédala, December 1952, MAE, 4.

4 See, for example, Colette Pétonnet's work on Rabat's Douar Doum. Pétonnet, "Espace, distance, dimension dans une société musulmane," *L'Homme,* no. 12 (April–June 1972): 47–84; and idem, *Espaces habités: ethnologie des banlieues.*

5 Robert, "Vers une politique," 8.

6 Pierre Mas and Pierre Pelletier, "L'habitat en nouvelle médina à Casablanca," Rabat, Service de l'urbanisme et de l'architecture, 1950, MH, R5. This study examined the Derb Chorfa, Carlotti, and El Ali districts, etc.

7 Memorandum on the improvement plan for the Carrières Centrales, Casablanca, ca. 1950, Ministère des Travaux publics, Service de l'urbanisme, Ministère de l'Habitat, Rabat. The first "relocation" experiments were carried out in Rabat and Fédala, with the El Alia housing development (built by the Hersent company according to Urban Planning Department plans). See Michel Écochard, "Note sur l'habitat," Direction de l'urbanisme, 1949, MAE, Cabinet civil, carton 131, Habitat et urbanisme, 1948–51, 7.

8 Écochard, "Note sur l'habitat," 7. See also Adam, *Casablanca*, 1:86.

9 Minutes of the Housing subcommittee, Moroccan section's July 1, 1949 meeting, MAE, délégué à la Résidence générale, 138, Commission des logements. The subcommittee also had a French section.

10 Écochard, "Note sur l'habitat," 8.

11 The ideal "neighborhood unit" for Écochard (who borrowed the term from British and American urban planning) accommodated 1,800 inhabitants, while a district was composed of five neighborhood units, that is, 9,000 inhabitants. Subsequently, essential facilities were completed. In 1955 Debroise would build the Carrières Centrales Vocational Training Center. The same year, Bailly and Schmidt would be commissioned to build the Youth Center, while Zevaco would build the Women's Education Center. Chemineau built the Carrières Centrales Dispensary (1956) and Lévy constructed the Post Office (1960).

12 Écochard, "Urbanisme et construction," 8.

13 Parinet, "L'habitat marocain," 12.

14 Écochard, "Urbanisme et construction," 8.

15 Meeting minutes of the Commission des Intérêts Locaux, the Casablanca Suburbs, April 9, 1952, MAE, 850, Comité régional d'urbanisme.

16 Sous-commission Travaux Voirie Plan d'Urbanisme, modifications to be made to Casablanca zoning, 1952, MAE, carton 850.

17 Jacques Delarozière, minutes of the Housing Commission's July 19, 1949, meeting established by the Direction of Interior Affairs, MAE, CDRG carton 138, Commission des logements, 1949–52.

18 Service de l'Urbanisme, memorandum on the improvement plan for the Carrières Centrales district, Casablanca, 1950, Ministère de l'Habitat, Rabat.

19 A. de Montmarin, "Les conceptions actuelles en matière d'habitat économique au Maroc," *Annales de l'Institut technique du bâtiment et des travaux publics*, no. 150 (June 1960): 618.

20 Each room measured between 8.5 and 12.5 square meters. There were 264 "small one-rooms" with kitchen and toilet, 200 "large one-rooms" and 542 "two-rooms."

21 S.E. El Mokri, minutes of the Housing Commission's July 19, 1949, meeting, MAE, CDRG carton 138, Commission des logements, 1949–52.

22 Ceiling height was discussed endlessly. Despite their desire to modernize Moroccan housing, the Moroccan members of the housing subcommittee followed local traditions in their insistence on a "sufficient cube of air and a ceiling of 3 to 3.5 meters." On the other hand, Parinet, recently back from the United States, defended a lower number (around 2.5 meters) on economic grounds, provided that "one foresees an extremely well analyzed ventilation system." Paul Parinet, "Missions de productivité: exposés de techniciens retour des USA," lecture at the Casablanca Chamber of Industry and Commerce, March 19, 1952, in *Construire* 15 (April 4, 1952): 322. In future public projects, standards would be lowered and ceiling heights often limited to 2.5 meters.

23 Approximately one thousand houses and thirty-eight shops were finished by late 1952, followed by seven hundred more in 1953. Délégation aux affaires urbaines de Casablanca, "Note sur l'habitat musulman et l'habitat israélite à Casablanca," February 1953. MAE, Cabinet civil, carton 122, dossier habitat marocain. In 1956 the development numbered 2,200 houses. It would receive an additional 3,300 during the 1960s.

Standard Design Solutions in Carrières Centrales

In 1949, the Housing Department purchased one hundred hectares of land with the aim of rehousing the 32,000 residents of the Carrières Centrales *bidonvilles*.[7] The initial core of the shantytown had sprung up in 1922, in a quarry close to the construction site of the Roches Noires power station. It was to keep its name of Karyan Central over the next two decades, despite shifting location on several occasions,[8] and in 1945 it entered a new growth phase. One of the first projects put forward by the Protectorate's Housing Commission, set up in 1949, involved sanitizing the area and equipping it with facilities including water supply, sewage, communal lavatories, drinking fountains, washhouses, showers, and streetlights.[9]

In 1949, Écochard opposed an initiative by the municipal authority to build twelve-square-meter dwellings without any facilities, and instead proposed a plan to redevelop the area by means of industrialized methods.[10] The first phase of his plan was dedicated to creating a five-unit residential neighborhood for some nine thousand occupants, with administrative, commercial, and social facilities.[11] The specific characteristics of Moroccan commerce were taken into account in an effort to create a familiar setting for the rural migrant population, and a new market and *kissaria** were planned to complement the existing souk and *fonduk*. This scheme formed part of a long-term strategy for creating "satellite towns" with an average population of 30,000,[12] and constituted the preliminary stage of a broader program to redevelop the surrounding area, which finally went ahead in 1951.

It remained to be decided what housing types should be adopted in the preliminary project, and discussion focused on individual or collective housing.[13] Écochard was in favor of a strategy developed in an experimental project in Port-Lyautey, where the architects had "set the building on its side instead of standing it up."[14] This was the solution that was eventually decided on, since it came closest to traditional Moroccan housing in that it provided for high density and did not pose the same problems as collective housing with respect to private spaces. However, the Planning Department recommended that the initial form of single-story blocks should only be maintained for one or two generations, after which extra levels should be added. This issue of additional levels was debated once again in 1951, with Écochard expressing strong reservations. On the other hand, Abbès Bennani, who was a Moroccan member of the Commission des Intérêts Locaux (a committee representing local residents and businesses), argued in favor of such an approach, declaring that this type of extension was already an established "local custom."[15] The municipal authority eventually agreed to ease regulations on additional stories, declaring that "this kind of structure with multiple levels and patios has already been tested out, notably in the SOCICA workers' housing development, and has proved entirely satisfactory."[16] The issue nonetheless continued to be hotly disputed during each phase of construction.

The "typical unit" was laid out on eight-by-eight-meter plots, which had long been considered sufficient for "standard two-room dwellings."[17] The units were made up of single- and two-room units opening onto a patio that contained a canopy-covered kitchen and a lavatory with a special tap for ablutions. As in the Ain Chock project, the units were carefully positioned east and south for maximum exposure, thereby using sunlight to "limit the risk of tuberculosis."[18] Furthermore, the main rooms all faced south, toward the patio, which provided another source of light:

> The rear wall of the main rooms also serves as a boundary wall for the adjoining patio. This means that the dwellings are set out in strips that are doubled, tripled, and most often quadrupled. The central strips are accessed by blind alleys measuring two meters wide; this is a totally acceptable solution for single-story buildings, and has the added advantage of extending the street system at minimal cost.[19]

The range of housing types in the 1952 program included a "small one-room dwelling," a "large one-room dwelling," and a "two-room dwelling," all incorporating a twenty-two-square-meter patio and a canopy-covered kitchen.[20] The shape of the rooms was the subject of extensive debate: traditional Moroccan houses are characterized by long, narrow rooms used day and night, but the Moroccan representatives on the Housing Commission were of the view that "this old formula should not be adopted as a rule of thumb."[21] It was thus decided that the layout should be more or less square. For the first time, ceiling height was set at 2.8 meters, which came closer to European norms.[22] Once construction was completed, the Housing Department entrusted 50 percent of the units to the Compagnie immobilière franco-marocaine (C.I.F.M.), which then placed them on the rental market.[23] The Moroccan railroad company purchased a quarter of them, and the remainder was sold off to industrial firms or owner-occupiers. In the final analysis, however, the original objective of the scheme was not achieved, since a number of surveys confirmed that former occupants of the Carrières Centrales *bidonville* only accounted for a minority of residents in the new neighborhood.

As early as 1954, that is, a year after the first residents had moved in, a significant number of patios had already been covered over, thereby depriving the rooms of light and ventilation; similarly, a large proportion of the owner-occupiers had begun to construct rooftop extensions for subletting purposes. These trends had serious health implications, given the extremely narrow streets that separated the dwellings. This was particularly troublesome, since the main aim of the project had been to improve standards of hygiene. An assessment survey carried out in the same year drew attention to further problems:

> The "Écochard" grid, which originally contained two-room units laid out at right angles, has proved difficult to construct using mechanical means. The basic unit has

Opposite
Carrières Centrales, 1951–55. General plan, in *Encyclopédie de l'urbanisme*, 1958.

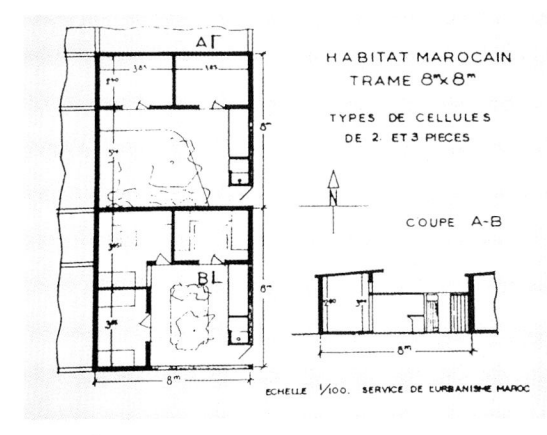

Michel Écochard, group of units at the Carrières Centrales, laid on an 8m-by-8m grid, c. 1951.

Pierre Pelletier, layout of a unit, Carrières Centrales 1952.

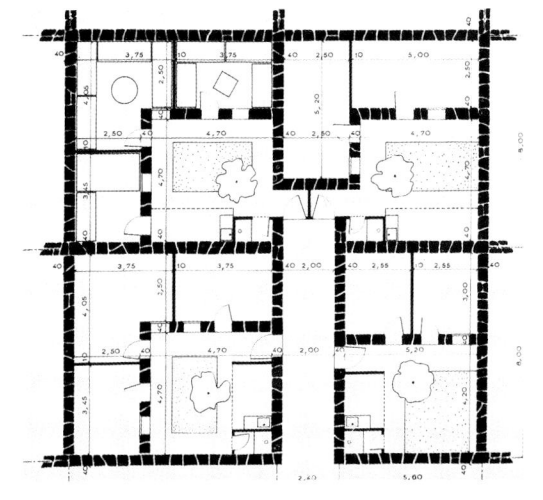

Compagnie immobilière franco-marocaine, housing schemes, Carrières Centrales, 1952–53, patio of a dwelling, in *Encyclopédie de l'urbanisme*, 1958.

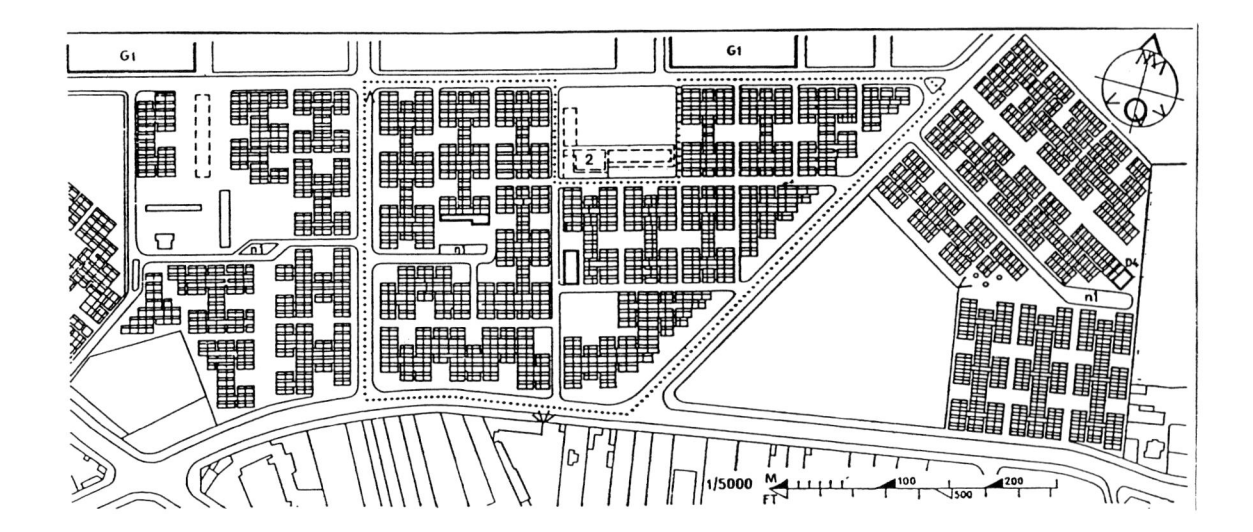

Compagnie immobilière franco-marocaine, housing schemes, Carrières Centrales, 1952–53. Plan of the three built projects, in *Encyclopédie de l'urbanisme*, 1958.

24 Louis Renaudin, *L'habitat en Afrique du nord* (Paris: Commissariat Général au Plan, February 1954), 87.

25 "Exposé de M. Durand, directeur général de la CIFM," *Annales de l'Institut technique du bâtiment et des travaux publics*, no. 82 (October 1954): 953. The program applied to 1,825 homes: 345 "one-rooms," 1,459 "two-rooms," and 24 "three-rooms." The average surface area of the rooms was 9.36 square meters.

26 Regarding this issue, see Durand and Kuhn's very thorough articles in *Annales de l'Institut technique du bâtiment et des travaux publics*, no. 82 (October 1954) : "Exposé de Monsieur Durand, Directeur de la CIFM," 952; and "Exposé de Monsieur Kuhn, Chef de service à la Société marocaine d'Entreprises Electriques et Travaux Publics," 959.

27 "OTH Afrique," in "Le Maroc moderne: architecture et urbanisme."

28 Maguy Mortier, "Les Carrières centrales," *Maroc-Monde* (Casablanca), January 15, 1954.

29 "Réalisations nouvelles dans le domaine de l'habitat musulman, la Compagnie Immobilière Algérienne," *Documents algériens, Habitat Musulman*, no. 48 (December 31, 1955).

thus been modified so that both rooms are placed side by side. The original 8-meter-by-8-meter grid turned out to be too large, since it contained a sizable courtyard on which leaseholders would set up a mini-*bidonville*. It has therefore been concluded that it is preferable to adopt the 6-meter-by-8-meter plan that can accommodate 100 houses (i.e., 400 residents) per hectare.[24]

The benefits of this type of rapid development outstripped the drawbacks, in view of the pressing need to rehouse *bidonville* dwellers. Using the same grid, the engineers of O.T.H. Afrique company (which had been commissioned to build the first housing development) began work on a C.I.F.M.-sponsored program in 1952 for the Ryad, Koudiat, and Saada subdivisions that lay south of the initial Carrières Centrales development. The houses were conceived as single-story units with patios, and building components were mass-produced, using only one type of front door, one type of plumbing facility, and so on, which caused the managing director of the C.I.F.M. to tout the project's "industrial qualities."[25] Walls were cast on-site using metal formwork—a procedure that was facilitated by the row layout of the buildings. Work proceeded at a pace of nine rooms a day, and was compared to "the car body–making process, in which careful attention is paid to perfecting all the finer details, such as interior capacity and modern comforts."[26]

This program was an adaptation of the Housing Department's master plan, with the two-room units set on seven-by-seven-meter plots, though east and south orientation remained an essential feature of all the dwellings. Washbasins and showers were included in the scheme, as were lavatories that were specially adapted to Moroccan customs (a tap "above an ablution basin"),[27] which ensured a level of comfort superior to that in the units designed by the Housing Department. The patios, which were laid with tiles, each included a small garden measuring twelve square meters and an outside kitchen sheltered by a canopy. A number of observers commented on what they termed the development's resemblance to a "horizontal beehive." Although a decision had been made in 1955 to release the units on the rental market, most of them were in fact sold to the tenants. These included a large number of public servants, such as firemen and administrative clerks, but very few former *bidonville* dwellers.[28] News of this innovative project traveled as far as Algeria, where it served as a prototype for the Petit Lac development in Oran, in 1955, followed by the Maison Carrée[29] project in Algiers. However, the repetitive uniformity of the schemes was swiftly criticized. In 1960 the civil engineer Gérard

Blachère wrote: "If we are not careful, we will end up churning out hopelessly ugly and featureless developments. We already have some outstanding examples of what should not be built, notably the Carrières Centrales project in Casablanca, where rows and rows of grimly identical houses stretch out as far as the eye can see."[30]

As residents set about injecting a little life—and chaos—into the ordered monotony of the Carrières Centrales, the C.I.F.M. embarked on construction of a similar development for the petty officers of the *Mokhazni*.*[31] It was built in 1952 on a barren stretch of coastline right by the El Hank lighthouse and is composed of a walled complex comprising a hundred units. At the time, it was the only Moroccan housing development constructed on a site near the city center, since its future residents were employed for colonial policing purposes and were therefore considered "trustworthy."

Alexandre Courtois was commissioned to build the Moroccan phosphate workers' development of Derb Comima in the less central neighborhood of Ben M'Sick. This contains 1,400 units which, like the previous projects, are also arranged at right angles around a small courtyard. It was termed a "neighborhood unit with services," and the design included dwellings for "married workers" and an "annex" for single men.[32]

Despite these large-scale projects, the *bidonville* issue remained far from resolved, especially as the parties concerned failed to reach consensus. Delarozière stipulated that the 1954 program should concentrate on providing "4,400 standard two-room dwellings" and that "9,500 shacks should be moved to a serviced site with drinking fountains and public toilets."[33] However, this was challenged by the prefecture of Casablanca, who called into question housing provisions for Muslims in the Écochard plan. In particular, they used Gouin's argument that "extensive development of Moroccan housing zones on the city outskirts would threaten the safety of European quarters," and cited critics who believed that these zones tended to grow dangerously overpopulated. The old medina, which was being "steadily vacated by residents, of their own free will," did not "seem to pose a serious threat, nor [did] Derb Ghallef, which was developing into an upmarket area," but the western *bidonvilles* and Carrières Centrales had to be contained. The methods con-

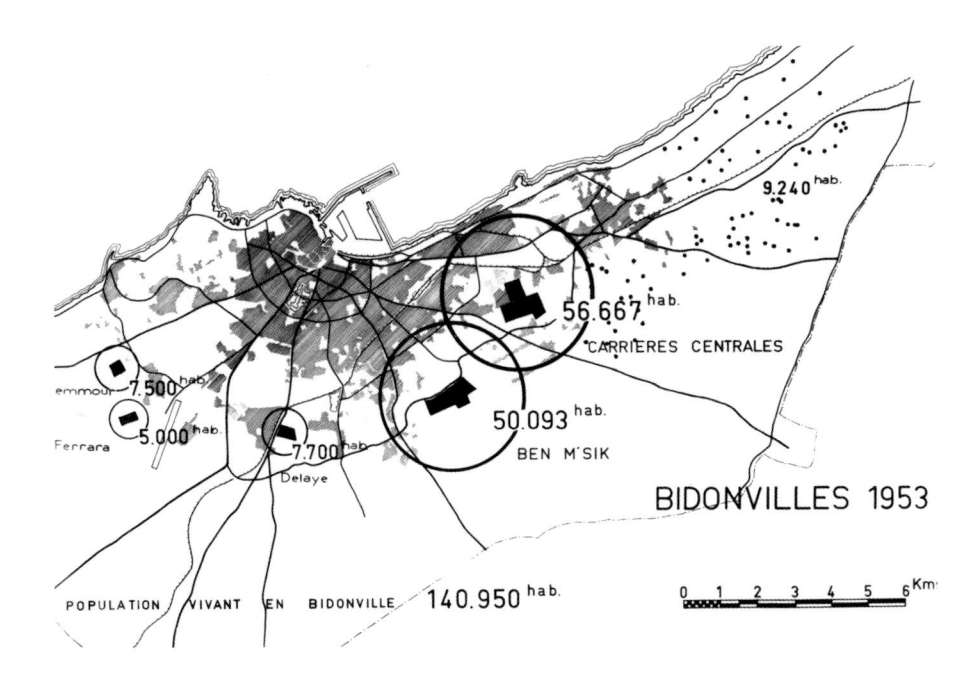

30 Gérard Blachère, "L'habitat modeste en Afrique du Nord et au Sahara," *Cahiers du Centre Scientifique et Technique du Bâtiment* 45, no. 365 (August 1960): 11. Blachère was an influential engineer at the Scientific and Technical Center for Building (Centre Scientifique et Technique du Bâtiment).

31 Paul Ripoche (C.I.F.M. financial director), memorandum on European housing (response to the December 1952 Écochard report), May 1953, MAE, SGP, carton 241, logements habitat. Almost four hundred homes would be built in the Makhzen development in 1954.

32 The phosphate workers' development comprised seven housing blocks containing 196 apartments ranging in size from one to three rooms. It was also equipped with a "social center and village chief's office," a clinic, a shower facility, a Moorish café, and a few stores. *Le Maroc Moderne Architecture et Urbanisme*, 1954.

33 Delarozière, "Urbanisme."

Town Planning Department, map of the Casablanca *bidonvilles*, 1953.

ceived for doing so were military-like, namely, "sectioning off the main Moroccan areas by roads that were "as wide as possible" and were bordered on both sides by empty strips of land."[34] In 1955, the administration emphasized the "need to space out building schemes to prevent the satellite developments of Ain Chock and Sidi Othman from one day joining up with the new medina, as this would result in a single Moroccan area totaling over 400,000 residents."[35]

The residency was rather ambiguous in its attitude toward the *bidonvilles*. A prime example is when Mohammed Khaled Saad-el-Dine was forbidden to speak about this issue at the congress of the International Union of Architects held in Rabat in 1951. The reason behind this decision, which was endorsed by Écochard, was that "a Muslim should not be offered the opportunity to initiate debate on the *bidonvilles*." Instead, discussion hinged merely on "two basic presentations" given by Écochard and Goupil.[36]

The "Sanitation Grid"—An Emergency Solution

The tone employed in the correspondence dated around 1950 that was sent between the various Protectorate departments is indicative of the authorities' concern over what amounted to a public health crisis. Since 1949, Écochard's team had been studying the issue of "decongesting the medinas and freeing up space there." In addition, it had begun to address ways of dealing with the housing problem created by the influx of rural migrants into the *bidonvilles* (as we have seen, the initial solution in this respect was to provide "temporary housing for *bidonville* dwellers," despite the reluctance expressed over such a project). In a study carried out on the new medina, Écochard's colleagues Pierre Pelletier and Pierre Mas noted how health standards were being thoroughly breached. In particular, they pointed out that in each of the "two- and three-story houses, the street-facing windows" were "always bricked up or had permanently closed shutters." In conclusion, they stated that a typical dwelling in the new medina represented "an infinitely greater health risk than a *bidonville* shack," and that the practice of covering over courtyards that were supposed to provide twenty square meters of open space further aggravated the problem.[37]

In an effort to resolve the situation, the Housing Department decided to take up the same kind of solutions that had been used for Rabat in the 1930s, when a similar crisis had occurred. The Douar Debbagh program, which involved equipping the *bidonvilles* with temporary amenities until proper housing could be provided, served as a major point of reference in this respect. In 1950, Écochard put forward proposals for a two-stage program of this kind. The initial phase involved putting in place "an infrastructure (street system, sewage, etc.) for improved *bidonvilles*," and the second stage was dedicated to "gradually adding 'permanent' dwellings"[38] as funding became available. This concept was known as the *trame sanitaire* [sanitation grid] and was defined as follows in 1953:

> By creating a sanitation grid, certain services can be provided in sectors where residents are awaiting permanent housing. These services include roads, water supply, and sewage, as well as basic municipal facilities. Minimum standards of health and hygiene can thus be met, in the hope that residents will undertake construction of permanent dwellings on their own initiative.[39]

The immediate priority was to acquire sites on which a basic infrastructure could be set up. Counting on the element of surprise to buy at a low price and to circumvent speculation, Girard, director of the Public Works Department, requested authorization from the residency for the Housing Department to purchase as many sites as possible that had been earmarked for Muslim housing.[40] In 1949, the municipal authority granted a site in Derb Jdid for the purpose of group-

---

[34] "Note au sujet des modifications qu'il serait possible d'apporter au plan d'urbanisme de Casablanca conçu par M. Écochard," Casablanca, Préfecture, May 5, 1954, Ministère de l'Habitat, Rabat, D 898.

[35] "Problème de l'habitat Marocain," unsigned memorandum, ca. 1955, MAE, 138, Cabinet Civil, dossier Bidonvilles.

[36] Director of the Civilian Cabinet, memorandum, August 4, 1951, MAE, 138, Cabinet Civil, 5.

[37] Mas and Pelletier, *L'habitat en nouvelle médina à Casablanca*, 21.

[38] Michel Écochard, "Note sur l'habitat," direction de l'Urbanisme, MAE, délégué à la Résidence générale, 131, Habitat et urbanisme, 1948–51, 5; and idem, "Urbanisme et construction pour le plus grand nombre," 10.

[39] Service du contrôle des municipalités, response to G. Bidault, February 1953, MAE, Cabinet Civil, dossier Bidonvilles. Bidault, the minister of Foreign Affairs, was worried about the viability of this strategy.

[40] Director of Public Works to delegate to the Residency General, October 22, 1949, MAE, délégué à la Résidence générale, 131, Habitat et urbanisme, 1948–51.

[41] A. de Montmarin, "Les nouvelles solutions en matière d'habitat; leur application au Derb Jdid," *BESM* (April 1959): 441; and idem, "Les conceptions actuelles en matière d'habitat économique au Maroc," 150.

[42] "Au Maroc; qu'a-t-il été fait, sur le plan municipal, pour améliorer les conditions de vie dans les médinas et les quartiers marocains?," *Construire* (1951): 158–59. Jean Robert remarked that in 1952 "all the funding was used to maintain that which had been neglected during the war." Robert, *Vers une politique populaire de l'habitat marocain*, 22.

"Housing for the greatest number." Display "grid" presented by the Moroccan group to C.I.A.M. at Aix-en-Provence, 1953. Photo of part of the Carrières Centrales *bidonville*.

ing together "most of the *bidonvilles* scattered over the western sector of the city, comprising Oasis, Beauséjour, and Anfa, among others." This "organized *bidonville*"[41] was laid on a gridded plan and included a school, a health center, and an administrative building, along with drinking fountains and streetlights. In the following decade, however, the authority reduced its funding of *bidonville* servicing and redevelopment.[42]

Another experimental project was launched to provide "improved" *nouallas** for recent rural migrants. These round huts closely resembled the traditional dwellings of the rural poor and were constructed on eight-by-eight-meter lots with a small garden. Meanwhile, the lack of Moroccan private investors was criticized for the first time in an article describing the various publicly subsidized schemes:

> It is to be hoped that affluent Moroccans who have hitherto been loathe to invest in the construction of basic housing will endeavor to help the state in the mammoth task that it is currently facing alone. In much the same way as private sector financing has played a vital role in European housing development, let us sincerely hope that affluent Moroccans will also devote part of their income to providing housing for their fellow countrymen.[43]

Due to the lack of funds for rehousing schemes, the Planning Department decided in 1953 to merely "upgrade" all the existing *bidonvilles* by providing a water supply and drainage facilities. This led to a political outcry, but the authorities remained unyielding. From then on, therefore, the Protectorate departments were no longer directly involved in the actual construction process; instead, their role was restricted to purchasing sites and materials and supposedly supplying financial aid when this was deemed to be warranted. As a result of this cautious policy, only 8,711 *bidonville* shacks were rehoused out of a total 40,000.

Various solutions were proposed to cater to the diverse socioeconomic groups in the *bidonvilles*. The Service de l'Habitat (Housing Department) advocated constructing "showcase homes (along the lines of those at Sidi Bernoussi)" in areas under development; it also recommended offering either "plots equipped with sewage, lavatories, and a water supply" or "tracts of land with boundary walls and even foundations (for the more affluent Moroccans)." A "resettlement area" was planned so that people who could not afford to build a permanent dwelling could at least "set up their shack there."[44] Less impoverished *bidonville* dwellers were offered loans, and mutual aid systems were encouraged whereby community members would help one another build their own homes. These were known as castor (beaver) schemes, in allusion to this eponymous animal's building skills.[45] In an experiment of this type carried out in 1954 in the Carrières Centrales, 302 applicants received a piece of land, building materials, and ten-year state loans.[46] Four hundred such dwellings were constructed in the area, and the Moroccan railroad company sponsored a similar program for a workers' development in Ain Sebaa.[47] However, instead of complying with the rules, "most participants in the mutual aid program hired a bricklayer or workman," and were thus considered to be "false beneficiaries."[48] This practice was nonetheless tolerated on the basis that it would "reduce unemployment . . . in the building sector,"[49] and even drew praise from C.I.F.M. executives who noted that it only took one month "for a castor builder assisted by three laborers to build a two-room 'Écochard dwelling.'" In an effort to cope with the extensive problems caused by insalubrious conditions in the medinas and rural migration zones, the Protectorate also offered incentives for private construction firms such as the wholly Moroccan-owned Sadni group,[50] which received "state subsidies as well as technical advice from the Housing Department."[51]

Transporting a *noualla*, c. 1952.

[43] "Au Maroc; qu'a-t-il été fait," 159.

[44] "Problème de l'habitat marocain," 14.

[45] In his response to a report by Écochard, Paul Ripoche insisted on the necessity of reducing the state's housing costs by developing a "*castor* system [that] enhances the value of the dwelling in the eyes of the beneficiary through the very contribution that he himself makes." In keeping with the work of Le Play and certain early-twentieth-century philanthropists, Ripoche affirmed that this system "facilitates the parceling out of urban real estate, an element of social stability." Ripoche, memorandum on European housing, 8.

[46] In 1954 the administration examined the possibility of providing financial assistance to the *castors* for the acquisition of building materials. Protectorate secretary general to director of finances, March 11, 1954, MAE, Secrétariat général politique, carton 241, logements habitat.

[47] Ripoche, memorandum on the report by Michel Écochard, December 1952, appendix entitled "Conditions de mise en œuvre des techniques Castor," 8. MAE, Secrétariat général politique, carton 241, logements habitat.

[48] R. Maneville, "L'expérience Castor aux Carrières centrales de Casablanca," *Notes marocaines*, no. 7 (1956): 4–5.

[49] Ripoche, memorandum on European housing.

[50] The company managers were Sadni and Abbes Bennani. In 1953 the group built the Jemaa development with the help of a loan institution. The approximately 1,000 individual homes in the development were built without an architect—the plans were those of the Housing Department. In 1954 the group would build 630 dwellings and begin 650 others, in the C.I.L. neighborhood and the M'Barka development. See Delarozière, "L'Urbanisme au Maroc."

[51] The state guaranteed their loans. The city "provided amenities for their properties and created associations, such as the one in Sidi Othman, which facilitated their ventures." Robert Hanztberg, "Le plan Écochard est-il applicable?", 2. Le problème des ceintures rouges," *La Vigie marocaine* (Casablanca), February 16, 1951.

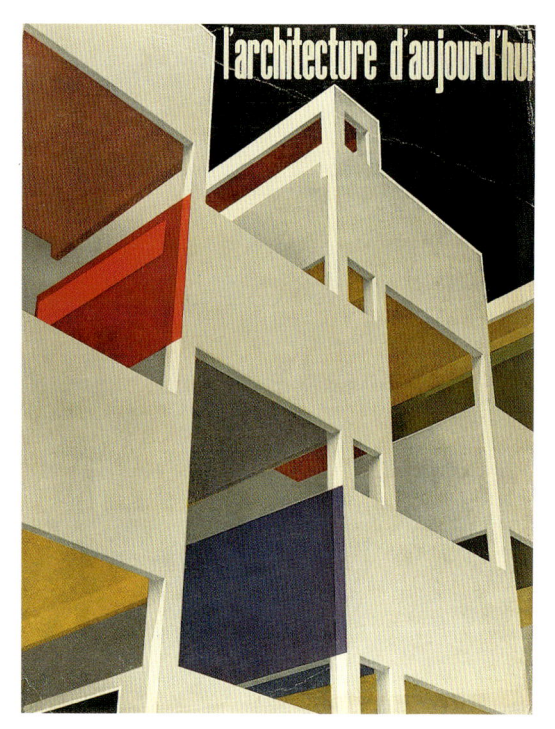

ATBAT-Afrique, Nid d'abeille building. Front cover of *L'Architecture d'aujourd'hui*, December 1954.

ATBAT's Modernized Casbahs Spark Debate throughout Europe

We regard these buildings in Morocco as the greatest achievement since Le Corbusier's Unité d'Habitation at Marseilles. Whereas the Unité was the summation of a technique of thinking about "habitat" which started forty years ago, the importance of the Moroccan buildings is that they are the first manifestation of a new way of thinking. For this reason they are presented as ideas; but it is their realization in built form that convinces us that here is a new universal.

Alison and Peter Smithson, 1955[52]

Since the 1920s, the Protectorate's policy had reflected the standpoint that only single-family dwellings with patios were suited to Moroccan Muslims. However, given the problems associated with this housing type, notably unauthorized rooftop development in the new medina, it was decided after the war that this growing population should be offered collective housing. It was a decision that fell in line with the views expressed by the Moroccan representatives on the Housing Commission, who had been campaigning for such a change in policy—proof, if it were required, that their opinion could no longer be ignored in matters concerning the Moroccan population. The representatives had "claimed that Moroccans wished to be housed in European-type buildings" and had demanded an end to construction programs that prevented residents from improving their social status. They also requested that the Beaux-Arts Department give up its policy of blocking modernization schemes in the medinas. Essentially, they were requesting that "housing be built in keeping with modern practices."[53] This was an important turning point and was approved, somewhat cautiously, by the Housing Department: "Mr. Delarozière has presented a model of a multistory building for Moroccan residents comprising European-style apartments, apart from one unenclosed room, which is designed as a substitute for the traditional courtyard or patio. This project ought to be undertaken on an experimental basis, given Si Lyajid's rather bold view that 'all Moroccans wish to be housed in European type buildings.'"[54]

In fact, several pilot projects of this kind were constructed fueling debate that extended well beyond Morocco. The most striking one was built by ATBAT-Afrique in Carrières Centrales in 1953. ATBAT-Afrique was the Moroccan subsidiary of the French design office ATBAT (Atelier des Bâtisseurs), which had been set up by the engineer Vladimir Bodiansky to execute the design of Le Corbusier's Unité d'Habitation in Marseilles. The group was led by Shadrach Woods and Georges Candilis, who had spent two years working on the Le Corbusier project.[55] The scheme consisted of three collective housing blocks that were radically innovative compared to other Moroccan buildings of the time, and which were to be set right in the heart of the Carrières Centrales spread of courtyard houses. Candilis argued that this form of housing was "suited to the natural, social, and economic environment of Morocco," since "approximately 70 percent of the *bidonville* population comes from regions south of the Atlas Mountains, where collective housing (Casbahs and mountain-slope villages) is already an established building type." In the display captions for the C.I.A.M. exhibition on "high-rise development," Candilis was careful to point out that the "Saharan Casbahs, *ksours*, fortified Atlas villages, and citadel-granaries reflect how people can live together in a close community and can share the same interests without jeopardizing domestic privacy."[56] He also emphasized the communal aspect of certain characteristics of traditional housing, such as the courtyard, which is a "veritable hearth, a living room, for it serves to bring people together, thus

---

[52] Alison and Peter Smithson, "Collective Housing in Morocco," *Architectural Design* 25, no. 1 (January 1955): 2.

[53] Minutes of the Housing Commission's July 19, 1949, meeting, established by the Housing Department, MAE, CDRG, carton 138, Commission des logements, 1949–52, 7. The Moroccan representatives were Si Jaffar Naciri (the Grand Vizier's delegate to the Public Works Management (Direction des Travaux publics), Hadj Omar El Ayadi (president of the Marrakech Chamber of Agriculture), M. Lyajid (president of the Rabat Chamber of Commerce and Industry), and Jacques Pérez (representative of various interests).

[54] Minutes of the Housing Commission's July 19, 1949, meeting, established by the Housing Department, MAE, CDRG, carton 138, Commission des logements, 1949–52.

[55] Candilis had resigned with bitterness from the studio, in the face of reproaches from Le Corbusier. Le Corbusier to Georges Candilis, Paris, May 3, 1951, FLC E (1) 11–12.

[56] Panel caption, "*La cité verticale*" exhibition, C.I.A.M. congress, Aix en Provence, 1953, gta/ETH. On the sources of the Casablanca experiments, see Monique Eleb, "An Alternative to Functionalist Universalism: Ecochard, Candilis, and ATBAT-Afrique," in Sarah Williams Goldhagen and Réjean Legault, eds., *Anxious Modernisms: Experimentations in Postwar Architectural Culture* (Cambridge, Mass.: MIT Press; Montreal: Canadian Centre for Architecture, 2000): 55–73.

Carrières Centrales, 1951–55. General view of the individual dwellings, high-rise building, and Nid d'abeille and Sémiramis buildings by ATBAT-Afrique. Photographed in 1955.

ATBAT-Afrique (Georges Candilis, Shadrach Woods, Vladimir Bodiansky, and Henri Piot). Three collective housing buildings, Carrières Centrales, 1952. General photo taken in 1955.

ATBAT-Afrique, Sémiramis building, 1952. North facade. Photographed in 1955.

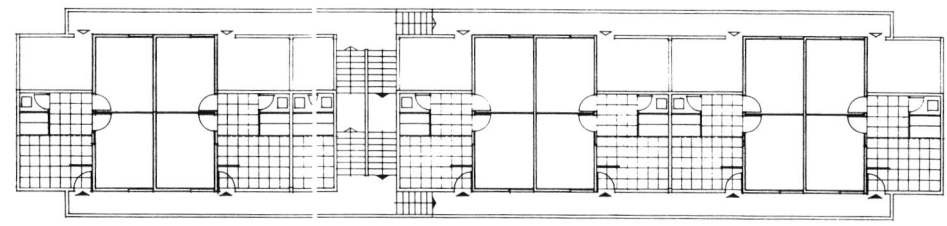

ATBAT-Afrique, Sémiramis building, Carrières Centrales, 1952. Standard floor plan, in *Candilis-Josic-Woods: A Decade of Architecture and Urban Design*, **1968.**

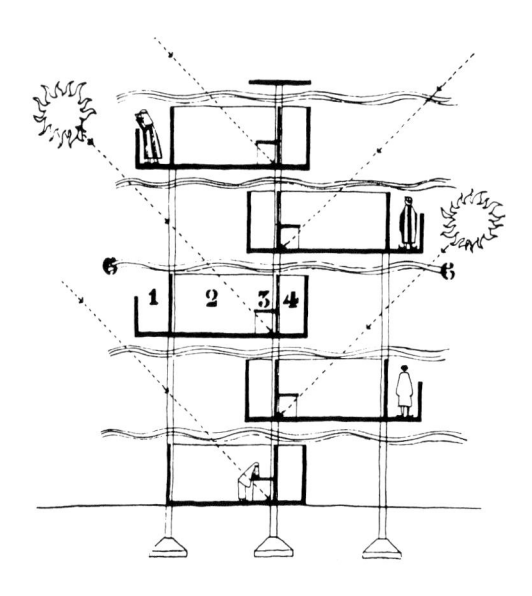

ATBAT-Afrique, Sémiramis building, 1952. Cross section of the double-height patios. "In the Sémiramis type, the floors of the courtyard-patios are out of line with one another, so that the largest part is double-height and the rest is single-height. The latter is given over to the cooking area, water tap, and lavatory. This solution provides effective protection against heat and humidity, while allowing for sufficient sunshine." *L'Architecture d'aujourd'hui*, February–March 1953.

responding to the function of 'meeting.'"⁵⁷ Écochard gave Candilis his recommendations, suggesting that the design should play on the stacking effect created by the eight-square-meter grid housing.⁵⁸ Bodiansky designed one of the buildings, creating a small and rather unexceptional tower block; the other two buildings, however, are clearly the product of innovative research into "standard prototype designs," especially as they contain "patios that also act as sun-traps, thereby letting light into the rooms."

One of these two buildings was named Sémiramis, recalling the hanging gardens of Babylon, as it has private patios positioned along the eastern and western facades. The units are split into two blocks, on account of the sloping site, and entry to them is through patios accessed by walkways situated at two-floor intervals. The other building is called Nid d'abeille (beehive) and was designed for a different type of occupant than Sémiramis, both in terms of religious practice and experience of urban life. According to Candilis, Sémiramis was explicitly designed for more conservative Muslims, and has "enclosed double-height patios" and a "facade with projecting access balconies."⁵⁹ In the Nid d'abeille, which is set at right angles to Sémiramis, access balconies are strapped to the northern facade, and slanting light is channeled down into the patios and onto the patio walls through large openings punched into the southern facade.⁶⁰ The development contains one hundred units in all, along with eight shops, and all details are geometrically fashioned, thus bearing witness to Candilis and Woods's extensive research into Casbah architecture. Even the staircases resemble those in traditional multistory buildings of the southern valleys, as Candilis was quick to point out when Écochard criticized the architects for making the stairs too steep and narrow.⁶¹

Candilis followed up this initial ATBAT-Afrique project with a series of designs featuring versions of his trademark semiduplex dwellings, though none of these designs were actually built. He also put forward proposals for three types of developments devised in keeping with the Protectorate's culture-specific housing policy: first, a "Muslim" housing block (with enclosed patios); second, a housing scheme for Jewish Moroccans with partially enclosed patios and a special room for menstruating women, in compliance with the custom of certain traditionalist Jewish families; and lastly, a housing type for Europeans (who were still treated as one single population group) that was more open to the exterior. Each proposal was characterized

57 "Habitat collectif marocain, étude ATBAT-Afrique," *L'Architecture d'aujourd'hui* 24, no. 46 (February–March 1953): 98.

58 After his Marseilles experience, Candilis had so much difficulty accepting the notion of a horizontal urban network that he drew the well-known sketch contrasting the horrors of an urban fabric of single-family homes to the virtues of the Unité d'Habitation. Georges Candilis, interview by the authors, Paris, January 2, 1991.

59 "Recherche pour des logements économiques, par ATBAT-Afrique," *L'Architecture d'aujourd'hui* 26, no. 60 (June 1955): 41.

60 Regarding this project (detailed by Henri Piot), as well as the work of ATBAT-Afrique, see ATBAT-Afrique, "Habitat collectif musulman à Casablanca," *L'Architecture d'aujourd'hui* 25, no. 57 (December 1954): 95–97; "Recherche pour des logements économiques, par ATBAT-Afrique, supervision de V. Bodiansky, G. Candilis et S. Woods, architectes, H. Piot, ingénieur," *L'Architecture d'aujourd'hui* 26, no. 60 (June 1955): 38–41; and *Candilis, Josic, Woods: une décennie d'architecture et d'urbanisme* (Paris: Eyrolles, 1968).

61 The title of an article in the daily *Maroc-Presse*, favorable to liberals of "French conscience," clearly expresses the astonishment felt in the face of this hybrid: "L'Habitat Marocain vient de réaliser une véritable gageure, un type de logement traditionnel avec patio dans des immeubles à étages" (The Moroccan Housing Service has just completed a truly far-fetched project, a kind of traditional courtyard dwelling in multistory apartment buildings), May 25, 1954, 6.

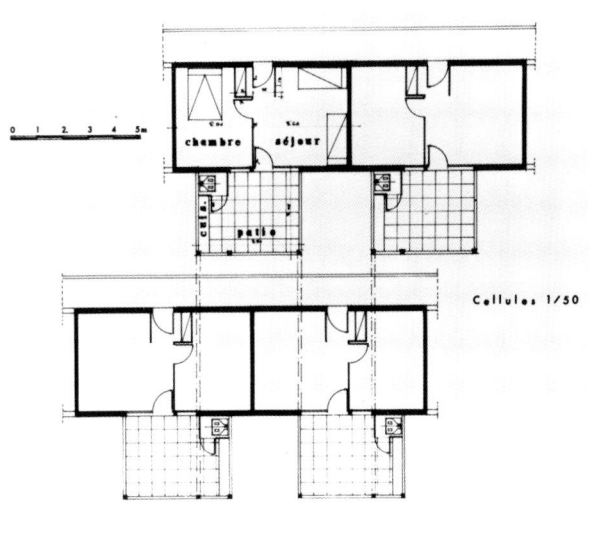

ATBAT-Afrique, Nid d'abeille building, Carrières Centrales, 1952. Each unit measures 35m² and comprises two rooms, a cooking area contained in a double-height patio, and a bathroom containing a sink, washtub, shower, and lavatory.

ATBAT-Afrique, Nid d'abeille building, Carrières Centrales, 1952. South facade. Photographed in 1955.

by a different facade type. Candilis then came up with a fourth project that was even more radical than the others insofar as it advocated a multiethnic society. In this scheme, the three culture-specific programs described above were combined in a mixed-use development for all three groups; even the facade designs were fused with one another. Candilis later claimed that this project was "fiercely opposed by racists" and acquired him a reputation as a proponent of "dangerous" views. It was at this point, he went on to say, that he felt "it was time to leave" Morocco.[62]

In 1952, the ATBAT projects were taken on by C.I.A.M., when Bodiansky launched a campaign for the United Nations Economic and Social Council to recognize the importance of "housing for the greatest number." The Moroccan example formed the central focus of his report, which Bodiansky presented to the United Nations in the same year, and which was supposed to have led to a U.N. seminar in Morocco.[63] A group of fifteen architects based in Morocco, including Candilis, Écochard, Élie Azagury, Pierre Mas, and Gaston Jaubert, participated in the 1953 Aix-en-Provence congress, which marked a turning point in C.I.A.M. debates. They brought two "grids" with them and presented their work in Morocco based on the four functions of the Athens Charter, as was the custom in all of the congresses since 1949.[64] The grids featured a series of photographs showing the striking contrast between the old towns and new quarters such as the Carrières Centrales, and provided details of the schemes undertaken by the Planning Department. They also included a presentation of the designs for patio and collective housing, as well as a comparative study of living conditions in the old medinas and *bidonvilles*.[65]

Mas and Écochard's GAMMA grid on "Moroccan Housing" was upstaged by the ATBAT-Afrique presentation on "housing for the greatest number," prepared by Candilis with the aid of Mas. Initially, only a small part of the Moroccan presentation was supposed to have dealt with the specific issues involved in the Carrières Centrales buildings, under the subheading "Vertical City." However, it seems that this decision was overturned during the preparatory stage of the exhibition, with Candilis's grid becoming the centerpiece of the presentation, and the analyses drawn up by the Town Planning Department being demoted to mere background material. Écochard was furious that Candilis had stolen the limelight in front of such a prestigious and demanding public.[66] Overall, the Moroccan contribution to the Aix congress caused quite a stir among the more radical participants, given that it lent support to Aldo van Eyck and the Smithsons' standpoint on identity and specificity. In 1991, Alison Smithson underlined how, by reassessing the notion of culture-specific housing, the North African experiments played a vital part in transforming the universalist viewpoint of mainstream modernism:

> Modern, hopeful France was in being in North Africa where there was none of the European middle generations' signs of deviation from the tenets of the Modern Movement . . . In North Africa, *espace, soleil* is plenty, and in the settlements, *verdure* . . . white cubic forms, private spaces adjoining the dwellings, the clarity of the *partis*: the Four Functions mattered and you could say still made sense.[67]

Alison Smithson also recalled the impact that these bright and optimistic design proposals had on Team X, which had only recently been set up, and the "new architectural language engendered by the forms of the habitat."[68] While this group of young rebels, an offshoot of C.I.A.M., was in the process of extending its activities, Alison Smithson and her husband, Peter Smithson, published a laudatory article on the ATBAT Carrières Centrales development in which they drew attention to the way "the slope of the ground is brilliantly utilized" and to the polychromy that contributed to "a spatial exercise of great refinement." They state in no uncertain terms that these buildings "[are] the greatest achievement since Le Corbusier's Unité d'Habitation at Marseilles" and further declare that the development

ATBAT-Afrique,
"Muslim," "European,"
"Jewish," and "Mixed"
housing projects, 1953.

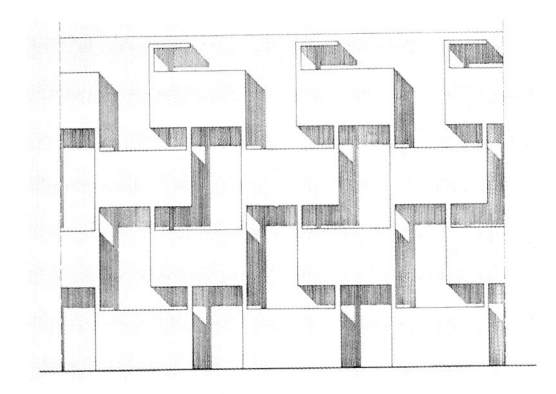

"Muslim housing" project. Elevation.

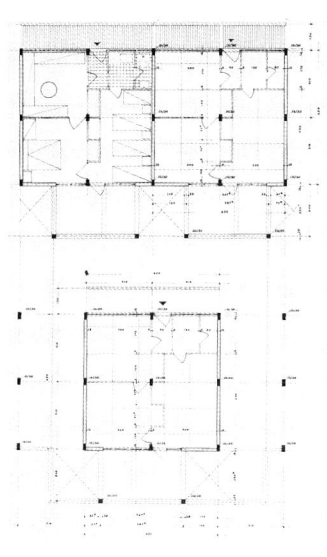

"Muslim housing" project. Plan.

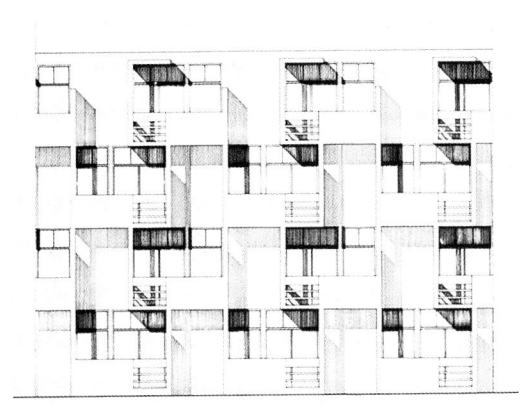

"European housing" project. Elevation.

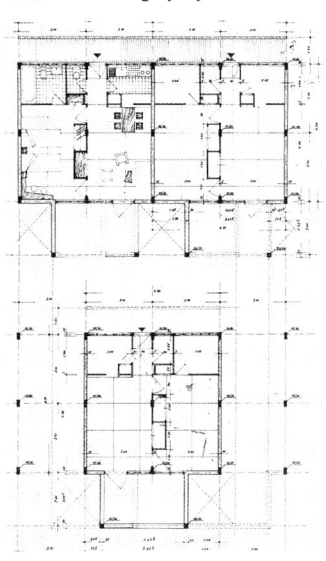

"European housing" project. Plan.

"Jewish housing" project. Model.

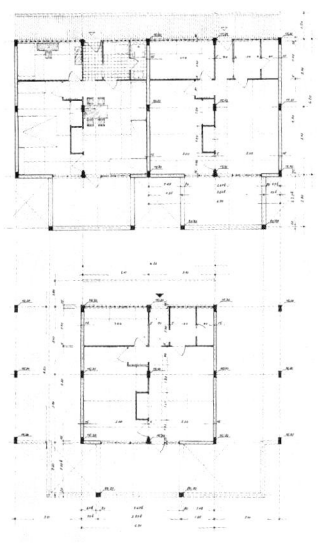

"Jewish housing" project. Plan.

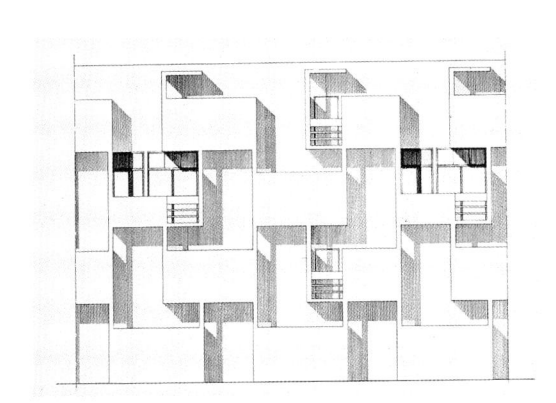

"Mixed" housing project. Elevation.

"Culture-Specific" Housing for Muslims 337

Traditional housing from beyond the Atlas mountains, and right, type 1 dwellings at Casablanca.

The work of **ATBAT-AFRIQUE** | Bodiansky
Candilis
Woods

COLLECTIVE HOUSING IN MOROCCO

described by A. and P. Smithson

Bodiansky

'The "habitat" has been the fundamental factor of well-being and of spiritual evolution of the human race, its constant amelioration constitutes the satisfaction of the mission of builders.'

Candilis

'Throughout the years ATBAT has studied the problems of "habitat" for the greatest number in all its aspects and peculiarities. It has not arrived at an all-round solution, but one solution for each case. It has found many solutions and many variants, but the spirit of search remains the same, the spirit of the greatest number with its laws and its disciplines.'

Detail of Type 2 A dwellings at Casablanca.

At CIAM X this summer, the subject under discussion will again be 'l'habitat,'* when it is hoped that the first steps of a CIAM approach to the problems of the dwelling will be formulated. At the 1953 Congress at Aix-en-Provence, though many schemes were presented from all parts of the world, the only really new contributions came from groups from Britain, Holland and Morocco, and these were all concerned with the organization of new forms of collective housing, which could be developed into larger urban patterns.

The essay on 'Modern Architecture in Holland' (*Architectural Design*, August, 1954), although it did not deal specifically with 'habitat,' did try to present the spirit in which the Dutch are working.

Our particular link with the Moroccan group (ATBAT-AFRIQUE), is that we found that through their own circumstances they were, like ourselves, working on the 'extension' of the dwelling. What we in Golden Lane † termed 'back-yard' they term 'patio,' drawing their knowledge of Arab needs from the area of greatest migration behind the Atlas mountains, where the established collective system includes the outdoor living space.

We regard these buildings in Morocco as the greatest achievement since Le Corbusier's Unité d'Habitation at Marseilles. Whereas the Unité was the summation of a technique of thinking about 'habitat' which started forty years ago, the importance of the Moroccan buildings is that they are the first manifestation of a new way of thinking.

For this reason they are presented as ideas; but it is their realization in built form that convinces us that here is a new universal.

Statement of Principle

It is impossible for each man to construct his house for himself.

It is for the architect to make it possible for the man to make the flat his home, the maisonette his 'habitat.'

Up to now, in Manual and in fact, the house is built down to the smallest detail and man is pressed into this dwelling—in spirit, the same from Scotland to the Gold Coast—and adapts himself as best he may to the life that the architecture furnishes him with.

The younger members of CIAM demand as a 'premier proposition de L'habitat' the voluntary effacement of the architecture.

We must prepare the 'habitat' only to the point at which man can take over.

We aim to provide a framework in which man can again be master of his house.

In Morocco they have made it a principle of 'habitat' that man shall have the liberty to adapt for himself.

---

* 'Habitat' is a word used by the French to describe not only the home but also its environment and everything appertaining to it.

† This refers to the rejected project by A. and P. Smithson for the City of London Golden Lane competition. A condensed version of it was included in the British contribution to the CIAM IX exhibition.

Georges Candilis and Shadrach Woods, *Trèfle Maroc* **housing type, 1954. Model.**

"[constitutes] the first manifestation of a new way of thinking," which in their view embodied a "new universal."[69]

Candilis and his team produced further variations on the Nid d'abeille and Sémiramis buildings in the Place Korte and Terrade quarters in Oran, as part of collective housing projects for Muslims.[70] These architects also perfected prototypes of dwellings for Moroccans along the lines of the *Trèfle* (cloverleaf) minimum housing designs that were later built in France and Algeria.[71] These designs subsequently served as a basis for the Candilis team's winning entry in the *Opération Million* competition, a program initiated by the French Ministry of Reconstruction and Urban Planning for low-cost mass housing that led to the construction of approximately 2,500 dwellings in Marseilles and greater Paris in the late 1950s.

The Carrières Centrales buildings therefore had a great impact, from both a theoretical and a pragmatic perspective. Although they may not have been quite as suited to the living conditions of Moroccan Muslims as Candilis claimed, they did nevertheless spark debate on adapting minimum housing for diverse populations. In addition, these photogenic buildings, which were featured in numerous French and European magazines, denoted a paradigm shift between the universalist approach of modern architecture and an ambition to adapt to local cultures and identities that characterized the Team X generation.[72] Yet in 1958, the French urban planner Robert Auzelle criticized the limitations of the Sémiramis designs. According to Auzelle, there was "inadequate privacy (especially a lack of insulation against sound, such as reverberations coming through the ceilings of the covered patios); also, the spacing between the buildings was alien to Islamic urban architecture," and "the rooms are badly proportioned as well as often being ill-suited to occupants' needs."[73] Michel Écochard drew attention to a further problem when he declared that "the patios, which are stacked and enclosed, will certainly be used as living space"[74]; this prediction was borne out by later modifications, as illustrated in contemporary photographs (see page 350). Moreover, while this form of patio design may be sculpturally effective, it fails to provide a place of communication between neighbors—an oversight that prompted André Adam to remark that "in her hanging patio, today's woman is like a caged bird."[75]

69 Alison and Peter Smithson, "Collective Housing in Morocco," 2. The projects were republished over ten years later in Alison Smithson, ed., *Team 10 Primer* (London: Studio Vista, 1968), 74–76.

70 *Candilis, Josic, Woods: une décennie d'architecture et d'urbanisme*, 129–30, 162.

71 One hundred thirty *Trèfle*- and *Nord-sud*-type dwellings were built on the Butte Mirauchaux in Oran, while sixty were built at Sidi Bel Abbès. Two hundred fifty *Trèfle*-type units were built for Emmaüs at Aulnay-sous-Bois, in 1954.

72 The Carrières Centrales buildings made the cover of *L'Architecture d'aujourd'hui* 25, no. 57 (December 1954).

73 "Maroc-Casablanca-Carrières centrales," in *Encyclopédie de l'urbanisme*, eds. Robert Auzelle and Ivan Jankovic (Paris: CSTB/Vincent et Fréal, 1958), plates 2/123–24.

74 Écochard, "Habitat musulman au Maroc," 37–38.

75 Adam, *Casablanca*, 1:137.

Muslims Gain Access to Collective Housing

Moroccans simply could not understand the Planning Department's stubborn adherence to a policy of building single-story apartments spread over a wide area, and so they continued to reiterate their demands for "European apartment types," expressing a desire for "modern conveniences."

Euloge Boissonnade, 1954[76]

Aware that there would not be enough land for a single-story spread of dwellings, the administration decided to increase the number of collective housing schemes for Moroccans.[77] Adam noted that these developments were not destined for "proletarians from the *bidonvilles* or immigrants just off the bus," but for "confirmed city-dwellers, and, more often than not, second-generation city-dwellers."[78] The fact that these new tenants had already become acclimatized to city life added a significant argument in favor of Écochard's long-term strategy for a progressive shift from low-rise schemes to high-rise functionalist slabs.

In 1953, Charles Lucas followed ATBAT's schemes with an "experimental European-type building" constructed for Muslims in the Carrières Centrales. It was, however, deemed too radical for a population that was seeking to attain European standards of comfort without sacrificing the traditional privacy of Muslim dwellings. Set in the heart of the Ryad development, it was characterized by access balconies and south-facing apartments equipped with showers and lavatories. It also offered other advantages at the time:

> It contains more housing per hectare for Muslims, and services costs are lower, as services are grouped in a core. This means less moving to and fro for the 250 tenants. Also, the kitchens are comfortable, the apartments are easy to maintain, and the rooms have large windows—a feature that has been overlooked up until now in housing programs for Moroccans."[79]

Further collective housing schemes were constructed in this neighborhood after 1954, and developments that complied with the Écochard guidelines were soon built in the vicinity of areas dedicated to individual dwellings, such as Ain Chock.[80] This high-rise trend rapidly spread to other Muslim quarters of the city, although local residents did not always agree with the planners' interpretation of their needs. As Candilis noted, for a number of militants and residents' representatives, culture-specific housing constituted a "new type of colonialism, or paternalism" that did not correspond to their demands for housing in ordinary, "low-cost slab buildings like everyone else."[81]

Hentsch and Studer's Volumetric Combinations

One of the most spectacular schemes of this period was built between 1953 and 1955 in Sidi Othman to designs drawn up by André Studer and Jean Hentsch, two Swiss architects who had gone into partnership. Studer, who had worked with Le Corbusier and had traveled extensively in Arizona and Mexico, initially proposed a pyramid building conceived as a "modern Casbah" that would "[take] into account the customs and traditions of people living in the country and on the mountainside."[82] However, the authorities considered this building type unfit for police surveillance, and the pyramid plan was replaced by nine slab buildings featuring an expressionist interpretation of Candilis's beloved hanging courtyards.[83] The development was financed by the Groupement Foncier Marocain (Moroccan Real-Estate Group) and included a small shopping area set apart from the housing. Pilotis rhythmically punctuate the lower levels of the buildings and bear the weight of patios that also form the access point to the service core. As in the ATBAT

---

76 Euloge Boissonnade, "Révolution dans la construction marocaine; plein succès de l'immeuble expérimental des Carrières centrales à Casablanca," *L'Écho d'Oran* (April 7, 1954).

77 From 1955 to 1960, 36 percent of the housing built by the Housing Department would be multifamily dwellings. See "État des logements," Ministry of Public Works, circonscription de l'Urbanisme et de l'Habitat, 1960, MH.

78 Adam, *Casablanca*, 1:139.

79 Boissonnade, "Révolution dans la construction marocaine."

80 Gremeret built a five-story apartment building at Place Koudiat for C.I.F.M. Four buildings were built by *castors* in 1957, with help from the Ministry of Urban Planning and Housing. In 1958, a five-story building was completed by Laure, and a two-story one by Azagury, both for the Ministry of Public Works. In 1956, over one thousand apartments in more modest multifamily dwellings were built by Gremeret within the framework of Écochard's general plan, as well as for the C.I.F.M. Two eighty-unit buildings were built by Azagury at Ain Chock in 1958 and 1959.

81 Candilis, interview, *Ingénieurs et architectes suisses*, 492.

82 André Studer, untitled plates of the architect's work, ca. 1975, private archive of the architect, Goeckhausen/Zürich.

83 *L'Architecture d'aujourd'hui*, no. 60 (June 1955): 38–39.

Jean Hentsch and André Studer, collective housing commissioned by the Groupement Foncier Marocain, Sidi Othman, 1955.

General view. There are four apartments on each floor, accessed by four staircases in the two five-story slab buildings and by a main stair in the small high-rise building.

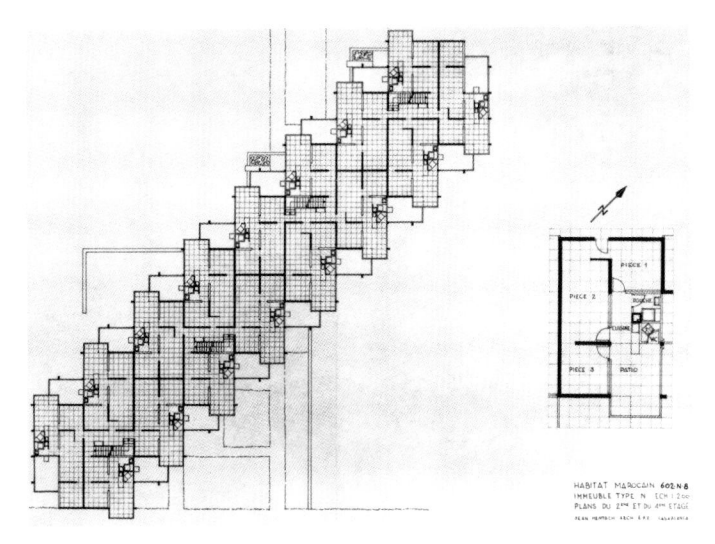

Jean Hentsch and André Studer, collective housing, Sidi Othman, 1955. Standard floor plan and plan of a three-room apartment in one of the slab buildings.
Each building contains units ranging from one- to four-room apartments. The two- and three-room units are the most common, though.

André Studer, "Arabersiedlung" project for the pyramidal housing for Muslims, 1954. Perspective.

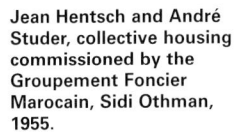

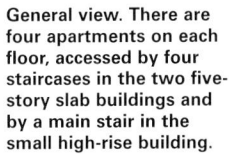

"Culture-Specific" Housing for Muslims 341

buildings, these outside spaces were designed in keeping with the cultural tradition of Moroccan housing, as the architect himself explained: "Each dwelling will have a 'traditional patio,' that is, a patio open to the sky and protected from public view, which functions as the center of the dwelling and which can be accessed from any of the rooms . . . Patios measuring 7.2 meters by 3 meters shall be aligned vertically and will branch out at right angles on alternate floors, thereby providing a 3-meter-by-3-meter space with one story of vertical clearance (containing the service area) and another space with two stories of vertical clearance."[84]

Although the underlying design concept of the development was rooted in a poetic and geometric interpretation of traditional building forms, the actual construction and layout of the apartments was conceived in an extremely modern way, with double exposures, large windows, and grouped services.[85] The buildings are of reinforced concrete with brick and plaster infill and are laid with terrazzo flooring. This development, in which Studer demonstrated his interest in harmonic proportions, was intended as a breeding ground for working up a prototype to be reproduced on adjacent plots with community facilities, though the prototype was never actually reproduced. Moreover, most of the patios were converted into living space once the occupants moved in. Hentsch and Studer worked on housing projects for U.S. military bases up until 1956, and also produced other "designs for Moroccan multifamily housing programs" in which they developed the themes explored in Sidi Othman.[86]

During this period, the Comité Interprofessional du Logement (C.I.L.) programs often featured a combination of collective housing and individual dwellings. The Moroccan development for the occupants of the Ben M'sick *bidonville*, built in 1953 between Avenue du Nil and Avenue Anoual in Sidi Othman, includes basic low-rent housing of both types.[87] The Caisse Marocaine d'Épargne and the Crédit Marocain helped fund this large-scale project, for which rents were to be deducted

---

84 "Immeubles à Casablanca, Jean Hentsch, étude André Studer," *L'Architecture d'aujourd'hui* 26, no. 60 (June 1955): 38. Construction was supervised by Jacques Zbinden.

85 See the following articles, published in Europe: "Wohnbauprojekte für Arabersiedlungen in Casablanca, Marokko," *Werk* 46, no. 1 (January 1956): 22–23; and "Housing at Casablanca," *Architectural Design* 26, no. 4 (April 1956): 136 (discussed above).

86 André Studer, interview by Jean-Louis Cohen, Gockhausen/Zürich, June 2, 1992.

87 Jacques Delarozière, memorandum on Moroccan housing in Casablanca, Urban Planning Department, March 1, 1953, MAE, Civilian Cabinet, carton 122, Habitat.

88 Casablanca Urban Affairs Delegation, memorandum on Muslim and Jewish housing in Casablanca, February 1953, MAE, Civilian Cabinet, carton 122, dossier Habitat musulman et israélite. In addition to the usual infrastructure and services, two mosques were built. Between 1962 and 1964 the architects Mauzit, Fougerat, and Charaï built schools for the C.I.F.M. and the public education authority.

89 Of 580 units planned, 414 were built during 1953 and 1954. Maguy Mortier, "Cité de Sidi Othman du service de l'Habitat," *Maroc-Monde* (Casablanca), January 15, 1954. The development's inauguration was reported on May 23, 1954, by *Le Petit Marocain*, *Maroc-Presse*, *Maroc-Soir*, and *La Vigie marocaine*.

Jean Hentsch and André Studer, collective housing, Sidi Othman, 1955. View of a slab building.

Erwin Hinnen, housing complex, Avenue du Nil and Avenue Anoual, Sidi Othman, 1953–54. General view.

Erwin Hinnen, housing complex, Avenue du Nil and Avenue Anoual, Sidi Othman, 1953–54. Elevation of a collective housing building as featured in the building permit. The two-story buildings contain some two hundred dwellings altogether. On each landing there are two units of 58m² made up of a large 9m² entrance hall closed off by screen walls leading into two rooms of 13.7m². Type B contains a loggia-patio (6.5m²), whereas type A has narrow balconies.

from residents' salaries.[88] The first-phase buildings were designed by Erwin Hinnen, whose scheme was approved by the Housing Department.[89] It comprises individual dwellings containing one- and two-room units laid out on an eight-by-eight-meter grid, as well as collective housing blocks set along the main roadways, covering three stories and containing approximately two hundred dwellings. Hinnen chose not to include kitchens in his scheme, as recent rural migrants continued to cook outside. Instead, this function was dedicated to the loggia-patios or balconies that were designed to accommodate a *kanoun.** Hinnen did incorporate a washroom, with a bathroom and lavatory, though, which is accessed from the entrance hallway.[90] Three different types of windows pierce each of the slab buildings. The developers promoted the relatively large floor area of the apartments and the attendant amenities in an effort to attract rural migrant tenants, who preferred single-family dwellings as a rule, since they had generally never experienced anything else.

A second phase of two thousand single-family dwellings—the M'Barka development—was completed in 1955. It has *hammams*, mosques, communal ovens, shops, and a movie theater, and is known as the "Moroccan Anfa," as it sits on a hill overlooking the city. The rental dwellings were offered with easy optional purchase terms, which clearly reveals that they were targeted at a more well-to-do population than those in the previous phase.[91]

By the late 1950s, a total of five thousand dwellings for twenty thousand people had been built in the area.[92] This scheme was the last of the major construction projects undertaken by the Protectorate and was finally completed by the independent Moroccan state. From 1953 on, a climate of political instability, triggered

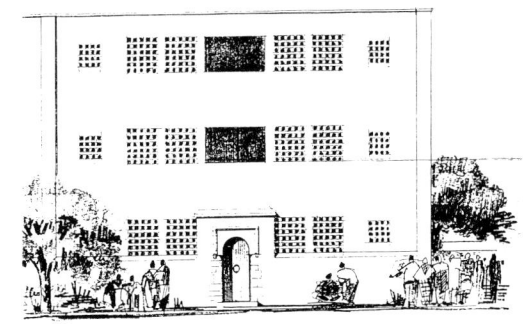

90 See *Le Maroc moderne*, and *L'œuvre du CIL au Maroc* (Casablanca: Éditions Bernard Rouget, 1954).

91 Euloge Boissonnade, "La cité M'Barka à Casablanca permettra de loger plusieurs milliers de Marocains," *Travaux nord-africains* (April 14, 1955): 1. This development was created by the Moroccan private developer Sadni. In 1957, the C.I.F.M. hired Mauzit to add an extension to the district, in collaboration with the O.T.H. This comprised 235 individual two-room dwellings, clustered in groups of four following, this time, a seven-by-eight-meter grid. The rooms opened onto a courtyard, subdivided into a little garden, kitchen corner, and lavatory.

92 In 1960, Paccanari would be hired by the Ksar El Bhar Tnine company to build 222 dwelling units in Sidi Othman. André Adam documents a total of 5,070 housing units in Sidi Othman, of which 4,452 were complete by late 1956. Adam, *Casablanca*, 1:110.

"Culture-Specific" Housing for Muslims 343

Gaston Jaubert and Pierre Coldefy, housing complex, Le Plateau, 1957. Curved facade. This building has six stories containing 262 units.

93 In 1952, 19.7 million francs were invested versus only 8 million in 1958. Adam, *Casablanca*, 1:51.

94 "Habitat collectif économique; résultats d'un concours organisé au Maroc," *L'Architecture d'aujourd'hui* 27, no. 70 (February–March 1957): 56.

95 Adam, *Casablanca*, 1:111.

by the growing nationalist movement, led to a drop in public building and a decline in European private investment. Overall, the construction industry slumped, falling by 50 percent a year before bottoming out in 1958.[93]

Morocco's Housing Dilemmas

The first housing complex built after independence was the Plateau project, which was the result of a competition staged in 1957 by the Ministère de l'Urbanisme et de l'Habitat (Ministry for Planning and Housing).[94] The brief specified that not only should the scheme provide a partial response to the chronic housing shortage but that it should also incorporate certain urban standards that had "been acquired by [the project's target population of] middle-class Moroccans who are now accustomed to a modern way of living."[95]

The program was for twenty slab buildings straddling Avenue Stendhal, southwest of Casablanca, and comprised just three categories ranging from two-room to four-room units. Gaston Jaubert and Pierre Coldefy's scheme won first prize, beating Émile Duhon and Chapon's entry, which included individual steam baths for each of the Moroccan Muslim dwellings.

Jaubert and Coldefy's design reads as a long, six-story, sinuous slab building, punched with doors providing access from one side of the building to the other, combined with smaller five-story slabs. The front of the main building features a highly graphic sawtooth pattern of spandrel panels, while the lower slabs are char-

Gaston Jaubert and Pierre Coldefy, housing complex, Le Plateau, 1957. Facade of the smaller buildings. These four-story buildings contain forty-eight units.

acterized by an alternating arrangement of ribbon windows, French windows, and screen walls. Three hundred forty-eight of the planned 1,760 units were completed by 1959.[96] Further construction phases took place over the following years, with one thousand dwellings built altogether, all of which complied with European standards of the period.

The budget was tight, and so the brief was to design "transitional dwellings with basic amenities, focusing on sunlight, proper ventilation, and unobstructed views."[97] Yet despite the lack of financial resources, the architects created as much usable floor space as possible. Communal access walkways lead directly into the three- and four-room units while the two-room dwellings have a small entrance hall. Depending on the size of the units, the kitchens either form part of the main room or take up an individual north-facing room. The service core runs along the access walkway at the rear of the building to free up space in the main rooms, which were carefully positioned so they could benefit from the best possible exposure. The bathrooms, which are often tiny in such a housing type, are surprisingly large in this carefully planned development that has stood the test of time.[98]

Although most of the low-rent housing of the period was funded by the state or by publicly funded corporations, industrial firms continued throughout the 1950s to commission workers' housing developments, which were usually located "right by the factories."[99]

[96] "Habitat collectif économique, le Plateau, Casablanca," *L'Architecture d'aujourd'hui* 30, no. 87 (December 1959–January 1960): 58–59. Coldefy had already tested this type of building in 1956, when he began an ensemble of 511 units for the C.I.F.M. on Boulevard Laurent Guerrero (today Yacoub el Mansour). The latter consisted of a single long curving building and six less specatular blocks, finished in 1958.

[97] "Habitat collectif économique," 59. See also Renée Diamant-Berger, *Gaston Jaubert: rythmes et volumes* (Marseilles: n.p., 1976), 15.

[98] Other architects intervened in the project later. In 1957, Azagury and Delanoé, as well as Laure, added buildings. In 1960, Abd-el-Kader Farès would build four buildings in the extension plateau. In 1959, Fleurant built a school for the French Cultural Mission.

[99] Bousquet built housing for the Moulins du Maghreb company, on Rue de l'École Industrielle, in 1946. Brion remained the specialist recognized by employers, and built thirty-eight dwellings near the Société des Chaux et Ciments factory, on Boulevard Colonna d'Ornano. He also built an "indigenous" housing development on the Route des Zénatas, for the Société Chérifienne d'engrais, in 1946. In 1953 Courtois received a commission for 216 units, at Derb Comima 2, for the Office Chérifien des phosphates. In 1956 Gourdain built forty-one dwelling units for Lesieur-Afrique, on Rue Rostand. Building permits listings, Wilaya of Greater Casablanca.

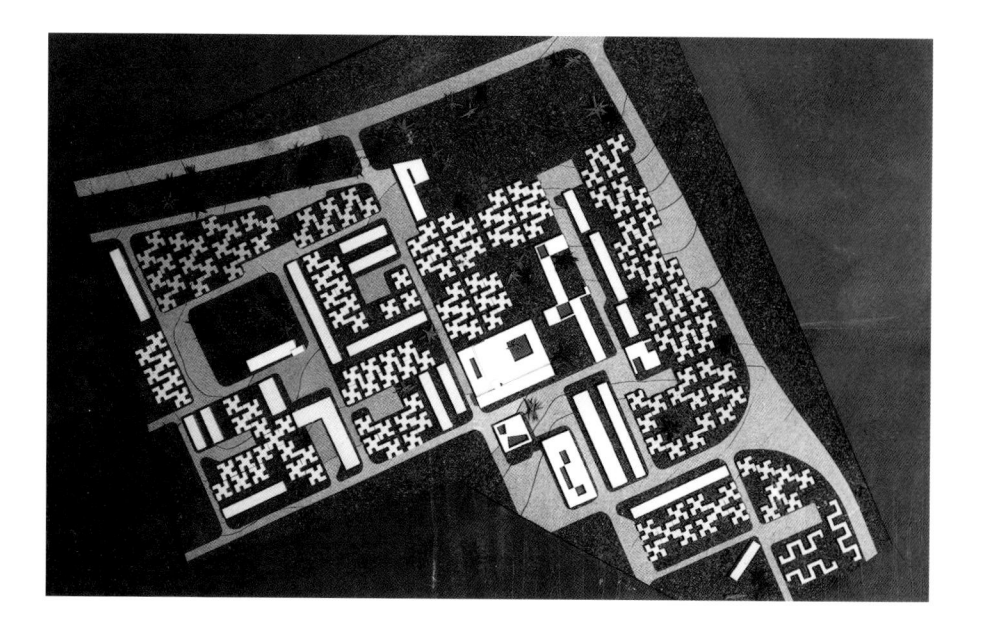

Élie Azagury, Derb Jdid housing scheme, 1958–62. Site model.

Derb Jdid—A New Village in the City

The Derb Jdid project is a genuine testing ground for low-cost housing. It is a prototype quarter that provides residents with clean and comfortable dwellings in the hope of replacing current bidonvilles. The valuable lessons that can be drawn from this experimental development will soon be applied in all housing programs throughout the kingdom.

A. de Montmarin, 1959[100]

100 De Montmarin, "Les nouvelles solutions en matière d'habitat," 447.

101 Adam, however, emphasized the absence of sewers. Adam, *Casablanca* 1:91.

Derb Jdid, known today as Hay Hassani, was a makeshift new quarter stretching west of the city on land bordering Anfa and the road to Azemmour. The municipal authority had grouped a number of *bidonvilles* on the site in the 1940s, and immediately after independence decided to create an improved *bidonville* there for rehousing purposes. The scheme knitted together groundwork research into culture-specific housing for the rural poor and, as such, had an ordered layout grid with several basic amenities.[101] In terms of health and hygiene, however, it was no better than anything else that had been built up until then, and there was no real protection against fire, though it was mistakenly argued that the width of the streets would prevent flames from spreading. By 1957, the derb was home to more than fifteen thousand people, including financially straitened families (a total of 7 percent), as well as more affluent families who had not yet adapted to city life.

The construction schedule had been set for 1959, and the design process was already under way when a fire broke out in June 1958, destroying the "temporary shacks." It was most probably started by the residents themselves to speed up events. Those who lost their homes were housed in makeshift cement-block structures composed of one-room dwellings with a yard and lean-to. Communal drinking fountains and lavatories were also provided. Poorer families were accommodated in temporary state-subsidized dwellings that were specifically designed to allow for extensions or additional levels. In just three months 1,800 of these were constructed. The quarter's redevelopment was led by the newly created Ministère des Travaux Publics (Public Works Ministry), assisted by Delarozière and Girard, alumni of Écochard's team. Moroccans gradually came on board too.

In 1957, a housing development for 25,000 residents was entrusted to Élie Azagury, who, in addition to conceiving the master plan, built the first three hundred units in the form of detached, semidetached, and collective housing. Azagury based his work in Derb Jdid on proposals that had been drawn up in 1952 for Muslim working-class housing, and which had since attracted the attention of planners in Rabat.[102] Working in association with Dominique Basciano, Azagury set to work on new plans for single-family dwellings that capitalized on the eight-by-eight-meter grid. Other private architects followed suit, as did some public-sector architects. By that time, this grid had become almost standard.[103] The dwellings were specifically designed so that stories could be added, since experience had proven that most residents tacked on an extra level sooner or later. The kitchen and services were brought inside, and the main rooms were arranged around the entrance hall. The distance separating each phase of construction grew gradually wider, the plans for two-meter-wide blind alleys leading off from the Carrières Centrales were shelved, and each unit included an open-air space such as a terrace or loggia. No state aid was allocated until all these guiding principles had been respected.[104]

Diverse building types were used to avoid long repetitive rows of single dwellings and to ensure a mix of classes. The architects constructed a number of two-story rental blocks and publicly subsidized freehold buildings, both types intended to accommodate two families. Some owners even constructed single-story buildings themselves, based on plans provided free of charge by the state. As for the shacks occupied by poorer residents, these were grouped in a sector equipped with communal drinking fountains and lavatories, and had only a basic road system.

The Azagury plan comprised single- and two-family dwellings conceived as two-story structures, as well as several three-story collective housing blocks. The minimum single-family dwellings were designed by various architects, such as Basciano, Gourdain, Michel, and Lévy, but nonetheless bear common features, apart from the room layout and positioning of the patio and courtyard.[105] Several two-room apartments containing a lavatory and "a loggia that can double up as a clothes drying area" were grouped in brick buildings fitted with screen walls. Three blocks went up first, "fitted with service areas and arranged around a core of community facilities."[106] Commercial amenities were spread throughout the development (including housing for shopkeepers), and a *kissaria* was set up in the center. Religious buildings, a healthcare facility, and a police station also formed part of the scheme, as did a youth center.

102 C. Vignaud, "Nouvelles cités d'habitation économique au Maroc," Rabat, circonscription de l'urbanisme et de l'habitat, 1952, MH, R 7.

103 Among the architects involved were Michel and Gourdain, Isaac Levy, and even one of the Suraqui brothers (who was to build shops and homes). Zéligson would build a school in 1963. But the Azagury team itself was to build over half of the dwellings in each category. Building permits listings, Wilaya of Greater Casablanca.

104 "A minimum width of 2.5 meters for each room and 9 square meters surface area." Vignaud, "Nouvelles cités d'habitation économique au Maroc."

105 Regarding the role of the patio, see de Montmarin, "Les conceptions actuelles en matière d'habitat économique au Maroc," 622, 623. The 9-square-meter rooms were 3.5 meters wide. Kitchens were 5 square meters, while bathrooms were 1.5 square meters. "Note sur l'évolution des programmes de construction et de lotissement de l'habitat," Rabat, Ministry of Public Works, 1958, MH. D 122, 4.

106 "Le Derb Jdid (Hay Hassani) Casablanca, Élie Azagury, architecte," *L'Architecture d'aujourd'hui* 30, no. 87 (December 1959–January 1960): 52.

Derb Jdid housing scheme, 1958–62. Aerial view c. 1965. The Basile types are shaped like swastikas; the Arsène types are grouped in a Greek-style figure; and the Porphyre type is a standard apartment building.

Élie Azagury, Basile-type building, c. 1959.

Élie Azagury, Basile type, 1958–1962. Standard floor plan.
The semidetached Basile type houses are grouped in buildings of eight units (43m² on the ground floor and 38m² on the first floor). Ground-floor occupants have a patio, whereas those living on the first floor all have a "service courtyard" connected to the kitchen. The windows overlook the street rather than the patio. This type was the first to be tried out.

107 Lots were leased for forty year terms to the least well-off residents, who benefited from ten-year loans. More comfortable residents used a loan, combined with an initial down payment, to finance the acquisition of a lot and the construction of a two-room home. Regarding sale conditions linked to the socioeconomic situation of residents, see de Montmarin, "Les conceptions actuelles en matière d'habitat économique au Maroc," 614, 625.

108 De Montmarin, "Les nouvelles solutions en matière d'habitat; leur application au Derb Jdid," 440.

109 De Montmarin, "Les nouvelles solutions en matière d'habitat; leur application au Derb Jdid," 440.

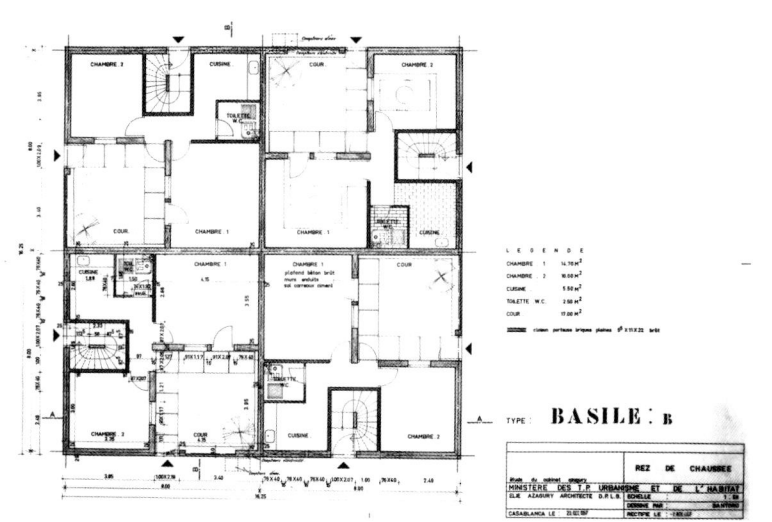

110 Beginning in 1958, Azagury contributed low-cost housing blocks, but also groups of single-family dwellings and the post office in 1964. In 1957 Sauvan built housing in the eastern extension. Dominique Basciano was commissioned to build the school in May 1958. The Coldefy/Riou team built two apartment buildings in 1960. Independently, Riou received a commission for over one thousand dwelling units in 1962. In 1968 André Adam indicated that "Sidi Bernoussi, one of the worker's housing districts projected in the Écochard plan, in the eastern industrial sector, has received 4,197 housing units, including 2,623 in the first phase." Adam, Casablanca, 1:110.

A total of 3,500 units of diverse types had been built by the late 1950s, and the state had started renting out lots equipped with amenities.[107] This system led the architects to look into ways of how the dwellings could later be converted. In view of the homeowners' meager resources, a certain degree of flexibility was required so that they could increase the usable floor area "as and when they [could] afford to do so,"[108] the idea being for residents to initially be provided with a single-story dwelling, which they could then improve in their own way, perhaps even building an extra floor either for their own use or to rent out. The Arsène and Basile units are a variant of this type, as they incorporate partitioning that can, in theory, be moved around.

This "truly experimental low-cost housing scheme" that taught "many invaluable lessons to the Ministry of Public Works"[109] eventually acquired all the facilities required in daily life. The neighborhood still forms a distinctly perceivable part of the city today, despite the fact that there are no longer any gardens and that every house has had a patio conversion or extra stories added.

Many of the architects who contributed to the design of Derb Jdid and other Moroccan housing developments simultaneously participated in the construction of the Sidi Bernoussi satellite development southeast of Ain Sebaa, in accordance with Écochard's master plan.[110] As in Derb Jdid, the collective housing blocks were set among the detached houses. Meanwhile, construction went ahead for the Basile and Emile low-cost housing types, together with a smaller, fine-tuned version of the Arsène type. Satellite City 2, another development with the same arrangement, would not, however, be completed until 1964.

Forty Years of Muslim-Specific Habitat

Conflict between the Eastern and Western worlds is deeply ingrained within every Casablancan. The industrial revolution is overturning Moroccan society, and Casablanca is the epicenter of the conflicts that derive from this.

Doris Bensimon-Donath, 1968[111]

Completed four decades after the Protectorate's preliminary urban experiments, the Derb Jdid program provides material for a comparative evaluation of Moroccan working-class housing schemes in Casablanca. During the interwar period, the administration, industrial firms, and architects such as Laprade, Cadet, Brion, and Laforgue set out to create mimetic housing in line with traditional rules governing spatial arrangement in Islamic societies. This concern for drawing on Moroccan architecture fell in line with Lyautey's political designs for Morocco (discussed in previous chapters), where special attention was paid to the "native Moroccan arts" in an effort to encourage their "protection." These traditional arts exerted a powerful influence over architects in Casablanca, who had to assimilate the existing languages of form.

While architects were often inspired by the residences of wealthy Moroccans and the monuments of imperial cities, as well as by public building design and luxury homes, the only interest they showed in more vernacular housing was on the rare occasions that they were commissioned to plan working-class developments. The Habous quarter, for instance, is one of the strikingly few schemes where smaller houses based on the traditional design of rural abodes and buildings of coastal towns were combined with larger dwellings conveying a more sophisticated urban architecture. It is worth noting that the most basic of the rural dwellings—as researched by Laprade—were adopted as prototypes for industrially produced units designed to provide light-filled, healthy accommodations for the rural poor seeking work in the city. In policies drawn up to cope with acute housing shortages,

[111] Doris Bensimon, "Note sur le livre d'André Adam," *Casablanca, Revue française de sociologie* 11, no. 1 (January–March 1970): 155.

Alexandre Courtois, courtyard and small garden in Derb Comima. Photographed in the early 1950s.

A new courtyard house at Derb Comima, c. 1952.

these prototypes served as a basis for constructing minimum housing for nomads and other disadvantaged groups. As it was though, in workers' housing programs set up by employers, focus on health and hygiene, building methods, and traditional design elements very often merely camouflaged what were in fact grim and unimaginative proposals. The housing debate came to a head in the 1950s, when young partisans of the modern movement discovered the cubic volumes of the Casbahs and fortified communal granaries, which they cited as vernacular precedents for modern-day collective housing.

A comparison of plans reveals a degree of continuity in the interior layout of single-family minimum dwellings—from the 1920s workers' housing programs right through to the era of "housing for the greatest number"—and thus contradicts the standard view that Écochard broke new ground. It is true that there can be no denying the common characteristics of these one- and two-room units that are arranged in a roughly identical pattern: rooms lit naturally by a courtyard, interior or communal lavatories, and kitchens covered with a canopy or confined to a small space built for that purpose. The hygienist approach also provided an element of continuity, for it enjoyed a fairly steady success, being unanimously supported by architects as well as by public and private builders. As previously mentioned, the early developments contained errors in the positioning of rooms, while the Écochard team went so far as to design blind alleys of only two meters in width. All in all, the most important factor that differentiated the earlier housing programs from the later ones was their political aspect inasmuch as 1950s schemes were politically responsive to the period, revealing a marked effort to incorporate Moroccan Muslims into Casablanca's *ville nouvelle*.

In spite of all these attempts to create "culture-specific" housing, the residents clearly resisted the schemes, as is demonstrated by the multiple alterations they made to them. Heedless of the benefits of decent ventilation and light-filled spaces, occupants converted the courtyards and sealed the doors and windows to render the dwelling more traditionally "introverted" (as well as to increase the usable floor area); in addition, they preferred to give up the interior kitchen in favor of an exterior *kanoun*. In the final analysis, it appears that the families living in these culture-specific abodes, which developers labeled "traditional" housing, but which in fact were merely reduced to caricature copies, sought in turn to adapt the dwellings to

Carrières Centrales. Photo taken in 1992 showing how the loggias have been sealed off in Nid d'abeille (left) and Sémiramis (background).

Comparison of two-story individual dwellings in different working-class developments. Drawings by Cristiana Mazzoni based on the building permits and architects' measured drawings.

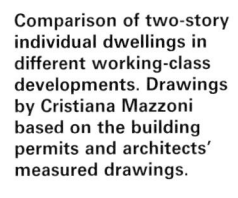

a. Dwellings in the new medina extension, c. 1932.

b. Paul Busuttil, dwellings for the Ain Chock development, c. 1949.

c. Élie Azagury, Arsène-type dwellings, Derb Jdid, 1958–62.

d. Élie Azagury, Basile-type dwellings, Derb Jdid, 1958–62.

e. Dominique Basciano, Christina-type dwellings, 1958–62.

In most of the two-story dwellings, the smaller units (often just a single-room dwelling with kitchen) were underprivileged, as they had no direct access to the courtyard but only a view looking down toward it. In some cases, notably in Derb Jdid, the architects endeavored to protect the privacy of occupants with courtyard access by not incorporating windows on the second floor. Nonetheless, the dwellings do have openings on the street side, even though this runs counter to tradition. The rooms began to be widened after 1945.

their needs, and often had to find substitutes for familiar elements. This principle applied whatever the housing type, since the more affluent Muslims also undertook what were often considerable alterations to protect their privacy. In this respect, it is to be noted that the Sémiramis building by ATBAT, which from the outset featured more "introverted" units, was less disfigured than the Nid d'abeille building, which comprises units of a more open design.

Écochard himself clearly foresaw that tenants would make unauthorized alterations. As early as 1953 he remarked, "If the local authorities do not strictly oversee the housing developments, residents will convert the patios, radically defacing the whole interior grid"; elsewhere, he pointed out that "high-rise buildings are similarly at risk."[112] In any event, the design solutions adopted for Moroccan housing failed to resolve the situation, especially as low-rise housing remained expensive, even in the outer parts of the city. Another key problem, as André Adam aptly notes, was that "the provision of improved housing encourages what is commonly

112 Écochard, "Habitat musulman au Maroc," 37.

Comparison of single-story individual dwellings in different working-class developments. Drawings by Cristiana Mazzoni based on the building permits and the authors' measured drawings.

a. Si Aomar Ben Kacem house, Bousbir quarter in the old medina, 1918. Drawing based on the building permit for extension works.

b. Auguste Cadet and Edmond Brion, Habous quarter in the new medina, house No. 2, block 15, 1922. Plan.

c. Albert Laprade, dwelling in the Habous quarter, 1917. Typical layout plan.

d. Auguste Cadet and Edmond Brion, prostitute's dwelling, Bousbir quarter (new medina), 1922. Measured drawing by Jacqueline Alluchon.

e. Proposed dwelling, new medina extension, 1934. Plan in *Chantiers nord-africains,* August 1934.

f. Edmond Brion, Cosuma workers' development, 1932–37. Building permit plan.

g. Antoine Marchisio, Ain Chock development, first-phase dwellings, 1946. Building permit plan.

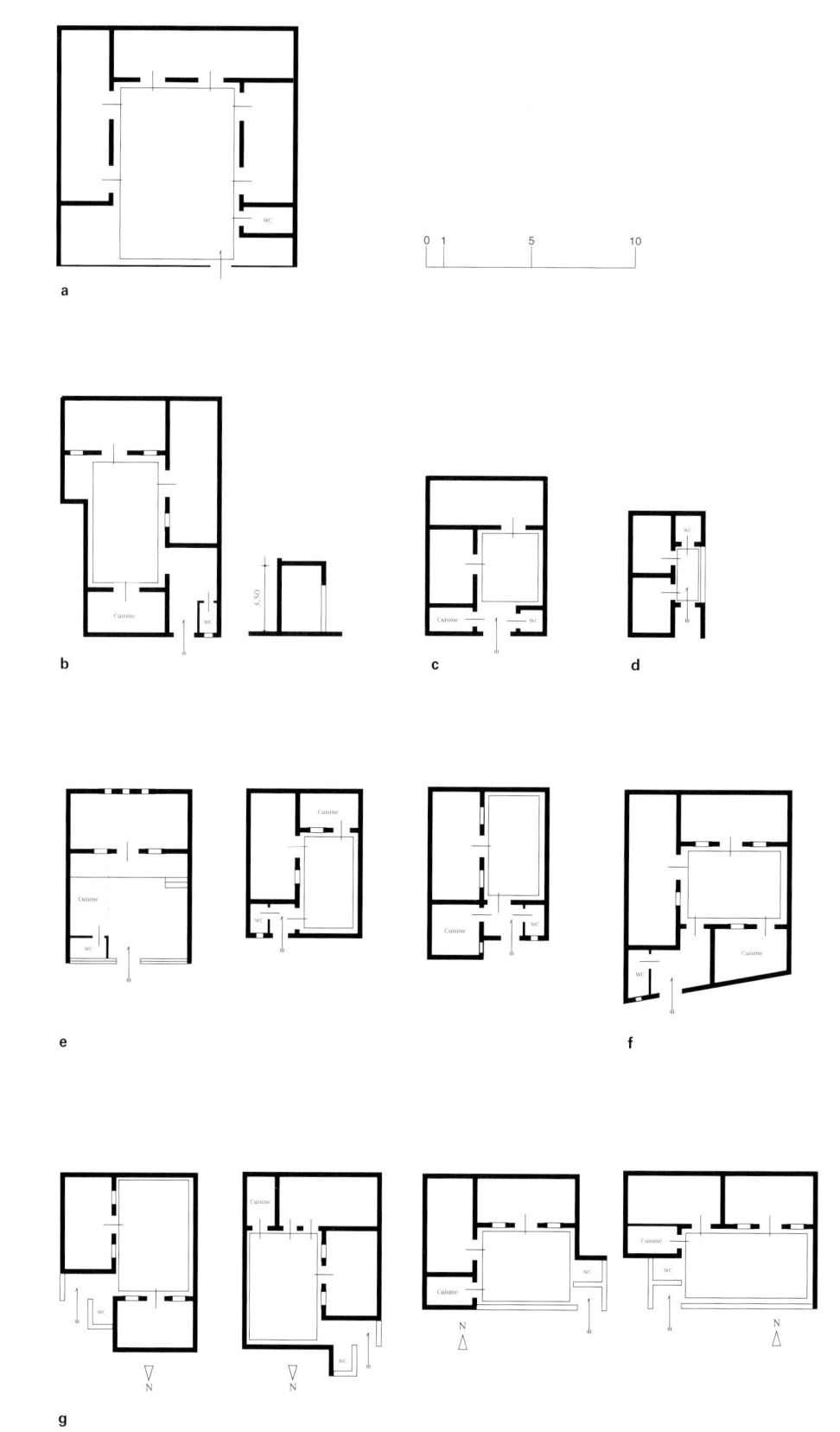

352 Casablanca

The bayonet entrance and direct entrance through the courtyard are standard. In general, the rooms are set out around the courtyards except in some of Busuttil's dwellings in Ain Chock, where the courtyards are located at the rear in relation to the entrance. In the latter case, the courtyards provide light and air but do not serve as circulation space. Hence they take on the same role as the European backyard.

The plots for the smaller houses in the workers' developments range from 40m^2 to 100m^2 (courtyard included). Michel Écochard's famous 8m by 8m plot (64m^2) also forms part of this category. The size of the rooms varies between 10m^2 and 20m^2, depending on the type of dwellings and number of occupants. It is to be noted that it is the floor area, rather than the number of rooms, that increases. The better-lit rooms can be used as reception rooms or guest rooms. The kitchen is usually a tiny room near the entrance, except in a few rare cases where it is an awning-covered space in the courtyard.

The rooms are generally laid out according to an L pattern around the courtyard, except for the smallest and largest dwellings, where the rooms are laid out in a U. The rooms in those dwellings set out in rows are aligned along the courtyard, which meant they could be installed by mechanical, and hence less costly, methods. This solution was also adopted in those projects where the issue of sunlight was not considered an essential variable, such as in the Koudiat and Saada developments. Sunlight was not properly considered as a variable until the 1950s.

The height of the rooms ranges from 3.5m to 2.8m. Between 1917 and 1952, they became more square, in line with European norms, rather than being very long and narrow.

h. Paul Busuttil, Ain Chock development, first-phase dwellings, 1946. Building permit plan.

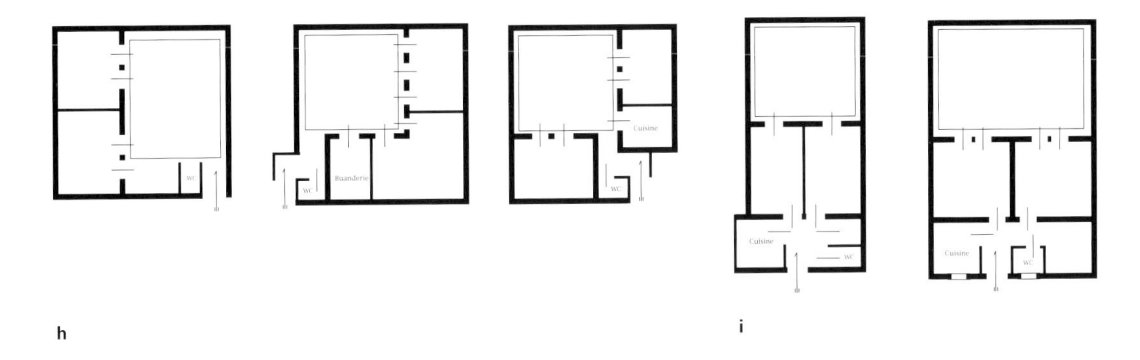

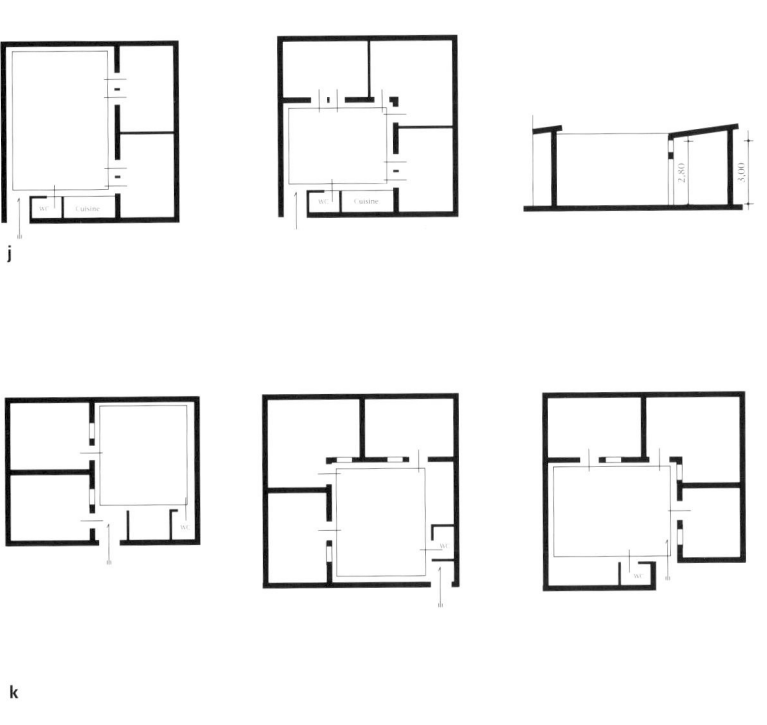

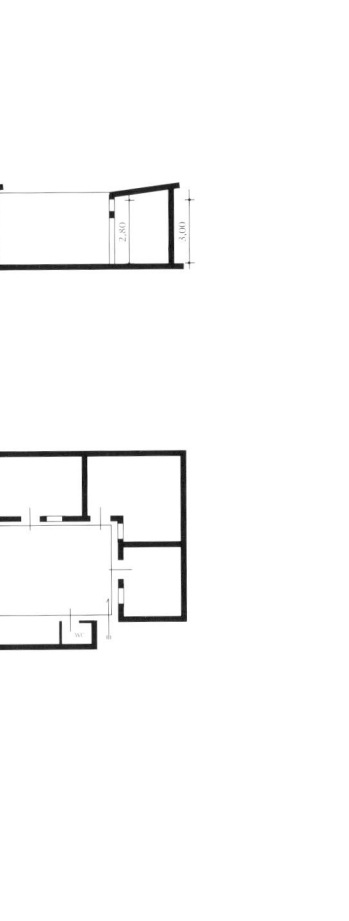

i. Paul Busuttil, Ain Chock development, second-phase dwellings, 1946. Building permit plan.

j. Town Planning Department, Carrières Centrales quarter, 1951.

k. Erwin Hinnen, dwellings, Sidi Othman development, 1953. Building permit plan. Master plan designed by Pierre Pelletier.

l. Town Planning Department, Koudiat and Saada developments, Carrières Centrales, 1952–53.

"Culture-Specific" Housing for Muslims 353

Carrières Centrales development. An example of how extra stories have been added to the patio houses (laid on a grid of 8m by 8m). Photographed in 1991.

known as the 'urban mirage,' whereby rural laborers migrate in the mistaken belief that they can find work, yet for the most part they never do find any."[113] The problem has yet to be resolved to this day, half a century after the Écochard plan.

As of 1956, most design teams began to seek ways of improving previous standard plans. The following memo drafted in 1958 by the Public Works Department outlined the solutions retained for Derb Jdid:

> We are witnessing a shift from low-level housing based on traditional urban and rural Moroccan styles to apartment buildings. A key characteristic of this new program type, which is composed of one-lot-deep rows, is that building space can be fully utilized. The only element still obstructing the way to the ultimate modern form of urban apartment blocks is the traditional patio.[114]

This latter, quietly asserted goal marked the end of the reign of the courtyard house. Both Moroccan populations were, to some extent, implicitly changed by living in a space structured according to the codes of another civilization, of another culture, and sometimes of another social class. As expounded by Mauss, Durkheim, Lévi-Strauss, and Althusser, internalizing material ideologies is achieved through gradual appropriation of objects, amenities, daily utensils, and lived-in space, as well as through education and even street life. At least Lyautey's strategic aim of preserving Moroccan Islamic culture proved extremely efficient for the emerging Moroccan middle class; the design of the new medina in Casablanca, for instance, is a pertinent example of the research conducted on relations between men and women and clearly shows how key traditions were maintained within Muslim cities, especially regarding the approach adopted toward public and private space. The Ain Chock development is another case in point, though it should be noted that the new medina and Ain Chock are the only developments of their type in Casablanca. Yet it is true that modern urban aspects of Casablanca have also proved essential in the learning process of rural migrants, who have been able to appropriate certain values of modern society, although these are tinged with colonialist attitudes.

Another function of *bidonvilles* was their acculturating role, as they provided a transitional space between rural and urban life. They also brought migrants into contact with new needs, almost in an experimental way.[115] In this respect it is worth

---

113 Adam, *Casablanca*, 1:102. See also idem, "L'occidentalisation de l'habitat dans les villes marocaines," in *Les influences occidentales dans les villes maghrebines à l'époque contemporaine* (Aix en Provence: Éditions de l'Université de Provence, 1974), 179–87.

114 "Note sur l'évolution des programmes de construction et de lotissement de l'habitat," Ministry of Public Works, 1958, MH, D 122, 3.

115 Comparison with the traditional French policy of the transformation, normalization, and acculturation of the working class merits further development here. One might consider, for example, certain Moroccan policies recalling the efforts of philanthropists, hygienists, low-cost housing administrators, as well as *Musée social* reformers to encourage among French workers practices conforming to bourgeois ideals. See especially the chapter entitled "Les lieux de l'apprentissage" in Eleb, *L'apprentissage du "chez soi,"* 21–38.

noting how throughout history, colonists, missionaries, and philanthropists have resorted to this type of transitional space when housing the local populace. The move from traditional to "modern" habitat results in certain deep-seated issues being called into question, such as social practices, gender relations, the relationship between parents and children, the specific codes concerning private and public space, and even views about religion and the sacred.[116] For instance, the inversion of accepted notions of private and public space in slab buildings can cause great confusion, for here corridors are often used for tasks that are usually confined to private courtyards in true Moroccan dwellings.

It must not be forgotten, however, that unlike in other cities governed by colonial rule, the Protectorate never resorted to violence to enforce a specific housing type on the native population; on the contrary, relatively few European-style apartment buildings were actually offered to Moroccans, and even then the prospective tenants were always given the choice of more traditional accommodations. This was true not just for Casablanca but for the whole of Morocco. What proved attractive to some social groups was the opportunity to appropriate all the outward signs of modernity through housing. Casablancan architects played an ambiguous role in this regard, initially reproducing kitsch exoticism before experimenting with hybrid forms,[117] apart from in the *ville nouvelle*, that is. There, the facades are showy and might be read as a dominating gesture in a country where houses are usually turned inward toward a courtyard, and where axial compositions and formal hierarchies such as vertical structures and domes are rare.

In 1954, the banker Louis Renaudin observed, "Official design schemes have shown a pronounced propensity to perpetuate the archaic form of local housing, whereas what is actually required is a coordinated program to gradually introduce designs that approach more modern standards."[118] He further pointed out that native Moroccans would eventually resent the "poor living conditions" offered in these housing projects, and that they would soon wish to live in "the type of housing currently reserved for Europeans." The Moroccan representatives on the Housing Commission who strongly supported a policy of offering modern collective housing to the Muslim population expressed a similar view: "The administration should not adhere more to tradition than the Moroccans themselves."[119] Other representatives accused the French of hindering the social development of the Moroccan working class by sponsoring programs that favored the traditional courtyard house over apartment buildings—a housing type that they viewed as a passport to the modern world. However, not all Moroccans were of the same opinion; their respective viewpoints depended on their cultural background, social rank, and regional origin, as well as on how they perceived the relationship between colonization and modernization, as Nathan Wachtel has observed: "In a textbook colonial society, the dominated population considers foreign intervention to be an aggressive subversion of their traditions and they may attempt to resist it; however, when colonial domination is viewed as less manifest, there tends to be voluntary acculturation, which is governed by the internal dynamics of the native people."[120]

Surrendering to the temptations of modernity was generally perceived as gaining access to a higher standard of living enjoyed by other cultures and inevitably led to psychological conflict. As Mohammed Boughali has aptly stated, "The choice between tradition and modernity creates a painful dilemma," inasmuch as "one is torn between both options, while having to remain true to oneself." He further points out how, in the early 1970s, "the traditionalist Moroccan working class nicknamed the rising younger generation 'our own backyard colonists,' which clearly confirms that they viewed modernization and colonization as being two sides of the same coin."[121]

---

116 Numerous works have shown how, in a wide variety of geographical contexts, cultural organization has been supported by the organization of the home. Among the classic works in this field are: Marcel Mauss, "Essai sur les variations saisonnières des sociétés eskimo," in Marcel Mauss, *Sociologie et anthropologie* (Paris: PUF, 1960): 387–477, first published as "Étude de morphologie sociale," *L'Année sociologique* 9 (1906): 39–132; and Pierre Bourdieu, "Trois études d'ethnologie kabyle: La maison ou le monde renversé," in *Outline of a Theory of Practice*, trans. Richard Nice (Cambridge and New York: Cambridge University Press, 1977), 9–151, first published as *Esquisse d'une théorie de la pratique* (Geneva: Droz, 1972). Other texts have highlighted the rupture constituted by the passage from a traditional habitat to one of a different culture that has been imposed. See: Claude Lévi-Strauss, *Tristes tropiques*, trans. John Russell (New York: Atheneum, 1961), first published as *Tristes tropiques* (Paris: Plon, 1955); and Pierre Bourdieu and Abdelmalek Sayad, Le *déracinement* (Paris: Minuit, 1964).

117 "Mestizo architectures," according to Saïd Mouline, in *Espaces urbains, espaces vécus, Signes du présent*, no. 3 (1988).

118 Renaudin, *L'habitat en Afrique du nord*, 95.

119 Si Hadj El Ayadi, member of the Housing Commission of the Direction of the Interior, statement made at the July 9, 1949, meeting, MAE, CDRG 138, dossier Maroc.

120 Nathan Wachtel, "L'acculturation," in *Faire de l'histoire*, eds. Jacques Le Goff and Pierre Nora (Paris: Gallimard, 1974), 1:128.

121 Mohammed Boughali, *La représentation de l'espace chez le marocain illettré* (Paris: Anthropos, 1974), 283–84.

Ambiguous Programs for Jewish Housing

The development and restructuring of business, coupled with the gradual abandonment of the mellah, led to a change in social distribution whereby the rich bourgeoisie was joined by a lower rank of shopkeepers and white-collar employees. This emerging, more Westernized class rapidly appropriated a modern lifestyle. Although the new bourgeois class made up only a small percentage of Moroccan Jews, Europeans hastily assumed that they represented the Moroccan Jewish population as a whole. However, the real situation was considerably more complex, for the social rise experienced by the emerging class served merely to accentuate the difference between rich and poor Jews, rather than uniting them, and mellah occupants remained at the bottom rung of the ladder. Recently arrived from backcountry villages or remote mountain communities, they made a living from semiskilled jobs or whatever work was available, even occasionally from begging . . . While it is true that an increasing number of individuals within this group managed to climb up a few rungs, their change in fortunes merely heightened the awareness of newfound class distinction, and those who succeeded in escaping from abject poverty were quick to sever links with their humble backgrounds. These individuals were middle managers who liked to present themselves as the young "elite" but who were in fact looked down on as upstarts by the "full-blooded bourgeoisie."

Doris Bensimon-Donath, 1968[122]

122 Bensimon-Donath, *Évolution du judaïsme marocain*, 53.

123 Michel Écochard, *Rapport préliminaire sur l'aménagement et l'extension de Casablanca*, 91.

124 Pierre Mas, interview by the authors, Paris, October 19, 1992. Thirty thousand to thirty-five thousand people were to be relocated.

125 Minutes of the Housing Commission's March 27, 1952, meeting, MAE, carton CDRG 138.

126 Casablanca Urban Affairs Delegation, memorandum on Jewish housing, November 21, 1952; and memorandum on Muslim and Jewish housing in Casablanca, February 1953, MAE, Civilian Cabinet, carton 122, dossier Habitat musulman et israélite.

127 Fines (head of the Civilian Cabinet), memorandum to Director of Interior Affairs Vallat, January 24, 1953, MAE, Civilian Cabinet, carton 122, dossier Habitat européen.

A specific housing program for working-class Jews had been under discussion in Casablanca since the 1930s, but did not actually come to fruition until 1950. In an assessment survey undertaken by Écochard in 1951, the Jewish population in the medina and surrounding neighborhood was estimated at 63,000, with 18,000 living in the old part that had been scheduled for demolition since 1922. Écochard recommended "demolishing the most insalubrious quarters," including the mellah, and suggested clearing open spaces in others. The occupants of the targeted demolition areas were not all necessarily considered eligible for low-rent housing, as "they will be able to find accommodations in neighborhoods close to the mellah due to the higher standard of living that they now enjoy. As for those people living in the mellah, they will seek to move to the [more salubrious] residential areas situated further west."[123]

In essence, the plan was to build housing that would not be predominately for Muslims close to the city's commercial center. Some of Casablanca's rabbis intervened so that families would be grouped in specific areas and not dispersed across the city.[124] Proposals for a "Jewish housing scheme," sited roughly ten kilometers outside the city to the southeast, on the Camp-Boulhaut road, were rejected both by the municipal authority and by the Jewish community, whose members considered the site to be too far from the commercial core and places of worship. Eventually, in 1952, the community's representative on the Housing Commission, Jacques Pérez, approved the Housing Department's plan for a project in El Hank, which was closer to the city center.[125] Consequently, eighty hectares of land located between the fairground and the El Hank headland (an area acquired by the municipal authority and the Protectorate in the early 1950s and renowned for its stench of sewer outlets, high humidity, and ocean mist) were set aside for housing forty thousand low-income Jewish families.[126] It is noteworthy that this middling site would later be rejected by the authorities in Rabat for rehousing eight thousand Europeans living in medinas, low-rent hotels, and *bidonvilles*, on the basis that since "the site is located too close to the ocean [it would have created] more disadvantages than advantages."[127] It was eventually decided that the scheme would cater only to those families who actually wished to move there, i.e., around 1,500.

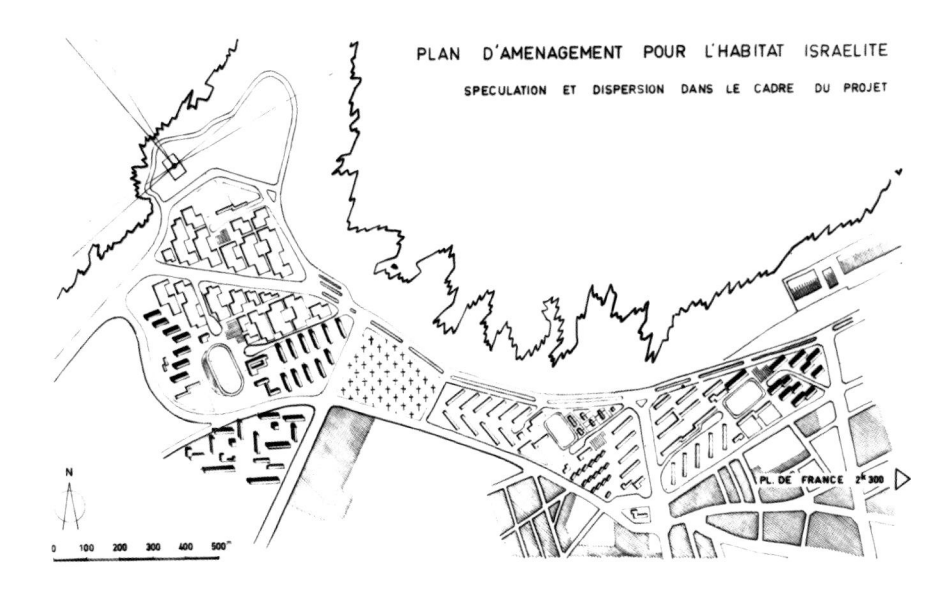

Town Planning Department, urban plan for the distribution of housing complexes devoted to the Jewish population, November 1951.

The issue of funding was broached, since the future residents certainly did not have the means to finance the scheme themselves. Banking on the solidarity of the Jewish community, Protectorate Finance Director Lamy suggested offering private companies sites at a reduced cost and low-interest loans of under 4 percent. This solution was approved, and Pérez tried to find companies willing to build at a low price. Defining a housing type proved difficult, as Moroccan Jews led different types of lifestyles, some close to the European way of life and others close to the Muslim one.[128] A number of journalists pointed out how these collective housing schemes implied a significant break with tradition for the Muslim and Jewish populations who needed to adapt to the change in lifestyle, and they applauded the "transitional features of the multistory dwellings."[129] Their opinion was not shared by the head of the Housing Department, who maintained that "on the contrary, Moroccan Jews are already accustomed to such a type of accommodations and have, moreover, made it known that they wish to be housed near the commercial hub."[130] Whatever the biased ideological views expressed by the journalists, the Housing Department maintained that sooner or later all sections of Casablancan society would be housed in "dwellings that had traditionally been referred to as European in style."[131]

Écochard's team thus decided in favor of collective housing; they were convinced it would be readily accepted, particularly as gender segregation did not play the same predominant role for Jews as it did for Muslims.[132] Thus, it was not a housing type that provided an especially "culture-specific" response; however, it has to be said that the project had no real basis for comparison, since the 1920s and 1930s buildings constructed by Jewish developers in central Casablanca featured a middle-class European layout, which obviously rendered them unsuitable as models of housing for the rural poor. Additionally, post-1930 architectural schemes completed in Palestine by European-trained functionalist architects patently demonstrated that the notion of specifically "Jewish" housing was difficult to translate into brick and mortar.[133] Hence, the buildings that were finally constructed according to a brief established by the Housing Department not only contained large windows but also balconies and loggias, "with kitchens, lavatories, washbasins, and patios, following a formula that strove to strike a balance between modern living conditions and traditional lifestyles."[134] This "culture-specific" housing drew heavily on standard plans for public housing, including a main room, which opened onto the other rooms in the dwelling, to which a patio was systematically added. In the following excerpt, it can be seen how Écochard sought to justify this program:

128 See Casablanca Urban Affairs Delegation, memorandum on Jewish housing, November 21, 1952.

129 "Habitat israélite," in *Le Maroc moderne: architecture et urbanisme.*

130 Paul Parinet, "L'habitat marocain," *L'Architecture française* 13, no. 131–32 (November–December 1952): 9.

131 C.I.F.M., *Avant-projet de programme de construction pour l'année* 56 (Casablanca: C.I.F.M., 1956), 21.

132 "The Jewish population rejects rudimentary formulas such as Écochard's grid and prefers multistory apartment buildings." Unsigned memorandum to the Protectorate secretary general regarding the question of the "relocation of families whose dwellings are located on the public thoroughfare," chemise "Habitat israélite à Casablanca, prolongement de l'avenue de la République," MAE, Secrétariat général politique, carton 237, Urbanisme.

133 Michael Levin, *White City: International Style Architecture in Israel* (Tel Aviv: The Tel Aviv Museum, 1984); and Winfried Nerdinger, ed., *Tel Aviv Modern Architecture 1930–1939* (Tübingen: Wasmuth, 1994).

134 Delegation on Casablancan Urban Affairs, memorandum on Jewish housing, November 21, 1952.

Louis Zéligson, collective housing building for Jewish residents, El Hank, 1950. Facade with balconies/loggias on the side opposite the ocean.

135 "Habitat de type israélite," *L'Architecture d'aujourd'hui* 26, no. 60 (June 1955): 41.

136 Joseph Goulven, "La maison juive au Mellah," *Le Maroc catholique* (December 1922): 480.

137 "Adjudication de gros-œuvre, architecte Zeligson," *Construire* (July 6, 1950).

138 "Habitat israélite à Casablanca," *L'Architecture française* 13, no. 131–32 (November–December 1952): 14.

139 Parinet, "L'habitat marocain," 9.

140 *Le Maroc moderne: architecture et urbanisme.*

141 Delegation on Casablancan Urban Affairs, "Note sur l'habitat musulman et l'habitat israélite à Casablanca," February 1953, MAE, Civilian Cabinet, carton 122, dossier habitat Marocain.

The Moroccan Jewish population is increasingly adopting a European way of life; however, certain traditions have remained that are dictated by ancestral customs and the African climate. The building thus comprises . . . double-height open patios that extend out from the main rooms. The units are single-story and are accessed by exterior corridors.[135]

In view of the high level of humidity in this quarter, only the service spaces could be situated on the seaward side of the developments, while plans for a screen of trees to shelter the site never materialized. The patios—intended, among other things, to accommodate the huts traditionally put up at the feast of Sukkot—were finally completed with only one story of vertical clearance. The architects apparently provided another cultural feature, which was noted by Goulven in the 1920s, namely the *hammam bird*, or *tabila*, a bath used for "ritual washing as prescribed by religious law."[136] The *hammam bird* is usually rectangular in shape and is adjoined to a short flight of steps, not unlike a lustral Greek bath. The plans also feature a minuscule washroom that can be used by women during menstruation. These cramped washrooms containing only minimal facilities constitute a somewhat derisory reference to the *hammam bird* tradition. On the other hand, Muslim housing schemes of the same category were not usually equipped with any washrooms at all, which is a rather telling attitude on the part of the French decision makers.

The first development in the scheme was built by Louis Zéligson in 1950 at the junction of Boulevard de la Corniche and Boulevard Calmel, opposite the El Hank lighthouse. It is a slab building made up of one hundred units with five stairwells facing inland, away from the sea breezes[137] and was to remain cut off from all other structures for almost half a century. A more ambitious project was launched at the other end of the site that had been allotted to the Jewish community, which was the result of a two-phase competition staged by the Housing Department in 1950. The following year, the winning team, composed of Rousseau, Zéligson, Lucaud, Morandi, and Aroutcheff (specialists in working-class housing), constructed an eight-building scheme at the intersection of Boulevard Moulay-Youssef and Boulevard Calmel, opposite the public swimming pool. Positioned like windbreaks, facing away from the ocean, the buildings reach five stories high and contain apartments accessed by walkways. Not only do the structures "all face south, to capitalize on natural light, thus reducing the need for heating in winter,"[138] they also proved less expensive to put up than the ones in the first program. In addition, they are situated in the heart of a large public park that encompasses a circular health center and kindergarten, together with a school designed by Joseph Suraqui in 1955. There are 160 units in all, ranging from one- to three-room dwellings that were delivered with a kitchen, a washroom (with running water but without a shower), a lavatory, and an outside kitchen-laundry-terrace. The kitchen and the living room open onto a loggia, part of which was designed as an open-air salon. The south-facing loggias are sheltered by horizontal brise-soleil, and these also help to conceal the kitchen-laundry. "The access galleries, stairs and smaller rooms [are confined to the north facade and] have very few openings."[139] Observers noted, "Each dwelling includes a terrace—an essential element in native Jewish lifestyle."[140]

In 1952 and 1953, the Protectorate acquired land edging the cemetery south of La Corniche, just up from the El Hank headland, and thirty-seven slab buildings comprising some three thousand units were constructed there between 1955 and 1960.[141] The first four of these buildings were erected in 1955, based on designs by the architect J. H. Laure, who was head of the Administrative Buildings Bureau in Rabat. Laure pointed out that, despite being built within a tight budget, "the units offer basic modern conveniences, and each residential unit includes a shower room

Léon Aroutcheff, Raymond Lucaud, Léonard Morandi, Marcel Rousseau, and Louis Zéligson, "Windbreak" apartment buildings for Jewish residents, 1951–52, Boulevard Moulay-Youssef and Boulevard Calmel. Aerial view in 1953.

Léon Aroutcheff, Raymond Lucaud, Léonard Morandi, Marcel Rousseau, and Louis Zéligson, "Windbreak" apartment buildings for Jewish residents, 1951–52. Plan of a three-room apartment, in *L'Architecture française*, 1952.

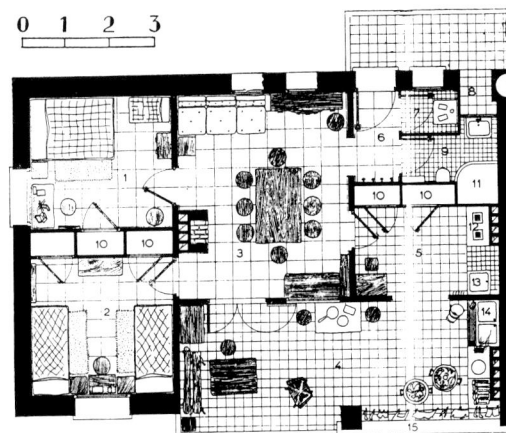

Léon Aroutcheff, Raymond Lucaud, Léonard Morandi, Marcel Rousseau and Louis Zéligson, "Windbreak" apartment buildings for Jewish residents, 1951–52. Walkways along the facade on the ocean side. Photographed in 1993.

"Culture-Specific" Housing for Muslims 359

J. H. Laure, housing complex, El Hank, 1953. Aerial view in October 1958.
Note the mix of slab buildings in the "Jewish" sector and patio houses in the Mokhaznis development.

J. H. Laure, housing complex, El Hank, 1953. Apartments bordering El Hank cemetery. Photograph taken in 1991.

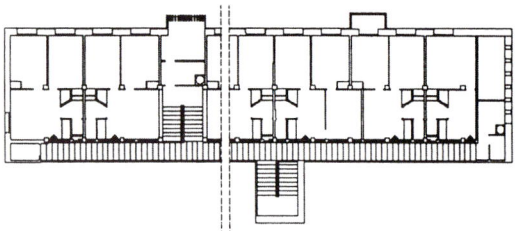

J. H. Laure, housing complex, El Hank, 1953. Standard floor plan. Drawing by Philippe Simon based on the building permit.
Each building contains sixty units—fifteen dwellings with two rooms, thirty-five with three rooms, and ten with four rooms.
There is a laundry room for every six units and a drying room for every three units, plus a waste chute every level (twelve units), as well as a storage room for push chairs and bicycles. The four-room apartments have a lounge, whereas the others have a communal room called "entrance-kitchen-eating" on the plan, which is accessed via the walkway. The bathroom (2.6m²) is large enough for a shower, but only has a squat lavatory and washbasin.

and a private lavatory."[142] A number of cost-cutting measures were introduced, such as rational building methods, carefully thought out storage space, reduced floor areas (for instance, the two-room units measure only twenty-five square meters), access walkways, grouped water outlets, and restricted circulation zones.[143] Nonetheless, the development did not escape criticism. *Maroc-Presse* spoke in highly disapproving terms of the poor ventilation in the living rooms—"four square openings each measuring only 60 centimeters and situated at ceiling height"—as well as the lack of skirting boards in a country where floors are traditionally washed down.[144] Above all, though, the article deplored the absence of clothes-drying rooms, as in the early buildings on Boulevard Calmel, which resulted in the spectacle of endless lines of washing hung out to dry; the journalist did acknowledge, however, that errors in the first four buildings could be corrected at a later stage.

The year 1954 marked the completion of the first phase of the Jewish housing program. The scheme, conceived as two buildings containing two hundred units designed by Joseph Suraqui, was financed by the S.I.H.I.C. (the Jewish Housing Building Company), which planned for twelve buildings in total. The first-phase blocks are noticeable for the square openings on their facades and their elegant

Joseph Suraqui, housing for Jewish residents in El Hank, commissioned by the Société Immobilière de l'Habitat Israélite de Casablanca, Boulevard Joffre and Boulevard Delavigne, 1954. General view.

The two buildings include about two hundred units. One building has four stairwells and the other has three.

Joseph Suraqui, apartments for Jewish residents, Rue La Bruyère, 1953–54. Rear facade. The slab building contains eight units, each of which comprises a living room and one or two bedrooms, a large kitchen, and a bathroom with shower. The lavatory is separate.

Joseph Suraqui, apartments for Jewish residents commissioned by the C.I.F.M., Rue La Bruyère, 1953–54. Photo taken in 1990 showing detail of the rear facade. Note how the stairwells leading up to two- and three-room apartments are crowned by a kind of pediment.

attic story, and were fashioned more in the mold of upscale apartment houses than low-cost housing. In the same period, Suraqui received another commission from the C.I.F.M. for a low-cost development on a site slightly less desolate than El Hank, and designed for slightly more affluent members of the Jewish population. Suraqui grouped the buildings in a long seven-story slab crowned with fully fitted roof terraces and punctuated by screen walls that protect the stairwells, kitchens, and bathrooms. The facades are turned around in terms of architectural hierarchy: entrances and utilities open onto a planted square, while the "rear" facade, grouping the entranceways and ancillary premises, becomes the front of the building. Living areas, washed with light from rows of square windows, are shielded from public view by an enclosed private garden. In general, developments such as these, designed by architects who were not working directly for the public administration, are more urban in style, less repetitive, and better equipped than the buildings in the El Hank scheme, which contain all the typical failings of large-scale complexes.

Regardless of the funding source, whether the state, private companies, associations, philanthropists, or community groups, no resources were available for constructing places of worship or any other community facilities, apart from primary

142 The prototype of a "Sixty-dwelling horizontal collective building" was presented at the Aix-en-Provence C.I.A.M. congress of 1953. Photothèque MH Rabat. Once perfected, this prototype of a bar building with open hallways and enclosed exterior stairwell would be employed in buildings at the Plateau, near the Jaubert and Coldefy buildings. The difference in quality is striking.

143 The size of living rooms was 8 to 11 square meters, that of the bedrooms 9 to 13 square meters, and that of the salon about 9 square meters. J. H. Laure, exhibition panel presented at the 1953 CIAM in Aix en Provence, Photothèque du ministère de l'Habitat, Rabat. According to Pierre Mas, Écochard had hoped to "personally undertake" this project. Mas to authors, October 7, 1996.

144 Marcel Herzog, "Les premiers immeubles destinés à l'habitat israélite à El Hank vont bientôt être achevés," *Maroc-Presse* (Casablanca), May 4, 1954.

schools. Consequently, the Protectorate reached the conclusion that these amenities had to be funded by religious or secular charities and private companies. This contrasted sharply with the housing policy for Muslims, but had much in common with the policy for Europeans.

Multiethnic Developments Replace Culture-Specific Habitat

With a view to alleviating the working-class housing shortage, the newly independent Moroccan government launched a housing development program in 1956 on the twenty-hectare El Hank site—the same plot that contained the initial slab units of the Jewish housing project. The program was for forty thousand residents,[145] and whereas the first buildings, completed in early 1956, were exclusively allotted to Moroccan Muslims, later building permits dating around the end of the same year, i.e., shortly after independence, featured the ethnically neutral title "Low-Rent Casablancan Housing." This implies that the later phases of the development were targeted at all populations regardless of origin—"Moroccans [Muslims and Jews] and non-Moroccans [Europeans and others]." These "low-rent" buildings were completed very swiftly by an "entirely Moroccan workforce (except for some supervisory staff)."[146]

"The needy, the homeless, and those who have been evicted from *bidonvilles*, squats, and tenements" were the social groups that were designated by the municipal authority and the Housing Ministry as the future residents of the El Hank development, which was to be managed by the C.I.F.M. The new Ministry of Public Works commissioned the O.T.H. Afrique company to produce plans for an apartment block type (a parallelepiped with access walkways and exterior stairwell) that could be adapted to buildings of thirty-six, forty-eight, or sixty residential units. The plans were signed by J. H. Laure, and permits for seven buildings were issued to Georges Delanoé, Élie Azagury, Isaac Lévy, and Léon Taieb in 1957, but none of these projects was ever built.[147] Technological and financial criteria became a prime concern, as was the case with other experiments in mass production that were carried out simultaneously on the French mainland, and architectural quality was relegated to the back seat.

The term *Garden City,* originally used by the architects for this neighborhood, no longer applied; only a few bits of scrappy lawn were slotted into the interstices between the shops and workshops, the two schools, kindergarten, social services offices, and the sports field, which had been added to the complex. Fortunately, the later buildings were accorded a more favorable exposure than those initially constructed on the site. However, providing shelter from the sun was just one of the issues to be addressed in this area which also has to contend with ocean mist and strong winds as well as unpleasant odors from the nearby sewer outlets. The buildings themselves contain apartments accessed by walkways and exterior stairwells, with small communal rooms adjoined by kitchenettes, closely resembling French public housing of the period. Nonetheless, the combined lavatory and washtub does bear overtones of the more rudimentary French public housing projects of the 1930s, such as the Plessis-Robinson Garden City to the south of Paris.

Delanoé's buildings, built in 1957 along Boulevard Moulay-Youssef on the eastern boundary of Écochard's development, cut more of an urban figure. The same year, the Ministry of Public Works commissioned Laure to build a development in the Plateau extension, and the following year he was asked by the same ministry to design ten slab units identical to those at El Hank. These were erected a few dozen meters from the ATBAT-Afrique buildings in the Carrières Centrales quarter, since named Hay Mohammadi in tribute to the local residents' courage in organizing an anticolonial march on December 7, 1952.[148] Despite—or perhaps

---

145 Delarozière, "Urbanisme."

146 Creugnet, "La cité-jardin de Casablanca" *Travaux Nord-Africains* (Algiers), March 28, 1957.

147 Delanoé requested a building permit for three buildings, Azagury for four, and Levy and Taieb for one. Building permit registers, Wilaya of Greater Casablanca.

148 It was in the Carrières Centrales that the Protectorate's December 1952 crackdown, launched in response to nationalists' actions, resulted in hundreds of deaths. Guy Delanoé, *Lyautey, Juin, Mohammed V: fin d'un protectorat*, 141–46. The ultra-colonialist Michel de la Varde saw the Carrières as a "Genghis-Khan-like town that horrifies all Casablancans." De la Varde, *Casablanca ville d'émeutes*, 18.

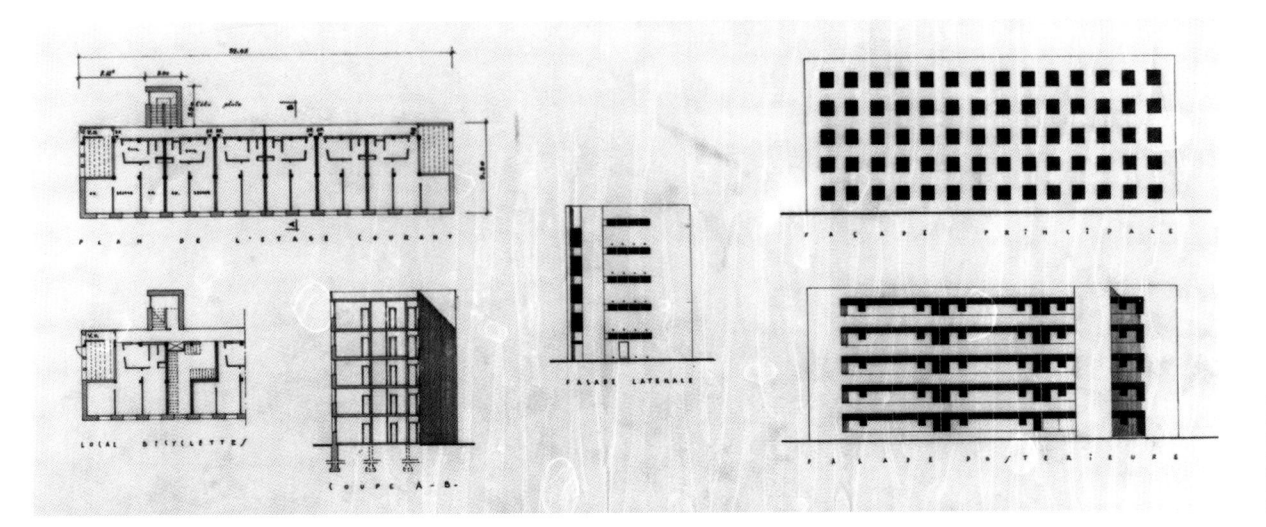

J. H. Laure, low-cost housing, Carrières Centrales and Hay Mohammadi, 1958. Plans and facades of a typical building.

because of—their poor architectural quality, these buildings were adopted as prototypes and were reproduced in other neighborhoods and cities, notably in Tangiers. It was a move that can be interpreted as a prequel to the "policy of constructing model buildings," initiated in the late 1960s in France by the Ministry for Housing and Planning.

Colette Pétonnet has studied the life of Muslim Moroccans in the above types of buildings and comments on their substandard quality not just in terms of architecture but also with respect to living conditions. In so doing, she calls into question the very notion of standardized architecture:

> We asked a Moroccan sociologist her opinion on the families she visits in those huge public housing buildings that lie on the outskirts of Casablanca, lost in the misty land that surrounds the El Hank lighthouse. She replied: "They are of two minds as to whether to set up a *kanoun* or to use the gas range; they aren't complaining, but they are very confused." They aren't complaining because they take what Allah gives them. As for being confused, how could they not be, coming straight from the *bidonvilles* as they do? Overnight, they find themselves without a *zriba* and are continually bumping into their neighbors along the access balcony and on the outside stairs. What is more, they cannot even walk into familiar surroundings once they open their own door.
>
> The apartments were originally designed for Jewish residents. There is a large entrance that also forms the kitchen and that has the same surface area as the two other rooms put together. Not only does one have to step over benches to get from one of the two rooms to the other, but the larger of them, which one enters first, is used for carrying out unclean tasks. This runs totally counter to Moroccan tradition. Moreover, women have no privacy, nor any means of communicating with one another discreetly, since all the corridors are laid out along the facade. As a result, they live in total seclusion. Even their very movements are hampered, given the way in which the household appliances are arranged. It is, in all respects, a true prison.
>
> Looking at Moroccan public housing, one would think it was the suburbs of Paris. There is the same chaos of people and objects. The staircase alone is proof of this. There are the same dirty walls that reach no higher than the average height of a man; there is the same human smell that is characteristic of confined spaces; and there are the same broken and nameless mailboxes that lie wide open, just like the ones we can see so often in French rehousing developments. All of this can only lead to the assumption that the Moroccan people have experienced a total loss of identity.[149]

149 Colette Pétonnet, "Espace, distance, dimension dans une société musulmane," 81–82.

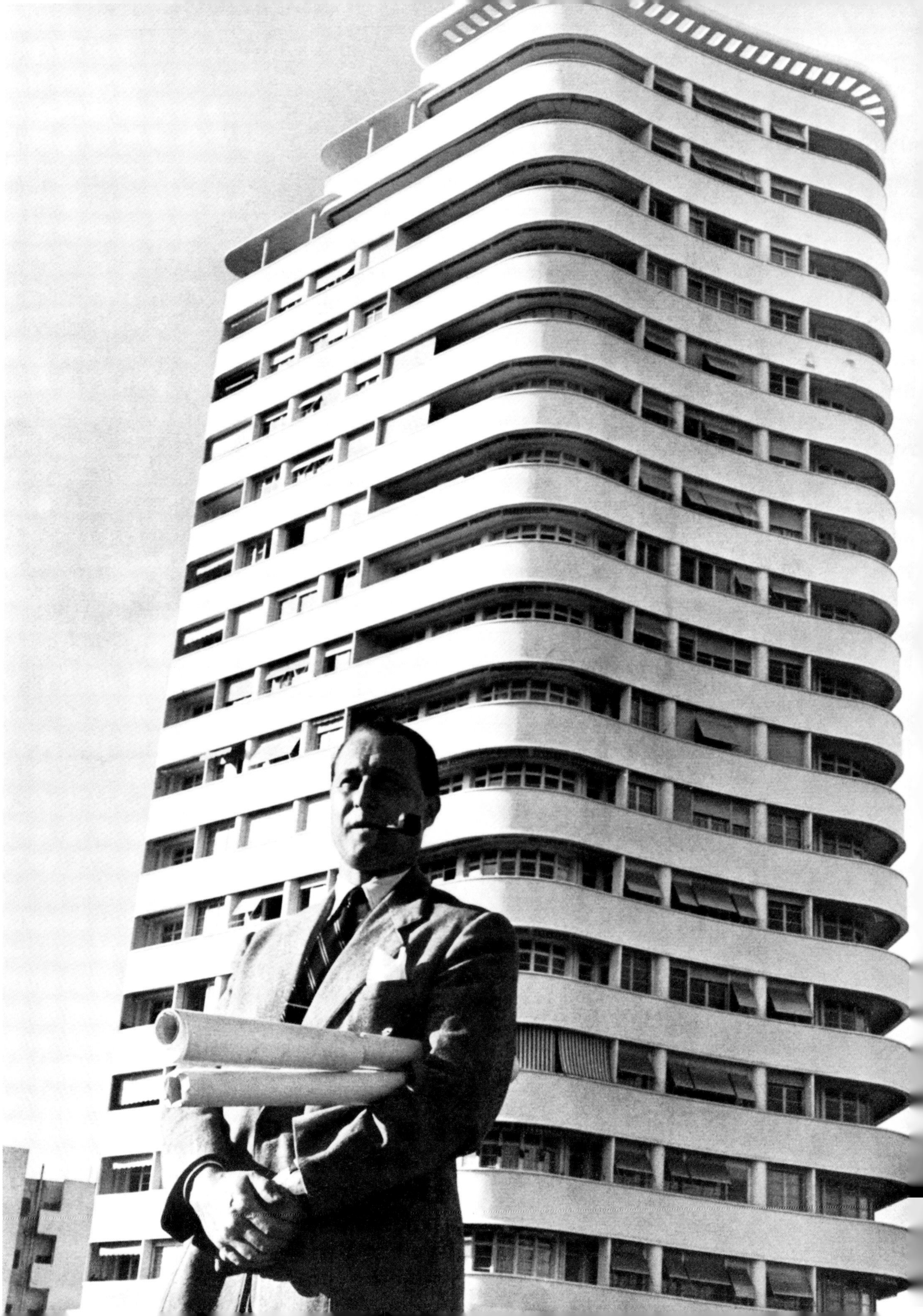

Housing the Europeans

Modernist Housing Schemes for North Africa

It may well be pleasant to live in a beautiful white-walled city of outstanding decorative art, but people still need a roof over their heads.

Maroc-Monde, 1953[1]

Although the number of European residents increased sharply during the 1940s, building output for this sector of the population remained proportionally low. Between 1942, which marked the creation of the Office Chérifien de l'Habitat (Sharifian Housing Office), or O.C.H., and 1950, approximately 2,150 European units were built, representing an average of just 240 per year.[2] The Town Planning Department was aware that it would be "impossible to meet the high housing demand, whatever the scale of works undertaken."[3] In 1949, it was estimated that one thousand units per year had to be built to accommodate the European intake, i.e., double that for the Moroccan community. The following year, Écochard calculated that a total of 35,000 units were required to resolve the overall chronic housing shortage.[4]

Bourgogne Garden City—From Block to Slab Housing

At the same time that the Ain Chock housing development was under construction for the Moroccan working class, the O.C.H. launched the largest public housing project conceived up until that point for the European population. It was a Garden City scheme, sited in the Bourgogne neighborhood, and had nothing in common with Ebenezer Howard's theories on urban decentralization. The residential buildings were to be of high quality and were chiefly dedicated to public servants and to military personnel. Work got under way in 1946 on several buildings, including one by Suraqui and one by Desmet, both on Boulevard des Régiments Coloniaux.[5] However, the true core of this quarter is made up of the buildings constructed the following year on a triangular plot. These had to comply with a number of specifications laid out in the development's brief. For example, the structures had to be low-rise, ranged in accordance with the existing street pattern, and grouped in open-angled blocks.

The diverse design languages of these buildings bear witness to the range of architects involved in the project[6]—Boyer, Michelet, Aroutcheff, Duhon, the

Opposite
Léonard Morandi in front of the Liberté building. Photo published in *Réalités,* January 1953.

Bourgogne quarter. Aerial view, postcard, c. 1950. Note the Chassagne building in the foreground and the Wates houses in the background.

1 M. Laurent, "Le problème crucial du logement à Casablanca," *Maroc-Monde* (Casablanca), March 28, 1953.

2 "From 1940 to 1949, the O.C.H. built 28 apartment buildings, 97 cabins, 140 villas, 95 Wates double villas in Casablanca, in other words 2,090 dwellings and 58 bachelor apartments." Girard, "Note sur l'habitat européen," March 2, 1953, MAE, Civilian Cabinet, carton 122, Habitat européen. Three times as many dwellings were built for Moroccans during the same time period.

3 Girard, "L'habitat au Maroc."

4 Écochard, "Urbanisme et construction pour le plus grand nombre," 5. This number took into account a very high density of occupancy—five persons per dwelling.

5 Fleurant and Renaudin built the corner buildings; Zéligson and Aroutcheff were responsible for a building on the nearby Rue Thimonnier; Zaleski worked on one on Rue de Catalogne. MAE, Ministry of Public Works, Circonscription de l'urbanisme et de l'habitat, 35, OCHE, 1946–52.

6 This intervention was closer to contemporary Parisian *Zones d'amenagement concerté* (mixed-use urban development zones), which combine urban unity with architectural diversity, than to Haussmannian developments.

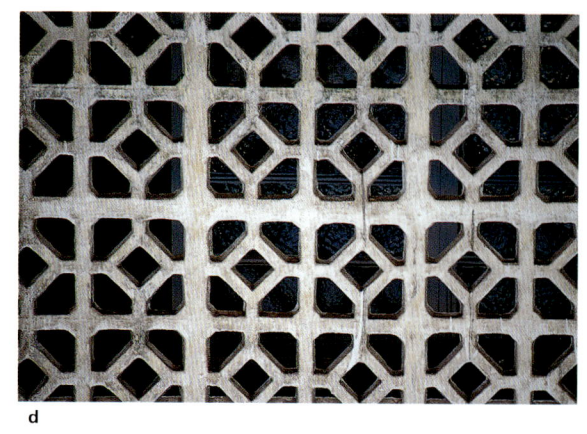

a. Ain Chock, c. 1946. Photo 1994.

b. Ain Chock, c. 1946. Photo 1994.

c. Pierre Chassagne, apartment building, Boulevard Foch (Bourgogne quarter), 1948. Photo 1996.

d. 21 Rue Bouardel (Bourgogne quarter), c. 1948. Photo 1993.

e. 19 Rue Bouardel (Bourgogne quarter), c. 1948. Photo 1994.

f. Pierre Chassagne, apartment building, Boulevard Foch (Bourgogne quarter), 1948. Photo 1996.

Pierre Chassagne, apartment building commissioned by O.C.H., Boulevard Joffre, 1948. Facade overlooking the boulevard. Photographed in 1995.

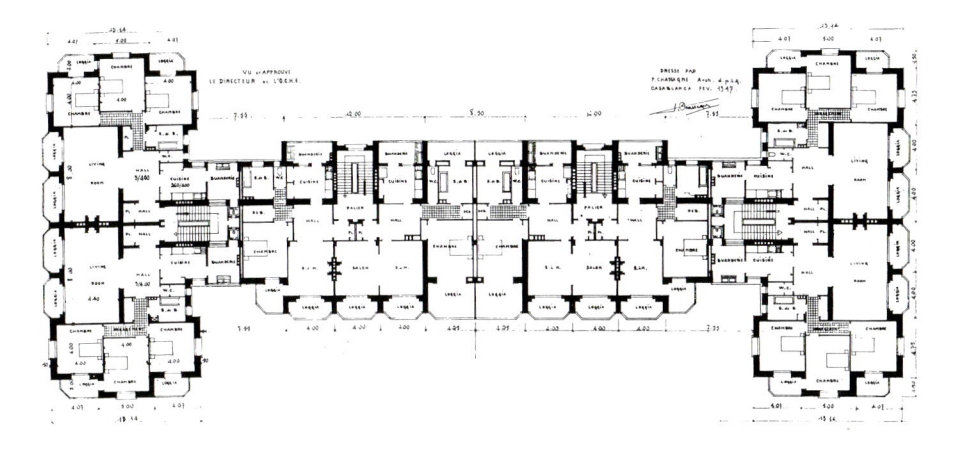

Pierre Chassagne, apartment building, Boulevard Joffre, 1948. Standard floor plan, in *L'Architecture française*, May 1950. Most of the service rooms in the apartments open onto the garden, while the main rooms overlook the boulevard or adjacent streets. Inside, the entrance leads into a hall which acts as a pivotal distribution point. Each room has a good-sized floor area and all the bathrooms receive natural light.

Gourdains, Renaudin, Sori, the veteran Bousquet, who was responsible for designing a kindergarten on the boulevard, and even Hinnen, who had relatively little experience in working on this type of program.[7] Regardless of personal style and doctrinal positions, all the architects conformed to the O.C.H. design charter, which generated a sense of overall cohesion. Each building contains only four or five stories; there are a limited number of apartments per landing; balconies and stairwells are washed with natural light; and screen walls were a requisite, even for those blocks built to a tight budget. In addition, *zillij* panels were used for the door surrounds to convey a modernized version of the neo-Moroccan theme that had lain dormant since the 1930s.[8]

The commission for the initial construction phase of the Bourgogne scheme was given to Boyer, who shortly before his death in 1947 built a service station at the apex of the triangular plot, along with three apartment blocks featuring wrap-style roof ridges with streamlined hip-joints. The development edges the Circular Boulevard leading to the sea and is heralded from this angle by a monumental six-story block constructed by Pierre Chassagne in 1948; designed in the form of an H,

7 "Permis de construire," *L'Entreprise au Maroc*, June 1948.

8 Weilenmann took up the use of *zillij* in the decoration around the door of his Rue Bouardel building. MAE, Ministry of Public Works, Circonscription de l'urbanism e et de l'habitat, 35, OCHE 1946–52.

9 Most of the bedrooms measured sixteen square meters (without the loggia), while the living rooms measured thirty-five square meters. The kitchens—over ten square meters—were connected to large laundry rooms and adjacent servants' bathrooms. The hallways were fitted with storage cabinets. "Immeuble de rapport, cité-jardin du quartier Bourgogne à Casablanca, P. Chassagne, architecte," *L'Architecture française* 10, no. 95–96 (November–December 1949): 62–64.

10 "Immeubles locatifs à Casablanca (OCH), Ed. et J. Gourdain architectes dplg," *L'Architecture française* 10, no. 95–96 (November–December 1949): 64–66.

11 Michel Écochard, *Quelques idées sur la politique de l'urbanisme et du logement au Maroc* (1948), MAE, carton 131, Habitat et urbanisme, 1948–51.

12 In practice, these prescriptions affected primarily state-controlled housing.

it can be read as a kind of city gate. Access is via four stairwells, and although it is mainly composed of large apartments, Chassagne did incorporate a number of studio and one-bedroom units for single tenants and young couples. Most of the living rooms and some of the bathrooms are adjoined by loggias and screen-walled balconies, which together with brise-soleil make for a highly sculpted facade.[9] In proposals for two buildings positioned around a children's playground on Rue Sauvage, architects Edmond and Jean Gourdain decided "to use screen walls extensively" to embellish the rear facade and also "to conceal the kitchens and laundry rooms from public view." A striking feature of this scheme is the deliberate concentration of water-serviced rooms on the northern side of the apartments, at the rear, "leaving the southern side free for living space."[10]

Multiple corner buildings provide a break in scale while reducing the impression of excessive density; at the time, this drew outspoken criticism from Écochard, who characterized all the hundred or so buildings of Bourgogne as the epitome of "a hackneyed academic style":

> This housing project was a perfect opportunity for the Protectorate to research original design solutions and new economic building methods. However, rather than contributing to innovations in architecture and planning, the O.C.H. encouraged a number of architects to indulge in intellectual laziness when they should have been seeking to create new forms for Morocco, even though these may already have been tried and tested elsewhere.[11]

This caustic criticism was leveled both at the excessive ground area taken up by the street system—a pet peeve of Écochard's—and the priority accorded to street alignment rather than optimal orientation. Furthermore, the interior layout principles stemmed from a more traditional design approach than those upheld by proponents of the modern movement, due largely to the fact that the program did not provide for minimum housing. Écochard further maintained that space was poorly utilized and that an alternative approach could have resulted in buildings "with the same amount of land and set in vast grounds." He also drew attention to what he termed "shopworn symmetrical design" and deplored the needlessly "complicated plans," which ruled out the possibility of using "standard formulae" to create "standardized living units."

It should be noted that as early as 1949 the Town Planning Department had adopted a similar stance when it stipulated that developments should not contain enclosed courtyards or include buildings ranged along streets—time-honored features of Casablancan architecture. It also banned open courtyards, another common design element. Projects began to hinge more and more on slab housing, and architects and planners became increasingly preoccupied with the issue of sunlight. Écochard thus recommended that slab buildings with a maximum ceiling height of three meters be constructed in neighborhoods that had hitherto been characterized by private villas. In addition, green space and children's playgrounds protected from traffic became standard elements.[12] In 1953 and 1954, pressure from Écochard's department resulted in the construction of a number of slab buildings, "rationally" oriented on a vacant plot in the Bourgogne neighborhood, close to the original triangular development. Today, with the benefit of hindsight, Écochard's scheme of slabs set in open ground appears hopelessly inadequate—both in terms of the quality of building design and of the surrounding open space—when compared to the developments Écochard took it upon himself to criticize. It was a scheme that formed the basis of the Bournazel development, which falls far short of the Bourgogne development, whose design qualities are apparent to this day.

Écochard's criticism was accompanied by a chorus of disapproval regarding the financial aspects of the project, mirroring the objections that had been voiced

Joseph Suraqui, apartment building commissioned by O.C.H., Boulevard des Régiments Coloniaux and Boulevard Joffre, 1946. Corner view. The building contains forty-two units, thirty-six of which are one-bedrooms. There are two bachelor apartments and two studio apartments with a kitchen, bathroom, laundry room, and storage room, and four two-bedrooms. The main entrance lobby has a spectacular circular staircase and *zillij* tilework.

Joseph Suraqui, apartment building, Boulevard des Régiments Coloniaux and Boulevard Joffre, 1946. The stairs. Photographed in 1997.

13 Girard, the director of Public Works, announced the housing survey to the delegate to the Residency General, October 31, 1949, MAE, délégué à la Résidence générale, carton 131, Habitat et urbanisme, 1948–51. See also the perforated cards of the housing quality surveys and the commentaries of the Direction of the Interior in MAE, Délégué à la Résidence générale, carton 132, Habitat européen, 1953. Delaroziére commented on the results of one survey: "For the Europeans, the survey of inadequately housed populations produced the number of 7,816 families for Casablanca." Delaroziére, "Urbanisme."

14 M. Costantini, letter to Resident-General Guillaume, February 24, 1953, MAE, Civilian Cabinet, carton 122, Habitat européen.

15 Finès to office of resident-general, MAE, Civilian Cabinet, carton 122, Habitat européen.

16 In an act that was completely unprecedented and contrary to the principles put into practice by the Housing Department, this endeavor provisionally (and after lengthy discussion) took the majority of funds necessary for the projects from money destined for Moroccan housing. The European section of the Service had been eliminated in 1949, as private initiatives were meant to replace public activity. Meeting minutes of the February 20, 1953, meeting with the C.I.F.M. and M. de Chalendar, MAE, Civilian Cabinet, carton 122, dossier Habitat européen.

about Ain Chock. The development was deemed too luxurious and not at all suited to the needs of a European population battling to cope with a chronic housing shortage; moreover, its street system was considered unnecessarily complex and costly. The impact of this criticism was compounded by a survey that drew attention to insalubrious conditions in many homes of the European population.[13] In 1953, the chairman of the Moroccan branch of the Fédération des associations familiales françaises addressed a petition to Resident-General Guillaume, stressing the urgent need to construct mid-range dwellings for families "who are forced to live in sheds or in overcrowded and unsanitary tenements."[14] The "growing discontent of the middle classes" prompted the Residency to contact the C.I.F.M. directly to provide "basic but salubrious two-bedroom lodgings" for low-income European families.[15] Hence plans were drawn up for "rudimentary five-story buildings that comply with the new standards recommended for publicly-subsidized collective housing."[16]

Housing the Europeans 369

17 Girard, "Note sur l'habitat européen."

18 The Protectorate secretary general's order of April 10, 1951, replaced the June 20, 1932, *dahir* (the first *dahir* regarding mortgage loans and construction supervision dated from July 4, 1928), MAE, Délégué à la Résidence générale, carton 131, Habitat et urbanisme, 1948–51.

19 Girard, "Résumé des considérations relatives à l'habitat européen," January 16, 1953, MAE, Civilian Cabinet, carton 122, Dossier habitat Maroc. Standard sizes for low-rent housing were: one room, 32m^2; two rooms, 46m^2; and three rooms, 57m^2. At the time, the norms in England were: 30m^2; 44m^2; and 51m^2, respectively; while in Germany they were: 28m^2; 38m^2; and 45m^2.

20 Godefroy, "Problèmes d'habitat de type européen," 46.

21 Courtois would be joined by Coldefy, who in 1964 built eight villas at the district's edge, along what was then Boulevard Gandhi.

22 The surface areas of the three-, four-, and five-room villas were 80m^2, 120m^2, and 140m^2, respectively. "Lotissement Beaulieu," in *Le Maroc moderne: architecture et urbanisme.*

Alexandre Courtois, Beaulieu housing complex, Boulevard des Crêtes, 1953–55. General aerial view in 1962.

Above left is the Plateau scheme.

A total of five thousand units were deemed necessary for the project, and as a result the state and commercial property developers set about drafting programs based on an unprecedented scale.[17] These programs proved less problematic than previous ones, given that French public housing prototypes could be readily adapted to the local climatic conditions. Furthermore, the housing problem was eased somewhat by the slowdown in European population growth, brought on by the political uncertainty that shrouded the dying days of the Protectorate. Nonetheless, the administration pushed ahead with its venture of funding low-rent collective housing and individual dwellings.[18] An especially attractive offer was extended to war veterans, whereby an architect-designed standard plan and on-site supervision could be purchased as an overall package. Analysis of the floor areas indicated on the plans reveals that there was a tendency to encourage the building of small, detached suburban homes. Furthermore, as previously mentioned, the inhabitants of Casablanca demanded a greater level of comfort than their counterparts in France, which resulted in large floor areas for units in such projects as the Beaulieu development, then under construction. In fact, the dwellings were so large in comparison to French public housing developments that, in 1953, Girard was compelled to remind architects of the standard floor areas prescribed by the Ministry for Reconstruction and Urban Planning. He further observed: "In most countries a fifty-square-meter unit is considered sufficient to comfortably accommodate four people, whereas here, seventy square meters is the established minimum, and even that is thought to be too small."[19]

From then on, floor area standards were more strictly applied in state-funded projects. Yet it is important to remember that European residents in Casablanca—a stable, employed segment of the population—held much more sway with regard to planning decisions than rural Moroccan newcomers. Also, other variables such as changes in living patterns (i.e., rural-urban shifts) had to be taken into account in housing policy. It was on this basis that Georges Godefroy (Écochard's head planner for Casablanca) focused both on architectural aesthetics and the social life

Alexandre Courtois, Beaulieu housing complex, Boulevard des Crêtes, 1953–55. "Block 14." Photographed in 1992.

The slab building contains forty bachelor apartments, each measuring 29m², as well as thirty two-bedroom apartments of 73m², and ten three-bedroom apartments of 100m². These last have eight bicycle sheds and four terraces for the drying of laundry.

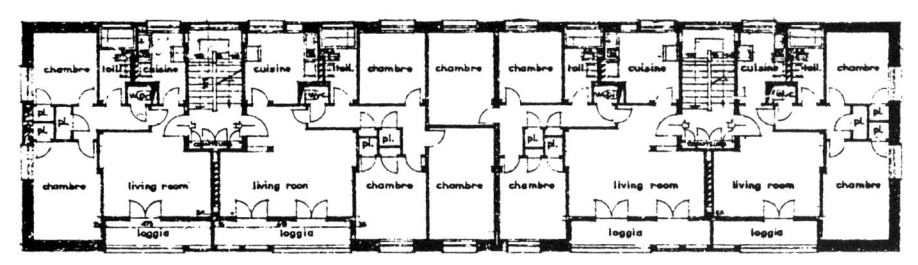

Alexandre Courtois, Beaulieu housing complex, Boulevard des Crêtes, 1953–55. Standard floor plan of "Block 10" as featured in the building permit.

Alexandre Courtois, Beaulieu housing complex, Boulevard des Crêtes, 1953–55. Playground.

Alexandre Courtois, Beaulieu housing complex, Boulevard des Crêtes, 1953–55. Circulation gallery in one of the slab buildings. Photographed in 1992.

The building includes eight studio apartments of 34m², sixteen one-bedroom apartments of 48m², and three two-bedroom units of 68m².

within the various neighborhoods.[20] However, both in Casablanca and elsewhere in Morocco, funds for the cultural facilities featured in the various plans were withheld until more affluent days, or were never allocated at all. On top of this, commercial facilities were limited to just a few small clusters of shops.

Toward Industrialization—From Beaulieu to Bournazel

Work began on several large developments for mid-to-low wage earners, including the remarkably successful Beaulieu project—a genuine *Siedlung* set among eucalyptus trees. Yet others, like the Bournazel project, were just as shoddy as the worst French public housing of the period, even though these schemes were closely tracked by the Town Planning Department.

The Beaulieu low-rent development, designed by Alexandre Courtois and built by the O.T.H. Afrique company between 1953 and 1955, occupies a site along Boulevard des Crêtes. Commissioned by the C.I.F.M., it was designed for singles, young couples, and families. The scheme includes five-story slab buildings, low-rise blocks, and several detached houses. Three slab units (comprising 240 dwellings fitted with shower rooms) were erected in the first phase, while the second phase was dedicated to two-, three-, and four-bedroom villas,[21] each with its own garden and outbuilding, measuring a generous fifty square meters.[22] The larger houses of this type were equipped with good-sized bathrooms as well as ancillary rooms containing showers and washbasins. The third phase was given over to the construction of six four-story slabs accessed by open walkways and set perpendicular to the considerably longer buildings of the first phase. All 160 units of this third construction phase were classified as low-rent housing, even though their usable floor areas exceeded those specified by public housing standards.

Six other slab buildings followed, as well as a circular covered market and a kindergarten, which is marked by square-shaped screens that are prevalent throughout Courtois's work, conveying a restrained geometric language. Fourteen buildings were constructed altogether, comprising four hundred blocks and thirty-

Housing the Europeans 371

Albert Lucas, Henri Grémeret, and Gaston Jaubert, Bournazel housing complex, 1956. Aerial view. Photographed in 1962.

23 The five-room units had a bathroom and water closet with shower. Private and public spaces were well separated, with a hierarchical arrangement of two bedrooms (9.2 to 12.6 square meters in size) and a large "living room" opening onto a loggia.

24 *L'œuvre du CIL au Maroc.*

25 In 1955, 4,500 people lived in the 371 villas and the sixteen apartment buildings that had been built, and they made use of the new neighborhood's two commercial centers and schools.

26 P. Guillet, "Le CILM de Casablanca inaugure son lotissement d'Ain Sebaa, fait connaître au public ses travaux et leur résultats," *Construire* 14 (1951): 961–64. See also "Réalisations à Casablanca, 1er trimestre 1951," *Construire* 14 (1951): 960.

27 Plans in Archives du Génie, CDG Maroc, Casablanca 18, Camp de Bournazel, 1945–50.

three villas set in open green space. The development's pergolas, trees, and well-tended flora make it seem more like a forest settlement than a large urban complex. The plans drawn up for the final-phase dwellings were very cutting-edge, and even prefigured some of the best interior layouts of 1970s French public housing.[23]

In 1951, the Comité Interprofessionnel du Logement (C.I.L.) built a development west of the Beaulieu scheme, in Anfa-Beauséjour, whose serviced plots were sold at cost to clients of "limited financial resources." This neighborhood, simply named the C.I.L., lies "behind Anfa hill, sheltered from the mist and sea breezes,"[24] and is composed of villas and apartment blocks. It has a Garden City atmosphere, which is partly due to its distance from the hustle and bustle of the city, as well as to its carefully designed road system in which main streets, secondary accesses, and blind alleys follow a clearly defined, hierarchic pattern. By means of this circulation system, Écochard's team was able to keep traffic away from the central green space.[25] The Germaine development, also constructed by the C.I.L. but on the other side of Casablanca, in Ain Sebaa, was dedicated more to working-class residents. It encompasses individual dwellings and apartment blocks, four of which serve as a buffer against the ocean mist and strong winds. Philippe Boniface led the official opening ceremony in November 1951, in the company of Écochard, who later recalled that the development had been "constructed according to the principles of the Athens Charter": "dwelling, work, recreation, and transportation."[26]

In 1954, the C.I.F.M. embarked on the Bournazel development, the largest housing scheme at the time in Casablanca, siting it on a former U.S. army base south of the Rabat freeway.[27] It was designed for white-collar employees and lower management and largely reflects the advanced thinking that was then being expressed at a number of events, including the fourth North African Congress of Building and

Public Works, during which the Casablancan architect Émile Duhon drew attention to cost-reduction guidelines for European housing. In Duhon's view, building "minimum units" called for "standardizing building methods," grouping services in a core, and eliminating corridor space. In addition, he emphasized the need to mass-produce construction components and elements such as bathrooms and service areas. Adopting a functionalist strategy, Duhon also recommended that furniture be taken into account in the interior layout, both in terms of its positioning and the space it would take up.[28]

The Bournazel development was designed by Albert Lucas, Henri Grémeret, and Gaston Jaubert, who based their scheme on rational building techniques and drew on prefabricated, mass-produced components, not just for the structural frames of the buildings, but also the finishes.[29] This preoccupation with mass production, regardless of the contextual framework, perhaps accounts for the scheme's visible lack of focus on the architecture itself. Its repetitive design can be attributed to the architects' preoccupation with "an aspect we consider primordial, namely, basic-form construction components."[30] As the design teams themselves even admitted, some of the methods used, notably the floor formwork, "led to substantial constraints during the planning stage."[31] As for the chairman of the C.I.F.M., he was thrilled that only one door type and two window types were used in the initial 1,666 units.

The program specified construction of 2,500 one- to four-bedroom units to accommodate some 10,000 residents; by 1957, 1,700 of these had been filled. The developers' aim was to create a full-scale town, which explains why the scheme was targeted at various classes. Jaubert and Grémeret were assigned two "deluxe" programs,[32] while Lucas, who teamed up with Courtois, designed "standard buildings" for the low-income program; it was the latter scheme that was most scrutinized by the media.[33]

Two shopping areas were included in the program, along with administrative buildings, schools, and artisan workshops, all of which were surrounded by sports fields and playgrounds. In addition, the development was located a safe distance away from traffic, which drew praise from critics.[34] Although the development was originally intended for European residents, Moroccans soon moved in, and Duhon built a *hammam* there in 1960. Yet in spite of all this, the long and repetitive slab buildings, dotted with tower blocks on a bald and dusty "green space," differed in no way whatsoever from the shabbiest and most segregated French housing complexes of the time.

28 Ways of grouping housing "cells" so as to eliminate costly stairhalls were discussed. Buildings of ten stories or more were encouraged, in order to avoid less economical, lower structures. "Rapport de la première commission au IVe Congrès nord-africain du Bâtiment et des Travaux-Publics, Tunis, 25–30 April 1950," *Construire* 13 (May 25, 1950): 471–72. The commission was composed of architects.

29 "We did our best to *type* to the limit the various construction components, in order to obtain large series of identical elements." R. Durand, "La cité Bournazel de Casablanca, étude et réalisation d'un ensemble de 1700 logements," *Annales de l'ITBTP*, no. 109 (January 1957): 7.

30 Pierre Lions, ibid., 30. Lions was the technical director of OTH-Afrique.

31 Durand, "La cité Bournazel," 8.

32 The three-room units measured 73 square meters, while the four-room units measured 90 square meters. Durand, "La cité Bournazel," 5.

33 "Cité d'habitation de Bournazel, à Casablanca, Albert Lucas, architecte," *L'Architecture française* 16, no. 163–64 (1955): 28.

34 Jaubert worked on the administrative and commercial center situated to the west, as well as on the schools, discussed below. Grémeret was responsible for the shopping complex and the artisanal workshops located to the east. Udo Kultermann ranked this operation among the most remarkable works of his contemporaries in *Architecture of Today: A Survey of New Building Throughout the World* (London: Zwemmer, 1958), 42.

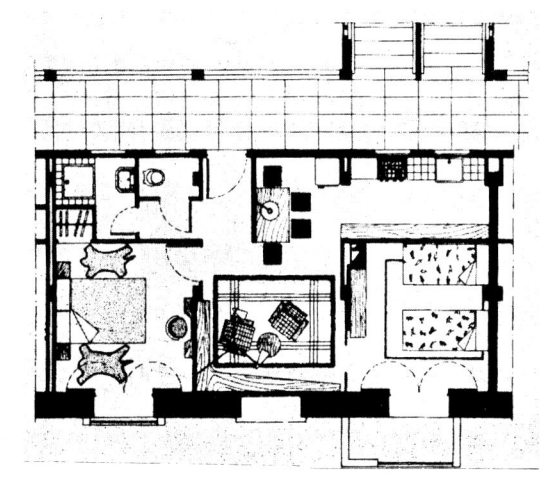

Albert Lucas, Bournazel housing complex, 1956. Facade of one of the east-west buildings, in *Annales de l'ITBTP*, January 1957.

There are two apartments on each floor of the east-west buildings, accessed by several staircases. Some of the apartments have two bedrooms, others three and four.

Albert Lucas, Bournazel housing complex, 1956. Plan of a two-bedroom apartment in one of the east-west buildings published in *Annales de l'ITBTP*, January 1957. In the two-bedroom unit, the living room opens onto the kitchen and children's bedroom. In the through-apartments, the utility rooms are grouped together and the kitchen is extended outside by a laundry room with a washtub on the loggia. There is only one shower, even in the four-bedroom units, and the living room is not much bigger than the largest bedroom.

35 See *Maroc-Demain* (Casablanca), November 24, 1951; " Cité des jeunes à Casablanca," *L'Architecture d'aujourd'hui* 24, no. 46 (February–March 1953): 41; "Recherches pour des logements économiques par ATBAT-Afrique," *L'Architecture d'aujourd'hui* 26, no. 60 (June 1955): 41; and "Logements pour jeunes ménages à Casablanca. R. Maddalena, architecte E.D.B.A.," *L'Architecture française* 13, no. 131–32 (November–December 1952): 22.

36 The rents were not to exceed 12 percent of average salaries. "Cité des Jeunes," in *Le Maroc moderne: architecture et urbanisme.*

37 *L'œuvre du CIL au Maroc.*

38 These included seven buildings (containing 61 apartments for singles and 212 units for young couples), which were supplemented by spaces for social services such as a "young woman's hall," a room for medical visits, and the offices of the Franco-Moroccan Mutual Aid Group.

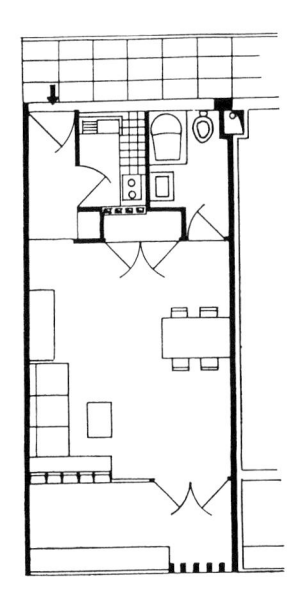

The Cité des Jeunes—Segregation by Status

When public decision-makers announced in 1955 that they intended to combine detached houses, small apartment blocks, and large slabs set in open ground, they were clearly endeavoring, somewhat late in the day, to combat neighborhood segregation. As described earlier, Casablanca's residential districts were not merely structured according to religious conviction, ethnic background, and nationality, but also by social station. Whereas a true mix had been achieved in some centrally located districts, in general, the working-class Spanish and Italians lived in the Maarif and Roches Noires, the mid-income Muslims in the new medina and Ain Chock, well-to-do Muslims in Le Polo, the European middle classes in Beauséjour and Beaulieu, and affluent Europeans and Jews in Anfa. Many shopkeepers and artisans from diverse backgrounds lived in the center of the *ville nouvelle,* except for Moroccan Muslims, who resided in ad hoc areas sited quite a way from their shops.

Division by age and status was also apparent. For instance, housing for young single residents and young married couples built both by the public sector and by private companies was set amid housing reserved for public servants. In view of this context, the competition staged in 1951 for the Cité des Jeunes in Casablanca received widespread attention, both in Morocco and in France.[35] The idea behind the program was hatched by Édouard Gouin, head of SOCICA and whose role within the municipal council has been described in an earlier chapter, with funding provided jointly by the employers' federation, the state, the Franco-Moroccan Mutual Aid Group, the C.I.L., and the young residents themselves. The thus-formed Cité des Jeunes companies were employee-shareholder limited liability companies, with the shareholders "considered priority tenants." These companies aimed to provide housing for low-income private-sector employees whose restricted financial resources were essentially due to "the discrepancy between their salaries and the cost of rented accommodations."[36]

A number of clear guiding principles were established to "provide affordable standardized units for low and average wage earners" while "blending the site with nature," "severing vehicular flows," and "orienting the buildings south and east."[37] Two developments of this type were built in Beauséjour[38] and Ain Sebaa, including

Léon Aroutcheff and Robert Jean, apartment buildings for single residents in Cité des Jeunes (C.I.L.), Avenue de l'Île-de-France, Beauséjour, 1952. Plan of type C housing, in *L'Architecture d'aujourd'hui*, February 1953.

Cité des Jeunes (C.I.L.). Facade of one of the buildings. Photographed in 1994. The buildings comprise twelve to fourteen units per floor, including 88 studio apartments of 34m² for single residents and 104 units of 55m² for young married couples.

apartment blocks designed by Aroutcheff and Jean (in partnership with Candilis and Woods), which comprise studio apartments for single residents and apartments for young couples with children. Exterior staircases and open walkways link the three levels; the apartments are devoid of partitions, thus freeing up space in the smaller apartments: "The entire apartment is open plan (except for the shower unit and kitchen), and is sectioned off by multifunctional furnishings to create individual spaces that include an entrance area, dining space, recreation area, work area, socializing space, lounge area and a sleeping zone."[39]

All the water-serviced rooms are grouped so that one shaft can be used for two apartments, a technique that was lauded as an innovation at the time. Each apartment was fitted with an en suite bathroom containing a minimal bath, while kitchen fixtures included cupboards and a range hood. The interior layout is particularly noteworthy: the architects used purpose-designed furniture such as sideboards, bookcases, cupboards, and wardrobes as partitioning, asserting that this served "to furnish the apartments while reducing usable floor space to the bare minimum." The apartment building was a true testing ground, helped perhaps by the fact that the developers were counting on the ability of young residents to adapt more swiftly to new design solutions. "Wide loggias, glazed walls, south-facing brise-soleil, and north-facing ventilation openings [were similarly included] to deal with Casablanca's unusual climate of burning hot summers, cold winters, and high humidity."[40]

Robert Maddalena, who was awarded second prize in the competition,[41] was entrusted with two programs in the project: the premises for the Franco-Moroccan Mutual Aid Group and three buildings called Cité 3 des Jeunes, which were to be composed of eighty-six "upgraded" apartments spread over three blocks and dedicated to lower management and young employees. "Upgraded" refers not so much to the size of the units (forty-nine square meters) as to their ancillary facilities of balconies and laundries, since these in effect increase the floor area by one-third. All the main rooms face south, and, to quote the *Le Maroc moderne* review, "the kitchen was delivered with a serving hatch and range hood." The same publication commented on how "access to the domestic quarters is tastefully discreet," together with the fact

39 "Notice descriptive des architectes," *L'œuvre du CIL au Maroc.*

40 *L'œuvre du CIL au Maroc.*

41 The other entrants in the competition were Basciano, Debroise, and Coldefy. "Quand le social rejoint l'économique," *Maroc-Demain* (Casablanca) November 24, 1951, 1, 4.

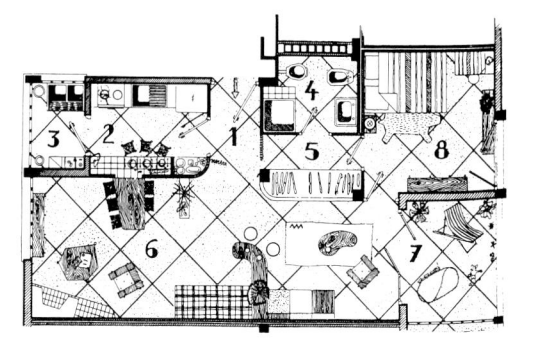

Robert Maddalena, "Improved housing" in Cité des Jeunes (C.I.L.), Avenue de l'Île-de-France, Beauséjour, 1952. Facade. Photographed in 1991. On the right is the staircase of one of the L-shaped buildings by Léon Aroutcheff and Robert Jean.

Robert Maddalena, "Improved housing" in Cité des Jeunes (C.I.L.). Plan of a unit for a young married couple with one child, in *L'Architecture française*, April 1952.

Housing the Europeans 375

that "the living room can be divided into two separate areas to accommodate sleeping arrangements."[42] The fireplace, "dressing area," and dining room with through views and a terrace were also presented at the time as indicators of the scheme's quality design, as was Maddalena's sound-insulation system.

The type of spatial distribution employed in the scheme was far ahead of the times and actually falls within the realm of 1990s thinking on high-standard apartment blocks. In an article dedicated to the same project, *Construire* recalled Écochard's slogan "cars have taken over the road, so now let housing turn them away." The journalist then goes on to say that as Casablanca's "major vehicular flows will skirt the housing settlements," it will be possible to "locate buildings in pleasant surroundings, thus dispensing with the prevalent 'mining village' type of the Maarif quarter."[43]

Luxurious Austerity in Military Housing

Housing programs for public servants also increased in number during this period, and were generally conceived as small apartment blocks or discreet slab units.[44] The largest of these projects was the Maréchal Lyautey development, constructed by Maurice Galamand for the Office chérifien de l'habitat militaire (Sharifian Military Housing Office) between 1949 and 1953. It is sited on a large plot in the Mers-Sultan district and is composed of five buildings that contain over two hundred one- to four-bedroom apartments. Bearing in mind that officers would be accustomed to individual dwellings and luxury interiors, Galamand favored spatial distribution and interior fixtures over floor area. The scheme responded to "new needs in family and domestic life, in that each unit contains a totally separate bedroom and more direct links between the kitchen and lounge area."[45]

The apartments are comfortable and spacious (the one-bedrooms measure a minimum of eighty-four square meters), and were delivered with fixtures and fittings. The development is located in the heart of central Casablanca, and its towering screen-wall facade was designed to contrast sharply with the neighboring low-rise buildings. It also has its own shopping facilities, school, and garage with one hundred parking spaces. French publications underlined the qualitative aspects of this comfortable housing block, focusing in particular on its "masterly layout and superb interior fixtures."[46]

In the meantime, the Army Engineer Corps designed and built slab housing on the outskirts of the city center for the peacekeeping forces that were called in during the mid-1950s to control the outbreak of national protests. One such example is the Jean Courtin barracks sited on the Circular Boulevard. The end of the Protectorate was thus marked by a stronger military presence, ironically mirroring the 1907 landings. In 1955, the army requisitioned two projects (Anfa II and Anfa III) to provide housing for the mobile police unit. These projects, which were supposed to form a huge condominium complex of twenty-six buildings, had been launched by the C.I.L. in the Hippodrome district, and were actually under construction at the time they were requisitioned.[47] The Anfa real-estate firm had been assigned the management of the project, and the commission had been won by Sucom (the Swiss Construction Company of Morocco), which began work on the site in 1953. As for the master plan of the neighborhood, this was done by Pierre Pelletier and W. Yvkoff from the Town Planning Department. The Anfa II and III schemes were designed by the Geneva-based architects A. Bordigoni and R. Fleury,[48] who took the new army housing brief into account when working on Anfa III, adding studio apartments to those intended for young couples and families.[49] This latter scheme encompassed eleven buildings that were constructed using prefabricated concrete components; completed in 1956,

---

42 *Le Maroc moderne: architecture et urbanisme*. In 1954, Maddalena would collaborate with the Urban Planning Service and the C.I.L. on the construction of seventy-five dwellings that constituted the beginnings of a Cité des Jeunes in the Germaine section of Ain Sebaa, five hundred meters from the sea. This housing block was built using the same techniques as the one at Anfa-Beauséjour. Girard, "Note sur l'habitat européen."

43 Guillet, "Le CILM de Casablanca inaugure son lotissement d'Ain Sebaa," 964.

44 See, for example, the 1953 project for the Housing Service in Bourgogne designed by Desmet, Jaubert, Maillard, and Candilis with ATBAT-Afrique. This development was composed of three buildings containing about one hundred economical units. Each apartment included double exposures, a loggia, and a large kitchen. Another example of average production is A. Planque and R. Deneux's group of three buildings on Rue de Jussieu, built in 1953 for civil servants in the Department of Public Education. See *L'Architecture d'aujourd'hui* 26, no. 60 (June 1955): 51. Alexandre Courtois's more ambitious Cité douanière for customs officers, on Boulevard Camille Desmoulins (1950), grouped housing blocks and a school building. All of the characteristic elements of Courtois's manner are legible in this scheme.

45 "Immeubles d'habitation pour l'Office Chérifien des logements militaires à Casablanca, M. Galamand architecte dplg," *L'Architecture française* 10, no. 95–96 (November–December 1949): 71.

46 "Groupe d'immeuble à Casablanca (Office chérifien des logements militaires)," *L'Architecture française* 13, no. 131–32 (November–December 1952): 18.

47 Requisition order, June 2, 1955, Archives du Génie, CDG Maroc, carton Casablanca 17.

48 The scheme comprised fifteen buildings containing almost two hundred apartments, including 9 two-room units of 50 to 52 square meters, 44 three-room units measuring 65 to 68 square meters, 135 four-room units of 78 to 98 square meters, and 11 five-room units measuring 101 to 116 square meters. Construction was supervised by A. Weilenmann. Archives du Génie, CDG Maroc, carton Casablanca 17.

49 Anfa III included 17 two-room units, 121 three-room units, 29 four-room units, and 19 five-room units. The 186 apartments for couples or families were supplemented with 30 studio units for singles (equipped with individual sinks and collective washrooms). Construction was supervised by R. Lucaud.

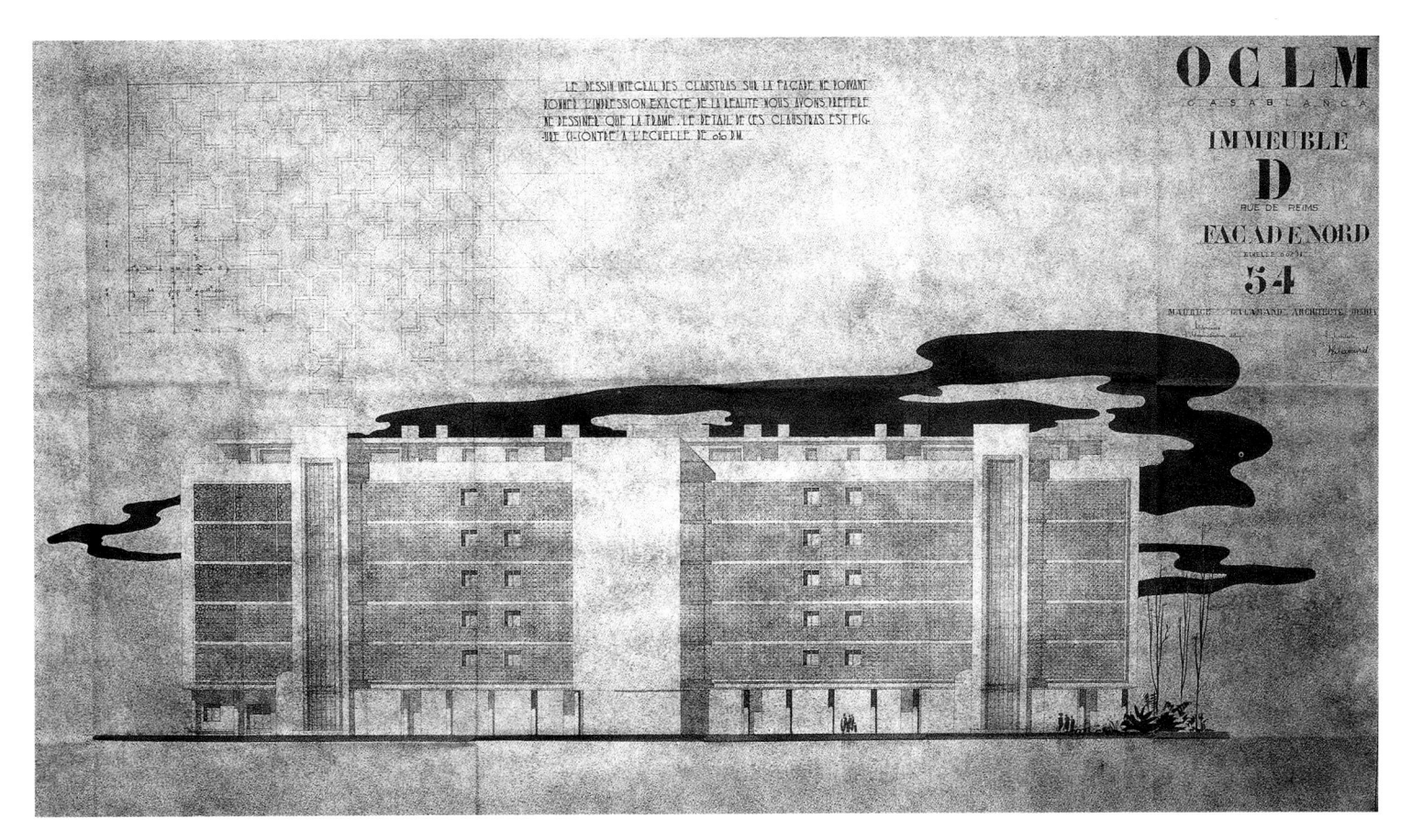

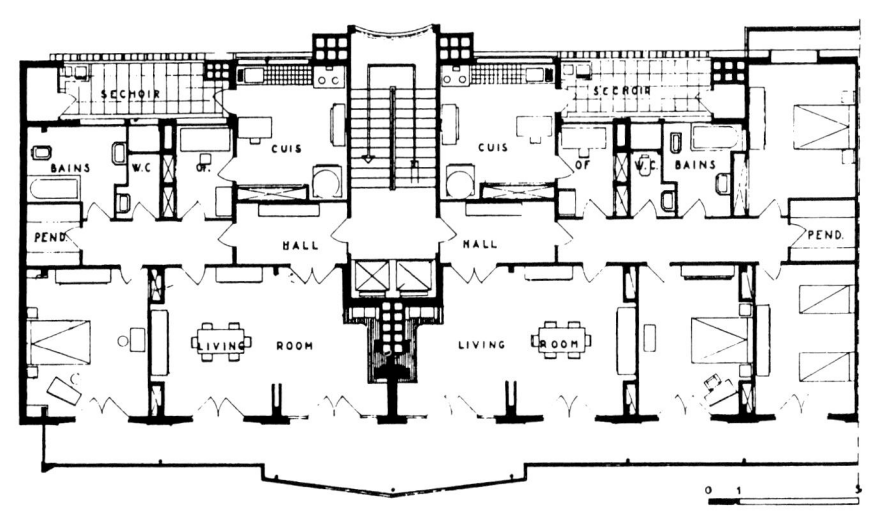

Maurice Galamand, Maréchal Lyautey housing development commissioned by the O.C.L.M., Rue de Damrémont, Rue de Commercy, Rue de Reims, and Rue Lamoricière, 1949–53. Plan of the two- and four-bedroom apartments, in *L'Architecture française*, May 1950.
The kitchen has an adjoining pantry and the hall, or "entrance/cloakroom," leads into the two living rooms. The bedrooms have a wardrobe and cupboard, and a storage room adjoins the laundry.

Maurice Galamand, Maréchal Lyautey housing development, 1949–53. North elevation as featured in the building permit.

A. Bordigoni, R. Fleury, and A. Weilenmann, Anfa II housing complex, Rue Yves de Gueux, 1954. Partial view. Photographed in 1996.

they fueled fierce debate over whether the use of prefabricated materials would result in job losses.[50] The program was widely disputed on a number of other levels, too: not only were there various complaints addressed by the initial co-owners (a number of whom had already moved in) about having to vacate the premises, but the Town Planning Department also failed to acknowledge that the buildings did not come up to modern standards, despite Sucom claiming that they did. The units' fixtures and fittings were considered below par in relation to other Casablancan housing schemes built in the same period, yet the project's cost exceeded that of Bournazel, a virtually identical scheme.[51] In spite of all these problems, the state nonetheless acquired the buildings in 1956.

Adapting Functionally to Different Lifestyles

"Culture-specific" and "class-specific" housing conflicted with the 1950s modernization trend toward universalism which formed the conceptual bedrock for the architects of the modern movement. In essence, these architects were aiming to relativize the differences between cultures with respect to "dwelling," favoring a move toward international architecture and a universal approach to meeting the needs of mankind. This explains how, in their work on European habitat outside France, Candilis and Woods reached the conclusion that the only norms that could possibly be applied were those in the Athens Charter. They observed that "apart from specific requirements such as protection against the heat and humidity, nothing should engender major differences in [architectural] design. Buildings are created by one set of people to achieve one set of goals, that is, allowing mankind to live in dwellings that share the same set of standards."[52] As it was, though, Candilis and Woods simultaneously carried out research on Muslim, Jewish, and European habitat, and successfully argued at the C.I.A.M. held in Aix-en-Provence that dwellings had to be attuned not

---

50 Columns, slabs, joists, load-bearing panels, as well as facade elements were all produced by S.T.I.C. Sucom wrote to the Protectorate secretary general with a description of the workforce employed in the Sidi Abderahman factory in order to counter journalistic attacks. According to its own account, the staff numbered five hundred Moroccan and sixty European workers. Sucom to Protectorate secretary general, July 12, 1955, Archives du Génie, CDG Maroc, carton Casablanca 17.

51 "While the exterior aspect of these buildings is not very felicitous, the apartments themselves are simply mediocre. We might cite the carpentry, the hardware, and the blinds, which are of altogether ordinary quality . . . The closets are narrow . . . There are no washbasins; the water closets are generally located within the bathrooms. There are no terraces. In a word, these apartments are of just barely average appearance, outfitted with only the indispensable minimum." P. Parinet and Clos, "Expertise des immeubles des groupes immobiliers Anfa II et III," Service de l'urbanisme et de l'habitat, June 24, 1955, Archives du Génie, CDG Maroc, carton Casablanca 17. The square meter costs of each project were, in the currency then used, 17,000 francs for Anfa and 14,400 francs for Bournazel. Inserting the toilet into the bathroom is considered by the French to be a feature of extreme low-cost housing.

52 Georges Candilis and Shadrach Woods, "Problèmes d'habitat européen hors de la métropole," L'Architecture d'aujourd'hui 24, no. 46 (February–March 1953): 87.

merely to climatic conditions, but also to local culture. It was at this time that they began to use the term *habitat* in lieu of housing. So new to the English-speaking architectural circles was the notion of habitat that in 1955 Alison and Peter Smithson found it necessary to define the term: "'Habitat' is a word used by the French to describe not only the home but its environment and everything appertaining to it."[53] In Candilis's and Woods's eyes, this was a sure means of providing an effective transition, since culture-specific architecture should actually encourage residents to gradually adopt modern living patterns, notably through the use of role models, as expounded in Écochard's theory of progressive shifts in domestic life. They also drew attention to the fact that modern architecture is a means of education because it generates specific bodily movements, such as those related to home comforts. Yet despite all this research, they nonetheless based their work on the dominant functionalist model, which ignores the anthropological aspect, or rather only accommodates it as a transitional feature. Following in the footsteps of many of their counterparts from the nineteenth century onward, Candilis and Woods were basically aspiring to render architecture "scientific," as is evidenced by their belief that since humankind shares the same fundamental needs, successful architecture hinges simply on providing for these.

Housing projects built in the 1950s for Moroccan Muslims were also characterized by developers' promotion of the model French nuclear family and accompanying living patterns. Habitat is therefore adapted to accommodate a family with two or three children, even though Moroccans generally have large families. It was assumed that these larger families would "make do," although decision makers nevertheless took overcrowding into account, thereby proving that they were fully aware the Moroccan family was not at all typically "nuclear." The only variables taken into consideration were hygiene (the limits of which have already been expounded) and privacy, while no thinking was devoted to gender issues, nor was any space assigned to receiving visitors. While this solution was partly due to the tight size of the apartments, the real fact of the matter was that the architects considered such features to be incompatible with the minimum housing concept. It is a strange twist of fate, then, that the ruling colonial powers selected the multifunctional vernacular language for interior layout precisely because of its affinities with minimum housing. In the end, the design teams' inability to respond to different housing needs and variations in family size casts a negative light on their work on housing composition and culture-specific programs. It is somewhat derisory, to say the least, that these types of programs amounted to nothing more than a standard housing type composed of a main room and courtyard.

Casablanca's architects were torn between two approaches: either applying the modernist theory of adapting buildings to structural "vital needs" of the human species at large, or adapting to the reality of different cultures. By introducing the social sciences, and more precisely anthropology, into the equation, the "culture-specific" strategy in effect overturned C.I.A.M. thinking derived from the "hard" sciences.[54] The result was that architects mixed both views—i.e., they sought to create culture-specific habitat, all the while drawing on the modern line of thinking that everyone should be accorded the same type of living space. Although Écochard pretended to provide for "all basic needs with respect to light, space, recreation, education, and work," he too subscribed to this type of schizophrenic procedure insofar as he adopted a modernist discourse for European schemes and an ethnological-cum-regional discourse for other programs.

[53] A. and P. Smithson, "Collective Housing in Morocco," 2.

[54] Eleb, "An Alternative to Functionalist Universalism: Écochard, Candilis, and ATBAT-Afrique," 55–73.

Honegger-Afrique, Cosyra apartment building, Boulevard Joffre and Boulevard d'Anfa, 1950. General view, c. 1952.

Honegger-Afrique, Cosyra apartment building. Entrance hall with ornamental pool and fresco by Jean-Marc Honegger. Photographed c. 1952.

The Lyrical Comforts of Apartment Houses

On one side there is the modern city flanked by five proud buildings—two banks, a hotel, the Galeries Lafayette department store, and the bus station. On the other side stands the native Moroccan town, hidden from sight by huge wooden fencing. The Orient we were expecting to see is concealed behind giant billboards.

Gabriel Bertrand, *La France Indépendante*, August 5, 1950[55]

Postwar design schemes for "standard-rent" buildings targeted at affluent Casablancan residents were underpinned by a quest for innovative, striking forms—the result of a new mind-set that Louis Delau had already encouraged his fellow citizens to adopt prior to the war:

> This is the front-stage box of an opera house or the poop deck of a steamboat. Whichever floor you are "hoisted" to, you find yourself in the dress circle or at the ship's rails. And it is not such a bad feeling at all, for this new style is inward-looking. To qualify the modern dwelling as aesthetic requires a certain amount of bias, it is true. But all it takes is to live in it to see that it is comfortable and inviting, in other words that it is fully geared to the general well-being. Its claim to beauty resides in its ensemble of ladderlike stories and facades that stretch over an entire block, an entire street, an entire neighborhood.[56]

Massive construction drives by developers combined with small-scale private projects alleviated the chronic housing conditions experienced by middle-class Casablancans, offering them a new degree of modern comfort. This real-estate boom attracted, among others, the Geneva-based Honegger brothers, who had originally trained as engineers and who practiced architecture in Casablanca between 1949 and 1959. In 1951, Jean-Jacques Honegger constructed a "modern building" at the junction of Boulevard d'Anfa and Boulevard Joffre, which is remarkable as much for its design language as for its technical prowess. It has a balcony-lined core set on

55 Bertrand, "Casablanca d'hier et d'aujourd'hui; I. Un brouillon pour demain."

56 Delau, "Casablanca."

pilotis, offering up glimpses of a fountain and a mural painting. The underlying aim of the scheme was to make "a building at an average cost, constructed in the modern spirit, and attuned to Moroccan climes."[57] The Honegger brothers subsequently completed several other buildings in the same neighborhood, as well as in the vicinity of the station, based on the same technique of formwork concrete floors laid with quick-drying cement. Unlike Sucom in the Anfa II project, here it was wisely decided to use mainly Moroccan labor and to invest very little in construction tools.[58]

The Honegger brothers' contribution rekindled interest in the use of concrete, for which Casablanca had been a testing ground since 1912. The non-load-bearing facades were designed using "a limited number of standardized, factory-made components, manufactured using the swift and economical instant-dry method."[59] The architects also incorporated vertical ribs, which allowed for a Perret-style profiling while serving to support the brise-soleil that crown the building. The two- and three-bedroom apartments have a double, and sometimes triple, exposure, while the living room (referred to as the "studio") is fitted with a fireplace and a south-facing balcony. Jean-Jacques Honegger commented on the buildings' design principles using the phraseology of the C.I.A.M. (in which he held the position of treasurer):

> Rational planning strictly prohibits courtyards, as these generate noise and offensive odors. It also precludes reentrant angles, which cast long shadows and create plunging views down into neighboring apartments. A residential area should be composed of buildings or groups of individual buildings, each forming a complete unit with four facades that are flooded with daylight.[60]

The Promise of Duplex Apartments

Double-height living units, which had already been introduced to Casablanca back in the 1930s,[61] began to become popular again in the 1950s, largely due to the Unité d'Habitation project in Marseilles. One case in point is the building constructed in 1952 by Gaston Jaubert on Rue de Mareuil, which was commissioned by the young physician Gaston Brami. Jaubert, who was a young architect at the time and a newcomer to Casablanca, designed sixteen apartments, stacking them on eight levels in a slight flouting of building codes so as to gain floor-to-ceiling height.[62] The apartments face southeast and northwest and are accessed by walkways at the rear of the building. The double-height living room, kitchen, and lavatory are all on the lower level, where a staircase leads to the bathroom and the two bedrooms; the master bedroom occupies an overhang and receives light from the living room. Jaubert placed the owner's apartment on the top floor and gave it a roof terrace.

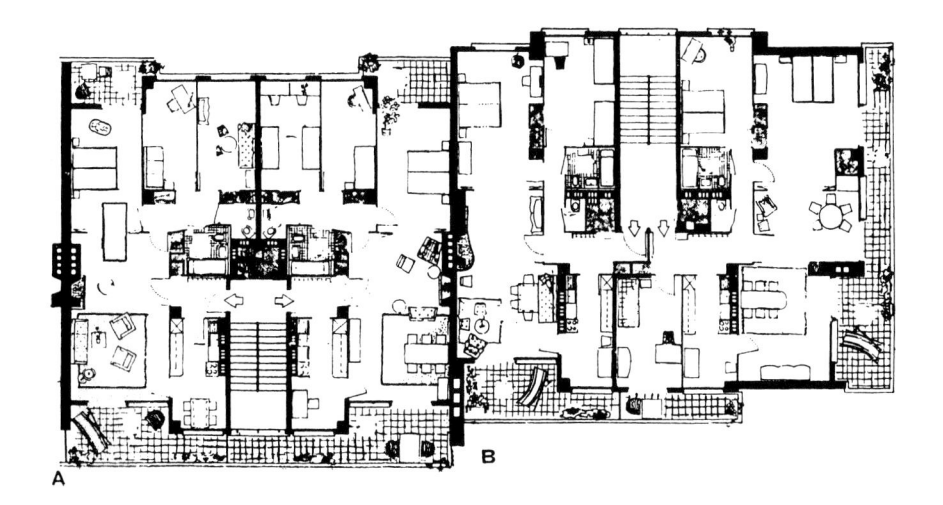

Honegger-Afrique, Cosyra apartment building. Photos of the building site in 1950, in *J.-J. Honegger raconte*, c. 1980.

57 "Immeubles d'habitation à Casablanca, J.-J. Honegger, architecte, P. Honegger, ingénieur," *L'Architecture d'aujourd'hui* 22, no. 35 (May 1951): 42.

58 Roland Crétegny (engineer at Honegger Afrique), interview by authors, Marly-le-Roy, May 1996.

59 The two brothers, Jean-Jacques and Pierre, were engineers. Jean-Marc was the son of Jean-Jacques. Mme. Schmidt, daughter and collaborator of Jean-Jacques Honegger, interview by Monique Eleb, Geneva, February 16, 1996. See also: *J.-J. Honegger raconte: Honegger-Frères (50e anniversaire)* (Geneva: Imprimerie G. de Buren, n.d. [ca. 1980]), 37, 43.

60 "L'union technique d'urbanisme," in *Maroc 1950*, 159.

61 In the late nineteenth century, this type of dwelling was known as a *hall anglais* (English hall), *hôtel dans l'immeuble* (mansion in apartment building), or *atelier d'artiste* (artist's studio). See Eleb and Debarre, *L'Invention de l'habitation moderne*, 76–91.

62 Gaston Jaubert, interview by Jean-Louis Cohen, Paris, February 12, 1990. See also: "Casablanca, immeuble d'habitation, G. Jaubert, architecte," *L'Architecture d'aujourd'hui* 26, no. 60 (June 1955): 50; Diamant-Berger, *Gaston Jaubert: rythmes et volumes*; and Gaston Brami, interview by the authors, Casablanca, May 23, 1998.

Honegger-Afrique, Cosyra apartment building. Standard floor plan, in *L'Architecture d'aujourd'hui*, May 1951.

Gaston Jaubert, Brami building, Rue de Mareuil, 1952. Facade view.

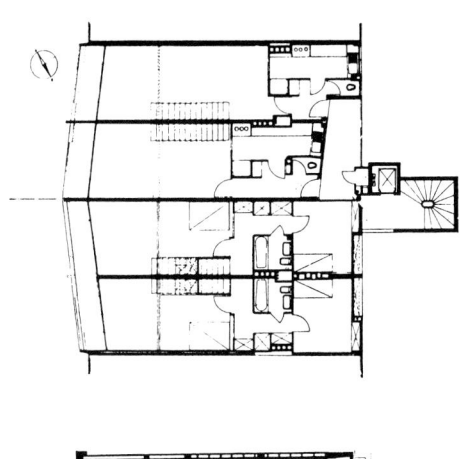

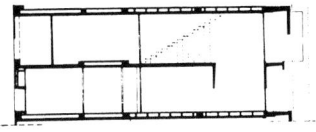

Gaston Jaubert, Brami building, Rue de Mareuil, 1952. Plans and section of a duplex apartment, in *L'Architecture d'aujourd'hui*, June 1955.

Brami building by Gaston Jaubert, Rue de Mareuil, 1952. Living room of a photographer in one of the duplexes.

The building's convex exterior is punctuated with elegant brise-soleil, making it one of the most photogenic buildings in Casablanca. The following year Jaubert designed the rather less flamboyant Atlanta building, which contains forty-two two-bedroom duplex apartments and for which he once again circumvented building codes.[63] The side staircase is fitted throughout with windows, creating a graphic play that is enhanced by the balconies and other openings. Overall, these two buildings by Jaubert can be said to contrast with the rather cautious modernism of other Casablancan buildings constructed around the same time.

Experimentation with the duplex apartment fascinated a number of architects. Candilis and Woods postulated a "semiduplex" type, in which they abandoned the double-height living room of the Unité d'Habitation in Marseilles (a project that

[63] "Immeuble Atlanta à Casablanca, G. Jaubert, architecte," *L'Architecture d'aujourd'hui* 26, no. 60 (June 1955): 49.

Gaston Jaubert, Gallinari building, known as Atlanta, Avenue Émile Zola, 1953. Plans for one of the duplexes, in *L'Architecture d'aujourd'hui*, June 1955.

Gaston Jaubert, Gallinari building, known as Atlanta, Avenue Émile Zola, 1953. General view.

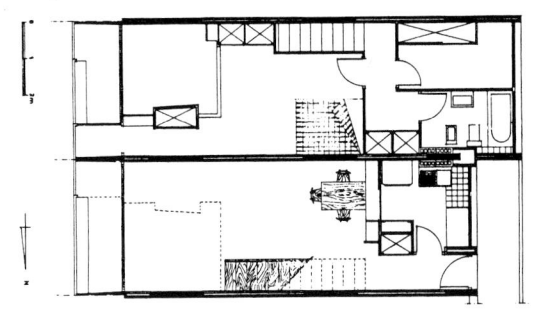

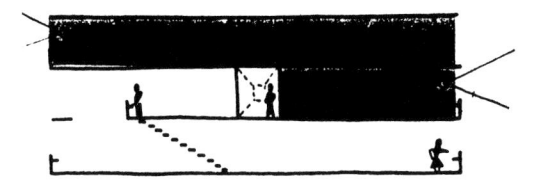

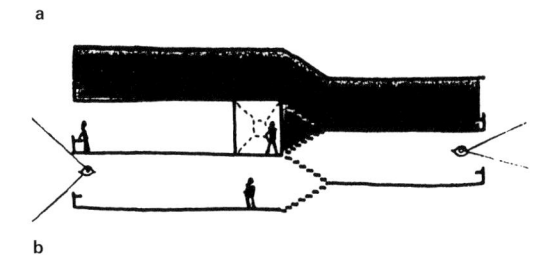

Georges Candilis and Shadrach Woods, dwelling studies, diagrammatic cross sections. Published in *L'Architecture d'aujourd'hui*, February–March 1953.

a. Le Corbusier, Unité d'habitation in Marseilles, 1946.

b. Georges Candilis and Shadrach Woods, Semi-duplex building, 1953.

64 Georges Candilis and Shadrach Woods, "Étude théorique de l'immeuble semi-duplex," *L'Architecture d'aujourd'hui* 24, no. 46 (February–March 1953): 87. This study was "dedicated to our master Le Corbusier, in testimony of [our] deep gratitude." Oscar Niemeyer had explored similar solutions in housing in Petropolis, Brazil. However, Candilis cited the experiments of the Russian constructivists (whose publications he owned) as the source of this principle. Georges Candilis, interview.

65 "Etude théorique de l'immeuble semi-duplex," 88.

66 The program of transgenerational cohabitation—between grown children, their parents, or grandparents—seeking to reconcile proximity to family with autonomy remains innovative and well suited to changing lifestyles today. It has retained the same relevance as multiple floors that permit people to "congregate" or "seclude themselves." See Monique Eleb and Anne-Marie Châtelet, "Les innovations en terme de programme," in *Urbanité, sociabilité, intimité: Des logements d'aujourd'hui* (Paris: Éditions de l'Épure, 1997): 213–17.

Candilis had worked on). They maintained that there is more "inhabitable" space when the height of the bedrooms and living room is increased by half a story, rather than by a whole one. Moreover, they moved the staircase out of the communal room. However, the designs contain the same focus on transparency as in the Unité, with double exposure in each apartment. Also, the bathroom and kitchen are grouped in the core of the building, thus allowing for a more economical infrastructure and freeing up the facade.[64]

Another notion raised by Candilis and Woods was that division of space by function provides the "basis for daily life" through hierarchic order: the communal room for socializing and the bedrooms for privacy. This micro Athens Charter presupposed grouping secondary functions in the heart of the building, thereby clearing the facades. These precepts were applied in the unbuilt project commissioned by the C.I.L. for a program in Anfa-Beauséjour that combined apartments and shops. With the help of Aroutcheff and Bodiansky, Candilis and Woods adapted their concepts to Casablancan climatic conditions, asserting that "cross ventilation provides rational solutions to dealing with the summer heat and high humidity." Additionally, "the wide loggias, brise-soleil, and glazed walls ensure that the apartments are kept cool in summer, and warm in winter."[65] The top-floor studios were designed to be paired if required. Not to be forgotten either is the interior street linking several floors; this means that apartments can be coupled up in an arrangement that facilitates "lodging older relatives or adolescents who can thereby retain their independence while living with their families."[66]

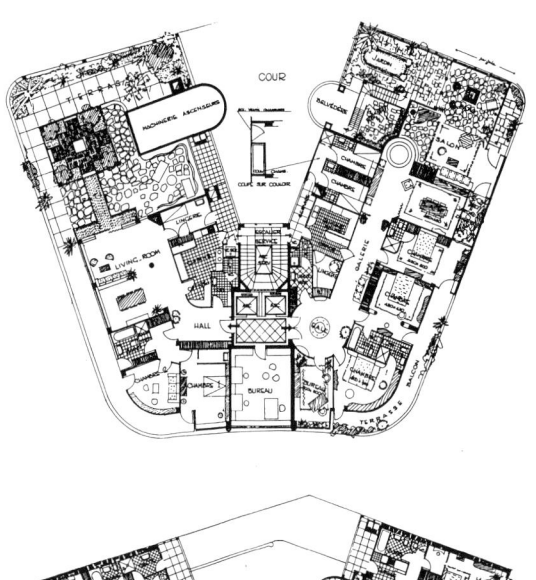

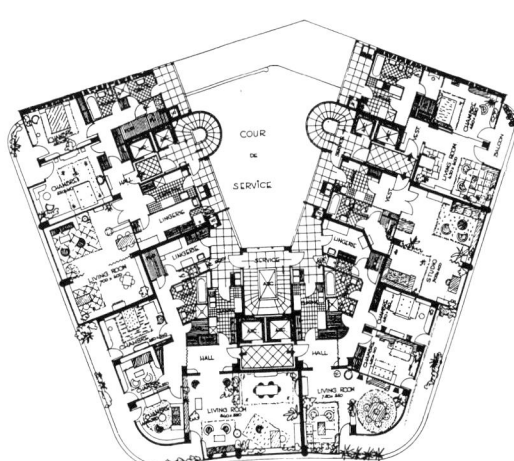

Léonard Morandi, Liberté building, Place de la Révolution Française, 1950. General view. Photographed in 1990.

Léonard Morandi, Liberté building. Standard floor plans and plan of the top floor, in *L'Architecture française,* May 1950. As in most plans of the time, the drawings are highly detailed, even showing the fringes of the rugs. This was useful for marking out the "corner areas" in the living rooms or for explicitly illustrating how comfortable the bedrooms were in terms of size. The top floor includes a three-bedroom apartment with a living room that extends into a patio, as well as a seven-room apartment with a pergola and belvedere. There are many service rooms, such as a linen room, pantry, cloakroom-cum-washroom and storage space. Each bedroom has an en-suite bathroom or a *cabinet de toilette*.

Flexible Designs for Residential High-Rises

A number of tower blocks were constructed on the Place de France as well as on Avenue D'Amade and the Circular Boulevard, joining Jabin's hitherto lone Moretti-Milone building to set a tone of verticality. Not surprisingly, visitors were systematically struck by the contrast between the fencing that concealed the medina and the central buildings under construction. Designs for such sky-high "giants" had already been drawn up back in the 1930s,[67] as well as in studies undertaken by Courtois. It was thanks to the technical skills of Morocco-based building firms that these types of designs could now become built works.

Casablanca's high-rise construction boom was exemplified by the Liberté building, whose markedly nautical design vocabulary did not fail to attract the attention of more than one reviewer. It was even accorded pride of place on the cover of *L'Architecture d'aujourd'hui*'s special edition on Morocco issued in 1951. The same year *Réalités* published a low-angle shot of it (the type of shot frequently used for New York), showing its architect, Léonard Morandi, proudly standing in the foreground.[68] In 1954 it figured as a symbol of violence in Mohamed Dahou's collage *Le Maroc aujourd'hui*, in which Dahou—a member of the Internationaliste lettriste, an emerging radical artistic group—clearly lets his anticolonial feelings show in a denunciation of French repression.[69] Built on the Place de la Révolution Française (a major crossroads of the Circular Boulevard), this testament to "the huge effort that France is making in Africa" was viewed as "the first large-scale African experiment in high-rise apartment blocks."[70] It stands eighteen stories high,

67 Dubois, "L'évolution de la construction à Casablanca."

68 "Casablanca, le développement prodigieux."

69 The collage is reproduced in Roberto Ohrt, *Phantom Avantgarde: eine Geschichte der Situationistischen Internationale und der modernen Kunst* (Hamburg: Nautilus, 1990), 92.

70 "Immeuble Liberté à Casablanca, L. Morandi, architecte dplg, Le Pape, ingénieur," *L'Architecture française* 10, no. 95–96 (November–December 1949): 69.

Charles Abella and Albert Lucas, Palais Mirabeau apartment building, Boulevard de la Résistance, 1954. General view.

reaching seventy-eight meters, which led the local press to question whether people could truly live comfortably so high up and with so many neighbors, even though the apartments offered all the modern comforts they might wish for. Although they felt proud to live in a city that was home to the tallest and most elegantly swathed building in Africa, some still harbored doubts about whether living in a high-rise block allowed for a quality lifestyle. It was pointed out, though, that the building's sunny exposure would "reduce heating costs": "The truncated V-shape site on which the building stands has a southern vanishing point, which means that it is positioned favorably in relation to the sun. The main rooms are all situated along the facade that overlooks the square and the avenues, and will thus be shielded against the ocean mist." [71] The building, which was clearly designed as a prestige block, as is confirmed by the number of elevators and high-quality fixtures,[72] was marketed as a condominium. The main ground-floor entrance leads to two floors of offices, while the side entrances provide access to the apartments. The core is given over to the larger apartments, which have between three and four bedrooms, and sometimes even more, whereas the wings of the building accommodate smaller units. The vast living rooms (between thirty-five and forty-two square meters) are rendered even larger by bay windows and balconies that "form terrace-gardens." Writing at the time, critics observed a hint of modernity in the large living room and the bedrooms of varying sizes, which were generally labeled as "small sleeping cells, designed in line with current trends."[73] Nonetheless, these bedrooms had attendant rooms, such as a bathroom and walk-in closet, thereby providing the degree of comfort expected by a bourgeois clientele. Morandi paid particular attention to flexible interior layouts, severing the service areas and their access corridors from the main rooms; these corridors can even be assigned to an adjoining apartment should the need arise. The top floor is marked by a large brise-soleil and houses two apartments with large terraces, coupled with an office space situated along the axis of the tower block. Lemaigre-Dubreuil, an entrepreneur and an active campaigner against Protectorate extremists, occupied one of these apartments prior to his assassination just outside the building in 1955.[74]

Contemporary preoccupation with flexible schemes fed the imagination of architects and developers alike, both parties being sensitive to housing market

---

[71] "Immeuble Liberté à Casablanca," *L'Architecture d'aujourd'hui*, no. 35 (May 1951): 44. See also "Immeuble Liberté, L. Morandi," in *Le Maroc moderne: architecture et urbanisme*. This building was designed, in Morandi's office, by Robert Maddalena.

[72] Six high-speed elevators served the building, as well as three stairways leading to apartment entryways and service balconies located in the building's interior courtyard. Thus, vertical circulation was duplicated. Individual garbage disposals led to incinerators equipped with septic ducts.

[73] "Immeuble Liberté à Casablanca, L. Morandi," 44. The bedrooms measured between 11 and 22.5 square meters. "Quelques aspects de l'immeuble Liberté," in *Maroc 1950*, 159.

[74] François Broche, *L'Assassinat de Lemaigre-Dubreuil: Casablanca le 11 juin 1955* (Paris: Balland, 1977).

trends. The Liberté building, along with the soaring Palais Mirabeau (built by Charles Abella and Albert Lucas on the Circular Boulevard) and the Océania block, constructed by Georges Renaudin on the Place Mirabeau, all reflect this key concern for flexibility, for, although they were primarily marketed as commercial space, their underlying design principles allowed for conversion:

> The layout was conceived to accommodate apartments either on purpose-designed floors or on the same level as the commercial premises. In leasehold terms, this type of layout has proved very popular, but it has given rise to some thorny problems with respect to selecting design solutions. All the floors were laid and completed before setting up any partitioning, so that the premises can be converted in line with needs. Floor heating . . . eliminates the need for radiators, which means that it is even easier to convert the property if required.[75]

The tradition of building specific structures for single occupants was maintained in high-rise construction, as is exemplified in Pierre Coldefy's building for the Société d'assurances générales, which he slotted between two other buildings on Boulevard de Lorraine in 1952. Conceived as a tower block, its design language bears overtones of Perret and Le Corbusier's work, as in the stout pilotis; these shoulder a facade steadily patterned by the screen walls of the loggias, which act as brise-soleil. There are three levels of garages, two floors of offices, and eight levels of apartments for single residents or childless couples, "complete with all the necessary home comforts."[76] The studio apartments contain a kitchenette and a large room, referred to as "living-room" on the plans. The floor area may be rather limited, but this is compensated for in the marble and mahogany finishes, which "endow this manufactured complex with all the airs of a traditional prestige

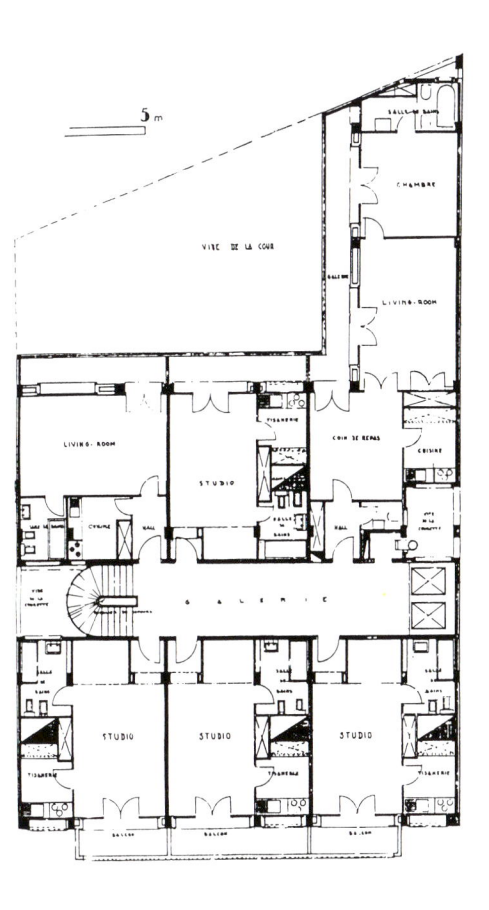

[75] "Immeuble Océania, place Mirabeau, G. Renaudin," in *Le Maroc moderne: architecture et urbanisme.*

[76] "Immeuble collectif à Casablanca, P. Coldefy architecte dplg," *L'Architecture française* 13, no. 131–32 (November–December 1953): 20.

Pierre Coldefy, Assurances Générales Incendie building, 40 Boulevard de Lorraine, 1953. Facade overlooking the boulevard. Photographed in 1994.

Pierre Coldefy, Assurances Générales Incendie building. Standard floor plan, in *L'Architecture Française*, April 1952. The building contains forty studio apartments and eight one-bedrooms.

Housing the Europeans 387

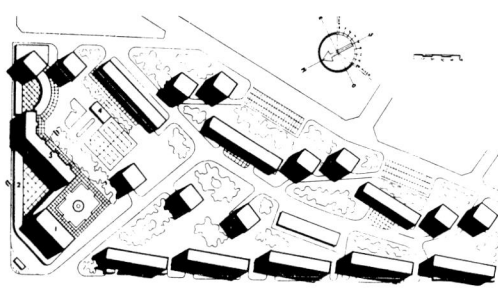

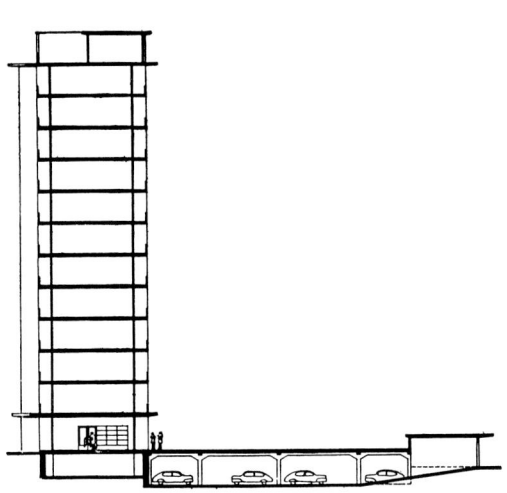

Gabus, Dubois, Marcel Desmet, Jean Maillard and Honegger-Afrique SA, Romandie building for the C.I.L., Boulevard Alexandre 1er, 1952. General view, 1952. Site plan and cross section, in *L'Architecture d'aujourd'hui*, May 1951.

77 "Immeuble Assurances Générales Incendie, P. Coldefy, architecte dplg," in *Le Maroc moderne: architecture et urbanisme*.

78 "Immeuble collectif à Casablanca," 20.

79 "Cité d'habitation à Casablanca, Gabus et Dubois, architectes, Desmet et Maillard, architectes d'opération," *L'Architecture d'aujourd'hui* 22, no. 35 (May 1951): 48.

80 It is from this idea project, intended in part for military housing, that the Anfa II and Anfa III projects discussed above evolved. "Cité d'habitation à Casablanca," 48.

81 A dense network of thirty-two companies (including Romandie-Plage, Romandie-Bel Air, etc.) was created in order to complete this urban project.

82 Here again, the privileging of bedrooms is apparent from their large size (each can accommodate a double bed) and from the fact that they open onto balconies (the living rooms have no terraces). "Un immeuble à Casablanca, Bailly et R. Schmidt," *L'Architecture française* 16, no. 163–64 (January–February 1956): 42.

dwelling."[77] As noted by a number of Parisian reviews, all eleven stories were completed in four months, "thanks to the use of factory-made units combined with mass-produced fixtures and construction components."[78]

The same concern for standardization led to the design of the Romandie tower, located southwest of the city center. It remains the sole living proof today of a broader project for middle-class housing, drawn up in 1951 by the Swiss-owned real-estate consortium Omnium Chérifien d'Investissement.[79] Intended to comprise twenty-one buildings ranging between ten and thirteen stories, the scheme was granted a site in the vicinity of the sports stadium, at the junction of Boulevard Louis Barthou and Boulevard Paul Dommer. The complex was to accommodate 1,600 public housing units, to be positioned in parallel rows, forming "a buffer against the winds and damp ocean breezes," and numerous amenities were planned at the base of the towers, including a swimming pool and tennis courts.[80] Only one thirteen-story tower block ever saw the light of day; designed as a T shape to plans drawn up by the Swiss architects Gabus and Dubois from Neuchâtel, it was assembled in-situ by Desmet and Maillard in 1952.[81] It includes prefabricated components produced by the Honegger brothers and mounted on a sturdy concrete framework. The tower was originally designed for offices, shops, and a hotel but now houses 175 apartments connected by wide communal circulation zones.

The thirteen-story tower block built by Bailly and Schmidt in 1955 on Avenue D'Amade (earmarked by Courtois for high-rise construction as early as 1944) is similarly striking, though for different reasons. Constructed by the real-estate firm Luxia, it was marketed as a fully fitted condominium complex, which was something of an innovation at the time for Casablanca since apartment blocks were usually built for rental purposes. The last two floors were set back from the rest, the top one accommodating a children's play area and a laundry equipped with tumble dryers.[82]

The thoroughfares laid out by Prost were likewise peppered with new high-rises. At the eastern tip of Boulevard de la Gare, the sixteen-story building constructed on the Place Albert 1er by G. Bardel, J. P. Sabatou, and A. Teillaud comprises luxury apartments, which were sold as condominiums. All of the main rooms are situated along the facade, while the service areas and stairs are grouped at the rear, around a courtyard.[83] Meanwhile, the Villas Paquet apartment block, at the start of the boulevard, was the only building designed along lines similar to the Liberté. Its sinuous, narrow projecting balconies cover seventeen stories in a skillful play of light and shadow. Constructed by Jacques Gouyon between 1951 and 1952, the building was designed in response to a brief that specified a mixed-use development of offices and apartment buildings. The apartments are accessed by three elevators and a freight elevator. All of the apartments, whatever their size, were thoughtfully designed with up-to-the-minute fixtures (thus explaining the rather paradoxical term *villa*). Sliding doors and a service gallery completed the overall impression of smart modern comfort. It is also worth noting that even though the building towers over the early low-rise blocks in the surrounding area, Gouyon nevertheless complied with Prost's arcade principle for the ground level.

These luxury high-rises in the city center brought together residential and office space by way of versatile design principles. In so doing, they often involved experimental projects that hinged either on testing cost-saving prefabrication systems or on developing construction methods that would enable the buildings to be adapted to different uses at a later stage. This flexible approach provides yet further proof of Casablanca's propensity to embrace more cutting-edge building techniques than those contemporaneously deployed in France. However, this being said, these prototypes were mostly to remain one-off ventures, given that post-independence investors would soon grow weary of risking their capital on projects that were as costly as they were ambitious.

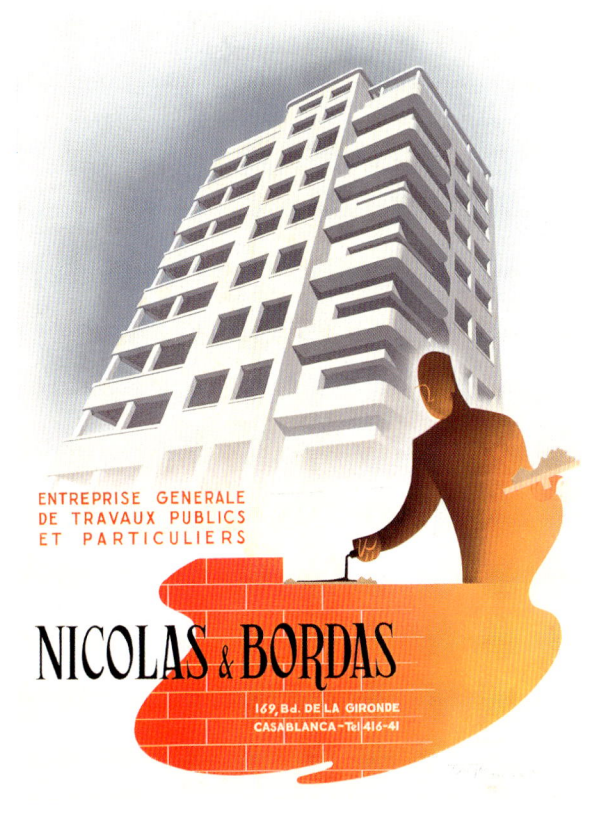

83 "Immeuble Albert Ier à Casablanca, G. Bardel, J.-P. Sabatou et A. Teillaud, architectes," *L'Architecture d'aujourd'hui* 22, no. 35 (May 1951): 23.

Jacques Gouyon, Villas Paquet apartment building, Boulevard de la Gare and Place Georges Mercié, 1952. View of the balconies. Photographed in 1994.

Nicolas & Bordas company, advertisement in *40 ans de présence française au Maroc*, 1952. The designer of the advertisement drew heavily on the high-rise building by Bardel, Sabatou and Teillaud in Place Albert 1er.

Screen walls and pergolas from 1950s buildings.

Émile Perollaz, Villa, Boulevard Alexandre 1er, 1951. Photo 1995.

Maurice Galamand, Maréchal Lyautey development, Rue de Damrémont, Rue de Commercy, Rue de Reims, and Rue Lamoricière, 1949–53. Photo 1989.

Erwin Hinnen, housing for Muslims, Avenue du Nil and Avenue Anoual, Sidi Othman, 1952. Photo 1994.

Private house, Allée des Cèdres and Allée des Cytises, Anfa supérieur. Photo 1996.

Pierre Coldefy, Assurances Générales Incendie building, 40 Boulevard de Lorraine, 1953. Photo 1990.

Pierre Coldefy, housing, Boulevard Laurent Guerrero, 1958. Photo 1996.

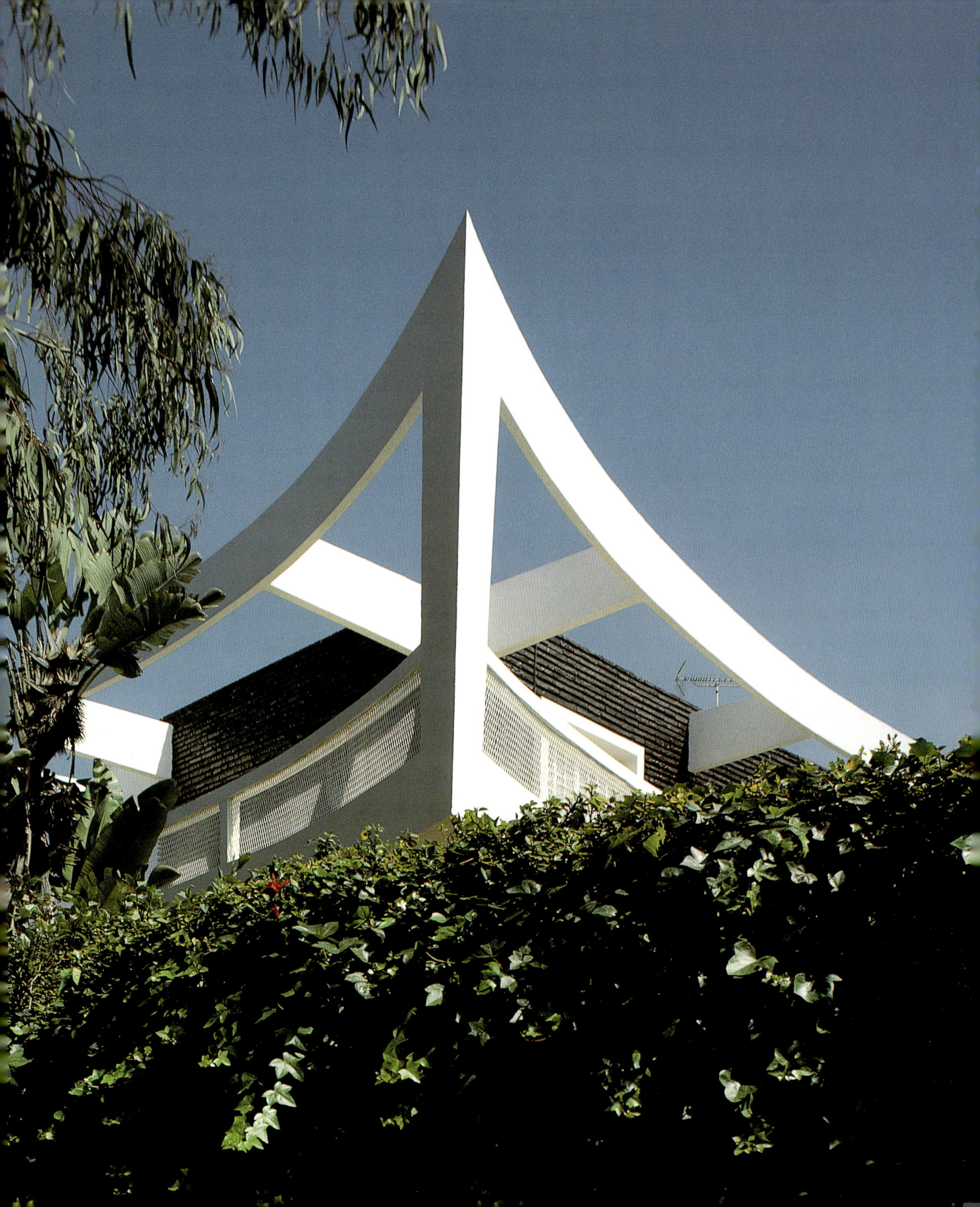

Villas, Beachside Resorts, and Movie Theaters: Hedonism at Work

Mediterranean Villas and a Californian Dreamscape

Modern architects enjoy greater freedom in Casablanca than in any French city, for they have a multitude of clients at their fingertips all seeking to break with traditional style.

Maisons et Jardins, 1953[1]

It is surprising (and disappointing) not to find more contemporary work of merit. Most of the architecture is a bit formal, static, and balanced, with an accent on round columns, heavy cornices, and stylized Beaux-Arts motifs. Much of the rest is an architectural cous-cous, cous-cous being the Moroccan equivalent of goulash or Irish stew.

G. E. Kidder Smith, 1950[2]

Postwar Casablanca was not only a buzzing metropolis full of workers toiling away, as illustrated in Jean Vidal's 1951 movie *Salut Casa!* (derived from the narrative structure of Walter Ruttmann's 1927 documentary *Berlin, Symphony of a Big City*), but was also a residential city in which the bourgeoisie had managed to carve out a sheltered lifestyle for itself despite growing political turmoil. In addition, it was a lively hub where cafés, movie theaters, and beaches offered entertainment to the younger generation who were looking for fun after the years of gloom. Whereas the bourgeoisie of metropolitan France turned their backs on modern architecture during this period, affluent Casablancan clients, open to new forms and ideas, commissioned private dwellings that were sumptuous yet functional and in keeping with the local context. Gaston Jaubert commented that his clients "were enamored of architecture and speculation,"[3] and in 1953, *Réalités* noted that "people are building wherever they can," and that "small, ultra-modern, hospital-white villas are springing up in all the gaps between dilapidated shacks."[4]

Clients in search of opulence did not have to look far to find Hollywood-style paradigms. The dream machine generated by the American movie business seemed all the more legitimate since Hollywood and Casablanca are on the same latitude, and hence share the same climate. Many thus perceived Los Angeles as a point of reference for Casablanca's future, and indeed it should be mentioned in this regard that the Protectorate's farming policy had been based on the Californian model since the 1930s.[5] American influence grew increasingly apparent: despite health

Opposite
Jean-François Zevaco, in association with Paul Messina, Villa Sami Suissa, 1947. Pergola overlooking Avenue Franklin Roosevelt, photographed in 1991.

[1] "Casablanca," *Maisons et Jardins* (August–September 1953): 53.

[2] G. E. Kidder Smith, "Report from Morocco," *The Architectural Forum* 92, no. 6 (June 1950): 68–72.

[3] Gaston Jaubert, interview by Jean-Louis Cohen, Paris, February 12, 1990.

[4] "Casablanca, le développement prodigieux," 49.

[5] At the time, study missions to the American Southwest and reports led to the launch of an irrigation program, and to the start-up of citrus cultivation following principles whose every detail was "blindly" based on the Californian model. Will D. Swearingen, *Moroccan Mirages: Agrarian Dreams and Deceptions, 1912–1986* (London: L. B. Tauris & Co, 1988): 59–77.

A street in Anfa with
a Buick, January 1954.

Opposite
a. Jean Michelet, villa, c. 1949. Plans published in *L'Architecture française*, May 1950. There is a service stair leading from the cellar and laundry room to the kitchen, along with two interior and exterior staircases which give independent access to the two floors.

b. Robert Maddalena, villa for a couple with two children, c. 1953. Plan published in *L'oeuvre du CIL au Maroc. Casablanca 950–954*.

c. Achille Dangleterre, villa, c. 1949. Ground-floor plan, in *L'Architecture française*, May 1950. The guest room forms a studio apartment that "can be accessed directly from the entrance." It was an essential requisite, used for receiving family from mainland France.

d. Gaston Jaubert, single-family house, Longchamp, 1951. Ground-floor plan, in *L'Architecture d'Aujourd'hui*, February–March 1953.

6 During the debate about this beverage in the French parliament, it came to light that the Coke extracts were imported from Morocco. Richard F. Kuysel, *Seducing the French: The Dilemna of Americanization* (Berkeley and Los Angeles: University of California Press, 1993), 55.

7 This American shelter magazine, aimed at housewives, was widely available at newsstands in the 1950s.

8 De Lacretelle, "Casa."

9 See, for example, "Deux villas à Casablanca, É. Duhon architecte dplg," *L'Architecture française* 10, no. 95–96 (November–December 1949): 88.

10 J. E. Chable, "Lieux dont on parle: Casablanca, édifice monumental et fragile."

11 The former were designed by Maddalena, Aroutcheff and Jean, Greslin, Duhon, Debroise, and Siroux, while the latter were the work of Archambault and Senlecq, Ewerth and Jaubert, Zevaco, and Mauzit. *L'œuvre du CIL au Maroc*.

12 In 1950, the C.I.L. had two "experimental" prefabricated villas built by Duhon at the "propriété Spaak" and Ferme bretonne. These were inaugurated on November 27, 1950, during the Habitat conference. MAE, carton SDRG 139.

13 "Maison familiale à Casablanca, J. Michelet, architecte dplg," *L'Architecture française* 10, no. 95–96 (November–December 1949): 85.

warnings issued by the French parliament in 1950, Coca-Cola became a readily available commodity,[6] while just thirty kilometers outside of town, the U.S. airbase of Nouaceur broadcast the first rock and roll songs and stocked all the latest household appliances, tempting local bourgeois women with dream kitchens straight out of *Good Housekeeping*.[7]

In 1949, Jacques de Lacretelle described Casablanca as "a city where everybody hurries and scurries," though at the same time he pointed out, "Casa's French population prefers initiative to luxury and has retained its pioneering spirit." He did not, however, pick up on the underlying shifts in local culture when he wrote: "No nabobs and very few *outward signs* of wealth. People don't give a hang about handsome palaces and American cars—they're quite happy with their Peugeots and Citroëns. All they ask for is a bit of office space."[8] Contrary to Lacretelle's take on the situation, Cadillacs and "up-to-the-minute" villas very soon formed part and parcel of the urban culture, in which hedonism at times verged on ostentation. Architects felt drawn to the American building language, and to Neutra and Schindler's houses in particular, perhaps because the latter schemes shared close affinities with Casablanca in terms of the climate and ocean setting. Nevertheless, despite the sometimes provocative expression of modernist ideals and formal 1950s symbols, luxury dwellings still continued to be built in the style of turn-of-the-century *hôtels particuliers* and upscale Parisian apartment buildings, whose high-quality spatial arrangements and layouts were, and perhaps still are, unsurpassable.

Unpretentious Innovation

Aside from a few rare deluxe residences, most houses fell within the mid-range bracket, sporting a low-key modernity expressed in cubelike shapes embellished with decorative elements such as pergolas and wrought-iron balconies. Styles hinged very much on client demand, as in the villas constructed by Michelet, Dangleterre, Maddalena, Planque, Gourdain, and Delanoé. Depending on the brief, these houses were designed in a "modern," "traditional," or "regionalist" vein, with

"Basque" and "Provençal" styles proving highly popular. A sort of syncretism arose, based on recycling motifs such as Spanish wrought-iron and Moroccan archways.[9] It was a principle repeated in countless Casablancan villas that came to represent a kind of comfortable and conformist adaptation to the local pattern, as indicated in *La Tribune de Genève*: "This style, which certainly has its enthusiasts, has served as the underlying design for a host of villas: an extravaganza in white mixed with a crossbreed of Mexican, Spanish, American, and Provençal genres and delicate Moroccan forms—arabesques, minarets, and pointed arches, and, thank God, that faint rustling of bougainvillea and geraniums whenever there is a water source nearby."[10] These dwellings were targeted at the more affluent members of the petite bourgeoisie and so were extremely comfortable. They not only contained ancillary utility rooms such as a pantry and a laundry, but also terraces, loggias, and pergolas, as well as garages, which had now become a standard feature due to the widespread use of cars.

Anfa-Beauséjour, a new quarter created in the early 1950s by the C.I.L., encapsulates this building type. Each house was delivered with "sanitary fittings and electricity, as well as a garden designed by a landscape architect." For reasons rooted more in social and economic issues than in aesthetic concerns, the villas were split into two categories: the "classic style" and the "daringly modernist,"[11] the latter often built to a fairly basic plan verging on minimum housing.[12] Jean Michelet's schemes best typify this category of accommodations characterized by large service spaces. One of his dwellings, dating from 1949, was designed to fulfill the dual function of family home and office,[13] a solution that was widely deployed for centrally located houses accommodating managerial staff. Elsewhere, Achille Dangleterre concentrated on popular outdoor features such as terraces and pergolas, so that occupants from northern latitudes could enjoy the full benefit of Casablanca's favorable climate.

More radical architects, like Azagury, Jaubert, Zevaco, Lévy, and German-born Ewerth, drew on modern architectural principles in their programs for the petite bourgeoisie. They established a sort of common language through pilotis, brise-soleil, and vast wall planes that played on the contrast between glass blocks, screens,

Gaston Jaubert, single-family house, Longchamp, 1951.

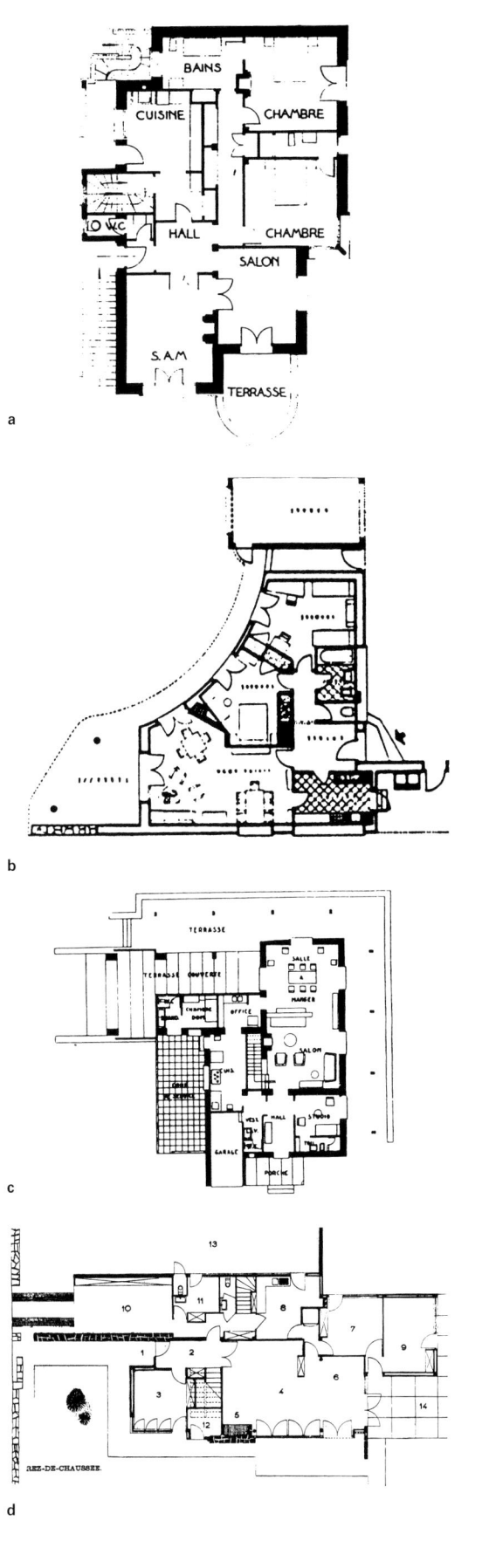

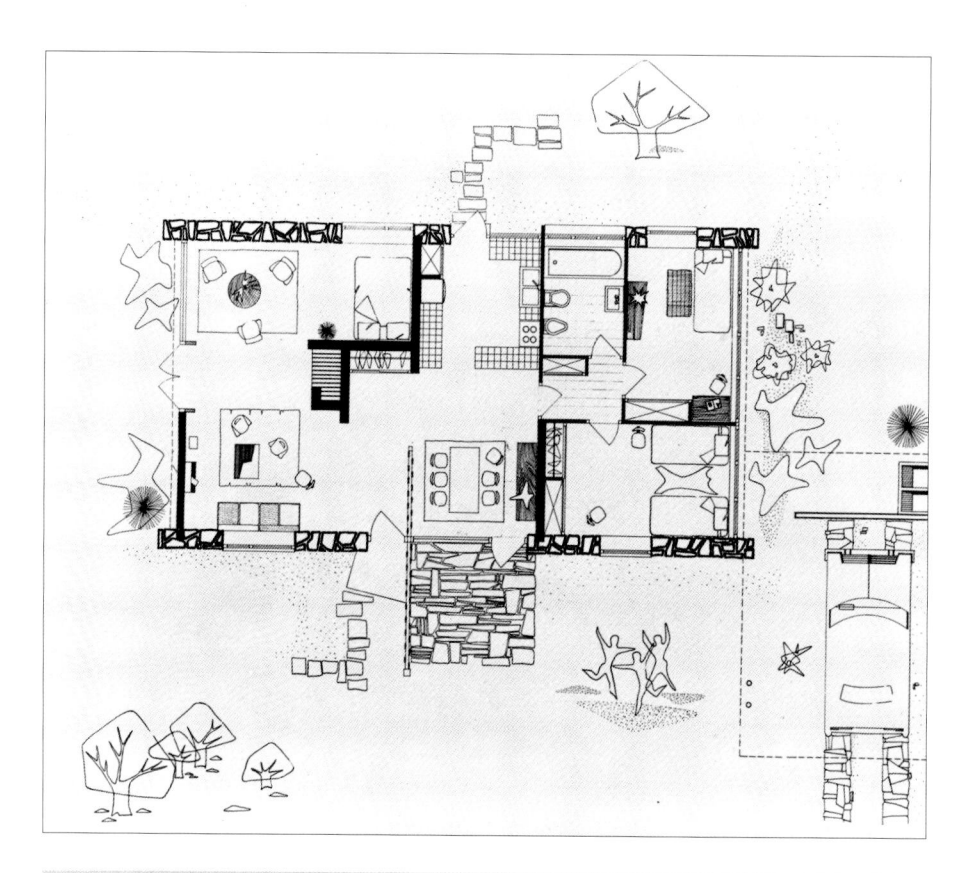

Élie Azagury, Villa Varaud, Rue du Chant des Oiseaux, c. 1954. Plan.

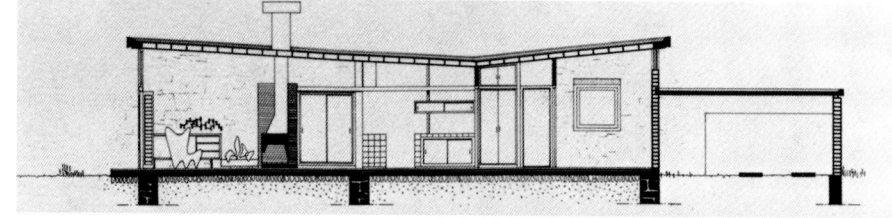

Élie Azagury, Villa Varaud, c. 1954. Cross section.

exposed stone, and rough concrete or plaster. In this way, a balance could be struck between satisfying the requirements of enlightened clients and complying with the principles of Neo-Brutalism, though these were nonetheless flavored with Mediterranean points of reference.[14] A recurrent element is the "reinforced-concrete brise-soleil, which takes the form of a pergola"[15] and steadily patterns many of the city's streets; this was borrowed as much from Le Corbusier's designs (notably in Algiers and Rio de Janeiro) as from southern California houses.

Azagury also tested concepts relating to the basic single-family dwelling, as demonstrated in his 1951 scheme for the tightly sited Villa Nahon, whose plan reads as a small house with an average-sized rear garden. The living room opens onto the garden and is split into a dining area (adjoining the kitchen) and a slightly lower lounge. All three bedrooms on the upper floor have a terrace, while outside, "the entrance facade is composed of a rectangle made from four different materials: a double brick wall clad in Venetian red; glass blocks; rough stone; and ivory-colored components."[16] As for the Villa Varaud, built by Azagury in 1954, it was conceived as a "minimum dwelling" whose single story covers barely one hundred square meters.[17] The interconnecting kitchen and dining room occupy a central position in the house, while the children's rooms and bathroom are tucked into the side wings. The master bedroom, which is next to the living room, is large enough to contain a "lounge area."

14 Regarding Neo-Brutalism, see Reyner Banham, *The New Brutalism: Ethic or Aesthetic?* (New York: Reinhold, 1966). This term was coined in early-1950s London.

15 Used notably by Élie Azagury and in a small house by Isaac Lévy. "Villa à Casablanca, I. Lévy architecte dplg," *L'Architecture française* 13, no. 131–32 (November–December 1952): 36.

16 "Maison à Casablanca, É. Azagury, architecte," *L'Architecture d'aujourd'hui* 22, no. 35 (May 1951): 53.

17 "Villa à Casablanca, É. Azagury, architecte," *L'Architecture d'aujourd'hui* 26, no. 60 (June 1955): 56.

18 "Villa à Casablanca. J.-F. Zevaco et P. Messina," in *Le Maroc moderne*.

19 "Villa à Casablanca," *L'Architecture d'aujourd'hui* 22, no. 35 (May 1951): 54.

20 Jean-François Zevaco, interview by authors, Casablanca, April 18, 1990.

21 Kidder Smith, "Report from Morocco," 72. Kidder Smith had published with Philip Goodwin *Brazil Builds: Architecture New and Old, 1652–1942* (New York: Museum of Modern Art, 1943) and had a perceptive vision of climate-specific architecture.

The first villa built by the young Jean-François Zevaco and his associate Paul Messina dates from 1949. Although somewhat small, it was nonetheless dubbed aggressively modern. Slotted between two semidetached dwellings, its street-facing facade reads as a near-blank wall with a large expanse of glazing that is sheltered by a deep loggia. The living room has a double exposure, yet is shielded from the street by a curved wall.[18] Zevaco and Messina opted for a bright color scheme that would stand out in this otherwise placid neighborhood—"lemon brise-soleil, gray sandstone walls, green screen on the left, orange screen on the right, red front door, white joinery, and black letter boxes."[19] According to Zevaco, such a profusion of color so alarmed "the local population and the [architectural] profession" that he was "refused commissions for quite a time."[20] But the reaction of G. E. Kidder Smith to this "flamboyant" house is quite enthusiastic: "Although there is a slight tendency to go overboard in the design and make it almost too rich, the house as a whole is one of the best in North Africa and one of the few to tackle the burning question of the sun."[21]

Rather less masterful are the villas by Léonard Morandi and Pierre Coldefy, whose designs fall within the sphere of starkly modern, comfortable dwellings. Morandi also sought to create an opposing pull between plastered facades and stone bases, as is evidenced by the two villas he built between 1951 and 1952. This

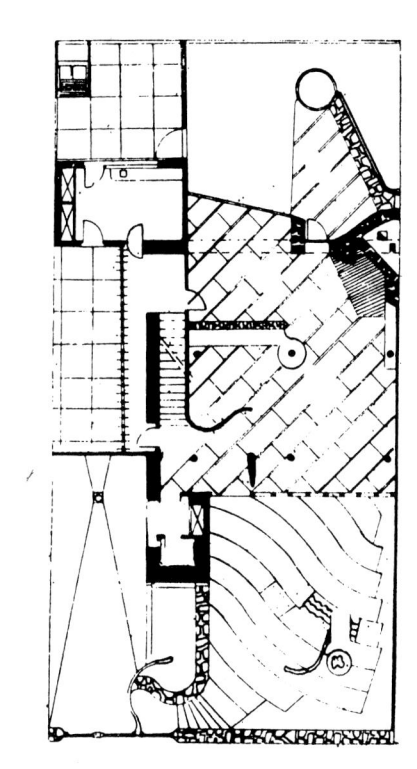

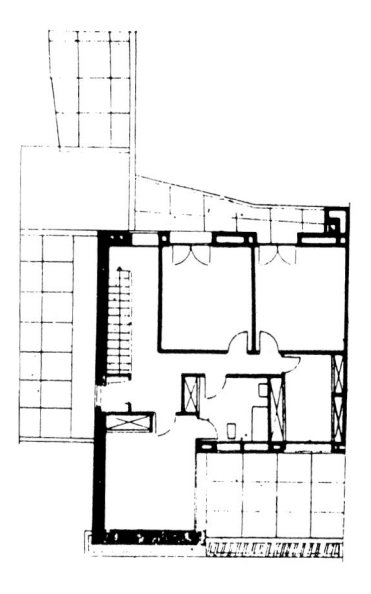

Jean-François Zevaco in association with Paul Messina, Villa Craig, Rue d'Auteuil, 1948. Photo of the entrance, in *L'Architecture française*, May 1950.

Jean-François Zevaco in association with Paul Messina, Villa Craig, Rue d'Auteuil, 1948. Ground- and first-floor plans.

One of the bedrooms faces south and overlooks "a terrace protected by a brise-soleil." On the west facade, "thick sandstone walls and a concrete-strip screen shield the bedroom from heat." "Villa à Casablanca, J.-F. Zevaco et P. Messina," *L'Architecture d'aujourd'hui* 22, no. 35 (May 1951): 54.

Villas, Beachside Resorts, and Movie Theaters

Léonard Morandi, Villa Dar Lugda, Anfa, c. 1951. Facade overlooking the street. Photographed in 1998.

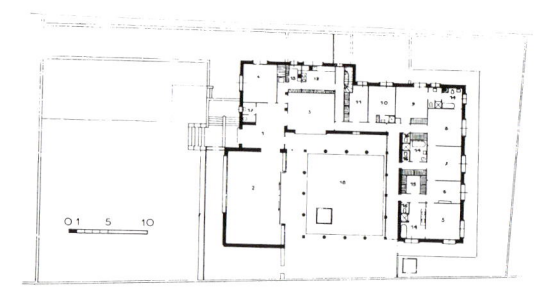

Léonard Morandi, Villa Dar Lugda, Anfa, c. 1951. First-floor plan, in *L'Architecture française*, April 1952.

Pierre Coldefy, architect's own house, Boulevard du Lido, 1955. General view.

is a stolid, affluent housing type, whose points of reference derived from the most firmly established stratum of Casablancan culture, i.e., the city's ceremonial, administrative, and institutional buildings. The Dar Lugda Villa in Anfa, designed by Morandi for his own use, shares a similar repertoire, but can be labeled more Mediterranean owing to its "inner patio-garden shielded from the wind, noise, and neighbors,"[22] with a connecting living room that boasts staggering sea views. As for Coldefy's designs, these include a single-story family dwelling that he built for himself in 1955, and whose vast glazed living room seems to merge with the garden. Both interior and exterior are faced with exposed stone—a material that was also used in the floors and on the walls, where it alternates with white plaster.

The Avant-Garde Sways toward Neutra and Aalto

A dozen or so boldly designed villas built in the 1950s made a strong impression on critics from Casablanca and Europe alike. Not only were their exteriors conceived as highly individualized sculptural works, but their layouts were also perfectly suited to the requirements of clients who were aspiring to a sophisticated lifestyle.

22 "Villa *Dar Lugda* à Anfa, Casablanca, L. Morandi architecte dplg," *L'Architecture française* 13, no. 131–32 (November–December 1952): 33.

The earliest of these dwellings (which could well be in California or Brazil) is the one designed by Jean-François Zevaco in 1949 for Sami Suissa, a real-estate developer. It is a prow-shaped building, since nicknamed the "Pagoda" or the "Butterfly," and it glides into the intersection between Boulevard d'Anfa and the seafront promenade,[23] its incisive white sunshields and balconies graphically framing the dark stone walls. Its reception rooms, hall, living room, and dining room can be converted into a single space by "two [sliding] glass panels,"[24] and the floors are laid with Belgian black marble in the main rooms and terrazzo in the others. At the time, its vast reception rooms, smoking room, and boudoir placed it within the realm of Parisian bourgeois dwellings, as did the villa's functional division of space: servants' quarters and garage with access ramp in the basement, reception spaces on the first floor, and private zones (bedrooms and bathrooms) on the second floor. In addition, a wall made of glass blocks running all the way around the building screens the symmetrically aligned swimming pool and garden from public view. This modern deluxe villa, sited in a prime city location, stirred up a great deal of controversy when it was built. The client gleefully recalls the public's jealous reaction

Jean-François Zevaco, in association with Paul Messina, Villa Sami Suissa, Boulevard Alexandre 1er, 1947. Photo taken in 1991 looking toward the garden.

23 Jean-François Zevaco commented on the "mentality" of Suissa, who situated his house at an intersection, on a lot more suitable for a gas station. Jean-François Zevaco, interview.

24 "Villa à Anfa, J.-F. Zevaco et P. Messina, architectes," *L'Architecture d'aujourd'hui* 22, no. 35 (May 1951): 57.

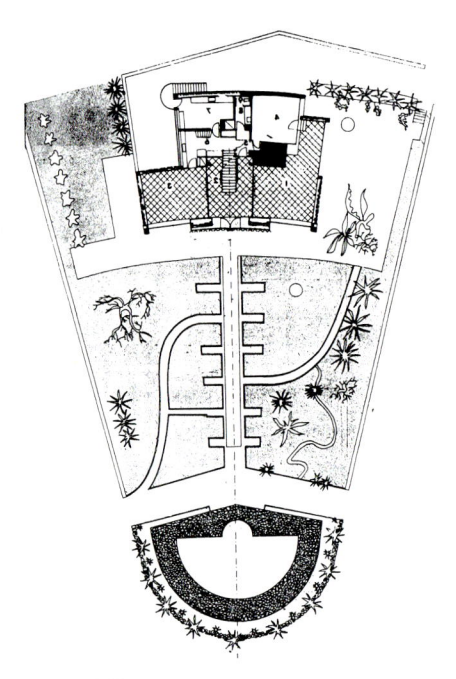

Jean-François Zevaco, in association with Paul Messina, Villa Sami Suissa, 1947. Plan of the ground floor and garden, in *L'Architecture d'aujourd'hui*, May 1951.

Jean-François Zevaco, in association with Paul Messina, Villa Sami Suissa, 1947. Perspective of the hall.

Jean-François Zevaco, in association with Paul Messina, Villa Sami Suissa, 1947. Elevation of hall partition.

25 Sami Suissa, interview by authors, Montreal, June 14, 1991.

26 Kidder Smith, "Report from Morocco," 72.

at the building's inauguration, while Zevaco professes to having lost many clients who were shocked by the dwelling's sharp forms. This all confirms just how daring the enterprise was.[25] Again, Kidder Smith was quick to grasp the villa's originality and to contrast it with the surrounding "cous-cous":

> The owner demanded a house that would be as prominent and attention-compelling as possible, and for a site that got a long triangular lot where normally a monument (or filling station) would be erected . . . The house is certainly calculated to stun one with its originality and, thus, superbly fulfills its program. Perhaps in the future we will witness tamer editions of the genius which produced it.[26]

Building designs also depended to a large degree on the personality of the client, as is demonstrated by the bold syntax employed in another of Anfa's most outstanding villas, this time on Boulevard Lido. In 1953 Terraz, a building contractor, commissioned Albert Planque in 1953 to build this single-story work, which is

Brise-soleil in 1950s villas.

Élie Azagury, Villa Schulmann, Lice d'Anfa, 1952. Photographed in 1991.

Albert Planque, Villa Roger Terraz, Boulevard du Lido, 1953. Photographed in 1994.

Wolfgang Ewerth, Villa Maurice Varsano, Sidi Maarouf, c. 1954. Photographed in 1996.

Albert Planque, Villa Roger Terraz, Boulevard du Lido, 1953. The terrace and brise-soleil. Photographed in 1994.

topped by a terrace, its jutting brise-soleil borne by a V-shaped support. The facade's stone cladding alternates with white stucco sections, while its interior arrangement corresponds to a tripartite distribution—reception space, private quarters, and service areas—so that each room opens onto a garden or patio. One particularly noteworthy feature is the master bedroom (with a large en suite bathroom and separate shower) that overlooks a covered patio. There is a large game room that extends into a terrace, and, as a final touch, the porthole windows of the basement swimming pool showers indicate a play on nautical vocabulary.[27]

In 1954, Wolfgang Ewerth constructed a villa for the cereals and sugar trader Maurice Varsano on a sizable, secluded plot in Ain Harrouda. It is remarkably rich in terms of spatial vocabulary, combining straight lines with curves, which wind around the swimming pool. In addition, its pilotis fulfill a function that is often missing in European houses, namely, channeling views from the entrance toward a

[27] After political uncertainty led the original client's family to flee, this house was completed for a new client who was seduced by its elegance.

Wolfgang Ewerth, Villa Maurice Varsano, Sidi Maarouf, c. 1954. Side facade.

Wolfgang Ewerth, Villa Maurice Varsano, Sidi Maarouf, c. 1954. Glazed entrance. Photographed in 1996.

Wolfgang Ewerth, Villa Maurice Varsano, Sidi Maarouf, c. 1954. View across the garden at night.

Wolfgang Ewerth, Villa Maurice Varsano, Sidi Maarouf, c. 1954. Living room.

Wolfgang Ewerth, Villa Maurice Varsano, Sidi Maarouf, c. 1954. Living room. Furniture by Jean Royère.

Wolfgang Ewerth,
Villa Girard, Anfa, 1955.
View of the villa under
construction.

Wolfgang Ewerth,
Villa Girard, Anfa, 1955.
View of completed villa.

Élie Azagury, Villa Schulmann, Lice d'Anfa, 1952. Entrance and brise-soleil.

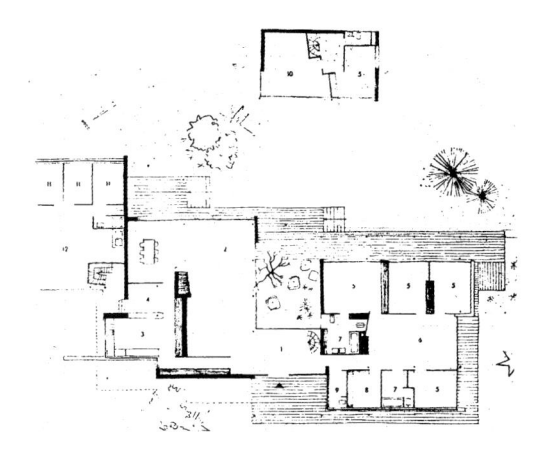

Élie Azagury, Villa Schulmann, Lice d'Anfa, 1952. Ground floor plan, in *L'Architecture d'aujourd'hui*, February–March 1953.
Rather than being enclosed by rooms or blank walls, the patio is marked out by a glazed wall, a bedroom wall, and a terrace that "acts as an extension to the owner's atelier and is sheltered by cantilevered sunshades." Sliding partitions separate the living room from a large playroom or children's "lounge." "Villa à Casablanca, É. Azagury architecte," *L'Architecture d'aujourd'hui* 24, no. 46 (February–March 1953): 86.

garden that is both interior and exterior. That it has a close link with California houses can be clearly detected in the sliding plate-glass windows, as well as in the relationship between the dwelling and the large swimming pool, which was intended for water polo games.[28] The interior is almost entirely open plan, while the decor and furniture, produced by the fashionable Paris designer Jean Royère, create a world of comfortable curves.[29] It constitutes a sort of manifesto of 1950s style, emphasized by the artwork. No less spectacular is the Villa Girard by Ewerth, likewise notable for its steel frame allowing for virtually no partitioning and superb sea views.[30]

Meanwhile, Élie Azagury adapted the traditional Moroccan inner patio to European use in one of his early villas, which dominates the city from the Anfa hill: "Here, the patio has been divested of its traditional Moroccan role to become a reception space in itself, running into the terrace that overhangs the garden and city."[31] The owner of this villa was Théo Schulmann, an interior decorator and son of a furniture maker. Schulmann had drawn up the program himself, and, on Azagury's return from Sweden, even agreed to become an agent for selling Scandinavian modern furniture. The local success of these products led to their being marketed in Paris, where they were also widely acclaimed.[32] The dwelling's *brise-soleil* grille, reused in Azagury's house for Luigi Lévy, which he built in 1955 in the Mers-Sultan district, was to become one of the architect's favorite design components.

Adopting an entirely new vocabulary, Azagury built the most dramatic manifestation of Casablancan Neo-Brutalism in a dwelling he designed in 1962 for his own use. The villa enjoys a commanding position atop Anfa hill and is fitted with

28 "Maisons tropicales, 35° latitude nord," *Plaisirs de France* (September 1958): 44–47.

29 Jean Royère (1902–81) designed and built flamboyant modernist interiors in Megève, as well as in Lebanon and Iran. See Marie-Claude Beaud et al., *Jean Royère: décorateur à Paris* (Paris: Musée des Arts décoratifs/Norma, 1999).

30 "Villa à Casablanca, Ewerth," *L'Architecture d'aujourd'hui* 26, no. 60 (June 1955): 58; "Villa G. in Casablanca-Anfa," *Die Innenarchitektur* (May 1957): 685–87; and Kultermann, *Architecture of Today*, 42, 210, 211.

31 "Villa à Casablanca, É. Azagury architecte," *L'Architecture d'aujourd'hui* 24, no. 46 (February–March 1953): 86.

32 Élie Azagury, interview by authors, Casablanca, April 17, 1990. Schulmann went on to create the firm Mobilier International in Paris.

Élie Azagury, second villa for the architect, 1962. Split-level living room and stairs.

The reading and music area is lit by a latticed window and a ribbon window. It overhangs the double-height living room, which receives natural light both from a French window and a large glass panel.

Élie Azagury, second villa for the architect, Rue Aspirant Henry Lemaignen, Ain Diab, c. 1962. Side facade. Photographed in 1990.

Élie Azagury, second villa for the architect, 1962. Living room and study on an intermediate level.

concrete beams that form a structural pattern along the facade, delineating stuccoed rectangles punctuated with an abstract arrangement of openings. Terraces extend out from mostly all the rooms, which at times protrude playfully from the central core. The visitor is led on a genuine *promenade architecturale* via an exposed staircase that weaves its way from room to room via half-story levels, resulting in a sense of spatial flow. Masterful interaction of shadow and light and of close and distant views engenders an atmosphere in which playful, lighthearted austerity contrasts with refined roughness.

Hybridized and Self-Effacing Modernity

A third type of deluxe villa was developed for clients who were reluctant to adopt avant-garde solutions. The creations of architects like Azagury, Zevaco, and Ewerth, showcased in Marc Lacroix's photographs, particularly shocked the propertied bourgeoisie, who turned instead toward a more reassuringly conventional building language. Casablanca's commercial architects were uncertain whether they should opt for restrained modernity or for a more regional style, and were torn between personal preferences, peer pressure, and the demands of their clients. For this particular category of housing, they therefore chose to reject the type of applied ornamentation used in less luxurious dwellings.

Erwin Hinnen's numerous dwellings west of the city can be said to belong to this reassuring building type, notably offering a perfect balance between local motifs and concessions to the slight nostalgia felt by the architect's bourgeois clients. As pointed out by *Maisons et Jardins*, unlike clients commissioning "young modern architects—disciples of Le Corbusier or Gropius who have designed their buildings to suit the scorching climate . . . many French settlers from the south of France have adopted the Provençal style so skillfully interpreted by Erwin Hinnen."[33] The elements that Hinnen worked into his designs were often, it is true, typically Provençal. He drew on "decorative tiling along the eaves, flat interlocking Spanish tiles, wrought-iron window grilles, archways, and exposed stone framework," just as he would have done if he were building on the Riviera. The only Moroccan touches are "minor details, such as the loggia lintel in the bedrooms and the central ornamental pool that adorns the patio." Observers clearly perceived this mix as a comforting form of compromise, sharply contrasting with the city's public architecture:

> Casablanca—a new city—is essentially a place where hotels and offices are conceived as skyscrapers built to reflect the latest architectural craze but where private housing is generally given a more personal touch, at least as far as the French are concerned. The fact that these people are mostly from the south perhaps explains why they nostalgically opt for distinctly Provençal architecture. One expert in this type of exported style is the architect Erwin Hinnen.[34]

Swiss-born Hinnen, an ardent admirer of the Mediterranean landscape, gave a picturesque interpretation of the principles of Beaux-Arts composition when he built his own villa, Les Chaumes, on the Crêtes hill, between 1949 and 1952. Here, the visitor is led through a Mexican-Moroccan patio into an interior largely open to rural views that cannot be seen from the street. The house he designed in 1950 for Tristan Vieljeux, a shipowner, is even more secluded. It is sited in the Oasis quarter, and its layout suggests a tranquil haven, as in many of Hinnen's staged arrangements. The entrance leads to a blank gable, after which a winding path guides the visitor into the house, which is coiled around a garden. The architect combined unexpected design elements with varied views in this introverted dwelling, which is a conversion of a 1920s house. The facades of the two main structural parts open onto a fountain and ornamental pool; the sculpted shells above the doors bear

33 "Casablanca," *Maisons et Jardins* (August–September 1953).

34 "À Casablanca, une maison à l'accent méridional de l'architecte Erwin Hinnen," *Maisons et jardins* (1955).

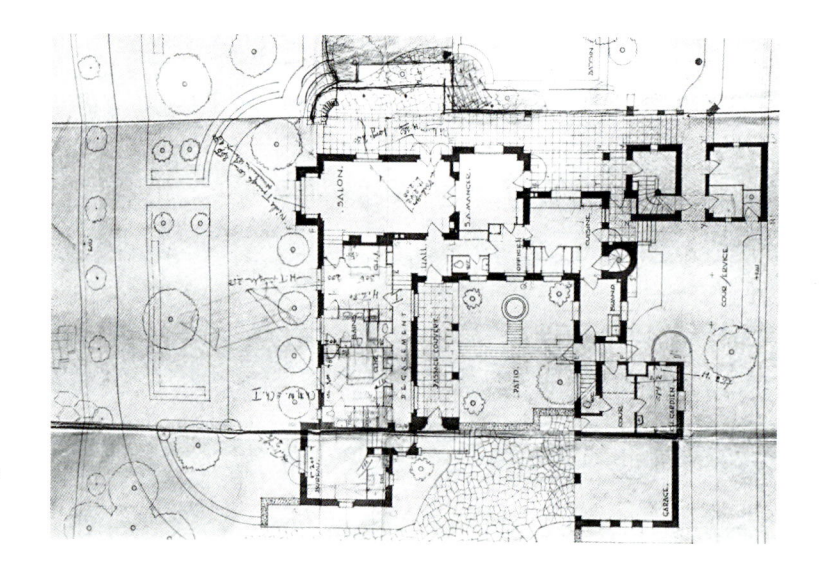

Erwin Hinnen, architect's own house, known as Les Chaumes, 413 Boulevard Panoramique, Les Crêtes, 1949–52. Plan.

Erwin Hinnen, architect's own house, 1949–52. Perspective view.

Erwin Hinnen, architect's own house, 1949–52. Patio-terrace. Photographed in 1994.

Erwin Hinnen, Vieljeux house, known as Saadia, Rue du Canonnier Carpentier, Oasis, 1950. Night view of the garden.

Erwin Hinnen, Vieljeux house, 1950. The garden. Photographed in 1994.

Villas, Beachside Resorts, and Movie Theaters 409

Auguste Cadet, architect's own home, Rue des Charmilles, Oasis, 1948. Garden facade.

Spanish overtones; the fountain is covered with star-shaped Moroccan *zillij*; and the neo-Gothic ramp leading to the upper story is imbued with the garden's subtropical fragrance, creating a heady, intimate atmosphere. The large four-meter-high salon in the dwelling's main wing opens onto both the garden and an enclosed patio, which also provides a source of light for the dining room. Hinnen chose to arrange the servants' quarters around an even more secluded courtyard.

The last contribution to neo-Moroccan domestic architecture is perhaps Auguste Cadet's own home, built by the architect in the Oasis district in 1948 and designed in a nostalgic manner at odds with the contemporary mainstream building output. The structure, which cannot be seen from the street, harbors a sequence of private patios arranged around a large living room and various bedrooms, and opens onto a vast *ryad** in the center of the plot. Elegant *zillij* panels and cedar ceilings clad the austere yet welcoming interior.[35]

Another point worthy of interest is the mestizo design logic developed by Ewerth, and which is still popular today in Casablanca. This involves wrapping a clearly European envelope around vast Moroccan-type salons. Ewerth's rather unusual villa designed for a Doctor B. in Anfa in 1962 is a case in point. It is laid like a pancake on spindly pilotis atop a hill, its Moroccan *zillij*-decorated salon opening out to panoramic views of the palm trees and ocean. This traditional salon is coupled with a modern living room, lit by a central glazed patio. The kitchen, which was delivered with all the latest appliances, such as a built-in oven and hotplate, was modern enough to satisfy even the most demanding American housewife. It is also interesting to note how Erwerth set contemporary technology side by side with a modern architectural language verging on kitsch. Such paradoxical twists created a by no means unattractive hybrid of modern living and features borrowed from the Moroccan vernacular.

[35] See the photograph album kept at the Académie d'Architecture, Paris.

Auguste Cadet, architect's own home, Rue des Charmilles, Oasis, 1948. *Ryad* in the garden. Photographed in 1996.

Wolfgang Ewerth, villa for Dr. B, Boulevard du Lido, 1963.

Wolfgang Ewerth, villa for Dr. B, 1963. Moroccan lounge with *zillij* tiles and sculpted ceiling.

Wolfgang Ewerth, villa for Dr. B, 1963. Kitchen.

Villas, Beachside Resorts, and Movie Theaters 411

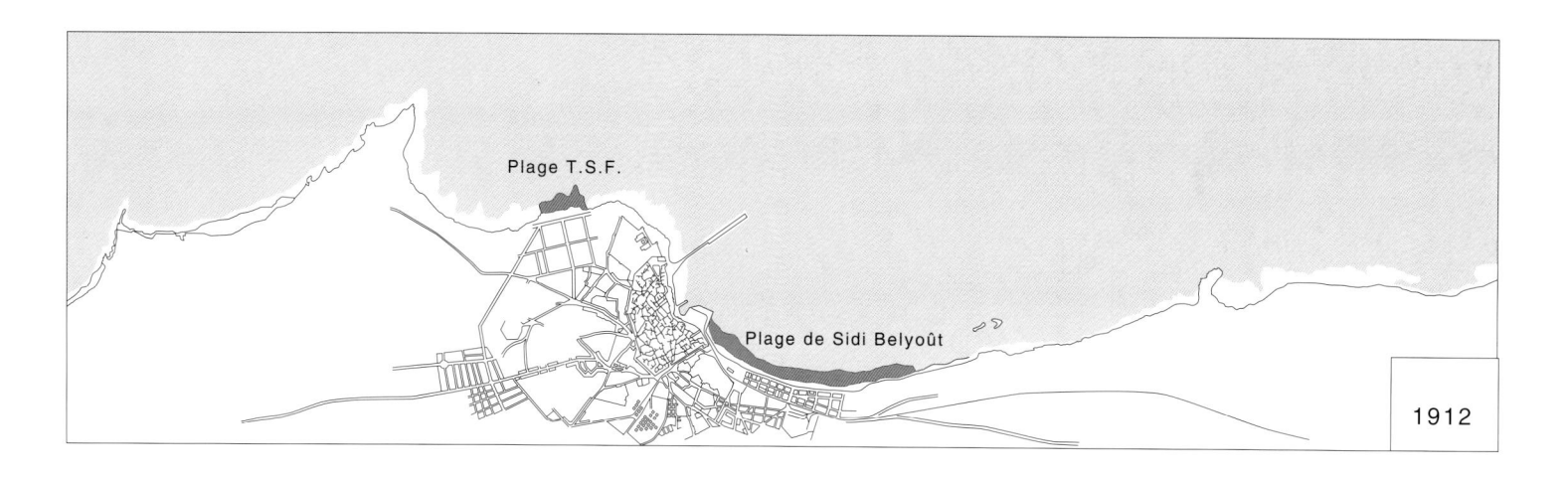

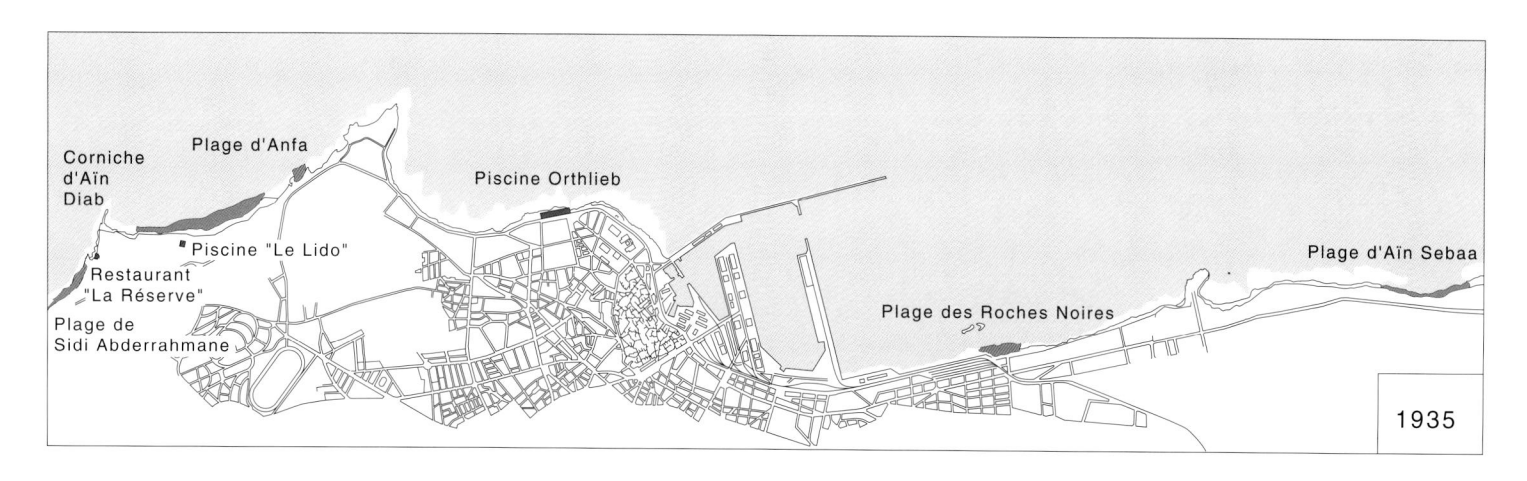

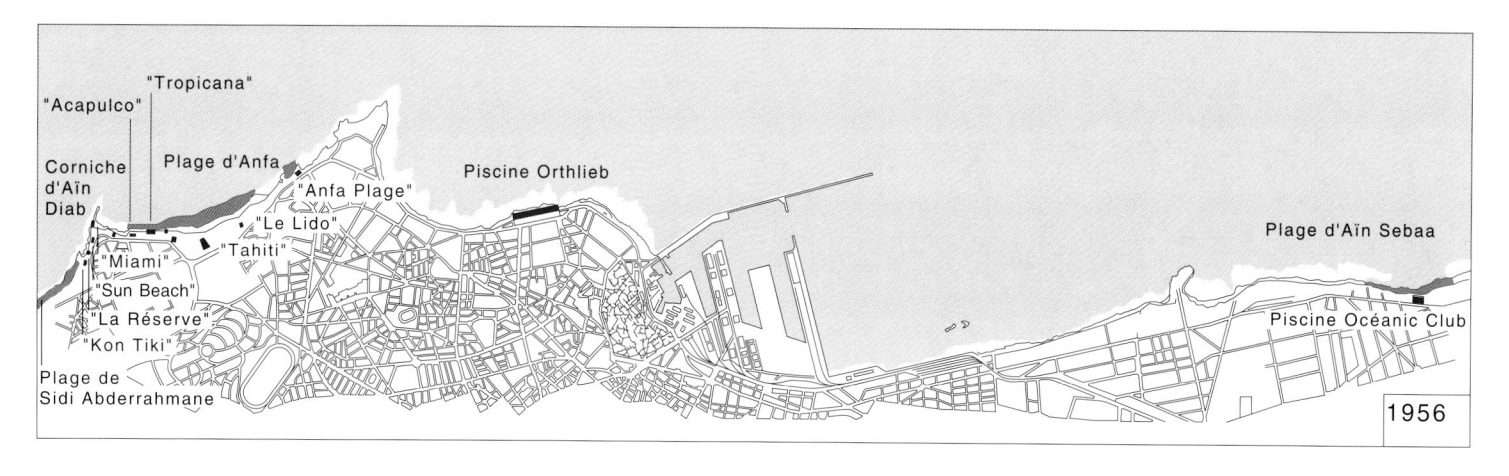

The sites of the beaches and pools along Casablanca's seafront and their displacement over time. Drawings by Philippe Simon.

La Corniche, Ain Diab, in the late 1950s. Looking toward the Lido café, the miniature golf course, and the beach.

Tropical Motifs for the Ain Diab Coastline

Silvery swimming pools sparkled like dead fish along the coast. Their names alone would have tanned a colony of albinos: Acapulco, Tahiti-Plage, Miami, Sun-Beach, and Kon-Tiki. A strip of light illuminated Ain Diab like stage footlights. The public was the ocean, plunged into darkness. The first rows were creating an uproar, while, on stage, nightclubs, pools, and bourgeois villas acted out their own scripts.

Tito Topin, 1983[36]

Sports were central to Casablancan life from 1945 onward, and the exploits of local heroes, such as Marcel Cerdan in the boxing ring or Just Fontaine and Ben Embarek on the soccer field soon became the talk of the town. Water sports also took off between 1945 and 1960. Serious water-pollution problems plagued the public swimming pool, which had been boarded up during the war, and the Ain Diab coastline became the latest fashionable haunt following major redevelopment work.[37] In 1944, Courtois had claimed there was "room for development in Ain Diab, where the top expanse of beach is linked to Anfa-Supérieur by an ensemble of gardens, stairways, and ramps that look onto the attractive Lido site."[38] By 1949, this part of the coast was already booming, as was noted in the tourist brochures:

> Small sandy beaches—a favorite spot for Casablancans—are dotted all along the shore. There is a fairly sheltered stretch of water, which is a good place for bathing, although it is subject to strong currents at times ... There are sand dunes and steep rocks, which are ideal for fishing. Bathing establishments, hotels, restaurants, and kindergartens have been set up, generating an influx of visitors.[39]

In 1953, the Lido pool restaurant that had been built in the 1930s was extended to include a miniature golf course and a Venetian-style gourmet restaurant and café called Le Doge, which overlooked "one of Casablanca's finest beaches"[40] and was generally regarded as one of the smartest establishments in town. Another pool was subsequently built in the Lido, containing a glazed covered bath for winter use, and

[36] Tito Topin, *55 de fièvre*, Série noire no. 1905 (Paris: Folio, 1988; first published, Paris: Gallimard, 1983) and idem, *Piano barjo* (Paris: Gallimard, 1983), 269.

[37] In 1939, it was classified as a "tourist site" in order to prevent construction. *BMO* (May–June 1939). However, with the exception of an amusement park built on Benhaïm beach before the war, it was endowed with few permanent installations. *BMO* (September–October 1939).

[38] Courtois, *Casablanca: projet d'aménagement et d'extension de la ville*, 40.

[39] *Casa-guide: renseignements sur la ville* (Casablanca: Éditions France-Afrique, 1949), 7.

[40] *La Quinzaine de Casablanca* (Casablanca), November 25–December 9, 1953.

Sun-Beach pool club in 1950, in Charles Penz and Bernard Rouget, *Photo-itinéraire de Casablanca*, 1950.

41 Topin, *55 de fièvre*, 83. Regarding this part of the Ain-Diab coast, as well as the Lido pool and its dramatic destruction by fire before independence, see Tito Topin's novel *Le Cœur et le chien* (Paris: Grasset, 1985), 303–9. Elsewhere, Topin "sees himself during the day, from one convertible to another, between the Réserve and the Lido." "Je me vois," in *Casablanca, fragments d'imaginaire*, vol. 9, eds. Bourdon and Folléas.

the ochre-red that had previously lent the place a Moroccan flavor was replaced by dazzling white, the color of modernity. The Lido remained a favorite meeting place for high-society sports lovers up until its demolition, and has been canonized by Tito Topin in his noir stories on 1950s Casablancan life:

> The Lido was laid on a concrete deck cast into the sand, cutting a daring figure of American baroque … Above the concrete base, cleansed of all makeup, rose its glass architecture brushed with an alternate palette of sky blue, earthy saffron, and sandy gold. Ocean breezes drifted ominously across, flattening the sand against the dunes, pushing the dust behind the hills and painting the Lido in a camaïeu of blue.[41]

The seasonal nature of the facilities in La Corniche—beach huts, chalets, and holiday camp tents—gradually gave way to more permanent amenities, and paying pools were constructed. A string of seawater pools was hollowed out of the rocks using dynamite, and the shoreline was peppered with exotic commercial signs. Bars and dance halls mushroomed along the roadside, although the land behind the Ain Diab promontory was left vacant, except for the Robitaillé housing subdivision built between Boulevard de Biarritz and La Corniche. Robitaillé's street names recall resorts such as Antibes on the Riviera and Quiberon in Britanny, indicating how the French *petite bourgeoisie* of Casablanca were clearly nostalgic for their country's beaches. The development turned into a full-scale village, complete with its own post office and school. The municipal authority planted a mimosa grove next to the Sidi Abderrahman marabout, which sits on a rocky outcrop accessible only at low tide. This grove proved highly popular both in summer and winter.

The bathing establishments with their sandy beaches were designed as social meeting places, and although their waterslides, volleyball courts, and large pools hollowed out of the rocks certainly tested one's fitness, the sensual side to life was also greatly emphasized. Riders would gallop along the beach in the froth of the sea from dawn to dusk, as the sounds of American jukeboxes drifted out from the dance floors and cabins. The first surfers created a setting worthy of a Californian or Hawaiian dream, while swimming and rock and roll eased the troubled atmosphere that marked the end of the Protectorate and helped the European bourgeoisie forget the looming threat of independence.

Each establishment had its own category of clientele, generating fierce social and racial divides amid the American- and tropical-themed billboards. Le Lac, an annex to La Réserve—a restaurant that opened just before 1939—attracted well-to-do customers, including businessmen and their families.[42] It was renamed Sun-Beach during the war, following its purchase by the Parisian journalist and champion diver Durand de Lompuy, alias Roland Lennad, and was fitted out with a volleyball court, a filtered seawater pool, a diving board, an ornamental portico, and rocks.[43] Lennad pulled all the necessary strings to get permission to open the club, which became a favorite spot for American GIs after the 1942 landings, especially as the seawater pool protected "swimmers from the treachery of the ocean."[44] Riding on his success, Lennad requested a tract of state-owned land and put up more buildings, surrounding the pool with an ensemble of spectator platforms, beach huts, a promenade deck, a fast-food café, and a restaurant. Lennad renamed Sun-Beach the Club des Clubs de Casablanca, or CCC, seeking to reproduce what he viewed as the sporty, socialite image of the elite Racing-Club in Paris. The establishment was run on a strict policy of exclusivity, as is demonstrated by its early 1950s membership register: out of a thousand members, there were three Muslims and ten Jews. The entrance requirements (character references from two members) enabled Lennad to bar certain ethnic groups, toward whom he openly displayed his aversion, as is graphically illustrated in his statement, "Do not forget that by protecting your Club against undesirable elements, you are protecting your own person."[45] As the owner of a swimming pool long renowned for being "off-limits to Jews and Arabs," he did not wish to see any "suspicious shade" of skin among his bathers, or so he wrote. In one of his novels, Tito Topin describes one Sun-Beach regular as a rich, racist "mummy's boy," protected by his mother's lover—a character based on Philippe Boniface, the real-life boss of the Casablanca region.[46]

Lennad's establishment was rooted in the worship of sports and had its own champion volleyball and water polo teams.[47] It was also closely linked to the European business world, and its members (who included the architect Hinnen) all sought commissions and services in one form or another. In addition, Lennad organized large themed parties and car rallies in an attempt to keep the Casablancans on their home ground during the summer. After converting the public swimming pool into a private club, he set up the Miami pool club especially for his American clientele, on a peninsula adjacent to Sun-Beach. Although this

Club des Clubs de Casablanca (Sun-Beach), front cover of the membership register, 1953.

42 Léandre Pola (club member and accountant), interview by the authors, Casablanca, December 19, 1995.

43 This pool was the first to be set up at sea level. The Lido's pool was farther from the sea.

44 Bernard Rouget and Charles Penz, *Casablanca: photo itinéraire* (Casablanca: Imprimerie de Fédala, 1950).

45 Robert Lennad, *Annuaire du CCC* (Casablanca: CCC, 1954), 48.

46 Topin, *55 de fièvre*, 108.

47 The prohibition against teenagers—called "juniors"—loitering aimlessly at poolside was characteristic of the atmosphere of emulation that Lennad wanted to create. The youths were admitted "only insofar as they register in one of our athletic divisions with the intention of participating in the free training sessions and the minor competitions." It was thus a matter "of not leaving idle at the pool young people whose moral education was in process." *Annuaire du CCC* (1952), 39.

Miami pool club, c. 1955. The pools are on the far right of the photo, hollowed into the rocks. The 800-meter-long dike opens directly onto the sea, with a viewing platform lashed by waves. The photo shows concrete sunbathing areas flanked by a fine-sand beach.

Aerial view of Sun Beach, 1962. Behind La Réserve restaurant is the Kon-Tiki pool club.

416 Casablanca

club was, in principle, open to everyone, selection was ensured by means of the entrance price, as would be the case with all the other clubs that later opened in the area.

La Corniche grew ever more popular, causing Lennad to compare Casablanca with Nice and Cannes. He dreamed of it "rising to the ranks of fashionable beach resort towns by developing the coastal site of Ain Diab."[48] However, persuading the European Casablancans that "summertime is extremely pleasant on the coast of Morocco" was not enough; it was also a matter of recasting the city's image: "The realization that Casablanca has the capacity to become a summer vacation resort may be the turning point in its expansion... With its European climate, year-round sunshine, medinas, hotels, and easy access, Casablanca could easily become a large summer tourist center if a suitable and affordable entertainment program were drawn up."[49] After Lennad's accidental death in 1955, Hinnen, the favorite architect of the European set, redeveloped the pool club. The road was widened to twice its original size, its verges leveled out and a link created with El Hank.

Tahiti-Plage, set up around 1952 by André Suire—a pioneer surfer as well as a pilot and parachutist—soon became the premier site in Ain Diab for swimming and other aquatic pursuits.[50] It broke with the slightly austere sea sport tradition that had dominated La Corniche up until then, rigged out in Polynesian trimmings and bearing a hint of African style—a design syntax that originated in Suire's long-standing love of the Pacific isles. He introduced the first surfboards to Casablanca, having brought them over from Polynesia, and five years after the club opened, he went into successful partnership with Paul Anselin. Suire oversaw the refurbishment of the pools and the design of the beach facilities—palm tree huts; black, ochre, and sky-blue canvases; and totemlike posts. Anselin took care of the management aspects and maintenance work on the pools. Moroccan laborers revamp the club on a yearly basis, but Suire's initial scheme has become

48 Roger Lennad, "Une grande création: la Corniche," in *Annuaire du CCC*, Casablanca (1954), 48.

49 Lennad, "Une grande création," 48.

50 Rouget and Penz, *Casablanca: photo itinéraire*.

General view of Tahiti pool club, 1954. Note the two adjacent pools and the restaurant with verandah and palm roof.

In the background are the changing cabins and on the far right is the Lido pool club. The El Hank lighthouse can be seen in the distance.

Aerial view of Tahiti pool club in the early 1950s. Note the huts between the Tahiti and the Lido.

51 Patrice Anselin (Tahiti-Plage director), interview by Monique Eleb, Casablanca, November 28, 1992.

52 Le Tonga was also a meeting place for young adults who favored nightclubs and jazz. See Topin, *55 de fièvre*, 110–14.

53 Patrice Anselin, interview. In 1963, during the opening of a new pool, the daily *La Nation* hailed the "irreproachable" attention to hygiene in this "example of an ultramodern beach-pool" accommodating 3,000 bathers. "La Corniche casablancaise améliore chaque année son standing," *La Nation* (Casablanca), May 17, 1963.

54 Since 1960, this Casablancan "ritual promenade" (*Guide Michelin*, 1950), has experienced significant modifications along its ocean side, but has remained unchanged along the interior. This despite projects like that of the Ministry of the Interior for "a district and site very much below their potential," in order to transform La Corniche into a tourist axis. Ministère de l'intérieur, "Casablanca, Secteur touristique du quartier d'Ain Diab" (Ministère de l'Intérieur, [c. 1970]), Ministère de l'Habitat, Rabat. This treatment contrasts with that of the coast between El Hank and the Great Mosque of Hassan II, into which massive investments have been made since 1980.

55 Topin, *55 de fièvre*, 123–24.

increasingly distorted.[51] Whereas the majority of pool designers in Ain Diab chose to link the beach directly with seawater pools, Suire and Anselin combined salt water with a number of natural springs (*Ain* meaning spring in Arabic), with a view to creating as authentic a setting as possible. Several years later, one of the huts, Le Tonga, was to house a gleaming Wurlitzer jukebox under its palm trees, tempting people to dance in the shadowy afternoon light to the strains of Elvis Presley and Little Richard, whose songs had been made popular by the radio station of Nouaceur, the U.S. military base. The radio station was a favorite among Casablancan teenagers.[52]

Just as the "Tahiti" style was hitting Saint-Tropez in the early 1960s, a decade behind Casablanca, Anselin decided to build ten palm-leaf chalets named after Polynesian islands. These mini-dwellings, which were equipped with deckchairs, recliners, and tables, were used by workers in the summer during their midday breaks and can be read as an urban alternative to the holiday cabin in Pont Blondin. They proved a huge success among the French bourgeoisie and Moroccan Jewish families, and very soon became just as much of a social hub as the city cafés; just being seen on the verandahs there denoted upward mobility, in the same way as being a member of the Sun-Beach meant that one was part of the wealthy elite. An extension program was launched later in the 1960s, with the surrounding rocks dynamited and thousands of tons of sand deposited to reclaim part of the land. Since then, the site has undergone constant repairs due to damage caused by the tides and damp winters, but has nonetheless managed to retain its tropical flavor to this very day, conveyed through wooden totems and palm-leaf huts.[53]

Aerial view of Tahiti pool club in the late 1950s. Note the former coastal path, converted into a boulevard with parking spaces. The photo also shows the first bungalows built on the site.

The 1960s also saw construction of the Tropicana pool club. It is located next to the Tahiti, and the two clubs sport a comparable design. Meanwhile, the owners of the Acapulco, at the other end of the beach next to the Miami club, decided to set up the first beach pool. Around the same time, the Kon-Tiki opened between the La Réserve restaurant and Sidi Abderrahman beach; it was fitted out in a similar way to Sun-Beach, but its three pools were all built entirely on reclaimed land.

Although the beaches belonging to these private establishments were developed and furnished by their owners, coastal development—a process that had been initiated back in the 1940s—was a joint scheme in that the Protectorate granted land (in general for a fifteen- or twenty-year period) provided there was a real investment plan. The development that took place in fact mirrored Casablanca's early precarious urban climate, with strips of wasteland interspersed with bars, nightclubs, and a gamut of restaurants that sprouted opposite the upscale pool clubs, in total disregard of visual cohesion.[54] Nonetheless, as finely described by Tito Topin, this beach suburb resort generated its own specific atmosphere, whether during the day or at dusk:

> The meager lampposts cast trembling shadows along the ground just like a Giacometti sculpture. Illuminated posters displayed enticing pin-ups slaking their thirst, drinking straight from the bottle. Shop, café, and hotel fronts flickered with neon lights, flickering even more when gusts of sand blew across. The seafront promenade, so alive in the daytime, lay strewn like a colored ribbon in the dust, as sad as a streamer after a party.[55]

Ain Sebaa beach, east of the coastal industrial zone, also underwent development in the 1950s, but made no great dent in Ain Diab's popularity, especially

Acapulco pool club, c. 1961.

La Corniche, Ain Diab, in the late 1950s.

Photo taken at sunset in springtime. Workers are restoring the Tahiti pool club.

among a community of mostly Italian and Spanish laborers and white-collar workers. The Guinguette Fleurie, the Jardin d'été, and the Parc Beaulieu, together with dance halls and fish restaurants, were set up for the adults, while the nearby zoo kept the children entertained. The Oceanic Club, fashioned in the same mold as the Ain Diab clubs, offered safe bathing facilities as of 1949 in a foreshore swimming pool. A full-scale suburb, made up of housing developments, schools, a post office, and a church, also sprang up further inland, near the factories.

As of the mid-1960s, La Corniche became fully privatized. Those Casablancans seeking free bathing facilities went to the reputedly dangerous Sidi Abderrahman beach, or to public beaches east of the Lido, although this part of La Corniche was also beginning to spawn pool clubs and other private establishments. Many Moroccan Muslims of diverse social backgrounds likewise began to use the beaches, thereby reducing segregation. In conclusion, although the city's various bathing points and facilities were initially curtailed given Casablanca's port function, they were eventually granted a vital role within the urban framework. Such development was rendered possible only by the combined efforts of civil engineers and enterprising businessmen, which was typical of Casablanca. It must not be forgotten, either, that they were catering to a public that craved sports, games, and partying.

Architectural Innovations in the 1950s

Pacheco showed us some photos of Casablanca's airfield and avenues. In one of them we saw him standing in a steward's uniform in front of a building whose blinding whiteness cut sharply against the blue of the sky. It was a sun-filled setting in which everything stood out intensely: the whites and the blues; the shadow outlined against the base of the building; the steward's sandy beige uniform; Pacheco's smile; and the fuselage of the tourist plane glittering in the background.

Patrick Modiano, 1990[56]

Morocco may be a product of France, but at the same time the fact that it is not subject to French law makes it a perfect proving ground for experiments that cannot be conducted in the metropolis. One notable example is construction, and rental apartment blocks in particular. There are no hard and fast rules laid down by the state with respect to this type of building, unlike in France, where the authorities have enacted such stringent legislation that private companies are unable to invest in construction; the state therefore does this in their stead, which implies that the latter has full control over the building industry— a most unfavorable and frustrating situation.

Albert Caquot, 1956[57]

Here, Caquot—an eminent civil engineer—underlines the innovative nature of contemporary Moroccan building practices compared to those in France. The contrast between the tightly regulated legislation of the metropolis and the autonomy granted to Moroccan-based architects and building firms was striking. Casablanca's postwar architectural course of experimental housing (in both social and technological terms) came at a time when a new generation of architects had begun to take

56 Patrick Modiano, *Fleurs de ruine* (Paris: Gallimard, 1990), 70.

57 Albert Caquot, remarks made in February 1956, *Annales de l'Institut technique du bâtiment et des travaux publics*, no. 109 (January 1957). Caquot was speaking of the Bournazel housing development—certainly not the most architecturally seductive work in Casablanca.

Jean-François Zevaco, Physical therapy center in Tit Mellil, 1953–60. View of the staircases.

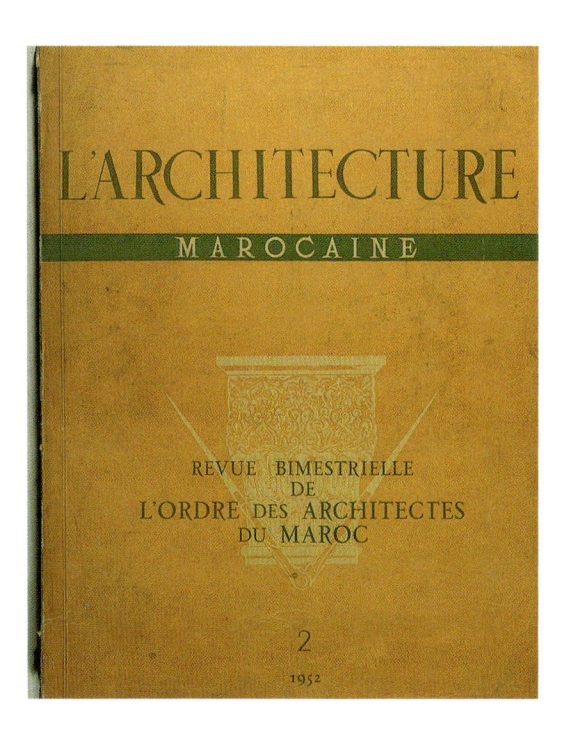

L'Architecture marocaine, a journal published by the Moroccan Order of Architects between 1950 and 1955.

58 Maddalena, "Sur l'évolution de l'architecture et de l'urbanisme au Maroc."

59 Azagury worked with Erskine on the Gyttorp housing for the Nobel dynamite factory workers. Peter Collymore, *The Architecture of Ralph Erskine* (London: Academy Editions, 1994), 44–45.

60 From 1950 to 1955, the Order published the journal *L'Architecture marocaine*.

61 The congress was supposed to take place from November 12 to 25, 1955, note Alger, February 20, 1955, gta/ETH, 42-JLS-9-21. Candilis still represented GAMMA in June 1954. "Arrangements for C.I.A.M. 10, September 1955 at Algiers," 1954, Éliane and Henri Tastemain, personal archives, Rabat.

62 Jean-Jacques Honegger, "Bilan et situation des groupes, période du 13 novembre 1947 au 30 juin 1955," gta/ETH, 42-AR-10-19/26.

63 A former student of Lods's and assistant of Écochard's, Tastemain resided in Rabat, where he had collaborated with Éliane Castelnau since 1948. Henri Tastemain, interview by authors, Paris, November 11, 1989.

64 "CIAM X Lapad août 1956, B7 commission report," gta/ETH.

65 Chemineau underlined the question of emerging Moroccan professionals, writing of the new "conjuncture" brought about by independence. Jean Chemineau to Pierre-A. Émery, Rabat, January 26, 1957, gta/ETH, 42-AR-17-112. In the future, Georges Delanoë, Louis Riou, and Édouard Delaporte would join in.

center stage. As Robert Maddalena points out, these architects enjoyed a privileged situation, in that they were freed from bureaucratic constraints and were backed by a clientele open to new forms: "It must be admitted that . . . in Morocco architects were, as a rule, afforded the rare opportunity of being able to work in total freedom and in a 'modern' spirit, as is commonly stated. They were not in any way bound by regional or archaeological restraints, since a clear caesura had been drawn between the end of the Middle Ages and the dawning of the twentieth century."[58]

Postwar Architectural Trends

The climate in which Casablanca's Beaux-Arts-trained architects worked in the 1920s and 1930s underwent a radical shift that was triggered by three factors: the launching of public programs, the arrival of the Écochard planning team, and the influence of young, usually Moroccan-born architects. Whether these specialists had left Morocco to study in Paris or, conversely, had fled a crushed France to come to a booming country spared the hardships of the war, they were united in their rejection of interwar Moroccan architecture, which they viewed as too monumental and picturesque. Only a handful of buildings by Boyer and Desmet seemed acceptable to them. Élie Azagury, for example, focused on the technical aspect of materials and the light Nordic architecture that he had discovered during a long spell in Ralph Erskine's practice in Stockholm; furthermore, he showed a keen interest in Richard Neutra's private houses, as did Gaston Jaubert.[59] Elsewhere, the influence of Le Corbusier and Oscar Niemeyer can be clearly perceived, as in Jean-François Zevaco's designs; it has to be said, though, that Zevaco's skillful, elegant works are as much seated in Beaux-Arts composition techniques as in modern concepts.

It is noteworthy that those architects who had at one time or another participated in meetings of the Groupe des Architectes Modernes Marocains (GAMMA) were not in fact united in a common design process. While some actively participated in less radical professional organizations—such as the Ordres des architectes (Order of Architects, modeled on the French system),[60] or the S.A.D.G. which brought together Beaux-Arts graduates—the major characteristic uniting GAMMA members was their rebuttal of prewar solutions rather than their adherence to C.I.A.M. doctrines, which were, in any case, overturned by critics after the Aix-en-Provence congress.

C.I.A.M. members thought of holding their tenth congress in Algiers in view of the work being conducted in Morocco and Algeria. The event, scheduled for November 1955, would have entailed "meetings with North African architects,"[61] but owing to the political situation, the venue was switched to Dubrovnik. Jean Chemineau, a Rabat-based architect and member of GAMMA since 1952, was appointed as the congress delegate for Morocco,[62] at a time when Morocco was veering increasingly toward independence. Chemineau's group prepared two grids for its Dubrovnik presentation, showing the design research in progress and intended as a follow-up to the findings that had made such an impact in Aix. However, as it turned out, although Chemineau, Henri Tastemain,[63] Azagury, and Louis Riou participated in the congress's task force on "Urbanism as a Component of Habitat," they did not present their grids; it was as if the impact of Écochard and Candilis's driving force had dried up.[64]

Chemineau sporadically continued to act as congress delegate up until the Otterlo congress of 1959, during which the C.I.A.M. was disbanded. By all accounts, Azagury's role in GAMMA's meetings grew increasingly important throughout the 1950s, all the more so as he was the only full-blooded Moroccan of the group, even though Zevaco was born in Casablanca.[65] He represented the group in Otterlo in 1959 and was elected first chairman of the Order of Architects in independent Morocco.

Alexandre Courtois, Banque Nationale du Commerce et de l'Industrie building, Place de France, 1950.

The building output of Moroccan modernists formed part of a broader framework, defined by Sigfried Giedion in 1954 when he came over to seek out examples of a new "regional approach." Giedion drew attention to Candilis and Woods's collective housing schemes and compared Écochard's work with that of Sert and Wiener in Cuba, likening the eight-by-eight-meter grid to the "units set in rows around the walls" of the ancient Egyptian village of Tel-el-Amarna.[66] As secretary general of C.I.A.M., Giedion was keenly aware of the increasingly rebellious climate within the organization's ranks. He realized that a page or two could be taken from Morocco's book on creating new housing concepts for developing countries, grounded in the use of local vernacular.

Sculpting Architectural Forms

Besides the housing programs described earlier, architects were invited by the Protectorate to enter competitions for the design of public facilities, and also received various commissions from private clients. Whatever the program—office buildings, hotels, garages, gas stations, or movie theaters—architects took on a new language in their search for modern sculptural forms.

Casablanca's urban structures of the 1950s, whether designed by radical GAMMA members or by other innovative designers, make up an original, albeit relatively unknown, chapter in the history of modern architecture. It was a time when academic architects, such as Alexandre Courtois, had to succumb to the pres-

[66] Sigfried Giedion, "The State of Contemporatry Architecture: (1) The Regional Approach," *Architectural Record* 155, no. 1 (January 1954): 135. Republished as, "The New Regionalism" in *Architecture, You, and Me: The Diary of a Development* (Cambridge, Mass.: Harvard University Press, 1958), 149.

67 "Immeuble de la place de France, A. Courtois et Ch. Favel," in *Le Maroc moderne.*
68. See the special issues of *L'Architecture marocaine* devoted to schools, no. 3 (1953) and no. 4 (1954).

68 See the special issues of *L'Architecture marocaine* devoted to schools, no. 3 (1953) and no. 4 (1954)

69 The Longchamp school is discussed in the context of international production in Alfred Roth, *Das neue Schulhaus* (Zurich: Girsberger, 1957), 143–48. Écochard would attempt to exclude Zevaco from school commissions following his work on a project in which the classrooms received natural light only from above. Pierre Mas, interview.

70 For this project, Jaubert was assisted by Brian Richards, a young British architect and future transportation specialist. Brian Richards, interview by Jean-Louis Cohen, London, June 4, 1992.

Alexandre Courtois, elementary school, Rond-Point de l'Europe, 1954. Photographed in 1991.

Élie Azagury, Longchamp elementary school, 1954. Facade overlooking the courtyard.

sure of the widely acclaimed "moderns" for fear of not responding to local demand. Courtois constructed the BNCI office/housing block in the early 1950s on the site where Boulevard de la Gare intersects with the Place de France. This sixteen-story prism, whose top floors are set back from the rest, complied with Courtois's ideas for the city center as well as with the legislation on arcades, while introducing a design aesthetic that breaks with the 1930s buildings.[67] Another Courtois scheme was for the slab housing unit designed for war veterans along Avenue D'Amade, overlooking Parc Lyautey. Here, the structure's brutal form casts a raw light over what had been touted as "the city's [southern] entrance." Elsewhere, Courtois adopted a cubist language allied with moderate use of screen walls in his plans for a number of schools and for Casablanca-Port station.

Schools were accorded a central role within the new residential districts. For instance, the public authorities of Rabat launched a competition in 1953 encouraging architects to come up with innovative designs and create a "classroom-type." Bodiansky submitted a scheme for this.[68] Meanwhile, Azagury worked on the Longchamp and La Villette schools, where he staged an interaction of materials and lighting forms, transposing North European design solutions to Morocco. Moreover, he called into question traditional classroom layout and focused on the patio motif.[69] Zevaco explored the multiple relationships between galleries, roof overhangs, and classrooms, while Gaston Jaubert's team set up a genuine nerve center in the heart of the Bournazel housing development. In this project, the school's large patio is girded by ramps that lead into the various classrooms, like a reassuring microcosm sheltered from the intensity of metropolitan life; it is, in fact, a modern interpretation of Boyer's design for the inner courtyards of the city hall.[70]

The specific urban culture of Casablanca in this period can perhaps best be

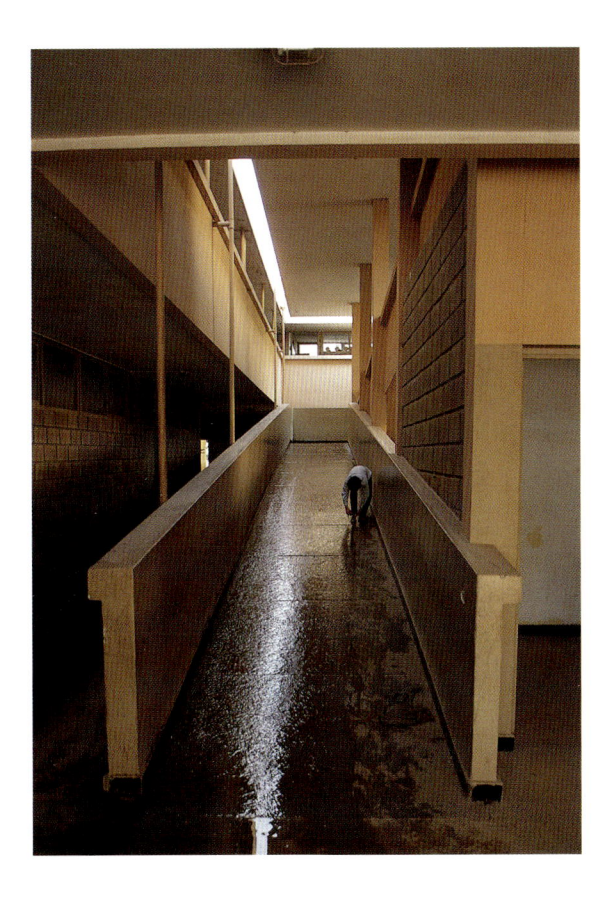

Gaston Jaubert, elementary school, Bournazel housing complex, 1956. Indoor ramp. Photographed in 1993.

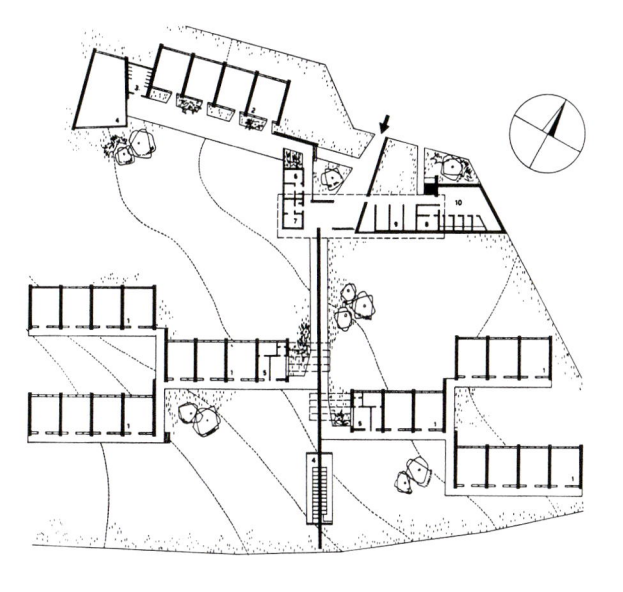

Élie Azagury, Longchamp elementary school, 1954. Plan published in Alfred Roth, *Das neue Schulhaus,* 1957.

Gaston Jaubert, elementary school, Bournazel housing complex, 1956. Patio and open-air amphitheater. Photographed in 1956.

Avenue de la République and Marhaba hotel (formerly Paquet hotel), Casablanca, 1955.

Émile Duhon, project for a hotel, Avenue de la République, 1948. Overall perspective. The built version would be called El Mansour Hotel.

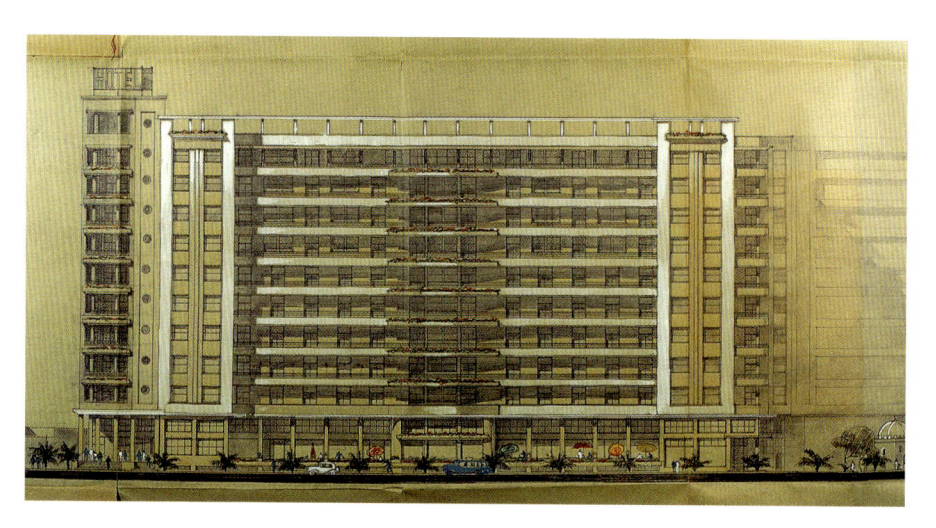

Edmond Brion, competition entry for a hotel on Avenue de la République, 1942. Elevation overlooking the avenue.

Alexandre Courtois, C.T.M. bus station and housing, Avenue de la République, 1951–55.

Robert Maddalena, electric transformer unit, commissioned by Société Marocaine de Distribution, Avenue Franklin Roosevelt, 1952.

Avenue de la République and El Mansour hotel looking from the elevator of the Hésperides building. Frames for the film *Six et douze* by Magid Khrich and Mohammed Tazi, 1968.

perceived in these types of public programs rather than in the office buildings that mushroomed throughout the center and out to the east toward the station. Monofunctional slab buildings began to make their mark along the new Avenue de la République[71] (a remote descendant of the Labonne scheme), the first being Émile Duhon's El Mansour hotel. This scheme was initially for a twenty-five story building, but its summit was lopped off before construction began. It was designed as part of an ensemble that included Erwin Hinnen's Saturne and Océanic buildings, as well as Albert Planque's Les Hespérides complex, conceived as strictly aligned shops protected by a continuous glass canopy and surmounted by office blocks. The Planque building is cleaved by a glazed elevator shaft that offers dramatic views down the avenue.[72] A second set of buildings, masterplanned by Godefroy, was intended to mark a break in the avenue's built front while introducing a new scale, first by means of Duhon's "tourist hotel," commissioned by the Paquet shipping company, and sec-

71 Debates regarding the avenue buildings occurred constantly in the Municipal Council. A first version of the regulation regarding these buildings was published in *BMO* (February 1950): 31–32. A modified version was published in *BMO* (December 1950): 40–45. It integrated the arcades' constraints with the practices of property owners associations.

72 A sequence shot from this elevator appears in Magid Khrich and Mohammed Tazi's film *Six et douze* (made in 1968 for the Moroccan Cinematographic Center).

Villas, Beachside Resorts, and Movie Theaters 427

Jean-François Zevaco, Société Civile Immobilière du Centre building, Rue Poincaré, 1949. Facade. Photographed in 1997.

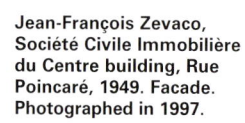

Jean-François Zevaco, Apartment and Volvo-Singer garage, commissioned by Société immobilière d'outremer Rue de Mareuil, 1950 (unfinished). View of the model, in *Évolution du Maroc en 1951*.

73 In 1954, a competition held for the Caisse Marocaine des Retraites (Moroccan Pension Bank) apartment building was won by Jean Forcioli. *L'Architecture marocaine*, no. 4 (1954): 91–108.

74 *Arts* (October 1948), quoted in Elisabeth Vitou, *Gabriel Guévrékian 1900–1970: une autre architecture moderne* (Paris: Connivences, 1987), 113. We have not suceeded in locating this building in Casablanca; it is possible that it was never built.

ond, via the Compagnie des Transports Marocains bus station by Alexandre Courtois, designed as slanting slabs set atop low-level commercial outlets.[73]

Interestingly, it is the more modest-scale commercial buildings that are, at times, more engaging. Such is the case with the Tragin building, designed in 1948 by Persian-born Gabriel Guévrékian, one of the C.I.A.M. founding members; Guévrékian used the Corbusian vertical brise-soleil in this scheme, which was a first for Casablanca.[74] In the building Zevaco constructed in 1949 on Rue Poincaré, for the Société Civile Immobilière du Centre (a real-estate developer), the architect offered another response to the treatment of natural light by incorporating a set of horizontal ribbon windows that striate the building's double facade—an experiment that was not taken up in Paris until the 1980s. Zevaco did not, however, complete his S.I.O.M. building, begun in 1950, whose V-shaped corner column still stands forlornly at a junction of Rue de Mareuil. In many of Zevaco's works, the architecture's functional substratum is intentionally blurred so that the structures become practically autonomous forms. For example, the curves of the Tit-Mellil air terminal, built in 1953 in the southeast of Casablanca, play out a silent scene and were perceived as a means of breaking with "the venerable tradition that has crafted all of Morocco's public edifices." This building's "skillful revolutionary" forms were deemed "truly beyond description": "No corners, as sinuous as a

Jean-François Zevaco and Dominique Basciano, clubhouse, Tit-Mellil airport, 1951. View from the runway. Photographed in 1998.

Jean-François Zevaco and Dominique Basciano, clubhouse, Tit-Mellil airport, 1951. Photo of the model, in *L'évolution du Maroc en 1951*.

Jean-François Zevaco, physical therapy center, Tit-Mellil, 1953–60.

Dominique Basciano, Socony Vacuum building, Rue de l'Horloge, 1954. General view. Photographed in 1998.

Georges Delanoé, Aquarium and Sea Fishing Institute, Boulevard Calmel, 1952.

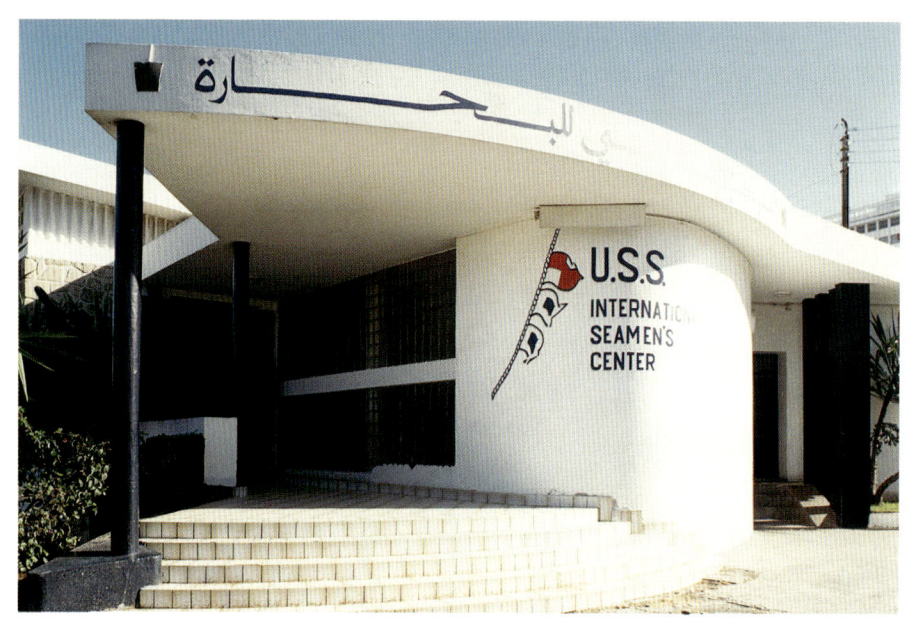

Georges Delanoé, USS Service Club, Boulevard du Chayla and Rue Dupleix, 1953. Photo 1996.

Élie Azagury, Henri Tastemain, and Isaac Lévy, Tea Office factory, 1956.

grand piano, with walls that at times are covered in glass from top to bottom, and at others adopt the form of vertical shutters to protect the interior from the blazing sun."[75] Tit-Mellil air terminal was given a strong Niemeyeresque flavor, much more so than any other building in Casablanca. Similarly, the physical therapy center built between 1953 and 1960 (again in Tit-Mellil) introduced a new register combining the poetic force of bare concrete and white walls, which was a style that would later become Zevaco's hallmark. In 1958, Michel Ragon underscored the "poetic expression" and "innovative spirit" inherent in these works.[76]

At times, Casablanca's role as a port city impacted the architectural style of the office buildings. The Socony Vacuum building, for instance, constructed by Dominique Basciano in 1954 on Rue de l'Horloge, is streamlined like a petrol tanker, while on the shore itself, the merchant navy school and porthole-spangled aquarium (by Georges Delanoé) called attention to the development of the port. In Delanoé's design for the U.S. navy club, the architect brought together nautical vocabulary and rough Brutalist stonework. Further east, the freight haulage depot and job center, constructed by Maurice Sori, punctuate a string of industrial facilities dotted all the way up to the Tea Office, which was built by Tastemain,

[75] "L'aérogare de Tit-Mellil sera la mieux équipée du Maroc," *Travaux nord-africains* (January 5, 1951).

[76] Michel Ragon, *Le Livre de l'architecture moderne* (Paris: Robert Laffont, 1958), 304.

Pierre Coldefy, Saint-Paul church, Avenue Denis Papin, 1954. General view.

André Studer, competition entry for Notre-Dame-de-Lourdes church, Boulevard Foch, 1954. Elevation.

Azagury, and Lévy, and which contains patent references to the work of the Perret brothers.

On the other side of the center, near the public swimming baths, is the parabolic trade-fair hall built of concrete by Maddalena and Lucaud. Its design is a clear indicator of how central Casablanca was shifting west at the time. Elsewhere, the physical presence of the Catholic church in the late years of the Protectorate grew increasingly apparent, as is evidenced by Coldefy's designs for the churches of Saint Paul and Saint Antoine in the Bourgogne and Maarif neighborhoods, respectively. In 1954, Dangleterre won the competition for the Notre-Dame-de-Lourdes church over André Studer, whose Wrightian project

Volvo garage, Boulevard de Lorraine, c. 1955. General view.

Volvo garage, Boulevard de Lorraine, c. 1955. View of the ground floor. Photographed in 1994.

would have stood out against Casablanca's urban landscape. In the built work, the cavernous arched structure overhangs the city's Circular Boulevard.

Construction of the *ville nouvelle* in the 1920s had coincided with the development of the motion-picture and automobile industries, whose architectural structures were accorded prime sites along Casablanca's thoroughfares. However, the solutions proposed in the 1950s offered a more dynamic response. Major existing garages such as Citroën and Auto-Hall had stories added, and Omar Benjelloun built the Volvo garage shortly after independence. Working in partnership with an engineer, Benjelloun designed this garage in the form of an aerodynamic white box whose glazed roof resembles a car radiator or a wireless radio perched on Y-shaped columns.

Villas, Beachside Resorts, and Movie Theaters 433

Gaston Jaubert, gas station, near Ain Sebaa zoo, 1951.

Georges Renaudin, Marcel Raygot garage, Boulevard Joffre and Rue de Coulanges, 1954. Photographed in 1997.

Gas stations, such as the one by Gaston Jaubert near Ain Sebaa zoo in 1951, were built to host a plethora of U.S. luxury cars, while the Circular Boulevard became home to a large number of buildings devoted to the motor industry. A noteworthy case in point is the 1952 New Yorker garage and the rather unusual mixed-use building designed by Renaudin in 1954, sited on the corner of Rue de Coulanges, whose shaped exterior columns inject a slightly futurist element into the urban fabric.

A Network of Movie Theaters

Casablanca's assimilation of American building language was all the more apparent in view of the transatlantic dialogue that had been struck up. The Casablanca hotel in Miami Beach is exemplary in this respect, its glass canopy borne aloft by caricature Arab figures, as if a single architectural vocabulary linked Florida's seaside resort with Ain Diab's Miami-Plage. There can be no doubt that this exchange was a direct product of the mass movie culture that was embraced during the postwar years.

Movie theaters formed Casablanca's real hub, serving as the meeting place for all ages and social groups. Not surprisingly, their exteriors were cast in a European mold, and fiction writers did not fail to include them in their descriptions of the city. For example, Michel Chaillou's visits to the Triomphe, Rialto, Vox, and Lux not only afforded him a number of erotic experiences, but also "improved his powers of imagination."[77] Tito Topin remembers his "head being filled with Indian war cries amid the jolting and pushing of donkey drivers" as he came out of the Régent or the Apollo, and recalls evening outings to the Triomphe, the Colisée, and the Empire. Elsewhere, he reminisces about the "Lux, where Virginia Mayo embraced James Cagney as if wondering whether he would make a good lover."[78] The Moroccans not only went to the host of theaters built for them in the new medina, but also to those in the Maarif, as recorded by Idriss El Khoury, who evokes the magic of the movies he saw in the 1950s at the Monte-Carlo, the Mondial, the Familia, and the Rex.[79] Specialized theaters also opened, such as the Cinévog, which focused on current affairs, thus mirroring the Cinéac theaters in Paris.

The design of postwar Casablancan movie halls remained dominated by Marius Boyer's Vox, an unbeatable yardstick. Some cavernous dens, such as the ABC and the Empire, were slipped beneath the porticoes of Boulevard de la Gare, and modern motifs were employed in the facades, most notably for the Lutétia, which is a theater of stepped-level design, integrated by Scob, Aroutcheff, and Jean into a building along Rue Poincaré.[80] Meanwhile, the interior furnishings and fittings of the theaters grew increasingly modern, at times verging on the spectacular, as was the case with the finely honed design for the Lynx's undulating ceiling, which Dominique Basciano produced in 1950.[81] Basciano subsequently built the Atlas on Rue Blanquefort (also in 1950), then the Rif, in 1958, along the Avenue des Forces Armées Royales, and in 1968 he was commissioned to revamp the Lux on Boulevard Lalla Yacout. As for the Liberté, built by Albert Planque along

77 Chaillou, "Instants en caravane"; and idem, *Mémoires de Melle*, 95, 120, 183.

78 Topin, "Je me vois"; and idem, *Piano barjo*, 194.

79 El Khoury, "Qui sommes nous pour ce monde blanc?"

80 "Cinéma Lutétia à Casablanca," *L'Architecture d'aujourd'hui* 22, no. 35 (May 1951): 19. A survey of theaters in Morocco, as well as in all of North Africa, would be a helpful complement to the pioneering work of Francis Lacloche, *Architectures de cinémas* (Paris: Éditions du Moniteur, 1981).

81 "Cinéma Lynx à Casablanca," *L'Architecture d'aujourd'hui* 15, no. 52 (January–February 1954): 51.

Léon Aroutcheff, Robert Jean and V. Scob, Lutétia cinema, rue Poincaré, 1950. Published in *L'évolution du Maroc en 1951*, 1951.

Dominique Basciano, Lynx movie theater, Avenue Mers-Sultan, 1951. View of the auditorium.

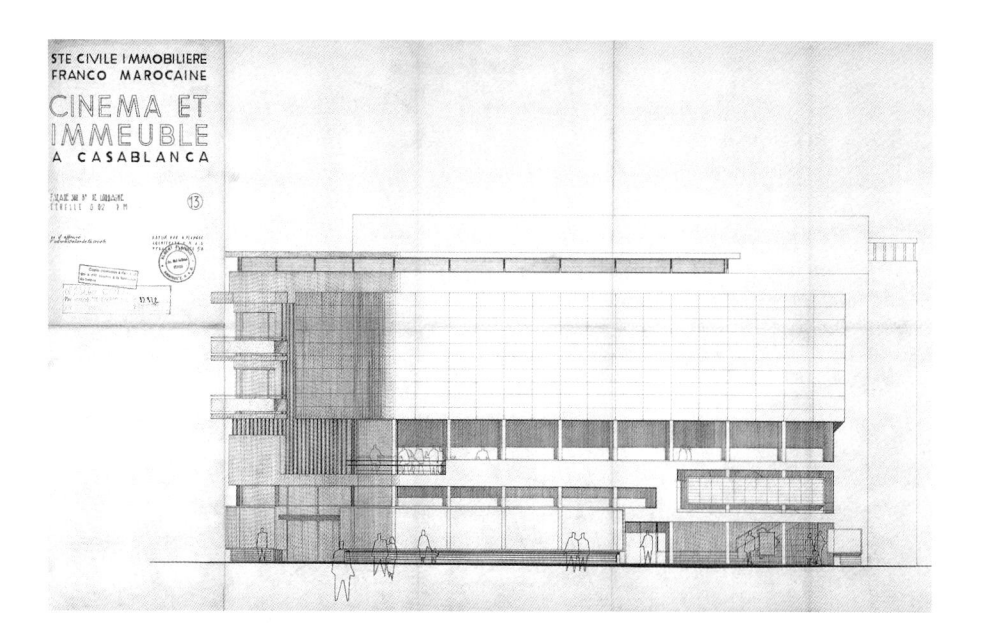

Albert Planque, Liberté cinema, Boulevard de la Liberté and Boulevard de Lorraine, 1954. Elevation on Boulevard de Lorraine. Building permit facade.

82 The competent modernization, since 1990, of a number of cinemas indicates that conditions inciting owners to maintain the buildings of the city center could convince members of the middle class already acculturated to the big city to reintroduce comfortable and well-designed dwellings into the center, assuring their durability through minimal maintenance.

83 Courtois, 1944, 40. In 1949 a debate on this recurring question was organized at the Tabarin. "La scène et l'urbanisme: les Casablancais méritent-ils un théâtre ?" November 21, 1949, *Construire* (November 23, 1949). The first identifiable project was one by Scob. "Musée et bibliothèque à Casablanca, V. Scob, architecte dplg," *L'Architecture française* 11, no. 105–6, (September–October 1950): 80–81.

84 *BMO* (May 1954): 25, 27.

85 *BMO* (July 1955): 35.

Boulevard de Lorraine in 1954, it was one of the city's only theaters (along with the Vox and the Triomphe) to be granted a purpose-built edifice. It reads as a large white structure whose scale breaks with the adjacent apartment houses, and its ground floor is given over to a Monoprix store.[82]

Casablanca's ever-growing number of movie theaters only served to underscore the municipality's reluctance to replace the city's temporary arts theater with a permanent building, despite an ongoing debate between 1949 and 1955 over a plan for a "civic theater and a venue for holding artistic, cultural, and commercial events," to quote Courtois.[83] The city councillors repeatedly refused to release funds, until Henri Croze eventually brought them up short with the following reminder: "Casablanca may be a new city, but it is nonetheless a city of taste [that is endeavoring to stave off] its philistine image." The go-ahead was finally given for a theater that could seat up to 1,500. The Muslim representative on the council, Hajaoui, requested that "Moroccan architecture be employed in the theater's interior, or at least for the auditorium or the academy," so that tourists could "discover a setting typical of the Morocco they had come to visit."[84] As for Jacques Bonan, he wished to see a scheme that was "sharply modern without bordering on the futuristic," specifying that "the structure's cladding should remain in keeping with the square."[85] As it happened, the colossal heaviness of Duhon's winning scheme, selected in 1955 (but which never got beyond project stage due to independence), in no way responded to the contextual specifications of the brief and would only have served to contrast with the elegant 1920s buildings.

The Casablancans' wavering support for the civic theater program reveals the local context of the project. Unlike Algiers, where a university had opened and where literary and artistic life had flourished since 1945, giving rise to new authors and other artists whose works were promoted through reviews and publications, the Casablancan intellectual scene was rather more restrained. The "liberals" in favor of independence were chiefly businessmen, doctors, and teachers. Moreover, Casablanca's architectural output, which can be ranked higher than that of Algiers, did not originate in any kind of deep-seated cultural outlook. Instead, it was the product of a socialite lifestyle led by a population that, while fond of novelty, expressed more interest in lighthearted activities such as sports and music than in intellectual pursuits.

Émile Duhon, competition entry for the civic theater and arts center, Place Administrative, 1955.

Achille Dangleterre, Marcel Cerdan grand stadium, 1953. View of the stands.

Villas, Beachside Resorts, and Movie Theaters

Policy after Independence

The city is like a vast shell, above all at night when under their fluorescent arc lamps the long thoroughfares are absolutely empty, and one gets the impression of a town just evacuated by retreating forces. In the daytime the place is still haunted by a shadowy présence française, *a ghost that refuses to be exorcised.*

Paul Bowles, 1966[86]

Although public housing programs continued after independence (as previously described), architects understandably lost commissions from European firms and private individuals, causing Simonne and Jean Lacouture to comment in 1958 on the "[scores of] unfinished buildings, their lopped walls stretching up to the sky."[87] However, construction as a whole was boosted, thanks to commissions for private dwellings, as well as to the policy adopted by the Moroccan government regarding educational facilities and health amenities. For instance, a "Mission Française" district school project was launched, based on the same parameters as the cultural program that had been put in place under colonial rule. Azagury and Zevaco played a leading part in this project, constructing several Brutalist complexes of reinforced concrete that received wide acclaim in Europe, notably via Marc Lacroix's photographs.[88] Renaudin, Coldefy, Fleurant, Maddalena, and Zéligson likewise worked on similar commissions, at least up until 1962, and designed various villas for the Moroccan bourgeoisie, who rapidly invested in the most sought-after residential areas. The new ruling class did not feel at all the same reserve about living in Anfa or the Crêtes as other Moroccans felt about living in the *ville nouvelle*. In this respect, Bowles noted in 1966, "The great majority of the inhabitants do not come into the center of the city at all, preferring to remain outside in the vast sordid quarters reserved for the poor." No doubt influenced by his hatred for Casablanca, Bowles states that the working-class quarters were marked by "a permanent contradiction between the way the city looks and what goes on in the streets," in that "the gestures of Moslem life are at variance with the commonplace European décor of Casablanca," rendering these quarters "very noticeable."[89]

The country's "Moroccanization process" had more of an impact on industry and public institutions (for instance, many Jewish residents left the country after the Alliance Israélite Universelle was downgraded) than it did on architectural offices. There are two key reasons for this: first, very few Moroccans graduated with degrees in architecture prior to the 1970s; and second, the leading Casablanca-based architects (notably Écochard's team) stayed in the city after independence was declared in 1956. They did not view the change in situation as problematic, since they felt closer affinities with the Moroccan nation than with a declining French empire.[90] Ironically, though, the sole major collective effort made by Casablancan architects took place several hundred kilometers away, in Agadir, following the earthquake of 1960. The master plan for this project was led by Pierre Mas and comprised contributions by GAMMA members, Écochard's veteran team, and individual schemes by architects based in Rabat and Casablanca. Sadly, though, no organic unity came out of it.[91] On another level, a shift in architectural focus occurred, due to the need to modernize other Moroccan towns that had been hitherto left out of the limelight, most notably Rabat, where many new public facilities were commissioned. This marked an end to Casablanca's fruitful reign.

In terms of housing, the policy adopted by the French Town Planning Department was fully maintained, notably for the eight-by-eight-meter grid and its variants, used up until 1980.[92] This perhaps explains why in the decade after independence, Mas continued to work in Rabat's central design office on schemes based on principles established between 1950 and 1952. In addition, a new housing law enacted

---

86 Bowles, "Casablanca," 75.

87 Lacouture, *Le Maroc à l'épreuve*, 8.

88 Udo Kultermann, *Neues Bauen in Afrika* (Tübingen: Ernst Wasmuth, 1963): 13, 114–15, 158–167; and idem, *New Directions in African Architecture*, trans. John Maass (New York: Braziller, 1969): 40–45, 64, 77, 84.

89 Bowles, "Casablanca," 78, 110.

90 Pierre Mas, interview.

91 See the issues of *A+U*, published during the 1960s in Morocco by the members of the GAMMA group and other young professionals. Also see Thierry Nadau, "La reconstruction d'Agadir ou le destin de l'architecture moderne au Maroc," in *Architectures françaises outre-mer*, eds. Culot and Thiveaud, 147–66.

92 It is interesting to note that the only government to include a *Habitat* portfolio was the one in power between December 7, 1955, and October 25, 1956. The portfolio was held by Mohamed ben Bouchaib, of the Istiqlal Democratic Party.

Jean-François Zevaco, school for the Mission Française, 1960.

in 1964 officially tied together the wealth of postwar experience and Écochard's methodology. Meanwhile, the new Muslim ruling class took on the building types, and the architects, of the European bourgeoisie. It can therefore be concluded that whereas most countries rejected colonial architectural methods and prototypes after regaining independence, this does not seem to have been wholly the case with Casablanca. Architectural culture emergent in the 1950s continued its course without any major hiccups almost up until the outbreak of postmodern themes in the 1980s, though sculptural forms did become slightly less restrained as of 1970.

The decision to continue the Protectorate's architectural policy forms merely one facet of the temporal nature of Casablanca's history of architecture and planning. Another such aspect can be perceived in the drawn-out pace at which urban projects have been completed. For example, the new central road system defined in the Labonne plan of the early 1930s only became fully operational in the 1960s, when the Avenue des Forces Armées Royales was eventually finished.[93] By the same token, the 1922 project to replace the mellah with monumental modern buildings did not actually come to fruition until the highly controversial scheme for the Casablanca (now Hyatt) hotel slab got off the ground. Infrastructural work cannot be said to have galloped along either, as is illustrated by the expressway linking the freeway to the port; mapped out in 1952, it was still only partially built in the late 1980s. Even as we embark upon the new millennium, a number of issues that have been identified now for decades remain unsolved. Redevelopment schemes for the medina and the Place de Verdun are still in project stage, fifty years after Alexandre Courtois' 1944 design scheme. In addition, the initial construction phase for the office skyscrapers promised for central Casablanca back in 1930 was not launched until 1998, on a plot edging the Maarif, which has generated huge traffic problems. Overall, then, design and construction phases in Casablanca seem to follow the "longue durée" pattern, despite all the efforts of Prost and Écochard to draw up programs quickly and efficiently.

93 Écochard still remained interested in this theme twelve years after his departure. Michel Écochard, "Casablanca, quartier de Sidi-Belyout et problèmes de circulation au Maroc," L'Architecture d'aujourd'hui 26, no. 60 (June 1965): 48.

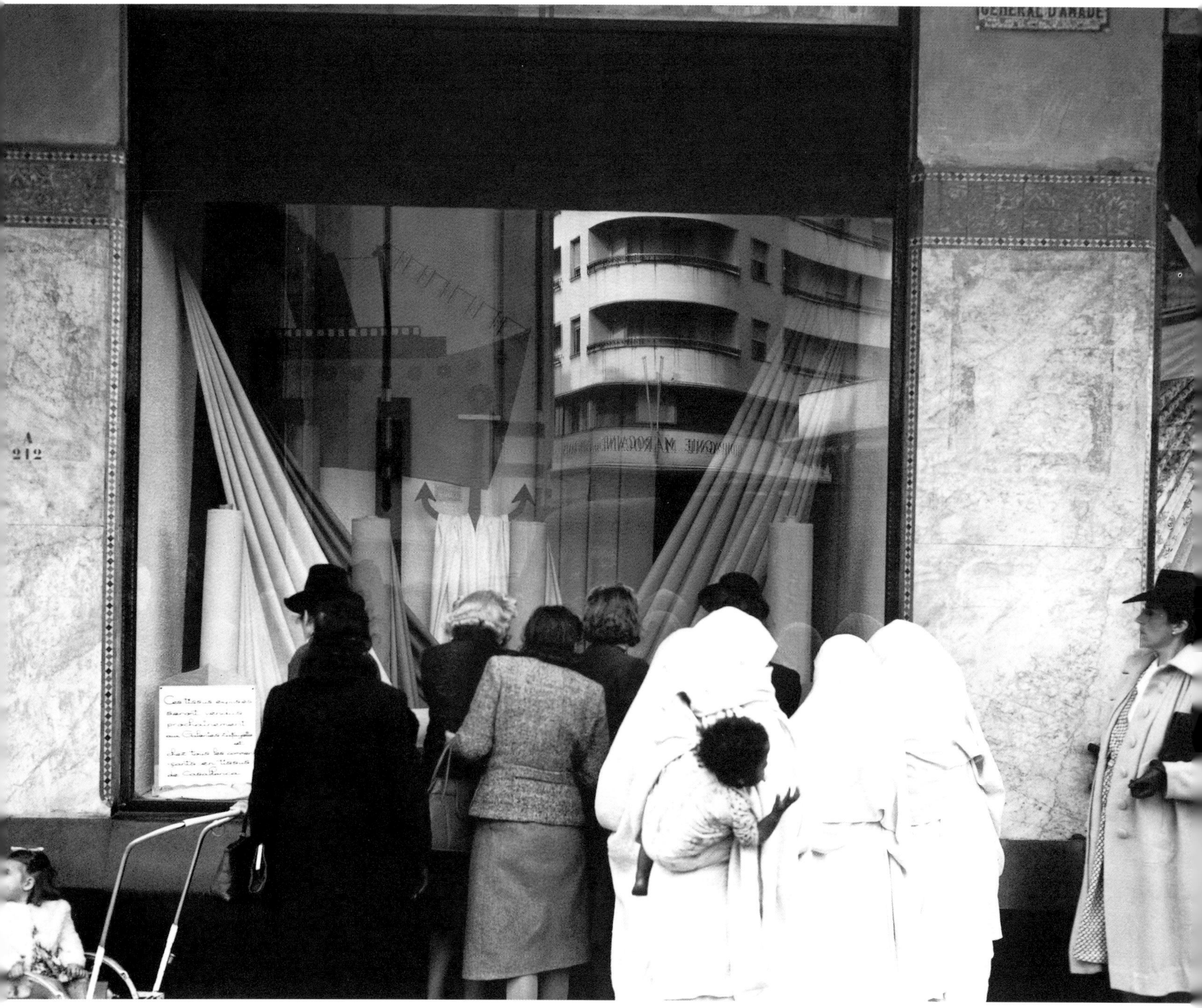

440 Casablanca

Epilogue

Up until 1956, Casablanca was heralded as a "French *ville nouvelle*," but in fact it can be considered a collective multinational work. In essence, it is characterized by a cross-fertilized urban grid whose initial components were fashioned by French players mindful both of European theories and of American types and techniques. Its architectural history is inscribed within a multipolar framework whose points of reference cannot merely be explained in terms of the conflicting relationship between the French metropolis and the Protectorate administration. Similarly, the fact that Casablanca's urban episodes have been extensively documented in French, European, and American reviews clearly indicates that its experimental status has been acknowledged well beyond France.

This book is based on the assumption that Casablanca's development was rooted in a conscious decision on the part of the French ruling powers to set up a city-scale testing ground in Morocco. By testing ground we mean not only the framework within which new solutions could emerge, but also the quest for new design concepts that were intended to be introduced into metropolitan France. A truly *experimental protocol* can thus be said to have developed at a number of levels, namely in the Prost plan, the Écochard plan, and in the majority of studies conducted on culture-specific housing—a protocol linking the conception of urban and architectural projects, their implementation, ultimate analysis, and application in France. This "testing ground" assumption has been confirmed by the unexpectedly high output of worldwide specialized analyses chronicling Casablanca's growth. The wealth of archive material is equally noteworthy and includes preparatory notes, key points of debate, project variants, status reports, and surveys on user satisfaction, all of which indicate a concern to carefully chart the course of each specific action.

While we are keenly aware that Casablanca served as a breeding ground for new building layouts, we have focused on culture-specific housing, notably in terms of how it became a key strategy of architectural modernization, having been previously regarded merely as a means of reproducing existing types and patterns. This is especially apparent in the experimental buildings constructed for the Moroccan population. Architects designed flexible housing types to respond to future developments, not only foreseeing the need to build additional stories in Moroccan dwellings, but also anticipating changes with respect to central buildings in which housing might replace offices. By taking this approach, their work prefigured late-twentieth-century preoccupations. Meanwhile, from an urban perspective, heterotopic spaces such as the

Opposite
U.S. goods displayed in the Galeries Lafayette (formerly Paris-Maroc) department store windows, March 1943. This photo, taken by the U.S. Signal Corps, provides an emblematic cross-sectional view of Casablancan society— bourgeois women with hats, a mother and child from the lower classes, and Moroccan women swathed in *haiks*. They are all gazing in wonder at the merchandise, which was practically impossible to come by during the war. The reflection of Edmond Brion's Bendahan building can be seen on the glass surface.

Habous or Bousbir, where the aim was to keep a check on the Moroccan populations, have since been replaced by new forms of social and ethnic divides on a regional level. At the same time, contrary to developments that have taken place in the housing sphere, the city's functional spaces conceived by Écochard cannot be said to rival the quality of the early squares, avenues, and arcades designed by Prost and his team.

A Pragmatic New Town

As we have endeavored to demonstrate, the hackneyed image of Casablanca having grown out of a barren site is an ideological viewpoint that does not hold up under analysis. In truth, the city's "founding" in 1907 was preceded by a long historical sedimentation process that had generated a specific urban culture and landscape well before colonization. The architects of Casablanca had to keep this urban legacy constantly in mind while drawing up plans for a commercial metropolis that can be likened more to Milan, New York, and Calcutta than it can to Rome, Washington, D.C., or New Delhi.

Not only is Casablanca the only complex new urban agglomeration to have been created in territories under French rule prior to the 1965 development of new towns in greater Paris, it also stands apart from twentieth-century utopian cities such as Chandigarh and Brasilia. Its pragmatic urbanism is grounded in a sensitive handling of the relationship between public space and private architectural works, breaking with the experience of towns developed dogmatically as grand monumental compositions or as experiments in functionalist zoning. As a city of trade, it was less impacted by the image of colonial power than Rabat, whose designation as capital had a liberating effect of sorts on Casablanca. Subsequently, its urban development grew ever closer to the hands-on English and Dutch approaches. The type of planning developed by Prost and his successors, which for a long time ruled out any form of social change, is in fact more akin to Patrick Geddes's "eu-topian" design strategy than to any form of utopia as such.[1]

The Place Administrative represented an attempt on the part of the Protectorate to convey its commanding role as powerhouse in a city where the grip of repression can still be felt. However, its conceptual urban language can be read as autarchic; in other words, it did not in any way serve as the mainspring for the city's general layout. On the contrary, right from its messy beginnings, Casablanca's urban fabric has been woven around the principle of juxtaposition: juxtaposition of military land with trade and recreational areas, and juxtaposition of districts based on social practices and the facilities required for such practices. This subsequently affected the way in which each population group developed its own forms of sociability. In this respect, it is also important to note how the city has grown through specific pseudopodia or tentacles more than through autonomous satellite towns, except in areas such as Anfa, dominated by the bourgeoisie, and Ain Chock, which is populated by Muslim workers. To a large extent, the metaphor of chaos, employed from the outset by the Protectorate to describe Casablanca, would remain pertinent, as endeavors to implement legislation and regulations were not always viewed favorably by local players and critics. While the early housing developments and the metallic waves of *bidonvilles* would seem to validate this long-term rejection of building principles and guidelines, it is clear that such precarious construction was in fact underpinned by an attempt to legitimize the process of bureaucratic and technical reordering, and was even deployed to this end by the city authorities themselves. The widespread negotiations that shaped most of the city were thus infinitely more complex than might be imagined.

Juxtaposition subsequently metamorphosed into fragmentation, with the city's various constituent parts resembling sequestered, truncated sections of an incomplete whole—commercial quarters waiting to be accorded specific centers, and

[1]. Patrick Geddes contrasts the "legitimate Eu-topia possible in the given city and characteristic of it" to "a vague Ou-topia, concretely realisable nowhere." Geddes, "Civics: As Applied Sociology I," in *The Ideal City*, 89.

sectors of the new medina totally lacking in any kind of clearly defined structure. This fragmentation reveals how Muslims were excluded from most of the colonial city; it was, moreover, a situation that was exacerbated by journalists and Protectorate officials, whose written accounts imply a sort of discursive distancing of Moroccans. This attitude is particularly apparent in documents relating to districts such as the Habous, in which Moroccan culture is described in purely folkloric terms. Likewise, there was clearly a refusal to acknowledge the specific class layering that is integral to Muslim society—for instance, it is only the poor classes and the aristocracy that are ever referred to. It was not until after 1945 that studies began to be conducted on Moroccan working-class quarters and the *bidonvilles*, thereby bringing public programs more in line with social reality.

Casablanca's Success Story
Although Casablanca has been the victim of colonial violence, its urban history goes beyond the oppression-exploitation-usurpation triad as defined by Albert Memmi. Rather, it is *inscribed* within a colonial context that was altered by way of the city's spatial arrangements. The picture of Casablanca as an example of an inequitable social order or as an outgrowth of colonial urban planning founded strictly on metropolitan concepts exported to Africa is hence challenged here.[2] As previously mentioned, Casablanca's urban "development" is due just as much to the groups making up Moroccan society—the Chaouia tribes, the *Fassi*,* the *Soussi*,* the Jews, and so on—as to the European population. The emergence of industrial values resulted in Casablanca assuming a pivotal role in the reshuffling of Morocco's internal trade links and existing hierarchies. Consequently, it was perceived as an arrogant den of vice and iniquity,[3] yet at the same time was envied by the *R'bati** and the Fassi who had to cede their commercial clout to the city during the Protectorate (although the Fassi have since regained their influence).

The *ville nouvelle* is the fruit of *multiple* energies. It is far from an exclusively French "creation," for numerous European players, the Germans in particular, contributed to its making. The end product is a modern city interlaced with different values and lifestyles and based on a constant challenging of cultures. Not to be forgotten either is how the city has been shaped by the urban discourse that took place between a varied range of social groups, resulting in building designs of the type that can be found in European and North American metropolises. Indeed, the question of whether to adopt the "benefits" of modernization or preserve the existing culture still remains topical in Casablanca today, in view of the ongoing flood of rural migrants.

Can we bestow the label of "success" on a city that was in essence founded on inequality and oppression? Before doing so, a wide spectrum of viewpoints needs to be considered. From the perspective of architecture and planning, Casablanca has spawned an extraordinarily versatile repertoire of forms and spatial arrangements, providing fertile ground for the development of pluralist modernist trends. In this respect alone, the methods are just as deserving of a place in the annals of twentieth-century architecture as the buildings themselves. From the general perspective of colonization, the cynical view of Casablanca as merely a source of profit for the metropolis—and its nationals—to the detriment of the "native population" is now irrelevant, in that the "French town" has become a shared space in which the Moroccans have at last found their rightful place. From the viewpoint of the liberals—campaigners for the coexistence of cultures—Casablanca represents the stage on which battle was waged against colonial brutality. And with regard to the colonized communities, divided among themselves and jockeying for social status, the city not only served as a remarkable stepping stone to modernization, with all its seductive appeal and opportunities, but also as a terrain for violence and wretchedness.

2. The figure of exportation is evoked in Christelle Robin, ed., *La ville européenne exportée* (Paris: Éditions de la Villette, 1995). Anthony King presents a more nuanced problematic. Anthony King, *Colonial Urban Development, Culture, Social Power and Environment* (London: Routledge & Kegan Paul, 1976); and idem, *Urbanism, Colonialism and the World Economy* (London and New York: Routledge, 1990).

3. In this sense, small-town Moroccans' perception of Casablanca is similar to provincials' view of Paris or New York.

4. Paul Bowles, "Casablanca," 75.

5. "European-style living meant, above all, material comfort and well-being." Doris Bensimon-Donath, *Évolution du judaïsme marocain*, 121.

6. In the same way the French working class rejected anything having an "antique" quality, a practice observed by Michel Verret, who reminds the reader that the bourgeoisie, in contrast, are antiques collectors. Michel Verret, *L'Espace ouvrier* (Paris: Armand Colin, 1979).

Issues of Acculturation

Like so many other colonial cities, Casablanca formed the backdrop to a structured acculturation process in terms of its various population groups. Such deliberate cultural conflict often resulted in a total breakdown of the initial culture, inciting a loss in values, self-contempt, or maiming identification with the colonizer. In Casablanca, however, acculturation also took on other forms, in that the colonized were by no means all victims. While the French were susceptible to the charms of Moroccan exoticism, some Muslims and Moroccan Jews were just as eager to embrace the exotic nature of the West, keen to possess Western clothes, housing, furniture, and other objects, to such an extent that they came to view their former lifestyle as irrelevant. Behavior and attitudes have gradually changed, and Moroccan society today (even the most traditional segment) has adopted and adapted to Western behavior and consumption patterns, juxtaposing old and new customs. A kind of interplay between values and bodily motions has arisen, explaining the ease with which Casablancans can change from a *jellaba* into tight pants or move from a living room into an Arab salon, demonstrating that the *habitus* of the first urban generation has apparently successfully survived the experience of Casablanca's development. As early as 1966, Paul Bowles commented on the city's "implicit hybridization": "In time, there will emerge here some sort of selectivity with regard to which facets of European life are to be accepted and which rejected as hazards to the existing culture."[4]

It can be said that Westernization has shaped the city's modernization, with housing and furnishings serving as a determining factor in the behavioral and cultural changes that have occurred. In town, meals are eaten not only on a divan or stretched out in front of a low table, but also seated on a chair, in front of a high table, with all the manners typical of Western civilization, the characteristic feature of changing populations being that they can readily switch from one type of behavior to another. For most Muslim Moroccans, their arrival in Casablanca has marked a twofold fracture. First, their familiar small village has been replaced by a new social structure molded by a different, secular outlook alien to most traditional Moroccans. Second, they have had to adapt to the dominion of industry, as well as to urban codes and behavioral patterns; it is to be noted that in all societies where such a phenomenon has occurred, the result has been widespread social rifts and even anomie.

Jewish acculturation began in Morocco as early as 1860 with the opening of French and English schools; this fell in line with the policy adopted by the Alliance Israélite Universelle of disseminating a democratic ideal to try to put an end to the way in which Jews were dominated by Muslim *dhimma*. The degree of Jewish commitment to architectural modernity was surprising to us. It can be perceived as a metaphor of adherence to the West, established through a close-knit relationship with some of the best architects, in the same way as adopting the French language and new urban quarters and houses can be seen to symbolize adherence to the modern world.[5] Such phenomena are particularly striking in Casablanca, which acted like a magnet during the twentieth century, just like Marrakech and Mogador before it. The commitment of some bourgeois and upwardly mobile Jews to modern trends and their rejection of the past confirms that they sought to wipe out all traces of precolonial dependence.[6]

Europeans, too, had to adapt to colonial patterns, even though not all of them necessarily approved of the inequality caused by such a system. Yet they also underwent an acculturation process, for however much they clung to their values and principles, these were nevertheless brought into contact with the Muslim Moroccan world. There is always the other side of the coin in any form of acculturation. Some cultural features of the dominated population are imitated on a daily basis by the dominators if such features are perceived to constitute an improvement to the latter's lifestyle. Casablanca's entire population, whether Moroccan or French, whether of the bourgeois, proletarian, or peasant classes, has had to adapt to new types of culture in the face of migration and accelerated urbanization. They have had to become accustomed to a city that is a world of its own, like Italian Renaissance towns that had their own range of values and tastes. As Adam has remarked, while terms such as *mellah* and *jutiya* sprang from Fès, as of 1960 Casablanca was also beginning to export some of its own place names, such as Bidonville.[7]

Each inhabitant has had to adapt to a city given over to cars, circulation flows, and zoning, in other words a totally alien way of living compared to the lifestyle of Casablancans in their native town or village. The problem encountered today by the privileged classes in their reading of Casablanca derives essentially from the city's multiple urban symbols, whose dimensions are difficult to measure for anyone who was not born there and who is thus not familiar with modern architecture. An apt example is the popularity of certain commercial districts among the middle classes from the 1980s onward, such as the Maarif, which was originally a working-class district whose architecture is nothing more than mediocre.[8] Consequently, these classes have abandoned the city center, although it is an unquestionable showcase of institutional and domestic monuments.

A Threatened Urban Heritage

During our work on this book, we at times felt that we had arrived in the aftermath of a battle, that the city's memory was gradually ebbing away. Between the start of our research period and initial publication, a frightening number of villas were demolished, triggered by the speculative greed that has gripped the city since 1907. As a result, some remarkable pieces of architecture have been wiped out, including buildings designed by Marius Boyer, along with the Galeries Lafayette department store (the former Magasins Paris-Maroc), the Vox cinema, and the civic theater; a large number of apartment buildings have also been given the death sentence. These demolitions, undertaken since the 1980s, underscore the fragility of Casablanca's urban fabric, which is further jeopardized by the fact that a rent freeze has halted all renovation programs for central apartment buildings. Elsewhere, areas formerly dedicated to villas have been earmarked as apartment block zones, and their preservation hangs on public opinion, which has not been particularly forthcoming to date. The fact that developers have been constantly pushing for parts of the city to be demolished acted as a strong incentive for us to complete and publish our research in order that it may do justice to those buildings in danger of extinction. Let us hope that our work will make the city's heritage better known, in order that the death threat looming over the architecture in the *ville nouvelle* may be lifted and an active conservation and restoration policy put in place.

Casablanca's urban heritage is in danger because it has been misread, misinterpreted, and misunderstood. At times it has even been construed by some Moroccan architects as the remains of a bygone domination. Yet, as we have sought to confirm, it would appear that the city's buildings are the product of a collective work undertaken by talented architectural and planning teams from a host of different backgrounds. Casablanca's architecture is the outgrowth of a certain mind-set and art of living, which for the most part evolved outside the confines of colonialism. Today, Casablanca's various population segments can relate to the architectural forms of their city whose myriad housing types cater to a wide range of uses. Casablanca is a fascinating urban creature that reflects the skills proper to each social group involved in its making. In addition, it provides telling evidence that truly creative twentieth-century urban planning is rooted far more in the fertile conflict of adventurous metropolises than in the utopian spaces of premeditated cities.

7. Adam, *Casablanca,* 1:86.

8. Idriss El Khoury thus sees the Maarif beginning "to degenerate, to forget its history, and to founder in dubious waters."

Research Methodology

This work is founded on the convergent use of numerous methods of observation and interpretation that have permitted the crossing of information gathered on the urban—and human—ground of Casablanca with the analysis of published sources. It was necessary to proceed simultaneously to the inventory and analysis of buildings whose presence was concretely evident in the city, but whose owners, architects, and conditions of construction were, for the most part, unknown. Concomitantly, in order to avoid clichés and hasty conclusions, it was essential to undertake an intersecting consideration of the architectural culture of France, Europe, and precolonial Morocco. This need for an assembly of all available information about the buildings accompanied all our research, to the point of becoming excessively intrusive at times. The appended architects' biographies attest to this collection of data.

Fieldwork
At the origin of our research, and confirming its initial feasibility even before the preliminary project outline of 1989, our investigation in the field took place in multiple phases. An initial exploration aimed at identifying the notable buildings in the city center led to the establishment of categories subsequently used during archival research. It focused on the major types of buildings constructed during the early stage of the city's development, as well as on outstanding edifices whose status as reference points was universally acknowledged. Generally identified by their owners' name, these constituted a part of Casablancans' accepted heritage. Identical work was undertaken for public buildings, privately owned monumental edifices (such as cinemas or garages), parks, and major axes of the road network.

The surveying of streets using successive city plans, the photographic documentation, and the search for relevant buildings in journals and archives were followed by visits to apartments and houses, from luxury villas to workers' housing estates. This was the most delicate phase, as entry into residents' intimate domain required a lengthy process of approach that varied depending on the type of dwelling. An entryway or sidewalk encounter with a tenant who took an interest in our work might lead to an impromptu apartment visit. But visiting major villas or traditional houses of the medina required an extended period of familiarization, as well as delicate introductions.

Interviews
The program of semistructured interviews regarding buildings, the conditions of their creation, and the lifestyles of their inhabitants focused on many different kinds of informants and protagonists of the city's history: architects, and their colleagues and families, owners, developers, sponsors, managers and administrators, as well as current occupants themselves. Approximately forty interviews were conducted, of which the principal examples are included in the list of sources. Our interviews generally consisted of two phases: first the interviewees' reconstruction of their biography and professional or familial involvement in the history of Casablanca, and then a discussion of relevant documents pertaining to buildings or neighborhoods (such as plans and photographs), which permitted a more precise recollection of their conditions of production and of their meaning. Among those interviewed were officials of the Town Planning Department and, notably, former colleagues of Michel Écochard.

Archival Research
In a continuous process of feedback, our fieldwork nourished and was nourished by our archival research. Materials gathered from publications and from Parisian collections provided information that required verification and completion in situ with the buildings, their architects, and their owners. In this way, a sizable amount of documentation—comprising building and lot plans, contemporary slides, and period photographs—was developed. These documents, entrusted to us by architects and their families, but also collected as assembled by Moroccan institutions (such as the photograph archive of the Ministère de l'Habitat) played a supporting role, particularly for precisely dating events such as the opening of a street or the completion of a building.

A significant portion of our research was devoted to the review of archival collections documenting the Moroccan activities of major decision makers and architects. The Lyautey, Henri Prost, Michel Écochard, and Auguste Perret collections, as well as documents maintained by Casablancan architects, were studied. Furthermore, collections useful for determining the international impact of experiments undertaken in Morocco—such as the C.I.A.M. archives and those of Sigfried Giedion at the Eidgenössische Technische Hochschule Zurich—were consulted. In Morocco, there was no lack of difficulty in accessing dispersed and, where available, generally uncataloged sources. The Protectorate archives, split between Nantes and Rabat, made invaluable discoveries possible.

The search for original and microfilmed building permit files presented significant difficulties due to their occasionally vague organization at the Wilaya du Grand Casablanca. The Agence Urbaine de Casablanca provided us with microfilms of approximately two hundred buildings and of a few developments, but did not allow direct access to the catalog. We could only partially consult building permit registers, many of which have been lost. Cross-referencing with professional publications, however, made a partial reconstruction of building permit lists possible. Ultimately, despite our efforts to achieve completeness in the domains of urbanism and construction, many of the materials analyzed long remained partial and discontinuous. Thus it was at times difficult to retrace diachronically, in completely rigorous fashion, a particular public policy over the entire duration of the Protectorate.

Bibliographic Research
The review of publications containing useful information and interpretations was carried out in several stages. We first consulted the principal historical works about Moroccan history and surveyed major interpretive materials pertaining to the history, geography, sociology, and economy of Casablanca. This was followed by more specific work on explicitly urbanistic and architectural sources—which proved to be surprisingly fertile. Alongside major French periodicals, the range of Moroccan publications revealed an unforeseen richness. Aside from technical journals such as *La Construction au Maroc*, *Bâtir*, and *Construire*, the *Réalisations* collection and that of journals such as *L'Architecture marocaine* and *Chantiers nord-africains* provided us with innumerable project documents and commentaries. Added to this material were

indispensable special issues of magazines rich in information about the building professions, such as *L'Afrique du nord illustrée*.

This very abundant corpus was supplemented by essays, political and historical analyses, novels, and guidebooks, which we analyzed using the psycho-sociological method of content analysis. The character of the Moroccan view of the city was difficult to establish other than through oral inquiry, as few available documents regarding this period in Casablanca were produced by Moroccans. Nonetheless, the opinions of Moroccan representatives on the city council, public surveys, and literary sources (both novels and essays) attest to their positions.

Study of Building Plans
Hundreds of plans brought to light through bibliographic research supplemented representations in building permits. We favored the study of the most frequently published and extensively discussed buildings, as well as those that, while not at the center of critical debate, seemed to be typical in character. The analysis of residential plans followed the methodology perfected in Monique Eleb's prior research on the genealogy of modern habitation. The study of relationships between the arrangement of domestic space, uses and mores was achieved through a reading of the architectural material, combined with an analysis and comparison of discourses from many different sources, be they accounts of clients and residents, of designers, or the numerous critical analyses published in journals.

Analysis of Urban Plans and Documents
Alongside the study of buildings, and in the absence of any usable descriptive publication or historical map collection, research into the sources of the history of urban street patterns was necessary. A corpus of master and detailed plans—linking numerous orders of urban representation with various moments in the city's brief history—was thus assembled. During the course our interpretive work, these representations frequently had to be compared. Early sketches of the first explorers, topographical surveys, and measured drawings used for situating projects all belong to the category of representations of materially vested, developed, parceled out, or built spaces. So too, of course, do the invaluable postcards and oblique and vertical aerial views for which Casablanca served as an early subject of experimentation beginning in 1907. Added to these documents are the military plans executed to document or prepare for operations—such as maps drawn by the secret services prior to the 1942 landings.

Strategic and regulatory documents—such as master plans, zoning plans, as well as building bulk plans and public projects—belong to the category of architectural and urban prescription. Documents of the Services de Rabat, as well as street plans, lot plans, and property maps drawn by local operators were particularly useful. All documents offering a selective reading of the city and its "curiosities," or its "monuments," belong to the category of symbolic interpretation. This group includes tourist maps found in guidebooks, schematic maps featuring the city's "centers of interest," along with various types of caricatures of its buildings featured in popular publications.

Analysis of Discursive Content
The texts most often studied here combine a discourse about architecture—whether scholarly or not—with a discourse about the social structure and the individual. It was thus necessary to clarify the points of articulation of these two referents through a content analysis. This classic (even banal) method seemed particularly appropriate, as it surpassed many others in gaining access to the beliefs, values, ideologies, and doctrines held by the speakers.

Architectural journals provided very specific, if partial, material for our analysis of architects' and critics' ideology as expressed in doctrinal debates, and for our evaluation of difference and convergence between positions expressed in Casablanca in respect to values or ideological themes and those of contemporary intellectuals and intellectual currents elsewhere. Here we were concerned as much with philosophical thought, with the interiorization of knowledge, with beliefs, as with conceptions of daily life and of individual interactions.

Lexical Analysis
The study of designations on plans and in texts furnished information that no other method could provide. The appearance of certain words, the frequency of their occurrence, as well as explicit discussions of their use or definition are guides to a more global comprehension of changes in mores and doctrine—whether architectural, urbanist, or political. Terms evolve as much as practices do. The evolution of language and of spatial arrangements provides clues that are complementary and that permit one to show the reciprocal adjustment between a changing society and the architects who design its habitat. In the field of urbanism, an analysis of the designations of spaces in the new city revealed how descriptive categories formulated in the cities of Europe were projected onto the North African context.

Plurality of Sources
The reading of discourses and plans complement and mutually articulate each other. If texts remain silent on certain subjects, at times plans are more explicit. Cross-referencing diverse sources brought to light gaps between architectural proposals and uses in habitat, as well as efforts at accommodation between architects aiming to understand or anticipate needs and residents seeking to enact, in the settings proposed, the lifestyle to which they aspired. The same holds true for efforts at inscribing government or class strategies within the network of urban streets. Factual information provided by journals and other texts was retained only on condition of corroboration by other sources such as plans, building permits, period photographs, and even, in rare cases, given the nature of our subject, drawings and paintings. Hypotheses put to the test in this manner were held to be verified when each constituent feature of the way space was conceptualized at a given moment reappeared in a convergent manner in plans as well as in texts.

Manuscript Sources

Public and Private Archives

Morocco
Public Archives
Agence urbaine de Casablanca

Casablanca building permits, 1918–50, microfiche collection

Bibliothèque Générale et Archives, Rabat

Archives du protectorat français au Maroc

Secrétariat général du protectorat, Service des études législatives (Plan de Casablanca, 1916–20, 1922–35, and 1931–32; Cessions de terrains du domaine municipal, 1930–33)

Secrétariat général du protectorat, Service des plans de villes (Casablanca, travaux, aménagement de rues et bâtiments; Casablanca, 1926–27)

Secrétariat général du protectorat, Logement (Habitat marocain 1936–50; Habitat indigène Casablanca, 1930–; Office chérifen de l'habitat 1944–48; Office chérifen des logements militaires 1947–50; Office chérifen de l'habitat européen 1946–52)

Secrétariat Général du Protectorat, Travaux publics (travaux du port de Casablanca)

Résidence générale, Bureau de la Presse (Urbanisme)

Ministère des travaux publics, Circonscription de l'urbanisme et de l'habitation de Casablanca (El Hank; Carrières centrales)

Centre cinématographique marocain, Rabat

Newsreel and documentary archives

Ministère de l'Habitat, Rabat

Reports and documents of the Service de l'urbanisme

Photographic archives

Archives de la Société pour la construction de la cité des entrepreneurs de Casablanca, Casablanca

Files of the SOCICA and the CILM housing developments

Wilaya du Grand Casablanca

Casablanca building permits, 1916–60, prints and microfiche collection; handwritten listings

Private Archives
Élie Azagury, Casablanca

Dominique Basciano, Casablanca

Gaspare Basciano, Casablanca

Patrice de Mazières, Rabat

Éliane and Henri Tastemain, Rabat

Jean-François Zevaco, Casablanca

France
Public Archives
Académie d'architecture, Paris

Auguste Cadet, Albert Laprade, Henri Prost, and Paul Tournon collections

Archives d'Architecture du XXe siècle, Institut français d'architecture, Paris

Georges Candilis, Michel Écochard, Albert Laprade, and Auguste Perret collections

Archives Nationales

Hubert Lyautey collection, 475 AP/52

École des Beaux Arts collection, Aj52

Ministère des Affaires étrangères, Centre des archives diplomatiques, Nantes

Consulat général à Casablanca: Tanger-légation collection, série A, boxes 666, 667, 668, 775

Protectorat français au Maroc

Délégué à la résidence générale, boxes 131, 132, 138, 139

Cabinet civil, boxes 5, 122, 135, 136, 138

Secrétariat général du protectorat, boxes 137, 198bis, 199, 228, 240, 241, 242

Direction de l'intérieur, boxes 302, 303

Région de Casablanca, boxes 848, 849, 850, 851, 853, 856

Photographic collection, series C and F

Service historique de l'armée de terre, Vincennes

Series 3H, boxes 78, 87, 114, 330, 568

Archives du Génie, Vincennes

CDG Maroc, boxes 1, 10, 15, 16, 18, 19, 20

Archives de la Marine, Vincennes

Series BB4, box 2458

Fondation Le Corbusier, Paris

Correspondence of Le Corbusier with Vladimir Bodiansky, Georges Candilis, Michel Écochard, and Marcel Lods, files E 1 (8), E 1 (12), E 2 (1), and E 2 (9)

Musée des années 30, Boulogne-Billancourt

Paul Landowski collection

Musée Social, Paris

Reports of the Section d'hygiène urbaine et rurale

Société française des architectes, Paris

Biographical catalog of the Société des architectes diplômés par le gouvernement

Private Archives
Éliane Bohin-Perrotte, Neuilly

Madame Jeanine Coldefy, Antibes

Roland Crétégny, Marly-le-Roy

Françoise Landowski, Sèvres

Pierre Suraqui, Paris

United States
Getty Research Institute for the History of Art and the Humanities, Los Angeles

Austin Wittlesey Photograph collection

Library of Congress, Washington, D.C.
Prints and Maps Division

National Archives, Washington, D.C.

Military Archives, Still Pictures Branch

OSS Archives, RG 226, box 3

Warner Brothers Archive, University of Southern California School of Cinema-Television, Los Angeles

Set design drawings for the film *Casablanca*

Warner Brothers Research Collection, Burbank Public Library, Burbank, Calif.

Albums of the film *Casablanca*

Switzerland
Eidgenössische technische Hochschule, Zurich.

C.I.A.M. collection; Sigfried Giedion and Jacqueline Tyrwhitt archives

André Studer Archives, Gockhausen/Zurich

Oral Sources: Interviews with Principal Figures and Witnesses

Patrice Anselin, Casablanca, November 28, 1992

Élie Azagury, Casablanca, April 17 and 19, 1990, November 25, 1992

Dominique Basciano, Casablanca, December 12, 1990

Gaspare Basciano, Casablanca, December 13 and 14, 1990

Gaston Brami, Casablanca, May 23, 1998

Georges Candilis, Paris, January 6, 1991

Jeanine Coldefy, Antibes, September 23, 1990

Roland Crétegny, Marly-le-Roy, May 11, 1996

Sété Guetta, Neuilly, December 14, 1996

Gaetano Guzzo, Casablanca, 1994, December 18, 1995

Pierre Hinnen, Villevieille, April 1998

India Heider-Bruckner, Casablanca, October 14, 1996

Claire-Lise Schmidt (Honegger), Geneva, February 16, 1996

Françoise Landowski, Sèvres, June 10, 1997

Patrice de Mazières, Rabat, July 29, 1994

Léonard Morandi, Paris, December 12, 1996

Mario Milone, Casablanca, August 2, 1994

Giulio Pediconi, Rome, June 28, 1997

André Peter, Casablanca, December 22, 1996, January 5, 1997

Louis Riou, Casablanca, August 4, 1994

Gaston Jaubert, Paris, February 12, 1990

Marc Lacroix, Biot, September 23, 1990

Léandre Pola, Casablanca, December 19, 1995

Brian Richards, London, June 4, 1992

Alison and Peter Smithson, London, June 4, 1992

André Studer, Gockhausen/Zurich, June 2, 1992

Sami Suissa, Montréal, June 14, 1991

Pierre Mas, Paris, October 19, 1992

Henri Souque, Paris, November 6, 1996

Éliane and Henri Tastemain, Paris, November 11, 1989, and Rabat, July 28, 1994

Jean-François Zevaco, Casablanca, April 18, 1990

Bibliography

Bibliographies

Adam, André. *Bibliographie critique de sociologie, d'ethnologie et de géographie humaine du Maroc: Travaux de langues anglaise, arabe, espagnole et française arrêtée au 31 decembre 1965*. Algiers: Centre de recherches anthropologiques, préhistoriques et ethnographiques, 1972.

Dethier, Jean, ed. *1200 références bibliographiques sur l'urbanisme, l'habitat, l'architecture et l'aménagement au Maroc*. Rabat: Direction de l'urbanisme et de l'habitat, 1970.

Dethier, Jean, ed. *1700 références bibliographiques complémentaires sur l'urbanisme, l'habitat, l'architecture et l'aménagement au Maroc*. Rabat: Direction de l'urbanisme et de l'habitat, 1971.

Groupe de recherche et d'études sur Casablanca. *Dossier bibliographique sur le Grand Casablanca*. Casablanca: Université Hassan II, Faculté des lettres et des sciences humaines, 1987.

Books, Research Papers, and Theses

Abitbol, Michel. *Les juifs d'Afrique du nord sous Vichy*. Paris: Maisonneuve et Larose, 1983.

Abrams, Charles. *Man's Struggle for Shelter in an Urbanizing World*. Cambridge, Mass.: MIT Press, 1970.

Abu-Lughod, Janet L. *Rabat: Urban Apartheid in Morocco*. Princeton: Princeton University Press, 1980.

Adam, André. *Casablanca: Essai sur la transformation de la société marocaine au contact de l'Occident*. Paris: Éditions du CNRS, 1968.

———. *Histoire de Casablanca (des origines à 1914)*. Annales de la Faculté des Lettres d'Aix en Provence, no. 88. Aix-en-Provence: Éditions Ophrys, 1968.

L'Afrique du nord, genres de vie et peuplement. Album no. 20. Paris: Librairie de l'enseignement, 1933.

Alaoui Fdili, Amine. "Casablanca 1913–1940: Un plan–une percée." Master's thesis, École d'Architecture Paris-Villemin, 1986.

Albert Greslin, architecte SAM, Casablanca. Madrid: Edarba, ca. 1930.

Alloula, Malek. "The Colonial Harem." Trans. Myrna and Wlad Godzich. *In Theory and History of Literature*, vol. 21. Minneapolis: University of Minnesota Press, 1986 (First published as: *Le Harem colonial: Images d'un sous-érotisme*. Paris: Garance, 1981).

Amade, General Albert-Gérard Léo d'. *Campagne de 1908–1909 en Chaouïa*. Comp. Captain Broussaud. Paris: R. Chapelot, 1911.

Arama, Maurice. *Itinéraires marocains: Regards de peintres*. Paris: Les Éditions du Jaguar, 1991.

Artbauer, Otto C. *Kreuz und quer durch Marokko: Kultur—und Sittenbilder aus dem Sultanat des Westens*. Stuttgart: Strecker und Schröder, 1911.

Assaraf, Robert. *Mohammed V et les Juifs du Maroc à l'époque de Vichy*. Paris: Plon, 1997.

Astier Loutfi, Martine. *Littérature et colonialisme: L'expansion coloniale vue dans la littérature romanesque française*. Paris and The Hague: Mouton, 1971.

Atlas de la Wilaya de Casablanca. Casablanca: GREC; Tours: Urbama, 1986–94.

Aubin, Eugène. *Le Maroc d'aujourd'hui*. Paris: Armand Colin, 1904.

Ayache, Albert. *Le Maroc: Bilan d'une colonisation*. Paris: Éditions sociales, 1956.

Azan, Paul. *Souvenirs de Casablanca*. Preface by General Albert-Gérard Léo d'Amade. Paris: Hachette, 1911.

Babin, Gustave. *Au Maroc*. Paris: Grasset, 1912.

Beauvoir, Simone de. *The Prime of Life*. Trans. Peter Green. Cleveland: World Publishing Co., 1962. (First published as: *La force de l'âge*. Paris: Gallimard, 1960).

Béguin, François, with Gildas Baudez, Denis Lesage, and Lucien Godin. *Arabisances: Décors architectural et tracés urbains en Afrique du Nord 1830–1950*. Paris: Dunod, 1983.

Bellocq, Mlle. "Les aérodromes de Casablanca." Postgraduate thesis, Faculté des lettres d'Aix-en Provence, Aix-en-Provence, 1953.

Ben Mlih, Abdellah. *Structures politiques du Maroc colonial*. Paris: L'Harmattan, 1990.

Bensimon-Donath, Doris. *Évolution du judaïsme marocain sous le Protectorat français, 1912–1956*. Paris and The Hague: Mouton et Cie, 1968.

Bensusan, Samuel Levy. *Morocco*. London: Adam & Charles Black, 1904.

Benzakour, Saad. *Essai sur la politique urbaine au Maroc, 1912–1925*. Casablanca: Les Éditions maghrébines, 1978.

Bernard, Augustin. *Une mission au Maroc: Rapport à M. le Gouverneur général de l'Algérie*. Paris: Publications du Comité du Maroc, 1904.

———. *La France au Maroc*. Paris: Armand Colin, 1917.

———. *Le Maroc*. Paris: Félix Alcan, 1918.

Bernard, Stéphane. *Le conflit franco-marocain 1943–1956*. Brussels: Éditions de l'Institut de sociologie de l'Université Libre de Bruxelles, 1963.

Berque, Jacques. *Le Maghreb entre deux guerres*. Paris: Éditions du Seuil, 1962.

Bertrand-Taquet, Alfred. *Exposition franco-marocaine de Casablanca 1915, Section métropolitaine, rapport général*. Paris: Comité français des expositions, 1915.

Besnard, René, and Camille Aymard. *L'œuvre française au Maroc, avril 1912–décembre 1913*. Preface by Joseph Caillaux. Paris: Hachette, 1914.

Bhabha, Homi K. *The Location of Culture*. London and New York: Routledge, 1993.

Bidwell, Robin. *Morocco under Colonial Rule*. London: F. Cass, 1973.

Bleuchot, Hervé. *Les libéraux français au Maroc (1947–1955)*. Aix-en-Provence: Éditions de l'Université de Provence, CNRS, 1973.

Boccara, Myriam. "Casablanca—histoires d'architectures." Master's thesis, Unité pédagogique d'architecture no. 8, Paris, 1985.

Bodiansky, Vladimir. *Housing for the Greater Number*. Geneva: United Nations, Economic and Social Council, 1951.

Bonnard, Abel. *Au Maroc*. Paris: Éditions Emile Paul Frères, 1927.

Bordeaux, Henri. *Un printemps au Maroc*. Paris: Plon, 1931.

Borély, Jules. *Mon plaisir au Maroc*. Paris: André Delpeuche, 1927.

Borély, Jules. *Le Maroc au pinceau*. Paris: Denoël, 1950.

Boughali, Mohammed. *La représentation de l'espace chez le Marocain illettré*. Paris: Anthropos, 1974.

Boulanger, Pierre. *Le cinéma colonial: De L'Atlantide à Lawrence d'Arabie*. Paris: Seghers, 1975.

Bourdieu, Pierre. *Outline of a Theory of Practice*. Trans. Richard Nice. Cambridge and New York: Cambridge University Press, 1977. (First published as: *Esquisse d'une théorie de la pratique*. Geneva: Droz, 1972).

Bourdieu, Pierre, and Abdelmalek Sayad. *Le déracinement*. Paris: Minuit, 1964.

Bourdon, Alain, and Didier Folléas, eds. *Casablanca: Fragments d'imaginaire*. Casablanca: Institut français de Casablanca, Éditions Le Fennec, 1997.

Bourdon, Georges. *Les journées de Casablanca, ce que j'ai vu au Maroc*. Paris: P. Lafitte, 1908.

Bowie, Leland Louis. "The Protégé System in Morocco 1880–1904." Paper, University of Michigan, Ann Arbor, 1970.

Bradel, Vincent. "Michel Écochard 1905–1985." Research paper, Institut français d'architecture, Paris, 1985.

Brasillach, Robert. *La conquérante*. Paris: Plon, 1943.

Braun, Georg, and Franz Hogenberg. *Civitates orbis terrarum*. Vol. 1. Cologne: Bertram Buchholtz, 1572.

Broche, François. *L'assassinat de Lemaigre-Dubreuil, Casablanca le 11 juin 1955*. Paris: Balland, 1977.

Brunschwig, Henri. *Mythes et réalités de l'impérialisme colonial français 1871–1914*. Paris: Armand Colin, 1960.

Burke, Edmund, III. *Prelude to Protectorate in Morocco: Precolonial Protest and Resistance, 1860–1912*. Chicago and London: University of Chicago Press, 1976.

Cadet, Auguste. *La Mahakma de Casablanca*. Paris: Paul Hartmann, 1953.

Candilis, Josic, Woods: *Une décennie d'architecture et d'urbanisme*. Paris: Eyrolles, 1968.

Caqueray, Gaston de. *Note pour l'histoire de Casablanca et de son port*. Paris: Publications du Comité de l'Afrique Française, 1937.

Casa-guide: Renseignements sur la ville. Casablanca: Éditions France-Afrique, 1949.

Casablanca et les Chaouïa. Vols. 1 and 2 of *Villes et tribus du Maroc: Documents et renseignements publiés sous les auspices de la Résidence générale*. Paris: Leroux, 1915.

Casinière, H. de la. *Les municipalités marocaines, leur développemt, leur législation*. Casablanca: Librairie Faraire, 1924.

Castellanos, Manuel Pablo. *Historia de Maruecos*. Tanger: Impr. hispano-Arábiga de la Misión Católico-española, 1898.

Catroux, General Diomède. *Lyautey le Marocain*. Paris: Hachette, 1952.

Celce, Georges. "Le port de Casablanca et l'économie marocaine." Ph.D. diss., Faculté de droit de Paris, Paris, 1950.

Célérier, Jean. *Le Maroc*. Paris: Armand Colin, 1939.

Çelik, Zeynep. *Displaying the Orient: Architecture of Islam at Nineteenth-Century World's Fairs*. Berkeley, Los Angeles, and Oxford: University of California Press, 1992.

Cerych, Ladislav. *Européens et Marocains 1930–1956: Sociologie d'une décolonisation*. Bruges: De Tempel, 1964.

Chaillou, Michel. *Mémoires de Melle*. Paris: Seuil, 1993.

Chouraqui, André. *La condition juridique de l'Israélite marocain*. Paris: Presse du livre français, 1950.

Chraïbi, Driss. *Le passé simple*. Paris: Denoël, 1954.

Chancel, Jules. *Lulu au Maroc*. Illustrations by L. Bombled. Paris: Ch. Delagrave, 1913.

Chénier, Louis de. *Recherches Historiques sur les Maures et histoire de l'Empire du Maroc*. 3 vols. Paris: published by the author, 1787.

Choay, Françoise. *The Rule and the Model: On the Theory of Architecture and Urbanism*. Ed. Denise Bratton. Cambridge, Mass.: MIT Press, 1996 (first published as: *La règle et le modèle*, Paris: Seuil, 1980).

Cinquième congrès nord-africain du bâtiment et des travaux publics. Casablanca: Éditions Construire, 1953.

Cohen, Jean-Louis, and Monique Eleb. "La constitution du dispositif portuaire urbain de Casablanca." Research paper, Laboratoire ACS/Plan Construction et Architecture, Paris, 1993. Typescript.

Colliez, André. *Notre protectorat marocain: La première étape 1912–1930*. Paris: Marcel Rivière, 1930.

Cormier, Anne. "Extensions-limites-espaces libres, les travaux de la section d'Hygiène urbaine et rurale du Musée social." Postgraduate thesis, École d'Architecture Paris-Villemin, Paris, 1987.

Cotte, Narcisse. *Le Maroc contemporain*. Paris: Charpentier, 1860.

Couette, Henri. *Casablanca et sa région*. Casablanca: Éditions Maroc-Presse, 1941,

Croze, Henri. *Souvenirs du vieux Maroc*. Paris: La Diffusion française, 1952

Culot, Maurice, et al. *Les Frères Perret: L'œuvre complète*. Paris: Norma/Institut français d'architecture, 2000.

Cuny, Marie-Thérèse. *La Petite Fille de Dar-el-Beïda*. Paris: Fixot, 1990.

Danger, René. *Cours d'urbanisme*. Paris: Eyrolles, 1933.

Delanoë, Guy. *Lyautey, Juin, Mohammed V: Fin d'un protectorat; mémoires historiques*. Paris: L'Harmattan, 1988.

Delau, Louis. *Le Maroc à la croisée des chemins*. Casablanca: Imprimeries réunies de la Vigie marocaine et du Petit Marocain, 1931.

Depaule, Jean-Charles, and Jean-Claude Arnaud. *À travers le mur*. Paris: Centre de création industrielle, 1985.

Dernouny, Mohamed, and Guy Léonard. *Casablanca: La parole et la trace*. Casablanca: Afrique-Orient, 1987.

Descamps, Henri. *L'architecture moderne au Maroc*. Vol. 1, *Édifices publics,* and Vol. 2, *Constructions particulières*. Paris: Librairie de la Construction moderne, 1930.

Deshen, Shlomo. *The Mellah Society: Jewish Community Life in Sherifian Morocco*. Revised and translated by the author. Chicago and London: University of Chicago Press, 1989

Diamant-Berger, Renée. *Gaston Jaubert: Rythmes et volumes*. Marseilles, 1976.

Diome, Marème, and André Guillerme. "Techniques et politiques économiques: Les travaux publics en Afrique du nord 1953–1962." Research paper, Plan urbain, Paris, 1987. Typescript.

Direction générale de l'instruction publique, des beaux-arts et des antiquités. *Historique 1912–1930*. Rabat: Résidence générale, 1931.

Dugard, Henry. *Le Maroc au lendemain de la guerre*. Paris: Payot, 1920.

Dujardin, Melle C. "Casablanca, centre d'affaires, étude de géographie économique marocaine." Postgraduate thesis, Faculté des lettres de Paris, Paris, 1950.

Duquaire, Henri. *Incertitudes marocaines*. Paris: Robert Laffont, 1946.

Durand, Emmanuel. *Traité de droit public marocain*. Paris: Lib. générale de droit et de jurisprudence R. Pichon and R. Durand-Auzias, 1955.

Écochard, Michel. *Casablanca: Le roman d'une ville*. Paris: Les Éditions de Paris, 1955.

El Malti, Mohammed. "The Architecture of Colonialism, Morocco, 1912–1932: An Inquiry into the Determinants of French Colonial Architecture." Ph.D. diss., University of Pennsylvania, Philadelphia, 1983.

Eleb, Monique, and Anne-Marie Châtelet. *L'Apprentissage du "chez-soi"*: Paris, le Groupe des maisons ouvrières, 1908. Marseilles: Parenthèses, 1994.

Eleb, Monique, and Anne Debarre. *Architectures de la vie privée: Maisons et mentalités XVIIe–XIXe siècles*. Brussels: Archives d'Architecture Moderne, 1989.

Eleb, Monique, and Anne Debarre. *L'Invention de l'habitation moderne, Paris, 1880–1914*. Brussels: Archives d'Architecture Moderne; Paris: Hazan, 1995.

Esme, Jean d'. *Ce Maroc que nous avons fait*. Paris: Hachette, 1955.

L'Essor industriel de Casablanca: Enquête sur les entreprises industrielles de Casablanca faite par la "Vigie marocaine." Casablanca: Éditions de La Vigie marocaine, 1914.

Étienne, Jean d', Louis Villème, and Stéphane Delisle. *L'Évolution sociale du Maroc*. Paris: Peyronnet & Cie, 1950.

Étude sur les populations habitant dans des cités construites par la Cie Immobilière franco-marocaine. Casablanca: Compagnie immobilière franco-marocaine, 1955.

Eyquem, Jean. *Les Ports de la zone française du Maroc: Leur rôle économique*. Algiers: Imprimerie Heintz, 1933.

Exposition franco-marocaine: Rapport général et rapport des sections. Paris: Plon, 1918.

Exposition franco-marocaine de Casablanca 1915: Catalogue général officiel et liste des récompenses. Paris: Plon, 1919.

Fannius, Jean. *Casa ou les heures françaises*. Paris: E. Figuière, 1936.

Farrère, Claude [Charles Bargone pseud.]. *Les hommes nouveaux*. 2nd ed. Color woodcuts by G. Géo-Fourrier, engraved by Auguste Mathieu. Paris: Horizons de France, 1928. (First published: Paris: Flammarion, 1922).

Ferry, Michel. *À vous . . . Casablanca: Incidences franco-marocaines*. Tangiers: Éditions internationales, 1956.

Fock, Gustav. *Wir Marokko-Deutschen in der Gewalt der Franzosen*. Berlin and Vienna: Ullstein, 1916.

Forestier, Jean Claude Nicolas. *Jardins: Carnet de plans et de dessins*. Paris: Émile Paul Frères, 1920.

———. "Des réserves à constituer au dedans et aux abords des villes capitales du Maroc: Remarques sur les jardins arabes et de l'utilité qu'il y aurait à en conserver les principaux caractères" (December, 1913). In Forestier, Jean Claude Nicolas. *Grandes villes et systèmes de parcs: Suivi de deux mémoires sur les villes impériales du Maroc et sur Buenos Aires*. Annot. by Dorothée Imbert et al. Paris: Norma, 1997, 159–219.

Frager, Marcel. *La ville neuve: Odyssée d'un écumeur*. Preface by Jean-José Frappa. Paris: Ollendorf, 1924.

Fuller, Maria Gubiena. "Colonizing Constructions: Italian Architecture, Urban Planning, and the Creation of Modern Society in the Colonies, 1869–1943." Ph.D. diss., University of California, Berkeley, 1994.

Gallissot, René. *Le patronat européen au Maroc (1931–1942)*. Rabat: Éditions techniques nord-africaines, 1964.

Gallotti, Jean. *Moorish Houses and Gardens of Morocco*. Illustrations by Albert Laprade. Photographs by Lucien Vogel, Félix, Vve P. R. Schmitt, G. Faure, and Canu. New York: William Helburn, Inc., 1926 (First published as: *Le jardin et la maison arabes au Maroc*. Paris: Éditions Albert Lévy, 1926).

Gargiani, Roberto. *Auguste Perret: La théorie et l'œuvre*. Paris: Gallimard-Electa, 1994.

Gaudin, Jean-Pierre. *L'avenir en plan: Technique et politique dans la prévision urbaine, 1900–1930*. Seyssel: Champ Vallon, 1985.

Geidel, Sylvie. "Etude des pratiques transformatrices dans le logement économique (Casablanca)." Master's thesis, École d'architecture Paris-Belleville, Paris, 1989.

Giedion, Sigfried. *Building in France, Building in Iron, Building in Ferro-Concrete*. Trans. J. Duncan Berry. Intro. Sokratis Georgiadis. Santa Monica, Calif.: The Getty Center for the History of Art and the Humanities. (First published as: *Bauen in Frankreich, bauen in Eisen, bauen in Eisenbeton*. Leipzig and Berlin: Klinkhardt & Biermann, 1928).

George, Pierre. *La ville: Le fait urbain à travers le monde*. Paris: Presses Universitaires de France, 1952.

Godard, Caroline. "Revivals, orientalisme, régionalisme: L'architecture néo-mauresque en Europe et en Afrique du nord." Master's thesis, École d'Architecture de Marseilles, Marseilles, 1983.

Goulven, Joseph. *Notice économique sur Casablanca et la région de la Chaouïa*. Casablanca: n.p., 1915.

———. *Le Maroc: Les ressources de ses régions, sa mise en valeur*. Preface by Auguste Terrier. Paris: Émile Larose, 1919.

———. *Les mellahs de Rabat-Salé*. Paris: Librairie orientaliste Paul Geuthner, 1927.

———. *Casablanca de 1889 à nos jours: Album de photographies rétrospectives et modernes montrant le développement de la ville*. Casablanca: Flandrin, 1928.

Gouraud, General Henri Joseph Eugène. *Au Maroc, 1911–1914: Souvenirs d'un Africain*. Paris: Plon, 1949.

Gouvernement chérifien. Les habitations salubres et à bon marché: Projets primés au concours des modèles d'habitations (août 1928). Casablanca: Imprimeries réunies, 1928.

Gråberg till Hemsö, Jakob. *Specchio geografico e statistico dell'impero di Marocco*. Genoa: Tip. Pellas, 1834.

Grandval, Gilbert. *Ma mission au Maroc*. Paris: Plon, 1956.

Grasset, Captain Alphonse-Louis. *À travers la Chaouïa*, Paris: Hachette, 1912.

Gresleri, Giuliano, Pier Giorgio Massaretti, and Stefano Zagnoni, eds. *Architettura italiana d'oltremare 1870–1940*. Venice: Marsilio, 1993.

Guigues, Léon. *Guide de l'Exposition franco-marocaine*. Casablanca: Imprimerie rapide, 1915.

Hall, Luella J. *The United States and Morocco*. Metuchen, N.J.: The Scarecrow Press, 1971.

Halstead, John P. *Rebirth of a Nation: The Origins and Rise of Moroccan Nationalism, 1912–1944*. Cambridge, Mass.: Harvard University Press, 1967.

Harris, Walter B. *The Land of an African Sultan: Travels in Morocco 1887, 1888, and 1889*. London: Sampson Low, Marston, Searle & Rivington, 1889.

Harris, Walter B. *The Morocco That Was*. London: W. Blackwood, 1921.

Hedgecoe, John, and Salma Samar Damluji. *Zillij: The Art of Moroccan Ceramics*. Reading: Garnet, 1992.

Hess, Jean. *Israël au Maroc*. Paris: J. Bosc & Cie, 1907.

Hilberseimer, Ludwig, and Julius Vischer. *Beton als Gestalter*. Stuttgart: Julius Hoffmann, 1928.

Hoisington, William A. *The Casablanca Connection: French Colonial Policy, 1936–1943*. Chapel Hill and London: The University of North Carolina Press, 1984.

———. *Lyautey and the French Conquest of Morocco*. New York: St. Martin's Press, 1995.

Hommes et destins: Dictionnaire biographique d'outre-mer. Paris: Académie des sciences d'outre-mer, 1975.
Hooker, Joseph Dalton, and John Ball. *Journal of a Tour in Morocco and the Great Atlas*. London: Macmillan and Co, 1878.

Houel, Christian. *Mes aventures marocaines*. Casablanca: Éditions Maroc-Demain, 1954.

Hubert, M. *L'évolution de Casablanca*. Rabat: Centre des hautes études d'administration musulmane, 1946.

Hubert, Paul. *L'administration municipale à Casablanca de 1907 à 1947*. Casablanca: 1949.

J.-J. Honegger raconte: Honegger-Frères (50e anniversaire). Geneva: Imprimerie G. de Buren, n.d. [c. 1980].

Johnson, Katherine Marshall. *Urban Government for the Prefecture of Casablanca*. New York, Washington, and London: Praeger, 1970.

———. *Urbanization in Morocco*. New York: Ford Foundation, 1971.

Joyant, Edmond. *Traité d'urbanisme*. Paris: Eyrolles, 1923.

Julien, Charles André. *Le Maroc face aux impérialismes: 1415–1956*. Paris: Éditions J. A., 1978.

Jussiaume, Eirik [Eirik Labonne, pseud.]. *Réflexions sur l'économie africaine*. Paris: Klincksieck, 1932.

Kaioua, Abdelkader. "L'espace industriel marocain de Kénitra à Casablanca." Ph.D. diss., Urbama, Tours, 1984.

Kalter, Johannes. *Aus marokkanischen Bürgerhäuser*. Stuttgart: Lindenmuseum, 1977.

King, Anthony. *The Bungalow: The Production of a Global Culture*. London: Routledge & Kegan Paul, 1984.

———. *Colonial Urban Development: Culture, Social Power, and Environment*. London: Routledge & Kegan Paul, 1976.

———. *Urbanism, Colonialism, and the World Economy*. London and New York: Routledge, 1990.

Knibiehler, Yvonne, Geneviève Emmery, and Françoise Leguay. *Des Français au Maroc: La présence et la mémoire (1912–1956)*. Paris: Denoël, 1992.

Kultermann, Udo. *Architecture of Today: A Survey of New Building Throughout the World*. Trans. E. H. W. Priefert. London: A. Zwemmer, 1958.

———. *Neues Bauen in Afrika*. Tübingen: Ernst Wasmuth, 1963.

———. *New Directions in African Architecture*. Trans. John Maass. New York: Braziller, 1969.

Kuysel, Richard F. *Seducing the French: The Dilemna of Americanization*. Berkeley and Los Angeles: University of California Press, 1993.

Labadie-Lagrave, H. *Le mensonge marocain: Contribution à l'histoire "vraie" du Maroc*. Casablanca: Imprimerie ouvrière, 1925.

Lacouture, Jean. *Profils perdus: 53 portraits de notre temps*. Paris: A. M. Métailié, 1983.

Lacouture, Jean, and Simonne Lacouture. *Le Maroc à l'épreuve*. Paris: Éditions du Seuil, 1958.

Lacroix-Rix, Annie. *Les Protectorats d'Afrique du nord entre la France et Washington, du débarquement à l'indépendance Maroc et Tunisie 1942–1956*. Paris: L'Harmattan, 1988.

Ladreit de Lacharrière, Jacques. *La création marocaine*. Paris: J. Peyronnet & Cie, 1930.

Lahbabi, Abdelouahab. *Famille et logement dans le Maroc colonial*. Master's thesis, École d'architecture de Rennes, Rennes, 1977.

Lahjomri, Abdeljlil. *L'image du Maroc dans la littérature française (de Loti à Montherlant)*. Algiers: Société nationale d'édition et de diffusion, 1973.

Lahure, Colonel Baron Auguste. *Lettres d'Afrique: Maroc et Sahara Occidental*. Brussels: Oscar Lamberty, 1905.

Lapeyre, Émile, and E. Marchand. *Casablanca, la Chaouia*. Preface by Jean Hersent. Paris: Larose, 1918.

Laprade, Albert. *Croquis Portugal Espagne Maroc*. Paris: Vincent, Fréal & Cie, 1958.

Laskier, Michael M. *The Alliance Israélite Universelle and the Jewish Communities of Morocco: 1862–1962*. Albany: State University of New York Press, 1983.

Le Corbusier. *The Athens Charter*. Trans. Anthony Eardley. New York: Grossman Publishers, 1973 (first published as: *La Charte d'Athènes*. Intro. by Jean Giraudoux. Paris: Plon, 1943).

Le Corbusier. *The Three Human Establishments*. Trans. Eulie Chowdury. Chandigarh: Punjab Government, Department of Town and Country Planning, 1979 (first published as: *Les Trois établissements humains*. Paris: Denoël, 1945).

Le Neveu, C. A. *Les empires coloniaux*. Paris: J. De Gigord, 1938.

Le Tourneau, Roger. *Fès avant le Protectorat: Étude économique et sociale d'une ville de l'occident musulman*. Casablanca: Société marocaine de librairie et d'édition, 1949.

Lebaut, René. *De Casablanca à Fez en aéroplane*. Paris: Librairie du Petit Journal, 1911.

Leclerc, Marc. *Au Maroc avec Lyautey (mai 1921)*. Paris: Armand Colin, 1927.

Leeuw, Hendrik de. *Sinful Cities of the Western World*. New York: Citadel, 1934.

Leftah, Mohammed. *Demoiselles de Numidie*. La Tour d'Aigues: Éditions de l'Aube, 1992.

Lempriere, William. *A Tour from Gibraltar to Tangier, Sallee, Mogodore, Santa Cruz, Tadoudant; and thence over Mount Atlas to Morocco, including a particular account of the Royal Haram, etc.* London: printed by J. Walter and sold by J. Johnson, 1791.

Leo Africanus, Johannes. *Description de l'Afrique*. Trans. A. Épaulard. 2 vols. Paris: Adrien-Maisonneuve, 1956 (originally published as: *Della descrittione dell'Africa et delle cose notabili che ivi sono*. Ed. Giovanni Battista Ramusio. Venice: 1550).

Lepp, Ignace. *Minuit sonne au Maroc*. Paris: Aubier, 1954.

Lévi-Strauss, Claude. *Tristes tropiques*. Trans. John Russell. New York: Atheneum, 1961 (first published as: *Tristes tropiques*. Paris: Plon, 1955).

Lewis, Wyndham. *Journey into Barbary: Morocco Writings and Drawings of Wyndham Lewish*. Ed. C. J. Fox. Santa Barbara, Calif.: Black Sparrow Press, 1983.

Loti, Pierre. *Au Maroc*. Paris: Calmann-Lévy, 1928.
Lyautey, General Louis Hubert Gonzalve, ed. *Rapport général sur la situation du Protectorat du Maroc au 31 juillet 1914*. Rabat: Résidence générale de la République française au Maroc, 1916.

Lyautey, General Louis Hubert Gonzalve. *Paroles d'action: Madagascar, Sud-Oranais, Oran, Maroc (1900–1926)*. Preface by Louis Barthou. Paris: Armand Colin, 1927.

Lyautey, General Louis Hubert Gonzalve. *Lyautey l'Africain: Textes et lettres du Maréchal Lyautey*. Paris: Plon, 1957.

Mac Orlan, Pierre. *Légionnaires: À la Légion étrangère espagnole, à la Légion étrangère française*. Paris: Éditions du Capitole, 1930.

Mac Orlan, Pierre. *Rues secrètes.* Paris: Gallimard, 1934.

Mahé, Yvonne. "L'extension des villes indigènes au Maroc." Ph.D. diss., Faculté de droit de Bordeaux, Bordeaux, Imprimerie J. Bière, 1936.

Mancuso, Franco. *Le Vicende dello zoning.* Milan: Il Saggiatore, 1978.

Marius Boyer: *Casablanca, travaux d'architecture.* Strasbourg: Edari, 1933.

Maroc 1950. Casablanca: Éditions Fontana, 1950.

Marrast, Joseph, ed. *L'Œuvre de Henri Prost architecture et urbanisme.* Paris: Académie d'Architecture, 1960.

Mas, Pierre. "Les phénomènes d'urbanisation et les bidonvilles du Maroc." Master's thesis, Institut d'urbanisme de l'université de Paris, Paris, 1950.

Mas, Pierre, and Pierre Pelletier. *L'habitat en nouvelle médina à Casablanca.* Rabat: Direction de l'intérieur, 1950.

Mathieu, Jean, and P. H. Maury. *La prostitution marocaine surveillée de Casablanca: Le quartier réservé.* N.p., n.d. [1951].

Maurois, André. *Lyautey.* Paris: Plon, 1931.

Mauss, Marcel. *Sociologie et anthropologie.* Paris: Presses universitaires de France, 1968.

Mazières, Nathalie de. "Un moment d'architecture, histoire d'une rencontre, Maroc, 1912–1933." Master's thesis, Unité pédagogique d'architecture no. 8, Paris, 1982.

Mernissi, Fatima. *Rêves de femme: Contes d'une enfance au harem.* Casablanca: Éditions Le Fennec, 1997.

Meunié, Dj. Jacques. *Greniers-citadelles au Maroc.* Paris: Arts et Métiers Graphiques, 1951.

Miège, Jean-Louis, and Eugène Hugues. *Les Européens à Casablanca au XIXe siècle (1856–1906).* Paris: Librairie Larose, Institut des Hautes Études Marocaines, 1954.

Miège, Jean-Louis, and Eugène Hugues. *Le Maroc et l'Europe (1830–1894).* 4 vols. Paris: 1961–63.

Modiano, Patrick. *Fleurs de ruine.* Paris: Gallimard, 1990.

Montagne, Robert. *Naissance du prolétariat marocain, enquête collective 1948–1950.* Paris: Peyronnet & Cie, n.d.

Montagne, Robert. *Révolution au Maroc.* Paris: France-Empire, 1953.

Montagne, Robert. *Villages et kasbahs berbères: Tableau de la vie sociale des Berbères sédentaires dans le sud du Maroc.* Paris: F. Alcan, 1930.

Mordal, Jacques [Hervé Cras, pseud.]. *La bataille de Casablanca (8, 9, 10 novembre 1942).* Paris: Plon, 1952.

Nehrkorn, Edmund. *Die Hölle von Casablanca: Erlebnisse eines Marokkodeutschen.* Bern: Ferd. Wyss Verlag, 1918.

Newman, Bernard. *Morocco Today.* London: Robert Hale Ltd, 1953.

Nolly, Émile [Captain Détanger, pseud.]. *Gens de guerre au Maroc.* Paris: Calmann-Lévy, 1912.

Nolly, Émile [Captain Détanger, pseud.]. *Le conquérant: Journal d'un "indésirable" au Maroc.* Paris: Calmann-Lévy, 1915.

O'Connor, Vincent Clarence Scott. *A Vision of Morocco, the Far West of Islam.* London: Thirnton Butterworth Ltd, 1923.

Ohrt, Roberto. *Phantom Avantgarde: Eine Geschichte der Situationistischen Internationale und der modernen Kunst.* Hamburg: Edition Nautilus, 1990.

Ollier, Claude. *Law and Order.* Trans. Ursule Molinaro. New York: Red Dust, 1971 (first published as: *Le maintien de l'ordre.* Paris: Gallimard, 1961).

Orieux, Jean. *Kasbahs en plein ciel.* Paris: Flammarion, 1951.

Ossendowski, Ferdinand Antoni. *Le Maroc enflammé.* Paris: Flammarion, 1927.

Osti, Giovanna. "Il Musée social di Parigi e gli inizi dell'urbanistica francese (1894–1914)." Master's thesis, Instituto Universitario di Architettura di Venezia, Venice, 1983.

Ouadda Idrissi, Mostapha. "L'architecture coloniale à Casablanca: Naissance et formes, politique urbaine sous le Protectorat, 1912–1956." Ph.D. diss., Université de Paris Panthéon-Sorbonne, Paris, 1983.

Oved, Georges. *La gauche française et le nationalisme marocain.* Paris: L'Harmattan, 1984.

Paccard, André. *Le Maroc et l'artisanat traditionnel islamique dans l'architecture.* Saint-Jorioz: Éditions Atelier 74, 1980.

Paul, James Albert. "Professionals and Politics in Morocco: A Historical Study of the Mediation of Power and the Creation of Ideology in the Context of European Imperialism." Ph.D. diss., New York University, New York, 1975.

Paul Tournon architecte 1881–1964. Paris: Éditions Dominique Vincent, 1976.

Penz, Charles. *Trentenaire de la Chambre de commerce et d'industrie de Casablanca 1921–1951.* Casablanca: Imprimerie rapide, 1951.

Penz, Charles, and Roger Coindreau. *Le Maroc: Maroc français, Maroc espagnol, Tanger.* Paris: Société d'éditions géographiques, maritimes et coloniales, 1949.

Penz, Charles, and Bernard Rouget. *Photo-itinéraire de Casablanca.* Preface by Philippe Boniface. Casablanca: Bernard Rouget, 1950.

Périgny, Comte Maurice de. *Au Maroc, Casablanca, Rabat, Meknès.* Paris: Pierre Roger & Cie, 1922.

Petites maisons, villas, bungalows. Paris: Albert Morancé, 1953.

Pétonnet, Colette. *Espaces habités: Ethnologie des banlieues.* Paris: Galilée, 1981.

Porch, Douglas. *The Conquest of Morocco.* New York: Knopf, 1983.

Powell, E. Alexander. *In Barbary: Tunisia, Algeria, Morocco, and the Sahara.* New York and London: Century, 1926.

Prost, Henri, and Gaston Monsarrat. *L'urbanisme au point de vue technique.* Paris: SAPE, 1927.

Rabinow, Paul. *French Modern: Norms and Forms of the Social Environment.* Cambridge, Mass.: MIT Press, 1989.

Rachik, Abderrahmane. *Ville et pouvoirs au Maroc.* Casablanca: Éditions Afrique Orient, 1995.

Ragon, Michel. *Le Livre de l'architecture moderne.* Paris: Robert Laffont, 1958.

Ragon, Michel, and Henri Tastemain. *Zevaco.* Paris: Éditions Cercle d'Art, 1999.

Rankin, Reginald. *In Morocco with General d'Amade.* London: Longmans, Green & Co., 1908.

Ratier, Jacques. "Les problèmes du bidonville des Carrières centrales à Casablanca." Internship paper, École Nationale d'Administration, Paris, 1949.

Raymond, André. *Grandes villes arabes à l'époque ottomane.* Paris: Sindbad, 1985.

Raymond, Jean. *L'urbanisme à la portée de tous.* Paris: Dunod, 1925.

Raymond, Jean. *Précis d'urbanisme moderne.* Paris: Dunod, 1934.

La Renaissance du Maroc: Dix ans de Protectorat 1912–1922. Rabat: Résidence générale de la République française au Maroc, 1923.

Renaudin, Louis. *L'habitat en Afrique du Nord.* Paris: Commissariat Général au Plan, February 1954.

Rey, A. *Souvenirs d'un voyage au Maroc.* Paris: Journal d'Algérie, 1844.

Richardson, James. *Travels in Morocco.* London: Charles J. Skeet, 1860.

Rivet, Daniel. *Lyautey et l'institution du Protectorat français au Maroc 1912–1925.* Paris: L'Harmattan, 1988.

Robin, Christelle, ed. *La ville européenne exportée.* Paris: Éditions de la Villette, 1995.

Rodinson, Maxime. *La Fascination de l'Islam.* Paris: François Maspero, 1980.

Rodrigue, Aron. *De l'instruction à l'émancipation.* Paris: Calmann-Lévy, 1989.

Roth, Alfred. *Das neue Schulhaus.* Zurich: Girsberger, 1957.

Ruiz Orsatti, Ricardo. *Relaciones hispano-marroquíes: Un gran amigo de España, el Sultán Mohammed-ben-Abdalá.* Madrid: Instituto de Estudios Politicos, 1944.

Sablayrolles, L. "L'urbanisme au Maroc, les moyens d'action, les résultats." Ph.D. diss., Faculté de droit, Toulouse, 1925.

Saïd, Edward. *Orientalism.* New York: Pantheon Books, 1978.

Saïd, Edward. *Culture and Imperialism.* New York: Knopf, 1993.

Saint-Aignan, Laurent, J.-E. *Prosper, Bousbir, ville réservée.* Rabat: Imprimerie Moncho et Laurent, 1950.

Saint-Aulaire, Auguste Félix Charles de Beaupoil, comte de. *Confession d'un vieux diplomate.* Paris: Flammarion, 1953.

Scham, Alan. *Lyautey in Morocco: Protectorate Administration 1912–1925.* Berkeley, Los Angeles, and London: University of California Press, 1970.

Sermaye, Jean. *L'Œuvre française en terre Marocaine.* Casablanca: Imprimeries Réunies, 1938.

Slaoui, Samir. "Analyse d'un bidonville au Maroc, les Carrières Centrales à Casablanca." Master's thesis, Unité pédagogique d'architecture no. 6, Paris, 1976.

Sloane, William Milligan. *Greater France in Africa*. New York and London: Charles Scribner's Sons, 1924.

Smithson, Alison, ed. *Team 10 Meetings 1953–1981*. New York: Rizzoli, 1991.

Soria y Mata, Arturo. *La cité linéaire: Nouvelle architecture de villes*. Paris: CERA/ENSBA, 1979 (first published as: La Ciudad lineal, Madrid: Imprenta de la Ciudad lineal, 1913).

Stöber, Georg. *"Habous Public" in Marokko, Zur wirtschaftlichen Bedeutung religiöser Stiftungen im 20. Jahrhundert*. Marburger geographische Schriften, no. 104. Marburg/Lahn: Marburger geographische Gesellschaft, 1986.

Studeny, Christophe. *L'invention de la vitesse: France, XVIIIe–XXe siècle*. Paris: Gallimard, 1995.

Stutfied, Hugh E. M. *El Maghreb: 1200 Miles' Ride through Marocco*. London: Sampson, Low, Marston, Searle, and Rivington, 1886.

Swearingen, Will D. *Moroccan Mirages: Agrarian Dreams and Deceptions, 1912–1986*. London: L. B. Tauris & Co, 1988.

Talamona, Maria-Ida. "Henri Prost architecte et urbaniste (1874–1959)." Postgraduate thesis, École des hautes études en sciences sociales, Paris, 1983.

Tarde, Alfred de. *Le Maroc, école d'énergie*. Paris: Plon, 1923.

Tarriot, Alfred. *Monographie de Casablanca de 1907 à 1914*. Casablanca: Imprimerie du Petit Marocain, 1924.

Terrasse, Henri. *Kasbahs berbères de l'Atlas et des oasis: Les grandes architectures du sud marocain*. Paris: Horizons de France, 1938.

Terrier, Auguste. *Le Maroc*. Paris: Larousse, 1931.

Tharaud, Jérome, and Jean Tharaud. *Le Maroc*. Paris: Flammarion, 1932.

Topin, Tito. *55 de fièvre*. Paris: Gallimard, 1983.

Topin, Tito. *Piano Barjo*. Paris: Gallimard, 1983.

Topin, Tito. *Le Cœur et le Chien*. Paris: Grasset, 1985.

Torres-Capell, Manuel. *Inicis de la urbanistica municipal de Barcelona 1750–1930*. Barcelona: Ajuntament de Barcelona, Corporacio metropolitana de Barcelona, 1985.

Tranchant de Lunel, Maurice. *Au pays du paradoxe*. Paris: Charpentier, 1924.

Tsur, Yaron, and Hagar Hillel. *Yehude Kazablankah: Iyunim be-modernizatsyah shel hanhagah Yehudit bi-tefutsah kolonyalit*. Ramat Aviv and Tel Aviv: ha-Universitah ha-Petuhah, 1985.

Tyrwhitt, Jacqueline, Jose-Luis Sert, and Ernesto N. Rogers, eds. *The Heart of the City: Towards the Humanization of Urban Life*. New York: Pellegrini and Cudahy, 1952.

Vacher, Hélène. *Projection coloniale et ville rationalisée: Le rôle de l'espace colonial dans la constitution de l'urbanisme en France, 1900–1931*. Aalborg: Aalborg University Press, 1997.

Vaillat, Léandre. *Le visage français du Maroc*. Paris: Horizons de France, 1931.

Vaillat, Léandre. *Le périple marocain*. Paris: Flammarion, 1934.

Van Beneden, C. *Madère, Les Iles Canaries, le Maroc*. Brussels: n.p., 1882.

Varde, Michel de la. *Casablanca ville d'émeutes*. Givors: André Martel, 1955.

Vidalenc, Georges. *Une œuvre française, le port de Casablanca*. Casablanca: Librairie Faraire, 1928.

Verret, Michel. *L'espace ouvrier*. Paris: Armand Colin, 1979.

Vitou, Elisabeth. *Gabriel Guévrékian 1900–1970: Une autre architecture moderne*. Paris: Connivences, 1987.

Vignaud, C. *Nouvelles cités d'habitation économique au Maroc*. Rabat: Circonscription de l'urbanisme et de l'habitat, 1952.

Wachtel, Nathan. *The Vision of the Vanquished: The Spanish Conquest of Peru through Indian Eyes, 1530–1570*. Trans. Ben and Siân Reynolds. New York: Barnes and Noble, 1977 (first published as: *La vision des vaincus: Les indiens du Pérou devant la conquête espagnole 1530–1570*. Paris: Gallimard, 1971).

Weisgerber, Dr. Félix. *Trois mois de campagne au Maroc: Étude géographique de la région parcourue*. Paris: Ernest Leroux, 1904.

Weisgerber, Dr. Félix. Preface by General d'Amade. *Casablanca et les Chaouia en 1900*. Casablanca: Imprimeries Réunies, 1935.

Weisgerber, Dr. Félix. *Au seuil du Maroc moderne*. Rabat: Éditions de la Porte, 1947.

Wharton, Edith. *In Morocco*. London and New York: Macmillan, 1920.

Wordell, M. T., and E. N. Seiler. *"Wildcats" over Casablanca*. Boston: Little, Brown, 1943.

Wright, Gwendolyn. *The Politics of Design in French Colonial Urbanism*. Chicago: The University of Chicago Press, 1991.

Zimmermann, Maurice. *Paysages et villes du Maroc*. Lyons: Imprimerie Express, 1923.

Zartman, I. William. *Morocco: Problems of New Power*. New York: Atherton Press, 1964.

Zurfluh, Jean-Michel. *Casablanca*. Casablanca: Soden, 1985.

Essays and Chapters of Books

Abitbol, Michel. "Colonialisme et relations judéo-musulmanes au Maroc." In *Relations judéo-musulmanes au Maroc: Perceptions et réalités*, ed. Michel Abitbol, 149–60. Paris: Stavit, 1997.

Adam, André. "(Al) Dar al-Bayda." In *The Encyclopaedia of Islam*, ed. H. A. R. Gibb, et al. Vol. 2, 116–17. Leiden: Brill, 1960.

Adam, André. "L'occidentalisation de l'habitat dans les villes marocaines." In *Les influences occidentales dans les villes maghrebines à l'époque contemporaine*, 179–87. Aix en Provence: Éditions de l'Université de Provence, 1974.

Augustin-Rey, Adolphe, Charles Barde, and Julien Pidoux. "Le remembrement urbain dans le Maroc français." In *La science des plans de ville*, 238–39. Paris and Lausanne: Payot, 1928.

Benzakour, Saad. "Casablanca ou le mythe urbain." In *Actes du colloque de Casablanca*, 39–74. Casablanca: Publications de la Faculté des lettres et des sciences de Casablanca, 1983.

Cambon, Victor. "L'aménagement et l'extension des villes." In *Conférences franco-marocaines*. Vol. 2, 203–16. Paris: Plon, 1917.

"Casablanca." In *Mémorial de Lyautey, l'œuvre de la France au Maroc: Livre d'or du Centenaire*, 193–246. Paris: n.p., 1954.

Casinière, H. de la. "Les grands travaux d'édilité au Maroc." In *Où en est l'urbanisme en France et à l'étranger*, ed. Société française des urbanistes, 296–312. Paris: Eyrolles, 1923.

Casinière, H. de la. "Les plans d'extension des villes et l'urbanisme au Maroc." In *Où en est l'urbanisme en France et à l'étranger*, ed. Société française des urbanistes, 202–11. Paris: Eyrolles, 1923.

Chaisemartin, Nathalie de. "Perspective de recherche sur le décor des façades des habitations privées dans le centre de Casablanca 1880/1930." In *Actes du colloque de Casablanca*, 15–34. Casablanca: Publications de la Faculté des lettres et des sciences de Casablanca, 1983.

Cohen, Jean-Louis, and Monique Eleb. "Casablanca: De la 'cité de l'énergie' à la ville fonctionnelle." In *Architectures françaises outre-mer*, ed. Maurice Culot and Jean-Marie Thiveaud, 108–45. Paris: Institut Français d'Architecture; Liège: Pierre Mardaga, 1992.

Durand, Emmanuel. "L'évolution de l'urbanisme dans le Protectorat du Maroc de 1923 à 1931." In *L'Urbanisme aux colonies et dans les pays tropicaux*. Vol. 1, ed. Jean Royer. 81–93. La Charité-sur-Loire: Urbanisme, 1932.

Eleb, Monique. "Immeubles et îlots du nouveau Casablanca: Reflets parisiens et horizons modernes." In *Paris s'exporte: Architecture modèle ou modèles d'architecture*, ed. André Lortie, 119–25. Paris: Pavillon de l'Arsenal; Picard, 1995.

Eleb, Monique. "An Alternative to Functionalist Universalism: Ecochard, Candilis, and ATBAT-Afrique." In *Anxious Modernisms: Experimentations in Postwar Architectural Culture*, ed. Sarah Williams Goldhagen and Réjean Legault, 55–73. Cambridge, Mass.: MIT Press; Montreal: Canadian Centre for Architecture, 2000.

Fargues, Philippe. "Le monde arabe: La citadelle domestique." In *Histoire de la famille*. Vol. 2, ed. André Burguière, 339–71. Paris: Armand-Colin, 1986.

Farrère, Claude. "Les Français au Maroc." In *Histoire populaire des colonies françaises: Le Maroc*. Paris: Éditions du Velin d'Or, 1932.

Favrot, Claude. "Une ville française moderne." In *Conférences franco-marocaines*. Vol. 2, 219–36. Paris: Plon, 1917.

Geertz, Clifford. "Suq: The Bazaar Economy in Sefrou." In *Meaning and Order in Moroccan Society*, ed. Clifford and Hildred Geertz and Lawrence Rosen, 123–313. Cambridge: Cambridge University Press, 1979.

Khatibi, Abdelkebir. "État et classes sociales au Maroc." In *Études sociologiques sur le Maroc*, 3–15. Rabat: Société d'études économiques, sociales et statistiques, 1971.

Khatibi, Abdelkebir. "Note descriptive sur les élites administratives et économiques marocaines." In *Annuaire de l'Afrique du Nord 1968*, 79–90. Paris: Éditions du CNRS, 1970.

Laprade, Albert. "Une ville créée spécialement pour les indigènes à Casablanca." In *L'Urbanisme aux colonies et dans les pays tropicaux*. Vol. 1, ed. Jean Royer, 94–99. La Charité-sur-Loire: Urbanisme, 1932.

Lourido Diaz, Ramón. "De nuevo sobre la creación de la ciudad marroquí Dar-al-Bayda' (Casablanca)." In *Homenaje al Prof. Darío Cabanelas Rodríguez, OFM con motivo de su LXX aniversario*, 405–17. Granada: Universidad de Granada, 1987.

Lucius, Jacques. "L'évolution économique récente du Maroc." In *Industrialisation de l'Afrique du nord*, ed. Gaston Leduc, 252–75. Paris: Armand Colin, 1952.

"Maroc-Casablanca-Carrières centrales." In *Encyclopédie d'urbanisme*, ed. Robert Auzelle and Ivan Jankovic, plates 2/123–24 and 2/125. Paris: CSTB; Vincent et Fréal, 1958.

Montagne, Robert. "Naissance et développement du prolétariat marocain." In *Industrialisation de l'Afrique du nord*, ed. Gaston Leduc, 199–222. Paris: Armand Colin, 1952.

Penz, Charles. "Histoire de Casablanca." In *Casablanca, porte du Maroc*, 43–50. Casablanca: Rotary-club de Casablanca, 1953.

"Port de Casablanca." In *Encyclopédie coloniale et maritime*, 330–34. Paris: Encyclopédie coloniale et maritime, 1942.

Prost, Henri. "Habitation et urbanisme dans l'Afrique du nord." In *Congrès de la santé publique et de la prévoyance sociale*, 224–33. Marseilles: Commission générale de l'exposition coloniale, 1922.

Prost, Henri. "Le développement de l'urbanisme dans le Protectorat du Maroc de 1914 à 1923." In *L'Urbanisme aux colonies et dans les pays tropicaux*. Vol. 1, ed. Jean Royer, 59–80. La Charité-sur-Loire: Urbanisme, 1932.

Talamona, Maria-Ida. "Henri Prost, du projet au zoning 1902–1912." In *L'usine et la ville 150 ans d'urbanisme 1936–1986*, ed. Jean-Pierre Épron, 51–55. Paris: Institut français d'architecture; Culture technique, 1986.

Wachtel, Nathan. "L'acculturation." In *Faire de l'histoire*. Vol. 1, ed. Jacques Le Goff and Pierre Nora. Paris: Gallimard, 1974.

Yver, G. "Dar al-Beda." In *Encyclopaedia of Islam*. Vol. 1, 915. Leiden and New York : E. J. Brill, 1987 (first published: Leiden: E .J. Brill, 1913–36).

Monographic Issues of Periodicals

"L'architecture au Maroc." *Réalisations* and *Le Maroc du nord au sud,* special joint issue (June 1939).

Bory, Paul, ed. "Le port de Casablanca et la naissance d'une grande ville," *Notre Maroc* 10 (June 1952).

"Casablanca." *Le Maroc du nord au sud* 3 (June 1938).

"Casablanca." *La Terre marocaine illustrée* (March 1, 1928).

"Casablanca: Grande ville et grand port de l'Empire français." *Revue de géographie marocaine* 23 (May 1939).

"Casablanca: Grande ville et grand port de l'Empire français." *Revue de géographie marocaine* 23 (January 1940).

Denoix, Sylvie, ed. "Biens communs, patrimoines collectifs et gestion communautaire dans les sociétés musulmanes." *Revue des mondes musulmans et de la Méditerranée* no. 79–80 (1997).

Écochard, Michel. "Urbanisme et construction pour le plus grand nombre." *Annales de l'Institut Technique du Bâtiment et des Travaux Publics* no. 148 (October 1950).

"L'évolution du Maroc en 1951." *Réalités marocaines* no. 3 (March 1951).

"France d'outre-mer." *L'Architecture d'aujourd'hui* 7, no. 3 (March 1936).

"Les grandes villes d'Afrique et de Madagascar, Casablanca." *Notes et Études Documentaire* no. 3 (June 14, 1971): 397–98.

"Maroc." *L'Architecture d'aujourd'hui* 22, no. 35 (May 1951).

"Maroc." *L'Architecture française* 11, no. 95–96 (May 1950).

"Maroc." *L'Architecture française* 13, no. 131–32 (November–December 1952).

"Le Maroc en 1932." *L'Afrique du Nord illustrée* 27 (1932).

"Le Maroc en 1938." *L'Afrique du Nord illustrée* 33 (1938).

"Le port de Casablanca, historique, description." *Réalisations* 5 (1938).

Major Articles in Periodicals

"À Casablanca, une maison à l'accent méridional de l'architecte Erwin Hinnen." *Maisons et jardins* no. 39 (September–October 1959).

"À propos d'urbanisme." *Maroc* (1950): 158.

Adam, André. "Le bidonville de Ben Msik à Casablanca." *Annales de l'IEO de la Faculté des Lettres d'Alger* 8 (1949): 61–199.

Adam, André. "Casablanca, grande ville marocaine." *Le Journal de Genève* (Geneva), September 4, 1951.

Adam, André. "La population marocaine de l'ancienne médina de Casablanca." *Bulletin économique et social du Maroc* no. 47 and 48 (1950): 183–85 and 14–26.

Adam, André. "La prolétarisation de l'habitat dans l'ancienne médina de Casablanca." *Bulletin économique et social du Maroc* no. 45 and 46 (1950): 245–56 and 44–50.

Adam, André. "Sur l'action du Galilée à Casablanca en août 1907." *Revue de l'Occident musulman et de la Méditerranée* no. 6 (1969): 9–22.

"Aéro-club et aérogare de Casablanca à Tit-Mellil, J. F. Zevaco, P. Messina et D. Basciano, architectes." *L'Architecture d'aujourd'hui* 24, no. 47 (May 1953): 60.

Anfreville de Jurquet de la Salle, L. d'. "Essai sur la climatologie et la démographie de Casablanca." *Bulletin de la Société de pathologie exotique* 12, no. 8 (1919): 525–30.

Anfreville de Jurquet de la Salle, L. d'. "Une grande ville vient de naître." *La Géographie* 53, no. 1 (January–February 1930): 25–38.

Antier, Jean-Jacques. "Promenade au Maroc: Casablanca la ville-champignon est aussi une capitale moderne; Bous-bir, visite nocturne au quartier réservé de Casablanca." *La Liberté normande* (Flers), August 25 and September 9, 1950.

Antraygues, R. "D'Anfa à Casablanca." *Bulletin de la Chambre de commerce et d'industrie de Casablanca* 14, no. 12 (December 1935): 549–59.

"Het arabische Casablanca." *De Telegraaf* (Amsterdam), December 30, 1934.

Arcos, R. d'. "L'urbanisme au Maroc." *Chantiers nord-africains* 1, no. 10 (October 1929): 583–84.

Arcos, R. d'. "Le Maroc à la recherche d'une formule d'architecture." *L'Art et les artistes* 24 (March 1930): 203–10.

"A. Arnone, immeuble de rapport, boulevard d'Anfa à Casablanca, J. Michelet architecte." *Réalisations* 1, no. 4 (June 1934): 99–101.

"Un aspect pittoresque de l'urbanisme marocain." *L'Afrique du Nord illustrée* 25, no. 492 (4 October 1930): 8.

ATBAT-Afrique. "Habitat européen au Maroc, 'immeuble entonnoir', orientation sud, étude faite par ATBAT-Afrique." *L'Architecture d'aujourd'hui* 24, no. 46 (February–March 1953): 76.

ATBAT-Afrique. "Habitat collectif musulman à Casablanca, ATBAT-Afrique." *L'Architecture d'aujourd'hui* 25, no. 57 (December 1954): 54–55.

Aujard, Robert. "Problème du logement au Maroc." *Bulletin économique et social du Maroc* 22, no. 79 (January 1959): 313–20.

B., J. "Lettre de la tradition: I. force de la tradition; II. Optimisme des bâtisseurs: Le Marhaba." *Cahiers du Sud* 326 (1954).

Balandier, Georges. "La situation coloniale: Approche théorique." *Cahiers internationaux de sociologie* 6, no. 11 (1951), 44–79.

"Le Bar Rustique à Casablanca, Suraqui frères architecte." *Réalisations* 2, no. 3 (December 1935): 81–82.

Barber, Noël. "The City of Fear." *Daily Mail* (London), July 15, 1954, 1 and 3.

Baron, Anne-Marie. "Densités de population des quartiers marocains à Casablanca." *Notes marocaines* 6 (1955): 3–11.

Benhima, Dr. Mohammed. "La cité du derb Jedid." *Bulletin économique et social du Maroc* 22, no. 80 (April 1959): 415–35.

Benoist, L. "Les nouveaux abattoirs de Casablanca (Maroc)." *Le Génie civil* 82, no. 5 (February 3, 1923): 98–100.

Benoît, Fernand. "L'évolution des villes et le décor architectural au Maroc." *La Renaissance de l'art* 14, no. 8 (August 1931): 239–44.

Benoît, Fernand. "100 ans d'urbanisme nord-africain." *L'Architecte* 9, no. 7 (July 1932): 61; no. 8 (August 1932): 69–72; no. 9 (September 1932): 80–84; and no. 10 (October 1932): 93–94.

Benoit-Lévy, Georges. "Une banlieue-jardin marocaine: Ain-Chock." *La Construction moderne* 70, no. 9 (September 1954): 319–24.

Bérenguier, Henri. "Monographie d'un quartier de Casablanca: Le derb Ghalef." *Bulletin économique et social du Maroc* 28, no. 63 (December 1954): 391–426.

Bernard, Ph. "Les plans du futur grand Casa." *Le Petit Marocain* (Casablanca), March 16, 17, 20, 21, 23, and 28, 1950.

Berque, Jacques. "Médinas, villeneuves et bidonvilles." *Les Cahiers de Tunisie* no. 21–22 (1959): 5–42.

Bertrand, Gabriel. "Casablanca d'hier et d'aujourd'hui, un brouillon pour demain." *La France indépendante* (Paris), August 5, 1950, 2.

Bertrand, Gabriel. "Casablanca d'hier et d'aujourd'hui, une capitale ou une sous-préfecture?" *La France indépendante* (Paris), September 9, 1950, 5.

Besnard, Philippe. "Impressions marocaines." *L'Action française* (Paris), June 14, 1937, 3–4.

"Les besoins en logements du Maroc." *Bulletin d'information du Maroc* (October 5, 1949): 5.

Blachère, Gérard. "L'habitat modeste en Afrique du Nord et au Sahara." *Cahiers du CSTB* no. 365, fasc. 45 (August 1960).

Bode, Léon. "Casablanca: Les problèmes de sa décentralisation industrielle et démographique." *Bulletin des ingénieurs du Maroc* (April–May 1951): 26–34.

Boissonnade, Euloge. "Révolution dans la construction marocaine, plein succès de l'immeuble expérimental des Carrières centrales à Casa." *L'Écho d'Oran* (Oran), April 7, 1954, 6.

Boissonnade, Euloge. "Dans le cadre de la lutte contre le terrorisme, un programme social constructif est en cours de réalisation à Casablanca." *L'Écho d'Oran* (Oran) 14 May 1954, 6.

Boissonnade, Euloge. "Le magnifique bilan du CIL au Maroc." *L'Écho d'Oran* (Oran), June 6, 7, 8, and 9, 1954.

Boissonnade, Euloge. "La cité M'Barka à Casablanca permettra de loger plusieurs milliers de Marocains." *Travaux nord-africains* (April 14, 1955): 1.

Boissonnade, Euloge. "Les architectes du Maroc protestent contre la création du Commissariat de l'habitat et de l'urbanisme." *Travaux nord-africains* (March 24, 1955): 1–2.

Borély, Jules. "L'architecture nouvelle et l'urbanisme au Maroc." *L'Art vivant* 6, no. 140 (October 15, 1930): 797–840.

Boujol, Pierre. "Renaissance de Casablanca." *Cahiers français d'information* (December 16, 1945): 16–17.

Bourdeix, Pierre. "L'urbanisme au Maroc." *Le Bâtiment* (August 27 and November 5, 1931): 20–23.

Bousquet, M. "Le port et la ville de Casablanca." *La Construction moderne* 35, no. 3 (December 7, 1919): 76–78.

Bousquet, M. "L'architecture marocaine." *La France Nouvelle* no. 10 (October 1928): 299–301.

Bowles, Paul. "Casablanca." Illustrations by Ronald Searle. *Holiday* 4, no. 3 (1966): 74–122.

"Brasserie-restaurant 'Le Roi de la bière' à Casablanca, M. Desmet architecte." *Réalisations* 2, no. 3 (December 1935): 77–80.

Bruant, Catherine. "Donat-Alfred Agache (1875–1959), l'architecte et le sociologue." *Les Études sociales* no. 122 (1994): 23–61.

Bruant, Catherine. "L'Orient de la science sociale." *Revue du monde musulman et de la Méditerranée* 73–74 (1994): 296–310.

Bruant, Catherine. "Un architecte à 'l'école d'énergie': Donat-Alfred Agache, du voyage à l'engagement social." *Revue du monde musulman et de la Méditerranée* 73–74 (1994): 100–117.

Brunfaut, Jules. "L'urbanisme au Maroc." *Bulletin de la classe des beaux-arts, Académie Royale de Belgique* 6, no. 10–12 (1925): 91–97.

Bughas, Bellaigue de. "L'actualité marocaine: Trois architectes casablancais travaillent aux plans d'un bloc culturel grandiose." *Travaux nord-africains* (February 15, 1951): 1–3.

C., A. "Les travaux du port de Casablanca (Maroc) et l'emprunt marocain." *Le Génie civil* 44, no. 23 (April 4, 1914): 458–60.

Cambo, J.-P. "Rayonnement et avenir économique de Casablanca." *Encyclopédie mensuelle d'Outremer* (November 1951): 306–9.

Cambon, Victor. "Les villes marocaines en 1927." *La Semaine coloniale* (1927): 19–24.

Candilis, Georges. "Entretien avec Georges Candilis." *Ingénieurs et architectes suisses* (December 7, 1994): 490–92.

Candilis, Georges, and Shadrach Woods. "Étude théorique de l'immeuble semi-duplex." *L'Architecture d'aujourd'hui* no. 46 (February–March 1953): 87–89.

"Une capitale mal située est une erreur capitale." *Combat-Maroc* (Casablanca, September 15, 1945).

"Casablanca." *L'Architecture d'aujourd'hui* no. 3 (September–October 1945): 64–72.

"Casablanca." *France Amérique Grande-Bretagne* (April 1946): 20–21.

"Casablanca." *Art présent* no. 10–11 (1949).

"Casablanca, la banque commerciale du Maroc." *Bâtir* (January 1933).

"Casablanca: City under a Pull of Fear." *New York Times Magazine* (September 11, 1955).

"Casablanca, grande ville marocaine." *Bulletin d'informations immobilières* (July 1949): 1 and 12.

"Casablanca: Le développement prodigieux d'une ville en pleine fièvre de croissance." *Réalités* no. 89 (June 1953): 48–55.

"Casablanca Population Totals 540000 Persons." *The Stars and Stripes* (Casablanca), July 22, 1943.

Carteau, Roger. "L'organisation à Casablanca de la délégation aux affaires urbaines." *La Vigie marocaine* (Casablanca), February 18, 1948, 2.

Casinière, H. de la. "Les villes nouvelles du Maroc." *L'Armée d'Afrique* 2, no. 20 (December 25, 1925): 86–92.

Cattedra, Raffaele. "Nascita e primi sviluppi di una città coloniale: Casablanca." *Storia urbana* 14, no. 53 (October–December 1990): 127–80.

Célérier, Jean. "Les fonctions économiques du port de Casablanca." *Revue de géographie marocaine* (1931).

Célérier, Jean. "Les conditions économiques du développement de Casablanca." *Revue de géographie marocaine* (May 1939).

Celle, R. de la. "Casablanca (Dar el-Beïda), ses vieux souks, sa nouvelle médina." *L'Afrique du Nord illustrée* 30, no. 751 (September 21, 1935): 2–3.

Celle, R. de la. "Maroc: Place de France." *L'Afrique du Nord illustrée* 30, no. 755 (October 19, 1935): 34–35.

"Centrale laitière du Maroc, Bernard Leclerc architecte." *L'Architecture française* 2 (September 1941): 22–23.

"Le centre de puériculture du Maârif à Casablanca, G. Renaudin, architecte dplg." *Réalisations* 3, no. 5 (March–June 1938): 141–45.

Chaban, André. "Les valeurs immobilières à Casablanca." *Notre Maroc* (January 1954): 97–100.

Chable, Jean-Edouard. "Lieux dont on parle, Casablanca, édifice monumental mais fragile." *La Tribune de Genève* (Geneva), January 11, 1955.

Chabot, T. de. "Comment on bâtit au Maroc." *La Terre marocaine illustrée* (February 15, 1930): 1078–82.

Chabot, T. de. "Faudra-t-il un jour démolir Casablanca?" *Chantiers nord-africains* 2, no. 10 (October 1930): 907–10.

Charbonneau, Dr. "Casablanca est-elle une ville humide ou non?" *L'Intransigeant marocain* (Casablanca), April 27, 1945, 1 and 3.

Charbonneau, General. "Casablanca et Safi (les ports africains)." *Tropique: Revue des troupes coloniales* (June 1948).

Charton, Albert. "Casablanca, ville industrielle." *Bulletin de la Société de Géographie du Maroc* (3rd trimester, 1922): 181–90.

Charton, Albert. "Une mission universitaire au Maroc, Casablanca." *Annales de Géographie* 23, no. 183 (May 15, 1924): 303–7.

Charton, Albert. "La politique des ports du Maroc." *Le Monde colonial illustré* 5, no. 52 (December 1927): 284.

"(Le) chauffage des immeubles de rapport au Maroc." *Réalisations* 3, no. 5 (March–June 1938): 125–26.

Chaux, Bouquet des. "Les ports marocains, 1. Port de Casablanca." *Annales des Ponts et Chaussées* 104, no. 3 (May–June 1934): 308–37.

Ciarlantini, Franco. "Casablanca e le medine del Marocco." *Il Resto del Carlino* (Bologna), May 31, 1935.

Ciarlantini, Franco. "Casablanca, vittoria della civiltà latina." *Il Mattino* (Naples), May 30, 1935.

Ciarlantini, Franco. "Italiani a Casablanca." *Il Messagero* (Rome), June 7, 1935.

Ciarlantini, Franco. "Luce di cultura italiana a Casablanca." *Il Resto del Carlino* (Bologna), June 6, 1935.

"Cinéma-théâtre 'Lynx' à Casablanca, D. Basciano, architecte." *L'Architecture d'aujourd'hui* 25, no. 52 (January–February 1954): 51.

"Cité d'habitation de Bournazel, à Casablanca, Albert Lucas, architecte, OTH bureau d'étude." *L'Architecture française* 16, no. 163–64 (1955): 28–32.

"Cité d'habitation pour jeunes ménages, CIL Casablanca, L. Aroutcheff, G. Candilis, R. Jean, ATBAT-Afrique." *L'Architecture d'aujourd'hui* no. 46 (February–March 1953): 90.

"Une cité ouvrière de 100.000 habitants va surgir aux portes de Casablanca." *Le Petit Marocain* (Casablanca), March 6, 1954, 4.

"Une cité ouvrière pour indigènes à Casablanca." *Construire* (February 15, 1939): 1.

"Cités ouvrières et quartiers de grand luxe . . . voici le grand Casablanca." *Maroc demain* (August 26, 1950): 1–4.

"La climatisation des locaux habités au Maroc." *Réalisations* 3, no. 5 (March–June 1938): 153–54.

"Club d'équitation à Casablanca, G. Jaubert, architecte et E. Di Gioacchino collab." *L'Architecture d'aujourd'hui*, no. 47 (May 1953): XV.

Cohen, Jean-Louis. "Casablanca, banco di prova per l'urbanistica dell'ampliamento (1920–1930)." *Casabella* no. 593 (September 1992): 30–37.

Cohen, Jean-Louis. "Casablanca, d'Agache à Prost: Un banc d'essai pour les techniques de l'extension." Quels dess(e)ins pour les villes? De quelques objets de planification pour l'urbanisme de l'entre-deux-guerres. Dossiers des séminaires Techniques, *Territoires et Sociétés*, no. 20–21 (October 1992): 108–19.

Cohen, Jean-Louis. "II Groupe des architectes modernes marocains e l'Habitat du plus grand nombre." *Gli ultimi C.I.A.M., Rassegna* no. 52 (December 1992): 58–69.

Cohen, Jean-Louis. "Henri Prost and Casablanca: The Art of Making Successful Cities (1912–1940)." *The New City* no. 3 (Fall 1996): 106–21.

Cohen, Jean-Louis, and Monique Eleb. "Casablanca 1950." *Le Moniteur Architecture* no. 40 (April 1993): 40–44.

Cohen, Jean-Louis, and Monique Eleb. "The Whiteness of the Surf." *ANY* no. 16 (1996): 16–19.

Colliez, André, and Henri Prost. "Une ville champignon française: Casablanca, son aménagement urbain." *Le Musée social* (February 1933): 55–56.

"Colonial, es-tu bien logé?" *France Outremer* no. 248 (May 1950): 123–37 and 157–64.

"La construction des bases américaines au Maroc." *Le Monde* (Paris), August 26, 1952, 3.

"Construction d'une villa à Casablanca." *Maisons et jardins* (February 1957).

Coste, Kirk Lucien. "Le claustra." *Réalisations* 2, no. 4 (February 1936): 111–17.

Courtois, Alexandre. "Casablanca, capitale d'Empire et porte du Maroc (un problème d'urbanisme posé par Casablanca)." *L'Entreprise au Maroc* (June 24, 1948): 5–6.

Couzinet, Paul. "L'urbanisme et l'aménagement des villes au Maroc." *Bulletin économique et social du Maroc* 7 (July 1945): 26–28.

Creugnet, Georges. "Casablanca, l'une des villes-champignons les plus actives du monde." *Travaux nord-africains* (September 20, 1951): 1.

Creugnet, Georges. "On construit à Casablanca le plus grand stade d'Afrique du nord." *Travaux nord-africains* (October 25, 1951): 1 and 5.

Creugnet, Georges. "La cité-jardin de Casablanca comprendra 35 immeubles totalisant 1980 logements." *Travaux nord-africains* (March 28, 1957): 1 and 3.

"La crise du logement au Maroc où 20000 familles sont sans foyer." *Les Échos* (Paris), March 29, 1949.

Cuénot, J. "Réalisations électriques: Immeuble de 'La Nationale' à Casablanca." *Réalisations* 1, no. 4 (June 1934): 109–15.

D. "Le nouvel Hôtel de ville de Casablanca." *Chantiers nord-africains* 3, no. 1 (January 1931): 69–73.

Dantin, C. "La centrale à ciment de Casablanca." *Le Génie civil* 68, no. 18 (April 29, 1916): 273–77.

Déchaud, E. "Une croisière de reconnaissance commerciale au Maroc." *Renseignements coloniaux et documents publiés par le Comité de l'Afrique française* 14, no. 4 (April 1904): 110–12.

Delau, Louis. "Casablanca et les Casablancais." *Revue de géographie marocaine* 23 (1940): 9–14.

Demagistri, F. "Le prodigieux développement de Casablanca, porte de l'Empire chérifien." *La Tribune de Genève* (Geneva), November 1938.

Demagistri, F. "Sous l'égide de la France, le prodigieux développement de Casablanca et sa féconde activité." *La Tribune de Genève* (Geneva), November 1941.

"Le derb Jdid (Hay Hassani), Casablanca, Élie Azagury." *L'Architecture d'aujourd'hui* no. 87 (December 1959): 52–57.

Derout, René. "Les étrangers dans la cité." *Maroc-Presse* (Casablanca), April 15–June 14, 1954.

Descamps, Henri. "L'architecture française au Maroc." *La Construction moderne* 45, no. 49 (September 7, 1930): 758–65.

Descamps, Henri. "L'architecture française au Maroc, l'urbanisme: L'œuvre de M. Prost." *La Construction moderne* 46, no. 4 (October 26, 1930): 50–55.

Descamps, Henri. "Urbanisme et architecture française au Maroc." *La Cité moderne* 12 (1931): 19–25.

Dessigny, Commandant Charles. "Casablanca, notice économique et administrative." *Bulletin de la Société de géographie d'Alger et d'Afrique du Nord* 16 (3rd trimester, 1911): 293–331.

Dethier, Jean. "60 ans d'urbanisme au Maroc: L'évolution des idées et des réalisations." *Bulletin économique et social du Maroc* no. 119–20 (1972): 5-56.

"Deux villas à Casablanca, E. Azagury, architecte." *L'Architecture d'aujourd'hui* no. 49 (October 1953): 24–25.

"Dispensaire antituberculeux Georges Orthlieb, G. Renaudin, architecte dplg." *Réalisations* 3, no. 5 (March–June 1938): 146–47.

"Dispensaire de la Maternelle, Boyer architecte." *Réalisations* 2, no. 1 (July 1935): 16–18.

"Dispensaire-école à Casablanca, Aroutcheff, Azagury, Erdely, Jaubert, architectes." *L'Architecture d'aujourd'hui* 18, no. 15 (November 1947): 4.

"Le drame marocain devant la conscience chrétienne (les événements de Casablanca à travers la presse française du Maroc)." *Cahiers du témoignage chrétien* no. 25 (1955): 1–71.

Drouin, Pierre. "Visages du Maroc au travail, II. Casablanca, l'Eldorado et son envers." *Le Monde* (Paris), June 5–6, 1949.

Du Taillis, Jean. "Les transformations de Casablanca, future capitale de la région marocaine des Chaouïas." *Le Tour du monde* 16 (1910): 257–60.

Ducatel, Charles. "Histoire de la tour de l'Horloge." *La Tribune des vieux Marocains* (February 1948): 11.

Dugard, Henry. "Le développement de Casablanca." *L'Europe nouvelle* no. 17 (April 26, 1919): 800–1.

Duncan, D. G. "L'église Sainte-Marguerite des Roches Noires." *Reflets de France* (1947): 14–15.

Durand, René, and René Kuhn. "Une réalisation en très grande série d'habitat indigène économique au Maroc." *Supplément aux Annales de l'Institut technique du bâtiment et des travaux publics* no. 82 (October 1954): 952–64.

Durand, René, and Pierre Lions. "La cité Bournazel de Casablanca: Étude et réalisation d'un ensemble de 1.700 logements." *Supplément aux Annales de l'Institut technique du bâtiment et des travaux publics* no. 107 (January 1957).

Dyé, A. Henri. "Les ports du Maroc." *Bulletin de la Société de géographie commerciale de Paris* 30 (May–June 1908).

Écochard, Michel. "Les quartiers industriels des villes du Maroc." *Urbanisme* 11–12 (1951): 25–39.

Écochard, Michel. "Problèmes d'urbanisme au Maroc." *Bulletin économique et social du Maroc* 15 (4th quarter, 1951).

Écochard, Michel. "Habitat musulman au Maroc." *L'Architecture d'aujourd'hui* no. 60 (June 1955): 36–40.

"Église du Sacré-Cœur de Casablanca." *Travaux* no. 244 (February 1955): 250–52.

Eleb, Monique. "Apartment buildings in Casablanca: Types and Lifestyles (1930–1950)." *The New City* no. 3 (Fall 1996): 94–105.

Eleb, Monique. "Casablanca tra arti decorative e funzionalismo." *Casabella* no. 593 (September 1992): 30–41.

Eleb, Monique. "Des Suisses à Casablanca: Une modernité adaptée." *Faces* no. 42–43 (Autumn 1997–Winter 1998): 90–96.

"En campagne avec l'armée chérifienne: Notes de voyage d'un médecin du Grand Vizir." *L'Illustration* no. 3134 (March 21, 1903): 178–82.

"En marge de l'action CIL, spéculation 'sociale' à Casablanca." *Maroc-Demain* (Casablanca), January 20, 1951, 1.

Escallier, Robert. "Espace urbain et flux migratoire: Le cas de la métropole économique marocaine, Casablanca." *Méditerranée* no. 1 (1980).

"L'étonnante métamorphose de Casablanca." *L'Illustration* no. 4487 (March 2, 1929): 222–25.

"Les événements du Maroc à Casablanca." *L'Illustration* no. 3363 (August 10, 1907): 83–85.

"Les événements du Maroc." *L'Illustration* no. 3364 (August 17, 1907): 98–101.

"Évolution de l'habitat marocain." *L'Architecture d'aujourd'hui* no. 46 (February–March 1953): 95–98.

"L'évolution du Makhzen, la famille Tazi." *Bulletin du comité de L'Afrique française* no. 2 (February 1904): 50–51.

"Exposition Internationale de Paris, 1937, Pavillon du Maroc." *Réalisations* no. 6 (June 1936): 172–75.

Farrère, Claude. "Une ville champignon." *L'Ouest* (Angers), December 12, 1920.

Faujès de Latour, E. de. "Trolleybus de Casablanca." *Le véhicule électrique* (December 1932).

"Fédala, Casablanca." *Le Maroc du Nord au Sud* 3 (1938).

Ferney, Pierre. "Au temps où Lyautey partait en guerre contre les 'boîtes à mouches.'" *Afrique-Magazine* (October 23, 1947): 7.

Forichon, Robert. "La législation de l'urbanisme au Maroc." *L'Architecture d'aujourd'hui* 35 (1951): 12–30.

Fries, Frank. "Les plans d'Alep et de Damas: Un banc d'essai pour l'urbanisme des frères Danger." *Revue du monde musulman et de la Méditerranée* 73–74 (1994): 311–25.

"La future cathédrale de Casablanca." *Chantiers nord-africains* 1, no. 5 (May 1929): 349.

G.-M., S. "L'urbanisme au Maroc: Que va-t-on faire pour les villes marocaines? (compte-rendu d'une conférence de M. Michel Écochard)." *Arts* (September 29, 1950): 8.

Galatoire-Malégarie, C. "Note sur l'œuvre marocaine de M. Gaston Delure, inspecteur général, ancien directeur général des Travaux publics du Maroc." *Annales des ponts et chaussées* 97, no. 4 (July–August 1927): 7–12.

Gallissot, René. "Le Maroc et la Crise." *Revue française d'histoire d'outre-mer* 63 (1976): 477–91.

Gallotti, Jean. "L'urbanisme aux colonies, à propos du récent congrès international de Vincennes." *L'Entreprise française*, October 25, 1931, 25–27.

Gallotti, Jean. "Urbanisme exotique." *Vu* (November 11, 1931): 2498–99.

Gallotti, Jean. "Esthétique et reconstruction: Une leçon de Lyautey." *Le Monde français* (June 1947): 355–68.

"Le garage de la société France-Auto Citroën à Casablanca, architecte Ravazé." *Chantiers nord-africains* 2, no. 9 (September 1930): 803.

"La garderie d'enfants d'Aïn Chock." *Bulletin d'information du Maroc* (March 15, 1948).

Gattefossé, Jean. "Sur l'origine lointaine de la ville de Casablanca." *Bulletin trimestriel du syndicat d'initiative de Casablanca et de sa région* no. 35 (October 1956): 27.

Gendre, F. "Les plans de Casablanca." *Revue de Géographie Marocaine* 23 (May 1939): 235–51.

Gendre, Lucien. "Urbanisme et accroissement géographique." *Confluent* no. 50 (April–June 1955).

Giedion, Sigfried. "The State of Contemporary Architecture: 1. The New Regional Approach." *Architectural Record* 115, no. 206 (January 1954): 132–37.

Gilbert, J. "Note sur la province de Chaouïa." *Bulletin de la Société de Géographie, 5th Series*, 7 (March 1867): 325–27.

Gillet, Georges. "La construction au Maroc au début du Protectorat." *Notre Maroc* 10 (December 1950): 27–40.

Godefroy, Georges. "Les problèmes démographiques marocains." *L'Architecture d'aujourd'hui* 26, no. 60 (June 1955): 34–35.

Gohier, Jean. "Michel Écochard ou l'urbanisme français à l'étranger." *Urbanisme* no. 211 (1986): 53–55.

Goulven, Joseph. "Villes d'Afrique, Casablanca la commerçante." *Renseignements coloniaux et documents publiés par le Comité de l'Afrique française et le Comité du Maroc* 24, no. 2 (February 1914): 75–81.

Goulven, Joseph. "Casablanca pendant un an de guerre." *Renseignements coloniaux et documents publiés par le Comité de l'Afrique française et le Comité du Maroc* 25, no. 8 (August 1915): 133–36.

Goulven, Joseph. "La vie chère à Casablanca, I. Le logement." *La Vigie marocaine* (Casablanca), November 13, 1915.

Goulven, Joseph. "Causeries urbaines, le mellah de Casablanca." *Le Petit Marocain* (Casablanca), December 18, 1921.

Goulven, Joseph. "L'assainissement de Casablanca." *Le Petit Marocain* (Casablanca), November 15 and 24, 1922.

Goulven, Joseph. "Propos du jour." *La Vigie marocaine* (Casablanca), November 3, 1922.

Goulven, Joseph. "Causeries urbaines." *Le Petit Marocain* (Casablanca) March 15, May 18, and September 28, 1923.

Goulven, Joseph. "Les biens austro-allemands à Casablanca." *Le Maroc catholique* (June 1924): 318–24.

Goulven, Joseph. "Histoire d'une ville: Casablanca." *Le Maroc catholique* (August 1924): 403–7; (September 1924): 444–54; (October 1924): 520–23; (November 1924): 551–56; (December 1924): 598–607.

Grand, Pierre. "Le développement industriel à Casablanca." *France-Maroc* (August 15, 1917): 21–24.

"Un groupe de huit immeubles à Casablanca, M. Desmet." *Chantiers nord-africains* 6, no. 7 (July 1934): 525–29.

"Un groupe d'immeubles modernes à Casablanca, A. Greslin architecte." *Chantiers nord-africains* 3, no. 3 (March 1931): 291–92.

"Groupes d'immeubles à Casablanca." *Chantiers nord-africains* 1, no. 9 (September 1929): 524–25.

Guillen, Pierre. "Les milieux d'affaires français et le Maroc à l'aube du XXe siècle: la fondation de la Compagnie Marocaine." *Revue Historique* 229 (April–June 1963): 397–422.

"Habitat collectif marocain à Casablanca." *L'Architecture d'aujourd'hui* 24, no. 46 (February–March 1953): 54–55.

"Garage à Casablanca, E. Hinnen architecte dplg." *L'Architecture française* 14, no. 137–38 (1953): 58–59.

"Habitat collectif musulman à Casablanca, ATBAT-Afrique: 3 immeubles-types." *L'Architecture d'aujourd'hui* 25, no. 57 (December 1954): 54–55.

"L'habitat indigène au Maroc." *Chantiers nord-africains* 6, no. 8 (August 1934): 649.

"(L') habitat pour le plus grand nombre: Un exemple-type, l'habitat au Maroc." *L'Architecture d'aujourd'hui* 24, no. 50–51 (December 1953).

Hantzberg, Robert. "Défense de la ville (Casablanca)." *La Vigie marocaine* (Casablanca), Febraury 15, 16, 17, 19, and 20, 1951.

Hantzberg, Robert. "Au printemps prochain, l'aérogare de Tit Mellil, d'une inspiration architecturale très moderne sera ouverte aux aviateurs et aux autres." *La Vigie marocaine* (Casablanca), December 7, 1951, 9.

Hantzberg, Robert. "Découverte du Maroc; inconnue au riche passé, mais combien vivante: Casablanca." *Maroc-Demain* (Casablanca), March 28, 1953, 5.

Hantzberg, Robert. "La nouvelle médina de Casablanca, ville dans la ville." *La Vigie marocaine* (Casablanca), June 24, 25, 27, 28, 30, and July 1 and 2, 1953.

Hantzberg, Robert. "Le plan Écochard pour l'aménagement du Grand Casablanca est-il applicable? Un handicap lourd à rattraper: celui d'un passé désordonné et anarchique"; "Le problème des ceintures rouges"; "Les zones d'habitat dispersé: une nouveauté qui suscite une vive opposition"; "Voici ce que seraient les zones d'habitat dispersé si le plan de zoning était adopté"; and "Ce plan présente certainement des défauts." *La Vigie marocaine* (Casablanca), February 25, 26, 27, 28, and 29, 1952.

"Henri Prost" (obituary). *L'Architecture française* no. 203–4 (August 1959).

"L'Hôtel-de-ville de Casablanca." *La Construction moderne* 42, no. 3 (April 1927): 318–20.

"Hôtel des services de police de Casablanca (concours)." *Réalisations* 2, no. 7–8 (November 1936): 196–97.

"L'hôtel des services de police de la ville de Casablanca (Maurice Sory dplg)." *Chantiers nord-africains* 8, no. 12 (December 1936): 618–19.

"Hôtel 'El Mansour' à Casablanca, Maroc, E.J. Duhon, architecte dplg." *L'Architecture française* 14, no. 139–40 (July–August 1953): 24–27.

"Hôtel Marhaba, Casablanca, E. J. Duhon, architecte dplg." *L'Architecture d'aujourd'hui* no. 61 (September 1955): 24–27.

"Housing at Casablanca." *Architectural Design* 26, no. 4 (April 1956): 136.

"Immeuble à Casablanca." *Chantiers nord-africains* 1, no. 7 (July 1929): 473–74.

"Un immeuble à Casablanca." *Chantiers nord-africains* 4, no. 12 (December 1932).

"Un immeuble à Casablanca, P. Bailly et R. Schmidt." *L'Architecture française* 16, no. 163–64 (January–February 1956): 42.

"Un immeuble de 11 étages à Casablanca, architecte P. Jabin." *Chantiers nord-africains* 6, no. 12 (December 1934): 922.

"Immeuble de la Fraternelle, boulevard de la Gare à Casablanca, M. Desmet architecte." *Réalisations* 2, no. 2 (October 1935): 42–51.

"Immeuble de la SIF, M. Desmet, architecte." *Réalisations* 2, no. 5 (April 1936): 132–35.

"Immeuble de la Soblanca à Casablanca." *Réalisations* 1, no. 6 (October 1934): 153–55.

"Immeuble de M. A. à Casablanca, V. Paccanari architecte TCB." *Réalisations* 4, no. 2 (September 1937): 52–53.

"Immeuble de rapport à Casablanca." *Réalisations* 1, no. 9 (February 1935): 243–45.

"Immeuble de rapport à Casablanca." *Réalisations* 2, no. 1 (July 1935): 12–15.

"Immeuble de rapport à Casablanca, G. Cottet, architecte." *Réalisations* 2, no. 7–8 (November 1938): 209–10.

"Immeuble de rapport à Casablanca, G. Renaudin, architecte dplg." *Réalisations* 3, no. 5 (May–June 1938): 139–40.

"Immeuble de rapport à Casablanca, J. G. Grel et G. Renaudin architectes dplg." *Réalisations* 4, no. 2 (September 1937): 47–51.

"Immeuble de rapport à Casablanca, P. Jabin." *Réalisations* 1, no. 5 (July 1934): 142–43.

"L'immeuble d'un grand quotidien et d'une imprimerie moderne à Casablanca." *Chantiers nord-africains* 4, no. 8 (August 1932): 647.

"Immeuble place de France à Casablanca, P. Jabin architecte." *Réalisations* 2, no. 2 (October 1935): 52–53.

"L'ingénieur Paul Les Enfant, bâtisseur du port de Casablanca." *Bulletin des Ingénieurs du Maroc* (July–August 1952): 7–17.

"Les innombrables visages de l'architecture casablancaise." *Chantiers nord-africains* 3, no. 10 (October 1931): 987–94; and 3, no. 12 (December 1931): 1207–11.

Itié, Georges. "Casablanca." *Le Grand Tourisme* (January 1929): 93–95.

Itié, Georges. "Notre ville (Casablanca)." *La vie marocaine illustrée* (January 1, 1932): 11–14.

J. D. "A propos de l'inauguration du hammam d'Aïn Chock." *Paris* (February 6, 1948): 4.

Jaclot, Charles. "Le port de Casablanca." *France-Maroc* 5, no. 61 (December 1921): 231–33.

Janon, René. "L'œuvre d'une municipalité marocaine: Casablanca." *Chantiers nord-africains* 4, no. 7 (July 1932): 563–67.

Jauréguiberry, J. "Les problèmes de la construction au Maroc, le soleil et l'habitation." *L'Afrique française* (October 1938): 241–44.

Jest, C. "Habitat du personnel journalier permanent de l'Office chérifien des Phosphates." *Bulletin économique et social du Maroc* (March 1958): 435–62.

Joly, Fernand. "Casablanca, éléments pour une étude de géographie urbaine." *Les Cahiers d'Outre-mer* 1, no. 2 (1948): 119–48.

"Un jour de tempête à Casablanca, la jetée assaillie par un raz-de-marée." *L'Illustration* no. 3658 (April 5, 1913): 305.

Joyant, Edmond. "Note sur la construction du réseau de routes du Maroc." *Annales des Ponts et Chaussées* no. 5 (May 1920): 105–26.

Joyant, Edmond. "Le plan d'aménagement de Casablanca (Maroc)." *Le Génie civil* 79, no. 2036 (August 20, 1921): 161–67.

Joyant, Edmond. "Législation des plans d'aménagement urbain du Maroc." *Annales des Ponts et Chaussées* no. 4 (April 1921): 96–110.

Joyant, Edmond. "L'urbanisme au Maroc." *La Technique sanitaire et municipale* (April 1922): 88–103.

Kahn, Réginald. "La mise en valeur du Maroc, mines et industries." *L'Illustration* no. 4056 (November 27, 1920): 396–98.

Kidder-Smith, G.E. "Report from Morocco," in *The Architectural Forum* 92, no. 6 (June 950): 64–72.

"L. Morandi, edificio Liberté en Casablanca." *Revista nacional de Arquitectura* (Montevideo) 11, no. 110–11 (1951).

L'Hérault, Jean de. "Extension de Casablanca; le plan Écochard devant la commission municipale." *L'Echo d'Oran*, (Oran), February 29, 1952, 6.

L'Hérault, Jean de. "Le drame du 'Grand Casablanca.'" *Journal général des travaux publics et du bâtiment* (March 29, 1952): 1 and 6.

L., M. "Casablanca, la fiévreuse." *Économie et humanisme* no. 93 (September–October 1955): 62–64.

Lacoste de l'Isle, R. "La vie de garnison à Casablanca." *L'Illustration* (February 29, 1908): 143–44.

Lacretelle, Jacques de. "Casa." *Le Figaro* (Paris), July 20, 1949.

"Ladenumbau 'L'Art et la table,' Casablanca." *Innenarchitektur* no. 11 (May 1957).

Ladreit de Lacharrière, Jacques. "L'œuvre française en Chaouïa." *Renseignements coloniaux et documents publiés par le comité de l'Afrique française et le comité du Maroc* 20, no. 9 (September 1910): 261–90; no. 10 (October 1910): 331–52; no. 11 (November 1910): 371–79; and no. 12 (December 1910): 403–8.

Ladreit de Lacharrière, Jacques. "Les vingt ans de Casablanca." *La Revue indigène* 22, no. 222–23 (July–August 1927): 127–29.

Laforgue, Adrien. "Les éléments construits dans l'architecture paysagiste." *Chantiers nord-africains* no. 4 (April 1938): 165–68.

Lambert, Étienne. "La construction à Casablanca." *La Terre marocaine* no. 16–17 (October 1–15, 1928): 312–19.

Lamy, A. "L'autre visage de Casablanca." *Maroc-magazine* (August 1936): 138–44.

Laprade, Albert. "Lyautey urbaniste." *Revue hebdomadaire* 37, no. 9 (September 1928): 216–30.

Laprade, Albert. "Souvenirs du temps de la guerre, contribution à la future histoire de Casablanca et de Rabat." *Le Maroc catholique* (September 1928): 498–501; (October 1928): 546–49; (November 1928): 597–600; (December 1928): 657–60.

Laprade, Albert. "Du temps de l'autre guerre; souvenirs d'un architecte." *Le Maroc*, May 21, 1939.

Laurent, M. "Le problème crucial du logement à Casablanca." *Maroc-Monde* (Casablanca), March 28, 1953, 1 and 6.

Le Châtelier, Alfred. "Au Maroc, la politique nécessaire." *La Revue bleue* (1908).

Le-Det, A. "Éléments du climat de Casablanca." *Revue de géographie marocaine* 3–4 (1963): 137–41.

Lefebvre, Jacques. "L'action des industriels marocains en faveur de leurs collaborateurs indigènes." *Cinq ans de politique constructive, Notre Maroc* (April 1942).

Le Masson, Henri. "Le poumon du Maroc, Casablanca." *France-Illustration* 6 (February 26, 1950): 197–200.

Lemoine, P. "Mission dans le Maroc occidental." *Renseignements coloniaux et documents publiés par le comité de l'Afrique française et le comité du Maroc* 15, no. 2 (February 1905): 68.

Lennad, Roland. "Nos grands reportages: Casablanca, résultat d'un effort prodigieux." *Le Populaire de Nantes* (Nantes), October 10, 1932.

Le Prévost, Jaques, and F. Creugnet. "Regards sur le grand Casablanca." *Le Maroc quotidien* (Casablanca), May 1, 2, 11, 12, 14, 15, 16, 19, and 29, 1949.

Le Prévost, Jacques. "Le Service de l'Urbanisme accouche d'un monstre: le Grand Casablanca"; "Un monstre de l'urbanisme: le Grand Casablanca: un retraité à la recherche d'un petit coin tranquille"; "Un monstre de l'urbanisme: le Grand Casablanca: 'car tel est mon bon plaisir'"; "L'enquête publique sur le plan Ecochard prolongée d'un mois; les fantaisies du service de l'urbanisme vivement critiquées"; "L'enquête sur le plan Écochard: il reste du terrain pour les millionnaires"; and "L'enquête sur le Grand Casa: des centaines de protestations condamnent le plan Ecochard." *Le Petit Marocain* (Casablanca), February 17, 20, 21, 27, and 29, and March 1, 1952.

Léris, Pierre. "Histoire immobilière de Casablanca." *La Terre marocaine illustrée* (March 1, 1928): 25–28.

Letellier, J. "Urbanisme et circulation." *La Vie marocaine illustrée* (October 15, 1931): 430–31.

"Le 'Lido' de Casablanca, architecte Maurice L'Herbier." *Chantiers nord-africains* 2, no. 9 (September 1930): 799–801.

"Le logement de la main d'œuvre indigène de l'Office Chérifien des Phosphates." *Bulletin d'information de la résidence générale* (August 1–15, 1939): 188–89.

Long, Charles. "Casablanca, métropole industrielle du Maroc." *Revue de géographie marocaine* 23 (May 1939): 183–89.

Loth, Gaston. "L'architecture des bâtiments administratifs au Maroc: I. Les postes et télégraphes." *L'Architecture* 37, no. 8 (August 10, 1924): 183–87.

Loth, Gaston. "L'urbanisme au Maroc." *L'Architecture* 37, no. 2 (February 25, 1924): 43–47.

Lourido Diaz, Ramón. "Documentos ineditos sobre el nacimiento de Dar-al-Bayda' (Casablanca) en el siglo XVIII." *Hespéris-Tamuda* 15 (1974): 119–46.

Maarec, A. "Un plan de Casablanca." *Le Petit Casablancais* (Casablanca), August 31, 1946, 1–2.

"Maisons de rapport au Maroc." *La Construction moderne* 36, no. 6 (November 7, 1920): 44 and pl. 23.

"Maisons tropicales, 35° latitude nord." *Plaisir de France* 20, no. 9 (September 1958): 44–47.

Maisonseul, Jean de. "Pour une architecture et un urbanisme nord-africains." *Revue d'Alger* no. 8 (1945): 352–58.

Maneville, Roger. "L'expérience 'Castor' aux Carrières centrales de Casablanca." *Notes marocaines* no. 7 (July 1956): 2–8.

Marc, Jean. "L'œuvre française au Maroc: Casablanca la nouvelle." *L'Exportateur français* (Paris), October 9, 1930.

"Marché de gros de Casablanca (concours)." *Réalisations* 2, no. 7–8 (November 1936): 198–99.

Marchisio, Antoine. "L'Architecture moderne au Maroc." *Aguedal* 1, no. 1 (May 1936): 63–64.

Marchisio, Antoine. "Architecture." *Aguedal* 2, no. 1 (1937): 75–77.

Marozeau, Jacques. "Maroc, constructions scolaires." *L'Architecture d'aujourd'hui* 26, no. 60 (June 1955): 60–63.

"Marruecos moderno." *Arquitectura* (Mexico) 5, no. 11 (1943): 14–25.

Mas, Pierre. "L'urbanisation actuelle du Maroc: les bidonvilles." *La Vie urbaine* no. 61 (1951): 185–221.

Mas, Pierre. "Problèmes d'habitat musulman au Maroc." *Bulletin économique et social du Maroc* 28, no. 62 (September 1954): 201–18.

Mas, Pierre. "Reprendre Casa." *Urbanisme* no. 211 (January 1986): 56.

Mauclair, Camille. "L'architecture au Maroc." *La Dépêche du Midi* (Toulouse), April 15, 1932.

McGurn, Barrett. "Casablanca, City of Fear." *New York Herald Tribune* (Paris), April 27, 1955.

Mazières, Nathalie de. "Homage to Écochard." *Environmental Design* no. 1 (1985): 22–25.

"La médina d'Aïn-Chock aux portes de Casablanca pourra recevoir 200000 habitants." *Les Annales coloniales* (August 15, 1949): 6.

"Les métamorphoses du port de Casablanca et leurs conséquences sur l'urbanisme." *La Vie marocaine illustrée* (January 11, 1933): 27.

Miège, Jean-Louis. "Deux plans inédits de Casablanca à la fin du XIXe siècle." *Notes marocaines* 3 (1953): 1–2.

———. "La nouvelle médina de Casablanca; le derb Carlotti." *Les Cahiers d'Outre-mer* 6, no. 23 (1953): 244–57.

———. "Les origines du développement de Casablanca au XIXe siècle." *Hespéris* (1st and 2nd trimesters, 1953): 199–226.

Migliorini, Elio. "Casablanca e il suo porto." *Bolletino della Reggia Societa geografica italiana* (March–April 1943): 78–95.

Mille, Pierre. "Le visage français au Maroc." *Les Nouvelles littéraires* (April 11, 1931): 1.

Mirtil, Marcel. "Le Mellah de Casablanca." *France-Maroc* no. 12 (December 15, 1918): 358–60.

Mohr, Paul. "Casablanca in Marokko." *Deutsche Rundschau für Geographie und Statistik* 27, no. 2 (November 1904): 71–78.

Montauzan, M. de. "L'organisation des villes nouvelles au Maroc." *La Construction moderne* 39, no. 13 (December 30, 1923): 148–50.

———. "Le développement des villes nouvelles au Maroc: Casablanca et Rabat." *La Construction moderne* 39, no. 25 (March 23, 1924): 289–92.

Montmarin, A. de. "Les nouvelles solutions en matière d'habitat: Leur application au derb Jdid." *Bulletin économique et social du Maroc* 22, no. 80 (April 1959): 437–47.

———. de. "Les conceptions actuelles en matière d'habitat économique et leur application à la reconstruction du derb Jdid à Casablanca." *Annales de l'Institut Technique du bâtiment et des travaux publics* no. 150 (June 1960): 613–29.

Morandi, Luigi. "La città crisalide." *Il Corriere d'Italia* (Rome), July 12, 1921.

Mouline, Saïd. "Architectures métissées." *Signes du présent* no. 3 (1988).

Mourey, Charles. "Le Maroc pendant la guerre et l'exposition de Casablanca." *Annales de géographie* 23–24, no. 132 (November 15, 1915): 437–42.

"Musée et bibliothèque à Casablanca, V. Scob, architecte dplg." *L'Architecture française* 11, no. 105–6 (September–October 1950): 80–81.

"Naissance et développement de la ville de Casablanca." *Notre Maroc* 10 (June 1952): 55–63.

"Nécrologie de Marius Boyer." *L'Entreprise au Maroc* (January 1, 1948): 1.

Nicolas, Janine. "Un quartier de Casablanca, le Maârif." *Cahiers d'outre-mer* no. 63 (July–September 1963): 281–85.

Noguès, General Charles. "Le Maroc, terre de tourisme, Casablanca." *Le Maroc du nord au sud* no. 4 (January 1937).

Noin, Daniel. "L'évolution récente de Casablanca." *Notes Marocaines* 16 (1961): 43–48.

Nonek, M. "Le Mellah casablancais." *Feuille d'avis de Vevey* (Vevey), August 27, 1936.

"Le nouvel immeuble de la Banque d'Etat du Maroc à Casablanca, 1937, Edmond Brion, architecte dplg." *Réalisations* 3, no. 4 (March 1938): 85–124.

"Le nouvel immeuble de la SMD à Casablanca, Fleurant architecte dplg." *Réalisations* 2, no. 4 (February 1936): 98–110.

"La nouvelle cité musulmane des Carrières Centrales à Casablanca." *Travaux publics et bâtiment* (September 15, 1951).

"La nouvelle halle aux poissons de Casablanca." *La Pêche maritime* (February 1939): 39–40.

Ohayon, J. "La grande pitié du ghetto casablancais." *La Vie juive* (Casablanca), January 31, 1936.

"Le palais d'une banque algérienne à Casablanca." *Chantiers nord-africains* 3, no. 5 (May 1931): 589–95.

"Le palais de son Excellence El Mokri, Boyer et Balois, architectes." *Chantiers nord-africains* 1, no. 7 (July 1929): 467–70.

Pasquali, Anna, and Gaetano Arcuri. "Casablanca: The Derb el Habous by A. Laprade or How to Build in the Arab Fashion." *Environmental Design* no. 1 (1985): 14–21.

Pauty, Edmond. "Casablanca et son plan." *Revue de géographie marocaine* 3, no. 4 (1945): 3–9.

"Pavillon de l'éducation physique à Casablanca, R. Lièvre architecte." *Réalisations* 4, no. 3 (January–February 1938): 67–68.

Pétonnet, Colette. "Espace, distance, dimension dans une société musulmane." *L'Homme* no.12 (April–June 1972): 47–84.

Pelletier, Pierre. "Problèmes de la circulation dans les villes créés, l'exemple de Casablanca." *Bulletin économique et social du Maroc* 19, no. 68 (1955): 493–512.

———. "Valeurs foncières et urbanisme au Maroc." *Bulletin économique et social du Maroc* 19, no. 65 (1955): 5–51.

Penz, Charles. "Note sur l'histoire ancienne de Casablanca." *Bulletin de l'enseignement public du Maroc* (1951): 43–44.

———. "Promenades littéraires, historiques et mythologiques dans les rues de Casablanca." *Notre Maroc* (January 1954): 17–21.

Petit, Charles. "Pages vécues, le véritable Casablanca." *Le Journal* (Paris), October 13, 1913.

Petit, René. "Images de Casablanca, ville champignon où le modernisme s'allie au plus pur exotisme." *Lyon-soir* (Lyons), September 28, 1941.

"Le petit Lycée de Casablanca, Armand Duffez." *Chantiers nord-africains* 8, no. 8 (August 1936): 416.

"Piscine municipale de Casablanca." *Réalisations* 2, no. 7–8 (November 1936): 185–94.

"Piscine municipale de Casablanca." *Réalisations* 2, supplement to no. 10 (April 1937): 229–38.

"La piscine municipale de Casablanca." *Réalisations* 3, no. 3 (January–February 1938): 82–83.

"Les piscines municipales à Casablanca." *Bulletin économique et social du Maroc* (July 1936): 254.

"Plan d'extension de la ville de Casablanca." *La correspondence de Presse* (Paris), April 18, 1951.

Plande, Dr. "Les stations-services à Casablanca." *Notre Maroc* (January 1954): 85–96.

"Le plan Écochard et les contre-propositions de la commission municipale (rapport sur les projets d'aménagement et d'extension de Casablanca, par MM. Gouin, Hajoui et Nahon)." *Maroc-Demain* (Casablanca), May 10, 1952.

Poix, E. "L'histoire et l'avenir de Casablanca." *Le Bâtiment* (Paris), May 10, 1931.

"Plus grand que tous ceux d'Europe, un immense aquarium va être construit à Casablanca." *Le Petit Marocain* (Casablanca), June 12, 1951.

Pommer, Richard. "The Flat Roof: A Modernist Controversy in Germany." *Art Journal* 43, no. 2 (Summer 1983): 158–69.

Porquerolle, L. "L'urbanisme au Maroc." *Travaux publics et bâtiment au Maroc* (November 13, 1930).

"Le port de Casablanca." *Le Sud-Ouest économique* no. 129 (1926).

"Le port de pêche de Casablanca et le marché aux poissons de Casablanca, Bars, Bouquet des Chaux, Bureau architectes." *L'Architecture d'aujourd'hui* 11, no. 3–4 (March–April 1940): 60–62.

"Les ports du Maroc: Voyage d'études de la mission Dyé." *La Dépêche coloniale illustrée* 6, no. 11 (June 15, 1906): 134–35.

Pouchol, E. "La circulation à Casablanca." *Revue de l'Automobile-club marocain* (December 1951): 28–33.

Pradeaux, R. "La piscine municipale de Casablanca." *Chantiers nord-africains* 9, no. 12 (December 1937): 529–35.

"La première réunion sportive et mondaine au Maroc: le concours hippique de Casablanca." *L'Illustration* no. 3658 (April 5, 1913): 304.

"Le présent et l'avenir du port de Casablanca." *La Construction moderne* 44 (December 21, 1928): 469–70; (December 28, 1928): 479–80; (January 4, 1929): 3.

"Problèmes d'habitat européen hors de la métropole." *L'Architecture d'aujourd'hui* 24, no. 46 (February–March 1953): 87.

Prost, Henri. "Le plan de Casablanca." *France-Maroc* (August 15, 1917): 5–12.

———. "L'urbanisme au Maroc." *L'Illustration économique et financière,* supplement (July 1925): 15–18.

———. "L'urbanisme au Maroc." *Chantiers nord-africains* 4, no. 2 (February 1932): 117–20.

Prunier. "Étude sur le territoire de Casablanca-Banlieue." *Bulletin économique du Maroc* no. 4 (1914): 5.

"Quand le social rejoint l'économique, la cité des jeunes (heureuse conjonction des efforts du patronat et des pouvoirs publics) abritera à Casablanca 300 foyers." *Maroc-Demain* (Casablanca), November 24, 1951, 1 and 4.

"Quatre habitations individuelles à Casablanca, Maroc, G. Jaubert architecte." *L'Architecture d'aujourd'hui* no. 63 (January 1955): 28–32.

Rabinow, Paul. "France in Morocco: Technocospolitanism and Middling Modernism." *Assemblage* no. 17 (1992): 53–57.

Raymond, Jean. "Aménagement des villes nouvelles, étude des redistributions." *France-Maroc* (February 1921): 33–36.

"Recherche pour des logements économiques, par ATBAT-Afrique, supervision de V. Bodiansky, G. Candilis et S. Woods, architectes, H. Piot, ingénieur." *L'Architecture d'aujourd'hui* 26, no. 60 (June 1955): 41.

Rémon, G. "Architecture moderne au Maroc, Albert Laprade, architecte." *Jardins et cottages* (1926): 161–74.

René-Leclerc, C. "Casablanca il y a dix ans." *France-Maroc* (August 15, 1917): 28–33.

———. "L'urbanisme et les villes marocaines." *Chantiers nord-africains* 2, no. 11 (November 1930): 1023–29.

René-Leclercq, C. "L'essor de Casablanca." *Annales de l'Institut colonial de Bordeaux* (October–November 1931): 133–37; and *L'Africain de Paris* (February 26, 1932).

Repaci, Leonida. "Frenesia di Casablanca." *Gazzetta del Popolo* (Rome), April 20, 1933.

"Report on the district of Dal el-Beida." *The Geographical Journal* 6, no. 1 (July–December 1895): 80–81.

Rey, Jean. "Casa la géante." *L'Ouest-journal* (Rennes), August 21, 1931.

R., J. "Vingt-huit garçonnières dans un immeuble." *Chantiers nord-africains* 4, no. 2 (February 1932): 151–52.

Roberti, Vero. "Nella 'ville champignon' dei Francesi; perchè da Casablanca non si vede tutto il Marocco." *Il Tempo* (Rome), April 6, 1949.

Rodari, André. "Casablanca, l'attrait de la profusion." *Le Journal de Genève* (Geneva), November 9–10, 1952, 1.

Rognon, G. "A temps nouveaux, solutions nouvelles; la crise des logements au Maroc peut être résolue par des procédés révolutionnaires." *Maroc-Demain* (Casablanca), March 21, 1953, 5–7.

Rohlfs, Gerhard. "Casablanca und der Deutsche Neumann." *Deutsche Rundschau für Geographie und Statistik* 17, no. 4 (November 1895): 155–57.

Rouch, J. "Le port de Casablanca." *Revue scientifique* 70 (1932): 72–83.

Royer, Jean. "Henri Prost, urbaniste." *Urbanisme* 34, no. 88 (July 1965): 11–16.

Rozael, Yves. "Révolution architecturale dans l'administration mais les pseudo-esthètes n'y mordent pas encore." *Maroc-Demain* (Casablanca), November 4, 1951, 1 and 8.

"Le salon de thé Trianon à Casablanca." *Chantiers nord-africains* 7, no. 2 (February 1935): 114.

Saboulin, Louis de. "À propos du Grand Casablanca, un précurseur: Me. Claude Favrot." *La Vigie marocaine*, (Casablanca), February 29, 1952.

———. "À propos du Grand Casablanca, le point de vue juridique." *La Vigie marocaine* (Casablanca), March 4, 1952.

Schwyter, Annemarie. "Im glückseligen Reich, II. Casablanca oder El Flus." *Tages-Anzeiger für Stadt und Kanton Zürich* (Zurich), January 22, 1954.

Segonds, Lieutenant Marie François. "Casablanca, monographie de la Chaouïa." *Bulletin de la Société de géographie d'Alger et d'Afrique du nord* (3rd trimester, 1910): 320–94 .

Serene, Jean. "Naissance d'une cité: Casablanca." *Maroc* 46 (March 1946): 15–16.

Sieburg, Friedrich. "Le rôle économique de Casablanca vu par un écrivain allemand." *Bulletin économique et social du Maroc* (July 1938): 205–7 (first published in *Frankfurter Zeitung,* June 24, 1938).

Smithson, Alison, and Peter Smithson. "Collective Housing in Morocco." *Architectural Design* 25, no. 1 (January 1955): 2–7.

"Sous l'égide de l'Entr'aide franco-marocaine, une cité des jeunes va naître à Casablanca." *Le Petit Marocain* (Casablanca), June 18, 1951.

Spender, J. A. "Casablanca: A Modern Miracle in Morocco." *News* (London), March 9, 1933.

"'Les Studios,' immeuble de rapport, M. Boyer architecte dplg." *Réalisations* 2, no. 1 (July 1935): 6–11.

Suquet-Bonnaud. "À l'actif de la France, les villes nouvelles du Maroc." *Urbanisme* 22, no. 25–26 (March 1953): 67–69.

Tard, M. "Casablanca, naissance et développement d'un port." *Le Petit Marocain* (Casablanca), October 25, 29, and 30, 1946.

Taylor, Brian Brace. "Planned Discontinuity: Modern Colonial Cities in Morocco." *Lotus International* no. 26 (1980): 52–66.

———. "Architectures en Afrique du nord." *Architecture, mouvement, continuité* no. 11 (April 1986): 108–17.

"Un théâtre-cinéma à Casablanca: Le Rialto." *Chantiers nord-africains* 3, no. 5 (May 1931): 597–601.

Toledano, Edward. "Go East, Young Man, to Casablanca." *The Reader's Digest* 53, no. 320 (December 1948): 17–19.

Toutlemonde, Georges. "Le port de Casablanca." *Le Génie civil* 105, no. 8 (August 25, 1934): 161–64.

"Trade Turning Casablanca to Boom Town." *New York Herald Tribune* (Paris), November 3, 1951.

"Tre scuole all'estero, arch. Mario Paniconi e Giulio Pediconi." *Architettura* 13, no. 8 (August 1935): 463–74.

"Trois immeubles modernes à Casablanca." *Chantiers nord-africains* 4, no. 9 (September 1932): 745.

"Urbanisation de Casablanca (1950–1953)." *L'Architecture d'aujourd'hui* 24, no. 46 (February–March 1953): 14–15.

"L'urbanisme à Casablanca: Belles demeures Casablancaises." *Notre Maroc* (January 1954): 59–66.

Vaillat, Léandre. "La nouvelle médina de Casablanca." *L'Illustration* no. 4752 (October 18, 1930): 225–26.

———. "Le décor de la vie: au Maroc, Casablanca." *Le Temps* (Paris), February 7, 1932.

Vandelle, R. L. "Pour la réalisation de la 'Ville Radieuse' de Le Corbusier." *Réalisations* 2, no. 6 (June 1936): 151–53.

Vattier, Jos. "Casablanca grand port français." *L'Écho d'Oran* (Oran), July 28, 1933.

———. "Buildings marocains." *L'Écho d'Oran* (Oran), September 16, 1933.

Vidalenc, Georges. "La croissance de Casablanca et les problèmes de la construction." *La Terre marocaine illustrée* (March 15, 1930): 2017–19.

"Villa à Casablanca, E. Azagury architecte." *L'Architecture d'aujourd'hui* 24, no. 46 (February–March 1953): 86.

"Villa à Casablanca, Georges Godefroy architecte." *L'Architecture d'aujourd'hui* 24, no. 62 (November 1953): 37.

"Villa Bareille à Casablanca (G. Cottet architecte)." *Réalisations* 2, no. 7–8 (November 1936): 208–9.

"(Une) villa entièrement électrifiée, la villa Azogué à Casablanca, Pertuzio Frères, architectes." *Réalisations* 2, no. 6 (June 1936): 162–66.

"Villa G. in Casablanca-Anfa (W. Ewerth)." *Innenarchitektur* no. 11 (May 1957).

"Villas modernes à Casablanca." *Chantiers nord-africains* 1, no. 1 (January 1929): 85.

"Villa de M. B. à Casablanca, M. Boyer architecte." *Réalisations* 2, no. 6 (June 1936): 167–69.

"Villa de M. F., boulevard d'Anfa à Casablanca, J. Michelet architecte." *Réalisations* 1, no. 4 (June 1934): 103–4.

Weisgerber, Dr. Félix. "Études géographiques sur le Maroc, 1. La province de Chaouïa, 2. Casablanca." *Bulletin de la Société de géographie de Paris* 1 (1st semester, 1900): 437–48.

"Wohnbauprojekte für Arabersiedlungen in Casablanca, Marokko." *Werk* 46, no. 1 (January 1956): 22–23.

Wright, Gwendolyn. "Tradition in the Service of Modernity: Architecture and Urbanism in French Colonial Policy, 1900–1930." *Journal of Modern History* 59 (June 1987): 291–316.

Y. "Le port de Casablanca." *Revue générale des sciences pures et appliquées* (April 15, 1914): 332–36.

Zischka, Anton. "Neue Wirtschafts-Magnete, das Wachstum 'exotischer' Städte." *Atlantis: Länder, Völker, Reisen* (March 1953): 93–99.

Filmography

Fictional Films about or Filmed in Casablanca

Les hommes nouveaux. Directed by Donatien and Édouard-Émile Violet. 1922. After the novel by Claude Farrère. With Georges Melchior, Marthe Ferrare, Donatien, and Lucienne Legrand.

Le roman d'un spahi. Directed by Michel Bernheim. 1936. After the novel by Pierre Loti. With Georges Rigaud, Mireille Balin, André Berval, Raymond Cordy, Pierre Larquey, Hélène Pépée, Jean Cyrano, and Lydia Chaliapine.

Les hommes nouveaux. Directed by Marcel L'Herbier. 1936. After the novel by Claude Farrère (1936). With Harry Baur, Gabriel Signoret, Nathalie Paley, Paul Amyot, Claude Sainval, and René Bergeron.

Casablanca. Directed by Michael Curtiz. 1942. After the play by Murray Burnett and Joan Alison. With Ingrid Bergman, Humphrey Bogart, Peter Lorre, Paul Henreid, Claude Rains, and Marcel Dalio. Filmed entirely in a Burbank studio.

A Night in Casablanca. Directed by Archie Mayo. 1946. With Groucho, Harpo, and Chico Marx, Siegfried Rumann, Dan Seymour, and Lisette Verea. A parody of Curtiz's *Casablanca*, filmed entirely in a Hollywood studio.

Minuit, rue de l'Horloge. Directed by Jean Lordier. 1947. After the novel by Jean-François Lamarche. With Nacira Chafik, Mohammed El Kamal, Jamal Badry, Gina Manès, Simone Sylvestre, and Leïla Farida. The negative of this film, which was never shown in theaters, was destroyed.

My Favorite Spy. Directed by Norman Z. McLeod. 1952. With Bob Hope, Hedy Lamarr, and Francis L. Sullivan. A parody of Curtiz's *Casablanca*, filmed entirely in Paramount's Hollywood studio.

La Môme vert de gris. Directed by Bernard Borderie. 1953. After the novel by Peter Cheney. With Eddy Constantine, Dominique Wilms, Howard Vernon, Philippe Hersent, Jean-Marc Tennberg, Dario Moreno, Maurice Ronet, Gaston Modot, and Paul Azaïs.

Casablanca, nid d'espions. Directed by Henri Decoin. 1963. With Sara Montiel, Maurice Ronet, and Franco Fabrizzi. In the same vein as Curtiz's *Casablanca*, but filmed entirely in a Madrid studio.

Le Pistonné. Directed by Claude Berri. 1970. With Guy Bedos, Yves Robert, Rosy Varte, Georges Géret, Jean-Pierre Marielle, Zorica Lozich, and Coluche. Set in Casablanca, shortly before independence.

Soleil de printemps. Directed by Latif Lahlou. 1970. With Amidou. Story of the dull existence of a minor Casablanca functionary.

Casablanca Express. Directed by Sergio Martino. 1988. With Glenn Ford. This film uses Casablanca (the Habous district and Cosuma workers' housing estate) as a stand-in for Algiers.

Documentaries

The first views of Casablanca were filmed from July to September 1907 by the cameraman Félix Mesguich, an Algerian who worked first for the Lumière brothers and later independently. Numerous newsreels were filmed by Pathé, Gaumont, the film services of the French army, and, after 1958, by Actualités Marocaines.

La Fugue de Mahmoud. Directed by Roger Leenhardt. 1951. A romanticized documentary about a Berber shepherd's initiation to modern agriculture.

Salut Casa! Directed by Jean Vidal. 1952. Twenty-four hours in the life of Casablanca: views of the old medina, street scenes, views of shantytowns and new housing developments. Michel Écochard's urbanism lecture. Two versions were dubbed, one in English and one in Spanish.

40 ans d'évolution marocaine. Directed by Serge Debecque and Henri Menjaud. 1952.

24 heures à Casablanca. By the Centre Cinématographique Marocain. 1955. Largely derived from *Salut Casa!* Includes a long sequence leading from Boulevard du IVe-Zouaves to Ain Chock.

De Chair et d'acier. Directed by Mohamed Afifi. 1959. Views of the fishing port and the loading of grain.

Casablanca porte de l'Afrique. Directed by Larbi Benchekroun. 1963. Aerial views of the city, the port, and the medina.

Le Logis des hommes. Directed by Larbi Bennani. 1964. On the rural exodus and working-class housing.

Six et douze. Directed by Magid Khrich and Mohamed Tazi. 1968. Views of and from post-1945 buildings. Depiction of urban circulation.

Biographies of Architects Active in Casablanca

The architects who shaped Casablanca were far from a homogeneous group. Certainly they differed in the period of their activity in the city and in Morocco. But they also varied in their geographic origin, training, relationship to public commissions, and their doctrinal orientation. Among the almost 140 professionals active between 1912 and 1920, precisely defined groups can, however, be identified.

The social background of graduates of the École Nationale Supérieure des Beaux-Arts in Paris is easy to trace in the École's admission files and was, for the most part, modest. Practically none of them were sons of architects—being so would have generally helped their careers in the metropolis. Perret and Jaubert number among the sons of contractors. Boyer's father was a city councillor in Marseilles, a fact that no doubt explains his son's civic engagement. Among the professionals and teachers number the fathers of Delanoë (a physician who had been granted awards by the Académie Française), Fleurant (a middle school teacher), Lièvre (a primary school teacher, like his mother), and Marrast (a musician). Balois and Vimort's fathers lived off small pensions. Most of the remaining identified fathers were small businessmen and tradesmen, be they a sewing machine salesman (Brion), a waiter (Chassagne), a packer (Delaporte), a traveling salesman (Desmet), a mole exterminator (Duhon), a shoe salesman (Gourdain), a cooper (Grel), or a grocer (Laprade). Sori's father was a horticulturalist, while Tournon's was a clerk.

Few men who had inherited wealth, then, and still fewer prodigies of the École des Beaux-Arts. The academic record of most of these architects was average. Prost, Courtois, and Tournon were laureates of the Grand Prix de Rome, though the third had no more than a fleeting presence in Casablanca. After the war, only Sachs received the Grand Prix. Of the seventy students whose records were studied, only about half won medals and very few won prizes. The studios of Pascal/Recoura, Paulin, Bernier/Scellier de Gisors, Esquié/Daumet/Jaussely, and Laloux furnished the largest contingents among the early arrivals in Casablanca. From Boyer to Azagury, the Héraud studio left its mark on the Casablancan profession for over thirty years. Similarly, the Pontrémoli studio was long a source of recruits. The most significant presence after 1945 was that of Perret studio graduates.

The background of other architects is more difficult to determine. Their diverse training—in Italian schools, as surveyors, or on the job—reflects the absence, prior to 1940, of regulations regarding professional accreditation. Based on the French model, as established by the Vichy regime, legislation put in place in 1941 permitted architects who had paid the "patente" (i.e., dues for a given number of years) to register in the newly created Ordre des Architectes du Maroc, or Order of Moroccan Architects. After the war, those holding formal architecture degrees were protected from the competition of "outsiders."

While a continuous stream of architects flowed into Casablanca from 1912 onward, major periods of migration can be identified. Thus in late 1922 Prost noted two distinct groups operating in the city: the "former functionaries of the Protectorate" (Bousquet, Grel, and Louis) and the "graduate architects or those soon to be so" (Delaporte, Boyer, Gourdain, Vimort, Desmarets, Fougère, as well as the Cadet, Brion, and Aulier group), that is, the core of the contingent that had arrived during World War I, and that would be active virtually up until independence. A second contingent of architects arrived during the mid-1920s and early 1930s, including some (such as Hinnen) who had great professional longevity. The third contingent was active from 1945 onward, and these architects benefited from the second boom in Casablanca real estate. A number of architects in this third group left Morocco at the time of independence, but some (such as Azagury, Basciano, and Zevaco) continue their practice in the city to this day. The sojourns of urban planners in Morocco were relatively brief—eight years in the case Prost and six in the case of Écochard. Only Courtois established roots in the city as soon as the office that he opened began to prosper. The many architects who had a limited presence in Casablanca—whether they endeavored to consolidate this presence (like Perret and Abella), or whether they were merely meteoric figures (like Tournon)—are discussed below. Investigations in some masonic archives have not yielded much information about the likely affiliation of several architects to the local lodges, and the connections it might have allowed to developers, contractors, and clients. The only clearly identifiable freemason is Chassagne.

The notes below are based on information gathered from the Archives Nationales, the Société des Architectes Diplômés par le Gouvernement (i.e., Beaux-Arts graduates), and the lists of the Ordre (into which almost all professionals who had paid professional dues prior to 1939 were integrated in 1945). A review of building permit registers kept at the Wilaya as well as lists published in (unfortunately, sporadically published) professional periodicals such as *La Construction au Maroc, L'Entreprise au Maroc,* and *Construire,* was essential. Research in the field, facilitated by interviews and the occasional surviving wall plaque bearing an architect's name on the buiding, made it possible to fill in missing information. See the list of sources and glossary for complete references.

Omissions and imprecisions—inevitable given the fragmentary character of the surviving information—remain. Future research will reduce their number. The biographical notices below list the architects' buildings and projects in Casablanca in chronological order, followed by their principal works outside of the city and of Morocco itself.

Charles-Paul Abella
Paris, July 14, 1879–May 22, 1961. ENSBA (admitted 1898; Scellier de Gisors/Bernier student; Second Grand Prix de Rome 1907; numerous awards; received diploma ca. 1909). After 1918 participated in the reconstruction of the Aisne region for the Ministry of Liberated Regions. His office was in Paris, and his participation in Casablanca was occasional.

Villa Pierre Mas, Avenue du Golfe, 1937 (supervising architect Gillet). La Vigie Marocaine building, Boulevard de la Gare, modification of the facade, 1953. Palais Mirabeau building, Boulevard de la Résistance, 1954 (with Lucas). Sources: AN AJ 52/400, Sadg, Wilaya, Delaire, *Construire.*

Isaac Abisror
No degree. Began paying dues in 1933. Licensed in 1941.

H. E. Adiba
No degree. Contractor and "consulting architect," arrived from Tunisia in 1914. Active until 1934 at least. Sources: Colette Zimeray.

Apartment building, Rue Colbert at Central market, ca. 1920. Villa, Ain Sebaa, 1935.

Pierre Ancelle
No degree. Active beginning in 1914.
Syndicat Immobilier de Casablanca building, corner of Boulevard de la Gare and Rue de l'Horloge, 1922 (with the de Montarnal brothers). Bourliaud building, corner of Rue Védrines and Rue Coli, 1928. Ancelle building,

corner of Rue Mirecourt and Boulevard de Lorraine, 1929. Apartment building, Rond-point Savorgnan de Brazza, 1929. Grisot building, corner of Rue Dupleix and Rue de l'Eglise. Société Urbaine Marocaine building, corner of Rue Lapérouse and Rue La Fayette, 1930. Bonnet building, Rue de Marseille. Dupuy Baroux building, Rue du Marabout. Sources: LM32, LCM.

Albert Archambeau
February 12, 1893. No degree. Present in 1934, began paying dues in 1936, licensed July 25, 1943. Registered in the Ordre in 1954.

Villa Gallinari, Rond-Point de France, 1936. Elias Hazan Synagogue, Rue de la Concorde, 1937. Villa Deconclois, Le Polo, 1940. Villa, Rue Rabelais. Source: Wilaya.

Léon Aroutcheff
Baku, January 18, 1915–March 17, 1977, Paris. ENSBA (admission 1937; Lefevre and Ferran student; awards in 1st class, received diploma February 27, 1945). Met É. Azagury at ENSBA and sheltered him in Paris during the Occupation. Present in Casablanca in 1945. Partners with Robert Jean and V. Scob.

O.C.H. building, Rue Jouffroy, 1948. Villa Tillie, Rue Franklin, 1948. Le Lutétia Cinema, Rue Poincaré, 1950 (with Robert Jean and V. Scob). Le Verdun Cinema, Boulevard de Bordeaux, ca. 1950. Opéra Cinema, corner of Rue Félix & Max Guedj, ca. 1950. Oceanographic station, 1950. Eight buildings for Jewish Habitat, corner of Boulevard Moulay-Youssef and Boulevard Calmel, 1951 (with Lucaud, Morandi, Rousseau, and Zéligson). Jewish Community School, corner of Boulevard des Régiments Coloniaux and Rue Séguin, 1951. Seven buildings for the Cité des Jeunes, C.I.L., Beauséjour, 1952–54. Villas for the C.I.L., Beauséjour and Germaine development, 1952. Villa André Brunet, corner of Rue Mac-Mahon and Rue Jules Grévy, 1953. Villa Van Gaver, corner of Rue d'Érymanthe and Rue Atalante, 1954. Sources: AN AJ 52/1283, Sadg, Wilaya, *Construire,* AA, AF.

René Arrivetx
Alger, January 27, 1883. No degree. Present in Casablanca in 1916, began paying dues in 1929, licensed on July 25, 1943. Built numerous "modern villas" in residential neighborhoods.

Villa Durand, Boulevard Circulaire, 1924. Hocine Tahari patio house, corner of Rue Voltaire and Rue Lacépède, 1926. Villa Ajoux, corner of Rue Lacépède and Rue Voltaire, 1928. Villa Hadj Mohamed Hadj, Rue Lacépède, 1928. Villa Bouchaïb ben Abdessalam, Avenue du Général Moinier, 1929. Costanza building, Rue Vignemal, 1929. Villa Renaud, Ain Sebaa, ca. 1932. Todaro building, corner of Rue de Commercy and Rue de Longwy, 1935. Pellegrino building, corner of Rue Lacépède and Rue J.-J. Rousseau, 1937. Todaro building, corner of Rue de Commercy and Boulevard du Maréchal Foch, 1947. Ritz Cinema, Rue Berthelot, 1949. Villa Chraïbi, Le Polo, 1953. Villas for the C.I.L., Beauséjour, 1952. Sources: LM32, Wilaya.

ATBAT-Afrique
Atelier de Bâtisseurs, or builders' studio, created by Le Corbusier and incorporating architects Georges Candilis and Shadrach Woods as well as engineers Vladimir Bodiansky and Henri Piot. Operated from 1951 to 1955. Also acted as as a consulting firm for the Cité des Jeunes and other projects. See Candilis.

Élie (Élias) Azagury
Casablanca, October 17, 1918. ENSBA (admission 1938; Héraud/Boutterin/Chappey and Beaudouin student, with the latter in Marseilles; awards in 2nd and 1st classes, received diploma November 13, 1946). Licensed on August 29, 1949. Worked for Marius Boyer and Louis Zéligson in Casablanca, for Auguste Perret, Paul Nelson, and Calsat in Paris, and for Ralph Erskine in Stockholm. Member of GAMMA, first postindependence president of the Ordre. Member of the U.A.M. Founded the Quadra group with Omar Alaoui and others.

Housing complex, Gyttorp, Sweden (for R. Erskine), 1946–48. Automatic garage, facade transformation, Rue des Ouled Ziane. Villa Sanchez, Les Crêtes, 1950. Villa Hazan, les Crêtes, 1952. Villa Cohen, Hippodrome, 1950. Villa Nahon, 1951. Villa Schulmann, Lice d'Anfa, 1952. Lévy house, Rue Amyot, Mers-Sultan, ca. 1955. Villa Édouard Roy, Avenue des Pléiades, 1954. Villa, Avenue Mers Sultan, ca. 1955. Villa Varaud, Rue du Chant des Oiseaux, 1954. Beach cabin, Bouznika, ca. 1955. Longchamp School, 1954 (with Isaac Lévy and Léon Aroutcheff). La Villette School, ca. 1954. Lyautey High School science pavilion, 1954 (with Isaac Lévy). Apartment building, Avenue du Général d'Amade, 1957. Development plan and working-class housing, Derb Jdid (Hay Hassani), 1958–62. Low-cost housing developments, Sidi Bernoussi, Ain Chock, and Tangiers, 1958–62. Office National du Thé factory, Rabat Road, ca. 1958 (with Henri Tastemain). Azagury Villa and Office, corner of Avenue de la Côte d'Emeraude and Rue Aspirant Henry Lemaignen, 1964. French Cultural Mission schools, Rue Denfert-Rocherau and Rue de Guise, 1963. Villa Nejma, Rue Abou Abd el Makoudi, ca. 1963. Courthouse and administrative complex, Agadir, 1961. Villa Mikou, Avenue Lucien Saint, 1975. Seaside resort, Cabo Negro, 1968. Caisse Nationale de Sécurité Sociale building, Rond-Point Chimicolor, 1980. Al Maghrib Bank, Boulevard Mohamed Zerktouni, 1994. Al Maghrib Bank, Agadir, 1997. Azagury house, Bouskoura, 1994–97. Al Maghrib Bank extension, Rue Idriss Lahrizi, 1997. Sources: AN AJ 52/1283, Wilaya, AA, EM, interviews.

Pierre-Félix Bailly
ENSBA (admission 1917; Lambert student; expelled from the school in 1920). Licensed May 16, 1947, registered in the Ordre in 1954. Partner of René Schmitt and Jean Balois.

Villa Friedmann, Rue Meyerbeer, 1948. Muslim school, Carrières centrales, c. 1954. Youth center, Carrières Centrales, 1955. Jules-Ferry Muslim Vocational Orientation Center, 1955. Bialong and Luxia buildings, Avenue du Général d'Amade and Rue de Longwy, 1951 (with René Schmitt). Sources: AN AJ 52/414, Wilaya, AF.

Jean Balois
Salins, October 23, 1892–July 26, 1967, Lamalou-les-Bains. ENSBA (EBA Dijon; admission 1913; Jaussely student). Arrived in Morocco in 1919. Worked for the City of Rabat's Architectural Department. Opened an office in Rabat. Partner of Marius Boyer from 1925 to 1929 and of Paul Perrotte from 1931 to 1934. Began paying dues in 1933, licensed July 25, 1943. Left Morocco in 1954.

Jules-Ferry School. Roches-Noires Schools. Jeanne d'Arc Institution Chapel, Boulevard Moulay-Youssef, 1936. Orain building, Rue du Marabout, 1932. Ouakline and Moynier buildings, Place de Verdun. Ettedgui-Mellul building, Avenue du Général Moinier, 1932 (with Perrotte). Villa Rousset, corner of Rue Jean-Jaurès and Rue de Tunis, 1931. Villa Donato, Mers-Sultan, ca. 1930. Wholesale Market Competition project, 1936 (with Perrotte). Muslim housing, new medina extension, 1937 (with Perrotte). Mers-Sultan Clinic, Parc Murdoch, ca. 1935. Four paired villas for Mme d'Hauteroches, Rue de Constantinople and Rue de la Grurie, 1936. Office building and service station for Shell Maroc and of the Parc Lyautey Building Society, Avenue du Général d'Amade and Boulevard de Lorraine, 1947. Villa, corner of Boulevard du Lido and Rue des Tamaris, 1948. Villa Brenalière, corner of Rue Perrault and Rue Lemercier, 1948. Bialong and Luxia buildings, Avenue du Général d'Amade and Avenue de Longwy, 1951 (with Bailly and Schmitt). Apartment building for the Duchesse de Guise and the Comte d'Harcourt, Rabat. Noguéras building, Rabat. Sources: AN AJ 52/575, CNA, *Bâtir,* LM32, LM38, *Réalisations,* AF.

Dominique (Domenico) Basciano
Tunis, January 2, 1911. ENSBA (admission March 13, 1933; Héraud/Boutterin/Chappey student; 1st class July 22, 1935, received diploma on February 21, 1939); Politecnico, Milan (Piero Portaluppi and Gio Ponti student, 1939–41). In Morocco beginning in 1922. Worked for Marius Boyer (1930–31). Licensed on March 12, 1949. Participated in numerous competitions. Extensive body of built work from 1960 onward.

Villa Tissot, Rue de Staël, 1952. Lynx Cinema, Avenue Mers-Sultan, 1950–51. Airport, Tit-Mellil, 1951 (with Jean-François Zevaco). Jeanne Hachette School, 1951 (with Jean-François Zevaco and Paul Messina). Villa Tissot, Rue de Staël, 1952. Prototype for an elementary school classroom, ca. 1954. G. Laperna (Socomy Vacuum) building, Rue de l'Horloge, 1954. School, Rue des Anglais, 1954–55. Rural School, Saint-Jean de Fédala, ca. 1955. School, Place Mirabeau, 1955. Internal Revenue Office building, Place Lyautey, 1954–55. Rif cinema, Avenue des Forces Armées Royales, 1958 (with Gaspare Basciano and Armand Riccignuolo). School, Carrières Centrales, 1958. Working-class housing, Derb Jdid (Hay Hassani), 1958–62. School, Sidi Bernoussi, ca. 1960. Atlas cinema, Rue Blanquefort, 1960. Italian professional school, 1963–65. Lux cinema, Boulevard de Marseille, 1968. Philip Stadium modernization, 1990–97. Sources: AN AJ 52/1284, Wilaya, AA, AF, AM, c.v., interview.

Gaspard (Gaspare) Basciano
Trapani, January 11, 1904–late 1995, Casablanca. Student of Ernesto Basile at the Accademia di Belle Arti in Palermo (1920–22). In Morocco from 1922 onward. Draftsman for Marius Boyer (1923–26 and 1927–36); Boyer student at the École des Beaux-Arts de Casablanca; student at the École des Arts Décoratifs de Paris (1926–27). Licensed November 10, 1949.

Architect's private mansion, 11 Rue Sarah-Bernhardt, 1932. Apartment building, 13 Rue Sarah-Bernhardt, 1930 (with Michelet). Numerous apartment buildings in the new medina and in Sidi Maarouf. Sources: Wilaya, c.v., interview.

Roger Belliot
Moroccan Radio-Television, Route de Marrakech. Maison de la Radio, Rabat.

Émile Bertin
Licensed December 24, 1948, registered in the Ordre in 1954.

Sefrioui et Bel Ghiti cinemas, Rue de la Douane, 1952. Source: Wilaya.

Biazzo
Liscia Frères building, Boulevard de Paris, 1929. Liscia Frères building, Rue Général Moinier, 1929. Todaro building, Boulevard Gambetta, 1929. Bosia Viari building, Rue Lamoriciere, 1931. Biazzo Raynal building, Rue Nationale, 1937. Source: Wilaya.

C. Blesson
Active in Casablanca from 1925 to 1939.

Élie Saada building, Rue de l'Aviateur Prom, 1927. Salerno building, Rue Franchet d'Espérey, 1929. Jeunehomme building, Boulevard de Lorraine, 1931. Sources: Wilaya, CNA.

Constant Bonnet
February 3, 1893. No degree. Began paying dues in 1928, licensed on July 25, 1943, registered in the Ordre in 1954.

Magne-Rouchaud building, corner of Rue de Bouskoura and Rue du Commandant Terves, 1929. Villa Lozana, Rue Jean Jaurès, 1930. Paired houses, corner of Rue Lacépède and Rue Mouret. Source: Wilaya.

Armand Bouchery
Lambersart, November 16, 1902–February 27, 1986, Poitiers. ENSBA (EBA Lille, admission 1922, Pontremoli student, received diploma). Licensed on July 25, 1943, registered in the Ordre in 1954. Partner of Maurice Sori. Source: AN.

Pierre Bousquet
Toulouse, April 29, 1885–1954. ENSBA (admission 1907; 2nd class 1907; Daumet and Jaussely student; 1st class 1908; numerous awards; received diploma June 9, 1911). Active in Casablanca from 1915; licensed on July 25, 1943; stopped practicing in 1952. Architecture Service of the Protectorate, Supervisor of Public Buildings in Casablanca. Later Municipal Architect of Casablanca.

Rabat, Casablanca, and Chaouia Pavilion, Exposition Franco-Marocaine, 1915. Municipal Market, Boulevard de la Gare, 1917. Commercial Stock Exchange, Boulevard de la Gare, 1918. Martinet building, Boulevard de la Gare, 1919. Apartment building, corner of Avenue de la Marine and Route de Rabat, 1921. Pasteur Institute and Hospital, ca. 1920. Lyautey High School, ca. 1922. Elementary school in La Foncière district, ca. 1925. Saint-François Church, ca. 1925. Housing for the Chemins de fer du Maroc, intersection of Rue Claude Debussy, Rue César Frank and Boulevard Denfert-Rochereau, ca. 1926. Clinic of Dr. Spéder, Rue d'Alger, 1928. Apartment building, corner of Rue d'Alger and Rue Mouret, ca. 1928. Newborn care center, Rue du Consulat de France, 1929. Société Française de Bienfaisance Nursery School, Rue Verlet Hanus, 1929. Banque Foncière du Maroc, corner of Rue Chevandier de Valdrôme and Rue Jean Bouin, 1929. Apartment building, corner of Rue Ouad Zan and Rue Chevandier de Valdrôme, ca. 1930. Architect's villa, Anfa, ca. 1930. Twenty-five workers' villas, ca. 1930 (with the contractor Ferrara). Auto-Hall garage, Boulevard de Marseille, 1930. Villa Bousquet, Rue Lacépède and Avenue du Général Moinier, 1933. Villa Werlhé, corner of Rue Bonaparte and Rue Victor Hugo, 1936. Talonneau service station, Rue de Dinant, 1937. Daycare center for the OCH, Boulevard Joffre, 1948. Moulins du Maghreb workers' housing, Rue de l'École Industrielle, 1946. Moulins du Maghreb mill, 1948. Coca-Cola plant, Rue de Camiran, 1950. Sources: AJ 52/416, Sadg, LM32, CM, *Construire*, Wilaya.

Marius Germinal Boyer
Marseilles, March 12, 1885–December 25, 1947, Casablanca. ENSBA (admission 1904; Héraud student; 2nd class 1904; 1st class 1908; Prix Américain 1910; received diploma ca. 1931; Premier Grand Massier, i.e., student representative, in 1913). Professor of architecture at the École des Beaux-Arts de Casablanca. Arrived in Casablanca in 1919, in partnership with Jean Balois from 1925 to 1929. During twenty-five years of activity, the office's production was considerable and extended well beyond Casablanca. Upon the death of Boyer, Émile Duhon took over the office.

Guedj building, Rue de l'Horloge, 1919. Hôtel Volubilis for Isaac Bessis, Rue de l'Aviateur Védrines, 1920 (with Lemonnier). El Glaoui building, corner of Boulevard de la Gare and Rue Nolly, 1922. Hôtel Atlas, 1922–23. El Glaoui Pavilion, Rampe d'Anfa, ca. 1922. Comptoir des Mines building, Rue Guynemer, 1923. Maré building, corner of Rue Guynemer and Rue Branly, 1923. La Vigie marocaine building, Boulevard de la Gare, 1924. Société Mobilière et Immobilière Franco-Marocaine building, corner of Rue de Marseille and Rue du Marabout, 1924. Bénazeraf villa, Avenue du Général d'Amade, ca. 1925. Officers' Club, Place Administrative, 1925. Villa of Grand Vizier El Mokri, Allée des Mûriers, Anfa Supérieur, 1928. Lévy-Bendayan building, corner of Boulevard de Marseille and Rue Lassalle, 1928. Pereire et Cohen building, Rue Aviateur Coli, 1928. Villa Raphaël Bénazéraf, Rue d'Alger, 1928. Le Glay and Houel paired villas, Avenue du Général Moinier, 1928. Bembarom et Hazan building, Rue Poincaré, 1928. Comptoir immobilier building, Rue de Bouskoura, ca. 1928. Apartment building of the Comte d'Harcourt, intersection of Rue des Ouled-Harriz, Rue Gay-Lussac, and Rue de Toul, 1928. Hôtel de Ville, Place Administrative, 1928–36. Basque house, Boulevard d'Anfa, ca. 1928. Villa Laurent, Boulevard Moulay-Youssef, 1928. Villa Canas, 1929. Nehlil building, Rue Aviateur Prom, 1929. Société Mutuelle Hypothécaire Sud-Américaine building, Rue de l'Aviateur Prom, 1929. Apartment building, Boulevard de Marseille and Rue Colbert, 1929. Villa Pierre Grand, corner of Rue Jean Jaurès, Rue Montesquieu, and Rue Alexandre Dumas, 1930. Gouvernet and Lorentz paired villas (called Les Tourelles), corner of Rue d'Alger and Boulevard du Général Gouraud, ca. 1930. Moses Asayag building, corner of Rue de l'Horloge and Rue de la Marine, 1930–32. Banque Commerciale du Maroc, Rue Galliéni, 1930. Boyer building, Rue du Commandant Terves, 1930. Boyer mansion, Rue d'Alger, ca. 1930. Villa Bonan, Boulevard Moulay-Youssef, 1930. Société Mobilière et Immobilière Franco-Marocaine building, Rue du Marabout, ca. 1930. Tobacco factory, Boulevard Bonaparte, 1932. Hôtel Transatlantique, Rue Colbert, ca. 1932. Apartment building, Rue de l'Aviation Française, 1933. Shell building, Boulevard de la Gare, 1934. Villa Bensimhon, Avenue Mers Sultan, 1935. Boyer apartment building (called Les Studios), corner of Avenue du Général d'Amade and Rue de Bouskoura, 1935. Villa Vannoni, corner of Boulevard Charles Lebrun and Rue Rodin, 1936. La Maternelle Dispensary, Boulevard des Régiments Coloniaux, 1936. Vox Cinema, Square Louis Gentil, ca.1935. Villa Plas, Rue Réaumur, 1937. Wallut service station, Route de Médiouna, 1937. Hôtel d'Anfa, Aire d'Anfa, ca. 1938. Liauzu garage, Rue de Pont-à-Mousson, 1948 (completed by Émile Duhon). OCH building and service station, corner of Boulevard Jouffroy and Rue Sauvage, 1947. Hôtel d'Anfa extension, 1948 (completed by Émile Duhon). Hôtel de Ville, Fédala, ca. 1936. Foncière et de la Seine building, Fès, 1932. Hôtel Transatlantique, Safi, 1938. Sources: AN AJ 52/416, G. Basciano, Wilaya, AA, *Bâtir*, LM32, LM38, Descamps, interviews.

Hubert Bride
Rennes, January 9, 1889. ENSBA (admission 1909; Chifflot student; 2nd class 1909; expelled in 1913). Arrived in Casablanca in 1915, active until 1920.

Compagnie Générale Transatlantique, Tobacco and Société d'Études de Casablanca Pavilions, Exposition Franco-Marocaine, 1915. Bride building, Rue des Ouled Ziane, 1916. Bessonneau building, Boulevard de la Gare, 1916–17. Apartment building, Rue de Madrid, 1917. Apartment building, 85 Rue de l'Horloge, ca. 1918. Apartment building for Soblanca, Place Centrale, 1920. Bessonneau building, corner of Boulevard de Lorraine and Boulevard Circulaire, 1920. Sources: AN AJ 52/416, Wilaya.

Edmond Brion
Soissons, May 23, 1885–June 9, 1973, Saint-Gervais. ENSBA (admission 1903; Paulin student; 2nd class 1903; 1st class 1908; awards, received diploma 1914). Active in Casablanca in 1918. In partnership with Auguste Cadet from 1920 until 1932. Authorized to practice July 25, 1943. In 1930 created the Moroccan group of the Sadg. Ceded his office to Jean Sachs in 1961.

Prior to 1932, see: Auguste Cadet.
Lafarge workers' housing development, Rue du Lieutenant Vidal, ca. 1932. Cosuma workers' housing development, Boulevard du Commandant Runser, 1932–37. Bendahan building, Rue Capitaine Maréchal at Place Edmond Doutté, 1935. Faure building, intersection of Rue Poeymirau, Rue Marguerite, and Boulevard de Marseille, 1936. Villa Ceccoli, Rue du Général Humbert, 1936. Villa Sala, Rue de Constantinople, 1936. Dispensary, Derb Sidna, 1937. Gras building, Place Bel Air, 1937. Pappalardo building, Rue Dupleix, 1937. Banque du Maroc, Boulevard de Paris, 1937. SOCICA housing development, Rue du Lieutenant Campi, Roches-Noires, 1940–42 and 1952. Société des Chaux et Ciments workers' housing development, Roches Noires, 1942. Project for a hotel, Avenue de la République, 1942. Mosque, Aïn Chock, 1945–46. Aiguebelle chocolate factory, Rue de Pauillac, 1946. Crédit lyonnais, corner of Boulevard de la Gare and Rue Berthelot, 1947. Moroccan war veterans' housing development, Aïn Chock, 1950. Société Immobilière Helvétia building, Place Amiral Sénès, 1948. Villa for Dr. Rollier, Rue Azéma, 1952. Société Chérifienne d'Engrais workers' housing development, Route des Zénatas, 1952. Mahakma du Cadi, new medina, 1954. Apartment building for the European personnel of the Société des Chaux et Ciments, Rue Michel de l'Hôpital, 1954. Sources: AN AJ 52/416, Sadg, CNA, *Construire*, LM32, LM38.

Georges Buan
Surveyor and developer. Active in Casablanca from 1912. Built a number of apartment buildings.

Villa Muñoz, corner of Rue de Londres and Rue de Castelnau, 1919. Faucherot building, corner of Avenue Mers Sultan and Rue de Terves, 1929 (with L. Beaufils). Polizzi building, Rue Sarah Bernhardt, 1929 (with L. Beaufils). Etedgui Synagogue, Rue de la Mission, ca. 1935. Artigues et Buan building, Rue de Tours, 1950. Sources: CNA, corresp. Jacques Etedgui, Wilaya.

Paul Busuttil
October 27, 1900. No degree. Began paying dues in 1926, licensed July 25, 1943. In partnership with Ignace Sansone until 1939.

Apartment building, Rue de l'Aviateur Védrines, 1928. Lévy et Charbon building, intersection of Avenue de la Marine, Rue Amiral Courbet and Rue de Tours, 1929. Villas Laberinto, Rue Claude Lorrain, 1929. Villas Mignot (three), corner of Avenue Mers Sultan and Rue de Provence, 1929. Villa Grégoire, corner of Rue de Malines and Rue de Namur, 1931. Eyraud building, Boulevard de Marseille, 1934. Apartment building, 79 Rue de Larache, 1936. Larrégieu building, corner of Avenue Poeymirau and Rue du Soldat Jouvencel, 1937. Bonsignore building, corner of Boulevard de la Liberté and Rue du Dauphiné, 1937. Housing, café, laundry facilities, and ovens for the OCH, Aïn Chock, beginning in 1949. Outdoor market, Aïn Chock, 1950. Camille Mathieu Muslim Vocational School, Rue Beni M'Guild, 1950. Eighteen paired villas for the Sécurité Publique, Les Crêtes, 1952. School, Avenue de l'Atlantide, Les Crêtes, 1955. Five apartment buildings for the CIFM, Rue de l'Hérault, Polo, 1955 (with Albert Lucas). Sources: Wilaya, AF.

Auguste Cadet
Lyons, May 17, 1881–March 13, 1956, Casablanca. ENSBA (admission 1902; Paulin student; 1st class 1905; received diploma 1911). Appointed to the Urban Planning Department in 1918. In partnership with Edmond Brion from 1930 to 1932. After 1935 established an office in the new medina, where most of his work would be developed. Licensed July 25, 1943. Married a Moroccan and converted to Islam.

With Edmond Brion:
Quartier des Habous, 1918–29. Société Marocaine de Distribution d'Eau, de Gaz et d'Électricité building, 1919–20. Central Pharmacy, Rues des Ouled Ziane, 1925. Michaut building, intersection of Rue de la Poste, Rue Poincaré, and Rue Clemenceau, 1927. Villa Gras, Rue Voltaire, 1928. Alexandre Bouvier and Société Marocaine Métallurgique building, corner of Rue de la Poste and Rue de Bouskoura, 1929. Grand Socco building and arcade, Sumica arcade, Boulevard de la Gare, 1929–32. Villa Goulven, Rue de Nieuport, 1929. Grand Bon Marché building, Boulevard de la Gare, 1931. Baille building, Rue de Bouskoura, ca. 1931. Tasso building, Rue des Ouled Harriz, 1931.

Alone within the partnership and on his own, beginning in 1932:

Architect's house, Rue du Parc, ca. 1930. Moulay Youssef Mosque, new medina, 1934–36. Sidi Mohammed Mosque, new medina, 1934–36. Mahakma of the pasha of Casablanca, 1941–52. Architect's house, Rue des Charmilles, Oasis, 1948–49. Sources: AN AJ 52/416, AA (Diverses réalisations modernes d'inspiration hispano-mauresque album, n.d.), Sadg; Wilaya, LM32, LM38; Michel Marty, "Auguste Cadet 1881–1956," in *Académie d'architecture, Portraits d'architectes, II* (Paris: Académie d'architecture, 1989), 67–69.

Georges Candilis
Bakou, April 11, 1913–May 18, 1995, Paris. (Athens Polytechnic School; briefly attended André Lurçat's studio at the ENSBA. From 1945 to 1951 worked with Le Corbusier. Active in Casablanca from 1951 to 1955, as part of ATBAT-Afrique (with Shadrach Woods). Later active in Paris, where Alexis Josic joined the team, building, among other projects, the new housing development at Le Mirail in Toulouse, 1961ff. Founding member of Team X, a reformist group within C.I.A.M..

Sémiramis and Nid d'abeille apartment buildings, Carrières Centrales, 1952. Housing for young families, Cité des Jeunes, CIL, 1952 (with Léon Aroutcheff and Robert Jean). Projects for "European," "Jewish," "Muslim," and "Mixed" habitat types, 1953. Seven model houses for Habitat Musulman, Ain Sebaa, 1953. Continuous habitat project, Route de Médiouna, 1954. Project for 1,500 housing units, for Sami Suissa, 1954 (with Élie Azagury). Strip housing project, for M. Guigui, Chemin des Crêtes, 1954. Sources: IFA, AA, interview.

Emmanuel Chaine
Present in Casablanca in 1934. Built a number of villas near the city center.

Villa, Rue Curie, ca. 1932. Warehouse, corner of Boulevard Circulaire and Route de Médiouna, ca. 1935.

Pierre Chassagne
Sauviat-sur-Vige, July 17, 1897–February 10, 1983, Béziers. ENSBA (admission 1917; Héraud student, 1st class 1923; awards; received diploma 1930). Head designer of the Boyer office from 1928 through the mid-1930s; Authorized to practice July 25, 1943. In partnership with Gustave Cottet after 1945.

Villa Bellanger, Rue du Mont Cinto, 1946. Three double villas for the CFM, Rue Colonel Scall, 1946. Apartment building for the OCH, Boulevard du Maréchal Foch, Bourgogne, 1947–48. Hammam, Ain Chock, 1948. Housing for the École Industrielle et Commerciale de Casablanca, 1950. Villa Nobles, Route de Bouskoura at Rue de Salins, 1950. Citroën garage, Boulevard Guerrero, 1951. Villa Chassagne, Rue Jules Ferry, 1952. Villa Vigroux, Riviera, 1952. Sources: AN AJ 52/579, Wilaya, AF, *Construire*.

Jean Chemineau
Paris, July 25, 1916–1964, Ville-d'Avray. ENSBA (admission 1937; Recoura/Mathon student; 1st class 1942; awards; received diploma February 15, 1944). Member of GAMMA, works for the Protectorate's Department of Public Health.

Dispensary, Boulevard Claude Perrault, 1950. Nine buildings for the Department of Public Works, Route de Mazagan, 1951 (with Jean Forcioli). Daycare center, Aïn Chock, 1956. Dispensary, Carrières Centrales, 1956. Church, Ouezzane. Muslim hospital, Ouezzane. Housing, Port-Lyautey. Caisse Centrale Marocaine de Crédit et de Prévoyance, Place Piétri, Rabat. High school, Agadir (with Édouard Delaporte and Jean Forcioli). Sources: AN AJ 52/1288, Wilaya, AA.

Pierre Coldefy
Decazeville, September 21, 1928–February 21, 1978, Nice. ENSBA (EBA Bordeaux; admission 1939; Hilt student; 1st class 1942; awards; received diploma June 12, 1945). Worked for the reconstruction in the region of Dunkirk (1946). Later joined the Courtois team. Licensed on February 14, 1950. Left Casablanca in 1966 for Nice, where he worked for the OTH and Paribas.

Reception room, Greek orthodox church, Rue de Namur, 1950. Apartment building, Rue de Cabris, 1950. Villa Salvaing, Route d'Azemmour, 1950. Hôtel de Sévigné, ca. 1951. Garage and service station, Boulevard de Bordeaux, 1952. Assurances Générales Incendie building, Boulevard de Lorraine, 1952. Maarif church, ca. 1952. Saint-Paul church, Boulevard Denis-Papin, Bourgogne, 1953. Villa Aubert, corner of Rue St-Servais and Rue de Porquerolles, 1953. Valentin Hauÿ Dispensary, near Boulevard des Crêtes, 1953. Esso service station, Boulevard de la Corniche, Aïn Diab, 1955. Apartment building for the Habous, above the Sumica arcade, Place Edmond Doutté, ca. 1955. Coldefy house, Boulevard du Lido, Anfa, 1955. CIFM housing, corner of Boulevard Laurent Guerrero and Rue du Préfet Laurent, 1956–58. Housing, le Plateau, 1957–59 (with Gaston Jaubert). Villa les Violettes, Boucle d'Anfa, 1959. Eight villas, Boulevard du Préfet Laurent, Beaulieu, 1964. Mission Française High School. Law Courts, Safi. René Descartes High School, Rabat. Participated in the reconstruction of Agadir. Sources: AJ 52/1288, Wilaya, Coldefy family.

Alexandre Cormier
Paris, August 11, 1890. (EBA Nice). Active in Casablanca in 1919, began paying dues in 1931; licensed on July 25, 1943. Built numerous industrial buildings.

Arenas, Boulevard d'Anfa, ca. 1922. Casablanca Velodrome, Boulevard Franklin Roosevelt, ca. 1922. La Princière pastry shop, Rue Galliéni. Offices and printing plants for *La Presse marocaine* and *Le Soir marocain*, Rue de l'Industrie. Vulcan-auto facilities, Rue Védrines, 1929. Beaumier building, corner of Boulevard de Marseille and Rue Gay-Lussac, 1929. Ambroselli building, Boulevard du Front de mer. Marc building, Rue Védrines. Augier building, Rue Clémenceau. Villa, Rue Monge, ca. 1931. Ludovic Galaup building, corner of Rue de Bouskoura and Boulevard de Paris, 1933. Scherrer building, Boulevard de Marseille. Villa Busset, corner of Boulevard Pétain and Rue de Londres. Graffenil Cinema, intersection of Rue Nationale, Rue Branly, and Rue Pégoud, 1936. Villa Pietro Alba, Franceville, 1941. Riquier garage and offices, corner of Boulevard de la Gare and Rue Hoyon, 1949. Sources: Wilaya, LM32, CNA, *Réalisations*.

Gustave Cottet
Algiers, December 19, 1896. (EBA Alger). Arrived from Algiers in 1919. In partnership with Pierre Chassagne after 1945. Built many more villas in the 1960s.

Crédit Marocain building, Avenue Mers-Sultan, 1928. Escot building, corner of Rue de l'Aviateur Prom and Rue de l'Aviateur Coli, 1929, transformation into Olympic Hôtel, 1931. Domerc building, corner of Rue Pellé and Rue de l'Industrie, 1929. Apartment building, 16 Rue Galliéni. Schriqui building, corner of Boulevard de Paris and Avenue Général Moinier. Amic garage, location unknown. Parnaud building and workshops, Boulevard Émile Zola. Villa Isaac Cohen, Boulevard Moulay Youssef, 1929. Villa Journel, Avenue du Général Moinier, 1929. M. Sicher building, corner of Rue de l'Aviateur Védrines and Rue de l'Industrie, 1930. Apartment building, Rond-point Mers-Sultan at Rue Franchet d'Esperey, ca. 1932. Villa Bareille, Rue Boïeldieu, ca. 1932. Villa Domerc, corner of Boulevard du Maréchal Foch and Rue d'Arras, 1933. Domerc building, corner of Rue Lapérouse and Rue Bascunano, 1934. Ansal building, Rue Colbert, 1937. Sources: Wilaya, LM32, *Réalisations*.

Henri Couette
Settled in Rabat, editor of the journal *Réalisations*.

Gilardi building, Rue de Pont-à-Mousson, 1929. Banchi building, corner of Boulevard du Maréchal Foch and Rue de Pont-à-Mousson, 1931.

Alexandre Courtois
Paris, March 7, 1904–April 3, 1974, Grenoble. ENSBA (admission 1923; Bigot studio, which he later directed; received diploma 1933; Second Grand Prix de Rome, 1930; First Grand Prix de Rome, 1933). Worked in Istanbul with Henri Prost. Arrived in Morocco in 1942 in order to design and build the BNCI headquarters. Commissioned by the Protectorate government in 1943. Licensed on March 30, 1946. President of the Conseil Supérieur de l'Ordre des Architectes du Maroc from 1952 until 1956. Editor of *L'Architecture marocaine*. His was one of the most important offices in Casablanca. He remained in Morocco until 1965.

Urban development and extension project for Casablanca, 1944. BNCI building, Place de France, 1942–50. CTM building and trucking depot, Avenue de la République, 1951–55. Casablanca-port railway station, Boulevard du IVe-Zouaves, ca. 1950. Elementary school, Square de l'Abbé de l'Épée, 1950. Police station, Boulevard Camille Desmoulins, 1950. School of the Cité Douanière, Boulevard Camille Desmoulins, 1951–52. Derb Comima workers' housing, 1952. Church and convent, CIL Beauséjour, 1953. Apartment building, 117–131 Avenue du Général d'Amade, 1956. School, Rond-Point de l'Europe, 1954. Housing and villa development for the CIFM, Boulevard des Crêtes, Beaulieu, 1953–55. Project for Habitat Israélite apartments, corner of Rue Diderot and Rue Fénelon, 1955. Market and newspaper stands, Oasis, 1955. Healthcare facility, Ben Ahmed, ca. 1953. Post office, Marrakech. Sources: AN, Wilaya, AA, AM, LMM, Alexandre Courtois Jr.

Henri Curton
Berlin, March 26, 1876. Active in Casablanca in 1916. Began paying dues in 1931.

Marcel Autiéro building, corner of Route de Mazagan and Rue Bourbonnais. Apartment building for Madame Gautier, Rue Aviateur Claude, 1926. Gautier office building, Avenue du Général Drude, 1929. Novella building, Rue Jacques Cartier, 1929. Villa Gautier, Place de la Fraternité, ca. 1930. Villa Delmas, Rue de la Dordogne, 1942. Apartment building for the OCH, Boulevard des Régiments Coloniaux, 1948. Sources: LM32, Wilaya.

Achille Dangleterre
December 29, 1907. Began paying dues in 1936. Licensed on December 24, 1946.

SIDEO factory, Boulevard Page, 1942. Office Chérifien des Phosphates offices, Rue Verdi, 1943. Villa Dangleterre, Les Crêtes, 1950. Office Chérifien des Phosphates housing, Rue Sergent Portelli, 1951. Marcel Cerdan (later Mohammed V) Stadium, 1953 (with the office of Hennebique and Ziegler, consulting engineers). Notre-Dame-de-Lourdes Church, Boulevard du Maréchal Foch, 1954. Sources: Wilaya, EM, LM54.

Robert Debroise
August 16, 1899. Architect-engineer. Began paying dues in 1928. Licensed on July 25, 1943.

Apartment building, 137 Avenue du Général d'Amade. Villas for the SMD, Rue Jeanne d'Arc, 1948. School, Boulevard d'Anfa, 1953. Vocational training center, Carrières Centrales, 1955. Sources: MAE, Wilaya.

Georges Delanoé
Montpellier, November 17, 1911–May 18, 1995, Antibes. ENSBA (EBA Strasbourg; admission 1931; Debat-Ponsan student; 1st class 1932; awards; received diploma 1940). Active in Casablanca in 1942. Licensed on July 25, 1943.

Hippolyte-Joseph Delaporte
Versailles, October 14, 1875–March 8, 1962, Marseilles. ENSBA (admission 1895; Laloux student; 1st class 1899; awards; received diploma 1902). Active in Versailles, and in Casablanca beginning in 1913. Municipal architect-surveyor from 1932 to 1946. Authorized to practice December 24, 1946.

Biographies of Architects 465

Magasins Paris-Maroc, Place de France, 1913–14 (concrete engineering and execution Perret Frères). Hôtel Excelsior, Place de France, 1914–16 (reinforced concrete engineering by Coignet). Villa, Boulevard d'Anfa, 1917. Magasins Paris-Maroc Annex, 1920, Rue Chevandier de Valdrôme, 1920 (with Perret Frères). Temporary theater, Boulevard de Paris, 1922. Architect's villa, Rue du Parc, ca. 1924. Robelin building, Boulevard d'Alsace, 1928. Villa du Garreau, corner of Avenue Mers-Sultan and Rue du Languedoc, 1929. Lebascle mansion, Boulevard Gouraud, 1929. Ferrieu house, 10, Rue du Parc, 1932. Fouronge house, 5 Rue Defly Dieudé, 1932. Cannestraro building, corner of Boulevard des Régiments coloniaux and Rue des Colonies, 1932. Maret building, 128 Boulevard de la Gare, 1932. Oil and soap factories, Route de Rabat, 1937. Villa Merlin, Rue des Aviateurs, 1937. Villa Louradour, Val Fleuri, 1952. Sources: AN AJ 52/403, IFA, Wilaya, Delaire, Souque interview.

Édouard Delaporte

Paris, November 14, 1909–July 6, 1983, Saint-Jeannet. ENSBA (admission 1935; Gromort student, 1st class 1937). Active in Rabat, built large hospital complexes for the Department of Public Health (with Jean Chemineau and Jean Forcioli).

Boys' High School, Boulevard de la Résistance, 1952. Chappe Telephone Exchange, ca. 1953. Technical Secondary School, 1955. Sources: AN, Wilaya, François Delaporte.

René Deneux

Paris, December 14, 1921. ENSBA (admission 1939; Tournon student; 1st class 1942; awards; received diploma 1945). Settled in Rabat, many projects built in partnership with Albert Planque.

Villas for the OCLM, corner of Rue Fontaine and Rue Burguiers, 1953. Sources: AN AJ 52/1289.

Georges-Ernest Desmarest

Paris, March 2, 1977–July 24, 1959, Saint-Lunaire. ENSBA (admission 1896; Deglane student; 1st class 1896; awards; received diploma 1902). Active in Paris beginning in 1907.

Apartment building, 51 Rue Jacques Cartier, 1919. Municipal slaughterhouses, Quartier de la Gare, 1922 (with Greslin). Apartment building, corner of Boulevard de Marseille and Rue Lassalle, ca. 1925. Sources: AN AJ 52/403, Sadg, Wilaya.

Marcel Desmet

Paris, June 24, 1892–May 1, 1973, Nice. ENSBA (EBA Lille; admission 1912; Pontrémoli student; 1st class 1924; awards; received diploma 1932). Active in Lille and the region, and then in Casablanca from 1932 until 1962. Licensed on July 25, 1943. Named vice president of the Ordre des architectes du Maroc. In partnership with Jean Maillard after 1945. Built numerous industrial buildings.

Built noted apartment buildings, shops, and cafés in Lille. Fraternelle du Nord apartment block, corner of Rue Savorgnan de Brazza and Rue Jacques Cartier, 1931–32. SIF building, Place de la Gare, 1935. Apartment building, 22 Boulevard de la Gare, 1934–35. Trianon pastry shop, 22 Boulevard de la Gare, 1935. Low-income housing, 349 Boulevard de la Gare, 1935. Villa Finoest, Rue Bara, 1936. Villa Joseph Partitucci, Rue des Hirondelles, 1937. Lesieur-Afrique workers' housing, Rue du Caporal Corbin, 1942. Apartment building for the OCH, corner of Boulevard des Régiments Coloniaux and Rue Maurice Leglay, 1948. Industrie Cotonnière du Maroc factory, Fédala, ca. 1948. Villa Mahieu, Rue des Mûriers, 1950. Apartment building for the OCI, Boulevard Alexandre 1er, 1952. Optiba building, Rue Dupleix, ca. 1953. Romandie building, CIL, 1952–53 (with Gabus and Dubois). Apartment buildings for the Department of Housing, Rue Maurice Leglay, 1953–55 (with Gaston Jaubert and ATBAT-Afrique, consulting engineers). Sources: AN AJ 52/582, Sadg, Wilaya, AA, *Réalisations. Architecture contemporaine: quelques réalisations de M. Desmet Marcel* (Strasbourg: Société française d'édition d'art, 1934).

Émile Duhon

Caudéran, November 23, 1911–November 21, 1983, Casablanca. ENSBA (admission 1935; Héraud student, 1st class 1938, prizes and awards; received diploma 1946). Licensed on December 3, 1946. President of the Sadg du Maroc in 1955. In partnership with Marius Boyer, whose office he took over in 1948. Extremely prolific, Duhon became architect to Mohammed V.

Hôtel d'Anfa extension, 1948 (Boyer project). Hôtel El Mansour, Avenue de la République, 1948–55. Apartment building for the OCH, Rue Jouffroy, Bourgogne, 1948. Ferrié building, Boulevard Ney, 1949. Experimental prefabricated villa for the CIL, Spaak and La Ferme Bretonne development, 1950. Duhon mansion, Rue Alfred de Musset, 1951. Urbaine et la Seine building, Avenue de la République, 1952. Villa Yves Mas, Allée des Pléiades, 1952. Villa Meunissier, Rue des Bouvreuils, 1952. Amic garage, Boulevard de Marseille, 1952. Villa Caravaca, Rue des Iris, 1952. Palmaro company office building, corner of Avenue du Général d'Amade and Rue du Lieutenant Bergé, 1952. Benjelloun service station, Rond-Point de la Révolution Française, 1954. Department of Finance building, corner of Boulevard du Général Gouraud and Place Administrative, 1955 (with D. Basciano). Six apartment buildings for H. M. Mohammed V, Boulevard Alexandre Mallet, 1956. Paquet Company (Marhaba) Hotel, Avenue de la République, ca. 1956. Paquet Company (Marhaba) Hotel, Mazagan, ca. 1952. Bureau of Comercialization and Export office building, Avenue des Forces Armées Royales, 1966. Sources: AJ 52/1290, Sadg, *Construire*, Wilaya, AF, MAE, Guzzo interview.

Liborio J. Durante

Began paying dues in 1920, licensed on July 25, 1943. Editor of *La Construction au Maroc* during the 1930s.

Apartment building for the OCH, Rue Bouardel, Bourgogne, 1948.

Michel Écochard

Paris, March 11, 1905–May 24, 1985. ENSBA (admission 1925; Bigot and Lemaresquier student; received diploma 1931). Member of the Sadg and C.I.A.M., founder of GAMMA. Established in Syria and Lebanon from 1931 to 1945. Protectorate Director of Town Planning from 1946 to 1952. Later worked in Pakistan, Guinea, Senegal, Iran, and Lebanon. Appointed chief architect for the French government; in 1967 he was appointed to the urbanism chair at the École des Beaux-Arts.

Museums, Antioch, 1931. Museum and French Institute, Damascus, 1936. Urban development plan for Damascus, 1934–36 (with the Danger brothers). Urban development plan for Beirut, 1941–48. Urban development and extension plan for Casablanca, 1949–52. Urban improvement studies for the new medina, Carrières Centrales, Avenue de la République and Place de France, 1949–52. Urban development and extension plans for Rabat, Fès, Meknès, and Oujda, 1946–52. Protestant high school, Beirut, 1955 (with Claude Le Cœur). University, Karachi, 1955–58 (with P. Riboulet and G. Thurnauer). School of the Marist brothers, Saida, 1959. National Museum, Kuwait, 1960–77. Urban development plan for Dakkar, 1963. Urban development plan for Damascus, 1968. Regional development scheme for Corsica, 1969. Urban development plan for Meshed, 1971. Plan for a new capital, Oman, 1973. Study of the city center, Tehran, 1978. Sources: AN, BGA, MAE, IFA, Sadg, Mas interview; V. Bradel, "Michel Écochard 1905–1985" (research paper, Paris, 1985); J. Gohier, "Michel Écochard ou l'urbanisme français à l'étranger 1905–1985," *Urbanisme* 211 (1986); M. Ghorayeb, "La transformation des structures des structures urbaines de Beyrouth pendant le Mandat français," Ph.D. diss., Université de Paris VIII, 2000.

Wolfgang Ewerth

November 4, 1905. German architect active in Casablanca from 1954 to 1975. Member of the Bund Deutscher Architekten from 1955 to 1976. In partnership with Chevalier.

Villa Maurice Varsano, Sidi Maarouf, 1954. Villa Girard, 1955. Villa Benjelloun, Rue d'Oslo, 1960. Villa Sefraoui, Anfa Supérieur, 1961. Villa of Dr. B., Boulevard du Lido, 1962. Villa of Dr. Driss Bennis, Rue des Grenadiers, 1962. Villa Armand Harroch, corner of Rue Gazy and Rue Paul Doumer, 1963. Villa Yahia El Medira, Rue Priol, 1963. Villa for the Elmar company, Boulevard Claude Perrault, 1963. Villa Hubert Fournier, Rue Parisis, 1963. Villa Patrice Anselin, Avenue Franklin Roosevelt, 1975. Villa Mohamed Bennis, corner of Boulevard Alexandre 1er and Rue du Lido, 1969. Sources: BDA Bonn, AA, Azagury and Heyder-Bruckner interviews.

Abd el Kader Farès

July 1922–October 9, 1979, Tangiers. ENSBA (received diploma in 1947). First Muslim Moroccan to graduate from the École des Beaux-Arts and to be registered in the Ordre. Built a number of projects for Moroccan clients in the new medina, later turning to larger multi-family dwellings. Appointed at the Ministry of Housing in 1957 and subsequently in charge of residential and educational programs. Later in charge of Morocco's government buildings abroad.

Larbi ben Mohammed Apartment building, corner of Boulevard de Bordeaux and Rue Adrienne Lecouvreur, 1951. Housing for the Ministry of Housing, Sidi Othman, 1960. Four apartment buildings for the Ministry of Housing, Plateau-Extension, 1960. Apartment buildings for the Ministry of Housing, Hay Mohammadi, 1961. Sources: Wilaya, EM, Azagury interview, Myriam Farès correspondence.

Louis Henri Fleurant

Compiègne, March 30, 1897–May 16, 1980, Montpellier. ENSBA (admission 1914; Redon-Tournaire student; 1st class 1923; awards; received diploma 1925). Active in Casablanca from 1927 to 1942 and again beginning in 1945. Named president of the regional council of the Ordre. Member of the Municipal Commission after 1945.

School, Rue Krantz, 1929. School for indigenous children, Ferme Blanche, 1929. Villa Masson, corner of Rue de La Haye and Boulevard de Londres, 1930. Villa Demillière, Boulevard de la Marne, ca. 1930. Villa S., ca. 1930. Villa Dolbeau, corner of Boulevard du Maréchal Foch and Rue Ollier, 1931. Villa Jouhaud, Rue de Paris, ca. 1932. First prize in the low-cost housing competition, 1932. Villa Fleurant, Boulevard Camille Desmoulins, 1937. Muslim School for Girls, new medina, 1937. Muslim housing, new medina extension, 1938. Cold storage laboratory, Ain Sebaa, ca. 1946. Société Marocaine de Distribution office building, Rue Savorgnan de Brazza, ca. 1948. Apartment building for the OCH, corner of Boulevard des Régiments Coloniaux and Rue du Tonkin, 1948. Maarif Tax Collection office, Rue de Roncevaux, 1949. Villa of Director of Municipal Services Grillet, ca. 1950. Société Chérifienne de Pneumatiques et Caoutchoucs building, Boulevard Émile Zola, 1950. Apartment building for the Department of Veterans' Affairs, Avenue Mangin, 1950. Amiral Courbet Real-Estate company building, Rue Amiral Courbet, 1950. Banque Paribas building, corner of Rue Lapébie and Avenue du Général d'Amade, 1951 (with Maddelena). Camiran Electrical Transformer Station, Rue Camiran, 1952 (with Lenormand; brise-soleil by Jean Prouvé). School, Maarif, 1952. Teachers' College, Ain Chock, 1957. Sources: AJ 52/584, Sadg, Wilaya, *Construire*, LM32, LM38, CNA, AF

Jean Claude Nicolas Forestier

Aix-les-Bains, January 9, 1861–October 26, 1930, Paris.

Landscape architect. École Polytechnique engineer; studied at the École Libre des Sciences Politiques (1882–83) and at the École Forestière de Nancy (1883). In charge of the Bois de Vincennes (1889), the Bois de Boulogne, and the Western sector of the Promenades de Paris (1898). He saved the Champ de Mars (1904), redeveloped the Avenue de Breteuil (1898), and re-created the Jardin de Bagatelle (beginning in 1904). Active in Barcelona, Buenos Aires, Seville, Havana. A driving force behind the Urban and Rural Hygiene Section of the Musée Social.

Mission on open spaces and urban extension of Moroccan cities, 1913. Project for the garden of the sultan's residence, 1916. Sources: IFA; B. Leclerc, ed., *Jean Claude Nicolas Forestier: du jardin au paysage urbain* (Paris: Picard, 1994).

René Fougère
Saint-Amand, July 7, 1882. ESA, later ENSBA (admission, 1905; Laloux/Lemaresquier student; 1st class 1909; awards; received diploma 1911). Active in Tangiers in 1911, and in Casablanca from 1914 until about 1930.

Cousin house, Rue de l'Horloge, 1917. Compagnie Algérienne building, corner of Rue de Tours and Rue Lapérouse, 1920. Villa Busquet, Boulevard de Londres, 1924. Hôtel Majestic, Boulevard de Marseille, ca. 1925. Brogne building, corner of Boulevard de la Gare and Rue Jacques Cartier, 1929. Sources: AN AJ 52/422, Sadg, Delaire.

Maurice Galamand
Licensed on July 25, 1943. Settles in Oujda. Member of the editorial board of *L'Architecture marocaine*.

Maréchal Foch (later Maréchal Lyautey) housing development for the Sharifian Army Housing Office, intersection of Rue Damrémont, Rue de Commercy, Rue de Reims, and Rue Lamoricière, 1949–53. Sources: BGA, AF.

Georges Gillet
Died in 1948. Engineering degree from the École Centrale des Arts et Manufactures, Paris (class of 1905). Active in Casablanca in 1913, directed the office of the Coignet Cement Construction Company. Opened his own office in 1921. President of the Casablanca Contractors' Association.

France-Auto garage (Citroën), corner of Boulevard de Paris and Avenue du Général d'Amade, 1929 (with Maurice-Jacques Ravazé [1885–1945], architect for Citroën). Fuel depots, Casablanca and Kénitra, 1928–29. Brasseries du Maroc extension, 1929–31. Supervised construction of Villa Pierre Mas, 1937 (for Charles Abella). Sources: Wilaya, LM32, LM38.

Natale Girola
December 24, 1905. Swiss. Licensed on July 25, 1943. Registered in the Ordre in 1954.

Robert Letour house, Boulevard Camille Desmoulins, 1934. Villa Mimram, corner of Avenue Lucien Saint and Boucle d'Anfa, 1935.

Georges Godefroy
Orléans, December 31, 1911. ENSBA (received diploma 1945). Inspector for the reconstruction of the Orléans region in 1945. Active in Morocco from 1949 to 1966. Created in 1949 and directs until 1953 the Town Planning Inspectorate for the Casablanca region. Then directed the Interregional Town Planning Inspectorate until 1966.
Coordination of the study for the Casablanca master plan, 1949–52. Urban improvement studies for the new medina, 1952–55. Plan for Muslim housing at the Carrières Centrales and Sidi Othman, 1949–52. Urban study for the Avenue de la République and Place de France, Sidi Belyout, 1949–52. Urban study for European housing at the CIL and Le Plateau, 1952–56. Villa, 1953. Sources: Godefroy corresp., G. Godefroy; "Les problèmes démographiques marocains," *L'Architecture d'aujourd'hui* 26, no. 60 (June 1955).

Edmond Gourdain
La-Fère-sur-Aisne, January 17, 1885–January 28, 1968, Compiègne. ENSBA (admission 1903; Daumet-Jaussely student; 1st class 1906; received diploma 1911). Active in Casablanca in 1913. Licensed on July 25, 1943. In partnership with his son Jean after 1945.

Paquet Company and Algerian pavilions, Exposition Franco-Marocaine, 1915. Double villas, Avenue Mers Sultan, 1917. Société Agricole du Maroc building, Boulevard de Lorraine, 1919. Apartment building, corner of Boulevard Lorraine and Rue de Belfort, 1920. Ferrara building, Boulevard de Marseille, 1920. Société Générale building, Boulevard de la Gare, 1921. Société Agricole building, 388 Boulevard de Lorraine, 1921. Hôtel Transatlantique, for Saboulin, 1921. Compagnie Générale Transatlantique building, corner of Boulevard de la Gare and Avenue de la Marine, 1929. Gourdain building, corner of Boulevard de la Gare and Rue Dumont d'Urville, 1929. Apartment building, corner of Rue de l'Horloge and Boulevard Poeymirau, 1930. Gautier commercial offices, Rue Lapérouse, 1931. Muslim housing, new medina extension, 1938. Apartment building for the OCH, corner of Rue Jouffroy and Rue Sauvage, 1948. School for Muslim girls, Roches Noires, 1950. Crédit Foncier d'Algérie et de Tunisie building, intersection of Boulevard de Marseille, Rue Nationale, and Rue Pégoud, 1953. Muslim school, Ben M'Sick, 1954. Serviceman's House, place Mirabeau, 1954. Lesieur-Afrique indigenous housing development, Rue Sous-lieutenant Rostand, Bel Air, 1954. Low-rent housing, Derb Jdid (Hay Hassani), 1958–62. Sources: AN AJ 52/423, Wilaya, LM32, LM38, AF.

Jean Gourdain
Casablanca, December 14, 1915. ENSBA (admission 1936; Tournon/Michau student; 1st class 1938; received diploma 1942). In partnership with his father, Edmond Gourdain, after 1945. Sources: AN AJ 52/1293.

Jacques Gouyon
Architect in Saint-Étienne, Casablanca, and Paris.

Murdoch real-estate company building, corner of Rue Murdoch and Rue Chevandier de Valdrôme, 1950. Villas Paquet apartment building, corner of Boulevard de la Gare and Place Georges Mercié, 1952. Sources: Wilaya, EM.

Joseph Gras
May 23, 1885. Began paying dues in 1924.

Villa, corner of Rue du Belvédère and Rue de Champagne, 1928. Project architect for the Rendu & Ponsard building, Avenue du Général d'Amade, 1930–31. Source: Wilaya.

Georges-Jean Grel
Caudéran, January 30, 1882–November 20, 1972, Bordeaux. ENSBA (EBA Bordeaux; admission 1902; Pascal student; received diploma 1910). Worked for Hermant and for Tauzin in Paris. Active in Mazagan from 1918 to 1924 and then in Casablanca until 1950. Often collaborated with Georges Renaudin from 1935 to 1939. Member of the Sadg. Distinguished member of the Municipal Commission during the 1930s.

Treasury Revenue Office, Place Administrative at Rue Chevandier de Valdrôme, 1925. Villa, corner of Rue d'Alger and Rue Duhaume, 1925. Braunschwig Israelite Hospital, Boulevard Moulay-Youssef, 1929. High school, Avenue du Général Moinier, 1929. Jewish school, Boulevard Fayolle, 1929. School for indigenous children, new medina, 1929. Lesca building, corner of Boulevard de Lorraine and Rue de Lunéville, 1929. Eyraud building, corner of Boulevard de Paris and Rue Chevandier de Valdrôme, 1930. Project for Terralia building, corner of Avenue du Général Moinier and Avenue du Général Gouraud, 1930. Villa Roucher, Boulevard Moulay-Youssef, 1934. Roucher building, 20 Boulevard Moulay-Youssef, 1932. Villa Cassou, Rue de la Haye, ca. 1932. Apartment building, Place des Aviateurs, ca. 1935 (with Renaudin). Girondet service station, Rond-Point du Général d'Amade, 1936 (with Renaudin). Apartment building, Avenue du Général Moinier, ca. 1936. Villa Monaigue, corner of Boulevard Le Nôtre and Rue Mansard, 1936 (with Renaudin). CFM railroad station, Marrakech, ca. 1923. Project for a hotel in Mazagan, 1923. Camp Boulhaut Post Office, 1923. Sources: AN, Sadg, Henri Bresler collection, Wilaya, Réalisations.

Henri Grémeret
ENSBA. Licensed on December 20, 1952; registered in the Ordre in 1954.

Housing and commercial facilities, Ain Chock, 1954–55. Housing for the CIFM, Place Koudiat, Carrières Centrales, 1955. Bournazel housing development, 1954–57 (with Albert Lucas and Gaston Jaubert). Sources: Wilaya, EM.

Albert Greslin
Versailles, May 24, 1888–November 30, 1966, Marseilles. Active in Casablanca beginning in 1917, in collaboration with Desmarest and later independently, until the 1960s. Began paying dues in 1931; licensed on December 25, 1943. Member of the Société des Architectes Modernes. Built countless small villas after 1950.

Municipal slaughterhouses, Rue du Médecin-major Ayrand, 1922 (with Desmarest). IMCAMA building, Rond-Point Lyautey, 1928. Demeure building, Boulevard de la Gare, ca. 1928. Fayolle building, corner of Rue de Bouskoura and Rue Poggi, 1929. Anginot building, Boulevard d'Alsace, ca. 1929. Villa Puech, Avenue de l'Hippodrome, ca. 1930. Villa Greslin, Rue Jeanne d'Arc, ca. 1930. Rodriguez building, Rue Girardon, 1934. Villa Boitel, Rue Rodin, 1936. St. Francis of Sales church, Maarif, ca. 1938. Villa Scaduto, Rue Dom Pérignon, 1952. Service station, corner of Rue de l'Aspirant Lafuente and Rue de Longwy, 1954. Villa, Beauséjour, 1954. Esso garage, Boulevard de Lorraine, 1955. Sources: Wilaya, LM32, LM38; *Albert Greslin: architecte SAM, Casablanca* (Madrid: Edarba, ca. 1930).

Jean Hentsch
Swiss. Graduate of the ETH Zurich. Active in Morocco between 1952 and 1956. Built Muslim housing in Agadir, as well as projects designed by André Studer (see entry for the latter).

El Itissal development, 1956. Sources: Wilaya, Studer interview.

Jacques Hentschel
Saint-Étienne, May 28, 1919. ENSBA (admission 1938; Tournon/Michaud student; 1st class 1944; received diploma 1947). Licensed on April 16, 1948. Registered in the Ordre in 1954.

School, Boulevard Émile Zola, 1949. Villa Di Guardo, Rue Guadet, 1949. Villa Daspremont, Rond-Point de Marseille, 1950. Villas, corner of Avenue Pierre Simonnet and Rue de Savoie, 1950. Van de Walle factory, Maarif extension, 1950. Lucky Land company office building, Ohana subdivision, Boulevard Moulay-Youssef, 1954. Sources: AN AJ 52/1294, Wilaya.

Erwin Hinnen
Lucerne, June 11, 1894–May 21, 1986, Le Canet. ENSBA (admission 1913; Pascal/Recoura student; 1st class 1918; awards; received diploma). Active in Casablanca from 1931 to 1974, with a parallel practice in Paris until 1939. In Switzerland 1939 to 1945. Authorized to practice on July 25, 1943.

Design for the Bendahan apartment building, Rue Bendahan, 1932. Socifrance building, corner of Boulevard de la Gare and Rue Chénier, 1934–35. Paired

Biographies of Architects 467

villas for the Platon brothers, corner of Allée des Mûriers and Allée des Mimosas, Anfa Supérieur, 1937. Villa Besson-Maufrangeas or Dar-es-Saada, 2 Aire d'Anfa, ca. 1935. Moretti Milone building, corner of Avenue Général Moinier and Rue Murdoch, 1937. Villa, 4 Aire d'Anfa, ca. 1938. Villa Theil, Anfa, 1938. Two villas for the Comptoir Français du Maroc, Boulevard Watin, 1945. Villa Mohammed Elzizi, Rue Arago, 1946. Brasseries du Maroc brewery plant, intersection of Rue d'Argonne, Rue de Rome, and Rue de Champagne, 1946. Apartment building for the OCH, Rue Bouardel, 1947. Villa Benitah, Boulevard du Lido, 1948. Villa de Lignac, Oasis, 1949. Villa Roger, Hippodrome, 1949. Architect's villa (called Les Chaumes), 413 Boulevard Panoramique, Les Crêtes, 1949–52. Vieljeux villa (called Saadia), and adjacent villas, Rue du Canonnier Carpentier, Oasis, 1950. Saturne and Océanic buildings, corner of Avenue de la République and Rue de Foucauld, 1950. Villa Sidoti, corner of Boulevard Barthou and Rue Dalayrac, 1951. Villa of Mme Isvy, corner of Boulevard Franklin Roosevelt and Rue E. Clopet. Police housing, Bournazel, 1951. Villa Pradel, Avenue de la Plage, 1953 . Villa Lévy-Lebhar, corner of Rue Page and Rue Oder, 1952. Villa Sander, Boulevard Claude Perrault, 1952. Benson's building for the Société Marocaine Foncière et Industrielle, Avenue de la République, 1953. CIL housing development, Avenue du Nil and Avenue Anoual, Sidi Othman, 1953–54. Manufacture Française de Lingerie factory, Rue de Zurich, 1954. Auto-Hall garage vertical addition, Boulevard de Marseille, 1954. Société Immobilière d'Anjou building, Avenue des Forces Armées Royales, 1960. Psychiatric clinic and villa of Dr. Pierson, Quartier du Palmier. Villa of the contractor Massot, corner of Boulevard du Lido and Rue Sergent-chef André Masset. Villa Vergne (called Gitana), Place de la Division Leclerc, Oasis. Villa, 246 Boulevard de Libye at Rue Necker. Villa Claire-joie, Rue 4, Lonchamp. Villa Messidor for the forwarding agent Kerguen, Anfa Supérieur. Villa Louisiane for the insurance executive Barbey, Boulevard du Lido. Villa Boussac, Rue Saint-Servan, Anfa. Villa Abbès Benjelloun, California. Brasserie de France restaurant building, Fédala. CTM trucking depot, Agadir. Sources: AN AJ 52/587, Wilaya, Maisonset jardins, Pierre Hinnen interview.

Jean-Jacques Honegger
Geneva, 1903–85, Geneva. Swiss civil engineer. In 1949 established the firm Honegger-Afrique SA with his brother. The company was active until 1959. Developed prefabricated construction systems with his son Jean-Marc and his nephew Gérard. His main client was René Berr, a Papiers Riz-Lacroix cigarette-paper shareholder.

Confort Quartier Racine building, or "Cosyra," corner of Boulevard du Maréchal Foch and Boulevard d'Anfa, 1951. Apartment building, corner of Boulevard du Maréchal Foch and Boulevard des Régiments Coloniaux. Honegger-Afrique SA offices, 123 Rue de la Villette. Luminex-Éclair offices, Rue du Sous-lieutenant Divot. Apartment building, Rue Saint-Saëns. Apartment building, Rue de Normandie. Angst villa, Les Crêtes. Villa Masson, Les Crêtes. Sources: Wilaya, AA, Crétegny interview.

Pierre Jabin
Blida, August 24, 1894–November 3, 1967, Nantes. Active in Casablanca in 1919. Began paying dues in 1926. In partnership with François Pénicaud. Rarely active after 1945.

Société Anonyme d'Entreprises Marocaines building and Colisée cinema, corner of Boulevard de la Liberté and Rue du Soldat Jouvencel, 1928. Brasserie le Petit Poucet, Boulevard de la Gare, 1929. Nouchy building, Boulevard de Lorraine, 1929. Pappalardo building, Boulevard de Lorraine, 1929. Benmergui building, corner of Rue de Bouskoura and Rue Galliéni, ca. 1930. Rialto cinema/theater, for Madame Adélaïde Gautier, Rue de l'Aviateur Roget, 1930. Comptoir Immobilier du Maroc building, Boulevard de Paris, 1930. Barizon building, Boulevard du Maréchal Foch, 1931. Brasserie La Coupole, Boulevard de la Gare, 1932. Primarios building, 140 Avenue Mers Sultan, 1932. Villa Cohen, Rue Curie, 1931–32. Circle of the association of graduates of the Alliance Israélite Universelle, Rue Lacépède, 1932. Moretti-Milone building, corner of Place de France and Boulevard du IVe-Zouaves, 1934–35. Villa Nathan Barrache, Boulevard d'Anfa, 1937. Colonel de Turenne Apartment building, corner of Rue de Nancy and Rue de Verdun, 1937. Liscia Frères building and Lux cinema, corner of Boulevard de Marseille and Rue de l'Aviateur Prom, 1937. Moretti building, 41 Rue Lapérouse, ca. 1938. Moretti building, 17 Rue d'Artois, ca. 1938. E. Décrion building, corner of Rue Blaise Pascal and Rue Ledru Rollin, 1939. Moretti building, corner of Rue Félix and Rue Max Guedj, 1939. Charles Legal store, 1954. La Coupole building, corner of Rue Roget and Boulevard de la Gare. Villa Taourel, Boulevard d'Anfa. Sources: Wilaya, LM32, LM38.

Gaston Jaubert
Salon de Provence, July 28, 1918. ENSBA (admission 1939; Arretche and Perret student, spent time at the Grenoble EBA; 1st class 1940; awards; received diploma 1943). Authorized to practice on June 30, 1951. Member of GAMMA.

Single-family house, Longchamp, 1950–51. Single-family house, Beauséjour, 1950–51. Apartment building of Dr. Gaston Brami, 25 Rue de Mareuil, 1952. SMPP service station, Casablanca Zoo, Ain Sebaa, 1952. Moussa building, corner of Rue d'Ajaccio and Rue Chiarelli, 1952. Gallinari building (called Atlanta), Avenue Émile Zola, 1953. L'Étrier equestrian club, 1953. Employees' apartment building for the Department of Housing, Rue Maurice Leglay, 1953–55 (with Desmet and ATBAT-Afrique, consulting engineers). Marcel Gout building, 37 Rue Savorgnan de Brazza, 1953. Apartment building, Bournazel housing development, 1956. Primary and technical schools, Bournazel, 1956 (with Woods and Richards). Housing development, Le Plateau, 1957–59 (execution with Coldefy). Jaubert house, Pélissane, 1960. Housing development, Salon de Provence. Port terminal, Fos sur Mer. Sources: AN AJ 52/1295, Wilaya, interviews; Renée Diamant-Berger, *Gaston Jaubert: rythmes et volumes* (Marseilles: 1976).

Louis Jourdan
May 22, 1880. Paid dues from 1931 to 1936.

Hôtel des Ambassadeurs, Place Georges Mercié, ca. 1925

Maurice Kunzi
Neuchâtel, December 28, 1878. ENSBA (admission 1901; Paulin student; 1st class 1904; received diploma 1907). Active in Casablanca from 1922 to 1934. Member of the Sadg. A vigorous defender of the status of the architect in Morocco. Sources: AN AJ 52/406, Sadg.

Adrien Laforgue
Montevideo, 1871–October 11, 1952, Rabat. Younger brother of symbolist poet Jules Laforgue, mostly active in Rabat from 1912 to his death.

Central post office, Place Administrative at Boulevard de Paris, 1918–20. Parcel post center, Boulevard de Paris, 1922. SIMAF building, Rue Georges Mercié, 1929. Workers' housing development for the Office Chérifien des Phosphates, Rue du Lieutenant Bruyant, 1929. Church of the Franciscans, Parc Lyautey, 1929. Numerous administrative buildings, Rabat. Sources: Wilaya, AM, de Mazières interview; *Adrien Laforgue: travaux d'architecture* (Strasbourg: EDARI, ca. 1934).

Albert Laprade
Buzençais, November 29, 1883–May 9, 1978, Paris. ENSBA (admission 1903; Cléret/Redon student; 1st class 1906; prizes and awards, Prix de Rome finalist 1909; received diploma 1907). Works for the General Residency, Rabat, from 1915 to 1919. Present in Casablanca from 1915 to 1917.

Parc Lyautey, 1917–19. Lighthouse superstructure, El Hank, 1916 (with the Municipal Services). Preliminary definition of street network and building typology of the new medina, 1917–19. Project for the urban development of the Anfa residential district, 1920. Project for the prostitution district, new medina, 1922. Military administration building, Place Administrative, 1922. Competition project for the Casablanca theater, 1922 (with Haller, engineer). General Residency building, Rabat, 1917–23 (with Jean Claude Nicolas Forestier, landscape architect). Citroën garage, Rue Marbeuf, Paris, 1929 (with Léon Bazin). Musée des Colonies, Paris, 1931 (with Léon Jaussely and Léon Bazin). Morocco pavilion at the *Exposition Coloniale Internationale*, Paris, 1931 (with R. Fournez). Barrage, Génissiat, 1939–50. Urban renewal of îlot insalubre XVI, Paris, 1940–50. Maison du Maroc, Cité Universitaire, Paris. Office building for the Prefecture of the Seine, Boulevard Morland, Paris. Sources: AN AJ 52/426, AA, IFA, Sadg, MH Rabat, A. Laprade, *Croquis Portugal Espagne Maroc* (Paris: Vincent, Fréal & Cie, 1958).

J.-H. Laure
Architect. Urban planning degree from the Institut d'Urbanisme de l'Université de Paris. Director of the Office of Administrative Buildings, Rabat, from 1954 to 1960. Studied and developed social housing building types.

Apartment building for Jewish residents (later "economical" housing), Rue des Îles d'Or, El Hank housing development, 1953–60. "Economical" apartment buildings, Plateau extension and Hay Mohammadi, 1956–60. Sources: Wilaya, MH Rabat, *Maroc-Presse*.

Paul Les Enfant
1894–1949. Engineer, graduate from the École Polytechnique in Paris. Designer of the port, piers, and fishing infrastructure development plan, 1930–39. Source: *Construire*.

Isaac Lévy
Tangiers, August 22, 1912–January 7, 1989, Pantin. ENSBA (admission 1936; Héraud and later Perret student; 1st class 1938; awards; received diploma 1947). Began paying dues in 1939, in Tangiers. Active in Casablanca beginning in 1947. Licensed on April 16, 1948. Many projects executed in partnership with Élie Azagury.

El Maleh-Ohayon mansion, Boulevard d'Anfa, 1950. Hôtel Trocadéro. Scali mansion, Rue d'Alger, 1951 (with Élie Azagury). Trucking depot, Boulevard Pasteur, ca. 1951. Villa Lévy, corner of Rue Amyot and Rue Lalande, 1952. Société Immobilière Mari building, corner of Boulevard de la Gare and Rue de l'Amiral Courbet, 1954 (with Louis Zéligson). Working-class housing, Derb Jdid (Hay Hassani), 1958–62. Jewish retirement home, El Hank, 1956 (with Cesare Pugliese). Sources: AN AJ 52/1297, Sadg, Wilaya.

Maurice L'Herbier
Architect, member of the Société Française des Architectes. Active in Casablanca from 1929 to 1934.

Alfano building, Rue d'Aumale, 1929. France-Maroc dance hall, El Hank, 1929. Villas Falcon, corner of Avenue Saint-Aulaire and Rue de Grenoble, 1929. Le Lido swimming pool, Ain Diab, 1930. Villa Addi, Avenue Mers-Sultan, 1931. Sources: Wilaya, CNA.

Robert Lièvre
Charleval, February 20, 1890–September 7, 1962, Fréjus. ENSBA (admission 1908; Paulin student; training interrupted). Active in Casablanca from 1918. Began paying dues in 1929. Licensed on December 26, 1952. Built numerous villas in Anfa Supérieur in the 1930s.

Fifty villas, Traverse de Médiouna, 1921. Private mansions, Rue du Parc and Rue Rouget-de-l'Isle, before

1925. Compagnie de Transports et de Tourisme du Maroc bus terminal, Place de France, 1926. Villas, corner of Rue de Franche-Comté and Boulevard Circulaire, 1927. Hôtel George V, Rue Sidi Belyoût, ca. 1927. Villa Violas, Rue de Constantine, 1928. Villa Teste (called L'Escale), Anfa Supérieur, ca. 1928. Parrain building, intersection of Boulevard de Lorraine, Rue de Bouskoura, and Rue Reitzer, 1928. Compagnie de Transports et de Tourisme du Maroc depot, Route de Mazagan, 1929. Froment building, Rue Gay-Lussac, 1929. Villa de Rueda, corner of Boulevard du Maréchal Foch and Rue d'Avignon, 1930. Urban development project for the port districts, 1930. Hôtel de Paris, corner of Rue Blaise Pascal and Rue Branly, ca. 1930. Lafitte building, Rue Dupleix, ca. 1930. Lièvre studio apartment building, 4 Rue Mouret, 1931. Lebascle building, corner of Avenue du Général d'Amade and Rue du Lieutenant Bergé, 1931. Lafitte building, Avenue du Général d'Amade, 1932. Physical Education Pavilion, Parc Lyautey, ca. 1936. Villa Lièvre, Anfa Supérieur, 1938. Studio apartment building for Mme Alessi, Rue d'Anizy, 1953. Armand Maré building, corner of Boulevard Ney and Rue de Soissons, 1953. Sources: AN AJ 52/428, Wilaya, CNA, LM32, LM38.

Sauveur and René Licari
February 2, 1903, and August 5, 1910. Architects and contractors. Sauveur was licensed in 1949. René paid dues in 1933 and requested registration in the Ordre in 1941.

Villa, 20–20 bis, Rue de Calais, 1915. Siot mansion, corner of Rue Jean Jaurès and Rue Lefèvre, 1936. Two double villas, Boulevard Claude Lorrain at Rue Régnault and Rue Rude, 1936. Licari building, Rue Franchet d'Espérey, 1937. L'Épée mansion, Rue Magellan, 1942. Reception center for the Department of Youth and Sport, Rue Chevreul, 1949. Hôtel Washington, Boulevard de Lorraine, 1954. Source: Wilaya.

Émile Louis
Lyons, January 22, 1883. ENSBA (admission 1906; Esquié/Jaussely student; received diploma 1912). Active in the Service of Civic Buildings of Marrakech from 1917 to 1918. In Casablanca in 1920 and until the 1950s. Licensed on August 31, 1945. Registered in the Ordre in 1954.

School, Rue de Tours, 1949. Girls' school, Ain Chock, 1949. Franco-Muslim and Qur'anic school, Ain Chock, 1949. School, Oasis, 1950. School, Bournazel Nord, 1950-1954. Sources: AN AJ 52/428, Sadg, Wilaya, *Construire*.

Albert Lucas
Licensed on March 12, 1949. Registered in the Ordre. In partnership with Paris-based Charles Abella.

Expansion of the Maarif Church, Rue du Jura, 1951. Apartment building for the CIL, Beauséjour, 1952. Office building, Boulevard Ney and Boulevard Émile Zola, 1952. Housing, Cité des Jeunes, Ain Sebaa, 1952. "European"-style apartment building for Muslims, Carrières Centrales, 1953. Apartment building for the CIFM, Grand Ensemble de Bournazel, 1954–57. La Vigie Marocaine building facade, Boulevard de la Gare (with Abella). Housing for the CIFM, Rue de l'Hérault, Polo, 1955 (with Busuttil). Sources: MAE, Wilaya.

Raymond Lucaud
Tonnay-sur-Charente, April 22, 1914. ENSBA (admission 1935; Laloux/Lemaresquier student; 1st class 1937; prizes and awards; Prix de Rome finalist; received diploma 1943). Licensed on May 3, 1947. Member of the Sadg du Maroc. Worked with Honegger after 1956.

International Fair of Casablanca, 1951 (with Robert Maddalena). Eight apartment buildings for Habitat Israélite, Boulevard Calmel, 1951 (with Rousseau, Zéligson, Morandi, and Aroutcheff). Soldiers' housing, Anfa III, 1955 (project architect). Hôtel d'Anfa swimming pool, ca. 1952. Apartment building for gendarmes, intersection of Rue Paul Doumer, Rue Mallet, and Rue Véga, 1956. School, El Hank, 1956. Sources: AN AJ 52/1297, Sadg, Wilaya.

Robert Maddalena
Paris, February 23, 1916–November 6, 1997, Nice. ENSBA (admission 1936; Patouillard/Demoriane student; 1st class 1939; received diploma). Active in Casablanca in 1948. Worked for Léonard Morandi on the Liberté building. Licensed on March 23, 1950. Left Morocco for Algeria in 1959. In the Côte d'Azur after 1962.

Senouf mansion, Boulevard Camille Desmoulins, 1950. "Improved apartments" and offices of the Entraide Franco-Marocaine, CIL Beauséjour, 1952–53. Apartment building, Cité des Jeunes, CIL Ain Sebaa, 1952. International Exhibition of Casablanca, 1951. Transformer station for the SMD, Boulevard Franklin Roosevelt, ca. 1952. Sources: AN AJ 52/1298, Wilaya, Mme Charlotte Maddalena.

Jean Maillard
Yport, September 17, 1909–January 2, 1990, Gy-en-Sologne. ENSBA (EBA Rouen; admission 1930; 1st class 1933; received diploma). Authorized to practice on March 18, 1948. Registered in the Ordre in 1954. In partnership with Marcel Desmet after 1945. Sources: AN, Wilaya.

Aldo (Angelo) Manassi
Milan, August 13, 1888. (Scuola Superiore d'Arte Applicata all'Industria, Milan; professor of drawing with a diploma from the Accademia di Brera, Milan, 1919). Active in Casablanca from 1921 to 1939.

Soto building, Place Guynemer, 1922. Ferrara building, Boulevard de Paris, 1924. S. Lévy building, Boulevard de la Gare, 1927. Manassi building, corner of Boulevard de Marseille and Rue de l'Industrie, 1927. Noulellis building, corner of Rue de l'Aviateur Védrines and Rue de l'Aviateur Coli, 1927. Ettedgui et Schriqui building, Boulevard de la Gare, 1927. A. Bitan and Hazan development, Rue Lacépède, 1928. Banon building, corner of Boulevard de la Gare and Rue de Foucauld, 1928. Ugazio building, corner of Boulevard de la Liberté and Rue Gay-Lussac, 1931. El Hadj Omar Tazi building, Rue du Capitaine Maréchal, 1931. Sidoti building, corner of Rue des Ouled Harriz and Rue de Commercy, 1931. Benarosch building, place des Cinq Parties du Monde, 1932. Sources: Acc. di Brera Archives, Wilaya, CNA, LM32, LM38.

Paul Manuguerra
April 11, 1899. Italian. Began paying dues in 1933. Licensed on September 29, 1949.

Dayan building, corner of Rue de l'Aviation Française and Boulevard du Maréchal Foch, 1931. Villas Balzano, corner of Boulevard de Londres and Rue de Castelnau, 1936. Hassan Benjelloun building, Rue Pellé, 1941. J. Allée building, Rue Blaise Pascal, 1938. Schéhérazade cinema, for Ahmed Sebti, Rue de l'École Industrielle, 1952. Villa Labretchéa, Avenue des Eucalyptus, ca. 1952. Villa Manuguerra, corner of Rue Bonaparte and Rue Jules Grévy, 1954. Ahmed Sebti building, Rue de l'Aviateur Roget, 1956. Source: Wilaya.

Antoine Marchisio
Cannes, November 25, 1885–February 4, 1954, Marrakech. ENSBA (admission 1904; Laloux student). In 1915 joined the team of Prost, whose position in the Department of Public Buildings he assumed in 1918. Head of Protectorate Architectural Services until 1947, he later settled in Marrakech.

Compagnie Algérienne bank building, Avenue du Général d'Amade, 1926 (with Henri Prost). Fishermans' housing development, Fédala, ca. 1936. Muslim housing development, Ain Chock, 1936–41 (design), ca. 1947 (construction). Hôtel de la Mamounia, Marrakech, 1928 (with Henri Prost). Department of Public Health, Rabat. Hôtel des Îles, Mogador, 1936. Collège des Orangers, Rabat. Oued el Abid Dam, Bin el Ouidane. Sources: Delaire, AA, AM.

Joseph Marrast
Paris, July 12, 1881–September 26, 1971, Brémontier-Cherval. ENSBA (admission 1900; Julien/Lambert student; 1st class 1903; awards; Prix de Rome finalist; received diploma 1911). Worked with Henri Prost from 1919 to 1922. Later member of the General Council of Buildings of France and of the Council of Civic Buildings.

Detailed plan for the Place Administrative, 1920. Casablanca Law Courts, 1920–23. Project for the City Hall, ca. 1923. Sources: AN AJ 52/429, Sadg, Delaire, Jean Denieuil.

Pierre Mas
Cannes, March 19, 1923–1999, Grenoble. Garden designer and urban planner (studied at the École Nationale d'Horticulture, 1940–43, and then in the landscape section of the ENH, 1946–47; subsequently studied at the Institut d'Urbanisme de l'Université de Paris, 1947–49). Écochard's assistant in the Town Planning Department beginning in 1949. Prepared studies on shantytowns, the new medina, and the Moroccan residential sectors of Casablanca. Active in the Town Planning and Housing Directorate and then in the reestablished Town Planning Department until 1965. Within the Department he directed the Central Bureau of Planning, which prepared, among other things, the plan for the post-1960 reconstruction of Agadir. Sources: MH Rabat, interview, correspondence.

Vladimir Mauzit
Kherson (Ukraine), August 8, 1920. ENSBA (admission 1941; expert student; 1st class 1944; received diploma 1947). Licensed on August 19, 1949.

Villas for the CIL, Anfa-Beauséjour, ca.1950. Dwellings, Sidi Bernoussi, 1958. Sources: AN AJ 52/1298, Wilaya.

Paul Michaud
Constantine, June 23, 1888. ENSBA (admission 1906; Godefroy/Laloux student; 1st class 1909; received diploma 1914). Active in Rabat from 1915 to 1962 and later in Imouzzer du Kandar, from 1963 to 1967. Returned to France in 1967. Architect for the Department, and later Ministry of Education.

Schools of the Gautier, Roches Noires, Mers-Sultan and Boulevard de Lorraine districts, 1922. Villa Marcel Rivollet, Boulevard de la Marne, 1929–30. Villa Marius Philibert, Avenue Jules Ferry at Place de la Chaouia, 1929. Villa Élise, 39 Avenue Jules Ferry. Lyautey High School extension, Avenue Pierre Simonet, 1950. Girls' High School, Boulevard Circulaire, 1955. City Center School. Layris-Vergé School. School, Oasis. Jewish School, Boulevard Moulay-Youssef. College, Mers-Sultan. Sources: AN AJ 52/430, Sadg, Wilaya, Descamps.

Émile Michel
Marseilles, November 26, 1874. ENSBA (admission 1894; Esquié student; 1st class 1898; received diploma 1905). Licensed on July 25, 1943. Registered in the Ordre in 1954.

Villa Rey, Rue de Stockholm, 1936. Villa Lebas, Rue de Rome, 1936. Amic building, Rue Blaise Pascal, 1941. Société Aramon building, Rue de l'Horloge, 1946. Housing, Derb Jdid, ca. 1960. Sources: AN AJ 52/408, Wilaya.

Jean Michelet
Maisons-Laffitte, August 2, 1901–March 11, 1996, La Garde. Active in Casablanca in 1926. Began paying dues in 1934. Licensed on July 25, 1943. Without a doubt the most prolific builder of villas in Casablanca's residential districts.

Desvaux building, corner of Boulevard de Lorraine and Rue Dumont d'Urville, 1929. Michelet building, Rue Sarah Bernhardt, 1929 (with G. Basciano). Villa Roux, Avenue Général Moinier, 1929. Villa Chambonnaud, Boulevard Le Nôtre, 1929. Apartment building of Dr. Roussel, 161 Rue Blaise Pascal, 1929. Artaud building, corner of Rue Védrines and Rue Prom, 1929. Villa Matton, corner of Boulevard du Maréchal Foch and Rue Bara, 1931. Villa Gallin, Rue Boileau, 1931. Villa Félici, Rue de Namur, 1931. Villa Payant, Anfa Supérieur, 1931. Apartment building, corner of Boulevard d'Anfa and Rue de l'Oise, ca.1933. Villa F., Boulevard d'Anfa, 1933. Villa Ange Mattéi, Rue Lemercier, 1934. Villa Poupignon and Villa Dugarreaux, Rue de Savoie, 1936. Villa Haering, Square de Douaumont, ca. 1936. Villa Genevois, Boulevard du Maréchal Foch, 1936. Val d'Anfa Clinic, corner of Avenue de l'Hippodrome and Rue de Longchamp, 1946. Apartment building for the OCH, Rue de Dijon, 1948. Beauséjour and Camp Turpin Schools, 1950. Villa Consturian, Boulevard Bonaparte, 1952. Nursery School, Ain Sebaa, 1955. Police station, Ain Diab, 1955. Sources: MAE, Wilaya, LM32, LM38, *Bâtir, Réalisations,* CNA, AF.

Joseph (Eugène-Charles-Jean-Joseph) de Montarnal
Moulins, 1867. ENSBA (admission 1888; Ginain/Scelliers de Gisors student; 1st class 1892; received diploma). Chief architect of the French Committee of Exhibitions. Involved in exhibitions in Amsterdam (1895), Brussels (1897), Glasgow (1901), Hanoi (1902), Saint Louis (1904), Liège (1905), Milan (1906), Bucarest (1906), Dublin (1907), London (1908), Saragossa (1908), Copenhagen (1909), Quito (1909), and Brussels (1910). Built apartment and office buildings in Paris, in particular 118 Rue Réaumur, 1898. Built the Paris representation of the Moroccan Protectorate, 21 Rue d'Argenteuil, 1918.

Jean-Marie-François de Montarnal
Saint-Ciré, 1873. ENSBA (admission 1893; Ginain/Scelliers de Gisors student; 1st class 1898; received diploma). Brother of Joseph.

Joint work of the Montarnal brothers in Morocco: general plan of the *Exposition Franco-Marocaine,* Casablanca, 1915. Projet for a workers' housing development, Les Roches-Noires, 1921. Syndicat Immobilier de Casablanca building, corner of Boulevard de la Gare and Rue de l'Horloge, 1922 (with Pierre Ancelle). Sources: AN, BGA, Sadg, Delaire.

Léonard Morandi
Corcelles, 1914. Swiss. ENSBA (Tony Garnier/Bourdeix student; received diploma in 1945). Active in Casablanca from 1948 to 1956 and later in Paris. Licensed on October 2, 1948.

Liberté building, Rond-Point de la Révolution Française, 1949–50 (with Le Pape, engineer). Pélissard offices, Rue Dumont d'Urville, 1950. Villa of Dr. Blanc, Rue de la Maternité, 1950. Villa Morandi (called Dar Lugda), Anfa Supérieur, ca. 1951. L'Union Insurance building, corner of Boulevard du Général Gouraud and Avenue du Général Moinier, 1951. Villa Boumendil, 70 Rue Jean Jaurès, ca. 1952. Crédit Marocain building, 27, Boulevard Moulay-Youssef, 1953. Le Lido swimming pool, renovation, 1954. Villa Fleureau, Avenue de Boulogne, 1952. Studio apartments for El Glaoui, Boulevard de la Gare, 1952. Chapel, Cité Ohana, Boulevard Moulay-Youssef, 1954. Sources: AA, AM, Wilaya, interview.

Valerio Paccanari
July 25, 1905. Swiss. Began paying dues in 1931.

Sulfates et Produits Chimiques indigenous housing development, Route de Camp Boulhaut, 1942. Société Immobilière Suisse building, corner of Rue Félix & Max Guedj, 1952 (with Weilenmann). Roger building, Rue Layris Verger, 1953. Source: Wilaya.

Mario Paniconi and Giulio Pediconi
Rome, May 1, 1904–1973, Rome; and Rome, January 31, 1906–September 19, 1999, Rome. Graduates of the Regia Scuola di Architettura de Rome, 1929 and 1930. As partners, they built the Fontana della Sfera in the Foro Mussolini, Rome 1933–34; the Istituto Nazionale delle Assicurazioni building and the Istituto Nazionale per la Previdenza Sociale at the EUR, Rome, 1939–43. Outside Italy, they built the Italian School of Salonica, and designed the Italian School in Grenoble.

Italian School, Les Roches Noires, 1934. Sources: AA, interview; Alessandra Muntoni, *Lo Studio Paniconi e Pediconi 1930–1984* (Rome: Officina, 1987).

Marcel (Claudius) Parizet
November 3, 1911. Licensed on December 24, 1946. Registered in the Ordre in 1954.

Housing and boutiques for the OCH, Ain Chock, 1949. Sources: MAE, Wilaya.

François Pénicaud
Limoges, February 27, 1884. ENSBA (admission 1907; Deglane student; awards; did not complete his studies). Licensed on July 25, 1943. Registered in the Ordre in 1954. In partnership with Pierre Jabin. Sources: AN AJ 52/432, MAE.

Auguste Perret
Ixelles, February 12, 1874–February 12, 1954, Paris. ENSBA (admission 1891; Guadet student; 1st class 1893; studies interrupted, 1901). A partner in the Perret Frères company, with his brothers Gustave and Claude. Taught in a studio he opened outside of the framework of the ENSBA, from 1924 to 1928. At Prost's request, taught at the ESA from 1930 to 1942, returning later to teach at the ENSBA. First president of the Ordre in 1942 and member of the Institut in 1943. A pioneering reinforced concrete construction company, Perret Frères was a presence in Casablanca from 1913 to 1920, retaining land in the city until the end of the 1920s. The Moroccan episode took place at a decisive moment in the trajectory of Perret's career—between the completion of the Théâtre des Champs-Élysées (1913) and the construction of the church at Raincy (1922).

Magasins Paris-Maroc, for Hippolyte Delaporte, 1913–14. Wallut warehouses, Boulevard Circulaire at Route de Médiouna, 1914–16. Perret Frères fonduk and workers' housing, Boulevard Circulaire, Quartier Gautier, ca. 1920. Paris-Maroc warehouses, Boulevard Circulaire, 1920. Magasins Paris-Maroc warehouse, Rue de Libourne, 1920. Hamelle warehouses, Route de Rabat, ca. 1920. Magasins Paris-Maroc annex, Rue Chevandier de Valdrôme, 1920 (with Hippolyte Delaporte). Sources: AN AJ 52 / 409, IFA; R. Gargiani, *Auguste Perret: la théorie et l'œuvre* (Paris: Gallimard-Electa, 1994); M. Culot, R. Legault, D. Peyceré, G. Ragot, *Les frères Perret: l'œuvre complète* (Paris:Norma/IFA, 2000).

Paul Perrotte
Caen, May 11, 1898–1954, Caen. ENSBA (admission 1920; Defrasse/Madeline student; 1st class 1922; awards; received diploma 1924). Worked on the Côte Basque and in Casablanca beginning in 1931. In partnership with Jean Balois until 1937. Licensed on July 25, 1943.

Ettedgui-Mellul building, Avenue du Général Moinier, 1932 (with Balois). Wholesale Market, 1936–39 (with Balois, for the competition). Muslim dwellings, new medina extension, 1938 (with Balois). Maurice Gaud Muslim Hospital, 1939–51 (with Renaudin and Sori). Dispensary for the OCH, Ain Chock, 1949. Viret building, corner of Rue de l'Aviation Française and Rue de Briey, 1952. School, Quartier de la Gare, 1950. Villa Grades, Rue des Trois Frères Witzmann, 1950. Villa Péjouan, Sept-Merveilles development, 1952. Muslim College, Les Crêtes, 1954–55. Teachers' College, Ain Sebaa, 1954–55. Sources: AN AJ 52/594, *Construire,* LM38, *Réalisations,* Perrotte family.

Émile Perrolaz
January 7, 1908. Swiss. Began paying dues in 1939. Licensed on December 24, 1956. Built numerous villas in Anfa, in a reticent modernist style.

Apartment building for the OCH, Bourgogne, 1948. Villa Boulevard Alexandre 1er, 1951. Ronnati building, Rue du Commandant Terves, 1955. Hygiene Center, Sidi Othman, 1956. Sources: MAE, Wilaya.

Louis-Paul Pertuzio and Félix-Joseph Pertuzio
Constantine, October 13, 1889; Constantine, April 27, 1887. No degrees. Active in Casablanca beginning in 1917. Félix-Joseph paid dues in 1926. Both were licensed to practice on July 25, 1943.

Sultan's Palace, Route de Médiouna, 1917. Zagoury building, corner of Boulevard de Marseille and Rue de l'Industrie, 1922. El Hadj Omar Tazi building, intersection of Rue Maréchal, Rue Poincaré, and Avenue du Général d'Amade, 1929. Schulmann building, Rue Gay-Lussac, 1929. El Hadj Omar Tazi building, corner of Rue Galliéni and Boulevard de Paris, ca. 1930. Pappalardo building, corner of Rue Savorgnan de Brazza and Rue Gay-Lussac, 1930. J.-P. Battaglia building, Boulevard de Lorraine, ca. 1931. Roig building, Rue de Bouskoura, ca. 1931. Villa Azogué, 1935. Boarding school, corner of Boulevard Jules Grévy and Boulevard Thiers, 1947. Saint-François d'Assise compound, ca. 1950. Albdelkrim Lahlou building, Rue de Strasbourg, 1952. Sources: MAE, Wilaya, LM32, LM38, *Réalisations,* CNA.

Albert Planque
Sallaumines, November 7, 1910–September 18, 1972, Annecy. Graduate of the École Nationale Supérieure des Arts Décoratifs, Paris. Licensed on July 25, 1943. Active in Rabat. Often in partnership with Robert Deneux.

Housing Fédala, 1946 (built out of ceramic cones, with Jacques Couëlle). Amic building, 4 Rue Nationale, 1948. Villa Desmarais, corner of Boulevard Alexandre 1er and Rue Meyerbeer, 1949. Villa Diaz, Allée des Treilles, 1952. Apartment building, Rue Savorgnan de Brazza, 1952 (with Deneux). Villa Ifrah, Boulevard d'Anfa, ca. 1952. Villa Henri Terraz, Boulevard du Lido, 1953. Apartment building, Rue de Chateaubriand, 1953. Liberté cinema and department store, corner of Boulevard de Lorraine and Boulevard de la Liberté, 1954. Apartment building for the Department of Education, Rue de Jussieu, 1953–55 (with Deneux). School, Rue de l'Yser, 1955 (with Deneux). Les Hespérides building, Avenue de la République, 1955. Project for the Kahane building, Boulevard Mohamed Zerktouni, 1969. Post office, Ain Sebaa (with Rouby). Chemins de fer du Maroc vacation center, Fédala (with Deneux and Hentschel). Sources: Wilaya, AA, EM, LMM.

François Pradier
February 6, 1897. Began paying dues in 1932. Licensed on July 25, 1943. Registered in the Ordre in 1954.

Giuseppe Privitera
April 2, 1893. Began paying dues in 1920. Licensed on September 23, 1949. Registered in the Ordre in 1954.

Henri Prost
Paris, February 24, 1874–July 17, 1959. ESA; ENSBA (admission 1893; Lambert student; Grand Prix de Rome 1902). During his stay at the Villa Médicis, he surveyed and drew Hagia Sophia, Constantinople. First prize winner in the Antwerp extension competition, 1910. With Eugène Hénard, Prost developed the first extension plan for Paris, 1912. From 1914 to 1922, he directed the Protectorate Department of City Planning in Rabat. He built very few buildings in Morocco. Director of the ESA, from 1929 to 1959.

Casablanca Urban Development Plan, 1917–22. Project for the Boulevard du IVe-Zouaves, 1914. Project for the Place Administrative, 1914. Project for urban development of the Place de France, 1923. Compagnie Algérienne building, Avenue du Général d'Amade, 1928 (with Antoine Marchisio). Hydroelectric plant, Said Machou, 1927. Hôtel de la Mamounia, Marrakech, 1928 (with Antoine Marchisio). Urban development plans for Fès, Marrakech, Meknès, and Rabat, 1914–22. Plan for the Var section of the Riviera, 1923. Paris Regional Plan, 1928–34. Metz Urban Development Plan, 1928–30. Algiers Regional Plan, 1932–39. Istanbul Urban Developmen Plan, 1936–51. Sources: AN, AA; J. Marrast, *L'Œuvre d'Henri Prost: architecture et urbanisme* (Paris: Académie d'architecture, 1960).

Angelo Rechichi
June 11, 1891. Italian. Graduate of the Accademia di Brera, Milan. Active in Casablanca in 1940–41.

Apartment building for officers, Avenue Émile Zola, ca. 1940.

René Renard
December 1, 1882. Began paying dues in 1930.

Caracalle building, Boulevard d'Anfa, 1929. Sources: MAE, Wilaya.

Georges Renaudin
April 18, 1902–1994, Breuillet. ENSBA (Laloux student; received diploma). Active in Casablanca in 1932. Frequently in partnership with Georges Grel from 1935 to 1939. Licensed on July 25, 1943.

Restaurant La Réserve, Ain Diab, 1933. Apartment building, Place des Aviateurs, ca. 1935 (with Grel). Société Peralta building, corner of Avenue du Général Moinier and Boulevard du Général Gouraud, 1936 (with Grel). Villa Monaigue, corner of Boulevard Le Nôtre and Rue Mansard, 1936 (with Grel). Antituberculosis dispensary, Rue de Jussieu, 1936. Girondet service station, Rond-Point du Général d'Amade, 1936 (with Grel). Villa for the Regional Indigenous Hospital, corner of Rue de Maupassant and Rue La Boétie, 1937. School, quartier de la Gare, 1937. Apartment building, corner of Rue Jean Jaurès and Rue Rabelais, ca. 1938. Guerrero building, corner of Boulevard du Maréchal Foch and Rue de l'Aspirant Lafuente, 1938. Maarif Pediatric Nursing Center, Rue Camille Desmoulins, ca. 1938. Georges Orthlieb Antituberculosis Dispensary, Rue Jenner, ca. 1938. Park of the Colombani Hospital, ca. 1938. Maurice Gaud Muslim Hospital, 1939–51 (with Perrotte and Sori). Océania building, Place Mirabeau, 1947. Amic building, Boulevard Denfert-Rochereau, 1948. Apartment building for the OCH, corner of Boulevard des Régiments Coloniaux and Rue Maurice Leglay, Bourgogne, 1948. Customs officers' barracks, Ain Bordja, 1950. Apartment building, corner of Avenue de la République and Rue de Foucauld, 1950. Palace auto garage, 304 Boulevard de la Gare, 1952 (incomplete). Hôtel Victoria, Avenue Poeymirau, 1952. Housing, CIL, Beauséjour, 1952. Marcel Raygot garage, corner of Boulevard du Maréchal Foch and Rue de Coulanges, 1954. Customs building, Place Lyautey at Boulevard du Général Gouraud, 1955. Sources: Wilaya, *Construire*, *Réalisations*.

Xavier Rendu
Sainte-Foy les Lyon, June 10, 1880–1941. ENSBA (admission 1901; Chédanne/Bénard/Redon student; 1st class 1904; awards; received diploma 1908). Active in Paris. Architect of the La Nationale insurance company from 1920 to 1937. In partnership with R. Ponsard.

La Nationale building, Avenue Mers Sultan and Avenue Général d'Amade, 1930–31. Sources: AN AJ 52/410, Sadg, Wilaya, Delaire.

Libero Ricci
March 30, 1904. Italian. Graduate of the Facoltà d'Ingeniaria in Rome. Licensed on October 10, 1949. Registered in the Ordre in 1954.

Ricci building, Rue Dupleix, 1938. Villa S. Benchaya, corner of Avenue de Londres and Rue de Castelnau, 1950. Sources: Wilaya.

Armand Rosario Riccignuolo
June 6, 1910. Italian. Began paying dues in 1930. Authorized to practice on November 10, 1949. Frequently in partnership with Dominique Basciano.

Todaro building, corner of Rue de Commercy and Rue Damrémont, 1939. Moretti-Milone building, Place de Verdun, 1940. Lignan et Azzaro building, Rue Dupleix, 1941. Casaire building, Rue Blaise Pascal, 1942. Project for the Moretti-Milone building, Boulevard d'Anfa, 1942. Néckerlé building, corner of Boulevard de la Gironde and Rue de la Dordogne, 1948. Sources: MAE, Wilaya.

Louis Riou
Brasparts, April 18, 1919. ENSBA (EBA Rennes; admission 1943; Perret student; 1st class 1946; awards; received diploma 1949). Authorized to practice on May 25, 1951. Active in Casablanca until 1998. Built numerous office and hospital buildings, as well as villas.

Villa Jean and Luce Senouf, Anfa, 1963–64. Sources: AN AJ 52/1302, interview.

Jean-François Robert
In partnership with R. Jeanin.

Renault building, corner of Rue Lapérouse and Rue Savorgnan de Brazza, ca. 1955. Hotel, corner of Boulevard de la Liberté and Rue d'Épinal, 1952. Source: Wilaya.

Marcel Rousseau
August 12, 1908. Began paying dues in 1927. Registered in the Ordre in 1941.

Apartment building for the Habitat Israélite, Boulevard Moulay-Youssef, 1950 (with Aroutcheff). Eight apartment buildings for the Habitat Israélite, Boulevard Calmel, 1951 (with Aroutcheff, Lucaud, Morandi, and Zéligson). Sources: MAE, *Construire*.

Jean Sachs
Paris, August 26, 1911. ENSBA (admission 1931; Pontrémoli/Bigot student; 1st class 1932; awards; 1st Second Grand Prix de Rome 1939; received diploma 1941). Licensed on August 31, 1945. In partnership with Brion during the 1950s. He took over Brion's office in 1961. Source: AN AJ52/1303.

Ignace Sansone
June 15, 1905. No degree. Began paying dues in 1926. Authorized to practice July 25, 1943. In partnership with Paul Busuttil until 1939.

Corcos Synagogue, corner of Rue Capitaine Ihler and Rue de Mazagan, 1928. Sansone building, corner of Boulevard de Lorraine and Rue de Verdun, 1929. Sources: MAE, Wilaya.

René Schmitt
Basel, September 28, 1912. ENSBA (admission 1934; Pontrémoli/Leconte student; 1st class 1937; received diploma 1942). Licensed on December 24, 1946. Registered in the Ordre in 1954. In partnership with Bailly and Balois.

Bialong et Luxia building, Avenue du Général d'Amade and Avenue de Longwy, 1951 (with Bailly). Sources: AN AJ52/1303, AF.

Maxime Siroux
ENSBA. Licensed on February 12, 1949. Registered in the Ordre in 1954.

Maurice Sori
Lille, October 10, 1900–ca. 1993, Casablanca. ENSBA (EBA Lille; admission 1928; Bigot student; 1st class 1925; awards; received diploma 1930). Licensed on July 25, 1943. Registered in the Ordre in 1943.

Central Police Station, Boulevard Jean Courtin, 1936–39. Muslim dwellings, new medina extension, 1938. Maurice Gaud Muslim Hospital, 1939–51 (with Perrotte and Renaudin). Villa Sori, 10 Rue Ambroise Thomas. Villa Botel, Boulevard du Lido at Route d'Ain Diab, 1948 (with Bouchery). Apartment building for the OCH, Rue Bouardel, 1948 (with Bouchery). Compagnie Marocaine des Carburants offices, Rue Jouandeau, 1948. Apartment building, Place de l'Amiral Senès at Avenue de la République, 1950. Trade unions headquarters, Avenue Pasteur, 1951. SMCM building, corner of Boulevard du IVe-Zouaves and Rue de Foucauld, 1953. Fire station, Ain Sebaa, 1955. Sources: AN AJ 52/598, MAE, Wilaya, AA, AF, *Réalisations*.

André M. Studer
Versailles, December 9, 1926. Swiss. Studied at Solothurn, and later at the ETH Zurich (from 1945 to 1951) where he met Jean Hentsch. Worked for Le Corbusier in 1948. During a 1952 trip to the United States, he met Frank Lloyd Wright and worked as a draftsman for Oscar Storonov. Became Sigfried Giedion's assistant. From 1954 to 1956 worked in Casablanca, where he designed projects marketed by Hentsch. Upon returning to Zurich, he worked for Haefeli, Moser, as well as Steiger, for whom he designed and built the Hochhaus zur Palme (1959–63). Working independently, he produced a large number of houses and small apartment buildings revealing an acute sensitivity to site.

Project for "Pyramidal Moroccan Dwellings" for the Groupement Foncier Marocain, Sidi Othman, 1954. "Moroccan Housing" development for the Groupement Foncier Marocain, Sidi Othman, 1953–55 (construction supervised by Jacques Zbinden). Architect's house, Gockhausen/Zurich, 1958. Ape habitat, Zurich Zoo, 1960. Center for religious education, Edlibach, 1965. Hospital for the Caritas organization, Bethlehem, 1961–67. Sources: Wilaya, AA, c.v., interview.

Joseph and Élias Suraqui
Oran, January 15, 1893–March 25, 1975, Paris; and Algiers, September 17, 1893–January 24, 1977, Lyons. Architects without degrees, members of the Société Professionnelle des Architectes Français. Joseph was a surveyor and held a diploma from the Union Professionnelle des Bâtiments de France. Active in Casablanca in 1923. Began paying dues in 1924. Authorized to practice on July 25, 1943. In partnership until 1950.

Gallinari building, corner of Boulevard de la Gare and Rue Roget, 1924. Villa Violetta, Boulevard Moulay-Youssef, ca. 1929. M. G. Braunschwig building, Boulevard de la Gare, 1927 (with D. Gimenez). Hassan et de la Salle building, Square Louis Gentil, at Avenue du Général Moinier and Rue Novo, 1928. Ernest de la Salle building, corner of Rue d'Alger and Rue de Verdun, 1928. Villa Salomon Kagan, corner of Rue Galliéni and Boulevard d'Anfa, 1928. Villa Moses Benzaquen, Boulevard Moulay-Youssef, 1928. Tolédano building, Boulevard de Paris, 1928. Braunschwig Fils docks, port of Casablanca, ca. 1928. Mordojay Cohen Mansion, Place de la Fraternité at Boulevard Moulay-Youssef, 1929. Coriat building, 58 Rue de l'Aviateur Coli, 1929. Benchetrit building, corner of place de Verdun and Rue du Capitaine Hervé, 1929. Ettedgui building, Rue de l'Industrie, 1929. Meffre building, Rue du Docteur Mauchamp, 1929. Lazare Hazan building, Rue du Docteur Mauchamp, 1930. Suraqui Frères building, Rue Chevandier de Valdrôme, 1930. Narcisse Leven School, 85 Boulevard Moulay-Youssef, ca. 1930. Villa Tolédano, Rue Régnier, 1931. Ernest de la Salle building, Rue Blaise Pascal. I., P., and M. Tolédano building, intersection of Avenue du Général d'Amade, Rue du Capitaine Maréchal, and Rue Chevandier de Valdrôme, 1930. Salomon Benalal building, intersection of Avenue Général Drude, Rue Védrines, and Rue Colbert, 1931. Moses Pinto building, corner of Place de Verdun and Rue Lacépède, 1931. Moses Pinto mansion, Place de la

Fraternité at Boulevard du Général Gouraud. Tabet building, corner of Boulevard de Paris and Rue Chevandier-de-Valdrôme. Apartment building, 99 Avenue Mers Sultan at Rue Condorcet. Apartment building, 164 Avenue Mers Sultan at Rue Condorcet.

After 1950, Joseph built: Apartment building for the OCH Européen, corner of Boulevard Joffre and Boulevard des Régiments Coloniaux, 1946. Apartment building for the OCH européen, corner of Rue Buffon and Rue Malherbe, 1952. Casa Ameublement building, Boulevard Leclerc, 1952. Apartment building, corner of Rue de l'Amiral Courbet and Rue Dupleix, 1954. Two apartment buildings for the Société Immobilière de l'Habitat Israélite (SIHIC), Boulevard Joffre and Boulevard des Mutilés, at Rue Berger and Rue Delavigne, 1954. Eight apartment buildings for the CIFM, corner of Rue Émile Augier and Rue La Bruyère, 1954. Villa Geidel, Boulevard Alexandre 1er, 1954. Jewish school, Boulevard Calmel, 1955. Élias builds: school, Boulevard des Régiments Coloniaux, 1950. Sources: Wilaya, Bâtir, CNA, Construire, EM, LM32, LM38, Réalisations, Suraqui family.

Vladimir Tamikovsky
Licensed on July 25, 1943. Registered in the Ordre in 1954.

Henri Tastemain
Paris, June 20, 1922. ENSBA (admission 1941; Larrieu/Perret student; 1st class 1945; awards and prizes; Prix de Rome finalist; received diploma 1950). Worked in the Department of Urban Planning in Rabat, 1948–49. Collaborated with Chemineau, in Rabat, 1949–50. Authorized to practice May 7, 1951. In partnership with Éliane Castelnau, Le Mont-Dore, 1923 (Perret student, received diploma 1954).

Project for Lyautey High School (with Zevaco and Azagury). Office National du Thé factory, c. 1958 (with Azagury and Lévy). Apartment building, Agadir, 1963. Journalism Institute, Rabat, 1980. Vacation village, M'Diq, 1971. University medical center, Rabat, 1972–80. Student residences, Rabat. National Agronomy Institute, Rabat. Airport, Tangiers. Sources: AN AJ 52/1304; Henri Tastemain, Éliane Castelnau, Constructions réalisées au Maroc de 1950 à 1964 (Rabat: published by the architects, 1964).

Ulysse Tonci
No degree. Likely the first European architect to settle in Casablanca.

Villa, 1913. Model of Casablanca, Exposition Franco-Marocaine, 1915. Paolo Lombardo house, 1917. Sources: MAE; L'Architecture usuelle, 1913.

Paul Tournon
Marseilles, February 19, 1881–December 22, 1964. ENSBA (admission 1901; Scellier de Gisors/Bernier student; 1st class 1903; numerous prizes; Second Grand Prix de Rome 1911; received diploma 1912). Professor at the ENSBA; he was its director during the Occupation. Vice-president of the governing body of the Ordre des Architectes. Member of the Institut. President of the Paris Circle of Catholics in the Fine Arts.

Cathedral (Church of Sacré-Cœur), corner of Rue d'Alger and Boulevard du Général Gouraud, 1930–52. Sources: AN AJ 52/436, Sadg, Delaire.

Albert Urban
ENSBA. Licensed on November 27, 1953. Registered in the Ordre in 1954.

M. (also R. L.) Vandelle
Architect and interior designer.

Abitabile building, traverse de Médiouna, 1922. Three artist studios, Place de Verdun, ca. 1930. Project for a synagogue, Rue Lacépède, 1931. Hôtel Guynemer, Rue Guynemer, ca. 1932. Sources: Wilaya, Descamps.

Georges Vargues
October 6, 1905. Dues paying since 1933. Licensed on July 25, 1943. Registered in the Ordre in 1954.

Housing and boutiques for the OCH, Ain Chock, beginning in 1949. Source: Wilaya.

Georges Vimort
Saint-Étienne, October 4, 1876–January 4, 1962. ENSBA (admission 1899; Paulin student; 1st class 1904; awards; received diploma 1906). Established in Paris. Worked in the Casablanca Region Architecture Service from 1917 to 1920. Architect of the École Coloniale in Paris from 1933 to 1942.

E. Ettedgui building, 104 Boulevard de Paris, at Rue de Bouskoura, 1919. Bank of West Africa headquarters and housing, Place Edmond Doutté, 1919. Société des Immeubles Urbains (Cercle de l'Union) building, Rue Chevandier de Valdrôme, 1920. Gratry offices and warehouse, 65, Rue des Ouled Ziane, ca. 1920 (with Louis Pertuzio). Project for the west side of Place de France, 1923. Sources: AN AJ 52/412, SADG, Wilaya, Delaire, CM.

Marcel Viremouneix
Château-Lévèque, August 2, 1912. ENSBA (EBA Bordeaux; admission 1932). Licensed on May 14, 1952. Registered in the Ordre in 1954.

Armin Weilenmann
January 22, 1907. Swiss. Graduate of the Technicum, Winterthur. Began paying dues in 1934. Licensed on July 25, 1943. Registered in the Ordre in 1954. Built a considerable number of houses in Derbs Carlotti, San Francisco, and Eskénazy.

Benjelloun brothers' twin villas, Boulevard Victor Hugo, 1936. Zagoury Community Hall, Rue Lacépède, 1937. Eskénazy spinning and weaving mill, corner of Rue de Sauternes and Rue d'Hendaye, 1942. Villa Mohammed Laraki, Le Polo, 1945. OCH building, Rue Bouardel, Bourgogne, 1948. Zagoury building, Rue Lacépède, 1949. Société Financière Franco-Chérifienne building, corner of Avenue du Général Moinier and Rue Murdoch, 1950. Société Immobilière Védrines building, Rue de l'Aviateur Védrines, 1952. Villa Weilenmann, Rue de Salins, 1953. Société Immobilière Suisse building, corner of Rue Félix and Rue Max Guedj, 1953 (with Paccanari). Anfa II development, Rue Yves de Gueux, 1954, (project architects A. Bordigoni and R. Fleury). Five buildings for the Groupe Immobilier Anfa, Boulevard Paul Doumer, 1954. Sources: MAE, Wilaya.

Charles Wolff
Active in Casablanca in 1913. Produced numerous early small projects, especially in the Maarif.

S. Coriat development, Rue des Ouled Harriz, 1918. Villa Guimont, Rue Galilée, 1918. José Simes House, Maarif, 1918. Six villas for Abdallah Hassan, Route de Mazagan, 1919. Six houses for Dr. Raoul, Boulevard Circulaire, 1920. Source: Wilaya.

Roger Yvetot
September 3, 1910. Licensed on December 24, 1946. Registered in the Ordre in 1954.

Dimitri Zaleski
September 23, 1893. Polish. Graduate of the Warsaw Polytechnic. Began paying dues in 1933. Licensed on July 25, 1943.

Michel Parra building, Rue de Tours, 1935. Villa Perez, corner of Avenue du Général d'Amade and Rue Réaumur, 1937. Lévy-Soussan and Samson Lévy mansions, Rue Murdoch, 1942. OCH building, Rue de Catalogne, Bourgogne, 1948. Lamira building, Boulevard du Général Gouraud, 1948. Zaleski building, Rue de Saint-Quentin, 1953. Sources: MAE, Wilaya.

Arnold Zarb
Graduate of ESA, Paris. Registered in the Ordre in 1954. Licensed to practice on November 28, 1953.

Church, corner of Rue des Roses and Rue des Cyclamen, Beauséjour, ca. 1955.

Louis Zéligson
Baku, February 14, 1900–July 26, 1966, Casablanca. Began paying dues in 1932. Licensed on July 25, 1943. Built many villas in Anfa, through the 1960s.

Villa Ettedgui, Rue de Douaumont, 1937. Villa May Zukar, Rue Boileau, 1937. Mohammed Ayoub house, corner of Boulevard du Maréchal Foch and Rue d'Avignon, 1937. Chemical laboratory, Rue Murdoch, 1946. Laredo building, Rue La Fayette, 1946. Apartment building for the OCH, Rue Sauvage, 1948. Senouf studio apartments, corner of Rue de Lille and Rue de Provins, 1948. Villa Vultaggio, Rue des Tabors, 1950. Apartment building for the Habitat israélite, corner of Boulevard de la Corniche and Boulevard Calmel, El Hank, 1950. Eight apartment buildings for the Habitat Israélite, corner of Boulevard Moulay-Youssef and Boulevard Calmel, 1951 (with Aroutcheff, Lucaud, Morandi, and Rousseau). Société Immobilière Mari building, corner of Boulevard de la Gare and Rue de l'Amiral Courbet, 1954 (with Lévy). Muslim school, Souk el Arba, ca. 1954. Ben Aomar (also called Ryad) cinema, Avenue Abdelmoumen, 1960. Sources: MAE, Wilaya, Construire, AF.

Jean-François Zevaco
Casablanca, August 8, 1916. ENSBA (1st in the 1937 admission; Pontrémoli/Leconte student; 1st class 1945; awards and prizes; received diploma 1945). Spent the war years in Marseilles, in Beaudouin's studio. Licensed on April 2, 1947. Member of the UAM. In partnership with Paul Messina until 1954.

Villa Sami Suissa (called La Pagode), Boulevard Alexandre 1er, 1947–49 . Villa Gilardi, Rue d'Auteuil, 1948–49. SCI du Centre building, Rue Poincaré, 1948. Villa Landau, Rue de Douaumont, 1948–50. Villa Rességnier, Rue de Boulogne, 1950. Rosilio service station, corner of Rue Claude Lorrain and Rue Régnault, 1951. SIOM building and garage, Rue de Mareuil, 1950 (not completed). Vincent Timsit factory, Route de Rabat, 1952. Villa Robic, CIL Beauséjour, 1952 (with Dominique Basciano). Villa Craig, Rue d'Auteuil, 1953. Reeducation center, Tit Mellil, 1953–60. Tit Mellil airport, 1951–53 (with Dominique Basciano). Post office, Ain Chock, ca. 1955. Project for a youth center, Derb Ghallef, 1955. Project for a womens' education center, Carrières centrales, 1955. Georges Bizet School, 1962. Théophile Gautier school, 1960–63. Automobile showroom, Avenue des Forces Armées Royales, 1968. Food market, Rue d'Agadir, 1972–75. Villa Sebti, 1972–74. New pedestrian layout of Rue du Prince Moulay Abdallah, 1974. Place des Nations-Unies improvements, ca. 1974. Villa Zevaco, Rue H, Ain Diab, 1975–79. Villa Zniber, Anfa, 1990. Service station, Marrakech, 1958. Courthouse, Mohammedia, 1958–62. Affordable housing, Marrakech, 1959–61. Post office, Agadir, 1963. Sources: AN AJ 52/130, Wilaya, AA, interviews; Michel Ragon, Henri Tastemain, Zevaco (Paris: Éditions Cercle d'Art, 1999).

Abbreviations and Institutional Acronyms

AA: *L'Architecture d'aujourd'hui*

AF: *L'Architecture française*

AM: *L'Architecture marocaine*

AN: Archives nationales

ATBAT: Atelier des bâtisseurs

BDIM: *Bulletin d'informations du Maroc*

BESM: *Bulletin économique et social du Maroc*

BGA: Bibliothèque générale et archives, Rabat

BMO: *Bulletin municipal officiel*

BNCI: Banque nationale pour le commerce et l'industry

BO: *Bulletin officiel du Protectorat chérifien*

CCI: Chambre de commerce et d'industrie

CDRG: Cabinet du délégué à la Résidence générale

CFM: Chemins de fer marocains

C.I.A.M.: Congrès internationaux d'architecture moderne

C.I.F.M.: Compagnie immobilière franco-marocaine

C.I.L.: Comité interprofessionel du logement

C.I.L.M.: Comité interprofessionel du logement au Maroc

CM: Commission municipale de Casablanca

CNA: *Chantiers nord-africains*

CRU: Centre de recherche d'urbanisme

CSTB: Centre scientifique et technique du bâtiment

Cosuma or Cosumar: Compagnie sucrière marocaine

CTM: Compagnie de transports marocains

CUH: Circonscription de l'urbanisme et de l'habitat

c.v.: curriculum vitae

Delaire: Edmond Delaire, David de Penanrun, and Louis Roux. *Les Architectes élèves de l'École des Beaux-Arts*, 2nd ed. Paris: Librairie de la Construction moderne, 1907.

Descamps: Henri Descamps. *L'Architecture moderne au Maroc.* Paris: Librairie de la Construction moderne, 1930.

DRG: Délégué à la Résidence générale

DTP: Direction (directeur) des travaux publics

DUP: Déclaration d'utilité publique

EM: *L'Entreprise au Maroc*

ENSBA: École nationale supérieure des beaux-arts

ESA: École spéciale d'architecture

GAMMA: Groupe d'architectes modernes marocains

gta/ETH Zurich: Institut für Geschichte und Theorie der Architektur, Eidgenössische Technische Hochschule, Zurich

H.B.M.: Habitations à bon marché

IFA: Institut français d'architecture

ITBTP: Institut du bâtiment et des travaux publics

LM32: *Le Maroc en 1932*

LM38: *Le Maroc en 1938*

LM54: *Le Maroc en 1954*

LMM: *Le Maroc moderne*

MAE: Centre d'archives du Ministère des affaires étrangères, Nantes

MH: Ministère de l'habitat, Rabat

OCH: Office chérifien de l'habitat

OCHE: Office chérifien de l'habitat européen

O.C.L.M.: Office chérifien des logements militaires

O.T.H.: Omnium technique du bâtiment

Sadg: Société des architectes diplômés par le gouvernement

SGP: Secrétariat général du Protectorat

SIHIC: Société immobilière de l'habitat israélite de Casablanca

SMD: Société marocaine de distribution

Soblanca: Société générale pour le développement de Casablanca

Soceca: Société chérifienne de la cité ouvrière indigène de Casabalanca

Sucom: Société suisse de construction du Maroc

SUMICA: Société universelle de mines, industrie, commerce et agriculture

U.A.M.: Union des artistes modernes

U.S.A.F.: United States Air Force

Wilaya: Wilaya du Grand Casablanca

Glossary of Moroccan Terms

The following terms are identified in the text in *italics*, followed by an asterisk.

Bab: gate

bît: room

bît ed-diaf: reception room, guest room

Casbah: fortress or fortified house

Chaouïa: the region in which Casablanca is located

dahir: decree

Dar-el-Makhzen: seat of the royal administration

derb: quarter, or village; often used in a pejorative way by the administration and the press.

Derb el-Baladiya: municipal housing

Dhimma: status of non-Muslim minorities

Dhimmi: individual protected under the terms of Dhimma status

Fassi: resident of Fès, or from a family originating in Fès

fonduk: warehouse

habous: possession(s) bequeathed to a foundation for religious or philanthropic purposes

harim: unbuildable land lot

jama: mosque

jutiya: flea market

kanoun: brazier

kechla: barracks

khalifa: deputy to a Pacha

kissaria: cloth market

m'allem (plural: m'allemîn): master artisan

Makhzen: royal administration

medina: city, town

mellah: Jewish quarter

Mokhazni: agent of the Makhzen

noualla: hut of branches or reeds

oued: river

qaida: tradition

qubba: cupola surmounting the tomb of a holy man

rah'ba: barracks

R'bati: resident of Rabat, or from a family originating in Rabat

ryad: enclosed garden with a longitudinal water pool

Soussi: resident of the Sous valley, or from a family originating in the Sous valley

sqala: battery of artillery

tenkira (plural: tnaker): hut, shanty

zellij or zelliges: cut ceramic tiles

zriba: enclosed land

Index

Buildings

Page numbers in italics refer to illustrations.

air terminal, Tit-Mellil, 428, *429*, 431
Allée, 193
Alliance Israélite Universelle, 32, 46
Anfa International Club, 32
Aquarium and Sea Fishing Institute, *430*
Arsène building type, *347*, 348
Artaud, 143
arts center, civic, 436, *437*, 445
Asayag, 180, *181–83*, *196*, *197*, 202
Assurances Générales Incendie, *387*, 387–88, *391*
Atlanta, 383, *385*
Auto-Hall garage, 252, *253*, 433

Bab el-Kebir (Bab es-Souk), 28, *29*, 30, 32, 43–44, 48
Bab el-Mersa, 28, 30, 34, *35*
Bab Marrakech, 28, 43, *280*, 283
Bab sidi Belyout (Bab ej-Jdid), 28, 30
Baille, *187*
Bank of the British West Indies, *91*
Banon, *145*, *200*
Banque Commerciale du Maroc, *212*, 255, *256*
Banque de l'Afrique Occidentale, 255
Banque d'État du Maroc, *61*, *115*, 256
Banque Nationale pour le Commerce et l'Industrie (BNCI), *283*, *423*, 424
Barizon, *60*
barracks, housing, 227, *227*
Basile building type, *347*–48, *348*, *351*
Belvisi, *145*
Bendahan, 123, 168, *186–87*, *187*, *196*, 441
Bennarosh, 160
Bessonneau, *88*, *118*, 119, *146*
Blondin Bridge, 45
BNCI (Banque Nationale pour le Commerce et l'Industrie), *283*, *423*, 424
Boyer (Les Studios), 190–92, *191*, 201, 201–2, *270*, 283
Boyer project (unbuilt), *132*
Brami, 381, *382–83*
Braunschwig, *145*
Brazza complex (Fraternelle du Nord), *178*, 180, *184*, 184, *279*
Bridge, Blondin, 45
bus station, Compagnie des Transports Marocains (CTM), 427, *428*

cafés, cabarets, and brasseries
    Bijou-Concert, *40*
    Brik's Bar, *266*
    Café des Roches, *262*
    Café du Commerce, 46–*47*, 48, *62*
    Eden-concert, *40*
    Eldorado music hall, *72*
    Excelsior Hotel, *62*
    Glacier, *44*
    Grand Café de Paris, *46*
    Guingette Fleurie, *420*
    Jardin d'éte, *420*
    La Coupole brasserie, 255
    La Réserve restaurant, *265*, *412*, *415*, *416*, *419*
    Le Doge, *413*
    Lido, *413*, *413*
    Moulin-Rouge, *40*
    Parc Beaulieu, *420*
    Parisiana-Bar, *40*
    Potinière, *266*
    Roi de la bière, *38*
caserne, la, 227, *227*
cathedral, Sacré Cœur, 108–9, *108–9*
Cerdan grand stadium, *437*
Chaux et Ciments, *271*, 345n
Christina building type, *351*
churches, 108–9, *108–9*, *176*, 432, *432*

Citroën garage, 252, *253*, 433
city hall (Hôtel de Ville), 104, *105*, 111
civic arts center, 436, *437*, 445
clock tower (Tour de l'Horloge), 43, *43*, 48, *61*, 110, *117*, *277*
Compagnie Algérienne, 123, *162*, *168*, 255, *256*
Compagnie des Transports Marocains (CTM), *115*
Compagnie des Transports Marocains (CTM) bus station, 427, *428*
Compagnie Générale Transatlantique, *166*
Coriat, *142*
Cosyra, *380*, *381*
customs warehouses, *52*
cycling stadium, 266

Dar-el-Makhzen, 28, 32
Dayan, *193*
Décrion, *199*
Delande terminal, *126*
Delpit terminal, *126*
department stores
    Galerie Lafayette (formerly Paris-Maroc), *10*, 13, 135, *380*, *441*, 445
    Grands Bazars Marocains, *119*
    Magasins Paris-Maroc (later Galeries Layfayette), *50*, 60–63, *61–63*, 67, *114*, 120, *168*, 255, *284*
    Monoprix, 436
depot, freight haulage, 431
Domerc, 193, *193*

electric transformer unit, *427*
El Glaoui, 137, *138*
El Hank Lighthouse, 111, *111*, 329, 358, 363, *417*
El-Kebir Mosque, 23, 30, *31*
Emile building type, 348
er-Rah'ba (grain market), 30
Escot, 164, *165*
Ettedgui and Shriqui, 164, *165*
Ettedgui (Balois and Perrotte), *192*
Ettedgui synagogue, *249*
Eyraud, 202, *202*

factories
    Bata, 311
    canning, 126
    carpet, 32
    cement, *307*
    Chaux et Ciments, *271*, 345n
    Grand Socco, 44
    Lafarge cement works, *319*
    late nineteenth-century, 32
    Magnier, 60
    Poliet et Chausson, *244*
    Roches Noires, 60, 239, *242*, 244
    sugar, *307*
Faucherot, 197–98
Fernau garden, 34
Fiat garage, 252
fonduks, 32, 44, 55, 76, 93, 113, 216, 220, 326
forts, 38, *39*
Fraternelle du Nord (Brazza complex), *178*, 180, *184*, *184*, *279*
freight haulage depot, 431

Galerie Lafayette. *See* department stores
Gallinari, *143*
Gallinari (Atlanta), 383, *385*
garages, 79
    Auto-Hall, 252, *253*, 433
    Citroën, 252, *253*, 433
    Fiat, 252
    Marcel Raygot, *434*
    New Yorker, *434*
    Volvo, 8, 433, *433*
    Volvo-Singer, *428*
gardens
    Fernau, 34
    Lamb, 34
    Place de France, *121*
    public garden, 41, *41*, 48
    ville nouvelle, 56
gas station, Ain Sebaa, *434*, 434
grain market (er-Rah'ba), 30
Grand Bon Marché, 164, *166*
Grand colonial villa, 58, *59*
Grands Bazars Marocains, *119*
Grand Socco building, *145*
Grand Socco Factory, 44
Guedj, *144*
Hassan and De la Salle, 164, *164*
Hespérides, 427, *427*
Hôtel de Ville (City Hall), 104, *105*, 111
hotels
    Casablanca (Hyatt), 439

Central, 56
El Mansour, *426–27*, 427
Excelsior, 60–62, *61–62*, *115*, *117*, 120, 169
Guynemer, *174*
Hôtel d'Anfa, *258*, *271*, 276
Marhaba (Paquet), *426*, 427
Palace, 49
Plaza, *277*
Rue de la Douane, 93
Volubilis, 255
houses. *See also* villas
    Ansado-Gautier-Lapeen, *58*, 59
    Banon, 56
    Benjelloun, *33*
    Boyer, *160*
    Coldefy, *398*
    Delaporte, 154, *155*
    Dinouri, *222*
    Ficke, *59*, 92–93
    Ifergan, 56
    Les Tourelles, *148*
    Lièvre, 156
    Mendeli Moulay Thami, *207*
    Rue 15, Bousbir, *55*
    Vieljeux (Saadia), 407, *409*, 410
    ville nouvelle, 56, *57*
    Wates, *290*, 365
    Xantopoulos, 32
housing developments. *See* Index of Places, Streets, and Districts

Ihler Fort, 38, *39*
IMCAMA, *134*, *136*, *146*, *270*

Jama-el-kebir (mosque), 23, 30, *31*
Jama-ould-el-hamra (mosque), 30
Jutiya (flea market), 30, *30*

Kechla (army barracks), 30
Kergomard Orphanage, 93
kissaria (cloth market), 32, 137, 215, 220, 242, 326

la caserne, 227, *227*
Lafarge cement works, *319*
Lafitte, 180
Lamb garden, 34
law courts, 98, *99*, *102*, *163*
law courts, Muslim (Mahakma), 299, *299*
Lebascle, 199, *199*
Les Studios, 190–92, *191*, 201, 201–2, *270*, 283
Lévi and Charbon, *136*, 137, *183*
Lévy-Bendayan, 8, 140–42, *141*, 202
Liberté, *385*, 385–87, *389*
lighthouse, El Hank, 111, *111*
Liscia, *176*, 190, *190*, *196*, 197

Magasins Paris-Maroc. *See* department stores
Magne-Rouchaud, 144, *145*
Magnier factory, 60
Mahakma (Muslim Law Courts), 299, *299*
Makhzen prison, 108
marabouts
    Sidi Abderrahman, 415
    Sidi Belyout, 30, 54, 116
Maret, *173*
markets
    central, *67*, 68, 215–16
    er-Rah'ba (grain market), 30
    fish, 126
    indoor (Ain Chock), 298
    Jutiya (flea market), 30
    kissaria (cloth market), 32, 137, 215, 220, 242, 326
    main food market (Perrotte), 258
    new indigenous town, 218, *219*
    Wadi Bouskoura, 30
    wholesale, *259*
Mas, 44
merchant navy school, 431
military administration building, 98
Military Circle, 98, *99*
mills. *See* factories
Monoprix, 436
Moretti-Milone, *179*, 187–88, *188*, *196*, *277*, *283*, 283–84, 385
mosques
    El-Kebir, 23, 30, *31*
    Ould-el-Hamra, 30, 215
movie theaters. *See* theaters

Nationale, *178*, 185, 185–86, *197*, 197
New Yorker garage, *434*
Nid d'Abeille ("beehive"), *332–33*, 335, *335*, 339, *350*, 351
nightclubs. *See* cafés, cabarets, and brasseries

Notre-Dame-de-Lourdes Church, 432, *432*
Notre-Dame des Archanges Church, *176*
nouallas (straw huts), 28, *28*, 90, 233, 236, 240, 243, 292, 331, *331*
Noulellis, 164, *165*

Océania, 387
Océanic, 427
OCH (Office Chérifien de l'Habitat), *367*, *369*
Orphanage, Pauline Kergomard, 93
Ould-el-Hamra mosque, 30, 215

Palace, Sultan's, *158*, 218, *218*, 225
Palais Mirabeau, *386*, 387
Pappalardo, 137
Paris-Maroc. *See* department stores
Parrain, *140*
Pauline Kergomard Orphanage, 93
Petit Marocain headquarters, 256
physical therapy center (Tit Mellil), *421*, *429*, 431
Pinto, 193
Planque, 427
police station, 258, *259*
Poliet et Chausson factory, 244
pool clubs
    Acapulco, *412*, 413, *419*, 419
    Kon-Tiki, *412*, 413, *416*, 419
    Lido, 266, *266*, *412*, 413–14, *417*, 420
    Miami, *412*, 413, 415, *416*, 417, 435
    Oceanic, *412*, 420
    Orthlieb (public), 265–67, *267–68*, 358, *412*
    Sun-Beach (Club des Clubs de Casablanca), *412*, 413, *414–15*, 415, *416*, 418–19
    Tahiti-Plage, 8, *412*, 413, *417–19*, 417–19
    Tropicana, *412*, 419
Porphyre building type, *347*
Portuguese Prison, *23*, *107*
post office, 98, *100–101*, 252
power station, Roche Noires, 326
prisons
    Makhzen, 108
    Portuguese, *23*, *107*
Provost Fort, 38, *39*, 216
public garden, 41, *41*, 48

qubba, Sidi Kairouâni, *31*

railroad stations, 48, 116, 118
    Casablanca-Port, 424
    Casablanca-Voyageurs, 8, 251–52, *252*
    Central, 424
    New Medina, 284
Raygot garage, *434*
restaurants. *See* cafés, cabarets, and brasseries
Roig, 164, *165*
Romandie, 388, *388*

Sacré Cœur cathedral, 108–9, *108–9*
Saint Antoine Church, 432
Saint Paul Church, 432, *432*
Saturne, 427
schools
    Ain Chock, 298
    Bournazel, 424, *425*
    experimental (by Bodiansky), *318*
    high school (Avenue Mers-Sultan), 257
    Italian, 257–58, *259*
    La Villette, 424
    Longchamp, 424, *424–25*
    Mission Française, 438
    Rond-Point de l'Europe, *424*
    Spanish Franciscan, 32
Sémiramis, *333–34*, 335, 339, *350*, 351
Shell building, 257, *258*, *279*
Sidi Abderrahman marabout, 415
Sidi Belyout marabout, 30, 54, 116
Sidi Kairouâni Qubba, *31*
SIF, 194, *195*
silo, storage (port), 126, *127*
SIMAF, 173, *173*
slaughterhouses, 244, 251, *252*
Société Centrale Immobilière, *176*, 190, *190*, *196*, 197
Société Civile Immobilière du Centre, 428, *428*
Société d'Assurances Générales, *387*, 387–88, *391*
Société Immobilière de l'Habitat Israélite de Casablanca (SIHIC), 360–61, *361*
Société Urbaine Marocaine, *143*, 143–44
Socifrance, 123, *168*, 188–90, *189*, *283*
Socony Vacuum, *430*, 431
Spanish Circle, 32
Spanish Franciscan school, 32
stadium, cycling, 266
stadium, Marcel Cerdan grand, *437*

stadium, sports, 388
Studios, The, 190–92, *191*, *201*, 201–2, *270*, 283
Sultan's Palace, *158*, 218, *218*, 225
SUMICA, 139, *139*
Suraqui, 213
swimming pools. *See* pool clubs
synagogues, 28, *249*
Syndicat Immobilier de Casablanca, 135, *135*

Tazi, 139, *139*, *168*
Tea Office factory, 431, *431*
Terralia (unbuilt), *200*
theaters. *See also* cafés, cabarets, and brasseries
    ABC, 435
    Apollo, 435
    Atlas, 435
    civic, 436, *437*, 445
    Colisée, 142, 255, 435
    Eldorado, 90
    Empire, 255, 435
    Familia, 435
    Liberté, 435–36, *436*
    Lutétia, 435, *435*
    Lux, 190, 435
    Lynx, 435, *435*
    Mondial, 435
    Monte-Carlo, 435
    Opéra-Comique, 90
    Place Adminstrative, 96, *99*
    Régent, 255, 435
    Rex, 435
    Rialto, 251, *254*, 255, 275, 435
    Rif, 435
    Temporary, 103, *103*
    Théâtre des Champs-Elysées, 63, 65
    Toledano, 144, 197
    Triomphe, 255, 435, 436
    Vox, *10*, 255, *255*, 435, 436, 445
Tit-Mellil air terminal, 428, *429*, 431
tobacco plant, 32
Toledano, 144, 197
trade-fair hall, 432
Tragin, 428
Trèfle building type, 339

Ugazio, *161*

Vigie Marocaine headquarters, 256
villas, 14, 149–59, 203–11, 392–411. *See also* houses
    Andaloussi, 206, *207*
    Assaban, 155–56, *157*
    Azagury, 405, *406*, 407
    Bénazéraf, 151, *152*, *153*
    Bensimhon, *209*, 210
    Bonan, 154–55
    Boulevard Moulay-Youssef, 123
    Brandt development, 93n
    Cadet, 410, *410*
    Cohen, 154, *176*, 203, *203*
    Craig, *397*
    Dar es-Saada, 210, *211*, *277*
    Dar Lugda, 398, *398*
    Dr. B., 410, *411*
    El Mokri, *149*, *150*, 151, *160*
    F., *204*
    Ficke, 93
    Girard, *404*, 405
    Grand, Pierre, *208*, 209
    Grand colonial villa, *58*, 59
    Grégoire, *206*
    Laurent, 155
    Le Glay, 154, *163*
    L'Escale, 151, 154, *154*
    Les Chaumes, 407, *408*
    Lévy, 405
    Lozana, *162*
    Masson, *167*
    Mimran, 175
    Nahon, 396
    Perollaz, *390*
    Petite Source, *160*
    Pierre Mas, 210, *210*
    Rivollet, *204*
    S., *204*
    Sami Suissa, *393*, 399, *399*
    Schulmann, *401*, 405, *405*
    Terraz, 400, *401*
    Teste, *154*, 156
    Theil, *205*
    Varado, *396*, 396
    Varsano, 401, *401–3*, 405
    Violetta, 154, *160*, *163*
Villas Paquet, 389, *389*
Volvo garage, 8, *428*

wall, city, *29*, 113
warehouses, 113
    customs, *52*
    Spanish tiles storehouse, *94*
Wallut, 63–65
Windbreak apartments, *359*

People

Page numbers in italics refer to illustrations.
Page numbers in boldface refer to biographical sketches.

Abella, Charles-Paul, 210, *210*, *386*, 387, **462**
Abisror, Isaac, **462**
Adam, André, 13, 14, 22n, 286–87, 299, 319, 321, 339, 340, 351, 445
Adiba, H. E., **462**
Africanus, Johannes Leo, 21, 22, 34
Agache, Donat-Alfred, 74, *75*, 79n
Alami-Bennis, Meryem, 8
Alaoui-Fdili, Ahmed, 8
Alluchon, Jacqueline, 8
Alphonse V, 21
Althusser, Louis, 354
Amade, General Albert d', 37, 38, 40, 42, 46, 129
Ancelle, Pierre, 135, *135*, *143*, 143–44, **462–63**
Andaloussi, Rachid Ben Brahim, 8

Anfreville de Jurquet de la Salle, L. d', 47
Anselin, Patrice, 8
Anselin, Paul, 417–18
Anselin, Sylvie, 8
Archambeau, Albert, **463**
Aroutcheff, Léon, 358, *359*, 365, *374–75*, 375, 384, 435, 463
Arrivetx, René, 95n, 204, 230, 244n, **463**
Artbauer, Otto, 40
Atatürk, Mustapha Kemal, 85
Aujame, Roger, 318
Aulier, 94
Auzelle, Robert, 339
Azagury, Élie (Élias), 7, 259, 318, 336, 345n, *346*, 346–47, *348*, 351, 362, 395–96, *396*, 401, 405, *405–6*, 407, 422, 424, *425*, 431, 432, 438, **463**
Azan, Paul, 32, 34, 40

Baille, Fernand, 93, 95n
Bailly, Pierre-Félix, 388, **463**
Baker, Josephine, 192, *275*
Balandier, Georges, 289
Ballande, Sub-Lieutenant, 36–37
Balois, Jean, 93, 137, *138*, *148*, *150*, 151, 154–55, *155*, 160, 192, *192*, 230, *230*, **463**
Banham, Reyner, 17, 124
Banon family, 56, 121
Barbedor, 46
Bardel, G., 389
Bardet, Gaston, 128, *128*
Barillet, Louis, 109
Barjot, Admiral Pierre, 305
Basciano, Dominique (Domenico), 7, 347, *351*, 429–30, 431, 435, **463**
Basciano, Gaspard (Gaspare), 7, 259, **463**
Battaglia, Joseph-Paul, 95n
Beaufils, L., 197
Beaumier, 24
Beauvoir, Simone de, 226
Belliot, Roger, **463**
Belouali, Lahcen, 8
Belvisi, 144, 151
Benazéraf, Raphaël, 8, 151
Ben Barka, Souheil, 8
Ben Cherifa, Mohammed, 8
Bendahan, Haïm, 123, 216
Bendayan, Carlos, 8
Ben El Fellah, Noureddine, 8
Ben El M'sick, Si Abd el Kerim, 237n
Ben Embarek, 413
Benhaïm, Raymond, 9
Benjamin, Walter, 17

Benjelloun, Omar, 8, 433
Benmussa, Cécile, 8
Bennani, Abbès, 327
Bennani, Souad, 8
Benoit, Fernand, 113, 129
Benoit-Lévy, Georges, 298
Bensimon-Donath, Doris, 92n, 170, 349, 356
Bensusan, Samuel Levy, 35
Benzaquen, Amelia, 8
Benzaquen, Gilles, 8
Benzaquen, Sophie, 8
Berger, Vincent, 171
Béros, Georges, 236–37
Berque, Jacques, 124, 215, 320
Berry, Walter, 129
Berthet, Marcel, 122
Berti, Victor, 82n
Bertin, Émile, *463*
Bertrand, Gabriel, 380
Besson-Maufrangeas, Mrs., 210
Béthouart, General Marie Émile, 276
Biagio, Nigita, 95n
Bianchi, 180
Biarnay, Samuel, 216
Biazzo, *176*, **463**
Bickert, Armand, 121
Bienvenu, Dr., 65
Bills, Emily, 9
Blachère, Gérard, 328–29
Blanchard, Germain, 9
Blesson, C., **463**
Blondin, Lieutenant, *45*
Boccara, Myriam, 8
Bodiansky, Vladimir, 304, 318, *318*, 332, *333*, 335–36, 384, 424
Bogart, Humphrey, 279
Bohin-Perrotte, Madame, 7–8
Boirry, Camille, *126*
Boissonnade, Euloge, 340
Bonan, Jacques, 436
Boniface, Philippe, 303, 372, 415
Bonnet, Constant, *145*, *162*, **463**
Bordigoni, A., 376, *378*
Bosman, Jos, 9
Bouchery, Armand, **464**
Boughali, Mohammed, 355
Bouhaya, Abdellah, 8
Boukait, Abddelatif, 8
Boukobza, Anne, 8
Bourdon, Georges, 36n, 42
Bourron, Amédée-Jules, 48, 62, 170
Boushaba, Jamal, 8
Bousquet, Pierre, 82n, 119, 233, *233*, 252, *253*, 257, 345n, 367, **464**
Bowles, Paul, 109, 275, 438, 444
Boyer, Marius Germinal, *92*, 94, 104, *105*, 119, *131–33*, 131–33, 137, *138*, 140–42, *141*, 144, *147–50*, 148, 151, *152–53*, 154–55, *155*, *160*, *163*, 166, *174*, 175, *178*, 180, *181–83*, 190–92, *191*, *196*, 197, *201*, 201–2, *208–9*, 209–10, *212*, 230, *230*, 239, *239*, 244n, *255–56*, 255–59, *258*, *259*, 271, 279, *279*, 283, 365, 422, 424, 435, 445, **464**
Brami, Gaston, 381
Brandt, Frédéric, 93n
Branly, Elisabeth, 109
Brasillach, Robert, 89, 94, 236
Brau, Louis, 82n
Braun, Georg, 22, *22*
Bride, Hubert, 82n, *88*, 94, *118*, 119, *146*, **464**
Brindeau, Édouard, 259, *269*
Brion, Edmond, 94, 139, *139*, *145*, 164, 166, *166*, 187, *187*, *196*, 218, 222–23, 225, *226*, *234*, 240–46, *241–43*, *246–47*, 256, *257*, 268–69, *296*, 297–99, *307*, 345n, 349, *426*, *440*, **464**
Broadhurst, Ron, 9
Buan, Georges, 46, *75*, 197, *249*, **464**
Busuttil, Paul, *136*, 137, *183*, 202, *202*, *206*, *295*, 295–98, *298*, 351–53, **464**
Butler, 44

Cadet, Auguste, 94, 139, *139*, *145*, 164, 166, *166*, 218, 220, 222–25, *226*, 246, *298*, 299, 349, 410, *410*, **464–65**
Cagney, James, 435
Calmel, Jean, 263
Cambon, Victor, 54, 55, 76, 84, 262
Candilis, Georges, 7, 12, 318, *318*, 332, *333*, 335–36, *339*, 339–40, *374*, 375, 378–79, 383–84, *384*, 422–23, **465**
Caquot, Albert, 421
Casinière, H. de la, 85
Cazanove, C. de, 67

Celle, R. de la, 169
Cerdan, Marcel, 413
Chable, Jean-Édouard, 285
Chaillou, Michel, 255, 266, 435
Chaine, Emmanuel, *176*, **465**
Chaix, Paul, 53–54
Chancel, Jules, 37
Chapon, 344
Charton, Albert, 124
Chaslin, François, 9
Chassagne, Pierre, 298, *298*, *366–67*, 367–68, **465**
Chefnoury, Sylvain, 259
Chemetoff, Alexandre, 8
Chemineau, Jean, 318, 422, **465**
Chénier, Louis de, 22
Chevrillon, André, 128
Choay, Françoise, 79
Chraïbi, Driss, 287
Churchill, Winston, 276, *277*
Clark, General, *279*
Claudius-Petit, Eugène, 289
Clavel, Sylvie, 9
Cobb, John, 32
Cogné, François-Victor, 104
Cohen-Olivar, Danièle, 8
Coignet, Edmond, 82n
Coldefy, Madame Pierre, 8
Coldefy, Pierre, 344, *344*, *345*, 387, *387*, *391*, 397–98, *398*, 432, *432*, 438, **465**
Colliez, André, 53, 72
Cooper, Gary, 276
Cormier, Alexandre, 203, 266, **465**
Coste, Kirk Lucien, 175, *177*
Cotereau, Jean, 156, 158, 175, 198, 212
Cotte, Narcisse, 21, 23, 95n
Cottet, Gustave, 164, *165*, 193, *193*, *213*, **465**
Couëlle, Jacques, 290
Couette, Henri, 180, 465
Courtois, Alexandre, 14, 110, 132, 279–84, *280–82*, 301, 304, 316, 329, 349, *370–71*, 371, 373, 385, 388, 413, *423*, 423–24, *424*, *427*, 428, 436, 439, **465**
Crétegny, Roland, 8
Creugnet, Georges, 289
Croze, Henri, 263, 436
Culot, Maurice, 8
Curtiz, Michael, 11
Curton, Henri, 95n, **465**

Dahou, Mohamed, 385
Dangleterre, Achille, 394–95, *395*, 432, *437*, **465**
Darsi, Fatima, 8
Darsi, Naima, 8
Debarre, Anne, 9
Debroise, Robert, **465**
De Gaulle, Charles, 276, *277*
Delanoë, Georges, 345n, 362, 394, *430*, 431, **465–66**
Delaporte, Édouard, 466
Delaporte, Hippolyte-Joseph, 60–63, *61–63*, 82n, 94, *103*, 154, *155*, *173*, 465–66
Delarozière, Jacques, 317, 321, 329, 332, 346
Delattre, Martine, 7
Delau, Louis, 170–73, 270, 380
Deloncle, 232, *232*
Delure, Gaston, 51, 53–54, 73–74, *126*, *126*
Deneux, René, **466**
Depaule, Jean-Charles, 9
Deschamps, Henri, 98, 159, 175, 209, 212–13, 223–24
Desmarest, Georges-Ernest, 251, *252*, 466
Desmet, Marcel, 9, 139, *139*, 171, *178*, 180, 184, *184*, 194, *195*, *199*, 200, 231, *231*, 279, 365, 388, *388*, 422, **466**
Dessigny, Charles, 41–44, 48, 60, 65, 68, 95
Dethier, Jean, 8
Devaulchier, Claudine, 9
Dib, Mohammed, 227
Dietrich, Marlene, 276
Don Fernando, Infante, 21
Drouin, Pierre, 288, 293
Drude, General, 37, 38, 104
Druet, Nicolas, 9
al-Duayf, Mohammed, 22
Dubois, Léon, 289, 388, *388*
Dugard, Henry, 60
Duhon, Émile, 344, 365, 373, *426*, 427, 436, *437*, **466**
Dumas, Léon, *176*
Durante, Liborio J., **466**
Durkheim, Émile, 354
Duvivier, Julien, 276
Dyé, A. Henri, 32, 51n

Écochard, Michel, 12, 14, 110, 132, 239, 244, 270–71, 284, 297, 299, *300*, 301–21, *305–9*, *311–12*, *316*, *320–21*, 325–26, *327*, 329–31, 335–36, 340, 346, 350–51, 354, 356–58, 362, 368, 370, 372, 376, 379, 422–23, 438–39, 441–42, **466**
El Amrani, Abdessatar, 8
El Awad, Hafid, 8
Elbaz, Rosine, 8
Elbaz, Victor, 8
El Bezzi, Jabrane, 8
Eleb, Jean-Charles, 9
El Mokhtar, Baadi, 8
Emery, Pierre-André, 318
Epstein, Julius, 279
Epstein, Philip, 279
Erskine, Ralph, 422
Essaïan, Elisabeth, 9
Étévé, Lieutenant, *40*
Ewerth, Wolfgang, 395–96, 401, *401*, *402–4*, 405, 407, 410, *411*, **466**
Expert, Roger-Henri, 210
Eyck, Aldo van, 336

Falandry, Gérard, 8
Fannan, Mustapha, 8
Farès, Abd el Kader, 345n, **466**
Farrère, Claude, 11, 48, 167, 169, 198, 209, 276
Favrot, Claude, 68, *68*, 72, 118, 215, 216
Fernau, Edmund, 34
Fernau, G., 44, 48
Fernau, H., 44, 48
Ferrara, G., 95n, 233
Ferrieu, Prosper, 23, 48
Fichet, Corrado, 259
Ficke, Karl, 44, 59, *59*, 92–93
Fleurant, Louis Henri, *167*, 204, 230, 345n, 365n, 438, **466**
Fleury, R., 376
Fontaine, Just, 413
Forestier, Jean Claude Nicolas, 74, *74*, 77, 79n, 106, 216, *218*, 313, **466–67**
Forster, Kurt W., 9
Foucault, Michel, 15
Fougère, René, 94, **467**
Frager, Marcel, 42
François, A., 53

Gabus, 388, *388*
Galamand, Maurice, 376, *377*, *390*, **467**
Gallotti, Jean, 167, 212–13, 223–24
Garel, Isabelle, 9
Garnier, Tony, 76, 96, 212, 232
Gaud, M., 233, 236, 243
Geddes, Patrick, 11, 442
Gentil, Louis, 121
Gide, André, 226
Giedion, Sigfried, 65, 318, 423
Gillet, Georges, 230, *253*, **467**
Gilsenan, Michael, 9
Gimenez, D., *145*
Girard, 291, 330, 346, 370
Giraud, Henri, 276, *277*
Girola, Natale, 175, **467**
Godefroy, Georges, 308, 370, 427, **467**
Gosset, P., 84
Gouin, Édouard, 244–46, 310, 329, 374
Goulven, Joseph, 45, 55, 56, 59, 92n, 263n, 264–65, 358
Goupil, Gaston, 330
Gourdain, Edmond, 82n, *92*, 94, 166, *166*, 347, 367–68, 394, **467**
Gourdain, Jean, 367–68, **467**
Gouvernet, 95n
Gouyon, Jacques, 389, *389*, **467**
Gråberg di Hemsö, Jacopo, 23
Grand, Pierre, 65n, 121, 209
Grandval, Gilbert, 317
Gras, Joseph, **467**
Grégoire, *240*
Grel, Georges-Jean, 131, *177*, 179, 192, *192*, *200*, **467**
Grémeret, Henri, *372*, 373, 467
Greslin, Albert, *92*, *134*, *136*, 137, *146*, **467**
Griffel, R. A., 89
Grillet, A., 308, 310–11
Gropius, Walter, 407
Guévrékian, Gabriel, 428
Guetta, Sété, 8
Guigues, Léon, 82
Guillaume, Augustin, 317, 369

Haddad, Rosemarie, 9
Hajaoui, 436
Haller, 103
Hamri, Driss, 8

Hantzberg, Robert, 312
Harris, Walter, 24, 34
Hassan II, 16
Hausman, Tami, 9
Haussmann, Georges-Eugène, 85
Hazan, Éric, 9
Hazan, Juliette, 9
Hénard, Eugène, 79, 295
Hentsch, Jean, 340, *341–42*, **467**
Hentschel, Jacques, **467**
Héré de Corny, Emmanuel, 97–98
Hersent, Georges, 51, 53, 82n
Hersent, Jean, 51, 53, 82n
Heyder-Bruckner, India, 8
Hinnen, Erwin, 171, *186*, 188, *189*, 193, 204, *205*, 210, 211, *277*, 343, *343*, 352–53, 367, *390*, 407, *408–9*, 410, 417, 427, **467–68**
Hoffmann, Joseph, 96, 212
Hogenberg, Franz, 22, *22*
Honegger, Jean-Jacques, 380–81, **468**
Honegger brothers, 380–81, 388, *388*
Hooker, Joseph Dalton, 24
Houel, Christian, 38, 43, 48
Howard, Ebenezer, 365
Hutin, Georges, 311
Hymans, Herbert, 9

Ifergan family, 56
Ihler, Captain, 38

Jabin, Pierre, 95n, 142, 151, 154, 156, *163*, *177*, *179*, 187, 188, *188*, 190, *190*, 193, *196*, 199, 203, *203*, 254, 255, *255*, 385, **468**
Jany, Alex, 266
Jaubert, Gaston, 7, *318*, 336, 344, *344*, *345*, *372*, 373, 381, *382–84*, 383, 393, *395*, 395–96, 422, 424, *425*, 434, **468**
Jaussely, Léon, 76, 79n, 80, 96
Jean, Robert, *374–75*, 375, 435
Jourdan, Louis, **468**
Joyant, Edmond, 54, 67, *83*, 85, 103, 131
Juin, Alphonse, 308, 317
Julien, Charles-André, 303
Julien, Léonard, 149, 151

Katz, Ariela, 9
Khaji, Fatima-Zohra, 8
Khmass, Idriss, 8
Khoury, Idriss El, 229, 435
Klee, Paul, 96
Klein, Richard, 9
Koch, Howard, 276
Kugler, Elizabeth, 9
Kunzi, Maurice, **468**

Labonne, Eirik, 16, 129, 132, 187, 303, 305, 308, 313–14, 317, 427, 439
Lacharrière, Jacques Ladreit de, 27, 34–35, 43, 51, 85, 251
Lacoste, Francis, 310, *315*
Lacouture, Jean, 289, 438
Lacouture, Simonne, 289, 438
Lacretelle, Jacques de, 285, 288, 394
Lacroix, Marc, 8, 407, 438
Laforgue, Adrien, 98, *100*, *101*, 173, *173*, 197, 230, *234*, 234, 252, 349, **468**
Lahbabi, Saïd, 8
Lahure, Auguste, 24, 28, 32
Lamb, 34, 44
Lambert, Étienne, 110
Lamy, 357
Landowski, Françoise, 8
Landowski, Paul, *104*
Lapeyre, Émile, 216, 261
Laprade, Albert, 72, 74, 78, 84n, 94, 98, 103, *103–4*, *106–7*, 108–10, *111*, 158, 161, 216, 218, *219–21*, 220, *224*, 224–25, 241, 246, 263–64, *264*, 313, 349, **468**
Larbaud, Valéry, 226
Laronce, 65
Laugier, Michel, 9
Laure, J. H., 358, 360, *360*, 362, *363*, **468**
Lazrak, Aziz, 8
Le Corbusier, 65, 129, 131, 149, 212, 258, 303, 306, 312n, 317, 332, 336, 340, *384*, 387, 396, 407, 422, 428
Lecouëdic, Daniel, 8
Leczinsky, Stanislas, 97
Leeuw, Hendrik de, 226
Lefebvre, Jacques, 245n
Lefrançois, Michèle, 9
Léglise, 179
Legrand, Édy, 288
Lemaigre-Dubreuil, Jacques, 386
Lempriere, William, 23

Lendrat, Eugène, 44, 48
Lennad, Roland, 415, 417
Léon, Paul, 79n
Léris, Pierre, 89, 268
Les Enfant, Paul, **468**
Le Stum, Sylvain, 9
Letrosne, Charles, 82n
Lévi-Strauss, Claude, 354
Levrat, Father, 8
Lévy, Isaac, 347, 362, 395–96, *431*, 432, **468**
Lévy, Luigi, 405
Lewis, Wyndham, 13
L'Herbier, Maurice, 266, *266*, **468**
Licari, René, **469**
Licari, Sauveur, *160*, **469**
Lièvre, Robert, 131, 140, *140*, 151, 154, *154*, 156, 180, 199, 199, *201*, 201–2, **468–69**
Lion, Yves, 9
Liscia brothers, 179
Lods, Marcel, 304
Lompuy, Durand de, 415
Londres, Albert, 226
Long, 69
Loos, Adolf, 192
Lorentz, Henri, 95n
Louis, Émile, 298, **469**
Lourido Diaz, Ramón, 22
Lucas, Albert, *372–73*, 373, *386*, 387, **469**
Lucas, Charles, 340
Lucaud, Raymond, 358, *359*, 432, **469**
Lurçat, André, 304
Lyajid, Si, 332
Lyautey, General Hubert-Gonzalve, 12–13, 16, 47, 51, 53–55, 72, 74, 78, 84, 96–98, *104*, 106, 109, 112–13, 116, 121, 128–29, 159, 167, 175, 269, 316, 349, 354

Macke, August, 96–97
Mac Orlan, Pierre, 11, 226, 235
Maddalena, Charlotte, 8
Maddalena, Robert, 289, 375, 375, 394, *395*, 422, *427*, 432, 438, **469**
Mahé, Yvonne, 233–34, 242–43
Maigrot, Émile, 258
Maillard, Jean, 388, *388*, **469**
Maisonseul, Jean de, 318
Majorelle, Jacques, 104
Mamez, Jean, 109
Manassi, Aldo (Angelo), *93*, 95n, *145*, 160–61, 164, 165, 252, **469**
Mandel, Georges, 275
Mangin, Charles, 37, 38
Manuguerra, Paul, 193–94, **469**
Manzana-Pissaro, Georges, *277*
Marc, Jean, 132, 227
Marchand, E., 216, 261
Marchand, Guillaume, 8
Marchisio, Antoine, 95, 104, 122–23, 132, 162, *256*, 269, 293–95, *294–95*, **469**
Maria, 179
Marmól Carvajal, Luis, 21
Marrast, Joseph, 94, 96, 97, 98, *102*, 104, *163*, **469**
Marx, Groucho, 279
Mas, Antoine, 44
Mas, Pierre, 7, 210, *297*, *314*, 315, 321, 330, 336, 438, **469**
Massot, *240*
Maurois, André, 106
Mauss, Marcel, 354
Mauzit, Vladimir, **469**
Maxence, Françoise, 9
May, Ernst, 295
Mazzoni, Cristiana, 9
Mélia, Jacques, 8
Memmi, Albert, 317, 443
Mercié, Georges, 40
Mercier, Louis-Sébastien, 17
Mérillon, General, 239
Messina, Paul, *392*, 397, *397*, *399*, 400
Michaud, Paul, 204, *204*, **469**
Michel, Émile, 347, **469**
Michelet, Jean, 143, 194, *194*, *198*, 199, 204, *204*, 365, 394–95, *395*, **469–70**
Miège, Jean-Louis, 13, 23
Milan, Germain, 290, *291*
Milyutin, Nikolai, 306
Millerand, Alexandre, 116
Milone, Mario, 8, 187, 193
Mirtil, Marcel, 121
Mninouche, Mohammed, 8
Modiano, Patrick, 421
Mohammed ben Abdallah, Sidi, 22
Mohammed V, 16
Mohr, Paul, 24, 34, 260
Moinier, General Charles, 40, 45

Mokri, Si El Hadj Mohammed el, 151
Monacelli, Gianfranco, 9
Monfried, Andrea, 9
Montagne, Robert, *319*, 321
Montarnal, Jean de, 232, *232*
Montarnal, Jean-Marie-François de, 82, 135, *135*, 232, *232*, **470**
Montarnal, Joseph (Eugène-Charles-Jean-Joseph) de, 135, *135*, **470**
Montefiore, Moses, 24
Montfort, Eugène, 156, 222–23
Montmarin, A. de, 346
Morand, Paul, 226
Morandi, Léonard, 7, 358, *359*, *364*, *385*, 385, 397–98, *398*, **470**
Moréno, Valérie, 8
Moretti, Raphaël, 187, 193
Moujahid, Abdelfettah, 8
Moulay Hassan, 28
Mouline, Saïd, 8
Murdoch, 48

Nachef, Michel, 8
Nahon, 311
Neumann, 34
Neutra, Richard, 304, 394, 422
Newman, Bernard, 13
Ng, Stuart, 9
Nicolas, Janine, 228
Niddam, Madame, 8
Niemeyer, Oscar, 422, 431
Noguès, Charles, 241, 275–76, 301
Nolly, Émile, 11, 34, 40–41, 260
Norris, Mary, 9
Noulellis, Georges, 8

Oleggini, Henri, 8
Opitz, Walter, 93n
Orthlieb, Georges, 266
Ouadi, Latifa, 8
Ouazzani, Rachid, 8

Paccanari, Valerio, **470**
Paniconi, Mario, 257, *259*
Pappalardo, Marius, *93*, 95n, 137
Parizet, Marcel (Claudius), 297, **470**
Parsons, Sarah, 9
Pascal, Blaise, 194
Pascucci, Ernest, 9
Patton, George, *279*
Pauty, Edmond, 171, 185, 187, 242, 284
Pediconi, Giulio, 7, 257, *259*
Pelletier, Pierre, *314*, 315, *327*, 330, 376
Pénicaud, François, **470**
Pérez, Jacques, 357
Périgny, Maurice de, 120, 216
Perollaz, Émile, *390*
Perotte, Paul, 258
Perret, Auguste, 12, 175, 231, *232*, 381, 387, 432, **470**
Perret Brothers, *62–64*, 62–65
Perrolaz, Émile, **470**
Perrotte, Paul, 171, 192, *192*, *259*, **470**
Pertuzio, Félix-Joseph, 95n, 139, *139*, *158*, 164, *165*, 206, *206*, 216, 470
Pertuzio, Louis-Paul, 95n, 139, *139*, *158*, 164, *165*, 206, *206*, 216, **470**
Pétain, Philippe, 275
Peter, André, 8
Peter, Jérome, 8
Pétonnet, Colette, 236, 363
Peyceré, David, 8
Piot, Henri, *333*
Planque, Albert, *291*, 394, 400, *401*, 427, 435, *436*, **470**
Plumet, Charles, 210
Pola, Jo, 8
Pola, Léandre, 8
Ponsard, R., *178*, 185, *185*, *197*
Pottecher, Odile, 303n
Pradier, François, **470**
Privitera, Giuseppe, **470**
Prost, Henri, 12, 14, 16, 48, 73, 74, *76–81*, 76–81, 84–85, 92, 95–96, 96, 98, 102, *103*, 104, 106, 108, *110*, 111–16, *114*, *116*, 119–23, *122*, 128, 131–32, 149, *162*, 215–16, *217*, 225, 228, 255, *256*, 268–70, *269*, 280, 282, 284, 289, 303–4, 306, 313, 388–89, 439, 441–42, **470–71**
Provost, Major, 38
Puaux, Gabriel, 303

Quessada, 311

Rabaud, Jean, 230
Ragon, Michel, 431

Ragot, Gilles, 8
Rankin, Reginald, 32, 34
Ravazé, Maurice-Jacques, 252, *253*
Rechichi, Angelo, **471**
Reclus, Élysée, 24
Redont, Édouard, 82n
Reese, Thomas F., 9
Rémon, Georges, 161
Renard, René, **471**
Renaud, J., 35
Renaudin, Georges, 171, 192, *192*, 197, *265*, 365n, 367, 387, 434, 438, **471**
Renaudin, Louis, 355
Rendu, Xavier, *178*, 185, *185*, *197*, **471**
Rey, J. B. M., 23
Ribot, Alexandre, 37n
Ricard, Bruno, 9
Ricci, Libero, **471**
Riccignuolo, Armand Rosario, **471**
Richards, Brian, 7, *318*
Riou, Louis, 7, 422, **471**
Risler, Georges, 72–74
Rivet, Daniel, 13, 37
Rivollet, Marcel, 131, 204, 230, 236, 238
Robelin, Jacques, 8
Robert, Jean-François, *325*, **471**
Rochdi, Mohammed, 8
Rodinson, Maxime, 13
Rohlfs, Gerhard, 24
Roosevelt, Franklin D., 210, 276, *277*
Rosenthal, Léonard, 137
Rothschild, Henri de, 42
Roucher, Maurice, 238
Rousseau, Marcel, 358, *359*, **471**
Roux-Spitz, Michel, 210
Royère, Jean, 405
Rumpf, Francis, 8
Ruttmann, Walter, 393

Saad-el-Dine, Mohammed Khaled, 330
Sabalot, 244
Sabatier, A. H., 230, 235
Sabatou, J. P., 389
Saboulin, Louis de, 263
Sachs, Jean, **471**
Sadrane, Mustapha, 8
Sahuc, Pierre, 242–43
Sahyoun, Isabelle, 8
Said, Edward, 13
Saïdi, Mohammed, 8
Saint-Éxupéry, Antoine de, 301
Salmón, Juan Miguel, 22–23
Salzedo, Raphaël, 9
Sanguy, C., 292
Sansone, Ignace, *136*, 137, *183*, 202, *202*, *206*, **471**
Sarrat, Édouard, 212
Sauvage, Henri, 180, 210
Schindler, Rudolf Maria, 394
Schlumberger, Captain, *25*, 27, 35
Schmidt, Michel, 388
Schmidt-Honegger, Madame, 8
Schmitt, René, **471**
Schulmann, Théo, 405
Scob, V., 435
Sears, Steve, 9
Segonds, Marie François, 42–43
Seliner, 256
Selva, Jean, 95n
Selva, Louis, 95n
Sert, Jose Luis, 423
Sicaud, G., 233, 236, 243
Sieburg, Friedrich, 170–71, 235, 236
Simon, Philippe, 9
Siroux, Maxime, **471**
Sitte, Camillo, 96
Slimani, Abderrahman, 8
Smith, G. E. Kidder, 267, 393, 397, 400
Smithson, Alison, 7, 332, 336–38, *338*, 379
Smithson, Peter, 7, 332, 336–38, *338*, 379
Sori, Maurice, *240*, 258, *259*, 367, 431, **471**
Soria y Mata, Arturo, 306
Soubreville, A., *149*
Spécioso brothers, 179
Studer, André, 7, 340, *341–42*, 432, *432*, **471**
Sturges, Abigail, 9
Subes, Raymond, 109
Suire, André, 417–18
Suraqui, Claire, 8
Suraqui, Élias, *92*, 95n, *142–44*, 143, 145, 154, *160*, *162–64*, 164, 173, *178*, 193, 197, *213*, **471–72**
Suraqui, Joseph, *92*, 95n, *142–44*, 143, 145, 154, *160*, *162–64*, 164, 173, *178*, 193, 197, *213*, 358, 360–61, 361, 365, 369, **471–72**

Suraqui, Pierre, 8
Tabat, 248
Taieb, Léon, 362
Talamona, Marida, 8
Tamikovsky, Vladimir, **472**
Tarde, Guillaume de, 77, 118
Tardif, Albert, 14, 46, 48, *49*, 55, 72–73, 79, 121, 261
Tarriot, Alfred, 121
Tastemain, Éliane, 7, **472**
Tastemain, Henri, 7, 318, 422, 431, *431*, **472**
Tazi, Omar, 139
Teillaud, A., 389
Terpak, Fran, 9
Terrasse, Henri, 314–15
Terraz, Roger, 400
Terrenoud, Georges, 122
Terrier, Auguste, 85
Teste, Maurice, *149*, 150, 154, 263
Teste, Théo, 151, 154, 263
Tharaud, Jean, 198
Tharaud, Jérôme, 198
Tirard, Paul, 51, 77
Tolila, 246
Tolly, Maurice de, 167
Tonci, Ulysse, 46, *58*, 59, 84, **472**
Topin, Tito, 414, 415, 419, 435
Tordjman, Eugène, 122
Toufiq, Ahmed, 8
Tournon, Paul, *108*, 108–9, *109*, **472**
Tournon-Branly, Florence, 109
Tournon-Branly, Marion, 8
Tranchant de Lunel, Maurice, 82n, 97
Trouvé, Joëlle, 9
Trystam, Jean-Paul, 288

Urban, Albert, **472**
Uyttenhove, Pieter, 9

Vaillat, Léandre, 12, 129, 172–73, 175, 212–13, 217–18, 224
Vallat, Marcel, 308, 316
Vallery brothers, 266
Vandelle, M.(R. L.), *174*, 230, **472**
Vargues, Georges, 297, 472
Varsano, Maurice, 401, 405
Veyre, Gabriel, 44
Vidal, Jean, 393
Vidalenc, Georges, 45–46, 95
Vieljeux, Tristan, 407
Vimort, Georges, *91*, 94, 121, *121*, 142, **472**
Violeau, Jean-Louis, 9
Viremouneix, Marcel, **472**

Wachtel, Nathan, 15n, 355
Waintrub, Alexander, 9
Weilenmann, Armin, *378*, **472**
Weisgerber, Félix, 26–28, *27*, 34, 46
Wiener, Lester-Paul, 423
Wolff, Charles, **472**
Woods, Shadrach, 332, *333*, 335, *339*, 374, 375, 378–79, 383–84, *384*, 423
Wright, Frank Lloyd, 154, 432
Wright, Gwendolyn, 9

Xantopoulos, 32

Yahya, Lahcen, 8
Yoshiwara, 225
Yvkoff, W., 376

Zagury, Yehia, 122
Zaleski, Dimitri, 365n, **472**
Zarb, Arnold, **472**
Zehrfuss, Bernard, 318
Zéligson, Louis, 347n, 358, *358*, *359*, 365n, 438, **472**
Zemmouri, Si Mohamed Ben Abderrahman, 237
Zevaco, Jean-François, 7, 259, 318, *392*, 395–97, *397*, 399–400, *399–400*, 407, *421*, 422, 424, 428, *428–29*, 431, 438, *439*, **472**
Zrika, Abdallah, 224

Places, Streets, and Districts

Page numbers in italics refer to illustrations. The index refers generally to the initial (pre-1956) names; for current names, see recent maps.

2e-Tirailleurs, Boulevard du, 122
IVe-Zouaves, Avenue du, *10*, 93, *114*, *115–17*, 119, 121, *123*, *179*, 188, *188*, 215, 260, *277*
15, Rue, 55

Adminstrative, Place. See Place Administrative
Agadir, 16
Agadir, Rue d', *134*, 136
Ain Chock, 241, 282–83, 287, *287*, 290, 292, *293–98*, 293–99, 327, 330, 340, *351*, *352–53*, 354, 365, *366*, 369, 374, 442
Ain Diab beach, 261, 263–65, *265*, *420*
Ain-Diab coastal road, 150–51, *412*
Ain Diab promontory, 414
Ain Diab Village Resort, 264
Ain Diab waterfront, *413*, 413–20, 435
Ain Harrouda, 401
Ain Sebaa beach, 261, 263, *412*, 419–20
Ain Sebaa quarter, 292n, 310, 331, 348, 372, 375
Ain Sebaa zoo, 434, *434*
airfields
    Camp Cazes, 301
    Nouaceur, 301, 394, 418
    Tit-Mellil, 301, *429*
Albert 1er, Place, 389
Alexandre 1er, Boulevard, *388*, *390*, 399
Alexandre Dumas, Rue, *208*
Alger, Rue d', *148*, 149, *152*, *153*, 154, *160*
Amiral Courbet, rue de l', *60*, 137
Anafé. *See* Anfa, historic
Anfa, Boulevard d', 90, 91, 123, 151, 194, *195*, *198*, 199, 204, *204*, 380, *380–81*, 399
Anfa, historic, 21–22, *22*, 34, 47
Anfa, Lice d', *401*, 405
Anfa beach, *412*
Anfa-Beauséjour quarter, 372, 384, 395
Anfa hill, 90, 372, 405
Anfa quarter, 38, 79n, *123*, 204, *205*, *210–11*, 258, 264, 271, 287, 292, 310, 331, 346, 374, 384, 398, 401, *404*, 410, 438, 442
Anfa seafront (Anfa-Plage), *264*, 266, *266*
Anfa-Supérieur, 38, 49, *149–50*, 149–51, 159, *391*, 413
Anoual, Avenue, 342, *343*, 390
Aspirant Henry Lemaignen, Rue, *406*
Auteuil, Rue d', *397*
Auxerre, Rue d', *290*
Aviateur Coli, Rue de l', *142*, 143, 146, 164, *165*
Aviateurs, Place des, 192, *192*
Aviation bidonville, 237
Aviation Française, Rue de l', *174*
Azemmour road, 310, 346

Bab el-Kebir square, 30
Bascunano, Rue, 193, *193*
beaches, 260–65, 412–20
Beaulieu district, 374
Beauséjour district, 292, 331, 374–75, *374–75*
Bel Alia district, *315*
Bendahan, Rue, *187*
Ben Jdia district, 237
Ben M'Sick bidonville, 237, 293, 319, 329, 342
Berrechid, 44
Biarritz, Boulevard de, 415
Bidonville quarter, 90, *235*, 235–38, 325, 445
Blaise Pascal, Rue, 193–94
Blanquefort, Rue, 435
Bordeaux, Boulevard de, 157
Bossuet, Rue, 164
Bouardel, Rue, 366
Bourgogne quarter, 290, 365–66, 365–70, 432
Bousbir district, 46, 48, 55, *225–26*, 225–26, 442
Bouskoura, Rue de, 144, *145*, *160*, *191*, *201*, 216, 313
Briey, Rue de, 38

Calais, Rue de, *160*
Calmel, Boulevard, *267*, *268*, 358, 360, *430*
Camp-Boulhaut road, 311, 357
Camp Cazes airfield, 301
Canonnier Carpentier, Rue du, *409*
Capitaine Ihler, Rue du, 43
Capitaine Maréchal, Rue du, *139*, *168*
Caporal-Beaux, Rue du, 227, *227*
Carrières Carlotti, *314*
Carrières Centrales (Hay Mohammadi), 237, 291, 292, *307*, *315*, *317*, *324*, *326–28*, 326–29, *330*, 331–40, *333–35*, 340, 347, *350*, *352–53*, 354, 362, *363*

Casa-Fédala Industrial Complex, 305–6, *306*, 316
Catalogne, Rue de, 365n
Cavaliers de Courcy, Rue des, *207*
Cèdres, Allée des, 391
cemetery, Muslim, 36, 54
central business district, 16
Chant des Oiseaux, Rue du, *396*
Chapon, Rue, 140, *140*
Charmilles, Rue des, *123*, *410*
Chayla, Boulevard du, *430*
Chénier, Rue, 188, *189*
Chevalier Bayard, Rue du, *259*
Chevandier de Valdrôme, Rue, *213*
Chorfa Tolba quarter, *315*
Circular Boulevard, *64*, 65n, 68, 73, 108, 123, 131, *145*, 367, 385, 387, 433–34
Cité Municipale, 224
Claude Debussy, Rue, *233*
Claude Perrault, Boulevard, 108
Colbert, Rue, *147*
Colonna d'Ornano, Boulevard, 345n
Commandant Provost, Rue du, 43–44, 48
Commandant Terves, Rue, 144, *145*
Commerce, Place du, 30, *46–47*
Commercy, Rue du, *390*
Corniche, Boulevard de la, 265–66, 358
Corniche, La (waterfront), *413*, 413–20, *420*
Côte d'Émeraude, Avenue de la, *123*
Coulanges, Rue de, *434*, *434*
Crêtes, Boulevard des, 293, *370–71*, 371
Crêtes hill, 407, *408*, 438
Curie, Rue, *176*, *203*
Cytises, Allée des, *391*

Damrémont, Rue, *132*, *390*
Dar-el-Makhzen, Rue, 30
Delavigne, Boulevard, *361*
Delure breakwater, 301
Denis Papin, Avenue, *432*
Derb Baladiya, 236, *315*
Derb Bouchentouf, *315*
Derb Carlotti, 224–25, *225*, *315*
Derb Comima, 329, *349*
Derb el-Baladiya, 224, *225*
Derb el-Hagib, 216
Derb el Miter, *315*
Derb Ghallef, 90, 216, 228–29, 237, 329
Derb Hajib, *315*
Derb Jdid (Hay Hassani), 287, 330–31, *346*, 346–49, *347*, *351*, 354
Derb Koréa, *315*
Derb Martinet, *315*
Derb Sidna (Soltane), 216
Douane, Rue de la, 48, 93, *207*
Dumont d'Urville, Rue, *176*
Dupleix, Rue, *430*

École Industrielle, Rue de l', 345n
Edmond Doutté, Place, 38, *91*, *186–87*, 187
El Afou district, *315*
El Hank cemetery, 358
El Hank headland, 263, *263*, 311, 357–58
El Hank quarter, 60, 65, 110, *111*, 357–63, *358*, *360*, 362, 417
Émile Zola, Avenue, *384*
Eugène Landrat, Rue, *259*
Europe, Rond-Point de l' (traffic circle), *424*

factory quarter, *271*
Fédala, 51, 290, 301, 304–6, 316
Fédala beach, 261–63
Ferme-Blanche quarter, 237
Fernau district, 65
Ferrieu district, 65
Foch, Boulevard, 180, *366*, *432*
Foncière district, 113
Forces Armées Royales, Avenue des, 435, 439. *See also* République, Avenue de la
France, Place de. *See* Place de France
Franchet d'Esperey, Rue, *213*
Franklin Roosevelt, Avenue, *393*, *427*

Gadoueville (mud town), 235
Gallieni, Rue, 112, *123*, *147*, 164–65, *256*
Gare, Boulevard de la, *67*, *88*, 112, *118*, 118–19, 123, *123*, 135, *135*, 137, *138–39*, 139, *143*, 145–46, 164, *165–66*, 166, 173, *184*, 188, *189*, 199, 200, 231, *231*, 252, *255*, 256–57, *258*, 268–69, *279*, *283*, 284, *389*, 424, 435
Gare, Place de la, 194, *195*
Gay-Lussac, Rue, *161*
Général d'Amade, Avenue du, 68, *111*, 112, 123, *139*, *145*, *168*, *178*, 185, *190*, *191*, 199, *201*, 252, *256*, 269, *270*, 385, 388, 424
Général d'Amade, Rond-Point du (traffic circle), *280*, 283
Général Drude, Avenue du, 58, 59, 216, 268
Général Gouraud, Boulevard du, *123*, 200
Général Moinier, Avenue, *56*, 154, *164*, *177*, *192*, 192–93
Georges Mercié, Place, *389*
Georges Mercié, Rue, 112, *123*, *173*, 268
Golf, Avenue du, *210*
Gourand, Boulevard, 148
Grand Place. *See* Place Administrative
Grand Socco, 21, *43*, 44
Grand Socco, Place du, 65, 67
Guynemer, Place, *212*
Guynemer, Rue, *174*

Habous quarter, 14, 206, *214*, 215–24, *219*, 222–25, 242, 246, 290, 299, *299*, 315, 349, 442–43
Haye, Rue de La, *167*
Hay Hassani. *See* Derb Jdid
Hay Mohammadi. *See* Carrières Centrales
Hippodrome, Avenue de l', 151
Horloge, Rue de l', 48, *61*, 67, 72, 82, 118, *135*, 137, *138*, 159, *182–83*, *430*, 431
Horloge district, 113
housing developments
  Anfa II, *378*, 381
  Asayag villas, 231–32
  Beaulieu, *370–71*, 370–72
  Bou Jniba Phosphates, 243
  Bournazel, 292, 368, 371–74, *373*, 424, *425*
  Carnaud, 234
  Chaux et Ciments, 232
  CIFM (Compagnie Immobilière Franco-Marocaine), *327–28*, 327–28
  CIL (Comité Interprofessionnel du Logement), 372, 384
  Ciments Lafarge, 234, 243, 246, *307*
  Cité des Jeunes, *374–75*, 374–76
  Cité Industrielle, 232
  Comptoir Lorrain, 38
  Cosuma, *241–43*, 241–44, 246
  Fayolle, 38
  Fernaus, 44
  Germaine, 372
  Habous, 161
  Haim Cohen, 38
  HBM (Habitations à bon marché), 229–31, *230–31*, 238
  Khouribga phosphate, 234, *234*, *247*
  Koudiat, 328, *352–53*
  Maréchal Lyautey, *375*, *390*
  M'Barka, 343
  Mers-Sultan, 38
  Moroccan railroad company, 291, 327, 331
  Nathan brothers, 38
  Neumann, 34
  Oasis, 38
  Pavin-Lafarge, 234
  Perret (unbuilt), 231
  Plateau, Le, *345*, *345*, 370
  Poliet et Chausson, 234
  Racine, 38
  Robitaillé, 414–15
  Ryad subdivision, 328, 340
  Saada, 328, *352–53*
  SOCICA, 245–46, *245–47*, 291, 327
  Société pour le Développement de Casabalanca, 48

Île-de-France, Avenue de l', *374–75*
Imam Ghazali, Rue, *222*
indigenous town, new, 215–16, *217*, 218, *219–20*

Jacques Cartier, Rue, *184*
Jean Courtin, Boulevard, *259*
Jean Jaurès, Rue, *208*, 209
Joffre, Boulevard, *361*, *367*, *369*, 380, *380–81*, *434*

Kébir Fassi district, *315*

La Bruyère, Rue, *361*
Lacépède, Rue, 193
La Corniche waterfront, *413*, 413–20, *420*
Lalla Yacout, Boulevard, 435
Lamoricière, Rue, *390*
Lapérouse, Rue, *143*, 193, *193*
Larache, Rue de, *33*
Lassalle, Rue, 38, 137, 140
Laurent Guerrero, Boulevard, *391*
Leclerc, Boulevard, 38
Léon l'Africain, Rue, *182–83*
Le Polo, 310, 374
Liberté, Boulevard de la, *161*, *436*
Liberté quarter, 55–56, 79, 142, 170, 227

Libourne, Rue de, 65n
Lido, Boulevard du, *123*, *398*, 400, *401*, *411*
Lido waterfront, 413
Lieutenant Bergé, Rue du, 140, *140*, 199
Lieutenant Bruyant, Rue du, *234*
Lieutenant Campi, Rue du, 245–46
Lieutenant Vidal, Rue du, *234*
Londres, Boulevard de, 59, *167*
Longchamp, *395*, 424–25
Lorraine, Boulevard de, 38, *134*, *136*, *147*, *387*, *391*, *433*, *436*, *436*
Louis Barthou, Boulevard, 388
Louis-Gentil Square, 164, 173, *255*
Lusitania quarter, 170
Lyautey, Rond-Point (traffic circle), *134*, *136*, *146*

Maarif district, 90, 170, 228–29, *228–29*, 237, 374, 432, 435, 439, 445
Maarif extension district, 232
Magnier factory, 60
Malines, Rue de, *206*
Marché, Rue du, 48
Mareuil, Rue de, 381, *383*, 428, *428*
Marine, Avenue de la, 30, 33, *137*, *166*, 180, *182–83*
Marinié, Rue, *247*
market square, 119
Marne, Boulevard de la, *204*
Marrakech, Route de, *287*, 293
Marronniers, Allée des, *123*
Marseille, Boulevard de, *112*, 140, 190, *190*, *196*, 202, *202*, 253
Mazagan, road to, 228
medina, new, 90, *158*, 215–26, *217*, 218, *219–20*, *221*, *225*, 235, 237, 270, 282, *282*, 284, 289, 299, 314–15, 330, 332, 354, 374, 435
medina, new extension, 238–41, *240*, *271*, *351*
medina, old, *10*, *21*, 28, 30, 32, *32–33*, *39*, 46, 54, 60, 65, *66*, 79n, 81, 96, 113, 115, 116, 170, *207*, 215–16, 224, 237, 242, *249*, 255, 270, *278*, 279, *280*, 284, 329, 439
Médiouna, Route de, 38, 44, 55–56, *64*, 82, 216, 218, 224, 239, 268, 313
Médiouna, Traverse de, *59*
mellah district, 28, *28*, *36*, 37, 45–46, 65, 91, 92n, *120*, 120–23, 170, 246, *248*, 301, 356
Mers-Sultan, Avenue, *178*, *185*, 209, 257, 435
Mers-Sultan, Rond-point (traffic circle), *213*
Mers-Sultan district, 55–60, 90, 93, 149, 151, 206, 285, 405
Mirabeau, Place, 387
Mission, Rue de la, *249*
Mogador, Rue de, *33*
Moinier Avenue, 68
Monge, Rue, *208*
Montesquieu, Rue, *208*
Moulay-Youssef, Boulevard, 108, 123–24, *123–24*, 149, 155, *155*, *160*, 266, 270, 358, 362
Mouret, Rue, *201*, 201–2
Murdoch, Rue, 193

Nancy, Rue de, 38
new indigenous town, 215–16, *217*, 218, *219–20*
new medina extension, 238–41, *240*, *271*, *351*
Nil, Avenue du, 342, *343*, *390*
Nolly, Rue, 137, *138*
Nouaceur air base, 301, 394, 418
noualla districts, 90, 233
Novo, Rue, *164*

Oasis district, *123*, 331, *410*
Oise, Rue de l', *194*, *195*, *198*
Oran, 339
Oudjari, Rue, 164, *165*
Ould-el-Hamra mosque square, 215

Panoramique, Boulevard, *408*
Parc, Rue du, *155*
Paris, Boulevard de, *56*, *111*, 144, *176*, 197, 252, *253*, *257*
parks
  "forest," 313
  Lyautey, 84, *106–7*, 106–8, 137, 151, 199, 424
  Murdoch, 48, *160*
Pasteur, Boulevard, 187–88
Patton traffic circle, *279*
Paul Dommer, Boulevard, 388
Place Administrative (Grand Place; Place de la Victoire), 68, *78*, 95–108, *96–97*, *99–105*, 111, 115, 161, 175, 185–86, 203, 256, 283, 442
Place Albert 1er, 389
Place de France, 14, 44, *50*, *61–63*, 67, *67*, 96, *114*, 116, *117*, 118–23, *120*, 128–29, 137, 151, 168, 169, 187–88, *188–89*, 193, 246, *248*, *256*, 281, *283*, 283–84, 301, 311, 314, 385, *423*, 424

Index 479

Place de la Gare, 194, *195*
Place de la Révolution Française, 385, *385*
Place de la Victoire. *See* Place Administrative
Place des Aviateurs, 192, *192*
Place de Verdun, 91–92, 193, 281, 283–84, 439
Place du Commerce, 30, *46–47*
Place du Grand Socco, 65, 67
Place Edmond Doutté, 38, *91, 186–87*, 187
Place Georges Mercié, *389*
Place Guynemer, *212*
Place Korte quarter, 339
Place Mirabeau, 387
Poincaré, Rue, *139*, 428, *428*, 435, *435*
Polo, Le, 310, 374
Pont-à-Mousson, Rue de, 180, *270*
port, harbor, and wharves, 14, 34–36, 44, *51–52*, 53–54, *66*, 73, 82–84, 93, 113, *115*, 115–16, *124–32*, *125–28*, *130–32*, 149, 187, 251, 266, 301, *302–3*, 305–6
Porte de la Marine, 45, 301
Port-Lyautey, 326
Prom, Rue, 143, 164, *178*, 190, *190*, 196
Provost, Rue du Commandant, 43–44, 48

Rabat, Route de (Rabat Road), 48, 65n, 67–68, *68*, 94, 232
Rabat freeway (Cassablanca-Rabat), *307*, 313, 372
Rabelais, Rue, 197
racetrack, 149
Racine quarter, 231
Régiments Coloniaux, Boulevard de, 365, *369*
Reims, Rue de, *132*, *390*
Reitzer, Rue, 140, *140*
République, Avenue de la, *10*, *283*, *303*, 313–14, *426–27*, 427. *See also* Forces Armées Royales, Avenue des
Résistance, Boulevard de la, *386*
Révolution Française, Place de la, 385, *385*
Roches Noires beach, 261–63, 326, *412*
Roches Noires quarter, 38, 44, 48, 79n, 90, *94*, 126, 170, *232*, 232–33, 239, 242, 244, 257–58, *259*, 271, *319*, 374
Roget, Rue, 59, *143*, *254*

Sauvage, Rue, 368
Savorgnan de Brazza, Rue, *178*, *184*
seafront promenade, 399
Sidi Abderrahmane beach, 263, 313, *412*, 419, 420
Sidi Bel Abbès, 339n
Sidi Belyout beach, *260–61*, 260–61, *412*
Sidi Belyout cemetery, 46, 128
Sidi Belyout quarter, 230, 310
Sidi Bernoussi quarter, 287, 331, 348
Sidi Maarouf, *401–3*
Sidi Othman, 330, 340, 342, *343*, *352–53*, *390*
Sour-ej-Jdid, 28, 38
Spagnol district, *315*
Sports, Rond-point des (traffic circle), *177*
Stendhal, Avenue, 345
subdivisions. *See* housing developments

Tanger, Rue de, 248
Terrade quarter, 339
Terves, Rue Commandant, 144, *145*
Thimonnier, Rue, 365n
Tit Mellil, *421*, 431
Tit-Mellil airfield, 301
Tnaker quarter, 28, *28*, 46
Tours, Rue de, *137*
TSF (Télégraphie sans fil) beach, *412*
TSF quarter, 261, 264, 266

Védrines, Rue, 143, 164, *165*, 255
Verdun, Place de, 91–92, 193, 281, 283–84, 439

Wadi Bouskoura, *21*, 44
Wadi Nfifikh, 45
workers' housing. *See* housing developments

Yves de Gueux, Rue, *378*

Zénatas, Route des, 345n

Illustration Credits

Académie d'architecture, Paris : 66, 79, 80, 96, 101b, 102tl, 109, 110, 114, 116, 149, 150t, 217, 218b, 256b, 299r, 410t
Agence urbaine de Casablanca : 136ml, 140l, 143r, 145l, 145b (a-d), 165l, 165tr, 189br, 191bl, 193, 199m, 201t, 202
Jacqueline Alluchon, Casablanca : 156tr, 226l, 298bl
Patrice Anselin, Casablanca : 418, 419t
Élie Azagury, Casablanca : 346, 347, 396l, 396m, 405l, 406t, 406bl, 406b
Gaspare Basciano, Casablanca : 215, 259br
Photos by Roland Beaufre, Paris : 153tl, 153bl, 153r, 157t, 157b
Beinecke Library, Yale University : 22
Bibliothèque de documentation internationale contemporaine, Nanterre : 126
Bibliothèque générale et archives, Rabat : 61b, 67, 84, 88, 91, 99, 101h, 106, 112t, 112m, 118t, 115l, 118mr, 120b, 122, 130b, 133, 219l, 225t, 228, 232l, 232b, 238, 244, 250, 255bl, 260, 269b, 288b, 294t, 377l
Bibliothèque nationale de France : 154tl, 206t, 266
Myriam Boccara, Paris : 131, 132t, 141ml
Éliane Bohin-Perrotte, Neuilly : 226
Henri Bresler, Paris : 178r, 200
Centre cinématographique marocain, Rabat : 316r, 427r
Photos by Jean-Louis Cohen : 29t, 33t, 33b, 56, 58, 59, 60, 94, 102ml, 102tr, 102b, 105tl, 105b, 107t, 107b, 124, 134, 136t, 138tr, 138br, 139t, 140r, 141r, 141bl, 146 (a-c), 147 (d-f), 148, 150ml, 152t, 152br, 160 (b-h), 161, 162 (a-c), 163 (d-i), 165bl, 165br, 166tl, 166br, 167, 172l, 172 r, 174t, 174b, 175 (a-c), 176 (d-f), 178 (a-f), 181, 182b, 184r, 185t, 187br, 188r, 189tl, 189bl, 190r, 191ti, 192tl, 194r, 195tl, 195tr, 195bl, 196l, 196tr, 196mr, 196br, 197, 199t, 203, 207t, 207bl, 207br, 211b, 212, 213t, 213b, 222, 227, 229, 233, 234t, 234b, 242, 247tr, 247b, 249, 253b, 256t, 257t, 258b, 265, 290, 298br, 350, 354, 359bl, 360bl, 361r, 366 (a-f), 367t, 369b, 371t, 371br, 374r, 375t, 378, 385l, 389r, 390t, 390ml, 390r, 391m, 391b, 392, 398tr, 399, 401tl, 401tr, 401ml, 401mr, 402b, 409b, 410b, 424t, 425t, 438, 429r, 430tl, 428b, 433m, 434m
Jeanine Coldefy, Antibes : 387l, 398m
Collection Albert Kahn, Archives départementales des Hauts-de-Seine, Boulogne-Billancourt : 103t
Alexandre Courtois, Bayonne : 280t, 280m, 281, 282t, 371mr
Roland Crétegny, Marly-le-Roy : 381l, 381r
Eidgenössische technische Hochschule, Zurich, Jacqueline Tyrwhitt collection : 274, 307t, 307bl, 317, 330 ; Sigfried Giedion archive : 333b
Photos by Marcelin Flandrin, Casablanca : 23, 29b, 107m, 261
Getty Research Institute for the History of Art and the Humanities, Los Angeles : 30, 31t, 32, 82, 158, 168, 288t, 338
Pierre Hinnen, Villevieille : 205t, 205b
L'Illustration, Paris : 26, 36b, 37, 53
Institut français d'architecture, Paris : 49, 50, 62t, 62b, 63t, 64b, 64r, 64m, 64b, 73, 74, 75b, 76, 103b, 104b, 111t, 111b, 154br, 186, 214, 218, 220t, 220m, 223m, 223b, 232l, 264, 337, 338
Institut géographique national, Saint-Mandé : 25t, 25b, 39b, 70-71, 322-323
Photos by Marc Lacroix, Cadaqués : cover, 108, 302t, 302mr, 302-303b, 318, 341t, 342, 344, 345, 382t, 383, 384r, 391t, 402t, 403t, 403bl, 403br, 404t, 404b, 409t, 411t, 411bl, 411br, 413, 416t, 417, 419b, 420, 421, 423, 425t, 426t, 427t, 427ml, 429br, 430tr, 432t, 433t, 434t, 435r, 437t, 437b, 439
Library of Congress, Washington, D.C. : 86-87, 272-273
Patrice de Mazières, Rabat : 100h, 100b
Drawings by Cristiana Mazzoni : 138l, 141tl, 152l, 154ml, 155tl, 183b, 185tl, 189br, 191br, 201br, 221 (a-g), 225b, 351, 352 (a-g), 353 (h-l)
Ministère de l'habitat, Rabat, Photographic archive : 240, 241, 271t, 283, 286, 287, 297, 302ml, 303mr, 309t, 311t, 312t, 312m, 312b, 313, 314t, 314b, 319t, 324, 326, 327t, 327m, 329, 335bl, 348t, 348b, 356, 358, 359tl, 359tr, 360tr, 370, 372, 388r, 394, 416b, 424b, 431
Ministère des Affaires étrangères, Centre des archives diplomatiques, Nantes : 10, 43l, 43r, 46l, 47, 52b, 55l, 57b, 68, 69, 117, 121, 248, 255tr, 270, 293, 296t, 315, 331, 386, 436b
Valérie Moréno, Casablanca : 160a
Musée de l'Air et de l'Espace, Le Bourget : 20, 40-41t, 44
Musée des années 30, Boulogne-Billancourt : 104t
National Archives, Washington, D.C., Military Archives, Still Pictures Branch : 127t, 210, 211t, 252t, 259bl, 267, 275, 276m, 277b, 279, 291, 426m, 440
Office national des chemins de fer marocains, Rabat : 252b
Giulio Pediconi, Rome : 259tr
Private collections, all rights reserved : 27, 28l, 28r, 31b, 35, 39r, 41r, 51, 57t, 58bl, 58br, 75t, 81, 83, 92, 93, 97, 104tr, 118ml, 127b, 128, 130t, 132b, 135, 136mr, 136b, 139b, 140mr, 155mr, 155bl, 164, 182l, 183r, 184l, 185bl, 187tl, 187tr, 188l, 190l, 192l, 192mr, 194l, 195br, 198, 199br, 201bl, 204t, 204b, 206l, 206mr, 208t, 208b, 209l, 209r, 224t, 224m, 226r, 230, 231l, 231r, 235, 236, 239, 240t, 243, 247tl, 253t, 254t, 254bl, 254br, 258t, 259tl, 262t, 262b, 263, 268t, 268t, 269r, 276t, 277tl, 277tr, 282t, 294, 295tl, 295mr, 296b, 298tl, 299t, 300, 305, 306, 307bl, 309b, 311b, 316l, 319b, 320, 321, 327b, 328, 332, 333t, 334t, 334m, 334br, 335br, 349r, 349l, 359br, 363, 364, 365, 367b, 373l, 373r, 374l, 375r, 377b, 381t, 381br, 382b, 384tl, 384ml, 385r, 387r, 388l, 389r, 395mr, 395br, 397l, 397tr, 397mr, 398tl, 400tl, 405r, 422, 425tr, 428l, 429bl, 435l,
André Peter, Casablanca : 46r
Joseph Pola, Casablanca : 89
Léandre Pola, Casablanca : 415
Jacques Robelin, Casablanca : 408t, 408m
Photos Roger-Viollet, Paris : 52r, 51t, 120t
Photo by Bernard Rouget : 414
Francis et Michèle Rumpf, Clamart (former collection of Victor Forbin) : 36t, 38
Service historique de l'Armée de terre, Vincennes : 78
Drawings by Philippe Simon : 123, 125, 360tl, 412
Soceca, Casablanca : 245, 246, 343l, 343r
La Source Library, Rabat : 77
André Studer, Gockhausen/Zurich : 341bl, 341br, 432m
Pierre Suraqui, Paris : 142l, 142r, 143l, 361t, 361ml, 369t
Warner Brothers Archive, School of Cinema and Television, University of Southern California, Los Angeles : 278m, 278b
Warner Brothers Research Collection, Burbank Public Library, Burbank : 278t
Wilaya du Grand Casablanca : 55b, 115bl, 115br, 119, 254tl, 255br, 295tr, 371ml, 436
Jean-François Zevaco, Casablanca : 400tr, 400mr
The reproductions have been made by Michel Nachef in Rabat, Raphaël Salzedo in Nantes, and Jean-Louis Cohen in Paris and elsewhere.